Jrkutsk

Lake Baikal

Khabarovsk

SAKHALIN

HEILUNGKIANG

MARITIME PROV.

KURIL IS.

•Ulan Bator
(Urga)

M O N G O L I A

•Harbin

HOKKAIDO
•Sapporo

KIRIN
Ch'ang-ch'un
(Hsinching)

Amur R.

Vladivostok

SEA OF

JAPAN

I N N E R   M O N G O L I A

Mukden

LIAONING

Yalu R.

NORTH
KOREA

Sendai

Shanhaikuan

Ta-t'ung•
•Peking
Tientsin•

HOPEI

Ta-lien
(Dairen)

P'yŏngyang

HONSHŪ

Tōkyō•
Nagoya•

•Seoul
SOUTH
KOREA

Kyōto•
•Osaka

J A P A N

NINGSIA

SHANSI

SHANTUNG

YELLOW SEA

Pusan

SHIKOKU

how
NSU

SHENSI

Loyang Kaifeng
•Sian
HONAN

Yellow R.

KIANGSU

Nagasaki• KYŪSHŪ

W K
ING
MTS.

AWAN

Han R.

HUPEI

Nanking•
ANHWEI

Wu-han
(Hankow)

Soochow
•Shanghai

EAST CHINA

SEA

RYŪKYŪ ISLANDS

P A C I F I C

ngtu
ungking

Yangtze R.

Hangchow•
•Ningpo
CHEKIANG

O C E A N

Changsha•

HUNAN

KIANGSI

KWEICHOW

Foochow•
FUKIEN

KWANGSI

Hsi (West) R.

KWANGTUNG
•Canton

Taipei•

TAIWAN

•Hanoi
ORTH
VIETNAM

HAINAN

Great Wall

Modern Grand Canal

Provincial boundaries in
China proper

OS

•Hué

SOUTH CHINA SEA

PHILIPPINE

•Manila

D)I A

SOUTH
VIETNAM

ISLANDS

•Saigon

Sanderson

East Asia

Tradition & Transformation   *New Impression*

Houghton Mifflin Company · Boston

Dallas

Geneva, Illinois

Hopewell, New Jersey

Palo Alto

London

East Asia

Tradition & Transformation   *New Impression*

John K. Fairbank, *Professor Emeritus*

Edwin O. Reischauer

Albert M. Craig

Harvard University

Printed in the U.S.A.

Library of Congress Catalogue Card Number: 77–77994

ISBN: 0–395–25812–X

To Serge Elisséeff

Director of the Harvard-Yenching Institute 1934–1956

Contents

Maps and Charts

Preface

In this book we have reworked, updated, and condensed the contents of our two earlier volumes: *East Asia: The Great Tradition* (1960) and *East Asia: The Modern Transformation* (1965). Since these volumes are almost twice the length of the present book, they include many more details and are not really superseded by it. But for the general reader and for many courses, the present work should be more satisfactory. This new impression has been updated in a number of minor respects, particularly in the first and last chapters.

The original two volumes grew out of the collaboration of J. K. Fairbank and E. O. Reischauer in a lecture course at Harvard which was begun in 1939 and further developed after World War II. When Mr. Reischauer left Harvard in 1961 to assume the American Ambassadorship in Tōkyō, A. M. Craig, who had meanwhile joined the course, kindly provided the remainder of the Japanese section of the second volume. The three authors have profited from one another's stimulus and criticism, and each has made extensive contributions to the portions of the book that the others wrote. The following listing, however, indicates the primary responsibilities for the various chapters:

> Chapter 1: Fairbank and Reischauer
> Chapters 2–6: Reischauer
> Chapters 7–10: Fairbank
> Chapters 11–15: Reischauer
> Chapter 16: Fairbank
> Chapters 17–18: Reischauer
> Chapters 19–21: Fairbank
> Chapters 22–23: Craig
> Chapters 24–25: Fairbank
> Chapter 26: Craig
> Chapters 27–28: Fairbank

During the several decades since we began our studies of East Asian history, the peoples of China, Japan, Korea, and Vietnam have experienced great disasters of warfare and invasion and have achieved great feats of national survival and regeneration. Present realities are complex and not easily summarized. Japan has only started to adjust to its new position as an economic superpower; the vast changes in the People's Republic of China have until recently been beyond the observation of Americans; Korea remains a divided country; and the people of Vietnam are still recuperating from the devastation of war. But clearly each of these four countries has now entered a new age. Their peoples may well feel that the past has been but the prologue to a hopeful future.

As historians we do not aim to deal in detail with the present, nor do we attempt to peer into the future. But we do assert that an understanding of history is essential for perspective on the present and for judgment about the future. History gives meaning to changes that otherwise might not seem significant or might be seriously misunderstood.

In writing a history of a third of mankind during a period of more than three milleniums, we have naturally relied on the work of a host of other scholars, both Asian and Western. Some have given us personal help and advice; far more have aided us through their writings. We are deeply grateful to all of them, but it would be impractical to attempt to list even the more important of these colleagues in our effort. Nor is it feasible to offer here a bibliography on this vast subject; any bibliography small enough to be included in this volume would have to be absurdly sketchy and soon would be quite out of date. The two preceding volumes listed some of those who had given us specific personal aid. Here we limit ourselves to expressing our special thanks to three persons who gave us extensive help on the manuscript for the present volume: the late Professor Edward A. Kracke on Chapters 5 and 6 on Chinese history, Professor Alexander B. Woodside on Vietnam, and Professor Edward W. Wagner on Korea. Meanwhile, in developing the illustrations for all these volumes, but especially concerning China, we have been profoundly indebted to Wilma Fairbank.

We also feel a special debt of gratitude to Professor Serge Elisséeff, native of Russia and citizen of France, for his great work as teacher and pioneer in developing East Asian studies at Harvard between 1932 and 1957. We are happy to have the opportunity to dedicate to him this distillation of our long-continued efforts.

John K. Fairbank
Edwin O. Reischauer
Albert M. Craig

The Pronunciation of Chinese, Japanese, Korean, and Vietnamese

The Romanization systems used in this book are those generally considered standard in the English-speaking world: Wade-Giles for Chinese (with the omission of a few unnecessary diacritical marks); Hepburn for Japanese; McCune-Reischauer for Korean; and the "national language" (*quoc ngu*) Romanization for Vietnamese. There is one major exception to this rule, however. Common Chinese geographical names are normally given according to the Chinese Post Office system, which often follows southern Chinese pronunciations and not the Peking pronunciation of standard Northern Chinese (Mandarin or *kuan-hua*). For example, the city that has been the capital of China for most of the past five and a half centuries is generally Romanized Peking and pronounced accordingly in the West, but the Wade-Giles Romanization of the name would be Pei-ching, and the real pronunciation is something like Bay-jing.

The Chinese, Japanese, and Korean systems of Romanization have points of similarity and therefore can be considered together. The following guide to their pronunciations is a nontechnical presentation which ignores many fine points but will be adequate for the general reader.

Vowels. The basic vowels, *a, e, i, o,* and *u,* in Chinese, Korean, and Japanese transcriptions are pronounced as in Italian, German, and Spanish.

    a as in f*a*ther
    e as in *e*nd
    i as the first *e* in *e*ve
    o as in *o*ld (but with less of the *ou* sound of English)
    u as in r*u*de

There are, however, some exceptions in CHINESE:

    e (except when following *i* or *y*) is pronounced like the *u* in *u*p
    ih is pronounced something like the *ir* in st*ir*
    o is often pronounced more like the *o* of s*o*ft

u when it follows *ss* or *tz* is sometimes hardly pronounced (and in Japanese too it is often barely audible; e.g., *desu = des'*)

Dipthongs and long vowels:

In CHINESE two vowels coming together are pronounced always as dipthongs, that is, run together (*ai* as the *i* in *i*ce; *ou* as the *o* in *o*bey; *ao* as the *ow* in c*ow*).

In JAPANESE only *ai* and *ei* (like the *a* in *a*le) are diphthongs; other vowels coming together are pronounced as separate syllables. Long vowels (*ō* and *ū*) are formed like the corresponding short vowels (*o* and *u*) but are held much longer. This distinction between long and short vowels is very important in Japanese.

In KOREAN *ae* is like the *a* in *a*dd; *oe* like the *ö* of German; and *ŭi* like the *uee* in q*uee*r.

Other vowels:

ŏ in Korean is like the *u* of b*u*t

ŭ in Korean is something like the *oo* in f*oo*t

ü in Chinese is like the *ü* of German or *u* of French

Consonants.   The consonants and the semi-vowels *w* and *y* in Chinese, Korean, and Japanese transcriptions are generally pronounced as they are in English. The following are the chief exceptions:

In the paired aspirated consonants (*ch'*, *k'*, *p'*, *t'*, *ts'*, *tz'*) and unaspirated consonants (*ch*, *k*, *p*, *t*, *ts*, *tz*) of CHINESE and KOREAN (the last two in each listing do not occur in Korean), the aspirated forms are more like the corresponding English consonants, which are usually aspirated, that is, are accompanied by a marked exhalation of air, and the unaspirated forms are closer to the corresponding consonants in French.* To the ears of English-speaking persons, however, the unaspirated consonants of Chinese often sound like the corresponding voiced consonants and are usually so pronounced as *j*, *k* as *g*, *p* as *b*, *t* as *d*, *ts* and *tz* as *dz*.

IN CHINESE:

hs (which occurs only before *i* and *ü*) is pronounced rather like *sh* (which occurs before *a*, *e*, and *u*)

j is pronounced something like *r* (*jen* sounds like *run*)

ss (which occurs only before the lightly pronounced *u*) is not to be distinguished from *s*

Vietnamese.   The "national language" system for Vietnamese was invented in the 1600's by Portuguese and Italian missionaries, who transcribed Vietnamese sounds into the Latin alphabet for the first time with the aid of copious

---

* The use of ' in Japanese transcriptions has nothing to do with aspiration. It follows *n* when the *n* is part of the preceding syllable and not the initial consonant for the vowel which follows.

diacritical marks. The French colonial government encouraged the use of this system in Vietnam at the end of the 1800's, causing the Vietnamese people to abandon their use of Chinese and Vietnamese (*nom*) characters but not to abandon their borrowing of Chinese words, which continues. Unfortunately it has not been possible to reproduce Vietnamese diacritical marks lavishly in this book. As a result, it is difficult to give the reader pronunciation guidelines, since the correct pronunciation of vowels, as well as of tones, is dependent upon these diacritical marks. For example, the vowel *o* with a conical hat-shaped diacritical mark above it is pronounced as in the English word *no;* with a diacritical slash to the right of it it is pronounced like the *u* without the *r* in the English word *fur;* without any diacritical mark at all it is pronounced like the *aw* in *law* or *gnaw.* Among the consonant combinations which give Western readers the most difficulty, *ng* at the beginning of a Vietnamese word (Nguyen) is like the *ng* buried in the English word *singer;* *t* is like an English *t* with no aspiration, (as in *stop*) whereas *th* is like an English *t* with strong aspiration (as in *top*); similarly, *k* is like an English *k* with no aspiration (as in *sky*) but *kh* is like an English *k* with much friction (as in *key*); *nh* at the end of a Vietnamese word (*minh*) is like the English *ng* in *sing,* but at the beginning of a word is like the *ny* in *canyon; qu* at the beginning of a word is like the *qu* in *quite; x* at the beginning of word is like the *s* in *saw; gi* (*Giap*) is like the *z* in *zoo* (at least in the north).

Correspondence in Pronunciation.   Words and names of Chinese origin, as used in Korean, Vienamese, and Japanese, are pronounced somewhat differently from Chinese. Actually, the Korean and Vietnamese forms are sometimes closer to ancient Chinese than are the modern Chinese. Korean, Vietnamese, and Japanese all preserve certain consonantal finals to syllables that have been lost in standard modern Chinese (though they are retained in the southern coastal "dialects"). The general nature of the correspondence in pronunciation for words and names of Chinese origin in the four languages can be seen in the following chart of the cardinal points, which are used in place names in all four countries and also appear in the names of the Korean political factions. (There are also native Japanese words for the cardinal points, much used in place names, which have no relationship to these Chinese-derived words.) The names of the cardinal points are given below in their traditional East Asian order:

	CHINESE	KOREAN	VIETNAMESE	JAPANESE
EAST	*tung*	*tong*	*dong*	*tō*
WEST	*hsi*	*sŏ*	*tay*	*sai*
SOUTH	*nan*	*nam*	*nam*	*nan*
NORTH	*pei*	*puk*	*bac*	*hoku*

1. The Setting
of East Asian History

The Objectives of this Study

When Europeans traveled far to the east to reach Cathay, Japan, and the Indies, they naturally gave those distant regions the general name "Far East." Americans who reached China, Japan, and Southeast Asia across the Pacific could, with equal logic, have called that area the "Far West." For the people who live there, however, it is neither "East" nor "West" and certainly not "Far." A better term for the area is "East Asia," which does not imply the outdated notion that Europe is the center of the civilized world.

The Extent of East Asia. East Asia can be defined in three ways: in geographic terms as the area east of the great mountain and desert barrier that bisects Asia; in racial terms as the habitat of Mongoloid man (except for the Eskimo and American Indian branches of that race); and in cultural terms as the domain of a civilization rooted in that of ancient China. In this book the last definition is naturally the most important. We concentrate on the histories of China, Japan, Korea, and Vietnam, countries that derived much of their higher culture and their primary system of writing from ancient China. In this sense, East Asia is "the Chinese culture area."

There are two other large areas that are, for the most part, east of the great barrier and basically Mongoloid in population. One is Inner Asia, particularly Mongolia, Sinkiang (Chinese Turkestan), and Tibet. The nomadic peoples of these regions have seen their histories interwoven with that of China through commerce, war, and conquest. In the other area, Southeast Asia, much of the higher culture stemmed more from India than from China. In recent centuries, however, this region too has become increasingly linked with the rest of East Asia, economically, culturally, and strategically.

For the peoples of the West the most important facts about East Asia are, first, the vast numbers of people who live there; second, the rapid growth and change that they are experiencing; and third, their very different ways of life, which distinguish them culturally from Westerners. In population and power, ancient China was the equal of the Roman Empire. Today China holds almost one-quarter of the human race—some 800 million people. More than 100 million Japanese live in a country smaller than California. In the last few decades it has become apparent that, in a rapidly shrinking world, relations with the third of humanity that lives in East Asia can directly affect the lives of Westerners. Three wars, the first against the Japanese, the second against the North Koreans and Chinese, the third in Vietnam, have made this quite clear to the American public.

The Need for Historical Understanding.   Mutual understanding between Westerners and the peoples of East Asia is needed to form a basis for harmonious relations. But understanding must be based on a knowledge and appreciation of the other peoples' different customs, attitudes, ideals, and forms of self-expression. These are not easy to grasp from a distance. The cultural gap is enormous. Rapidly growing contacts during the past century have tended to lessen the cultural gap, but other factors have widened the gulf: first, a great upsurge of national consciousness and patriotic pride among the peoples of East Asia; second, a growing discrepancy in material standards of living; and third, a different experience of war and revolution. In part because of accidents of history and geography, Westerners have achieved a far more favorable balance between population and natural resources than has been the case in East Asia, and this economic gap perpetuates and sometimes heightens the cultural differences. Americans in particular have not suffered warfare in their homeland as East Asians have, and the great changes in the lives of most Western people have been evolutionary, not revolutionary. Not only their inherited culture but also their experience in modern times have set them apart from the East Asian peoples.

The quest for peace is not the only reason for learning more about East Asia. For the humanist interested in art, literature, philosophy, and religion, the ancient societies of China, Japan, Korea, and Vietnam hold a mirror up to Western culture. They demonstrate alternative systems of value and belief, different traditions of aesthetic experience, and different forms of literary expression. For the social scientist, whether in anthropology, sociology, economics, political science, or history, the human record in East Asia, in certain periods and in certain fields, is far fuller than that of the West.

East Asia can best be understood through its history for a number of reasons. One is that the peoples of East Asia, more than those of the rest of the world, see themselves in historical perspective. They are strongly aware of their heritage. To approach them through their history is to look at them as they see themselves. Secondly, the distinctive aesthetic, intellectual, and institutional achievements of the peoples of East Asia can best be studied as they evolved. They should be looked at separately from the rapidly changing cultures of contemporary East Asia. Only as one looks at the long flow of East Asian history can one perceive the direction of its motion and understand what is happening there now.

The essence of the present turmoil in East Asia is the interaction between new forces, many of which were derived from the West, and traditional habits and modes of thinking. Our story divides naturally into two major phases: the evolution of traditional East Asian civilization in relative isolation over three thousand years, and the upheavals and transformation of that civilization in recent times partly in response to contact with the modern Western world.

Land, Peoples, and Languages

The Natural Environment.   One determining influence on East Asian civilization has been its relative isolation from the other great civilizations of mankind. Separated by great distances and formidable mountains and deserts, it developed distinctive cultural patterns that have been retained in large part until today. For example, the modern writing systems of all the rest of the world derive ultimately from a single series of inventions made in West Asia. Only in East Asia is there a writing system—the Chinese—which is based on entirely different principles.

Western civilization grew up in closely connected areas such as Mesopotamia, Egypt, and Greece. Only after it had spread to include most of Europe, North Africa, and Western Asia did it divide into its two present halves, Western Christian civilization and Islamic civilization. The Indus Valley in Northwest India (now a part of Pakistan) was the second great center of early civilization. Alexander's invasion of the Indus Valley in 327 B.C. is but one example of the close early contact between the ancient West and India.

The home of early East Asian civilization in North China was very much more isolated than were these other early centers. On one side stretched the seemingly boundless Pacific. On the other side rose the tremendous central massif of Asia—the Himalayas, the Tibetan Plateau, more than ten thousand feet high, and the huge mountain chains that radiate from this roof of the world. North of this massif lie the vast deserts and steppes of Central Asia—cold, inhospitable, and all but impassable for early man until he domesticated the horse and camel. South of the massif the rugged mountains and jungles of Southwest China and Southeast Asia are an even more formidable barrier. In ancient times this tremendous impediment of terrain and climate stretching

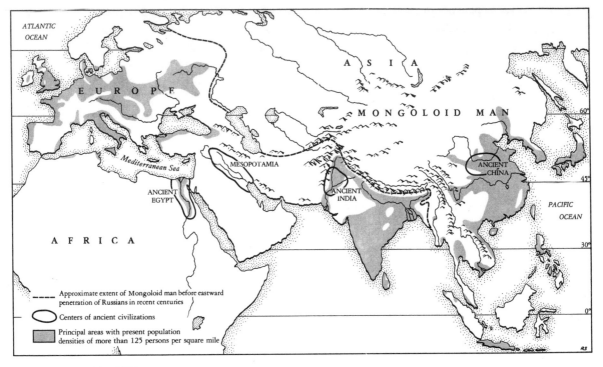

EURASIA

from the arctic wastes of Siberia to the jungles of Malaysia inhibited the free movement of men. Even today this barrier is crossed by only two railway lines and only a very few roads.

Climate also contributed to East Asia's cultural distinctiveness. Europe and West Asia have their weather determined largely by the Atlantic Ocean and receive the bulk of their rainfall in the cooler months. North Europe has relatively little sunshine, while the Mediterranean areas and West Asia receive relatively little rainfall. As a result the soils in Europe and West Asia are for the most part not cultivated very intensively. Usually only one crop can be grown each year.

The climate of East Asia, like that of India, is determined largely by the great land mass of Asia. In winter the air over Central Asia, far removed from the ameliorating influence of water, becomes very cold and heavy, flowing outward and bringing cool, dry weather to the southern and eastern fringes of the continent. In the summer the reverse takes place. The air over Central Asia warms up and rises, and moist oceanic air rushes in to take its place, dropping a heavy load of water on the continental fringes. As a result of these monsoon winds, most of East Asia and much of India have ample rainfall during the best growing months. This abundant water supply combined with the hot sunshine customary at these latitudes, far to the south of

Europe, permit intensive cultivation and, in many places, two crops per year.

This distinctive climate gave East Asia an agricultural pattern quite different from that of the West. Many of the principal crops and animals of East Asia, notably rice, the soy bean, the chicken, the water buffalo, and the pig, seem to have come from hot and humid Southeast Asia. In the West, cattle raising and sheep herding became a fundamental part of the economy, but in the more intensive agriculture of East Asia domesticated animals were used less and manpower more. The chief cereal of the West has been wheat, while that of most of East Asia and much of India has been rice, which grows best in flooded fields and is well adapted to the hot, wet summers of this area. Producing a much larger yield per acre than wheat, rice supports a heavier population on the land. Thus, right from the start of agriculture, there seems to have been a significant difference in the ratio between people and land in East Asia and India on the one hand, and in West Asia and Europe on the other. Even in recent times, when industrialization had added so heavily to the population of Europe, largely preindustrial East Asia and India continued to have greater densities of population.

The Peoples.   The area from the great Asian barrier eastward is for the most part the domain of Mongoloid man, while the area west of the barrier, including the greater part of India, most of the area of Islamic civilization, and the full zone of Western civilization, is the home of white or Caucasoid man. Negroid man, the third major racial type, occupies a discontinuous band of southerly areas in Africa, spots along the southern edges of Asia, and on the islands of Melanesia.

The origin of the races of mankind is still an unknown story. One of the predecessors of modern man in East Asia is Peking Man, whose skeletal remains were discovered in a cave near Peking in 1927. Living about 400,000 years B.C., he had tools, used fire, and was a hunter. He also had certain physical features that are more characteristic of Mongoloid man than of the other modern races. More recently a still earlier precursor of Mongoloid man, dating back some 600,000 years, has been found at a site in Lan-t'ien, near Sian in northwest China.

When the curtain rises on the first act of recorded history in East Asia, we find the Mongoloids already in a solid block covering almost the whole area. Their relative shortness of limb, which facilitates the retention of body heat, and their fleshy, narrow eyelids, which protect the eyes from snow glare, are thought by some to be the result of an original cold habitat in Northeast Asia. The range of skin color among Mongoloids, from very light in the North to dark brown in southern areas such as Indonesia, is clearly a product of environment, as is the comparable color range in the so-called white race. The other distinctive features of Mongoloid man are straight black hair, relatively flat faces, and dark eyes.

Mongoloids are not limited to East Asia. Some Mongoloids spilled westward north of the great barrier. The Eskimos represent a relatively recent incursion of the Mongoloid race into North America, while the American Indians themselves are thought to have come originally from Siberia by way of Alaska. Archaeology suggests the spread of the Mongoloids from the north and central parts of East Asia southward and outward to the offshore islands. The movement of the Thai people some seven centuries ago from Southwest China to their present home in Thailand was part of this great movement.

The Mongoloids were not, however, the sole occupants of this part of the world; the peripheral areas of East Asia contain many survivors of non-Mongoloid races. The most interesting of these are the Ainu, at present restricted to the northern extremities of Japan, who show certain traits of Caucasoid man. For example, they have considerable facial and body hair, a feature notably lacking in most Mongoloids.

The Sinitic Languages.   The significant human divisions within East Asia, as in the West, are primarily linguistic rather than racial. In both East Asia and the West there is a common misconception that these linguistic differences correspond to racial divisions, but in fact there is no more a Chinese or Japanese race than there is a German or Hungarian race.

The largest linguistic division in East Asia is the Sinitic (or Sino-Tibetan) family of languages, which is comparable to the great Indo-European family that spreads over most of Europe and much of the Islamic and Indian zones of civilization. The Sinitic family of languages occupies a very solid block in the center of East Asia, covering all of China proper, Tibet, Thailand, Laos, most of Burma, and perhaps Vietnam. Except for the Tibetans, all the members of this language group appear to have been farmers since the Neolithic period, sedentary occupants of their part of the world, contrasting with the early Indo-Europeans, who often were nomadic, herding peoples and therefore wandered far afield.

Within the Sinitic group, Chinese is by far the largest linguistic subdivision. Chinese-speaking people have been in North China since the earliest recorded times. They have spread by emigration and also have assimilated culturally and linguistically allied groups. In time they came to occupy almost the whole of China proper and more recently Manchuria, much of Inner Mongolia, parts of Sinkiang, most of Taiwan (Formosa), as well as Chinese sectors in Southeast Asia, particularly Malaysia, where Chinese now constitute more than 40 per cent of the population, and Singapore, where they are the great majority.

In the course of this expansion the Chinese language divided into several mutually unintelligible languages, as distinct from one another as Spanish is from Italian, or Swedish from German. Chinese proper, which has been called Mandarin, is spoken as a mother tongue by more people than any other lan-

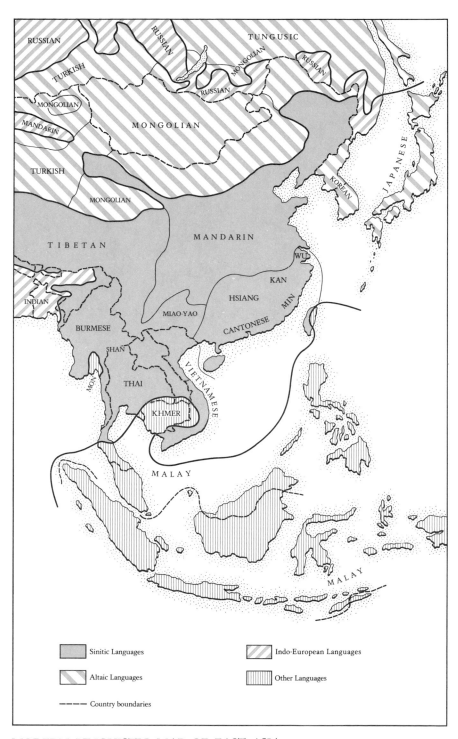

RUSSIAN

TURKISH

MONGOLIAN

MANDARIN

TURKISH

MONGOLIAN

RUSSIAN

TUNGUSIC

MONGOLIAN

RUSSIAN

RUSSIAN

MONGOLIAN

JAPANESE

KOREAN

TIBETAN

MANDARIN

WU

KAN

HSIANG

MIN

INDIAN

MIAO-YAO

CANTONESE

BURMESE

SHAN

MON

THAI

VIETNAMESE

KHMER

MALAY

MALAY

	Sinitic Languages		Indo-European Languages
	Altaic Languages		Other Languages

– – – Country boundaries

MODERN LINGUISTIC MAP OF EAST ASIA

guage in the world. Its various dialects cover all North China and most of Central and Southwest China. Along the coast from Shanghai southward to the Vietnam border, the Chinese-type tongues, usually miscalled "the Chinese dialects," are all quite distinct from Mandarin. There are the Wu "dialect" of the Shanghai area; the Min "dialect" of Fukien, subdivided into Fukienese and the Amoy "dialect"; Hakka in several widely scattered areas; and finally, Cantonese. These various coastal "dialects" are also the languages of Taiwan and the Chinese communities in Southeast Asia. Cantonese is the language of most Chinese communities in the United States.

In addition to the Chinese languages, there are several other groups of Sinitic tongues spoken by peoples in Southwest China and contiguous areas. The Tibeto-Burmese group includes the Tibetan dialects, Burmese, and several others. The Thai group of Thailand and Laos, and Vietnamese, the language of modern Vietnam, are usually included among the Sinitic languages.

The Altaic and Other Language Groups.   North of the Sinitic bloc is a large group of Mongoloid peoples who speak languages of a family as distinct from the Sinitic tongues as from the Indo-European. This linguistic family has been named Altaic after the Altai Mountains in Mongolia. These peoples, like early Indo-Europeans but in sharp contrast with their sedentary neighbors to the south, were nomadic, horse-riding sheepherders. They have moved about a great deal; indeed, some have wandered entirely out of East Asia.

Turkish, Mongolian, and Tungusic are usually considered to be the three major Altaic language groups. Turkish-speaking groups now inhabit Turkey and the greater part of Central Asia, although in the course of their wanderings, they absorbed a sometimes preponderant quantity of Caucasoid blood. The Mongols occupy much of Mongolia and many isolated pockets in Central and West Asia. Tungusic-speaking tribes, such as the Manchus, once constituted the chief population of Manchuria and the Siberian areas to the north. Since Korean and Japanese show close structural resemblances to the definitely Altaic languages, the Koreans and Japanese may be two eastern extensions of Altaic-speaking peoples into predominately agricultural areas.

A third great linguistic family of East Asia is the Austronesian, which includes the languages of Malaysia, Indonesia, the Philippines, and the tongues of the aborigines of Taiwan. The Khmer of Cambodia probably represents still another linguistic family.

In ancient times Indo-European languages were used in some of the pastoral northwestern areas of East Asia. Until the ninth century Sinkiang was inhabited by blondish peoples, speaking Iranian or now extinct Indo-European languages. Westward-moving waves of Turkish-speaking peoples eventually blotted out these languages. Thus, an Indo-European element disappeared from East Asia a millennium ago and was reintroduced only in the last few centuries by Russian colonization in Siberia.

China's Geographical Setting

China is geographically a less united area than either the traditional zone of Western civilization or India because it lacks the easy communications made possible by the Mediterranean or by the great plains of the other regions. The North China Plain is much smaller than the plain that extends across North India, to say nothing of the still greater North European Plain or the American Middle West.

China is broken up into a sort of checkerboard by two intersecting sets of parallel mountain chains. One major inland chain runs from southwestern China northeastward through Shansi and western Manchuria. A parallel coastal range extends from Canton northward to the Yangtze and then re-appears in the Shantung Peninsula and again in the mountains along the Korean-Manchurian border. Intersecting these two southwest-to-northeast ranges, three parallel mountain chains spaced at roughly equal intervals protrude from west to east toward the Pacific. The southernmost chain creates the watershed dividing the West River system of the Canton region from the Yangtze Valley. In the extreme north another east-west range divides North China from the Mongolian plateau. Between these two the important Tsinling range, the eastward extension of the massive Kunlun of northern Tibet, creates the watershed between the Yangtze and the Yellow Rivers and (together with the Huai River) marks the boundary between North and South China. This cross-hatching of mountain ranges has created a number of distinct geographical regions. It has given rise to problems of economic and political unity and has determined military strategy.

River Systems. The great rivers of China water the centers of habitation which lie within the mountain ranges. The Yellow River (Huang Ho) is some 2700 miles in length. After it enters the North China Plain about 500 miles from the sea, it crosses a broad flood plain built up over the ages by its own silt. The river bed here slopes only about one foot per mile. In the summer flood season the waters from the great treeless mountain ranges to the west bring with them a heavy deposit of yellow silt which gives the river its name. Since the Yellow River constantly builds up its own bed, from earliest times Chinese administrators have had to construct dikes to keep it within its channel. Ordinarily the waters of "China's Sorrow" move across the plain within these dikes between ten and forty feet above the level of the surrounding land. A single breach in the dikes may spread a few inches or feet of water over hundreds of square miles and cut millions of farmers off from their sustenance. Years may elapse before flood-ravaged lands can be cultivated again. Meanwhile famine will have followed upon the flood. Only since 1949 have afforestation and dam building begun to conquer this age-old problem.

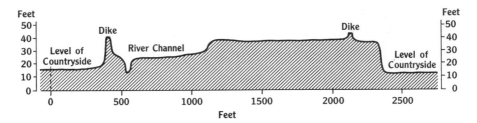

PROFILE OF THE YELLOW RIVER. *This diagram is a cross section with the vertical aspect greatly exaggerated. It shows how during flood season the river rises between its dikes above the level of the countryside.*

The vastness of the Yellow River problem has been graphically demonstrated by the historic shifts of its bed from the north to the south of the Shantung promontory and back again. From 1191 to 1852 its waters for the most part entered the ocean south of the peninsula; from 1852 to 1938 on the north; and from 1938 to 1947 again to the south. The present channel enters the ocean near Tientsin.

The Yangtze is a larger river than the Yellow. It is 3200 miles in length, with a catchment basin twice as large and receiving twice as much rainfall. It is also navigable, as the Yellow River is not. Steamers as large as 10,000 tons can in season ascend 630 miles to Hankow and smaller vessels another 1000 miles. In flood season the river rushes through the famous Yangtze gorges above Hankow at fourteen knots, and special steamers are required to make the ascent. Joined by a great network of tributaries, the Yangtze itself carries an enormous volume of silt into the China Sea, extending the Shanghai delta at the rate of about one mile in seventy years. Big lakes serve as storage basins for the lower Yangtze. Even so, the rainy season may raise the water level as much as forty or fifty feet between the dikes. Disastrous floods are not infrequent.

Climate.   China lies far south of most of Europe. Peking is south of both Naples and Madrid; Canton is in the same latitude as the Sahara Desert. China is further south than the eastern half of the United States, with Peking corresponding to Philadelphia, Shanghai to Mobile, and Canton to Havana, Cuba. The greater land mass to which China belongs gives it a more markedly continental climate, with much lower winter and somewhat higher summer temperatures than at corresponding latitudes in the United States. Peking in July can be as hot as Cairo and in January as cold as Stockholm.

China is a battleground between cold, dry, continental air and warm, humid, oceanic air, which brings it most of its rainfall. During the summer this sea air reaches further into the continent, sometimes as far as Mongolia. Most of the South receives more than sixty inches of rainfall a year. This ample water supply can be used not only for irrigating rice fields but also for transportation. Navigable streams and canals cover most of the central and lower Yangtze basin. In marked contrast, the Northwest receives less than the twenty inches minimum rainfall necessary for farming unirrigated lands and has little or no water transportation.

One important climatic boundary is the Tsinling Mountains. South of the Tsinling rainfall for the most part is over forty inches, making possible the irrigated rice economy that supports two-thirds of the Chinese people. North of this boundary stretch brown, parched lands used for dry field farming and traversed by cart or wheelbarrow tracks. (See page 908.) Another climatic boundary is between the farming areas of China proper and the steppe lands to the north that are too lightly watered to support any sort of agriculture. This has been sharply demarcated by the Great Wall, which the Chinese erected to defend themselves from their northern neighbors, pastoral, Altaic-speaking nomads.

Geologists speculate that in the last Ice Age the frozen interior of Asia sent forth tremendous winds which deposited the fine loess soil that covers about 100,000 square miles of Northwest China. The Yellow River has spread some of this soil over the North China Plain as alluvium. Fortunately the loess makes a fertile soil. In a region of light rainfall, it has remained unleached; that is, its mineral substances have not been percolated out by the constant passage of water through it. North China, however, despite its fertile loess, balances dangerously on the edge of famine. The growing season is short; precipitation is light and highly variable. Until the introduction of irrigation by electric pump, the Northern peasant faced a constant threat of drought. In the last 1800 years more than 1800 famines have been recorded.

South China soils have been leached by the heavier rainfall of that area. Moreover, only 15 per cent of its uplands are flat enough for cultivation. But since most of the area produces two crops a year, South China has a denser population than the North and higher standards of nutrition.

China's Traditional Economy and Society

China's greatest natural resource has always been her agricultural land. It is understandable therefore that climate and terrain have helped shape the economic and social institutions of Chinese life. Although the historical records of China, like those of most other countries, generally neglect the life of the common people, we can sketch certain features that have been typical of the life of the Chinese masses. First of all, China's vast population, now roughly four times that of the United States, must get its food supply from a cultivated area about one-half the size of that of the United States. The 80 per cent of the populace who live upon the soil and till it have been barely able to produce a food surplus adequate to maintain the other 20 per cent.

They have not been able to afford the raising of animals for food, aside from the scavengers, pigs and chickens. And because of the lack of animals, peasants have largely depended on human excrement, or "night soil," for fertilizer. At best, Chinese agriculture has always been a precarious business.

Secondly, China's economic life has been labor-intensive, that is, strongly dependent upon human muscle-power. The agricultural cycle requires the lavish use of human energy. In growing rice, for example, seed is thickly scattered in nursery beds. Meanwhile winter crops are harvested in the main fields, which are then cultivated and flooded in preparation for the rice. When the rice seedlings are about eight inches high after a month's growth, they are transplanted by hand to the main paddy fields, an activity roughly equivalent to the planting of the American wheat and corn crops by hand. Mechanization is difficult, not least because other work must be found for so many hands.

Similarly, the famous silk industry requires endless labor. A pound of silk-worms at hatching may number about 700,000 individual worms. Fed mulberry leaves by hand and carefully tended for five weeks until their maturity, the pound of worms will grow to a weight of some five tons, consuming about twelve tons of mulberry leaves in the process, but producing in the end only about 150 pounds of silk. The semimechanized reeling of silk cocoons to get their thread is only the last step after an enormous application of hand labor. The other traditional household industry of South China, tea production, involves a comparable use of hands to pick, sort, roast, pick over, re-sort, re-roast, and package the tea leaves.

The labor-intensive nature of the economy has been typified by the moving of irrigation water by human muscle, customarily with a simple foot treadle or even more simply by a bucket on ropes held by two persons. Transportation also has customarily been labor-intensive, using porters with carrying poles on mountain paths, men pushing wheelbarrows over the plains, boatmen sculling sampans on the waterways, chair-bearers with their palanquins in the cities (supplanted in recent times by rickshaw coolies and later by pedicab drivers). Even now bicycles seem to carry as many people as do motor vehicles.

Chinese farming from ancient times has applied large amounts of labor and, when possible, large amounts of water to small plots of land. Landowning has therefore been the main goal of economic endeavor and investment. Problems of landlordism and agricultural taxation have preoccupied both populace and officialdom in every generation. Moreover, the farmer's lack of capital and storage facilities kept him at the mercy of the middleman, who bought cheaply in the harvest season and lent capital in the off-season to the impoverished cultivator at rates of 2 per cent or more a month. Tenancy led to further exploitation. The farmer might have to pay as much as half his crop to the landlord.

Transportation of produce to market has always been a problem. A decentralized market pattern has therefore been typical, each village community

TRANSPLANTING RICE. *With their bundles of rice seedlings, which have already been grown in a seed bed, these farmers wade backward ankle-deep in the flooded fields to transplant the seedlings by hand in orderly rows. Communication paths are on top of the field dikes. The bridge crosses the irrigation canal. From* P'ei-wen-chai keng-chih t'u, *an early eighteenth-century work extolling the imperial patronage of agriculture.*

exchanging its produce by barter at the local market town. A market center and its surrounding villages within walking distance formed a unit that could of course be wiped out by natural calamities such as flood or drought, but conversely could live almost by itself as long as nature was kind. Thus the fragmented and cellular nature of the traditional market center and village economy enabled them to survive with a high degree of inertia, or persistence in established channels, in spite of wars, invasions, and great social changes in the cities and administrative centers where history was recorded. While the recent decades of revolutionary effort have brought great changes—for

MAKING SILK. *Silk culture requires a maximum investment of hand
labor. The silkworms are hatched from eggs and must be kept in
the right condition of temperature and moisture. During their
growth period they must be fed several times a day with fine-cut
leaves from specially cultivated mulberry trees. The man and
woman on the left are sorting the silk cocoons. A later stage
requires that the strands of silk be unraveled from the cocoons in a
pan of hot water. The woman in the picture on the right is
collecting strands on a reel. This occupation also is suited to the
lavish application of labor in a subsidiary handicraft industry
within a farm household. These pictures show only two out
of a dozen stages in the complex process of silk production.
(Chinese woodcuts from the* T'ien-kung k'ai-wu *of 1637.)*

example, dams to accumulate water, more irrigation canals to distribute it,
electrification to pump it onto the fields, afforestation, and improved crops—
these improvements have only begun to remake Chinese life.

The Social Heritage.   While it would be misleading to generalize in brief
terms about a society as large, ancient, and varied as that of China, there are

IRRIGATED AGRICULTURE. *Two men walk the treadles of a square-pallet chain-pump to lift water onto the fields, and another uses a windlass to distribute water to the various crops shown around the edge of the picture. (From* T'ien-kung k'ai-wu, *1637.) Electric pumps now do this work.*

still a few major points for an outside observer to keep in mind. First of all, the family, rather than the individual, the state, or the church, has formed the most significant unit in Chinese society. Each individual's family was his chief source of economic sustenance, security, education, social contact, and recreation. Through ancestor worship, it was even his main religious focus. Of the five famous Confucian relationships—between ruler and subject, father and son, husband and wife, elder brother and younger brother, and friend and friend—three were determined by kinship. China's whole ethical system tended to be family-centered, not oriented toward God or the state.

The Chinese kinship group was extensive, reaching out in each direction to the fifth generation. The ideal was to have all the living generations reside in one great household, divided among the various courtyards of a big compound. Actually this was seldom achieved except by the rich. A typical household seems to have averaged around five persons and was in fact a family of a type familiar in the West, rather than the ideal extended Chinese family.

The family system was both hierarchic and authoritarian. The status of each person depended on his position by birth or marriage. Gradations of kinship were carefully spelled out in a complex terminology. The patriarchal father was the center of authority. At least in theory he controlled the family property and he arranged his children's and grandchildren's marriages. As an index of the subordination of the individual to the family, filial piety was the most admired of virtues. (See page 45.) The arrangement of marriages by the respective families, for which a good deal can no doubt be said when wise matchmakers were used, symbolized more clearly than anything else the individual's subordination. Marriage was more a union of families than of individuals.

Women traditionally obeyed their fathers in youth, their husbands in middle life, and their sons in old age. They were expected not to remarry if widowed, but men could take secondary wives and concubines into the household. Except for a dowry, women had no property rights and on marriage entered their husbands' families as humble newcomers. This tradition suggests the great potential for change that awaited China's modern revolution.

This authoritarian family pattern provided a basis for social order in political as well as in domestic life. The role of the emperor and his officials was merely that of the father writ large. A district magistrate was called the "father and mother" of the people.

In a pluralistic society, like that of the modern West, the many forces of church and state, capital and labor, government and private enterprise are balanced under a rule of law. Instead, in Chinese life the personal virtues of probity and loyalty, sincerity and benevolence, inculcated by the family system, provided the norms for social conduct. Law was a necessary tool of administration; but personal morality was the foundation of society. Far from being anarchic because of the weakness of the legal concept, Chinese society was firmly knit together by Confucianism. This great ethical institution occupied in China much of the place filled by both law and religion in the West.

As in most large-scale peasant societies, there was a wide gulf in power and prestige between the rulers and the ruled. Society was traditionally divided into four classes, which in descending order were the scholar-administrator (or warrior-aristocrat in ancient times), the farmer, the artisan, and the merchant. The scholar-administrator, as an educated man, was presumed to be morally superior. Exercising the supreme authority of the emperor, the paterfamilias of all Chinese society, the scholar-administrator came to dominate all aspects of public life, and also left us the voluminous record of Chinese history, which was naturally written from his ruling-class point of view.

2. Early China: The Birth of a Civilization

The Archaeological Record

Agriculture seems to have started in North China in the region of the great bend of the Yellow River, in a fringe area between wooded highlands on the west and swampy lowlands on the east, where hunter-fisher folk could domesticate animals and begin to cultivate plants for food. It then spread along the middle and lower course of the Yellow River and out over the North China Plain, which, despite severe winters, was well suited to agriculture in primitive times. In fact, this center of early Chinese civilization resembled in some ways the homes of other ancient civilizations—the flood plains of the Nile in Egypt, the Tigris and Euphrates in Mesopotamia, and the Indus in modern Pakistan. In each case, rainfall was too light to produce forests that had to be removed before tilling could begin, and the great river, if adequately controlled, provided ample water and replenished the soil's fertility with periodic floods.

It is significant that the North China Plain is the part of agricultural East Asia most accessible by land from India and West Asia. As far as we now know, many basic elements of ancient civilization appeared much earlier in West Asia and the Indus Valley than in East Asia and therefore may have spread slowly across the steppes and mountains of Central Asia to the North China Plain. Examples are the cultivation of grains like wheat; domestication of animals such as sheep, cattle, and horses; the wheel and chariot; bronze and iron.

Recent finds, on the other hand, have shown that pottery goes back as far in East Asia as anywhere in the world—perhaps some 10,000 years—and that bronze may have been produced even earlier in northern Thailand than in the Middle East. Rice, the chief cereal of East Asia today, is of Southeast Asian origin, and its cultivation was well established in the Yangtze Valley by prehistoric times. The prehistoric Chinese also produced silk, which spread to the West very much later. Some important domestic animals were of different derivation—pigs, chickens, and dogs for food and the water buffalo for rice cultivation. The basic agricultural tool of East Asia has always been the hoe, in contrast to the plow of the West. The most characteristic Paleolithic remains are stone choppers; in the rest of the "old world" they are chipped stone axes. Neolithic remains in East Asia are typified by halfmoon-shaped stone knives and grey pottery with mat and cord markings, both quite different from Western Eurasian artifacts.

There is, thus, good reason to assume that in East Asia agriculture and early civilization developed quite independently of Western Eurasia. The culture that arose around the bend of the Yellow River in northwest China was probably based on this East Asian culture but seems to have also received enrichment from regions to the West. However, there is no evidence that these influences were brought by invaders or migrants, and the Neolithic peoples of North China and possibly their Paleolithic predecessors appear to have been the direct ancestors of the modern Chinese. Even at this early time the culture of North China showed distinctive East Asian features.

The Painted and Black Pottery Cultures.   Two distinct cultures, named for their characteristic pottery, occupied North China in late Neolithic times. They were first thought to show a clash between West Asian and local influences, but more recent studies have proved that the Black Pottery culture in large part followed the Painted, occupying most of its area.

The Painted Pottery culture, which is also known as Yang-shao from a type site in northwest Honan, is found throughout North China, except for Shantung province in the extreme east, and it lingered on longest in Kansu province in the northwest. Its most famous site is the partly excavated village at Pan-p'o near Sian (the ancient Ch'ang-an), which dates from the fifth millennium B.C. The culture is typified by large bulbous pots, painted in red and black, usually with bold geometric designs. While it bears some resemblance to the painted pottery of West Asia, one cannot assume that it was merely a cultural borrowing from the West, because there is no clear archaeological trail by which it could have come.

The Black Pottery culture, also called Lung-shan from type sites in Shantung, covered the same area as the Painted, except for the extreme northwest, and also extended into Shantung and the middle and lower Yangtze valleys. It is typified by a very thin, shiny, black pottery. This culture showed that since the time of the Painted Pottery new influences from West Asia, such as domesticated sheep and horses and the potter's wheel, had reached North China. It also showed strong cultural continuity with the following bronze

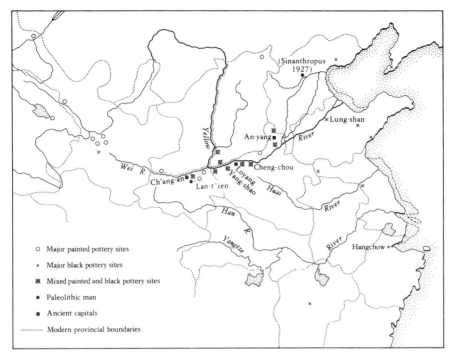

NORTH CHINA IN PREHISTORIC TIMES

age. For example, it shared the same hollow-legged tripods, a common system of divination, and town walls of pounded earth, much like those that still may be found in North China today.

The Bronze Age.   Bronze casting by the piece-mold process, different from the method used in ancient West Asia, made its appearance in China by the middle of the second millennium B.C., if not earlier. The first known sites are found spread out in Honan south of the Yellow River from its great bend eastward, but the only bronzes they contain are small weapons. A second stage is typified by a site near Cheng-chou in the same area, which was a formidable capital city, surrounded by a pounded earth wall more than twenty feet high and a mile square. Outside the walls were two bronze foundries which produced elaborate ritual vessels.

The third bronze stage is best represented by a site near An-yang in the part of Honan north of the Yellow River. It was discovered by Chinese scholars who in 1899 became intrigued by what appeared to be ancient writing scratched onto the "dragon bones" that Peking apothecary shops were grinding up for medicine. They traced these bones to their source near An-yang and on further study discovered that they bore the earliest known form of Chinese writing and corroborated much of the early historical tradition.

The inscriptions contained the names of virtually all of the traditional rulers of an ancient dynasty known as the Shang and a wealth of detail about the latter half of the dynasty, when the capital was said to have been at An-yang (roughly from about 1400 to 1050 B.C.). Clearly the archaeological record and historical traditions flowed together at this point. Scholars, who at the time looked with complete skepticism on the Shang Dynasty, had to reverse course and accept its existence as verified history.

Early Chinese Traditions

The oldest remaining Chinese books, dating from the first half of the first millennium before Christ, do not tell us much about previous ages. In the next few centuries, however, the Chinese wrote a great deal about the beginnings of their civilization and its early history. In fact, as one approaches the time of Christ, the Chinese writers have more and more to tell about earlier and earlier periods. Their works, of course, tell us more about the beliefs and customs of the period in which they were written than of the history of earlier ages. Still, they contain much material on earlier mythology and traditions and undoubtedly some solid bits of history.

From these works and the archaeological record emerges a shadowy picture of a once matriarchal but increasingly patriarchal society, divided into tribal or clan-like units. From the clan name, the *hsing* or family name had already developed in ancient times. Then, as now, it always preceded a man's personal name, instead of following it as in the European tradition. There was a strong emphasis on exogamy, that is, marriage outside one's clan, which has persisted throughout Chinese history, so that even today Chinese feel that persons of the same surname, even though not actually related, should not marry.

Religious ideas centered on the clan and its deities, often identified as ancestors. Ancestor worship has remained ever since a characteristic of Chinese civilization. As was natural in an agricultural society, there was also strong emphasis on heaven as a controlling factor in agriculture, on the fertility of the soil, on grain gods, and on cosmological and calendrical lore. Authority was strongly religious, and the ruler was in a sense the chief priest and also calendar maker.

The Chinese early developed a strong feeling of history and the ideal of political unity. Unaware of the great cultures to the west, they considered China the unique land of civilization, surrounded on all sides by the "four barbarians." They therefore called it Chung-kuo, literally the "Central Country" but commonly translated the "Middle Kingdom." Chung-kuo is still the Chinese name for their land. The term *t'ien-hsia,* meaning "all under heaven," meant the world but came to be used for the Chinese Empire. Information and speculation about earlier ages was organized into a strict historical sequence of events attributed to rulers of a politically and culturally unified China that constituted the whole of civilization.

The Culture Heroes.   There are several versions of this early pseudohistory. The usual sequence is of three early rulers (*huang*) or possibly fraternal groups of rulers, followed by five emperors (*ti*), followed by three dynasties, which take us well into historical times. The three rulers and five emperors are often called "culture heroes," because to them and to lesser figures like them are attributed the early achievements of civilization, such as the discovery of fire, the origination of fishing, hunting, and agriculture, the devising of the calendar, the development of medicine, and the invention of writing. The wife of the first of the five emperors is credited with the development of sericulture, for silk production is typically the work of women.

The last two of the five emperors, Yao and Shun, are best known for having passed on their rule, not to sons, but to worthy ministers. Yao selected Shun, and Shun a man named Yü. The three together are known as the three model emperors. Yü is also famed as the hero who drained off the flood waters of the North China Plain and divided the empire into nine provinces. A Chinese reflection of the worldwide flood legend can be detected in this story.

The Early Dynasties.   With Yü also commences a somewhat more credible aspect of the tradition. He started a dynasty called the Hsia, which has been assigned the dates 2205–1766 B.C. (or 1994–1523 B.C. according to another source). The Hsia rulers are credited with reigns of reasonable length, in contrast to the Methuselah-like spans of the culture heroes.

The last Hsia emperor was so depraved that people revolted under the leadership of a man who founded a new dynasty, named Shang. The Shang, which is traditionally given the dates of 1766–1122 B.C. or 1523–1027 B.C., has been proven by archaeology to be fully historical, for the An-yang finds indubitably correspond to the second half of the dynasty and the Cheng-chou finds presumably to its earlier centuries. This raises the question of what actual facts may lie behind the tradition of the Hsia dynasty. Might it not correspond to the earliest bronze age, or perhaps the Black Pottery culture which preceded it?

The last of the Shang emperors was said to be a debauched tyrannical ruler—an allegation which the bone inscriptions from An-yang tend to substantiate. One of those who suffered most at his hands was a subject known to history as King Wen (Wen Wang) of the principality of Chou. His son and successor, King Wu (Wu Wang) eventually revolted, according to the tradition in either 1122 or 1027 B.C., and founded the third dynasty, which he called Chou after the name of his principality. His brother, the Duke of

Chou (Chou Kung), became the consolidator of the dynasty, as the wise and saintly councilor of King Wu's young son and heir.

While the story of the founding of the Chou bears the marks of later idealization, much of the record of the early centuries of the Chou is acceptable as history, because our earliest surviving books do date from this period. After 841 B.C. the traditional dating seems quite reliable, and in the next century we begin to encounter our first fully verifiable events—eclipses of the sun that did occur just when the Chinese records date them.

The Chinese Writing System

The outstanding feature of the late Shang finds at An-yang is the writing they contain; not only is it unmistakably the Chinese language but it is also an early form of the Chinese writing system that still dominates East Asian civilization. Some symbols are recognizable even to the untutored eye as identical with characters appearing in newspapers today. It is much as if the Arabic-speaking inhabitants of Egypt or Iraq were able to recognize in hieroglyphics or cuneiform the same language they now use and could point out occasional words that any schoolboy could read. The Chinese have always felt a complete cultural and racial identity with the ancient inhabitants of their land, and here is striking proof that they are right in doing so. They have good reason to feel a greater sense of direct continuity from the Shang than Westerners feel from the early Egyptians and Mesopotamians, or even the ancient Greeks and Romans.

One of the characteristics of the Sinitic languages, to which Chinese belongs, is that a relatively high percentage of their words are monosyllables. This is truer of ancient Chinese than of modern. Another feature of Chinese and most other Sinitic languages is the absence of inflections. The Chinese word *shan,* for instance, can mean "mountains" as well as "mountain." In the case of verbs, the difference from the languages of the West is even more marked. There are no variations like "go," "went," "gone," or even "look," "looks," "looked." Another feature of most Sinitic languages is their tonal character. Monosyllabic words which otherwise sound alike are distinguished from one another by the tone in which they are spoken, something like the differing inflections we use in conversation: "What's your name?" "Name?" "Yes, name." In modern Mandarin there are four tones. *Ma* pronounced in the first of these, for example, is an informal word for "mother," but in the second tone it means "hemp," in the third "horse," and in the fourth "to curse."

Chinese Characters. The monosyllabic and uninflected nature of the Chinese language helps account for the retention by the Chinese of a

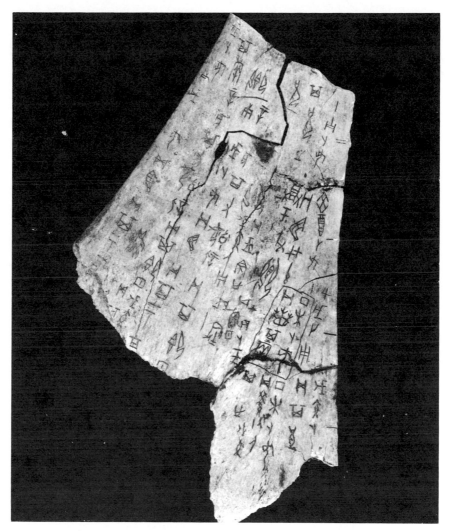

AN INSCRIBED AN-YANG BONE.

writing system which, like that of ancient Egypt, originated from pictographs but, unlike hieroglyphics, always remained true to the basic principle that each monosyllabic word should have its unique symbol, or character. Inflections would long ago have forced the Chinese to a more flexible phonetic system of writing.

The Chinese writing system encountered in the An-yang finds had already undergone a long development and had progressed far beyond simple pictographs. Antecedents for this writing, in fact, seem to exist in sites of the fifth millenium B.C. The writing usually ran from top to bottom, as remained the rule until recent years. The more than two thousand characters found in the Shang remains look for the most part quite different from modern Chinese characters, but almost all have been clearly identified with later forms, and all the principles to be found in the eight or nine thousand characters commonly used in modern times (dictionaries list up to fifty thousand characters and variants) were present in the Shang writing.

The many pictographs, though often very stylized, were for the most part more recognizable as pictures in Shang times than are their modern forms. For example, the character for "sun" (now 日) originally was a circle with a line in it; that for "moon" (now 月) was still quite recognizably a crescent moon; and "tree" 木 was written in Shang times 朿 , a sketch representing both the branches and the roots of a tree. Some pictographs were quite complicated, as, for example, one of the words for "sacrifice," which showed two hands holding a bird upside down over a symbol that meant "the spirits."

There was, in addition, a large number of ideographs, that is, sketches of ideas rather than actual pictures. Perhaps the numbers "one" 一 , "two" 二 , and "three" 三 should be put in this category. "Above" 上 , originally a shorter line above a longer line, and "below" 下 , analogously formed, certainly belong to this group. So also do more complex characters, like those for "grove" or "forest" 林 , which is made up of two trees, and "bright" 明 , composed of the characters for "sun" and "moon." Many of the ideographs are very picturesque: a woman under a roof 安 means "peace" and a woman beside a child 好 means "good" or "to like."

A third category of characters was derived at least in part according to phonetic principles. Already by the Shang period many words were written with pictographs that actually represented some more easily depictable homophone, or word of identical pronunciation. Thus 來, which originally was a picture of some sort of grain, presumably pronounced *lai,* is the character used for the word *lai,* meaning "come."

A large subdivision of the phonetic category consists of compound characters made up of phonetics and significs. The phonetics are characters used to indicate the approximate sound of the compound character, and the significs, usually placed to the left or above the phonetic, show the category of meaning to which the word belongs. Thus hundreds of characters for words associated in some way with trees or wood, such as "maple," "pear," "branch," "to plant," "shelf," "spear," and "ladder," are made up of the character for "tree" combined with some other character used purely for its phonetic value.

The great majority of currently used characters belong to this compound type, and the significs in such characters have become the basis for the commonest system for classifying characters. In this system, 214 characters, largely made up of those commonly used as significs, are selected as "radicals," or classifiers, under which all characters are grouped and listed in

ORACLE BONE TEXT   MODERN CHINESE   LITERAL TRANSLATION

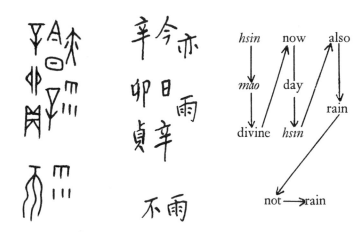

SHANG INSCRIPTION ON BONE. *The characters are to be read from top to bottom, but the lines in this particular case read from left to right. The meaning of the text is: "[On the day]* hsin-mao, *it is divined whether on this* hsin *day it will rain—or not rain."*
Most of the characters in this text are clearly identifiable from their modern forms. The second character in the second column is a picture of the sun with a spot in it, while the second character in the third column as well as the lower right-hand character show rain falling from a cloud. The upper right-hand character, showing a man's armpits (the two spots under the arms), was at this time a homophone for the undepictable word "also."

accordance with the number of brush strokes needed to write the rest of the character. Thus the word for "ladder" is classified under "tree" (radical 75) plus seven additional strokes. This is a very cumbersome system of classification as compared with alphabetic spelling, and many characters fit in only very poorly, but at least it achieves some order in what is otherwise an ocean of unique symbols.

Advantages and Disadvantages of the Writing System.   The Chinese writing system has certain drawbacks when compared with the simpler phonetic systems of the West. It obviously takes a great deal more time and effort to master. The individual characters tend to be rather complex. The average character may require some twelve or thirteen brush strokes to write, and a few take as many as twenty-five. At least two or three thousand characters must be memorized before one can read even simple texts. The emphasis on rote memory work to learn all these characters may have had a limiting influence in Chinese education, putting a premium on memorizing ability

The complexity of the system made literacy more difficult to achieve than it was in cultures with simpler writing systems, and thus helped limit upper-class life to the relative few who could find the time for protracted study. The writing system has become an increasing handicap in modern times as the need for widespread literacy has increased. Even though the Chinese invented printing, characters have made printing a much more difficult technique than in the West and so far all efforts to construct a Chinese typewriter that is anything less than a small printing press or electronic brain have proved unsuccessful. The recent simplification of some of the more commonly used characters, though helpful, has not solved the basic problems inherent in the writing system.

On the other hand, the Chinese writing system has certain merits that the Western systems lack. The very complexity of the characters and their graphic qualities give them aesthetic values far beyond mere phonetic scripts. Calligraphy is a great art in East Asia and the ancestor of all the graphic arts, for the writing brush is also the brush of the painter. A distinguished hand has always been considered the mark of a well educated man.

The characters themselves also have a sort of vitality lacking in phonetic scripts. Once they have been learned, who can forget that the character for "peace" is a woman under a roof and the character for "bright" a combination of "sun" and "moon"? Chinese characters seem to carry with them richer substance and subtler overtones than the oral words they were designed to represent, thus lending themselves to a terse vividness in both prose and poetry that is quite unattainable in our phonetically-bound writing systems. Once mastered, they can also be read more rapidly than a phonetic script.

It is easy to imbue the character with magic qualities, as the ancient Chinese undoubtedly did. The written word always took precedence over the spoken. Chinese history is full of famous documents—memorials to the throne, essays, and poems—but few great speeches. Everything written, and particularly that which survived from antiquity, was considered to be of almost sacred value. Such attitudes may help account for the high store the peoples of East Asia have placed on book learning and formal education. It may seem ironic but it is no accident that literacy rates in East Asia tend to run much higher than in other areas of comparable economic level but simpler writing systems.

Another great advantage of the Chinese writing system is that it easily surmounts differences of dialect or even more fundamental linguistic barriers. All literate Chinese, even if they speak mutually unintelligible "dialects," can read the same books and feel that classical written Chinese is their own language. If they had had a phonetic system of writing, they might have broken up into separate national groups, as did the Italians, French, Spanish, and Portuguese. The stature of China as the largest national grouping in the world is to be explained at least in part by the writing system.

The larger unity of East Asian civilization has also depended on it in great part. A love and veneration for Chinese characters has been a strong link between the various countries. Until a century ago, most books written in Korea and Vietnam and many of those written in Japan were in classical Chinese, not in the national languages. Even today educated Chinese, Japanese, and Koreans can recognize thousands of words written in characters in books from the other two countries, even if they all pronounce these words quite differently. If China had had a phonetic system of writing, East Asia would certainly not have become so distinct a unit in world civilization.

Shang Culture

Next to writing, the most remarkable finds at An-yang and other Shang sites are bronzes, consisting largely of weapons or elaborate ceremonial vessels, often of imposing size. The vessels are covered with rich designs in sharply incised lines or high relief, suggesting clay or wooden prototypes. Their beauty is enhanced by patination of varied shades of green produced by the chemical action of the soil in which they lay. The quality of bronze casting in the late Shang was extremely fine and has never been surpassed anywhere in the world. The designs appear to be entirely East Asian. There are bronze tripods, for example, which hark back to the hollow-legged tripods of the Black Pottery culture. Some vessels were cast in the shape of animals, such as the elephant, which still inhabited North China in this period when the climate was somewhat warmer and wetter than it is today.

The chief design element on the bronzes is the *t'ao-t'ieh* or animal mask. It is a frontal view of an animal head, such as a water buffalo or ram, portrayed with angular lines in a highly conventional manner. Similar designs are found at An-yang on bone artifacts and marble sculptures. The whole Shang approach to the problem of design is quite distinct from anything known in the prehistoric or ancient West, where animals were normally portrayed in profile. There are, however, parallels in other East Asian countries, in the South Pacific, and among the Indians of the Pacific Northwest. This has given rise to the concept of a Pacific Basin type of design, of which the Shang offers the earliest example.

Inscriptions occur on some early bronzes, but most Shang writing has been found incised on the "dragon bones." These are actually the undershells of tortoises, the scapulae or shoulder blades of cattle, and other flattish bones. Since they were used in a method of divination, also practiced in the Black Pottery culture, they are often called "oracle bones" and this method of divination, scapulimancy. A small groove was carved on one side of the bone and heat was then applied near this thin spot, producing cracks from which the diviner somehow derived "yes" or "no" answers to his questions.

About a tenth of the "oracle bones" have inscribed on them the questions asked, and a few also have the answer and sometimes even the eventual outcome. The questions cover such matters as sacrifices to the deities, the weather, crops, war, hunting expeditions, aid or injury by an ancestor to his living descendants, and the luck of the next ten-day period, which already had been established as the East Asian "week." We can see how significant an activity divination was from the fact that the chief ministers of the rulers all seem to have been diviners. Sacrifices were also extremely important. Usually animals were used, but sometimes liquor, probably a sort of beer, was poured on the ground in libation. Sacrifices were made to various nature deities, the cardinal points, and to Ti or Shang Ti (Supreme Ti), who may have been a "first ancestor" of the Shang people.

The Shang State and Society.   The Shang economy was mainly agricultural. The Shang also had sheep and cattle but already seem to have had the traditional Chinese abhorrence for milk and milk products. Since bronze was rare and costly, agricultural tools were made of wood or stone. Cowrie shells were used as a sort of primitive money. These shells from southern waters have left their mark on the writing system: many characters having to do with wealth and trade have the "shell" signific. Jade was highly prized, as it has been throughout Chinese history. (See Plate 1.)

Succession among the Shang rulers was often from brother to brother (thirteen cases) rather than from father to son (seventeen cases). Two of the successive capitals of these rulers were undoubtedly the cities unearthed near Cheng-chou and An-yang. How far beyond their walls they actually ruled is not known. Shang cultural remains are found scattered over a wide area in North China from the great bend of the Yellow River to central Shantung; but much of this area may have been ruled by vassal or even rival states, and the effective area of Shang control may have been fairly small. The Shang rulers were frequently at war with nearby neighbors and marauding herdsmen.

On the other hand, the state was big enough to field armies of three thousand to five thousand men, and the remains at Cheng-chou and An-yang are impressive. The style of architecture was essentially the same as that of modern China, contrasting with the stone architecture of the ancient West. The roof was carried by rows of wooden pillars, and the walls, at first made of pounded earth but in later times usually of brick, were merely non-structural screens. The pillars rested on individual foundation stones set on

SHANG AND EARLY CHOU BRONZE RITUAL VESSELS.
The left vessel, of ku *shape, is from the Shang; the
upper right, of* yu *shape, from the Shang or early Chou;
the lower right, of* kuang *shape, from the early Chou.
The upper right, vessel has a* t'ao-t'ieh *(animal mask)
of a water buffalo with upward curving horns, the
lower vessel a* t'ao-t'ieh *of a ram with in-curving horns.
Note the elephant above the* t'ao-t'ieh.

a platform of pounded earth. As is still the custom in North China, buildings were carefully oriented to face south.

Unlike the palace buildings, the houses of the common people appear to have been crude pit dwellings, as in Neolithic times. The gap between ruler and ruled is further illustrated by the grandiose scale of the royal tombs at An-yang. These were great pits, as much as forty-three feet deep and covering up to five thousand square feet, subsequently filled with beaten earth. It was customary to bury with the corpse articles of use and value, presumably for the benefit of the deceased in some afterlife. In the tombs have been found war chariots, which show that Shang was part of the war chariot culture that in the middle of the second millennium B.C. swept over the civilized world all the way from Greece to China.

Many bodies of both aristocrats and humble followers were also buried with the rulers, and there were other forms of human sacrifice, usually in multiples of ten and sometimes hundreds at a time. Some historians have concluded that the Shang was a slave society. In any case, the cleavage between ruler and ruled was very great. The Shang sovereigns, who may have started as little more than chief shamans mediating between the people and their ancestors and deities, developed during the roughly five centuries of Shang ascendancy into rulers of very great authority. Thus the tendency of the Chinese to establish and accept a unified, authoritarian state goes back to very early times.

Origins of the Authoritarian Pattern.   The early Chinese pattern of political absolutism has given rise to some interesting theories. A virtual monopoly of bronze metallurgy, bronze weapons, and chariots probably gave the ruling class great power over the other members of the state in Shang times. Certain broader factors may also have been operative. As we have seen, the family pattern of China lends itself to authoritarianism. The development of an absolute centralized state may also have been fostered by the constant need the Chinese felt for unified defense against their nomadic neighbors, as is illustrated by the Great Wall.

Some scholars have seen the need for huge cooperative efforts to keep the Yellow River within bounds and to provide for necessary drainage and irrigation as another source for the authoritarian state in China. A few men had to direct the work of a great many in order to complete these undertakings. Wherever such water-control efforts were necessary on a large scale, it is argued, a despotic or "Oriental" type of society developed, with absolutist monarchs supported by a bureaucratic official class ruling over dense peasant populations, as was the situation in ancient Egypt and Mesopotamia.

The myth that Yü, the founder of the Hsia dynasty, controlled the flood waters of China fits this theory well, and great coordinated efforts at water control did take place in the years leading up to the founding of the first great Chinese Empire. But this was about a millennium after the Shang, who themselves depended on rainfall rather than irrigation for agriculture. The water-control theory thus cannot explain the centralized absolutism of the Shang state, although it may help explain the continuance and strengthening of this pattern in later times.

The Early Chou

The Chou State. The Chou people, who conquered the Shang around 1050 B.C., lived in the Wei Valley west of the great bend of the Yellow River. Their capital was near the modern city of Sian. While the Chou were themselves an agricultural people, they lived close to the sheep-herding barbarians of the Northwest and were culturally quite distinct from the Shang. The old Neolithic Black Pottery culture seems to have persisted in the Wei Valley almost to the time of the conquest.

The Chou apparently had become vassals of the Shang, protecting the western marches of the realm, but under three successive leaders, King Wen, King Wu, and the latter's brother, the Duke of Chou, they destroyed the Shang and overran all of North China. In fact, the wide spread of early Chou remains suggests that they conquered a much larger area than the Shang had ever dominated, stretching from the Wei Valley to the eastern extremity of Shantung and from southern Manchuria to the middle and lower Yangtze Valley.

The primitive communications of the time by chariot or wagon made it impossible to administer directly so large an area. The Duke of Chou established a secondary capital at the modern Loyang in the old heartland of the Shang, but otherwise the Chou rulers delegated authority to a large number of vassals. These were for the most part their descendants or relatives, but included unrelated henchmen and local aristocrats who had acknowledged Chou suzerainty. In time these vassals became graded in a strict hierarchy of prestige with titles usually translated duke, marquis, count, viscount, and baron. Each principality was in essence a small city-state, consisting of a walled town and its surrounding countryside. How many such states there were is not known. In the eighth century, however, after many had been absorbed by others but new peripheral ones had also been added, the number seems to have been about two hundred.

Each lord, while supposedly recognizing Chou suzerainty, enjoyed autonomy within his realm. The system has often been called "feudal," and the East Asians use the same term for it as for medieval Western and Japanese feudalism. It seems dubious, however, that "feudalism" is the right word. Much of our view of the early Chou is colored by the attitudes of later Chinese thinkers, who took the early Chou as a sort of "golden age" and read back into it their own desires for political unity and organization and the emphasis on ritual, propriety, and morality that they felt should be the governing principles in politics. The resultant picture does bear some resemblances to Western feudalism, but the actualities were probably far different. Effective control depended more on bonds of blood or pseudo-blood relationships than on feudal legal principles. The Chou system was probably closer to the system of rule through satraps in West Asia of the same period than to the feudal organization of Europe two millenniums later.

The Chou, like the Shang, had a sharply divided class society, in which the hereditary lord, supported by his aristocratic warriors, ruled over the peasant masses and the outright slaves, who were used largely as domestic servants. Later writers claimed that in the early Chou eight peasant families, each with its own field, would cultivate among them a central field for the support of the lord. This system has been called the "well field" system, because the character for "well" 井 depicts the pattern of nine fields that made a unit. This is obviously a later idealization, but it may reflect a period when agricultural property and its produce were communally shared.

Chou Culture. The cultural backwardness of the Chou conquerors is attested by the fact that in the early Chou period much of the Shang culture continued almost without a break. Imposing bronze ritual vessels continued to be cast, many with lengthy inscriptions, but the designs sometimes were cruder than those of the Shang, and as the period progressed the details became weaker and plainer, perhaps because they had lost their original religious significance and had become merely traditional. The writing system continued its uninterrupted evolution, and scapulimancy was still practiced, although in time other forms of divination took its place.

Unlike the practice during the Shang, succession was from father to son (the Duke of Chou's failure to ascend the throne is a key case in point), and the kings were buried under massive, square earthen pyramids. The chief Chou deity was T'ien, which came to mean "Heaven" but was obviously anthropomorphic in origin, since the character for T'ien was originally a rough sketch of a man. The Chou kings called themselves the "Son of Heaven" and justified their conquest on the grounds that they had received the "Mandate of Heaven." The chief ceremonial activity of the kings centered around their ancestor "Heaven," while each community conducted sacrifices to the life-giving soil. Later dynasties continued these ancient rituals up until the twentieth century, and a round altar of Heaven and a square altar of Earth, both imposing structures, still stand in Peking.

3. Classic China: The Golden Age of Chinese Thought

The Later Chou

We do not know how long the early Chou maintained effective control over their wide conquests—perhaps not for long or only sporadically. The original bonds of loyalty between the kings and their vassals probably weakened over time. In 841 B.C., the tenth Chou king was driven out of his capital by its citizens, and an interregnum of thirteen years ensued. Marxist Chinese historians make much of this event as the first popular uprising in Chinese history. It produced considerable disruption, and perhaps this accounts for the fact that traditional Chinese dating becomes reliable only after that date.

The next king managed to resuscitate Chou power and is said to have led armies of 3000 chariots and 30,000 men, as compared with the 350 chariots used in the original conquest. In 770 B.C., however, what remained of Chou power was extinguished when "barbarians" in alliance with rebel Chinese principalities destroyed the capital. Tradition says that the thirteenth king, by lighting the beacon fires, had repeatedly summoned his vassals' troops merely to amuse a favorite concubine, and now when help was really needed no one responded. The royal line was re-established at the subsidiary capital of Loyang to the east, but the Chou kings never again exercised any real political or military power, retaining only certain religious and ceremonial functions until their final extinction in 256 B.C.

The period before 770 B.C. is called the Western Chou from the location of the capital, and the period after 770, the Eastern Chou. The Chinese, despite a strong emphasis on the decimal system in counting (they had little use for dozens, the seven-day week, and the like), have not traditionally counted time by centuries. Instead they have divided history into dynastic segments, such as the Western Chou and the Eastern Chou. The Chinese further subdivide part of the Eastern Chou into two shorter periods, the names of which will be explained later. These are the "Spring and Autumn" period, usually dated 722–481, and the "Warring States" period, commonly dated 403–221. The chronological chart included in this volume will help the reader coordinate the Chinese dynasties and periods with the Western system of counting years.

Technological and Economic Growth.   Later Chinese, imbued with the ideal of a unified empire, have looked back on the Eastern Chou as a period of hopeless disunity. But it was an age of dynamic growth, bursting energy, and tremendous creativity. Possibly the very lack of central authority and the multiplicity of rival states served as stimuli. In many ways the Eastern Chou is the most exciting and romantic phase of Chinese history.

In the eighth century B.C., China was still technologically behind West Asia, but by the end of the period it had largely caught up and already was the most populous land on earth. The seven largest of the Chinese states together may have had in the neighborhood of 20 million people—quite comparable to the whole of West Asia and the Mediterranean area. Iron, which had appeared about a millennium earlier in the West, became common in China by the fifth century B.C. Iron replaced bronze for weapons, and iron farming tools and the ox-drawn plow brought an agricultural revolution to China. Hitherto unfarmed areas in North China were brought under the plow, and the remaining islands of "barbarian" peoples were absorbed into the dominant culture. Grain yields were also greatly expanded by large-scale irrigation and other water-control projects, and great effort was devoted to the construction of transport canals, indicating the growth of the economic unit and the rising need to move large quantities of tax grains and other commodities over long distances.

The growth of production was accompanied by a rapid development of trade and a tremendous increase in wealth. As the Chou period progresses one hears more and more of wealthy merchants of all types. This newly risen class proved disruptive to the old aristocratic order, which perhaps in self-defense, propagated a theory that society consists of four classes: the warrior-administrators at the top, the peasants or primary producers next, the artisans or secondary producers third, and last of all the merchants, whose economic value seemed dubious to the aristocrats. However unrealistic this theory was even in late Chou times, it remained East Asian dogma for the next two millenniums.

While bolts of silk and ingots of precious metal had come into early use as media of exchange and continued to be used until modern times, copper coinage became prevalent at this time. At first the coins were in the shape of small agricultural tools in the western parts of the country and small knives in the east, but before the end of the Chou era the copper cash, a small round coin with a square hole for stringing purposes, had come into use, and it remained the standard Chinese coin until late in the nineteenth century. The late Chou also saw the appearance of other characteristic features of Chinese civilization, such as chopsticks and lacquer.

The States of the Eastern Chou Period.   Hand in hand with technological and economic progress went a steady growth of the effective political unit, as the great water-control activity of the latter centuries of the era clearly shows. Among the welter of petty city-states that covered the North China Plain, some ten already stood out by the eighth century B.C. as larger and more efficient units. These states, however, lost their leadership in later centuries to those on the periphery of the Chou cultural area. Crowded together in the center, they had less room for growth, and they were probably more constrained by tradition from making innovations in political, military, and economic techniques. The states of Lu and Sung, for example, despite the proud tradition that their rulers were descended from the Duke of Chou and the Shang royal line respectively, and despite their prominence in the early years of the Eastern Chou, gradually degenerated to the status of satellites of the peripheral states.

Ch'i was typical of the border states. Located on the eastern edge of the North China Plain, it extended its sway over the greater part of the hilly Shantung Peninsula, increasing its area sixfold in the seventh and sixth centuries B.C. and winning control over an area comparable to a modern Chinese province. On the north, in modern Shansi Province, the state of Chin carved out a comparable domain. Beyond it to the northeast, in the area around the modern Peking, was Yen, from which has been derived the literary name for Peking: Yen-ching, or the "Yen capital." In the west, Ch'in, regarded as semi-"barbarian" by the others, replaced the Chou in the Wei Valley.

In the south, the semi-"barbarian" state of Ch'u had by the eighth century built up a vast domain along the middle reaches of the Yangtze River. From the start it rejected the empty pretense of Chou rule by calling its own rulers *wang,* or "kings." To its east the state of Wu had by the sixth century come to dominate the area around the lower Yangtze. Recent archaeological discoveries indicate that it grew from an early Chou outpost among "barbarian" peoples. On the coastal region beyond Wu appeared the powerful state of Yüeh. Situated in a region of great lakes and navigable rivers, these three southern states were water powers, with fleets as well as armies. Wu is the origin of the name "Wu dialect" for the language of the Shanghai area, and in Yüeh we have the first appearance of a name that clung to the edge of the

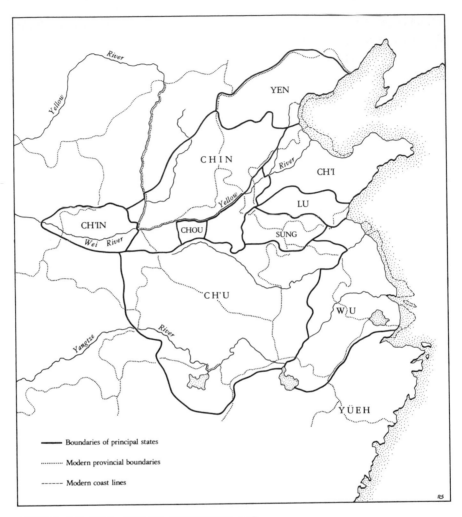

CHINA IN THE SIXTH CENTURY B.C.

advancing southern boundary of the Chinese cultural area, coming to rest
eventually in Vietnam, or "Yüeh South."

The regions ruled by the great peripheral states fell for the most part
within the area of the early Chou conquests, but they were in part inhabited
by what people in the Chinese heartland considered to be "barbarians." On
the north and west these "barbarians" presumably were pastoral folk, some
perhaps already Chinese-speaking. In the south, they were agricultural people
like the Chinese but were said to speak unintelligible tongues (though
these were probably related Sinitic languages) and they clearly had many
other distinctive cultural features. The incorporation of these "barbarian"
peoples into the Chinese cultural area during the Eastern Chou period was
the start of the great process of acculturation by which the originally non-

Chinese peoples of the Yangtze Valley and South China were gradually drawn into the main stream of Chinese civilization, except for a few still unassimilated remnants in the extreme southwest.

Political and Social Innovation.   The early Chou city-states were highly aristocratic societies. Their ruling lords claimed a sort of religious legitimacy as the maintainers of sacrifices to the common ancestors, and their warrior henchmen were largely their own relatives. But as technology advanced, wealth increased, trade grew, population rose, and the political unit expanded, this old form of aristocratic, almost tribal organization became outmoded. Many of the individual states became too large and complex for such family-like control.

The old communal use of land was gradually replaced by private ownership, and powerful new families, whose wealth was based on the lands they owned or on commerce, replaced the old aristocracy of close relatives of the lords. Newly risen families of this sort sometimes even overthrew and replaced the old rulers. One famous example of this was the split up of the northern state of Chin into the successor states of Han, Wei, and Chao. This occurred in 453 B.C. and was officially recognized by the Chou king in 403. Both dates are used as the start of the "Warring States" period.

If large domains were to be kept under control and if subjects were not to challenge the authority of their lords, there had to be stronger and more effective methods of rule than were used in the old aristocratic society. The result was the development of more impersonal political institutions and a greater centralization of power. Several important innovations of this sort are attributed to Duke Huan (685–643 B.C.) of the eastern state of Ch'i and his able minister Kuan-tzu, to whom a later book of this name is popularly attributed. They are said to have divided the population of Ch'i into geographic units controlled by the central government, instituted a uniform tax system, and reorganized the military forces by requiring that the various geographic subunits provide levies for a central army, instead of relying on such household units as the hereditary aristocracy might bring into the field. Ch'i is also said to have had an active economic policy, attempting to control prices, regulate weights and measures, and encourage trade. The first state monopolies of salt and iron production, which were to become major economic supports of centralized government in China, are also traditionally attributed to Kuan-tzu.

It is hard to say how many of these innovations actually date back to the seventh century B.C. or took place first in Ch'i. State monopolies probably did not develop that early, but all the reforms attributed to Kuan-tzu were important innovations that had appeared in China by the latter part of the Chou period. Unquestionably a major aspect of the centralization of power was the establishment of a uniform, centrally controlled system of local government and the development of a clear system of agricultural taxes. Another key factor was the appearance of bureaucratic administrators to replace the old related aristocrats as the aides of the ruler. Kuan-tzu himself is the first clear example of such a bureaucrat. Written law codes also came to replace the old system of personal rule on the basis of accepted tradition. The first known to history was that of Duke Wen (445–396) of Wei, one of the three successor states of Chin.

Military Development.   Meanwhile the scale and nature of warfare had also changed. In earlier times, strict rules of combat had apparently been observed, and there was a strong feeling that, even if subjugated, other noble lines should not be extinguished. Through this emphasis on legitimacy, the weaker central states may have sought to check the menace of the peripheral powers. But now warfare became much larger in scale and more ruthless. Conquered states were obliterated and turned into centrally controlled provinces of the victor. In the fourth and third centuries, all the principal states followed the lead of Ch'u in assuming the title of king for their rulers, thus indicating that they no longer recognized even the theory of Chou supremacy. While chariots continued in use until the late Chou, cheap iron weapons had led to a great increase in the size of fighting forces. Peasant foot soldiers replaced the aristocratic charioteers, who had been armed with expensive bronze weapons, as the backbone of the armies, which now numbered in the tens of thousands.

Another military innovation was the use of cavalry. Horseback riding, first developed by the pastoral peoples of Central and West Asia, had significant cultural influences on the Chinese wholly aside from its military impact. The greater mobility made possible by horseback riding speeded up communications between the agricultural civilizations of West and East Asia. This may account for the more rapid flow at this time of Western inventions and ideas to China, thus helping to close the technological gap that had once existed. Even in the field of the visual arts, for example, the Western emphasis on portrayal in silhouette, as transmitted by the intermediary nomads, came to replace the old Shang approach to design.

The use of the horse made the pastoral northern neighbors of China a greater military threat than they had been before. One result of this was the erection by the northern Chinese states of long walls, which when later unified became the Great Wall of China. Another result was the replacement of chariots by cavalry in Chinese armies. This change was perhaps hastened by the introduction of the crossbow, probably a local invention, which, together with the old native composite bow, made the cavalry a formidable force. Still another result of horseback riding was the introduction of close-fitting jackets and trousers, which were more convenient than the full sleeves and flowing robes of the traditional garb. The Chinese thus started on their way

Mounted archer design in silhouette, stamped on a late Chou tile.

to becoming the first great agricultural people to clothe both men and women in trousers.

The Search for Political Stability. The states of the Eastern Chou period, in the face of fading Chou authority and the growing ferocity of warfare, made many efforts to minimize fighting and stabilize the political situation. Bilateral or multilateral interstate conferences were held with considerable frequency; disarmament proposals were discussed; treaties were signed and alliances formed. Marriages between princely lines were an important means of strengthening alliances, while hostages were widely used to insure the loyalty of a satellite state.

The semi-"barbarian" state of Ch'u in the south posed a special threat to the states of the North China Plain, and they frequently leagued together against Ch'u. This league first took effective shape in 651, when Duke Huan of Ch'i was recognized as hegemon of the confederation. The system of hegemony, however, gave China only brief and sporadic stability, lasting no longer than the lifetime of each strong man who was able to establish himself as hegemon. After Duke Huan, the next to achieve this status was the duke of Chin in 632. The original purpose of the system was completely lost when the king of Ch'u became the third hegemon before the turn of the century. At times during the sixth century B.C. some stability was achieved through a formalized balance of power between Chin in the north and Ch'u in the south. Wu meanwhile had been rising rapidly on Ch'u's eastern frontier and in 482 won recognition as the paramount military power of China, only to be crushed and annexed in 473 by Yüeh, the most "barbarian" of all the states.

There were no further attempts to organize an interstate order in ancient China. Brute conquest had become the order of the day. After the breakup of Chin in 453 B.C., the chief contenders for supremacy were Ch'i in the east, Ch'in in the west, and Ch'u in the south. Ch'u exterminated Yüeh in 334 and the small central state of Lu in 249. Ch'i, surviving a usurpation of the throne, annexed the central state of Sung in 286, and Ch'in calmly exterminated Chou itself in 256. Finally, in a series of great campaigns between 230 and 221 B.C., Ch'in conquered all the remaining independent states, unifying China for the first time and opening a new phase in its history.

The Age of the Philosophers and the Classics

The Early Philosophers.   The Eastern Chou was a period of great economic growth, social change, and political development. The failure of old authority, both temporal and spiritual, as well as the current innovations, posed new problems. Time-worn traditions had to be discarded and new guiding values found. Men's minds could wander at will and did range more freely than ever again in East Asian history.

One is struck by the parallel in time between this intellectual outburst in China and the heyday of the Greek philosophers, the Hebraic prophets, and the historical Buddha and other early religious leaders in India. Throughout the whole civilized world it was a time of prodigious philosophical activity. One reason for this may have been mutual intellectual stimulation between the great centers of civilization in this age of accelerated communications. Another may have been that all these areas had by this time become wealthy enough to support large numbers of thinkers. Moreover, the increased pace of human invention was shattering traditional points of view, and therefore men everywhere were beginning consciously to grapple with the fundamental problems of the meaning and purpose of life and society. The challenge was the same, but the answers varied greatly, setting the civilizations of the Mediterranean, South Asia, and East Asia off in decidedly different directions. The contrasting philosophical attitudes developed during this great age of intellectual ferment still stand out among the factors that differentiate these major cultural zones.

Chinese philosophical interest from this time on centered primarily on man as a social and political animal. It was overwhelmingly "humanistic," or perhaps one should say "social," because the emphasis was more on society than on the individual. This was in sharp contrast to the emphasis on the divine and otherworldly in the traditional philosophies of India and the Mediterranean world. It is difficult to determine why Chinese thought took this particular direction. Possibly political and social problems posed themselves more vividly to Chinese minds because the interstate anarchy of the Chou period existed within a single large cultural unit.

The early Chinese philosophers, in any case, were first of all practical politicians. They were part of the new class of bureaucrats, produced by the spread of literacy and the needs of an increasingly complex political system. Such men often wandered from state to state, offering their services where they would be most appreciated. Great thinkers among them, whether successful or not as practical politicians, attracted followers and thus became teachers. Their disciples gradually formed into schools of philosophy, and from these schools the sayings of the original masters, as reworked and supplemented by many later hands, eventually emerged as the philosophical books of Chou times.

The Classics. Although the philosophers were often daring innovators, many of them looked to supposedly golden ages of the past for their inspiration, as have many other thinkers elsewhere in the world. In a civilization particularly concerned with the problems of society, it was natural that history, as the repository of human experience, should become the special focus of attention. This interest in the past, together with the peculiar Chinese respect for the written word, produced a tremendous veneration for the writings of earlier times. This, of course, has been a common trait throughout the world, but it seems to have been particularly strong among the Chinese. Confucius and other ancient Chinese philosophers looked upon the writings of earlier ages as classics from which they drew their own teachings, and this idea persisted in East Asia until recent times. For over two thousand years Chinese scholars, when faced with new problems, tried to wring the answers from reinterpretations of the classics.

To the Chinese, with their love of order and classification, "the Classics" is not just a vague term for ancient literature in general but means a clearly specified set of books associated with the dominant Confucian tradition. These works, together with the vast body of commentaries that has grown up around them, constitute the first of the traditional four divisions of Chinese literature. The various listings of the Classics were all made after Chou times and consequently contain works of diverse epochs, but the Five Classics, the earliest and most important listing, dating from the second century B.C., include the most ancient and most venerated works.

The first of the Five Classics is the *Classic of Songs* (*Shih ching,* also known as the *Book of Poetry*), which consists of 305 songs dating from the tenth to the seventh centuries B.C. Some are love songs, others political poems or ritual hymns, but all are characterized by such patterns of meter, rhythm, and rhyme that they clearly are not just folk songs but the products of a sophisticated literary tradition. Poetry was obviously an important part of Chinese culture even at this early time, and the ability to recite and also to compose poetry has remained ever since the mark of the educated man.

The *Classic of Documents* (*Shu ching,* also known as the *Book of History*) contains semihistorical documents and speeches dating from the early centuries of the Chou period, but a large part of the text is now known to consist of later forgeries. The development of two differing versions of the *Shu ching* in the second century B.C. and the problem of the forged portions of the work have led to endless philological and philosophical controversy ever since.

The *Classic of Changes* (*I ching,* also known as the *Book of Divination*) is another work of mixed age. It is built up around the eight trigrams and sixty-four hexagrams which developed as a system of divination alternative to scapulimancy. The eight trigrams, which are frequently portrayed in East Asian art, are all the possible permutations of three-line combinations of complete or broken lines. If six lines are used instead of three, the possible combinations number sixty-four. Probably by drawing odd or even numbers of stalks of the milfoil plant, a specific trigram or hexagram could be selected, and the *Classic of Changes* would then be consulted on this hexagram. It was, in other words, a diviner's handbook.

The *Spring and Autumn Annals* (*Ch'un ch'iu*) is a brief chronological record of major events that occurred in the state of Lu or were reported there. The period it covers from 722 to 481 B.C. became known as the "Spring and Autumn" period. The text is terse and entirely factual, but Confucius, according to tradition, and certainly later philosophers read great philosophical significance into the choice of words used to describe each event. The tradition that Confucius himself compiled this work, however, is undoubtedly false.

The last of the Five Classics, the *Record of Rituals* (*Li chi,* also known as the *Book of Rites*), is a compilation made in the second century B.C. out of earlier materials dealing with rites and rituals. These were, as we shall see, key elements in the whole Confucian concept of social order, and this classic clearly stems from the Confucian tradition. The others, too, became so closely identified with Confucianism that all five are commonly called the Confucian Classics.

More than a thousand years after the end of the Chou, four relatively short works were selected from the vast mass of classical literature as the supreme embodiment of Confucian teachings. These, known as the Four Books, included two chapters taken from the *Record of Rituals:* the *Great Learning* (*Ta hsüeh*) and the *Doctrine of the Mean* (*Chung yung*). The other two works were the *Analects* (*Lun-yü,* literally meaning "Conversations") of Confucius himself and a comparable work of his greatest successor, the *Mencius* (*Meng-tzu*). The *Analects* and *Mencius* together with the Five Classics and a few other early works are also commonly classified as the

A carved white jade showing the yin-yang *symbol (see page 49) surrounded by the eight trigrams.*

Thirteen Classics. In this grouping, the *Spring and Autumn Annals* counts as three works because of its three so-called commentaries. Two are simple exegetical works, but the third, the *Tso chuan* (*Tradition of Tso*), is an elaborate political history, containing much imaginative reconstruction of detail but constituting nevertheless the chief historical source for the period.

The writings of non-Confucian philosophers were never included among the Classics, and various other ancient works of comparable historical or literary interest to the Classics failed to win official acceptance. The most outstanding poetic collection of the late Chou period was the *Elegies of Ch'u* (*Ch'u tz'u*), made up largely of poems by Ch'ü Yüan, an aristocrat of the southern state of Ch'u who lived at the beginning of the third century B.C. His *Li sao* includes a fanciful flight through time and space that shows a rich imagination quite absent from the *Classic of Songs* and perhaps characteristic of the semi-"barbarian" peoples of the South.

Confucianism and Taoism

Confucius. It is fitting that the first man we know to have been a pro-fessional teacher and philosopher in China should always have been recog-nized in East Asia as the greatest of all teachers and philosophers. We call him Confucius, the Latinized form of K'ung-fu-tzu (the *tzu* meant "Mas-ter"). He lived around 551–479 B.C., and what we know of him is largely drawn from the *Analects.* This work consists for the most part of Confucius' answers to questions, prefaced by the phrase, "The Master said." It was written by disciples or perhaps by disciples of disciples and includes many later additions.

Confucius was a native of the tradition-bound central state of Lu. He aspired to high political office and wandered in vain from state to state in search of appointment. Thus, in his chosen role as a practical politician, he was a failure; in his incidental occupation as a teacher, however, time proved him an unparalleled success. At first glance the concepts Confucius taught seem unexciting and flat. He showed the bias of his day in his para-mount interest in political problems. While he fully recognized the spirits and Heaven (T'ien), sometimes showing a sense of mission derived from the latter, he was obviously not much interested in the suprahuman realm. To an inquiry about death, he replied, "Not yet understanding life, how can you understand death?" Even in the political sphere, he merely claimed to be a devoted student of antiquity and transmitter of the wisdom of the past. The disorder of his own day, he felt, could be corrected if men would return to the political and social order supposedly created by the founders of the Chou dynasty, King Wen and the Duke of Chou.

To return to the ancient Way, Confucius felt, men must play their assigned roles in a fixed society of authority. The idea is succinctly expressed in the statement: "Let the ruler be a ruler and the subject a subject; let the father be a father and the son a son." Later this concept was expressed by the term "the rectification of names" (*cheng ming*), by which Confucians really meant that society should be made to conform with theory.

All this sounds ultraconservative, but Confucius was in fact a great, though probably unconscious, innovator in his basic concept that good government was fundamentally a matter of ethics. He did not question the hereditary right of the lords to rule, but he insisted that their first duty was to set a proper example of sound ethical conduct. In a day when might was right, he argued that the ruler's virtue and the contentment of the people, rather than power, should be the true measures of political success. Chinese thought before Confucius might be characterized as premoral; it centered on auguries and sacrifices. Confucius was China's first great moral-ist, the founder of a great ethical tradition in a civilization which above all others came to concentrate on ethical values.

FILIAL PIETY. *Later Confucianists emphasized filial piety as a cardinal virtue. A famous story, illustrated (top) in this Han stone engraving (second century* A.D.*), tells of "Old Lai-tzu," who in order to show his seventy-year-old parents that seventy is not old, amuses them by dressing and playing like a small child. "Old Lai-tzu" became one of the Twenty-Four Stories of Filial Piety, memorized by every youngster. Dressed like a child (right), he plays with toys (a Sung painting by Chao Meng-chien, 1199–1295), and in a Shanghai woodblock of 1873 (left) he amuses his parents by purposely stumbling with his buckets.*

Confucius' ideal was the *chün-tzu,* literally "ruler's son" or "aristocrat," a term which at his hand changed its meaning from "a noble" to "a man of nobility." It is perhaps best translated as "gentleman" in the sense of a cultivated man or superior man. He had a great deal to say about the virtues the "gentleman" should possess. These were uprightness or inner integrity (*chih*), righteousness (*i*), conscientiousness toward others or loyalty (*chung*), altruism or reciprocity (*shu*), and above all, love or human-heartedness (*jen*).

The necessary qualities of the "gentleman," Confucius felt, were not limited to these inner virtues. He must also have *wen*, meaning "culture" or possibly "polish," and *li*, literally "ritual," that is, an understanding of proper etiquette and social usage. Confucius was not interested in producing "diamonds in the rough." As he says, "Uprightness uncontrolled by etiquette becomes rudeness." Like Aristotle, he felt that proper music helped produce the proper ethical attitudes. His emphasis on the *li* of antiquity contributed to the tremendous importance of ritual and etiquette in later Confucianism and the reliance in East Asia on inculcating inner attitudes through the practice of external forms—a sound pedagogical principle that may be too little honored in the contemporary West.

The judicious balancing of inner virtues and external polish is characteristic of the moderation of Confucius in all his ideas. Great philosophers and religious leaders in India and in the West have commonly dealt in absolutes; that is, they have tended to emphasize logical and mathematical absolutes. Confucius was a relativist, thinking in social and human terms. He set the East Asian pattern of compromise, of always seeking the middle path. As the *Mencius* so aptly says, "Confucius did not go to extremes."

Moderation and balance may help explain the eventual triumph of Confucianism. Its basic political conservatism made it popular with most subsequent rulers in East Asia, and its high ethical principles gave political authority a stronger foundation than mere hereditary right and served as a constant stimulus for the improvement of government. Another basic reason for its success was its timeliness. A bureaucracy of the educated was slowly growing up in China in response to political needs, and this functional group required a philosophy, which Confucius admirably supplied. While never questioning the legitimacy of hereditary power, Confucius assumed that men of superior learning, whatever their original social status, had the right to tell the rulers how they should conduct themselves and their government. Confucius thus propounded the idea of a "career open to talent" —a concept that was essentially revolutionary and an implicit challenge to hereditary power.

Taoism. Next to Confucianism, the most important stream in Chinese thought is Taoism (pronounced *dowism*). It was in large part a philosophy of retreat and withdrawal on the part of thinkers who were appalled by perpetual warfare, instability, and death and so turned away from the struggle for power, status, and wealth. In the face of infinite time and space, they accepted the unimportance of individuality except as human beings are individual manifestations of vast cosmic forces. This philosophy constituted a protest of common men against the growing despotism of rulers. It also expressed the rebellion of the very uncommon man of intellect or sensitivity against the growing rigidity of the moralists, who were following in the footsteps of Confucius. Where both the moralists and the rulers sought to bring men into conformity with social patterns, the Taoists stoutly championed the independence of each individual, whose only concern, they maintained, should be to fit into the great pattern of nature. This was the *Tao,* literally the "Road" or "Way," a term used by Confucius to describe the social system he advocated but given a metaphysical interpretation in Taoism.

Some scholars have associated early Taoism with the state of Ch'u in the Yangtze Valley, suggesting that it may represent an enrichment of Chinese thought derived in part from "barbarian" sources. Its attempt to fit human life into nature's rhythms may also represent a philosophical expression of the interest of the early Chinese in nature deities, fertility cults, and the ruler's role as mediator between nature and man. Taoist mysticism, which may have been at the core of the movement, might also have derived from the early shamans. The latter, through self-induced trances, had communicated directly with the spirits; the Taoists, through "sitting and forgetting" and "fasts of the mind," experienced trance-like ecstasies in which they achieved the state of the "true man" and directly apprehended the oneness of the universe. Such practices may have been influenced by Indian yoga, for the Taoists, like the Indians, emphasized breathing exercises.

Our chief knowledge of Taoism of the Chou period is derived from three books of unknown authorship and somewhat doubtful date. The most venerated of these is the *Lao-tzu* or *Tao te ching (The Way and Power Classic).* It is a composite text, probably dating from the third century B.C., though attributed to a presumably mythical sage known as Lao-tzu, or the "Old Master," whose traditional dates have been fixed to give him a slight edge in seniority over Confucius. Terse and cryptic in style, the *Tao te ching* has given itself to diverse interpretations by later Chinese thinkers and a startling variety of translations into Western languages.

The second text is the *Chuang-tzu,* also probably of the third century B.C. but attributed to a man of this name of the late fourth century. Consisting of delightful parables, metaphors, and poetic passages, it is a work of high literary merit and represents the most important formulation of early Taoist thought. The third work, the *Lieh-tzu,* which in content and style is much like the *Chuang-tzu,* is variously attributed to the same period or to the third century A.D.

Like all mystics, the Taoists found it difficult to express their basic ideas in words. As they said, "The one who knows does not speak, and the one who speaks does not know." The *Tao* is founded on a nameless, formless "Non-being" which is, in essence, the totality of the natural processes. Despite constant flux, the *Tao* is unitary, having no distinctions of big or little, good or bad, life or death. The relativity of all things and the dependence of any quality on its opposite are constant Taoist themes. As they say, "Water, which is life to fish, is death to man," and "It is only because everyone recognizes beauty as beauty that we have the idea of ugliness."

The man who can transcend mundane human distinctions and become one with the *Tao* is "beyond all harm" and achieves "tranquillity in the midst of strife." The key to merging with the *Tao* is *wu-wei* or "doing nothing." By this the Taoists did not mean complete inaction but rather doing what comes naturally: "Do nothing and nothing will be not done." If left to itself, the universe proceeds smoothly according to its own harmonies. Man's efforts to change or improve nature only destroy these harmonies and produce chaos. There is a knack to all spontaneous accomplishment which conscious effort only mars. The sage knows no ambition and therefore experiences no failure. He does not even attempt to teach others. By this criterion, our Taoist authors are themselves clearly imperfect.

The Taoists were sufficiently in tune with the prevailing interests of the day to draw their own picture of a perfect society. Like other Chinese philosophers, they looked back to a golden age, but for them this past was a time of perfect knowledge, before the ancients even realized that "things had come into existence," much less had recognized the "distinction" between things or reached the consequent expression of "approval and disapproval." The concept of good and bad and the embodiment of this concept in rituals, they felt, were the real sources of human misery. The Confucian sages thus were the unwitting villains of history. The virtues they had invented were the reasons for the existence of vice. Law was the source of crime; without wealth there could be no stealing.

Primitivity was the ideal of the Taoists. Knowledge can only corrupt. In the *Chuang-tzu* we find the parable of Primitivity, whose two friends, Change and Uncertainty, decided to give him the usual seven apertures that are needed for seeing, hearing, breathing, and eating; this they did with success, boring one a day, but Primitivity died in the process. The Taoists laud the peasant who, though he knew of the water wheel, chose to carry water up from a well on his back, realizing that ingenious devices would lead to a devious mind. The political ideal of the Taoists was a small state from which the cocks and dogs of a nearby state could be heard, but whose people were so content that none had ever bothered to visit this neighboring village. Over such a primitive, passive society the Taoist sage would rule, without effort and without benevolence, accomplishing everything by doing nothing.

Taoism, as a school of philosophy, suffered serious debasement in later centuries, but its basic attitudes remained strong throughout Chinese history. It obviously supplied things which otherwise were weak or lacking in Chinese society. Growing political conformity and heavy Confucian morality were not conducive to aesthetic expression. The Chinese, however, have always had a strong aesthetic urge, which the individual freedom of Taoism and its mystical union with nature encouraged. Chinese artists and poets, however closely identified with the Confucian tradition, have usually been Taoists at heart.

Taoism, in fact, has served as an admirable balance to the dominant concepts of Chinese culture. The centralization of power placed sharp limits on human freedom; Confucian morality and insistence on social conformity were even more restrictive. But in Taoism the individual could achieve self-expression; his intellect was free to wander at will. Since neither Confucianism nor Taoism were jealously exclusive religions in the Western sense, the individual and even the whole of society could be Confucian and Taoist at the same time, achieving perhaps a healthier psychological balance on these two bases than could have been achieved on only one. The man in power was usually a Confucian positivist, seeking to save society. The same man out of power became a Taoist quietist, intent on blending with nature around him. The active bureaucrat of the morning became the dreamy poet or nature lover of the evening. This balanced dualism in philosophy and in personality has persisted until the modern day.

Other Philosophic Schools

The Naturalists and the Logicians.   Confucianism and Taoism were by no means the only philosophies that flourished in late Chou times. With a characteristic love of categorizing, the Chinese have dubbed the proliferation of philosophical teachings in this period "The Hundred Schools."

One school, which might be called the Naturalists, consisted of men who attempted to explain nature's working on the basis of certain cosmic principles. One of their concepts was the basic dualism of nature: *yang* is male, light, hot, active; *yin* is female, dark, cold, passive. Unlike the dualism of the Mediterranean world, in which good and evil are in perpetual conflict, *yin* and *yang* are mutually complementary and balancing. The greater *yang* grows, the sooner it will yield to *yin*; the sun at noon is starting to give way to night. The interdependence of the two principles was well symbolized by an interlocking figure (see page 43), which today is used as the central element in the flag of the Republic of Korea. Actually, the *yin-yang* concept often seems more useful than Western dualism for analyzing nature and also human affairs. It neatly fits the rhythms of day and night, summer and winter, and the balancing roles of male and female. To apply it to the subject matter of this chapter, one might say that Confucianism is the *yang* of Chinese thought and Taoism the *yin*.

Another basic concept of the Naturalists was that all nature is made up of varying combinations of the "five elements" or "five powers": wood, metal, fire, water, and earth. The parallel to the four elements of the Greeks (earth, fire, air, and water) is striking. The "five elements" concept led in time to the development of an extensive pseudoscience that persisted through later ages. Cosmic correlations were worked out among the five elements and other categories of five: colors, tastes, sounds, planets, directions (including the center), and so on. With the addition of numerology and astrology, the possibilities became infinite. The ancient calendar signs were also incorporated into the system. These were the ten "heavenly stems" and twelve "earthly branches" (associated with the signs of the zodiac). When combined together in a sequence of pairs of characters, these formed the traditional cycle of sixty, which was used for counting time in periods of sixty days and sixty years. As applied to the lay of the land and the proper locations for houses, graves, and the like, this pseudoscience became geomancy (*feng-shui,* literally meaning "wind and water").

Another group of philosophers, the Logicians or School of Names, like the Sophists of Greece, were groping toward a system of logic by analyzing the meaning of words. For example, one of their most famous propositions propounded in the fourth century B.C. was that "a white horse is not a horse," presumably meaning that the adjective "white," in this phrase, makes "white horse" no longer applicable to the universal concept "horse." The ideas of the Logicians were condemned by later Chinese as frivolous and unprofitable.

Mo-tzu.   Confucianism's chief early competitor was the school of Mo-tzu, who was born around or soon after the death of Confucius. His teachings are found in a work known as the *Mo-tzu,* which contains essays, as well as dialogues like those in the *Analects.* Mo-tzu's concentrated attacks on Confucianism suggest that he may have represented a heretical offshoot of that school, while his interest in logic may have given rise to the school of Logicians.

In most matters Mo-tzu took a more extreme stand than Confucius. Where the latter advocated that men of learning should guide the rulers, Mo-tzu saw no reason why hereditary princes should not relinquish their thrones to their obvious superiors. While Confucius had been a traditionalist at heart, Mo-tzu was strictly a utilitarian. He advocated measures to enrich the country, increase the population, and bring order to the state. Anything that did not contribute to these ends he attacked with vehemence. Food, clothing, and housing should be limited to bare necessities. He had no use for any aesthetic expression and advocated the suppression of all emotions. Music and all the ceremonial *li* of the Confucianists were wasteful. In particular, Mo-tzu inveighed against elaborate funerals and the three-year period of mourning for one's parents, which were part of the Confucian system. Warfare was the greatest waste of all. His solution to the problems it poses was to develop the defense until offense became impractical. The history of the next two centuries presents overwhelming evidence of the failure of Mo-tzu's pacifistic views, and later ages esteemed his writings far less than they did the *Sun-tzu,* the late Chou classic on the military arts.

Mo-tzu did favor sacrifices to the spirits as bringing worldly blessings, and he accepted a moral Heaven which would provide the final sanction for his teachings by meting out appropriate rewards and punishments. There was thus a definitely authoritarian strain in his teachings. From his large following he demanded strict obedience, and he bequeathed his authority to a line of Grand Masters of the school. Not unnaturally, he envisioned a rigidly disciplined state, in which the subordinate at each level would follow the lead of his superior in all matters.

Mo-tzu's panacea for achieving his utilitarian utopia was the doctrine of universal love. The Confucians, accepting the family system and the complexities of society, were developing at this time a theory of graded love, dependent on the specific relationships among individuals. Mo-tzu felt that the interests of all would be better served if "everyone would love every other person as much as he loves himself."

It is an interesting question why Mo-tzu's school did not survive the third century B.C. He had a better organized following than Confucius, and for a while his ideas may have had greater currency. The Westerner recognizes in his "universal love," utilitarianism, pacifism, awareness of the otherworldly, and interest in problems of logic, concepts that could have greatly enriched Chinese thought. But Mo-tzu's ideas may have seemed too extreme to the Chinese of his time. They did not care for his austere utilitarianism and complete lack of psychological subtlety; they preferred the moderate but practical graded love of the Confucians to his lofty but seemingly impractical "universal love."

Mencius and Hsün-tzu.   A philosopher who succeeded where Mo-tzu failed in passing on his doctrines to later ages was Meng-tzu, known to the West in the Latinized form, Mencius. His book, the *Mencius,* was in the twelfth century elevated to the status of a classic, second only to the *Analects.* A long work of great literary merit and deep psychological perception, the *Mencius* has left a profound mark on East Asian civilization.

Mencius, who lived around 370–290 B.C., came from an area near Lu. Like Confucius, he wandered from state to state seeking high government office without success. But he and his large retinue of disciples were well received by a series of rulers, whom Mencius treated with surprising disdain. Mencius considered himself merely a transmitter of Confucius' Way of the ancients, but in fact he added important new emphases. One was that man is by nature good. Anyone, he pointed out, will spontaneously feel alarm and pity if he suddenly sees a child about to fall into a well. (Such reasoning by example and analogy is typical of Mencius and most of the philosophers of his day.) This inborn goodness can be developed by inner self-cultivation and also by education. Men should consciously strive to extend their love to those beyond the narrow family circle, which spontaneously evokes this feeling.

In the political field, Mencius was even more insistent than Confucius that government was primarily an exercise in ethics. He identified Mo-tzu's utilitarianism with gross opportunism and maintained that the guiding principle of government should be not profit but what is right. He confidently believed that if any ruler showed himself to be a fully moral man the whole land would inevitably gravitate into his hands. This was the real "Kingly Way." The rule of the truly moral king, he argued, is characterized by his benevolence toward his people. He provides schooling for them and above all sees to their economic well-being. Mencius extolled the communal ownership of property under the "well field" system, as he interpreted this supposedly ancient institution. There is no way to become a true king, he reasoned, except by providing for the well-being of the people and thus winning their support. In fact, the "Mandate of Heaven," the basic justification for the ruler's power, manifests itself only through the acceptance of a ruler by his people; if the people kill or depose him it is clear that he has lost Heaven's support. In this way, Mencius took the argument that the Chou had used to justify their overthrow of the Shang and turned it into a justification of any successful rebellion.

Mencius' contributions to the main stream of Chinese thought were second only to those of Confucius. His concept of the goodness of human nature, which meant, in essence, that all men are created morally equal, contributed much to the egalitarianism of subsequent Chinese society. His insistence that government must be on behalf of the people and requires their tacit consent helps account for the high political ideals the Chinese were able to maintain throughout much of their history.

Hsün-tzu (about 300–237 B.C.) was another Confucianist who left a deep mark on Chinese civilization, though he was condemned by later men as unorthodox. In his day, however, he was a great success both as a politician and teacher, and sections of his book, the *Hsün-tzu,* which is made up of well-organized essays, were incorporated into the *Record of Rituals.*

Hsün-tzu flatly contradicted Mencius' basic tenet that man is naturally good. Human nature, he argued, is derived from an impersonal, amoral

Heaven; man's emotions and natural desires lead to conflict and therefore are bad. The cure for this situation is improvement through education. The teacher is all-important and therefore to be revered. The process of learning "begins with reciting the Classics and ends in learning the *li.*" Hsün-tzu's concept of "the Classics" and *li* as the repository of all essential wisdom, the key role he assigned formal education and teachers, and his flat disbelief in spirits, all became accepted ideas in the Confucian mainstream. His emphasis on education, rituals, a hierarchic order, and strict rule through admonishments and punishments also seem to have contributed to a growing authoritarian trend in government.

The Legalists. These authoritarian tendencies and Hsün-tzu's pessimistic evaluation of human nature were developed further by a group of philosophers and practical politicians known as the Legalists, who for the most part were closely associated with the state of Ch'in. A leading thinker of this school, Han-fei-tzu (died 233 B.C.), and a prominent Ch'in statesman identified with it, Li Ssu (died 208 B.C.), were both disciples of Hsün-tzu. The Legalists may also have been influenced by Mo-tzu's utilitarian doctrine and his insistence on absolute obedience, as well as by the Taoist concept of an amoral natural order and their contempt for conventional ethics and book learning. Legalist ideas found fullest exposition in the *Han-fei-tzu*, which contains some essays by the philosopher of this name.

The Legalists believed that severe laws and harsh punishments, though hateful to the people, are the only means of bringing them the order and security for which they yearn. The people are like the baby who howls when its boil is lanced. The appeal of other philosophers to the Way of the ancients was dismissed by the Legalists: different times require different methods. Since the people are stupidly selfish and the bureaucrats untrustworthy self-seekers, the ruler cannot rely on their moral virtues but must control all alike by clearly defined rewards and punishments—in other words, by a detailed code of penal laws. Men should be judged not by their motives but by their accomplishments. Anyone who fails to achieve what he is assigned to do must be punished. People are to be made mutually responsible for one another's actions, and those who fail to denounce a transgressor are to be considered guilty of the same crime. If the penalties are made harsh, the people will be forced into such complete obedience that there will, in fact, be no penalties.

Right, to the Legalists, consisted simply in what the ruler desired. Though denying all hereditary rights except those of the ruler, they assumed hereditary kingship, and their whole philosophy was designed to aid the ruler in consolidating his position and power. They took for granted that the ruler's objective would be the creation of a prosperous and militarily strong state.

Merchants, intellectuals, and other unproductive and unmartial groups should not be tolerated. All aspects of life should be so regulated as to produce maximum wealth and military might for the state.

In recent years, the Legalists have often been called totalitarians. The name might be fully justified if they had had the technical means of popular control and propaganda of their twentieth-century counterparts. In terms of their own day, they were reactionary in their unquestioning acceptance of royal absolutism and an agrarian society of an earlier age. At the same time, they were undoubtedly part of the wave of the future in their emphasis on a universal system of law and impersonal, uniform relations between the government and the people it ruled. This emphasis, after all, was in large part the product of the needs of the larger, more complex political units of the day.

While the concept of law is one of the glories of Western civilization, in China, Legalism has been a despised term for more than two millenniums. This is because the Legalist concept of law fell far short of the Roman. Whereas Western law has been conceived of as a human embodiment of some higher order of God or nature, the law of the Legalists represented only the ruler's fiat. China developed little civil law to protect the citizen; law remained largely administrative and penal, something the people attempted to avoid as much as possible. Whereas Westerners have felt it safer to be ruled by impersonal laws rather than by fallible judges, the Chinese, presumably following Mencius in his estimate of human nature, have felt it safer to be ruled by ethically-minded adminstrators rather than by impersonal and, in their estimate, purely arbitrary laws.

Despite the condemnation of later ages, Legalism left a lasting mark on Chinese civilization. Through the triumph of Ch'in and the imperial system that Ch'in originated, it became an important part of the Chinese political tradition, partially accounting for the highly centralized government of later times and its harsh and often arbitrary rule. Legalism naturally leads us to the great political transition in Chinese history of the late third century B.C., when Ch'in unified the whole country and founded the Chinese Empire.

4. The First Chinese Empire:
The Ch'in and Han Dynasties

Ch'in Creates the Empire

Ch'in's capital region was the Wei Valley, where previously the Chou had risen to power. The defense of this area was simple, because easy access to it from the rest of China was limited to the narrow strip of land between river and hills at the great bend of the Yellow River. The Wei Valley also was a peripheral area where there was room for growth at the expense of the nomads on the northwest and the less advanced agricultural peoples to the southwest. Ch'in annexed two semi-"barbarian" states in the Szechwan Basin in 318 B.C. Contact with the "barbarians" also maintained the martial arts. Ch'in, for example, developed cavalry in the fourth century B.C. Ch'in also faced a simpler water-control problem in the Wei Valley than did the states which sought to control the Yellow River. In the third century B.C. it built an irrigation and transport canal that greatly increased the productivity and population of the Wei Valley, and Ch'in engineers are credited with the marvelous irrigation system of the Chengtu Plain in Szechwan.

Another reason for Ch'in's triumph was its wholehearted application of the new techniques of political and military organization that the Legalists advocated. The first great surge forward took place under the leadership of Shang Yang, whose name has been incorrectly linked with a third-century Legalist work, the *Book of Lord Shang.* A native of East China, Shang Yang was the leading official of Ch'in from 361 until his disgrace and death in 338 B.C. He is said to have instituted a strict system of rewards and punishments, forced all persons into "productive" occupations, set up a system of mutual responsibility and spying among the people, and attempted to replace the old hereditary aristocracy by a new, purely honorary aristocracy based on military achievements.

The most important of Shang Yang's reforms was the effort to bring all the territory of the state under the direct control of the central government. For some time in Ch'in and some of the other larger states, newly acquired territories had been made into districts (*hsien,* sometimes translated "subprefectures" or "counties"). Each of these probably represented an old administrative unit of a walled town and its supporting countryside. Also, along the borders large military units had been set up under the name of commanderies (*chün*). In 350 Shang Yang divided the whole of Ch'in for the first time into thirty-one districts. These various measures, which centralized political control and maximized military power, enabled Ch'in to defeat a coalition of rival states. It then went on in 256 to exterminate Chou.

Unification under the First Emperor.   The unification of China was accomplished by a Ch'in king who ascended the throne as a boy in 246 B.C. He was assisted in his rule first by Lü Pu-wei, who had originally made his fortune as a merchant, and after Lü's downfall in 237 by Hsün-tzu's former disciple Li Ssu. The final unification came with amazing speed. Between 230 and 221, Han, Chao, Wei, Ch'u, Yen, and Ch'i fell in rapid succession. By 221 the King of Ch'in had created what he believed was a universal and everlasting empire. Grandiloquently he adopted the title *Shih Huang-ti,* "First Emperor," using for the new term "emperor" two words that previously had been used for deities and mythological early rulers.

It might have seemed natural for the First Emperor to parcel out his conquests among his relatives and generals as satrapies, as was the system in the newly risen empires of India and West Asia. On Li Ssu's advice, however, he applied the centralized system of Ch'in to the whole of his conquests, dividing the land into thirty-six (later forty-two) commanderies and these into districts. He also applied the Ch'in system of equal, impersonal laws and taxation to the whole land. He confiscated the arms of the states he had conquered and collected their hereditary aristocracies at his capital in the Wei Valley near the site of the ancient Chou capital. Here he built a great palace and erected a mausoleum within a veritable man-made mountain. Life-size ceramic figures of warriors, retainers, and horses by the thousands have recently been found nearby.

Not content with the conquest of the whole Chinese cultural area, the First Emperor sent his armies south, where they incorporated into the empire large numbers of the "barbarian" peoples of what is now South China and penetrated to the coast near modern Canton and into the northern part of the present Vietnam. Along the northwestern frontier the Ch'in armies drove back their old nomadic rivals, who in this period were themselves forming for the first time a large political union. To secure the border against the pastoral peoples of the steppe, the First Emperor had huge levies of forced laborers unite the walls built by the northern states into a single defense system stretching fourteen hundred miles from southwestern Kansu along the southern edge of Mongolia to southern Manchuria. This Great Wall was designed to be a permanent barrier separating the agricultural Chinese from the nomadic "barbarians." Properly manned, it could hold up raiding parties of nomad horsemen until adequate defense forces could be concentrated against them. Under later dynasties new walls were erected north or south of the old ones, depending on military and climatic conditions, and the simple earth construction of the Ch'in wall was later changed to more imposing brick, but the Great Wall always remained essentially the same unified defense system the Ch'in first created.

To consolidate his vast conquests, the First Emperor laid out a radiating system of roads, unified weights and measures, standardized the coinage, and even standardized the axle lengths of wagons. This last measure was important for communications in Northwest China, where wagon wheels cut miniature canyons through the loess soil. Li Ssu is also said to have standardized the writing system, for previously many different types of calligraphy had flourished in the politically divided land. As a result of his efforts and of the unifying influence of a centralized state, both the Chinese characters and the formal style of Chinese composition became standardized by the second century B.C. in what are essentially their modern forms.

The Ch'in rulers looked upon the writings of the philosophers, the ancient classics these men extolled, and the histories of the other princely states as subversive to their own system and therefore tried to wipe them out. Li Ssu started a literary inquisition in 213 B.C. in what has come to be called the "Burning of the Books." All books except useful ones, such as those on agriculture, medicine, and divination, as well as the collections in the hands of the central government, were to be destroyed and recalcitrant scholars banished or executed. Reportedly several hundred were actually buried alive. For this desecration of the written word, Li Ssu has won the opprobrium of later ages. His policy did indeed help put an end to the golden age of Chinese thought, but there were even more important factors at work, such as the violent wars that bracketed the brief supremacy of the Ch'in and the centralized empire itself, which had little room for cultural diversity. A great break resulted between pre-Ch'in and post-Ch'in philosophy, and the vigor and richness of Chou thought was seldom if ever again matched in Chinese history.

The Failure of Ch'in. Although the First Emperor thought that he had founded a dynasty that would endure "ten thousand generations," it survived his own death in 210 B.C. by only four years. His success had been

*The First Emperor of the Ch'in attempts to recover the Chou ritual
bronzes. (A Han stone engraving from the Wu family funerary
shrines in Shantung, second century A.D.) The emperor stands on
the bank of a river directing his men who are hauling on ropes
to bring the bronze vessel up from the river bottom, but suddenly
a dragon's head emerges from the vessel and snaps the ropes.*

too sudden and his rule too severe. The upper classes of the states he had
conquered were still pulled by loyalties to the old royal lines, and the best
educated groups throughout the country were repelled by his effort to suppress the old philosophies. The common people felt heavily burdened by his
drafting of men for campaigns abroad and unprecedented building programs at home: palaces, roads, canals, and the Great Wall. In proving the
efficacy of Legalist concepts of rule, Ch'in also demonstrated the validity of
one of Mencius' ideas: that government ultimately depends upon the tacit
consent of the governed. The Chinese people simply deserted Ch'in, and the
invincible empire collapsed.

The First Emperor had overcentralized the government, and a failure of
leadership at the top immediately affected the whole. Though a prodigious
worker and indefatigable traveler, he seems to have been a megalomaniac

who hid his movements under an elaborate cloak of mystery. He also was obsessed with the idea of achieving physical immortality through magical practices, which was a rising Taoist concept of the time, and he visited magicians along the Shantung coast and dispatched expeditions to seek the "islands of the immortals" in the Eastern Sea. When he died, Li Ssu and others engineered the suicide of the heir apparent and the enthronement of a young and inexperienced son of the former ruler as the Second Emperor. Li Ssu himself soon fell prey to court intrigues, the Second Emperor was destroyed in turn, and by 206 B.C. Ch'in had disappeared entirely.

The First Emperor thus failed completely in founding a lasting dynasty, but the imperial system he created was to continue, though with occasional breaks, for more than two millenniums, proving to be the world's most durable political system. He has been excoriated as a tyrant throughout most of Chinese history, but Chinese scholars today quite rightly consider him the founder of China as a unified country. The name Ch'in quite fittingly is the origin of the Western name for China.

Han Receives the Mandate

The Founding of the Han.   In 209 B.C., only a year after the First Emperor's death, a revolt broke out in the old Ch'u area, and rebellions followed in quick succession throughout the empire. Most of the rebel bands were led by turncoat soldiers or bandits, who commonly espoused the cause of the royal line of one or another of the states Ch'in had destroyed. When the leading rebel, Hsiang Yü, a descendant of Ch'u generals, finally wiped out the last of the Ch'in armies in 206, he enthroned a Ch'u prince as emperor, let the rest of the land be divided among supporters of the other royal lines, and declared himself Hegemon King. The old Chou system, however, could not be revived. Another rebel general, Liu Pang, who had seized the Wei Valley in 207, challenged Hsiang Yü, destroyed him in 202, and set himself up as emperor. He established his capital at Ch'ang-an near the old Ch'in capital in the Wei Valley and took for his dynastic name, Han, derived from a major tributary of the Yangtze River.

Liu Pang succeeded, where the First Emperor had failed, in creating a lasting dynasty. His descendants reigned for more than two centuries until 8 A.D. and then, after a brief usurpation, resurrected the dynasty as the Later Han, which lasted from 25 until 220 A.D. Corresponding roughly in time to the heyday of Rome, the two Han empires also paralleled Rome in power, prestige, and historical significance. Even today the Chinese refer to themselves as "men of Han," and the Japanese and Koreans call the Chinese writing system "the Han characters."

Liu Pang, like most later Chinese emperors, is best known not by his personal name but by his posthumous title, which is Kao Tsu ("High

Progenitor"). His success can be attributed to several factors: he could build on the work of the Ch'in; the wars that had swept all of China had further cut people off from the traditions of the Chou; and he himself represented an even more complete break with the past. Unlike the First Emperor, who was the scion of a long princely line, or the aristocratic Hsiang Yü, Kao Tsu had no contact with the aristocratic past but was of rough, plebeian origin. Most important, he was shrewd enough to move more slowly in consolidating his empire and push his subjects less hard. He reduced the severity of punishments and lessened the tax burden. As a result, the Chinese people gave a loyalty to Han they had denied Ch'in. In other words, Han won the Mandate of Heaven, as Mencius understood the term.

The early Han rulers for the most part continued the Ch'in system of government, but Kao Tsu made one notable and perhaps necessary retreat from centralized rule. He made some of his relatives and generals kings or marquises of vassal principalities. Subsequently, however, he eliminated the nonrelated kings and before his death in 195 B.C. established the rule that henceforth only members of the imperial clan could hold this rank. His successors whittled away the power of the remaining kings by reducing their territories, by dividing realms among the sons of the kings, and eventually by appointing officials of the central government to control each kingdom. The menace of the kings was eliminated in 154 B.C. when seven of the largest were destroyed. Kingdoms and marquisates continued throughout the dynasty, but at the end there were only 20 kingdoms as compared with 103 commanderies, and 241 marquisates as compared with 1314 districts.

A second menace to Han rule, and one which was to arise repeatedly in later Chinese history, was posed by the families of the empresses. Chinese emperors had many consorts, but when a child of one of them was made heir apparent that consort usually was recognized as empress, and on the accession of her son she, as the Empress Dowager, often became a dominant figure at court. This happened when Kao Tsu's empress became the real ruler of China on his death and came close to usurping the throne. Members of her family, surnamed Lü, dominated the court until her death in 180 B.C., whereupon they were massacred by loyal supporters of the Han line.

A third menace to the Han came from the pastoral peoples of the North, who at this time were known to the Chinese as the Hsiung-nu, an early form of the name later known to the West as Hun. By the third century B.C. these probably Turkish-speaking people had created a tribal federation that spread from western Manchuria through Mongolia and southern Siberia into Chinese Turkestan as far as the Pamirs, and their bands of mounted archers repeatedly raided and looted North China. Kao Tsu, after suffering a severe defeat at their hands, attempted to buy them off by giving their emperor a Chinese princess in marriage and sending annual tribute, but Hsiung-nu depredations continued.

Government and Society. Despite all these difficulties, the Han rulers gradually established a firm and highly centralized government, and the whole country prospered greatly after centuries of almost uninterrupted warfare. By the first century B.C. the bureaucracy is said to have consisted of 130,285 officials. They and other persons of distinction held ranks in eighteen grades, which entitled them to reduced sentences for crimes and, in the higher brackets, to exemption from taxation. Although this bureaucracy can rightly be described as huge, it was small compared to the country it administered. A census of 2 A.D. reported a population of 59,594,978. Traditional Chinese population figures are notably unreliable. They were essentially tax registers, which might be falsified downward in an effort to escape tax responsibilities or upward to indicate administrative efficiency. But it seems safe to conclude that the Han ruled over a greater mass of people than ever recognized Rome's authority.

The Han administration was not constituted to provide what we today would consider the full services of government. It devoted attention primarily to the lavish support of the emperor and his relatives and the defense of the dynasty. The people were of major concern to the government only as taxpayers and *corvée* labor or as potential rebels. *Corvée* labor was a more important support of the central administration than were taxes. The government usually required each farmer to spend a month every year in local work on roads, canals, palaces, and imperial tombs, and various less frequent periods for military duties, frontier-guarding, and service at the capital. So long as the people met their tax and labor schedules and avoided all subversive activities, they were usually left free to administer their own village affairs and carry out their own customary justice. The government thus was a relatively small, highly centralized body that floated on a sea of semi-isolated peasant communities. The point of contact between the two was the district town, where a district magistrate and perhaps two or three other central government appointees dealt with the village heads, landed magnates, and other local leaders.

The ruling elite was in no sense a hereditary aristocracy like that of the Chou period. Even the families of the kings and marquises rose and fell with astonishing rapidity. The bureaucracy and the whole upper class consisted simply of those persons with sufficient talent, education, or wealth to play a part in the central government. The merchant class, however, was specifically excluded from leadership. The Han, like the Ch'in before it, and like most other despotisms based on agricultural taxes, had a strong prejudice against merchants. The class of wealth and education from which the bureaucracy was largely recruited, therefore, was primarily the richer landowners.

Except for the imperial clan at the top and a small number of slaves at the bottom, society seems to have been made up of two main groups: tax-

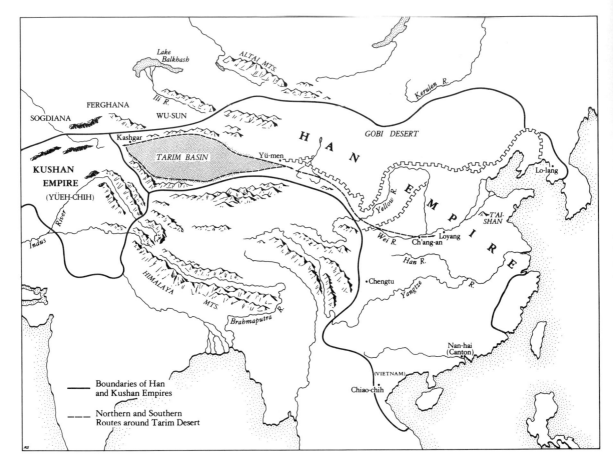

THE HAN EMPIRE

paying peasants and rich landowners. The latter were to some extent tax-exempt, provided the bulk of officialdom, and, as local leaders, served as the link between central government and the countryside. This remained the basic composition of Chinese society for the next two millenniums. These two groups were not castes as in India or even strict classes in the medieval European sense. A spin of the wheel of fortune could plunge a political leader into slavery or elevate a commoner like Liu Pang to the throne.

The Apogee of Han Power.   The first sixty years of Han rule were a period of national recuperation and dynastic consolidation. Then followed a sudden expansive burst of Chinese power such as had taken place under the First Emperor and was to be repeated under all of the stronger dynasties of later times. This occurred during the long reign of Wu Ti ("Martial Emperor"), which lasted from 141 to 87 B.C.

The government of the Chinese Empire has tended to alternate between periods of personal administration by dynamic emperors and periods in which the high bureaucrats were dominant. Under the former, policies could be more vigorously pursued, but, since the emperor was beyond criticism, there could be no check on his follies. Wu Ti was no exception to this rule. He reinstituted a major program of canal construction, connecting the capital directly with the Yellow River and thereby greatly facilitating the transportation of tax grain from East China to Ch'ang-an. He also embarked upon a long series of foreign conquests, while dealing harshly and unjustly with his generals and officials and being himself frequently the dupe of magicians.

Wu Ti greatly extended the Han Empire, filling it out to a much closer approximation of what appears on more recent maps as the Chinese Empire. He conquered native states along the southern coast in Chekiang and Fukien and moved their populations inland. In 111 B.C. he destroyed and annexed the semi-Sinicized state of Nan-yüeh (South Yüeh) in modern Kwangtung, Kwangsi, and northern Vietnam, inaugurating a thousand years of Chinese rule over the region around the modern Hanoi. In 108 he overthrew the semi-Sinicized state of Chosŏn in northern Korea and southern Manchuria, setting up at P'yŏngyang, the present capital of North Korea, the commandery of Lo-lang, which was to remain a flourishing outpost of the Chinese Empire until 313 A.D.

Wu Ti's greatest campaigns were against the Hsiung-nu on the northwest. These were in part defensive, for these highly mobile, warlike people constantly harassed North China. Wu Ti, however, may also have desired to control the lucrative trade with West Asia that passed through Central Asia, and he perhaps had the "Alexander complex," which lured some early Chinese leaders to distant conquests. Between 129 and 119 B.C. he dispatched a series of great armies, some numbering as many as 150,000 men, against the Hsiung-nu and managed to destroy their power south of the Gobi Desert, which bisects Mongolia.

Wu Ti's Hsiung-nu policy was not merely military. He also sought to find allies against them. As early as 139 B.C. he dispatched an officer, Chang Ch'ien, to make an alliance with a Central Asian people known as the Yüeh-chih. Probably an Indo-European people, the Yüeh-chih had been driven out of western Kansu by the Hsiung-nu and in Chang Ch'ien's time had moved all the way to Afghanistan and were on the point of invading India, where they subsequently set up the Kushan Empire. Chang Ch'ien, despite long years of captivity at the hands of the Hsiung-nu, finally reached the Yüeh-chih, but they had no interest in becoming embroiled again in wars in East Asia. He returned to China in 126 B.C. but was dispatched on a similar mission in 115 to another Indo-European people who occupied the Ili Valley of Central Asia. Although this effort also failed, Chang Ch'ien's two expeditions greatly increased Chinese knowledge of and interest in the regions to the west.

HAN MILITARY DEFENSE.
*Miniature of a three-story Han
watchtower, earthenware with
green glaze, from a tomb in
Honan. Note the horses at the
door and the watchmen on the
upper levels.*

Wu Ti also tried to outflank the Hsiung-nu. He set up two commanderies
between Tibet and Mongolia in what is now the western panhandle of
Kansu and populated this area with 700,000 Chinese colonists. To protect
this western protrusion of Chinese-speaking people, he extended the Great
Wall westward as far as Yü-men ("Jade Gate"). Han rule was subsequently
extended over the Indo-European populations of the small agricultural oases
around the rim of the Tarim Basin in the heart of Central Asia, and the
region was placed under a Protector General. These oases were important
way stations on the ancient trade route between East and West. Chinese
armies in 104 and 102 B.C. even crossed the mighty Pamirs to Ferghana
in what is now Russian Turkestan.

The wars against the Hsiung-nu continued after Wu Ti's death, and
eventually in 52 B.C. the ruler of the southern half of the Hsiung-nu horde
submitted to Han. In 42 B.C. a Chinese army again crossed the Pamirs and

penetrated as far as the former Greek kingdom of Sogdiana, where it crushed a force that may have included captive Roman soldiers. Thus Chinese armies, marching across all but impenetrable deserts and mountains, extended Han military might farther from their capital (over two thousand miles) than Roman legions ever reached from Rome, despite the much easier maritime communications of the Mediterranean area.

Han Thought and Scholarship

None of the pre-Ch'in schools of thought survived into Han times as distinct and mutually exclusive philosophical systems. This is the clearest evidence of how completely the successive triumphs of Ch'in and Han had destroyed the traditions of the past. But elements of the old thought survived piece-meal. Among these were the concepts of the late Chou Naturalists of *yin* and *yang* dualism and the "five elements." Closely allied with these ideas was the notion that unusual natural phenomena were portents which reflected the character of the ruler or foretold the future.

From such ideas there developed in the time of Wu Ti the practice of counting years by arbitrary "year periods" (*nien-hao*) chosen largely for their magical potency. A "year period" might last a long time if conditions were stable or might be abandoned within a few months if some disaster struck or a particularly propitious omen occurred. The result has been a chaotic method of counting years, which has made the Chinese all the more dependent on dynasties for reckoning time. Despite the drawbacks of this system, it still is widely used in East Asia. The only later advance has been to make year periods coincide with reigns, an innovation adopted by the Chinese in 1368 and by the Japanese in 1868.

The Taoist tradition survived the political upheaval of the late third century better than most schools of thought, but in the process the philosophy of the *Tao te ching* and the *Chuang-tzu* was almost lost among more primitive beliefs, particularly the search for long life and eventually for physical immortalitiy. There was great interest in finding an elixir of life and in transmuting baser elements into gold, which apparently was the start of alchemy in the world. There was also much emphasis in this search for immortality on dietary regimens, such as the avoidance of cereals, and yoga-like breathing exercises. Various popular nature or ancestral cults also survived and developed a rich mythology, increasingly identified with Taoism. The old aristocratic cults had, of course, been obliterated, but their memory continued. In 110 B.C. Wu Ti was persuaded to revive them in mysterious form and on a grandiose scale, performing the sacrifice to Heaven on the summit of T'ai-shan, a sacred mountain in Shantung, and the sacrifice to Earth on a low hill at its foot.

At a higher intellectual level, men of scholarly bent busied themselves with the recovery of the writings of earlier times. After the Ch'in ban on philosophical and historical works was formally lifted in 191 B.C., some older scholars were apparently able to reconstitute certain texts from memory, while others were discovered hidden in walls. The result was sometimes two different versions of the same text, as for the *Classic of Documents,* which had an "old text," found in pre-Ch'in calligraphy, as well as the currently reconstituted text in the new standardized writing.

Han scholars showed little philosophic perception, lumping all the old writings together as equally valid expressions of the thought of antiquity. But they tried to bring order into the ancient writings by devising categories such as the Five Classics, and they devoted great efforts to attempting to explain these only imperfectly understood ancient writings. Their exegetical works, or commentaries, were the start of what has been ever since one of the major intellectual activities of China. The first great systematic dictionary, the *Explanation of Writing (Shuo wen)*, also appeared around 100 A.D. In it more than nine thousand characters are listed under 540 radicals.

Han books were often decidedly eclectic in their philosophic content, as in the case of the *Huai-nan-tzu,* a compilation of cosmological, Taoist, and other lore, made under the patronage of a grandson of Kao Tsu. While most Han writing was scholarly or didactic, one important poetic genre developed during the period. This was the *fu,* which because of its irregularity of meter and rhyme has sometimes been called "prose poetry." Closely akin to the *Li sao* of Ch'ü Yüan, the *fu* were featured by long descriptions, rich in imagery and hyperbole, of capitals of China or beautiful landscapes.

The Writing of History.   The greatest literary achievement of Han times was in the field of historical writing. This is not surprising in a civilization that has so emphasized the record of the past. The Chinese have made history one of the four main categories of literature, the others being the classics and their commentaries, philosophical writings, and belles-lettres.

The *Historical Records (Shih chi)* of Ssu-ma Ch'ien (died about 85 B.C.) represents a great step forward in Chinese historical scholarship. A court astrologer, Ssu-ma Ch'ien claimed to be simply completing a history started by his father, but this may have been partly a pious excuse for what was in reality a most presumptuous undertaking—the continuation and amplification of what was supposed to be Confucius' greatest accomplishment, that is, the arrangement of the record of the past in proper form. Ssu-ma Ch'ien was obviously a man of great daring as well as prodigious learning. In 99 B.C. he came to the defense of a prominent Chinese general who had been forced to surrender to the Hsiung-nu, and Wu Ti repaid him for his audacity by having him castrated.

Ssu-ma Ch'ien not only set the pattern for most later Chinese historical works but also determined their style and scholarly approach. He limited

*The archer Yi shooting nine of the ten sun crows which threaten to
burn up the earth—a drought myth. Stone engraving on the wall of
the Wu family shrines.*

himself to a concise and straightforward statement of the facts as he knew
them, quoting with a minimum of alterations those sources which he felt to
be the most reliable. His book, therefore, is for the most part a complicated
patchwork of passages and paraphrases from earlier books and documents.
He thus set a standard for historical scholarship in China that was probably
not equaled in the West until relatively modern times.

Ssu-ma Ch'ien was attempting to write universal history and came as close
to succeeding as any man has. The *Historical Records,* which consist of 130
solid chapters, is a text of over 700,000 characters. Because of the concise-
ness of classical Chinese, this represents a work of close to ten times the
content of the volume the reader has in hand. The first twelve chapters are
"Basic Annals," which contain the main record of events from the time of
the "culture heroes" through the kings of the three dynasties and the emperors of the Ch'in and Han dynasties up to Wu Ti. The next ten chapters
are chronological tables of Chou princely houses and princes and high officials of the Han. Then follow eight essays on subjects that do not lend themselves to chronological treatment, such as rituals, music, the calendar,

astrology, rivers and canals, and economic matters. The following thirty chapters are devoted to the records of the various states of Chou times. The last seventy chapters consist of biographies of important men and a few brief essays on other peoples and lands.

Many later Chinese historians followed Ssu-ma Ch'ien's model. Pan Ku (died 92 A.D.), together with his father and sister, compiled the second great history of this type, the *History of the Han*. A work of one hundred chapters, it differed from the pattern of the *Historical Records* largely in that it was limited to a single dynasty, the Earlier Han, and naturally has no section corresponding to that on the various states of Chou. Pan Ku also added very useful essays on literature and geography. The *History of the Han* became the prototype for all the later dynastic histories, which treat either one major dynasty or a group of smaller ones. The number of officially accepted "standard histories" of this sort had been twenty-four for some centuries until the President of the Chinese Republic accepted a "new" history of the Mongol dynasty in 1921.

The Triumph of Confucianism.   Wu Ti was almost as thoroughly a Legalist monarch as the First Emperor had been. It is commonly said, however, that during his reign Confucianism became the predominant philosophy of the Chinese court. Actually the triumph of Confucianism was a slow process, continuing over the whole Han period, and the Confucianism that won out was a curious synthesis of ancient philosophies and current superstitions, and not at all the pure, ethical teachings of Confucius and Mencius. But for all the eclecticism of Han thought, men of scholarly bent seem to have identified themselves increasingly with the Confucian tradition. This may have been because Confucianism was very specifically a philosophy for bureaucrats and educated men. Its very name suggested this: "the learning of the literati," or rather "weaklings," as the term *ju* originally meant. It was not so much that Confucian philosophy won over Han thinkers as that Han scholars gradually adopted Confucius as their ideal prototype.

At the same time scholarly men who identified themselves with the Confucian tradition were being brought into what had started out as a purely Legalist type of government. Kao Tsu, though himself untutored, had seen the need to utilize men of education in his government, and his successors had even held examinations to select qualified scholars for government service. By Wu Ti's time there was enough of a Confucian bias in the central government for the ruler to ban students of Legalist philosophy from the court. Two so-called Confucian scholars who rose to considerable influence under Wu Ti were Kung-sun Hung (died 121 B.C.) and his junior contemporary Tung Chung-shu. Both men were chiefly noted for their ability to interpret omens and for their analysis of the *Spring and Autumn Annals* as a book which supposedly indicated the moral judgments of Confucius through its choice of words. The pseudoscientific reasoning about the relationship between the "five elements" and historic events in Tung Chung-shu's writings on the *Spring and Autumn Annals* is a far cry from the thought of Confucius and Mencius.

In 136 B.C. Wu Ti set up at court five Erudites of the Five Classics, which were by then identified with the Confucian tradition, and in 124 B.C. he assigned fifty official students to these five Erudites, thus creating a sort of state university. This school is said to have grown to three thousand students in the second half of the first century B.C., and by 1 A.D. a hundred men a year were entering government service through the examinations administered by the official scholars. Thus, from Wu Ti's time on, a considerable portion of the lower bureaucracy was produced through a definitely Confucianist education at government expense.

Confucian precepts about proper rituals and etiquette were also gradually incorporated into law—a development quite at variance with the original Confucian emphasis on ethics in place of law. Confucianism was also beginning to be recognized as the official philosophy of the state. Great conferences of scholars were held under imperial auspices in 51 B.C. and again in 79 A.D. to determine the true interpretation of the Confucian Classics. In 175 A.D. the government had the approved version of the Classics carved on large stone tablets, which were erected at the capital. Meanwhile, in 58 A.D. all government schools were ordered to make sacrifices to Confucius.

The incorporation of Confucianism into the Legalist state was in many ways a strange phenomenon, but it helps explain the superior lasting power of the Chinese imperial system over all other empires. The land, though won by the sword, could be governed only by the writing brush. The Legalist conqueror needed the efficient civil administrator, and a place of responsibility and honor was, accordingly, created for him in the government. As a result, men of education became supporters rather than opponents of the state. More important, a start was made toward the development of an efficient bureaucracy through a system of education and selection of prospective officials. China in short was already beginning to develop a modern type of civil service system based on merit. It was almost two thousand years before the West adopted a system similar to, and in part inspired by, that of China.

It was fortunate for the Chinese that the Confucian tradition became the chief intellectual force among the educated classes. Although Han Confucianism was a strange mixture of ideas, the ethical concepts of the Chou founders of the school gradually reasserted themselves over the syncretic beliefs of the early Han scholars. The ruthless depotism that the Ch'in had created on Legalist principles, therefore, came increasingly into the hands of men who stressed moral virtues. The balance eventually achieved between the Legalist empire and its Confucian administrators once again illustrates the

Rubbing of a Han stamped tile showing a banquet scene. Note the full-sleeved flowing robes and kneeling position, no longer characteristic of China but still seen in Japan.

usefulness of the *yin-yang* concept of complementary, as opposed to conflicting, dualism. The Legalist victory, while seeming to destroy Confucianism, in reality created the stable society in which it could flourish. The Confucian victory, far from destroying Legalism, made the Legalist empire all but indestructible.

The Dynastic Cycle

The Chinese have traditionally interpreted their past as a series of dynastic cycles in which successive dynasties repeated a boringly repetitious story: a heroic founding, a period of great power, then a long decline, and finally total collapse. The Chinese practice of compiling history in dynastic chunks has contributed to this picture, as has their concept that the best that man could hope for was to recreate some golden age of antiquity. As a result, the tremendous growth and development of Chinese civilization has been all but hidden behind this apparent circular motion in human affairs, and the later history of China is made into a series of more or less successful attempts to repeat the story of the Earlier Han.

It must be admitted that there is some validity to the Chinese concept of a dynastic cycle, at least as a superficial political pattern that overlies more fundamental technological, economic, social, and cultural developments. The two Han dynasties both lasted about two centuries; the great dynasties of later times, existing under more advanced conditions, each tended to run about three centuries. And within each dynastic period, such matters as fiscal conditions, administrative efficiency, and military power showed remarkably parallel trends.

Personal Factors. Chinese historians, influenced by the Confucian insistence on the ethical basis of government, have always emphasized personal factors in explaining the dynastic cycle. Founders of dynasties, who, like Kao Tsu, successfully claimed the Mandate of Heaven, were not portrayed just as strong men but as supermen. The last rulers, who lost the Mandate, were not considered just unfortunate or weak but were often described as evil and debauched, like the last kings of the Hsia and Shang. Actually, the imperial lines invariably did degenerate. The dynastic founder naturally had to be a man of great ability and force. Later rulers, raised in a luxurious and intrigue-ridden court, were more likely to be weaklings. Usually the dynasty produced at least one later strong man who either brought the regime to new power, as did Wu Ti, or gave it a sort of second start; but in general all the imperial lines showed a downward trend in ability.

The quality of the men around the throne was on the whole more important than that of the emperors themselves. Here the picture is less clear. Struggles over the succession and court intrigues between rival factions characterized the history of all the dynasties almost from beginning to end. In some of the later dynasties, factional quarrels at times centered on basic matters of policy, but throughout most of Chinese history they were simply struggles over power and rewards. In the latter years of a dynasty, when the central government was weakening for other reasons, the effect of such factional quarrels, *coups d'état,* and palace revolutions was naturally more deleterious than in the dynasty's heyday.

The most persistent factional problem was posed by the families of the empresses, as in the case of Kao Tsu's widow, who almost took the throne for her Lü family. High officials, generals, or great landed families might also take advantage of the weakness of an emperor or the disruption of his court to make themselves virtually independent power holders and in the end break up the empire.

Another type of factional struggle that was endemic in all dynasties was that between civil bureaucrats and eunuchs. The eunuchs were at court to guard and administer the imperial harem, but their functions spread to other fields, including the military. As men of low social origin without descendants who could rival the imperial line, they were the natural allies of emperors, who might need their help to curb overly ambitious or greedy officials. The bureaucrats naturally looked with keen disfavor on influential eunuchs, who lacked their own education, came from a different social background, and were their rivals for power and rewards at court. It was a eunuch who destroyed the Ch'in statesman Li Ssu in 208 B.C., and in 47 B.C. another eunuch got rid of his bureaucratic rivals at court. Since the writing of history was in the hands of bureaucrats, we find the eunuchs uniformly condemned by historians for their misrule.

Economic and Administrative Factors. Despite the Chinese emphasis on individual morality and personality, the dynastic cycle is better explained in terms of problems of fiscal stability, administrative efficiency, and military power. All the great dynasties had an initial period of prosperity. The group that had seized the throne was relatively small and closely knit. The wars that had brought it to power had eliminated most of its rivals, and therefore the wealth of the nation poured largely into its coffers. The country prospered in its newly established peace, the population increased rapidly, and the treasuries and granaries of the central government were full.

But the excess of *yang* led to the rise of *yin.* The affluent central government built great palaces, roads, canals, and walls. The very military successes of the empire established far-flung defense lines that were costly to maintain. The imperial clan, the nobility, and the high bureaucracy grew in numbers and became accustomed to an ever more luxurious mode of life. More and more lands and their peasant-cultivators were used for the personal support of the ruling class and fewer and fewer tax-paying contributors remained to support the central administration. Because of constantly increasing expenditures and often a slight decline in income, every dynasty began to experience serious financial difficulties within a century of its founding.

Economic and administrative reforms were then carried out which sometimes halted the financial decline for a while. The downward trend, however, eventually reasserted itself. Economic and administrative difficulties accumulated. Official self-seeking and corruption became worse, leading to a decline in administrative efficiency and an intensification of factional quarrels at court. The potential rivals of the imperial family became politically and economically more independent of the central government and challenged it with greater impunity. To meet government deficits, the burden on the tax-paying peasant was increased to the breaking point. Because of the government's financial difficulties, canals and dikes were allowed to fall into disrepair, making floods and droughts more probable. Crop failures that once could have been offset by stores from the government granaries now resulted in famines, and these led to banditry and eventually to peasant uprisings. Inadequately maintained frontier defenses began to crumble. Provincial officials and their armies began to defect, and the central government started to go to pieces. Then followed the wars that liquidated the old regime and cleared the slate for a new dynastic beginning.

This downward economic and administrative spiral can be perceived in the histories of most of the long-lived dynasties. It was particularly clear in the Earlier Han. Wu Ti's canal-building program and foreign wars brought the dynasty to the height of its power but also produced a fiscal crisis. New revenues were desperately needed for the greatly expanded costs of government. Wu Ti's whole reign (141–87 B.C.) was characterized by a long series of efforts to redeem the finances of the dynasty.

The most important of Wu Ti's economic measures was the reinstitution of state monopolies, or rather licensing systems, for the production and sale of certain commodities from which large profits could be made with minimal effort. He restored the government monopoly on minting copper coinage, and in 119 B.C. he reintroduced the old Ch'in monopolies on salt and iron, later adding a monopoly on liquor. Such monopolies, though common throughout Chinese history, always remained highly controversial. As early as 81 B.C. a great court conference was held to discuss their propriety, and the largely condemnatory conclusions were put into book form a generation later under the title of *Discourses on Salt and Iron*.

In 110 B.C. Wu Ti introduced the so-called "leveling" system, by which the government purchased surplus produce in times or areas of glut to sell in periods or places of deficiency. This system may have helped stabilize prices, but the motive was profit for the treasury. Wu Ti also managed to tax commerce to some extent by special imposts, but others of his reforms were very unsound. He commuted some punishments to money fines; he sold court ranks for cash; and he debased the currency, making smaller coins and forcing worthless deerskin certificates on the wealthy.

Wang Mang's Usurpation.   Wu Ti's fiscal efforts were on the whole successful and the government remained solvent for the next few decades. But meanwhile a serious problem had developed. The population had grown to such a point that the average peasant had less land to cultivate than had his ancestors. Moreover, a much larger proportion of the peasants were now on the virtually untaxed estates of the great landowners, and therefore the tax-paying peasants elsewhere were forced to carry a heavier load than before, on a smaller agricultural base. State revenues were declining and with them all the institutions of central government. A series of large-scale revolts commenced in 22 B.C.

At this critical juncture, Wang Mang, the nephew of an empress, rose

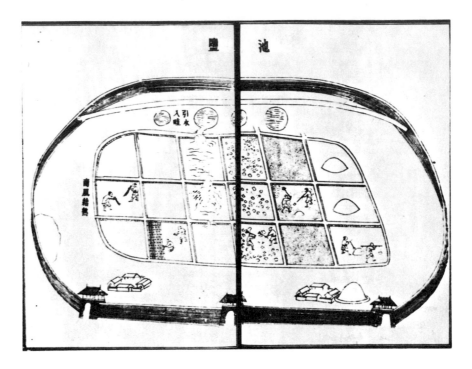

THE SALT MONOPOLY. *Since salt was a necessity and its production
easily monopolized, its production and distribution were ordinarily
controlled by government licensing for the benefit of the
central government treasury. This picture from an encyclopedia
of 1637 (the* T'ien-kung k'ai-wu) *shows, from left to right, flat salt
"pans" being smoothed, sea water being let in for evaporation,
and the remaining salt pulverized and then collected in mounds
for transportation, all within walls and gates for control purposes.*

to power and by vigorous reforms sought desperately to stem the tide.
Eventually he usurped the throne in 8 A.D. and substituted his Hsin
("New") dynasty for the Han. (The date was January 10, 9 A.D., in the
Western calendar, but the Chinese lunar calendar starts the year later in
the winter.) Wang Mang seems to have been a sincere Confucian, and he
saw his reforms as recreating the golden age of the Duke of Chou. With
the aid of Confucian scholars, he focused attention on certain ancient texts
that had hitherto been little studied, and he contributed greatly to the
ultimate triumph of Confucianism. But his reforms actually were more in
the Legalist tradition and were largely a revival or amplification of Wu Ti's
policies. He built up the monopolies, reinvigorated the "leveling" system,
and debased the coinage. He also instituted a policy of agricultural loans
to peasants.

Wang Mang's most daring reform was a frontal assault on the major economic problem of his day. So many peasants lived on the tax-free estates that not enough of them remained as taxpayers supporting the central government. He therefore decreed an end to the great private estates by ordering in 9 A.D. that the land be "nationalized" and parceled out among tax-paying peasants and that private slavery be stopped. Such a drastic policy would have been extremely hard to carry out even in Wu Ti's time. Now, a century later, it was entirely beyond the power of the central government to enforce. While Wang Mang has been condemned by traditional Chinese historians for his usurpation, his effort to "nationalize" the land and free the slaves has won him the anachronistic title of "China's first socialist" and the praise of Marxist historians.

Wang Mang's daring effort to turn back the dynastic cycle and recreate the conditions that had existed at the beginning of the dynasty may have hastened the collapse of the central government. Already undermined by slow fiscal and administrative erosion, it now lost the support of the powerful families whose lands Wang Mang had sought to expropriate. A series of bad harvests and the breakdown of the water-control system also produced famines. A great peasant uprising broke out in Shantung in 18 A.D. and soon spread throughout the land. The rebels, who called themselves the Red Eyebrows from a mark used to distinguish them, had originated from a secret society with Taoist tendencies. As in many later popular uprisings that featured the closing years of dynasties, economic necessity was the real motivating force, but popular religious beliefs helped give the rebellion solidarity and lasting force. Meanwhile, the frontier defenses had crumbled, and the border states had reasserted their independence. The nomads invaded the border regions, the capital was sacked by rebels, and Wang Mang died at their hands in 23 A.D. The great centralized government that Kao Tsu had founded had finally collapsed in complete ruin.

The Later Han

The Reconstitution of the Empire.   Although the Red Eyebrows had laid waste the land, they, like the leaders of many popular rebellions, lacked the administrative experience and understanding to substitute a central government of their own for the one they were destroying. The task of re-creating the central power fell to the hands of better educated men. Various descendants of the Han emperors, usually great landowners themselves, had also risen in revolt, and one of them, Liu Hsiu, finally emerged victorious from the free-for-all that followed Wang Mang's downfall. He declared himself emperor in 25 A.D. and re-established the Han dynastic name, but since his capital was at Loyang to the east of Ch'ang-an, his dynasty is known as the Eastern Han as well as Later Han.

Liu Hsiu, who is better known by his posthumous title of Kuang Wu Ti

("Shining Martial Emperor"), unified and pacified the land by 37 A.D. and recreated a powerful central administration on the pattern of the Earlier Han. He was able to do this because he did not face the insoluble financial problem that had proved too much for Wang Mang. The wars had wiped out the Earlier Han aristocracy and some of the other great landholders. The new dynasty, moreover, was not as yet burdened with a large imperial clan and ruling class.

Kuang Wu Ti reconquered South China and northern Vietnam, and under his successor, Ming Ti ("Enlightened Emperor," 57–75 A.D.), a determined effort was made to restore Chinese control over Central Asia and the pastoral peoples of the north. Pan Ch'ao, the brother of the historian Pan Ku, was dispatched to Central Asia in 73 A.D. and eventually brought the whole of the Tarim Basin under his control, serving as the Protector General of the Western Regions from 91 A.D. until his death in 102. During this time he led an army across the Pamir Mountains and dispatched a lieutenant across intervening Parthia to the eastern regions of the Roman Empire.

In the meantime the Hsiung-nu had divided into northern and southern confederacies, and the southern group had submitted to the Later Han. In 89 A.D. Chinese armies marched across the Gobi Desert in Mongolia and administered a great defeat to the northern Hsiung-nu, which probably helped start them on their western migrations that were to bring them, under the name of Huns, to the southern Russian steppes in the late fourth century and into the heart of Europe a half-century later.

Cultural Growth.   Control over Central Asia during the two Han dynasties permitted a greatly increased flow of overland trade with the western regions. Contact by sea and a trickle of maritime trade with India and the Roman Orient also developed during these centuries. A group of jugglers appeared at the Chinese court in 120 A.D. claiming to be from the Roman Empire, and some merchants in 166 claimed, no doubt speciously, to be emissaries of Marcus Aurelius Antoninus. The Chinese obtained through this trade fine horses from Central Asia and various luxury goods from South and West Asia. They especially valued glass objects from the Mediterranean area. But Chinese silk was in even greater demand in the Roman Empire. In fact, so much silk was exported from China to the West that it contributed to an economically injurious drain of specie from Rome, and the route by which it came through Central Asia has been called the "Silk Road." The greater demand for Chinese goods abroad than for foreign goods in China was to remain characteristic of China's trade until the nineteenth century, in large part because of superior Chinese technology as compared with other areas during most of this period.

Stone engraving from the Wu family shrines (see pages 58 and 67). The upper register shows, left to right, guests arriving and then being served a banquet while sitting on the floor and watching acrobats perform. A gaming board is above the food trays. On the lower register servants prepare the banquet.

Trade with western areas brought to China various foreign influences in art and music and new agricultural products. The high level of Han astronomical and mathematical learning may have reflected stimulation from India or West Asia. But already by Han times the flow of cultural influences from China westward may have exceeded the flow toward China. Han textile techniques were centuries ahead of those of West Asia and Europe; in the Later Han the water-powered mill was invented; during the Han period the Chinese developed the shoulder collar that so greatly increased the efficiency of horses as draft animals; and at about the same time the technique of iron casting began to spread from China to the western regions.

Two of the greatest of all Chinese inventions, paper and porcelain, had their beginnings during the Han period. Pure rag paper dating from about 100 A.D. has been found in the remains of Han outposts in Central Asia. Naturally, paper soon replaced cumbersome wooden and bamboo slips for writing and also reduced the use of expensive silk cloth for this purpose. But it took more than a thousand years for the knowledge of paper-making to spread to Europe. Pottery glazes were already common during the Han, and toward the end of this period a sort of proto-porcelain appeared. The Chinese, in other words, were beginning to invent china. During the next several centuries they gradually developed the fine porcelains that the rest of the world eagerly imported and eventually copied in modern times.

Ch'ang-an and Loyang, no doubt, were cities that rivaled Rome, but little has survived from these great Han capitals. Their wooden architecture was too perishable and later inhabitants too numerous and destructive. Rich Han remains, however, are still to be found in Han tombs. From tombs at the Lo-lang commandery in Korea have emerged fine lacquer pieces made in distant Szechwan. (See Plate 3.)

Dynastic Decline.   Despite the cultural brilliance of the period, the Later Han was never able to achieve the financial strength of the Earlier Han at its height. Too many of the large private estates of the first century B.C. had survived into Later Han times to allow the new dynasty the same clean slate, economically and administratively, that Kao Tsu and his successors had enjoyed. The position of the great landowners was quite secure. Land taxes in Han times were usually only about one-thirtieth of the yield, while rents ran about one-half. Thus they paid only an inconsequential land tax and could protect their wealth by holding high court posts. Although the central government repeatedly made efforts to build up an efficient bureaucracy based on merit, the great majority of the officials achieved their positions through inheritance, patronage, or the open manipulation of the official examinations by those in charge.

The financial and administrative weakness of the Later Han is reflected by the numbers of people on the tax registers. At their height in 105 A.D. the Later Han census roles did not quite reach the figures for the Earlier Han, and the decrease in tax-paying, *corvée*-serving peasants was greatest in North China and the northern border regions, where they were most needed for miltary defense and to support the capital. To maintain itself, the central government was forced to levy increasingly heavy taxes on the dwindling number of tax-paying peasants in North China. The burden eventually became unbearable, and many peasants fled to the less rigorously taxed South or into the estates of the great landowners, where the rents were less crushing than the taxes on free peasants. The result of such absconding was an inevitable increase in taxation on those who remained. The hard-pressed peasants thus were forced into banditry or open revolt, which further weakened the dynasty's finances. This downward spiral, once started, was not easily stopped.

As in the Earlier Han, the first major challenges to the imperial clan came from the relatives of empresses, but the emperors managed to suppress them with the aid of powerful eunuchs. The Tou family was put down in 89 A.D. and the Liang were exterminated in 160. The other great court families, supported by the students of the government university, who were said to number thirty thousand at the time, attempted to prevent the triumphant eunuchs from monopolizing power, but the latter struck back, imprisoning hundreds of officials and students in 166 and killing or imprisoning thousands of them again in 169.

The great purges carried out by the eunuchs were both symptomatic of administrative decline and contributory to a further disintegration of the government. By 184 two great rebellions had broken out, in East China and in Szechwan. Both were led by Taoist religious leaders of faith-healing sects. That in the East was called the "Way of the Great Peace" (T'ai P'ing Tao), but was popularly known as the Yellow Turbans for the yellow head cloths the rebels wore. In Szechwan the rebels were known as the Five Pecks of Rice band, because of the dues paid their cult masters. These popular Taoist rebellions raged for three decades, seriously disrupting the country.

The End of the First Chinese Empire

The Division of the Empire. The *coup de grâce* was given the Han by its own generals, as was often the case in later dynasties. The collapse of the tax-paying peasantry entailed the ruin of the *corvée* labor system and the peasant draft army associated with it. The professional armies that took its place tended to become the private forces of the rich, land-owning generals who commanded them. After the outbreak of the popular revolts, the generals became virtually independent warlords and soon completely overshadowed the central government. Gradually a three-way division of power developed among the leading generals, with Ts'ao Ts'ao, the son of an adopted son of a eunuch, in the North, Liu Pei in Szechwan, and Sun Ch'üan in the region of the lower Yangtze and the South. This division was geographically a natural one and was to reappear at various times in later Chinese history.

When Ts'ao Ts'ao died in 220 A.D., his son usurped the Han throne, naming his dynasty the Wei. The Later Han dynasty had been little more than a legal fiction for the past three decades, but this act brought it to an official end. The following year Liu Pei also assumed the imperial title, taking the dynastic name of Han, since he was a descendant of the old imperial line. His dynasty is called the Shu Han after the state of Shu which had once existed in Szechwan. In 222 Sun Ch'üan in the South followed suit, adopting the dynastic name of Wu after the Chou state that had once ruled the lower Yangtze Valley. The half-century during which China was divided between these three states is known as the Three Kingdoms (*San-kuo*) period.

The Breakdown of the System.   According to the theory of the dynastic cycle one of the three succession states or some new rebel group should presently have reunited the country and started another two-century cycle of united rule, but nothing of the sort happened. Something much more profound than a mere administrative breakdown was occurring in China. The whole Han system of political and economic organization was going to pieces in somewhat the same way that the Roman Empire was starting to

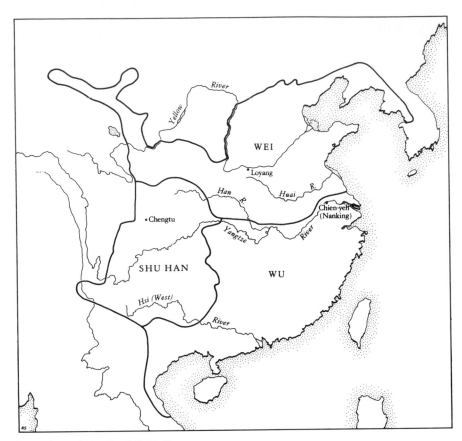

THE THREE KINGDOMS

disintegrate at much the same time. Existing at quite comparable technological levels, both Han and Rome proved incapable of adjusting to the
increase in population, the growth of wealth, and the development of complex institutions that their great centralized rule had made possible.

The decline of the first Chinese Empire can be traced back to the financial
difficulties at the time of Wu Ti. It became marked during the late first
century B.C., when the great families consolidated their hold on their large
estates. Kuang Wu Ti, in recreating the centralized state of the Later Han,
had to make a greater compromise with large private holdings than had the
emperors of the Earlier Han. From then on the decline was rapid, and the
Later Han took no effective measures to check it. In fact, the centralized
administration was its own worst enemy. Emperors awarded to their relatives,
favorites, and outstanding generals and administrators huge grants of land
and peasants in perpetuity. The great officials were unendingly avaricious
in rewarding themselves and their relatives in similar fashion.

By the late second century the great local families were simply too rich
and powerful to be curbed by the central government; in fact, they con-

trolled it, and the division of the country into three separate empires after 220 A.D. was merely formal recognition of the fact that a truly united government was no longer possible. Nor was any of the three succession states an effectively united empire. All were more or less at the mercy of their own great families and generals. They and the dynasties that followed all sought to revive the Han imperial system, but none could achieve more than a pale imitation of it. Most of them were merely one-man dynasties, created by a strong general and lost within a generation or two by his heirs.

The Three Kingdoms period was a time of incessant warfare, which has seemed exciting and romantic to later Chinese. Finally in 263, Wei managed to destroy and annex Shu Han, but two years later, a Wei general usurped the Wei throne from Ts'ao Ts'ao's heirs and founded the Chin dynasty. Known to history as Chin Wu Ti ("Martial Emperor" of the Chin), he conquered the southern state of Wu in 280, uniting the country briefly, and he strove valiantly to restore the old Han system. No one man, however, could turn back the tides of history. The official census was down to 16,163,863, a sure sign that a large part of the population was beyond effective control or taxation by the government, and Chin Wu Ti made no real attempt to break up the estates and get the peasants back on the tax registers. The Chin, in fact, proved to be a typical one-man dynasty. Soon after Chin Wu Ti's death in 290, it fell apart in civil war.

"Barbarian" Invasions. A new aspect of the disintegration of the imperial system now became apparent. China was all but defenseless against the pastoral peoples of the North. The pendulum of conquest, after swinging outward into the steppe land for centuries, was now beginning to swing back into China. This drastic shift in power relationship between the Chinese and the nomads can be explained in part by our useful concept of *yin-yang* dualism. The very subjugation of the pastoral peoples by the Han had sown the seeds for the "barbarian" conquest of China. Hsiung-nu bands that had surrendered were settled as semiagricultural tribal groups on the northern borders of China. The "barbarians," because of their horsemanship and martial traditions, also became important elements in the Chinese armies. Thus, the borderland and the whole Chinese defense system became permeated with semi-Sinicized "barbarians." The situation was not unlike that of late Roman times in Europe, when the borderlands and defense forces passed in large part into the hands of the Germanic "barbarians."

As the Chinese Empire disintegrated, the semiagricultural "barbarians" to the north and the still purely pastoral tribes beyond them found no difficulty in penetrating deep into China in their search for better pasture or booty. In 304 a Hsiung-nu band in North China declared its independence, and in 316 its armies sacked Loyang, the Chin capital, slaughtering thirty thousand of its inhabitants. For more than a century after that North China was fought over, despoiled, and ruled by rival "barbarian" groups. Only the mountain ramparts of Szechwan and the large river systems of the Yangtze Valley and the South preserved these regions from the ravages of the northern horsemen.

Huge numbers of Chinese, naturally, attempted to escape the depredations of the "barbarians" and the generally chaotic conditions in North China, fleeing southward to the safety of Szechwan and the area south of the Yangtze. As a result, the Chinese population in the South multiplied several times over between the third and fifth centuries, and the absorption of the non-Chinese peoples of the area was accelerated.

The Succession States of the South.   The year after the fall of Loyang, a Chin prince in South China declared himself emperor at Nanking. His dynasty is known as the Eastern Chin, in contrast to the first Chin dynasty, which is called the Western Chin. The capital at Nanking (appropriately meaning "Southern Capital," though this is actually a much later name for the city), grew into a great metropolis where the luxurious ways of the Han were continued. The government, however, was weak and continually at the mercy of its great generals, who repeatedly seemed on the point of snuffing out the dynasty. The Eastern Chin was obsessed with the idea of reconquering the North, but its various wars against the "barbarians" brought no permanent gains, and it was plagued at home by revolts and *coups d'état.*

Finally in 420 a general, Liu Yü, usurped the throne and founded the Sung dynasty, usually called the Liu Sung to distinguish it from the great Sung dynasty of later history. The next century and a half witnessed dismal repetitions of the same story. There were constant and usually unsuccessful wars with the "barbarian" states of the North, and one general after another seized the throne from the weak heirs of the preceding usurper. Usurpations followed in quick succession: the Southern Ch'i dynasty in 479, the Liang in 502, and the Ch'en in 557.

For more than three centuries, one dynastic founder after another had attempted to restore the great centralized empire of the Han, but all had failed. No dynasty had been more than a mere shadow of the old empire, perpetuating at most the conditions of ineffectual central government and complete dominance by the great families that had characterized the dying days of Han rule. A broken-down Han could be maintained for a while, much as Byzantium continued a degenerated Roman tradition for a much longer period in the West, but Han itself could not be revived—at least not by the Chinese alone. The later history of the Chinese Empire was to grow out of the amalgam of "barbarians" and Chinese in North China, as the later history of Europe grew out of the union of Latins and Germans.

5. The Regeneration of the Empire

The Challenge to the Chinese System

The Six Dynasties Period. The epoch following the fall of the Later Han is called the Six Dynasties period (*Liu ch'ao*) after the six successive dynasties that had their capitals at Nanking between 222 and 589. This span of three and a half centuries is commonly treated as a single slice of history —a sort of dynastic cycle in reverse, in that it runs from unity through prolonged disunity back to unity again. During this period foreign peoples and influences challenged Chinese civilization more fundamentally than it was ever to be challenged again until the nineteenth century. Eventually the Chinese overcame this crisis by incorporating the challengers into the Chinese system. Out of this synthesis grew a new and richer Chinese civilization and a revivified empire that outshone the most glorious days of Han.

The challenge to classic Chinese civilization was posed most dramatically as a "barbarian" threat, for invaders overran North China and an alien religion, Indian Buddhism, menaced the ideological basis of Chinese society, but the challenge was more internal than external in origin. Only because the Han political system had collapsed of its own inner contradictions were the "barbarians" able to pour into China. Only because the Han synthesis of Confucian ideology, pseudoscientific superstitions, and Legalist practices had proved spiritually unsatisfying and politically inadequate were the Chinese receptive to Buddhism. In fact, thinking men first deserted Confucianism for Taoism before turning to Buddhism.

The Later Han and its aftermath saw the breakdown of a whole social order. Conditions were not unlike those in the Roman Empire at a slightly later date. They might even be described as protofeudal. As the central government weakened, the bulk of the land and its peasant cultivators gravitated into the hands of great landowners. These drew together for self-protection into extended family groups. They also consolidated their control over their subordinates. Tenant farmers gradually declined in status into virtual serfs. Impoverished peasants, fleeing the government tax collectors or the "barbarians," gave themselves and their services to powerful landowners in return for economic security and protection, becoming hereditary dependents or "guests" (*k'o*) of their patrons. Those among the dependents and serfs who had martial inclinations became the personal soldiers of the great landlords, and private armies replaced the former peasant levies. Each great family came to possess its own fortified manors and fortresses. The "barbarian" invasions, the constant wars and usurpations, and the movement of whole family groups to the South as organized military and economic units contributed to the militarization of society.

The large self-sufficient manor became the chief economic unit, and trade consequently languished. Administrative centers declined in size, and trading cities were drastically reduced. Copper coinage virtually went out of use in some regions, and barter, which had always persisted in rural areas, became again the rule throughout the country.

The Upsurge of Taoism.   The Confucian bureaucrat found only a shrinking role in the new society, and his scholasticism and preoccupation with rituals and the past proved of little help in meeting the problems of the day. During the Later Han the Confucian tradition had dominated society as never before, but as central government disintegrated, thinking men turned away from Confucianism's social teachings and began to look inward. Since society and government now seemed hopelessly degenerate, men again became interested in the old Taoist problem of the individual's relationship to nature and his personal perfection or salvation. This Taoist current of thought had no doubt always existed, particularly among the common people, but now it rose prominently to the surface of Chinese society. Wang Ch'ung (died about 100 A.D.), perhaps the most original thinker of Han times, had presaged the turning of educated men away from Confucianism in his iconoclastic and skeptical *Disquisitions* (*Lun heng*). The precocious Wang Pi (226–249), the most brilliant man of his day, showed the new interest in Taoism in his great commentaries on the *Tao te ching* and the *Classic of Changes*.

The outstanding expression of the Neo-Taoist intellectual current of the third century was called *ch'ing-t'an,* translated as "pure discussions" or "purity debates." The men in this tradition held themselves disdainfully aloof from unsavory politics and all other mundane matters. Their answer to the social and political disillusionment of the time was to develop their own aesthetic sensibilities and give individualistic expression to their every impulse. Typical of such men were the Seven Sages of the Bamboo Grove, a group of wealthy and eccentric recluses, living at the Western Chin capital, who loved to engage in philosophical debate, compose poetry, play the lute, enjoy nature, and drink to excess. A similar but even more eccentric group was the Eight Understanding Ones who lived at Nanking in the fourth century. In turning their backs on government, such men robbed society of some of its natural leaders, thus contributing to the general breakdown.

Another aspect of the Taoist resurgence was the growing interest in alchemy as a method of obtaining an elixir of life. A monumental work on alchemy, the *Pao-p'u-tzu,* appeared in the early fourth century. The search for elixirs probably led to the experimental eating of all sorts of organic and inorganic substances, which may have contributed to the extraordinarily catholic tastes of the Chinese and the richness of their culinary art. It also contributed to the development of medicinal knowledge through the discovery of many beneficial drugs and led to even broader protoscientific inquiry. One reason why later Chinese thinkers turned away from scientific experimentation was its association in their minds with Taoism.

A more widespread Taoist immortality cult centered on concepts of inner hygiene. By eschewing wine, meat, and cereals and by breathing exercises, practitioners supposedly cleansed the three "cinnabar fields" in their bodies, nurtured the 36,000 internal gods, and suppressed the three worms that were the causes of disease, old age, and death. This cult, which flourished between the third and sixth centuries, eventually evolved into the breathing exercises and general hygiene systems that are still popular among Chinese.

Popular Taoist Religion. The most spectacular aspect of the upsurge of Taoism was its development as an organized popular religion. Very possibly the whole concept of collective worship and religious organization was derived from Buddhism, which was seeping into China at this time. Certainly many of the books of the huge Taoist canon that was later developed were nothing more than close imitations of Buddhist texts.

The revolts of the Yellow Turbans and the Five Pecks of Rice band in 184 A.D. were the first clear signs that Taoism had given birth to organized popular religions. Faith-healing was at the heart of both these religious movements. Popular Taoism in time developed an enormous pantheon, headed by a triad of deities and at the lower levels composed of immortals and historic human beings. It also borrowed heavily from Buddhism, eventually accepting the concept of the indestructible soul, an afterlife in heaven rather than corporeal immortality, and the value of good works as a means of reaching heaven and avoiding hell. In later centuries the distinctions between popular Taoism and popular Buddhism became vague, and the two tended to merge in a confused mass of mythology, superstitions, and magical practices.

After the suppression of the Yellow Turbans and the Five Pecks of Rice band near the end of the Later Han, the Taoist religions were never again reconstituted as effectively centralized churches, but individual parishes remained, and the movement flourished under their atomized leadership. The local priest was supported by gifts received at religious ceremonies and by the traditional tithes of five pecks of rice from his parishioners. Taoist monasteries and convents also developed in obvious imitation of Buddhist monasticism, but the monks were commonly allowed to marry, and the intellectual and moral standards of their communities tended to be very low. Taoist sects also appeared in great numbers, again under the influence of sectarian Chinese Buddhism.

Various efforts were made to unify the Taoist sects and parishes, but with no great success. An emperor of the "barbarian" Northern Wei dynasty was persuaded to proclaim Taoism the official religion of the state in 444, and various later rulers accorded it official recognition. In 1019 the hereditary leader of one of the Taoist sects, who claimed descent from Chang Ling, the second-century founder of the Five Pecks of Rice band, was granted a great tract of land in Kiangsi in South China and was invested as "Heavenly Master." In the late thirteenth century the Chang family was accorded official recognition as the leader of the Taoist church and during the next century was given a certain degree of official control over the Taoist priests of the whole land. The so-called Taoist "popes" of this line maintained some of their holdings and at least the theory of their leadership until 1927.

The Coming of Buddhism

Indian Buddhism.   The resurgence of Taoism in China at a time of political disruption is quite understandable; the even greater popularity of Buddhism is more surprising. The Indian religion flatly contradicted the dearest concepts and ideals of the Chinese. It constituted an even more direct challenge to Chinese civilization than did Western culture in the nineteenth century, and its adoption represented the greatest borrowing from abroad that the Chinese were to know before modern times. Buddhism is the chief cultural link between the peoples of East and South Asia, but its contrasting histories in India and China highlight the differences rather than the similarities between these two spiritual and psychological ends of the earth.

Indian Buddhism was based on a series of premises that the ancient Chinese would never have understood. It assumed that life was essentially painful. It also assumed that life was unending, since one existence was tied to the next by *karma,* a term literally meaning "act" but implying causality. Birth leads to old age, death, and further births in an endless chain of causality, which explains the differences in status and the seeming injustices one sees in the world. The Indian Buddhist, unlike the Chinese Confucian, was not interested in correcting these injustices and perfecting the social order but in escaping the painful cycle of existence.

The historic Buddha, known as Sakyamuni, lived around 500 B.C. in what is now the southern edge of Nepal north of India. Distressed by the suffering he saw around him, he abandoned his family and adopted an ascetic way of life, but found that this led nowhere. Subsequently, sitting in meditation, he achieved enlightenment, discovering the "Middle Way" between the extremes of self-indulgence and self-mortification. He thus became the Buddha, "the Enlightened One," and began to preach his wonderful discovery to a devoted band of disciples.

The essence of the Buddha's ideas was expressed in the Four Noble Truths: life is painful; the origin of pain is desire; the cessation of pain is to be sought by ending desire; and the way to this goal is through his Noble Eightfold Path—that is, his rules for right living. These constituted, from the Chinese point of view, an extremely ascetic way of life. The end objective was Nirvana, which was not the achievement of godhood or the salvation of the soul in the Western sense but merely the breaking of the chain of existence through the ending of all desires. Although literally meaning "emptiness," Nirvana was felt to be not simply extinction but something more, like the peaceful merging of a drop of water into the sea.

Buddhism early developed into a monastic church, and around the first century B.C. its hitherto oral teachings began to be written down in two closely related Indo-European languages. The Pali scriptures have been preserved in Ceylon, and the Sanskrit scriptures have been preserved largely through translations into Chinese and Tibetan. The Buddhist canon, known as the Tripitaka, or "three baskets," is traditionally divided into the *Vinayas* or "disciplines" for monastic life, the *Sutras* or "discourses," which constitute the major teachings, and the *Abhidharmas* or scholastic elaborations of the teachings. It is a huge collection of writings. The Chinese Tripitaka, for example, consists of more than sixteen hundred works in over five thousand sections.

The Spread and Development of Buddhism.   Buddhism is a universal religion, in which all men are equal in the Buddhist "law," or teachings. Like Christianity and Islam, the two great universal religions of the Mediterranean area, it spread widely. Indian traders and travelers carried it by sea throughout Southeast Asia and to South China. It also spread among the Greek kingdoms left over by Alexander's conquests on the northwestern frontiers of the Indian subcontinent. Gandhara in the border region between the present Pakistan and Afghanistan became a particular stronghold of Buddhism. The greatest monarch of the Kushan Empire of the Yüeh-chih, who ruled around 100 A.D. from North India to the Tarim Basin, also was an ardent patron of Buddhism. He championed the faith in Central Asia, and from there it spread into North China. A third wave of Buddhist propagation rolled northward a few centuries later, through Tibet and on into Mongolia. This was a late and degenerate form of Buddhism, which contained a large element of Hinduism and soon absorbed the popular demon worship of Tibet. The resultant Lamaism and the theocratic society it produced in Tibet and Mongolia bear small resemblance to the original teachings of the Buddha.

Even the purer forms of Buddhism divided at an early date into two major trends. These are usually known as Mahayana or the Greater Vehicle and Hinayana or the Lesser Vehicle, also called Theravada, "the doctrine of the Elders." Theravada, which remained closer to original Buddhism, is still the religion of Ceylon, Burma, Thailand, and Cambodia, while the Buddhism of China, Korea, Japan, and Vietnam stems largely from Mahayana.

The Greater Vehicle was "greater" in the sense of its all-inclusiveness. Since it distinguished between absolute and relative truth, it could tolerate even contradictory ideas as representing various degrees of relative truth accommodated to the different levels of understanding of its believers. Mahayana developed a vast body of metaphysical speculation and a huge pantheon. In place of the godless religion of the historical Buddha, the Mahayanists have myriads of godlike Buddhas in eons of time. They also developed a new type of deity, the Bodhisattva or "Enlightened Existence," who, though he has achieved the enlightenment of a Buddha, stays back in this world to help others to salvation before passing on into Nirvana himself.

Because of the concept of Bodhisattvas dedicated to saving other weaker creatures, the emphasis in Mahayana Buddhism shifted from enlightenment through "one's own strength" to salvation through "the strength of another." Faith was all that was necessary. The *Lotus Sutra,* a popular Mahayanist scripture, predicts the eventual salvation of all animal life. (Buddhism recognizes no division between humans and animals.) Naturally Bodhisattvas became the great popular gods of Mahayana Buddhism. For example, the Buddha Amitabha (Chinese: O-mi-t'o Fo; Japanese: Amida Butsu), who was a Bodhisattva in origin, became the great savior as the "Deity of the Western Paradise." Similarly Avalokitesvara (Chinese: Kuan-yin; Japanese: Kannon), gradually changing in sex, emerged as the benign "Goddess of Mercy." Mahayana thus provided compassionate, comforting gods for every human need.

Nirvana also gradually changed its meaning, at least for the less sophisticated Mahayanist believers. Increasingly, it came to mean salvation in a very definite afterlife in paradise. Descriptions and portrayals of this paradise became quite specific and those of hell even more graphic and gruesomely convincing. The Bodhisattva ideal of aid to others led to a strong emphasis

*The Bodhisattva Kuan-yin carved
in stone, from the Northern
Chou dynasty (557–581* A.D.*).*

in Mahayana on charity—on good works to help others and to contribute to one's own salvation. Buddhism thus was turned somewhat from its original antisocial contemplative bent. The concept of charity made social work important; the possibility of salvation through faith made monasticism, celibacy, and asceticism less necessary.

The Introduction of Buddhism to China.   Many of these developments in Mahayana took place after Buddhism reached China, but the tolerance for other religious concepts and the wide inclusiveness of early Mahayana made it from the start more palatable to Chinese than the original religion would have been. Appearing to the Chinese at first as a variant of Taoism, it had a powerful appeal to a "barbarianized" North China and a demoralized South. To the superstitious it was a potent new magic, to the educated a stimulating new set of ideas. It was the first organized universal faith the Chinese had encountered. It had behind it the fruits of another great culture—the metaphysics and early science of India, a noble literature, a beautiful religious art, aesthetically satisfying ceremonials, the appeal of the peaceful

*Nine-story brick pagoda erected at Cheng-ting in Hopei in 659 A.D.
and rebuilt in 1668.*

monastic life in a troubled age, and the promise of personal salvation at a
time when there seemed to be no solution to man's worldly problems.

According to tradition, Buddhism was first introduced to China as the
result of a dream in 64 A.D. of the second emperor of the Later Han, Ming
Ti. The story is apocryphal, but already at this time there was a Buddhist
group at a noble's court in the lower Yangtze Valley, and by the next
century Buddhism had become entrenched in what is now North Vietnam.
Soon stupas, the Buddhist reliquary towers, were being erected by converts
in various parts of China. Modified by Chinese architectural concepts, these

stupas in time developed into the stone, brick, or wooden pagodas that have become so typical a part of the scenery of East Asia.

The first transmitters of Buddhism may have been traders, but the religion was soon being propagated more actively by missionaries. A Parthian prince, known to history by his Chinese name, An Shih-kao, was active as a missionary and translator of scriptures at Loyang during the latter part of the second century. An even greater transmitter of the faith was Kumarajiva, who was born in Central Asia to an Indian father, captured by a Chinese expedition around 382, and brought to China, where he headed a great translation project. No fewer than fifty-two of the ninety-eight scriptures he translated are still extant.

Chinese converts eventually became more important than the missionaries in transmitting the Indian religion to China. We have the names of close to two hundred East Asian monks, nine of them Koreans, who between the third and eighth centuries essayed the long and perilous trip to India to imbibe the Buddhist teachings at their source. This was the first great student migration of East Asian history. Fa-hsien, who left for India by way of Central Asia in 399 and returned by sea in 414, is particularly famous for the record of his trip that he left. Since the Indians, lacking much interest in history, rarely bothered to record dates, the carefully dated accounts of Fa-hsien and the other Chinese Buddhist pilgrims have proved invaluable in establishing Indian and Central Asian chronology. The most famous of the Buddhist pilgrims was Hsüan-tsang, who made the round trip to India between 629 and 645 by way of Central Asia. The account of his travels, the *Record of the Western Regions,* is the most important work of its sort. A third Chinese pilgrim, I-ching, who between 671 and 695 made the round trip to India by the southern route, compiled records of more than fifty other pilgrims.

Buddhism, unlike Christianity in the Roman Empire, apparently was taken up by the rich before it spread downward to the poor. At first it seems to have made more rapid progress in the "barbarian" North than in the South, perhaps because the non-Chinese rulers of this area felt no prejudice against it as a foreign religion. The greatest imperial patrons of the new religion were the emperors of the "barbarian" Northern Wei dynasty (386–534). Two groups of Buddhist cave temples, at Yün-kang near their first capital in northern Shansi and at Lung-men near their second capital of Loyang, contain some of the finest artistic remains of early Chinese Buddhism. By the sixth century, however, the South was as thoroughly permeated by Buddhism as the North.

Part of Buddhism's success was due to its readiness to compromise with Taoism and Confucianism, tolerating the former as an inferior level of truth and the latter as a political and social philosophy that was not incompatible with its own basic teachings. Ever since, there has been a strong tendency

*Stone bas-relief of the empress as a donor with attendants, from
the Lung-men rock temples (near Loyang) of the Northern Wei
dynasty (about 522 A.D.).*

among the Chinese to synthesize "the three religions" or to maintain them
side by side. At this time, however, Buddhism was definitely the dominant
member of the trio, and a great proportion of the higher intellectual capacities and artistic genius of the Chinese was devoted to the translation and
interpretation of its scriptures and the building and beautifying of its temples
and monasteries.

The whole epoch from the fourth century to the ninth might well be
called the Buddhist age of both Chinese and Asian history. During this
period, Buddhism blanketed the whole of the Asian continent, except for
Siberia and West Asia, giving to this vast area a degree of cultural unity
that has never again been matched. This, however, was but a brief moment
of religious unity. Buddhism began to decline in India as early as the sixth
century and by the fifteenth had virtually disappeared. It was wiped out in
Central Asia in the ninth century by the inroads of Islam. Meanwhile, the
Hinayana of Southeast Asia and the Mahayana of East Asia had begun to
drift apart, and a serious decline had commenced in Chinese Buddhism.

The "Barbarians" Restore the Empire

The Strength of the Imperial Tradition.   To an observer of world history in the fourth century it might have appeared that Rome would always endure but that the days of the Chinese Empire were over. North China, the heartland of the empire, was completely overrun by "barbarians"; South China was obviously incapable of restoring imperial unity; and the whole land was being swept by a foreign religion which had an otherworldly emphasis and a celibate, monastic ideal that cut at the roots of Chinese philosophy and the family-centered social system.

The Chinese Empire, however, was eventually reconstituted, while Rome faded into a mere memory. The "barbarian" conquerors of the North were no different from the "barbarian" conquerors of Rome in their hope that they could appropriate for themselves the empire they were defeating. They differed from their Western counterparts in that they eventually succeeded in this effort, recreating by the middle of the fifth century a fair facsimile of the old empire, which started a process that led by the seventh century to a Chinese Empire richer and stronger than Han had ever been. The contrast with the steadily sinking fortunes of Rome is striking and constitutes a sharp parting of the historical ways between the peoples at the two ends of the Eurasian continent.

There is no certain answer to the question why the Chinese Empire was restored but not the Roman. One reason may be that the southern dynasties maintained the old imperial tradition more fully than did Greek Byzantium and had a stronger influence on the North than Byzantium did on Italy or France because of the greater geographic compactness of China. Another reason may have been the superiority of the Han imperial ideal to the Roman. The concept of just and ethical rule by an emperor whose possession of the Mandate of Heaven demonstrated the support of his people and who exercised his power through a bureaucracy of educated men, chosen not by birth or by chance but because of merit, may have been more understandable to people of this age than was the Roman ideal of rule through impersonal law. The Chinese writing system also probably made for greater cultural continuity than did the Latin and Greek scripts of the West. The "barbarians" had to learn Chinese if they were to read and write, since Chinese characters could not be easily applied to their languages. Moreover, even the Chinese whose spoken "dialects" were mutually unintelligible had the written language in common. And finally, the very size and density of the Chinese population probably led to a more rapid and complete absorption of the "barbarian" invaders than happened in Europe. Since Chinese agriculture was more intensive than that of Europe, it produced a denser population, and the invaders thus were more rapidly submerged in the large numbers of Chinese around them.

The "Five Barbarians" and the Sixteen Kingdoms.   The Chinese traditionally describe the fourth-century invaders of North China as the "Five Barbarians." These were the Turkish Hsiung-nu and another Turkish group; the Hsien-pei (or Hsien-pi), a Mongolian people from the northeast; and two groups of Tibetans from the west. The Hsien-pei overran the edges of the North China Plain as early as 281, and the Tibetans started their depredations in 296, but the main inundation came after the revolt of the Hsiung-nu in North China in 304.

During the period from 304 to 439 the Chinese throne in North China was claimed by a number of contending "barbarian" and Chinese groups, which historians have fittingly dubbed the Sixteen Kingdoms. The Hsiung-nu band that destroyed Loyang in 316 adopted the dynastic name of Chao. This kingdom is usually called the Earlier Chao in contrast to the Later Chao of one of their rebellious generals, Shih Lo, who destroyed the Earlier Chao in 329. Shih Lo attempted to restore a more strictly tribal rule than that of the more Sinicized Earlier Chao, and he treated the Chinese with great severity. Finally in 349 the people rose up and destroyed his successors.

Meanwhile a Chinese general had set up an Earlier Liang dynasty in the western panhandle of Kansu and Hsien-pei tribes had created the Earlier Yen in the Peking area, while in 351 a strong Tibetan leader, Fu Chien, set up the highly Sinicized state of Earlier Ch'in at the old historic capital of Ch'ang-an. Earlier Ch'in conquered Earlier Yen in 370, establishing a brief period of comparative peace and unity in North China.

This peace was shattered by the usurpation of the throne at Ch'ang-an in 384 by a Tibetan general, who founded the Later Ch'in, and in rapid succession Hsien-pei tribes founded Later Yen in the northeast and Western Yen in Shansi, while Tibetan groups founded Later Liang in the Kansu panhandle and Western Ch'in in the far west. All these were very short-lived kingdoms, and they were followed in turn by six other equally transitory so-called dynasties.

The Northern Wei.   Finally one "barbarian" tribe managed to establish a more lasting government and unify the North. This was the T'o-pa tribe of Hsien-pei, which had moved into northern Shansi as the Hsiung-nu had moved southward. The T'o-pa declared themselves the independent state of Wei (called the Northern Wei) in 386 and succeeded in pushing back some newly risen pastoral rivals on the northern steppes. By 439 they had also destroyed their "barbarian" rivals in China and had unified the North.

After the Northern Wei had incorporated under their rule the densely populated agricultural lands of the North China Plain, a subtle change began to take place in this originally "barbarian" empire. Like the Earlier Ch'in, the strongest of the previous "barbarian" dynasties, the Northern Wei from the start had been a semi-Sinicized state, but now the process of

CHINA AROUND 500 A.D.

cultural absorption was accelerated. The agricultural lands were not divided among the T'o-pa tribesmen but were administered in the traditional Chinese manner, and the T'o-pa themselves were relegated to the status of a soldiery.

By the late fifth century, the process of acculturation had gone so far that the Northern Wei court embarked on a conscious policy of Sinification. In 493–494 the capital was moved from the present Ta-t'ung in northern Shansi to Loyang, which had been the capital of the Later Han and Western Chin. At about the same time, Chinese was made the only official court language, and the T'o-pa aristocrats were ordered to adopt Chinese dress, customs, and surnames and were encouraged to intermarry with the local population.

The complete Sinification of the court led to serious revolts in 524 by the still partly tribal military forces. The central government also found itself increasingly the prey of its own great families. In 534–535 it was divided under puppet emperors into Eastern and Western Wei dynasties, and through usurpations these became Northern Ch'i in 550 and Northern

Chou in 557. The latter, based in the Wei Valley with its capital at Ch'ang-an, once again proved the military superiority of this area by conquering Northern Ch'i in 577.

The Sui and T'ang Dynasties

Sui Recreates the Unified Empire.   Four years later Yang Chien, a general of mixed Chinese and Hsien-pei blood, usurped the throne, founding the Sui dynasty. By this time, however, the "barbarians" had become so absorbed into the population and culture of North China that the distinction between "barbarian" and Chinese was largely theoretical. Quite fittingly, this mixed inheritor of both Chinese and "barbarian" traditions conquered the Ch'en dynasty of the South in 589, thus restoring the unified Chinese Empire.

The role of the Sui was much like that of the Ch'in eight centuries earlier. The founder of the dynasty reunited the empire, but his successor failed to hold it. Like their Ch'in predecessors, the Sui rulers may have been overly ambitious. They attempted to achieve too much in too short a time, overstraining the endurance and loyalty of their new subjects. This was particularly true of the second ruler, Yang Ti ("Zealous Emperor," 604–618). Under the two Sui emperors, however, China was started on its second great imperial period. A strong centralized government was re-established for all China; the Great Wall was reconstructed; long canals were dug, making possible the great prosperity of the following centuries; huge palaces were erected; and the prestige of the Chinese Empire was fully restored.

Once again, the pendulum of conquest swung outward from China into the lands of the "barbarians." The *yin* of "barbarian" rule in China, by infusing new blood and new martial ardor into China, had produced once again the *yang* of Chinese imperial conquest. Chinese control was re-established over northern Vietnam and expeditions were sent against the Cham state in southern Vietnam and to Taiwan. In the north, the T'u-chüeh, the earliest known form of the name Turk, had overthrown their nomad masters but had split into eastern and western confederations in 581. The Eastern Turks now acknowledged the suzerainty of China, and in 609 Sui also conquered a mixed Tibetan and Hsien-pei state (called T'u-yü-hun) in northern Tibet.

Yang Ti, however, alienated his people because of his endless wars and the tremendous labor needed for the construction of canals, walls, and palaces. The prestige of the dynasty was also seriously tarnished by a disastrous campaign in 612 against the Korean kingdom of Koguryŏ in North Korea and South Manchuria. Serious revolts broke out, forcing him to terminate inconclusively his campaigns of 613 and 614 against Koguryŏ.

Stone relief from the tomb of the T'ang emperor T'ai Tsung (626–649), depicting one of his battle chargers attended by a bearded "barbarian" groom.

In 615 he was badly defeated by the Eastern Turks, who had hitherto been his loyal vassals. The empire then started to disintegrate, and Yang Ti fled to South China, where he was assassinated in 618.

The World Empire of T'ang. The man who emerged victorious from the free-for-all that followed the collapse of Sui was Li Shih-min, who was a prominent official and general of mixed Chinese and "barbarian" blood from Shansi in the North. He captured the capital, Ch'ang-an, in 617 and the next year founded the T'ang dynasty, placing his father on the throne. After eliminating his brothers, he had his father abdicate in 626 and thereafter ruled in his own name until 649. He is known to history as T'ai Tsung ("Grand Ancestor") and his reign (626–649) is considered the first great high point of the T'ang dynasty. The whole T'ang dynasty, like the Earlier Han, is regarded as one of the two golden ages of the Chinese Empire.

In 630 T'ai Tsung subjugated the Eastern Turks, and in great campaigns in 639–640 and 647–648 he wrested the Tarim Basin from the Western Turks. He was aided in this victory by the Turkish Uighur tribes, which at this time broke away from the Western Turkish Empire to become the loyal allies of the T'ang and their chief source of military power in Central Asia. Chinese suzerainty was gradually extended beyond the Pamirs over the states of the Oxus Valley. In 657 the Western Turkish Empire was finally broken up, and various Turkish groups were pushed southward into India and westward into West Asia and Europe.

Tibet, which had been unified for the first time in 607, also came under Chinese suzerainty, and from there a Chinese emissary, leading Tibetan troops, pacified a part of North India, bringing back to Ch'ang-an in 648 a captive Indian princeling. This incident was the only military encounter between China and India before recent years, and its uniqueness illustrates the effectiveness of the mountain barrier between these two great masses of humanity. T'ai Tsung's armies were twice repulsed by the Korean state of Koguryŏ, but in 668 his successor, Kao Tsung ("High Ancestor," 649–683), succeeded with the help of the southeastern Korean kingdom of Silla in crushing a coalition of Koguryŏ, Paekche (in southwest Korea), and Japan. Thereafter a unified Korea under Silla remained a loyal vassal of T'ang.

T'ang power extended over a vast area from southern Siberia to Southeast Asia and westward through Tibet and Central Asia to the Caspian Sea. Around the borders of China proper clustered vassal states, controlled by six protectorates. Four of these were named for the cardinal points, as in An-hsi ("the pacified west") in the Tarim Basin, An-tung ("the pacified east") in the Korean area, and An-nan ("the pacified south"), from which Annam, the usual Chinese name for Vietnam, was derived. Beyond these vassal states were others, such as Japan and various kingdoms in Southeast, South, and West Asia, which recognized a vague Chinese suzerainty by occasionally presenting tribute. T'ang rule thus, from the Chinese point of view, was virtually worldwide.

The T'ang, like the Han before it, was almost brought to an end by an empress. The Empress Wu dominated Kao Tsung's later years and after his death ruled for a while through puppet emperors. Then in 690 she assumed the title for herself—the only time a woman ever did this in China—and changed the dynastic name to Chou. As a usurper, and a woman at that, she has been severely condemned by Chinese historians, but actually she was a strong and able ruler, and she greatly furthered the supremacy of the merit bureaucracy over the aristocracy. The Empress Wu was set aside in her eighties in a palace *coup d'état* in 705, but after a few years of confusion another able ruler came to the throne in 712. He is known to history as Hsüan Tsung ("Mysterious Ancestor") or Ming Huang ("Enlightened Emperor"), and his long reign (712–756) represents the second blossoming of the dynasty.

Actually T'ang was by this time a far more populous and richer empire

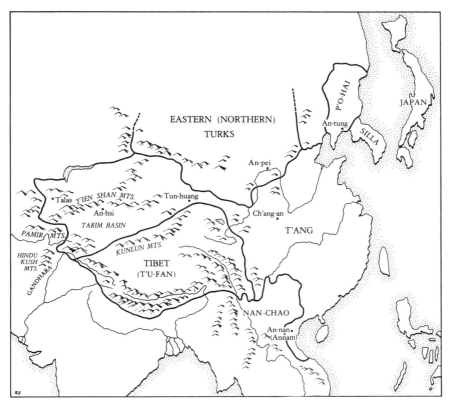

THE T'ANG EMPIRE IN THE EARLY EIGHTH CENTURY

than it had been in the days of T'ai Tsung. But it had also started to show signs of decay. Financial problems multiplied, and the pendulum of conquest started to swing back against China. In 747 Kao Hsien-chih, a Korean general in the service of T'ang, led an army across the Pamirs and the Hindu Kush to break up an attempted juncture between the Arabs and the Tibetans, but this was the last highwater mark of T'ang power. In 751 he was disastrously defeated by the Arabs at Talas, north of Ferghana, and Hsüan Tsung's reign ended a few years later in rebellion and an apparent breakup of the empire. With the aid of its "barbarian" allies, the dynasty was restored and continued for another century and a half, but it never again showed its earlier power and verve.

The Revival of Centralized Rule

The Landholding and Military Systems.   The reunification of China by force of arms in the sixth century and the conquest of a far-flung empire in the seventh were merely the surface manifestations of a much more profound process—the restoration of a stable centralized government. For centuries the powerful independent families of the South and the tribal divisions of the "barbarians" of the North had made centralized rule impossible. Buddhism, moreover, had introduced a new element of economic disruption. Rich monasteries became great landowners and thus joined the great families as contenders with the central government for the fruit of the peasants' toil. The greatest achievement of the Northern Wei, Sui, and T'ang was the development of institutions that overcame these divisive forces.

In the fifth century the Northern Wei began to solve the basic problem that had destroyed the Han. They returned, in a sense, to Wang Mang's effort to nationalize the land. Since land taxes were light and the main tax burden, especially *corvée* labor, was borne by the free peasantry on a per capita basis, a government, in order to prosper, had to keep as many peasants as possible in a tax-paying status and out of serfdom or slavery on the great estates. In 485 the Northern Wei instituted an "equal field" system, according to which all able-bodied adult peasants were supposed to be assigned agricultural lands of equal dimensions. Only a small part of this could be held permanently as crop lands in mulberry trees for feeding silkworms or in other tree crops. The rest was to be returned to the government at a person's death or his passing of the age limit. Although the "equal field" system was not designed to deprive the great families of their holdings and was applied only to free peasants, it did help to stop the flow of lands and peasants into private hands and to stabilize the financial foundations of the central government.

The Northern Wei also reinstituted a system by which the people were divided into groups that were mutually responsible for one another's conduct and tax payments. This sort of collective-guarantee system had been used in one form or another since antiquity, and it was continued in more recent times as the *pao-chia* system for maintaining local order. This system sets neighbors to watching neighbors, since they are all held accountable for one another.

During this period also, self-supporting military colonies of soldier-farmers were set up along the northern frontier. Similar colonies had been created during the Han, but from the Six Dynasties period on they became a permanent element in the defense of the empire. Another important military institution—the militia system—was inaugurated by the Western Wei (535–557) and Northern Chou (557–581), the successor states to Northern Wei in the Ch'ang-an area. Able-bodied peasants were given military training and organized into regular forces like the tribal soldiery. Under the T'ang this militia service became part of the tax burden that peasants bore as landholders under the "equal field" system.

During the Sui and T'ang dynasties the "equal field" system was greatly elaborated. The Sui applied it to the whole country and forced the great families to fit into the system by assigning their holdings as "rank lands," scaling downward from a maximum of about 1370 acres for the highest rank. In the T'ang the great families and officials were assigned similar "rank lands" and in addition "office lands" varying in size according to the specific government positions they held. Organs of local government were supported by "office fields." The bulk of the land, however, was divided equally among the peasants. Each able-bodied male between the ages of eighteen and fifty-nine was supposed to receive about 13.7 acres, of which only one-fifth could be permanently owned "mulberry" land. On this economic base, he was to pay the government in taxes a fixed amount of grain; a certain amount of silk or hemp, depending on the type of textile produced in his region; and twenty days per year of *corvée* labor for the central government and other periods of labor for the local organs of government. This *corvée* labor was sometimes commuted into textile or money taxes. In addition, certain able-bodied peasants who were exempted from other taxes and levies had to render periodic military service, usually without pay and at their own expense.

To operate this complicated landholding system, a careful census and land register were necessary for the whole country. Remaining examples of such surveys show that every piece of land was indeed allotted by specific category to individual taxpayers. This was perhaps as complicated a system of landholding and taxation as was to be found anywhere in the world before the late nineteenth century, but it worked reasonably well for about a century, supporting the Chinese Empire during an outstanding epoch.

T'ang Prosperity.   During the early T'ang, the central government had an ample tax income, which was equaled by expenditures only after the imperial clan and the organs of government had undergone a long period of growth. With their characteristic genius for organization, the Chinese at this time developed units of measure of approximately equal value for the principal commodities in the economy. Thus, a string of one thousand cash, an "ounce" of silver, a "bushel" of grain, a "bolt" of silk, and a "weight" of silk floss were all roughly equivalent in value. Counting by this standard "unit" of value, the tax income of the central government, according to one of several such listings, amounted to over 52 million "units." In addition, the central government enjoyed as a part of the tax system the free labor and military service of its millions of peasants.

The government unquestionably was far more affluent than it had ever been under the Han. Advances in technology and administration were probably responsible for part of this gain, but the chief reason was the great growth in population of the Yangtze Valley during the intervening centuries. Although the government remained in the Northwest and in the hands of a military aristocracy from that region, the chief breadbasket was no longer the dry wheat and millet lands of the Wei Valley and the North

China Plain but the rich rice-growing paddy fields of the lower Yangtze region.

This situation explains the great canal-building activity of the Sui. An efficient transport system was necessary between the South and the capital and frontier areas in the North to enable the empire to take full advantage of its rich southern provinces. Yang Ti, by connecting various older canals and building new ones, constructed by 610 a Grand Canal system stretching from the Hangchow area south of the Yangtze to the Yellow River and from there westward to Ch'ang-an and northward to the Peking area. The modern Grand Canal was identical with this first system as far north as the Huai River but then cut directly across the North China Plain to Peking.

In theory the "equal field" system rested on the periodic redistribution of the bulk of the farm land among the tax-paying peasants, but it is doubtful that there was ever much actual redistribution. The population grew quickly because of domestic peace, and the peasantry thus increased faster than the land resources. The result was that most peasants received from their fathers less than their full quota of land, and most of this came to be registered as permanent possessions. At the same time, cumulative imperial grants, as in the Later Han, reduced the total quantity of land available to the tax-paying peasants. By the first half of the eighth century the whole system was obviously breaking down. The collapse of the T'ang government toward the close of Hsüan Tsung's reign may be attributed in part to the failure of the landholding and tax system. In any case, the system was abandoned at this time and was never again attempted on the same scale.

The Bureaucracy and the Examination System. A dependable bureaucracy was indispensable for the centralized government. After the Han system of government schools and examinations had decayed, the Wei and Western Chin dynasties of the third century attempted to secure efficient administrators by having local authorities classify men of merit in nine grades and recommend the best for government service, but the powerful local families perverted the system by putting their own members and henchmen at the top of the lists, which became in time merely rankings of social status.

It was not until the Sui and T'ang that Chinese rulers were able to reconstitute a system for recruitment of officials that would help preserve the central government from the complete domination of the rich, aristocratic families. The first Sui ruler restored the old Han emphasis on Confucian traditions as being the most suitable ideological basis for a centralized government. He also reinstituted—though on a much more elaborate scale—the Han system of examinations for would-be bureaucrats based on a Confucian curriculum, and he reasserted the principle that the officials of the prefectures and districts should not be local aristocrats but appointees from the central government.

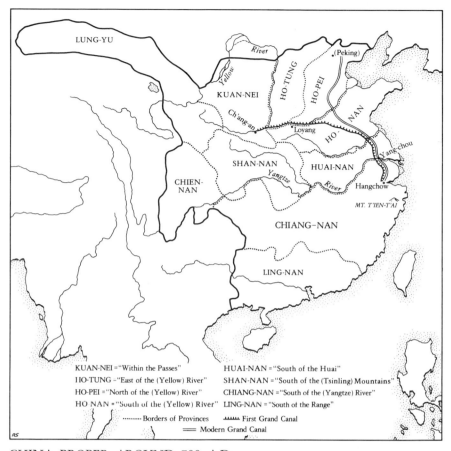

KUAN-NEI = "Within the Passes"   HUAI-NAN = "South of the Huai"
HO-TUNG = "East of the (Yellow) River"   SHAN-NAN = "South of the (Tsinling) Mountains"
HO-PEI = "North of the (Yellow) River"   CHIANG-NAN = "South of the (Yangtze) River"
HO NAN = "South of the (Yellow) River"   LING-NAN = "South of the Range"
········· Borders of Provinces   ⊥⊥⊥⊥⊥ First Grand Canal
═══ Modern Grand Canal

CHINA PROPER AROUND 700 A.D.

T'ang continued and expanded the government schools and examination
system of the Sui. There was a series of specialized national schools at the
capital, and the prefectures and districts also maintained institutions where
local students could pursue their studies. Government examinations were
held for the students of the capital schools and for nominees from the local
governments. The Ministry of Rites administered these examinations amidst
elaborate rituals. There were several different categories of examination
degrees, such as "flowering talent" (*hsiu-ts'ai*) for current political problems,
"presented scholar" (*chin-shih,* implying presentation to the emperor) for
letters, and also examinations in classics, law, calligraphy, and mathematics.
The last three, however, were considered merely technical skills leading to
low positions, and in time the *chin-shih* degree became the most prestigious
and the chief route to high government office. Before appointment, those
who had passed the *chin-shih* examination faced a second series of examinations, administered by the Ministry of Personnel, in which they were judged
not only on their written answers but on their personal appearance and

speaking ability. For officials in service, there were also merit examinations, which amounted to a civil service rating system.

This elaborate system developed only slowly and did not reach its height until the eighth century. Even then, it was strongly weighted in favor of the rich and powerful. To prepare for the examinations took years of classical studies, which only the rich could afford. The capital schools were primarily for the aristocracy, and candidates recommended by local governments were likely to be from the privileged classes. Moreover, high officials always had the privilege of recommending their sons and protégés for official rank and position without their passing through the examination system.

Nevertheless, the T'ang examination system helped create a bureaucracy of merit that went far beyond anything the Han had known. With the exception of the first group of T'ang leaders, who achieved power through the sword, and the leaders during the last years of dynastic collapse, the great majority of the men who reached the top posts in the bureaucracy (and apparently the majority of those in the middle grades also) first distinguished themselves by winning the *chin-shih* degree.

The T'ang system was the true start of the civil service merit system that is one of the greatest achievements of Chinese civilization. Since the examinations became the most obvious route to political and financial success, all who wished to participate in national leadership were led to seek the same classical, literary type of education, thus producing an intellectually unified nation. One is reminded of the classical education that produced a successful ruling class for the British Empire in modern times. Since Confucian ideology lay at the basis of Chinese education, the ruling class was thoroughly imbued with ethical principles, concepts of loyalty to existing authority, and a strong sense of the value of rituals and decorum. Men of intellectual ability, singularly favored as they were by the system, became the strongest supporters of the government, instead of its critics, as has happened in so many other societies. The system even won the support of the lower classes for the established order, because there was always the possibility that a man of humble birth might pass the *chin-shih* examination and eventually become one of the emperor's chief ministers.

Of course, the examination system had its weaknesses too. The resulting prestige of scholarship, combined with the traditional prestige of political office, helped perpetuate a division of Chinese society by education into two major strata long after the power of the medieval aristocracy had faded. The emphasis on literary, historical, and scholarly subject matter in the examinations may also have given the ruling groups an overly scholastic, literary, and antiquarian bent, to the detriment of other more practical qualities. The system, while helping to produce extraordinary stability in China over the next millennium, may also have contributed to a slowing down of change and progress.

The Structure of Government. The Sui abolished the old commanderies (*chün*) and divided the country into a more uniform system of districts (*hsien*), grouped together in prefectures (*chou*). The T'ang added to this system by grouping prefectures together as provinces, called "circuits" (*tao*), of which there were originally ten and later fifteen.

To bind the empire together, T'ang also created an elaborate system of post-stations on the roads and waterways that radiated out from the capital. Commonly located at ten-mile intervals, these post-stations maintained inns for official travelers provided with government tallies and furnished them with horses or boats. The post-station system remained thereafter a standard part of Chinese government. T'ang also established barriers on the principal trade routes and strictly controlled city marketplaces as a way to tax and regulate trade. Despite this interest in taxes on trade, however, it showed the traditional Chinese scorn for merchants.

In T'ang times the top organs of the central government were the Imperial Secretariat, the Imperial Chancellery, and the Department of State Affairs. The first was the chief originator of government policies and imperial orders; the second, a stronghold of bureaucratic power, had the right to review these orders, thus serving as a check on the emperor's authority; the third carried out the orders agreed upon by the other two. This three-way division of power and the collegial sharing of leadership among high officials in each of these bodies ensured a division and balance of power in the high bureaucracy beneath the throne. Under the Department of State Affairs were Six Ministries or Boards *(Pu)*: Personnel, Revenue, Rites, Military, Justice, and Public Works. This sixfold division of adminstration persisted in Chinese government down to the twentieth century.

An office that deserves special mention was the Board of Censors. It had the duty of ferreting out cases of treason or misgovernment and reporting them directly to the emperor. Its members were also to point out to the emperor (at no little risk to themselves) any imperfections in his conduct. The Board of Censors remained an important organ in the Chinese imperial government in later dynasties.

Ch'ang-an was both the focus and symbol of the highly centralized T'ang Empire. The eastern terminus of the great overland trade routes across Central Asia as well as the capital of the largest empire the world had yet seen, Ch'ang-an was thronged with people from all over Asia. The population of the capital district, including the city, its suburbs, and a little surrounding countryside, rose to 1,960,186. Its walls formed a great rectangle of slightly more than five by six miles. The city was laid out in modern checkerboard fashion. Broad and straight north-south and east-west thoroughfares divided it into 110 blocks, each of which was an administrative "village," with its own internal alleyways. A 500-foot-wide central thoroughfare led from the central southern gate of the city to the Imperial City (government head-

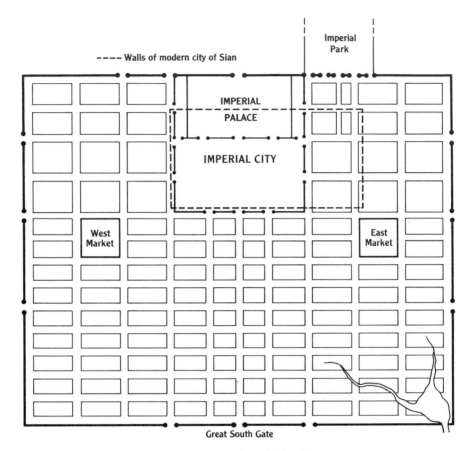

PLAN OF CH'ANG-AN DURING THE T'ANG

quarters) and beyond it the Imperial Palace at the north, dividing the city into eastern and western administrative halves, each with a large government-operated marketplace.

The whole plan and organization of Ch'ang-an illustrate the strict and careful control that the early T'ang maintained over society. The size and grandeur of the city suggest the dynasty's power and wealth. China during the seventh century towered high above all other political units of the time. During the Han dynasty China had drawn abreast of the Mediterranean world. Now it was starting on what was to prove to be almost a millennium of pre-eminence as the strongest, richest, and in many ways most advanced country in the world.

The Absorption of Buddhism

The Development of Sects.   Just as the Chinese incorporated the "barbarians" into a new and greater Chinese Empire, they also gradually absorbed

Buddhism, deriving cultural enrichment from it but neutralizing its challenge to Chinese values. Buddhism flourished economically and intellectually under the imperial patronage of the Northern Wei and in the early T'ang. It perhaps reached its apogee in China around 700 under the zealous patronage of the Empress Wu, who had once been a nun. The Buddhism that flourished from the fifth to the eighth centuries, however, was being steadily reshaped into a set of ideas and institutions that bore little resemblance to primitive Buddhism but fitted easily into the Chinese system.

The Indian love of philosophical speculation had given rise to numerous schools of thought; the Chinese love of classification now resulted in the organization of some of these different philosophical tendencies into sects. Some sects were direct philosophic transplants from India, as in the case of Fa-hsiang (Japanese: Hossō), brought back in 645 by the great traveler Hsüan-tsang. Those sects that prospered most, however, stressed elements that were native to Chinese thinking. One of these was T'ien-t'ai (Japanese: Tendai), founded by Chih-i (538–597) and named for its mountain head-quarters in Chekiang. Its popularity was based on its typically Chinese eclecticism, love of compromise, and skill at classification. It developed the Mahayana concept of relative truths, organizing the vast body of conflicting Buddhist doctrines into different levels of truth, each valid in its own way. T'ien-t'ai became the leading sect in the eighth and ninth centuries and helped establish the *Lotus Sutra* as the most popular scripture of East Asian Buddhism.

Another sect that came to the fore at much the same time was Chen-yen, the "True Word" (Japanese: Shingon). This was an esoteric or secret doctrine, strongly influenced by the Tantric cults of Hinduism. It taught that ultimate reality could not be expressed by words but was best suggested by magic signs and symbols. The incantations, magic formulas, and ceremonials that Chen-yen emphasized were readily appreciated by the Chinese, who were familiar with such things from Taoism and from the Confucian emphasis on ritual. Chen-yen masses for the dead, in particular, became extremely popular, because they fitted in well with traditional ancestor worship. Chen-yen's schematic cosmological drawings, known as *mandala* (Japanese: mandara), had great influence on later Chinese Buddhist art.

The Mayahana concept of salvation through faith also became the basis of a strong sectarian movement known as "Pure Land" (Ching-t'u; Japanese: Jōdo), a name for the Western Paradise of Amida. This sect stressed the simple act of faith of calling on the Buddha's name (*nien-fo;* Japanese: *nembutsu*). By the fifth century these ideas were entrenched in China. Popular rebellions from Sui times on drew spiritual inspiration from such forms of Buddhism, rather than from Taoism. The "Pure Land" sect appealed to the common man and became numerically the greatest force in East Asian Buddhism.

The last of the sectarian movements proved ultimately the most significant.

This was the Meditation sect, or Ch'an, better known by its Japanese name, Zen. It appeared in China in early T'ang times but did not become prominent until the ninth century. Zen was close to primitive Buddhism in its stress on meditation and intuitive insight or "enlightenment," but it derived perhaps even more from philosophical Taoism, which had also stressed these qualities. It taught that the only true reality was the Buddha nature within each person's heart. Though it derived a sense of the otherworldly and the infinite from India, this mysticism was applied in typically Chinese fashion to the mundane life of the individual. The meditative life became in China a life of hard work and rugged self-reliance. Zen's antischolastic, antitextual bias was pure Taoism. Instead of texts, it stressed oral instruction, particularly through the posing of outwardly nonsensical questions meant to shock the student out of his dependence on ordinary logic. In its love of nature and rustic simplicity, Zen was merely the old Taoist tradition in a new guise, and it therefore quite naturally became a major inspiration for artistic and poetic creativeness.

Although Zen never formed a well-organized church in China, its discipline of meditation and emphasis on self-reliance gave it much greater strength than the other sects derived from their monastic rules or intricate philosophies. Zen was the only type of Buddhism that continued a vigorous intellectual life after the T'ang. Gradually, the rest of Chinese Buddhism was absorbed either by Zen or by the popular "Pure Land" sect, and in time even these two lost their distinctiveness, merging in the vague mixture of superstitions into which Chinese Buddhism eventually degenerated.

Buddhism's Role in Society.   While the Chinese were modifying Buddhist ideas, they also were remolding its institutions to better fit Chinese society. Buddhist monasteries began to take on social functions as inns, public baths, and even primitive banking institutions. They also took over the burial of the dead until recent times. Celibacy, which was regarded by the Chinese as the most antisocial aspect of Buddhism, was in time relaxed to permit the marriage of the clergy and thus the continuation of the family.

The rich holdings of the great Buddhist monasteries presented the Chinese state with the only true church problem it ever faced. Monasteries were built and endowed by rulers or prosperous individuals and tended to accumulate more riches through further gifts of land or treasure from pious believers. They also expanded their holdings through usury and the various other legal or illegal methods by which the great families amassed their landholdings. Thus they constituted in the eyes of the rulers a fiscal menace to the state, removing land and men from the tax registers. The idea therefore developed that the number of monasteries and monks and the size of their holdings should be limited. This was paralleled by the concept that, if Buddhism were indeed of value to society, it should not only be regulated by the state but also supported by it as a sort of spiritual branch of the administration. Nothing could have been further from the original role of Indian Buddhism.

The southern dynasties could no more control the Buddhist monasteries than they could the great families, but in the North a regulatory system did develop. By the fourth century, rulers were appointing "bishops" to control the church, and the Northern Wei fixed limits on monasteries and their lands. The T'ang had the theory that there should be one official monastery, with thirty monks, per prefecture and by 729 had inaugurated a clerical census every three years to help enforce this system. By 747 the government itself was issuing ordination permits to limit the number of new monks. Attempts to control the number of monasteries and monks, however, always failed in the long run. Devout rulers and government officials were constantly breaking their own regulations, and secret ordinations were common.

Occasionally the effort to regulate the Buddhist church escalated into harsh persecution. Many Chinese resented Buddhism as a foreign religion or abhorred some of its practices, such as self-mutilation and cremation as well as celibacy, which were felt to threaten family continuity and to violate the body one had received from one's ancestors. The jealousy of Taoist priests was also sometimes a contributing factor. But the chief reason for Buddhist persecutions was the financial need of the government. Persecutions were chiefly efforts to return the lands and monks of the monasteries to the tax registers and seize their gilt-bronze images and other wealth for the imperial treasury. Individual believers were not seriously bothered.

There was a persecution of Buddhism under the Northern Wei in 446 and another, including Taoism, under the Northern Chou in 574. The greatest and most significant persecution occurred in 841–845 under a half-insane T'ang emperor who had become a fanatic Taoist. According to the official accounts, 4600 monasteries and 40,000 shrines were destroyed, and 260,000 monks and nuns and their 150,000 slaves were returned to the tax registers. This persecution proved a crippling blow to Buddhism because the Indian religion was already losing its inner vitality. The examination system had again focused attention on the Classics and Confucian ideas, and the upper classes, as a result, were losing interest in Buddhism. Zen continued its growth and influence for a few more centuries, but the other forms of Buddhism rapidly fell into decay.

Fortunately, before the intellectual and artistic glories of Chinese Buddhism were irretrievably lost, it left a permanent shrine at Tun-huang near the western extremity of the Kansu panhandle in the far northwest. Here, among the elaborately decorated, rock-hewn temples known as the "Caves of the Thousand Buddhas," a great Buddhist library was sealed shut around 1035 to save it from raiding Tibetans. Not reopened until 1900; this library, with its thousands of manuscripts, many in various Central Asian languages, proved to be a unique repository of the Buddhist age in China.

T'ang paintings of Buddhist deities, saints, and angels on the walls and ceiling of a grotto at Tun-huang.

Although Buddhism was a major component of Chinese culture during one of its most brilliant epochs, it left relatively little permanent impress on Chinese civilization. Its lasting contributions tend to be additions to traditional Chinese culture rather than fundamental alterations of native values. It was the source of much of the popular religion and mythology of the common people. It added a metaphysical dimension to Chinese thought and greatly enriched Chinese literature and art. It thus embellished Chinese culture, but it did not remold the whole civilization, as did Christianity in Europe.

The Growth of Chinese Culture

Contacts with the Outside World.   During the Six Dynasties period and the early T'ang, China was pervaded by a spirit of cultural tolerance. The "barbarian" invasions left the North wide open to foreign influences; Buddhism was both a vehicle for and a stimulus to close cultural contacts with distant areas; interregional trade by sea and by land was growing far beyond anything known in Han times; and the early T'ang Empire brought the Chinese into direct contact with the great centers of civilization in India and West Asia. Never again until the twentieth century was China to prove so responsive to foreign influences.

Foreign contacts brought many new agricultural products and some inventions. Tea, for example, was introduced from Southeast Asia. Valued at first as a medicine and as a stimulant for meditation, it had by late T'ang times come into more general use and subsequently spread from China to become the world's most popular drink. The chair was also introduced from the west and over the centuries gradually replaced sitting pads and mats. More technological advances came from China itself. The earlier inventions of paper and porcelaneous ware were greatly developed, and gunpowder was discovered, though it was still used only for fireworks. Another invention was the wheelbarrow, which became a major means of transportation on China's narrow footpaths but did not spread to the West for many centuries. Coal came into use as early as the fourth century in North China, though it was still a marvel to the European Marco Polo in the thirteenth century.

Trade and foreign embassies brought thousands of foreigners to the T'ang capital, and these people brought with them their many religions. Zoroastrianism (or Mazdaism), the fire-worshipping religion of Persia, reached China by the sixth century. Manichaeism, which included Zoroastrian and Christian elements, came in the early T'ang, as did the Nestorian branch of Christianity. A great stone stele was erected at the Nestorian church in Ch'ang-an in 781 and rediscovered only in the seventeenth century. All three of these religions from the west were virtually wiped out in the religious persecutions of 841–845, but two others survived. Judaism continued in small isolated communities until the nineteenth century, and Islam grew steadily until it embraced many millions, largely in Chinese Turkestan and in the northwest and southwest corners of China proper.

T'ang, as the greatest empire of its day, was assiduously imitated by many neighboring peoples. Never before or again did such a large proportion of mankind look to China not only as the paramount military power of the time but as the obvious model for government and culture.

The first unified Tibetan government, established in the seventh century, and the state of Nan-chao, founded by Thai groups in Yunnan around 740, were both directly inspired by the T'ang system of rule. The T'ang political and cultural pattern was even more fully adopted by the peoples to the east. The various kingdoms of Korea had for centuries shown strong Chinese influence, and Silla, after uniting the peninsula in 668, became a veritable replica of the T'ang in miniature. The Tungusic kingdom of P'o-hai, which flourished in the woodlands of southern and eastern Manchuria and northeastern Korea from 713 to 926, also closely copied certain T'ang institutions. The efforts of the Japanese in the seventh and eighth centuries to create another small T'ang in their remote islands was an even more remarkable example.

The Arts.   Buddhist psalmody had a profound influence on Chinese music, and during this period the music and instruments of Central Asia virtually displaced the older musical traditions of China. In art, and particularly in sculpture, foreign Buddhist influence was also strong. In fact, the Buddhist demand for religious images made this the greatest age of Chinese sculpture. What had been a minor art form in earlier periods rose to great heights for a few centuries, and then declined with Buddhism after the T'ang.

Chinese Buddhist sculptures, as preserved in such successive shrines as the rock temples of Yün-kang, Lung-men, and Tun-huang, show diverse artistic strains. Some influences came directly from India, but the most important artistic traditions in North China during the Six Dynasties period were those of Central Asian Buddhism, which had been derived in turn from the strongly Hellenistic Buddhist art of Gandhara and surrounding areas in what is now northwest Pakistan and Afghanistan. The early Buddhist sculpture of China, however, was quite different from the Greek in spirit, as was to be expected in a deeply religious art. The human figures, far from being naturalistic, were stiff, austere abstractions of deity, and Greek realism was limited to such superficial elements as the folds of their clothing, By the T'ang, however, Chinese humanistic interests had made the Buddhist concept of deity more intimate, and this change was reflected in sculpture. Images became much plumper and more lifelike, closely approximating T'ang concepts of human beauty. There was also great secular sculpture during this period, and large numbers of beautiful pottery figures of dancing girls, camels, horses, Central Asian grooms, and the like were made for burial in tombs.

Little remains of the Buddhist painting of the Six Dynasties and T'ang periods, except for the murals of the Tun-huang caves, but the Buddhist influence on Chinese painting was tremendous. Though most of the artistic genius of China during this time was probably devoted to religious art, secular painting also flourished, and South China saw the beginnings of artistic trends which were to grow into the great painting traditions of the late T'ang and following periods. Though, again, little remains today of this secular art, Ku K'ai-chih, who flourished around 400 A.D., is honored as the first great figure in Chinese painting, while Wang Hsi-chih (321–379) is considered the greatest name in calligraphy. (See Plate 4.)

Except for brick and stone pagodas, not much remains of either the secular or religious architecture of the T'ang or earlier periods. Buddhist temples built in the Chinese style in Japan during the seventh and eighth centuries, however, have survived, giving us some idea of the classic simplicity and balance of Chinese architectural forms at this time (see pages 343–344).

Giant guardian deities carved in a cliff at Lung-men around 672–676 A.D. *Note the square holes and niches made to support the wooden structures that once enclosed these images.*

Seventh-century pottery figure of a lady polo player, about ten inches high.

CHINA'S OLDEST WOODEN BUILDING. *Front elevation and cross section of the main hall of the Fo-kuang-ssu ("Monastery of the Buddha's Halo") on Mount Wu-t'ai, dating from the T'ang dynasty.*

Literature and Scholarship.   During the Buddhist age a large proportion of the best literary and scholarly talent naturally was devoted to Buddhist works, which later generations of Chinese have generally ignored, but there was also much endeavor along more traditional lines. Literary writing for the most part continued to be an essentially aristocratic art. The *fu* poetic form remained in fashion during the Six Dynasties period and was paralleled in prose by an elaborate balanced style that featured carefully paired verbal patterns, commonly in four- and six-syllable phrases (*p'ien-t'i-wen*). The most important verse form of the Six Dynasties period was the *shih,* a lyric in five-syllable meter, which first appeared in the late Han. It was typically Taoist in its laments over the corruption of the world and its assertation of the individual's independence of society. The greatest *shih* master of the time, T'ao Ch'ien (also known as T'ao Yüan-ming, 376–427), was a southerner who in characteristic Taoist fashion found his personal elixir in wine.

Works of literary criticism began to appear as early as the third century, and in the sixth Hsiao T'ung (501–531), the heir apparent to the Liang throne in the South, compiled the *Literary Selections* (*Wen hsüan*), China's most famous anthology. There was no falling off in the output of standard histories, commentaries on the classics, and other traditional types of scholarship. Around the year 500 there appeared a curious work much used in later Chinese elementary instruction. This was the *Thousand-Character Classic,* which summarizes Chinese history and Confucian philosophical views in a thousand characters, none of which is repeated.

One new aspect of Chinese scholarship, which in later periods grew to colossal proportions, was the compiling of works of an encyclopedic nature.

These were of many different types, but one of the commonest, usually called local gazetteers, concerned the history, natural features, and political and social institutions of a single local administrative unit, such as a district or prefecture. The earliest surviving work of this sort dates from the fourth century.

All these new literary and scholarly trends grew out of earlier Chinese traditions and were continued and expanded under the T'ang. In higher culture the Six Dynasties period thus represented no great break with the past and led on smoothly into the T'ang and later periods. This was perhaps because of the broad overlapping in time of the old and the new. The continuing Han cultural tradition of succession states in South China and the rising new semi-"barbarian," semi-Buddhist culture of the North remained for a long time contemporaneous. Despite the challenge to Chinese society of "barbarian" invaders and a foreign religion, there was much greater cultural continuity between Han and T'ang than between Rome and medieval Europe.

6. The Late T'ang and Sung:

The Flowering of Chinese Culture

The Transition from Classic to Early Modern China

To divide a dynasty between two major periods goes against the whole cyclic interpretation of Chinese history. The traditionalist may be especially outraged when the dynasty so divided is the T'ang, perhaps the most resplendent in all Chinese history. But this is necessary if we are to see the more fundamental trends that underlay the dynastic cycle.

We are accustomed to thinking of great cultural and social changes as occurring during times of military defeat or political breakdown. But nothing produces change more inevitably than growth, and growth in population, production, trade, culture, and institutions takes place more easily in peaceful times than during periods of disruption. This is what happened during the T'ang. The Sui and early T'ang saw the re-creation of the classic empire, though in a more perfected form. A century of relative peace and prosperity then brought growth that lifted China to a significantly higher level than that attained by the Han. There was an institutional and cultural breakthrough, which in turn produced more growth.

The Six Dynasties period and early T'ang were in many ways the last phase of ancient Chinese history; the late T'ang and the Sung (960–1279) which followed it formed the first phase of later Chinese history. One might, in fact, call this period the "early modern" phase, for the culture which evolved at this time was to remain characteristic of China until the opening decades of the twentieth century. Much of what has proved most typical of China during the past millennium appeared at least in embryo by late T'ang times and came into early bloom under the Sung.

The cultural and institutional level achieved during the late T'ang and Sung was not greatly changed during the next several hundred years. This period proved to be a plateau in time, with the Chinese at first well above Western attainments but in later times technologically below them. In post-Sung times, China seems to have changed more slowly than in earlier centuries and certainly much less rapidly than the Occident, where the rate of change accelerated in modern times.

The period of transition between late classic China and the early modern period centered around the eighth century. The decay of the T'ang dynasty at this time and the start of a long swing of the pendulum of conquest back against China were typical of the dynastic cycle and earlier trends in relations with the northern "barbarians," but there were also other more subtle changes in progress which were to remake Chinese society and culture. The intellectual leadership, for example, started to reject Buddhism and return to Confucianism, but with such decidedly new emphases that post-T'ang Chinese philosophy is usually called Neo-Confucianism. The Chinese also re-emphasized the strongly secular bias that has distinguished East Asian civilization from the civilizations of South Asia and the West during the past millennium. Moreover, in their rejection of foreign religions and in their losing battle with the "barbarians," they gradually lost the cosmopolitanism and cultural tolerance they had shown in the Six Dynasties period and early T'ang and became much more narrowly ethnocentric.

In the eighth century a fundamental change also was made from a per capita based system of taxation to taxation of land areas, and this together with a tremendous increase in both domestic and international trade during the T'ang period made the government's subsequent financial and administrative problems quite different from those of earlier dynasties. These economic changes also contributed to a great shift in society. Until the early T'ang the ruling class had been composed of powerful aristocratic families, largely of military origin. But gradually leadership devolved upon a much broader class of landowners, often with mercantile backgrounds, who have commonly been called the "gentry."

With the decline of the old aristocracy came the real triumph of the bureaucratic system. Or, to put it the other way, with the appearance of the fully developed examination system in the T'ang, the decline of aristocratic society commenced. Until the seventh century the organized bureaucracy, itself drawn largely from a hereditary aristocracy, had been used to buttress the rule of a military empire of aristocratic traditions. In post-T'ang times, Chinese or "barbarian" warriors continued to found dynasties by force of arms, but for the most part government and culture became dominated by bureaucrats who owed their position more to their own talents than to birth. This meant the acceptance of a basically egalitarian ideal that had always been implicit in Confucianism but did not really triumph in Chinese society until the late

T'ang and Sung. It also meant the shift from an essentially military leadership to one that was basically civilian. By Sung times the civilian point of view had become predominant, and there was a growing contempt for the military profession.

A parallel change was the displacement of the center of gravity in China. While the capital usually remained in the North, where the major defense problem existed, the lower Yangtze Valley became the economic heart of the country, and men from this region increasingly dominated both the culture and the government. The cultural center of gravity also moved from rural China to the cities. The new gentry class did not necessarily live on its agricultural holdings and lead a rural life, but often joined the officials and merchants in the cities and towns, leaving junior members to manage estates in the countryside.

The higher culture was naturally affected by all these trends. There was a growing sophistication of scholarship, literature, and art and a tremendous expansion in scope and sheer quantity of production. Most of this activity grew out of earlier traditions, but it was richly creative, producing the artistic and literary forms which have seemed most typically Chinese ever since. In fact, the patterns set during the late T'ang and Sung in art and literature, as well as in society and government, were to dominate Chinese civilization until the early twentieth century. In this sense, the period from the eighth to the thirteenth centuries was a second golden age of Chinese culture.

The Late T'ang

The Degeneration of the System.   Naturally, the great changes outlined above took place slowly, and some of them had only just begun by the late T'ang. Still, the reign of Hsüan Tsung (712–756) was perhaps the key period in the transition from ancient to early modern China. It was also, and more obviously, the crucial turning point in the dynastic cycle, which revolved as inexorably during the T'ang as in the Han.

Under Hsüan Tsung the dynasty reached its second great peak. In wealth, grandeur, and cultural brilliance his reign far outshone that of T'ai Tsung a century earlier. But the costs of maintaining the imperial family and the government had multiplied many times over, and income had by no means kept pace. The whole system of government was operating less smoothly and was beginning to break down in such vital sectors as taxation and military defense, much as had happened in the Han. The "equal field" system (see pages 100–101) slowed the descent but could not stop it.

The rapid increase of population and the habit of emperors of rewarding their ministers with grants of lands and people—as many as fifteen hundred households at a time—made it impossible to redistribute the land to the peasants and assign each family an adequate share, as was called for in the "equal field" system. The tax burden, including *corvée* labor and military service, fell on a progressively shrinking proportion of the peasantry, whose holdings were growing steadily smaller. When the burden became unbearable, peasants would flee their farms or transfer their holdings through shady deals to the estate of some wealthy man, where the 50 per cent of produce paid in rent would actually be less oppressive than the government taxes. This only aggravated the situation for the remaining free peasants.

As the "equal field" system collapsed, the yield from the per capita tax system associated with it declined drastically, and the government had to find substitute forms of income. For example, the very light land tax, which applied to the estates as well as to peasant holdings, was gradually increased, commercial taxes were developed, and a tax on all households, divided into nine categories according to wealth, was instituted. Such tax reforms, however, could not save the *corvée* and militia systems. Bit by bit *corvée* labor was eliminated from the key function of transporting tax grain up the Grand Canal to the North. By 723, some 120,000 mercenaries had taken the place of the militia in the capital guards, and professionals had also begun to replace the militia in the frontier armies. Although both the *corvée* and militia systems were to continue in use in various forms until recent times, they were never again as important to the central government as they had been up through the seventh century.

While these changes in part represented an institutional advance connected with a developing money economy, they entailed some grave difficulties. Paid workers and mercenaries meant increased government expenses. Moreover, professional soldiers, who were commonly recruited from the dregs of society or from "barbarian" tribes, might not prove ardent defenders of China, and because of their long terms of service they frequently developed a primary loyalty to their generals rather than to the dynasty. This situation allowed ambitious generals to become virtually independent local warlords.

The defeat in 751 of Kao Hsien-chih by the Arabs at Talas west of the Pamirs was a turning point in East Asian history. It marked the end of Chinese control over Central Asia and the beginning of five centuries of steady military decline for the Chinese Empire. It also marked the beginning of Islamic penetration of Central Asia. At much the same time the Turkish language also began to replace the Indo-European tongues in the oasis states of the Tarim Basin.

Not long after the defeat at Talas, T'ang collapsed internally. Regional commanders had by Hsüan Tsung's time become more or less permanent officials controlling the civil as well as military affairs of ten large border regions. One of these regional commanders, a man of Turkish origin named

An Lu-shan, came to control three regions and won power at court through the patronage of Hsüan Tsung's favorite consort, Yang Kuei-fei ("Consort" Yang), who adopted him as her legal son. An Lu-shan came into conflict with Yang Kuei-fei's brother over control of the central government and revolted in 755. He captured the capital, and the fleeing emperor was forced by his discontented soldiers to execute Yang Kuei-fei and her brother, who were blamed for the catastrophe. This pathetic story has been a favorite theme for Chinese poets and writers. An Lu-shan was killed by his own son in 757, and the same fate befell his successor, another "barbarian" general. Meanwhile Hsüan Tsung had abdicated, but loyal armies, with the aid of the Uighur Turks, managed to restore order to the country by 762. The earlier grandeur of T'ang, however, was never restored.

Political Disunity and Fiscal Reforms.   The rebellion of An Lu-shan was a serious blow to centralized government, as was reflected in the drop of the official census figures from 52,880,488 in 754 to a mere 16,900,000 in 764. The dynasty also remained entirely dependent on foreign troops and never again exercised any real power outside of China proper. The Uighurs continued to dominate much of Central Asia, until they were supplanted around 840 by the Kirghiz. T'ang control over China proper also weakened. The system of regional commanders was extended to the whole country, and many of the commanders turned their areas into personal satrapies. Their positions in some cases became virtually hereditary, and on occasion they openly rebelled against the court.

The central government was wracked too by internal dissensions. Already in Hsüan Tsung's reign there had been a growing struggle for power between the old T'ang aristocracy and the newer bureaucracy. A century of successful use of the examination system and the strong patronage of the Empress Wu had made the bureaucrats powerful enough to challenge the old sources of power. After An Lu-shan's revolt the now dominant bureaucracy itself broke up into quarreling factions. The eunuchs, as in the Later Han, also became powerful, contending with the bureaucrats for leadership, and they dominated most of the T'ang rulers during the ninth century.

Despite these conditions the T'ang managed to survive for a century and a half after An Lu-shan's revolt. The central government, moreover, was not as feeble nor were conditions as chaotic as has usually been supposed. Such matters are always relative. The Japanese monk Ennin, during his stay in China between 838 and 847, described in his diary a prosperous and well-ordered society with a degree of bureaucratic meticulousness and centralized control that probably was not matched in other parts of the world until much later times.

One fundamental reason for this situation was the new financial basis of government developed during the restoration that followed An Lu-shan's revolt. The transport of grain from the Yangtze Valley to the capital was improved and put fully into the hands of professional workers. The old system of government monopolies was revived, and those in salt, tea, and liquor became important sources of revenue. In 780 various land, personal, and household taxes were consolidated into the so-called Double Tax, levied twice a year on land areas, regardless of ownership, rather than on peasants as individuals.

This reform capped an epoch-making transition which had been a century under way. Thenceforth in Chinese history land areas rather than individuals were the basic units of agricultural taxation, and the collecting of taxes became much simpler. The central government could be less concerned about the development of private holdings, for such holdings no longer represented a menace to the financial underpinnings of the state. In fact, the whole landholding system of China changed. Landowners no longer needed to be politically powerful in order to protect the virtually tax-free status of their estates but could simply be landlords of tenant-operated, tax-paying farms. This was, in other words, the beginning of the type of landlordism that was to characterize China's rural economy from then until the twentieth century.

The Final Breakup: The Five Dynasties Period.   A simpler landholding and tax system than in earlier times, together with a more diversified fiscal foundation for government and an improved administration based on the examination system, may account for the ability of the T'ang and later dynasties to run a cycle of three centuries, compared to the two-century cycle of the Earlier and Later Han. But it was inevitable that sooner or later the long enfeebled T'ang would collapse completely. The final breakup started with great uprisings in the North in 874. One of the rebel leaders, Huang Ch'ao, an unsuccessful candidate in the government examinations, even captured the capital, but the revolt was finally suppressed in 884 by a general of Turkish origin. All semblance of control over the regional commanders had been lost, however, during the revolt, and in 907 one of them, who once had been a supporter of Huang Ch'ao, usurped the throne, bringing the T'ang to a formal end.

There ensued a more complete but much briefer disintegration of centralized rule than had followed the collapse of the Later Han. Central and South China and parts of the North were divided among a number of former regional commanders, each claiming to be the emperor of China. There were, in all, fourteen such kingdoms, though the official histories have grouped them together as the "Ten Kingdoms." Meanwhile in North China, five ephemeral dynasties, for which the Five Dynasties period (907–960) is named, followed one aonther in rapid succession, as a series of ambitious generals usurped the throne and tried without success to found lasting regimes. None lasted more than sixteen years. The last, the Later Chou (951–960),

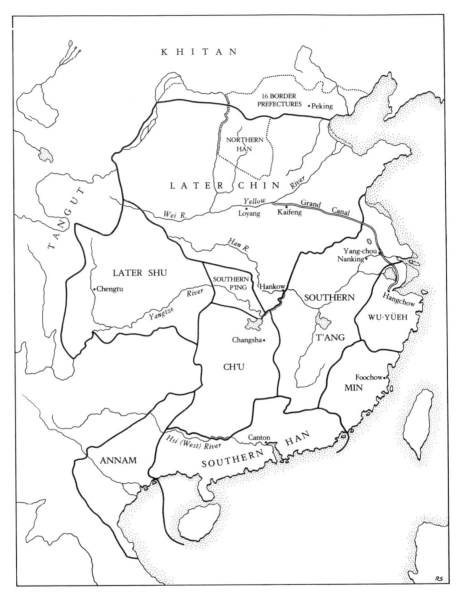

CHINA AROUND 940 A.D.

is remembered chiefly for a great persecution of Buddhism it carried out in order to strengthen its financial position.

Three of the five usurping generals were "barbarians"—two Turkish and one perhaps an Iranian. Thus once again the Chinese Empire had drawn "barbarian" soldiers into its heart. Meanwhile tribal "barbarians" were pressing in again on China's borders. The Khitan Mongols of southern Manchuria, in return for helping the Later Chin (936–946), the third of the "Five Dynasties," achieve the throne, were given sixteen border prefectures around the present Peking. Although they subsequently destroyed Later Chin and over-ran North China, they proved unable to hold onto it. Their control of the sixteen border prefectures, however, has given their Liao dynasty (947–1125) a place in official Chinese histories. Incidentally in Kitai, a later form of Khitan, we find the Russian name for China as well as the origin of Cathay, the medieval European term for the country.

The Sung Dynasty

The Founding of the Sung.   The most significant fact about the disunity of the Five Dynasties period is that it lasted only half a century, in contrast to the three-and-a-half centuries of political division during the Six Dynasties period. Perhaps the traditions and techniques of centralized rule had become so much stronger by the tenth century that a long multiple division of the country was no longer possible. In any case, it should be noted that China was never again divided into a number of competing political units for even so long as half a century. Foreign conquest was to divide it between a purely Chinese South and a "barbarian"-ruled North, but not until the collapse of the old system in the early twentieth century was the empire again broken up into a number of independent or autonomous units. In other words, China since the T'ang has proved to be a virtually indestructible political unit.

In 960, only fifty-three years after the end of the T'ang, another general, Chao K'uang-yin, carried out the sixth usurpation of the throne in the North, and this time the effort succeeded. Known to history as T'ai Tsu ("Grand Progenitor"), he founded the Sung dynasty, which was to last until 1279. Before his death in 976 he had extended his rule over all but two of the other Chinese states, and these last two were incorporated into the empire in 978 and 979 by his brother and successor T'ai Tsung ("Grand Ancestor," 976–997).

T'ai Tsu's successs in establishing a lasting dynasty can be attributed in large part to the determination with which he tackled the gravest political problem of his day—the almost unrestricted power of local military commanders. He managed to transfer his own leading generals to minor posts or to retire them with suitable rewards. In the provinces he limited the regional commanders to a single prefecture and, as they died or retired, replaced them with civil officials from the central bureaucracy. He also followed a policy of transferring the best military units to the capital armies, and he placed all military forces directly under the central government. In these various ways he assured the central government of preponderant military power and eliminated the warlordism that had destroyed the T'ang and kept China unstable and divided during the Five Dynasties period.

T'ai Tsu's success in carrying out these military reforms, however, may have contributed to what became the Sung's greatest problem—military weakness in the face of the "barbarian" menace. The Sung never achieved the military prowess of the Han and T'ang. It was unable to reincorporate Northern Vietnam (Annam) into the empire or extend its control over any part of Central Asia or the northern steppe. It even failed to win back the sixteen prefectures lost to the Khitan Liao in 926, and in 1004 it agreed to pay the Liao an annual sum of 300,000 units of silk and silver. On the northwest, Sung was hard pressed by Tangut tribes of Tibetans. These had established a strong state in the Kansu panhandle and the Ordos region inside the northern loop of the Yellow River, and in 1038 they assumed the Chinese dynastic name of Hsia (called in history the Hsi Hsia, or "Western Hsia"). After a serious defeat, the Sung started in 1044 to pay an annual sum to the Hsi Hsia too. Thereafter a three-way military and diplomatic stalemate developed between the Sung and their two predatory northern neighbors.

The Government and Civil Service.   T'ai Tsu and his successors set up at the capital a series of administrative offices that were more directly under the personal control of the emperor than the T'ang organs of government had been. For example, two minor offices, close to the throne, which had appeared in the second half of the T'ang, were now made into major government agencies and continued to have an important role in later Chinese history. The first was the Board of Academicians, originally a sort of document-drafting body, which now became a major advisory group to the emperor. The other was the Bureau of Military Affairs. The Secretariat-Chancellery continued the names of two of the three highest bodies of the T'ang, and under it operated the six ministries and lesser administrative offices, as they had under the Department of State Affairs in the T'ang. Two other important organs of government were the Board of Censors, which in time developed an elaborate system for checking on all the operations of government, and the Finance Commission, which handled the treasury, taxes, monopolies, and other financial matters. The Sung, unlike the T'ang, kept close and direct control over the entire tax yield of the empire. Because of this and also because of general economic growth, the government's income in the early eleventh century was three times that of the T'ang at its height, and a huge surplus was soon built up.

The administration of the whole empire in the Sung was more thoroughly centralized at the capital than ever before in Chinese history. The capital, as during most of the Five Dynasties, was at Kaifeng. Located near the juncture of the Grand Canal system with the Yellow River, it was still in the old northern heartland of China but almost three hundred miles closer than Ch'ang-an to the rich rice-producing areas of the lower Yangtze. The Sung continued unchanged the T'ang system of prefectures and districts but increased the number of provinces or "circuits" (*tao,* later called *lu*). These were given greater supervisory authority over the prefectures than the T'ang

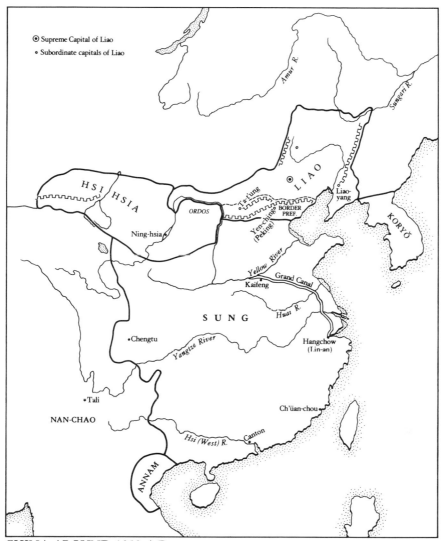

CHINA AROUND 1050 A.D.

"circuits" had possessed, and in order to insure that they would not fall under military dominance, as had happened in the T'ang, they were given functions and areas of supervision clearly differentiated from those of the military authorities.

The conscious effort of T'ai Tsu and his successors to gather the reins of administration into their own hands and concentrate control of the whole country at the capital made the Chinese government thenceforth not only more centralized but also, in a way, more autocratic. The following millennium of Chinese history, therefore, is often called the age of "autocracy," as opposed to the preceding "aristocratic" age. The term, however, is misleading. Despite the right of rebellion implicit in the theory of the "Mandate of

Heaven," the Chinese Empire had always been basically autocratic in theory and fully autocratic in practice under strong rulers. What had changed primarily was that it had become more efficient, and therefore more successfully centralized, because its officialdom had changed in nature from aristocrats to bureaucrats.

The chief strength of the Sung government was the quality of its higher civil service. This in turn depended in large part on the examination system, which had been so greatly developed during the T'ang and now attained its most perfected form. The palace eunuchs around the emperor and other nonbureaucratic groups were successfully barred from political power. The high standards of government service at this time are indicated by the practice of prohibiting close official contact among high bureaucrats related by blood or marriage and by rules barring relatives of empresses and other imperial consorts as well as members of the imperial clan from holding any of the important positions.

The higher civil service was built up by the transfer of able men from lower posts, by permitting high officials to nominate relatives for appointment to junior positions, and even by the sale of offices. By far the most important source of higher civil servants, however, was the examination system. Between 997 and 1124 an average of well over two hundred men a year entered the civil service through the examinations, constituting probably a slight majority of the twelve thousand or more higher civil officials. Moreover the men with examination degrees virtually monopolized the highest posts in the bureaucracy.

There were various categories of examinations, but the *chin-shih* in letters, which was the only examination that put much emphasis on originality and skill in reasoning rather than on mere memory, was most esteemed and all but eclipsed the others by the late eleventh century. To insure that there would be no favoritism in the grading of examinations, the identity of the individual examinee was carefully concealed by the use of numbers instead of names and the examination papers were copied so that the handwriting could not be recognized.

After 1065 the examinations were held regularly every three years. There were three successive levels of examinations. First came the examinations held by the individual prefectures or government schools. Scholars who passed these, reportedly varying between 1 and 10 per cent of the candidates, went on to an examination given by the central government at the capital. About 10 per cent of these were passed and were then subjected to a "palace examination," which rejected a few more and gave rankings to the others that helped determine their initial appointment to office. Unsuccessful candidates usually took the examinations time after time. As a result, those who passed might range in age from the late teens to the seventies, though they probably averaged around thirty-five.

The promotion of officials depended on several factors—the length of their tenure of office, a system of merit ratings, special examinations for certain specific assignments, a candidate's rank in the original examinations, and the sponsorship of higher officials. According to the sponsorship system, certain higher officials had ths duty of nominating for promotion promising junior officials who might otherwise be overlooked. The protégé could not be a relative of the sponsor, but the latter was responsible for his protégés and could be punished for their misdeeds.

The civil service system succeeded in bringing a large measure of talent into government. It also helped keep men of ability out of subversive activities by opening a more attractive door to them. The degree to which the examination system discovered new talent is suggested by the lists of successful candidates in 1148 and 1256, which reveal that more than half of the men came from families with no record of civil service status in the paternal line during the three preceding generations.

In large part because of the civil service system perfected under the Sung, the Chinese government became so stable that Chao K'uang-yin's usurpation in 960 was to prove to be the last in Chinese history. In earlier periods emperors had repeatedly been robbed of the throne by their great generals, empresses, or other powerful subordinates. After 960 this never happened again. Dynasties continued to be destroyed by foreign conquest or popular revolution, and members of the imperial family stole the throne from one another, but no subject ever again succeeded in usurping the imperial prerogative.

Economic Problems. While the Sung was more prosperous than any previous dynasty had ever been, the usual administrative decline and financial difficulties of the old dynastic cycle had reappeared by the end of its first century. Government income had risen rapidly during the first six decades to a high point in 1021 of 150,850,000 units, each roughly equivalent in value to a string of a thousand cash, but thereafter receipts gradually dropped off, until by 1065 government income had fallen by nearly a quarter.

One underlying cause for this decline may have been the increase in population. In a basically agrarian economy, population growth swelled tax resources up to a certain point, but beyond that point it tended to outrun the increase in yield from the limited land resources. As a consequence, the more mouths there were to feed, the less surplus remained for the tax collectors. Another factor may have been the increasing concentration of farm land in the hands of the bigger landowners. Although taxes had been levied since the middle T'ang primarily by land areas rather than on a per capita basis, the burden still fell most heavily on the small peasant, who had the least financial resources. Population increases meant smaller farms and overworked soil, with the result that many small peasants were reduced to pauperism or were driven into tenancy on the holdings of the landlord class. The latter, though theoretically subject to the same taxes as the peasants, frequently enjoyed exemptions or were able to escape part of the burden through their government connections, and thus the state's income tended to decline as landlord holdings increased.

Government expenditures, however, could not be tailored to fit declining receipts. As in past dynasties, the costs of government steadily grew as the court became larger and more luxurious, government organs proliferated, and the bureaucracy expanded. Some historians have attributed the financial difficulties of the Sung to the appeasement payments paid to the Liao and Hsi Hsia, but this was only a minor factor. While the payments came to total 1,500,000 units of silk and silver, this never amounted to even 2 per cent of the government budget. A much more serious drain was military expenditures. The professional armies that had replaced the comparatively inexpensive militia system of the T'ang had proved not only ineffective but costly. Ill-equipped with horses and recruited largely from among paupers, the Sung forces were no match for the spirited cavalry of the northern "barbarians." The only answer seemed to be to increase the size of the military, until by 1041 it numbered 1,259,000 men and absorbed close to 80 per cent of the government budget.

The Reforms of Wang An-shih.   Because of its financial difficulties, the government allowed official salaries to become inadequate, which in turn hurt morale, encouraged the misuse of office, and may have stimulated the growth of the bureaucratic factionalism that bedeviled the remaining years of the Sung. A more fundamental reason for this factionalism, however, was that the bureaucrats, rather than aristocratic families, empresses, or eunuchs, were now in control of the government and they faced very difficult financial problems and a precarious military situation. They not unnaturally became deeply divided over policy issues, but there was no mechanism for resolving these policy differences, except through factional strife and imperial whim.

In 1069 the new young emperor, Shen Tsung ("Inspired Ancestor," 1067–1085), appointed as Chief Councilor the able but opinionated Wang An-shih (1021–1086). Wang was the champion of a reformist faction that was opposed by the traditionalists, who supported established bureaucratic procedures as they had developed in recent decades. He immediately embarked on a series of sweeping reforms to bolster the government's finances and strengthen its armies.

Wang plunged the government into economic manipulations of a sort that had not been tried for several centuries. He had the government buy the specialized products of one area for sale in other regions, thereby helping to stabilize prices and making a profit for the government. He instituted government loans to peasants at 20 or 30 per cent, a very low rate for the time, thereby possibly helping poorer farmers to maintain themselves but certainly diverting the profits of moneylending from private usurers to the treasury. He had new land surveys made to eliminate old inequities and established a graduated scale of land taxes according to the productivity of the soil. He commuted the remaining *corvée* services into taxes. He also had all personal wealth assessed for tax purposes, attempted to regulate prices, extended relatively cheap credit to small enterprisers through government pawnshops, and carried out needed water control.

On the military side, Wang An-shih revived under the name of *pao-chia* the old collective-guarantee methods of the Six Dynasties period, and decreed that the various units under this system were to provide at their own expense certain quotas of trained and armed militia. To build up a cavalry, he had horses procured at government expense and assigned to the peasant families of North China, in return for which one member of each family was to serve with his horse in cavalry militia in time of need.

Wang also expanded the number of government schools to compete with the endowed private academies (*shu-yüan*) that dominated education at this time, and he insisted that the government examinations should be less tests of memory and literary ability and should be directed more toward practical problems of policy and administration. Like Wang Mang in Han times, he claimed the support of the Classics for his reforms.

Wang An-shih, again like Wang Mang, has been both castigated and praised as a socialist, but he was no more motivated by concepts of social equality than was his famous predecessor. Some of his reforms, such as the graduated land tax, cheaper credit systems, and the complete abandonment of the *corvée,* obviously were steps forward economically and administratively. Other measures, such as price regulating, government commodity controls, and the collective-guarantee and militia systems, were merely revivals of earlier institutions. The reforms naturally roused the determined opposition of the groups they hurt—large landowners, big merchants, and moneylenders. The bulk of the bureaucracy, drawn as it was from the landowning class, was also in opposition. Most of the great scholar-statesmen of the day, such as Ssu-ma Kuang, Ou-yang Hsiu, and Su Tung-p'o, were ranged against the innovations, and Wang has been roundly condemned by traditional Chinese historians.

This bureaucratic and scholastic opposition, however, was probably not basically a matter of class interests. It more fundamentally reflected the natural administrative inertia of a bureaucratized state—a growing inflexibility which was to characterize the Chinese government from this time on. The reforms also had produced considerable confusion and transgressed various checks and balances in the established system. For these various reasons, even though the reforms were not really very revolutionary

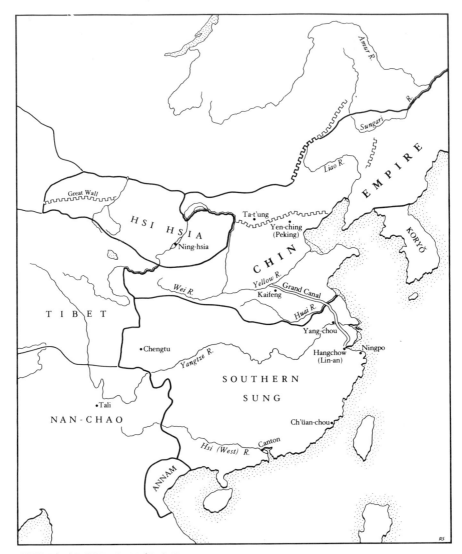

CHINA AROUND 1140 A.D.

and were often merely a reversion to older practices, they stirred up intense partisan politics during the next several decades, and partisan debate has raged ever since. On Shen Tsung's death in 1085, the traditionalists came back to power and vitiated Wang's reforms. Thereafter reformists and traditionalists alternated in power, nullifying through their bitter struggles whatever financial and military benefits the reforms might have produced, until this bureaucratic battle was itself submerged in a greater disaster.

The Southern Sung. The emperor Hui Tsung ("Excellent Ancestor," 1100–1125), a great patron of the arts and himself a talented painter, presided over a culturally brilliant and luxurious court that further strained government finances. (See Plate 5.) During the latter years of his reign, the empire was wracked by popular uprisings, but the chief blow came from outside. Beyond the Liao, Tungusic tribes known as the Jurchen (Ju-chen in Chinese) had gradually risen to power in northeastern Manchuria. In 1114 the Jurchen rebelled against the Liao and the next year adopted the Chinese dynastic name of Chin (1115–1234), meaning "Golden." The Sung, intent on regaining the sixteen border prefectures lost to the Liao two centuries earlier, unwisely allied themselves with the Chin against the Liao. The Chinese armies, however, met with no success, while the Jurchen hordes completely destroyed the Liao by 1125. When Sung showed itself dissatisfied with its meager share of the spoils, the Jurchen swept on to capture Kaifeng in 1126 and pursued the Chinese armies across the Yangtze. The many rivers and canals of the South, however, made it unfavorable terrain for their cavalry, and they eventually withdrew from the South, though they retained their hold over most of North China.

A son of Hui Tsung, known to history as Kao Tsung ("High Ancestor," 1127–1162), managed to restore Sung rule in the South, establishing his capital in 1138 at the modern Hangchow in Chekiang. Henceforth the Sung Empire was limited to the area south of the Huai River and consequently is known as the Southern Sung (1127–1279), as opposed to the Northern Sung (960–1126), which had ruled from the North over almost the whole of China proper.

For a while the Southern Sung fought desperately to recapture the North under the able general Yüeh Fei (also pronounced Yo Fei), who has been extolled by modern patriots as a symbol of national resistance to foreign domination. A peace party under Ch'in Kuei, however, eventually won out, executed Yüeh Fei, and concluded a treaty with the Chin in 1141. This treaty stipulated that the Sung was the vassal of the Chin and should pay an annual tribute of 500,000 units of silver and silk. An unsuccessful attempt by the Chin to conquer the South led to the reduction of the sum by 100,000 units in 1165 and the dropping of the Sung's status of outright vassalage, but an even less successful effort by the Sung to conquer the Chin led in 1208 to an increased annual payment of 600,000 units and a special indemnity of 3,000,000 units.

While the Southern Sung was geographically a rump state and its government remained torn between war and peace factions, it was in most ways a wealthier country than the Northern Sung had ever been. It occupied what had become the economic heartland of China, and this was a period of rapid economic growth. The Southern Sung had a much higher military budget than the Northern Sung and supported a larger bureaucracy. Its capital at Hangchow was a far grander city than Kaifeng had been. Even after Hangchow had passed its peak and had fallen into the hands of "barbarians," it struck Marco Polo as "beyond dispute the finest and noblest city" in the world.

The Southern Sung during its century and a half of existence was no more impervious to the dynastic cycle than previous dynasties had been. The administrative decline continued throughout the period. Even so, the government, because of its sound financial base and strong civil service, showed no sign of collapsing from inner pressures. As in the case of the Northern Sung, it was destroyed only by a powerful foreign enemy, the Mongols, and only after many years of large-scale warfare.

The Commercial Revolution

The political history of China shows a steady military decline from the high point of empire in the eighth century to the eventual conquest of all China by the Mongols in the thirteenth; but this was nonetheless a period of significant institutional and cultural growth. Underlying this growth was such a great expansion of the Chinese economy, and particularly its commercial aspects, that it might not be inappropriate to call it the "commercial revolution" of China. This rapid growth brought China up to an economic level that was distinctly higher than that of earlier ages and produced economic and social patterns that remained in many ways unchanged into the nineteenth century.

One of the reasons for this spectacular development of the economy was probably a general increase in population. Chinese census figures, as we have seen, are generally more indicative of administrative than of demographic conditions, but they suggest a considerable growth in population at this time. In fact, the population of the South seems to have tripled between the eighth and the eleventh centuries, and the total population of China may have passed the 100 million mark during the Northern Sung.

Technological Advances.   There also appears to have been a considerable increase in agricultural productivity during the Sung period. For example, the introduction in the early eleventh century of a more quickly maturing strain of rice from Champa in South Vietnam greatly increased agricultural yields in the South by making double cropping possible. Another factor was the large number of major water-control projects undertaken during the Sung, which added significantly to the total area devoted to irrigated paddy fields. The cultivation of tea on hillsides also increased, and around the twelfth century cotton began to be a common crop, expanding the textile resources of the country.

There were also technological advances in fields other than agriculture. Already highly developed skills, as in textiles, lacquer production, and porcelain making, were further perfected. The abacus came into use in

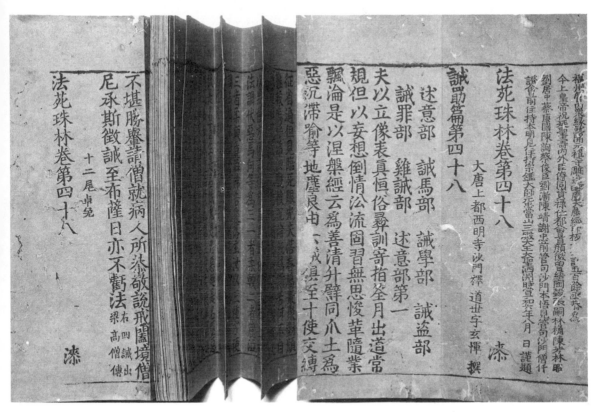

SUNG PRINTED BOOK. *Page from a Buddhist book compiled in 668 A.D. and printed in 1124, more than three centuries before the Gutenberg Bible. The vertical lines are to be read from right to left. The small type on the right lists the reasons for the project and also its patrons. The first large line of type gives the chapter heading, followed by a smaller line identifying the author.*

late Sung times and ever since has been the chief calculating device of East Asian merchants. Another step forward in technology was the use of gunpowder for explosive weapons. By the early eleventh century, mines, a type of hand grenade, and other explosive projectiles had been developed, helping the Chinese to compensate for the weakness of their cavalry.

The most important technological advance, though it contributed only indirectly to economic growth, was the development of printing. This great invention was originally motivated by the desire to establish and spread authentic versions of important books. It may have been inspired by the practice of making "rubbings" from texts carved on stone tablets. This was done by making a thin, dampened sheet of paper adhere closely to the stone and rubbing the higher surfaces of it with lampblack, thus producing a primitive sort of block print with white characters on a black background. The actual technique of printing, however, probably grew out of large carved seals for official use. By the seventh century these had developed into full-page woodblock pictures or texts. A series of consecutive printed blocks produced whole books in scroll form. When such a long sheet of consecutive printed blocks was folded at regular intervals and then stitched together on one side, the result was the standard Chinese printed book with its continuous double-folded pages.

A whole Buddhist sutra had been printed in China by 868, and in the middle of the tenth century the printing of all of the Classics and the whole of the Buddhist Tripitaka was undertaken by some of the independent regimes in Szechwan and South China. During the Sung, printing became extremely widespread, and printed books of all types appeared in large numbers.

Because of the huge number of Chinese characters, the Chinese usually found it simplest to have a whole block of wood carved as a unit for printing. When in the fifteenth century this invention reached the West by way of Central Asia and the Middle East, the Europeans quickly discarded woodblocks for movable type, because of the small number of writing symbols they employed. But movable type in wood, porcelain, and copper had actually been developed long before in East Asia, appearing in China around 1030 and being much utilized in Korea during the first half of the fifteenth century.

The Growth of Trade.   The most important reason for the great economic growth of the eighth to thirteenth centuries was probably the tremendous expansion of trade, which permitted much greater local specialization and therefore increased overall production. The early T'ang, with the traditional Chinese contempt for commerce, had attempted to control and restrict trade, but during the late T'ang and Sung it broke out of this government strait jacket. It spread beyond the old government marketplaces, and by Sung times the main streets of the cities were lined with shops, as in modern China. Great commercial cities also began to appear for the first time—that is, great population centers which, unlike earlier Chinese cities, were not largely centers of political administration but were primarily great emporiums of trade.

The interregional exchange of goods in earlier times had been conducted in large part by the government through taxation, the operation of monopolies, and other measures of economic control, with private traders serving mainly as dealers in luxury goods. During the late T'ang and Sung, however, there was so great a development of private trade that it came to overshadow the government's operations. Wholesalers or brokers gathered the local surplus of agricultural or manufactured goods for sale to transport merchants. The latter ranged from itinerant peddlers to large-scale, monopolistic operators, served by an extensive network of inns. The large transport merchants disposed of their goods through local brokers to a multitude of individual shops and peddlers.

The growth of commerce was accompanied by a proliferation of trade guilds. These were known as *hang* (later called *hong* by Westerners), because they had grown out of the merchant associations grouped by streets (*hang*) in the marketplaces of early T'ang times. The more important guilds were usually those that transported and sold such basic commodities as grain, salt, tea, or silk or had the banking functions of storing and lending money. The scale of operation of the larger guilds is indicated by the case of a guild of one hundred grain transport merchants in the capital region during the eleventh century which reportedly did an annual business worth 10 million units.

Foreign Trade.   Growth in foreign trade was one of the clearest indications of the mercantile expansion of the time and presumably was a major stimulant to the whole commercial revolution. Trade with the West by way of Central Asia had gone on since Han times, and now there was a great increase in overland trade with China's immediate neighbors to the north and northwest. The peoples of these areas had acquired a taste for Chinese products, such as silk and tea, and the incorporation of millions of Chinese into the empires of the Liao, Hsi Hsia, and Chin greatly heightened the demand for these goods. Profits from these exports made it possible for the Sung both to make appeasement payments to the northern empires and to purchase from the steppe lands the horses needed for China's defense.

Overseas trade seems to have been an even greater stimulus to the economic development of China at this time. A significant maritime trade with India and the Middle East had existed since the Later Han, but in the eighth century it began to grow very rapidly, ushering in what might be called the first period of great oceanic commerce in the history of the world. The entrance of the Europeans in the early sixteenth century into this lucrative trade along the southern littoral of Asia was to mark the beginning of the oceanic phase of Western history.

Improvements in the techniques of shipbuilding and navigation help account for the increase in maritime commerce. Large vessels, relying on both sails and oars, had come into use, and a system of transverse watertight bulkheads had been developed, making ships much less likely to sink. The Chinese had known of magnetic polarity at least as early as the third century A.D., and a Chinese text clearly indicates that the compass was in use in this southern trade by 1119, several decades before it was introduced to Europe by the Arabs. Another factor in the growth of oceanic commerce may have been the outburst of energy in West Asia following the rise of Islam. In fact, the overseas trade of China was at first largely in the hands of Muslim Iranians and Arabs. But the greatest spur to this trade was probably the unprecedented prosperity of China under the T'ang and Sung, which inevitably drew traders to Chinese ports and created an insistent demand for Chinese manufactures all the way from Japan to East Africa.

The rise of oceanic commerce in time altered the orientation of China toward the outside world. The eastern and southern coasts, which had once been distant and unimportant regions, gradually became the chief areas of foreign trade and contact, while the northwestern provinces, once the front door of China, started to sink to the status of a remote hinterland. During the Sung, overseas trade was concentrated at a few large ports along the south coast and on the lower Yangtze, where it was supervised by the Superintendencies of Merchant Shipping. The system of limiting foreign trade to certain official ports where custom duties could be collected had started in the eighth century, and during the Sung these custom duties became an important source of government income. The bulk of foreign trade flowed through Canton during the late T'ang and the Northern Sung, but, under the Southern Sung, Ch'üan-chou (Marco Polo's Zayton), situated near the great tea- and porcelain-producing areas in Fukien, became the leading port.

Koreans seem to have dominated the trade with Korea and Japan in the ninth century, and Arabs and Iranians controlled most of the trade with South and West Asia. These foreigners, who occupied designated quarters in the port cities, lived under their own customary laws, under a system analogous to the extraterritoriality of modern times but without its implications of foreign cultural superiority. The West Asians brought Islam with them and erected mosques. The foreign trade communities seem to have been quite large, and already in the eighth century the records tell of "thousands" of foreigners in Canton and in Yang-chou, a great city on the lower Yangtze. Gradually during the Sung, the Chinese began to take a larger part in overseas trade and by late Sung times had come to dominate commerce with Korea and Japan. Thus the originally land-locked Chinese were becoming a more maritime people, and their ships began to venture overseas and in time all the way to Africa.

The nature of China's foreign trade at this time indicates the leading role China had come to occupy in the world's economy. Except for fine cotton textiles, China's imports were largely raw materials—horses and hides from the steppe lands, and gems, spices, ivory, and other luxury goods from the tropics. On the other hand, except for some minerals, Chinese exports were largely manufactured goods. Books, paintings, and art objects were eagerly sought in areas such as Korea and Japan, which had derived their higher culture from China; Chinese copper cash was in great demand throughout East and Southeast Asia; and silk textiles and porcelains were highly prized everywhere. Fragments of Sung porcelains are to be found as far afield as Zanzibar, and the ruins of the medieval trading cities of the Persian Gulf and Egypt are said to be littered with them.

The Advanced Money Economy.   One of the clearest signs of the economic growth that took place in China during the late T'ang and Sung was the great expansion of the currency system. Copper cash had appeared as early as the late Chou and had been used extensively ever since, but there was now a huge increase in the quantity of currency minted, a great development in the complexity of the currency system, and a corresponding rise in the role of money in trade and government finance.

Annual tax receipts in cash, as opposed to textiles or grain, had amounted to only 2 million strings of a thousand cash each in 749, but by 1065 the Sung was receiving 37 million strings of currency a year in payment of taxes, and in the Southern Sung the government's income in money completely overshadowed its grain and textile receipts. The early T'ang, like most previous Chinese regimes, had relied almost exclusively on agricultural taxes, but during the Northern Sung income from government monopolies and various commercial taxes began to outbalance agricultural taxes, and in the Southern Sung state revenue came overwhelmingly from commercial sources. Although later dynasties were to prove more dependent than the Sung on agricultural taxes, the great development of commercial sources of revenue during the Sung gave to Chinese regimes from this time on a second major financial support and therefore greater fiscal stability than earlier dynasties had enjoyed.

The rapid growth in the use of money during the late T'ang and Sung put a heavy strain on China's currency resources. Under the T'ang, the minting of cash had averaged between 130,000 and 310,000 strings per year. By the late tenth century production was around 880,000, and in the eleventh century it rose to as much as 1,830,000 strings a year. Even then the demand for cash commonly outstripped production. To meet this demand the government sometimes tried to limit the use of copper to coinage or attempted a sort of debasement by reducing the number of coins in a string of cash. It also attempted to bar the export of cash and, when this proved ineffective, to place a 50 per cent export duty on coinage. In border areas such as Szechwan and Shansi it even experimented with iron coins in a vain effort to erect a sort of "iron curtain" between China and the purses of its "barbarian" neighbors. The use of gold and silver—gold dust by weight and silver in the form of ingots of supposedly standard weight and purity—helped relieve the pressure on copper coinage, but curiously the Chinese only rarely minted these precious metals.

The most interesting solution to the currency problem, and the one that best illustrates the growth of an advanced money economy, was the development of paper currency. Both the government and the great transport merchants faced the problem of transferring large sums of money over great distances. Copper cash were too bulky for convenient transfer, and consequently various types of paper credit and paper money were developed to meet the need. As early as 811 the T'ang was issuing so-called "flying cash" to pay for goods acquired in distant areas. These money drafts were reimbursable at the capital. The system proliferated under the Sung, which put out many separate issues of this sort. Because of their convenience, such government money drafts were exchanged between merchants who wished to transfer credits.

Meanwhile, another type of paper money was being developed by private bankers, who issued certificates of deposit which could be cashed for a 3 per cent service charge. Such certificates, because of their convenience, came to circulate freely at face value. Those issued by the bankers of Chengtu in Szechwan were among the most famous, and when they were taken over by the government in 1024 they became the world's first genuine paper money. Issued in denominations of between two hundred and a thousand cash (or one string), these government notes were subject to the usual 3 per cent service charge, and they were limited to three years' validity because of the deterioration of the paper.

The Chengtu paper money was at first limited to 1,256,000 strings in value and in the early days was soundly backed by 360,000 strings of cash. The Sung also put out various other local issues of paper money. When in financial trouble, however, the government could not resist the temptation of printing more paper money than it could redeem, thus starting what was to become in time a worldwide phenomenon. In currency development and in many other features of the economy, the Sung achieved a level that was not always equaled and was not significantly surpassed in China before the nineteenth century.

Society and Culture

The Gentry Class.   China's commercial revolution did not produce as great a change in society and government as did the later commercial revolution of Europe. This was probably because it took place within a highly organized, bureaucratic empire which easily adjusted to and drew new strength from this economic growth, whereas the feudal social and political institutions of Europe were quite incapable of accommodating great changes in the economy and therefore collapsed, leading to far more basic alterations of society in Europe than occurred in China. On the other hand, very significant changes in society and culture did accompany the great economic growth of the eighth to the thirteenth centuries in China.

Since the society that emerged at that time was to remain characteristic of China until the nineteenth century and since it included many features that appear characteristic of modern urban civilization, it can in a sense be considered "early modern." In any case, while the twelfth-century culture of Europe seems only a rather remote ancestor of the nineteenth-century West, the twelfth-century civilization of China appears to be only a younger and more exuberant stage of the China that the West came to know in the nineteenth century.

One of the major factors in the transformation of the highly aristocratic society of the Six Dynasties period and early T'ang into the essentially nonaristocratic and more egalitarian society of the Sung was the shift in the landholding and tax system. Before this change the land was divided for the most part between the free peasants, who gave virtually the whole of their surplus produce and labor as taxes to the government, and the estates of great families, who could protect their lands from most taxes, could count on the political and military support of their subordinates on their estates, and could influence government because of their wealth and independent base of power. After the change, the government no longer opposed the private accumulation of agricultural land, and so private holdings could be preserved without exceptional power and influence. As a result large numbers of small and medium landowners appeared. On the other hand, the new simplified tax system made it more difficult for the old aristocrats to maintain their tax-free status.

The rapid rise of commerce and a money economy also made the old type of self-sufficient estate no longer an efficient economic unit, and at the same time the political power of the great landowner was diminished by the growing role of the examination system in producing political leadership and the increasing concentration of power in the hands of the emperors and their bureaucracy. Gradually the old aristocracy merged into a much broader gentry or landlord class, scattered parcels of land became a more common landholding pattern than large estates, and the farmers living on the property of the landlords took on the character of tenants rather than of retainers.

The new gentry class depended much less on agricultural wealth than had the old aristocracy. Actually agriculture seems to have become economically a losing proposition from Sung times on. Because of the prestige of owning land and its relative safety from government confiscation, surplus capital was usually invested in land, but the wealth of the gentry landowners seems to have been often of merchant origin, and it could best be protected by high government office. Another reason why the gentry was not simply a landowning class was that its wealth could be effectively translated into power in the central government only through education and the achievement of high political office by way of the examination system. The gentry as a class gained national political influence directly from intellectual accomplishments and only indirectly from wealth and property.

Still another contrast with the old aristocracy was that by Sung times hereditary status had become relatively unimportant. Social mobility had greatly increased in an economically more diversified society and had become justified by a greater acceptance of egalitarian principles. Thus the whole tone of society was different, and this in turn affected the spirit of the higher culture.

The Urbanization of Society.   Another feature of the new society was its growing urbanization. At the beginning of the twelfth century there were fifty-two large urban prefectures with more than 100,000 households, compared to twenty-six in the middle of the eighth century. The real urbanization of Chinese culture, however, was not so much a matter of numbers as it was the domination of society from this time on by city and town dwellers. The new gentry, unlike the old aristocracy, lived to a large extent in cities and towns, being thus more like absentee landlords than country squires. Since nearly all officials and rich merchants also lived in cities and towns, a large proportion of the leadership group was concentrated in urban areas. The higher culture, therefore, naturally became heavily urbanized, developing interests and attitudes that seem more characteristic of city people than of rural populations.

The triumph of the civilian as opposed to the military point of view was one of the chief characteristics of the new urban culture. While the Chinese until the early T'ang had exulted in military power as much as other strong peoples, from the time of the Sung, Chinese civilization has been characterized by an overwhelming emphasis on civil accomplishments and a contempt for the martial life, as also appears to be the case in modern urban societies in the West. Military service, it was felt, was fit only for the dregs of society; or, as the Chinese put it, the best men were no more to be used for soldiers than the best iron for nails. It is significant that of the four great dynasties since the T'ang only the two "barbarian" ones conquered far afield.

In an urban environment, the higher culture became much more sophisticated and diversified than before, and a broader swath of the population participated in it. The urban way of life and citified amusements naturally came to the fore. While rural pleasures such as hunting and horseback riding have persisted among certain groups in the West until the present, most cultivated Chinese turned their backs on such rustic pastimes almost a millennium ago. At the same time, and somewhat paradoxically, the Chinese began to show the romanticized love of the beauties of nature characteristic of the West as it began to urbanize.

City life in the Sung was free and luxurious. Cities were no longer

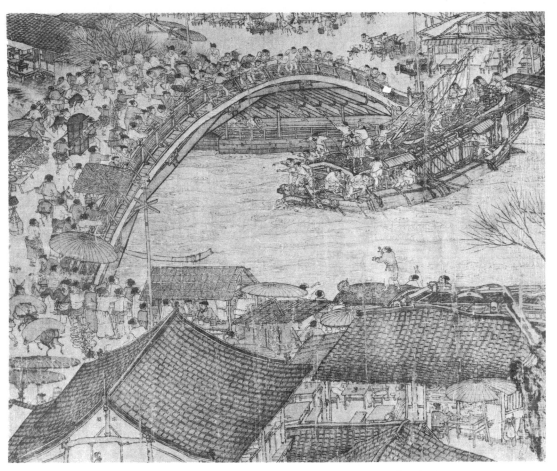

*Scene from "Spring Festival on the River," a long scroll painting
from the twelfth century. Note the street stalls, a sedan chair on the
bridge, and boatmen lowering their mast to pass under the bridge.*

conglomerations of walled villages dominated by the imperial palace or
some other center of political authority. Amusement quarters, instead, were
now the centers of social life. Here were to be found countless wine and
tea shops, restaurants specializing in various types of cuisine, and houses
featuring professional female entertainers comparable to the geisha of a
later period in Japan. Both these houses and the restaurants frequently
shaded off into brothels. There were also theaters, puppet shows, jugglers,
storytellers, and various other entertainments.

The evils of urban society also first made themselves felt in this age.
Absentee landlords and tenancy created problems in Chinese agriculture
that continued until contemporary times. Widespread pauperism also ap-

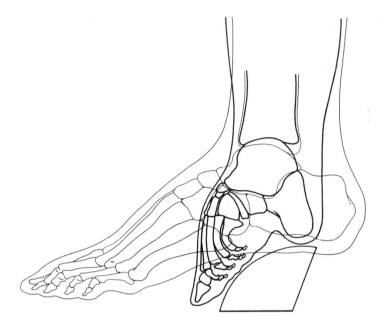

A BOUND FOOT. *This diagram shows the twisted and cramped bone structure of a bound ("lily") foot, as compared with that of a normal foot. Bound tightly with cloth from the age of five, a little girl's foot grew painfully into this deformed but erotically admired shape.*

peared among the city proletariat. Private charity agencies came into being in the late T'ang, performing such services as caring for orphans and indigent old people or burying dead paupers. These institutions were nationalized and greatly extended in the early twelfth century. The Sung army was the chief means of taking care of the unemployed, but the government also provided work relief and special granaries for the support of the poor.

A change in the position of women may also have been associated with the urbanization of culture. Women had always been subservient to men, but the concentration of the upper classes in cities, where the work of women was less essential than on the farm, may have contributed to a further decline in the status of women over the next few centuries. This change is suggested by the growth at this time of the institution of concubinage, the strengthening of the social rules against the remarriage of widows, and the custom introduced among the upper classes of binding the feet of women. When still quite young, girls would have their feet tightly wrapped and gradually bent until the arch was broken and the toes, except for the big toe, were turned under. This produced a "lily-foot" only about half the normal size, virtually crippling girls for life and thus accentuating the wealth of the men who could afford such useless play-things. While foot-binding and the resultant stiff walk of Chinese women have appeared repugnant to foreign observers, bound feet developed strong erotic associations for Chinese men. The custom gradually spread through-out society and lasted down to the present century.

Artistic Trends.   Despite the far conquests of the T'ang and the wide commercial contacts of the Sung, the culture of the eighth to thirteenth centuries showed relatively few new foreign influences. It was characterized instead by a rich and sophisticated reworking of native traditions. This was as true in the arts as in other fields. Architecture remained close to its original post-and-lintel construction, though multistoried buildings became more common and the original straight lines of the tile roofs increasingly curved upward at their ends. Religious sculpture, which had flourished under the influence of Buddhism, achieved a high point of realism in the Sung and then rapidly declined. (See Plate 14.) The industrial arts all prospered greatly, and the celadons and other porcelain wares of the Sung became world famous.

Painting, however, showed the richest development, and ever since the Sung most Chinese have felt, with good reason, that it is the greatest of their fine arts. Drawing from a rich, continuous tradition stretching well back into the Han period, Chinese canons of painting became fully established during the Sung, and painting itself reached a level of per-fection that was probably not surpassed in later dynasties. Looked at closely, subsequent Chinese painting reveals great variety and vitality but, scanned more broadly, it seems to be largely variations on themes already well developed by Sung times.

Buddhist painting, with its strong iconographic elements, remained prominent through the Sung, though it was fast losing place to purely secular art. In the latter, the emphasis shifted from figures and depictions of human events to landscapes, in which the human element was at most a small detail, or to vignettes of nature, such as a spray of bamboo. The approach was impressionistic rather than realistically complete. Color was felt to be unimportant and monochrome paintings predominated. The artist was selective in detail and concentrated on what he felt was the true essence of his subject. A landscape represented nature as a whole; a spray of bamboo was a microcosm of the universe. The Taoist or Zen inspiration of this art is obvious. (See Plate 7.)

The genius of Sung painting is revealed by the fact that, as compared with the art of medieval or Renaissance Europe, it seems to us extremely modern. The whole Sung attitude toward art also appears essentially modern. It was no longer the handmaiden of religion. Paintings were not merely icons or architectural adornments but were valued for their own aesthetic

*Detail of an eleventh-century ink and tint painting on silk by
Kuo Hsi.*

qualities. Painters were not nameless craftsmen but were known and
respected artists—usually men of broad education and high social status.
(See Plate 5.)

The names of famous late T'ang and Sung artists are legion. Among
the greatest were Wu Tao-hsüan (or Wu Tao-tzu) of Hsüan Tsung's
time, Mi Fu (or Mi Fei, 1051–1107) of the Northern Sung, and the
Southern Sung landscapists Ma Yüan and Hsia Kuei. The Chinese love of
classification was applied to art, and there was much written about Southern
and Northern schools of landscape painting. There was also a great
antiquarian interest in art and archaeology. Great public and private collections were assembled. Famous collectors affixed their seals to important
paintings as indications of authenticity as well as ownership, thereby
increasing rather than detracting from the value of the works. (See Plate 9.)
Detailed catalogues and learned critiques of art were written. The antiquarian
interest also stimulated the faking of antiques, a minor art in itself.

Literature.   While the ability to paint was a prized talent among the elite
of China, beautiful calligraphy and literary skill, especially the ability to

Landscape painted on a round fan by Ma Yüan in the late twelfth or early thirteenth century.

compose poetry, were virtual necessities. The written word had always been accorded great respect, and the development of the highly literary examinations as the chief doorway to fame and fortune further enhanced its prestige. There was a great increase in the tenth century in private schools and academies (*shu-yüan*), and the spread of printing naturally contributed to the availability of written materials of all sorts and thus to a general spread of literature and learning.

The lyric poetry known as *shih,* which had been popular since the Six Dynasties period, flourished in the T'ang, becoming freer and less bound by form. It perhaps reached its apogee in the eighth century at the hands of Li Po (or Li T'ai-po, 701–762) and Tu Fu (712–770). Li Po was a Taoist wine lover and carefree, though melancholy, wanderer. The apochryphal story of his death characterized his attitudes: he is said to have drowned while boating when he reached out in drunken ecstasy for the reflection of the moon in the water. Tu Fu was more the grave Confucian moralist, deeply aware of the suffering of humanity and the injustices of life.

Literally thousands of other T'ang and Sung poets have left their names to posterity. Po Chü-i (772–846), who wrote in a simple style not far removed from the vernacular, became vastly popular throughout East Asia. By Sung times the *shih,* through constant repetition of its themes, had become more stereotyped and lost some of its vigor, but there were still great poets of this form, such as Su Shih (better known as Su Tung-p'o, 1036–1101), who was also a famous calligrapher, great prose stylist, and philosopher.

As the *shih* declined in freshness, a new form of poetry, the *tz'u,* which originated in the lyrics of popular songs, rose to prominence. The *tz'u* had a great variety of patterns and made free use of the colloquial language. At first it was looked down on by literary men, but by the Sung all the major poets, including Su Tung-p'o, wrote *tz'u.* But this form too in time became more stereotyped, and a new type of song lyric, *san-ch'ü,* began to take its place and became the favorite song form of the succeeding Mongol and Ming periods.

The late T'ang and Sung was also the golden age of formal prose writing. Han Yü (768–824), rejecting the ornate, balanced prose style that had flourished since the Six Dynasties, returned to a simple and straightforward style. It was, however, slightly archaic and tended to fall back on ancient models, in this way widening the gulf between literary and colloquial Chinese. But the fight to free prose writing from cramping artificialities was continued. Ou-yang Hsiu (1007–1072), a leading historian and thinker of his day as well as a composer of *tz'u,* felt that writers should be entirely free to express ideas in whatever form seemed best. Back of such a concept, no doubt, was the rising use of the vernacular for philosophic writings and for the recorded dialogues of Zen masters.

This period also saw the beginnings of two entirely new literary currents —popular theater and romances or tales. Though traditionally depreciated by well-educated Chinese as plebeian and vulgar, these were in time to achieve great literary heights, growing into the full-fledged drama and novels of later periods. The appearance of these popular literary forms at this time is clearly to be associated with such factors as the spread of literacy and the general urbanization of Chinese culture.

An outstanding characteristic of the literature of the late T'ang and Sung is that most of the great poets, prose writers, and scholars were also officials, even if sometimes relatively unsuccessful ones, as in the case of Li Po and Tu Fu. Conversely, most of the great statesmen were also distinguished men of letters. Wang An-shih was a poet of note as well as the leading political personality of his day. In earlier periods, the roles of poet, scholar, and statesman had been relatively distinct; but the ideal Confucian type that had evolved by the Sung was that of the "universal man" who was scholar, poet, and statesman all at the same time, and possibly philosopher and painter as well.

Scholarship. The late T'ang and Sung saw a tremendous expansion and enrichment of earlier forms of scholarship. Standard histories were compiled with even greater enthusiasm and care than before and were supplemented by new types of historical work. The historical record had grown to such enormous size that a new effort at a single comprehensive history of China's past seemed necessary. The *Tzu-chih t'ung-chien,* by Ssu-ma Kuang (1018–1086), a statesman and leading opponent of Wang An-shih, was the first effort at a comprehensive history since Ssu-ma Ch'ien's time. It is a strictly chronological presentation covering the years 403 B.C. to 959 A.D. in 294 chapters. Its name reveals the whole philosophy of the Chinese historian, for it literally means *The Comprehensive Mirror for Aid in Government.*

The materials of this bulky book were abridged and reworked in the twelfth century under the direction of the famous philosopher Chu Hsi. In the resulting *Outline and Details of the Comprehensive Mirror,* the main points of history were sorted out from the supporting factual data, and a great deal of emphasis was given to moral judgments. *Narratives from Beginning to End from the Comprehensive Mirror* by Yüan Shu (1131–1205) was another reworking of the same materials but was divided up by major incidents more in the manner of the modern historical writings of the West. These three works became the chief introductions to history for later generations of Chinese students.

The earlier tendency toward encyclopedic compilations was also greatly developed during this period. The *Comprehensive Compendium (T'ung tien),* completed in 801, and the *Selected T'ang Documents (T'ang hui yao),* a great collection of materials on T'ang government and economics, completed in 961 on the basis of earlier compilations, became the prototypes for whole new categories of encyclopedic works, which thenceforth supplanted the standard histories as the chief sources of information on the political institutions and economic developments of the past.

Neo-Confucianism

New Currents of Thought. In intellectual attitudes and formal philosophy, the late T'ang and Sung saw the clear appearance of patterns that were to remain characteristic of China until the nineteenth century. The philosophical synthesis, known in the West as Neo-Confucianism, which emerged from the intellectual ferment of these centuries was to be the almost unchanging core of Chinese thought from then until its collapse under the impact of Western thought and revolutionary political and social changes in the twentieth century.

Two basic factors lay behind the revived interest in Confucian philosophy. One was the turning inward of the Chinese during their long losing battle with the northern "barbarians." In the early T'ang the Chinese, confident in their power, were inquisitive and tolerant toward the outside world. When the first ambassadors from the Islamic caliphate came to China in 713 and refused on religious grounds to prostrate themselves before the emperor in the traditional kowtow, the Chinese readily waived the requirement, in significant contrast to their rigidity on this point with European embassies in recent centuries. By the late T'ang, however, a growing fear and resentment of the "barbarians" was becoming evident. Buddhism had always been criticized on the grounds that it was a foreign religion, but now attacks of this type became more common and had greater influence. A sign of the times was a famous memorial presented to the throne in 819 by the great scholar and essayist Han Yü, criticizing the emperor for paying honor to the supposed fingerbone of the Buddha. Two decades later came the great persecution of 841–846.

The other basic reason for restored interest in Confucianism was the obvious success of the old Chinese political ideal. The political disillusionment of the Six Dynasties period had now receded into the dim past. The need for an educated officialdom in the revived bureaucratic state had led to the re-creation of the examination system and a re-emphasis on the Confucian writings and ideas on which the examinations focused. Confucian concepts, of course, had never died out even at the height of the Buddhist age, but after the reunification of the empire they grew steadily in strength and popularity. By the ninth century the educated classes were so thoroughly imbued with Confucianism that they increasingly rejected the antipolitical concepts of Taoism and condemned what they regarded to be the antisocial aspects of Buddhism.

The Neo-Confucian upsurge, however, was not simply the continuation of Confucian concepts as they had existed in the Chou or Han. It was in part an exciting rediscovery, in part a creative new movement. It was obvious to scholars that the society in which they lived was quite different from that described in the Classics. The Neo-Confucians hoped to recapture the original vision—to recreate the ideal Confucian society that they believed had existed in ancient times—but they did so in terms of the attitudes and interests of their own day.

The Neo-Confucian thinkers were strongly influenced by some of the Buddhist concepts that had been so important in Chinese thinking for the past few centuries. Many of them had been students of Buddhism or Taoism before they turned to Confucianism, and some had even lived in Zen monasteries. Buddhism had conditioned men to think in metaphysical terms, and one of the things that was new about Neo-Confucianism was that it developed a metaphysics for Confucianism, freely utilizing Buddhist ideas and Taoist terminology.

Neo-Confucianism thus was drawn from the diverse intellectual currents of the day, just as Han Confucianism had been eclectic in its time. Essentially, however, it was a rejection of the Taoist search for immortality and the Buddhist concern with the divine and the afterlife. It returned to the ancient Chinese emphasis on mundane social and political matters, particularly ethics, and it reasserted the old agnostic, nontheistic tendencies of Chinese thought.

The Neo-Confucianists and Their Thought. Han Yü, the distinguished prose stylist and critic of Buddhism in the ninth century, might be called the first of the great Neo-Confucianists. The eleventh and twelfth centuries, however, were the period of greatest philosophical ferment, when many different schools of thought appeared. For example, Lu Chiu-yüan (or Lu Hsiang-shan, 1139–1192) developed a Zen-like emphasis on personal intuition that was to reach its height under the Ming. In the eleventh century, the great reformer Wang An-shih represented a pragmatic, activist type of Confucianism, while his contemporaries, the scholar Ou-yang Hsiu and the poet Su Tung-p'o, were leaders of other important philosophical trends.

Among the opponents of Wang An-shih there was one particular school of philosophy which was eventually to win out as Neo-Confucian orthodoxy. The first major figure in this line of thought was Chou Tun-i (1012–1073), who took from the essentially non-Confucian *Classic of Changes* the term *T'ai chi,* or "Supreme Ultimate," and devised a cosmological chart showing how *yin* and *yang* and the five elements derived from it. The brothers Ch'eng Hao (1031–1085) and Ch'eng I (1032–1107) elaborated this metaphysics. Ch'eng I was also largely responsible for selecting two works which in a sense had been rediscovered by Han Yü—the *Mencius* and the *Great Learning* from the *Record of Rituals*—and adding to them another chapter from the latter work, the *Doctrine of the Mean,* and the *Analects* of Confucius to form the category known as the Four Books, which became thereafter the central scriptures of Confucianism and the core texts for traditional Chinese education.

The final synthesizer and organizer of this school was Chu Hsi (1130–1200), who has been compared with Aquinas and was in any case the perfect Confucianist. He was a famous historian, as we have seen, and played briefly a dramatic role as statesman, but above all he was a great commentator on the Classics and China's leading philosopher after the classic age. He put his stamp so heavily on Neo-Confucian thought that in East Asia it has often been known as Chu Hsi-ism.

In the Neo-Confucian metaphysics of Chu Hsi's school, all varieties of things were thought to have their respective *li,* or fundamental principles of form, and their *ch'i,* literally "ether," or what we might call "matter." While *li* provides the pattern of a house, actual houses are made out of the *ch'i* of wood or bricks. All the many *li* are part of the limitless, time-less, unitary Supreme Ultimate, which "is not cut into pieces; it is merely like the moon reflecting itself in ten thousand streams."

The influence of Buddhist concepts is obvious. The Sung Neo-Confucianists were close enough to Buddhism to put much emphasis on this sort of metaphysics, and they carefully elaborated and schematized the relationships between the Supreme Ultimate, *yin* and *yang,* and the five elements and developed cyclical theories of change reminiscent of Buddhist ideas. But the heart of Neo-Confucianism, like that of all earlier Confucianism, was the application of its ideas to ethics and to social and political institutions. To later generations, who were ready to accept Sung metaphysics without question, perhaps in part out of apathy, the ethical and social concepts of the school were what was truly important.

The old conflict between Mencius' belief that man is by nature good and thus only needs teaching and self-development and Hsün-tzu's view that man is by nature evil and thus needs strict control and indoctrination came to a head during the Sung. Chu Hsi and his school settled the argument in Mencius' favor. The *li* of man's nature, they argued, is of course pure and good. It is the origin of the five basic virtues, which can be translated as love, uprightness, propriety, knowledge, and reliability. But the pearl of man's *li* is always found in the mire of his *ch'i.* It needs polishing to be given its full potential luster. Thus, education is desirable, though self-cultivation is even more important.

Confucianism, as it has been known during the past millennium, came into full flower under the Sung Neo-Confucianists. The emphases were essentially those of Mencius and of the scholar-bureaucrats of Sung times. There was the particularistic, family-centered ethic, stressing the five human relationships first spelled out in the *Mencius.* These were between the ruler and his minister or subject, between father and son, husband and wife, elder brother and younger brother, and friend and friend. It should be noted that, except for the last, all of these were relations of authority and obedience. Next there was the Confucian political ideal of benevolent paternalism. The state was regarded as the family writ large. The authority of the ruler, like that of the father, was considered to be essentially ethical, as Mencius had insisted. Finally there was the bureaucratic ideal, institutionalized in the civil service and the examination system. Moral, scholarly men, trained in the classical principles of right conduct and good government, should guide and administer society. They bore a responsibility to put public service above private interest and to advise the Son of Heaven with rectitude, even at personal risk.

Cultural Stability. After Chu Hsi's death, his Neo-Confucian synthesis gradually became established as a rigid orthodoxy. By 1313 his commentaries on the classics had been made the standard ones to which all answers in the civil service examinations had to conform. Thus Chu Hsi's great scholarship and philosophic comprehensiveness became a check on further Chinese intellectual development. Strengthened by the traditional respect for both the past and the written word, Chu Hsi-ism, once established as orthodoxy, proved to be a sort of intellectual strait jacket, reinforcing the growing rigidity of Chinese society.

Neo-Confucianism thus helped create the uniquely stable and traditionalist society of early modern China—a society which changed so little, in comparison with Europe, that both Occidentals and Chinese came to accept the myth that China has always been "unchanging." The relative slowness of cultural and institutional change in China after the Sung left the country weak in the nineteenth century before the cultural onslaught of the West, which had grown so spectacularly during that same period. China's comparative inertia during these centuries, therefore, is usually viewed as an historic tragedy, if not a cause for national shame. It can, however, be looked at in an entirely different perspective. For the successive generations of Chinese who lived during this long period, the high degree of political, social, and spiritual stability that they enjoyed was probably preferable to the constant turmoil of life and thought during these same centuries in Europe. Modern man, living in the notably unstable world civilization that has grown out of the rapidly changing culture of the West, may also look with envy at the peace and stability of China between the thirteenth and nineteenth centuries.

The question remains how China was able to achieve so long a period of cultural stability. The chief reason may have been the balance between political, social, and intellectual forces that China had achieved by the thirteenth century—a sort of perfection within the bounds of the ideas and the technology of that time. The balance was so firm that it took massive blows from the outside to destroy it in the nineteenth and twentieth centuries. The Chinese are perhaps right.to view with great pride the golden age of their culture which produced a degree of stability no other high civilization has ever been able to approach.

7. China and the "Barbarians": The Mongol Empire

From the thirteenth to the nineteenth centuries the Chinese way of life showed great stability. Three ruling houses held power during three dynastic periods: Yüan (1271–1368), Ming (1368–1644), and Ch'ing (1644–1912). Disorder occurred principally during the years of dynastic decline and change, in the fourteenth, seventeenth, and nineteenth centuries.

Yet this stable political record has a puzzling aspect. The Yüan and the Ch'ing were non-Chinese dynasties of conquest who ruled over the immensely more populous Middle Kingdom as legitimate holders of the imperial power. Plainly, the Chinese Empire included not merely the agricultural area within the Great Wall but also the peripheral regions of Inner Asia, especially Mongolia and Manchuria. A strong Chinese dynasty, such as the Han, T'ang, or Ming, would dominate these regions. But periodically, the *yang* of Chinese expansion would give way to the *yin* of "barbarian" invasion. Tribal peoples outside the Wall would seize power and rule part of the empire. Yet invariably they would make use of its traditional political institutions, which supported centralized imperial rule through a great and largely Chinese bureaucracy. The stability of the Chinese political order lay partly in its capacity to let non-Chinese, when they were strong enough, rule over it without changing its fundamental features.

The chart of Central Asian peoples and kingdoms on page 153 indicates the names and habitats of the major groups of "barbarians" who have appeared and disappeared in the grasslands on China's northern horizon

CENTRAL ASIAN PEOPLES AND KINGDOMS

(Note: The data below are not by any means permanently established, many points being still in dispute among scholars.)

People	*Language Group*	*Period and Region*
Hsiung-nu (Huns?)	Turkish	Founded first steppe empire in third century B.C.; conquered by Han in first century B.C. and first century A.D.
Yüeh-chih	Probably Indo-European	Second century B.C., sought by Han China as allies against Hsiung-nu; migrated from Kansu to Ili to Bactria, thence to Northwest India and set up Kushan Kingdom.
Hsien-pei	Mongolian	Third century A.D., in eastern Mongolia; invaded China in fourth century A.D.
Tabgach (T'o-pa)	Largely Mongolian	Founded Northern Wei dynasty, 386–534 A.D., in North China.
Turks (T'u-chüeh)	Turkish	Empire established c. 552; split into Eastern Empire (c. 600–744) on the Orkhon River, and Western Empire, in contact with Sassanians in Persia; groups penetrated India and Europe after 659.
Uighurs	Turkish	Conquered Eastern Turks and set up empire on the Orkhon River, 744–840; forced out by Kirghiz, set up empire in Tarim basin (Turfan) during 840 and after.
Khitan (Ch'i-tan)	Mongolian	Founded Liao dynasty in North China and adjacent area, 947–1125; driven west by Jurchen; set up Kara-Khitai (Western Liao) Empire in East Turkestan, 1124–1211.
Jurchen (Ju-chen, ancestors of the Manchus)	Tungusic	Founded Chin dynasty in North China, 1122–1234.
Tanguts	Tibetan	Founded Hsi Hsia Kingdom in Northwest China, 1038–1227.
Mongols	Mongolian	Founded Yüan dynasty over all China, 1271–1368.

throughout history. A westward drift characterizes this record, one people after another being driven by the Chinese or by their own nomadic successors toward the west. The earlier peoples belonged generally to the Turkish-speaking language group, while the Mongolian-speaking peoples became dominant later. From these tribes of the steppe emerged periodically leadership groups and fighting forces that succeeded in ruling part or all of China.

This ever-present "barbarian" influence on China's political life was based upon a major geographical fact—the close juxtaposition of the steppe and the sown areas, of two irreducibly different ways of life and two contrasting types of social organization suited to these different geographical regions. Underlying this contrast was the difference in rainfall. The aridity of the Inner Asian steppe, from which no rivers flow out to the sea, has made extensive agriculture impossible. Lacking adequate water resources, the high uplands of Tibet and the grasslands of Mongolia have had a very sparse population. The "barbarians" lived in areas roughly twice the size of China, but had perhaps no more than one-fortieth of the population. The source of "barbarian" power is therefore a very interesting question. The military superiority of the "barbarians" was frequently demonstrated when their mounted archers came within the Wall. But what lay behind this capacity to produce fierce and mobile fighting men?

The Society of the Steppe

In the grasslands, life was sustained primarily by the raising of animals rather than crops. The full nomad lived on a sheep-and-horse economy. Sheepskins formed his clothing. The wool made felt for his tents. He ate mutton and from the milk of his horses and sheep made cheese and butter. His women gathered dung for fuel. He used his horses for transport and the management of his flocks, and also for hunting and warfare, supplemented by camels for crossing deserts and by oxen for pulling his carts. His pastoral economy had little need of agriculture so long as it could maintain a minimal trade with settled areas in order to secure grain and also textiles, tea and other "luxuries," and metals to make weapons. Thus the nomad of the open steppe was self-sufficient in the short run, but could not be wholly cut off from commercial centers.

Since cities could not flourish on the grasslands, there were strict limits to culture and technology. Wealth was stored in the silver ornaments worn by the women. The chief art form was the so-called Scythian or animal style of metal work found all across the Eurasian steppe from the lower Volga and the Caspian Sea to the Amur River. Literacy and literature remained undeveloped. The religion of the tribes was a primitive shamanism, practiced by medicine men, not unlike that of those far-distant cousins

LIFE ON THE STEPPE. *A Mongol camp near the Altai Mountains with yurts, sheep, horses, pasture, and a brackish lake of surface water (on right).*

of the Tungusic peoples, the American Indians. The one great deity of the steppe was the Eternal Heaven.

The nomad's migration was not an aimless wandering but occurred on a seasonal basis, usually to move his flocks and herds from summer pasture on the open plain to winter pasture in some more sheltered area such as a mountain valley, and back again. His essential rights were those of movement for pasture rather than of land control for agriculture. The tribal chieftain sought the right to perform a cycle of migration using certain grasslands at certain seasons. He had little interest in the settled activities of plowing, reaping, house construction, and road building. He remained precariously dependent upon nature, for a severe winter could destroy his flocks. The seminomads, who lived on the fringes of sedentary agricultural societies, shared this constant economic instability. Their lack of accumulated resources gave both types of nomads a periodic incentive not only for increased trade but for military expansion. The nomads were the have-nots of antiquity, always poor in comparison with peoples in more thickly populated farming regions.

"SCYTHIAN" BRONZE. *A horned herbivore attacked by a feline beast. Bronzes in this so-called "Scythian," "Sino-Siberian," or "animal" style have been found throughout the northern areas of Asia which were accessible to the steppe peoples.*

Unlike peasants, who could seldom leave their fields without loss of production, the herders and huntsmen of the steppe could be quickly mobilized. From boyhood they spent their lives in the saddle. Their energies could be turned in a moment from the care of their flocks or the pursuit of game to the destruction of enemies. Their active outdoor life produced a type of individual (not unlike the early American cowboy) who was independent, self-reliant, and omnicompetent. The herdsman-hunter-warrior of the steppe had to be ready for anything. His capacity for warfare was increased by the fact that his women managed the camp and could handle all the problems of nomad life except war and politics.

The social organization of the tribes contributed to their military strength. Their clans were under chieftains who rose through personal prowess. When old or weak, they would be displaced. Personal relations of fealty and protection were reciprocally maintained between major and minor chieftains as well as among warriors, and so a strong personality could rise rather quickly to the top of a hierarchy of personal relationships.

Nomad striking power came from a combination of many factors. One technical element was the iron stirrup, which came into use in the early centuries A.D. and gave the cavalryman a firmer basis for mounted archery. Securely mounted on a well-trained horse and armed with a compound bow small enough for use from the saddle, he now had a tactical military superiority over the peasant foot soldier. For the next thousand years (ca. 400–1400), until the introduction of firearms, the balance of military technology in Asia remained in favor of the horseman.

The Great Wall boundary, where cultivator and herdsman met, remained unstable. Rainfall was marginal and farming met periodic disaster. Chinese trade with the nomad—in grain, silk, and later tea—in exchange for horses, easily became intermixed with politics. Seminomads on this frontier might settle down as Chinese vassals and even become Sinicized. Conversely, if Chinese rule proved ineffective, the mixed Sino-"barbarian" populace of the frontier might give allegiance to a rising nomad leader. The secret of such a leader's rise lay usually in his capacity to learn Chinese ways of administrative organization, so that he could set up a hybrid regime based on control of merchants, farmers, and tribal warriors. Chinese inevitably played a part in the rise of such a "barbarian" ruler on the frontier. In this uneasy partnership the alien rulers functioned in special roles—as fighters and power-holders.

The Khitan Empire. The Liao Empire of the Khitan tribes (947–1125) illustrates the characteristic features of a dual state. Their empire extended over much of Manchuria, Mongolia, and the northeast corner of China proper. Thus it included an agricultural area in North China and southern Manchuria, grasslands in western Manchuria and Mongolia, and the forested valleys of eastern and northern Manchuria. The non-Chinese part of this kingdom included several tribal groups. In eastern Manchuria were the Tungus (ancestors of the Manchus), who lived by a combination of hunting and agriculture together with pig-raising. On the Mongolian steppe to the west were Turkish tribes, full nomads who had neither agriculture nor pigs, but many sheep, horses, and camels. In between were the semi-nomadic Khitan people, who lived by a mixed economy in which agricultural crops, camels, pigs, horses, and oxen all played a part. These Khitan tribes in the central region of mixed economy led the way in building the empire, beginning with a nucleus of eighteen tribes which eventually grew to a total of fifty-four.

Khitan society was headed by one clan, divided into eight main lineages, who regularly got their wives from another major clan. Non-Khitan tribes were incorporated into the society as was also the settled Chinese population of agricultural villages and cities. The status of the Chinese varied all the way from slavery, through various forms of bondage and partial freedom, to complete freedom. At the bottom of the social scale were the conquered peoples of the state of P'o-hai (713–926) in eastern Manchuria.

Unlike the Chinese clan system, in which an unbroken line is maintained indefinitely, most of the Khitan clans lacked clan names and tended to lose their identity after several generations. Ancestral sacrifices were maintained only by the ruling clan, following the Chinese example. Marriage followed the tribal custom, which was quite at variance with Chinese practices. That is, a man might marry his mother's or his father's sister, or his brother's widow, in complete disregard of the Chinese rules of generation.

By 907 the Khitan had formed a tribal confederation comparable to that of the Hsiung-nu of earlier times. In that year the chieftain declared himself emperor of the Khitan. Soon he set up a dynasty with his son as heir apparent but was involved in constant warfare, not least with his own brothers. As the empire expanded, it firmly adopted the Chinese system of hereditary monarchy.

Next to their capacity for central leadership, the Khitan owed their empire to their cavalry. The ruler's mounted archers were organized in his *ordo,* which formed his camp bodyguard and was the prototype of what Westerners later called a "horde." As early as 922 he had some two thousand braves in this elite guard drawn from all the tribes. Beginning as a bodyguard like those of Western emperors, this elite cavalry grew to include some fifty to seventy thousand horsemen.

In warfare the cavalryman might use three horses (leading two remounts). He wore some armor and in battle used two kinds of bows and carried an ax, a sword, a rope, and dried food. Training was in the form of hunting exercises in units of five or ten horsemen, strictly disciplined to follow their leaders. On the open plain, the Khitan warriors developed a clock-like precision of organization based on units of tens, hundreds, and thousands, with a vanguard, wings, a center, and an imperial guard. Their army was preceded by a scouting force, perhaps ten thousand strong, and they used night patrols and complicated signals consisting of beacons, drums, horns, banners, shouted code names, gongs, and even birdcalls. They avoided close combat with superior numbers but would cut off the enemy's supplies and use tactics of ambush and maneuver. In siege operations they made the Chinese populace fill in moats and used Chinese catapults to break down walls. In storming a city they would drive Chinese captives ahead against their own townsmen and relatives.

The Liao Dynasty.   By 947, the Khitan had extended their power southward over the sixteen prefectures in North China already mentioned and had captured towns and cities. In that year they adopted a Chinese dynastic title, as the Liao dynasty. Taking advantage of the collapse of the T'ang, they had now created a dual state of "barbarian" elements in the north and Chinese in the south. In this they had essential help from Chinese advisers who joined their cause, bringing with them the culture of cities and the methods of bureaucratic government.

The Liao administration was organized under five capitals, among which the Supreme Capital was north of the Wall. Each capital was the center of a circuit with a hierarchy of territorial units below it and with its own military commanderies, forts and fortified cities to protect it. Each half of the dual government had its own prime minister, chancellery, and ministers. The heads of both governments held office at the Supreme Capital. The government of the southern region inherited forms of the T'ang, such as the Six Ministries and the Board of Censors. The Chinese examination system was adopted after 988 to determine eligibility of Chinese for office. In making the Liao monarchy into a Chinese type of ruling institution, the Khitan took over the Chinese custom of naming year periods, selected an heir apparent, made Confucius the supreme sage of the state, practiced Confucian ancestor worship, used the Chinese language and script as their administrative *lingua franca,* and even wore Chinese clothes when in the southern region.

To offset this Sinification, the Khitan retained their own tribal organization and rites and, in the main, their own style of food and clothing. Unlike earlier "barbarian" invaders they consciously avoided taking over the Chinese spoken language as their own tongue, lest they be submerged in the sea of Chinese. They developed two forms of writing for their own type of Mongolian speech, the smaller one being alphabetical and the larger one based on Chinese characters. (See page 161.) The two Khitan scripts were used for administration, but no true literature developed in them.

The Liao Empire seems never to have had a population of more than about 4 million, very small in comparison with the Northern Sung. Indeed, the actual Khitan population was only about 750,000. Constituting only one-fifth of the population of their empire, the ruling Khitan tribesmen had to be on their mettle to maintain control. In the end they were overwhelmed not by Chinese but by another tribal people at their rear.

The Hsi Hsia Kingdom. The Sung had been able to withstand the Liao partly because a three-way division of power had developed in the northwest. A Tibetan people, the Tanguts, had built in the area of modern Kansu a kingdom known as Hsi Hsia, or West Hsia. Their capital at Ning-hsia, on the Yellow River, stood between Mongolia and the Central Asian trade route to the west. They had a semioasis economy, combining irrigated agriculture with pastoralism and trade. After sending tribute to the Sung, the Tangut ruler in 1038 declared his independence, proclaiming himself emperor of the Hsia. He had a new writing system invented for his people which used extremely intricate Chinese-type characters to record the Tangut speech. The resulting literature remains today still largely undeciphered. The Tanguts modeled their government and education on that of China but made Buddhism their state religion.

The Chin Dynasty of the Jurchen. The Jurchen tribes of northern Manchuria were Khitan vassals who became restive because they were prevented from moving down into the attractive southern region of Manchuria. They rose to power after an outstanding leader unified them in 1115, declared himself emperor, and quickly seized the Supreme Capital.

The Liao collapsed, but a remnant of the regime fled westward and set up another nomad empire. This was the Kara-Khitai, or "Black Khitan," which styled itself the Western Liao Empire (1124–1211). It established its control over the oases both east and west of the Pamirs, from the borders of the Hsi Hsia in Kansu across to the Amu-Daria (the Oxus River of Western antiquity), but was finally overwhelmed by the Mongols in 1211.

The Jurchen, unlike the Liao, were not confined to the northern borders of China but overran most of North China and captured the Sung capital Kaifeng in 1126. Their armies pushed all the way south to the Yangtze but the boundary with the Southern Sung was eventually stabilized roughly along the Huai River, at the approximate northern limit of major rice cultivation (see map, page 130).

The Jurchen named their dynasty the Chin ("Golden," 1122–1234), after a river in their homeland. Compared with the Chinese population they ruled, they were proportionally even fewer than the Khitan had been. They inherited the dual administration and hybrid culture of the Khitan rulers but were inevitably drawn further into the Chinese pattern. At their main capital, Yen-ching, on the site of modern Peking, they built up a Chinese-type bureaucratic state, divided into nineteen small provinces and subdivided into prefectures and subprefectures (*hsien*) on the model of the Sung and governed by the Six Ministries in the style of the T'ang. Chinese officials eventually outnumbered non-Chinese three to two.

The Jurchen, like the Khitan, sought both to rule over a large mass of Chinese subjects and to preserve their own culture in the face of the Chinese tradition. These post-T'ang non-Chinese peoples are in this respect reminiscent of the European tribal peoples who asserted their nationality as Frenchmen or Germans against the tradition of the Roman Empire. Thus the Jurchen used the Khitan alphabetic script and also devised two styles of Jurchen script, one alphabetic and one in characters derived from Chinese (see page 161).

At first, the Jurchen tribesmen, together with Khitan and other non-Chinese allies, were kept in readiness for instantaneous warfare, but this nation-at-arms, once settled in farming households on Chinese soil, could not remain effective warriors. Through economic relations with Chinese, they often became tenants on their land and sometimes paupers. Intermarriage between the two peoples was eventually permitted. Peace with the Southern Sung in 1141 confirmed the nominal suzerainty of the Chin and facilitated extensive trade. While Jurchen nobles fought among themselves over the succession, their Chinese subjects creatively pursued the arts of peace, in printing, scholarship, painting, literature and also the theater. The Chin rulers themselves came to follow Confucian norms, studying the Classics and writing Chinese poetry. After 1189, the Chin became involved on two fronts in exhausting wars with the Mongols and

	CHARACTER SCRIPTS				ALPHABETIC SCRIPTS			
Chinese	Khitan	Jurchen	Hsi Hsia	'Phags-pa	Syriac	Uighur	Mongolian	Manchu

SCRIPTS USED OR CREATED BY INNER ASIAN PEOPLES. *These examples are given to show form without any reference to meaning. For each type of script two columns are shown. All of them usually read from top to bottom and from right to left, although there are sometimes exceptions. For example, Syriac and Uighur almost always read from top to bottom in the Far East and in Central Asia, but they normally read horizontally from right to left in the Near East. The scripts in non-Chinese characters are believed to have been developed mainly on the model of Chinese, but are still largely undeciphered. The alphabetic scripts (except 'Phags-pa) trace back indirectly to Aramaic, which had a common origin with our own alphabet. The 'Phags-pa script was derived from the Tibetan which ultimately was derived from the Sanskrit.*

the Southern Sung. They inflated their paper currency, which they had inherited from the Northern Sung, with the usual unfortunate consequences. By 1215, under Mongol pressure, they were forced to move their capital south from Peking to Kaifeng, where the Mongols extinguished the Chin dynasty in 1234.

The Mongol Empire

In the history of the Northern Wei, the Liao, and the Chin we can see a number of repetitive features which become still clearer in the periods of Mongol and Manchu conquest: (1) Invaders seized power in North China usually during periods of disorder. (2) The "barbarians" enlisted Chinese advice and aid, especially from Chinese of the border region. (3) The superior "barbarian" cavalry was supplied with more and better horses from the steppe than could be maintained in an agricultural region. (4) Through a policy of tolerance, if not appeasement, local Chinese leaders were attracted and used to enlist a larger corps of Chinese tax collectors and administrators. (5) The invaders made use of the Chinese institutions of government and also let the traditional administration and Chinese social and cultural life continue. (6) But for themselves the invaders maintained a homeland of their own beyond the Wall in order to preserve their own conscious existence as a people and avoid absorption. (7) A dual, Sino-"barbarian" administration was conducted at the local level, largely by Chinese under the supervision of the conquerors. (8) The invaders also employed other foreigners in their administration. (9) They preserved control through military force held in reserve—including both a territorial army into which Chinese could be recruited, and units of the invading horde, which garrisoned the capital and key areas. (10) Toward tribal peoples in Inner Asia, dynasties of conquest developed a divide-and-rule policy. (11) In the long run, the invaders in the midst of overwhelming numbers of Chinese subjects would begin to borrow elements of Chinese culture: food, clothing, names, and even the language. (12) The result was eventual absorption or expulsion. All these features were illustrated during the Mongol conquest.

The Mongol people lived in small groups of a few families, each family in its felt tent, or yurt. At times of seasonal migration these scattered units might form larger groups of several hundred yurts. The basic social and political units were patriarchal clans. Spiritual life was focused on loyalty to clan, expressed in a cult of the hearth. A group of clans, bound together by blood relationships, formed a larger tribal unit. Within this social framework, two members of different clans might become "sworn brothers." Meanwhile, polygamy heightened the demand for wives to be acquired from outside the clan. Consequently, wives were often obtained by seizure, which fostered feuds, raids of vengeance, and petty warfare. As a result clan groups would become vassals of other clans, and whole tribes subordinate to other tribes, enhancing their power. A hierarchy of feudal-type relations of fealty and protection among "lords," "knights," "commoners," and "serfs" (to borrow European terms which are not entirely appropriate) thus developed among the Mongols. Through these personal relationships a strong personality might rise to a commanding leadership.

The Career of Chinggis Khan. When Chinggis Khan (also spelled Genghis, Jenghiz, etc.) was born, about 1167 (some say earlier), the Mongolian-speaking tribes still lacked a common name. He became their great organizer and unifier. His personal name was Temüjin. He was of aristocratic birth but his father had been slain when he was a boy, and he struggled through hard times to avenge him. He rose only slowly, for the establishment of personal loyalties was a gradual process. Rebelling against his overlord, he subjugated first one tribe and then another. Finally, in 1206 at a great meeting of the Mongol tribes on the Kerulen River, he was confirmed in the title of Chinggis Khan, which seems to have connoted "universal ruler." From the few accounts written long afterward by Persian, Chinese, and Arab chroniclers, we can see Chinggis' methods of organization. To secure a religious sanction, he asserted his own divine mission, delegated to him by the Eternal Heaven. His political structure was organized on the family principle, families forming clans, clans forming tribes, and so on. He drew up as a permanent basis of rule, superior to the Khan himself, an imperial code of laws or Great Yasa, first promulgated in 1206 and further developed before his death in 1227. While no complete text has survived, we know that it formulated the basic rules of organization. One source of the strength of this untutored nomad chieftain lay in his ability to learn from others. In building a civil administration, he used Uighur Turks, who were a commercial people, many of them Nestorian Christians, centered around the oasis of Turfan. The Mongols adapted the alphabetic Uighur script to write down Mongolian speech.

Chinggis' personal bodyguard eventually grew to an elite corps of 10,000, recruited from the sons of clan leaders, generals, and kinsmen. From this group, comparable to a modern officer training corps, Chinggis chose his generals and top administrators. The army was organized in units of tens, hundreds, and thousands, with clan members carefully intermixed. The whole force in 1227 amounted to about 129,000 men, a huge army by nomad standards but small for China. The total population of the Mongols cannot have exceeded 2,500,000 and perhaps was closer to 1,000,000 at this time. The Mongol cavalry fought under hereditary, aristocratic leaders. Clad in leather and furs, leading extra horses as remounts, living in the saddle as long as ten days and nights at a time, these troops could cover incredible distances, such as 270 miles during three days in Hungary. Since the troops lived mainly on their plunder, bases of potential supply ahead of them were a constant incentive for expansion.

In battle the Mongols used flying horse columns to encircle and compress the enemy just as they compressed the game caught in the ring of a great hunt on the steppe. Their heavy bows, more powerful than the English longbow, could kill at six hundred feet. As masters of deception, they would get their enemies to pursue, and then turn back, surround, and cut them up. "In this sort of warfare," Marco Polo remarked, "the adversary imagines he has gained a victory, when in fact he has lost the battle." In another tactic, heavy forces concealed on the wings would wait for the enemy to be enticed through the center and so expose his flanks. Through mobility and coordination, crushing force could be concentrated against a weak point. The Mongols thus brought offensive power to its height in the age before firearms. They were also masters of espionage and psychological warfare. From spies among merchants on the trade routes, the Mongols learned about their victims. By putting cities to the sword, they let terror run ahead of them. To capitalize on this terrorism, they also spread fair promises of toleration for religious minorities and freedom for merchants, providing all surrendered without delay.

Chinggis subjugated the Hsi Hsia kingdom in the northwest of China between 1205 and 1209, and it was finally extinguished in 1227. His first campaign against the Chin Empire in 1211–1215 destroyed their capital and also gained the services of Chinese who knew how to besiege cities and to govern them. The most famous of these was a descendant of the Khitan royal house, Yeh-lü Ch'u-ts'ai (1190–1244), who persuaded his new masters that it would be more profitable *not* to turn North China into an empty pasture! Instead he taught them to levy taxes on agriculture and foster the existing mines and industries. Chinggis then overran the Turkish empire of Khorezm (in Russian Turkestan) in 1219–1221. He acquired not only rich, irrigated oasis-cities like Bokhara and Samarkand, centers of handicraft production, caravan trade, and Islamic culture, but also the services of Muslim merchants and financiers. Turkish tribes were also incorporated into the Mongol horde.

Thus Chinggis before his death in 1227 had established the basis of a far-flung Eurasian empire by conquering its inner zone across Central Asia. Many have speculated as to Chinggis' true personality. For all his ability, his motives apparently were simple. "Man's highest joy," he reportedly said, "is in victory: to conquer one's enemies, to pursue them, to deprive them of their possessions, to make their beloved weep, to ride on their horses, and to embrace their wives and daughters." Both in Europe and in Asia the Mongols have been remembered for their wanton aggressiveness, and this trait was certainly present in Chinggis.

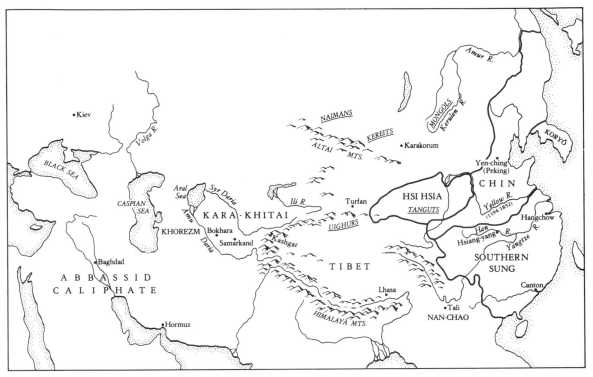

ASIA ON THE EVE OF THE MONGOL CONQUESTS (AROUND 1200)

The Four Khanates. In the tribal fashion, Chinggis divided the empire among the four sons of his principal wife. After his numerous grandsons had helped to expand it, the empire was composed of four main khanates (the asterisks denote grandsons of Chinggis):

(a) *Great Khan* (East Asia): Ögödei (third son of Chinggis), 1229–1241; Möngke (Mangu),* 1251–1259; Khubilai,* 1260–1294 (ruled over all China after 1279); Mongols expelled from China by Ming, 1368.

(b) *Khanate of Chaghadai (Djakhatai,* in Turkestan): Chaghadai (second son of Chinggis), 1227–1242; western part incorporated after 1370 in empire of Timur or Tamerlane (1336–1405).

(c) *Khanate of Persia* (Il-khans): built up by Hülegü*; capture of Baghdad, 1258; dissolution after 1335.

(d) *Khanate of Kipchak* (Golden Horde) ·on lower Volga: built up by Batu,* 1227–1255; dominated Russia; conquered by Tamerlane and broken up in fifteenth century.

In their expansion over most of the known world, mixed Mongol-Turkish armies overran Persia by 1231 and extinguished the Abbassid Caliphate at

Baghdad in 1258. While their forces in East Asia were completing the conquest of North China (by 1241) and Korea (finally conquered in 1258), the West Asian armies erupted westward. Under Batu they burned Moscow, seized Kiev, and invaded Poland, Bohemia, Hungary, and the Danube Valley (1241). At the western end of the great Eurasian steppe, they reached the Adriatic Sea. But Batu received news of the death of the "Great Khan" Ögödei in 1241 in Mongolia and withdrew his army so as to participate in the choice of a successor. Western Christendom, disunited and unprepared, was saved by Mongol domestic politics.

Batu's successors of the Golden Horde ruled for two hundred years in South Russia. The so-called Il-khans (meaning vassal khans) ruled for a century in Persia. The three agricultural areas—South Russia, Persia, China—were peripheral to the central communications zone of the grasslands of Mongolia and the oases of Turkestan. Thus the khanate of Chaghadai was the strategic center of politics and rivalry. In this region the Mongol post stations on the routes across Central Asia provided shelter and supply as well as protection against banditry. Over these routes moved traders and travelers while the official post moved goods and persons on government business and gave the rulers intelligence of events. Tough Mongol couriers, using relays of horses, could cover two hundred miles a day.

Imperial unity was fostered at first by the participation of all four khan-ates in each conquest. But the descendants of Chinggis soon yielded to centrifugal forces within their far-flung domains. Mongol rulers in West Asia accepted Islam while in China they became Buddhist believers and Confucian statesmen. The Chinese, Persian, and Russian states had their separate languages, cultures, official systems, court politics, and local needs, all bound to create disunity among the relatively few Mongol-Turkish over-lords. The local bureaucratic administrations were oriented inward, toward their domestic problems. The Mongols' conglomerate superstate held to-gether for only a century.

Conquest of the Southern Sung.   The Mongols' takeover in China occupied more than a generation up to 1279 and left a correspondingly deep im-press on Chinese life. The Southern Sung repeated its earlier mistake of aiding Chin against Liao by joining the Mongols against the Chin, thus helping to remove the buffer between themselves and their eventual con-querors. Yet the conquest of South China took several decades, which is clear evidence of the strength of the Southern Sung—a much more difficult conquest for the Mongols than the empires of West Asia.

The invaders' strategy was to outflank the Southern Sung on the west. In 1253 they took over the non-Chinese kingdom of Nan-chao with its capital at Tali in Yunnan, making this region for the first time an integral part of China. The conquest of the Southern Sung was completed under

Chinggis' ablest grandson, Khubilai (1215–1294), who became Great Khan in 1260 and ruled for thirty-four years. Khubilai built up Peking as his winter capital. His forces moved down the Yangtze and took the Sung capital at Hangchow. Next they took Canton, southwest of which the remnants of the big Sung fleet (most of which had already defected to the Mongols) were finally destroyed in 1279. Khubilai, in 1271, had adopted the Chinese dynastic name of Yüan, meaning "The First Beginning" or "The Origin," the first dynastic name not derived from a place name.

Conquest having become a way of life, Mongol envoys and expeditions went on to penetrate outlying parts of East Asia, using the naval power inherited from the Sung. Large but unsuccessful armadas comprised of thousands of vessels were sent against Japan in 1274 and 1281. At least four land expeditions invaded Vietnam and five penetrated Burma. Envoys visited Ceylon and South India by sea. In the 1280's ten states of Southern Asia sent tribute. In 1292 a Mongol fleet attacked Java but without permanent success. This continued effort to conquer the known world is all the more remarkable in view of Khubilai's long struggle with the rebellious leader of a western branch of the imperial clan. This rival, a grandson of Chinggis' successor, Ögödei, revolted in 1268, seized the khanate of Chaghadai, and remained until his death in 1301 a continual threat to the Great Khan in China.

China under Mongol Rule

Only gradually did the Mongols face the fact that conquered Chinese villagers, merchants, and city artisans could not be incorporated into the Mongol tribal society. Yeh-lü Ch'u-ts'ai, as chief minister in the conquered parts of North China after 1230, set up schools and held examinations to recruit Chinese into a bureaucracy. But the Mongols, like the Jurchen, found they could not use the rather simple dual type of divided Sino-"barbarian" administration that the Liao had developed. The Yüan therefore continued the administrative structure of the T'ang and Sung, particularly the sixfold division under the Six Ministries at the capital. During the thirteen hundred years from the early T'ang to 1906, this basic structure remained the same. The Yüan also continued a threefold division of central government among civil administrative, military, and supervisory (censorial) branches. Innovation was greater in provincial administration, where they followed the Chin example and made provincial governments into direct extensions of the central chancellery, an important step in perfecting the Chinese imperial structure.

The Mongol conquerors faced the age-old problem of how to rule in a Chinese fashion and still retain power. The Chinese populace had to be persuaded to acquiesce in foreign rule. To accomplish this, an alien dynasty had to maintain local order, give Chinese talent the opportunity to rise in bureaucratic political life, and lead the scholar-official class by fostering Confucian ideology and culture. For this exacting task the rank and file of Mongols were unprepared. Much of their success in the early Yüan era must therefore be ascribed to the commanding personality of Khubilai and his use of Confucian principles and collaborators.

The Mongols differed from their subjects in very striking ways, not only in language and status. For costume, they preferred the leather and furs of steppe horsemen. For food they liked mare's milk and cheese, and for liquor the fermented drink made of mare's milk. Bred on the almost waterless grasslands, the Mongols were unaccustomed to washing. They lacked even surnames. Their different moral code gave greater (and in Chinese eyes, immoral) freedom to women. Moreover, the Mongols' non-Chinese traits were constantly reinforced by their contact with a vast area outside China. They were the only *full* nomads to achieve a dynasty of conquest. The gap between them and the Chinese was thus greater culturally to begin with and was more strongly perpetuated politically. To make the division between conquerors and conquered even more complete, the recruiting of Southern Chinese talent for the Yüan bureaucracy was impeded by the heritage of Sung hatred for the plundering "barbarian." Later Chinese chroniclers, who have always had the last word on their conquerors, depicted the Mongols as primitive savages capable only of destruction and orgiastic excess. One later Chinese account states, "They smell so heavily that one cannot approach them. They wash themselves in urine."

In the face of native hostility, the Mongols in China as elsewhere employed many foreigners, particularly Muslims from Central and Western Asia. As Marco Polo recorded, "You see the Great Khan had not succeeded to the dominion of Cathay by hereditary right, but held it by conquest; and thus, having no confidence in the natives, he put all authority into the hands of Tartars, Saracens, or Christians, who were attached to his household and devoted to his service, and were foreigners in Cathay." The Mongols set up a hierarchy of social classes: they were the top class, and their non-Chinese collaborators second, followed by the Chinese of the North who had capitulated earlier, and, at the bottom, by those of the South, who of course outnumbered all the rest. Meanwhile the Mongol ruling class remained separate from Chinese life with separate systems of law for Chinese and for Mongols. The Great Khan kept his summer residence north of the Wall at Shang-tu (Coleridge's "Xanadu," meaning "Superior Capital"). His alien rule injected a heightened degree of centralized and ruthless despotism into the traditional Chinese Empire.

Life Under the Yüan Dynasty.   Khubilai on his accession had protected the Confucian temples, and he soon revived the state cult of Confucius.

Later he exempted Confucian scholars from taxation. But on the more fundamental issue of recruitment for government service, Khubilai did not seek out the talent of South China. The examination system had ceased to function in the North after 1237 and in the South after 1274. Its revival was delayed until 1315. Chinese clerks of course staffed the bureaucracy, but Confucian scholars did not often rise to the top.

The scholar class was antagonized also by the Mongols' patronage of foreign religions. In Persia many had embraced Islam, and in Central Asia, Nestorian Christianity. In China religious establishments of the Buddhist, Taoist, Nestorian, and Islamic faiths, like the Confucian temples, were all exempted from taxation. The Chin and Yüan periods saw many new Taoist monasteries built in North China. This multiple religious growth was a distinct setback for the Neo-Confucian doctrines of the Chu Hsi school.

The superstitious Mongols, with their background of shamanism, tended to accept the debased form of Buddhism that had developed in Tibet, namely Lamaism. Buddhism was introduced into Tibet according to tradition from northwest India in the eighth century. Once introduced, it was influenced by the native Tibetan cult known as Bon, which made much of magic and divination. The fusion which resulted is called Lamaism (the term "lama" means "superior one"). In the thirteenth century it spread rapidly into Mongolia and also China, with imperial support.

Khubilai was hailed by the Buddhist clergy in China as an ideal Buddhist monarch. Under his patronage the number of Buddhist establishments, including the great mountain retreats at Mount Wu-t'ai in Shansi, rose to 42,000 with 213,000 monks and nuns, a great many being Lamaists. All this patronage of a religious cult could not be offset, in the eyes of the Confucian scholar class, by the emperor's performance of Confucian ritual. He lacked the personnel and the policies to patronize Chinese accomplishments in literature, the arts, and thought. Instead of performing this function of upper-class leadership in China, the Mongols maintained a cosmopolitan regime, under which the Chinese bureaucratic class was given little scope.

In fostering the people's livelihood, on the other hand, Khubilai had some temporary success. The landholding element of the Southern Sung was not dispossessed, taxation of land and labor and the usual government monopolies were developed, and trade was facilitated by the far-flung contact with the rest of Asia. Arab and Persian seafarers and merchants frequented the great port cities like Canton and Ch'üan-chou (Zayton). Foreign trade by land was chiefly conducted by Muslim merchants of Central Asian origin. Their corporate groups not only served as trading associations but also became tax-farmers for their Mongol patrons. These merchant "companies," whose members guaranteed one another, played a key role in collecting the agrarian surplus of the Yüan Empire and channeling some of this accumulated capital into an expanded commerce. They also shared in the inordinate graft and corruption which accompanied Mongol rule. Commerce was aided eventually by a unified nation-wide system of paper currency. Marco Polo, coming from a much less economically advanced Europe, was amazed at this use of paper for money.

Khubilai moved the Great Khan's capital from Karakorum in Outer Mongolia to Peking, where the main entrance through the Great Wall leads down to the North China Plain. There he built a new city called Khanbaligh (Marco Polo's "Cambaluc"), meaning in Turkish, "city of the Khan." Within it was a palace enclosed by double walls and complete with parks, treasuries, a lake and a big hill dredged from it. (See page 181.) To feed the new capital, grain was transported from the lower Yangtze by extending the Grand Canal north to Peking from the Yellow River. On the stone embankments of this second Grand Canal system ran a paved highroad from Hangchow to Peking, a distance of eleven hundred miles, which took forty days to traverse.

Khubilai's grandson Temür, who succeeded him in 1294, maintained a strong central administration, but after his death in 1307 the Mongols' hold on China rapidly weakened. In the next twenty-six years, seven rulers occupied the throne. Open civil war began after 1328. Meanwhile paper money, which had earlier stimulated trade, was now issued in increasing quantities without backing, and so paper notes were no longer accepted for tax payments and steadily depreciated. In addition, the Yellow River was causing recurrent floods which ruined the well-watered productive areas of northern Anhwei and Kiangsu and southern Shantung. Financial, moral, and political bankruptcy thus came hand in hand.

The First Direct Contact with the West.   The Mongol Empire's control over the Central Asian trade routes permitted the travel of many Europeans to the court of China. Marco Polo was only one of many who brought back direct word of "Cathay" (the name derived from "Khitai" and referring specifically to North China). The century from about 1240 to about 1340 was an interlude between earlier and later eras in which Arab-Turkish control of Central Asia and the Near East kept a barrier between China and the West. During this Mongol century, European travelers reached Cathay by several routes: either through South Russia and Ili across the steppe, a hard journey; or across the Black Sea and through the Central Asian oases of the ancient Silk Route, the way taken by Italian merchants like the Polos; or by sea to Syria and the Latin states set up by the crusades, and thence through Baghdad and Central Asia; or, finally, by the sea route through the Indian Ocean and around Southeast Asia to the ports of South China, a passage made difficult by Arab obstruction. Over these routes, thronged by people of West Asia, many Europeans reached China and a few left accounts of their travels. They recorded the presence of many Greek Orthodox Christians at the Great Khan's court, mainly captured Russian artisans or soldiers.

Contact between medieval Christendom and East Asia was facilitated by the fact that the heretical Nestorian Christian faith had earlier penetrated the region from Persia. Although it had died out in China, it was revived among the Khitan and Jurchen and became widespread among the Uighur Turks and several Mongol tribes. Khubilai's own mother was a Nestorian Christian. The Nestorian church had some twenty-five metropolitan sees; in 1275 its patriarch at Baghdad created an archbishopric at Peking. Though deemed heretical, the Nestorian church had contact with the papacy.

Meanwhile, Western Christendom was absorbed in the fervor of the crusades. The stage was thus set for diplomatic relations between Western Christendom, the Mongols, and Islam. Saracen envoys sought French and English help against Mongol expansion in the Near East and, after the Mongols' conquest of Persia and Baghdad, their Il-khans sent at least seven embassies to the West between 1267 and 1291 to get help against Islam. On its part the papacy, when the Mongol threat to Europe had receded after 1241, sent a notable series of Franciscan monks on diplomatic and evangelical missions to Persia, Mongolia, and China, evidently to explore the possibility of obtaining Mongol help against the Saracens. While no diplomatic result was achieved by these envoys between East and West, the papal missionary effort finally established a Roman Catholic outpost in China under John of Montecorvino. Under the Great Khan's protection he preached, built a church with help from an Italian merchant, and taught 150 choirboys, whose Gregorian chants pleased the imperial ear. Six thousand converts were baptized in Peking in 1304, many of them probably non-Chinese. Roman Catholic missions made increasing progress toward the end of the Yüan period in China only to be snuffed out afterwards.

Western merchants must have greatly outnumbered the friars who crossed Asia, but Marco Polo was the only one to leave a record. He set out in 1271 with his father and uncle, Venetian merchants on their second trip to China. After reaching Shang-tu ("Xanadu") and Peking ("Cambaluc"), Marco spent seventeen years in Khubilai's service (1275–1292), returning to Venice in 1295. His *Description of the World* was dictated to a professional romance writer in a Genoese prison. It is not a travelogue but a systematic, scientific treatise, well informed and objective. (The original has not survived, but about 120 manuscripts, containing many variations, have been found in Italian, Latin, French, and other languages.) No other traveler has ever had so great a tale to tell as Marco Polo. His was the first connected exposition of the geography, economic life, and government of China to be laid before the European public. It was more than could be believed, for the China of the late thirteenth century was

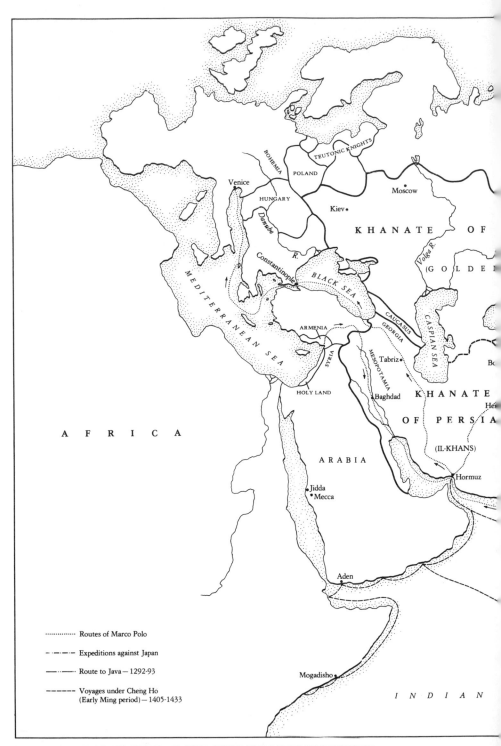

THE MONGOL EMPIRE (LATE THIRTEENTH CENTURY)

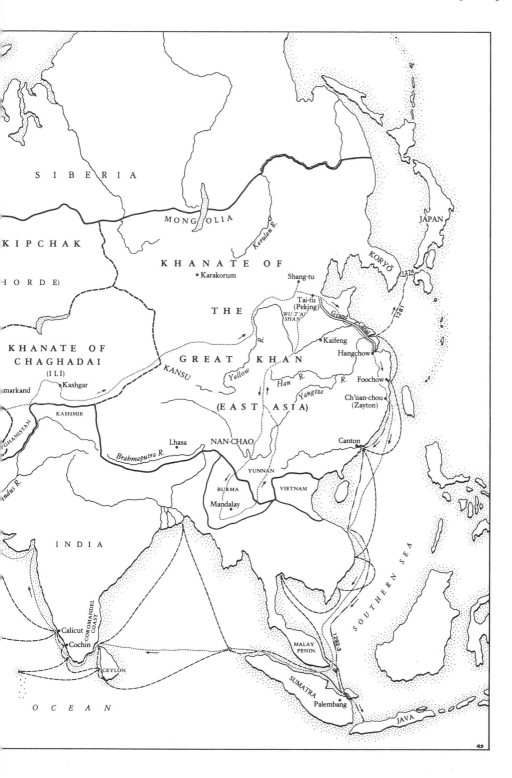

SIBERIA

MONGOLIA

KIPCHAK

(HORDE)

KHANATE OF

THE

• Karakorum

Kerulen R.

Shang-tu

Tai-tu
(Peking)

WU-T'AI
SHAN

Grand Canal

KOREA

JAPAN

1274

1281

KHANATE OF
CHAGHADAI
(ILI)

Kashgar

GREAT KHAN

KANSU

Yellow R.

Han R.

Kaifeng

Hangchow

R.   Foochow

markand

KASHMIR

(EAST ASIA)

Yangtze

Ch'üan-chou
(Zayton)

AFGHANISTAN

Lhasa

NAN-CHAO

Brahmaputra R.

Canton

Indus R.

YUNNAN

INDIA

BURMA

Mandalay

VIETNAM

SOUTHERN SEA

Calicut

COROMANDEL
COAST

Cochin

CEYLON

MALAY
PENIN.

1292-3

SUMATRA

Palembang

JAVA

OCEAN

RS

superior to Europe not only in size but also in culture and technology. Marco Polo in late medieval times became a byword for the incredible. Yet his influence persisted. Columbus had a copy of Polo's book and made notations in it. Time vindicated the Venetian. His burnable "black stones" dug from mountains, for example, proved to be coal. In the nineteenth century his itineraries were verified in detail.

Polo had his East Asian counterpart in Rabban Sauma, a Nestorian monk born in Peking. He crossed Central Asia to the Il-khan's court in 1278 and was sent to Europe to seek Christian help against Islam. In 1287 Sauma went through Constantinople to Naples, Rome, and Paris. He saw the Kings of France and England, expounded the Nestorian creed to the College of Cardinals and celebrated the Eucharist before the Pope in order to show that, while the language might differ, the ritual was the same.

European contact under the Mongols was minuscule compared with the contact between China and West Asia. Mongol conquest greatly facilitated Arab trade. This trade now went both by caravan from Baghdad to Peking and by ship from Hormuz on the Persian Gulf to Zayton (the Arab name for Ch'üan-chou in Fukien) and the other South China ports. Of all the medieval travelers, the Arabs, though largely unknown to Europe, were most conversant with East Asia. The fullest travel narrative of the Mongol period is by Ibn Batuta, who roamed across Southern Asia in the period 1325–1355, settling down and having families in several places as he circulated along the routes of Arab trade. He claims to have met a certain Arab in China and the Arab's brother on the Sahara Desert.

In the period of Mongol power Russia, Persia, and Mesopotamia received a Chinese cultural impact. Coming at the end of a millennium during which Chinese technological achievements had generally surpassed those of the rest of the world, the Mongol century saw a flow of many things from China westward—gunpowder, paper money, printing, porcelain, textiles, playing cards, medical discoveries, and art motifs, to mention only a few. This cultural influence was strongest in Persia and the Arab world, from which it often reached Europe indirectly. In return, China was most influenced by the Arab-Turkish culture. Islam took permanent root in the Middle Kingdom, while Christianity did not. In Kansu and Yunnan, the Muslim faith has remained strong ever since. In seaports like Canton and Ch'üan-chou Arab communities were allowed to live under their own legal customs and responsible headmen.

Chinese Culture under the Mongols. Despite this century of contact, things foreign remained superficial in China, as did the Mongol conquerors themselves. Some traditional institutions such as the examination system were only partially maintained, but they were not supplanted. The attraction of China's culture was so strong that a number of Central Asians—

ILLUSTRATION FROM THE SHUI-HU-CHUAN. *Outlaws, led by one
of their number who wields an ax, ambush an official (with black
hat, on horse) and his entourage, in order to rescue a comrade
who is being led to execution. From a Ming woodblock of a type
easily reproduced for wide distribution.*

Tanguts and Uighurs, Nestorian Christians, and Muslims—made their
mark as Confucian scholars or as typically Chinese painters and calligraphers. Compiling of the official dynastic histories of the Sung, Liao, and
Chin went forward under a Mongol as head of the bureau of historiography.
Chinese scholarship did not flourish notably, but neither did it wither away.
The great traditions of landscape and nature painting were brilliantly
maintained.

Two new literary forms, the drama and the novel, were connected with
the increased use, during this period, of the written vernacular (*pai-hua*)
in place of the traditional literary language. Both had to use a form closer

to everyday speech in order to reach the wider urban audiences of the day. The Yüan administration itself used a more vernacular style in its documents so that these would be more easily intelligible to the many officials who lacked a Chinese classical education. Chinese scholars on their part, finding less opportunity in official life and less patronage of classical studies, turned their talents to purely literary endeavor. Playwriting had begun to flourish in the twelfth century, both at Peking under the Chin and at Hangchow under the Southern Sung. Titles of nearly a thousand plays survive from this period. From the Yüan there exist the printed librettos of many plays. Their themes, typically Chinese, involve conflicts of human passion with the social bonds of filial piety, fidelity, or loyalty.

The Chinese drama was semioperatic, with orchestral music to accompany a great deal of singing and dancing. Scenery and realistic properties were not used, as in Elizabethan England. In their place was developed a great variety of conventions—stylized movements of the hands, sleeves, eyes, and feet, as in stepping over an imaginary doorsill, climbing nonexistent steps, or mounting an imaginary charger. Female roles generally came to be played by men, whose falsetto singing, dancing, and delicate gestures were especially appreciated. Romantic plots, technical virtuosity, humorous dialogue, brilliant costuming, and violent action all combined to create an urban art of wide popularity.

While the drama grew up primarily at the capital cities, the novel was created by professional storytellers among the populace. The Buddhist wonder stories of T'ang times grew into historical or purely imaginative love and adventure tales, which professional storytellers developed into long, loosely constructed sagas. Prompt-books for itinerant storytellers were the earliest written form of these episodic tales, and when gradually filled in with details by many different hands, became the early novels. Most are of prodigious length. The heroes usually are not scholar-bureaucrats but men of low class or military origin. All the novels are written in a style close to the vernacular of the day. The later ones were usually the work of single authors, men of education and literary talent, though they often concealed their identity. (The principal novels are discussed more fully on pages 235–237.) Although most of the major novels attained their mature form, or were actually first composed, in the Ming and Ch'ing periods, their roots go back to the Yüan or earlier.

The novel became the kind of literature that the majority of literate Chinese could most readily appreciate. Though customarily disesteemed by the scholar trained in the Classics, it became a principal literary form, with wide influence as a repository and mirror of social values. The emergence of both the novel and the drama in the Yüan period illustrates the vitality of Chinese culture as well as the frustration of the scholar class under the Mongols.

8. State and Society under the Ming

Chinese "Culturalism"

The Ming period from 1368 to 1644 is one of the great eras of orderly government and social stability in human history. A population averaging around 100 million lived during 276 years in comparative peace. The subsequent change from Ming to Ch'ing rule was relatively easy. The decline of Ming power and the Manchu capture of Peking in 1644 were followed by the Manchu conquest of all China. But this warfare and its devastation seem limited in comparison with the organized looting and massacres of contemporary European armies during the Thirty Years' War of 1618–1648. In any case, so stable was the political and social order of the Ming that it persisted, basically unaltered, under the alien Ch'ing dynasty for another 267 years from 1644 to 1912. Thus from the middle of the fourteenth century to the beginning of the twentieth, China followed traditional ways.

Unfortunately for the Chinese people of recent times, this remarkable stability was maintained during those very centuries that saw the dynamic rise of modern Europe — the Renaissance, the Reformation, the growth of national states, their expansion into the New World and over the earth, followed by the French Revolution and the Industrial Revolution. None of these fundamental Western transformations of the last six centuries had a real counterpart in China's own experience. China remained outside the turbulent stream of Western history, which was moving to engulf the world, and consequently by the nineteenth century had fallen behind the

West in many aspects of material culture and technology as well as in economic and political organization. This long period of stability in East Asian civilization left it comparatively "backward" or "underdeveloped." But this comparison with the expanding West should not stigmatize the Ming and Ch'ing periods as retrogressive or overshadow their real achievements. As we learn more about these centuries, we may expect to find many evidences of innovation and growth. Chinese society was far from unchanging, but the pace was slower and the degree of change less than in the West.

One factor creating stability was the Chinese view of history as "change within tradition." The leaders of society were devoted to tradition; anything that happened in the present had to be fitted into the rich pattern of experience inherited from the past. Instead of the ideal of progress, which Westerners today have inherited from the nineteenth century, the Chinese of the Ming and Ch'ing saw their ideal models far in the past.

This turning back for inspiration to the great ages of Han, T'ang, and Sung was accompanied by a deep resentment against the Mongols. Alien rule had inspired hostility toward alien things in general. Gradually this view hardened into a lack of interest in anything beyond the pale of Chinese civilization. This turning away from the outside world was accompanied by a growing introspection within Chinese life. We have already seen this in the antiquarian interest in art and in the burst of historical scholarship in the Sung. From that time on a degree of mingled fear and contempt for the outside world and a narrow concentration on the exclusively Chinese way of life produced a growing ethnocentrism. Eventually it dominated China's foreign relations and gave her an intellectual and psychological immunity to foreign stimuli.

This attitude had much in common with modern nationalism. But there were differences. A nationalist group asserts its own distinctiveness and superiority because it fears not only political but also cultural inundation by some other group. Nationalism thus seems closely tied to a general feeling of competition and insecurity. It is commonly asserted by a cultural subunit, particularly a linguistic subgroup, against other subunits within the same culture, as in the rise of national states within the common culture of Western Christendom. The Chinese, by contrast, showed no sign of a feeling of cultural inferiority. Political subjugation may have been feared, but cultural conquest was unimaginable. Thus Chinese xenophobia was combined with a complete confidence in cultural superiority. China reacted not as a cultural subunit, but as a large ethnocentric universe which remained quite sure of its cultural superiority even when relatively inferior in military power to fringe elements of its universe. Because of these similarities to and differences from nationalism, we call this earlier Chinese attitude "culturalism," to suggest that in the Chinese view the significant unit was really the whole civilization rather than the narrower political unit of a nation within a larger cultural whole.

Underlying this devotion to the Chinese way of life was one primary political fact, that the whole Middle Kingdom remained an administrative unit under a central government. This remarkable cohesiveness, compared with the constant disunity among the relatively smaller European states, cannot be attributed to geography. It normally took a month or so for the emperor's writ to be carried by horse to the borders of the realm in Kwang-tung, Yunnan, Central Asia, or the Northeast, farther than any distances in Western Europe. China's inveterate unity must be explained on institutional grounds, by the habits of thought and action that had become established in the society. The Chinese state was regarded as coterminous with Chinese culture. There was such a close identification of the entire way of life with the unified empire that the one implied the other. It was as if the Roman Empire had persisted in the West and had prevented the rise of France, England, and the other nations. The identity of culture and polity made the Chinese leadership of the Ming and Ch'ing periods uninterested in, and at times hostile to, things foreign. Culturalism thus was a pervasive attitude throughout the period.

Government under the Ming

The Founding of the Ming Dynasty.   The weakening of Mongol rule was hastened by fratricidal rivalry within the imperial clan. Fifteen years of frequent famine in North China after 1333 were capped by severe floods of the Yellow River. Flood and famine depleted the granaries. During the 1340's, uprisings occurred sporadically in nearly every province. In 1351–1353 several major rebel leaders emerged, and a typical interdynastic contest began among them to determine who should survive as the fittest to inherit the Mandate of Heaven. Some of these men claimed descent from the Sung emperors, some invoked a religious sanction by prophesying the advent of the Bodhisattva Maitreya, the Buddha of the Future, and others had the help of secret societies. The most famous of all secret societies has been the White Lotus Society. Its origin as a sect of T'ien-t'ai Buddhism has been traced back directly to the first half of the twelfth century. As with any group that opposed the ruling dynasty, this society had to be secret in order to survive.

The eventual winner among all these Chinese rebel heroes was Chu Yüan-chang (1328–1398), whose name ranks with that of Liu Pang, the founder of the Han, as a humble commoner who through native ability in a time of opportunity became the Son of Heaven. He was born in the Huai River region northwest of Nanking. Left an orphan, he entered a Buddhist monastery as a novice, which gave him a chance to become literate. For a time he even begged for a living. But in 1352, at the age of twenty-five, he joined a rebel band. (Probably he also joined the White Lotus Society, but he later denied this—it was an unwise precedent to leave in the historical record.)

Chu and his band crossed the Yangtze and in 1356 seized Nanking, a strategic base close to the key economic area of the Yangtze delta. By 1367, after defeating rival regimes both upstream and downstream, he controlled all the Yangtze Valley. Meanwhile, the Mongol commanders, instead of attacking the Chinese rebels, fought among themselves. In 1368 Chu Yüan-chang seized Peking but continued to use Nanking as his capital. He proclaimed himself the first emperor of the Ming ("Brilliant") dynasty, and chose Hung-wu ("Vast military power") as the name of the "year period," but, by keeping it for his whole reign, the first Ming emperor transformed it into his reign title. This set a fashion throughout the Ming and Ch'ing, of using only one year-period name during a whole reign, so that emperors of this era are generally known by their reign titles.

A second strong ruler was Yung-lo (reigned 1403–1424). The fourth son of Hung-wu, he had his base of power in Peking, where he rebelled against his nephew, Hung-wu's grandson, who had inherited the throne at Nanking. He waged a devastating civil war until he finally captured Nanking, and as a usurper at the age of forty-three took as his reign title Yung-lo ("Perpetual Happiness").

Nanking had been built up by Hung-wu as the imperial capital, with a city wall sixty feet high and over twenty miles around, the longest city wall in the world. Yung-lo in 1421 moved the Ming capital to Peking, leaving Nanking as the subsidiary capital. He rebuilt Peking on a more extensive plan than that of the Mongols. The main city walls, forty feet high and more than fourteen miles around, formed a square with nine gates, each one protected by an outer gate. In the center stood the walls of the Imperial City, some five miles in perimeter. Within it, in turn, were the high red walls of the Forbidden City, the imperial palace itself, surrounded by a moat about two miles around. Running from south to north through the palace, on the main axis of the whole capital, are the imposing throne halls with their gold-tiled roofs, each one rising from a terrace of white marble. Much of this great architectural creation of the Ming still stands today as an unparalleled monument of empire. The walls of the southern city of Peking with their seven additional gates were added in the sixteenth century.

Ming Despotism. The seventeen Ming emperors reigned during a series of recognizable phases: (1) the inaugural era of founding and consolidation under Hung-wu (1368–1398); (2) the vigorous building and expansion under Yung-lo (1403–1424) and his successors, which, however, by the

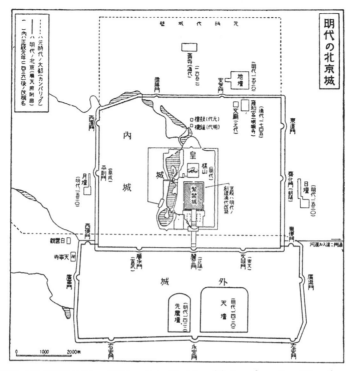

PEKING UNDER THE MING AND CH'ING. *Top and center: Site of Yüan capital, Tai-tu, of which the northern walls were razed by the Ming. Center: Inner City surrounds Imperial City which encloses lakes on left and Forbidden City or Palace on main axis, with Prospect Hill (dredged from lakes) on north. Bottom: Outer city (under the Manchus, the "Chinese City") with Altars of Heaven (right) and of Agriculture (left). Outside the main city on east, north, and west, respectively, are Altars of the Sun, Earth, and Moon. (From Wada Sei,* Tōyō bunkashi taikei.*)*

middle of the century had overstrained the imperial resources; (3) a century of gradual decline of imperial power both at home and abroad; (4) in the latter part of the sixteenth century a period of reform; and (5) by the early seventeenth century an intensification of evils and final collapse.

This profile was studied intensively by moralistic Confucian scholars in the late Ming, who saw the Chinese state collapsing. They and their successors in the Ch'ing made a moral interpretation of the dynastic decline, analyzing the personal failings of successive emperors, the errors of their officials, and the factionalism which rent the bureaucracy. Today, our basic political criticism might be that the emperor was subject to no higher law or constitutional checks. Power was concentrated in him personally. He had to be either a benevolent despot or tyrant, or else let his power be exercised by others as favorites on an irregular, unstable, personal basis. The Ming government had to have a great man at its head or face disaster.

Because the founder of the Ming, ruling for thirty-two years, left his imprint so strongly upon the dynasty, his personality was of special significance. Hung-wu was represented in his portraits as a man with an ugly, porcine face. He had had a hard life in his youth, and as emperor remained lonely and austere. He made a fetish of frugality and became subject to fears and suspicions, sometimes to delusions and violent outbursts of temper. He became very cruel and inflicted terrible tortures for slight offenses. In his final will he wrote: "For thirty-one years I have labored to discharge Heaven's will, tormented by worries and fears, without relaxing for a day." Perhaps this rather paranoid temperament of the founder helps to explain the growth of the Ming despotism. Hung-wu's concentration of power in his own hands may also have derived from his experience as a self-made conqueror of pre-eminent capacity. He institutionalized his personal role.

In 1380, suppressing a widespread plot attributed to his chief minister, Hung-wu abolished the central administrative organ of past dynasties, the Imperial Secretariat. Henceforth the emperor's rule was to be personal and direct. This institutional change gave the emperors of the Ming and also the Ch'ing periods a more autocratic role. In his personal administration Hung-wu, however, made use of Grand Secretaries, who handled the flow of official memorials (as many as a hundred a day) and drafted the imperial edicts in reply. Eventually they became institutionalized informally as the Grand Secretariat, a sort of cabinet, superior to the Six Ministries. But the Grand Secretaries remained merely aides of the ruler, unable to take executive action on their own initiative.

One group who eventually acquired considerable power were the eunuchs. Hung-wu had warned vigorously against this very possibility. He erected in the palace a metal tablet three feet high reading, "Eunuchs must have nothing to do with administration." He limited their numbers, ranks, titles, and style of clothing, forbade their handling documents, dismissed those who commented on government affairs, and decreed that they should remain illiterate. Nevertheless the eunuch institution remained an integral part of the Inner Court, based on the emperor's need of male descendants and his consequent maintenance of a harem. Later emperors grew up in the Inner Court, often personally devoted to eunuchs who had been their childhood companions or preceptors. The eunuchs' ranks and duties proliferated within the palace, and their influence gradually extended into the entire administration. In the 1420's a palace school was set up for them. The number of eunuchs increased to thousands. In a central office in

THREE MING EMPERORS. *Left: The founder Chu Yüan-chang who reigned as the Hung-wu emperor, 1368–1398. Center: The consolidator, the Yung-lo emperor, 1403–1424. Right: A source of disaster, the Wan-li emperor, 1573–1620.*

Peking (the Eastern Yard), they kept secret files on official personnel, accessible only to the emperor. They became, in effect, a separate echelon of administration, not unlike a present-day security system. This was because eunuchs, as palace inmates, lacking family loyalties and completely dependent upon their master, had a unique inside position, closer to the imperial person than any of the scholar-officials. Eunuchs consequently gained great influence as trusted agents of the emperor, even becoming commanders of military forces or inspectors in the provinces. The Ming saw a constant struggle for power between the eunuchs and the Grand Secretaries within the palace, and also between these groups of the Inner Court and the top officials of the imperial bureaucracy, or Outer Court, at the capital.

The arbitrariness of the emperor's rule was visibly demonstrated in another custom, the corporal punishment of high officials at the court. Hung-wu had early followed the Mongol precedent of having officials publicly and ceremoniously beaten with the bamboo. He had a dozen officials executed at various times on suspicion of having inserted derogatory puns in their congratulatory memorials. Such treatment contravened the Confucian doctrine that punishments are for the unlettered masses while the superior man is to be moved by the power of the ruler's moral example. The Ming regime, famous for exalting the letter of the Classics, became notorious for contravening their spirit.

Another phenomenon of the Ming court was factionalism. Cliques of officials became violently involved in one dispute after another, hating their opponents, appointing members of their own faction to office when they could, accusing those in power when they were not. However, the unconfined power of the emperor and the factionalism of officials were active mainly at the level of the imperial bureaucracy, which was spread very thinly over the empire. At the local level was a stable social order in which the emperor's power was held in reserve and seldom exercised.

The Structure of Government.   The Ming emperors retained the inherited structure of central government: first, a civil bureaucracy under the Six Ministries and other organs; second, a centralized military hierarchy; and third, a separate hierarchy of censors. In Western eyes the Board of Censors is perhaps the most interesting of the three. Its chief bureau at the capital had a staff of 110 "investigating censors." In addition, each ministry had a special censorial staff that watched its operations. Censors drawn from the general civil bureaucracy were typically younger officials of rather low rank, selected for personal qualities of probity. When sent into the provinces, often on one-year tours of duty, they investigated the conduct of justice and of ceremonies, the condition of granaries and of schools, and received reports from officials and complaints from the public. Their power came from their having direct access to the throne, both to impeach other officials and to remonstrate (at their peril) with the emperor. These broad powers were limited by the fact that censors usually returned to the regular civil bureaucracy after a tenure of nine years or less; like all officials, they depended upon the imperial whim. Protected neither by life tenure nor by immunity from their master's wrath, these "eyes and ears of the emperor" were in reality bureaucrats like all their fellows, concerned for their own safety, dependent upon favorable merit ratings from their superiors, and sometimes open to bribery or intimidation.

This threefold administration of the Ming and Ch'ing has an interesting comparability with the recent regimes of the Kuomintang and the Chinese Communist Party. Since 1928, China has been governed through the three principal echelons of party, army, and government. The modern governing parties in China may be viewed as the successors of the dynastic families, from whom the rulers were chosen and to whom they answered. The party apparatus, running parallel to army and civil administration, has also inherited some of the ancient censorial functions. This Chinese trinity is not a separation or balance of powers, like that under the Constitution of the United States, but perhaps we may call it a system of balanced administration. The military forces kept the regime in power, the civil bureaucracy carried on the government, and the censors (and also the eunuchs) kept watch on everything.

The territorial civil administration of the Ming was divided into 15 provinces, which the Ch'ing later increased, by subdivision, to 18. Each province was divided into local units composed of still smaller units—prefectures, of which there were, generally speaking, 159 in the Ming Empire; subprefectures or departments, of which there were 234; and counties (hsien), which totalled 1171. Under the Ch'ing these totals expanded to roughly 183 prefectures and 1470 counties (also called districts). The local administrative hierarchy of magistrates, according to the law of avoidance, were never permitted to serve in their own native provinces lest they be seduced into collusion with kinfolk and local friends. These officials in ascending order were the hsien magistrate, the subprefect, and the prefect. Their administration was headed by a provincial administrative commissioner. There was also a judicial commissioner or judge, with his own staff. A third top official was the provincial military commander. Thus each province was under a collegial group of officers who represented the same threefold administrative, military, and supervisory functions as in the capital. A governor was eventually added as a coordinator at the top of each province. The administrative hierarchy was also watched, as already noted, by censors on tour.

The Ming military system developed by Hung-wu was based on guards units of 5600 men. Each unit was divided into five subunits of 1120 men, who were registered professional soldiers. By 1393 there were 493 guards units under the Ministry of War, stationed at strategic spots on the Inner Asian frontier and the seacoast, along the Grand Canal and at the capital, under five main regional commands. The original guards units had thus become garrisons, independent of the local civil administration. The positions of the registered soldiers were hereditary, and many were given land on which to farm for their livelihood, in the hope of realizing the ancient ideal of a self-supporting army of farmer-soldiers. But inevitably, these Chinese garrisons, even more than Khitan, Jurchen, or Mongol troops, found it difficult to remain effective soldiers in a nonwarlike society.

As at the capital, new administrative organs in the provinces began informally and later became institutionalized. Among these were the intendants of circuit (*tao-t'ai,* Anglicized as taotai), first appointed to handle special functions connected with the salt monopoly, police,. customs, river conservancy, or the like. Eventually, the provinces were each divided for these various purposes into a number of circuits, which formed a new

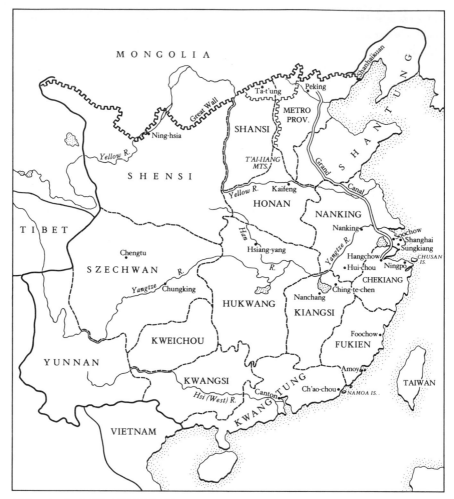

CHINA UNDER THE MING

administrative level between the provincial and the prefectural levels. Another development was the sending of new traveling inspectors and special commissioners from the capital to check corruption and misgovernment. Such officials were given certain administrative, censorial, and military powers within designated areas, so as to introduce a more unified executive capacity into the territorial administration. From them developed, by the middle of the Ming era, the office of provincial governor, already mentioned, as well as that of governor-general, an official normally in charge of two provinces.

Land, People, and Taxes. The Ming government's control over the land and the people was signalized by the drawing up of detailed registers of land and of population. In 1393 the population registers gave an estimated total of 10 million households and 60 million persons. This registration, not based on a modern type of census, produced a total no greater than that of the Han period. We can only wonder whether the population in 1393 may not have been double this figure. The land registers in 1393 recorded a total of roughly 129 million acres of land in use, less than half the estimated acreage of cultivated land in recent times. Each holding was classified according to type and productivity and was taxed accordingly.

Taxation followed the tradition which went back to the Double Tax of the eighth century (see pages 120–121). The Ming Summer Tax was collected in the eighth month on the supplementary crops grown during the winter and harvested in early summer. The Autumn Grain Tax was collected in the second month on produce grown during the previous summer and harvested in the autumn, above all on the great rice crop of the Yangtze Valley. The usual government monopoly taxes on tea and salt were also maintained. The Ming continued to issue paper money, as the Sung and Yüan had done, but made it unconvertible into metal currency (copper cash or silver bullion), so that it became worthless and had to be abandoned by 1450.

Households were classified into three, five, or nine grades (there were many complexities) and were obliged to provide labor service according to the number of registered adult males between sixteen and sixty years of age. One kind of labor service was to bear local responsibilities in connection with tax collections and public works. This service was organized under the *li-chia* system. Ideally, each 110 neighboring households formed a unit (*li* or village). Within this unit each year one of the ten leading families superintended one-tenth of the 100 remaining households to form a *chia* or section, which bore the responsibility for local labor service during the year. The others served in rotation over a ten-year period. Thus the *li-chia* system had common features with but was separate and distinct from the *pao-chia* system of mutual guarantee which had been inherited from the Sung (pages 100 and 129). Another kind of labor service, also apportioned among the male adults, involved prescribed tasks in the big government offices (*ya-men,* Anglicized as yamen), or else money payments for supplies for the yamen. Still other forms of labor service, apportioned among the populace, required service at the government post stations and in the local militia.

The Ming legal system showed the same pattern of reapplying traditional principles with a new thoroughness. A comprehensive body of administrative and criminal law was first published in 1397.

Yet the early Ming government remained, by modern standards, superficial. It claimed the prerogative of organizing and controlling all aspects of society. But in practice it did not interfere with the Chinese people in their daily lives. There were in the provinces only about two thousand principal posts. If one adds minor incumbents, the total of civil officials in the Ch'ing Empire as late as 1800 was only around twenty thousand. The control of the country by such a small number of mandarins, as Chinese officials came to be called by Westerners, was feasible only because of the functions performed by the dominant elite in each locality, that is, the degree-holders or gentry.

Society and Culture under the Ming

The Examination System.   In the Ming revival of a purely Chinese rule over China, the animating spirit had been to return to the pre-Mongol institutions of the T'ang and Sung. This soon built up the importance of the examination system. Under the Ming and Ch'ing there were three main levels of examination activity: First were preliminary examinations in the county (*hsien*), which qualified one to compete in examinations held during two out of every three years at the prefectural city (*fu*). This gave one the lowest principal degree, that of licentiate or bachelor, called by the ancient name of *hsiu-ts'ai,* "flowering talent." This admitted one to the privileged class of literati, who enjoyed exemption from labor service and corporal punishments. In order to retain this lower-gentry status, the degree-holder had to pass routine examinations, usually every three years. For the second level another preliminary test led to the great triennial examinations at the provincial capitals, where thousands of candidates would spend several days incarcerated with brush and paper in the long rows of individual cells at the examination field. One out of every one to two hundred competitors became a provincial graduate or "recommended man" (*chü-jen*), eligible to compete at the third level in the triennial metropolitan examinations at Peking. If successful at the capital, he became a metropolitan graduate or "presented scholar" (*chin-shih*), went to the palace for a final test by the emperor himself, and then received his official ranking and appointment to a post.

The bureaucratic system flexibly permitted some men to advance without examination. One means was the inheritance privilege, by which a son of an official of high rank could receive degree status and sometimes even official position in consideration of his father's merit. Another means under the Ming and Ch'ing, as in all previous dynasties, was to let men secure degree status by purchase. This was done by making a contribution to the imperial treasury. Generally the purchaser was allowed to obtain only degree status, not an actual official post. This admitted him to the gentry class, but not into officialdom. Thus degrees acquired by purchase, clearly designated as such, admitted certain men of wealth, mostly merchants or landlords, to the scholarly elite, giving them, in return for their

THE IMPERIAL GOVERNMENT'S EXAMINATION SYSTEM. *Thousands of cells standing in a vast enclosure at Nanking, as in other provincial capitals.*

payments, a qualified recognition within a framework that still gave the genuine scholar the highest prestige. The sale of degree status in this fashion was partly a safety valve, letting ambitious nonintellectuals into the establishment, and partly a source of revenue, which tempted a dynasty particularly in time of need. In the nineteenth century roughly a third of the lowest level degree-holders got them by purchase.

Generally speaking, the examination system brought in the great bulk of the bureaucracy and succeeded in recruiting the best talent of the country for government service. Quotas limited the number who could succeed in each county and province, so as to ensure geographical representation. Candidates' papers were sometimes copied, without their names, before being read in order to ensure anonymity and impartiality. For the provincial examinations, the examiners were sent out from the capital. The system was managed by the Ministry of Rites, instead of the Ministry of Personnel which supervised the officials' later careers. All these practices ensured the impartial universality of the selection process.

One weakness of the system was its restriction of subject matter to the Four Books, which had been selected as the essence of Confucianism in the Sung, and the Five Classics, again as interpreted by the Sung scholars of the school of Chu Hsi (see pages 149–150). In its passion for formal organization, the Ming adopted finally in 1487 a set form for writing examination papers under eight main headings, with not over seven hundred characters in all and with much use of balance and antithesis. This was the famous "eight-legged essay" style, later denounced as imposing a tyranny of literary structure over thought.

The institutions which prepared examination candidates included so-called government schools, which were ordered to be set up at the county and prefectural levels. But their chief function was to enroll the scholars and hold periodical examinations, not to provide organized instruction or residence facilities. The actual preparation of scholars began in the family or sometimes in a clan school. This gave the advantage to youths from extended families that could afford tutors, specifically from scholar-official families, in which parental example and family tradition provided incentive and guidance.

The chief primer, memorized by many millions during the Ming and Ch'ing eras, was the *Three-Character Classic* produced in the thirteenth century. It gave in jingle form a concise summary of basic knowledge and doctrine in 356 alternately rhyming lines, each of three characters. The opening lines, when understood, convey the prime doctrine of Mencius that human nature is fundamentally good, an idea universally accepted in China, which was to prove a stumbling block to Western missionaries convinced of original sin. Thus the process of elementary learning was at the same time a process of philosophical indoctrination.

Scholarship.   At the top of the intellectual pyramid under the Ming stood the Hanlin Academy, a carefully selected body of outstanding metropolitan graduates, who performed important literary tasks for the court. The ethnocentric reaction of the early Ming centered in this citadel of Confucian doctrine. In addition some 300 private academies (*shu-yüan*) were founded in various parts of the country, on the model of the Sung, as centers of scholarly study, discussion, and compilation, usually under the patronage of high officials or rich merchants; some also received imperial encouragement. They brought together eminent scholars, students who received free maintenance and tuition, and small libraries. Academies also published scholarly works and stored the wooden printing blocks.

The emperor's sponsorship of letters and the arts was an important means of maintaining his position as head of the Confucian state and culture. This tradition produced in 1407 the great *Encyclopedia of the Yung-lo Period* in 11,095 volumes—a compilation of all the principal

三字經

章炳麟重訂

人之初 性本善 性相近 習相遠
苟不教 性乃遷 教之道 貴以專
昔孟母 擇鄰處 子不學 斷機杼

孟母姓仉曾三遷其居以教孟子孟子廢學母斷

織以警之孟子懼旦夕勤學卒成大儒

荀季和 有義方 教八子 名俱揚

荀季和東漢時潁陰人名淑桓帝時補朗陵侯相

蒞事明理稱爲神君子八人並有才名時謂之八

THE THREE-CHARACTER CLASSIC (SAN-TZU CHING). *The first page of a modern edition, with the title of the book at the upper right-hand corner and the text itself starting on the third line. The commentary appears in smaller type.*

works on history, government, ethics, geography, etc., inherited from previous ages. Compiled by more than two thousand scholars, it was too large to print. Fewer than four hundred manuscript volumes have survived. The next two centuries saw a continued flood of publication sponsored by the court, by officials, and by academies and families. To try to describe this literature, its great compilations, the myriad monographic treatises, the many genres of belles-lettres, would be no easier than to attempt to describe the literature of all Europe in the same period. To cite one example, after several smaller works had led the way, one scholar (Li Shih-chen) spent twenty-six years compiling an illustrated *materia medica* which described almost two thousand animal, vegetable, and mineral drugs and gave over eight thousand prescriptions. Completed in 1578, it described smallpox inoculation and the uses of mercury, iodine, chaulmoogra oil, ephedrine, and other items of a rich pharmacopoeia upon which the modern world is still drawing. Again, a well-illustrated handbook of industrial technology (by Sung Ying-hsing, printed in 1637; see pages 14, 15, and 74), describes methods and instruments used in producing rice, silk, salt, pottery, metals, coal, paper, weapons, and many other products of China's premodern technology.

The vitality of Ming scholarship reflected processes of social growth of the same sort that had flowered in the Sung. Two centuries of domestic peace under the Ming brought substantial economic growth—big increases

*The Ming official and philosopher,
Wang Yang-ming (Wang Shou-
jen), 1472–1529.*

in farm production and population as well as in trade and industry. City
life flourished accordingly, accompanied by more printing and distribution
of books, more widespread education, and a more refined and also more
democratized urban culture. Out of this came a larger scholar class as well
as an enlarged bureaucracy; yet the problems of Chinese life also proliferated and taxed the powers of Confucian thinkers to maintain an
integrated view of society and define the scholar's role in it.

The Ming philosopher most influential on later generations in China
and Japan was Wang Yang-ming (1472–1529), a successful high official
who went beyond the orthodoxy of Chu Hsi by advocating both spiritual
enlightenment through meditative self-examination and a vigorous ethical
activism within society. Wang carried further a line of Sung thought (see
page 149), the Neo-Confucian school of Idealism or of the Mind which had
stemmed from a contemporary of Chu Hsi as a minority school opposed
to the dominant Chu Hsi school of Rationalism. In general, this School of
the Mind was inclined to deny the dualism of Chu Hsi's system, the sharp
distinction between Heaven and man and therefore between "Heavenly
Principle" (*t'ien-li*) and "human desire." Instead, it viewed them both as
parts of a single realm, which brought it closer to Buddhism. Building on
this tradition, Wang Yang-ming's teaching represented a sort of Zen
revolt within Confucianism: it put greater stress on meditation and intuitive knowledge. Chu Hsi's interpretation of the classical phrase (from
the *Great Learning*) about the "extension of knowledge through the

investigation of things" could thus be revised. Wang advocated instead "the extension of intuitive knowledge," which could be achieved through the investigation of one's own inner mind, the *li* within one. The process for doing this, as in Zen Buddhism, was essentially meditation, leading to a sort of enlightenment. But Confucian self-cultivation sought to eliminate not all desires, as in a Buddhist nonattachment to the world, but only selfish desires, the better to achieve one's dutiful harmony with others and with all creation. This led Wang to stress the "unity of knowledge and conduct." As he put it, "Knowledge is the beginning of conduct; conduct is the completion of knowledge." This has remained a Chinese and Japanese ideal down to the present day.

The Gentry Class. The metropolitan graduates totaled only 25,000 men during the whole Ming period. But the degree-holders of the lower ranks probably numbered at any one time about half a million. These degree-holders of all ranks have been known in Chinese as "officials and scholars" (*shen-shih*). In English the term gentry has been applied to them, but this term requires careful definition. It is ambiguous, for it is applied both to individuals and to families, and may have either a political-social or an economic connotation. Strictly defined, the gentry were individual degree-holders. Yet in China where the family overshadowed the individual, the existence of gentry families (i.e., families that had members who were degree-holders) was to be expected. Individuals became gentry by securing degrees. Yet, in a crowded society based on farming, where landowning was a chief economic support for scholarly study, landlord-gentry families were very common. Degree-holders and landlords overlapped to a considerable but imprecise extent.

The peculiar strength of Confucian government lay in the fact that the gentry performed so many public functions in the local community without official remuneration. They commonly lived in their big houses in the market towns but also maintained contacts or establishments in the administrative cities. As men of influence, they assumed responsibility for many activities which today are performed by officials. They raised funds for and supervised public works, such as the building and maintenance of irrigation ditches and canals with their dikes and dams, and roads with their bridges and ferries. They took responsibility for public morals, maintaining the local Confucian temples and ceremonies. They supported schools and academies. They compiled the local histories or gazetteers. In time of plenty they sponsored orphanages and care for the aged. In time of disaster they provided relief. In the face of disorder, they might get permission to organize local militia as defense forces. In most of these activities they received official encouragement or recognition but not specific appointment to office or any pay. A loose comparison might be made

GENTRY IDEALS. *From an eighteenth-century work* (Pin-feng kuang-i) *illustrating the rewards of virtue. The caption (not shown) for the illustration on the left says: "In the tenth month winter cold sets in. The diligent have ample food and clothing. They feast with wine, play games, and entertain relatives. Parents live in comfort while sons pursue learning." The illustration on the right is for the eleventh month and shows a winter scene. Within their apartments women who have done their weaving sit warmly clothed around a brazier enjoying wine. On the street people who have been indolent suffer from the cold.*

with other classes that have functioned in very different societies, such as the equestrian order of ancient Rome, the modern American business class, or other nonofficial groups that have provided local community leadership.

The interest of the government was to maintain morale and a type of public spirit among the gentry, as opposed to selfish opportunism. To this end the Confucian doctrines were recited in the local Confucian temples and the Son of Heaven issued his moral exhortations. The six imperial injunctions of Hung-wu were ordered posted in all villages in 1397. These said, in effect, "Be filial, be respectful to elders and ancestors, teach your children, and peacefully pursue your livelihood." Thus the great tradition of learning, under the patronage of the head of the state, was used to indoctrinate the common people, while the gentry class as the local elite in turn provided leadership in the orderly life of the villages. Though not aristocratic in a hereditary sense, this was indeed an elitist system, for the degree-holders with their immediate families formed certainly no more than 2 per cent of the population but held the highest social authority outside the small official class itself.

Foreign Relations

The Tribute System.   Upon gaining the throne, Hung-wu immediately tried to re-establish the grand design of the Chinese state in his foreign relations as well as at home. He sent envoys to the peripheral states, Korea, Japan, Annam (Vietnam), Champa, Tibet, and others, announcing his accession. Tribute missions soon came from these states and from others to which Mongol expeditions had been sent almost a century earlier, on the established routes of China's overseas trade.

The suzerain-vassal relationship between the ruler of China and rulers of other countries expressed the traditional "culturalism" in which China was assumed to be not only the largest and oldest among the states of the world but indeed their parent and the source of their civilization. Tribute relations involved not only performance of the kowtow, the "three kneelings and nine prostrations," but also many other aspects of interstate relations: the exchange of envoys and conduct of diplomatic relations, repatriation and extradition of persons, regulation of Sino-foreign trade, and special Chinese efforts at self-defense through intimidating, cajoling, or subsidizing foreign tribes and rulers. In short, the fitting of foreign potentates into a hierarchy of superior and inferior, and the expression of this in ritual observances, was merely an extension to the outer world of the "Confucian" social order which the ruler of China sought to maintain at home. The vassal king was given an official patent of appointment and a seal to use on his memorials, which were to be dated by the Chinese ruler's year period. The Son of Heaven affected a paternal interest in the orderly government of the tributary state, confirming the succession of new rulers, sometimes offering military protection against attack, usually conferring the boon of trade with China, and in any case sending down moral homilies and exhortations. This was not an aggressive imperialism. Rather, it was a defensive expression of culturalism: foreign rulers, if they wished contact with the Middle Kingdom, had to accept its terms and acknowledge the universal supremacy of the Son of Heaven. Trade with China might be of great value. Tribute formalities were the price to be paid. Like so many grand designs, this one failed of perfect execution. Yet Chinese chroniclers, by maintaining the forms of tribute at least in the

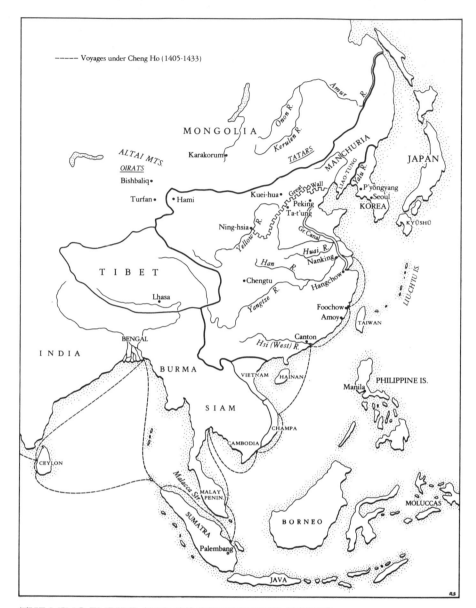

- - - - - Voyages under Cheng Ho (1405-1433)

THE MING EMPIRE AND ITS FOREIGN RELATIONS

record, made it seem important. It was often regarded quite differently by the tributaries.

The tribute system served many purposes. To get the "king of Japan" to curb Japanese pirates who were raiding Chinese ports, Hung-wu sent three missions to Japan in 1369–1372, using various inducements—repatriation of captured pirates, threatening rescripts from himself, and Chinese monks as envoys, but all to no avail. Japanese piracy continued. Though tribute missions came, they were not always submissive, nor were they from the Japanese sovereign. "You stupid eastern barbarians!" wrote Hung-wu to the Ashikaga shogun, the feudal ruler of Japan. "Living so far across the sea...you are haughty and disloyal; you permit your subjects to do evil." The Japanese replied in kind: "Heaven and Earth are vast; they are not monopolized by one ruler."

The high point of tributary activity under Yung-lo saw a brief period of professed Japanese fealty to China, expressed in very dutiful terms but regarded by the Japanese feudal rulers as merely a means of monopolizing the lucrative Chinese trade for themselves. Yung-lo in 1403 reopened the three Superintendencies of Merchant Shipping in the southern coastal provinces, which had been closed in 1374, and built hostels at each to entertain tribute envoys. Japanese missions now came annually for several years. In the usual fashion the Chinese court prepared a series of numbered paper passport tallies, tore them from their stub books, and sent them to the vassal ruler, retaining the stub books. When a mission came to the designated Chinese port to bring tribute and to trade, its ships, goods and persons were all specifically limited by statute. They were recorded on one of the numbered tallies, which could be verified by its fitting into the stub books. Thus all envoys were given bona fides, and imposters were checked. The Japanese shogun could maintain his trade monopoly and the Chinese could identify pirates. Between 1433 and 1549, eleven large Japanese missions, usually of several hundred persons, came to the Chinese court under the tally system, by way of Ningpo. Innumerable problems arose—rivalry in Japan to get possession of the official tallies, conflicts in China with disorderly Japanese warriors, prolonged haggling at Peking over the prices to be paid for trade goods, which included copper ore and sulphur by the hundreds of tons and Japanese swords by the thousand. Members of missions also carried their own goods for private trade. In addition, they received gifts from the emperor, as did the shogun, in lavish quantity.

The Maritime Expeditions.   One of Yung-lo's major undertakings was to incorporate the states of South and Southeast Asia into the tribute system. While his motives still remain a matter of speculation, this ambitious venture was marked by seven great maritime expeditions which were begun in 1405, and continued until 1433. They were led for the most part by a Muslim court eunuch named Cheng Ho, who came originally from Yunnan and as a Muslim was well fitted to deal with the Islamic rulers of South Asia. (See map, pages 172–173.) The first fleet sailed in 1405–1407 with sixty-two vessels carrying 28,000 men, and reached India, as did also the second and third. The fourth voyage in 1413–1415 reached Aden and the head of Asian circum-navigation at Hormuz on the Persian Gulf. A fifth voyage also went as far as Aden. The seventh voyage started out with 27,500 men and reached Hormuz again in 1431–1433. Chinese vessels visited far down the east coast of Africa, where chinaware and copper cash had been known for centuries. Seven Chinese reached Mecca.

The world had never seen such large-scale feats of seamanship. These Chinese armadas sailed all across the Indian Ocean almost a century before the Portuguese in 1498 reached India by sailing around Africa, and a century and a half before the Spanish Armada of 1588 made Western history by its short voyage around England. Cheng Ho's voyages were made possible by the development of Chinese shipbuilding and techniques of navigation on the Asian sea routes. His seagoing junks were of considerable size, some over four hundred feet in length, with four decks and up to a dozen watertight compartments. They navigated by detailed sailing directions and also used the compass. These remarkable expeditions penetrated to the sources of China's maritime trade not only along the Southeast Asian coasts but also in Ceylon, on both coasts of southern India, and in the Middle East and East Africa. In addition to customary tributaries, like Vietnam and Siam, some fifty new places were visited, and their rulers enrolled as tributaries. Missions from Hormuz and the African coast came to China four times, from Bengal eleven times. Rulers in Sumatra and Ceylon were brought back by force. Back also came ostriches, zebras, and giraffes, the latter touted as the auspicious "unicorn" of Chinese fable.

These spectacular maritime expeditions expressed the exuberance of an era of great vitality. For the eunuch leaders, they brought adventure, fame, and presumably profit. Commercial interests were also no doubt at work on the well-established routes of earlier trade, where Chinese migration had already created large overseas Chinese communities in Southeast Asian ports. Another motive seems to have been broadly political, to bring all the known world within the Chinese tributary scheme of things. Far-distant places trading by land were regularly enrolled as tributaries. Why not those trading by sea? This grandiose concept had been in the minds of Mongol emperors and was implicit in the idea of the universal rule of the Son of Heaven.

Speculation as to the causes of the Ming expeditions raises the question of why they were suddenly stopped and never resumed or imitated later. One reason for their cessation was their great cost, at a time when the early Ming campaigns against the Mongols and the building of Peking had begun to deplete the imperial coffers. The great fleets could be criticized as expensive adventures, largely unproductive except for pageantry and strange tales. They were also promoted particularly by court eunuchs, whose activities were opposed by the scholar-officials—so much so that Cheng Ho's feats were practically suppressed in the historical record.

These demonstrations of the early Ming capacity for maritime expansion were all the more dramatic because Chinese ideas of government and official policies were fundamentally indifferent, if not actually opposed, to such an expansion. The contrast between capacity and performance, if looked at by our modern world of trade and overseas expansion, is truly striking.

Chinese seapower, based upon the fishing fleets and trading junks of Canton, Amoy, Ch'üan-chou, and Ningpo, had been steadily increasing. China was on the verge of becoming a naval power that could dominate East Asia. The Ming fleets were developing the nautical and logistic capacity to bring military force and trading goods in overwhelming volume to any point in the Eastern seas. But after 1433 this beginning was cut short. No Henry the Navigator came to the Chinese throne. The Ming court, unlike that of contemporary Portugal, had no sustained interest in seafaring, no grasp of the possibilities of seapower. The Ming voyages were not followed up but remained isolated *tours de force,* mere exploits.

Ming Anticommercialism.   This contrast throws light on the nature of Chinese society. Cheng Ho lived and sailed a century and a half before Sir Francis Drake and the other captains of Queen Elizabeth began to lay the foundations of the British Empire. The Chinese Empire was then greater than all of Europe in size and in the volume of her domestic, if not also her foreign, commerce. Yet Ming China, having shown her capacity to do so, failed to become a maritime power. Through this default, the Eastern seas and even the China coast soon came to be dominated by a succession of non-Chinese seafaring peoples—the Japanese, the Portuguese and Spanish, the Dutch, and finally the British and Americans. Out of this commercial and naval domination of East Asian waters emerged eventually those forces of imperialistic expansion which finally humbled the traditional Chinese Empire and led to its disintegration. Cheng Ho, as a court eunuch and high dignitary, lacked precisely those motives which later inspired the merchant-adventurers of Europe. His power and advancement, even as he cruised the Indian Ocean, still depended upon the emperor. Cheng Ho was an organizer, a commander, a diplomat, and an able courtier, but he was not a trader. No chartered companies grew out of his expeditions, empowered like the Virginia Company or the East India Company to found colonies or establish governments overseas. The migration of Chinese into Southeast Asia was already under way, and the Chinese in that area would always outnumber the Europeans who might come there. But the Chinese state remained uninterested in these commercial and colonial possibilities overseas. The Ming and Ch'ing governments got their major sustenance from the land tax, not from trade taxes. They refused to join in the great commercial revolution which was beginning to sweep the world.

To understand this anticommercialism we may suggest several approaches, institutional, economic, ideological, and strategic. The institutional explanation goes back to the early environment of ancient China on the North China Plain far from the sea, where the official class came into being as tax-gatherers, fostering agriculture and gathering its products to maintain themselves and the state. In this agrarian-bureaucratic society merchants were kept subordinate to officialdom and utilized by it. The economic interests that did grow up were centered in domestic, not foreign, commerce simply because the Chinese subcontinent, then as now, was so relatively self-sufficient. But after the growth of commerce during the T'ang, Sung, and Yüan, why did the Ming and Ch'ing governments revert to the traditional agrarian-centered attitudes of an earlier era? Perhaps one reason was the culturalism we have already mentioned, in particular the establishment of the Neo-Confucian orthodoxy as the matrix of Ming thought. This revived the classical values, including the ancient disesteem of commerce. Foreign trade was left to powerful eunuchs, which made it all the more distasteful to the official class. Another explanation was presumably strategic—the Ming determination to prevent a repetition of the Mongol conquest.

The Mongol Problem. Hung-wu's preoccupation with breaking the Mongol power remained the chief focus of early Ming foreign relations. His aim was not to subjugate the whole of Mongolia but rather to destroy the unity of the tribes, which gave them their striking power. Even before China had been unified, Ming armies crossed the steppe to break up the Mongol forces, twice seizing Karakorum. Mongol chieftains pacified by defeat, intimidation, purchase, or other means were put in charge of Mongol settlements on the border and given titles, honors, emoluments, and opportunities for trade. Using a divide-and-rule policy, the Chinese tried to keep the seminomads of Inner Mongolia as border allies against the fully nomadic and mobile tribes of Outer Mongolia.

In the Central Asian khanate of Chaghadai, the last great successor of Chinggis, the conquerer Timur, known to Europe as Tamerlane (1336–1405), rose to power in 1369. From his capital of Samarkand, he expanded violently in all directions, overrunning Persia and Mesopotamia, defeating the Golden Horde in southern Russia, even briefly invading northern India. Tamerlane had some contact with the Chinese court and conceived the ambition to take it over. When he died in 1405, he had a vast army already on the way eastward to conquer China and make it an Islamic state. His death, however, marked the end of the Mongol era, particularly of the Mongol capacity to keep Central Asia united and so to threaten the agricultural civilizations that bordered on it. The end of a united Central Asia also diminished the trade and contact across it between East and

West. Under the Ming and Ch'ing, this land route was severed, and the tribes of Mongolia became more dependent on trade with China alone.

By the early fifteenth century the Mongol tribes were split (see map, page 196): in eastern Mongolia were the Tatars (*Ta-tan* in Chinese, corrupted by Europeans to "Tartars"), in western Mongolia, the Oirats. Chinese strategy was to play each off against the other. The Yung-lo emperor rose to power by leading expeditions against the Mongols and also by finding allies among them on the border. After his usurpation in 1403, Yung-lo personally led five expeditions far out across the steppe. In 1410 he mobilized over 100,000 men with 30,000 cartloads of supplies, overawed the Oirats, gave them gifts and secured their neutrality, crossed the Kerulen River, and defeated the Tatars. However, when the Oirats expanded eastward in 1414, Yung-lo led an army back to the Kerulen and this time defeated the Oirats. Both these Ming expeditions used cannon. Soon the Tatars ventured to raid the border. In 1422 Yung-lo led forth another host of 235,000 men with a supply train of 117,000 carts and 340,000 donkeys. The Tatars escaped westward, however, and further campaigns in 1423 and 1424 were unable to catch them.

Already Yung-lo's removal of the capital in 1421 from Nanking to Peking had symbolized the Ming preoccupation with defense against the Mongols. Imperial strategy centered on the frontier, where Peking stands guard near the principal gateway (the Nan-k'ou Pass) leading from Mongolia down onto the North China Plain. The capital of the great Ming Empire thus was located a scant forty miles from the traditional northern boundary of China, the Great Wall. This site has been used by dynasties oriented toward Inner Asia—the Liao, Yüan, Ming, and Ch'ing, as well as the Chinese People's Republic since 1949. Southern capitals have been used by regimes originating in the south or oriented toward overseas trade—Hangchow under the Southern Sung; Nanking in the early Ming, under the Taiping rebels (1853–1864), and under the Nationalist Government after 1927. Peking was far from the centers of Chinese population and production. Its strategic vulnerability to nomad inroads and its dependence on grain shipments from the lower Yangtze via the Grand Canal, are startling facts—too startling to be mere accidents. The explanation is that the capital of China had to serve also as the capital of the non-Chinese areas of Inner Asia. The "barbarians" were a constant military and therefore political component of the Chinese Empire; its capital was drawn outward to the border of China as a result.

The Ming expeditions to chastise the Mongols had been part of the effort to keep them harmless by carrot-and-stick methods. The Oirats, for example, had established tribute relations in 1408 and sent missions almost every year, which became a thinly veiled means of keeping them pacified through subsidies, a sort of tribute in reverse. Their annual missions to Peking sometimes totaled two or three thousand persons, including several hundred merchants from Central Asia. Passing through the Great Wall at Ta-t'ung in northern Shansi, this host had to be quartered and banqueted by the local authorities, for, like cultural delegations invited to Peking today, tribute missions were guests of the Middle Kingdom. As tribute, the Oirats presented their chief native product, horses, and received in return imperial "gifts in reply," mainly silk and satin textiles. A few days of free trade in the market followed the presentation of tribute within the Forbidden City. In this context of profitable exchange, the "barbarians" acquiesced in the "three kneelings and nine prostrations" as a traditional court ceremony. While gaining the nomads' submission, China had to suffer their depredations on the route between the border and the capital, and their drunken roistering at Peking. For the Mongols, the trip spelled glamour and profit, from fees paid them by the Muslim traders to whom their tribute missions gave cover. Many bearers of "tribute" were actually merchants claiming to represent distant and sometimes nonexistent potentates. The Ming *Collected Statutes* listed thirty-eight countries of the Western Regions which submitted tribute by way of Hami, the natural funnel for the caravan trade. Among them, for example, the Kingdom of Rum in Asia Minor (i.e., the long defunct Roman East) was recorded as presenting tribute as late as 1618. The Ming viewed this thin trickle of Central Asian tributary trade as having political rather than fiscal value, as it kept troublesome warriors quiet on the frontier.

In the late 1430's, just as the overseas expeditions came to an end, the Inner Asian frontier saw a violent recrudescence of the Mongol threat. A new chieftain of the Oirats subjugated Hami, then extended his influence over the tribes to the east all the way to Korea, and in late 1449 mobilized his horde along the border, threw off the forms of tribute, and approached Ta-t'ung. The Ming emperor, a product of palace life, was under the ill-advised domination of his chief eunuch, who took the emperor into the field and foolishly advanced toward Ta-t'ung to do battle. The Oirats advanced, defeated, pursued, and destroyed the Chinese force, and captured the emperor. But when they came to Peking, they found that the war minister and others had prepared a defense with cannon, enthroned a new emperor, and affected no interest in the former one. After several days before the walls, the Oirats went back to Mongolia. Next year they sent back the useless emperor and soon resumed their profitable tribute relations.

Ming-Mongol relations during the next century were a mixture of border raids and tribute missions. In 1550 a new leader, Altan Khan of the eastern Mongols, united a large striking force, came through the Wall from the northeast, and pillaged around Peking again for several days before withdrawing. Ming defenses of walls, beacon towers, and military agricultural colonies on the frontier were offset by Chinese deserters who aided the raiders. Such Chinese helped Altan Khan try to establish a settled administration. He built a capital city at Kuei-hua outside the Wall, northwest of Ta-t'ung. Eventually in the 1570's he was pacified and given the hopeful title of "Obedient and Righteous Prince" (Shun-i Wang). Until the rise of the Manchu Empire, however, Mongol free-booting continued to harass the Chinese border.

Troubles with Japan. From the cost of the Japanese and the Mongol tribute missions, we can see why the Ming court may have preferred to let the tribute system rest in comparative abeyance overseas after the first half of the fifteenth century. The expense of maintaining, transporting, and bestowing gifts upon hundreds of functionaries and merchants who came to Peking was not compensated by the trade they conducted. Missions from Southeast Asia grew fewer and fewer. The Ryūkyū Islands alone remained a regular maritime tributary on a biennial basis, serving actually as an indirect channel for Sino-Japanese trade. In this context of fading grandeur and frontier disorder, the first Europeans to reach China by sea, Portuguese adventurers in 1514, seemed to the Chinese only a small increment in a general growth of piracy and unwanted relations on the China coast (see Chapter 16).

In Japan a growing maritime capacity had produced overseas adventurers a full century before the Elizabethan age glorified the somewhat comparable exploits of gentleman-pirates from England. Like Drake and Hawkins, the Japanese could trade or loot by turns, as opportunity offered. Their bigger ships could carry three hundred men. Landing suddenly and attacking villages with their great swords, the pirates would seize provisions, hostages, and loot and make their getaway. Although known in Chinese records as "Japanese pirates" (*Wo-k'ou,* or in Japanese, *Wakō,* a term with pejorative connotations of "dwarf"), these raiders actually included many Chinese. Unlike the Mongol raids, the disloyal Chinese in these forays were not so much advisers as principal participants. By the latter decades of Ming rule, Chinese actually formed the majority among the "Japanese pirates."

The Ming response to this growing disorder, the prohibition of maritime trade, reflected the court's agrarian-minded and land-based unconcern for foreign commerce in general. The prohibition had the effect of forcing crews and captains into smuggling or buccaneering for a livelihood. Pirate raids after 1550 became actual invasions. The pirates based themselves on Chusan Island south of Shanghai, which was later to be the British base in 1840, and in 1552 they attacked inland cities in Chekiang, while others went up the Yangtze. In defense, Ming pirate-suppressors bought over the leading renegades with rewards and pardons and attacked the pirate lair on Chusan. But the scourge increased. Japanese harassment of the South China coast declined only with the political reunification of Japan in the late sixteenth century (see Chapter 13). However, this reunification concentrated Japan's military energies in a form even more menacing and exhausting to the Ming court.

Peking learned of Japan's intent to invade China by way of Korea through spies in Japan as well as from Korea. In 1592, when the Japanese attack on Korea came, the court debated whether to send a fleet from the southern provinces to attack Japan, or to put an army on the Korean frontier, or to negotiate for peace. In the end the court decided it had to fulfill its suzerain duty to aid Korea in order to defend Southern Manchuria and North China. Ming forces did not cross the Yalu until after the whole peninsula was in Japanese hands. The Chinese attacked P'yongyang in mid 1592, were badly defeated, and started negotiations to gain time. Early in 1593 they surprised the Japanese, drove them out of P'yongyang, and advanced to the outskirts of the capital, Seoul, but were ambushed and again defeated. The short swords of the Chinese cavalry proved no match for the long swords, spears, and guns of the Japanese infantry. Negotiations and exhausting conflict continued until the Japanese finally withdrew in 1598 (after a second invasion in force in 1597). The total Ming expenditure to meet the first Japanese invasion of Korea must have come to over 10 million taels, with a comparable sum required later to meet the second invasion. The administration was already close to bankruptcy, after constant subsidies to the Mongols and rebuilding of Peking palaces. Japan's invasions of Korea were a final strain on Peking's dwindling resources and prepared the way for the rise, after 1600, of bandits within and "barbarian" invaders from without.

The Ming Economy

Economic Growth. In studying China's economic history, we must constantly distinguish between the imperial regime and the country as a whole. We have noted the court's anticommercial attitude and approach to final bankruptcy. But if we look at the late Ming economy as a whole, we find much evidence of growth in almost all its aspects—population, area of cultivated land, volume of foreign trade, production of handicraft and industrial goods, and even, perhaps, in the use of money.

Tax grain (called by Western writers "tribute rice") had to be transported from the rice baskets of the Huai River and lower Yangtze to feed the new capital at Peking. Sea transport around Shantung was increasingly hindered by Japanese pirates, and was in any case expensive. Yung-lo therefore dug out the unused "Connecting Canal" in western Shantung that Khubilai Khan had first constructed as part of the second Grand Canal system, and installed fifteen locks. Three thousand or more shallow boats were now used on the canal route, and after 1415 sea transport was given up. But transport of tax grain to collecting depots on the canal, still part of the labor-service obligation of the peasantry, became a heavy burden on them. Yung-lo's successors therefore placed the task of transportation entirely on certain military transport divisions of the local garrisons, which had to be increased from 120,000 to 160,000 men. From the 1430's this new system supplied usually over 3 million Chinese bushels (say roughly 200,000 tons), and sometimes over 5 million, to the capital every year.

Trade between North and South China was stimulated by the growth of Peking and the canal system. Trade on the Yangtze and in South China also increased. For example, merchants in the southernmost part of modern Anhwei spread their operations widely into other provinces. Called, from an old place name, "Hsin-an merchants," they traded in all manner of commodities—porcelains from the nearby production center at Ching-te-chen in Kiangsi, teas and silks locally produced, salt, timber, and comestibles. Naturally they developed the close relations with officialdom that such extensive operations required for their protection.

Specialized handicraft production grew up for this enlarging market and even some larger-scale manufacturing. At Ching-te-chen the imperial kilns produced great quantities of porcelain for the palace and also for upper-class use and even for export. The particular clay now known as kaolin (named for *Kao-ling,* "High Ridge," a hill east of Ching-te-chen; a hydrous silicate of alumina), when properly prepared with other substances and heated to about 1400 degrees Centigrade, becomes white, translucent, and so hard that steel will not scratch it. This porcelain was a truly superior product in the eyes of Europeans, who lacked the technique and who properly called it "chinaware." Again, Soochow became a national center of trade, finance, and processing industries, particularly the weaving and dyeing of silk. The nearby Sungkiang region, inland from Shanghai, became a late Ming center for cotton cloth production, using raw cotton from other provinces both north and south, and sending its product back for sale there. Canton iron pans (shallow cooking pans for use directly over fire) were exported widely throughout China, overseas, and to Central Asia.

This domestic commercial growth led to the setting up in the sixteenth century of numerous regional guilds with guild halls in major centers, especially Peking. These bodies were created chiefly by officials and merchants who came from a common region—a province, prefecture, county, or city—so as to have a convenient center of contact and mutual aid in a distant place, pre-eminently at the capital.

Meanwhile China's maritime trade developed steadily in the late Ming outside the framework of the tribute system. Missions from Southeast and South Asia became fewer, while Chinese merchants who went overseas became more numerous. In short, foreign trade was no longer brought to

China principally by intermediaries, like the Arabs, but was now carried by Chinese merchants who went abroad with Chinese products and on their return with foreign wares entered easily into the stream of China's coast-wise junk traffic. The government did little to encourage this trade and sometimes banned it, but it continued to grow.

The Single-Whip Reform.   The traditional taxes on land and labor under-went a gradual reform during the sixteenth century, which reduced them to money payments and simplified them by combining many small items into one. The whole movement has become known as the "Single-Whip" reform. (The name is a pun, since *i-t'iao-pien,* meaning "combination in one item," sounds also like "a single whip.")

The evils in the land and labor taxes had begun with the falsification of local records. As we have seen on pages 186–187, both landholdings and households early in the Ming period were classified into grades and remained supposedly subject to reclassification every ten years or so. Each man's tax burden depended first of all on his classification in the local registers. But responsibility for management of the system was placed on the leading households—the wealthier families, who thus had an opportunity to escape their allotted burden by falsifying the records. By collusion and bribery, these interested parties could reduce their own tax liability, providing they could increase that of the poorer households to meet the overall tax quota of the area. Many methods could be used: concealing the number of male adults, removing land from the record altogether, registering land under the name of a servant or tenant, or registering private land as government land or private persons as officials. Because of the special privileges enjoyed by wealthier families, smaller households often sought their protection, transferring the nominal ownership of their land in order to escape the tax burden, for a consideration paid privately to the large household. As a result, the official registers within a few generations became meaningless, while taxation became chaotic—a racket levied by the powerful upon the weak. Revenue collections ran short, the government above suffered loss, and the poorer peasants beneath were milked harder than ever, while the large households and petty officials in between benefited from their mutual arrangements. Since this middle stratum of leading families in the countryside provided many of the degree-holders through examination or purchase, they became all the more a "landlord-gentry" ruling class.

The confusion of this situation was compounded by the variety of taxes. The forms of landholding were complex: rights to the subsoil might be held by one person but rights to the use of the surface by another, who might lease the use of the surface to a tenant, who could sublet in turn. Tenantry assumed many forms. The labor service charges became even more complex. They were apportioned on the basis of a factor less stable than land, namely, the number of male adults, and might vary according to local needs and by decision of the local powerholders. As the institution became more corrupt, demands for labor services bore so hard on the poorer peasantry that first households, then sections (*chia*) of villages, and finally whole villages (*li*) began to abscond. Since tax quotas were seldom diminished, this increased still further the burden on those left behind. Finally, as more and more items became commuted to money payments, the tax collectors had every opportunity to add surtaxes and extra fees, commute labor into silver inequitably, and maintain assessments after the need for the original services had passed. The result was a limitless web of money taxes entangling the peasantry, levied in all seasons of the year for myriad nominal or alleged purposes, inequitably assessed and imperfectly recorded, according to no general scheme and under no superior control or direction.

The Single-Whip reform was carried out gradually by many hard-pressed provincial officials in one area after another, in a desperate effort to maintain a reliable tax structure and regular collections. It occurred chiefly in the period 1522–1619, that is, in the final century of effective Ming administration. It consisted of two principal tendencies—to combine all the various items of taxation under one or a few headings and to collect them in silver. One basic reform was to simplify the land classification so that in place of as many as a hundred different land tax rates, there were only two or three rates. Another reform was to unify the land taxes, combining sometimes thirty or forty different taxes into two or three items. Labor services were similarly unified. Next, the two major categories of land tax and labor service were sometimes combined to make a single item. Finally, dates of collection were unified, as well as the apparatus for it, which reduced the opportunities for extortion and fraud.

The resulting fiscal situation was probably no simpler than it would be to have a separate income tax law for each county in the United States. The Single-Whip reform was only a partial step toward a modernized tax structure. After the reform, the government used its tax receipts in silver to pay wages to hired laborers, who performed the labor service tasks formerly required of the common people. Communities were no longer required to transport their tax grain to a government granary. The reform also abolished the former indirect payment of taxes through the section and village heads. Instead, the taxpayer now put his tax silver directly into the government collector's silver chest in front of the local yamen and got an official receipt.

Several earlier dynasties had begun by relying at first on taxes and services in kind, only to have the system deteriorate, until a reform simplified it by a greater recourse to tax collections in money. In the late Ming this increased use of money was related to the vigorous economic growth already mentioned and in particular to the inflow of silver from abroad.

The End of Ming Rule

Even if we make allowance for human frailty among historians—their capacity to find in the voluminous record of history the evidence they may seek for almost any interpretation of events—still the drama of the late Ming has all the classic features of a dynastic decline: effete and feckless rulers, corrupt favorites misusing their power, factional jealousies among officials, fiscal bankruptcy, natural disasters, the rise of rebellion and, finally, foreign invasion. These evils in the last decades of Ming rule were highlighted by the fact that they followed a vigorous reform effort under Chang Chü-cheng, one of the great ministers of the era, who rose to supreme power as senior Grand Secretary during the first decade (1573–1582) of the Wan-li reign. Chang was on good terms with the Outer Court and influential with the young emperor. He tried to increase the land tax revenue by getting exempted lands taxed again. He tried to restrict the ever-growing perquisites and privileges of the official class and the imperial family. Yet Chang, for all his efforts, could not check the emperor's greed. After his death in 1582, Wan-li, reigning for another thirty-eight years until 1620, became utterly irresponsible. He avoided seeing his ministers for years on end, refused to conduct business or make needed appointments, let evils flourish, and squandered the state's resources. The fifteen-year-old emperor who ascended the throne in 1620 was a dimwit interested mainly in carpentry. He let his nurse's close friend, the eunuch Wei Chung-hsien (1568–1627), who had been butler in his mother's apartments, take over the government. Wei brought the eunuch evil to its highest point. Backed by a small eunuch army to control the palace and a network of spies throughout the empire, he recruited unprincipled opportunists among the bureaucracy, purged his enemies in official life, and levied extortionate new taxes in the provinces.

Factionalism: The Tung-lin Party.   The Confucian resistance to these evils was carried on mainly by a group of scholars, whose long struggle and eventual failure make a poignant chapter in the annals of Chinese politics. Tung-lin (literally, "Eastern Forest") was the name of an academy at Wusih on the lower Yangtze. Led by a dozen scholar-ex-officials, most of whom had been dismissed during factional controversies at the court, its members lectured at affiliated academies nearby, and soon spread their influence among scholars and officials elsewhere in a moral crusade to reassert the traditional principles of Confucian conduct. They condemned the philosophical eclecticism that had grown popular in the sixteenth century since the time of Wang Yang-ming, and that seemed to confuse Confucianism, Buddhism and Taoism. They stressed the supreme importance of moral integrity and denounced various holders of power, both Grand Secretaries and eunuchs.

The Tung-lin reformers of course had an incomplete monopoly on virtue. By 1610 they were being denounced in turn as a *tang* (the modern word for "party"), that is, an organized clique of the sort traditionally anathematized as subversive of imperial authority and bureaucratic harmony. The factional struggle was conducted in terms less of state policies than of the moral qualities of ministers. Denouncing and being denounced, the Tung-lin crusaders had their ups and downs. They became dominant in the years 1620–1623, just before the eunuch Wei Chung-hsien achieved complete power. In 1624 a Tung-lin leader accused Wei of twenty-four high crimes, including murders and a forced abortion of the empress. Wei mobilized the enemies of the reformers and retaliated with terror. Blacklists were compiled of some seven hundred Tung-lin supporters. Leading figures were denounced, condemned, dismissed, disgraced, imprisoned, tortured, and beaten to death. The Tung-lin group had been practically wiped out by the time Wei fell from power in 1627. This eunuch's manipulation of the sacred office of the Son of Heaven for evil ends had completed the moral degradation of the Ming regime.

The Rise of Rebellion. Yet the Ming collapse was perhaps due less to misgovernment than to nongovernment, less to eunuch immorality than to the regime's failure to keep up with its problems. The real problem was not that tax burdens were oppressive but that tax revenues were inadequate. The administration suffered less from tyranny than from paralysis.

When Shensi in the Northwest was hard hit by famine in 1628, a postal employee named Li Tzu-ch'eng was thrown out of his job by unwise government economics. Li joined his uncle, who was already a bandit, and made his lair on the edge of the North China Plain in the mountains of southern Shansi, the same area where the Japanese during World War II proved unable to dislodge the Chinese irregular forces. Li Tzu-ch'eng raided Honan and Szechwan, acquiring more followers, and eventually some of the forms of an organized government. At least two scholars joined him and advised him how to win popular support. They spread songs and stories about his heroic qualities, helped him distribute food to the starving, appoint officials, proclaim a dynasty, confer titles, and even issue his own coinage. By 1643 Li Tzu-ch'eng held much of Hupei, Honan, and Shensi. Early in 1644 he descended on Peking from the northwest, just as the last Ming emperor hanged himself on Prospect Hill, overlooking the Forbidden City.

Meanwhile Li's chief rival, another rebel named Chang Hsien-chung, had acquired a great reputation more as a killer than as an organizer of men. From about 1630 he had raided widely through North China, plundering with hit-and-run tactics. Finally in 1644 he invaded Szechwan and set up a government, complete with Six Ministries and a Grand Secretariat, headed by genuine metropolitan graduates who held examinations and minted money. But Chang's main concern was stamping out opposition with terror tactics, used especially against the gentry. He lost gentry support, and the Manchus killed him in 1647.

Thus the Ming dynasty was destroyed by Chinese rebels before it was superseded by "barbarian" invaders. But the Manchu conquerors preserved and used the major institutions of government that had functioned for more than two centuries under the Ming. The downfall of Ming rule must therefore be attributed less to the structure of these institutions than to their malfunctioning under the accumulated stresses that typify the end of a dynastic cycle.

9. Traditional China at Its Height under the Ch'ing

The Rise of the Manchu Dynasty

The Ch'ing dynasty began in the early seventeenth century, contemporary with the American colonies, and lasted until 1911. Thus it spanned the greater part of modern times and yet was dominated by a regime and social order that changed relatively little. The Ch'ing period saw both the zenith and the nadir of the traditional Chinese state. In the eighteenth century the population and territory of the empire were the largest they had ever been, and the finesse and stability of administration were at a high point. Yet the nineteenth century brought unmitigated disaster.

Here we are concerned only with the first act in this drama, the success of the Manchus in presiding over the Chinese state and society up to the beginning of the nineteenth century. In studying their achievement, however, we cannot help wondering to what extent their very success in maintaining the traditional order may have been a factor in its later collapse. So well established was the Chinese tradition that a thoroughgoing change of institutions and values could not easily be imagined. The Manchus were more successful as inheritors than as innovators; it was not in them to remake the Chinese scheme of things.

The success story of the Manchus was like that of the Mongols under Chinggis Khan: a powerful leader at a propitious time united his people, giving them a common name, and set them on the march until his descendants ruled all China. The Manchu nation-at-arms sprang from Jurchen tribes of the same Tungusic stock as the founders of the Chin dynasty (1122–1234). They rose to power on the fringe of Chinese culture and

administration where they could learn both from their predecessors the
Mongols and from China on a selective basis without being completely
subjugated or Sinicized.

Southernmost Manchuria, or Liaotung ("East of the Liao River," including the Liaotung Peninsula), had been part of ancient China, suited
to the same kind of intensive agriculture as North China and administered
within the Han Empire. It communicated easily by sea with the Shantung
peninsula and under the Ming was part of Shantung province. But Liaotung, being vulnerable strategically, was a hostage to fortune. No natural
barriers defended it from the north. On the other hand, like all Manchuria,
it could easily be cut off from land contact with China at Shanhaikuan
("the mountain-sea pass"), where the Great Wall meets the coast. Anyone
who can hold a few miles of level land between mountain and ocean there
can control access to or from Manchuria like a cork in a bottle. Consequently Liaotung, though Chinese, was a place where Chinese and "barbarians" interpenetrated, where strong "barbarians" could control an agricultural Chinese population, and so rival the ruling dynasty.

The Chinese defense against this was to rely not on static walls but on
human relations, to establish China's political hegemony over the tribes by
"subduing them with a loose rein" (*chi-mi*). Hung-wu created commanderies on the Mongol border and Yung-lo extended this system to the tribes
of Manchuria also. In the Yung-lo period alone 178 commanderies were
set up, an index of the Chinese divide-and-rule tactics. These commanderies
were tribal military units under their own hereditary tribal leaders. These
chieftains were given official titles and seals and expected to send yearly
tribute. A chieftain's family might be given a Chinese surname and his
daughter might be taken into the imperial harem. Surnames of course facilitated compilation of genealogies and fostered concepts of legitimacy and
inheritance. Meanwhile the bestowal of honors and decorations from the
emperor, like those still conferred throughout the British Commonwealth,
served to bind the "barbarians" into the empire. Another policy was to let
a tribal chieftain become an absentee, moving his own residence into the
pleasanter circumstances of a Chinese town or even the capital, and so
become Sinicized.

The first Jurchen commandery was established on the northeast of Liaotung in 1403. As the Manchurian tribes grew in numbers, groups of two
hundred to six hundred tribesmen at a time would parade annually to
Peking, harassing the populace en route. The Ming opened a horse market
on the northern border of south Manchuria near Mukden (modern Shen-
yang) so as to obviate this travel inside the Wall. It was on this frontier
that the Manchu power arose as the Ming grew weak. China's defense
required the Sinicizing of the "barbarian" to make him a loyal subject of
the empire; yet this process gave the "barbarian" his chance to combine

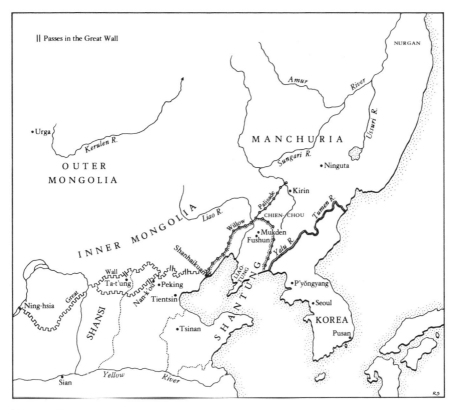

THE RISE OF THE MANCHUS

his native fighting strength with all that he could learn of Chinese ways. The result in Manchuria was a formidable synthesis of institutions and a new state power.

The Creation of a Sinicized Manchu State.   Nurhachi (1559–1626), the founder of the Manchu state, followed the tradition of Chinggis Khan in fighting his way to power on the pretext of avenging the deaths of his father and grandfather. They had been killed in a fight which involved the Chinese commander of Liaotung and an allied Jurchen chief, who therefore became Nurhachi's immediate target. While accepting the Chinese appointment to succeed his father, Nurhachi is said to have mobilized his family and tribe and exterminated this rival by 1586. He fortified his home, married the daughter of one powerful chief and the granddaughter of another, suppressed bandits, and earned Chinese commendation. Through thirty years of negotiation, arrangements of marriages and alliances, and sporadic warfare, Nurhachi united the four main Jurchen tribes to the north and rose to a position where he could defy the Ming. Meanwhile, he traded at the horse market and dealt in the supposedly medicinal root ginseng, which already formed a valuable luxury export from Manchuria for aging Chinese in need of rejuvenation. On the northeast border of Liaotung, Nurhachi built a fortified castle which had three or four concentric walls. These provided an innermost castle for himself and his clan, a middle fortress of some three hundred dwellings for his generals and close followers, and an outer fortress for thousands of troops and their families. Chinese technicians and advisers helped him. One Chinese was Nurhachi's adviser for thirty years.

Avoiding conflict with the Ming and the Mongol tribes to the west, Nurhachi concentrated on uniting his own people. His greatest achievement was to develop new administrative institutions, especially the "banner" system, which came into being gradually after 1601. Companies of three hundred warriors were grouped at first under four banners, colored yellow, white, blue, and red. Four more were later added, of the same colors but bordered with red, except for the red banner, which was bordered with white. Under these eight banners all the tribesmen were enrolled and thus a transition was made from tribal to bureaucratic organization. All the people, including their captured Chinese slaves or bondservants, were now registered under their respective banners and taxed and mobilized through them as administrative units of the new state. Instead of hereditary chieftains, the banners soon had appointed officers as well as clerks to keep their accounts. As the new state conquered nearby peoples and gained adherents, eight Chinese and eight Mongol banners were added, making a total of twenty-four. By 1644 there were 278 Manchu companies, 120 Mongol, and 165 Chinese, making an army of about 169,000, with the Manchus forming less than half the total.

Banners and their component companies did not fight as units. Rather, each company contributed a certain quota of men to make up the needed task force. For the expedition of 1634 into Inner Mongolia, for instance, each company provided twenty cavalrymen and eight guards, making a force of about 11,000. The banners differed from the Ming garrisons in that bannermen were allotted lands scattered in diverse places and intermixed with holdings of nonbannermen. The banners thus were not attached to one place, even though they had their own lands and got sustenance from them.

Another of Nurhachi's achievements was to develop a writing system for administrative purposes. He had his interpreter write Jurchen words in a modified Mongolian alphabet to which diacritical marks (dots and circles) were later added beside the letters. The *Mencius* was soon available in written Manchu. Thus the new writing made possible a rapid borrowing of the Confucian ideology of the state.

In 1616 Nurhachi took the title of emperor of the Later Chin, as though to continue the Chin dynasty of 1122–1234. In 1618 he openly attacked the Ming, took part of Liaotung, and developed a civil administration with Chinese help. In 1625 Nurhachi moved his capital southeast to Mukden. After his death in 1626 he was given the posthumous title of T'ai Tsu ("Grand Progenitor"). He was followed by three other capable leaders: his eighth son, Abahai (1592–1643), his fourteenth son, Dorgon (1612–1650), who dutifully refused the imperial title in favor of Abahai's six-year-old son but actually ruled as regent, and finally Nurhachi's great-grandson the K'ang-hsi emperor, under whose sixty-one-year reign from 1661 to 1722 the dynasty was firmly established.

To establish their leadership, the early Manchu rulers first had to subordinate clan government by group decision to a new principle of monarchy. The imperial clan leaders were brought into a state council and subordinated to it. Eventually the Manchu imperial clan was kept out of administration entirely, but its members nonetheless were concentrated at the capital. Their primary state function was to put a strong ruler on the throne and avoid the twin evils of government by women and by eunuchs.

On their part, the Manchu rulers absorbed the Confucian style of government far better than had their Mongol predecessors. Their success depended upon organizing state power in a Chinese fashion and using Chinese collaborators. As bureaucracy supplanted tribalism, literate clerks and administrators were recruited from among the Chinese of Liaotung, who numbered about 3 million, some ten times the estimated number of the Manchus at this time. These Chinese were attracted by the prospect of taking part in a strong and successful "Confucian" type of government. In 1631 the Six Ministries were set up at Mukden, a simulacrum of those at Peking. A censorate and other offices were also established, all on the Ming model.

The joint Sino-"barbarian" nature of the Manchu regime in its formative years is indicated by the number of Liaotung Chinese who rose in the Manchu service. For example, three Ming officers from Liaotung went over to the Manchus about 1633. Later, all three led armies to conquer South China. All three were made princes. One of these Chinese had twenty-three sons, of whom eleven became generals under the Ch'ing and three became state councilors.

The Manchu Conquest.   By building up their military and administrative capacities, the early Manchu rulers had made themselves leading contenders for the throne at Peking. Abahai attacked Korea in 1627 and again in 1636–1637, making it a vassal state. He led expeditions through the passes in the Great Wall to descend on North China in 1629, 1632, and 1634. He defeated the Inner Mongols and made them his vassals. Four expeditions brought the Amur region under his control. During this furious expansion, Abahai in 1636 renamed his dynasty the Ch'ing ("Pure").

The key figure in the Manchu conquest of China in 1644 was a Ming general, Wu San-kuei (1612–1678), who was a native of Liaotung. As the rebel Li Tzu-ch'eng (see page 209) approached Peking, the Ming emperor summoned Wu to the rescue. The capital fell before his arrival, however, and Li Tzu-ch'eng advanced against him. Instead of surrendering to a Chinese bandit rebel, Wu preferred to surrender to the Manchu, Dorgon, whose banners were waiting east of the pass. He did so and together they defeated Li, drove him from Peking and wiped him out. Thus the non-Chinese rebels on the frontier were able with Chinese assistance to eliminate the rebels within the country. Seizure of the throne proved easier from outside the Wall than from within. The Manchu state, in its defensible external base, had been able to develop as a rival imperial regime, while rebels within China had hardly been able to rise above the bandit level.

For three decades after the capture of Peking, Wu San-kuei helped install the Manchu dynasty while gaining great power for himself. He built up his own satrapy in Yunnan and Kweichow, developed his own trade monopolies, and yet milked the central Ch'ing treasury to support his armies. Two other satrapies were built up by Liaotung Chinese generals in Kwangtung and in Fukien. For many years South China thus remained under the Manchus' Chinese collaborators, whose local power rivaled that of Peking. When Wu rebelled against the Ch'ing in 1673, the other two satraps soon followed suit, in the so-called Revolt of the Three Feudatories (*San-fan*). This major civil war caught the nineteen-year-old K'ang-hsi emperor by surprise and threatened to oust the Manchu dynasty. It was not suppressed until 1681.

The last part of China to be taken over was the island of Taiwan, as it is known in both Chinese and Japanese, or Formosa ("The Beautiful"), as it was christened by the Portuguese. Although frequented by traders and pirates and colonized from Fukien, Taiwan had not been brought under Ming administration. From 1624 to 1662 the Dutch East India Company from Batavia (modern Djakarta) maintained several posts on the island. The last anti-Manchu resistance was maintained in Taiwan by Cheng Ch'eng-kung (1624–1662) and his family. This man's father had risen as an adventurer in maritime trade and piracy. He was in contact with the Portuguese at Macao (who baptized him a Christian), the Spanish at Manila, and the Japanese at Hirado, where he acquired a Japanese wife who bore him Cheng Ch'eng-kung. The son became a favorite of the refugee Ming court at Nanking and then at Foochow and received from it the imperial surname Chu and hence the popular title *Kuo-hsing-yeh* ("Lord of the Imperial Surname"), from which the Dutch derived "Koxinga." From 1646 to 1658 he controlled much of the Fukien coast, basing himself on the Amoy region, including Quemoy.

The Ch'ing tactics in dealing with Koxinga's maritime power were in

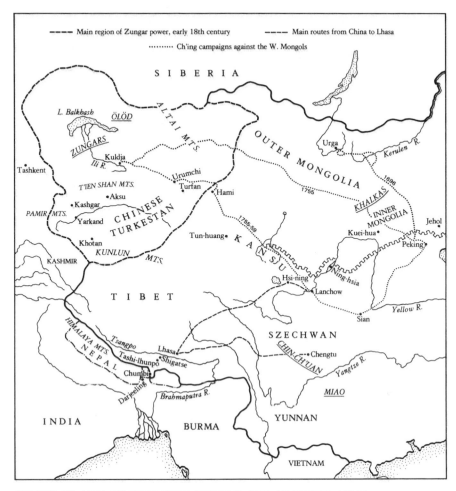

Main region of Zungar power, early 18th century   Main routes from China to Lhasa

Ch'ing campaigns against the W. Mongols

CENTRAL ASIA UNDER THE CH'ING (TO AROUND 1800)

the landbound tradition of the past. Echoing the Ming tactics toward Japanese pirates, they restricted foreign trade. Koxinga retaliated with a massive attempt to seize Nanking. Defeated, he descended on Taiwan in 1661 with some nine hundred ships and expelled the Dutch, who sent a fleet to help the Ch'ing against him in 1663–1664. After Koxinga's death, a son maintained his regime. The Ch'ing now resorted to a drastic policy of trying to force the population along the Chinese coast to evacuate the islands and move inland a distance of ten miles or more, behind a patrolled barrier, so as to cut Taiwan off from its mainland sources of manpower, food, and trading silk. The Taiwan regime was little damaged by these efforts, but finally became involved in supporting the Revolt of the Three Feudatories. After suppressing this, the Ch'ing occupied the island in 1683. Thus the Manchu conquest, in spite of the sudden success of 1644, actually occupied two generations, from 1618 to 1683.

The Ch'ing Empire in Inner Asia.   Until modern times control over China could not easily be maintained without control over Inner Asia. From the beginning the Ch'ing had set to work to incorporate the Mongols of Inner Mongolia into their new state. This led them in the late seventeenth century to the conquest of Outer Mongolia and in the eighteenth to the conquest of Ili and Chinese Turkestan and a protectorate over Tibet.

The Manchus had begun by defeating the Inner Mongols and then enrolling them as vassals and yet simultaneously as allies in the Mongol banners. The dynasty gave scope and opportunity for Mongol talent. The Ch'ing also strengthened the devices by which the Ming Chinese had kept the Mongols in check—assigning the tribes to fixed geographic areas, confirming new chiefs in their successsion, conferring titles and honors, supervising intertribal councils and postal communications, permitting a regulated trade at fixed markets, and bestowing the customary gifts on regular tribute missions. In short, the Ch'ing continued to make use of China's advantage as the source of culture, commerce, and luxuries; they maintained the Son of Heaven's role as the source of legitimacy, honors, and favors. This divide-and-rule policy used Inner Mongols against Outer Mongols, the principle of legitimacy against usurpers, imperial allies against rebels, and so prevented the accumulation of power by any one Mongol leader. To operate this complex system, the Manchus set up a Superintendency of Dependencies (*Li-fan yüan*), a Manchu innovation on the same level as the traditional Six Ministries.

The administration of this system required constant care and occasional fighting. In the late seventeenth century a descendant of the Mongol chieftain who had captured the Ming emperor in 1449 rose to power in the grasslands north of Chinese Turkestan, the region of the Altai Mountains and the Ili River valley, a common route of access to West Asia. This new leader was Galdan, khan of the Zungars, one of the tribes of the Western Mongols. Galdan had been educated as a lama at Lhasa, and he received valuable moral support from Tibet. In the 1670's he took over the oases and Muslim population of Chinese Turkestan as far east as Hami. Eventually he crossed Outer Mongolia and pillaged the Eastern Mongols as far as the Kerulen River. The K'ang-hsi emperor of the Ch'ing mobilized accordingly, and at length in 1696, like Yung-lo of the Ming, he personally led some eighty thousand troops in several columns to the Kerulen River. Galdan's power was destroyed in a great battle south of Urga, in which the Ch'ing use of artillery foreshadowed the end of a millennium of nomad cavalry power.

The final settlement came in the 1750's. After a long series of Mongol tribal rebellions, murders, usurpations, invasions, and migrations, Ch'ing forces occupied the Ili region three successive times in the years 1755– 1757, practically wiped out the Zungars, and in 1758–1759 also sup-

CONQUESTS OF THE EMPEROR OF CHINA. *To celebrate the conquest of Ili and Chinese Turkestan, Emperor Ch'ien-lung had sixteen drawings by Catholic missionaries at Peking sent to Paris for copperplate engraving. This one (1772) shows a Manchu army camp in 1758. In the central pavilion the commander, with his officers on either side, receives a kneeling delegation, while wrestlers, lancers, and archers perform.*

pressed a Muslim rising in Chinese Turkestan and established control over Aksu, Yarkand, Kashgar, and the other oases. Following the precedent of the Han, T'ang, and Yüan, this was the fourth major period in which the Son of Heaven in China ruled over the Tarim basin as far as the Pamir massif.

Incorporation of Tibet in the Empire. In the process of subduing the Western Mongols, the Ch'ing rulers also had to establish their control over Tibet, because the Lamaist church centered at Lhasa had become a potent influence not only in Tibetan life but also among the Mongols. For several centuries the Tibetans had played a role on the periphery of the Chinese Empire. During the T'ang they emerged as a small but strong military power capable of making devastating raids into India or into China as far as Ch'ang-an. In the Yüan period the vogue of the Lamaist faith had spread rapidly among the Mongols (see pages 98, 111, and 169). The early Ming had regularly recorded tributary relations with Tibet, and Yung-lo in particular received Tibetan envoys, conferred titles, and confirmed appointments. During the Ming, however, a reform movement had arisen in the Tibetan church: one lama who did not come to China was Tsong-kha-pa (1357–1419), a great religious reformer who aimed at restoring monastic discipline within Tibetan Buddhism by such measures as enforcing celibacy and prescribing the various routines of meetings, confession, retreat, and other aspects of monastic life. His reform movement is generally known from the color of the vestments of its adherents as the Yellow Sect, as distinct from the older Red Sect. During the late Ming its influence spread over Mongolia, and so the Mongols became involved in the politico-religious competition between the established Red Sect of Lamaism and the new reforming Yellow Sect.

According to the Lamaist belief in reincarnation, Tsong-kha-pa's successors as head of the Yellow Sect were found in new-born infants. When his third successor went to Mongolia, a powerful prince of the Eastern Mongols gave him the impressive title of Dalai ("All-Embracing") Lama, and when he died there in 1588, his successor was found reincarnated in a Mongol baby. In this way the Eastern and Western Mongols and the two Tibetan sects all were drawn into religious power politics. The second dignitary in the Yellow Sect was the Tashi Lama, generally known as the Panchen Lama, of the great monastery called Tashi-lhunpo, west of Lhasa. A third figure emerged about 1600 as a permanent patriarch of the church in Outer Mongolia, the so-called "Living Buddha" (in Mongolian, *Hutukhtu*) at Urga, modern Ulan Bator.

Order was eventually imposed upon this Inner Asian field of religious politics when, first, the Dalai Lama became the temporal ruler of Tibet, and second, the Ch'ing rulers of China established a protectorate over him. Though long recognized as head of the Yellow Sect, the Dalai Lama achieved his temporal power in Tibet only by degrees and by making skillful use of Mongol and Manchu support. Even before the Manchu conquest of China, a Western Mongol tribe had intervened at Lhasa in 1641 on behalf of the Yellow Sect. It crushed the Red Sect supporters, unified the country under foreign Mongol rule, and put the fifth Dalai Lama (1617–1682) on his spiritual throne in Lhasa, where he rebuilt his great palace, the Potala.

When the K'ang-hsi emperor confronted the Western Mongols, he naturally regarded the Dalai Lama as one key to the control of Mongolia, where Lamaist monasteries were already absorbing large numbers of young men into the peaceful life of the church. The upshot of K'ang-hsi's concern was another Mongol intervention at Lhasa, with Ch'ing moral support, in 1705. This was followed by anti-Ch'ing counterintervention by the Zungar

CH'ING PATRONAGE OF LAMAISM. *Above: The Potala, the monastery or palace of the Dalai Lama at Lhasa, rebuilt by the Fifth Dalai Lama (1617–1682). Below: The miniature Potala erected by the Ch'ing emperors at their summer residence at Jehol (Ch'eng-te) north of Peking, as an aid in their relations with the Mongols as well as Tibet.*

tribe of the Western Mongols which in turn inspired in 1720 the first direct Ch'ing intervention in force. Soon a violent Tibetan civil war in 1727–1728 brought in a second Ch'ing army of fifteen thousand. The Dalai Lama's administration was now taken under the supervision of two Ch'ing imperial residents (*amban*) and a garrison. The third Ch'ing intervention was precipitated by a revival of Zungar intrigue and multiple murders in 1750. The Ch'ing solution to this breakdown of political control was to establish the Dalai Lama finally in a position of full temporal power under a continued Ch'ing protectorate. He ruled thenceforth through a council of four ministers under the supervision of the imperial residents and a Ch'ing garrison of fifteen hundred men. Thus after a good deal of trial and error, the political power in Tibet was firmly incorporated in that of the Ch'ing Empire.

Ch'ing Rule over China

The Preservation of Manchu Power. The Manchus' basic problem in China was to preserve themselves as a cohesive minority capable of keeping its grip on power. Since their numbers totaled at most 2 per cent of the population of their empire, this was a formidable task. They had to preserve their special status, privileges, and emoluments, keep themselves separate from the Chinese, and so maintain their racial consciousness and identity.

One method to maintain the ruling family's power was to build up its material resources. Its own revenues accumulated from extensive landholdings, special taxes, and investments rivaled the ordinary state revenues but were kept under separate and secret management of the Imperial Household Department. Such funds supported not only the palace but also the imperial clan, which was governed through a special office and organized in twelve main ranks from princes on down. The rank inherited by a son was one grade lower than that of his father, giving the son an incentive to prove himself. There was also the Manchu aristocracy, ranked in thirty-one grades of nobility, who received investiture and stipends from the throne.

The remainder of the Manchus were all bannermen, given land to till and also stipends, and exempted from Chinese local jurisdiction. For all the Manchus there was a ban on engaging in trade or labor, intermarrying with Chinese, or following Chinese customs. The traditional clan system was preserved and education in the Manchu language was compulsory. On the other hand, all Chinese were required to braid their hair in a queue and shave the rest of their heads like the Manchus, as a symbol of submission.

To preserve Manchu military control there were the banner forces. On the official rolls these grew from some 169,000 in 1644 to about 350,000 listed in the eighteenth century, although this listed strength was not maintained in practice. The banner forces were distributed in a network under Manchu generals-in-chief, whom Westerners called "Tartar generals." Garrisons were located in three sectors—first, twenty-five small posts around Peking; second, in strategic spots in the northwest against incursions from Central Asia; and third, in major Chinese centers of population (Chengtu, Nanking, Hangchow, Foochow, Canton), and at strategic spots in the South. The banner garrisons, of about 4000 men, were each set apart with their families in their own fortified residential quarter of a city, instead of being outside it like their Mongol predecessors of the thirteenth century.

The remnants of the Ming military system and additional Chinese levies were absorbed into a Chinese constabulary, the "Army of the Green Standard." In the late seventeenth century it totaled 594,000 men, and by the early nineteenth century 640,000 men in 1202 battalions, decentralized in scattered small units and posts. As a local police force designed to suppress banditry, its troops were seldom concentrated and never expected to have the offensive power of the bannermen. In general, the military command was carefully divided—between Chinese and Manchus, between the Ministry of War and troops at the capital and the garrisons in the provinces, and between the high civil and military officials all over the empire. Together with the meagre funds for army maintenance, this prevented the growth of any military power independent of the court.

As a major way of preserving themselves and their control of China, the Manchus also maintained their homeland as a base separate from Chinese life and culture. Sinification seemed to be overtaking them after the conquest: Manchus in China were learning the Chinese language, while Chinese from Liaotung were pushing northward in Manchuria. To stop this, north and central Manchuria were closed to Chinese immigration in 1668. The Willow Palisade (a ditch with willows planted along it, begun by the Ming) was extended several hundred miles from Shanhaikuan to the north of Mukden and then down to the Yalu, to mark the statutory limit of Chinese settlement. Most of Manchuria, with its hunting lands, forests, and streams, was thus preserved for the tribal peoples. One pecuniary motive in closing off this area came from the official ginseng monopoly. This theoretically medicinal root was gathered in the hills along the Ussuri and other streams and special officials annually sold licenses to some ten thousand ginseng collectors, following the general model of the salt monopoly system.

How could a limited number of Manchus rule a people some fifty times as numerous? Modern Chinese have felt humiliated by this historic fact. There are several lines of explanation. First, non-Chinese like the Manchus were as much a part of the great "Chinese" Empire of East Asia as were the Chinese themselves. The small "barbarian" Inner Asian component of this empire was specialized for fighting and for holding power. The Man-

MANCHU RULERS ON VACATION. *Beaters have maneuvered a stag into being fair game for the emperor's bow, while courtiers look on.*

chus were just numerous enough to provide the imperial clan, the top supervisors and the garrisons for an empire embracing both China and Inner Asia. Like Europeans in their nineteenth-century colonies, the Manchus bore the burden of governing and were also exhausted by it. Others have stressed a different aspect—that China under the Ch'ing was still ruled about 90 per cent by Chinese, that the Ch'ing regime was from the first not purely Manchu but a Manchu-Chinese synthesis, that the Manchu rulers stayed in power only by becoming as Chinese as their subjects.

These two views are not incompatible with each other, nor with a further consideration, that the Chinese state was an autocracy in which political life was monopolized by the bureaucracy so that the mass of Chinese had little to do with it in any case, no matter who was in power. The imperial government was superficial, confined to the upper layer of society, not present in the villages. The Chinese polity was a synthesis of state and culture. Its state sector was highly centralized while the culture was thoroughly diffused among the populace. The state could be dominated by an alien autocracy, while China's cultural life continued firmly rooted among the people.

The Ch'ing Administration.   In ruling China within the Wall, the Ch'ing altered the Ming administrative structure only to insert Manchu power and dynastic control into the established edifice. The three ingredients of Ch'ing rule were ultimate military force, kept in reserve; ultimate political power, exercised by the Son of Heaven; and Manchu supervision of Chinese collaborators in administration. The Manchu rulers from the first conciliated the Chinese upper strata of landlord-gentry families, local scholar-gentry leaders of community life, and Ming officials. Local landlords and administrators were generally let alone, providing they submitted. The Manchus raised no flag of social or agrarian revolution. On the contrary, they buried the Ming emperor with honors at Peking and claimed they had come to suppress the anti-Ming rebels and bring China peace and order. This persuaded most local officials in the North to accept the new dynasty. A leading example of this class was Hung Ch'eng-ch'ou (1593–1665), a metropolitan graduate who had risen to be Ming governor-general of five provinces. Transferred in 1639 to subdue the Manchus, he was captured by them and well treated. After Peking fell, he was made a Grand Secretary and from 1645 to 1659 Hung played a principal administrative role in mobilizing the resources needed for the Ch'ing campaigns in South China.

The Peking administration after 1644 became a Manchu-Chinese dyarchy. Of the six Grand Secretaries, three were Chinese and three Manchu. The Six Ministries each had two presidents, one Manchu and one Chinese, and four vice presidents, two Manchu and two Chinese. Since this produced a collegial body in place of one minister at the head, the Six Ministries under the Ch'ing have been called by Western writers the "Six Boards." Manchus (together with some Mongols) were similarly interlarded among Chinese at the top of the provincial administrations. In the early years primary reliance was placed on Chinese who were either bannermen or actually bondservants (originally household slaves) of the Manchus. The Ch'ing completed their system of dual control by appointing equal numbers of Manchus and Chinese to the Board of Censors. In the provinces fifty-six

CHINA PROPER UNDER THE EARLY CH'ING (TO AROUND 1800)

censors were divided under fifteen circuits. Manchus and Chinese worked side by side. In general the dyarchy was made secure by using many Chinese bannermen loyal to the Ch'ing among the Chinese appointees.

The Ch'ing divided three of the fifteen Ming provinces to make a total of eighteen within the Wall. A single governor was now put over every province (except Chihli and Szechwan) on top of the territorial hierarchy—namely, county (*hsien*) magistrates, subprefects, prefects, intendants of circuit (or taotais), and the four heads of province-wide administrations, civil service, judiciary, examination system, and salt monopoly). A governor-general, often called "viceroy" by Europeans, was put over every two provinces, with some exceptions. Important business from all provinces that were under both a governor and a governor-general had to come to the emperor from the two officials jointly. Provinces were typically administered by a

Chinese governor and a Manchu governor-general working together. Each had his own troops, but the chief provincial force was usually of bannermen under a Manchu general.

The bracketing of Manchus and Chinese at first created a problem of interpretation and translation. The early Ch'ing regime was bilingual. Chinese interpreters, usually Chinese bannermen, were at first appointed to assist all high Manchu officials. Until its last days, the Ch'ing continued to go through the formality of elaborately translating Chinese documents at Peking into Manchu, but the need for bilingual procedures collapsed rather early, for the Manchus learned Chinese. The Manchu dictionary compiled under K'ang-hsi to help keep the language in use served chiefly to embalm it for posterity. Meanwhile, local government throughout the Ch'ing period was carried on in Chinese; local magistrates were almost all Chinese.

Ch'ing Absolutism.   The gathering of power into the emperor's hands was a continuing tendency during the Yüan, Ming, and Ch'ing periods. Under the Ch'ing all important and many unimportant decisions, executive, legislative, and judicial, had to come from the emperor himself. A further step in this centralization of power in the emperor's person was taken under K'ang-hsi's successor Yung-cheng, who reigned from 1723 to 1736, and perhaps grew in part out of the circumstances of his accession to the throne.

K'ang-hsi from the age of thirteen had produced uncounted daughters and thirty-five sons, of whom twenty grew up. When the son who had been designated heir apparent grew mentally unbalanced, intrigue arose among his brothers over the succession. Yung-cheng became emperor by having military support on the spot at Peking when K'ang-hsi died and boldly announcing his own accession. It was rumored by the jealous opposition that he had disregarded his father's wishes, perhaps even killed him. At any rate, Yung-cheng took every means to safeguard his imperial power. Five of his brothers died in prison, and their supporters were victimized. He further divorced the imperial princes from control of the banner forces. He forbade the naming of an heir apparent, leaving the succession to the emperor's deathbed decision. Yung-cheng made widespread use of spies and secrecy in administration. He arranged that "palace memorials," a new type of document, should be opened only by himself and returned directly to the senders, so that he could get secret reports direct from trusted officials all over the empire.

The main Ch'ing addition to the Ming administrative machine was made in 1729 when Yung-cheng set up a Grand Council (*Chün-chi Ch'u*) as the top organ of policy decision. The Grand Secretariat (*Nei-ko*) continued to handle most routine business while the new Grand Council (literally, "Military Plans Office," sometimes called "Privy Council")

worked directly with the emperor on urgent matters, using less formal documents and less complex procedures. Among the Grand Councilors, usually
five or six, there were often two or three who were concurrently Grand
Secretaries, providing some identity between the two bodies. The council
met with the emperor every day at dawn. Its business was handled by
thirty-two specially selected secretaries, half Manchu and half Chinese.

The emperor was a hard-working and hard-worked man. Yung-cheng
wrote his personal comments on an inordinate mass of documents. Ch'ien-
lung, during most of his long reign from 1736 to 1795, was equally con-
scientious. "Ten or more of my comrades," wrote one of the Grand Council
secretaries, "world take turns every five or six days on early morning duty
and even so would feel fatigued. How did the emperor do it day after day?"

The Unity of State and Culture.   The insertion of a Manchu controlling
element into the inherited administration was only the first requirement for
successful Manchu rule. The second was the wide recruitment of Chinese
talent through the examinations. This ramified and exacting system of successively higher competitions winnowed out both the weak and the unorthodox. Under the Ch'ing, county (*hsien*) examinations, held two years out
of every three, provided each time a total of about twenty-five thousand
degree-holders at the lowest regular level. In the triennial examinations at
provincial capitals, there were usually about fourteen hundred successful
provincial graduates and something over two hundred successful metropolitan graduates (*chin-shih*) in the subsequent tests at Peking. The latter,
normally in their mid-thirties, were the pick of the land, bearers of a title
twelve hundred years old, and fit for appointment as county magistrates.

By presiding over the palace examinations at the summit of the system,
the emperor personified a sage-teacher who rewarded assiduous and loyal
scholars. Once admitted to the elite, scholar-officials still looked to their
imperial master as the font of ethical instruction and the patron of learning
and the arts. The real test for the Manchu emperors was whether they could
become such patrons of Chinese scholarship that the state and culture
would remain unified, under the sole headship of the Son of Heaven. To
rule the Middle Kingdom called for cultural as well as political and military leadership.

Both these aspects of leadership were well typified by the K'ang-hsi
emperor (reigned 1661–1722). Inheriting the throne at the age of seven,
he began to rule in person at thirteen. By the time he was twenty-seven,
he had met the crisis of the Revolt of the Three Feudatories and won an
eight-year civil war (1673–1681). He led great armies into Mongolia
(page 220) and fostered the warrior-huntsman tradition among the Manchus, building up his summer capital at Jehol, north of the Wall. As ruler
of China he made six great tours to the south as far as the lower Yangtze

PEKING STREET SCENE. *From a scroll celebrating the K'ang-hsi emperor's birthday (1713). Note harrows, one-man and two-man carrying poles, Peking carts, shop lanterns, and pennants.*

provinces, the stronghold of the scholar-gentry. On these imperial progressions he devoted special attention to the efforts to check the flooding of the Huai and Yellow River systems and maintain the grain transport by canal to Peking. The sixteen moral maxims that he laid down in 1670, which became known as the *Sacred Edict,* were to be expounded semimonthly by officials and gentry in the villages to inculcate proper conduct.

K'ang-hsi's chief ideological success was with the Chinese scholar class. He was well-versed in the Classics himself and had strong intellectual interests. A number of leading scholars refused all cooperation with the Manchus, but in 1679 K'ang-hsi held a special examination to select the compilers of the *Ming History* and succeeded in getting 152 top scholars to take it, out of 188 whom he invited. He also selected Chinese scholars, calligraphers, and artists to serve within the palace. Important works were produced under his patronage, often with a preface by him. These included the famous *K'ang-hsi Dictionary,* an administrative geography of the empire, and the complete works of Chu Hsi. He also supported a massive encyclopedia, *Synthesis of Books and Illustrations of Ancient and Modern Times* (*Ku-chin t'u-shu chi-ch'eng*), a good deal larger than the *Encyclo-*

paedia Britannica. It was finally printed in five thousand volumes. Thus the Manchu emperor had become as ardent and magnificent a patron of scholarship as any Ming emperor had ever been.

Control over the local populace was not merely a physical matter of inculcating fear of punishments, but included cultural measures and a good deal of moral exhortation. There were the network of official granaries to control famine; the academies and local "schools" to spread classical learning; the system of official honors to be paid to the aged and virtuous; official sacrifices to local spirits; and official lecturers who expounded the *Sacred Edict.*

The mixture of Confucian and Legalist devices is best illustrated by the system of mutual responsibility for groups of neighboring families. As we have seen (pages 53–54 and 187), this originally Legalist institution was used by the Ch'in and had been inherited by the Han, Northern Wei, T'ang, and Sung with more variations in terminology than in practice. Known by Sung times as the *pao-chia* system, it was particularly suited to a static agrarian society rooted in the land. The Ming had used mutual responsibility within village units to maintain order by identifying all persons and encouraging neighbors to inform on all suspected evildoers.

The Ch'ing perfected the *pao-chia* structure. Ideally, one hundred households formed a *chia,* and ten *chia* a *pao.* The headmen of each were selected by the villagers, and could not be gentry. They became responsible for the local registry of population and for seeing that each household kept on its door placard the correct information as to who dwelt within. This was less a form of "self-government" than an officially imposed but unofficial arm of the state. Through it the government and local ruling elite used the family system for police purposes.

Culture in Late Imperial China

Scholarship: The School of "Empirical Research." The major fact confronting Chinese scholars of the seventeenth century was the failure of Chinese rule under the Ming and the re-emergence of "barbarian" conquerors. The dynastic change-over, occupying most of the century, raised many moral problems, such as how to uphold Confucian ideals against eunuch corruption at the late Ming court and whether to transfer one's loyalty from the old dynasty to the new. Scholars of the late Ming, who still worshiped the culture of T'ang and Sung and abominated the Mongol tyranny, were deeply disturbed by the repetition of alien conquest. They rejected any idea that the non-Chinese warrior peoples outside the Middle Kingdom could have an organic political function as potential holders of power over it. Many remained staunchly loyal to the Ming and refused to serve under the Manchus. Instead they held the traditional assumption that foreign aggression was made possible only by domestic disorder and they sought to discover the reasons for the moral decline which alone, they felt, had opened the door to "barbarian" invaders.

One leader in this new scholarship was Ku Yen-wu (1613–1682), a Ming loyalist who fought against the Manchus, was persecuted by personal enemies, and from about 1650 lived a life of intermittent travel and study. This took him widely over North China and brought him into intimate contact with problems of farming, trade, and banking, and even industry and mining. His travel notes and researches resulted in a major geographical work and also a widely-read collection of essays on many topics.

Refusing to serve the Ch'ing, Ku developed a trenchant thesis as to the cause of the Ming collapse. He blamed the sterile and abstract philosophizing of the dominant Ming school of Sung Neo-Confucianism—the so-called "Sung Learning" or "Rationalism" of Chu Hsi. He also attacked particularly the metaphysical branch of Neo-Confucianism, which had been further developed by the influential Wang Yang-ming (see pages 192–193). Ku correctly discerned in Wang's idealistic stress on intuition and self-cultivation the actual influence of Ch'an (Zen) Buddhism, rather than of the Classics. He attacked the routine acceptance of preconceived ideas which had resulted, and their propagation through the Four Books and the examination system as a prefabricated, orthodox interpretation of the Classics. This, he felt, had so confined Chinese thinking within set patterns that it had become incapable of facing political realities or of saving China from "barbarian" conquest. The "eight-legged essay" had done more harm, he claimed, than the First Emperor's burning of the books.

To remedy this intellectual failure of the Chinese scholar class, Ku advocated the pursuit of "knowledge of practical use to society." But this attack on the "Sung Learning" was by no means an attack on the Classics. To the contrary, Ku Yen-wu was the chief founder of the great Ch'ing school of Han Learning, which sought to restudy the classical inheritance by going back to writings of the pre-Sung period. The commentaries of the Han scholars, who had been closer in time to the sages and lacked the metaphysical preconceptions of Neo-Confucianism, were thought to be a more accurate reflection of the wisdom of the Classics. The Sung Learning, as the established orthodoxy now under attack, gave ground only slowly, but the fresh ideas of the Ch'ing period came mainly from adherents of the new Han Learning.

This new approach brought with it the use of the inductive method, assembling evidence from a broad range of sources, not from a few selected texts, and making new hypotheses to test against the evidence. This was applied first in the field of phonetics (studying the rhymes of ancient poetry to determine the ancient pronunciations) and led into broader studies of philology, etymology, and textual criticism. It was called the method of "empirical research" and greatly enlarged the subject matter of classical studies. Indeed, studies of this sort made it possible to determine the authenticity of ancient texts. One great scholar, for example, after studying the *Classic of Documents* for thirty years, proved by textual analysis and historical reasoning that the so-called "old text" of this venerated classic, accepted for over one thousand years and used in the official examinations, was really a forgery. Thus the Han Learning, through the many scholars who came after Ku Yen-wu, achieved a new critical mastery of the great corpus of Chinese classical literature.

This work has been hailed by some as a growth in premodern China of the scientific method, but this term can apply only to the limited field of literary studies, not to natural science and technology. The many protoscientific discoveries and inventions in China were associated more with the nature-loving Taoists than with the scholarly Confucians. The promising beginnings of nature lore in China were never consciously rationalized and institutionalized like modern science in the West. Ch'ing scholars continued to be divorced from the practical inquiries and manipulations of the workshop.

The Ch'ing reappraisal of Neo-Confucianism had its effect on formal philosophy. Tai Chen (1724–1777), for example, attacked Chu Hsi's dualism, which consisted of the two elements of form (*li*) and material stuff or ether (*ch'i*), as based on a misreading of the Classics. The Sung philosophers, having been misled by Taoist and Buddhist concepts, had accepted the *li* as transcendent, superimposed on man's physical nature, and setting proper limits to his physical desires. Instead, Tai Chen asserted that *li* is the immanent, internal structure of things, inherent in the processes of life, including the desires. He denied the Neo-Confucian contention that one can grasp the *li* through introspective meditation and achieve sudden enlightenment. Instead, he argued that the *li* exists objectively and can be grasped only through study, by "wide learning, careful investigation, exact thinking, clear reasoning, and sincere conduct." Although a few words cannot do justice to Ch'ing philosophy, it is plain that systematic thinkers like Tai Chen were modifying the great Sung tradition, not subverting it. Their contribution was still "change within tradition."

The Official Domination of Learning.   Much of the intellectual activity of the eighteenth century was carried on in the shadow of the imperial institution. Yung-cheng subsidized academies to give employment to scholars. Ch'ien-lung, who reigned from 1736 to 1795 and actually held power for sixty-three years, sponsored some fifty-seven large publications compiled by a host of learned editors. Ch'ing scholarship was dependent upon official life, even if indirectly. For example, Tai Chen, the son of a cloth merchant, found his livelihood mainly as tutor or editor in the homes of leading officials. He was one of the leading scholars appointed by Ch'ien-

IMPERIAL PATRONAGE OF LEARNING: THE FU-WEN ACADEMY.
*This woodcut shows the orderly arrangement of academy
buildings in a natural setting, on the Peak of Myriad Pines in the
Phoenix Mountains beside a lake in Chekiang. Subsidized by
Emperor Yung-cheng in 1733, the academy was visited by Emperor
Ch'ien-lung on his fourth southern tour, when he composed
poems for the scholars to match.*

lung in 1773 to compile a great imperial manuscript library called *The
Complete Library of the Four Treasuries* (*Ssu-k'u ch'üan-shu*), that is, the
four branches of literature—the Classics, history, philosophy, and belles-
lettres. This marked a high point in the tradition of bringing together a
number of works previously produced, sometimes on a common theme, and
republishing them as a collection. Ch'ien-lung's super-collection of the *Four
Treasuries* employed as many as fifteen thousand copyists and lasted nearly
twenty years. The compilers began by copying rare works from the great
Ming *Encyclopedia of the Yung-lo Period* (see page 190). But where the
Yung-lo collection had produced 11,095 manuscript volumes, the *Four
Treasuries* now comprised more than 36,000 volumes, containing about
3450 complete works. Seven manuscript sets were made. A printed cata-
logue gave comments on about 10,230 titles.

The emperor's domination of the Chinese learned world was demonstrated in the literary inquisition which for some fifteen years paralleled the compilation of the *Four Treasuries.* The searching out of all major writings afforded an opportunity to suppress objectionable works. Some 2300 works were listed for total suppression and another 350 for partial suppression. The aim was to destroy writings that were anti-Ch'ing or rebellious, that insulted previous "barbarian" dynasties, or that dealt with frontier or defense problems. All the works of certain authors, even inscriptions by them on monuments, were destroyed, as were works that seemed heterodox in general, or merely unliterary. "Although there is nothing that shows evidence of treason in this work," wrote the censors in one case, "still the words are in many cases lying nonsense, fishing for praise. It should be burned." This literary despotism may be illustrated by one case among many, that of an unfortunate dictionary-maker who disrespectfully printed in full the forbidden characters for the personal names of Confucius and the Ch'ing emperors. He and twenty-one members of his family were arrested and sent to Peking. He was executed; two sons and three grandsons were sent into slavery.

The Cultured Life.   In pre-empting intellectual talent for official projects, the Ch'ing government drew upon the gentry class. The common people did not bulk large in the cultural record. For them, Taoism and Buddhism still supplied the principal explanations of the cosmos, and the family and village still were the focus of their lives. But it is not yet possible to reconstruct the daily life of the Chinese villager in the premodern centuries. We know most about the ruling class who lived off the peasantry usually as landlords. They were an educated, urban upper class, who had the means and leisure to enjoy their own private gardens or collections of *objets d'art,* and practice their own calligraphy and painting. They also, without boasting about it, read novels and joined the city crowd at the theater. Porcelains from the imperial kilns at Ching-te-chen in Kiangsi, which reached their height of perfection with Ming blue-and-white and Ch'ing polychrome wares, were of course prized by Chinese connoisseurs long before they became a European vogue. These inheritors of the great cultural tradition were first of all collectors, connoisseurs, and critics, with a strong antiquarian interest. Their amateur ideal was a natural result of their classical education. Their purpose was humanistic, to perceive the principles and proper values of the tradition. (See Plate 13.)

This life of culture, though widespread, centered in the commercial cities of the lower Yangtze delta, in direct descent from the Southern Sung. Hangchow was famous for its beautiful West Lake, its wooded hills, and many temples. Soochow women were the empire's most beautiful. The proverb went, "Above is paradise; here below, Soochow and Hangchow."

One major avocation of cultivated men was painting, in which the trends already well established in the Ming period were continued in the Ch'ing. The names of over one thousand Ming painters have come down to us and of course many more from the Ch'ing. The Ming emperors patronized artists, and Hsüan-te (who ruled from 1426 to 1435) was himself a talented painter. (See Plates 9–10.) One conservative style followed the landscape painting of the Southern Sung, with the misty distances, the angular pine trees, and broken cliffs of masters like Ma Yüan and Hsia Kuei. Another community of painters centered at Soochow. The amateur ideal of these scholar-gentlemen-artists was expressed by the wealthy critic Tung Ch'i-ch'ang (1555–1636), who summed up the view that painting together with poetry and calligraphy were the highest expressions of the human spirit, reflecting man's communion with the forces of nature. Mastery of technique and the taste to avoid the vulgar or sentimental both had to be gained through close study of the old masters. This view combined the appreciation of nature with the study of tradition. The artist paid minute attention to method. The famous seventeenth-century *Mustard Seed Garden Painting Manual,* for example, illustrated the painter's vocabulary of techniques. Tung and his fellow critics appraised and classified the whole inheritance of Chinese painting. Under the Ch'ing, private collections were absorbed into the palace at Peking, where Ch'ien-lung, with great zeal if not taste, made an imperial collection of some eight thousand paintings.

Chinese painting is only the most obvious of the humanistic arts that embody the spirit of Taoism and Buddhism rather than Confucianism. The institutions of political and economic organization, so heavily stressed in this volume, formed the framework of Chinese life but by no means summed it up. The public scene was dominated by the Sage, to be sure, but not the private thoughts of most individuals. Consequently, the day-to-day life of the upper class may be approached more closely through some of the books they read for amusement.

Literature.   One widely read work was *Strange Stories from a Chinese Studio* by P'u Sung-ling (1640–1715), which continued the T'ang tradition of tales of the marvelous and supernatural. Consider, for example, the typical story of a lonely young man visited alternately by two beautiful girls, each more eager than the other to please him in every way, who turn out, after he is nearly dead from exhaustion, to be actually a ghost in human form and a fox-fairy (fox-fairies are mischievous creatures who live as foxes in their holes but often appear among mankind in the form of beautiful women). In such a story neither the situation nor the action is in the Confucian vein, to say nothing of the actors. But since the author wrote in a classical style with a wealth of literary allusions, it was intelligible only to the educated elite, with whom it was actually very popular.

是一是二不
那不離儒
可墨多何
熏閣思
那羅延居
題并書

CH'IEN-LUNG AS A CHINESE RULER. *Surrounded by a scholar's* objets d'art, *the emperor is shown with his portrait.*

For a broader public, the vernacular novels supplied a wealth of fiction, romantic in theme and realistic in detail. The plots derived in part from the late Sung and Yüan, but most of the great novels were written during the Ming. One of the most popular, *Shui-hu chuan* (translated as *All Men Are Brothers* and as *Water Margin*), originated in legends concerning a bandit who lived about 1121. With thirty-six companions he probably had his lair in a great marsh near the juncture of the Yellow River and the Grand Canal. Professional storytellers developed the exploits of this band in a narrative interspersed with verses to be sung by the raconteur. Playwrights of the Yüan also used these themes. Several story sequences were recorded about 1300 in a prompt-book by members of the storytellers' guild. By this time the bandits had become "faithful and just" heroes, champions of the oppressed common people, victimized by evil and corrupt officials, and their number had grown to 108. *Shui-hu chuan* in its final written form was the work of several authors in succession and was a truly popular novel, developed gradually in response to public taste during several centuries— an example of the extensive literature of protest which the Confucian system called forth but tried to ignore. (See page 176.)

The first great realistic novel, created by a single (although still un-

known) author, was *Chin P'ing Mei* (translated as *Golden Lotus*), written
in the late Ming. Its story of the pursuit of pleasure in an everyday urban
life avoids overtones of popular legend, heroic adventure, or the supernatural, and treats women characters convincingly as individuals. Its value as
a reflection of social manners and family life is not obscured by the fact
that it is also pornographic.

The Chinese family system has its greatest monument in *The Dream of
the Red Chamber* (*Hung-lou meng*) by Ts'ao Hsüeh-ch'in, whose forebears
had grown rich in the service of the Manchus. The founder of the family
had been captured by the Manchus and enslaved as a bondservant under the
imperial household. His descendants held lucrative posts so that Ts'ao's
grandfather was wealthy enough to play host to K'ang-hsi on four of his
southern tours. He was both a calligrapher and writer and also a patron of
literature who printed fine imperial editions of T'ang poetry. Small wonder
that his debts survived him! The Yung-cheng emperor collected some of
these debts owed to the imperial court by confiscating the family property
in 1728. At the time the household comprised 114 persons, including servants, with some thirteen residences in Nanking and about 300 acres of
land. Ts'ao lived meagerly with his early memories of this vanished household. He portrayed in his novel, written mainly in the 1750's, the varieties
of personality and of incident, the strengths and weaknesses of character,
which attended the gradual decline of a well-to-do gentry family. The
frustrated love story of two cousins forms only the most tragic of several
interwoven themes.

While the professional storytellers' tales in the marketplace had gradually been developed by talented writers into the vernacular (*pai-hua*)
novels, the drama remained less developed and less widely read as literature.
Its combination of singing, dancing, violent action, and earthy humor left
little chance for the few spoken lines of the libretto to develop into a
literary form of interest to the scholar class.

Present-day impressions of the culture of late imperial China will be
modified as studies of these five-and-one-half centuries approach the thoroughness and detail already achieved in studies of the same centuries in
Japan. Yet our overall impression of the Ming and Ch'ing is of a rich
culture so firmly imbedded in its inherited tradition that it is more critical
than creative and, in some cases, even repetitive and decadent. In architecture, for example, the grandeur of the palace buildings at Peking derives
from an ancient and well-proved formula—white marble terraces, red pillars and beams supporting massive gold-tiled roofs. Under the broad eaves
the beams are brilliantly colored, yet their construction betrays the decadence of the architectural style. T'ang and Sung buildings had carried
the weight of the heavy tiled roof down to the pillars through a complex
series of large wooden brackets. The large, twin-armed brackets of the

T'ang style, still visible at Nara in Japan, were both functional and decorative, lending rhythm and grace to the wooden construction by which an imposing roof was supported on a few columns. By Ming and Ch'ing times, however, the brackets had become smaller and more numerous, set in a continuous series and performing no more function than a cornice— in short, vestigial ornaments instead of important structural components.

The Beginning of Dynastic Decline

Military Deterioration.   Certain preliminary signs of decline had appeared by 1800 in at least three forms—military ineffectiveness of the banner forces, corruption at the top of the bureaucracy, and difficulties of livelihood among a greatly increased population. The banner forces which had dominated continental East Asia for almost two centuries were losing their vigor. Under Ch'ien-lung, the Ten Great Campaigns were much celebrated in the official annals, yet most of them were in a different category from the early Manchu conquests.

The Ten Great Campaigns included three already mentioned—two against the Zungars and the pacification of Turkestan, strategic achievements of the 1750's which enlarged the area of Ch'ing control in Central Asia. But the other seven campaigns were more in the nature of police actions on frontiers already established—two wars to suppress rebels in Szechwan, another to suppress rebels in Taiwan (1787–1788), and four expeditions abroad to chastise the Burmese (1766–1770), the Vietnamese (1788–1789), and the warlike Gurkhas in Nepal on the border between Tibet and India (1790–1972), the last counting as two. Ch'ien-lung's generals, almost all Manchus, led busy lives. For example, Fu-k'ang-an (died 1796) commanded forces in Szechwan, Kansu, Taiwan, and against the Gurkhas. To fight the Gurkhas, who had invaded Tibet, he led an army over a thousand miles across the roof of the world in 1792 and drove the invaders back through the Himalayan passes into their homeland of Nepal, which thereafter sent tribute to Peking every five years until 1908.

All these later campaigns took place on the periphery of the empire, were conducted by a group of professional Manchu generals, and required large expenditures of funds, often through the hands of these generals. For example, the rebels in the mountains on the Szechwan-Yunnan border, although they totaled fewer than thirty thousand households, built thousands of stone forts in the rocky defiles of their homeland and were eventually dislodged only with cannon. The second campaign against them took five years and seventy million taels of silver, equal to more than two years of the cash revenues normally received at Peking. Until the mid-Ch'ing campaigns are thoroughly studied, we can only speculate as to the corrupt pecuniary motives that may have played a part in their prosecution. The large alloca-

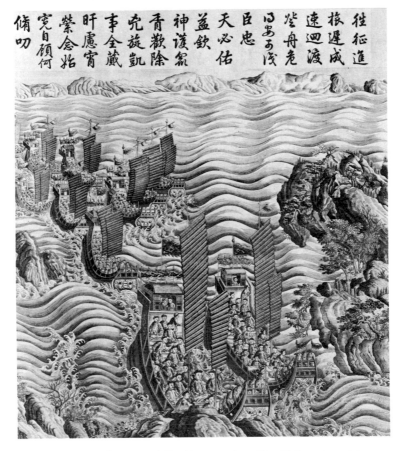

備　寬　縈　旰　軍　肯　神　益　天　臣　何　速　根
叩　日　絆　宵　全　歡　護　欽　必　忠　安　迴　遟　往
　　顧　始　　蕆　除　宇　　佑　　可　渡　戍　征
　　何　　　　　凱　　　　　　陵　　危　　進

*The great Manchu general, Fu-k'ang-an, invading Taiwan to suppress
a Triad Society rebellion, 1787. Emperor Ch'ien-lung's autographed
poem celebrates the victory.*

tions of imperial funds necessary in each case may have created a vested
interest in the prolongation of operations. Fu-k'ang-an, we know, was not
only governor-general over various provinces continuously from 1780 to
1795, but also a henchman of Ho-shen (1750–1799).

Ho-shen was the classic type of evil courtier, reminiscent of infamous
eunuchs of earlier times. His rise was a symptom of the emperor's senes-
cence. With great prudence the Manchus had succeeded in forestalling the
rise of most of the evils which had beset the leadership of earlier dynasties.
Imperial princes, military commanders on the frontier, new "barbarian"
invaders, great landed families entrenched in the provinces, eunuchs at the
court, empresses and their relatives, even factionalism among the officials—
all had been sedulously guarded against, so that the centralized power of
the state might remain undiminished in the emperor's hands. The one thing
that could not be prevented was the aging of the emperor himself. When

Ch'ien-lung was sixty-five he became much impressed by a handsome twenty-five-year-old bodyguard, a clever and unscrupulous Manchu who became his favorite and chief minister and plundered the state for the next twenty years. Ho-shen rose like a meteor in one year from the fifth rank to Grand Councilor. Thereafter he got his hands on the principal posts in charge of revenue and personnel, betrothed his son to the emperor's youngest daughter, and entrenched himself in as many as twenty different positions at a time. He built up his clique of similarly corrupt henchmen all over the empire and levied a squeeze upon the whole officialdom. The private wealth attributed to him by his enemies after his fall was alleged to be worth some one-and-a-half billion dollars.

With Ho-shen leading the way at Peking, we can more easily understand how military corruption went hand-in-hand with its civilian counterpart. The banner forces became gradually ill-supplied, poorly trained, and demoralized. Officers and troops on stipends were both under the pressure of rising prices. Impoverished bannermen who tried to subsist on rice stipends in their garrisons were forced to become artisans, petty traders, or evildoers to eke out a living. Finally, after more than a century of comparative peace within China, the deterioration of the Manchu military machine was startlingly exposed in a big peasant rebellion.

The White Lotus Rebellion.   In the mountainous border region bounded by Hupei, Szechwan, and Shensi, the relatively inaccessible area between the upper waters of the Han River and the Yangtze gorges, a great uprising, called the White Lotus Rebellion, occurred during the years 1796–1804. Here a migration of poor settlers from the crowded lowlands had created new communities on infertile mountain soil, on the margin of subsistence. Though encouraged by the government, this immigration had not been accompanied by an equal extension of civil administration, communications, or military control. The expression of discontent, evidently aroused by the exactions of petty tax collectors, was led by men who claimed the mantle of the ancient White Lotus Society (see page 179), a religious cult that had been active in the late Yüan and Ming periods. It now promised its followers the advent of the Buddha, the restoration of the Ming, and personal salvation from suffering in this world and the next. Once started, the rebellion became violently anti-Manchu, but it achieved no further ideological development and did not create a government administration or claim a dynastic title. During its early years the rising was an inconclusive contest between ill-organized bands of rebels and inefficient imperial forces who struggled for control of the mountain villages and thus of the sinews of local military power—the supplies of men and food. However, the corrupt administration dominated by Ho-shen, who held power until the retired Ch'ien-lung emperor died early in 1799, hamstrung the military effort.

The suppression of the White Lotus Rebellion, after both sides had harassed the local scene for several years, showed many classic features. The first requirement was to restore discipline and morale to the banner forces. This became possible after the Chia-ch'ing emperor came into effective power in 1799 and supported more vigorous Manchu commanders. A systematic program was also pursued of "strengthening the walls and clearing the countryside," that is, collecting the farming populace in hundreds of walled or stockaded villages and removing all food supplies from the open fields. The local manpower, thus concentrated, was organized into garrisons of self-defense corps paid and fed partly by the government. Recruitment of this militia was made easier by the devastation and poverty that the rebellion had brought. Some militia were also trained as a striking force to pursue the rebels. With its campaign of pursuit and extermination, the government combined a policy of conciliation, trying to split followers from leaders by offering amnesty to the rank and file who surrendered and putting a price on the heads of rebel commanders. The Ch'ing suppression thus was many-sided, starving the rebels of food and new recruits, organizing military strength among the villages, and encouraging desertion from the rebel ranks. This program was eventually effective, and the banner forces, after their initial failure, somewhat redeemed themselves. But the Manchu fighting man had lost his reputation for invincibility. The government's victory, such as it was, was really due to its use of some three hundred thousand local militia, whom the government subsequently had to try to disarm.

Population Growth.   Behind this popular rising at the turn of the century lay an era of unparalleled domestic peace, prosperity, and population increase. The growth of numbers, however, eventually destroyed both the prosperity and the peace which had made it possible. The official population estimates record a year-by-year increase from 142 million in 1741 to 432 million in 1851. Such an increase might be possible in a new country where immigration and industrialization were both at work, but in an ancient and thickly populated agricultural state like early modern China such figures are amazing.

The ritualistic, rather than statistical, nature of the Ch'ing population figures seems evident from the way they were compiled and reported. From 1741 this was done by the *pao-chia* headmen in the villages. Population figures recorded on the door placards of each household were only one of their many concerns. They also had to report on local irregularities of all sorts—such as burglary, gambling, harboring criminals, illegal coinage, illicit sale of salt, gang activities, or the presence of strangers. Moreover, procedures were neither uniform nor reliable for reporting births, deaths, females, children, non-Chinese minority peoples, and migrants. Premodern

China did not, in short, achieve a modern census. On the contrary, annual reporting of population figures became routinized and ritualized. Some provinces reported regular increases year after year, often a fixed percentage, say 0.3 or 0.5 per cent, over the previous year. As Ch'ien-lung remarked, "The number increases the same year after year. This is absurd."

This literary nature of the Ch'ing figures suggests that the steep curve of increase should be flattened out, that the Chinese population was greater at the beginning and probably less at the end of the Ch'ing period than the figures indicate. For example, the totals of population estimated in the Ming do not exceed 60 million, the figure reached by the Han dynasty some fifteen hundred years earlier. We may guess that the Ming population actually approached 150 million by 1600 and this total was inherited by the Ch'ing. In the early eighteenth century came an important administrative change that combined the head tax and the land tax and decreed that the quotas of these taxes to be collected in the provinces should remain fixed forever at the levels of 1711. This may have reversed the incentives in the estimating of population totals. Where formerly an official in charge of an area might have held his estimates down to avoid raising his tax quota, normally set according to population and land totals, now he might aim to please the throne by reporting a prosperous increase of the people under his care. Imperial demands for careful reporting called forth great increases. By 1800 the total population may have been about 300 million, rather than the 350 million reported to the emperor.

Even so, this was an extraordinary growth in an ancient farming country where industrialization had not yet commenced. Historians have accounted for it mainly by citing the domestic peace and order of the eighteenth century and the increase of food supply through cultivating more land and planting faster-ripening types of rice. In ancient times, after transplanting from nursery beds into paddy fields, rice had required about 150 days to reach maturity. Importation and development of earlier-ripening varieties from Champa (in what is now South Vietnam) had gradually reduced this growing time to 100, then to 60, 40, and, in the nineteenth century, even 30 days. This made possible double- and even triple-cropping. Another factor was the use of new food crops. Maize, sweet potatoes, tobacco, and peanuts all were introduced into China from the Americas in the sixteenth or early seventeenth century. The sweet potato became the poor man's food of South China, for it could be grown on sandy soil, useless for rice, and provided more food energy per unit of land than most crops. Other factors in population growth presumably lay in the area of hygienic practices affecting public health, in the increase of foreign trade and of handicraft production and trade attending it, and in other domestic economic developments as yet unexplored.

Whatever the causes of China's demographic growth, it was not paralleled by comparable growth of the Ch'ing administration. The populace may have doubled, but not the official class and its services for the people, nor the military forces which maintained peace and order. On the contrary, the Ch'ing government in all its aspects seems to have grown less effective just at a time when its domestic problems were increasing. The two developments were of course interrelated. Bad government and unsolved problems exacerbated each other in a vicious downward spiral, such as China's long history had seen so often before. This time, however, because of new factors from abroad, the process was to culminate during the late nineteenth and early twentieth centuries in an unprecedented crisis for the whole traditional system of government and society. The process was complicated, some say "distorted," by the intrusion of the West.

Early Western Contact

The expansion of Europe is an oft-told tale. In the parochial Western perspective, the Europeans going out to conquer the globe in early modern times were impelled by their superior culture, which stemmed from the Greco-Roman and Judeo-Christian traditions and created the modern European nations. Europeans trace the rise of their modern power to the growth of towns after the Dark Ages that were contemporary with the glory of T'ang. They stress the influence of the Crusades, the growth of a merchant class, the commerce of Venice and Genoa with the eastern Mediterranean, and the Italian-Iberian rivalry to control the spice trade from the Indies. In a Chinese perspective, the Europeans on their northwest Eurasian peninsulas seem have-not peoples, too far north (between 35 and 55 degrees) to produce much rice, sugar, tea, or cotton and so impelled to trade and drawn like many barbarians before them to the Middle Kingdom.

From any point of view, it is plain that China under the T'ang and Sung and right down to Marco Polo's day was a far greater civilization in both size and accomplishment than its contemporary, medieval Europe. As one index, consider how the main flow of influences over the long course of history had been from China to Europe, not the other way: first, the silk trade across Central Asia to Rome, then the great series of inventions emanating from China—paper and printing that spread literacy, porcelain (chinaware) so easy to keep hygienically clean, the crossbow used by the Han armies, cast-iron, canal lock-gates, the wheelbarrow, the stern-post rudder to steer ships at sea, the compass to navigate them, gunpowder, and all the rest. This material technology was paralleled by the Chinese primacy in the methods of bureaucratic government, including civil service examinations, to say nothing of such arts as painting. In short, the expansion of the Europeans reflected not only their greed, curiosity, zeal and patriotism but also in some ways their backwardness.

Portuguese adventurers, from a tiny nation of perhaps one and a half million persons, set the tone for Sino-European relations. After rounding Africa in 1498, they took Malacca on the Malay Peninsula in 1511 and by 1514 reached the southeast coast of China, where only pirates, like those from Japan, had previously caused trouble. Their assertion of equality with the Chinese seemed unjustified. Many arrived in Chinese junks with Chinese pilots. Most Europeans of the time were unaccustomed to daily bathing, and they commonly emerged from their cramped and fetid ships' quarters not only with more body hair than most Asians but also with more body odor.

The first Portuguese explorers in China's waters accomplished little to prove Europe's cultural equality. In 1517 the Portuguese sent an embassy from the "King of Portugal" to the "King of China." On reaching Canton the mission fired a salute of cannon in proper Western style, which outraged the Chinese sense of etiquette and required an immediate apology. The envoys were housed in the office of the Superintendent of Trading Ships, like any tribute mission, and were taken to Peking in the usual Chinese manner. Meanwhile other Portuguese built an island fortress outside the Canton River mouth and mounted cannon in *their* usual fashion. Hindering trade and flouting Chinese law, these semipirates were accused of robbery, blackmail, and buying Chinese children from Chinese kidnappers. All Portuguese were expelled from Canton in 1522, and their first envoy died in prison there. Not until mid-century did they get local Chinese permission to base their trade on the small peninsula of Macao. The peninsula was walled off by Chinese authorities, who continued (until 1887) to collect land and customs taxes while letting the Portuguese run their own local government. Meanwhile in late Ming times the Portuguese in Asia were generally eclipsed by the Dutch, who took Malacca in 1641 but devoted their main effort to the East Indies.

The Jesuit Success Story.   The Europeans met the Chinese on two fronts —trade and evangelism—but the religious contact was at first more active than the commercial. During the Ming decline and Ch'ing conquest, a handful of Jesuit missionaries became versed in Chinese culture, secured the patronage of high officials, and gained court positions at Peking.

The greatest of these Jesuit pioneers, Matteo Ricci (Chinese name, Li Ma-tou; 1552–1610), was assigned to China in 1582. Ricci was an Italian of impressive personality, tall and vigorous, with a curly beard, blue eyes, and a bell-like voice. Guided by their experience in India and Japan, where they gained admittance earlier than in China, Ricci and his colleagues accommodated their message to the local scene. In China as in Japan they worked from the top down, appealing to the upper-class elite. They adopted Chinese forms as far as possible, avoiding all open connection with the

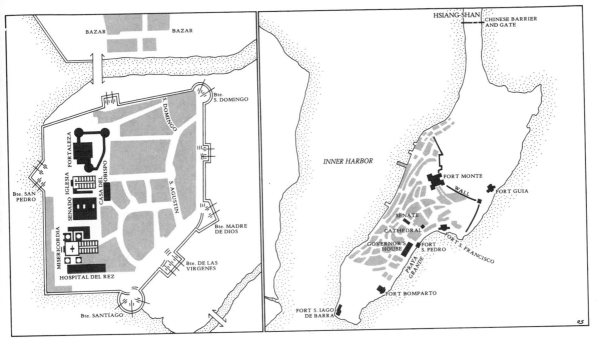

LEFT: THE PORTUGUESE STRONGHOLD AT MALACCA.
RIGHT: MACAO IN THE 1840'S.

Portuguese traders at Macao. They soon abandoned the Buddhist monk's costume for the Confucian scholar's gown. Instead of preaching, they held conversations with Chinese scholars, arousing their curiosity with demonstrations of prisms, clocks, and geographic knowledge. Above all they became fluent in Mandarin, or standard North Chinese, and literate in the Chinese Classics. This enabled Ricci to represent Christianity as a system of wisdom and ethics compatible with Han Confucianism.

By 1601 Ricci, like a Chinese man of talent, had secured the patronage of high officials and was able to establish his residence at Peking. When he presented two clocks and a clavichord, which caught the emperor's fancy, he and his colleagues were brought into the palace to show how these mechanisms operated. Ricci finally got himself out of the category of tribute-bearer and was given an imperial stipend as a scholar. Within a few years he and his colleagues had made some two hundred Christian converts, including even ministers of state.

Ricci's successors found that they could make themselves most useful by applying their Western knowledge of astronomy to the revision of the Chinese calendar. The Son of Heaven had a special responsibility to maintain a calendar which would accurately foretell the positions of the heavenly bodies and the timing of the seasons—no easy matter. In the astronomical bureau at Peking, the Muslim astronomers, as well as the old-style Chinese astronomers with whom they competed, were behind the times and in 1610 predicted an eclipse several hours wrong. Such errors gave the Jesuits their opportunity. The German Jesuit, Johannes Adam Schall von Bell (1591–1666), who came to China in 1622, was a trained astronomer and secured a position in the palace, where he first celebrated mass in 1632.

By the last years of the Ming, the Jesuits had made numerous converts among the imperial family, and the emperor was gradually coming under Christian influence. The mission brought to Peking a Western library of some seven thousand volumes on which to base writings in Chinese. During the seventeenth century with the aid of devoted Chinese scholars they produced some 380 such works. These writings were mainly on Christianity, but included treatises on astronomy, mathematics, geography, medicine, meteorology, mechanics, pharmacology, anatomy, zoology, logic, and European government and education.

The decay of the Ming regime made the dynasty, for many Chinese scholars, no longer a worthy focus of their loyalty. The combination of Western science and Christian moral teaching attracted a number of outstanding converts, who were capable of collaborating in truly bicultural endeavors. The most famous convert was Hsü Kuang-ch'i (Christian name, Paul Hsü; 1562–1633), who became a Christian even before he passed the highest examination and entered the Hanlin Academy in 1604. With Ricci he completed the translation of the first six books of Euclid's geometry. Hsü was made a Grand Secretary in 1632. He gave the missionaries an entrée into high official circles and helped them to present Christianity through Chinese writings that had literary polish. Both Paul Hsü and Adam Schall also helped the Ming court obtain Western arms. To fight off the Manchus, Schall in 1636 set up a foundry and cast some twenty big guns. Western technology, in short, gained acceptance more readily than Western religion.

After the Manchu conquest of 1644, the Ch'ing kept Schall as chief astronomer. The young emperor for several years saw much of him, called him "grandpa," and permitted the building of a Christian church at Peking. During the middle decades of the long reign of K'ang-hsi the Jesuit mission at Peking reached the height of its influence. The missionaries enjoyed intimate contact with the emperor, seeing him sometimes almost daily. They once gave him a new drug, "Jesuit's bark" or quinine, and were commissioned to survey and map the Chinese Empire using Western methods. Their position was that of courtiers to the emperor, performing the kowtow with complete servility like other officials, displaying knowledge with finesse, presenting gifts and making friends at court.

Sino-European Cultural Relations. The Jesuits were pioneers in contact between two great cultures. Facing two ways, they eventually suffered

THE JESUITS IN PEKING AS DEPICTED IN EUROPE. *1. Ricci and his
chief convert. Left: "Fr. Matteo Ricci of Macerata, of the Society of
Jesus, the first propagator of the Christian Religion in the
Kingdom of China." Right: "Paul Li {error for Hsü}, Great Colao
{i.e., Grand Secretary} of the Chinese, propagator of the Christian
Law."*

*2. Fr. Adam Schall with his astronomical instruments. Director of
the Imperial Board of Astronomy, he wears on his cap the colored
button and on his gown the "mandarin square" of a Ch'ing
civil official. Illustrations published in 1673.*

attack on both fronts. Significantly, however, the main attack came from
their European competitors.

Europe, having initiated the contact with China, received at first the
greater impact from it. The image of China conveyed through the influential Jesuit writings from Peking figured in the Enlightenment as an example
of an ancient society which had a natural morality quite independent of
revealed religion. In the philosophical debate over the relationship between
morality and religion, the China depicted by the Jesuits was cited approv-
ingly by Voltaire and the Deists, and also by the Physiocrats. Eighteenth-

EMPEROR CH'IEN-LUNG RECEIVES MONGOL HORSES. *Painted by the Jesuit lay brother G. Castiglione (Chinese name: Lang Shih-ning, 1688–1766), who reached Peking in 1715 and was court painter to three emperors.*

JESUIT ARCHITECTURE AT CH'IEN-LUNG'S SUMMER PALACE. *This European engraving (ca. 1786) of the Hall of Peaceful Seas (Hai Yen T'ang) shows Chinese-style tile roof surmounting pilasters and "Chinese rococo" details, combined with Western perspective and staircases reminiscent of an Italian villa.*

century Europe enjoyed a vogue of things Chinese, not only an idealized image of rational Confucian ethics and benevolent despotism in government but also a craze for *chinoiserie,* the Chinese style in architecture, porcelain, furniture, and decoration.

At Peking the Jesuits continued to serve the emperor as astronomers, interpreters, cartographers, painters, engravers, architects, and engineers—the first technical experts from West to East. At the old summer palace near Peking, the Yüan Ming Yüan, they designed baroque buildings and banks of fountains for a miniature Versailles, as part of a minor European vogue at the court. But the Jesuits were primarily missionaries, and their effort to apply the universal principles of Christianity to the concrete realities of China led them into the path of cultural accommodation—in short, Sinification. Accommodation in fact had been the secret of the Jesuit success in Asia generally. In China, as Paul Hsü put it, Christianity "does away with Buddhism and completes Confucianism." Christian faith could be added to Confucian practice. The cornerstones of this position were the acceptance of the Confucian canon in its textual form in the Classics as "ancient wisdom"; the rejection of much of the great corpus of Chinese interpretation and comment upon the Classics, constituting principally what we now call Neo-Confucianism, as unsound and misguided; and an attack upon Taoism and Buddhism as idolatry.

This Jesuit compromise did not go unchallenged by missionaries in the field. Should the ritual performed in veneration of ancestors before the family altar be regarded merely as a "civil rite" and therefore permissible to Christians, or was it really "pagan worship," which could not be allowed? What about the state cult of Confucius and a magistrate's prayers for rain? To many theologians it seemed plain that the Jesuits' compromises went too far, that in making Christianity acceptable to Chinese classical scholars the early Jesuits had destroyed its essential monotheistic articles of faith. Since the pagan world, after all, had no idea of the true God as a spiritual substance, its classical expressions could not be used to describe Him.

By the 1640's the controversy over the rites to be permitted had been referred to Rome by mendicant friars of the Dominican and Franciscan orders from the Philippines who got a foothold in Fukien. They had an utterly different approach to mission work, based on their experience in less culturally resistant lands like Mexico and the Philippines, where there were no powerful local bureaucracies to prevent a direct and uncompromising evangelism among the common people. Consequently they followed the order of poverty and preached in the streets, disregarding most of the lessons the Jesuits had learned. By 1701 there were in China fifty-nine Jesuits, twenty-nine Franciscans, eighteen Dominicans, fifteen secular priests, mainly from the French Society for Foreign Missions, and six Augustinians. The Jesuits alone had 70 mission residences and 208 churches or chapels.

The total Christian community was estimated at 300,000, but its leadership was split. The "Rites Controversy" boiled along for a full century (ca. 1640–1742), both within and between the various orders and missions in China and their supporters in Europe, eventually even between the Pope and the Ch'ing emperor.

The Confucian scholars' hostility to Christianity, meanwhile, was based on several points of view—rational skepticism about such doctrines as original sin, the virgin birth, and the divinity of Jesus; a culturalistic defense of Taoism, Buddhism, and the Confucian teachings; and a positive aversion to such alleged Christian practices as sexual promiscuity, kidnaping of children, and extraction of the eyes and hearts of the dead. The leading Chinese opponent of Christianity, Yang Kuang-hsien (1597–1669), was a highly emotional but articulate xenophobe. Appealing to Chinese pride, he cited Jesuit writings that depicted the Chinese as minor descendants of the Hebrews who had anciently worshiped God but had lost the true way until Ricci's arrival. He also accused Father Schall of having cast evil spells on the recently deceased Shun-chih emperor. This alarmed the Manchu court, which had an inherited belief in the spells of shamans. Schall, sentenced to death, was saved by a providential earthquake, indicative of cosmic disapproval of the sentence, but five Chinese Christian astronomers were executed. Christianity remained suspect because of its convert's private organization in an esoteric cult, like a secret society but with foreign connections, truly subversive.

The Jesuits' eclipse was precipitated by action in Europe. During a controversy at Paris in 1700 the Jesuits at Peking in self-defense secured a rescript from K'ang-hsi which supported their view of the Chinese rites. This threw the fat in the fire, for K'ang-hsi had now been brought to pronounce on theology, the prerogative of the Pope. Christian priests, representing the interests of Portugal and France, or of the rival orders, now began to destroy the hard-won Christian position at Peking. In the trial of strength between emperor and Pope, the Jesuits were largely on the side of the emperor. K'ang-hsi sent Jesuits to Rome with sixty-nine documents to lay before the Pope. But the Pope responded with a bull of 1715 reaffirming the anti-Jesuit position.

The Jesuit compromise with Chinese practice had been accepted at the court of Peking for over a century, and K'ang-hsi had found the missionaries useful and reliable throughout his long reign. The papal attack on the Jesuits came now as an affront, difficult to believe, impossible to accept. K'ang-hsi sent a Jesuit emissary to Rome via Russia, but the only papal reply was a heightened denunciation. After 1722 the Yung-cheng emperor turned against the missionaries, who had been unable to avoid involvement in palace politics, and began an active suppression of Christianity in China. Many churches were seized for civil purposes, and missionaries were forced into hiding, except at Peking. In 1724 Yung-cheng added a commentary to his father's *Sacred Edict* to denounce Christianity as a heterodox sect, which remained the Ch'ing policy for over a century. In 1742 another papal bull settled the Rites Controversy for the next two centuries. It required (until 1938) a strict oath by Catholic missionaries to forbid all Christian practice of "the Rites and Ceremonies of China." Under Ch'ien-lung, missionaries outside Peking suffered continued persecution. They were obliged to live and travel in disguise and to keep out of cities. Congregations shrank. The anti-Christian folklore became implanted in the popular mind.

Early Sino-Russian Relations.   European contact with China by sea and the Jesuit letters from Peking overshadowed in Western thinking the other early approach to China that was made by the Russians overland across Siberia. On this route the Russians of course faced much greater logistic problems. The Westerners' ships could bring them to Malacca or Canton in full force, self-sufficient, mobile, with their own armament, and without the necessity of passing through foreign kingdoms. Sea power could bring great force to bear suddenly. The carracks of the Portuguese or the East Indiamen of the Dutch and English could also carry more goods than camel caravans.

Characteristically, the Russian colonizing expansion across the endless stretches of Siberia was slow and gradual but also relatively permanent. The Russians reached the Pacific by 1637, almost as early as the English founding of New England, but their penetration of East Asia subsequently lagged far behind the Westerners who came by sea. British fleets might descend upon East Asia like a typhoon, irresistible but impermanent. Russian colonists advanced like a glacier. Americans today have inherited the West European tradition of sea contact with the Far East. The Russian tradition is different.

Beginning with the penetration of the Ob River basin about 1580, the Russians traversed the closely adjoining upper waters of the great rivers (Ob, Yenisei, and Lena) that flow northward to the Arctic. Climate and terrain were inhospitable and there were no centers of population. The administration of this vast region set up by officials from Moscow was parasitic, collecting its tribute of furs and skins from the local tribes through a network of fortified out-stations joined by post routes. Since the food supply was precarious, the Russian explorers sought a grain-growing area, and inevitably were attracted to the Amur River, on which barges in summer and sledges in winter could reach more productive country and, eventually, the sea. After 1643, Cossack raiding parties from Yakutsk began to go down the Amur, fighting the local tribes and establishing fortified posts. Other Cossack expeditions, coming from Yeniseisk by way

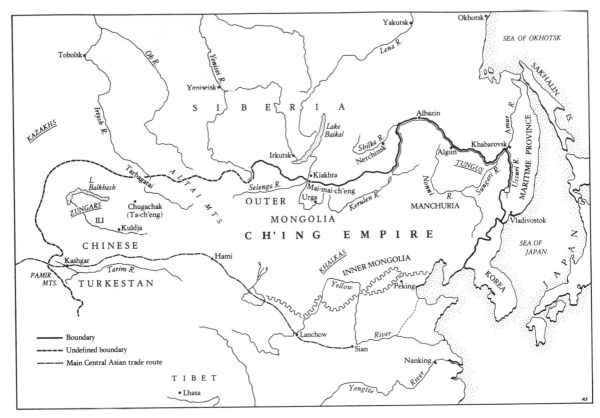

EARLY RUSSIAN-CHINESE CONTACT

of Lake Baikal, founded in 1656 a post at Nerchinsk on the main tributary of the Amur. A permanent outpost and a fortress were established to the east at Albazin in 1665.

These posts within the Amur watershed brought the Russians into conflict with the Ch'ing Empire. The tribes of northern Manchuria appealed to their overlords of the new dynasty at Peking. However, during the first generation of Manchu-Russian relations, the Ch'ing rulers were not in a strong position. Their conquest of China was not really completed until 1681, and meanwhile their hegemony over the Mongols was formidably challenged by the rise of the Zungar tribe in the far northwestern Ili region. Western Mongol tribes were already in contact with the Russians on their north in Siberia, and Eastern Mongols were already trading with the Russians at Nerchinsk. The K'ang-hsi emperor's aim, therefore, was not only to eject the Russians from the Amur but also to forestall their growing closer to the Mongols.

Diplomatic relations had begun informally as early as 1619. A more formal attempt was made in 1654 when the tsar sent an envoy to Peking with a letter to the emperor of China. The envoy's aim was to get trade without acknowledging Chinese suzerainty; he therefore refused to perform the kowtow. The officials in charge of him were not interested in trade, and the Russian envoy's stubborn demand for the European type of inter-state equality threatened the ideological basis of Ch'ing power over East Asia. He was sent away without being received at court. Another Russian envoy was the colorful N. G. Spathar-Milescu ("Spathar" was actually a title), an intellectual Greek educated in Constantinople who had had wide experience in Western Europe. He reached Peking in 1676 bearing credentials for the first time in Latin and got the Jesuits to serve as interpreters. He was sent away for refusing to kneel when receiving the emperor's presents for the tsar.

After the consolidation of his rule within China in the early 1680's, K'ang-hsi proceeded systematically to develop post routes by land and water from South Manchuria to the Amur region, setting up stations, establishing granaries and military colonies, and creating a naval force to operate on the Manchurian river system. The Russians were soon ejected from the lower Amur. A superior Ch'ing army laid siege to the one remaining small fortress of Albazin. Under this pressure the Russian court decided to negotiate and sent an ambassador to Nerchinsk. The time was favorable, for the Ch'ing position was still threatened by the Western Mongols. Following the precedent of Spathar-Milescu, K'ang-hsi deputed two Jesuits to act as interpreters and advisers in negotiating with the Russians. After much confusion, suspicion, and bargaining, during which the two Jesuits crossed the river repeatedly between the rival camps, agreement was reached, and the Jesuits drew up official copies of a treaty in Latin, with other copies in Manchu, Chinese, Mongolian, and Russian. This treaty of Nerchinsk of 1689 was in terms of equality. It checked the Russian advance into the Amur region but gave Russia a stable basis for trade by caravan at Peking. The Russians agreed to destroy Albazin and withdraw from the Amur watershed. The treaty delimited the North Manchurian boundary but left its western end, between Mongolia and Siberia, uncertain.

By the Treaty of Nerchinsk, K'ang-hsi had forestalled Russian aid to the Eastern Mongols. In the decade after 1689 he achieved the final defeat of Galdan (see page 218) and began to assert his control over the Western Mongols. Russian trade caravans now crossed Mongolia via Urga to Peking under official passports, usually accompanied by envoys with a semicommercial, semidiplomatic status. Under the Superintendency of Dependencies (*Li-fan Yüan*), this early caravan trade fitted into the Chinese tributary pattern. Missions were nominally limited to two hundred persons, and eventually were conducted under a system of numbered tallies. At Peking they were kept under guard in a Russian Hostel similar to the Hostel for Tributary Envoys. Russian envoys performed the kowtow.

Sino-Russian relations continued to be important in the complex Ch'ing strategy for the control of Inner Asia. In the early eighteenth century the Zungars still fought, traded, and negotiated with the Russians, who under Peter the Great were encroaching steadily on their western frontier. On their part the Russians wanted a permanent commercial-diplomatic foothold in Peking, with their own interpreters, independent of the Jesuits. This effort resulted in a Russian Orthodox ecclesiastical mission, whose ostensible purpose was to minister to the spiritual needs of a small Russian emigré community at the Ch'ing capital. In the 1690's Moscow began to use it as a pretext for sending Russian Orthodox priests to Peking along with the trading caravans. The Yung-cheng emperor after 1722 welcomed the establishment of the Russian ecclesiastical mission to offset that of the Jesuits. He also wanted to prevent a Russian-Zungar alliance in the west and to eliminate Russian influence among the Eastern Mongols.

These Russian commercial interests and Manchu strategic interests produced another important settlement in 1727. The Russian ambassador brought fifteen hundred troops and a retinue of one hundred persons. After negotiating for six months in Peking, he withdrew to Kiakhta on the Mongol-Siberian border north of Urga. The treaty signed there delimited the boundary between Russia and the Ch'ing Empire and Russia was definitely excluded from Mongolia. In return the Russians gained a regular trade at Kiakhta. The Russians were allowed to send official caravans triennially to Peking and to maintain there a Russian Orthodox ecclesiastic-diplomatic mission, building their own church and sending language students. But whereas a score of Russian missions had reached Peking in the century before 1730, only half a dozen came in the century following. The Ch'ing court was not interested in trade but wanted political stability, and for this the best policy was isolation. Ch'ing realism was illustrated in two embassies sent to secure Russia's neutrality toward the Western Mongols, one to Moscow in 1731, the other to St. Petersburg in 1732. The Manchu envoys performed the short kowtow, kneeling and bowing three times, a ceremony which the Russian court expected of Oriental envoys, just as the Ch'ing expected Russian envoys to perform the kowtow in Peking. This realistic Ch'ing diplomacy was successful. By 1760, Ch'ing power had been firmly established over Tibet, the Western Mongol menace had been destroyed in Turkestan, and Russian contact was being held in check on distant frontiers.

The Canton Trade.   The Ch'ing foreign policy of stability through limitation of contact was less easy to achieve in the maritime trade at Canton. In the eighteenth century China faced new and more powerful forms of European expansion. The British East India Company, like its Dutch counterpart and like the other chartered companies that settled Virginia or Massachusetts Bay, was a private association that brought extensive capital resources under a central control, yet by its royal charter acquired wide powers of government abroad, monopolizing the national trade in certain areas. It built and armed its outposts, exercised jurisdiction over its countrymen there, developed navies as well as carrying fleets, and had in fact the prerogatives of both a merchant and a government. Eventually it ruled India, until the end of its charter in 1858. The expanding British trade with China was based on India, where the commercial spirit remained dominant in the Company's activities. When the British public developed a great demand for China teas, England, India, and China soon became joined in a triangular trade. And so the revenue of British India began to depend partly on commerce at Canton.

A British factory or trading post was established at Canton in 1699. During the next sixty years the Anglo-Chinese trade gradually became institutionalized into what we may call the Canton system. In this evolution, the British finally concentrated all their business at Canton, and their export trade came to center on teas and silks. During the eighteenth century, the tea trade became a great vested interest which stimulated further developments—the British effort to monopolize it for profit at home and to finance it abroad through trade from India to China, and the Ch'ing effort to regulate it at Canton and profit from it at Peking.

On the Chinese side, maritime trade increased so greatly during the Ch'ing period that it outgrew the framework of the tribute system. The European trade at Canton was only one of the two great commercial interests that expanded outside the system—the other was the trade of Chinese merchants with Southeast Asia. These Chinese traders had actually led the way in expanding beyond the tribute system and the Westerners merely moved into channels they had created. In this Chinese "junk" trade (as the Europeans called it, "junk" being a Malay word for "ship"), the Chinese vessels compared in size with their European counterparts and far outnumbered them. The biggest junks might be of 1000 tons burden, carrying a crew of 180 men. An average-sized junk of 150 tons, high-sterned, with lateen sails held out by battens to take a following wind, could make six or even eight knots, which compared well with the East Indiamen. Hundreds if not thousands of these sturdy merchantmen plied annually between Amoy or Canton and the Straits of Malacca, south in winter and north in summer. They followed detailed sailing directions through numerous ports of call. Since this trade with Southeast Asia was carried in Chinese vessels, it could not be regulated under the old forms of tribute. Instead, the Ch'ing officials used a traditional device. They appointed merchant firms (*hang,* anglicized as "hong"; see page 135) to be licensed brokers responsible for the conduct of the trade.

In a similar way the Chinese merchants that handled Canton's trade with the Europeans gradually became organized into a merchant guild called by Westerners the Cohong (from *kung-hang,* meaning "officially author-ized merchants"). It consisted of half-a-dozen to a dozen firms who were given a monopoly of the Western trade. This was the same type of regula-tory mechanism used for trade within China—a guild monopoly, licensed by and responsible to the officials, with little room left for free private enterprise. In charge of taxing the foreign trade at Canton was a high officer specially deputed from the Imperial Household Department at Peking, whom the foreigners called the "Hoppo." The Chinese merchant firms or hong merchants paid large fees to the Hoppo and bore responsibility for the foreign ships and traders. Every ship entering Canton was guaranteed or "secured" by one of them acting as its "security merchant." On the foreign side, the British East India Company's Canton committee took responsibility for all British vessels and persons. In this way by 1760 the British and other European trade was brought under Chinese control.

The foreign merchants were restricted by numerous regulations (not to bring in foreign wives, not to ride in sedan chairs, etc.). They were kept outside the city walls of Canton, confined to the riverbank area known as the "Thirteen Factories," that is, the establishments of foreign business agents or "factors." Their trade was legally confined to the Cohong. Mean-while, all foreigners remained subject to the procedures of Chinese criminal law, which gave the individual few civil rights and might subject him to arbitrary imprisonment and torture.

The picturesque life and trade at Canton became a legend. For the young Western trader ensconced in the Thirteen Factories, there was the prospect of large profits in exotic surroundings and occasional contact with famous hong merchants. The concentration on trade made it hardly necessary to speak more than pidgin (i.e., "business") English, a lingua franca using a limited number of foreign words in Chinese word order, which can still be heard in Hong Kong. The young men quickly made fortunes, if they did not die of the ague, but they learned little of Chinese culture. Anglo-Chinese relations at Canton were relatively easy, handled by a trading company, not a sovereign government, without raising the question of equality between sovereign states.

Canton had thus been drawn into world trade, though the Chinese Em-pire remained intellectually unaware of it and politically cut off. Breaking down the traditional Chinese indifference to trade expansion seemed less urgent to the East India Company, conservatively intent on current profits, than to government leaders seeking outlets for British manufactures. Al-ready free trade was being advocated in place of mercantilism, East or West. In 1784 enterprising young Americans began to compete at Canton. Private traders were agitating for access to the Indian market and abolition of the Company's monopoly. This was the background of the Macartney embassy of 1793.

Though paid for by the East India Company, this embassy came from the King of England in a ship of war to Tientsin. Macartney asked for permission to trade at Ningpo, Tientsin, and other northern places, access to one or more island depots where British goods might be stored and ships refitted, and a regular printed tariff instead of the Chinese system of personal presents or "squeeze" in addition to more formal fees. From the beginning, the embassy struck the problem of fitting into the tribute system. It brought magnificent presents which the Chinese officials labeled "tribute presents." They also urged Macartney to practice the kowtow, which he stoutly refused to do. The emperor issued an edict commending King George III for his "respectful spirit of submission" but pointing out that "our celestial empire possesses all things in prolific abundance." From this direct contact the British gained some knowledge of China but no change in the Canton system. The dogma of tribute was confirmed in the Chinese records. A Dutch embassy of 1795 reinforced this idea, for the Dutch envoys found themselves lined up with those of the outlying dominions at the Chinese New Year, and performed the kowtow on numerous occasions.

Behind the failure of the Macartney embassy lay the vested interests of the merchants and officials at Canton. So strong was this interest and so cautious did the Company become in its last years that the Canton system continued unchanged by any diplomatic effort. The Amherst embassy in 1816 was less well prepared than Macartney's and had the misfortune of arriving just as the British were fighting with Nepal, a Chinese tributary. Amherst when he reached Peking was misrepresented by his Chinese escorts and querulously ordered away by the emperor without an audience.

By the second quarter of the nineteenth century, when European expansion was about to take on a new and overwhelming vigor, the West had no more contact with Peking than in the seventeenth century. The Ch'ing rulers, inheritors of China's imperial tradition, had perfected their institutions of domestic control and had stabilized their relations with non-Chinese in Ili, at Lhasa, at Kiakhta, and at Canton. Europe and even North America had achieved contact with China, but the first three centuries of this contact had been successfully contained. The Chinese way of life remained essentially undisturbed.

10. Vietnam: A Variant of the Chinese Pattern

The Sphere of Chinese Civilization

Where Europe's seas and peninsulas led outward in many directions, making for diversity and expansion, the huge mass of China remained for the most part landlocked and self-contained. For many reasons China's maritime expansion was rather limited and late in comparison with that of the Europeans. Until recent times China's major foreign contacts were made largely by land, and only the immediate continental borderlands seemed to the Chinese of much importance.

To the north and west of China the steppes and deserts of Mongolia and Turkestan and the cold, dry plateau of Tibet supported a life of pastoral nomadism fundamentally different from the intensive agriculture of China. The Mongolian, Turkish, Manchu, and Tibetan tongues were quite unlike Chinese and could not be written in Chinese characters. Inner Asia was thus culturally unassimilable although strategically unavoidable, a constant factor on the fringe of Chinese life. This produced a symbiotic relationship in which the nomad tribes were marginal participants in the Chinese economy and polity. Only those limited parts of the north and west where a Chinese type of agriculture was possible were eventually filled with Chinese immigrants and fully incorporated into the Chinese society. This happened over the centuries in the great central plain of Manchuria, the better watered parts of Inner Mongolia, the eastern valleys of the Tibetan highland, and some of the oases of Chinese Turkestan.

The situation to the south of ancient China was quite different. Here there was no climatic barrier to the spread of intensive agriculture and

Chinese patterns of life. The peoples of the Yangtze Valley and of the South China lowland or plains areas, who were linguistically and culturally related to the ancient Chinese, were fully absorbed into the Chinese Empire at an early date. Only in Vietnam did China's cultural influence eventually extend beyond her political control. The Vietnamese language is probably related to Chinese, the literate culture of the country is largely of Chinese origin, and the land was for long periods under Chinese rule, but despite these facts the Vietnamese since the tenth century have remained politically distinct from China, even while assiduously copying Chinese models.

The other lands of Southeast Asia beyond Vietnam were never absorbed into the East Asian cultural sphere, but derived much of their civilization from Hindu and Buddhist India. One of the mysteries of early East Asian history is why the Chinese did not take greater advantage of the monsoon winds of the South China Sea to transport their influence into Southeast Asia. These seasonal winds, blowing north in July and south in January, facilitated the early European trade after 1500 and had always been available to take Chinese shipping to the straits of Malacca or Java and bring it back. Yet the historical record shows that sea trade between South and Southeast Asia—from the east coast of India across the Bay of Bengal, and later from the west coast of India and the Persian Gulf all the way across the Indian Ocean to the Spice Islands—very early became and steadily remained more important than the sea trade down to Southeast Asia from China. By the first century A.D. this Indian Ocean trade was already sizable and was known to the Chinese, yet they became only marginal participants in it.

It seems plain that the early Chinese were not interested in long-distance maritime trading or expansion overseas. The Indian commercial and religious influences which were present in Southeast Asia in the early centuries A.D. were later supplemented or supplanted by the Islamic diaspora and Arab trade, which made Indonesia and Malaya largely Muslim. Portuguese, Dutch, and British colonialism followed in succession after 1500. Throughout these many centuries traders, missionaries, and advisers came to Southeast Asia from India and the Arab world, and eventually from the maritime nations of Europe—all of which were farther from the Southeast Asian scene than China. There could be no more striking demonstration of the Chinese impulse to stay at home at the center of civilization in the Middle Kingdom. Despite the recent emigration of great numbers of Chinese to all the countries of Southeast Asia, their settlements have remained cultural islands in essentially alien civilizations, except in the city-state of Singapore where the Chinese population predominates.

To the east of China, the development of Korea was closely parallel to that of Vietnam. It too derived its higher civilization (writing system, Confucian learning, political institutions, major art forms, etc.) from China and was at times under Chinese rule. But it was geographically more separate from China than was Vietnam, and its Altaic language, which differed radically from Chinese, provided a strong linguistic barrier. Like the Vietnamese, the Koreans usually acknowledged Chinese suzerainty and closely modeled their political and social institutions after those of China, but they retained a clear sense of separate identity.

Beyond Korea to the east, the Japanese produced a still more distinctive variant of East Asian civilization. While their higher culture was virtually all of Chinese origin, their sense of separate identity was even more defined than that of the Vietnamese or Koreans. Strong linguistic barriers separated the Japanese from the Chinese, and thanks to their isolated island position, they were never conquered by China. While the Japanese also on occasion recognized a vague Chinese suzerainty and attempted to model their institutions after those of China, the civilization they developed showed a much weaker Chinese imprint and came to contrast sharply with that of China in many of its basic patterns.

A comparative study of the four national subunits that exist in East Asian civilization—China, Vietnam, Korea, and Japan—can be as revealing as a study of the much more numerous Western national entities. Certain common traits set them off from other civilizations and particularly from their neighbors in South Asia. At the same time, the four are probably more unlike one another than are the various national subunits of the West in such basic matters as cuisine, dress, domestic architecture and living arrangements. They also represent three clearly different types of historical development and institutional structure. One is that of China itself—the great central and largely self-developed unit. The next is represented by Vietnam and Korea, where Chinese political and social patterns were faithfully applied to much smaller units in somewhat different geographic and cultural settings, resulting in significant parallels and contrasts with China. The third type is Japan, where the higher civilization of China was adopted wholesale but at a distance which prevented continuous contact and in a setting so different that the outcome was often radically distinct from what existed in China.

Early Development of Vietnam

From prehistoric times men had undoubtedly made their way from one river valley settlement to another along the coasts of southern Asia, just as they did from one oasis or grassland to another across Inner Asia, leaving only a fragmentary record. Thus the "Scythian," "Sino-Siberian," or "animal" style of metal work, found all across the Eurasian steppe from the lower Volga to the Amur (see pages 38, 156), seems to have been present along with Chinese influence in the early Dong-Son culture, named for a bronze-

*Bronze sculpture of a warrior
from Dong-Son.*

age site in North Vietnam. Other sites of this period have recently been
found not far to the west in Thailand. If we trace the Vietnamese people
back to this bronze-age culture, we place them among the Mongoloid
peoples who in prehistoric times migrated from South China into the Southeast Asian peninsula. The Vietnamese spoken language with its use of tones
has affinities to the monosyllabic, tonal Thai group of languages but also

has many elements of Mon-Khmer (Cambodian) mixed in. Like the Burmese and the Thai, the Vietnamese originated in the north and expanded southward; but of the three peoples, they received the most from China and the least from India.

The rich Tongking rice-bowl of the Red River delta around Hanoi is the heart of North Vietnam. It is separated from South China by low mountains and jungle, which form a not impassable but well-defined barrier. Chinese control was first extended to this region in the period of China's earliest unification, near the end of the third century B.C. The Chinese then called it Nam-viet, or, in Mandarin Chinese, Nan-yüeh, "South Yüeh," a name long associated with the southern frontier of China's culture. A Chinese type of rice culture and bureaucratic administration could be set up more easily in the regions around modern Canton and Hanoi, on the watered plains of river deltas, than in the mountain regions of South China, which were at first bypassed in the southward extension of Chinese power. During most of the second century down to 111 B.C., North Vietnam was under a secessionist Chinese state, called Nan-yüeh, centered at Canton.

The Han annexation of this state in 111 B.C. firmly established over the North Vietnam region a Chinese government under three commanderies, equipped with the Chinese writing system, Confucian classical studies, and a Chinese officialdom, all of which overlay the indigenous culture of the villages. This Chinese conquest of North Vietnam in the second century B.C. had two important results. The Red River delta became the first region in Southeast Asia to support a densely populated, centralized society based on rice culture. Where the earlier economy of hunting, fishing, and primitive slash-and-burn or hoe agriculture had produced little surplus, intensive rice culture with the metal plow and draft animals now raised living standards and supported an urban culture. Second, the Chinese Empire actually incorporated North Vietnam for a full millennium (111 B.C.–939 A.D.). But this expansion of Chinese society was a matter of military-administrative absorption by land. It did not use the sea and reach the rest of Southeast Asia.

Thus a Chinese type of administration and indeed most of the literate culture of ancient China spread over the North Vietnam area—much as it spread over South China—building up the agrarian-based civilization of the irrigated plains but leaving the highland peoples of the mountain fringes relatively untouched. For fully a thousand years the two delta regions of Canton and Tongking, north and south of the low mountain barrier, remained the southernmost part of the Chinese empire.

Vietnam's Position on a Cultural Boundary. Although Vietnam's higher culture and politics bore the Chinese imprint, the life of the people had traits in common with other parts of Southeast Asia. From prehistoric times

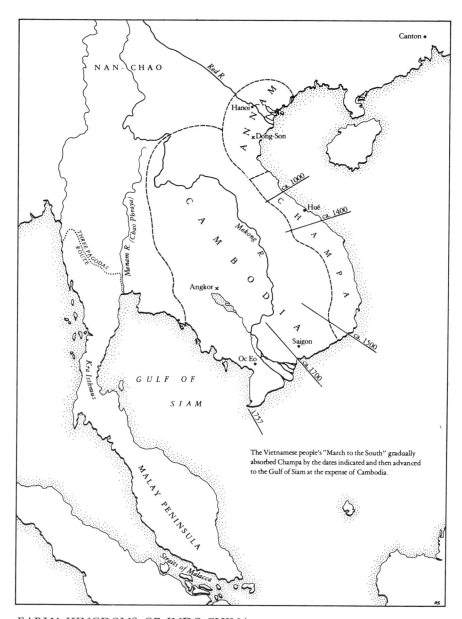

EARLY KINGDOMS OF INDO-CHINA

the Southeast Asian style of life was differentiated from that of India and China. While its technology, which included irrigated rice culture, the use of the ox, water buffalo, and elephant, metal working, and skill in seafaring, overlapped with that of India or China or both, its social customs were more distinctive, including chewing betel nut, tatooing, and totemism, and its social structure gave high status to women. Other cultural traits in bewildering variety were imported and superimposed on the original pattern.

Cultural imports in Vietnam came largely from China, but almost every-where in continental Southeast Asia—especially in Burma, Siam, and Cam-bodia—Indian influences came to predominate in law, politics, and religion. Thus the Vietnamese lived on a cultural boundary and their sense of identity with and eventually of separateness from China was continually nourished by their contact with peoples on the south and west who fell outside the sphere of Chinese civilization.

This contact was first of all with the highland peoples, later called by the French "montagnards," who were thinly spread among the mountains that encircle the Tongking basin and closely parallel the southern coastal strip of North Vietnam. Living in the comparative poverty of a slash-and-burn, dry rice agriculture, these upland peoples remained linguistically sepa-rate, unassimilated, and outside the literate and urban-centered culture of the lowlands. They were a modest source of trade, and unlike the horsemen of the Mongolian grasslands, they remained in their village communities, too isolated and fragmented to be a military problem except when invaded. Rulers in Vietnam usually tried to bring them into nominal tributary relations.

The Indianized kingdom of Champa situated on the coast of South Viet-nam was a recurrent military problem throughout Vietnamese history down to at least the fifteenth century. The Chams were a seafaring people with linguistic and other ties to Indonesia. Their kingdom remained decentralized in small coastal enclaves, and specialized both in maritime trade and in the piracy that flourished with it. Champa over the centuries was repeatedly em-broiled with Vietnam and was gradually absorbed by Vietnamese expansion from the north. This warfare on the expanding southern frontier was a constant motif in Vietnamese history.

In the four centuries of disunity between the collapse of the Han Empire in 220 A.D. and the Sui and T'ang reunification of China completed in 618, North Vietnam experienced civil warfare, much as did the rest of China. But where North China suffered the actual invasion of Inner Asian tribes-men, North Vietnam on the opposite frontier of the empire was mainly influenced by trade and religion coming from India. The early trade route between the Roman Empire and India had now been extended eastward across the Indian Ocean to Malaya, where goods were transshipped across the narrow waist of the peninsula and entered channels of sea trade between Sumatra, Java, Champa, and other areas in Southeast Asia. Buddhist monks and pilgrims, both Chinese and Indian, traversed these routes, bringing a knowledge of Sanskrit and Indian ideas of law and government, as well as religion.

Under the vigorous imperial government of the T'ang (618–907), the Red River delta and the coastal strip of North Vietnam down to about the seventeenth parallel, were ruled by a Chinese bureaucracy under the protectorate general of An-nan ("the pacified south," locally pronounced Annam). In addition to the political features of imperial Confucianism—classical studies, the examination system, the official orthodoxy—North Vietnam was also profoundly influenced by the Mahayana form of Buddhism then flourishing in the rest of China, Korea, and Japan. This was still another factor differentiating this southernmost extension of East Asian civilization from the rest of Southeast Asia, including Cambodia and Laos, where the Theravada (Hinayana) form of Buddhism eventually came to predominate. The Mahayana offered the believer a broader interpretation of the Buddha's teachings, many Bodhisattvas to worship, and greater opportunities for laymen and women to participate in the religious community. These and other features gave it more widespread appeal than Theravada Buddhism. On the other hand, under the Chinese system of state supervision of religion, Buddhism in Vietnam as in China eventually came under government supervision and control. In Vietnam even more than in China it was assimilated with Taoism and Confucianism into a compound which the Vietnamese called the "three religions." In contrast to practices in Theravada lands, the Mahayana priesthood in Vietnam was less sharply separated from the rest of society, monasticism was less powerfully developed, and an integrated, countrywide network of temples and monasteries was not allowed to grow up and gain power independent of the state. Thus confined and dominated, Buddhism played less of a role in Vietnamese society than it did in Burma, Thailand, and Cambodia.

On this cultural frontier where so many influences met, distinctive styles of Vietnamese art and architecture appeared in the stupas, pagodas, and stone reliefs of religious monuments. These styles reflected a synthesis of influences from Central Asia by way of China and from India and Indonesia by way of the sea route and Champa. For example, contact was maintained over the sea trade route with the Buddhist center at Srivijaya in Sumatra.

Independence from China.   By the close of the T'ang era, a local Vietnamese upper class with a strong sense of national identity had grown up under the framework of Chinese imperial government. The disorders in South China that accompanied the long decline of T'ang central power finally resulted in the independence of Vietnam as a state in 939. Chinese rule was occasionally reimposed thereafter, but never for very long. Instead of direct Chinese rule, tributary status became the norm. This had also happened in North Korea after the period of direct Chinese rule there (108 B.C.–313 A.D.), but our picture of Vietnam's social development is not yet so clear as that of Korea (see Chapter 11).

The principal hero to emerge in this period of Vietnamese history was Dinh Bo Linh, who unified the country and took the title of emperor in

968, overcoming the fragmentation of local family regimes. He soon enrolled as a tributary of the new Sung dynasty in China, and his militant
successors intermittently attacked Champa on the south and defended themselves against occasional incursions from the north. In this warlike era the
Buddhist clergy sustained the arts of peace. Their pagodas served as centers
of learning and welfare as well as devotion.

The new Vietnamese state was chiefly constructed during the later Li
dynasty (1010–1225), the fourth of the fifteen dynasties usually distinguished during the whole of Vietnamese history (see chart). For two centuries it maintained a unified Chinese-type regime based on the Red River
delta, where centrally managed irrigation and diking were needed equally
against winter drought and summer floods. Its salaried bureaucracy was
recruited in Chinese style through an examination system.

The Tran dynasty which followed (1225–1400) had to defend itself
against Mongol invasions from China. The Mongols not only took over
Southwest China, speeding up the migration of the Thai people from the
medieval kingdom of Nan-chao in Yunnan into present-day Thailand, but
also sent several expeditions into Southeast Asia after their final conquest
of Sung China in 1279. Among other things, they invaded Champa in 1283
and Vietnam in 1257, 1285, and 1287, but with only transitory success,
although on the west they conquered and ruled part of North and Central
Burma until 1303. The Mongols seized Hanoi three times, but each time
they were obliged to withdraw and accept tribute instead of ruling over
Vietnam—a pattern that continued under the Ming and Ch'ing.

In the late fourteenth century when the first Ming ruler was renovating
the tribute system, Hanoi was under attack from Champa, and by 1400 the
Vietnamese Tran dynasty had fallen to a usurper. The Ming emperor
Yung-lo, vigorously expansionist, decided to intervene, restore order, and
make Vietnam a province of China again. His armies conquered Hanoi
easily enough in 1406, but Chinese imperial rule was shakily based on a
bureaucracy staffed with many Chinese who had failed elsewhere and with
Vietnamese who remained patriots at heart. Supplies for the Ming occupation force and contact with it also proved costly and inadequate. A varied
and vigorous program of sinicization in government, education, and religion
was accompanied by rapacious economic exploitation. In 1418 a Vietnamese
war for independence broke out and harassed the Chinese regime with increasing effect. By 1427 the new emperor at Peking was disillusioned with
Vietnam and tired of the military cost. He evacuated 86,000 troops and
officials and accepted again the old tributary relationship.

The leader of the Vietnamese resistance, Le Loi, set up the Later Le
dynasty (1428–1789). His dynasty proved to be unusually long-lived by
Chinese standards and in time showed a corresponding degree of political
decay. It regularly sent tribute to Peking, but being much farther away than

PRINCIPLE REGIMES IN VIETNAM

Regime	Capital	Period
Later Li Dynasty	Hanoi	1010–1225
Tran Dynasty	Hanoi	1225–1400
Later Le Dynasty	Hanoi	1428–1789
Mac Dynasty (in Tongking)	Hanoi	1527–1592
	Cao-Bang	1592–1677
Trinh Family of Tongking	Hanoi	1539–1787
	(from 1592)	
Nguyen Family of Hué	Hué	1558–1777
Tay-son Rulers	Saigon	
	Hué	
	Hanoi	1788–1802
Nguyen Dynasty	Hué	1802–1945

was Korea, it could assert a greater degree of autonomy: "We have our own mountains and rivers," Le Loi said, "our own customs and traditions." Vietnam, unlike Korea, called itself "great" (Dai Viet) like a Chinese dynasty and its ruler an "emperor" like the emperor of China. (When sending tribute to China, however, the Vietnamese ruler prudently called himself "king.") Throughout its history moreover, Vietnam was constantly expanding to the south, as Korea could not, and so continually incorporated new non-Chinese influences. A detailed comparison with Korea would probably reveal more differences than similarities.

Growth of the Vietnamese State. The strongest emperor of the Later Le dynasty, Le Thanh-ton ("Sage Ancestor," 1460–1497), with his capital at Hanoi, built his central administration on the T'ang-Ming model in great detail. He divided the empire into 13 provinces or "circuits," subdivided into 52 prefectures, 178 counties, and 50 departments. He held triennial examinations and had nine ranks of civil and military officials, each rank subdivided. Triennially they officially registered the population and revised the tax quotas. The emperor planted military colonies on the expanding southern frontier. He promulgated a code of penal and civil administrative laws, and also a moral code in twenty-four articles or precepts to be read periodically and explained in every village. From the patronage of letters and virtue at the capital to the maintenance of welfare and public works in the provinces, the whole government was modeled on that of China, with dynastic chronicles and other compilations written in Chinese. Like the founder of the Ming, Le Thanh-ton asserted the power of the monarch by getting rid of an oligarchy of entrenched high officials and imperial councilors and strengthening instead the bureaucratic processes of the government. The high degree of similarity between the recorded Vietnamese and Chinese systems of state-and-culture underlines the interesting but as-yet-unanswered question of how much the two societies differed in substance, behind the official façade of Chinese structures and terminology.

One important difference sprang from the fact that the Vietnamese imitation of the Chinese central government was imposed not on an empire but on an area the size of a Chinese province. As a result, the Vietnamese government tended to be overstaffed and many offices withered into mere sinecures. Moreover, since the official structure and regulations were borrowed, it was less easy to change them; the mandarinate was even more conservative than in China and many archaic terms and forms, long since discarded by the Chinese, were still retained. In addition, the borrowing of China's higher culture, literature, dress, and code of conduct set the China-oriented Vietnamese ruling class more starkly apart from its own people with their tropical Southeast Asian life style. Features of the earlier Vietnamese culture, like the higher status of women—for example, the greater rights of wives and daughters to inherit and hold property—found expression in legal codes because these customs were still alive among the people.

Vietnam's continual southward expansion was stimulated by the piratical raids of Champa, whose seafaring people had suffered repeated invasions from both Vietnam and Cambodia and had repeatedly struck back. Some fourteen dynasties had ruled Champa from the second century A.D. to 1471. They had usually enrolled as tributaries of China and often sought Chinese help against their neighbors. Meantime the Vietnamese, expanding their rule southward along the narrow strip of arable coastal land, had also suffered many vicissitudes in periodic wars with Champa. But by the fourteenth century they had acquired Hué, and in 1471 they finally conquered Champa, except for a vestigial remnant which survived in the far south till 1720. (See map, page 263.)

Unfortunately, the peculiarly elongated, narrow waist of this new and greater Vietnam, where the mountains came down close to the coast, made unity difficult to maintain and dissidence easy to defend. Though the Later Le dynasty reigned from 1428 to 1789, under it the actual ruling power became fragmented. The Mac family ruled as a dynasty in North Vietnam (also called Tongking, the "eastern capital" area) from 1527 to 1592 and were recognized by China. Later under the powerless Later Le dynasty, which China continued to recognize south of Tongking, power was divided between two great ruling families: there was a long civil war from 1620 to 1674 between the Trinh family (1539–1787) in the north based at Hanoi and the Nguyen family (1558–1777) in the south-central region based at Hué. The latter blocked the narrow coastal corridor with two great walls north of Hué on about the seventeenth parallel. Stalemated in civil war by 1674, the two family regimes continued to rule separate governments for another century, setting a long precedent for the political division of Vietnam between northern and southern regimes. The Nguyen family regime continued to press south in conflict with Cambodia, taking over border regions which Vietnamese settlers had infiltrated. It added two provinces in the Saigon area by 1700 and two more in the southern tip of the peninsula by 1750, opening up the whole Mekong delta region.

Both the northern (Trinh) and the southern (Nguyen) family regimes were headed by "princes" who professed continued loyalty to the "emperor" (Vietnamese: *hoang-de;* Chinese: *huang-ti*) of the Later Le dynasty. Both governments built up their administrations in the Chinese style, classifying landholdings for tax purposes according to productivity, registering the populace, conscripting a territorial army, encouraging cultivation, setting tax quotas, regulating the salt trade and mining, printing the Confucian Classics, and selecting officials by an examination system. Each provincial administration was under a governor, treasurer, and judge. The northern regime, more firmly in the Chinese tradition, led the way in producing its own histories in Chinese, while banning the import of books from China, and also in producing poetry in the rather cumbersome native writing system known as *nom* or *chu nom.* This was a system of transcribing spoken Vietnamese with Chinese-like characters created for the purpose, usually by combining a Chinese character that had phonetic value with one that had signific value so as to make one Vietnamese character—much as many Inner Asian neighbors of China had attempted to do in the past, with indifferent success (see table of scripts on page 161.)

The seventeen thousand or so villages that comprised early modern Vietnam retained an ancient ideal of village-owned, communal property. Local leadership was in the hands of the village council of notables, a continuing but informal elite who owed their position by common consensus to family headship, wealth as landlords, achievement in the examinations, or personal qualities. The village council assigned the use of the communal lands (usually less than a fifth of the total in use) to needy and deserving persons. The councils also generally chose the village chiefs, though they then had to be appointed by the court. Tax collection and the other activities of the village chiefs thus depended on the consent of the local elite. At the wider provincial level, the loyal orientation of these ruling-class elements toward the court was equally essential to maintain the stability of dynastic rule. The inveterate tendency on their part to acquire larger and larger private landed estates signaled trouble, as in China, both for the common villagers below and for the central government above.

There were many basic differences between the Vietnamese and Chinese cultures, in spoken language, ethnic origins, folklore, and customs; but the Chinese-style family system and elitist government were vigorously and profitably maintained by the Vietnamese ruling class. Vietnam's social prob-

金石奇緣 第一回

VIETNAMESE CHU NOM WRITING. *Characters of Vietnamese invention are interspersed with Chinese characters, which however may have non-Chinese meanings and be used for sound only. (From the drama, "The Marvelous Union of Gold and Jade.")*

lems were also reminiscent of China's: overtaxed and overconscripted peasants might desert their villages in desperation; local leaders might build up regional power against the central government. While the state cult of Confucius tended to become stereotyped in Vietnam, there was a revival of Buddhism in the seventeenth and eighteenth centuries, nourished from China but expressed in new syncretic Vietnamese sects, for religious life in Vietnam tended toward syncretism even more than in China.

The Chinese Pattern Challenged and Reaffirmed

Western Contact. Until the mid-nineteenth century Vietnam's relations with Europeans were only of peripheral concern. They began in the sixteenth century when Portuguese traders came to buy raw silk at Vietnamese ports frequented by Japanese and Chinese merchants. The Portuguese were

followed by Jesuits who, barred from Japan, arrived in 1615. Though proscribed by the Trinh rulers in the north, the missionaries maintained
precarious relations with the Nguyen in the south, who were then more
interested in Western trade and arms. Christian converts were occasionally
massacred and missionaries persecuted. But the Christian community came
to play a role in politics, and the missionaries at times were influential, both
at court through their medical and scientific abilities and among the populace as occasional supporters of rebellion.

Like their confreres in China, the Jesuits in Vietnam began to write down
the sounds of the spoken language in the Latin alphabet. This romanized
system of writing, called *quoc-ngu* (corresponding to the Chinese characters
kuo-yü, "the national language"), eventually became the modern form of
written Vietnamese. It won out over the earlier, cumbersome *chu nom*
system. However, while a vernacular literature began to be produced in
the romanized *quoc-ngu,* Chinese writing in characters continued in use for
official and scholarly purposes until the early twentieth century.

The ambitious French support of Catholic missions through the Société
des Missions Etrangères after 1658 was inspired by the celebrated French
Jesuit pioneer, Alexandre de Rhodes, who had inaugurated a mission to
North Vietnam in 1627 and later printed Christian works in *quoc-ngu.*
The French Society was harassed by local persecutions and the jealousy of
other Christian powers and societies, but it persevered in the Nguyen territories in the south and created a tradition of French interest in Vietnam.
The French East India Company also tried to develop trade there, although
both Dutch and British efforts during the seventeenth century had ended in
failure. Against this background of continual effort and small success,
French missionaries met a great opportunity in the late eighteenth century.

The Tay-son Rebellion.   In 1771 there began a widespread peasant rising,
the significance of which is only beginning to be appraised. It was led by
three brothers, who had the surname Nguyen, like so many other Vietnamese, but who are generally called Tay-son from the name of a place on the
plateau south of Hué. They took the Saigon area by 1778 and Hué and
Hanoi in 1786, thus ending the local rule of the Nguyen and Trinh families. The Tay-son brothers divided the country into three parts, south,
center, and north. Since the ruler of the moribund Le dynasty had sought
Chinese help against the rebellion, a Chinese expeditionary force invaded
North Vietnam in 1788 ostensibly to restore the Le claimant to his throne.
To counter this invasion, the northern and most gifted of the Tay-son
brothers was proclaimed the Quang-trung emperor in 1788. The Ch'ing
army, after it took Hanoi, was attacked and driven out within a fortnight,
whereupon the new emperor at once sent envoys to Peking to secure recognition as a tributary in the traditional fashion.

Quang-trung reigned vigorously from 1788 until his death at forty in 1792. Being one of the first Vietnamese rulers to assume power as the peasant leader of a peasant uprising, he was inclined to innovate rather than simply imitate the Chinese model. For example, he tried to give his revolutionary army a dominant role in Vietnamese politics at the expense of the Chinese-type civil service. He went further and tried to abolish the use of classical Chinese at his court and even created a special government office to translate the Chinese Classics into *chu nom*. While sending tribute to Peking, he simultaneously fostered piratical raids on South China. The Tay-son rebellion and the regime that briefly came out of it foreshadowed a new national spirit, antitraditional and antiforeign (in particular, anti-Chinese). In some ways the Tay-son movement was comparable to the Taiping rebellion of the 1850's in China. Similarly, it lacked staying power and succumbed to a revival of traditional forces which found Western support.

The young Nguyen Anh, the surviving heir of the Nguyen family, which had been violently thrown out of power in 1777, joined forces with a priest of the French Society named Pigneau de Behaine. Though with different ambitions, the priest and the young pretender were refugees together. In 1787 Pigneau, with Nguyen Anh's small son, got to Versailles and proposed to Louis XVI that France should put Nguyen Anh back in power. In the latter's name he hopefully concluded a treaty of alliance between France and Cochin China (the French name for South Vietnam) and succeeded without much official help in raising enough support to send ships in 1789 with a few hundred volunteer troops and supplies from the French foothold of Pondichery in India. This French assistance proved of strategic value in consolidating Nguyen Anh's power at Saigon, which he had just recaptured. The French volunteers trained his army and navy and built forts on the best French (Vauban) design, while Pigneau handled his foreign relations.

With continued hard fighting, Nguyen Anh eventually took both Hué and Hanoi, and in 1802 proclaimed himself Emperor Gia-long of a unified Vietnam, thereby founding the Nguyen dynasty which lasted until 1945. This was the first time that the Mekong delta region of the south (Cochin China) had been included in a regime ruling the center and north also. The capital was moved from ancient Hanoi to Hué. In the preceding two centuries or more of civil war and division, regional administration had developed in each half of the country, but the symbolic fiction of unity under the Later Le dynasty had never been abandoned. Now that the whole area of modern Vietnam was unified, its government could be reconstructed and strengthened.

Gia-long at first showed some interest in Westernization, with the help of some four hundred French comrades-in-arms who had supported his reunification of the country. In fact, several Frenchmen became high mandarins in Vietnam. But France under Napoleon was too preoccupied in

Europe to exploit this opportunity for closer relations, and the Nguyen rulers were too patriotic and preoccupied with local problems to show much interest in Europe.

Persistence of the Chinese Pattern. The new dynasty, though on the threshold of greater contact with the West, sought to strengthen itself by putting traditional ideals into practice. Somewhat in the manner of a classic Chinese "restoration," it sedulously modeled its government upon the institutions of China in the heyday of the Ming and Ch'ing. Both Gia-long (1802–1820) and Minh-mang (1820–1841) were vigorous imitators of the Ch'ing and copied much of the formal structure and official terminology of the contemporary government at Peking. Though protected by an imposing citadel with twenty-four bastions designed in the European fashion, the capital Hué was principally a small replica of Peking, the walled palace or Forbidden City, lying within the walls of an imperial city, which was within the walls of the capital city as a whole. There were Six Ministries, a Hanlin Academy, and a Censorate, which had the same statutory functions and even the same names in Chinese characters as their Chinese counterparts. The emperor ruled from among the harem and eunuchs of his inner court in the palace, which transmitted orders to the "outer court" or heads of the bureaucracy at the capital. The thirty-one provinces in the three major regions of North, Central, and South Vietnam were subdivided territorially into a hierarchy of subunits much as in China. Many features of Chinese administration were carefully copied—tax collections twice a year, five-year census registrations, *corveé* labor, public granaries, allowances added to salaries to "keep integrity," even the demoralizing sale of offices. Gia-long's law code of 1812 was copied exactly from that of the Ch'ing. Emperor Minh-mang further strengthened his central government in 1839 by making his officials dependent solely upon stipends, instead of on personal income from village lands formerly allotted them. He also built up the old Mandarin Road from the Chinese border to Saigon. Over it the imperial post carried examination candidates, officials, and communications from stage to stage for some 750 miles.

Chinese influence was transmitted to Vietnam partly through a special group of descendants of Ming loyalist refugees who had fled southward during the Manchu conquest of China in the seventeenth century and had been allowed to set up their own villages in Central and South Vietnam, separate from the local population. These "Ming incense" people (*Minh-huong,* those who kept alive the altar fires of the defunct dynasty) intermarried with the Vietnamese, and their sons often entered the official class. Unlike later immigrants who formed Overseas Chinese trading communities under their own headmen and were kept separate from Vietnamese life, some of the Ming loyalists' descendants became cultural middlemen, loyal to the court at Hué but able to represent it at Peking, where their mastery of the Chinese Classics and spoken language enabled them to keep abreast of Chinese institutional developments. These bicultural envoys to Peking gave their Vietnamese rulers day-by-day accounts of conditions in China and brought back important publications. Some emissaries were accepted at Peking as "tribute scholars" and maintained there at Chinese government expense for years like scholars from Liu-ch'iu, Korea, and other tributaries.

Aided by this channel of contact, Minh-mang sponsored a vigorous Confucian revival, which was naturally xenophobic toward the West. He instituted examinations for the *tien-si* degree (Chinese: *chin-shih,* metropolitan graduate) in 1822, and renamed the lower degrees to correspond with the current Chinese titles. Chinese classical studies were encouraged and large geographies and histories compiled. For the better coordination of his small replica of the Peking bureaucracy, he set up in 1829–1830 a Grand Secretariat (*noi cac;* the Chinese *nei-ko*) such as China had developed in the early Ming. In 1834–1835 he followed this up by creating a Privy Council (*co mat vien;* Chinese: *Chi-mi-yüan*) of high officials to handle military and other crises, much as the Yung-cheng emperor had done in 1729. Minh-mang emulated K'ang-hsi in putting out his own ten-point version of a *Sacred Edict* exhorting his subjects to respect the Confucian virtues and relationships. A vernacular poetry also flourished at his court as well as outside it, but this and the native Vietnamese art motifs and other Indian-influenced cultural elements all coexisted with a court ideology, bureaucratic structure, and ritual copied in detail from China.

In their foreign relations the early Nguyen dynasty rulers faced two ways. Toward China they continued to be enrolled as Ch'ing tributaries and between 1803 and 1853 sent some fourteen regular missions to Peking. But meantime toward local rulers within their own smaller area, they claimed to be Sons of Heaven themselves. The culturally alien Cambodians were called "barbarians." In addressing the weak rulers of Laos, the Nguyen court styled itself *trung quoc* (Chinese: *chung-kuo*), "the central country," borrowing the ancient Chinese term that became the modern name for China. Foreign tribute presents, foreign trade taxes and luxury goods were siphoned into an Imperial Household Department, which served as the court's private treasury, just as the Manchus had arranged at Peking.

The vigor of Minh-mang's "restoration" efforts at building up central power was an index of the troubles he faced domestically. These have not yet been thoroughly analyzed but several sources of weakness are evident. Small peasant risings were frequent. We may imagine that, as in China, population increase may have reduced living standards. Yet the conscription of labor for the imperial service was a basic element in the building of the new capital at Hué and in the maintenance of roads and water control in the provinces. The new southern provinces of the Saigon area, though less densely populated than the Hanoi region, saw a great economic gap between large landholders and a rootless and impoverished peasantry. In this frontier region, migration and land-grabbing had not been accompanied by an adequate extension of a trained officialdom and administrative regulations. At the same time the south, evidently backward in education, was very poorly represented in the examination system.

Being committed as a Confucian ruler to dominate ideology as well as organization, Minh-mang strictly controlled the numbers of the Buddhist priesthood, the award of ordination certificates to its novitiates, and the building of new temples and endowment of old ones. Thus controlled and patronized, the Buddhist establishment in Vietnam remained small in size and weak in influence, no rival to the government bureaucracy.

Roman Catholic Christianity, on the other hand, became a major threat to the Confucian monarchy. The French influence in Vietnam strongly supported it. Among both the missionaries and the French adventurers who had helped Gia-long were Catholic partisans who got into Vietnamese politics. Some missionaries supported the chief satrap of the Saigon region, Le Van Duyet, an opponent of Minh-mang who sought Western arms from them. By 1825, five years after his accession, the emperor was convinced that the Christian teaching demanded a loyalty incompatible with the Vietnamese state system, and he issued his first edict proscribing it as heterodox. There were already 300,000 or more Catholic converts in the small area of Vietnam, as many as there had ever been in all of China. When Christians were involved in a rebellion in 1833, the emperor began a program of suppression, including the imprisonment and execution of missionaries. This would eventually give French empire-seekers their *casus belli.* To counter the foreign religion ideologically, Minh-mang appointed local scholars to lecture on the Confucian teaching in areas most influenced by Christianity.

Despite these defensive efforts, Minh-mang was not a purblind xenophobe. Well before the time of the early Westernizer in Siam, King Mongkut (1851–1868), and far ahead of the Chinese and Koreans, he studied the West and tried to deal with the problems it presented. He bought Western steamships and in 1839 tried to build some. He argued against the prohibition of foreign trade on the grounds that it would ruin the Vietnamese sugar producers and prevent his country from learning about the West. As an acute observer of the Chinese scene, Minh-mang believed that the Chinese court had made a mistake in permitting the growth of the semiprivate vested interests in the Canton trade, and he favored a strict official control over foreign trade in Vietnam, which was naturally resented by the Europeans. By 1840 he observed that "at the Northern Court [i.e., Peking, Hué being the Southern Court] imperial princes and high officials all smoke opium.... If their own country is in such a state, how can they give laws to foreign countries?"

On the whole, Minh-mang seems to have known a good deal more about Europe than did the court at Peking. He persecuted Christianity only after he had personally read the Christian Bible in Chinese translation. In fact he tried in 1840 to send missions to Paris and London to work out some accommodation for Christianity, but the animosity of the Christian missionaries made them fruitless. Although the strongest of the Nguyen rulers, he could not avoid the basic conflict of cultures. A policy of resistance to foreign incursions was continued by his successors, Thieu-tri (reigned 1841–1847) and Tu-duc (reigned 1848–1883).

11. Early Korea: The Emergence of a Chinese Type of State

The Beginnings of Korean History

The Setting. Though dwarfed by China and only two-thirds the size of Vietnam, Korea is actually a country of average size and more than average population. One can emphasize its smallness by saying that it is scarcely larger than the single state of Minnesota, but it would be more meaningful to say that it is not much smaller than the combined areas of England, Scotland, and Wales. Its present population of close to 50 million is not much less than that of the traditional "great powers" of Western Europe.

The climate is much like that of North and Central China—hot and humid in summer but dry and very cold in winter. Nearly all of Korea is mountainous, and only a fifth of the land is suitable for cultivation. A big mountain barrier along the northern frontier effectively divides Korea from Manchuria, while a great north-and-south chain protrudes from these mountains southward along the east coast, forming the spiny backbone of the peninsula. The lower mountains, having been largely deforested, are relatively barren and jaggedly eroded masses of granite. The coastal strip on the east is narrow and has few good harbors, but the coastal plains on the west and south are much broader, producing the bulk of the rice crop on which the nation lives. The deeply indented coastlines on the west and south afford numerous harbors, though phenomenally high tides on the west coast complicate navigation.

The ancestors of the Koreans seem for the most part to have drifted into the peninsula from the north, and the movement of peoples from the Manchurian area into Korea continued well into historic times. The Koreans of today are physically much like the other Mongoloid peoples of Manchuria, North China, and Mongolia, being somewhat taller than the South Chinese and Japanese and having more prominent cheekbones. Their polysyllabic and highly inflected language also seems to tie them to the Altaic peoples of North Asia.

The archaeological record reveals two types of neolithic pottery: comb-marked pottery in coastal areas in the southwest, possibly showing water-borne influences from coastal China, and plain, reddish-brown pottery widely spread throughout the peninsula and clearly of overland provenance. Dolmens much like the megalithic chambers in Manchuria and Shantung (and further afield in Europe and Southeast Asia) are found throughout Korea, but are particularly numerous in the northwest, while a variant but probably derivative form exists in the south and finds echoes in western Japan, suggesting an outward flow of the dolmen culture from the continent.

The early Koreans were apparently tribal peoples who lived at first by fishing and hunting and then gradually turned to agriculture. Like the other early peoples of North Asia and Japan, they probably lived under hereditary aristocratic chieftains of a semireligious character. They stood in animistic awe of the phenomena of nature, considering them to possess spirits and believing that their own ancestors were totemic animals. They attempted to propitiate malevolent spirits through shamanistic mediums, who, as in ancient Japan, were usually women. Despite later overlays of Chinese civilization, female sorcerers (*mudang*) are still called upon in times of sickness and death.

The Chinese Colonies: Lo-lang.   The supposed founding of a Korean state in 2333 B.C. by Tan'gun, born of a union between the son of the divine creator and a female bear that had achieved human form, is, of course, pure mythology, as may also be the tradition that a scion of the Shang royal line of China, Kija (Ch'i-tzu in Chinese), fled to southern Manchuria where he founded the state of Chosŏn in 1122 B.C. But this latter tradition does reflect the gradual flow of cultural influences from China into Manchuria and Korea during the first millennium B.C. Agriculture and some knowledge of bronze and later iron seeped into Korea during this period, along with fresh waves of people pushed from Manchuria by the expanding power both of the Hsiung-nu and the Chinese. By the early third century B.C. the North China state of Yen seems to have exercised some control or influence over northern Korea and southern Manchuria, and early in the second century Wiman (or Wei Man in Chinese), fleeing to Korea after an unsuccessful uprising in North China, won control over the northern half of the peninsula, founding around 194 B.C. a Sinicized state called Chosŏn, with its capital at modern P'yŏngyang, still today the capital of North Korea.

China extended direct rule over Korea when Wu Ti of the Han conquered Chosŏn in 109–108 B.C. and set up four commanderies in the northern two-thirds of the peninsula. While three of these were abandoned by 75
B.C., the fourth, Lo-lang (Nangnang in Korean) at P'yŏngyang, the old
Chosŏn capital, continued to exercise a vague sort of suzerainty over the
whole of Korea. Lo-lang, which remained a rich outpost of Chinese civilization for four centuries, was divided into twenty-five districts with a recorded population of around 400,000. The tombs of its leading Chinese
families contain some of the finest remains of Han times, including superb
pieces of lacquerware. (See Plate 3.)

The Chinese colony in Korea survived even when cut off from China
itself for prolonged periods because of wars and dynastic decline. The
Chinese were still strong enough in Korea in the early third century A.D.
to found a second commandery, Tai-fang (Taebang in Korean) in the Han
River Valley in west central Korea. Shortly after the barbarian inundation
of North China in the early fourth century, however, the Chinese colonies
were overwhelmed by local Korean tribal states. Tradition dates the end of
Lo-lang in 313 A.D., and the fall of Tai-fang may have come soon after,
but there is evidence that rich Chinese families maintained some local authority in parts of Korea throughout much of the rest of the fourth century.

The historic role of the Chinese commanderies in Korea was much like
that of the contemporary Roman colonies in Britain. Although the later
Korean kingdoms were not the direct political heirs of these foreign colonies, they derived much of their higher culture from contacts with these
outposts of Chinese civilization. In fact, the cultural continuity between
the Han colonies and later Korean states seems to have been much greater
than that between Roman Britain and Anglo-Saxon England. This may
account for the greater rapidity with which the Koreans were able to
achieve a unified national state.

The Emergence of Native Kingdoms. As the Chinese colonies sank into
oblivion during the fourth century, three purely native kingdoms emerged
into the light of history and came to divide the peninsula among them.
These were Koguryŏ in the north, Paekche in the southwest, and Silla in
the southeast. According to tradition Silla was founded in 57 B.C., Paekche
in 37 B.C., and Koguryŏ in 18 B.C., but Silla and Paekche were in fact of
much later origin.

Koguryŏ, the first purely native state to develop in Korea, was originally
composed of five tribes which had broken off from the Tungusic Puyŏ
people (Fu-yü in Chinese) in central Manchuria. These tribes had moved
southward into the mountainous region north of the middle course of the
Yalu River (the Amnok in Korean), the present northern boundary of the
country. In this rugged terrain the Koguryŏ tribes maintained an aristocratic

society of mounted warriors, who lived in part off tribute and booty from surrounding agricultural peoples. The Koguryŏ tribes revolted against Chinese authority in 12 A.D. and thereafter remained in periodic warfare with the Chinese or non-Chinese rulers of the rich agricultural areas of southern Manchuria. Twice, in 244–245 and again in 342–343, their capital region on the Yalu was sacked by these stronger neighbors in retaliation for Koguryŏ forays. Despite these external pressures and constant internal upheavals, Koguryŏ remained in existence and gradually grew in strength. It was the extension of Koguryŏ power over the Lo-lang commandery that ended its existence as a recognized part of China in 313. During the fourth century, Koguryŏ spread over the northern two-thirds of the Korean peninsula and farther into Manchuria, and in the course of the fifth century it absorbed the remnants of the other Puyŏ tribes.

Southern Korea, which had never been directly ruled by China, was in early times inhabited by tribal peoples called the Han,* from whose name is derived the official name of the present South Korean state—Tae Han ("Great Han"). In the southwest were the Ma Han tribes, said to number fifty, while the Chin Han and Pyŏn Han, each said to number twelve tribes, were located respectively in the southeast and along the eastern end of the south coast. This last area was an early center of iron production as well as of trade with Japan.

During the first half of the fourth century a more centrally organized state named Paekche appeared in the area of the former Chinese commandery of Tai-fang in the valley of the Han River and extended its control over the whole former Ma Han area. The founders of this state appear to have been offshoots of the Puyŏ people who had fled southward from central Manchuria. Meanwhile the Chin Han area of the southeast seems to have fallen under the influence of Koguryŏ, but in the latter part of the fourth century there developed in this area an independent kingdom called Silla, which was at first closely allied with Koguryŏ. The Pyŏn Han area produced no comparable centralized kingdom, but six of its tribes formed a league known as Kaya. This league became loosely allied with the rising Japanese state of Yamato, either because of trade ties or possibly because the people of Kaya were closely related to tribes that had recently crossed over to Japan and therefore naturally sought aid from the islanders in their feuds with their immediate neighbors. The Japanese came to maintain a garrison in Kaya, which they called Mimana.

From the late fourth century until the second half of the seventh, most of the Korean peninsula was divided among the three states of Koguryŏ Paekche, and Silla. The Koreans, therefore, have named this the Three

---

*Written with a different character from that for the Han River of Korea and the Han dynasty of China.

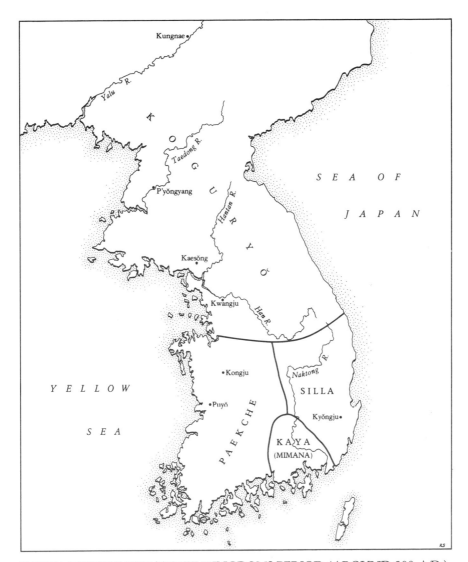

KOREA DURING THE THREE KINGDOMS PERIOD (AROUND 500 A.D.)

Kingdoms period, in obvious imitation of the name for the period of tripartite division in China in the third century.

The Three Kingdoms

The Rivalry Between Koguryŏ and Paekche. The elimination of the Chinese colonies in the fourth century did not diminish Chinese cultural influence in Korea. Although there were no longer any islands of purely Chinese culture, Chinese civilization now began to spread much more widely throughout the peninsula. The disturbed conditions in North China following the collapse of the Han dynasty sent repeated waves of Chinese refugees and Sinicized northern peoples into Korea, and the three native kingdoms eagerly sought contacts with China and readily accepted cultural innovations from their great neighbor in the hope of deriving some advantage in their violent competition with one another.

The incorporation of the Sinicized populations of the Lo-lang commandery and of parts of southern Manchuria into Koguryŏ naturally had a profound effect on its society and political organization. From the middle of the fourth century, Koguryŏ also maintained tributary relations with whichever was the chief state in North China, and in the fifth century it added relations with the successor dynasties in South China. Thus it was able to import Chinese culture directly from its source. In 372 a Buddhist monk dispatched by the Earlier Ch'in dynasty of North China officially introduced Buddhism to Koguryŏ, and gradually the new religion came to exert a great influence over the whole society. At about the same time a "university" was organized for the teaching of the Confucian classics, and Koguryŏ also began to develop a Chinese type of law code.

A further step in the Sinicization of Koguryŏ resulted from the moving of the capital in 427 from Kungnae on the Yalu River to P'yŏngyang, the former headquarters of the Lo-lang commandery. Thereafter the government became increasingly dependent on Chinese-type agricultural taxes and *corvée* labor, and it developed a complex Chinese style of bureaucratic government which, together with organized military garrisons, controlled the subject peoples in much the same way as the contemporary "barbarian" dynasties ruled in North China. While the old tribal society and cults inevitably started to degenerate, the state as a whole prospered, as is attested by the magnificent stone tombs of the kings and nobles around Kungnae and P'yŏngyang, which contain some of the finest Chinese-style wall paintings of the fourth and fifth centuries.

The state of Paekche, cut off by Koguryŏ from land contact with China, established tributary relations by sea with the southern Chinese dynasty of Eastern Chin, and Buddhism is said to have been officially introduced to Paekche from South China in 384. Not much is known of the government and culture of Paekche, but beautiful tiles and other remains suggest that Chinese-style arts and crafts were highly developed. The fact that Paekche played a major role in the successful transmission of Buddhism and Chinese culture to Japan indicates that the people of Paekche must have had a solid mastery of elements of Chinese civilization. Silla remained more cut off from China but did send an embassy to North China as early as 381.

The expansion of Koguryŏ southward during the fourth century and the consolidation of Paekche at the same time brought these two kingdoms into conflict over the area around the Han River. In 369 invading Koguryŏ forces were driven back by Paekche, which then invaded Koguryŏ and

*Detail of a wall painting in a tomb dating from the fifth century near
the early Koguryŏ capital at Kungnae on the Yalu River.*

killed its king in 371. Thus was inaugurated almost three centuries of warfare between these two kingdoms. Paekche had won the first round, and,
occupying the best agricultural regions of Korea, it was relatively populous
and rich, but during most of this protracted period of warfare it proved to
be less well organized and weaker than Koguryŏ. Perhaps the original
divisiveness of the many tribal units of the Ma Han area or the alien origin
of its ruling house undermined its solidarity. Paekche, in order to maintain
itself, was constantly forced to seek alliances either with Silla or with the
Japanese.

Under the leadership of Kwanggaet'o (391–413), a strong warrior king,
Koguryŏ expanded greatly in all directions, and for the next century it
was the paramount power in the peninsula. A stone monument erected in
414 at Kungnae on the north bank of the Yalu River describes Kwanggaet'o's exploits, including his wars with Paekche, the Kaya league, and its
Japanese allies. By 475 Koguryŏ forced Paekche to move its capital southward from the site of the modern town of Kwangju, a little south of the
Han River, to the modern Kongju, and in 538 Paekche was forced to
remove its capital still farther south to Puyŏ (the same name as that of the
Manchurian people.)

The Triumph of Silla. Silla, centered on its capital near the modern Kyŏngju in the extreme southeastern corner of the peninsula, was at first a relatively backward region, much less influenced by Chinese culture. In its early years it was hard pressed to maintain itself against Paekche and Japanese marauders from Kaya. In the long run, however, its tribal and aristocratic social structure, which was less eroded than that of the more Sinicized states of Koguryŏ and Paekche, seem to have given it greater cohesiveness and lasting power.

Silla was originally a confederation of six tribes controlled by a council of tribal leaders, but in the early sixth century, under the rule of Pŏphung (514–539), it began to consolidate as a stronger, more unified monarchy. The Chinese title of king (*wang*) had been adopted in 503, and Pŏphung, by accepting Buddhism as the state religion and identifying the authority of the king with the new religion, introduced a rationale for centralized authority over the old tribal units. In the course of the sixth century Silla adopted piecemeal various elements of the Chinese bureaucratic political system, thus developing both greater administrative efficiency and increased local control.

The old aristocratic, tribal habits of the Silla people were not wiped away by Chinese political concepts, however, but were overlaid, as it were, by a garment of Chinese bureaucratic institutions. This had probably been to some extent the case in both Koguryŏ and Paekche, and throughout Korean history, despite the growing Sinicization of external patterns, there was always a strong survival of a sense of hereditary, aristocratic privilege. As a consequence, there was, as compared with China, a clear weakness of monarchy and a certain degradation of the lower classes.

This surviving aristocratic tendency can best be seen in early Silla in the assignment of the seventeen Chinese-type grades of the government bureaucracy on the basis of hereditary "bone ranks." The top two "bone ranks," reserved for the very extensive royal clan, monopolized the top five grades of the bureaucracy, the next "bone rank" monopolized grades six through nine, the fourth rank held the remaining official grades, while families of the lowest three "bone ranks" were relegated to the role of commoners. Similarly, the core of Silla's military forces was not made up of peasant draftees, as in China, but of bands of youthful warriors (known as Hwarang-do), who were drawn from the aristocracy and emphasized comradeship as well as physical training and military arts.

The gold bracelets, belts, ear pendants, and crowns found in the tombs of the rulers and nobles of early Silla have a certain barbaric grandeur that indicates the relative weakness of Chinese influence in this corner of Korea. There are antler-like crowns covered with pendant decorations, some of which are identical with the "curved jewels" of Japan (see page 329). These decorative items in particular suggest that the wearers of early Silla were still

Fifth- or sixth-century pottery figure of a Silla mounted warrior.

Silla golden crown of the fifth or sixth century from near Kyŏngju.

Bronze Buddha (Maitreya, the Buddha of the Future) of the Three Kingdoms period (before 668).

close to the totemistic and animistic cults of the primitive Koreans.

The synthesis of Buddhism and Chinese political institutions with the native tribal society of Silla seems to have produced a sudden burst of energy in the sixth century. Allied with Paekche, Silla seized the upper basin of the Han River from Koguryŏ in 551 and then turned on its erstwhile ally and took from it the lower Han Valley. This gave Silla an outlet on the west coast of Korea, enabling it to begin direct contact with China across the Yellow Sea. In the next few years Silla established its control far up the east coast of Korea and in the south eliminated Kaya, which had been a troublesome Japanese foothold in the peninsula.

As a result of the reunification of China by the Sui dynasty in 589, Chinese military power once more began to penetrate into the peninsula. But now China faced Korean kingdoms that were far stronger than the state of Chosŏn had been when Wu Ti of the Han had overrun it in 108 B.C. In 598 Koguryŏ repulsed a large-scale attack by the Sui, and three great

Sui expeditions in 612–614 ended so disastrously that they contributed to the collapse of the dynasty. The T'ang dynasty, which succeeded the Sui in 618, was no more successful in a series of big expeditions between 644 and 659, but in 660 it changed its strategy, dispatching a large sea-borne force against Paekche. With the aid of Silla, the Chinese managed to destroy Paekche and in 663 repulsed a Japanese expedition sent to its aid. Meanwhile T'ang and Silla had turned on Koguryŏ, and in 668 they brought an end to this kingdom, which had lasted for almost seven centuries.

T'ang had expected to incorporate its Korean conquest into its empire, as the Han had done, but Silla, now aided by the conquered peoples of Koguryŏ and Paekche, managed within a decade to force the Chinese to withdraw from all of the peninsula south of its narrow waist in the P'yŏng-yang area. Eventually T'ang was forced to accept Silla as a tributary but autonomous state ruling over the southern two-thirds of the peninsula. A second period of Chinese colonial rule was thus averted, and Silla emerged as a unified state occupying the greater part of what today constitutes Korea.

Korea ever since its unification by Silla has remained a basically unified country, with only occasional and relatively brief periods of political division. Already in the seventh century it was essentially the same country it is today in geographic extent, race, language, and underlying culture, and the Koreans have had a strong sense of political continuity ever since. In the whole world only China among existing nations can claim a clearly longer history as a unified political entity.

The Silla Period

The Chinese Political Model.   The incorporation into Silla of the more Sinicized populations of Paekche and the southern part of Koguryŏ, together with increased direct contact with China, resulted in further borrowing of Chinese political institutions and culture. Annual tribute embassies were sent to the T'ang capital, and large numbers of students and Buddhist monks spent long periods of study in China. As a consequence, Silla became a thoroughly Buddhist country, and politically it was remade into a little T'ang—perhaps the most faithful of the many replicas of the great Chinese state that came to surround it on all sides.

Among the other imitations of T'ang in the borderlands of China, the Manchurian state of P'o-hai (Parhae in Korean) is usually considered by Koreans to be an integral part of their history. P'o-hai was founded in 713 in northern Manchuria by Koguryŏ survivors together with remnants of the Puyŏ people and various Tungusic tribes. It managed to achieve the same relationship with T'ang that Silla had as an autonomous tributary state, and it created a Chinese type of administration, built Chinese-style Buddhist monasteries, and produced a literature in the Chinese language. P'o-hai at its height controlled most of Manchuria and the northern third of Korea, and it traded extensively with China and Japan. It survived for more than two centuries but was extinguished in 926 by the Khitan, who were soon to found the Liao dynasty on the northern borders of China.

Silla's attempt to transplant the T'ang model to Korea embraced learning and religion as well as political institutions. An astronomical observatory, which still stands, was erected at the capital before 647, and a national "university" was founded in 682 for the teaching of Confucian texts. The country was divided in the Chinese manner into nine provinces, subdivided into prefectures and districts. Because the capital, Kyŏngju, was inconveniently located in the extreme southeast, five subsidiary capitals were established, but Kyŏngju remained the center of power and grew into a large city made up of grand houses roofed with tiles in the Chinese style.

An attempt was even made in 689 to convert the estates of the aristocrats into lands assigned them in the Chinese manner by the government, but the effort proved abortive and was completely abandoned in 757. Meanwhile an attempt was begun in 722 to assign lands to peasants in accordance with the land-holding and tax system of the early T'ang. Korean documents preserved in Japan show that land registers of the Chinese type were still being kept up as late as 755, but it is doubtful that the system had much success.

The adoption of Chinese political and economic institutions was probably in part necessitated by the decline of the old tribal society and the resultant loss of political cohesiveness. But the native sense of hereditary privilege remained strong enough to prevent a complete adoption of the Chinese political model. No serious effort was made to borrow the examination system that was emerging at this time in China as a shaping element in government and society. Instead, eligibility for government posts continued to be determined basically by the hereditary "bone ranks," and the government as a whole remained dominated by the royal clan and the other aristocratic clans. The court monopolized the production of fine industrial and art goods patterned on Chinese models. Despite the efforts to create a broad tax-paying peasantry of the Chinese type, most Korean peasants remained virtual serfs, whose labors went to the enrichment of the hereditary aristocracy rather than to the support of the central government.

Silla Culture.   The seventh century was the height of the Buddhist age in China, and it was the Indian religion, rather than Confucianism, that appealed most to the Koreans of this period. Coming with the prestige of Chinese civilization behind it and in the optimistic Mahayana form it had developed in China, it appeared to the Koreans to offer greater protective power and richer promise of both worldly and spiritual rewards than did the old native cults. The beautiful art that accompanied Buddhism also had

Stone pagoda at the Pulguksa ("Monastery of the Buddha Land"),
founded in 751 near Kyŏngju.

a direct appeal, and the Koreans, like the Japanese at this same time, showed an amazing capacity for mastering the most advanced Chinese artistic skills. The contrast is sharp with the much slower and less successful efforts of the newly Christianized peoples of Northern Europe to absorb the classic art of the Mediterranean that had become fused with Christianity.

Some of the many Korean monks who went to China to study proceeded on all the way to India, but others brought back to Korea the various sects of Chinese Buddhism. The simple teachings of the "Pure Land" sect of

*Eighth-century bas-reliefs
in the Sŏkkuram
grotto near Kyŏngju.*

salvation through faith became particularly popular, but in the latter part of the Silla period Zen (called Sŏn in Korean) also was influential. The Silla kings and nobles expended great sums on the erection of beautiful monasteries, and these in time became so rich and powerful that the government was forced to put restrictions on their holdings.

Many massive rectangular stone and brick pagodas of Silla date are to be found all over southern Korea, as well as large numbers of stone or bronze Buddhist images, as fine as anything produced in T'ang China. The great Buddhist images of the Pulguksa, a monastery founded in 751 a few miles south of Kyŏngju, and the large stone Buddha and bas-reliefs of the Sŏkkuram grotto, high on a ridge behind the monastery, are among the finest works of Buddhist art in T'ang style. A great bronze bell, eleven feet high and decorated with beautiful figures in low relief, now in the museum at Kyŏngju, is another outstanding relic of Silla Buddhism.

One limitation on cultural development in Silla, as in early Japan, was the lack of a writing system suitable for transcribing the native language. The only writing the early Koreans and Japanese knew was Chinese characters, but these were very ill adapted to writing their own polysyllabic and highly inflected native tongues. Consequently they were forced to do all of their writing in a foreign language. This situation may have contributed to the pervasiveness of Chinese influence in both countries, and in the case of Korea it resulted in time in the transformation of local place names and also personal names to Chinese-type names. As in China and Vietnam, personal names in Korea from Silla times on have consisted of a one-character (or occasionally two-character) surname, such as Kim, Pak, or Yi,* the three commonest, which together account for about half of the modern Korean population, followed by a one- or, more usually, two-character given name.

Despite the handicap of writing in a foreign language, there was a great deal of literary activity in Silla, such as the composition of historical records, Buddhist works, and Chinese poetry. Eventually a system called *idu* was developed for the transcription of native Korean words and names, syllable by syllable, in Chinese characters. This made possible the explanation of Chinese texts through Korean words and the writing down of poems composed in Korean, but only a few such poems have been preserved.

The Decline and Fall of Silla. The golden age of Silla, which followed the unification of Korea in 668, began to wane in the middle of the eighth century. By this time the old tribal society had seriously eroded. The royal clan, for example, had become so extensive that it had broken up into contending subunits, the "bone ranks" no longer gave much cohesion or organization to society, and the bands of aristocratic youthful warriors known as Hwarang-do had degenerated into groups of effeminate dilettantes. On the other hand, the borrowed Chinese political institutions had not succeeded in creating a real bureaucracy of merit and had in any case started to degenerate, much as these same institutions, after about a century or so of operation, tended to become more costly and less efficient in the successive dynasties of China. As the old sense of solidarity weakened, the clashes over wealth between families and over power between government officials became progressively fiercer, and the new bureaucratic institutions proved inadequate to counteract these tensions.

A sharp turning point in Silla's fortunes came in 780 when, after more than a decade of revolts, the king was assassinated. During the next century and a half, twenty kings from contending lines of the royal clan followed one another in a series of brief reigns, each usually winning the throne and losing it through violence. A succession dispute led to the founding of a short-lived rival state in the old Paekche area in 822, and other revolts followed. Rich families established local dominance, and even merchants built up political as well as financial power.

The most colorful man of commercial background was Chang Po-go,

*Because of an initial unpronounced *l,* Yi is often rendered as Lee in the West and even as Rhee. Pak is sometimes written as Park.

who rose to prominence as a leader of the Korean trade communities along the east coast of China, which seem to have dominated the commerce of the East China Sea at this time. Chang Po-go, after returning to Korea in 828, became a virtual merchant prince at his headquarters on an island off the southwestern tip of the peninsula. He was instrumental in putting one of the contending candidates on the Silla throne in 839, but, when he sought to marry the king's daughter, he ran afoul of deep aristocratic prejudices and was destroyed in 846.

Central authority had so declined by 889 that peasant uprisings began to sweep the country. Three years later the state of Later Paekche was set up in the southwest by a man of humble birth, and in 901 an illegitimate son of a Silla king established Later Koguryŏ in the north. One of his officers named Wang Kŏn, who was of merchant background, seized control of this new state in 918 and succeeded by 935 in absorbing the remains of Silla and then extinguished Later Paekche the next year, thus reunifying Korea.

Early Koryŏ

The Koryŏ Government. Wang Kŏn had renamed his state Koryŏ, an abbreviation of Koguryŏ and the origin of our name Korea. The Koryŏ dynasty was to last for more than four and a half centuries, from 918 to 1392, and during its first century marked another surge forward toward the establishment of the Chinese political pattern in Korea. The long years of rebellion and warfare in the latter part of the Silla period had swept away the old "bone rank" system and the whole tribal order, leaving the political ground clear for a new start in state building. The posthumous titles by which the Koryŏ kings are known are symbolic of the growing Chinese cultural imprint. Wang Kŏn, for example, is known as T'aejo, the Korean pronunciation of T'ai Tsu ("Grand Progenitor"), which was also the posthumous title of the roughly contemporary first emperor of the Sung.

The basic structure of the Koryŏ government took shape under T'aejo (918–943) and two of his successors, Kwangjong (949–975) and Sŏngjong (981–997), but the system continued to be revised and perfected throughout the eleventh century. The capital was at Kaesŏng, a little north of the mouth of the Han River. Kaesŏng was an imposing city even by Chinese standards, laid out in checkerboard fashion in the manner of Ch'ang-an and dominated by a great palace. A secondary "western capital" was established at P'yŏngyang, the old Koguryŏ capital, and lesser capitals at the old Silla capital Kyŏngju in the "east" and the modern Seoul in the "south." The institutions of the central government closely paralleled those of the T'ang and Sung, with three central boards like those of the T'ang, a Bureau of Military Affairs, the traditional Six Ministries, and a host of lesser administrative organs. In 958 a civil service examination system was set up on the Chinese model, and central government schools were established to teach Confucian texts and prepare students for the examinations. The central army was made a powerful, permanent force, and a system of national mobilization was developed for times of war.

Under T'aejo the borders were pushed northward from the P'yŏngyang area, but Koryŏ soon ran into the expanding power of the Khitan, who in 947 founded the Liao dynasty. Liao invaded Koryŏ in force in 993 and again in 1010, sacking the capital and compelling Koryŏ to accept its suzerainty. A third Liao invasion in 1018 was repulsed with heavy losses, and as a result Koryŏ was able to establish permanent control over the northern part of the peninsula all the way up to the lower Yalu River. Between 1033 and 1044 Koryŏ constructed a wall along its northern border from the mouth of the Yalu eastward to the coast of the Japan Sea somewhat north of the present Wŏnsan. Thus by the eleventh century all but the northeastern corner of modern Korea had come under the rule of a unified Korean government.

Society and the Economy.   Koryŏ's dynastic start had been highly successful, and it had developed an imposing Chinese form of centralized government. But beneath the surface it was a very different society from that of China. Although the "bone ranks" had disappeared, the Koreans remained much more sharply divided into hereditary classes than were the Chinese. At the top was a hereditary aristocracy made up of T'aejo's associates and other powerful families which, though of the old Silla aristocracy, had come to his support. Concentrated at the capital and monopolizing the higher posts in the government, these aristocratic families constituted a closed ruling group. While in theory the examination system opened access to the bureaucracy to others, in fact class prejudice, the lack of opportunity for long classical studies, and petty restrictions excluded commoners from the government. The sons of high aristocrats could receive government appointment without examination, and the schools leading to the examinations were for the most part open only to them. Military officers, though a quite separate bureaucracy from the civil and considered much inferior, also became a purely hereditary subaristocracy.

The nobles in theory received from the government the lands that supported them, in accordance with their government rank, position, and service, as in the early T'ang system, but in actuality these lands soon became their own private estates, and there was a tendency for the remaining public, tax-paying lands also to gravitate into their hands. As a consequence, the tax base of the central government was weak from the start and steadily grew weaker.

Although much of the land was absorbed into the great estates of the nobility, these families did not live on their lands but congregated at Kaesŏng. Both political leadership and political activity were more completely centralized at the capital than even in China, perhaps because of the relative smallness of Korea and its greater need for a centralized response to the threat posed by the mobile cavalry forces of seminomad empires like that of the Liao. There was a wide gulf between the capital officialdom and the rest of the nation. The aristocrats took positions in the provinces only rarely and reluctantly, leaving local government largely in the hands of petty local aristocrats, whom they controlled closely by a system of hostages.

The bulk of the population, whose production supported both the government through taxes and the aristocrats through rents, were commoners, known as *yangmin,* or "good people." Below the commoners were the "base people" (*ch'ŏnmin*), who were largely slaves but also included government workers in mines, porcelain factories, post stations, and other specialized employments, and sometimes also whole villages of peasants. Such hereditary groups of "base people" had existed since Silla times, but they seem to have been more numerous in the Koryŏ period.

As compared with late T'ang or Sung China, the economy of Koryŏ was backward. In the ninth century, Korean merchants had been important in the international trade of East Asia, but subsequently they sank into insignificance, and even at home the commercial classes had a negligible role. Except at the capital, there were virtually no permanent stores, and trade was carried out by peddlers and at periodic markets. The government started to mint coins in 996, but the bulk of trade continued to be by barter. The wealth of the nation was heavily concentrated at the capital through taxation and the surplus produce from private estates paid to their noble owners, and most manufacturing of fine industrial and art products was centered there and was devoted to supplying the court and its aristocracy. Envoys to Koryŏ from the Sung commented on the contrast between the palaces and great houses of the capital and the wretched hovels throughout the rest of Korea.

Koryŏ Culture.   Buddhism was at its height in Korea during the early Koryŏ period and had a large place in the life and culture of the aristocracy. T'aejo, in the "Ten Injunctions" he left his heirs, stated that the success of the dynasty depended entirely on the Buddha's protection. Monasteries were richly endowed with lands and sometimes became involved in banking functions, as was the case in China, or built up their own private forces to protect their property, as also happened in Japan at this time. Buddhist "National Teachers" seem to have had an advisory role in government. The monk Ŭich'ŏn, a son of a Koryŏ king, brought back from China the T'ien-t'ai sect (called Ch'ŏnt'ae in Korean) in the latter part of the eleventh century, and it soon became the dominant force in Koryŏ Buddhism.

About a century later, however, another monk developed the Chogye sect from Zen elements, and it then achieved predominance.

A sign of the vigor of Buddhism at this time was the printing of the entire Buddhist Tripitaka during the eleventh century. The woodblocks cut for this purpose over a sixty-year period were subsequently destroyed during the Mongol invasions in the thirteenth century, but this national tribulation inspired another great effort between 1236 and 1251 to cut a new set of blocks. More than 81,000 of these blocks, together with some older ones, are still stored at the Haeinsa, a monastery high on beautiful Mt. Kaya in southern Korea, forming a collection of early printing materials unique in the world.

By Koryŏ times Buddhism had become a mixture of sometimes contradictory Buddhist schools, and it had also come to include surviving shamanistic cults and many Taoist concepts of geomancy, which influenced the location of monasteries. In fact, Buddhism had become so confused a set of doctrines and so adulterated by entirely alien ideas that it began to lose its identity. This, together with the decline of Buddhism at this same time in China, may help explain the rapid degeneration of the Indian religion after the Koryŏ period. Although Korea has nominally been a Buddhist country for a millennium and a half, it is significant that the present flag of South Korea features symbols of pre-Buddhist Chinese philosophy—the two entwined "commas" of the complementary dualism of *yin* and *yang* surrounded by four of the eight trigrams of the *Classic of Changes*. (See pages 42, 43, and 49.)

Koryŏ Buddhist art shows a decline from the artistic excellence of the Silla period, and secular arts, such as landscape painting and porcelain making, took its place as the foci of aesthetic endeavor. The pale green Koryŏ celadons, with their graceful modeling and lovely designs executed in inlaid clays of white and grey, while very different from the Sung celadons that inspired them, are among the greatest triumphs of the potter's art in the world. (See Plates 11 and 12.)

There was increasing scholarly and literary activity during the Koryŏ period. In 1055 the first private Confucian school was founded, and others followed. Kim Pu-sik, a great scholar statesman, compiled in 1145 the *History of the Three Kingdoms,* the earliest remaining Korean historical work. This is the chief native literary source for early Korean history, and its account is supplemented only in minor detail by the *Memorabilia of the Three Kingdoms,* compiled by a thirteenth century monk.

Later Koryŏ

Military Domination over the Court. The system of centralized rule in the Chinese manner began to show signs of decay in the second half of the eleventh century, after a little over a century of successful operation; this had happened before in the Silla period and repeatedly in the successive dynasties of China. The steady encroachment of the private estates of the aristocracy on the tax base of the government and the internal rivalries of the noble families over power at court increasingly undermined the government's authority. The institution of kingship, as in the Silla period, remained relatively weak, and many of the occupants of the throne were no more than the pawns of court factions. During the middle decades of the eleventh century a Kim family, through intermarriage with the royal line, achieved a dominant position at court, but it was displaced by a Yi family, which built up great power until it was finally eliminated in a palace coup in 1126. Subsequently a Buddhist monk, Myoch'ŏng, won influence as a master of geomancy and *yin* and *yang*. When he failed in an effort to move the capital to P'yŏngyang, he revolted in 1135 but was soon suppressed by the scholar-statesman Kim Pu-sik.

A more serious challenge to the central government came from the military bureaucracy. Consistently less favored than the civil bureaucracy, it became deeply dissatisfied, and in 1170 and again in 1173 the palace guards under Chŏng Chung-bu carried out palace coups and massacred the civil bureaucrats. The military officers, however, soon fell out among themselves. Chŏng Chung-bu was eliminated, and other would-be leaders met the same fate. Meanwhile a great peasant uprising broke out in 1176, and for the next few decades slave and peasant revolts swept the land.

Finally in 1196 a military officer, Ch'oe Ch'ŭng-hŏn, managed to gain control over the court, and during the next few years he was able to stabilize the situation at the capital and bring back some order throughout the country. In the process, he built up a system of military rule which was to last for more than half a century. He based his power on a personally loyal elite corps of three thousand palace guards and a mass of slave soldiers, reassigned landholdings to favor his supporters, created private organs of government which actually controlled the state, and used successive kings as his puppets. His son, Ch'oe U, who succeeded him to power in 1219, brought some of the civil bureaucrats back into the government, though under his own complete control, thus further stabilizing the new system.

The usurpation of power but not of the throne by land-owning aristocrats and the subsequent seizure of leadership by a military family and its control of the state through its private organs of administration constituted a sharp departure from Chinese political norms. In part, this may have been because of the comparative weakness of the Sung dynasty and the intrusion between it and Korea first of the Liao dynasty and then the Chin, both of seminomadic "barbarian" origin. But this distortion of the Chinese model seems to have been more basically a re-emergence of older Korean patterns.

The sharp rivalries between aristocratic clans, the warrior bands on which the power of the Ch'oe family was founded, and the ties of kinship through which it consolidated its control over other military families were all reminiscent of the early Silla tribal, warrior society.

What was happening in Koryŏ was also closely parallel to what was happening in Japan at precisely the same time, as traits inherited from an earlier aristocratic, tribal, warrior society began to distort the political institutions the Japanese had borrowed from China and to prepare the way for what was to prove to be a fully feudal experience. But Koryŏ differed in one essential respect from Japan or from protofeudal Europe of a few centuries earlier. The Ch'oe and other great military families had no close links to the land or to the agricultural population. They owned great estates and assigned themselves the tax yields of other areas, but they did not manage these areas themselves or draw their military forces from them. They remained essentially private military power groups within a degenerated centralized government. This basic difference from the situation in Japan and in protofeudal Europe may have been because continuing pressure from the seminomadic empires of Manchuria and Mongolia made it necessary for the Koreans to maintain a centralized military force, instead of breaking up into a fragmented, locally-based feudal system.

The Mongol Conquest.   Koryŏ, as we have seen, was subjected to a series of invasions by the Khitan Liao dynasty between 993 and 1018, and in 1104 it first came into conflict with the Tungusic Jurchen people of Manchuria, who were rising rapidly in power. In 1115 the Jurchen founded the Chin dynasty, and soon thereafter they eliminated the Liao on the northern borders of China and conquered all of North China from the Sung. Koryŏ, which had accepted the suzerainty of China and had sent annual tribute missions to both the Sung in the South and to the Liao in the North now became tributary to the Chin too.

The rise of the Mongols in the early thirteenth century posed a greater threat to Korea than the Khitan or Jurchen had ever been. Jurchen from Manchuria, fleeing the Mongols, began to disrupt northern Korea as early as 1215, and in 1231 the Mongols invaded the peninsula in force. When they invested the capital, Koryŏ sued for peace, submitting to demands for an immense tribute and accepting Mongol military garrisons and governors throughout the country. But Ch'oe U in 1232 moved the court to Kanghwa Island off the west central coast of Korea, where it could be better protected from the formidable Mongol cavalry. For the next quarter-century the Koreans conducted guerrilla warfare against the Mongols, who repeatedly ravaged the land, carrying off more than 200,000 captives in their incursion of 1254 alone. Finally in 1258, the fourth and last of the Ch'oe dictators was assassinated, and the next year the court on Kanghwa submitted to the Mongols. Actually it did not move back to Kaesŏng until 1270, and sporadic resistance to the Mongols continued until 1273.

The Mongols, who had already overrun the greater part of Asia and much of Eastern Europe and were about to complete their conquest of China, established a firm grip on Korea. They annexed the northern part of the peninsula; by repeated marriages of Mongol princesses to Koryŏ kings they made the royal family virtually into a branch of the Mongol ruling house; they reorganized the government nomenclature to make clear Koryŏ's subservience to the Mongols; and they controlled the land through Mongol garrisons and officials. The Koryŏ aristocracy became strongly Mongolized in culture, and the royal family, which was often dominated by its Mongol princesses, even resided at times in Peking rather than in Korea.

The annual tribute fell heavily on the peasantry, and preparations for the two great Mongol expeditions against Japan in 1274 and 1281 proved particularly onerous. Both times the Koreans were called upon to build about nine hundred ships and to furnish great quantities of supplies and sizable military contingents. Thus the period of Mongol rule was a time of economic suffering for the common people and political and spiritual oppression for the upper classes. At the same time, the fact that Korea was part of an almost worldwide Mongol Empire meant that it was more open to cultural and technological influences from abroad than at other times. Among the diverse innovations of the period were the cultivation of cotton, the use of gunpowder, the borrowing of astronomical and mathematical knowledge from West Asia, and the strong impact of Neo-Confucian philosophy from China.

The Fall of Koryŏ. The firm hand of the Mongol overlords served to prop up the Koryŏ dynasty for about a century, but beneath the surface the foundations of the central government were crumbling. Agricultural lands continued to flow from the public domain into the estates of the nobles, and formerly tax-paying commoners were transformed into slaves or serfs of the great families. The government's revenues continued to shrink, and there were no longer adequate resources to pay the lesser government functionaries. Prolonged periods of invasion and civil war had resulted in some reshuffling of the social classes, and large numbers of former commoners had sunk to the status of "base people."

Another disruptive factor was the repeated incursions of Japanese pirates, which resembled the depredations of the Norsemen a few centuries earlier in Europe. Japanese piratical attacks started in the thirteenth century and by the middle of the fourteenth had reached serious proportions. The pirates not only despoiled coastal districts and towns, sometimes forcing the inhabitants to abandon these regions for safer inland locations, but also disrupted the vital transportation of grain taxes by sea.

The Koryŏ dynasty had come to rely so heavily on Mongol power that it did not long survive the collapse of the Mongol Empire. As Mongol power waned with the outbreak of rebellions in China in the 1340's, King Kongmin (1351–1374) began to reduce Mongol influence at court, restructured the government so that it would be less subservient to the Mongols, and restored control over the northern part of the peninsula. He also made strenuous efforts with the aid of a monk, Sin Ton, to regain for the government the lands and people that had been absorbed into the private estates. This policy naturally encountered opposition from the nobility, and Sin Ton was banished in 1371 and the king himself assassinated three years later.

Chinese rebel bands spilled over into Korea in 1359 and again in 1361, disrupting the northern part of the peninsula and even capturing Kaesŏng. A bitter debate broke out at the court between the advocates of an alliance with the newly founded Ming dynasty in China and supporters of the old ties with the Mongols. Eventually the pro-Mongol faction won out, but, when Ming forces appeared on the northern frontier of Koryŏ in 1388, Yi Sŏng-gye, the general dispatched against them, realized the folly of the undertaking and instead of attacking the Chinese marched back southward and seized the court. After consolidating his power for a few years, he usurped the throne in 1392, bringing the Koryŏ dynasty to an end after 474 years of rule.

12. Yi Dynasty Korea: A Model Confucian Society

The Perfected Chinese Pattern

Confucianism. The regime Yi Sŏng-gye founded in 1392 was to last until 1910—a total of 518 years, almost twice as long as any of the dynasties of imperial China. Yi Sŏng-gye quickly established tributary relations with the new Ming dynasty, receiving from it the ancient name of Chosŏn for his kingdom, although it has usually been known from his own name as the Yi dynasty. For five centuries the Yi dynasty remained in close contact with China and displayed unwavering loyalty to it. Tribute missions were at first sent every third year, but they gradually increased in number to three a year. Through them, continuing new waves of Chinese influence reached Korea, strengthening the already well established Chinese political and cultural patterns.

The Yi dynasty was the heyday of Confucianism in Korea. One reason for this was the restored emphasis on Confucianism in China itself since the latter part of the T'ang dynasty and the development and systematization of the philosophy at the hands of Chu Hsi and other great scholars during the Sung dynasty. Another was the closer contacts with China that Korea had developed first in the late Koryŏ period as a subordinate unit of the Mongol Empire centered at Peking and subsequently through the frequent tribute missions of the Yi Dynasty to the Ming. A final reason was that the increasing success of the Koreans in their use of the Chinese political pattern and especially their complete adoption at this time of the

Chinese examination system focused the attention of the whole ruling class on Confucian concepts and the texts which embodied them. Since the way to fame and success now lay through the mastery of Confucian scholarship and philosophy, successive generations of ambitious Korean boys assiduously studied their Chinese Confucian books in the hope of establishing a name for themselves and power and prestige for their families.

The Koreans in the early Yi dynasty adopted Confucianism with such enthusiasm that their value system and social practices were restructured along Chinese lines more fully than ever before. Since Korea was a relatively small country, and thus a more manageable and homogeneous unit than the sprawling Chinese Empire, it may have become more uniformly and fully permeated by Confucian ideas than China was itself. In fact, Korea became in many ways an almost model Confucian society, and it came to show some of the strengths and also some of the weaknesses of the Confucian polity in more extreme form than they appeared in China.

For example, the Koreans came to place even more stress on formal education than the Chinese did themselves. This may have been necessary because both the language and the subject matter of education were of foreign origin and therefore required more disciplined effort on the part of Korean boys than of Chinese. Probably as a result of this intensive study of Confucian texts, the Koreans also developed a very literal but sincere devotion to Confucian principles and an almost fanatical adherence to Confucian rituals. Filial piety was extolled and faithfully practiced, and the three-year period of mourning for parents was dutifully observed. The chastity of wives was strictly enforced, and the remarriage of widows severely condemned. Chinese literary arts were highly valued, and Confucian texts became the all-absorbing intellectual interest of the ruling class.

Another result of this emphasis on Confucian scholarship may have been a narrowing of the range of intellectual interests and a growing dogmatism of thought. The Confucianism of the early Yi dynasty court was at first more pragmatic than dogmatic, but eventually the Chu Hsi school of Neo-Confucianism became established as the only acceptable interpretation in the examinations. It was developed first by private scholars of the so-called "Mountain and Forest" (Sallim) tradition, largely in Kyŏngsang province in the southeast, but under the leadership of the scholar Kim Chong-jik (1431–1492) this school managed to make its teachings into a rigid court orthodoxy. Perhaps because Confucianism was a borrowed ideology, Chu Hsi's doctrines became in time even more narrowly restrictive in Korea than they were in China.

The intellectually limiting influence of Confucian orthodoxy did not manifest itself at once, and the fifteenth century was in fact a golden age of Korean intellectual endeavor. A host of important works of scholarship in the Chinese language appeared at this time. There were encyclopedias, geographies, a huge compendium on medicine, commentaries on Confucian texts, and, of course, histories, which occupied so central a position in Confucian scholarship. Among the great histories compiled during this period were the *History of Koryŏ* of 1451 and the *Complete Mirror of the Eastern Country* of 1484, both of which lived up to the best traditions of Chinese historical scholarship.

The rise of Confucianism meant a corresponding fall in the status of Buddhism. Buddhism had shown signs of increasing corruption and lessening intellectual vigor during the late Koryŏ period, and in the fifteenth century its decline became precipitous. Although the court continued at times to show it some favor, the government drastically limited the number of monasteries and monks and in 1425 forced the various sects to combine into two. While monasteries remained havens of refuge, usually in remote places, Korean Buddhism sank to the sad state of theological confusion and low social esteem which it occupies today.

The Government. The new dynastic beginning allowed Yi Sŏng-gye to make a fresh start in creating a Chinese political system, and the result was a much closer approximation of the Chinese model than either Silla or Koryŏ had ever achieved. Although he was a military man who had first distinguished himself by repulsing Jurchen raiders in the northeast and Japanese pirates in the south, he proved to be a statesman of unusual ability. Even before he usurped the throne, he had swept the state clean of rivals, redistributed the land to his supporters, and started to restructure the government. By the time he abdicated in 1398, to pass into history under his posthumous title of T'aejo ("Grand Progenitor"), the new regime was well started, and it was perfected under his son, the third king, T'aejong ("Grand Ancestor"; T'ai Tsung in Chinese), who ruled from 1400 to 1418, and by the latter's son Sejong (1418–1450).

The capital was established at Seoul on the Han River, where it has remained ever since, and the country was divided into eight provinces. The division in the late nineteenth century of all but the three central provinces into northern and southern halves produced the thirteen provinces of recent times. The provinces were subdivided in the Chinese manner into counties (the Chinese prefectures) or comparable administrative units. As in China, only a few higher offices in the local governments were filled by officials from the capital, and these, again as in later Chinese history, were never assigned to natives of the district. Under Sejong the present northern boundaries of Korea along the Yalu and Tumen Rivers were clearly established, and the regions along the northern frontier were brought under firm Korean control by the establishment of six garrison towns in the extreme northeast and four garrison counties along the upper Yalu River.

----- Divisions of Provinces into Northern and Southern halves

Tumen R.

HAMGYŎNG

S. N.

Yalu R.

P'YŎNGAN

N.

S.

P'yŏngyang

SEA OF

JAPAN

HWANGHAE

KANGWŎN

Kaesŏng

Seoul

KANGHWA
IS.

KYŎNGGI

CH'UNGCH'ŎNG

S. N.

YELLOW

SEA

KYŎNGSANG

N.

Kyŏngju

S.

Pulguksa

Haeinsa

CHŎLLA

N.

S.

Pusan

KOREA DURING THE YI DYNASTY

Audience Hall of the Kyŏngbok Palace at Seoul (a later reconstruction of a 1394 building).

The Ming criminal code was adopted in 1395, and two years later a native administrative code was added. After many revisions the law codes reached final form in 1485. The organs of the central government closely paralleled those of China. There was a State Council, a Royal Secretariat, and the traditional Six Ministries, as well as many lesser bureaus. The very special Chinese institution of the Censorate was particularly well developed. There were in fact two Boards of Censors, one designed to scrutinize and criticize the policies and actions of officials (*Sahŏnbu*) and the other for remonstrance against the king's actions (*Saganwŏn*). The Hall of Talented Scholars under Sejong served as a key instrument of cultural innovation (perhaps comparable to the Hanlin Academy of the Ming) but was becoming a political force when abolished by Sejo in 1456. Its dual function was assumed some twenty years later by the *Hongmun'gwan,* which soon developed into a third arm of the Censorate. The Office of Royal Lectures was a kind of top-level seminar in statecraft which met as often as three times a day and was centered on the reading of Chinese Confucian texts.

In time, however, it became a forum for increasingly acrimonious policy debates.

The Examination System.   The Chinese examination system had been used to some extent by Koryŏ in selecting its bureaucracy, but under the Yi dynasty it became, as it was in China, the chief route to high government office. Most villages in Korea developed their own little private schools to start promising students on the arduous Chinese classical education the examinations required, and schools at the secondary level were maintained by the government at the capital and in each district. The graduates of these secondary schools were entitled to take the triennial lower examinations, either in the Confucian classics or in Chinese literary arts, and one hundred were passed in each category. The literary examinations led to the highly prized *chinsa* degree (the *chin-shih* in Chinese).

Some of those who succeeded in the lower examinations then entered the capital University (Sŏnggyun'gwan) to study for the higher examinations. As the dynasty wore on, however, more and more candidates for this final degree proceeded to the examinations directly from the local schools. Many others first obtained lower government posts through family privilege and then tried to win the coveted final degree. The higher examinations were divided into preliminary screening examinations held in the provinces and a final capital examination at which thirty-three men were selected for immediate assignment to court rank and government posts, in general correspondence with their examination grades. All these examinations were at first held triennially, but extra examinations were often added, and in practice the final examinations came to be held even more frequently than once a year.

A sequence of military examinations paralleled the civil service examinations, eventually qualifying for the military bureaucracy considerably larger numbers than entered the higher civil bureaucracy. There were also government schools and special examinations for candidates for positions in such technical fields as medicine, law, astronomy, and foreign languages.

The examination system displayed some of the same virtues and faults it had in China. It produced a high bureaucracy chosen for personal intellectual ability rather than simply for social status, military prowess, or wealth. It made government service the great ideal of the upper class, although, as in China, high government office was also recognized as the surest road to wealth. It placed men of intellectual inclination and literary and philosophical training in charge of the mechanisms of government. At the same time, it led to much too exclusive an emphasis in education on scholarly and literary skills and antiquarian, historical interests. This tendency may have been even more inhibiting to intellectual originality and the development of practical abilities in Korea than it was in China, since scholarship had to be demonstrated in a foreign language and the historical orientation was that of a foreign country and society, known by most Koreans only through books. Despite these weaknesses, however, the examination system in Korea produced an initially successful bureaucratic form of government which continued, though in debased form, for five centuries, constituting probably the longest administrative cycle in world history.

Society and Culture

Class Structure. The wholehearted adoption of the examination system made Yi dynasty Korea much more fully Sinicized than the earlier Korean states had been, but one fundamental difference from China still remained. There were not just educational, and therefore economic, limitations to those who could hope to succeed in the examinations; there were also class barriers. In fact, Korean society retained its clear hereditary class divisions, which all along had contrasted sharply with the greater openness of Chinese society. Successful candidates in the civil service examination were limited for the most part to the hereditary ruling class, which came to be known as the *yangban,* a term meaning literally "the two groups"—that is, the civil and military branches of the bureaucracy. The military examinations were much more open, but assignment to the more important military posts remained generally restricted to this class. The specialist examinations were also limited to hereditary groups which filled these specialist roles in society. Thus the Koreans combined the concept of hereditary status with the selection of officialdom through examinations testing individual ability.

By dominating the examinations, the *yangban* families of course were able to monopolize political leadership and high government office, and they also came to own most of the land. In theory, all land was state-owned, although some was assigned to officials for their support or as rewards for their services, in keeping with the early T'ang system. T'aejo assigned his officials lands in the province of Kyŏnggi around the capital. He also elevated a few dozen of his chief supporters to the special category of "Merit Subjects" and gave them large grants of land and slaves and important special privileges. A bigger category of "Minor Merit Subjects" received lesser awards. T'aejo's successors, especially after succession disputes, which were frequent, rewarded their supporters in similar fashion. From the start it was recognized that these lands were hereditary property and might be confiscated later only as punishment for very serious offenses. As a result of these repeated generous distributions of land, much of the country became divided up into private landholdings owned by *yangban* families. Since these same families provided the members of the high officialdom of the central government, land ownership and political power became almost synonymous. Thus social status, land ownership, and political leadership were all concentrated in the hands of the *yangban* class.

The *yangban,* however, differed in several respects from the Koryŏ aristocracy they had replaced. They constituted a much broader social group, and they were not entirely concentrated at the capital. Leading families in the capital aristocracy and others in actual political power lived in Seoul, but most *yangban* families resided on their provincial holdings or at least had members of their families living in the countryside. The properties of the *yangban,* moreover, were not entirely tax-free, as most estates had been in earlier Korean history. Normally one-fifteenth of the rent received by the landowners was passed on to the central government as taxes. *Yangban* holdings moreover were not consolidated estates but were made up of small and scattered tracts of land. Thus in some ways the landholding pattern resembled the landlordism of China of post-Sung times, and the *yangban* had become roughly equivalent to the so-called "gentry" of China, except for the fact that they were a closed hereditary class.

While a wide and almost uncrossable gulf separated the *yangban* from the lower classes, there was no corresponding gulf between them and the king, who was regarded as little more than a "first among equals." As with their predecessors, the Yi kings lacked the semireligious aura and unique status of the Chinese Son of Heaven, to whom they were admitted subordinates. One sign of this difference was the whole system of "Merit Subjects," which showed the need of the kings for the support of powerful *yangban* families. Another sign was the relatively flourishing state of the Censorate under the Yi dynasty. Not only were there three boards of Censors, but their members often criticized the king and his officers with a temerity unheard of in China, making the boards at times into major decision-making bodies.

Below the *yangban* was a relatively small and legally undefined class which has been called the *chungin* or "middle people." These served as petty government functionaries and performed the various specialist roles in government. Though absolutely essential in the whole operation of government, they had little opportunity to rise to high policy posts. This essentially hereditary group clearly predated the founding of the Yi dynasty, but it received new recruits from among the large numbers of illegitimate offspring of *yangban.*

The bulk of the population was made up of commoners (*yangmin*), who were for the most part tax-paying, *corvée*-serving occupiers of government lands or else semiserfs on *yangban* holdings. They were more closely bound to the soil than in earlier times, but are thought to have been in general in a somewhat more favorable position than before, because the government guaranteed their rights to the land they cultivated. Rents were normally 50 per cent of the yield, but in 1444 the government made an attempt to fix a sliding scale of rents in accordance with the relative productivity of the soil.

Typical Chinese-type monochrome painting (of a fisherman and woodsman) from the middle Yi dynasty.

As in Koryŏ times the lowest class was called the "base people" (*ch'ŏnmin*). These were government or private slaves, workers in government industries, and certain professional categories, such as butchers (originally despised because of the Buddhist prohibition against the taking of animal life), actors, and *kisaeng,* who were female entertainers comparable to the Japanese geisha of a somewhat later date.

The Economy and Culture.   As during the Koryŏ period, Yi dynasty Korea lagged far behind China in economic development. The official disdain for commerce and merchants was part of the whole Chinese Confucian point of view, but it may have had a more stultifying effect on the economy in Korea than it did in China simply because Korea was a smaller and more

Korean gentleman in traditional horsehair black hat and white costume.

isolated country. Tribute relations with China brought in some luxury goods, and limited commercial contact existed with Japan, largely at Japanese insistence. Post roads and post stations were maintained for governmental purposes, but internal communication for the most part remained primitive. The government on occasion minted coins or even issued paper currency, but most trade was conducted by barter. Shops and commercial towns were slow to develop, and most manufacturing of fine artistic and industrial goods was still in the hands of the government at the capital.

Thus Korea, despite its Confucian scholarship and Chinese political institutions, remained a very different country from China. This was true not only of social structure and economic development but in other more visible ways. The mud walls and mushroom-shaped thatched roofs of the peasant homes contrasted sharply with the brick and tile-roofed houses of China. Unlike the Chinese, who by this time used chairs and slept on raised, heated beds made of brick or clay, the Koreans continued to sit and sleep directly on the floor, which was made of clay covered with oil paper and heated by flues from a fire fed from outside the house. In contrast with the slim trousers and close-cut jackets worn by most Chinese men and women, Korean men had loose-fitting, baggy trousers, while women wore very full skirts and short separate bodices. The stiff horsehair black hats of men, though derived from Chinese prototypes, and the slippers with up-turned toes, which suggest a Central Asian provenance, were also quite unlike what Chinese wore. Also in contrast with the black and dark blues that predominated in Chinese clothing, the Koreans so strictly observed the rules for white clothing for mourning that eventually the everyday costumes for men—peasants and city dwellers alike—became an impractical white, which necessitated endless laundering. Korean food, too, was very distinctive, centering around a very peppery cabbage pickle called *kimch'i.* Underlying all these superficial differences and the deeper social contrasts was a very distinctive Korean personality type, which seems to have been more volatile than that of the Chinese. The Korean language, moreover, was of a type entirely different from Chinese, and the latter was used in Korea only in written form and for purposes of scholarship and government. Model Confucian state though it may have been, Yi dynasty Korea was in no danger of being culturally absorbed into China.

Technology and the Arts. There were many technological innovations during the early Yi dynasty in a variety of fields. Advances occurred in mathematics, new astronomical instruments were made, and a rain gauge was invented in 1442. The most important technological innovation, however, was quite understandably related to Confucian scholarship. This was large-scale printing by movable type. Chinese had made use of movable type since the eleventh century, and some type had been cast in Korea as early as 1234, but the first extensive use of movable type anywhere in the world was in Korea in the fifteenth century. As part of the great scholarly activity of the time, the Korean court undertook between 1403 and 1484 eight ambitious printing projects by movable type.

The most remarkable intellectual achievement of the age was the invention of an excellent phonetic system for indicating the Korean pronunciation of Chinese characters and also for writing the native language. The system, known today as *han'gŭl* ("Korean letters"), was developed by the Hall of Talented Scholars in 1443 under the leadership of King Sejong himself. *Han'gŭl* is perhaps the most scientific system of writing in general use in any country. The basic vowels are indicated by vertical or horizontal straight lines, modified by short lines on one side or the other, a single short line for a simple vowel and two if it includes the *y* sound. Consonants are represented by angled lines, and aspirated consonants are shown by the addition of an extra line to the corresponding unaspirated form. The respective advantages of an alphabetic script and a syllabary are combined by bunching the individual letters into syllabic groups.

Although *han'gŭl* is a simple and almost perfect system for writing Korean, it was at first used only for explicating Chinese texts and for writing down native songs and poems. While it came in time to be used for

HAN'GŬL CHART

Vowel pairs: ㅏ a ㅑ ya, ㅓ ŏ ㅕ yŏ, ㅗ o ㅛ yo, ㅜ u
ㅠ yu, ㅡ ŭ ㅣ i.

Some consonant pairs: ㄱ k ㅋ k', ㄷ t ㅌ t', ㅂ p ㅍ p',
ㅈ ch ㅊ ch'.

Some other consonants: ㅅ s, ㄴ n, ㅁ m, ㅇ ng.

Syllables:* Chosŏn 조 선   Taedong 대 동

ch'ŏnmin 천 민   T'aejong 태 종

Puyŏ 부 여   *yangban* 양 반

P'yŏngyang 평 양

K, t, p and *ch* are voiced (*g, d, b,* and *j*) when occurring between vowels. The symbol ㅇ is used both for a final *ng* and to indicate the absence of an initial consonant. *Ae* is written ㅐ *(ai)*.

such humble purposes as the writing of stories for popular consumption and correspondence between women and other persons of little education, all serious scholarship and government documents continued to be written in Chinese, and the educated classes looked with disdain on *han'gŭl*. It was not until after Korea regained its independence from Japan in 1945 that *han'gŭl* came into its own. It can be either supplemented by Chinese characters or used alone, and it has proved to be as excellent a system for writing Korean in the twentieth century as it was when it was first invented.

The predominance of Confucianism during the Yi dynasty was reflected even in the arts. There was no Buddhist art of any distinction, and the chief artistic activity was in the fields of painting and calligraphy, which are close to the literary tradition. In subject matter and style the influence of Chinese painting and calligraphy was obvious. Korean painters came from two distinct social groups. *Yangban* artists, for whom calligraphy and painting represented socially approved skills and who fiercely insisted on their amateurism, tended to be academic in their interests and closely bound by Chinese models. Professional painters of the "middle people" class were employed primarily to paint ancestral portraits. In ceramics the Koryŏ celadon tradition was lost, and the potter's art became simpler and rougher but more widespread among the common people.

Political Disruption

The Struggle Between the Kings and the Confucian Scholars.   In typical
dynastic fashion, the Yi had a brilliant first century, but even before it was
over the government showed signs of decline. The kings, eager to win
yangban support, had been too generous in the creation of "Merit Subjects"
and the assignment of land to them, with the result that there were insuf-
ficient remaining lands to assign to new officials, government income became inadequate, and the tax burdens and *corvée* duties levied on the
peasants living on the remaining public lands became unbearably oppressive. Such conditions induced King Sejo (1455–1468) to make a determined effort to get the land back onto the tax registers and power at court
back into the king's hands. He set up a land survey system designed to
limit landholding to persons actually serving in official positions; he reduced the powers of some of the organs of the central government; he
even favored Buddhism as a means of offsetting the Confucian *yangban*
class. Such efforts to reduce the power of the *yangban* families were doomed
to failure, however. Even Sejo himself, in his search for support, created
new "Merit Subjects" on three separate occasions.

The year after Sejo died, his grandson Sŏngjong (1469–1494) came to
the throne. Being a mere child, he was subjected to heavy indoctrination
regarding the Confucian duties of a ruler and perhaps as a result was very
tolerant of criticism by his officials. With Sejo gone, there was a vacuum
in power at the top of the government, and some of the officials in the
censoring organs took advantage of this situation to dominate the court.
They were for the most part idealistic but doctrinaire young men under the
influence of the great Confucian scholar Kim Chong-jik. From their safe
 ⌐nd administratively unburdened refuge in the censoring bodies, they
launched sweeping condemnations of the older officials in administrative
posts who had cooperated with Sejo. Their chief ground of attack was that
Sejo had usurped the throne from his nephew in 1455, and this issue became a prime bone of contention in later factional disputes within the
bureaucracy. The unrestrained attacks by the censoring bodies drove the
older bureaucrats from office and made strong leadership in government
all but impossible. The government, while perhaps philosophically true to
Confucianism, remained weak and disrupted throughout Sŏngjong's reign.

Sŏngjong's son, Yŏnsan, who succeeded him in 1494, tolerated the situation for a few years, but in 1498 he turned on the Confucian critics of
government, executing, banishing, or dismissing some forty to fifty of the
disciples of Kim Chong-jik. In 1504 Yŏnsan started an even broader and
more vicious attack on presumptuous officials and others who had run
afoul of him, and this reign of terror was not ended until he was finally
dethroned by the remaining officials in 1506. Yŏnsan seems to have

suffered from paranoia during these later years and to have been given to gross debauchery, although one cannot be certain of the accuracy of the account of his misdeeds left by his enemies. In any case, he was denied by the officials a legitimate place in the list of Yi kings and is known to history only as Yŏnsan'gun or "Prince Yŏnsan."

Bureaucratic Factionalism. The *yangban* officials, back in control after Yŏnsan's fall, reinstituted the censoring organs as a means of inhibiting the despotic exercise of power, and the fight between the younger officials in these offices and the older responsible government administrators soon broke out again. The leader of the censoring officials now was a prominent Confucian scholar, Cho Kwang-jo. He and his supporters launched a furious attack upon the existing institutions and high officials in an effort to recreate the hypothetical ideal Confucian state of Chinese antiquity, although Cho did not hesitate to bypass the examination system and use the institution of recommendation to pack the government with his own supporters. Eventually his opponents, with the king's blessing, managed to fill the censoring organs with their own adherents, who then used these organs to have Cho and his supporters executed, banished or dismissed from office.

The pattern had now been set for successive strong men or bureaucratic groups to utilize the censoring organs as a base of power from which to destroy their opponents, and factional quarrels of this sort became endemic for the remainder of the Yi dynasty. The factions, which had first formed over philosophic and administrative disagreements, gradually turned into virtually hereditary groupings which refused to intermarry. The whole scholar-official class became involved from the highest officials down to the lowliest student candidates. The original grounds for dispute often became obscured, and factional groupings came to be pitted against one another, generation after generation, in what was quite openly a struggle for power, prestige, and the economic benefits of high office.

Factionalism is probably inevitable in any extensive bureaucracy, but it seems to have been more disruptive of the traditional Chinese type of government than of some others. Because of the Confucian emphasis on right conduct as the basis for political leadership, no distinction could be made between a man's policies and his moral worth: to attack one was to attack the other. Consequently opposing policies were not accepted as the product of honest differences of opinion but were commonly regarded as signs of moral depravity. Since the political system was considered to be merely a reflection of a universal moral order, there was no room for disagreement about it. There was no concept of agreeing to disagree. Majority decisions after clashes of opinion would not suffice; unanimity of opinion or at least consensus was necessary. Since practical issues were complex and often all but insoluble, there was always ample room for disagreement between even wise and loyal men. Moreover, the gap between Confucian ideals and political realities was inevitably wide. For example, the examination system was an admirably fair way to provide candidates for office, but actual appointments and subsequent promotions depended largely on the patronage of high officials, who were often in competition with one another for power.

Bureaucratic factionalism was a recurrent problem in China, reaching particularly dangerous levels there in the great disputes over the reforms of Wang An-shih in the Sung dynasty (see pages 128–130). But it never was as great a problem in China as it became in Yi dynasty Korea, in terms of both intensity and duration. One reason for this difference was probably the weakness of the monarchy in Korea. In China strong emperors or powerful central administrative organs acting in their name could usually decide between contending factions and could keep both sides somewhat under control. In Korea, after the deposing of Yŏnsan in 1506, there were no truly strong rulers or even strong central administrative bodies. Even lesser officials, as members of the privileged *yangban* class, stood in little awe of the throne or of high officials. The censoring organs and the Office of Royal Lectures made ideal rostrums for polemics and personal attacks. As a result, the sort of factionalism that appeared periodically in China as an aberration from good government became the political norm in Korea and was carried to great extremes, leading to numerous executions of fallen opponents and the purging of hundreds of officials at a time.

The factional disputants usually couched their arguments in terms of Confucian philosophy and propriety and denounced their opponents largely on ethical grounds. The historical record is filled with self-righteous attacks on an opponent's philosophical heresies, disloyalty, immorality, and above all his failures to live up to the strictures of Confucian etiquette. The proper period of mourning became an especially acrimonious subject of debate.

The long duration of factional struggles in Korea helps account for the factions becoming hereditary groupings, which did not happen in China. Another reason for this was the development of geographic bases for the factions in the provinces. Many *yangban* families, and particularly those out of power, lived on their lands, where factional leaders could gather about them relatives and disciples who would give them a permanent geographic base from which to wage their political vendettas at court.

Related to this phenomenon was the development of private academies, or *sŏwŏn,* named and patterned after the *shu-yüan* of Sung China. The first *sŏwŏn* was founded in 1543, and by the end of the century there were more than a hundred, largely in the south. They were usually located in

Abridged Chart of Yi Dynasty Factions

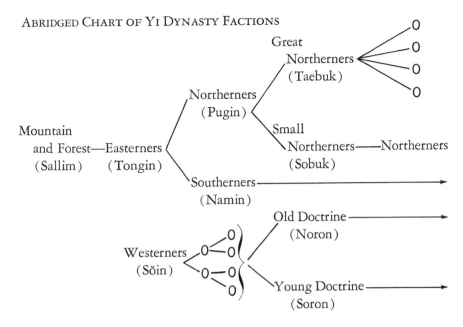

rural settings and were often endowed by the government. In their early years they contributed to a great reinvigoration of Confucian scholarship, and they gradually replaced the government schools as the chief educational institutions. But located in the provinces as they were, they often became associated with the various local bases for factions at court, and by dividing education along family and factional lines they contributed to the hardening of factional divisions.

By the latter part of the sixteenth century much of the bureaucracy had become divided into two great factions, known as the "Easterners" and the "Westerners" from the locations of the residences in Seoul of their respective leaders. The "Easterners" eventually emerged victorious but in 1591 split into "Northerners" and "Southerners," with first the latter and then the former in the ascendancy. The victorious "Northerners" then divided into "Great" and "Small" factions. The factional pot continued to boil and to dominate court politics. Needless to say, leadership in government remained weak and unstable.

Foreign Invasions.   While the factional struggles were mounting in intensity during the late sixteenth century, disaster struck from abroad in the form of a massive Japanese invasion. Until then the Yi dynasty had been relatively free from foreign encroachments. The Ashikaga shoguns had established some degree of authority in Japan in 1392, the year the Yi dynasty had been founded, and they managed to keep the Japanese pirates somewhat under control. The Koreans allowed Japanese traders and fishermen to use Pusan and two other southeastern ports in the peninsula, and there were few conflicts, except for an uprising of the Japanese residents in the three southern ports in 1510 and an attack by Japanese pirates in the southwest in 1555.

The reunification of Japan by Hideyoshi in 1590, however, changed the situation. Hideyoshi, falling prey to the Alexandrian desire for more worlds to conquer, invited Korea to join him in the conquest of China or to give him free passage. When the Koreans refused, Hideyoshi dispatched a force of about 160,000 men against them in 1592. The Japanese met little effective resistance because of the disruption of leadership in Korea and the inability of the Korean troops to stand up against the firearms of the Japanese. Within a month the invaders had captured Seoul, and they then fanned out over the whole country, except for the extreme southwest. One unit even crossed the Tumen River in the far north into what is now Manchuria.

The Ming, however, came to the aid of their tributary state, putting pressure on the Japanese from the north (see page 204). A more serious threat to them was posed by the Korean admiral Yi Sun-sin, who repeatedly defeated the Japanese naval forces and disrupted their communications with his "turtle ships," which had decks covered with iron plates and are claimed by some to have been the world's first armored warships. Guerrilla resistance also undermined the Japanese hold on the peninsula. Under these multiple assaults, the Japanese entered into truce talks with the Chinese and withdrew to a foothold in the south. The peace parleys dragged on for years, with the Japanese assuming that they were the victors and the Ming demanding their acceptance of vassalage. Finally Hideyoshi renewed the attack in 1597 with a huge new force which, however, achieved only limited success in the two southern provinces. When he died the next year the Japanese hastily returned home. The Tokugawa family, which came to power in Japan in 1600, restored amicable relations with Korea in 1606, and these continued unbroken until the second half of the nineteenth century.

The Japanese invasion, though brief, was an unmitigated disaster for Korea. Many cultural treasures and monuments were destroyed, the central government was further weakened, agriculture declined seriously, land registers were lost, and the whole tax system was disrupted. During this period of confusion such great amounts of previously tax-paying lands were incorporated into private *yangban* holdings or appropriated by members of the extensive royal family that the tax yield is said to have declined by more than two-thirds.

The Yi dynasty never fully recovered from the Japanese invasions, and recovery was made all the more difficult by new onslaughts—this time from the north. The campaigns in Korea had denuded southern Manchuria of its Chinese garrisons, helping to pave the way for the rise of the Manchus, who started to cross the border and raid northern Korea in the late sixteenth century. A serious revolt that broke out in Korea in 1624 opened the way for an invasion in force by the Manchus in 1627. Determined to secure their flanks in the impending decisive battle with the Ming, the Manchus again in 1636 invaded Korea with an army of 100,000 men and early the next year forced the Yi dynasty to switch allegiance from the Ming to their newly formed Ch'ing dynasty. Henceforth Korean tribute missions went to the Ch'ing, but loyalty to the Ming continued strong in Korean hearts to the very end of the Yi dynasty.

The Later Years of Yi Rule

Further Political Decline. The Japanese and Manchu invasions proved to be a major turning point in Korean history. The political structure was further distorted from its original Chinese pattern, and forces were set in motion that brought changes to the economy and perhaps to the social system as well.

During the years of warfare the Office of Border Defense emerged as the chief executive council in the central government. It created a new system of military training and in the course of the seventeenth century set up four permanent military bases, which together with the royal guards at Seoul were called the "Five-Camp System." Peasant draftees were little used, and the soldiery became for the most part volunteers. Taxes paid largely in textiles and imposed on commoners in lieu of military service became a major part of the tax burden. With the drastic decline of the old land tax, a great variety of new taxes were imposed which bore little relationship to the original system of taxation.

The "Westerners" faction seized power in a coup in 1623, executing or banishing its rivals, and similar coups followed throughout the century. The "Southerners" and "Westerners" seesawed in and out of power for two decades after 1674, but finally the "Westerners" won a decisive victory in 1694. They then, however, split into two major factions—the "Old Doctrine" and the "Young Doctrine." In the middle of the eighteenth century the "Old Doctrine" faction triumphed for a while, but before long its monopoly of power was broken, and King Yŏngjo worked out a balance between the four remaining factions—the "Old Doctrine," the "Young Doctrine," the "Northerners," and the "Southerners"—in which none of them was allowed a preponderance of high government posts.

In the seventeenth and eighteenth centuries the government of the Yi dynasty, though still modeled outwardly on that of China, had become in reality very different, and there was little relationship between the Confucian theories the ruling class professed and the actual way in which the government operated. Still, except for occasional palace coups, the country remained unified and for the most part at peace. During the long and relatively strong reigns of Yŏngjo (1724–1776) and his grandson Chŏngjo (1776–1800), the administration and the tax system operated with reasonable efficiency, the law codes were revised and brought up to date, historical records were printed, and encyclopedias and various other books on subjects felt to be related to government were compiled. A sign of the vigorous patronage of learning at the court was the casting between 1777 and 1795 of four fonts of movable type.

Economic and Social Change.   Korea during the late Yi dynasty remained economically a backward country as compared with China or even with Japan, which was surging ahead at this time. There was, nonetheless, considerable economic development in Korea, in part because of technological advances, particularly in agriculture. Wastelands were brought under cultivation, irrigation for rice fields was increased, and faster growing rice strains permitted the development of double cropping in much of the land, with summer crops of rice and winter crops of other cereals. The increase in agricultural production resulted in a considerable growth of population. By 1669 the registered population was close to 5 million, and it was well over 7 million by the middle of the eighteenth century. Already in 1669 Seoul was a relatively large city of close to 200,000.

Increased agricultural production and population may have served as spurs to commercial growth, but an equally important factor was the weakness of the central government, which prevented it from maintaining some of its earlier restrictions on trade, thus permitting more spontaneous economic development. Even before the invasions, contractors, in a sort of tax-farming operation, had collected for the government the local special products known as "tribute." At this time this "tribute" was commuted largely into grain levies, and the collectors gained greater freedom in their activities, developing into wholesalers who exchanged the grain they collected for the various commodities needed to supply the court and capital. Other merchants also developed more or less free of government restrictions, and Korean traders began to enter more actively into relations with Japan and to accompany tribute missions to Peking in order to exchange goods with the Chinese. The government artisans at the capital were cast free by the enfeebled court and developed into private craftsmen. Coinage at last began to be used commonly, and in time most taxes were commuted into cash payments. By the eighteenth century there was even some commercial capital at Seoul available for borrowing at interest. Thus slowly Korea began to experience the sort of commercial development that had occurred in China several centuries earlier and was appearing at a much more rapid pace in Japan at this same time.

The dislocation of the wars, the decline of government control, and the growth of the economy seem together to have brought about a steady erosion of the old class system and the development of a looser social structure, closer to that of China. The disruption of the wars permitted considerable crossing of class lines, and subsequently the bankruptcy of the government induced it to sell class status and even official positions to those who could pay for them. The growth of the population and the development of commercial wealth further disrupted the old class system. Merchants, once regarded as virtual outcasts, became men of influence, and great *yangban* families at the capital enhanced their incomes through commercial activities.

As a result of the great proliferation of the *yangban* class over the centuries and the long separation of the defeated factions from positions in the government, the *yangban* class began to separate into two rather distinct groups—the great families who retained their access to political power and the bulk of the *yangban* who gradually lost their distinctiveness from the commoners. Many no longer possessed lands and had themselves become simple farmers. Increasing numbers of commoners also seem to have been able to claim *yangban* status. Census registers from one area indicate that families claiming such status grew from less than one-tenth of the population in the late seventeenth century to about half by the middle of the nineteenth century.

The distinction between slaves and commoners was also fading. Slaves escaped their status by becoming professional soldiers, and the government artisans too became commoners when they transformed themselves into private craftsmen. Government slaves, which are said to have numbered 350,000 in 1484, were down to 190,000 in 1655 and to 27,000 by the middle of the eighteenth century. The same decline in numbers seems to have occurred among private slaves.

Intellectual Developments.   During the late Yi dynasty, higher cultural activities remained largely in the strait jacket of Chinese models, which limited originality and caused much of the artistic and literary work to be merely variations on Chinese themes. Nevertheless, the deep structural changes taking place in the economy and society began to have some impact even in this field. There were signs of disenchantment with the whole system of government and society, not only among the oppressed common people, but also among *yangban* factions long out of power, such as the "Southerners."

Foreign influences also contributed to these stirrings of change. Koreans on tribute missions to Peking began in the seventeenth century to come into contact with the Jesuit scholars there, and through these contacts some knowledge of both Catholic Christianity and Western science was transmitted to the peninsula. It is a sign of the degree of discontent in Korea that in the second half of the eighteenth century Christianity, which the Koreans called the "Western Learning" (*Sŏhak*), was embraced by a few *yangban*, even before the first Christian missionary, a Chinese named Chou Wen-mu, entered the country in 1795.

The government was horrified to discover that Christianity disapproved of ancestor worship and the rites of Confucian mourning. The religion was proscribed in 1785 and actively persecuted in 1791. A decade later the original Chinese missionary, Chou Wen-mu, and a number of Korean converts were executed, and Chŏng Yag-yong (or Chŏng Tasan; 1762–1836), a prominent scholar who was close to the Catholic movement, was banished to a remote island where he remained for eighteen years. Driven from the court, the religion spread in the provinces, nourished by clandestine Chinese Christian missionaries and after 1836 by French missionaries as well. More persecutions and executions followed in 1839 and again in 1866.

While the Christian faith maintained only a limited and underground existence in Korea, elements of Western scientific knowledge, acquired by the Koreans from the Jesuits in Peking and from Chinese books, had a much broader impact. These new ideas, together with the influence of the contemporary Chinese school of "empirical research," gave rise to a vigorous intellectual movement called "Practical Learning" (*Sirhak*). Among the chief figures in this movement were Chŏng Yag-yong and before him Yi Ik (1681–1763), who was fascinated by Western science but rejected Christianity. Both were adherents of the long-out-of-power "Southerners" faction.

The "Practical Learning" scholars turned their backs on the empty formalism and rituals of orthodox Confucianism and advocated practical measures to solve the problems of the day. They emphasized reform of the landholding system and government organization, technological innovations, scientific knowledge, agricultural production, the welfare of the common people, and greater social equality. Some of the "Practical Learning" scholars showed the usual Confucian limitations in their agrarian scorn for commerce, and all attempted to justify the reforms they advocated by what they professed to find in early Confucianism. However, their egalitarian tendencies, their interest in science and technology, and their advocacy of daring innovations may have helped prepare the way for the great changes in store for Korea in more recent times.

Another promising intellectual sign was the growing awareness of Korea as a separate entity from China. This was clear among many "Practical Learning" scholars and some others as well. It resulted in a burst of historical writing about Korea and studies of its geography and language. These beginnings of a national consciousness were perhaps stirred by the knowledge obtained from Jesuit sources of the world beyond China. At

A girl selling wine, painted by Sin Yun-bok (born 1758).

a more popular level also, there were stirrings of cultural independence from China. *Han'gŭl* at long last began to be used, not just for Korean poetry, but for prose stories written in Korean. Even in the field of art, the professional painters of the "middle people" class began to produce genre paintings of a sort quite independent of Chinese styles (see page 308), and Korean calligraphy began to show marked independence of Chinese models. Thus the ground was being prepared for the unbridled nationalism that was to sweep Korea in the twentieth century.

The Superannuation of the Yi Dynasty. Despite the pragmatic bent of the scholars of "Practical Learning" and the stirrings of national consciousness, Korean society and government remained set in old ways that were outmoded, ineffective, and strongly resistant to change. In fact, the most remarkable feature of the whole Yi dynasty period is the amazing persistence of the regime long after it had lost its first élan and ceased to address itself effectively to the pressing social and economic needs of its people.

A characteristic feature of the Chinese bureaucratic political system borrowed by the Koreans was its periodic rejuvenation through new dynastic starts. Korea in the early seventeenth century, after the havoc left by the Japanese and Manchu invasions, was in obvious need of such a fresh beginning, but the Yi dynasty continued for another three centuries. The long reigns of Yŏngjo and Chŏngjo in the eighteenth century brought increased stability and perhaps some improvement in the situation, but in the nineteenth century the downward course became more rapid again. The tax system grew even more confused and inadequate, the bureaucracy more corrupt, government less efficient, and the populace more discontented. The families of royal consorts came to dominate the government, and in the end the examination system became a largely meaningless formality, since family affiliations were now the deciding factor in determining the results.

As in China in times of dynastic decline, the people had no protection against bad harvests. Famine became endemic, pestilence and disorders followed in the wake of famine, and banditry was commonplace. In the single year of 1671 more Koreans are said to have died from famine and disease than during the whole of the Japanese invasions. In 1784 a half million people reportedly died of starvation. Floods ravaged the land in the early decades of the nineteenth century. In 1811–1812 there was a major peasant uprising in the northwest, and others followed in the next several years. A great popular uprising broke out in the southeast in 1862 and then spread throughout much of the land.

If one looks at the Yi dynasty from the vantage point of Chinese history, it seems strange that it could have lasted so long under these conditions. It may be that a badly degenerated bureaucratic state can be maintained longer in a small country like Korea than in a huge empire like China. Another difference from China may have been that foreign invaders did not hunger for the Korean throne as they did for the Chinese. Whereas the Manchus gave China a new dynastic start, they made Korea simply into a vassal state and served as an external prop for the Yi dynasty much as the Mongols had for Koryŏ. Perhaps the later Chinese dynasties too would have survived in almost endless decrepitude if the ebb and flow of power between foreign invaders and native rulers had not brought fresh dynastic beginnings. Significantly the end of the Yi itself was finally brought about at foreign hands— the Japanese in 1910.

As has been noted in earlier chapters, the Chinese achieved an extraordinary stability of political and social institutions from Sung times on. This they did by creating a marvelous balance between the economy, society, government, and the value system. Although running the danger of stagnation and immobility, China during these centuries was characterized more by inner strength and social harmony. In Korea, however, a comparable stability of institutions produced a much higher degree of cultural stagnation, political immobility, and social friction. Perhaps the Chinese philosophic and political system, when applied to a smaller and culturally more homogeneous country, engendered a deadening degree of uniformity, which China in its geographic spread, greater cultural and linguistic diversity, and more rapid changes of dynasty, was at least in part able to escape.

Another reason for the difference between Korea and China may have been that Confucian philosophy and the Chinese political system had originated with the Chinese but had only been borrowed by the Koreans. As the borrowers, the Koreans, even while maintaining a class structure that was the antithesis of Confucian egalitarian ideals, adhered to the minutiae of the Confucian system with a rigidity that exceeded that of the Chinese. It perhaps took even greater courage to be an innovator in Korea than in China itself. The dead weight of Chinese, as a foreign language, may also have inhibited creative endeavors. The strong orientation of scholarship and philosophy to China, rather than to Korea, also drew Korean leaders away from the practical problems of the society in which they lived into a world of written words concerning a remote time and a different place.

There were, as we have seen, stirrings of change in Korea in the eighteenth and early nineteenth centuries, but despite the efforts of the scholars of "Practical Learning," Korea remained mired in broken-down political and social institutions, while its leadership for the most part looked backward toward Chinese antiquity rather than forward toward unfolding Korean problems. Korea had become more stagnant and immobile than "unchanging" China had ever been. It was clearly in much greater need of rejuvenation. Thus by the nineteenth century the stage had been set for a very bitter period in Korean history.

13. Early Japan: The Absorption of Chinese Civilization

The Land and People

Geographic Influences. The early history of Japan paralleled that of Korea but thereafter the two diverged. While Korea became an interesting variant of the Chinese pattern, Japan, though sharing much culturally with China, Vietnam, and Korea, came to contrast sharply with them in social and political structure. Significantly, many of the differences between Japan and the other members of East Asian civilization turn out to be points of resemblance between Japan and the West. Feudalism is an outstanding example. So also is Japan's more rapid modernization during the past century, which has produced closer parallels to the contemporary Occident than are to be found in China or anywhere else in Asia.

The chief reason for Japan's distinctive role in East Asian civilization is probably its location as a relatively remote island country. The parallel with the British Isles, at the other end of the Eurasian land mass, is striking, but Japan's isolation from its neighbors is much greater. The Straits of Tsushima between Japan and Korea are approximately 115 miles wide, as compared to 21 miles for the Straits of Dover.

Unlike Korea and Vietnam, Japan was never invaded by Chinese armies. Chinese influences therefore penetrated to Japan less steadily and strongly, and changes came relatively slowly and resulted more from internal evolution or the voluntary adoption of foreign ways than from external pressure. As a result, more of the indigenous culture could be maintained. Old and outmoded habits and institutions could be lovingly preserved alongside the new. One spectacular example is the survival of the imperial family as the theoretical source of all political authority for a millennium after it had lost all real political power.

Relative isolation also made the Japanese more conscious of cultural borrowing than were other peoples. Foreign influences did not seep across land frontiers but came quite visibly by ship. Early in their history the Japanese developed the habit of cataloguing foreign influences and contrasting them with "native" characteristics. One result has been a frequent emphasis in Japanese history on primitive and therefore supposedly native Japanese traits. Another has been the myth that the Japanese have been merely a nation of cultural borrowers, although the truth seems to be that, because of their isolation, they have developed a larger proportion of their culture themselves than have most nations.

Japan is commonly described as a small country, which it is as compared with China or the United States. It is only the size of Montana, but a fairer comparison would be to the nations of Western Europe. Though smaller than France, Japan is larger than the British Isles, Italy, or the two Germanies combined. In population it is unquestionably a big country. For many centuries it has had a much larger population than any of the major powers of Western Europe, and today with a population of a little over 100 million it ranks sixth in the world.

This large population has been maintained even though the land is extremely mountainous, rising in central Honshū, the main island, to Fuji's 12,389-foot volcanic cone and the 10,000-foot peaks of the Japanese Alps. Less than one-fifth of the terrain is suitable for agriculture, though plentiful rainfall, hot summers, and intensive rice agriculture in irrigated fields have combined to make Japan one of the most productive lands per cultivated acre in the world. Most of agricultural Japan is made up of narrow river valleys and alluvial coastal plains separated from one another by stretches of rugged hills. Land communication therefore is not easy, but the surrounding seas have always provided links between the islands and along their coastlines as well as contact with the outside world. The seas also furnish the Japanese with abundant fish, which have provided the main source of protein in their diet.

The climate of Japan is salubrious, being generally similar to that of corresponding latitudes of the east coast of North America from the Gulf of Mexico to Maine. While extraordinarily deep winter snows blanket the northern part of the Japan Sea coast, relatively mild and sunny winters along the southern Pacific coast permit double cropping as far north as the Tōkyō area.

Racial and Cultural Origins.   The Japanese as we know them today are a homogeneous Mongoloid people, much like their near neighbors in Korea

JAPAN SUPERIMPOSED ON THE UNITED STATES

and China. The Japanese language is a polysyllabic, highly inflected language, similar to Korean and the Altaic tongues of North Asia. Thus, as in Korea, a very different type of language from Chinese has helped preserve Japan's cultural distinctiveness despite an inundation of Chinese influences.

The Japanese seem to have achieved their present physical and linguistic identity by the early centuries A.D. and perhaps much earlier. The dominant element unquestionably came from the near continent—that is, Korea and the regions to the north of it. The archaeological record shows this conclusively, and the movement of peoples from Korea into Japan continued well into historic times. However, other groups were probably absorbed into the mix. The Ainu, apparently the remnants of a proto-Caucasian people, were the chief inhabitants of the northern island of Hokkaidō until the past century and appear to have once occupied most of northern Japan. They probably contributed appreciably to the Japanese blood stream, perhaps accounting for the fact that many Japanese have more facial and body hair than their Mongoloid neighbors. Some early Japanese cultural traits and even elements of the language also suggest affinities with the Malay areas of Southeast Asia. This may have been the result, not of direct movements of people from Southeast Asia to Japan, but of cultural and possibly racial diffusion in early days from coastal South China southward to Southeast Asia and eastward to Korea and Japan.

At least two waves of paleolithic culture reached the islands—the first some 100,000 or 200,000 years ago. The earliest neolithic culture, named Jōmon for its characteristic "cord-pattern" pottery, spread throughout Japan about 6000 years ago. The Jōmon people lived in sunken pit dwellings and subsisted by hunting, fishing, and gathering nuts, roots, and shellfish. They left behind extensive shell mounds and a wealth of pottery, unsurpassed in its richness and imaginativeness of design by any other stone-age culture in the world.

In the third century B.C. a new culture displaced Jōmon in western Japan and by the end of the first century B.C. had spread as far east as the Kantō Plain. Named Yayoi from a type site, it was characterized by a simple wheel-made pottery, by agriculture, including rice cultivation using techniques of irrigation still in practice, and by the presence of both bronze and iron. The bronze artifacts, which seem to have been used largely for symbolic purposes, included mirrors of Chinese type and weapons and bells too thin to have been functional. The agriculture as well as the bronze and iron of the Yayoi culture were no doubt derived ultimately from China, and the presence in Yayoi sites of Chinese coins and mirrors of the Earlier Han dynasty are indisputable evidence of cultural contacts with China.

In the third century A.D. the Yayoi people of the Kinki, the historical capital region, began to erect large earthen tumuli over the tombs of their leaders, and this practice spread to Kyūshū and later to the Kantō area. The culture of the following centuries thus is known as the tomb culture. Some of the tumuli have a peculiar keyhole shape, square in front and round in the rear, and the largest, said to be the tomb of the Emperor Nintoku of the early fifth century, is about 120 feet high and 1500 feet long. On many of the mounds are found concentric circles made up of pottery cylinders, some of which are surmounted by simple but charming figures of men, animals, and houses. These are known as *haniwa*.

Many features associated with the tomb culture show strong new influences brought over from Korea either by new waves of invaders or through trade or military contacts. The tomb culture was obviously aristocratic, and its leaders were mounted warriors who carried long straight

Above: Pottery figure of the Jōmon period. Below: Haniwa horse and warrior.

iron swords and wore helmets, padded garments, and armor made of iron slats, all of which had close parallels in contemporary Korea and Manchuria. The "curved jewels" (*magatama*), found in the tombs of this period, are identical to those on the golden crowns of Silla.

The tomb culture, at the same time, was a clear outgrowth of the Yayoi culture and the direct ancestor of fully historical Japan. Its pottery was similar to that of Yayoi, though harder and more highly fired. Its agricultural techniques were the same, though iron was coming into common use for farm tools. Its houses were thatched structures raised off the ground, much like Japanese farm dwellings of more recent date. Gradually the tomb culture merged into the early historical Japan of the fifth and sixth centuries.

Ancient Japanese Society

Early Records. When pieced together, archaeological evidence, contemporary Chinese histories, and later Japanese accounts, which recorded the early myths and traditions, give a shadowy picture of the emergence of the Japanese state. The most important Chinese record (in the *Account of the Three Kingdoms,* compiled before 297 A.D.) details the route from Korea to Japan and describes the inhabitants of the islands. It portrays them as law-abiding people, fond of drink, concerned with divination and ritual purity, familiar with agriculture, expert at fishing and weaving, and living in a society of strict social differences indicated by tattooing or other bodily markings. The land is described as divided into one hundred "countries," varying in size from one thousand to seventy thousand households, some ruled by kings and others by queens—possibly a transition between matriarchy and patriarchy. The countries of the western part of the land were under the suzerainty of the unmarried queen Himiko of Yamatai, who was a sort of high priestess, and over whose grave a great mound was erected.

This and other Chinese histories record the coming of envoys from Japanese states to the Chinese court, the earliest in 57 A.D. A fifth-century Chinese history describes a Japanese ruler of the beginning of that century as having conquered fifty-five "countries" of hairy men (presumably Ainu) to the east, sixty-six "countries" to the west, and others across the sea to the north, meaning southern Korea.

The two most important Japanese accounts of early time are the *Record of Ancient Matters* (*Kojiki*), compiled in 712, and the *History of Japan* (*Nihon shoki* or *Nihongi*), compiled in 720. The authors of these works wove together often contradictory myths and traditions in an effort to enhance the prestige of the ruling family and create a picture of long-centralized rule and respectable antiquity comparable to that of China. While reasonably reliable on the later periods, their accounts give at best only vague hints about earlier happenings.

Both works start with creation myths centering around a divine brother and sister, who gave birth to the islands of Japan and a number of deities, including the Sun Goddess, Amaterasu. Her grandson, Ninigi, descended to earth and became the center of a cycle of myths localized in Kyūshū. He brought with him the Three Imperial Regalia, still the symbols of imperial authority in Japan. These are a bronze mirror (the symbol of the Sun Goddess and kept at Japan's greatest shrine at Ise), an iron sword, and a necklace of "curved jewels."

Ninigi's grandson (or great-grandson) moved up the Inland Sea, conquered the Kinki region, and established the Japanese state on the Yamato plain in that area. This was dated as happening in 660 B.C. Like later Japanese emperors, this first "emperor" became known by a posthumous title of Chinese type—in his case Jimmu, the "Divine Warrior." Subsequently, around 100 A.D., a martial prince conquered first the "barbarians" of Kyūshū and then those of the Kantō Plain, and about a century later an empress conquered Korea. Scribes from the Korean state of Paekche were installed at the court around 400 A.D. to keep records in Chinese.

Back of this largely mythological story lies some historical reality. Cultural waves did come from Korea to North Kyūshū and up the Inland Sea to the Kinki region. The latter did become the first and greatest center of tomb building, and the Yamato state of Japanese tradition may be the Yamatai of the Chinese texts under its priestess-queen, Himiko (meaning "Sun Princess"). The original Sun Goddess and occasional empresses fit in with the third-century Chinese picture of a transition from matriarchy to patriarchy. The conquests of Kyūshū and the Kantō by the Yamato state had taken place by the fifth century. There was a Japanese foothold in southern Korea. The reported introduction of Paekche scribes around 400 A.D. corresponds to a transition at that time from rulers with impossibly long reigns to emperors of normal life spans and believable activities. In fact, in the early fifth century the archaeological record, Chinese histories, and Japanese traditions merge into a single plausible story, which becomes convincing history by the late sixth century.

The Uji System.   The Japan that emerged slowly into the light of history was essentially a tribal society, like that of early Korea and perhaps somewhat comparable to the Germanic tribes of Roman times or to the later Scottish clans. It was divided into a great number of family or pseudofamily groups called *uji,* each under a hereditary chief and worshiping an *uji* god, commonly thought of as its ancestor. Subordinate to the aristocratic *uji* were occupational groupings known as *be,* organized as agricultural communities or performing other services, such as fishing, weaving, pottery making, and divining. Some *uji* had won supremacy over their less powerful neighbors, thus forming clusters of *uji.* It was probably groupings of

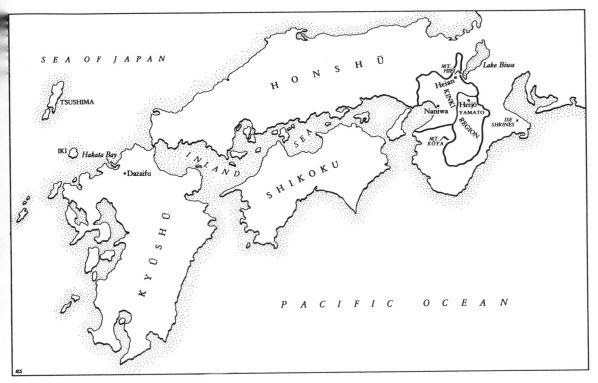

WEST JAPAN IN ANCIENT TIMES

this sort that constituted the hundred "countries" of the Chinese records of the third century. The many large tumuli scattered throughout much of Japan are good illustrations of the power and wealth held by such groupings.

The Yamato state was probably in origin such an *uji* cluster under its dominant sun-line *uji.* By the fifth century, however, it had won a vague supremacy over the other *uji* "countries." It classified these subordinate *uji* as either "country vassals" in charge of local areas or "attendant vassals" directly serving the sun line, and both types were bound to it by the establishment of real or fictive family ties. By the sixth century the sun line was treating these vassals as if they were appointive officials, and it also was expanding its own wealth and power at the expense of the local *uji* by creating directly subordinate agricultural *be* in their areas.

In an effort to put more order into the system, the Yamato court also organized the *uji* by ranks, reminiscent of the "bone ranks" of Silla. The two largest ranks, *Omi,* used for the lesser off-shoots of the sun line, and *Muraji,* used for the most important of the unrelated *uji,* were placed under a Great *Omi* and a Great *Muraji* respectively, and these two officers became in time the ruler's chief ministers.

Shintō.   Both the Chinese records and Japanese traditions make clear that there was no real line between religion and government in early Japan. No distinction was made between the *uji* chief's function as ruler over his people and his role as maintainer of the cult to the *uji* god. Even today the imperial family retains the sacerdotal functions of the early sun-line *uji* of Yamato. The political dominance of the sun line was expressed as the supremacy of its ancestral deity, the Sun Goddess, over other *uji* deities, and her worship grew from an *uji* cult into a national religion. The various other *uji* cults were integrated into an official mythology which made clear the supremacy of the Sun Goddess. By the eighth century there were more than three thousand officially recognized and ranked local shrines, about one-fourth of them supported by the government.

The *uji* cults were merely a manifestation of a broader current of animistic nature worship that underlay them. The early Japanese, awed by both the menacing and beneficent aspects of nature, thought of the various natural phenomena as spirits or deities, which they worshiped under the name of *kami.* Thus they paid reverence to waterfalls, mountains, great trees, unusual rocks, even pestiferous vermin, as well as their own progenitors, which they often identified with natural phenomena, as in the case of the Sun Goddess. Emperors and other humans who inspired awe easily entered the category of *kami.* Thus the so-called divinity of the Japanese imperial line was a far cry from what divinity came to mean in the West. The fertility of nature particularly attracted worship, as is illustrated by phallic cults and the prevalence of shrines to the God of Rice. Both *uji* gods and nature deities were commonly symbolized by objects such as mirrors, swords, or "curved jewels."

Nature worship and its associated *uji* cults came in later times to be called Shintō, the "Way of the Gods," to distinguish it from Buddhism. It was not, however, an organized religion, but rather a loose conglomeration of cults and attitudes. It had no organized philosophy or even a clear moral code, except for a concept of ritual purity. Exorcism, cleansing ceremonies, or ritual abstention were thought to remove ritual impurity incurred by physical dirtiness, sexual intercourse, menstruation, childbirth, sickness, wounds, or death. A priestly class which performed these rites or served as mediums and diviners probably represented the Japanese variant of the shamans of Korea and Northeast Asia. The modern Japanese insistence on cleanliness and fondness for bathing in hot springs and deep tubs may hark back to these early concepts of ritual purity.

Japan still today is dotted with a myriad of Shintō shrines. Some are great cult spots like the Ise Shrines of the Sun Goddess, which, though periodically rebuilt, reflect in their clean simple lines Japanese architecture of about the sixth century. Others are sleepy village shrines, set among towering trees and dedicated to the original local *uji* god. Many are no

Above: Main Building of the Inner Shrine (Naikū) at Ise. Although rebuilt every few years, the shrine buildings reflect an early architectural style. Below: A torii *in front of a small shrine.*

more than miniature box-like structures on mountain tops or other places of natural beauty. All are marked by the *torii,* a simple gateway made of two uprights and one or two crossbeams.

Worship at Shintō shrines is uncomplicated, consisting largely of the clapping of one's hands to attract the god's attention and then bowing and possibly making offerings. Ritual purity is achieved by washing out the mouth with water or by the waving of a sacred branch by a priest. Shrine festivals are gay affairs. Food and amusement booths set up along the approaches to a shrine give a carnival atmosphere, and the young men of the community, sometimes in boisterous intoxication, may take the deity out in a portable shrine to visit and purify individual homes and shops. Shintō thus remains a simple, somewhat primitive religion compared to the great faiths of Asia and Europe, but its attitudes and practices have remained a major component of Japanese culture throughout history.

The Adoption of the Chinese Pattern

Korean and Chinese Influences. The growing strength and institutional complexity of the Yamato state were probably in part the results of continuing contacts with the continent, particularly Korea. There was a steady flow of people from Korea to Japan that lasted up until the early ninth century. Many immigrants came as well organized groups, whose leaders took a prominent place at the Yamato court because of the knowledge and skills they possessed. More than a third of the 1182 aristocratic Japanese families listed in a genealogical register compiled in 815 claimed Korean origin or Chinese ancestry through descent from families in the Han colonies in Korea.

This flow of people was probably facilitated by the Japanese foothold in Kaya (Mimana) in South Korea while it lasted. The Japanese myths describe this foothold as the product of conquest, but it is more probable that it resulted from alliances by the people of that area with closely related groups which had earlier crossed over to Japan. The Japanese hold over Kaya appears to have been at its height in the late fourth century, but it was eliminated in 562, and subsequent attempts up until 663 to revive it all failed.

Among the many elements of continental civilization which came to Japan by way of Korea was Buddhism. It probably drifted into the islands over a period of time, but its official introduction is dated in 552 (though probably more accurately in 538), when the Korean state of Paekche presented an image and scriptures to the Yamato court. The new religion was opposed by conservative groups but was supported by the Soga *uji,* which held the post of Great *Omi.* After emerging victorious over their rivals in a succession war in 587, the Soga firmly established Buddhism at the court.

The subtleties of Buddhist philosophy were probably little appreciated by the Japanese of the time, but the continental religion appealed as possessing magical power superior to that of the native cults. It also became a vehicle for the transfer of much of Chinese culture to Japan, just as Christianity served as a vehicle for the transfer of Mediterranean civilization to North Europe.

Hitherto the cultural flow from the continent had been a slow unconscious process, but with the adoption of Buddhism the Japanese began to make a conscious attempt to transplant elements of the continental civilization. As a result, the rate of cultural borrowing increased sharply, ushering in a new age in Japanese history.

There were probably several reasons for this rather abrupt change. For one thing, China was beginning to exert a greater cultural pull than before. In 589 the Sui reunited the country after more than three and a half centuries of division, and in 618 the T'ang launched China on one of its greatest epochs. The Japanese too seem by this time to have attained a cultural level that permitted a more rapid rate of learning. Moreover the *uji* system, based as it was on familial and mythological ties, was proving inadequate to the needs of the time. It did not permit firm control over the local areas; the great court *uji* had come to overshadow the sun line itself, often disrupting the central government with their struggles for power; and succession wars were frequent because of the lack of a clear system of inheritance.

Prince Shōtoku.   The victory of the Soga in 587 made them supreme at the Yamato court. Their chief put his niece on the throne and appointed as regent her nephew, Prince Shōtoku (574–622), who was also half of Soga blood. Shōtoku and the Soga proceeded to carry out a series of important innovations that signaled their determination to shape Japanese society and government more after the pattern of China.

In 604 Shōtoku issued a set of precepts, known as the "Seventeen Article Constitution,"* which advocated such revolutionary Chinese ideas as the complete supremacy of the ruler, the centralization of government, and a bureaucracy of merit. It also enjoined reverence for Buddhism and extolled the Confucian virtues. The same year Shōtoku adopted the Chinese calendar. It was probably at this time that interest in the Chinese calendar and history induced the Japanese to count back 1260 years—a major Chinese cycle—to select the date 660 B.C. for the founding of the Japanese state.

In 603 Shōtoku adopted a major aspect of Chinese centralized bureaucratic rule—the system of personal court ranks for officials, assigned in accordance with the posts they held. These gradually replaced the heredi-

*It is thought by some to be a later forgery, but in any case it probably represents Shōtoku's ideas.

tary *uji* ranks as the major designations of status. The court rank system, in the permanent form it achieved by the middle of the eighth century, had eight numbered ranks, each divided into "senior" and "junior" classes, and the classes from the fourth rank on down were further divided into "upper" and "lower" grades. Every government post carried with it one of the twenty-six specific ranks, from the "Senior First Rank" down to the "Junior Eighth Rank Lower Grade."

The Japanese had sent embassies to China in earlier centuries, but Shōtoku reinstituted embassies on a much larger scale, sending one in 607, another the next year, and a third in 614. The importance of these embassies to the Japanese can be judged from their size and the extreme perils they braved. By the eighth century it was customary to build four new ships for each mission and some five hundred or six hundred men set sail on them. By this time Korean hostility had made the earlier route along the Korean coast unsafe, and the Japanese attempted to sail directly to China across the five hundred miles of open sea, without benefit of compass or much knowledge of the seasonal winds. Disasters were frequent, as can be seen in the graphic account of the clerical diarist Ennin, who accompanied the last embassy in 838.

The significance of the missions lay, not in their diplomatic achievements or incidental trade, but in what the Japanese participants learned in China. Students of all sorts accompanied the missions—Buddhist monks, scholars of Chinese history and literature, painters, musicians, and the like. Studying during the year the mission was in China or possibly for several years until the next mission brought them home, these men acquired knowledge and skills that were highly regarded at the Japanese court and contributed greatly to the cultural transformation of the country. (See Plate 17.)

The Taika Reforms.   After Shōtoku's death, the Soga alienated the other court families by their despotic rule and were eventually crushed in 645 in a *coup d'état* engineered by a prince, the future Emperor Tenchi (reigned 668–671), and a supporter who was given as a reward a new family name, Fujiwara. As Fujiwara no Kamatari* (614–669), he became the progenitor of a line of nobles that was to dominate the Japanese court for many centuries. Tenchi and Kamatari embarked on a second great wave of reforms based on the Chinese model of centralized government. Students returned from earlier embassies played an important role, and five more embassies were sent between 653 and 669. Taika, meaning "Great Change," was adopted as the name of the Chinese-type "year period" started in 645,

*As in other East Asian countries, the surname precedes the given name. The genitive *no,* making this name "Kamatari of Fujiwara," was dropped from names in later centuries.

and the reforms that were carried out over the next several years have usually been called the Taika Reforms.

A capital with Chinese-style buildings was erected at Naniwa (in the present Ōsaka) at the eastern end of the Inland Sea; central government ministries were set up; efforts were made to establish uniform rule over the provinces and to institute the centralized Chinese system of taxation; a census was carried out in 670 to facilitate this effort; and law codes of Chinese type were drawn up. These reforms were made piecemeal, with pragmatic compromises with existing institutions and the power of the various *uji*. Many of the laws may have existed only on paper, but slowly the Japanese state began to be reshaped into the image of the T'ang government.

Tenchi's successors carried on his reforms, and the new centralized system of rule was eventually embodied in the Taihō law codes, which went into effect in 702, and was symbolized by the establishment for the first time in 710 of a supposedly permanent capital. This was Heijō, commonly known by its later name of Nara, located at the northern end of the small Nara (or Yamato) Plain. The period from 710 to 784 when Nara was the capital is usually considered the high point of the Chinese political pattern in Japan.

The Nara Period

Government. Ch'ang-an, the T'ang capital, was both the symbol and the seat of China's centralized government. The Japanese did their best to create a comparable capital city. Nara was laid out in the same checkerboard fashion as a rectangle roughly three by two and two-thirds miles (Ch'ang-an was six by five miles), with the imperial palace at the northern end. Tile-roofed palace buildings and imposing Buddhist monasteries were erected. But even this reduced scale was far too grandiose for the needs of Japan in the eighth century. No city walls were built, since there were no enemies to ward off, and the western half of the city never materialized. After the center of government was moved, the whole city withered away, and modern Nara later grew up beside the Buddhist monasteries and Shintō shrines that had clustered around the capital.

A second effort at capital building proved more lasting. Kammu (781–806), who was the strongest emperor of the whole period, decided to leave Nara, perhaps because of the oppressive influence of its great monasteries. After an abortive effort in 784 to establish his capital a few miles to the north, he built in 794 a new city, called Heian, at the northern end of the small Kyōto Plain, just north of the Nara Plain. Laid out again in checkerboard fashion but on a slightly larger scale—three by three and one-third miles—Heian too lacked city walls or a western half. But it

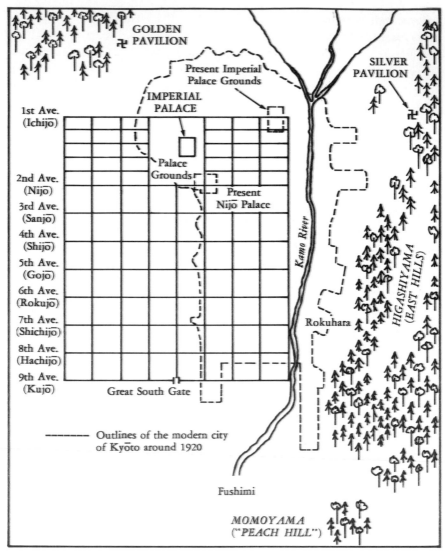

THE HEIAN CAPITAL (KYŌTO)

survived to become the modern city of Kyōto, which remained the official capital of Japan until 1868 and still maintains the original checkerboard layout of its main thoroughfares.

The new system of government was meticulously spelled out in the Taihō and later law codes, which were closely modeled on those of China. The basic concept in these was that the Yamato ruler was to be a Chinese-type emperor, concentrating in his hands all authority and power over a centralized state. Since Shōtoku's time he had been called *Tennō,* or "Heavenly Sovereign," a Chinese type of title. The change in the emperor's role, however, was much greater in theory than in actuality. The emperors continued to be dominated for the most part by the great court families around them, and their dual ritual functions as Shintō cult chiefs and Chinese-type rulers made their position so ceremonially onerous that early abdication became a common practice already in the eighth century and remained the rule until the nineteenth. But feminine rule, which had been frequent in the past, was abandoned under Chinese influence. During this period a Buddhist monk, through his influence over the reigning empress, made a bid for the throne, and after she died in 770 and he was exiled, no woman ascended the throne again for the next nine centuries.

Under the emperor, the Japanese central government was a simpler and more logical organization than its T'ang prototype, since it was not the product of evolution but of conscious adaptation. It departed from the Chinese pattern wherever the Japanese felt the need. At the top was a Grand Council of State headed by three Ministers. Below it were eight ministries, not the six of China, in order to include a Central Secretariat and a Ministry of the Imperial Household. Parallel to the secular Grand Council of State was an Office of Deities to supervise the emperor's cult functions and regulate the many Shintō shrines.

The court rituals and ceremonials were largely of Chinese origin. Orchestral music and stately dances borrowed from China were an important part of them. Including Central Asian and Indian influences, these T'ang dances and music (known as *gagaku* in Japan) are still maintained at the Japanese court, constituting the oldest fully authenticated musical and dance traditions in the world.

The whole country was reorganized into Chinese-type provinces, which were subdivided into districts and these into village units. By the ninth century there were sixty-six provinces, grouped into a capital region (later called Kinki) and circuits (*dō*, the Chinese *tao*), according to the routes by which they were reached. Of these the Tōkaidō, or "Eastern Sea Route," along the coast to the Kantō Plain, was to become the most famous. Dazaifu in North Kyūshū, which had developed earlier as an administrative subcenter, exercised some control over all of Kyūshū.

Governors and other officials dispatched from the capital controlled the provinces, but the officials in the districts and villages were local leaders. All rice lands were in theory government property and were supposed to be divided equally among the cultivators on the basis of detailed land and population records. Peasants paid equal taxes in the form of grain produce, textile produce, and *corvée* labor, which was the most onerous part of the tax burden. Military service was in theory included in the labor tax, but in actuality the Japanese, lacking powerful foreign enemies, never developed a Chinese type of draft army, and the palace guard groups remained the preserve of the aristocracy.

Society. According to the law codes, the Japanese seem to have taken over almost *in toto* the T'ang pattern of centralized bureaucratic government and its very complex system of landholding and taxation. The realities were probably much more of a compromise with the earlier *uji* society. But there was undoubtedly a great consolidation and extension of the power of the central government during the seventh and eighth centuries. The area of effective rule was expanded, as southern Kyūshū was fully incorporated into the state and a series of campaigns during the late eighth and early ninth centuries broke the power of the Ainu in North Honshū. A succession war in 672 and an uprising against the would-be monkish usurper in 764 were the last serious internal disturbances for almost two centuries. Eighth-century registers show a meticulous effort to carry out the system of equally divided rice fields, and there was a substantial flow of taxes from these fields to the capital, which continued, though at a slowly diminishing rate, for several centuries. The political forms and official titles established at this time survived until the nineteenth century, forming at least the theoretical framework and nomenclature for a millennium of political evolution.

Nara Japan, however, was in many ways vastly different from T'ang China. By comparison it was still economically backward. For example, the government issued copper cash in 708 and on some subsequent occasions, in imitation of the Chinese government, but barter remained the rule. The old court *uji* had been transformed into a broader court aristocracy (known as the *kuge*), but class lines remained sharp, and the great Chinese concept of a bureaucracy of educational merit was simply ignored. A central university of the Chinese type was created but was used largely to educate the sons of the court aristocrats, not as a channel for a wider recruitment of bureaucratic talent.

The court aristocracy fell into three distinct levels, with corresponding court ranks, while the descendants of the *uji* aristocracy in the provinces, who had been reduced to posts at the district level, were for the most part relegated to a separate series of "outer" ranks. Below them the peasantry probably achieved some rise in status and rights in their transformation from serf-like members of *be,* subservient to local *uji,* to citizens who paid taxes directly to the central government and had their rights to their lands guaranteed by this government.

The supposed nationalization of all agricultural lands and the taxation of all peasants was probably not carried through as sweepingly as the law codes imply. Much of the agricultural wealth of the old *uji* aristocracy probably remained undisturbed. In keeping with the T'ang system, the highest ranks of the aristocracy retained the income from their lands simply because of their ranks and the lesser aristocracy the income from smaller tracts because of their official positions. Thus some elements of

*Left: Late seventh-century Buddhist wooden image at a nunnery
attached to the Hōryūji near Nara. Right: Eighth-century bronze
trinity in the Yakushiji ("Temple of the Buddha of Medicine")
near Nara.*

the aristocratic *uji* system probably survived under the veneer of Chinese
institutions of centralized government. But the reorganization of the
Japanese state from the time of Prince Shōtoku through the Nara period
did reduce drastically the wealth and the once autonomous power of the
provincial *uji,* as both archaeology and the historical record clearly show.

Buddhist Art. The political transformation of Japan was accompanied
by a great leap forward in technology and culture. As we have seen,
Buddhism was the first aspect of continental civilization consciously
adopted by the Japanese, and the arts associated with it were prominent
among the early borrowings. They seem to have been easier for the Japanese to absorb than were political and philosophic ideas, because no
difficult barrier of language stood in the way.

  Some of the early Buddhist images in Japan were brought from Korea
or were the products of Korean immigrants, but already in the seventh

century the Japanese themselves were producing works of consummate beauty, and the full-bodied Buddhist images and realistic portrait statues of the Nara period are among the finest works of East Asian art of this epoch. Japanese sculptors, unlike Chinese and Koreans, made little use of stone but skillfully employed bronze, wood, clay and lacquer.

The Japanese mastered Chinese architectural and bridge building techniques and a host of other skills. The Buddhist temples built in Japan during the seventh and eighth centuries are the best remaining examples of classic T'ang architecture. The Golden Hall and pagoda of the Hōryūji, a monastery founded by Shōtoku on the western edge of the Nara Plain but apparently rebuilt a few decades later, are probably the oldest wooden buildings in the world. The Golden Hall is crowded with beautiful images from Shōtoku's time, and its walls are covered by frescoes (seriously damaged by a fire in 1949), which are reminiscent of the paintings in Buddhist cave temples in India. The Nara capital was graced by a number of great temples with stately tile-roofed halls and towering pagodas, some of which are still standing.

Much of Buddhism's early appeal in Japan depended on its reputation as a magical protector of the state and also of individual families. In a way reminiscent of the *uji* cults of an earlier age, families established protective family temples. The Tōdaiji in Nara served that function for the central government and the imperial family. Emperors devoutly built and endowed monasteries, and around 770 the court printed a million Buddhist charms, many of which remain as the earliest examples of printing in the world.

The emperor Shōmu (reigned 724–749, died 756) was the most enthusiastic of all the imperial patrons of Buddhism. He set out to create a state cult of Buddhism which would parallel the centralized civil government. In 741 he ordered the establishment of an official branch monastery and nunnery in each province, and in 752 he dedicated at the Tōdaiji in the capital a gigantic fifty-three-foot, seated bronze image of Vairocana, the supreme and universal Buddha. Marred by later damages and repairs, it is no longer a great artistic work, but it is still one of the largest bronze figures in the world. The ritual objects used in the dedication ceremony together with Shōmu's personal belongings remain in a large storehouse nearby (called the Shōsōin), constituting a unique treasure of eighth-century musical instruments, painted screens, textiles, rugs, weapons, and the like, many of them imported from China or from even further afield in Asia.

The Spread of Buddhism.   Buddhism at first had been concentrated largely at the capital and had generally been limited to the ruling class. But in the eighth and ninth centuries it gradually spread to all parts of the country, and Buddhist ideas began to influence the whole of society. The new religion brought with it a new concept of the afterlife and new ethical values of

Eighth-century Lecture Hall of the Tōshōdaiji ("Temple Brought from the T'ang") near Nara.

charity and service. The decline in tomb burials after the seventh century and the adoption of cremation can be attributed to Buddhist influence. Buddhist injunctions against the taking of life may also help account for the decided decline in warlike ferocity among the Japanese at this time, the substitution of banishment for execution, and a growing prejudice against the eating of meat, though not of fish.

The question arises why Buddhism could succeed so rapidly when a native religion was already well entrenched in Japan. The answer probably lies in part in the fact that Shintō and Buddhism operated at such different philosophical levels that they did not come into serious conflict, in part in Buddhism's ability to adapt to and absorb the beliefs it encountered as it spread, as had already been demonstrated in China. Shintō gods and cults could be accommodated to Buddhism as subordinate local manifestations of Buddhist deities and universal Buddhist principles. Even the Sun Goddess came to be identified with Vairocana, whose alternative name of Dainichi, or "Great Sun," aided this concept. The growing subordination of Shintō to Buddhism was elaborated and systematized under the name of Dual Shintō

*Late seventh-century
wooden pagoda at the
Yakushiji near Nara.*

by monks of the Shingon ("True Word") sect in the twelfth century. Not until the nineteenth century was Shintō disentangled again from Buddhism.

During the seventh and eighth centuries some of the major philosophical schools of Buddhism, which had been transmitted from India to China, were introduced to Japan. The Japanese, following the Chinese in their love of classification, have labeled these the Six Nara Sects. The last of these was brought by a Chinese monk, Chien-chen (Ganjin in Japanese), who after five unsuccessful efforts finally reached Japan in 754, a blind old man.

Four of the Nara sects still exist as separate entities, but all were soon overshadowed by two new sects introduced in the early ninth century. Their success may have been in part due to the court's desire for religious counterweights to the great monasteries of the older sects that had grown up around Nara, but probably owed more to the fact that the new sects represented trends in Buddhism that had greater appeal in Japan than did Indian philosophical niceties. Both new sects were introduced by student monks who accompanied the embassy to China of 804.

Eighth-century lacquer statue of the Chinese missionary priest Chien-chen (Ganjin).

Kōbō Daishi returned to Japan in 806 with the Shingon sect. Its emphasis on incantations, magic formulas, ceremonials, and masses for the dead proved as popular in Japan as in China. The complicated iconography of its statues and paintings of Buddhist deities and its elaborate *mandara,* which are schematic representations of Shingon philosophical concepts, also had a great impact on the religious art of the time. Kōbō Daishi's monastic center on Mt. Kōya, south of the Nara Plain, is still one of Japan's most impressive Buddhist establishments, and he remains Japan's most popular religious hero, about whom a vast body of myth and tradition has formed.

Dengyō Daishi returned from China in 805 with the Tendai Sect (T'ien-t'ai in Chinese). Its typically East Asian eclecticism and its classification of conflicting Buddhist doctrines as different levels of truth, each valid in its own way, appealed as much to Japanese as to Chinese. The Tendai monastic headquarters was at the Enryakuji, near the summit of Mt. Hiei a few miles northeast of Kyōto, where it came to be regarded as the spiritual protector of the capital. The third Enryakuji abbot, the traveler diarist Ennin, assured the later dominance of Tendai by combining its original teachings with the esoteric practices of the Shingon sect. Out of Tendai's diversity were to emerge most of the sectarian movements of later periods.

Writing and Literature. The adoption of the Chinese pattern naturally included the borrowing of the Chinese writing system. But the pictographic and ideographic Chinese characters were ill-adapted to writing other languages, particularly the polysyllabic and highly inflected languages of Japan and Korea. It was a major historical tragedy for both countries that they did not learn about phonetic systems of transcription until after the use of Chinese characters had become firmly established.

Chinese characters, each standing for a specific meaning and sound, could be borrowed as a whole. In fact, thousands of Chinese words were gradually incorporated in this way into Japanese. But for native Japanese words, the Chinese writing system was entirely inadequate. The early Japanese, like the Koreans, solved the problem simply by writing in the Chinese language, though on occasion they would laboriously spell out Japanese names and words syllable by syllable with Chinese characters used phonetically. It is a tribute to the diligence of the early Japanese that they were able to carry out such sweeping political and cultural changes in the seventh and eighth centuries through the medium of a radically different foreign language and a vastly difficult writing system.

With the Chinese writing system came the Chinese emphasis on the written record of the past as an aid in government, which resulted in the two great history works already mentioned, the *Record of Ancient Matters* of 712 and the *History of Japan* of 720. The latter was followed by five successive Chinese-type histories which take the record up to 887. Together with the *History of Japan,* these are known as the *Six National Histories.* Among other serious scholarly writings inspired by Chinese prototypes were local records (*fudoki*), started in 713, which were accounts of the geography, economy, legends, and political institutions of each province.

The Japanese also took on Chinese attitudes toward the literary arts, and a distinguished hand in Chinese calligraphy and a pleasing style in Chinese composition or native poetry became the essential marks of a person of breeding. An anthology of 120 Chinese poems by Japanese still remains from the Nara period, but it is overshadowed in size and quality by a great compendium of 4516 poems in Japanese, called the *Collection of Myriad Leaves* (*Man'yōshū*). The great majority of the poems in this collection are so-called "short poems" (*tanka*) of 31 syllables, divided into phrases of 5-7-5-7-7 syllables. Though a very restricted literary medium, the "short poem" has remained the favorite Japanese poetic form ever since. Normally a "short poem" suggests a natural scene and then by a deft turn changes this into a surge of emotion. Commonly depending for interest on plays on words or literary allusions, "short poems" can only rarely be translated both artistically and accurately. The following, from the ninth century, however, is simple enough to lend itself to literal translation, though its very simplicity may make it atypical:

Haru tateba	*When spring comes*
kiyuru koori no	*the melting ice*
nokori naku	*leaves no trace;*
Kimi ga kokoro mo	*Would that your heart too*
ware ni tokenan	*melted thus toward me.*

The Modification of the Chinese Pattern

One can only marvel at the success of the Japanese in creating a fair facsimile of the Chinese political system and in moving from what was a relatively primitive society in the fifth century to a high degree of cultural sophistication by the eighth. The achievement is all the more surprising in that it was done without the stimulus of conquest from abroad and despite the wide expanse of open sea between Japan and China and the high barriers of language and writing. It stands in contrast to the much slower and less successful efforts of the North Europeans at this same time to master Mediterranean civilization. Part of the difference no doubt was because China, Japan's cultural model, was in full vigor, while the Roman model in the West was sinking into sad decay.

As we have seen, however, the Japanese copy of the Chinese political system was from the start far from exact. There had been no real effort to get away from a sharply divided class society or to create a real bureaucracy. Even in China centralized bureaucratic rule tended to show signs of serious decline within a century of its inauguration and to break down completely within two or three. Without any real bureaucracy, there was even less to stop the erosion of the system in Japan. In fact, it evolved into something quite different from the original Chinese model. That this should have happened is less surprising than that the Chinese system operated successfully as long as it did and left a heavy residue of ideas and institutions that have influenced Japan ever since.

The Nara period is usually thought of as the time when the Chinese pattern prevailed and the Heian period which followed it, when the capital was at Heian, or Kyōto, as the time of a return to a more native pattern. Actually the periods do not coincide quite so neatly with the trends. The Heian period is usually dated from 794 to 1185 (although Kyōto remained the capital until 1868), and its early decades probably witnessed the high point of Chinese cultural influence in Japan. As we have seen, both the Tendai and Shingon sects were introduced in the early ninth century, and a great embassy went to China as late as 838.

In the course of the ninth century, however, there was a slow but major shift in the tide of Japanese history. Chinese institutions in Japan were becoming so modified that new borrowings from the continent seemed somewhat irrelevant. The Japanese aristocrats were now so at home in the continental culture that they felt free to depart from Chinese norms as they saw fit. Another factor was that by the ninth century T'ang was in serious dynastic decline. This was cited as a major reason for the decision not to send an embassy to China in 894. Trips were still made to China by monks and merchants traveling on Korean and Chinese ships, but the declining interest in learning from China reduced the cultural significance of these contacts for the next few centuries.

The Estate System. Meanwhile profound changes were taking place within Japan. From the start, aristocratic families had claim to the income from extensive holdings on the basis of rank, office, or services, and these tended to become their permanent possessions. The same was true of lands assigned to Buddhist monasteries and great Shintō shrines. Such private holdings constantly grew, in part at the expense of public tax lands, but more as a result of the opening up of new rice paddies, for which the wealthy families and institutions were best able to undertake the substantial costs of drainage and irrigation. The court encouraged such reclamation of new land, permitting in 723 the retention of reclaimed fields for a generation or more, and making ownership permanent in 743.

The value of a private holding, of course, depended largely on its degree of tax exemption and independence from the central government. From the start these lands had enjoyed some exemptions from taxation, and these tended to expand. Owners hoped to win not just freedom from various sorts of taxes but protection from civil and criminal jurisdiction and eventually immunity from entry and inspection by government officials. One of the best ways to achieve these various degrees of independence was to commend holdings to powerful court families or religious institutions, whose prestige at court could ensure protection from government officials. Thus parcels of privately owned land tended to cluster together to form large private estates under the patronage and protection of powerful families and institutions. Such estates (called *shōen*) began to form in the eighth century, and they spread throughout Japan during the next four centuries until there were literally thousands of them. Unlike the manors of Europe, the estates were not unified pieces of land centering around a manor house and grazing land used in common (there were no dairy herds and few draft animals) but were made up of scattered tracts of agricultural land administered as a unit.

The central figure in the estate system was the proprietor, who was likely to be an aristocrat of influence either locally or at court. Above him might be a patron, who normally was one of the most prestigious of the court nobles or a great religious institution. Below the proprietor were the local estate managers, below these in turn the small holders who did the actual farming, and below them their dependent workers. All but the last category had their respective rights to parts of the income from the estate. These income rights, which were called *shiki,* meaning "function" or "office," were usually specified in documents and were both divisible and inheritable—by women as well as men. The resemblance of this system to the system of multiple rights attached to a single piece of land in feudal Europe is striking but perhaps not surprising. Both were survivals of elements of an earlier centralized administrative and legal system—the Roman in Europe—after centralized control itself had waned.

The public tax-paying domain did not disappear entirely into private estates. Much of the land, perhaps as much as half, was still outside them as late as the twelfth century. The administration of these public lands, however, gradually took on many of the features of the administration of the estates. There was no effort to redistribute land among the tax-paying peasants after the middle of the ninth century, and gradually the unit of taxation shifted from the individual male peasant to the land itself. Even at the height of the Chinese system, courtiers had gone with reluctance to provincial posts and even then largely for the income rather than the prestige or power. Increasingly in the ninth century it became the custom for governors to send deputies in their place and to regard a provincial appointment merely as a source of revenue. In fact, the right to select governors for certain provinces became itself in time a sort of possession, like the "patronage" over an estate. Minor court aristocrats, who went out to the provinces to make their fortunes as deputies or lesser officials, succeeded in making their posts hereditary and took on functions on the public lands comparable to those of the proprietors or managers of estates.

The whole economy and society of Japan thus was moving far from the Chinese pattern of centralized political control and back toward private and personalized relations reminiscent of the *uji* period. Each group, instead of being directly related to the central government, was more narrowly oriented toward the group immediately above it. On the estates, landless peasants worked for small holders, who were controlled by estate managers, who were answerable to proprietors, who in turn might be beholden to patrons. The names and theories were different on government lands, but the realities were becoming much the same. The local produce that flowed to the capital increasingly went into the hands of the great religious institutions and court families, members of which held posts as proprietors or patrons of estates or exercised the patronage of appointment to the provincial governments. Thus the chief ties, political as well as economic, between the provinces and the capital came to be through the great noble families and the powerful central religious institutions, rather than through the central government itself.

The great families and religious institutions of the capital area, though still associated with one another through the framework of the old centralized government, had in a sense become its multiple successors in the exercise of real power. This can be seen in their development of what amounted to small private family or institutional governments. The Fujiwara family, descended from Kamatari, the leader of the *coup d'état* of 645, is a good case in point. It resembled in a way the great *uji* of earlier times, having a family head, significantly called *uji* chief, and possessing a family temple and Shintō shrine at the old Nara capital. To administer its complex family affairs and the dozens of estates it owned throughout the country, it had a family government, headed by the family head and consisting of a series of bureaus, including an "administrative office" (*mandokoro*).

The Modification of Political Institutions. The reshaping of society and the economy through the development of estates was a long slow process spreading over the eighth to the thirteenth centuries, but it was far enough advanced by the ninth to begin to have a visible effect on the outward forms of the central government. As the tax yield declined or was diverted into private hands and the area of effective control by the government shrank, the government was slowly starved both of economic sustenance and of functions to perform. But it did not wither away, as might have happened in a country more subject to foreign pressures. Maintained by the wealthy families around it, the central government became in large part an elaborate stage for their rivalries. It also continued to be regarded by the real holders of power as the ultimate source of all titles, ranks, and claims to legitimacy.

As the substance of administration ebbed from the offices of government, their rituals and ceremonies loomed all the more important and were maintained by the courtiers with meticulous attention to precedent. All the posts and titles of government were carefully preserved but increasingly became the inherited possessions of family lines. Eventually what had been actual governmental functions in the eighth century degenerated into purely honorary hereditary titles awarded regardless of the incumbent's age or ability, and subsequently some of these titles became little more than surnames or personal names.

In place of the now needlessly elaborate organs of state, simpler political institutions grew up in the ninth century to handle the remaining duties of the central government. Audit Officers, first appointed in 790 to audit the accounts of retiring local administrators, supplanted a variety of offices as the chief supervisors of the government's tax income and the most effective channel of control between the capital and the provincial governments. A Bureau of Archivists, established in 810, grew into the chief organ for drafting imperial decrees. Police Commissioners, first appointed around 820 in the capital, developed into the only effective organ of the central government for maintaining law and order and came in the process to administer a sort of customary law that was growing up around the old Chinese-type law codes. Together with some aristocratic provincial militia groups, they also became the only remnants of the Chinese concept of a centralized army.

The appointment of Audit Officers in 790 was the first of many efforts by the central government to stop the erosion of its income and powers. A century later two successive emperors tried hard to stem the tide but achieved little except to inspire the compilation in 927 of an elaboration of the old law codes.

The Fujiwara and the Retired Emperors.   The greatest change in the central government in the ninth century was the establishment of almost complete control over the imperial family by a branch of one of the great court families—the Fujiwara. It was able to do this in part through providing empresses and imperial concubines, in part because it was emerging as the family which owned the largest number of estates throughout Japan. Its head, Yoshifusa, put his seven-year-old imperial grandson on the throne in 858 and assumed for himself the post of regent. This was the first instance of a small child being made emperor and the first time the regent had not been a member of the imperial family. The next Fujiwara chief similarly served as regent for a child emperor and then continued in this capacity for an adult who came to the throne in 884, taking for this purpose the specially created title of *kampaku.*

After Yoshifusa had established the supremacy of the Fujiwara, members of the family continued to monopolize nearly all of the high government offices, to supply most of the imperial consorts, and to place sons of Fujiwara mothers on the throne. In fact, they so dominated the court that the period from 858 to 1160 is commonly called the Fujiwara period. The height of Fujiwara glory came under Michinaga (966–1027). The extent of his control over the imperial family can be seen from the fact that four emperors married his daughters, two were his nephews, and three his grandsons. His family "administrative office," rather than the organs of the central government, was the real center of power at the capital. Despite their great power, however, the Fujiwara never made the slightest move toward usurping the throne. The concept of hereditary authority and the special religious aura of the imperial line were too strong. It gradually became accepted, however, that the emperors reigned but did not rule.

Since the Fujiwara were content to derive their authority in theory from the imperial line, they could always be challenged by a vigorous emperor. For example, a retired emperor who did not happen to be born of a Fujiwara mother attempted to oppose Fujiwara domination by appointing Sugawara no Michizane, a lesser aristocrat but a renowned scholar, to a high post in 899, but two years later the Fujiwara chief managed to have this rival sent off into virtual exile in Kyūshū. Again in 1069 an emperor not born of a Fujiwara mother founded a Records Office in an attempt to confiscate all estates formed since 1045, but the effort was frustrated by the Fujiwara.

A more successful attempt to recapture power was carried out by the

Emperor Shirakawa, who, after his abdication in 1086, successfully contested the supremacy of the Fujiwara by utilizing minor aristocrats who had made their reputations as scholars or in provincial administrations. This form of rule by retired emperors, which is known as *insei,* was continued by other retired emperors for a century after Shirakawa's death in 1129 and was sporadically revived for another century after that.

Meanwhile, however, the whole central government was declining rapidly and there was progressively less power for the Fujiwara and retired emperors to fight over. During the eleventh century, dwindling revenues resulted in the neglect of government buildings, which fell into serious decay. Lawlessness was becoming prevalent in the provinces, and acts of violence were occurring even in the capital. Deep rivalries divided and weakened the Fujiwara family, while the chief success the retired emperors had during their period of power was in further despoiling the public domain by turning much of it into estates owned by the imperial family.

The Culture of the Fujiwara Period

The gradual disintegration of the institutions of central government and the subsequent decline of law and order have given to the period from the tenth to the twelfth centuries an aura of decay and impending catastrophe. Such attitudes were commonly expressed in the writings of the time. But these centuries were in fact a period of great economic and cultural growth throughout the country. The estate system seems to have proved as conducive to economic and cultural development as had the more centralized but also more constrained system that had preceded it. The opening of new agricultural lands and the increase of the population in distant areas such as the Kantō and North Honshū were signs of economic growth as well as reasons for the decline of the centralized government. Communications actually improved, and the flow of goods throughout Japan was much greater by the twelfth century than it had been in the eighth. Many features of continental civilization that had been limited largely to the capital area in the eighth century had become widely diffused throughout Japan by the twelfth. A beautiful temple building, erected in 1124 at Hiraizumi in North Honshū by a locally powerful branch of the Fujiwara family, illustrates the high levels of provincial wealth and artistic achievement even in this remote area.

In the capital the court nobles, supported by their many estates, lived in luxury. Lacking real duties to perform in a government largely empty of meaningful functions, they led lives that were in many ways shallow, centering around symbols rather than realities. They occupied themselves in an endless round of ritual observances and dilettantish pastimes, such as judging the merits of flowers, roots, or shells or composing poems as a wine cup floated to each person in turn down a miniature winding waterway. The emphasis was strongly aesthetic: what counted was the proper costume, the right ceremonial act, the successful turn of phrase in a poem, and the appropriate expression of refined taste. Love-making was a major art in a society in which the institution of marriage was not sharply defined.

While full of Chinese elements, Fujiwara court culture was almost entirely free of any new efforts to imitate Chinese patterns. It was a complete and natural blend of now thoroughly assimilated Chinese elements and native tendencies. In this sense it was completely Japanese. In contrast to the stern asceticism and military virtues of later times, Fujiwara culture seems effete and effeminate. But its aesthetic sensitivity and creativity were to remain characteristic of all later Japanese civilization.

Buddhism. During the Fujiwara period Buddhism in Japan, which up until the ninth century had depended heavily on successive waves of influence from the continent, developed into Japanese Buddhism. At court the emphasis on elaborate rituals in secular life was paralleled by a corresponding emphasis on Buddhist rituals, for which the esoteric cults of the Shingon and Tendai sects provided ample scope. At the same time, Buddhism, in spreading outward from the capital and downward in society and in amalgamating with the Shintō cults, lost some of its original emphasis as the magical protector of the state, becoming instead more of a vehicle of faith and hope for the common people.

This new and more popular Buddhism was based on Pure Land doctrines introduced from China in the ninth century, but now greatly developed by the Japanese themselves. The central concept was that the present was a degenerate age, known as "the latter period of the law," and that rebirth into the Pure Land Paradise of the Buddha Amida, who had vowed the salvation of all living creatures, could now be achieved only through faith. Salvation thus depended on the "strength of another," not on "one's own strength," and it could best be achieved through calling on the Buddha's name by chanting "Hail to the Buddha Amida" over and over. During the tenth century such ideas were popularized by priests who preached in the streets, but the most important figure in the new Buddhism was a more scholarly figure, Genshin (942–1017), whose *Essentials of Salvation* contained detailed descriptions of the horrors of hell and the bliss of paradise.

During this period Buddhism also became incorporated into the institutional life of Japan in a way it never had on the continent. In the course of the ninth century the government abandoned its effort to limit the size of the clergy by regulating ordinations, and the organized church grew without restrictions. The sectarian divisions of earlier times, which had been based primarily on philosophical differences, hardened into clear administrative hierarchies of mother and branch monasteries. Buddhist monasteries increasingly drew support from their own lands, and the great monastic establishments of the capital region vied with the powerful families as proprietors and patrons of estates throughout the country. Monasteries also began to form armed bands from among their younger priests and workers on their estates in order to protect their interests. The turbulence of the monks in the capital area and the armed rivalries between some of the great monasteries became legendary. Repeatedly after the late eleventh century priestly armies threatened the authorities in the capital, and the retired emperor Shirakawa quipped that the only things he could not control were the Kamo River (flowing through Kyōto), the fall of the dice, and the monastic armies. Thus the Buddhist church achieved a far greater economic and secular role in Japan than it ever had in China or Korea.

Art.   The Japanese during the Fujiwara period continued to use the basic Chinese artistic idiom but began to express through it typically Japanese tastes. The balanced, formal architecture of the T'ang was replaced in palace architecture by more airy pavilions connected by covered passageways and artfully placed in a natural setting of gardens and ponds. This style was to grow into the Japanese domestic architecture of more modern times.

In Buddhist sculpture and painting the emphasis was on the complex iconography of the ritualistic, esoteric sects and on representations of Amida and his Pure Land, but there also developed in painting a style of simple, flowing lines and flat colored surfaces quite unlike Chinese prototypes and fittingly called "Yamato pictures" (*Yamato-e*). Commonly such paintings were organized into picture scrolls, which in a continuous drawing or series of drawings told a story. The earliest remaining example illustrates the famous court novel, *The Tale of Genji* (*Genji monogatari*), but others portray monastic traditions or famous historical events. (See Plates 15–16.)

The appearance at this time of hereditary families of artists, commonly maintained by adoption when heredity failed to produce talent, provides another example of how the continental civilization was fitted into a completely familial pattern. The same happened in the various other specialized fields of endeavor, such as scholarship, calendar making, music, calligraphy, and the like.

The Kana Writing System.   During the ninth and tenth centuries it became customary for Japanese to read Chinese texts in native Japanese words and according to the Japanese word order. This, of course, was a sign of declining competence in the Chinese language, and by the tenth century much of the Chinese composed in Japan, which is known as *kambun* or "Han writing," had become so heavily Japanized that it can be understood today only by persons who know both Chinese and Japanese.

A more important development at this time was the appearance of purely phonetic scripts for writing Japanese. The poems of the *Collection of*

Scene from a humorous scroll painting, attributed to Toba Sōjō,
showing a frog as a Buddhist image, a monkey, fox, and rabbit
in clerical garb, a fox as an aristocratic court lady with attendants,
and a rabbit in a layman's black hat.

Myriad Leaves had been spelled out syllable by syllable in Chinese characters used phonetically. In the course of the ninth century these characters were simplified to be nothing more than phonetic symbols, each representing a syllable. There were two systems, both called *kana.* Whole characters written cursively in abbreviated form became known as *hiragana* and selected parts of characters as *katakana.* The two systems were not fully standardized until the late nineteenth century, and variant forms are still sometimes used in handwriting.

The *kana* syllabaries were excellent ways to write the Japanese of the time, but because of the prestige of Chinese, well educated people continued to attempt to write in that language for most serious purposes, though with increasing admixtures of Japanese elements. Even those who wrote in Japanese were always tempted to insert Chinese words written in characters. The eventual outgrowth of both tendencies was the present mixed style of writing, in which Chinese characters are used for borrowed Chinese words and for those Japanese words (or at least their stems) which can be equated in meaning with specific Chinese characters, while *kana* is used for the inflections and other elements not easily represented by characters. Such a mixed style was evolving already in the eleventh century and thenceforth competed with the two other systems of writing—straight Chinese (or what the Japanese thought was Chinese) for documents and scholarly writing and pure Japanese in *kana* for poems and some prose texts.

The contemporary mixed style is probably the most difficult writing system in common use anywhere in the world. Each Chinese character may be

EXAMPLES OF THE DERIVATION OF KANA

Chinese character	安	以	加	多	奴	保
Original meaning	peace	take	add	many	slave	protect
Chinese pronunciation	*an*	*i*	*chia*	*to*	*nu*	*pao*
Katakana			カ	タ	ヌ	ホ
Hiragana	あ	い	か		ぬ	ほ
Phonetic value in Japanese	*a*	*i*	*ka*	*ta*	*nu*	*ho*

read according to the Japanese approximation of its Chinese pronunciation (there is often more than one Japanese pronunciation, depending on the period and location in China from which the Chinese pronunciation was first learned). The same character could also have the pronunciation of one of several Japanese words that might be equated with it in meaning. A strictly phonetic system of writing would be preferable. But to return to writing in pure *kana* or, better still, to shift to the much simpler "Roman" alphabet (*rōmaji* in Japanese) would not be easy. This is because of the huge number of homophones in written Japanese, largely derived from Chinese words. Since Japanese is phonetically much simpler than Chinese, many words that are distinct in Chinese are pronounced alike in Japanese. For example, twenty different Chinese syllables, each differentiated further by four tones —a total of eighty separate sounds—all boil down to the single sound *kō* in Japanese. Though such homophones are easily confused in speech, they are quite distinct when written in characters. Thus a shift to purely phonetic writing in Japan would necessitate a massive alteration of the scholarly and technical vocabulary.

Literature. The *kana* syllabaries greatly facilitated writing in Japanese. The emphasis at court on the composition of poetry in Japanese continued, and a second anthology of about eleven hundred poems was compiled on imperial order in 905. Called the *Ancient and Modern Collection* (*Kokinshū*), it became the model for twenty more imperial anthologies compiled up to 1439. A preface to the *Ancient and Modern Collection* is one of the earliest examples of serious prose writing in pure Japanese, and the author of this preface also wrote a poetic travel diary, the *Tosa Diary*, in Japanese. Many other diaries were written at this time in either Japanese or Chinese, and the Japanese have ever since shown themselves to be inveterate diarists.

Around the year 1000, during the ascendancy of Fujiwara no Michinaga, there was a veritable outburst of literary activity in Japanese. This was largely the work of court ladies, whose lesser mastery of Chinese characters led them to write in Japanese—with great beauty—while most of their male counterparts continued to write proudly in Chinese—with artistically undistinguished results. Lady Sei Shōnagon's *Pillow Book*, compiled at this time, is a miscellany of witty and sometimes caustic comments on the court life about her. Other ladies wrote diaries or novels, all liberally sprinkled with poems. The greatest work was the massive *Tale of Genji* by Lady Murasaki, which recounts with great psychological subtlety and aesthetic sensitivity the life and loves of an imaginary Prince Genji, and in the process gives us a detailed picture of the court life of the time. *The Tale of Genji* has exerted immeasurable literary influence throughout Japanese history and in Arthur Waley's masterful translation has become one of the great world classics.

In the late eleventh and twelfth centuries a new literary genre appeared. This was romanticized accounts of the period of Fujiwara dominance at court. The *Tale of Splendor* (*Eiga monogatari*) covers the period 889 to 1092 in chronological sequence and the *Great Mirror* (*Ōkagami*) the period from 850 to 1025 in biographic style. The shift from the official court histories written in Chinese, which came to an end in 887, to these more literary efforts at history writing in Japanese and centering on the Fujiwara, illustrates how far the Japanese had strayed from the Chinese patterns they had earlier adopted.

14. Feudal Japan: A Departure from the Chinese Pattern

The Rise of the Provincial Warrior Class

The Roots of Feudalism. For all its cultural brilliance, the Fujiwara court was not the direct ancestor of later Japanese society. It had grown too effete to continue its dominance. Instead it served as the transmitter of the now fully assimilated residue of Chinese civilization to another more vigorous group. This was the provincial warrior class, in whose hands the future of Japan was to lie.

The estate system gave the people in the provinces fiscal and legal protection against the officers of the central government, but it did not provide them local security. As the power of the central government and its provincial representatives waned, armed struggles between local groups over lands or offices increased in frequency, and piracy became endemic on the Inland Sea. To counter such conditions, provincial authorities during the ninth century acquired the right to maintain armed guards and in time were given military titles. Similarly managers or local proprietors of private estates developed armed bands to defend their interests. Thus military functions began to merge with political and economic roles. As such guard groups drew together for mutual security, they began to provide a lateral integration of local society to accompany the vertical integration of the provincial estates with the great families or religious institutions of the capital area.

Defense groupings of this sort grew up gradually between the ninth and twelfth centuries. They tended to be familial in organization, composed of head and branch families, but for geographic and other reasons nonrelated subordinates, known as "house men" (*kenin*), increasingly joined in. As these groups became more powerful and influential, they were able to provide not just physical security but also protection for the property rights of their members. In time they even became able to reward loyal members with new rights.

The mutual defense groups tended to form around lines of particular hereditary prestige. These were usually minor offshoots of the Fujiwara family or of the imperial line itself. On repeated occasions after 814, excess members of the imperial line were cut off from it and given the family names of Minamoto (also known as Genji) or Taira (also called Heike). Unable to achieve high office at court, these men would go out to the provinces in order to make their fortunes as provincial officials or estate proprietors and managers. Coming with the prestige of the court and imperial descent, they tended to form a top layer in the provincial aristocracy above the descendants of the old provincial *uji*.

The local armed bands thus were led by the most prestigious members of the local aristocracy, and they were in fact made up almost exclusively of the upper crust of provincial society. This was because the military technology of the day made fighting an expensive and therefore aristocratic profession. As in Europe at that time, the central figure was a mounted, armored knight with his supporting footmen. Unlike his European counterpart, however, the Japanese mounted warrior relied not on a lance but on bow and arrows and a curved sword—the finest blade in the world. His armor, made of thin strips of steel held together by brightly colored thongs, might look flimsy compared to European armor, but its lightness and flexibility probably made it more practical. As in Europe, warfare was conducted primarily as a series of individual encounters between knights, rather than through coordinated mass movements of troops.

The provincial warrior aristocracy that emerged during these centuries is known as the *bushi* ("warrior") or *samurai* ("retainer") class. It was made up in large part of the descendants of the old provincial *uji* aristocracy and clearly inherited the latter's military traditions, which perhaps had never been lost, despite the long-standing overlay of a Chinese-type of centralized civil government. As this provincial warrior class moved to the center of the historical stage during the twelfth century, it led Japan into a type of social and political organization more like that of feudal Europe than the Chinese centralized bureaucratic state. Military power absorbed into it political and economic authority, and all three became defined primarily in terms of rights to land, while personal lord-and-vassal relationships, often expressed in familial terms, became central to political integration.

Both Japanese and Western feudalism seem to have resulted from a mixture of two basic ingredients: administrative and legal institutions

A sixteenth-century suit of armor (little changed from the twelfth century).

surviving from a more centralized state and a system of personal bonds of loyalty. In Japan these two were derived respectively from the Chinese type of organization of the Nara period and the earlier familial pattern of *uji* society; in the West from Roman law and the German tribal war bands. The two basic ingredients have frequently been present together in human history, but apparently only rarely in the proper proportions to produce a fully feudal system. The Japanese is the only well documented case besides that of Europe.

The Rise of the Minamoto and Taira.   Two large-scale struggles between provincial warrior bands broke out almost simultaneously in the middle of the tenth century. In the Kantō region a Taira leader seized two provinces before being destroyed by his rivals in 940. The next year in the Inland Sea area a descendant of the Fujiwara was brought down after a decade of disorders. In the eleventh century a branch of the Minamoto won great power and prestige in East Japan, destroying in 1031 a rival Taira group in the Kantō area and then eliminating two powerful rival families in North Honshū in successive wars between 1051 and 1088. Warrior bands in East Japan seem to have been larger and stronger than elsewhere in the country, perhaps because of the remoteness of the area, the regional cohesiveness of the Kantō Plain as the largest agricultural area in Japan, and the stronger survival of military traditions there as a result of the long campaigns against the Ainu.

While the warrior bands in their struggles sought to have their rivals branded as "rebels" against the court, their clashes had little effect on Kyōto, except to stop temporarily the flow of income from the estates involved. However, provincial warriors were increasingly used in the capital as Police Commissioners and members of the palace guard groups, and as early as 889 the Bureau of Archivists organized its own defense unit out of such men. As we have seen, the great central monasteries developed armed forces made up in part of men drawn from their estates, and the great families did the same. Certain Minamoto warriors came to be known as the "claws and teeth" of the main Fujiwara family, while a Taira line, after eliminating a strong Minamoto leader in West Japan in 1108, became prominent at the capital as the military supporters of the retired emperors. Because of such military services at court, the leaders of these warrior bands were able to achieve court ranks and posts and by the twelfth century had sufficient influence to be able to serve as patrons of estates, to whom other local leaders might commend their holdings or from whom they might receive rights to lands in return for services.

In this way, provincial military leaders were assuming an increasing role in the old central government. This process was greatly accelerated when two successive small wars at the capital in the middle of the twelfth century suddenly revealed the dominant power these military men actually commanded. On the death of a retired emperor in 1156, a sharp struggle for control of the court broke out between two of his sons, supported respectively by rival claimants to the headship of the Fujiwara and the mixed groups of Minamoto and Taira warriors each side could muster. One group was headed by Taira no Kiyomori (1118–1181), whose main seat of power was in the Inland Sea area. The other group was headed by Minamoto no Tameyoshi, the leader of the Minamoto family that had won ascendancy in the Kantō area. Kiyomori's group emerged victorious and executed most of the remaining leaders of the other band. One of Tameyoshi's sons, Yoshitomo, had sided with the winning clique in 1156. He became dissatisfied with his share in the rewards and, supported by dissident elements among the Fujiwara, seized the capital in the winter of 1159–1160, but he and his supporters were soon destroyed by Kiyomori. These two brief military clashes, called the Hōgen and Heiji Wars from the names of the "year periods" in which they occurred, left Kiyomori and his warrior band in undisputed military control of Kyōto. A superb picture scroll of the Heiji War gives a nearly contemporary portrayal of some of its chief incidents. (See Plates 15 and 16.)

Taira Rule.   Kiyomori, who had long been prominent at court, settled down to the now time-honored practice of providing titular superiors with wives and dominating them without replacing them. Emperors, retired emperors, and Fujiwara regents and *kampaku* continued to maintain their respective pretenses to authority, but Kiyomori was the real source of power, ensconced in his palace at Rokuhara on the southeastern edge of the city. He gained title to many more estates in western Japan, promoted his relatives to high positions in the central government, rewarded his henchmen with governorships and posts on estates in the provinces, married his daughter to the emperor, and in 1180 had the satisfaction of placing his own infant grandson on the throne. Thus he dominated the court, despite determined opposition by the retired emperor. He had little control, however, over the great religious institutions of the capital region and still less over the remaining warrior bands in the provinces.

The role of Kiyomori and his immediate family as a new layer of court aristocrats may, in fact, have weakened the bonds of loyalty of their warrior associates in the provinces. In any case, when a disappointed imperial prince issued a call for military support in 1180, much of eastern Japan responded. Yoritomo (1147–1199), a surviving son of the former Minamoto leader, Yoshitomo, raised the standard of revolt in the mountainous Izu Peninsula, where he had lived in exile, and many of the warriors of the Kantō region rallied to him. Minamoto prestige was still strong in the area, and to these men a local military leader probably seemed more likely to respect and protect their interests and property rights as local officials and administrators of estates than would a distant leader like Kiyomori, immersed in the life of a court noble.

Yoritomo extended his control over the Kantō area, and his younger brother, Yoshitsune, then seized the capital area for him and pursued the Taira down the Inland Sea to its western end, where he finally annihilated them in 1185 at Dan-no-ura in a naval battle. Four years later Yoritomo destroyed the Fujiwara family of Hiraizumi in the north, bringing the whole of Japan under his military control.

The Kamakura Period

The Minamoto and Their Vassals.   The Minamoto triumph over the Taira in 1185 signified a long step forward in the domination of Japan by the provincial warrior class and the development of a feudal society. Where Kiyomori's military control had not extended effectively to many parts of Japan, Yoritomo's military dominance was nationwide. Where Kiyomori had exercised his authority from Kyōto and largely through the old civil government, in the fashion of the Fujiwara before him, Yoritomo created a separate governmental structure, intertwined with the old civil administra-

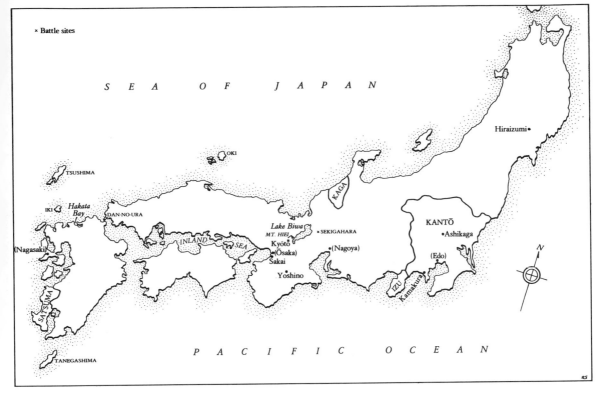

× Battle sites

SEA   OF   JAPAN

Hiraizumi•

OKI

TSUSHIMA

IKI   Hakata
Bay   DAN-NO-URA

KANTŌ
•Ashikaga

Lake Biwa
MT. HIEI   × SEKIGAHARA
Kyōto
(Nagoya)
(Nagasaki)   INLAND   SEA   •(Ōsaka)   (Edo)
Sakai
Yoshino

SATSUMA   IZU
Kamakura

TANEGASHIMA   PACIFIC   OCEAN

N

MEDIEVAL JAPAN

tion but independent of it and separately based at Kamakura, a seaside
town in the Kantō, the seat of his military power.

After the Minamoto victory in 1185 the court bestowed on Yoritomo
high court posts and ranks and special titles to signify his military control
over the country. Eventually in 1192 he was given the title of *Seii-tai-
shōgun* ("Barbarian-Quelling Generalissimo"), once assigned leaders of
expeditions against the Ainu, but henceforth used in its shortened form of
shogun to denote supreme military command over all Japan. Since the post
of shogun was in theory purely military, Yoritomo's administration, or
shogunate, like that of later shoguns, was known as the *bakufu,* or "tent
government," in distinction to the Kyōto civil government.

Appointment to high office by the court was useful to Yoritomo in
providing him with legitimacy, but his real power rested on his personal
band of warrior vassals, called "honorable house men" (*gokenin*), which
he had built up in the Kantō. The confiscation of lands from the defeated
adherents of the Taira in 1185 gave Yoritomo ownership or control over
large numbers of estates throughout the country, and he also came to exercise powers of appointment to provincial posts in no less than sixteen
provinces. Thus he could reward his vassals with new appointments in the

estates and provincial governments. At the same time many warriors originally outside the Kantō band sought to protect their positions by commending their properties to Yoritomo and accepting vassalage as his "honorable
house men." Thus, although the ultimate right to posts in the provinces or
estates and income from them derived from the Kyōto court, Yoritomo
came to be directly responsible for the protection of many of these posts
and appointments to some of them.

In 1185 Yoritomo extended and systematized this old method of achieving power through patronage by appointing in each estate an additional
official called a steward (*jitō*) to assist in its administration and collect a
small military levy. In this way, he inserted his vassals into estates where
they had not been before and asserted his right to a share in taxation and
administration entirely outside the structure of the civil government. The
stewards, who often were incumbent managers given this additional title,
were assigned a part of the produce of their estates specifically as their
rights (*shiki*) for performing this new function in behalf of the Kamakura
shogunate. Like most other positions and incomes at this time, those of the
stewards were of course passed on through inheritance along with the duties
of vassalage to the Minamoto.

In 1185 Yoritomo also appointed leading vassals as protectors (*shugo*)
over one or more provinces, with responsibility for assigning local vassals
to guard duties and leading them in time of war. Thus through his vassals
scattered throughout the country as stewards and protectors, Yoritomo established direct administrative control over most parts of Japan and also
established small but effective provincial armies.

Because of the resistance of the retired emperors to these infringements
on the powers of the civil government, this new system was applied at first
only imperfectly in western Japan, but an opportunity to extend it more
fully came in 1221. In that year the retired emperor, supported by some of
the warriors and monasteries of the capital area, attempted an armed "rebellion" against Kamakura. This was easily crushed in what is known as the
Shōkyū War. The retired emperor was exiled from Kyōto, and most of the
other ringleaders were executed. The Kamakura shogunate confiscated more
than three thousand estates in central and western Japan owned by members
of the losing side, awarded ownership or posts in these to its own members,
and extended the steward system systematically to the whole nation. It placed
two deputies (*tandai*) in Kyōto, where they exercised respectful but firm control over the court from the old Taira headquarters at Rokuhara.

The Organs of Government.   To oversee the system he had created, Yoritomo set up at his headquarters in Kamakura a simple set of offices reminiscent of the family governments of the Fujiwara period. Already in 1180 he

had established a Retainers Office to supervise the military duties, rewards, and punishments of his vassals. An Administrative Office (so named in 1191) was a central administrative and policy-making organ, headed by a minor Kyōto aristocrat versed in law. An Office of Inquiry served as a final court of appeal, kept land and judicial records, and enforced legal decisions. All these offices operated as committees, issuing only unanimous decisions This prevented any one member from becoming an independent source of authority and gave all the protection of collective responsibility. Ever since this time the Japanese, whenever possible, have shown a strong preference for collective leadership and great skill in its operation.

Since the old Taihō Code had little applicability to the actual social conditions and land-owning system of the time, the law the Office of Inquiry administered was essentially customary law that had grown up among the warriors in the provinces. In 1232 the Kamakura government drew up the Jōei Code as a set of general legal and administrative principles to guide its members. This was the first codification of "feudal law" in Japan. Since the civil government had little power to carry out legal decisions, the court nobles as well as the warriors looked to Kamakura for justice, and its law became for all practical purposes the basic law of the land.

The system of government created by Yoritomo was a curious hybrid. It had a feudal core of a single large lord-vassal group, spread thinly throughout Japan, in control if not in possession of most of the estates, combining military, political, and economic functions of leadership, and possessing unchallengeable military power. But this band lived, as it were, in the shell of the old civil administration. The whole panoply of the imperial civil government remained, and the shogunate was in theory merely its military arm. Yoritomo and his vassals continued to sport titles and posts derived from the civil government. The imperial family and court aristocracy, as well as religious institutions, still owned great numbers of estates and drew revenue from them. Some land even remained in the public domain, paying taxes to the Kyōto government as well as supporting the warriors who held posts in the provincial administrations. Because of this combination of feudal and prefeudal elements in the Kamakura system, it is usually regarded as having been only protofeudal.

Yoritomo's system of rule, however, fitted the needs of the time very well. It lasted with relatively little change from 1185 to 1333—a period of history appropriately known as the Kamakura period. After the establishment of effective control by Kamakura throughout the country following the Shōkyū War of 1221, Japan enjoyed a century of internal peace and order perhaps unparalleled in its earlier history. Certainly the Kamakura system provided the most effective centralized control over all parts of the country that Japan had as yet known.

The Hōjō Regents.   The Kamakura system survived despite two great challenges, the one internal and the other external. In theory it depended entirely on the personal loyalty of some two thousand scattered families of vassals to their lord, the head of the Minamoto family. The latter, however, disappeared quite early in the period. Yoritomo eliminated his brother Yoshitsune and other close relatives out of jealousy and suspicion. At the time of his death in 1199 he left only two sons, neither of any great ability, and they were soon pushed aside by the Hōjō family of Yoritomo's widow Masako.

The Hōjō, ironically of Taira descent, had served as Yoritomo's keepers in his Izu exile but had joined his cause. Masako and her father, Tokimasa, forced Yoritomo's incompetent eldest son to abdicate in 1203 in favor of his brother, who was assassinated in 1219, bringing the main line of the Minamoto family to an end. By this time Masako's brother, Yoshitoki (1163–1224), was dominant at Kamakura, but neither he nor his successors made any effort to usurp the post of shogun. Instead they exercised their power through puppet leaders, as the Fujiwara had in Kyōto. A Fujiwara infant, descended through his mother from Yoritomo, was brought to Kamakura and made titular shogun in 1226. In 1252 an imperial prince was chosen to fill the position. It is a tribute to the solidity of the system Yoritomo had constructed that although in theory it depended entirely on the personal loyalty of the vassals to him and his heirs, it survived the extinction of his line and operated successfully with a purely symbolic object of loyalty.

The Kamakura period was thus a period of rule more by the Hōjō family than by the Minamoto. Tokimasa had taken the post of chief of the Administrative Office, and the title of this post, *shikken*, held by successive Hōjō, came to signify "shogunal regent." Yoshitoki's son, Yasutoki (1183–1242), was the great consolidator of the Kamakura shogunate and of Hōjō power. He created a Council of State in 1225 to broaden participation in the government and made an uncle a "co-signer" of government decrees to share responsibility with him. Thereafter until the fall of Kamakura in 1333, two senior Hōjō occupied the paired posts of "shogunal regent" and "co-signer," while two slightly junior members of the family occupied the paired posts of deputies in Kyōto. Thus, the Hōjō as a family demonstrated great success at collective leadership.

The Mongol Invasions.   The external threat to the Kamakura system came from the Mongols, who had overrun much of Asia and part of Europe, had fully incorporated Korea into their empire by 1258, and were to complete their conquest of China in 1279. Khubilai, who ruled from Peking over the main eastern domains of the Mongols, demanded Japan's submission in 1266. The Kyōto court was terrified, but the Hōjō leader haughtily refused.

Section of a picture scroll painted around 1293 depicting the Mongol invasion of 1274. It shows Mongol bowmen, a Japanese knight, and a bomb bursting in the air.

Finally in 1274 Khubilai dispatched a mixed Mongol and Korean force of about thirty thousand men from Korean ports to Hakata Bay in North Kyūshū. The local knights Kamakura mustered against these invaders were individually well armored and formidable fighting men, but the Mongols had much larger numbers, excelled at massed cavalry tactics, which had proved irresistible everywhere they had gone, and had superior weapons, such as catapults that flung gunpowder missiles. Before battle could be decisively joined, however, the Mongols sailed back to Korea in the face of unfavorable weather.

Khubilai renewed the attack in 1281, this time with a force of some 140,000 Mongols, Chinese, and Koreans, dispatched from ports in both China and Korea—probably the greatest overseas expedition the world had yet seen. Kamakura meanwhile had kept its retainers in western Japan on the alert and busy erecting a wall around Hakata Bay. With the aid of this wall, the defenders managed to keep the invaders contained on a narrow beachhead for almost two months, while smaller, more mobile Japanese boats played havoc with the Mongol junks. Then a typhoon struck, destroying much of the Mongol fleet and forcing the remainder of the Mongol force—perhaps less than half—to withdraw in defeat. The *kamikaze*, or "divine wind," of this typhoon has loomed large in the historical memory of the Japanese, confirming them in their belief that Japan was indeed a unique and "divine" country.

Early Feudal Culture

The Feudal Ethic.   The feudal period in Japan is sometimes viewed, as it is in Europe, as a dark cultural trough between an ordered antiquity and brilliant modern age, but this concept is quite incorrect. Not only did the Kamakura system provide a more efficient central control over all Japan than had existed before, but the whole economy stood high above earlier levels. Centers of paper making, iron casting, pottery making, and the like, spread more widely throughout the country, and there was a marked increase in trade with the continent. While the life of the court aristocrats became economically more constrained and culturally less creative, the culture they had helped develop spread much more widely throughout Japan. At the same time, the provincial warriors emerged as leaders in a vigorous new culture, quite different in some ways from what had preceded it and even further removed from Chinese norms than Fujiwara life had been.

This was particularly true in the field of ethics, as the warrior ethos contrasted sharply with the gentle but ostentatious aestheticism of the Fujiwara courtiers and the civilian, bureaucratic spirit of Sung China. The Kamakura warriors lived a life close to the land and to warfare. They were by profession leaders of the farming community and also soldiers. Life for them was simple and frugality a major virtue. Martial arts were all important— horsemanship, archery, and above all swordsmanship. They were proud of their armor and made a veritable cult of their swords. Bravery and the stoical acceptance of physical hardship were fundamental to their life style. All this required self-discipline and character building—concepts that became central to the whole warrior ethic. Death was preferred to surrender. The practice of suicide in defeat may have started to avoid torture, but it became institutionalized by the twelfth century as a matter of honor in the form of *seppuku,* or "disembowelment" (commonly known in the West as *harakiri,* "belly slitting"), which because of the lingering, painful death it produced demonstrated a warrior's disdain for suffering.

Loyalty was central to the whole system, because the feudal structure depended entirely on the personal loyalty of the vassal to his lord or to the group, when the lord was himself merely a symbol of group solidarity. In a society in which all status was inherited, living up to the honor and obligations of one's ancestry loomed particularly large. Strong emphasis was placed on fidelity to one's word and the concept of honor. A vassal owed his lord complete, unquestioning loyalty, even to death. He was to sacrifice his own family, if need be, for his lord, and sometimes did so. The contrast was marked with China, where the first loyalty usually remained to one's own family. But loyalty, of course, remained the weakest as well as the most critical link in the feudal system. Treachery was all too common at times of crisis.

The Japanese feudal ethic differed in some important ways from that of Europe. The bond of loyalty, for example, was seen not so much in legal or contractual terms, as it was in Europe, as in ethical absolutes. The difference may have been the result of the Roman emphasis on law in the West and the Chinese concept that good government is essentially a matter of ethical conduct—of moral example and absolute obedience. The Japanese also had nothing comparable to the Western cult of chivalry, in which women were regarded as weak, romantic figures to be courted and protected. In Japanese feudal society, women not only could inherit both property and positions in the system but were expected to demonstrate the same bravery, stoicism, and loyalty as their men. Another difference from feudal Europe was that the warriors, while often illiterate themselves, showed deep respect for scholarship and the arts. Probably because of the strong Chinese emphasis on writing and learning, warriors even in this age of the sword took pride in literary accomplishments or at least respected them.

This stronger emphasis on learning and cultural achievements together with the greater wealth and more effective organization of twelfth-century Japan, as compared with early feudal Europe of the ninth and tenth centuries, may account for the much greater transfer of the higher culture of earlier periods to feudal Japan. Many artistic and literary trends continued unchanged. But there was, at the same time, a sharp break in basic spirit between Kamakura Japan and earlier periods. Certain of the new elements in Japanese culture which first became clear in the twelfth and thirteenth centuries were to remain characteristic of Japan until the present day. The ethical code of the warriors has been an active force in Japanese society until recent times. The agrarian bias and the emphasis on loyalty, bravery, stoicism, frugality, and the martial arts of early feudalism all survived until modern times. So also did the cult of the sword and the concept that suicide was an honorable and admirable way out. While the world of the Fujiwara diaries and novels is so remote from modern Japanese as to be hardly comprehensible, the tales of the twelfth-century wars and the attitudes of Kamakura warriors are perfectly understandable and still strike responsive chords.

The Popular Faith Sects.   The early feudal period in Japan, as in Europe, was a time of religious fervor. There was a great resurgence of vigor in Buddhism, which led to the founding of a number of new sects, largely in revolt against the older, established sects. This religious awakening has commonly been interpreted as a pessimistic reaction to the decline of the old central government and the resulting military disturbances, which made people feel that the degenerate period of the "latter end of the law" had arrived and that only faith in the Buddha could bring salvation. But the ferment in Buddhism was probably more a sign of its spread to new classes and its further assimilation into Japanese life. The Pure Land doctrines of salvation through faith in the Buddha Amida had started to spread in the Fujiwara period but now achieved great popularity among the common people, who found this an understandable and attractive concept. At the same time, the rising warrior class found solace and support in the meditative aspects of Buddhism, known as Zen. It is significant that the new sects, unlike the older ones, which had been centered on the court aristocracy, were oriented toward either the lower classes or the warriors.

Feudalism is often viewed in retrospect as an extremely repressive system, but in twelfth- and thirteenth-century Japan it seems actually to have given the lower classes a more important and secure position than they had enjoyed before. In any case, the common man, who is almost nonexistent in Fujiwara literature, appears prominently in the picture scrolls and even in the literature of the Kamakura period, and in the faith sects of Buddhism he found a medium of self-expression. Commoners were among the religious leaders of these sects, and their message was directed primarily to the man in the street and paddy field. The leaders of these sects wrote in simple Japanese, rather than classical Chinese, the earlier language of Japanese Buddhism; they encouraged the translation of the scriptures into the vernacular; and they showed strong egalitarian tendencies in contrast to the aristocratic nature of the earlier Buddhist sects. Since salvation through faith was open to everyone—even women—all people were in a sense equal.

The first of the new sects was named the Pure Land *(Jōdo)* Sect for Amida's Pure Land Paradise. It was founded in 1175 by Hōnen (1133–1212). His emphasis on salvation through calling on the Buddha's name obviated the need for temples, priests, and rituals. The traditional sects were outraged and in 1207 managed to have Hōnen temporarily banished from Kyōto.

One of Hōnen's followers, Shinran (1173–1262), further popularized his ideas and carried them to their logical conclusion. He insisted that a single sincere utterance of the Buddha's name sufficed for salvation, condemned self-conscious virtue as undermining simple faith, verged toward monotheism in his concentration on the single Buddha Amida, discarded most of the scriptures, repudiated the monastic church, and encouraged priests to marry and lead normal lives among their congregations. His branch of the movement, in typical reformist style, grew into the separate True Pure Land Sect, or as it is usually known the True Sect *(Shinshū)*. Its practice of marriage of the clergy spread in time to most sects, and it became the largest branch of Japanese Buddhism, followed by the Pure Land Sect. The Eastern and Western Honganji ("Temples of the Original Vow") in Kyōto are the impressive headquarters of the two main branches of the True Sect.

*A segment of a picture scroll of the late Kamakura period, depicting
the life of a popular Buddhist religious leader, Ippen Shōnin
(1239–1289).*

Another major sect of the popular faith movement was founded in 1253
by Nichiren (1222–1282), a man of humble origin from the Kantō. He
stressed the Lotus Sutra, rather than Amida, as the object of faith and
taught his followers to chant "Hail to the Lotus Sutra of the Wonderful
Law." His movement was fittingly named the Lotus Sect, but it came to be
known by his name as the Nichiren Sect. He was a passionate, street-
preaching revivalist, who harshly condemned all other types of Buddhism.
He predicted dire consequences unless the Japanese embraced his views,
and the Mongol invasions were seen as fulfilling his prophecies. He
showed a strong nationalistic bent, and his name, which means "Sun Lotus,"
can also be taken to mean "Japanese Buddhism."

It is worth noting that the popular faith sects developed striking parallels to Christianity, just when Japanese feudal institutions were producing
political and social parallels with Europe. One cannot but wonder if there
are some causal links between these respective institutions and beliefs. In
any case, the emphasis in the new sects on salvation through faith in a
single object of worship (either Amida or the Lotus Sutra) and an after-

life in a very definite paradise was much more similar to basic Christian concepts than to original Buddhism. The organization of the church around congregations rather than monasteries, the marriage of the clergy, the translation of scriptures, and the nationalistic tinge of Nicheren, all remind one also of Christian developments during the Reformation.

Zen.   Elements of Zen, the meditative type of Buddhism, had been present in Japanese Buddhism for centuries, but it was introduced as a sectarian movement at this time by monks returning from studies in China, where it had become the dominant form of the religion. Eisai (1141–1215) brought back from China the Rinzai Sect of Zen in 1191 and Dōgen (1200–1253) the Sōtō Sect in 1227. Eisai incidentally is also known as the introducer of tea to Japan.

Zen, as we have seen, stemmed from one of the earliest and most fundamental aspects of Indian Buddhism but had in China incorporated the Taoist emphasis on individual character and a closeness to nature, together with Taoism's anti-intellectual and antitextual bias. Zen stressed the transmission of truth from master to disciple (rather than through scholastic study), rigorous methods of meditation, strict discipline of character, individualistic independence of authority, and salvation in the more traditional Buddhist sense of enlightenment (*satori*) through self-understanding and self-discipline. In the Sōtō Sect the emphasis was on *zazen,* or "sitting in meditation," as a means of attaining *satori*, while in Rinzai a special emphasis was put on the *kōan,* an insoluble or even nonsense problem designed to jar the meditator into sudden intuitive enlightenment. While Zen's meditative practices made it seem quietistic, its discipline produced rugged individualists who could easily be men of action.

All this had a special appeal to the relatively untutored Kamakura warriors with their great need for stoicism and self-discipline. When Eisai, like Hōnen, was expelled from Kyōto, he won the patronage of the shogunate at Kamakura. In time five official Zen temples were established at Kamakura and at Kyōto, and these and other Zen temples became increasingly important as centers of art, literature, and learning at this time of declining cultural activity at the Kyōto court. Warrior leaders came to draw on the Zen priesthood for both scribes and high advisers, and they themselves sometimes retired to Zen monasteries when they wished to escape the pressures of secular life. In fact, the warriors as a whole seem to have drawn special spiritual and psychological strength from Zen, which contributed to the strength of character, firmness of will, and imperviousness to suffering on which they prided themselves.

Literature and Art.   The literature and art of the Kamakura period reflect the duality between a continuing but gradually waning court aristocracy

Wooden guardian deity dating from around 1200, at the Kōfukuji,a monastery near Nara.

and the rising warrior class. Some of the literary activity of the early feudal period was simply a continuation of Fujiwara literary trends. There was, in fact, a fresh revival of the overworked "short poem." The wandering monk Saigyō (1118–1190) proved to be one of Japan's greatest poets in this medium, while *The New Ancient and Modern Collection,* completed in 1205, was the greatest of the later imperial anthologies. Novels and diaries continued to be written, but the most famous prose work to emerge from Kyōto society was the *Record of a Ten-Foot-Square Hut,* attributed to Kamo no Chōmei (1151–1213) and describing his life as a recluse after he retired in disappointment from the court.

In contrast to the refined and gently melancholy works of the Kyōto courtiers, the tales of the exploits of the warrior class, which began to appear at this time, overflow with vigor and vitality. Even their language is different and much more modern, showing a heavy admixture of Chinese words and influences of the Kantō dialect. These stirring war tales, though historically accurate in broad outline, are full of imaginative detail. They had a great vogue at this time, often being chanted to the accompaniment of the lute, and they have remained immensely popular ever since and a major inspiration in later literature and drama.

The greatest of the war tales, dating probably from the early Kamakura period, is the *Tale of the House of Taira,* telling of the wars between the Taira and the Minamoto. Two shorter works of about the same time, the

*Scene from the "Scroll of the Hungry Spirits," dating from the Kama-
kura period. It depicts souls damned to perpetual hunger, scav-
enging in the streets. Around them are ordinary citizens, including
two ladies on the left and a monk in the center holding a rosary.*

Tale of the Hōgen War and the *Tale of the Heiji War* treat these limited
parts of the story, while the whole saga was reworked again in the middle
of the thirteenth century as the *Record of the Rise and Fall of the Minamoto and Taira.* The *Mirror of the Eastland,* based largely on the official
records of the Kamakura shogunate, is the major historical source for the
period from 1180 to 1266.

The revived vigor of Buddhism was reflected in a second great flourishing of Buddhist sculpture, which drew heavily on the traditions of the
Nara period. Unkei and other great sculptors produced marvelous life-like
statues, while the religious fervor of the age is illustrated by the one
thousand identical, many-armed images in the "Hall of Thirty-Three Bays"
in Kyōto and the beautiful fifty-two-foot bronze Great Buddha erected in
Kamakura in the middle of the thirteenth century.

The styles of painting of the Fujiwara period were continued, but the
subject matter of the picture scrolls shows the influence of Kamakura society. War scenes are common, as in the scroll depicting the Mongol invasion and the three scrolls illustrating the *Tale of the Heiji War.* Many
other scrolls illustrated the histories of monasteries, portrayed the lives of
Buddhist saints, such as Hōnen, or revealed the terrors of damnation.

The Ashikaga Period

The Collapse of the Kamakura Shogunate. A century after the victory of the Kamakura military band, it was still sufficiently intact to rise magnificently to the Mongol challenge, but the strenuous defense efforts these onslaughts necessitated put a serious strain on both the economic position and the loyalty of Kamakura's retainers and thus accentuated internal weaknesses already appearing in the system. This was particularly true because, unlike earlier wars, the Mongol invasions left no spoils to be divided among the victors to renew their loyalty to the system.

As with most ruling classes, the Kamakura warriors over the years became more luxurious in their habits, despite repeated sumptuary regulations issued by the shogunate. At the same time, their economic position tended to decline. This was because the full status and duties of a vassal might be inherited by all his sons, but his landholdings and income, which did not increase, had to be divided among them. As the class grew in numbers, its per capita income inevitably shrank, making it increasingly difficult for some warriors to maintain the necessary equipment of a knight. Some became so impoverished that in 1297 the shogunate issued an order cancelling the debts and mortgages of its retainers. Such acts came to be known as *tokusei*, or "virtuous government," but they had no lasting effect, because they merely worsened the terms of borrowing for the retainers.

The passage of time also proved corrosive to the cohesiveness and the personal loyalty on which the whole Kamakura system depended. It was gradually undercut first by geographic spread and then, with each successive generation, by the dimming of memories of the twelfth-century campaigns in which the bonds of loyalty had been forged. Shared interests with other local warriors began to loom larger than ties to distant Kamakura and its purely symbolic shogun. Loyalty might be felt more strongly to personally known local leaders, sometimes particularly prominent stewards, but more commonly provincial protectors. Such local strong men gradually came to form a new class of feudal leaders, occupying an intermediary position between the shogunate and its retainers. The old nation-wide warrior band was gradually being replaced by a large number of local leader-follower groupings.

In 1333 the weakening Kamakura shogunate finally fell victim to these divisive tendencies. The incident that destroyed the system grew out of the ambition of the Emperor Go-Daigo (1318–1339) to keep the succession in his branch of the imperial family (two rival lines had developed in the second half of the thirteenth century) and to restore actual political power to the emperors. When Kamakura attempted to force Go-Daigo to abdicate in 1331, he launched a revolt, supported by the great monasteries of the capital region and some local military leaders, such as Kusunoki Masashige, who by turning traitor to Kamakura and espousing Go-Daigo's cause won for himself the undying reputation of being the greatest of all Japanese "loyalists." The Kamakura forces captured Go-Daigo and sent him into exile, but various military groups, motivated probably by local rivalries and ambitions, joined the revolt. Go-Daigo escaped, and the Kamakura general sent to recapture him in 1333 suddenly switched sides, seizing Kyōto in the emperor's name. This man, Ashikaga Takauji (1305–1358), a prominent provincial protector of the Kantō, apparently wished to replace the Hōjō in power, but East Japan now erupted in revolt, and another prominent Kantō vassal captured Kamakura, destroying the Hōjō and their government.

During the next three years Go-Daigo sought to restore imperial control over Japan, recreating some of the old civil organs of government and assigning the leading generals to governorships. This brave attempt (known from the "year period" as the Kemmu Restoration) proved to be only an anachronistic interlude in Japanese feudal history. The clock could not be turned back to the age of Yoritomo, much less to the Nara period. No one, least of all a nonmilitary man, could control the many lord-and-retainer groupings into which the military class of Japan was dividing. When Go-Daigo sided with Ashikaga Takauji's rivals, the latter turned against the emperor, seized Kyōto in 1336, and set up a new emperor from the other line. Go-Daigo escaped and established a second imperial court at Yoshino in the mountains south of Nara. The more than half-century (1336–1392) that this rival court survived is known as either the Yoshino period or the period of the Northern and Southern Courts (*Nambokuchō*).

The Ashikaga Shogunate.   Takauji took the title of shogun in 1338 and attempted to recreate a unified political system centered on Kyōto, but although his descendants did manage to retain the title until 1573, their shogunate was a far cry from that of Kamakura. In fact, it represented a distinctly different stage in the development of Japanese feudalism.

Unlike Yoritomo, Takauji had become shogun, not as the unchallenged leader of a triumphant, unified warrior band, but merely as the most successful among a number of ambitious military leaders. He and his successors never laid claim to the direct loyalty of the bulk of the warrior class, as Yoritomo had, but recognized that the warriors were in fact divided into many separate lord-and-retainer groupings. All they attempted to do was to extend their control over these lords. Actually they did not succeed even in this restricted effort. Their shogunate never achieved full military control over all Japan, and warfare remained endemic throughout most of the period.

The Ashikaga shogunate was at best an uncertain coalition of major military families, which recognized only grudgingly the overlordship of the Ashikaga. In theory these other families derived from the shogunate their positions as protectors over one or more provinces, but in actuality their power rested on the estates they themselves controlled and on the personal loyalty of the lesser warrior families in their regions. They so fully appropriated local political as well as military authority that the practice of appointing civil governors was dropped. While these regional military leaders were not full territorial lords like the *daimyō* of later times, they were clearly their forerunners and have often been called "protector daimyo" (*shugo-daimyō*).

The Ashikaga established a façade of centralized government, consisting of various administrative and judicial boards, some of them the same at least in name that Kamakura had used, but these and other administrative organs were little more than an outward expression of the loose coalition between the Ashikaga and some of the chief protector families, particularly those of the central region around Kyōto. Some of these families were descended from the Ashikaga or related to them by marriage or by old bonds of loyalty. Residing usually in the capital, rather than in their respective provinces, these central protector families formed the inner core of the Ashikaga shogunate, while more distant provincial protectors remained peripheral and to a large extent independent of it.

An Administrator, traditionally drawn from one of three protector families, shared power with the shogun in Kyōto. Next to this post ranked the head of the Retainers Office, drawn from one of four other families. At Kamakura there was a Kantō Administrator, a post held by a branch of the Ashikaga family, and in Kyūshū and the far north there were deputies (*tandai*). Behind this formal structure of a centralized government, however, the realities remained very different. The Ashikaga depended for their income on their own landholdings and such trade taxes as they were able to impose around Kyōto, while their power rested on the balance of forces they were able to achieve with their leading vassals.

The existence between 1336 and 1392 of the rival southern court of Go-Daigo and his descendants at Yoshino opened the way for countless local wars and vendettas between claimants to estates and local power, fought in the name of one or the other imperial line. However, in 1392 the third Ashikaga shogun, Yoshimitsu (1358–1408), finally managed to force Go-Daigo's line to return to Kyōto, with the promise that it would alternate on the throne with the northern line—a promise that was never fulfilled. Yoshimitsu had meanwhile been eliminating his most serious military rivals, and, with the defeat of the powerful Ōuchi family of west Japan in 1399, his power was for the moment unchallenged. The next three decades were the only period of real peace and stability during the whole Ashikaga shogunate. The Ashikaga had in 1378 established their headquarters in the Muromachi district of Kyōto, and the period after the reunification of the two courts in 1392 is often called the Muromachi period.

The temporary order created by Yoshimitsu began to disintegrate after the death of his grandson in 1428. In 1439 the shogun joined with the Uesugi family of the Kantō in eliminating the Kantō branch of the Ashikaga and transferring the post of Kantō Administrator to the Uesugi. A succession dispute in the Ashikaga family led to the outbreak of open warfare in 1467 between two major groupings of the great families, led respectively by the Hosokawa and the Yamana. Known as the Ōnin War, this military free-for-all lasted until 1477, laying waste Kyōto and leaving the shogun and his government powerless vestiges of what had been at best only a partial restoration of central political authority.

The Kamakura shogunate had been a feudal, military government living within the shell of the old imperial government and landholding system, but Go-Daigo's bid for power had brought the warriors in force into Kyōto, where they contended for power and in the process all but destroyed the shell of civil government, while in the provinces they stifled central authority. Whatever central authority emanated from Kyōto was that of the shogunate rather than the imperial government. Already before the collapse of Kamakura, the stewards had so expanded their rights to the income from their estates that in many cases this income had become divided into halves which gave support respectively to the original Kyōto owners and to the local stewards. Under Takauji it became generally accepted that the provincial protectors had the right to half of the total income for military purposes, thus further cutting into the revenues received by the court and its aristocracy. This income continued to dwindle as the incessant wars of the Ashikaga period gave ample opportunity to local strong men to reduce the remaining property rights of the Kyōto aristocracy. Starved of sustenance, many of the old court families withered away, and the great main line of the Fujiwara family, split since 1252 into five branches named after the streets in Kyōto on which they lived or for their hereditary government posts, sank into political impotence, although it continued to occupy the chief civil positions around the throne until the nineteenth century. Even the imperial family, deprived of many of its estates as the result of Go-Daigo's unrealistic attempt to regain power, relapsed into political passivity.

Meanwhile the warriors had been consolidating family power. The constant warfare of the period necessitated a gradual shift from the Kamakura practice of dividing patrimonies to a system of inheritance of all or most of a family's holdings and authority by a single heir. Unlike primogeniture in European feudalism, in Japan the father retained the right to choose any of his sons as heir and, if lacking one, to adopt a son, who commonly was a son-in-law or a member of a collateral branch of the family.

MAJOR DAIMYO OF THE 15TH AND 16TH CENTURIES

The Emergence of the Daimyo System. The Ōnin War of 1467–1477
proved to be merely the opener of a century of constant warfare unparalleled in Japanese history, but much like conditions in feudal Europe. Local
wars raged all over Japan between rival claimants to land and local leadership. The Ashikaga shoguns lost all control over the provincial lords and
became so enfeebled that the virtual deposition of the last of them in 1573
passed almost unnoticed. The period between 1467 and 1568 is appropriately called the age of the Warring States (*Sengoku*), and in its crucible
of constant warfare was forged a new form of Japanese feudalism, most
closely parallel to that of Europe.

The drastic decline of shogunal power merely reflected the rising power
of local military leaders, who began to develop into true territorial lords in
complete control of well defined geographic areas and populations. From
this time on these local lords can properly be termed daimyo, though those
of this century are often called the "warring states daimyo" (*sengoku-
daimyō*), in contrast to those of a later and more peaceful age. Some of the
daimyo families, such as the Shimazu of Satsuma in southern Kyūshū and
the restored Ōuchi of west Japan, were the descendants of prominent old
families, but many more were from newly risen warrior lines which had
overthrown the local protectors in a process the Japanese have called "the
inferior overcoming the superior." The provincial protectors proved to be
very vulnerable during this time of constant warfare, because their authority
commonly did not coincide in geographic extent with the lands and vassals
that actually supported them, and these were often interspersed with lands
and warrior groups not under their control. The emerging daimyo by con-

trast carved out clearly defined areas of complete control, and thus were less vulnerable to attack and better able to mobilize their forces.

In the process of consolidating their domains, the daimyo wiped out the last vestiges of the old estates and the remaining income these had paid to the court aristocracy. This plunged the imperial court and its aristocratic families into serious economic want. At times in the first half of the sixteenth century the court was so poor that it could not carry out even the most basic court ceremonies, such as enthronements. What income it had was largely derived from the largess of affluent military men or fees from Kyōto merchant groups seeking the supposed protection of the court's continuing prestige.

As the estates disappeared, the peasant population became organized for the most part into semiautonomous, tax-paying villages. These were more natural and unified areas than the old estates had been, centering frequently on sources of water used in common for irrigation or on the ancient local shrines, some dating back to the *uji* period. These villages continued to serve as the chief administrative units of rural Japan up until recent decades.

The daimyo commonly drew up "house codes," which combined moral maxims with an outline of the basic laws and administrative system of their domains. All the military families in a domain had to be completely subservient vassals of the daimyo. The more important might receive from him their original lands or new ones as subfiefs, in which they could have their own "rear vassals." They held these subfiefs at their lord's sufferance, however, and, unlike the vassals of European feudalism, they did not hold allegiance also to another lord for other lands. The lesser warrior families became little more than a salaried officer class, administering the daimyo's domain and leading his armies. In part this change reflected a shift in military technology. Large bodies of foot soldiers (*ashigaru* or "light foot"), armed with pikes, had replaced the mounted knight as the backbone of military power. Warfare was no longer a matter of multiple individual combat but of massed soldiery.

A daimyo's prestige was measured by the size of the area he controlled and his wealth in terms of the rice production and tax yield of its villages. The daimyo also controlled and taxed the artisans and merchants in his domain and utilized the latter as the transport corps of his army. All resources were devoted to maximizing military power, and those domains that were most efficiently organized were able not only to flout central authority but to bite off pieces from their weaker neighbors or swallow them whole.

While the authority of the central government all but vanished during the period of the Warring States, it had been replaced by a much more complete and efficient administrative control at the local level than had ever existed before. To the Europeans, who first arrived in Japan in the middle of the sixteenth century, the daimyo appeared to be little "kings." Thus the daimyo domains were developing into firm building blocks out of which a much more solid centralized political structure could in time be constructed.

The daimyo domains that emerged during this century of warfare were of varying sizes, and some areas remained fragmented among a number of smaller warrior families. The great monasteries retained their extensive estates, protected by their own military men, and, with the growing importance of the common foot soldier in warfare, commoners, supported by petty local warriors, were also sometimes able to challenge feudal power. Rioting villagers and townsmen had begun to be a serious problem as early as 1428, sometimes forcing the cancellation of their debts under the name of "virtuous government" (*tokusei*). The town of Sakai, today a part of the great metropolis of Ōsaka at the eastern end of the Inland Sea, managed to develop a limited degree of autonomy. The adherents of the True Sect won military control over the province of Kaga on the west coast in 1488 and retained it for almost a century, while other members of this sect, commonly called the "Single Minded" (Ikkō) sect because of its religious fanaticism, were able to exercise military control over other smaller areas from time to time.

The protracted fighting and endless intrigues of the Warring States period has made it a romantic age, which has often drawn the attention of later authors and modern film makers. In the course of all this fighting, most of the great families of the middle years of the Ashikaga period, such as the Yamana, Uesugi, and the Ashikaga themselves, were eliminated by newly risen rivals or drastically reduced in power and wealth. The Ōuchi of western Japan were replaced in 1557 by their former vassals, the Mōri. The Hosokawa survived only through a distantly related line in Kyūshū. Of all the great military families of the early Ashikaga period, only the Shimazu in their remote fastness in southern Kyūshū survived to play an important role in later times.

High Feudal Society

Economic Growth.   One might assume that the constant warfare of the Ashikaga period might have slowed or even reversed economic development, but this was not the case. In fact, political decentralization seems to have stimulated the economy. This was because the provincial warrior families and emerging territorial lords were naturally concerned with increasing local production and thus their own income or tax yield. Under this sort of locally-oriented political leadership, new lands were opened to cultivation, irrigation was extended, agricultural techniques were improved, and specialized local cash crops were increased. As a consequence there appears to have been a doubling or tripling of production per acre in parts of the country during this period. Specialization in economic functions also became more common, as the basic economic unit grew from the relatively small estate to the much larger local domain, and there was a great increase in handicraft production and of trade both locally and between regions. These stirrings of economic growth were already noticeable in the late thirteenth century but became much more marked in the fourteenth and fifteenth.

One clear sign of economic development was the proliferation of local markets, held once in each ten-day "week," under the patronage of influential shrines or temples or some local feudal leader. Another sign was the gradual appearance of trade towns at ports or around great religious institutions. The clearest sign of economic growth was the gradual shift between the twelfth and fifteenth centuries from barter to the use of money in trade. In the eighth and ninth centuries the Chinese-type civil government had, in imitation of China, issued copper coins, but the people had not become accustomed to their use. Now there was a genuine demand for money, and, in the lack of an effective central government to mint coins, these were supplied for the most part by importing copper cash from China, supplemented in time by paper money orders for the transfer of large sums. A money economy led to the develoment of pawnshops and other types of moneylenders, including Buddhist institutions. As we have seen, the indebtedness of the steward class had become so serious by late Kamakura times that the government ordered the cancellation of their debts, and similar debt cancellations were frequent in the Ashikaga period.

The many political authorities of feudal Japan were all eager to erect barriers to tax the trade that passed through their areas. To protect themselves against such multiple taxation and the other economic hazards of an unsettled time, the producers or transporters of certain goods, such as paper, salt, and the rice beer called *sake,* and the members of certain trades, such as carpenters or actors, grouped together into guilds (*za*), analogous to the medieval guilds of Europe. Under the patronage of a prestigious religious institution, the Kyōto court, or a local feudal authority, to which they paid fees, the guilds succeeded in establishing protection from extortion by other authorities and some degree of local monopoly under which their trade or profession could flourish. The center of industrial and commercial activity was Kyōto, which, despite the wars that ravaged it, remained a city of a few hundred thousand. As the feudal lords developed complete territorial mastery, however, the merchant groupings fell increasingly under their control, and the guild organization was gradually replaced by "official merchants" closely supervised by the daimyo and serving the needs of his government, thus setting the pattern of political control over economic activities that has remained characteristic of Japan ever since.

Overseas Trade. Unlike the countries of late feudal Europe, Japan lacked the economic stimulation of close neighbors, but, despite its relative isolation, international trade increased greatly during this period. Japanese traders had been venturing abroad since the eleventh century, and the casting of the Great Buddha of Kamakura in the thirteenth century seems to have been financed in part from foreign trade. Japanese merchant adventurers, whose activities often shaded off into piracy, were a scourge to the Koreans already in the early fourteenth century and a few decades later became a serious nuisance to the Chinese as well. Known simply as "Japanese pirates" (*Wakō*), these warrior-merchant adventurers from the coastal communities of western Japan often seized what they wanted when the restrictive trade policies of the Koreans and Chinese denied them the trade they sought.

The Koreans managed to lessen the pressures of Japanese piracy by making an agreement in 1443 for a generous flow of official trade—some fifty ships a year. The number was subsequently increased, and the Japanese were given the right to maintain permanent trading settlements in three port towns in southern Korea. The Ming dynasty in China after 1368 also tried to control Japanese piracy through official agreements. Yoshimitsu, after consolidating his control over the country, responded to Chinese requests by agreeing in 1404 to the sending of one official trade mission every ten years. To regulate this trade, the Chinese government issued booklets of tallies, which the missions were to carry with them. To fit into Chinese concepts of the world order, the Japanese traders were regarded as bearers of tribute to China, and the Ming issued to Yoshimitsu a patent as the "King of Japan" and "subject" of the Ming. Yoshimitsu's acceptance of this investiture has brought down on his head the uniform condemnation of Japanese historians.

The official tally trade never lived up to the expectations of either the Chinese, who saw in it a way to control Japanese piracy, or the Japanese, who were only seeking trade profits. The Japanese, instead of sending a mission once every ten years, seem to have sent six between 1404 and 1410 before breaking off the agreement. It was revived in 1432, and while only eleven missions went between then and 1549, many more ships went in each mission than were authorized, and these were in fact not under the control of the Ashikaga but were dispatched by Buddhist monasteries, Shintō shrines, and local lords. The Ōuchi family of west Japan actually captured the tallies in 1469 and thereafter controlled the official trade.

Meanwhile illegal trade and piracy expanded greatly, undoubtedly accounting for the greater part of the flow of goods between China and Japan. The records of the tally trade, however, give a good picture of the nature of this flow. Japanese exports were not merely raw materials, such as sulphur and copper, but also fine manufactured goods, such as painted folding fans, apparently a Japanese invention, picture scrolls, and especially the highly prized swords of Japan. No less than 37,000 swords are said to have been exported to China by the embassy of 1483 alone. In return Japan imported silks, porcelains, books, paintings, and, above all else, copper cash. The mission of 1453 alone is recorded as having brought back 50 million coins. Clearly international trade was becoming important in the economy of Japan, and the country, once so far behind the continent in technology, was drawing abreast of China.

Zen Culture.   The great economic growth of Japan during the political confusion of the Ashikaga period was paralleled by a remarkable cultural flowering. This was the product of several factors: the fusion of the vigor of the warrior class with the refinement of the old Kyōto aristocracy, the merging of these traditional Japanese cultural flows with the philosophy and aesthetic attitudes of Zen, and strong new cultural influences introduced from China by Zen monks. Thus several hitherto distinct cultural streams flowed together, forming a strong new current which was to dominate Japan culturally until modern times.

The shogun's court in Kyōto was the center of this cultural activity, and the later shoguns are more renowned as cultural leaders than as statesmen or warriors. Even Yoshimitsu is best known for the coterie of artists, scholars, and literary men he presided over at his monastic retreat, the Golden Pavilion (Kinkakuji), which he built in 1397 in the Northern Hills (Kitayama) of Kyōto. The eighth shogun, Yoshimasa (1443–1473; died 1490), living after the Ashikaga had lost most of their power, was at least able to parallel Yoshimitsu's cultural achievements. In 1483 he built in the Eastern Hills (Higashiyama) of Kyōto his own monastic head-quarters, known as the Silver Pavilion (Ginkakuji). These two shogunal retreats have given the names Kitayama to the middle period of Ashikaga culture (1392–1467) and Higashiyama to the later phase (1467–1568).

Zen monks played a prominent role at the court of the shoguns, and official patronage was given to the five great Zen temples of Kyōto and Kamakura. The Enryakuji, the Tendai center on Mt. Hiei, and other great old monasteries remained rich and powerful, but they had become intellectually moribund and morally lax. Homosexuality, for example, was common, as it was among the whole warrior class of Japan. Meanwhile intellectual and cultural leadership had passed to the newer Zen monasteries. The Zen master Musō Kokushi (1275–1351) set the pattern by exercising great influence over Takauji and persuading him to erect a network of Zen monasteries throughout the country and to send a trading ship to China to raise funds for the building of a great monastery in Kyōto, the Tenryūji. Other Zen monks continued to serve as shogunal advisers, as chief intermediaries in the official relationship with China, and as drafters

The Silver Pavilion and garden built by Yoshimasa in 1483.

of the shoguns' messages to the Ming emperors. They also were the leading artists, scholars, and literary men of the day and often the arbiters of aesthetic taste.

The cultural dominance of Zen monks was so great that the whole culture of the Ashikaga period may appropriately be called Zen culture. Zen culture, however, is no more easy to define than is Zen philosophy. Words such as *yūgen,* "mystery," which the Japanese have commonly used to describe it, leave the subject still mysterious. Drawing on Zen philosophy and the associated arts that had been developed in Sung China, Zen culture blended these with the delicate sensitivity, impressionism, and love of form and ritual of the Kyōto court and the rugged strength of personality of the warrior tradition. The originally Taoist sense of man's identity with nature and the Zen desire for an intuitive understanding of the basic principles of the universe merged with the native Japanese sensitivity to the beauty and wonder of nature; the intuitive indirection of Zen fused with the Japanese tendency toward allusion and suggestion; and Zen and warrior discipline and restraint combined with the older Japanese love of form and ritual. The result was a disciplined tranquillity and sophisticated simplicity that bordered at times on self-conscious aestheticism. Universal truth and beauty were to be perceived through some small but carefully created symbol. The little was preferred to the big, the intimate to the impressive, the simple to the complex, the natural to the artificial, the old and misshapen to the new and perfect. The emphasis on the small and simple could degenerate into a snobbish pose of mock simplicity, but it admirably fitted the relative poverty of feudal Japan and significantly has a revived appeal today in Japan and also in the West in this more affluent and complex age.

Zen culture is perhaps best presented not by verbal description but in Zen fashion by example. The tea ceremony is one of the most characteristic expressions of Ashikaga taste. It is a gathering of a few lovers of art in a simple, bare room close to the beauties of nature. The tea is prepared in slow, graceful motions and drunk in similar fashion from a bowl—by preference a simple, seemingly coarse type of pottery. The bowl and other articles used are then admired and discussed. Spiritual calm is the effect produced as much as aesthetic appreciation. Developed in the course of the fifteenth century, the tea ceremony reached final shape under Sen no Rikyū (1521–1591). In modern times it has become embalmed as one of the social graces every well-bred bride should master. Flower arrangement, which emphasizes not the artificial, massed bunching of flowers, which is the Western tradition, but a naturalistic arrangement of a few flowers or sprigs, is a similar Zen art, which in modern times has undergone the same fate at the hands of mass society.

Art.   The greatest of the Zen arts was the Sung style of landscape painting, in which the artist seeks to portray the essence of nature by eliminating minor detail and accenting with bold brush strokes what he sees to be essential. Or, again, he may select some small aspect of nature to serve as a microcosm epitomizing the whole. In these paintings, man and his handiwork—temples, bridges, boats—usually appear as minor details, blending into the great pattern of nature. The Japanese Zen painters produced works hardly distinguishable from those of China, and yet, instead of being merely imitative, they are often great masterpieces themselves. The greatest of the Zen artists was probably Sesshū (1420–1506). (See page 387.) The hereditary Kano school of artists painting in this tradition stemmed from the

*Autumn landscape in India
ink on paper by Sesshū
(1420–1506).*

late fifteenth century and remained the dominant "official" school until the nineteenth century.

Stately, heavy-roofed Zen temples were a common architectural expression of the Ashikaga period, but the smaller, lighter Silver and Golden Pavilions better typify the spirit of the time. These were closer to domestic architecture, in which modern Japanese tastes were beginning to make their appearance. These tastes showed a preference for natural wood finishes instead of painted interiors, and twisted tree trunks rather than artificially shaped lumber. Thick rush floor mats called *tatami* were sometimes spread over the whole floor area of each room, and the *tokonoma* was developing into a standard feature of domestic architecture. This is a recessed alcove for the display of one or at the most a few choice art objects, instead of the masses of *objets d'art* which traditionally crowd Western rooms.

The fifteenth-century "rock garden" of the Ryōanji in Kyōto.

Most important was the emphasis on the setting of a building—that is, the surrounding garden. Landscape architecture, deriving originally from China, was developed in the Ashikaga period into one of Japan's most distinctive and today most influential art forms. The Golden and Silver Pavilions were really gardens graced by a single unpretentious building. The Zen temples all looked out on carefully planned and executed gardens. The effort was not to shape nature to fit man's propensity for geometric regularity, but to reproduce in small the untamed magnificence of nature. Musō Kokushi was one of the first great masters of landscape architecture in Japan and is credited with the beautiful Tenryūji gardens. The essence of the Zen spirit is perhaps to be found in the "rock garden" of the Ryōanji in Kyōto, in which nothing but a few rocks and well-raked white sand suggest the grandeur of a vast seascape.

Literature. Zen monks were less dominant in the literature of the Ashikaga period than in the art. This may have been because their writings,

A temple garden near Kyōto (the Sambōin of the Daigoji).

known as "the literature of the Five Monasteries," were largely in classical Chinese and therefore outside the mainstream of Japanese literature.

The Ashikaga period witnessed a reviving interest in ancient customs, early Japanese literature, and the history of Japan. The first critical and analytic Japanese history, the *Jottings of a Fool,* by the monk Jien, had appeared in 1220, and at the beginning of the Ashikaga period, Kitabatake Chikafusa, a warrior supporter of Go-Daigo, continued this tradition in the *Record of the Legitimate Succession of the Divine Emperors,* which championed Go-Daigo's cause and helped establish the nationalistic doctrine that Japan's unique superiority derived from its unbroken line of emperors. There were also stirrings in Shintō. The great old shrines, such as that at Ise, which had lost their financial support from the now destitute court, developed popular organizations of supporters who made pilgrimages to these shrines. A priestly family in Kyōto named Yoshida also developed in the fifteenth century a new syncretic Shintō philosophy, called Yoshida Shintō, which was based on forged texts claiming that Buddhism and Confucianism were derivatives from fundamental Shintō truths.

Photograph of masked Nō actor performing a dance, with musicians in back and the traditional pine tree painted on the back wall.

Many of the literary trends of Ashikaga times were simply the continuation of earlier currents. *Grasses of Idleness* (*Tsurezuregusa*) by a courtier named Yoshida Kenkō (1283–1350) was reminiscent of the *Record of a Ten-Foot-Square Hut* of the Kamakura period. Similarly the *Record of the Great Peace,* which tells of the endless warfare between 1318 and 1367, was written in the manner of the earlier war tales. The *Otogi-zōshi* ("Companion Booklets") were comic, romantic, or wondrous popular stories, which had evolved from the Buddhist cautionary tales, historical romances, and novels of the Fujiwara period. In poetry, the "chain poem" (*renga*), in which two or more poets took turns composing alternate three- and two-line units, were an outgrowth of the earlier "short poem." "Chain poems" represented a further development of the Japanese tendency toward a subtle and complex associative technique, and at the hands of masters they could be sustained poetic efforts of much greater scope than the "short poems," but they could also degenerate into little more than word games.

The most significant and original literary development of the Ashikaga period was the *Nō* drama. Earlier symbolic court dances and mimetic performances among the people had evolved by the fourteenth century into simple plays, and these developed at Yoshimitsu's court into the Nō drama, chiefly at the hands of Kan'ami (1333–1384) and his son Seami (1363–1443). Nō is not unlike the drama of ancient Greece. It is performed on an almost bare stage by a chief actor and assistant, both elaborately costumed and masked, and perhaps a few subsidiary characters. There is always a chorus which fills in the narrative, and both actors and chorus chant their lines to the accompaniment of rhythmic, orchestral music. The librettos are largely in poetry or highly poetic prose. Action is restrained and very stylized, and the climax of the play is always a symbolic dance performed by the chief actor.

In presentations, Nō dramas were usually interspersed with comic interludes, called *Kyōgen,* or "Crazy Words," which were burlesques of contemporary feudal society. The Nō dramas themselves normally dealt with Shintō gods or famous figures in Buddhist or secular history. They often centered on the concept of salvation through faith of the popular faith sects, and the usual possession of the chief actor by the spirit of a deity or deceased person is reminiscent of the shamanistic mediums of ancient Japanese folk religion. Thus Nō is not specifically Zen in inspiration, but it offers a good example of the refined and disciplined spirit of Zen aesthetics and of the cultural creativity of the Ashikaga period.

15. Tokugawa Japan:
A Centralized Feudal State

Political Reunification

By the middle of the sixteenth century, certain changes were occurring in the Japanese economy and society that were similar to developments which are normally associated with the breakdown of feudalism in Europe. Domestic commerce and international trade were expanding rapidly; in fact, Japanese merchant-pirates not only ranged widely along the coasts of China but had become active throughout the waters and coastal communities of Southeast Asia. The functional line between warriors and peasants was being lost as a result of the development of massed foot-soldier armies. As a consequence, religious groups of commoners were able to challenge feudal rule in parts of Japan, while the old warrior class was becoming transformed into a professional military and administrative bureaucracy. The close ties of the aristocratic warriors to the land, which had characterized feudalism in both Europe and Japan, were disappearing, since the samurai, as the warriors were generally coming to be known, were being gathered by the various daimyo around their castle headquarters, while the peasantry was being organized into semiautonomous tax-paying villages, ruled directly by the lords. The multiple overlapping jurisdictions which had been common in earlier feudalism were also being eliminated as the political authority of the individual daimyo became more direct and absolute throughout his realm.

In Western Europe such conditions were accompanied by political centralization under the leadership of national kings at the expense of feudal institutions. In Japan a much more rapid and in some ways more thorough centralization of political power occurred in the late sixteenth century, but through the use of a basically feudal pattern. The daimyo domains, which had become quite efficient units of local control, were used to build a surprisingly uniform and solid national political structure. This use of long familiar institutions is perhaps one reason for the great speed with which the Japanese were able to create effective national unity after so many centuries of disruption. Other factors may have been the cultural and ethnic uniformity within Japan resulting from its isolated location, the strong tradition of national unity inherited from earlier times, and the whole East Asian assumption that a unified state was the natural setting for society.

Japan's centralized feudalism, while seeming almost a contradiction in terms from the point of view of the European feudal experience, proved to be an extraordinarily stable political system, which served well for almost three centuries. This long success was perhaps made possible because the relative remoteness of the islands permitted Japan to isolate itself from external pressures for most of the period. In any case, this apparently anomalous use of feudal institutions to create centralized political power constituted the third major stage in Japanese feudalism, contrasting with the single lord-vassal band of the Kamakura system and the constantly warring, multiple lord-vassal groupings of the Ashikaga period. Although the corresponding phase in European history was represented by the essentially postfeudal early modern monarchies, the Japanese did not necessarily fall behind in institutional development, despite their more old-fashioned feudal framework. Japan in the seventeenth century was perhaps more effectively united than any European state, and Japanese levels of efficiency in political administration and economic integration were probably not exceeded anywhere in Europe before the nineteenth century.

The Coming of the Portuguese.   While isolation helped make possible the long perpetuation of the centralized feudal system, international influences seem to have contributed initially to the reunification of Japan. Less than a half-century after the Portuguese had found their way around Africa to India in 1498, some of them reached Tanegashima, an island off the southern tip of Kyūshū, apparently in 1543. Two years later Portuguese traders started visiting west Japanese ports regularly, and in 1549 the famous Jesuit, Francis Xavier, initiated the Christian missionary movement in Japan.

The Portuguese, with their own feudal background, found the martial skills and sense of feudal honor of the Japanese more admirable than the traits of other Asian peoples they had encountered. The Japanese at first were not much attracted by Christianity, which seemed to them merely a variation of the popular faith sects of Buddhism. Nevertheless, they were eager for the profits of trade, and some Kyūshū daimyo, noting the respect of the Portuguese merchants for the Jesuits, showered favors on the missionaries in an effort to attract trade to their domains. A few, motivated perhaps by a desire as much for economic as for spiritual gain, embraced Christianity and forced the people in their domains to follow suit. The small Ōmura daimyo, who was converted as early as 1562, founded the port of Nagasaki on the west coast of Kyūshū and in 1571 made it the center of the Portuguese trade. In 1579 he actually assigned control of the town to the Jesuits. The much greater Ōtomo daimyo of northern Kyūshū was converted in 1578.

The religious intolerance of the missionaries soon stirred up opposition among the Buddhist clergy, and this in turn led to sporadic persecutions of Christians by the political authorities, but the religion spread rapidly in Kyūshū and also in the Kyōto area. In fact, the Japanese, with their consciousness of having learned much from abroad—that is, from China—proved more open to Western ideas as well as goods than were other Asian societies. Japan became the Jesuits' most promising missionary field in Asia, and it is estimated that there were 150,000 Japanese converts around 1582, some 300,000 by the end of the century, and perhaps as many as 500,000 in 1615, thus constituting a greater percentage of the population than Christians do today.

Eventually the bond between Japanese Christians and their loyalty to a distant, alien pope led Japanese leaders to view Christianity as a potentially subversive force. In a sense foreign trade too was disruptive to agrarian-based feudalism. Other aspects of the contact with the West, however, were probably more enriching and stimulating than disruptive. The trade brought new plants, such as tobacco from the Americas, and fascinating new goods, such as clocks and spectacles. There was a veritable craze for European things; modish Japanese sometimes even adopted European dress; and certain Portuguese words, such as *pan* for "bread," entered the Japanese vocabulary. Many of the painted folding screens popular in this period portray the strange foreigners and their ships. Since the Portuguese arrived in Japan from the south and seemed to the Japanese to be swarthy southerners, these paintings are called "Screens of the Southern Barbarians" (*Namban-byōbu*). (See Plate 18.)

The greatest and most lasting European influence in Japan at this time proved to be on military technology, and through it on political organization. The arquebuses of the Portuguese were the first firearms the Japanese had encountered, but they immediately saw their value. Cannon were first used in warfare in Japan about 1558, and within two decades the firepower of musketeer corps had become the decisive factor in battles in the field. The richer daimyo who could afford the new weapons became still more dominant over their weaker and less modernized rivals and thus moved swiftly toward a consolidation of political power.

Outer walls and gate (lower left) and inner walls and central tower (upper right) of Himeji castle, west of Ōsaka, dating from the late sixteenth century.

Another result of European military technology was the appearance of great castles. Stockades and little castles, which hitherto had been scattered on strategic high points, were replaced by a single large central castle in a daimyo's domain. Many castles of this type were built all over Japan in the last quarter of the sixteenth century. They were more like sixteenth-century fortresses in the West than like medieval European castles, consisting of concentric circles of broad moats and great earth-backed walls, quite impervious to the cannonfire of the day. The castle buildings themselves were relatively flimsy, decorative wooden structures with white-washed mud walls. Around the central castle were clustered the residences of the daimyo's retainers and a commercial town, which was the economic heart of the domain. Such sixteenth-century castle towns were the origin of most of the great and middle-sized cities of modern Japan.

The Conquests of Oda Nobunaga and Hideyoshi. Three successive military leaders—Oda Nobunaga (1534–1582), Hideyoshi (1536–1598), and

Tokugawa Ieyasu (1542–1616)—building on each other's work, unified Japan and created the lasting pattern of centralized feudalism. Their technique was to develop a strong coalition of daimyo under their own hegemony, win control over the central capital area, with its imperial court symbolizing political legitimacy, and then extend their authority over the other coalitions of daimyo.

Oda Nobunaga was the heir of a newly risen minor daimyo in the area east of Kyōto around the modern city of Nagoya. In 1568 he seized Kyōto, ostensibly in support of a claimant to the position of shogun, but he drove this last shogun out of Kyōto in 1573, thus ending the Ashikaga shogunate. Protected on the east by an alliance with another fast-rising daimyo, Tokugawa Ieyasu, Nobunaga set about consolidating his power in the capital region, destroying in 1571 the Enryakuji, the great Tendai center on Mt. Hiei; forcing other centers of monastic power into submission; crushing various local daimyo; subduing the True Sect adherents of Kaga on the west coast; and finally in 1580, after a ten-year war, capturing the great castle headquarters of the sect in the modern Osaka. Nobunaga's long battle against Buddhist secular power led him to take a friendly attitude toward the Christians, thus permitting the phenomenal success at this time of the missionaries in the capital area.

Nobunaga confiscated the lands of those he conquered and either absorbed these into his own domain or assigned them to his vassal daimyo. He also centralized power more thoroughly. In 1571 he started a survey of the agricultural lands he controlled; in 1576 he began to confiscate the weapons of the peasantry; and he also standardized weights and measures. In 1576 he commenced construction of a great castle headquarters at Azuchi on the east shore of Lake Biwa east of Kyōto. Nobunaga did not succeed in asserting his authority over all of Japan, however. His armies were still locked in struggle with the Mōri of the extreme western end of Honshū when in 1582 he was killed in Kyōto by a treacherous vassal.

The leader of Nobunaga's armies against the Mōri was his ablest general, Hideyoshi. This man exemplified the rise of the nonaristocratic foot soldier, for he was of such humble origin that he had no family name by birth, though he later adopted the surname of Toyotomi. He had been appointed to be one of the four guardians of Nobunaga's heir, an infant grandson, but he soon managed to establish his own hegemony over Nobunaga's coalition of daimyo in central Japan and then set about eliminating the remaining daimyo groupings in the peripheral areas. In 1585 he subdued the island of Shikoku, and after an inconclusive battle in 1584, Tokugawa Ieyasu in the east accepted vassalage under him in 1586. The same year Hideyoshi invaded Kyūshū with an army of 280,000 men, forcing even the powerful Shimazu of the extreme south to accept his suzerainty. Then in 1590 he destroyed the Hōjō of the Kantō (a newly risen family not descended from the Hōjō of the Kamakura period). Meanwhile the Date of the Sendai area and the other great daimyo of the north had been overawed into submission. Thus by 1590 Japan had once again been reunited politically.

Like many successful generals before him, Hideyoshi dreamed of more worlds to conquer, which in East Asia meant, of course, China. He may also have been motivated by the practical objective of giving outlet abroad to the excess military spirit and power that centuries of incessant warfare had built up in Japan. When Korea refused his armies free passage, he dispatched to the peninsula in 1592 an invading force of 160,000 men— an army considerably smaller than those he had used against either the Shimazu or the Hōjō. The Japanese, with their firearms, quickly overran Korea but then withdrew southward in the face of massive Chinese armies (see pages 204 and 316). After long but unsuccessful negotiations, Hideyoshi renewed the war in 1597, but upon his death the next year, the Japanese armies withdrew precipitously. He himself never went to Korea but left the campaigns to his chief vassals. While the invasion had a devastating effect on Korea, it had little lasting influence on Japan, except for the technological and artistic stimulus of Korean porcelain makers and printers brought back to Japan by the retreating Japanese army.

Hideyoshi's Government. Hideyoshi extended and systematized the methods of rule he had inherited from Nobunaga. Like Nobunaga, he did not take the title of shogun—he was considered ineligible since he was not of Minamoto descent—but again like Nobunaga he drew on the prestige and legitimacy of the imperial court and in return gave it far more generous economic treatment than it had received for some centuries. He managed to claim descent from the Fujiwara family and on this basis assumed in 1585 the old title of *kampaku,* used for a Fujiwara regent of an adult emperor.

Hideyoshi's actual authority, however, rested on his military might and the lord-vassal relationship with the daimyo. As the power center of his regime, he built a great castle on the site of the castle headquarters that Nobunaga had captured from the True Sect. Around this castle developed the port city of Ōsaka. He also built in 1594 a great palace for himself at Momoyama, a little south of Kyōto. His own extensive domains centered on these two headquarters and in the rich rice lands the Oda had controlled to the east in the Nagoya area. Around this central region were grouped the domains of his most trustworthy vassals, while beyond them in more peripheral areas extended the relatively large domains of the other daimyo who had more recently accepted his suzerainty. To assure his control over the daimyo, he kept their wives and heirs as hostages at his headquarters, and he moved some of the daimyo to new domains, where the common people would feel less loyalty to them. For example, Tokugawa Ieyasu was moved to the small village of Edo (the modern Tokyo) in the Kantō, where he was given a huge domain confiscated from the Hōjō and their allies. Ieyasu's domain, in fact, was even larger in tax yield than that of Hideyoshi himself.

The organs of Hideyoshi's central government were at best rudimentary. Some of his vassal daimyo were assigned administrative titles and functions, but not until 1598, the year of his death, did he create a more elaborate system of three five-man boards made up of leading vassals. Hideyoshi's rule was basically personal and maintained by a heavy-handed threat of overwhelming military power. The daimyo domains constituted the autonomous units of local government and the supporting components of his armies. He did not tax them directly but forced them to bear heavy military burdens and the costs of his ambitious construction projects. Despite this seemingly decentralized system of local autonomy, he actually conducted himself as the *de facto* ruler of the country, demanding strict obedience from his vassal daimyo, controlling the major cities directly, regulating foreign trade by requiring his vermilion seal for overseas expeditions, and minting copper, silver, and gold coinage.

In 1585 Hideyoshi started a new cadastral survey of agricultural areas to ascertain and regularize tax yields. All lands were registered uniformly according to their productivity by *koku* (4.96 bushels) of rice. A daimyo by definition had to have a domain of at least 10,000 *koku* (49,600 bushels) yield.

As a man who himself had risen from the bottom of society to supreme political control, Hideyoshi was probably quite aware of how unstable this sort of social mobility could make a feudal system. He therefore drew a new and largely artificial class line between the samurai class and commoners. Families that remained active in agriculture in the villages, however aristocratic their origins, were classified as peasants and thus clearly separated from the professional military retainers who served Hideyoshi or his vassal daimyo. This distinction was reinforced by a nationwide "sword hunt," started in 1588, to deny the peasantry all arms. Hideyoshi also issued a series of laws designed to freeze the social classes, preventing military retainers from leaving their lords' service to become merchants or farmers and prohibiting farmers from deserting their fields to become merchants or laborers.

Hideyoshi was eager to maintain trade with the Europeans, but his desire for stability made him view Christianity with disfavor. He was suspicious that it might serve as the basis for subversive cooperation among the Kyūshū daimyo. In 1587 he suddenly ordered all the missionaries banished from Japan, although the order was not rigorously enforced, and he also commanded his vassals to secure his permission before embracing Christianity. The arrival of Spanish Franciscans in 1592 and their subsequent bickering with the Portuguese Jesuits further deepened his suspicions. So also did the close association of Christian missionaries and European soldiers in establishing colonial outposts, as in Manila in the Philippines. In 1597 he abruptly enforced his ban by crucifying nine missionaries and seventeen of their Japanese followers.

Nobunaga and Hideyoshi presided over one of the most exuberant periods in all Japanese history in terms of artistic expression and life style. In sharp contrast to Zen concepts of aesthetics, their tastes ran to the imposing and even gaudy. They built monumental and sumptuous castles and palaces adorned with elaborate carved or lacquered woodwork and sliding panels and screens decorated lavishly with gold leaf and bold paintings by the leading artists of the day. Even the "tea ceremony" Hideyoshi held in Kyōto in 1587 was a veritable public art festival, attended by thousands over a ten-day period and featuring art exhibits and dramatic and dancing performances.

The Tokugawa Shogunate

Ieyasu Founds the Shogunate.   Hideyoshi, like Nobunaga, left only an infant heir, Hideyori, whom he had placed under the joint regency of Tokugawa Ieyasu and four other of his leading vassals. Since Ieyasu was by far the most powerful, with a domain of 2,557,000 *koku* and no less than thirty-eight rear vassals of daimyo rank (more than 10,000 *koku*), many of the other daimyo began to look to him as their *de facto* lord, but a coalition of western daimyo resisted his domination. Ieyasu crushed his opponents in 1600 at Sekigahara in the low pass between the capital area and the plain around Nagoya, confiscated the domains of some eighty-seven daimyo, reduced the lands of others, and exacted written oaths of fealty from all who remained. Then in 1603 he legitimized his hegemony by having the court assign him the old title of shogun, thus founding the Tokugawa shogunate that was to last more than two and a half centuries until 1868.

Ieyasu permitted Hideyori to retain Ōsaka castle and a relatively large domain of 650,000 *koku.* He realized, however, that the heir of Hideyoshi constituted a possible rallying point for resistance. He therefore trumped up an excuse for laying siege to Ōsaka castle in 1614, renewed the attack in 1615, and seizing this stronghold, destroyed Hideyori and his supporters.

Warned by the inability of Nobunaga and Hideyoshi to pass on their power to their heirs, Ieyasu took steps to insure that his death would not lead to a quick transfer of hegemony to some rival family. In 1605, two years after assuming the title of shogun, he resigned in favor of one of his adult sons, Hidetada, chosen more for his steadiness than for his brilliance. Leaving the Edo castle to Hidetada, Ieyasu ruled Japan from then until his death in 1616 from the modern Shizuoka in the area where the Tokugawa had first arisen. Hidetada followed Ieyasu's lead by resigning the post of shogun in 1623 in favor of his adult son Iemitsu, who ruled as shogun until his death in 1651. Under these first three shoguns, the Tokugawa system of government took full shape.

Ieyasu and his descendants built on the achievements of Nobunaga and Hideyoshi, utilizing their basic method of ruling the nation through a tightly controlled coalition of ostensibly autonomous daimyo. They did not proceed to a more complete political unification of Japan, which their over-whelming military power might have made possible, probably because there seemed no need for this. Japan's geographic isolation secured it against serious foreign pressures, and Tokugawa power and prestige faced no challenge at home. In fact, Ieyasu had gained by far the most complete and efficient control over all parts of the country that Japan had ever seen. In one sense, however, the Tokugawa system was regressive. It rested almost exclusively on agricultural taxes, whereas in the preceding centuries the ruling classes had increasingly drawn support also from commerce and even international trade. But the peace created by the Tokugawa made agricultural income adequate to the needs of government, at least initially.

The Daimyo System.   The daimyo domains, which were known as *han*, fluctuated in number from 245 to 295 but tended to average around 265. They varied greatly in size from the minimal ones of 10,000 *koku* to 22 great domains of over 200,000 koku. During the seventeenth century in particular, *han* were sometimes confiscated, when a daimyo lacked an heir or was judged to have misruled, and many of the smaller daimyo were moved, together with their retainers, from one domain to another, thus receiving "promotions" or "demotions" in the size of their domains.

Tokugawa power centered in the shogun's own lands which constituted in a sense a super-daimyo domain. It grew to a whopping 6,480,000 *koku,* embracing about a quarter of the agricultural production of the whole country and somewhat more of its population. It was located largely in the Kantō, around Kyōto, and along the south coastal region in between. In addition the shogun directly ruled the major cities, such as Edo, Kyōto, Ōsaka, and Nagasaki, and owned the most important mines. His direct retainers, or samurai, were divided into two main categories. Some five thousand "bannermen" were senior retainers, the more important of whom held fiefs, although of less than daimyo size. The remainder together with some seventeen thousand lesser retainers, called *gokenin* or "honorable house men" as in the Kamakura period, received hereditary salaries. The government was based at Edo, where Ieyasu completed in 1606 the greatest of all the castles. Its outer moats made a rough circle two miles in diameter, and its inner portions still constitute the spacious and beautiful moats, walls, and grounds of the present imperial palace in the heart of Tōkyō.

The shogunal domain was buttressed by those of some twenty-three collateral Tokugawa families, known as "related *han*" (*shimpan*). Some of these were relatively large *han* which formed an outer line of defense. The three major ones, founded by three of Ieyasu's sons, were strategically situated east of Edo at Mito (350,000 *koku*), between Edo and Kyōto at Nagoya (619,500 *koku*), and southwest of Kyōto at Wakayama (555,000 *koku*). These three major collateral lines, known as the "Three Houses," were designated to supply an heir to the shogunal post if the main line ran out. Many of the other collateral daimyo were given the earlier family name of Matsudaira. Together the collateral lines controlled some 3,370,000 *koku* of rice produce.

Interspersed with the shogun's domain and the *han* of the collateral daimyo, but also scattered further afield at strategic spots, were the domains of the *fudai* daimyo ("house daimyo"), who were families first raised to daimyo status by Ieyasu or his successors and were for the most part descendants of men who had already been Ieyasu's vassals before his victory in 1600. Although the *fudai* grew to number 145, their domains were relatively small, and only one, the Ii, enfeoffed east of Kyōto, ranked as a great daimyo (originally 350,000 *koku*). The aggregate holdings of the *fudai* were about 6,700,000 *koku*.

A third category of daimyo was the *tozama,* or "outer" daimyo, the descendants of already established lords who became vassals of Ieyasu only after 1600. Some, such as Shimazu (770,800 *koku*), centered in the province of Satsuma in southern Kyūshū, and Mōri (369,000), centered in the province of Chōshū in western Honshū, had been his enemies at that time and continued a well-concealed tradition of hostility toward the Tokugawa throughout the period. Others, like Maeda at Kanazawa in Kaga on the west coast, the largest of all the daimyo (1,022,700 *koku*), had been his allies. The "outer" daimyo declined gradually to ninety-seven in number, but their domains were mostly large, totaling around 9,800,000 *koku.* Almost all were located in the peripheral parts of Japan in the north or in the west, where they would be less of a menace to the great central power block of the Tokugawa.

The bulk of the retainers of the daimyo, like those of the shogun, were salaried, but the more important ones were enfeoffed. In some peripheral domains, there was a class of petty "village samurai," who were self-supporting farmers. Most samurai, however, were gathered at the daimyo's headquarters.

The daimyo were in theory autonomous within their domains and free of taxation by the shogun's government. In actuality, however, they bore heavy financial burdens, and their freedom of action was severely constrained. As in Hideyoshi's system, they had all the responsibility for local

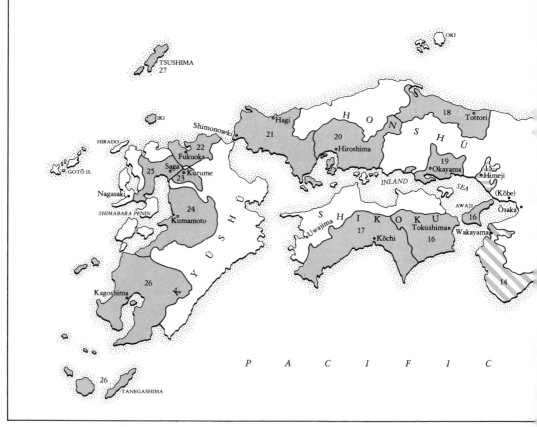

1 TSUGARU	15 SAKAKIBARA
2 SATAKE	16 HACHISUKA
3 NAMBU	17 YAMANOUCHI (TOSA)
4 SAKAI	18 IKEDA
5 DATE	19 IKEDA
6 UESUGI	20 ASANO
7 HOSHINA (MATSUDAIRA)	21 MŌRI (CHŌSHŪ)
8 TOKUGAWA (MITO)	22 KURODA
9 MAEDA (KAGA)	23 ARIMA
10 TOKUGAWA (OWARI)	24 HOSOKAWA
11 MATSUDAIRA (ECHIZEN)	25 NABESHIMA (HIZEN)
12 II (HIKONE)	26 SHIMAZU (SATSUMA)
13 TŌDŌ	27 SŌ
14 TOKUGAWA (KII)	

MAJOR DAIMYO DOMAINS

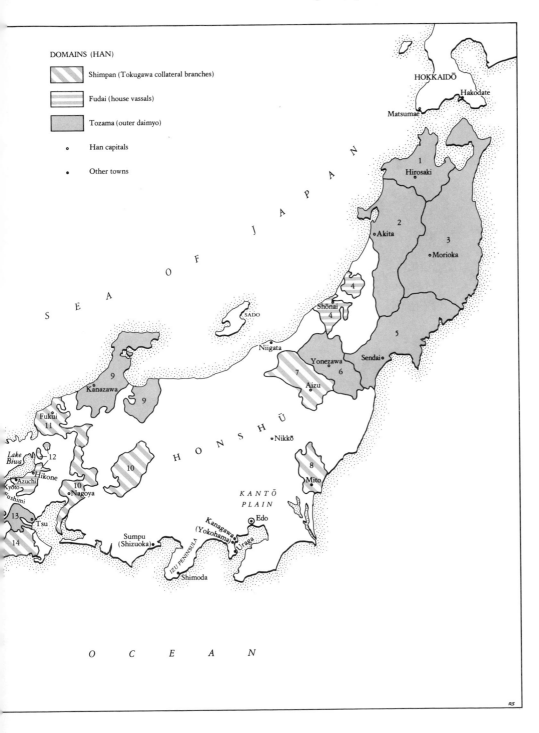

DOMAINS (HAN)

Shimpan (Tokugawa collateral branches)

Fudai (house vassals)

Tozama (outer daimyo)

o   Han capitals

•   Other towns

HOKKAIDŌ

Hakodate

Matsumae

SEA OF JAPAN

1
Hirosaki

2
Akita

3
Morioka

4
Shōnai
4

5

SADO

Niigata

Yonezawa

6

Sendai

7

Aizu

9
Kanazawa

9

Fukui
11

Lake Biwa
12

Azuchi

Hikone

10

• Nikkō

8
Mito

Kyoto
Fushimi

13

Tsu

10
Nagoya

KANTŌ PLAIN

14

Sumpu
(Shizuoka)

Kanagawa
(Yokohama)

Edo

Uraga

IZU PENINSULA

Shimoda

HONSHŪ

O   C   E   A   N

RS

*A two-page woodblock print of a daimyo (in a palanquin) and his
entourage passing the gate of a daimyo mansion on the way to
the shogun's castle on New Year's Day. In the foreground is the
head of another procession. The traditional pine and bamboo
decorations in front of the gate are still displayed at New Year's.
The text at the top is a poem in good classical Chinese describing
the scene. From* Illustrations of Famous Places in Edo *(Edo
meisho zue), printed in 1834 and 1836.*

government, were required to provide component parts for the shogun's army,
and were repeatedly called upon for expensive construction services, such
as the building of the Edo castle. They might be punished by the diminution or confiscation of their domains if they were judged guilty of disloyalty
or serious misgovernment. Edo's laws were considered the supreme law of
the land. In 1615 Ieyasu issued a code, revised in 1635, called *Laws for
the Military Houses,* which regulated the lives of the military class, limited
the military establishments and fortifications of the daimyo, prevented them
from entering into alliances with one another, and set up many other restrictions on their activities.

The Tokugawa sought to bind the major daimyo families to them
through marriage, but their chief methods for insuring the loyalty of their
vassals were two old feudal institutions: the holding of hostages and periodic attendance and service of the vassal at the lord's court. From the
start the daimyo had voluntarily sent their wives and heirs to Edo as hostages, and this system was made mandatory in 1633. Barriers on the roads

leading into Edo kept a watch for women leaving the city or guns entering, for either might signify a plot against the regime. Attendance by the daimyo at the shogun's court also started on a voluntary basis but was made into a rigid compulsory system after 1635. Called "alternate attendance" (*sankin kōtai*), this system required most daimyo to spend alternate years in Edo.

Both the hostage and the "alternate attendance" systems required each daimyo to maintain one or more costly residences in Edo. Daimyo processions going to or from Edo, sometimes consisting of several thousand people, became a colorful feature of the time, especially along the Tō-kaidō, the great coastal road between Kyōto and Edo. The large expenditures for these expeditions and for the Edo residences of the daimyo, often amounting to more than half of a daimyo's income, seriously weakened the daimyo financially, making revolt all the less probable. Long residence in Edo also transformed the daimyo families over time from local warriors into courtiers, further lessening their threat to the regime. And the constant flow of a large proportion of the ruling class between Edo and the provinces created a greater degree of cultural, intellectual, and ideological conformity in Japan than any other country in the world could boast before the nineteenth century.

The Shogun's Government.   The shogunal government, or *bakufu,* had a double function: it administered the shogun's super-domain, and it also controlled the daimyo and set national policy, ostensibly in behalf of the emperor's civil government in Kyōto. The Tokugawa treated the emperor generously and with respect, as the ultimate source of their own legitimacy, but maintained a firm control over his court. The palace was rebuilt, and the emperor and his nobles were assigned 187,000 *koku* in support. In 1615 Ieyasua promulgated a code of laws for the court and its nobility which made clear their purely symbolic and cultural role and gave the shogunate control over all court appointments. A Kyōto Deputy and garrison were established at the Nijō castle in Kyōto to assure Edo's mastery over the situation there and in west Japan.

The shogun's own government was staffed by the *fudai,* or "house," daimyo and his personal retainers. Positions were assigned in accordance with family status, but within these bounds men were selected for their talent, and exceptionally able or favored administrators were occasionally promoted in both post and feudal status. At the top were two councils. The senior one, called the "elders," which was usually made up of from four to six larger "house" daimyo, had authority over national affairs, including the control of the daimyo and the court. The "elders" took monthly turns as officer in charge, and one of the group in time came to be recognized as the head of the council, but the post of Great Elder, a sort of prime minister, was usually filled only in time of crisis. The junior council, called the "young elders," also consisting usually of from four to six smaller "house" daimyo, had charge of the shogun's "bannermen" and lesser retainers, the shogun's own military forces, and his household staff.

Beneath these councils was a great proliferation of offices, usually headed in typical Japanese fashion by paired officials or a group who shared responsibility and power. Chamberlains exercised considerable influence at the shogunal court, especially in the middle years of the Tokugawa. Four Commissioners of Finance supervised the income of the shogunate and oversaw the work of the forty-odd intendants who administered and collected taxes from the shogun's domain. Four Commissioners of Temples and Shrines supervised the Buddhist monasteries and Shintō shrines of the land, whose total holdings had been reduced to a mere 600,000 *koku*. Paired Town Commissioners controlled each of the major cities, and those at Nagasaki supervised foreign trade as well. Four inspector generals and lesser inspectors checked on the activities of the daimyo and served as police officers. Some slight degree of order was given to the jumble of laws and edicts issued over the years by occasional codifications, which had become necessary by the middle of the eighteenth century.

The daimyo domains tended to mirror the shogunate both in administrative organization and in laws. A daimyo's chief retainers, usually called "house elders," constituted a top council, and lesser samurai occupied the middle and lower posts in the system, first in accordance with their specific family status and only secondarily in accordance with their abilities.

Social Classes.   The Tokugawa followed Hideyoshi's lead in seeking to insure political stability by limiting social mobility. The Chinese concept of a natural social order consisting of a clear hierarchy of classes proved useful in imposing artificial limitations on social change. The Tokugawa, in fact, adopted the ancient Chinese theory that there were four natural classes, which in descending order were: 1) the warrior-bureaucrats, in place of the scholar-bureaucrats of China; 2) the peasants or primary producers; 3) the artisans or secondary producers; and 4) the merchants, whose contribution to society was least valued.

The highest of the four recognized classes consisted of the shogun, daimyo, and their retainers. The daimyo fell into categories by origin and wealth, and the retainers into a great number of levels running from richly enfeoffed "house elders" and "bannermen" down to common foot soldiers with only subsistence salaries. All had specific hereditary status and incomes which were changed only under unusual circumstances, and they occupied posts in the shogunal or *han* governments commensurate with their hereditary status, from high councilors down to gate guards. Together they constituted around 6 per cent of the total population—a far higher percentage than that of the feudal aristocracy of Europe. Many samurai were in income and function hardly aristocrats, but they all felt great pride in their status, symbolized by the wearing of two swords, one long and the other shorter. Any samurai was considered to be far above any commoner and at least in theory had the right to kill a disrespectful commoner on the spot.

The line between the samurai and commoners was strictly maintained, but below it class lines were largely theoretical. Artisans and merchants were not really differentiated and tended to form a single "townsmen" (*chōnin*) category. The concept that the merchants were the lowest class of society was patently absurd, because many were men of great wealth, and increasingly this group took the lead in cultural life. Peasants were by function distinct from townsmen but commonly migrated to the city or engaged in artisan or merchant activities in the countryside. Village society was divided between leading, land-owning families, often the descendants of former warrior lines, which were usually in control of the autonomous village governments, and humbler peasants who had little or no land of their own. Agricultural taxes were high—up to 40 to 50 per cent of the yield—but, since these supported not just the shogun and daimyo and their administrations but the whole broad samurai class, they are not to be compared to taxes in other societies where the upper classes derived their income from resources other than taxes.

Outside of the theoretical four-class system existed the tiny group of court aristocrats, a much larger category of Buddhist monks and Shintō priests, and a group of "outcasts" (known as *eta*) at the bottom of society, who are best compared to the "base people" of Korean history. Living largely in the Kyōto area and west Japan, these "outcasts" constituted around 2 per cent of the population. They seem to have originated in pre-Tokugawa times from persons defeated in warfare, criminals, and groups whose professions, such as butchery or leatherwork, were considered demeaning, since they violated Buddhist dictates against the taking of animal life.

At all levels of society the family (or "house," *ie*), rather than the individual, was considered the basic unit, carrying with it not just property rights but specific social status, which the individual family head simply fulfilled. Most families were grouped into administrative units. Among the lower samurai these were functional groups, and among peasants and sometimes townsmen they were groups of mutual responsibility for taxes and legal liability.

Forcing all people into the rigid Tokugawa social mold was not easy after the social fluidity and confusion of the sixteenth century, and frictions developed, especially at the points of contact between classes. Particularly troublesome was the problem of members of the samurai class who had lost their specific niches in the system, perhaps through the elimination of their lord, or through a failure to fit in, because of personality or inclination. As late as 1651 such masterless samurai, known as *rōnin* ("wave men"), were the center of a plot against the shogunate.

Isolation. The Tokugawa might not have been able to maintain so stable a system of rule or such great social rigidity if they had not also isolated Japan from the upsetting foreign influences that had poured in during the sixteenth century. Actually Ieyasu, like his predecessors, was eager for commerce with the outside world. He tried to persuade China to agree to official trade through licensed ships and, when frustrated in this effort, created instead in 1604 a government-supervised monopoly in Chinese silk. Desirous of attracting European trade to his home region, he allowed the Spanish Franciscans to establish a mission at Edo. He also permitted the Dutch in 1609 and the English four years later to set up trading posts at Hirado, an island off the northwest coast of Kyūshū. He learned from these nonproselytizing Protestants and also from his foreign trade adviser, Will Adams, an English pilot of a Dutch vessel stranded in Japan in 1600, that there were Europeans who were perfectly ready to trade without conducting missionary activities.

Like Hideyoshi, Ieyasu viewed Christianity as essentially subversive, and as early as 1606 he started issuing anti-Christian decrees. His successor, Hidetada, banned all missionary activity in 1612 and commanded the "house" daimyo and all people in the shogun's domain to renounce the religion. In 1614 a minor Christian daimyo was exiled to Manila and more than two-thirds of the 156 European missionaries then in the country were expelled, although more continued to slip in. Four missionaries were executed in 1617 and 120 missionaries and converts in 1622. The daimyo were forced to join in the persecution, including even the great Date of the North, who had sent a large mission to the papacy by way of Mexico in 1613. By 1629 it had become customary to force suspected Christians to step on some Christian symbol, such as a bronze plaque portraying Christ or Mary, and to execute or force into apostasy through torture those who refused to step on this "treading picture" (*fumi-e*). The Catholic church recognizes 3125 martyrdoms in Japan between 1597 and 1660.

The persecution of Christianity came to a climax in 1637–1638 when some twenty thousand Christian peasants, supported by "masterless samurai," rose in revolt in western Kyūshū because of oppressive taxation. They fended off a much larger shogunal army from an old castle on the Shimabara Peninsula but were finally crushed and slaughtered. Except for the survival of a few isolated communities of crypto-Christians, the Shimabara revolt marked the virtual end of Christianity in Japan. Starting in 1640, all Japanese were forced to register at local Buddhist temples as a means of keeping check on their religious affiliations.

The fury of the anti-Christian persecution, together with the Tokugawa policy of closely regulating foreign trade as part of their control system, eventually carried the shogunate into almost complete national isolation. In 1616 European ships were limited to the two ports of Nagasaki and Hirado, and in 1623 the English gave up their trading contacts with Japan as unprofitable. The next year the Spanish were expelled because of complicity in missionary activities. In 1635 all Japanese were prohibited on pain of death from going abroad or from returning home if already overseas, for fear that they might bring back Christian doctrines. To help enforce this ban, a prohibition was placed on the building of ships of more than 500 *koku* capacity, thus limiting Japan to smaller vessels suitable only for coastal transport. These measures brought to a sudden halt more than a century of tremendous overseas activity and left large groups of Japanese traders and fighting men stranded throughout Southeast Asia, to be absorbed into the native populations. A single Japanese community in the Philippines is said to have numbered three thousand in the early seventeenth century.

As an aftermath of the Shimabara revolt, the Portuguese were expelled in 1639, and their envoys were executed when they returned the next year. This left only the Dutch among the Europeans still trading with Japan, and their representatives were moved in 1641 from Hirado to the tiny island of Deshima in Nagasaki harbor, where they were kept as virtual prisoners. Chinese merchants were also allowed to trade at Nagasaki, but under strict controls. Two other foreign trade contacts were also permitted—one with Korea through the Sō daimyo of Tsushima, the islands in the straits between the two countries, and the other by way of "tributary" missions to China from the king of Ryūkyū (Liu-ch'iu in Chinese, and now known as Okinawa), the island chain stretching south of Kyūshū, which the Shimazu daimyo of Satsuma had subjugated in 1609 and made a closely controlled vassal domain.

Substantial amounts of silver and copper and later dried marine products were exported through Nagasaki in return largely for Chinese goods, but this trade had relatively little effect on the Japanese economy as a whole. While Chinese intellectual influences through imported books remained strong, all other foreign influences were virtually eliminated. Political and social pressures from abroad were reduced to zero, and a strict ban was maintained on all Western books and on Chinese books mentioning Christianity. The isolation of the country, although artificially created and maintained, was perhaps more complete than it had been in any period since primitive times. Through the Dutch and Chinese at Nagasaki, the authorities kept watch on developments in the outside world, but for most practical purposes Japan developed over the next century and a half almost as if the rest of the world did not exist.

In this cocoon-like isolation, the hitherto rapid rate of technological, political, and social change that had marked the sixteenth century slowed down precisely at the time when change was accelerating in the West. The Japanese, who had been technologically and institutionally abreast of the Europeans in many respects and ahead in some at the start of the seventeenth century, fell drastically behind. This might be viewed as a national tragedy for which the Japanese paid bitterly in their frenetic efforts to catch up in the nineteenth and twentieth centuries. At the same time, the Tokugawa period was a time of great cultural creativity. By turning inward on their own resources, the Japanese had a chance to develop fully their own identity and culture, producing in the process distinctive personality traits, social skills, and artistic achievements that constituted an invaluable national heritage.

Social and Economic Development

The Transformation of the Samurai Class.   The pattern of social organization and political rule that had been established in the first half of the seventeenth century hardened into well-accepted practice by the end of the century and continued with only minor modifications until the middle of the nineteenth century. For exactly two and a quarter centuries after the suppression of the Shimabara revolt in 1638, there was no significant political change or any warfare in Japan—only occasional riots by villagers or townsmen or perhaps a political assassination. This was probably the longest period of complete peace and political stability that any sizable body of people has ever enjoyed. And yet it was a time not of stagnation but of very dynamic economic and cultural growth. After centuries of warfare and disunity, peace alone proved a strong stimulus to change, as did also the thorough centralization of controls that the Tokugawa had instituted.

The impact of peace and political unity was felt perhaps most strongly by the samurai class itself. To rule a land at peace, the Tokugawa needed educated administrators more than rough soldiers. The writing brush replaced the sword as the chief implement of the samurai, as they rapidly evolved from a body of fighting men into an urbanized class of well educated bureaucrats and petty government functionaries. Numerous enough to have furnished the mass armies of a country in constant civil war, they provided in time of peace a superabundance of would-be administrators, which proved a needlessly heavy burden on government finances.

The samurai remained organized for the most part into military units and made a fetish of their two swords, but warfare had become a matter of theory, not practice. Schools were founded in the various domains to teach the military arts, but gunnery and the use of firearms, which had proved the decisive military techniques, were largely ignored in favor of the medieval military disciplines of swordsmanship and archery, which were favored for their character-building qualities as much as for their military value. From this grew the emphasis on other character-building martial arts, such as the wrestling-fighting technique of *jūdō* and its modern variant *karate*.

The samurai value system, which had been a natural outgrowth of a feudal warrior society, gradually became transformed into a self-conscious philosophy. The feudal ethical principles of unquestioning loyalty to one's lord, fierce defense of one's own status and honor, and strict fulfillment of all obligations became codified as *Bushidō*, the "Way of the Warrior." Social realities, however, were moving away from the feudal conditions that had created this value system, as is illustrated by the prohibition in 1663 of suicide by retainers in order to "follow their lord in death." The famous incident of the "Forty-Seven *Rōnin*" of 1702 illustrates the same point. A minor daimyo, humiliated by a shogunate official, drew his sword within the Edo castle, for which offense he was forced to commit suicide and his domain was confiscated. His retainers, now made "masterless samurai," disarmed official suspicion by two years of dissolute living but then fulfilled the medieval code of ethics by assassinating the Edo official in vengeance for their lord. The public was thrilled, and the event became Japan's favorite dramatic theme, but the authorities coldly forced the forty-seven to commit suicide. Law and order triumphed over loyalty.

Confucianism.   As the samurai turned increasingly into a hereditary civil bureaucracy, Confucianism, which in China had developed into the philosophy of a bureaucratic ruling class, began to take on a new meaning and an increased appeal. In a country at peace, the Confucian concept of political leadership as dependent not so much on brute military force as on ethical example and moral suasion became important. It was largely through Confucian learning that the rude warrior class of the beginning of the seventeenth century was transformed by the end of the century into a literate officialdom, deeply steeped in ethical precepts.

The Neo-Confucian philosophy of the Sung dynasty (see pages 147–151) had been introduced by Zen monks during the Ashikaga period, but in the seventeenth century it burst out of its monastic confines. Fujiwara Seika (1561–1619) forsook Buddhist orders to become Japan's first lay Confucian philosopher, and his disciple, Hayashi Razan (1583–1657), served as an adviser to Ieyasu on legal and historical matters. In 1630 the Hayashi family founded a school at Edo which grew into the official Confucian University under its hereditary leadership. Similar Confucian schools were also founded in many of the domains. Together they helped spread the Chinese concept of an essentially secular society, based on a natural, moral order, and epitomized by a centralized state, administered by an educated, ethically upright bureaucracy.

The Confucian emphasis on filial piety and loyalty and its concepts of a hierarchy of classes fitted early seventeenth-century Japan, but there was nonetheless a basic clash between the military, hereditary origins of the samurai class and the civil, bureaucratic ideal of government imbedded in Confucianism. This heightened the tensions already developing between the feudal value system the samurai had inherited and the social and political realities in which they operated. Confucianism emphasized centralized, imperial, civil rule, rather than a feudal, military hegemony, which was the origin of the Tokugawa system. It stressed uniform bureaucratic relationships in government, rather than the personal bonds of loyalty on which feudalism was based. It maintained that individual learning and moral excellence were the qualifications for political leadership, not hereditary status.

The resulting tensions were perhaps in part disruptive but in more ways creative. Confucian concepts provided an alternate pattern of political organization to the shogunate, which contributed to the transformation of Japan during the nineteenth century. They helped Tokugawa society move slowly toward the recognition of personal merit as well as family status. Most official posts came to carry specific salaries in addition to the incumbent's hereditary stipend, and in time a system of supplementary stipends was developed to permit particularly able administrators to qualify in status and income for higher posts. Despite these relaxations of the hereditary system, however, demands for recognition of merit over birth grew toward the end of the period.

The conflict between Chinese political and philosophic principles and Japanese social realities may help explain the development in Tokugawa society of greater pressures on the individual for conformity and stricter and more artificial rules of conduct than existed in China. These in turn may account for the tenseness that seems to characterize Japanese personality and the great Japanese emphasis on self-discipline and will power. In any case, whatever the causes, the Japanese of the Tokugawa period seem to have developed an extremely strong sense of honor, duty, and obligation and a dogged determination to live up to all that society expected of them. These qualities gradually spread from the samurai to other classes. The mixed feudal and Confucian values of the Tokugawa period thus left Japan a legacy of extraordinary formalism and rigidity on the one hand but also of strong inner discipline and personal drive on the other.

The contradictions between Confucian ideas and the inherited Japanese tradition may also have helped keep Japanese thought from becoming as limited by an official orthodoxy as happened in China and Korea. The multiplicity of locally autonomous regimes, of course, was another important reason for intellectual diversity. The Chu Hsi (Shushi in Japanese) school of Neo-Confucianism was established as orthodoxy by the shogunate, but heterodox Confucian schools also flourished, as well as much pragmatic economic and scientific thought.

Shintō too continued its role in the life of the people through the great historic shrines and the many small local ones with their periodic festivals. The Tokugawa even added a major cult of their own. Ieyasu's spirit was enshrined by his grandson Iemitsu in a great complex of shrines and temples set in a magnificent setting of giant cryptomeria trees at Nikkō on the northern edge of the Kantō Plain.

Buddhism also had its place. The anti-Christian edict of 1640 forced all Japanese to register as parishioners of some local Buddhist temple, which also performed for them such rites as marriages and funerals and maintained the family graves. The shogun and daimyo also built and patronized new Buddhist temples in their respective capitals. Today's parks at Ueno and Shiba are the vestigial remains of the chief shogunal temples of Edo. The unifiers of Japan, however, had drastically reduced the wealth and political power of the Buddhist church, and the shift of interest of the samurai class to Confucianism now robbed Buddhism of much of its intellectual and cultural vigor. Thus during the Tokugawa period, the Japanese, like the Chinese and Koreans before them, became an essentially secular society, dominated by the philosophy of Neo-Confucianism.

The Growth of Commerce.   Despite Japan's relative isolation from world trade, the prolonged Tokugawa peace produced an almost explosive expansion of commerce. This was furthered by the centralization of political controls and ironically by the agrarian orientation of the ruling class and its disdain for trade, which Confucian concepts had further strengthened. Relying basically on agricultural taxes, the shogunate and domains taxed commerce less heavily, thus permitting it to grow more easily.

The system of "alternate attendance" at Edo also contributed greatly to the commercialization of the economy and the development of a single broad national market. The "alternate attendance" system forced the daimyo to expend much of their income to maintain residences with large staffs at Edo and to pay for the annual movement of themselves and great numbers of their retainers between their domains and Edo. This required large money resources that could be provided only by the sale of local products outside of their domains. For this purpose some domains developed monopolies over local agricultural, marine, forest, or handicraft specialities. Sugar cane in the southernmost islands of the Shimazu domain of Satsuma is a good example. Most domains, however, had to rely on the sale of surplus rice to the central cities.

There was a rapid growth of cities and towns throughout Japan. The roughly 6 per cent of the population that constituted the samurai class was largely concentrated at Edo and in the various daimyo castle towns. Merchants and providers of other services were required in comparable numbers in the cities and towns to supply the needs of this large upper class. As a consequence, although in the past Kyōto had been the only city of significance, as both the capital and the center of commerce, Japan now became a land of many large and small cities. Edo in the eighteenth century approached a million in population and was possibly the largest city in the world at that time, as it is again today under the name of Tōkyō. Ōsaka, which because of its location at the head of the Inland Sea became a major center of commerce, paralleled Kyōto in size at about 400,000. The castle towns of the daimyo ran from a few thousand inhabitants for a small daimyo to close to 100,000 for such large domain capitals as Kanazawa (Maeda) and Nagoya (Tokugawa).

Barter all but disappeared in this commercial urban economy, and an adequate supply of currency, of course, became essential. The shogunate from the start minted gold coins and copper cash and later silver coins too. A great deal of commercial paper also developed. The individual daimyo used rice and silver certificates as paper money within their domains—some 1600 different issues have been identified—and commercial notes and money orders of private merchants and bankers were widely used for large transactions, thus greatly expanding the monetary resources of the country. The great variety of currency and repeated debasement of the coinage by the shogunate, however, always kept the monetary situation complex.

Most of the domains of western Japan maintained commercial offices and warehouses in Ōsaka to dispose of their excess produce and acquire needed commodities. At first these were run by their own retainers, but in time they were entrusted largely to men of merchant origin. Rice markets grew up in both Ōsaka and Edo and by the eighteenth century were dealing in futures, much like the contemporary wheat markets of London and Amsterdam. A widespread system of coastal shipping developed in order to supply the two great centers of commerce and consumption at Edo and Ōsaka. This, together with the many roads and post stations needed for the large-scale movement of men in the "alternate attendance" system, gave Japan a complex and well-developed communications network, though land transport was still quite backward, since a shogunate ban on wheeled vehicles necessitated the use of pack horses and human porters.

The Townsmen.   The shogunate and domains controlled the merchants in their respective areas as they saw fit. Some were designated as "honorable service merchants" (*goyō shōnin*), who helped supply the shogunal or daimyo households. Arbitrary monetary contributions might be exacted from merchants in time of need, and unbecoming acts or displays of wealth by members of this theoretically lowest class might result in complete confiscation of their property. Frequently the authorities recognized various monopoly guilds of local merchants, from which they collected fees, and by the end of the seventeenth century a variety of great wholesale guilds in

Wholesale sake *firms located along a canal, from* Illustrations of Famous Places in Edo *of 1834 and 1836.*

Ōsaka and Edo had developed with official sanction. In 1721 the shogunate even started licensing merchant associations (*kabu nakama*, which literally means "stock companies"), and the practice increased later in the century as the shogunate's finances deteriorated. Similarly the daimyo domains, in increasing financial desperation, turned to *han* commercial monopolies in an effort to bolster their finances.

Thus the ruling classes held the merchants down socially and sometimes controlled their economic activities in order to extract fees from them, but by and large, with feudal and Confucian contempt for commerce, they turned their backs on trade, leaving it largely in the hands of the urban merchants. Except for relatively light taxes for urban services, there was no direct taxation, and government fees were not very heavy. Since the three largest cities and the major centers of trade were all within the shogun's great central domain, the bulk of the more important merchants were under shogunal jurisdiction. This was a great advantage for them, because the shogunate, controlling as it did the whole economic heartland of Japan and possessing large agricultural resources as compared to its samurai population, was a relatively lenient master, and it also afforded the merchants of its area considerable protection in their dealings with the daimyo domains. While Tokugawa merchants did not have the freedom or prestige of their counterparts in Europe at this time, they were much more protected from arbitrary confiscation or ruinous taxation and controls than were merchants in most parts of Asia. Thus they could afford to make longer-range investments of capital.

A number of great merchant houses developed during the Tokugawa period. The house of Mitsui started in the province of Ise in *sake* brewing, added pawnbrokerage and moneylending, opened a dry goods store in Edo in 1673, established branches in Kyōto and Ōsaka, became official banker to the shogunate in 1691 and the banking agent of several daimyo, and survived to become in modern times one of the largest private economic enterprises in the world. The Kōnoike house, also starting in *sake* brewing, entered into moneylending and shipping at Ōsaka after 1616 and became the financial agent for many *han*. Sumitomo, starting in iron goods and drugs in Kyōto, became a major trader and refiner of copper and still is an important component of Japanese industry. (See Plate 22.)

The great spurt in urban and commercial growth produced by peace and centralization had largely run its course by the early eighteenth century. Thereafter the pace slackened, but the social effects of the commercial explosion continued and actually grew stronger. Tied as the samurai class was to income from agriculture, which grew less rapidly than commerce and handicrafts, its share of national wealth declined, although its members increased somewhat and its standards of consumption greatly. Most daimyo and many samurai came to live well beyond their means. As a consequence they fell heavily in debt to urban merchants and moneylenders. This situation was already severe by the end of the seventeenth century, and it grew steadily worse during the remainder of the period.

The indebtedness of the top social class to the lowest class obviously undermined the whole theory and spirit of the Tokugawa system. So also did the urban milieu in which the samurai lived. Already transformed from warriors into civil bureaucrats, they now found themselves living in an environment in which the economic patterns and cultural tone were increasingly set by the despised merchant class. One philosopher likened the samurai, with their constant comings and goings to and from Edo, to transients residing in an inn owned and operated by the townsmen. The domains could attempt to extricate themselves from debt by commercial operations and the reduction of their retainers' stipends in the guise of loans. This last measure, of course, only worsened the plight of the samurai. The poorer ones, who in any case received only minimal stipends in rice, were frequently forced to eke out their inadequate income by cottage industries, such as the making of straw sandals.

The Peasantry.   Change came more slowly to the rural villages where the bulk of the population lived. Nevertheless peace and unity, together with

Plate 1   *Jade disk of the late Chou period (fifth–third centuries* B.C.*)*.

Plate 2 *Gilt bronze lamp from a Former Han tomb.*

Plate 3 *A lacquer-painted basket discovered in a Han tomb in Lo-lang, Korea.*

Plate 4   *Detail of a painting of an emperor and attendants of the*
     Six Dynasties period, attributed to the T'ang painter
     Yen Li-pen (seventh century).

Plates 5–7 SECTIONS OF THREE SUNG SCROLL PAINTINGS.
*Upper left: Women ironing silk, attributed to the emperor
Hui Tsung (reigned 1100–1125). Lower left: The first Han
emperor's army marching to Ch'ang-an. Above: Landscape by
Hsü Tao-ning (died ca. 1066). The fishermen at the extreme
right and left toast each other with raised wine cups.*

Plates 8–10 *Upper left: Detail of a Sung painting of a Han lady (Wen chi), ransomed from the nomads. Below: Afghan hounds painted by the Ming emperor Hsüan-te in 1427, with seals of the painter and successive owners. Right: Portrait group of a Ming family.*

Plate 14   *Kuan-yin bodhisattva of the Sung period.*

Plates 11–13 *Below: Korean celadon vase and wine pot of the Koryŏ period. Right: Ming vase of blue and white porcelain (Hsüan-te period, 1426–1435).*

Plates 15–16 *Details from "The Burning of the Sanjō Palace,"
a thirteenth-century Japanese scroll painting, illustrating an account
of the Heiji War of the twelfth century.*

Plates 17–18 *Above: Section of a late twelfth-century Japanese scroll of the adventures of Kibi, an envoy to T'ang China. (Kibi's knowledge of Chinese literature is being tested in a special examination hall.) Below: Portuguese landing in Japan (a "Screen of the Southern Barbarians").*

Plate 19 *Detail of a seventeenth-century Japanese painting of
samurai visiting the gay quarters.*

鈴木春信画

Plate 20　*Woodblock print by Harunobu (1724–1770).*

Plates 21–22   *Above: Woodblock print of Mt. Fuji by Hokusai (1760–1849). Below: Mitsui dry goods shop in Edo by Hiroshige (1797–1858).*

Plates 23–24 *Above: Tōkyō Olympics in 1964. Below: Parade passing T'ien-an men in Peking during the Cultural Revolution.*

specialization of crops, expanded acreage, improved irrigation, better seeds and tools, increased use of fertilizers, and more double cropping, resulted in a considerable expansion of agricultural production. The Japanese peasant was becoming the most technologically advanced farmer in Asia. There was a great increase in commercial crops, such at cotton, tobacco, and mulberry leaves for silkworms, and cereal production seems to have doubled between 1600 and 1720. Thereafter agriculture expanded less rapidly as it approached the narrow limits set by geography.

The Japanese population grew with the economy but not as rapidly. It stood at about 30 million at the time of the first census in 1721, which is thought to have been a 50 per cent increase over the estimated 20 million for 1600 and was well above the population of any European country at that time. In the second half of the Tokugawa period the population grew hardly at all, despite a continued, even if slower, growth of the economy. As a consequence, there was a clear rise in living standards throughout the Tokugawa period, even for the peasantry. What had once been luxurious city ways became commonplace in the countryside too. Thus during these centuries, the Japanese economy outpaced the population.

Why this happened in Japan, as it was happening at much the same time in Western Europe, is not clear, although it may be connected with the feudal social pattern, in which there is room in each family for only one heir and therefore, unlike other traditional societies, a large family is a burden rather than an asset. One rural response was the practice of infanticide, known by the agricultural term of "thinning" (*mabiki*). In any case, the rise of the Japanese economy above mere subsistence levels permitted the development of relatively high standards of literacy, economic institutions, and government services, and these high standards helped make possible Japan's successful modernization in the nineteenth century.

Despite generally improving economic conditions, however, the economic position of large parts of the peasantry seems to have deteriorated during the second half of the Tokugawa period. This was reflected in the rising number of famines and also of "peasant uprisings," which usually were peaceful demonstrations against increased taxes or misgovernment and turned to violence only late in the period.

The root cause of this situation seems to have been a growing imbalance in the distribution of rural wealth. Farming units had once been made up typically of several collateral and servitor families grouped around a central family, providing it with labor and depending on it for security in a largely subsistence agriculture. As a result of the commercialization of the whole economy, the geographic specialization of crops, and the development of village industries in *sake* brewing, cotton spinning, weaving, dyeing, and the like, this pattern began to dissolve. Subsistence farming was replaced by specialized cash crops, which made all peasants more vulnerable to outside economic vagaries. At the same time, the large farm units began to break up into smaller family-size units, as the richer families found it more advantageous to concentrate their own efforts on their best piece of agricultural land, rent out the remainder to tenants, and then invest their profits in village industries, which brought in a larger return than agriculture. Meanwhile the former dependent families, now cut free as tenants, farmed the less fertile fields but commonly bore a disproportionately heavy portion of the taxes, assigned by the richer families which dominated the autonomous village governments. Thus the richer peasants became richer, and the poorer ones lost their former security of association with them.

This whole transition was slow and uneven, coming much earlier in the central and economically more advanced areas, especially the regions around Kyōto and Ōsaka, than in more peripheral areas. Its effects were not limited to the increase of rural unrest. By the early nineteenth century poor peasants were becoming accustomed to working for wages on the farms of richer peasants or in village industries. Thus they were forming a reservoir for urban factory labor when Japan subsequently industrialized. Many richer peasants had turned into aggressive rural entrepreneurs. Often well-educated, such peasant entrepreneurs led a second great wave of commercial expansion in the late eighteenth and early nineteenth centuries, invading even the urban strongholds of the great merchant houses. A harbinger of the future was the silk-weaving town of Kiryū on the northern edge of the Kantō Plain, which had dormitories for workers already in the eighteenth century and five thousand looms by the middle of the nineteenth.

Tokugawa Culture

Confucian Scholarship.   Cultural and intellectual developments during the Tokugawa period tended to separate into two fairly distinct streams, the one dominated by the samurai class and the other by the townsmen. The samurai, proud of their feudal heritage and immersed in Chinese Confucianism, did not prove to be very innovative in the fields of literature and art, but the needs of bureaucratic rule and the stimulus of Chinese learning produced an outburst of scholarly and philosophical activity among them. Classical Chinese became once again the language of most serious writing and the prime subject of samurai education in the many *han* and private academies that were founded, especially after 1700. Many samurai mastered a grammatically correct and even elegant Chinese written style, although then as now almost no Japanese knew the spoken language or even the real Chinese pronunciations for the characters, which were read according to the greatly modified Japanese pronunciations for them.

History writing—the vital core of Chinese scholarship—naturally attracted major attention. The Hayashi family of official shogunal Confucian scholars completed in 1670 the *Comprehensive Mirror of Our Country,* a chronological history based on Chinese models. The *Veritable Records of the Tokugawa,* a massive chronological compendium of shogunal activities based on Chinese prototypes, was compiled between 1809 and 1849. Meanwhile Tokugawa Mitsukuni (1628–1700), the daimyo of Mito and a grandson of Ieyasu, had started a large project known as the *History of Great Japan,* which was partially completed in 1720 but did not reach final form until 1906. Many individual scholars, such as Arai Hakuseki (1657–1725), who was a leading shogunate official, also produced important historical works.

In addition to the Hayashi family in Edo, there was a great number of samurai scholars at Edo and in the various domains who propagated the orthodox Chu Hsi school of philosophy. Among them, Kaibara Ekken (1630–1714) of northern Kyūshū helped spread these ideas to the lower classes by writing in Japanese. Some samurai scholars, however, protected by their respective daimyo from Edo's periodic insistence on orthodoxy, followed other lines of Chinese Confucianism.

Nakae Tōju (1606–1648) was inclined to the Idealist School of the Ming Confucianist, Wang Yang-ming (Ōyōmei in Japanese; see pages 192–193. His disciple, Kumazawa Banzan (1619–1691), a "masterless samurai" who rose to become the chief official of the important "outer" domain of Okayama in western Honshū, advocated the return of the samurai to the soil and a more austere form of life. Wang Yang-ming's emphasis on the individual's intuitive moral sense, on personal discipline, and on action rather than words appealed to the samurai, since these concepts, which were probably at least in part of Zen inspiration even in China, had become part of the samurai heritage through Zen influence during the Ashikaga period. It is significant that some of the men most active in transforming Japan in the second half of the nineteenth century were influenced by the Wang Yang-ming school of thought.

Another heterodox school, called "Ancient Learning" (*Kogaku*), followed the lead of contemporary Ch'ing scholars in attempting to get back of the Sung philosophers to earlier Confucianism. Yamaga Sokō (1622–1685), a "masterless samurai," contributed to the development of the "Way of the Warrior" as a comprehensive philosophy. Itō Jinsai (1627–1705), who actually came from a merchant family in Kyōto, stressed the virtues taught in the early Confucian works, especially the *Analects* and *Mencius,* and Ogyū Sorai (1666–1728), the son of a doctor in the shogun's service, went back to the still earlier Five Classics, but at the same time was an advocate of utilitarian policies, greater shogunal absolutism, and more recognition for men of individual talent.

Perhaps because Confucian theory and Japanese political and social realities did not fit together very well, Tokugawa thinkers on the whole seem to have remained somewhat more pragmatic than their counterparts at this time in China and Korea. Good examples of this are to be found in the work of the great mathematician, Seki Takakazu (1642–1708), and the cartographer, Inō Tadataka (1745–1818). Many Confucian thinkers paid attention to the practical economic problems that were bothering the shogunate and domains. While most intellectuals remained tied to the agrarian biases of feudalism and Confucianism, some developed iconoclastic ideas. Kaiho Seiryō (1755–1817), for example, ridiculed the samurai disdain for the profit motive and advocated that government frankly exploit commerce.

In time, scholarly activities also spread to the merchant class and even to the peasantry, as is illustrated by the many technical books on agriculture that appeared from 1697 on. Rural society even produced a peasant sage, Ninomiya Sontoku (1787–1856), a very successful farmer from near Edo, who helped institute practical agricultural reforms in the area and taught mutual cooperation and long-term planning for the peasant community.

"Dutch Learning."   By the eighteenth century the fear of Christianity had so receded that it became permissible again to show interest in Europe and its technology. For example, the great Edo statesman and scholar, Arai Hakuseki, manifested frank admiration for Western science in his book *A Report on the Occident*, which was based on his interviews with an Italian priest who had smuggled himself into Japan in 1708 and had, of course, been promptly imprisoned. In 1720 the shogunate relaxed its ban on Western books, except for those treating Christianity, and scholars began to go to Nagasaki to learn Dutch from the official interpreters who dealt with the Dutch merchants there. As a consequence, the whole study of Europe and its science came to be known as "Dutch Learning" (*Rangaku*). The presence between 1769 and 1786 at the Dutch trading post in Nagasaki of two scholarly Europeans, the Swedish physician Thunberg and the Dutchman Titsingh, proved a great stimulus. Western medicine had an especial appeal as being clearly more scientific and effective than Chinese medical theory and practice. The Shimazu domain in southern Kyūshū established a medical school as early as 1774, and in the same year Sugita Gempaku (1733–1817), after prodigious efforts, produced a translation of a Dutch medical work. In 1783 another physician, Ōtsuki Gentaku (1757–1827), published *An Introduction to Dutch Learning*, which was a great help to other scholars in their study of the Dutch language and Western science.

"Dutch Learning" opened doors to many new and admittedly useful fields besides medicine, such as cartography, botany, and more modern gunnery. Some scholars, such as Hiraga Gennai (1728?–1779), showed a wide range of scientific interest, and some even wandered into what were felt to be subversive areas of thought. Hayashi Shihei (1738–1793), who in 1786 wrote *A Discussion of the Military Problems of a Maritime Country,* was im-

Woodblock print by Hayashi Shihei, based on a sketch he made while being entertained by the Dutch at Nagasaki. The empty chair is the one he vacated to make the sketch.

prisoned for criticizing the shogunate for the weakness of its defenses against the Russians in the North. Honda Toshiaki (1744–1821) attacked the whole isolation policy, and Satō Nobuhiro (1769–1850) advocated a more centralized form of government. Actually such men had little influence on political developements in Japan, but the existence by the nineteenth century of a considerable body of scholarly men able to read Dutch and knowledgeable about the Occident and its science was a tremendous advantage to the Japanese when they decided in the middle of the century to attempt to catch up technologically with the West.

"National Learning" and Shintō. The emphasis on history in Confucian scholarship drew attention to Japan's pre-Tokugawa and pre-Confucian traditions. Tokugawa Mitsukuni's *History of Great Japan* followed the lead of Kitabatake Chikafusa of the fourteenth century in ascribing Japan's greatness to its divinely descended, unbroken line of emperors. Yamazaki Ansai (1618–1682), an orthodox Confucianist, equated the Shintō foundation myths with Chinese cosmology and nationalistically asserted that, if Confucius or Mencius were to lead invading armies, it was the duty of Japanese to repel even these founding sages of Confucianism. Many other Confucian

scholars, despite their strong orientation toward Chinese civilization, also looked to Japan's antiquity for "unique" national virtues.

These trends were strengthened by a largely literary movement called "National Learning" *(Kokugaku)*. Two Shintō priests, Kada Azumamaro (1668–1736) and Kamo Mabuchi (1697–1769), drew attention once again to ancient Japanese poetry, and Kamo's disciple, Motoori Norinaga (1730–1801), a merchant's son and himself a physician, devoted more than thirty years to writing a great *Commentary on the Record of Ancient Matters (Kojiki den)*, Japan's earliest historical work. Inspired by men of this type, many scholars as well as dilettantes took up the study of the ancient language and early literature. While the main thrust of "National Learning" was literary and philological, Motoori and his predecessors had imbued it also with a strong nationalistic content. They rejected the secular rationalism of Confucianism and sought the true, unsullied Japanese spirit in early mythology, ancient poetry, and purely Japanese prose works such as *The Tale of Genji*. Hirata Atsutane (1776–1843), a physician of samurai origin, while unconsciously eclectic in his inclusion of Confucian, Taoist, Buddhist, and even Western ideas in his brand of "National Learning," aggressively asserted Japan's national superiority as the land of the gods.

The emphasis on ancient Japanese virtues and the imperial line easily led to doctrines subversive to the Tokugawa system. A teacher at the imperial court and his noble pupils were punished in 1758 for subversive tendencies, and two other teachers were executed in Edo in 1767. At the same time, these attitudes, when combined with the deep awareness of national identity fostered by the self-conscious policy of isolation, produced by the nineteenth century a strong national consciousness not unlike the nationalism that had developed in the West.

Revived interest in Japan's early history and literature may also have contributed to the appearance among the peasants in the early nineteenth century of several popular religious movements that were eclectic in content but basically Shintō in emphasis. Usually called Shintō sects, these actually independent religions commonly promised immediate worldly benefits for the believers and sometimes stressed faith healing. Some of these "sects" are still strong. Tenrikyō, the "Teaching of Heavenly Truth," founded by a peasant woman in 1838, has today a great center in a town (renamed Tenri) a little south of Nara, complete with a university, museums, and a large religious headquarters.

Urban Culture.   While commoners contributed to the intellectual life of the Tokugawa period, townsmen fully dominated many other aspects of the culture. The rapidly increasing wealth of the cities offered possibilities for social innovation and aesthetic creativity. The commercial port of Ōsaka and the townsmen quarters of Kyōto and Edo permitted social and cultural opportunities undreamed of in samurai or village society. A distinctive townsmen's style of life developed and with it new emphases in culture.

Most townsmen of any standing were literate, as were the richer peasants. In some domains commoners were permitted to attend the official domain schools, but there was in addition a great network of small private schools for commoners—more than ten thousand are known to have existed— usually called "temple schools," not for their religious affiliations but because of their usual location in Buddhist temples. Since virtually all samurai were educated, this made for a quite literate society. It has been estimated that by the middle of the nineteenth century roughly 45 per cent of the male population could read and write and perhaps 15 per cent of the women—figures not far behind the most advanced countries of the West at that time.

The urban merchants were basically sober, hard working, and disciplined, much like the samurai and peasants. The great merchant houses developed family codes similar to those of the samurai houses and a keen sense of honor, discipline, and obligation, derived largely from samurai ethics. There were also merchant philosophers. Ishida Baigan (1685–1744), a peasant by origin who worked his way up in a Kyōto merchant house, developed a philosophy he called "Learning of the Mind" (*Shingaku*), in which he taught that honest and diligent merchants, as stewards of the country's wealth, performed a national function comparable to that of the samurai. This concept, like that of "the calling" in Protestant thought in the West, gave moral legitimacy to merchants, who in a closed, class society, were denied an equal social status. It also provided a rationale for moneymaking and for dynamic achievement within one's status, which proved extremely important in Japan's modernization in the nineteenth century. It seems likely that there is a causal relationship between the parallel feudal backgrounds of Japan and Europe and their modern goal- rather than status-oriented ethics.

For all the sobriety of Tokugawa merchants, their urban culture showed great vigor and panache. The city man tended to be quick-witted and cocky, contemptuous of the stolid peasant and disdainful of the haughty but poor samurai. Since profits were the measure of success, he was extremely money-conscious and fond of luxuries. Ceremonies became ever more elaborate; novelty was highly esteemed; fashion was important—the latest feminine fashions in hair styles or sleeve lengths, or masculine styles set by leading actors or recognized dandies.

The urban merchant reserved his home for his serious moneymaking activities and his family. The long, warrior-dominated feudal age had left women entirely subordinate to men throughout Japanese society. Marriages were arranged for the interests of the family, not for romantic love, and women were kept at home to bear children and perform the household duties. The townsmen went elsewhere for their diversions. Amusement quarters in the cities, provided with restaurants, theaters, and houses of prostitution, served as the centers of social life and aesthetic activity. Here the merchant could relax from his serious role as businessman and family head to enjoy the company of gay companions and women not constrained by the prevailing social codes. (See Plate 19.)

The women of the amusement quarters were usually indentured servants, sold by impoverished parents, but the more beautiful and gifted were trained in singing, dancing, and conversational skills to become talented courtesans, known in more modern times as *geisha,* or "accomplished persons." They were divided into many categories, and those in the higher grades were considered the setters of feminine styles. They were also assiduously courted by wealthy patrons, who not infrequently purchased their freedom and set them up as their recognized mistresses or even legal wives.

The social and cultural activity centering around the amusement quarters provided an exuberant release from the rigidities of the Tokugawa system. Even samurai, themselves confirmed urban dwellers by this time, were attracted by it, participating in increasing numbers, though always in theory incognito. Borderline groups, such as "masterless samurai," who were free of shogunal or domain discipline, entered in more wholeheartedly. Thus there developed a compartmentalization of urban life between family and business or government service on the one hand and leisure and amusements on the other. Modern city life in Japan still shows the residue of this division. But there were inevitable clashes between the two, as was shown by efforts of the authorities to curb activities in the amusement quarters and still more by the conflicts that went on in the hearts of those who participated in this double life. A favorite theme of the literature and drama of the period was the clash between duty (*giri*) and emotion, or "human feelings" (*ninjō*). In a typical case, a young man's love for a courtesan, running counter to his duty to family and society, could be resolved only by the double suicide of the ill-fated lovers.

It took several decades after the founding of the Tokugawa shogunate for these urban social phenomena to develop, but the second half of the seventeenth century saw a sudden flowering of townsmen culture. The period is usually known as Genroku from the name of a "year period" (1688–1704). The center of townsmen culture at this time was Ōsaka, for Kyōto was now losing its cultural lead and Edo was still a raw, new city, dominated by its heavy samurai population. By the latter part of the eighteenth century, however, Edo had become the cultural as well as the political center of the nation.

The urban culture of the Tokugawa period tended at times toward flamboyance, but it was saved from ostentatious display and garish vulgarity by two factors—the watchful eyes of a repressive government, which was quick to issue sumptuary laws, and the simple, almost austere aesthetic canons inherited from the Ashikaga period. The result was an extraordinarily sophisticated blend of verve and daring with an underlying sense of restraint and discipline. The aesthetic tastes produced by this blend still persist in Japan and have recently proved to have a wide appeal in many other countries.

Literature.   Numerous publishing houses flourished throughout the Tokugawa period, issuing a flood of printed books from inspirational essays to pornography. Printing had been known in Japan since the eighth century but had been used only sparingly and usually for weighty works of scholarship. Korean printers brought back by Hideyoshi's armies as well as a mission press founded by the Jesuits may have helped revive interest in printing in the late sixteenth century, but the basic reason for the great increase in printing was the development of a large literate public. Most popular books were printed in the *kana* syllabary or with *kana* readings beside Chinese characters. At first there was some use of movable type, but this technique was soon abandoned in favor of woodblock printing—that is, the use of a single carved block of wood for each printed page—which permitted the inclusion of illustrations that helped attract readers.

Early Tokugawa popular writings were largely uplifting tracts, known as "*kana* booklets," on religion, morality, or history, but these in time became enlivened by amusing anecdotes and other realistic touches. Practical but interesting guidebooks to amusement quarters, with descriptions of the more prominent courtesans and actors, also appeared. Such more popular works were called "fleeting-world booklets" (*ukiyo-zōshi*), for the term "fleeting world" (*ukiyo,* literally "floating world"), which reflected the Buddhist emphasis on the transience and vanity of life, had acquired the connotations of "up-to-date" and "stylish."

From such beginnings, Ihara (or Ibara) Saikaku (1642–1693), an Ōsaka townsman, developed character portrayals of amusing townsmen types. His first important work, *An Amorous Man,* published in 1682, created an entirely new literary genre. He followed this with comparable books, such as *An Amorous Woman, The Everlasting Storehouses of Japan,* and *Twenty Examples of Unfilial Conduct in this Land.* Saikaku was a master of allusive and poetic diction and of the plays on words that Japanese love, but he was also extremely realistic. His chief interest was the moneygrubbing, self-made businessman and his less disciplined, spendthrift heirs. Saikaku's cynicism came as a refreshing departure from the heavy moralizing of earlier writers. "Money," he wrote, "is the townsman's pedigree."

Ejima Kiseki (1667–1736) wrote critiques of actors and courtesans and, after breaking with his Kyōto publishers, the Hachimonjiya ("Figure of Eight Store"), turned to sketches of merchant families, as in his *Characters of Modern Sons.* His basic theme was that "parents toil, their children idle, and the grandchildren beg." Among later Tokugawa authors, Takizawa Bakin (1767–1848), the son of a masterless samurai, was a prolific writer of long, didactic novels much influenced by Chinese models and samurai morality. A more interesting figure was Jippensha Ikku (1766–1831), a samurai by origin, whose immensely popular *Shank's Mare Travels* (*Hizakurige*), which appeared serially, was a picaresque novel about two wandering rogues whose misadventures are a parody of samurai pretensions.

Even in poetry, the Tokugawa period produced a distinctive new form. The initial three 5-7-5 syllable lines of a certain type of "chain poem" developed into an independent seventeen-syllable form called *haiku.* Unlike the classic "short poem," the *haiku* was up-to-date in both vocabulary and concepts, and its brevity fitted the wit that was so appreciated by the townsmen. The following example, chosen for ease of literal translation, illustrates some of the technique and spirit of *haiku:*

Tsuki ni e o	*To the moon, a handle*
sashitaraba yoki	*add—a good*
uchiwa kana	*fan indeed!*

Haiku composition became a craze among all classes. One of the earliest and probably the greatest *haiku* master was Matsuo Bashō (1644–1694), a former samurai who became an aesthetic wanderer. His most famous work, *The Narrow Road of Oku,* is a poetic account of a trip to northern Honshū.

The Theater.   In the field of drama the samurai class patronized and kept alive the *Nō* of the Ashikaga period, but the townsmen developed new forms. One was the puppet theater, which was called *Jōruri* from a popular form of recitation to a three-stringed banjo-like instrument. The puppets at first were small and operated by men out of sight but grew to be about two-thirds life size, each operated by three men, with further assistants, all in plain view of the audience but supposedly rendered invisible by black shrouds. At the side of the stage, a chanter, with musical accompaniments recited the story, taking the parts of all stage characters. This form of theater, called Bunraku, can still be seen today.

The *Jōruri* dramatic form was developed in the late seventeenth century chiefly by two men, Takemoto Gidayū (1651–1714), who founded a very successful puppet theater in Ōsaka, and Chikamatsu Monzaemon (1653–1724), a man of samurai origin who was the chief writer for this theater. Other theaters and authors soon appeared, and the competition between them became keen. Chikamatsu, living a century after Shakespeare, was in a

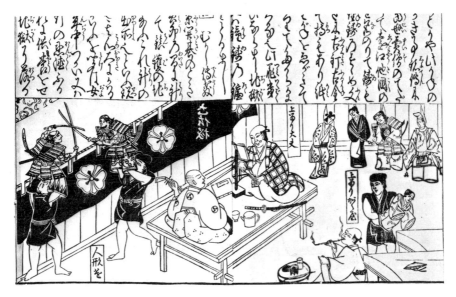

Illustration from a book printed in 1690 showing the backstage of an early puppet theater. On the left are the puppets and their manipulators, in the center the reciter and his accompanist, and at the right puppets hung up for future use. The text above is of an encyclopedic nature.

sense the creator of the modern Japanese theater. He never departed from a conventional poetic meter and a highly ornate style for narrative passages, but he developed a fine dramatic structure and turned his attention to the portrayal of character and psychological analysis. Many of his plays were loose, episodic, thrill-packed reworkings of earlier historical and literary themes, although in time he took up recent political events, only thinly disguised by being placed in earlier periods. His most popular work was *The Battles of Koxinga* about the famous Chinese-Japanese pirate known as *Kuo-hsing-yeh* (1624–1662; see page 216). This play ran for seventeen consecutive months when it was first produced. Chikamatsu's more interesting works are his twenty-four contemporary domestic plays, which dealt in a highly realistic fashion with life problems the townsmen knew from intimate experience, such as the clash of duty and emotion that might lead to double suicide. Several of his plays were based on well-known contemporary scandals in Osaka society.

A popular theater with live actors had developed early in the seventeenth century but had been so sex-oriented and mixed with prostitution that the authorities had permanently banned women from the stage. Male impersonators of female roles developed to take their place, but this form of theater, known as *Kabuki,* was at first eclipsed by the puppet stage and only began to win out in popularity in the eighteenth century. *Kabuki* borrowed the

*Woodblock print of 1740 by Okamura Masanobu showing a Kabuki
theater in Edo. Note on the left the runway through the audience
to the stage.*

violence and exaggerated gestures of *Jōruri* and also its repertoire, adapting
the plays of Chikamatsu and other *Jōruri* dramatists to its use and developing new plays from *Nō* dramas or recent events, placed for safety from the
authorities in an earlier historical setting. The most popular of all *Kabuki*
plays was *The Treasury of Loyal Retainers* (*Chūshin-gura*), based on the
1702 incident of the Forty-Seven *Rōnin. Kabuki,* like *Nō,* utilized instrumental accompaniments and an on-stage chorus to chant narrative sections.
It also showed the influence of *Nō* in the dances that highlighted many
plays. But it was at the same time far more realistic. Stage settings became
extraordinarily close to reality, the revolving stage was developed for rapid
shifts of scene, and a runway down through the audience permitted "roadway" scenes and a sense of intimacy between the audience and actors.
Kabuki is still very much alive in Japan today.

Art. The grandiose, ornate type of architecture developed in the late
sixteenth century was continued in the Tokugawa period and is well represented by the baroque grandeur of the shrines and temples dedicated to
Ieyasu at Nikkō and the decor of the rooms of the Nijō castle, the Tokugawa headquarters in Kyōto. The more sophisticated, restrained trends of
the Ashikaga period were also continued in the Katsura detached palace in
Kyōto, with its extensive but very beautiful garden, and at a more modest

level provided the prevailing spirit of most domestic architecture and landscape gardening.

With the decline of Buddhist intellectual and religious vigor, most religious sculpture became uninspired and imitative, as had happened earlier in China and Korea, and what vigor remained in the sculptor's tradition was devoted largely to ornamental architectural details and small ivory carvings (*netsuke*) used for the fastenings of tobacco pouches and the like. The industrial arts, however, all developed greatly. The Korean potters brought back by Hideyoshi's armies helped start Japan on a glorious period of porcelain making, and there was great activity in lacquer wares and in silk brocade work, centering at Kyōto.

Painting remained probably the most vigorous field of artistic expression. Under the Kano school of painters, the Ashikaga traditions of painting in the Chinese style were maintained, and new Chinese influences gave rise in the eighteenth century to the so-called Southern (*Nanga*) or Literati (*Bunjinga*) school of painting, which followed in name as well as in style Chinese prototypes of the Ming and Ch'ing periods.

At the same time strong new native artistic traditions arose, which were increasingly to dominate the artistic expression of the age. For example, some artists strayed far from Chinese canons by freely manipulating the traditional elements of landscape painting to form bold, almost abstract design effects. Their favorite mediums were lacquer ware and large folding screens. The greatest artist in this style was Ogata Kōrin (1658–1716). Other artists, possibly influenced by the down-to-earth tastes of the townsmen, moved toward greater realism. Hanabusa Itchō (1652–1724), also a *haiku* poet, based his realism on the "Yamato pictures" style of the late classic period, while Maruyama Ōkyo (1733–1795) adopted Western principles of perspective. Shiba Kōkan (1738–1818) went further in the European style, experimenting with copper plate etchings, oil paints, and even Occidental subject matter.

The most significant artistic developments of the Tokugawa period grew directly out of the interests and way of life of the townsmen. These were the realistic paintings, called "pictures of the fleeting world" (*ukiyo-e*), of courtesans and city life, and the colored woodblock prints developed from this style. Simple monochrome woodblock prints had been used for centuries in China for religious pictures and book illustrations and came into common use in publications in Japan in the seventeenth century, but they were now developed into extremely complex, multicolored reproductions of paintings. With meticulous accuracy a wood carver would make from the artist's original painting a large number of different blocks—sometimes several dozen for a single picture—to reproduce each color and shading to be superimposed on one another in the final print. Woodblock pictures of this type thus represented a triumph of technical skill and at the

Kitchen scene, a polychrome woodblock print by Utamaro.

same time the first effort in the world to produce in full color great works of art at a reasonable price for sale to a broad public.

Hishikawa Moronobu (died 1694) was one of the greatest *ukiyo-e* painters and the first of the great woodblock artists. Suzuki Harunobu (1724–1774) was the first master of the multicolor techniques. Sharaku, who was active briefly around 1794–1795, produced an amazing series of caricatures of actors. Kitagawa Utamaro (1753–1806) was famous for his beautiful women. The last great woodblock artists turned more to famous scenes and landscapes. Katsushika Hokusai (1760–1849), who showed the influence of Western concepts of perspective, is famous for his "Thirty-Six Views of Mount Fuji," while Andō Hiroshige (1797–1858) is best known for his "Fifty-Three Post Stations on the Tōkaidō." Considered vulgar and plebeian during the Tokugawa period, woodblock prints were the first form of Japanese art to attract wide attention and admiration in the West. (See Plates 20, 21, and 22.)

The Erosion of the Tokugawa System

The "Dynastic Cycle" in Tokugawa Japan.   After the Tokugawa system had been well established by the middle of the seventeenth century, the chief historical developments in Japan were in the fields of economic growth, social evolution, and cultural innovation. Political incidents and change were by comparison minor and seemed more a matter of decline than progress, as political institutions derived from the experience of the sixteenth century proved less and less adequate to the conditions and problems of the eighteenth and nineteenth. In a country that was undergoing a tremendous commercial development and dynamic, even if partially concealed, social change, government remained entirely in the hands of a feudal aristocracy, devoted to the warrior traditions of the past and desperately attempting to maintain its agrarian basis of support. The consequence was a long but losing battle for the political authorities.

A strong sense of frustration permeated the ruling class in the second half of the Tokugawa period. Although the country as a whole was growing steadily more prosperous and the new urban culture was vibrantly vigorous, the two classes of most concern to the government were declining in relative economic position and in some cases even in absolute terms. The shogunate and domain governments were becoming heavily indebted to the merchant class, and the resulting cuts in the stipends of their retainers reduced many samurai to poverty. The growing division between the rich and poor peasants was leading to economic insecurity and serious want for many in the countryside.

Thus the history of the Tokugawa period, from the perspective of the government, showed some of the characteristics of the "dynastic cycle" of China. There was a strong beginning, but after about a century of relatively untroubled rule, government finances were badly undermined, the morale of the ruling class was eroding, and the whole theory of society and government appeared to be challenged. But the comparison with the Chinese dynastic cycle should not be pressed. Political control remained firm and relatively effective throughout the Tokugawa period, and the unprecedented peace and order of the period were broken only by minor incidents of no national significance or by natural calamities beyond man's control. In 1657 much of Edo was destroyed by the first of many fires that ravaged the city. In 1703 Fuji erupted disastrously, though for the last time, and in 1783 occurred an even more destructive eruption of Asama, a still very active volcano in central Honshū. Crop failures periodically produced famine conditions in parts of the country. But all this did not affect the basic system itself. Political administration remained stable and largely routine, highlighted only by periodic but increasingly unrealistic efforts to return to the ethical values and economic and social conditions of the early seventeenth century.

Alternating Decline and Reform.   The first three shoguns were strong, able rulers, but, as was typical of Chinese dynasties, most of the later leaders were weaker or more inept men. The fifth shogun, Tsunayoshi (1680–1709), left a particularly unfavorable reputation. After the Great Elder was assassinated by a "younger elder" in 1684, Tsunayoshi ruled largely through his Grand Chamberlain, Yanagizawa Yoshiyasu (1658–1714), a favorite whom he raised from relative obscurity to be a 150,000-*koku* daimyo. He was naturally criticized for this and also for resorting to currency debasement in the face of mounting financial problems and for his many capriciously disruptive policies, such as his Buddhist-inspired protection and patronage of animals, particularly dogs, for which he won the sobriquet of the "Dog Shogun."

Following Tsunayoshi's death, the great scholar Arai Hakuseki was the chief shaper of government policy from 1709 to 1716. He attempted to cut shogunal expenses, recreate a sound currency, and restore among the samurai the high morale and discipline of the early Tokugawa period. This effort was continued on a more significant scale by the eighth shogun, Yoshimune (1716–1745; died 1751), who had been brought in to fill the post from the collateral Tokugawa line at Wakayama. His efforts, which are considered the first of the major rallies aimed at restoring the original vigor of the system, have been called the Kyōhō Reforms from the name of the "year period." Yoshimune set an example of simplicity and uprightness, issued a plethora of moral and sumptuary laws, and strove to revive the old martial spirit and at the same time to further learning and a sense of responsible leadership. He initiated administrative reforms, inaugurating a census in 1721 and codifying the Tokugawa laws. But the results proved for the most part disappointing even to him. His policies basically worked against the needed adjustments to the economic and social realities of the time. With his agrarian bias, he managed to increase agricultural production while depressing the rest of the economy. The resultant fall in rice prices hurt the very groups he was most concerned about, the samurai and peasants, because their incomes were largely in rice. In terms of Tokugawa ethics, Yoshimune was a great hero, but, in terms of Japan's economic and social evolution, he was a wrong-way leader.

Under the tenth shogun, Ieharu (1760–1786), the chief determiner of government policy was Tanuma Okitsugu (1719–1788), another favorite of modest origin, who was raised to be a 57,000-*koku* daimyo. Tanuma has been roundly condemned as a corrupt traitor to the Tokugawa ethical system, but he was at the same time an able pragmatist, more in tune with the basic economic currents of the time. He further expanded agricultural production, but he also encouraged foreign trade at Nagasaki, which Yoshimune had reduced. He tightened up the traditional shogunal monopolies in gold, silver, and copper and added new ones. More significantly, he expanded the practice of licensing merchant associations and began to develop taxes on commerce, though in a haphazard fashion. To bolster shogunal finances, he again resorted to the debasement of the currency, but he added a useful set of silver coins to the existing coinage. His period of leadership may have been characterized by decline in the traditional morality, but it was also a time of great economic growth and development.

The death of Ieharu in 1786 led to Tanuma's immediate downfall and a vigorous attempt to "return to Yoshimune." The new dominant official at Edo was Matsudaira Sadanobu, a grandson of Yoshimune and the daimyo of one of the major Tokugawa collateral lines. Sadanobu's efforts, known as the Kansei Reforms, centered on strict financial retrenchment, strong sumptuary laws, limitations on commerce, and the restoration of the morale and prestige of the samurai class. He canceled the debts incurred by the direct shogunal retainers after 1785 and like Yoshimune cut back again on foreign trade. Sadanobu's reform efforts, running as they did against the vigorously expanding commercial economy, collapsed even more rapidly than those of Yoshimune.

The young shogun, Ienari (1787–1831; died 1841), on coming of age in 1793, dropped Sadanobu and thereafter let shogunal finances and the national economy drift. The shogunate itself remained financially afloat through repeated currency debasements, which yielded quick profits for Edo but of course led to economic confusion and a rapid rise in prices. Most domains fell badly into debt, sometimes coming to owe ten to twenty times as much as their annual incomes, and poorer samurai were increasingly forced to supplement their incomes by handicraft or commercial activities. Such conditions were aggravated by serious crop failures and famines between 1822 and 1836, and a pervading sense of crisis developed.

When the already retired shogun Ienari died in 1841, another determined effort to turn the clock back was launched under the leadership of one of the "elders," Mizuno Tadakuni (1793–1851). Mizuno's policies, usually called the Tempō Reforms, were the same old nostrums of financial retrenchment, sumptuary laws, currency reform, and moral exhortation. He also attempted to force all peasants who had migrated to the cities without proper papers of authorization to return to their villages, exacted huge forced loans from some seven hundred urban merchant houses, suddenly abolished in 1841 all the government-licensed merchant associations, and decreed a 20 per cent cut in all prices and wages. The result was economic chaos, and most of the reforms soon had to be dropped, as was Mizuno himself in 1843. Meanwhile many of the domains were carrying out their own Tempō Reforms. Started in some cases in the 1830's, these *han* reforms, implemented as they were in smaller, more manageable, and less commercialized areas, sometimes proved more successful in restoring a domain's finances than the shogunate efforts had been.

Japan in the Mid-Nineteenth Century.   Many historians, influenced by the pattern of the Chinese "dynastic cycle" and still more by modern Western history, have argued that Japan by the middle of the nineteenth century stood on the brink of "dynastic" collapse and even a bourgeois revolution. Growing disequilibriums in income, decreased morale, if not efficiency, among the ruling groups, and heightened economic expectations had produced a steady upcreep in popular disturbances among the peasantry and even among city dwellers. City rioting first appeared in Edo in 1732, became more serious in Tanuma's time, and took a somewhat revolutionary turn in 1837, when Ōshio, a former official in the city government of Ōsaka, led an attack on Ōsaka castle in an effort to win relief for the city poor. Natural disasters, as in the crop failures of the 1820's and 1830's, may also have become more politically disruptive toward the end of the period.

There were also many new trends that could prove subversive to the Tokugawa system. The military effectiveness of the samurai had declined seriously, and their sense of personal loyalty to the shogun or daimyo had become more a loyalty to the system, in which individual men were little more than symbols. There was a rising awareness of the supreme national symbol of the emperor and a growing demand for the recognition of individual talent in addition to hereditary status. The commercial economy and urban society and culture had expanded far beyond the narrow feudal confines of the early seventeenth century. The aggressive entrepreneurial spirit of urban merchants and rich peasants, with its strong overtones of an achievement- rather than status-oriented ethic, was not at all in line with the emphasis of the ruling class on an unchanging agrarian economy and society. There was a growing diversity of intellectual trends among all classes, including a rising interest in Western science. By the 1840's there was also a mounting apprehension over the now greatly increased military power of the Western nations and their aggressive actions in neighboring countries.

Thus the Tokugawa system was under many pressures that had not existed in the seventeenth century, but one should not assume from this that it was about to collapse of its own weight, like an undermined Chinese dynasty, or that Japan was about to be swept in the European fashion by a bourgeois revolution. Japan in 1850 was still free of any serious external pressures. While social tensions had indeed developed, perhaps most severely among impoverished samurai and peasants, and many imperfections and illogicalities strained the social and political system, the samurai Confucian ethic still pervaded the nation, and the whole Tokugawa political structure still stood firm. If Japan had continued free of foreign encroachment, the Tokugawa system might well have continued for quite some time longer without major change. At the same time, severe strains between the theories and realities of government and society and a pervasive ferment beneath the surface calm made Japan more prepared for rapid change than were either China or Korea.

16. Invasion and Rebellion in Nineteenth-Century China

Traditional China's Resistance to Change

In the middle decades of the nineteenth century, China, Japan, Vietnam, and Korea were each in turn confronted by the expanding Western nations and forced into greater contact with them. The Victorian era, so exhilarating for Englishmen, brought dismay and disaster to the peoples of East Asia. This was especially true in the great Chinese Empire, which had slipped into the downward phase of a dynastic cycle just as the Western powers began to beat upon the gates. Domestic and foreign troubles came hand in hand, as the nineteenth century advanced, each abetting the other. One chief problem for the student of this period is to discern the complex interaction between the rise of rebellion within China and the impact of the Western invasion from without. How far one process "caused" the other is an all-but-meaningless question, inasmuch as both went on for an entire century, mutually interacting from moment to moment.

The main fact influencing China's modern transformation was that China's center of gravity lay deep within. Her long history as the ancient center of East Asian civilization had given her people an inborn sense of superiority to all outsiders. The inertia and persistence of traditional patterns and both material and intellectual self-sufficiency all made China comparatively resistant and unresponsive to the challenge of the West. In Japan an economic and social ferment was already at work. Partly in response to Western contact, this ferment would develop into a full-scale political and social transformation. Within the much larger Ch'ing Empire no such transformation occurred. Scholars are still debating why it was so long delayed.

435

The Ruling Class and Its Agrarian Outlook.   One cause of China's inertia
was the world view or self-image of the ruling class which intervened between the great mass of the peasantry and the rather small imperial government. This Chinese ruling stratum of the Ming and Ch'ing eras was, to be
sure, a composite of several types of persons—rent-collecting landowners,
merchants, degree-holding literati, officials not in office. All together they
formed the local elite in the market towns of the countryside and in the
administrative centers, the local ally of the Manchu dynasty.

The ruling class was knit together and set apart from the peasantry by its
possession of literacy and the higher culture that went with it. It derived
strength from the extended family system, indeed, the upper class consisted
of large successful families that sought by every means to preserve themselves and their status. The leading elders of a clan lineage or common-
descent group (*tsu* or *tsung-tsu*) managed its common property, recorded
its genealogy and performed the rites of ancestor reverence in the clan temple, dispensed welfare aid, provided schooling for talented sons, and disciplined its wayward members to keep them out of the magistrate's court and
jail. Marriages were arranged between families, and not by the individuals
concerned, with an eye to sustaining the family-clan structure. It did, of
course, cut across class lines and relate poor families to rich, providing
channels of contact and cohesion between the landlord families and the
tenant families within a clan. This facilitated upward mobility into the
ruling class but a downward pull was exerted by the parceling of landholdings divided up among a family's sons in an era of population growth.
In general, the kinship relations of the local elite seem to have given it
balance and continuity, allowing just enough mobility to keep the underprivileged but talented and energetic members within the system.

The ideal of this gentry elite was agrarian rather than urban, frugal
rather than expansive. The Confucian teachings extolled the cultivation of
the land and decried the parasitic manipulations of merchants. "Acknowledgment of limits leads to happiness" was an old adage. Ideally, one should
be content amid one's fields, close to nature, almost like the Taoist worthies
who lived their lives hearing the dogs bark in the next village but never
going there.

This bucolic and nostalgic view of the world was kept vigorously alive
by the fact that the local elite were mainly supported by landholding and
were oriented to seek advancement through the examination system. Confucianism taught that self-cultivation, especially through learning based on
study of the Classics, would enable one to be a superior man and possibly,
through the government examinations, to become a degree-holder and even
an official. This ideal was kept alive by the way in which the examination
system accommodated even nonscholars who were rich enough to buy their
way into it and thereby supported the system. The lower-level degree-holders,

lower gentry not yet qualified for appointment to office, included two types: the great majority were genuine scholars who had passed the preliminary examinations (and were called *sheng-yüan*). But about a third were usually degree-holders by purchase (*chien-sheng*) whose "contributions" had been rewarded by degree status. As in earlier dynasties, a few degrees were also acquired by inheritance or by recommendation. As of 1800 this lower level totaled altogether something more than a million persons and formed a reservoir from which emerged the upper stratum of higher gentry and officials. The upper level, consisting of persons qualified for appointment to office, together with officials in office and in retirement, totaled somewhere around 125,000 persons and had special privileges which set them apart from the lower level. Thus the examination system was flexible, permitting upward mobility into the ruling class for people who could pay their way, and yet ensuring in normal times that the scholars, being the great majority especially at the higher levels, would predominate and set the tone among the actual holders of power. This in turn ensured the continued domination of orthodox ideals.

China's Premodern Economy.   Western contact came earliest in the form of commerce; trade was important long before diplomatic relations or Western ideas. Yet the Chinese economy, like the ruling class, was slow to respond. This was because of its large size and great self-sufficiency. In the early nineteenth century some 300 million people lived in rural China, at least four-fifths of the population. Their capital wealth consisted chiefly of the land itself, improved over the centuries by an arduous investment of labor to create paddy fields with embankments and irrigation channels; terraces even in the Northwest, where irrigation was often impossible; waterways both for transport and for irrigation, with dikes and sluiceways and the equipment of foot treadles, buckets, and wheels for moving water onto the soil. This farm economy represented a great investment of past labor and presupposed a continued heavy application of manpower to keep it working. Other types of capital equipment—draft animals, tools, buildings, storage facilities—were rather meager. Unexploited natural resources, assuming no revolution in technology, were limited. Labor resources, on the other hand, were plentiful. Rapid population growth in the eighteenth century had put a high proportion of the populace in the younger age brackets. Thus land was limited and capital scarce, while labor was plentiful and generally skilled in the traditional methods of production. There was little means or incentive for labor-saving innovation in technology. Innovation was also inhibited by the sharp functional distinction between handworkers and brain-workers, who lived at different social levels. Farmers and artisans remained generally illiterate, while men of learning seldom came up against the practical, mechanical problems of field and shop.

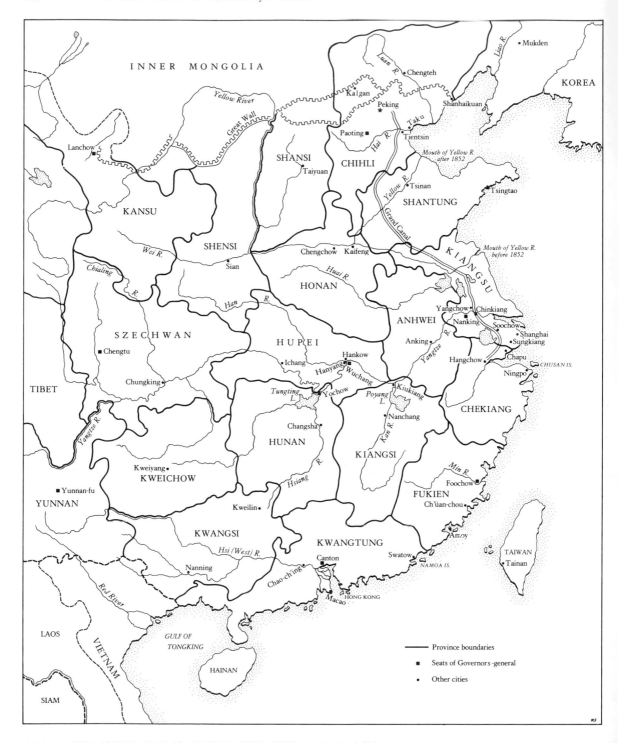

ADMINISTRATIVE AREAS UNDER THE CH'ING DYNASTY

On the commercial level, local trade centered in the market towns, of which there were several score in each province. At their periodic markets, which were held generally every three or four days, were collected the products from each market town's outlying villages, typically a dozen or so hamlets within a day's round-trip transport distance by beast, barrow, or carrying-pole or by sampan on a waterway. Peddlers and traveling merchants brought to the market those few essential commodities which the peasant could not produce himself, primarily salt, metals, and paper, also simple luxury goods, textiles, pottery, tea, and the produce of city craftsmen or of other regions.

On this cellular pattern of local trade within market areas was superimposed an extensive interregional trade in special products such as copper, porcelain, furs, cotton, silk, or timber. China's domestic trade serviced the world's largest single market. The European trade at Canton was only a small offshoot of it.

Water transport was the great facility on which interregional trade depended. Brick tea (tea formed into bricks for transport) went up the Yangtze and its tributary the Han River and thence by caravan to Mongolia and Russia. North China and the Yangtze delta exchanged commodities by way of the Grand Canal as well as the coastal route. The teas of Fukien and the silks of Anhwei went to Canton by the Kan River route through Kiangsi. All manner of Szechwan products came down the Yangtze, while the junk fleets plying along the coast, especially from Ningpo northward all the way to Manchuria and from Amoy down to Southeast Asia, formed another extensive transport network. They took soybeans and beancake out of Manchuria and brought subtropical products to the North. This carrying trade on China's water routes was to prove the Westerner's main point of ingress into the Chinese economy, for here the introduction of the steamship could quickly alter the inherited technology.

On the other hand, foreign contact could not quickly change the patterns of the great domestic economy. Exports like tea and silk were products of traditional labor-intensive farm handicrafts, not easily susceptible to modernization. Both the demand of the local population for imported goods and the supply of capital for trade remained sharply limited. There was little creation of credit and only a limited supply of currency in the form of copper cash and silver bullion. Merchants were dominated by officials, on whom they depended for protection, or else they became semiofficials themselves, showing the spirit of monopolistic tax-gatherers rather than of risk-taking investors in productive enterprise.

On the governmental level in the early nineteenth century there was no leadership in the direction of economic development. The classical doctrines of the state gave little thought to economic growth and stressed the frugal use of agrarian taxes rather than the creation of new wealth. It was assumed that there was a fixed volume of trade. Customs were levied on exports at the same rates as on imports. There was no mercantilist concept of maximizing the national wealth through exports. Official monopolies and license systems reduced competition.

In sum, the Chinese economy around 1800 was not only at a different stage of development from that of Europe, it was also differently constructed and was thought of in entirely different terms. First, China regarded herself as—and in fact was—a relatively self-sufficient economic entity. Trade, both foreign and domestic, was neither formally encouraged nor heavily taxed. Second, China had not yet institutionalized science and invention, as Europe was in the process of doing, and so the development of new technology was negligible. Third, lacking the stimuli of both foreign trade and new technology and suffering from the government's readiness to monopolize or tax exorbitantly any newly profitable economic undertaking, the type of entrepreneurship so important in Britain's industrialization was quite impossible in the Middle Kingdom. Capital accumulation was precarious except under the wing of officialdom. Legal safeguards, an investment market, and the forms of the joint-stock company were all lacking. Finally, the application of abundant manpower to all processes— irrigation, rice culture, transport, handicrafts, and the like—had reached a high degree of efficiency in the use of resources but was at a stationary level of technology. Population growth tended to eat up any increase in production. Production, in short, was generally absorbed completely in consumption, in an endless circular flow just to keep people alive, so that net saving and investment were all but impossible.

The Inertia of Government.   A similar unresponsiveness to foreign stimuli characterized the Ch'ing administration, beginning with the fact that it had to be quite passive at the local level because it was spread so thin. The typical county magistrate had charge of an area of three hundred square miles and a population of a quarter of a million people. A minor official in the government, faced with a large administrative task, he was in no position to coerce a defiant populace or the local gentry, or initiate new policies, nor would his philosophy of government have permitted him to attempt such things. The local magistrate was aided by his private secretaries or advisers and by personal servants whom he brought with him and paid himself. With their help he had to deal with the local yamen staff of semipermanent government clerks and various underlings—runners, jailers, police, and miscellaneous attendants. The magistrate was caught up in a web of responsibility for all that occurred within his area. His jurisdiction was territorial and complete rather than functional and specialized.

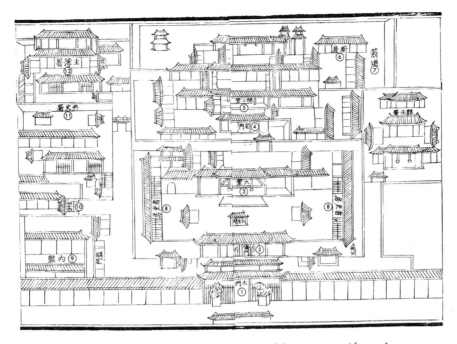

YAMEN OF THE SHANGHAI DISTRICT MAGISTRATE (from the
Shanghai gazetteer of 1871). *On the main axis, reading upward,
are the (1) main entrance, (2) ceremonial gate, (3) main hall,
(4) residence gate (to the magistrate's personal quarters) and his
(5) meditation hall, and (6) kitchen (right top), adjoining (7) an
archery butt. Right and left of the main hall are (8) clerks' offices.
Far right is the small yamen of the assistant district magistrate.
At left, reading upward, are (9) jail, (10) "ever-normal" granary,
(11) jail warden's office, and (12) registrar's office.*

Since his own virtuous conduct was supposed to set the example, he was to
blame or praise, almost in a ritual manner, for all that took place within
his jurisdiction, just as was the emperor within the empire. This doctrine of
what we might call ritual responsibility made officials seek by all means to
avoid the appearance of trouble. Looking forward to transfer to a new post
within three years, local officials were more interested in avoiding immediate
embarrassment within their areas than in fostering their long-term development. To have to suppress disorder and so acknowledge its existence
might be more disastrous to one's personal career than to have it continue
unreported. Better to buy off bandits by enlisting them in the local militia
than to oppose them publicly. The result was a deeply ingrained tendency
to compromise, to harmonize the elements of the local scene, not to change
them. The spirit of Chinese official life was therefore passive. Officials
waited for things to happen, hoping they would not.

The government structure of checks and balances was designed to keep the ship of state on its traditional course, not to steer it in new directions. Even at the very top, the personal rule of the emperor was passive. His function was to serve as a glorified clearing-house rather than to initiate policy. Business was initiated in memorials addressed to the emperor; it was concluded by edicts from him. The volume of business became so great that the emperor was forced more and more to be a mere transmitter and selector of proposals rather than a maker of them. Here was one reason for the Chinese state's incapacity to change when confronted by the Western challenge: leadership was stultified below and worn out at the top. Officials on the spot in the provinces could not easily innovate, while the emperor in Peking was much too busy to do so. The broad responsibilities of the bureaucracy were not matched by a capacity for local initiative and innovation; the cumbersome safeguards which preserved the imperial power robbed it of adaptability.

Enfeeblement by Corruption. Fiscal administration further limited the government's responsiveness, because it permitted a growth of organized corruption that by the middle of the nineteenth century robbed the Ch'ing dynasty of its financial resources. Officials were still tax-farmers, expected to maintain both their public offices and their private establishments out of the revenues they collected. This confusion of public and private funds, as it would be considered today, reflected the very personal nature of the official's administration and responsibility, and also the fact that his revenues were not collected entirely in money (some being in kind or in labor), were not accounted for in a system of budgeting and auditing, and were produced by the infinitely complex interplay of personal relationships, haggling, and bargaining that characterized the old China on all levels. The actual amounts of tax payments were not fixed but resulted in each case from an interplay of interests, including those of the taxpayer, the tax collector, and his superiors, as well as the state. The custom of receiving unofficial fees or "squeeze" was well established. Genuine "corruption" appeared only when the customary limits of squeeze were exceeded.

Central government revenue figures give us only the most superficial view of how the ruling class and government together lived off the peasantry. In times of peace and good crop weather, all three might make ends meet. But with any decline in the self-denying Confucian morality of the ruling class, the interests of the government and the local elite tended inevitably to diverge. The instinct of the local landlord class was constantly to increase their private exactions. If unchecked this would make the government responsible for ever-increasing burdens upon the populace and lose it the Mandate of Heaven. The official quotas collected and reports made to Peking were thus a façade behind which the triangular struggle between landlords, officials, and populace went on without ceasing.

For example, in the lower Yangtze Valley, a chief area of surplus rice production, the land tax included chiefly two items. First was the fixed land-and-capitation tax, a combination of a tax on acreage and a tax originally levied on males between sixteen and sixty, but which had become since the early 1700's purely a fiscal quota of revenue to be collected from each administrative area. The second item, also to be collected by quota, was the grain tribute for Peking, either in kind or in money. The collecting officers not only added to the established quotas a number of further charges, but also found ways to profit through the process of collection. In general this profit was achieved by bold-faced methods, whereby several pecks might be discounted, i.e., "squeezed," from each bushel of rice; or silver payments substituted for the rice might be demanded at higher than the current market price; or copper payments in lieu of silver might be demanded at more than the current copper-silver exchange rate. The extra charges and discounts might total ten times the stated tax. These personal takings of the tax collectors usually had to be split with certain local gentry who cooperated in the system and with the higher officials. Collectors, gentry, and higher officials formed a corporation, living on the "sweat and blood" of the farmer. The underlings and clerks got their squeeze by manipulating a variety of charges for porterage, inspection, stamping, gate money, and the like.

In all this institutionalized corruption, the most significant feature was the alliance between the officials and the "big households." In general, big landlords, who usually had gentry status, paid their taxes at lower rates than the middle and poor peasants. This made the tax system "regressive," bearing more heavily on the poor, rather than "progressive," like a modern income tax. The wealthier a family was, the better arrangement it could make with the officials. Gentry degree-holders in the community, even if they were not landlords, through their access to officialdom could similarly oblige the tax collectors to give them favorable arrangements. That the well-to-do paid at lower rates than the poor can be documented in each province. Where a big house might pay four thousand cash to discharge a tax of one bushel, a small village household might have to pay twenty thousand. Yamen runners were usually ready to help landlords by coercing defaulting tenants. The consequence was that the poorer households sought the protection of the bigger, so as to make their payments on the latter's more favorable terms. On their part, the big gentry households were happy to make these payments on behalf of their smaller neighbors and take a profit on the transaction. Big establishments that paid taxes for others were known as "tax-farming households." Thus the landlord gentry got their middlemen's profit, the state was defrauded of revenue, and the little people were defenseless against the dominant landlord-official combination.

In the preceding we have offered different explanations of China's peasant impoverishment in the early nineteenth century: one, that the farming masses lacked the economic resources (especially capital and technology) to improve their lot; second, that the corrupt maldistribution of their product left them exploited by the landlord-official ruling class. These explanations are of course not incompatible. Future research will highlight many regional variations in the diverse and as yet barely studied Chinese landscape.

Scholarship and Thought

The "New Text" and "Statecraft" Schools.   After the White Lotus Rebellion (1796–1804; see Chapter 9), the customary symptoms of dynastic decline could not be lost upon the scholar-official class, who were from their training particularly aware of, and believers in, the operation of a dynastic cycle. Corruption and rebellion had shortened the life span of earlier dynasties. How could the Ch'ing escape?

This concern prompted a new growth of scholarship. By the nineteenth century the Han Learning (see page 231) had become firmly established as a new orthodoxy, but now two new trends became important. One was a continuation of the "new text" school of classical criticism. The orthodox Han Learning, as its name implies, studied texts of the Later Han period, when the "ancient text" versions of the Classics were allegedly discovered and in time became accepted as orthodox. However, in the late seventeenth century, the so-called "ancient text" of the *Classic of Documents* (also known as the *Book of History*) had been shown to be a forgery. Now bold and vigorous scholars began to question other "ancient text" versions of the Classics and found in them further proofs of forgery or editorial tampering. Thus the "new text" school, paradoxically, espoused the older texts which had been recovered and accepted in the Earlier Han, alleging that they were older and more authentic than the orthodox "ancient texts" accepted ever since the Later Han period. At the same time it found in these "new text" versions of the Classics, especially in the *Kung-yang Commentary* on the *Spring and Autumn Annals* (*Ch'un-ch'iu*), radically new meanings which had implications for the hitherto taboo subject of politics and seemed relevant to the course of events in the nineteenth century. In brief, the concept of change in the *Kung-yang Commentary* could be used as a basis for advocating institutional reform. This prepared the way for a wholesale attack at the end of the century upon the classical tradition, which would open the door for reform and indeed revolution at the very center of the tradition itself. Until the 1890's, however, the "new text" movement was still gradually gathering momentum. (For its later history, see page 631.)

The other new trend of the early nineteenth century was likewise a revival of an earlier approach. This was the school of "statecraft" *(ching-shih)*, which aimed at the application of scholarship to the problems of government administration in reaction against intuitive knowledge, speculative philosophy, and formalism. This revival of concern with the policies and processes of administration was stimulated by the evidences of dynastic decline. The dominant tradition of Ch'ing scholarship, confined to the study of classical antiquity and especially philology, had provided detailed information on the imperial institutions of earlier eras, including the sacrifices, funeral dress, conveyances, and even the styles of headgear, but it offered little wisdom on how to meet the pressing problems of government in the late Ch'ing period. As the portents of decline became more obvious, reflective minds began again, as they had during the disorder of the Ming-Ch'ing changeover in the seventeenth century, to blame the impracticality of the scholars and their absorption in dry-as-dust and useless book-learning. The writings of Ku Yen-wu (see page 231) provided a special stimulus. The slogan of the new movement was "learning of practical use to society" *(ching-shih chih yung)*. Its leaders set themselves the task of studying how to maintain the economic and political institutions of the empire.

The efforts of the school of "statecraft" are illustrated in the career of Wei Yüan (1794–1857), a wide-ranging and practical-minded scholar-administrator from Hunan. He had studied the Neo-Confucianism of the Sung and the Han Learning at Peking, and his criticism of these orthodox traditions contributed to the rise of the "new text" movement. He also became a leading advocate of the application of the scholar's talents to the urgent practical problems of administration. When the Grand Canal became blocked, Wei Yüan in 1825 wrote a treatise advocating the transport of rice to Peking by sea. His admirer, a reforming governor of Kiangsu, put this plan into effect in 1826, for one year only, sending fifteen hundred shiploads to Tientsin. During the 1830's Wei helped the reform of the North Huai salt monoply. Later, in 1850, Wei himself administered part of this salt region, with exemplary results. Thus he was a scholar with practical experience.

In 1826 Wei Yüan was invited to edit a work called *Collected Essays on Statecraft under the Reigning Dynasty (Huang-ch'ao ching-shih wen-pien)* in which were reprinted over two thousand essays on economic and other administrative topics. This became the prototype for an entire genre of such collections, of which more than a dozen continuations or supplements later appeared, in order to make readily accessible the ideas of scholar-officials concerned with governmental problems. Wei Yüan next secured a post under the Grand Secretariat at Peking, with access to the archives, where he saw the vast sea of unpublished proposals, studies, reports, and decisions accumulated under the Ch'ing administration. He began to compile a large work of recent history on the campaigns of the Ch'ing period, the *Record of Imperial Military Exploits (Sheng-wu chi)*, in which he set forth the impressive record of Ch'ing subjugation of China, Mongolia, Tibet, Sinkiang, and Taiwan and defeat of the Russians, Burmese, Vietnamese, and the White Lotus rebels. He completed this work in 1842, the very moment of unprecedented disaster at the hands of the British.

There were others like Wei Yüan concerned with current policy, but unfortunately they were a small leaven in a large mass. The Ch'ing dynasty's consistent policy of wooing the scholars, while at the same time suppressing dissent and forbidding scholarly discussion of official policy outside government channels, had diverted the early vigor of political thought, manifested in the period of the Manchu conquest, into orthodox textual research or fact-gathering for its own sake. Skepticism and criticism had been largely confined to matters of etymology and exegesis of the Classics. The scholarly talent of the day was absorbed in narrow bibliographical or purely classical literary activities. This may be illustrated in the case of Juan Yüan (1764–1849), a famous bibliophile and promoter of scholarly enterprises, who served as governor-general at Canton in the crucial decade from 1817 to 1826. Juan Yüan had been several times a governor and governor-general, had founded several libraries and academies, and had published at least a dozen large works—catalogues of art objects, anthologies of poetry, dictionaries and commentaries on the Thirteen Classics, collections of rare works, and the like. During his decade at Canton, when the disastrous conflict with Britain was taking shape there, Juan Yüan established another academy, edited the provincial gazetteer, printed in 366 volumes a collection of 180 works of classical commentary, published some fifty chapters of his own poems, prose, and bibliographical notes, and brought out an anthology of Kiangsu poets in 183 chapters. He also made important contributions to the study of Chinese painting, mathematics, and ancient inscriptions on stone and bronze. All this time he was the top official in charge of China's relations with the West. Small wonder that his policy toward the Westerners at Canton was generally one of compromise and passivity.

China's Image of the West. With scholar-officials like the orthodox and assiduous Juan Yüan setting the example, there was little opportunity or incentive for trained minds to pursue a curious interest in the overseas peoples. The inherited lore of the Ming era, when Cheng Ho sailed west and Europeans first came to China, was laboriously copied out—errors, garbles, and all—and set forth as information about the Europeans of 1800, one outdated source being copied into another in endless succession. Aside from this lore, the only other source of information was the Westerners themselves who came to Canton; but they were few in number and more accessible to merchants than to scholars. In the absence of more precise

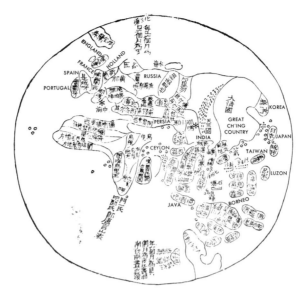

CHINA'S PREMODERN VIEW OF WORLD GEOGRAPHY. (English captions superimposed) *Round map is "A General Sketch of the Four Seas," from the widely used* Hai-kuo wen-chien lu, *ca. 1730. Among many anomalies, the Black Sea is labeled "Dead Sea," the Indian Ocean almost disappears, and both places marked* ***** *are labeled No-ma ("Rome"). Square map is Wei Yüan's map of Europe from* Hai-kuo t'u-chih, *1844. In it, Germany is "now divided in 24 parts," Italy into "9 countries," England is large and Denmark expanded. "Sweden" (Shui-tien) and "Switzerland" (Shui-shih) are confused, both being simply "Shui country." Such maps gave Commissioner Lin his view of East and West.*

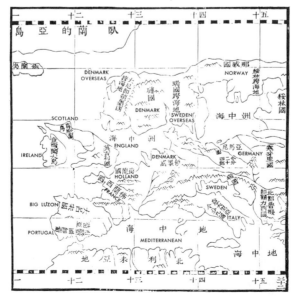

information, Chinese observers of the early nineteenth century applied to the Europeans and Americans many of the stereotypes that had been developed during millenniums of contact with neighboring peoples in Asia. Just as the pastoral tribes of the Inner Asian steppe constantly waxed and waned, changing their names and locations, so the Western peoples whose traders came to Canton, as recorded in Chinese writings, shifted about and changed identity like phantoms. Their names had become thoroughly confused. In the Kwangtung provincial gazetteer, edited under Juan Yüan in 1819–1822, the account of the Spaniards in the Philippines was sandwiched in between Quilon (in southern India) and the Moluccas, and dealt with the Ming period only. Portugal was stated to be near Malacca. England was another name for Holland, or alternatively a dependency of Holland. France was originally Buddhist, and later became Catholic (it had become a common belief in China that Christianity was an offshoot of Buddhism). Finally, France was said to be the same as Portugal.

One is left with the impression that the scholars were not interested in learning about the West. When exceptional men like Wei Yüan sought to do so, they had to seek translations of Western writings. The facts were not to be found in China. The expansive West caught China by surprise, and ways of handling foreign relations which had worked reasonably well for four centuries suddenly became useless.

The Collapse of the Canton System

Country Trade and Private Traders.   Private enterprise in India was from the first an indispensable extension of the East India Company's operations, necessary to connect them with the local Asian sources of trade and revenue. This enterprise took the form of the so-called Country trade, that is, trade conducted by private individuals within the commercial domain of the Company's charter. Country trade grew up first within and around India, where the British Company sold bills of exchange, payable in Calcutta or London, to the Country traders, both British and Indian, and so were able to use the traders' profits as a means of making Company remittances. The Country trade expanded eastward in response to greater opportunities for profit. The supply of Bengal opium, for example, was monopolized by the Company, sold by it at auction, bought by Country traders, and exported by them, mainly at first to the Straits of Malacca and Indonesia. The Country trade was facilitated by private firms of Englishmen and Scotsmen, who formed "agency houses" which not only invested in shipments themselves, but also handled cargoes, ships, warehouses, insurance, and sales for other private parties on a commission basis. They were the cutting edge of the commercial, financial, and industrial expansion of Britain and the modern international economy.

"ILLUSTRATIONS OF TRIBUTARIES" FOR THE CH'IEN-LUNG
EMPEROR. *"A 'Barbarian' from Sweden" (left) and "An English-man" (from* Huang-Ch'ing chih-kung t'u, *Palace edition, 1761).*

   The Country trade from India was soon extended to China. Enterprising
British subjects as early as the 1780's had begun to remain at Canton as
nominal representatives of other European governments, in order to avoid
the control of the British East India Company. This became an established
custom—in 1823, for example, James Matheson was Danish consul and
Thomas Dent was Sardinian consul. To succeed in this kind of private
business required little capital but a great deal of enterprise and ingenuity.
Thus Dent, Matheson, and the other "private English" at Canton soon
began to acquire fleets, set up insurance companies, and carry on banking
operations. The private traders were the Far Eastern correspondents, friends,
and often relatives of merchants in the similar but bigger agency houses in
India, which had become well established after the Company ceased to
monopolize British trade in India in 1813. These houses in turn, like those
at Canton, dealt with the hub of Britain's worldwide economic expansion
in London. In this expansion, the Country trade by providing (after about
1817) three-quarters of the British imports at Canton, accomplished two
things at once: it gave an outlet for Indian produce, remitting profits to
India, and it continued to finance the East India Company's purchase of
China's teas, which were as usual profitably taxed by the British government in London.
   A similar growth of commercial interests occurred on the Chinese side,
although they have not yet been as fully studied. Canton was an outlet for
tea and for silk and cotton textiles, mainly produced by handicraft industries on the farms of South China. Cotton textiles went chiefly in the form
of "nankeens," named for Nanking, because the main center of the Chinese

cotton textile industry was in the nearby region of Soochow and Sungkiang. These exports for the West were taken from the total Chinese domestic production, for which the principal market remained the Chinese public. Until well into the nineteenth century the chief import of the Country trade from India was raw cotton to supply China's own textile industry. The hong merchants served as funnels through which flowed out consignments of tea and silk collected by traveling merchants in the producing regions of Central China. The transport route by barge and by coolie carrier through Kiangsi to Canton was greatly developed. Despite its comparatively small volume, the Canton trade had become important as a center of growth, both in the accumulation of capital and in the creation of commercial mechanisms and an articulate commercial interest. The "Canton interest," in the person of merchant firms and imperial officials who profited from the Canton monopoly of Western trade, became a factor in Chinese policy considerations.

The Rise of the Opium Trade.   The origin of a British opium trade between India and China lay partly in the growth of opium-smoking in China. Because opium is a habit-forming narcotic, it was a social evil even more serious than the gin that was considered an evil in contemporary Britain. The opium poppy had long been known in China and its product used as a drug, but the "smoking" (actually, inhaling water vapor) of opium began only after tobacco-smoking had spread to China from America by way of Manila in the seventeenth century. During the late eighteenth century, about a thousand chests of opium a year were being imported from India to China. From 1800 to 1821, the average was about forty-five hundred chests a year, but the annual total grew by 1838 to some forty thousand chests. (A chest usually contained 133 pounds.) The spread of opium addiction can no doubt be associated with other trends already noted—population pressure, the probable lowering of living standards, and the increase of corruption in government and of rebelliousness among the people. The spirit of the age, in short, was one of demoralization. Opium-smoking as a symptom of this frame of mind spread particularly among yamen underlings and soldiers, two groups who represented the government in contact with the populace.

Behind the growth of the opium trade also lay the basic fact that British India had become dependent upon it for 5 to 10 per cent of its revenues. While Bengal opium was cultivated under Company control and sold officially to private traders at auctions in Calcutta, opium in western India was grown not under Company control and at first competed with the Bengal product; but by the 1830's the Company had got control of the ports of shipment, like Bombay, which enabled it to levy a transit tax and profit accordingly. In the meantime, the competition between Bengal and

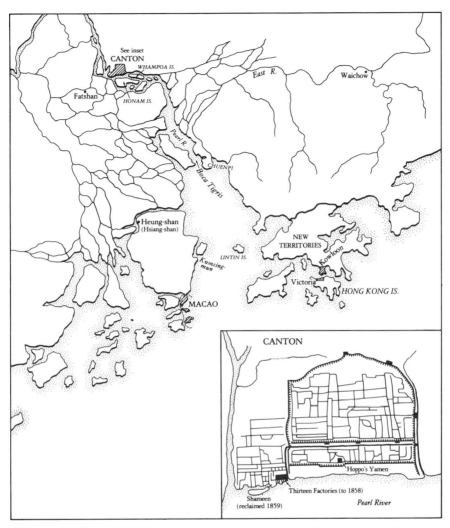

THE CANTON ESTUARY AND OUTER WATERS (19TH CENTURY)

western India had stimulated the production of more opium at lower prices.

Opium traders in China could make big profits, as prices fluctuated according to supply. A chest might sell for one thousand or even two thousand Mexican dollars before 1821, and for seven hundred to one thousand in the period of increased supply thereafter. This speculative trade created intense competition. Foreign merchants began to use the earliest type of clipper ships to get ahead of their rivals. They delivered cargoes to "receiving ships," which were heavily armed floating warehouses. The Chinese opium traders were organized in brokerage houses, usually composed of a score or more of partners, whose funds made up the capital for investment. Their smuggling boats, well armed and manned by sixty or seventy oarsmen (which gave them their Chinese names of "scrambling dragons" or "fast crabs") would normally take delivery of opium chests from the foreigners' receiving ships. By the 1830's one to two hundred such Chinese boats were taking deliveries from about twenty-five foreign receiving ships in the waters outside Canton. At first the domestic distribution of opium was along the routes of inland trade to the west and especially to the north of Canton, toward Central China, but eventually a new phase began with distribution by foreign ships on the coast of China northeast of Canton.

The incapacity of the Chinese government to stop the trade was illustrated by the opposite courses followed in Ch'ing policy and official practice. Selling and smoking opium had been prohibited by imperial edict as early as 1729, its importation or domestic production in 1796, and after 1800 these bans were frequently repeated. But official connivance had grown as the trade had grown. Opium paid its way, becoming a new source of corruption. To greed was added fear, for the opium distributors tied in with the secret societies, and could oppose with force those officials who would not accept bribes. The higher officials issued edicts of prohibition, while the lower officials connived at the trade, passing some of their ill-gotten gains on to their superiors, no doubt right up to the court. As the higher authorities became more vulnerable to exposure, blackmail, or censure, they found it safest to drive the contraband trade out of their immediate jurisdiction. In 1821 Governor-General Juan Yüan forced the receiving ships to leave the river anchorage below Canton and move outside to Lintin Island. Foreign traders began to seek outlets to the northeast at Namoa Island and Chinchew (Ch'üan-chou). This "coast trade," even less controllable than that in the Canton delta, began during the 1830's to import as much as Canton.

The opium trade was pushed from both sides. Not only had Britain's commercial expansion become dependent on opium; the trade had become entrenched in China as a powerfully organized smuggling system which corrupted the government as the number of addicts grew. The imperial household at Peking had been accustomed for over a century to drawing revenue from the Canton trade. Opium had merely increased the unofficial revenue and also strengthened the "Canton interest." Similarly, the British opium interest was a recent addition to the long-continued British desire for commercial expansion in China. It gave further impetus to British demands that had long been formulated.

To the list of British grievances was now added the financial inadequacy of the hong merchants. The most famous of these was the head of the Wu family firm, Houqua, who made a great fortune, trading and even investing abroad through his American friends of the Boston firm of Russell and Company. But Houqua was exceptional. Most of the hong merchants, constantly pressed for "contributions" to the government and short of capital themselves, regularly went into debt to the East India Company, which advanced the capital to buy up the next season's teas and silks. There was no legal machinery, however, for collecting debts owed to foreign merchants, and so unpaid hong merchant debts accumulated.

There was also the Western repugnance at the arbitary arrest and torture of accused persons, as practiced under Chinese criminal law. Antithetic assumptions concerning the rights and responsibilities of the individual underlay the Anglo-Saxon and the Chinese legal traditions, and so the British at Canton had refused to submit to Chinese jurisdiction in homicide cases after 1784, and the Americans after 1821. In practice a degree of extraterritoriality (forcign legal jurisdiction over foreign nationals) had grown up, but it was not explicitly assured from the Chinese side.

The British Crown Supplants the Company.   Crisis came in 1834 when the proponents of free trade secured the abolition of the East India Company's monopoly of British trade with China and the British government sent an official Superintendent of Trade to Canton to oversee the commerce in place of the Company. This Scotsman (Lord Napier) had had no experience in diplomacy or in Asia. He was sent without adequate instructions, preparations, or support to attempt an all but impossible task: the opening of equal relations between Britain and China, which would bring to an end the ancient Chinese tribute system. The local officials predictably refused his demand for correspondence between them as equals. Soon they stopped the British trade, their usual device for curbing foreign merchants. Napier then circulated handbills in Chinese denouncing the Ch'ing officials' disregard for trade and its benefits. The officials in return cut off all supplies to the British. Lord Napier's two frigates forced their way through the principal mouth of the river and exchanged cannon fire with the Chinese forts. The emperor ordered that the English be made to submit or be expelled by force.

This wrathful confrontation was now somewhat palliated by the hong merchants on one side and the British free traders on the other, who pressed for a compromise. Napier retired to Macao, where he died of illness in October 1834, and for the next four years his successors pursued a "quiescent policy," while two schools of thought developed as to what the British policy should be. A majority group of merchants, headed by Jardine, Matheson and Company (a successor of earlier firms, which has retained this name since 1832), demanded that a British naval force repair the insults to Lord Napier and secure the opening of more ports. The rival group of merchants headed by Dent and Company preferred to reap the profits of trade quietly. The Canton officials demanded that England appoint a chief merchant to take responsibility.

By 1836 the Canton system had thus fallen apart. Trade was no longer confined to Canton, the Cohong no longer monopolized the Chinese side of it (in particular, the opium imports), the hong merchants were frequently insolvent, the Company monopoly had given way to competing private traders, and its function of controlling the British merchants had been assumed by an official who objected to taking orders from the hong merchants. The volume of trade and its lawlessness were both increasing.

The Opium War

No episode in modern history has provided more occasion for the charge of "imperialist aggression" than the First Anglo-Chinese War of 1839–1842—a war that was precipitated by the Chinese government's effort to suppress a pernicious contraband trade in opium, concluded by the superior firepower of British warships, and followed by humiliating treaties that gave Westerners special privileges in China. As patriotic Chinese of all camps have reviewed the story in recent times, it has given substance to their feeling of grievance at the forceful intrusion of the West and the subjection of China to "semicolonial" status for almost a century thereafter.

In addition to looking at the Opium War from this point of view, it is also necessary to see it in the context of major trends of modern history. By the nineteenth century, the Chinese position on foreign relations, like the contemporary seclusion policy of Japan, was out-of-date and no longer supportable. An industrializing West, moving rapidly ahead in technology, organizational skills, and military power, could no longer be dealt with like the Europe of the eighteenth century. A vast discrepancy in power relations had developed, and this would inevitably lead to a great change in China's relations with the outside world. Sooner or later the old order of tribute relations would have had to give way, not only because of China's relative military weakness, but also because of the currents of ideas—concepts of scientific learning, individual freedom, and economic growth, for example—which were beginning to sweep over the modern world. In demanding diplomatic equality and commercial opportunity, Britain represented all the Western states, which would sooner or later have demanded the same things if Britain had not. It was an accident of history that the dynamic British commercial interest in the China trade centered not only on tea but also on opium. If the main Chinese demand had continued to be for Indian raw cotton, or at any rate if there had been no market for opium in late-Ch'ing China, as there had been none earlier, then there would have been no "opium war." Yet probably some kind of Sino-foreign war would have come, given the irresistible vigor of Western expansion and the immovable inertia of Chinese institutions.

The Anti-Opium Movement.   The British resort to warfare was precipitated when the Ch'ing court finally faced the opium-trade menace to its vital interests and strove, too late, to catch up with the situation at Canton. The anti-opium movement was a moral crusade which, as often happens in such cases, coincided with concrete interests.

Until the 1830's, neither the growth of addiction among yamen underlings and soldiers, nor the increase of barefaced smuggling and official connivance had roused Peking to a sustained effort at suppression. But meanwhile another problem had arisen. The opium inflow seemed to be causing an outflow or "drain" of silver that in turn seemed to be upsetting China's bimetallic currency system. The exchange rate began to change between the copper cash used in everyday transactions and the silver bullion (in the unit of weight and fineness known as the tael) used in government fiscal operations. Silver became dearer in terms of copper. This was a real crisis for the government because it imposed hardship at all levels—peasants had to pay more coppers to meet taxes, while tax collectors meeting their quotas in silver had less copper cash left over as private squeeze. In actuality, several factors lay behind this situation: first, a debasement of the copper coinage due to reductions in the size and weight of the copper cash by around one-third; second, the volume of cash officially minted every year was increased, and counterfeiting of cheap cash and hoarding of silver further increased this problem; finally, an actual outflow or "drain" of silver began sometime after 1821. Until then, China had consistently been a net recipient of silver in foreign trade—from Japan, Manila, England, the United States, India, and elsewhere. But, at least by the 1830's, China began to suffer a net loss of silver, mainly taken out to India as bullion to pay for opium. An apparent drain was noted long before the balance actually shifted, because Chinese observers saw silver paid out for opium but did not see its subsequent return to pay for tea exports. As a result they jumped to a simplified conclusion. In 1825 a censor connected the silver outflow specifically with the opium inflow, and soon it was generally accepted that the fiscal crisis caused by the shift in the copper-silver exchange rate was due to a drain of silver caused by the opium trade.

So great was the opium evil by this time that extirpation seemed an immensely formidable task. Some realists, especially a group connected with the academy that Juan Yüan had founded at Canton, counseled a policy of compromise: to continue to oppose smoking by scholars, officials, and soldiers, but to legalize the opium import under a tariff so as to discourage smuggling and at the same time to prevent the outflow of silver by letting opium imports be purchased only by bartering Chinese goods, not silver. In May 1836, while Juan Yüan was a Grand Secretary in Peking, this proposal was presented to the emperor, referred to Canton, and soon became known to the foreign traders, who for some time anticipated that legalization would occur. The Canton authorities gave their support to the proposal in September 1836. In Peking, however, the argument had meantime gone the other way and the legalization movement was dead within four months after it started. In 1837–1838 suppression of the Chinese part of the trade at Canton was attempted more vigorously, but smuggling continued on the coast and imports reached a new peak. In the latter half of 1838 a great debate of memorials from high officials all over the empire proved inconclusive. But the emperor at the end of 1838 finally decided on a root-and-branch attack upon the evil all along the line: against cultivators, distributors, and consumers, all of whom would be subject to the death penalty. This statute, issued in 1839, also provided the death penalty for foreign importers.

By this time the anti-opium campaign at Canton had destroyed opium dens, executed dealers, and depressed the trade, which in the winter of 1838–1839 was almost at a standstill. But this stimulated the coast trade and induced the foreign importers to take a more active and forceful role in armed smuggling operations. The position of the British government meantime was that it could not interfere "either by aiding or restraining the pursuits of the smugglers." Suppression would have to be effected by the Ch'ing government.

In the confused events of this period, one point stands out—that the Chinese government was attempting to do two things at once: suppress the opium evil and maintain the tribute system of foreign relations. The Canton authorities refused time after time to communicate with the superintendent of British trade except through the hong merchants, and demanded that the character "petition" head his letters, as it would those from an inferior to a superior. Any kind of trade agreement or cooperative effort between the two governments thus remained impossible. Two worlds stood in opposition. The Chinese struggle against the opium trade went forward in the context of the British struggle against the tribute system.

Commissioner Lin at Canton.   The man selected to exterminate the opium evil, Lin Tse-hsü (1785–1850), was a practitioner of the school of "statecraft" and an incorrupt and effective administrator. After he reached Canton on March 10, 1839, he pioneered in obtaining translations from Western sources, for example, a passage from Vattel's *Law of Nations* concerning a nation's right to control its foreign trade. He also addressed two eloquent letters (never delivered) to Queen Victoria: "Suppose there were people from another country who carried opium for sale to England and seduced your people into buying and smoking it; certainly you would deeply hate it and be bitterly aroused. . . ."

Lin's program was to wipe out the Canton network of Chinese opium importers and distributors, and this he practically accomplished. It was not his aim to use force against the foreign traders, much less start a war with the British. But he soon found it necessary to coerce them into surrendering their opium stocks, and for this purpose on March 24 he confined the foreign community of about 350 men in the Thirteen Factories. Deprived of their servants but not of supplies, the foreigners spent six weeks in this detention. Lin released them when the British merchants delivered up their opium stocks, which he then publicly destroyed. Thus he secured delivery of some twenty thousand chests of British opium, but two things made this a hollow victory: first, the opium market had collapsed, while the supply on hand in China or in prospect from India had risen to some fifty thousand chests, so that the merchants' interest lay in getting whatever price they could; and second, the British superintendent of trade took personal responsibility for the surrender of the opium on behalf of the British government. As Matheson put it to Jardine at the time, "The Chinese have fallen into the snare of rendering themselves directly liable to the British Crown." Lin's coercion of British subjects and officials was entirely in keeping with the unequal nature of the traditional tribute system; but from the viewpoint of the modern international world it gave the British government a *casus belli*.

The traditional order in China's foreign relations was further brought into question in July 1839 when drunken English sailors killed a Chinese villager, who became a symbol in the dispute over legal jurisdiction. The Chinese authorities demanded that a culprit be delivered up. The British refused to admit Chinese criminal jurisdiction over British subjects. As the dispute widened, it highlighted the Sino-Western conflict over diplomatic relations and legal jurisdiction as well as over the opium trade.

Under pressure, the British community retreated successively from Canton to Macao and then in August 1839 to Hong Kong, a largely uninhabited island about thirty square miles in area, separated from the mainland peninsula of Kowloon by one of the world's best deep-water harbors. Hostilities began gradually, in small affrays intermixed with negotiations. The first naval battle was in November 1839. But the Canton trade survived even during wartime. The American firm of Russell and Company, working closely with their hong merchant friend, Houqua, handled much of the season's tea exports under the American flag on behalf of the British. Meanwhile, the coast trade in opium continued, well armed, beyond the reach of Commissioner Lin. When a British expeditionary force arrived in the summer of 1840, seized Chusan Island south of Shanghai, and then negotiated below Tientsin close to the capital, it was evident that Lin Tse-hsü had not succeeded in his twin efforts to suppress the opium evil and maintain the Canton system. In September the emperor recalled him in disgrace, while Britain prepared for a settlement by force of arms.

War and Negotiation. The Ch'ing dynasty's unpreparedness for warfare was due both to the technological backwardness of its armed forces and to the decay of military administration. The army's training stressed form without content, a meaningless posturing with swords and spears. To make up a force against bandits or rebels, small detachments would be collected from a number of different garrisons. This prevented the development of large units as striking forces with high morale and continuous leadership. Troops were commonly rebellious. Without training or discipline, they lacked skill and courage in the field and would run before the enemy could arrive, being fearless only toward the helpless common people.

The decline of Ch'ing power was even more evident on the sea than on the land. The naval tradition included no concept of a mobile striking force constantly ready and able to apply sea power. Instead, each coastal province maintained flotillas of war junks to suppress disorder in certain assigned areas of coastal waters. Under separate provincial commands, trained neither for deep-water cruising nor for joint maneuvers, the Chinese "water forces" were a sort of water-borne constabulary. Pirates could therefore save themselves by using the same tactic as bandits—fleeing across jurisdictional boundaries, so that the province they had victimized would be unable to pursue them while the province they entered would have as yet no reason to do so. Chinese naval vessels remained small— about three hundred tons burden and one hundred feet in length, with one hundred men aboard and half a dozen cannon—in a period when trading junks might carry one thousand tons. They were in no condition to defend China against a nineteenth-century Western navy.

To chastise the Ch'ing government, Britain sent a small mobile force of a few thousand men with the latest devices of warfare, such as flat-bottomed, shallow-draft iron steamers that could defy wind, tide, fire-rafts, and fortresses. Chinese war junks with their archers and antiquated cannon proved as ineffective as the coastal batteries with their fixed emplacements and poor gunnery. The British reduction of Chinese strong points all along the coast from Canton to Shanghai was not difficult (see next page). The real problem was how to capitalize on this military superiority so as to create a new order in China's foreign relations. Britain had no territorial ambitions except for a commercial base like Hong Kong. Neither was it her aim to attack the Chinese populace, who, except at Canton, generally remained passive spectators of the fighting and supplied a coolie corps to work for the invaders' wages. But to make the Son of Heaven agree to a new status for the Westerners in China meant the end of an age-old set of beliefs and practices—in short, the destruction of the tribute system.

In the first phase of the war in 1840–1841, Lin's successor, a wealthy Manchu grandee, signed in January 1841 an abortive convention, which would have ceded Hong Kong, given diplomatic equality and an indemnity to Britain, and reopened Canton. But both governments spurned this attempted settlement. In May 1841, after the season's teas had been shipped,

THE FATE OF CHINA'S TRADITIONAL WATER FORCES. *Supported by boats from British warships, the East India Company's iron-hulled, paddle-wheel steamer* Nemesis—*184 feet long, 120 horsepower, with two 32-pounders on pivots fore and aft, but drawing only 6 feet of water—attacks a Chinese fleet in shallow water near Chuenpi on January 7, 1841.*

a small British force of twenty-four hundred troops attacked Canton, but withdrew from outside the city walls after securing a "ransom" of $6 million. Since local militia, mobilized under gentry leadership at official instigation, were threatening the British when they withdrew, this incident (at the village of San-yüan-li) was hailed as a victory of the Cantonese populace over the British forces. Some historians have viewed it as the first evidence of a modern spirit of nationalism among the Chinese masses.

In the second phase of the war in 1841–1842, the British seized positions all along the coast, in Amoy harbor, on Chusan Island (which they had earlier evacuated), and at Ningpo. Reinforced in the spring of 1842, they occupied Shanghai, took Chinkiang, where the Grand Canal crosses the Yangtze, and advanced to the outskirts of Nanking, having defeated every form of Ch'ing resistance. This resistance had had many aspects—the stoppage of British (but not other) trade, mobilization of militia at Canton, blocking of harbors and river mouths, building of war junks, and the assembling of troops from many provinces. In March 1842 a Chinese surprise attack was made on the British-held city of Ningpo. But this Chinese offensive in the traditional style was ineffective in command, organization, and armament alike. In defense, on the other hand, the garrisons of Manchu bannermen resisted the British with hopeless courage.

The new British plenipotentiary, Sir Henry Pottinger, negotiated only after the British attack had forced the Ch'ing court to consent to an entire new deal in Anglo-Chinese relations. The Manchu dynasty capitulated in order to preserve itself. As descendants of alien conquerors, the rulers at Peking were sensitive to the collaboration which so many "Chinese traitors" were giving to the invaders. Secret societies were active both in opium smuggling and at Hong Kong. Continued defeat by British arms would weaken the dynasty's hold on China. It had to make concessions to the British invaders in order to maintain its rule over the Chinese people. The Chinese reformer Lin Tse-hsü had failed to suppress the opium evil. Now another Manchu grandee, Ch'i-ying (died 1858), was sent to appease the British.

The First Treaty Settlement.   Ch'i-ying signed the Treaty of Nanking with Pottinger on August 29, 1842. It prepared the way for a new order by abolishing the Cohong monopoly of foreign trade at Canton, promising a "fair and regular tariff," ceding Hong Kong to Britain, and opening five ports to British residence and trade—Canton, Amoy, Foochow, Ningpo, and Shanghai. An indemnity of 21 million Mexican dollars was to cover hong merchant debts, pay for the confiscated opium, and reimburse the British Indian government for the cost of the war. But three further treaties were necessary in 1843–1844 to complete the first settlement: the British Supplementary Treaty (October 8, 1843), amplified by the American Treaty (July 3, 1844) and by the French Treaty (October 24, 1844). Because of the "most-favored-nation" clause—a promise to each power that it would receive whatever privileges might later be given another—these treaties reinforced one another to form a single system of treaty law. Since China did most of the giving of privileges, the system has properly been called "unequal." It was not created in a day, however, and actually took eighteen years of continued trade, diplomacy, and eventually warfare to become established.

The first settlement was thus only an entering wedge. It placed British consuls in five ports where British residents were under their consul's legal jurisdiction, that is, they had the right of extraterritoriality. The protection of Western legal procedures covered not only the persons of merchants and missionaries but also their goods and property and sometimes extended in practice to their Chinese servants and assistants. Thus, Western and Chinese enterprises were relatively secure from the arbitrary exactions of officials. The printed treaty tariff, based on the rates of the old imperial tariff, ranged, very roughly, between 4 and 10 per cent. Chinese trade monopolies or guilds, like the Canton Cohong, were forbidden in the name of free trade. The American treaty, negotiated by Caleb Cushing and Ch'i-ying, improved upon the British in the provisions for extraterritoriality and gave Americans without a struggle all the privileges that Britain had fought for.

THE "OPENING" OF EAST ASIA:
PRINCIPAL TREATIES IN THE "UNEQUAL" TREATY SYSTEM, 1842–1943

Characteristic features: treaty ports, extraterritoriality,
most-favored-nation clause, tariff fixed by treaty.

Beginning	*Development*	*Termination*
CHINA		
Nanking (British) 1842, plus Suppl. Treaty of Hu-men-chai ("The Bogue") 1843	Wanghia (American) 1844, Whampoa (French) 1844	Germany, Austria-Hungary 1919, USSR 1924
	Tientsin (Br., Fr., Am., Russian) 1858	Tariff autonomy 1930 (ff. Washington treaties 1922, recognition treaties 1928)
	Chefoo Convention (Br.) 1876, ratified 1885	
	Boxer protocol 1901	New equal treaties (Am. and Br.) 1943
JAPAN		
Kanagawa, Perry (Am.) 1854 (Br. 1854, Russian 1855)	Harris (Am.) 1858	Brit. revision treaty 1894; extraterritoriality ended 1899; tariff autonomy 1911
VIETNAM		
Saigon (Fr.) 1874 (earlier Fr. 1862)	Hué (Fr.) 1883, protectorate confirmed (1885 China recognizes French protectorate)	"Freedom within French Union" 1946, independence of Repub. of Vietnam 1954
KOREA		
Kanghwa (Jap.) 1876	Shufeldt (Am.) 1882	(Japanese protectorate 1905, annexation 1910) Repub. of (So. Korea) 1948

Western Influence Through the Early Treaty Ports

Western contact, with its inevitable undermining of the traditional order, proceeded by stages from the first war and subsequent treaties, in 1840–

1844, to a second set of wars and treaties in 1856–1860. During this period the Ch'ing statesmen, whether Manchu or Chinese, found out too late what they were dealing with. The lead in learning about the Western invaders had been taken by Commissioner Lin at Canton. He turned the translations he had secured over to his friend, the scholar-official Wei Yüan, who produced in 1844 his *Illustrated Gazetteer of the Countries Overseas* (*Hai-kuo t'u-chih*). This collection of materials on world geography and Western conditions also contained a discussion of how to handle the "barbarian" problem. Wei Yüan's strategic thinking was a mixture of old and new. He combined the ancient theme of "using barbarians to control barbarians" (e.g., the French and Americans to control the British) with the new concept of "learning their superior technology in order to control them," specifically warships, firearms, and methods of maintaining and training soldiers. From this concept was to come the movement for the strengthening (*tzu-ch'iang,* literally "self-strengthening") of the Chinese state by borrowing Western devices and technology, a direct application, to the problem of Western aggression, of those ideas of "statecraft" which Wei Yüan and others had already advocated in dealing with domestic problems. The desire for knowledge of the West could be justified by quoting the Chou dynasty classic on the art of war, the *Sun-tzu*: "Know yourself, know your opponent; in a hundred battles, win a hundred victories." Unfortunately China was too big a country, with too many tradition-bound scholars annually moving into official life from the great reservoir of inland provinces, to be easily stirred by a marginal sea-frontier contact with foreign ideas. The stimulus of the Western example was largely confined to Hong Kong and the treaty ports.

Merchants and Missionaries.   The British requests for legalization of the opium trade were refused by Peking, but the trade continued and expanded along the coast as far north as Shanghai without being mentioned in the treaties. Outside the five treaty ports there grew up double that number of "receiving stations," centers of unadvertised but regular and generally peaceable trade between the foreign opium importers and the Chinese opium distributors. Opium addiction increased. In the 1850's the import rose to fifty thousand and even sixty thousand chests a year, double the figure of the early 1830's at Canton. American opium merchants like Russell and Company, who had competed with the Indian supply at Canton by bringing opium from Turkey, now could compete directly with Jardine and Dent by acting as agents for shipments from India. American as well as Chinese, English, Scottish, and Indian Parsee fortunes were made from the trade. Cultivation of the poppy increased rapidly within China, foreshadowing the eventual supplanting of the Indian import. But during the mid-century decades, the few big firms, with their fast clippers, well-armed

TEA PRODUCTION AT A GLANCE. *Picked on the hillside (top left),
tea leaves are dried, sorted, roasted, trampled, packed, weighed, and
otherwise processed through successive stages until purchased by
the three foreigners in top hats and tail coats (bottom left) and
conveyed to their vessels (far right).*

receiving ships, accumulated capital, and superior facilities, maintained an
oligopoly. Tea exports rose above 100 million pounds, silk increased similarly, but both were paid for mainly by the funds received for opium
imports. The Chinese market for textiles and other British manufactures
remained disappointingly limited, mainly because of the self-sufficiency and
poverty of the Chinese peasantry, who still made their own textiles and had
little money for purchases. This was not realized by the foreign merchants,
perched on the rim of a vast subcontinent, and they continued to believe
that the mills of Lancashire could be kept busy for a generation if only
each "Chinaman" would add one inch to his shirt-tail.

The treaty ports, particularly Shanghai, represented an aggressive and
highly dynamic new order based on organized competition. Some two
hundred firms, mainly British and American, though united in chambers
of commerce at Shanghai and Canton, lived or died by competing in all
aspects of trade. Yet the five ports and Hong Kong formed a single community, protected by gunboats, mainly British, and inhabited by a young
and mobile population. A similar degree of organized competition and a
similarly expansive hope for the conversion of the "heathen" masses of
China animated the early Protestant missionaries, who met similar frustration because of the slowness of the Chinese response. After the dissolution

of the Jesuit order in 1773, French Lazarist fathers had taken the Jesuits' place at Peking. While leaving the missionaries untouched there, the Ch'ing government tried with some success to suppress Christianity elsewhere. From 1801 to 1829 only a few new missionaries were able to enter the country, except for the first Protestant pioneer, Robert Morrison, who lived in Canton from 1807 under the wing of the East India Company. Protestant missions had come out of that spiritual accompaniment of the rigors of industrialization, the evangelical movement in late-eighteenth-century Britain and parallel developments in New England. Robert Morrison succeeded in studying Chinese and translating the Bible. To avoid hostility at Canton, his colleagues opened an Anglo-Chinese training college at Malacca in 1818.

The first American Protestants, who reached Canton in 1830, were sent by the American Board of Commissioners for Foreign Missions, an agency founded in 1810 by several denominations but which eventually represented the Congregational churches. They founded an important monthly journal, *The Chinese Repository* (1832–1851) and one of its editors, S. Wells Williams, compiled an influential general account of China, *The Middle Kingdom* (1848). Peter Parker inaugurated medical missions by opening an eye hospital at Canton. Both Williams and Parker later served their government in diplomacy, just as Morrison and other British missionaries aided theirs. At first, however, their chief concentration was on spreading the word of the gospel in Chinese, particularly through tracts such as those written by the first convert, Liang A-fa (1789–1855). Intent on making the gospel available, they began to experiment with romanization (or transcription, i.e., writing the sounds of Chinese in the Roman alphabet). Yet for a long time converts remained very few, measured in tens rather than hundreds.

Meantime the revival of Roman Catholic missions went on both at the ports and in the interior. As the modern patron of Catholic missions, the French government secured from the Ch'ing emperor the issuance of imperial edicts of toleration, in 1844 and 1846, which made Christianity no longer a banned religion and restored certain churches. By working through its native hierarchy of Chinese priests and communicants, the Catholic Church was able to achieve a widespread growth. The Society of Jesus, which was restored in 1814, set up its main center at Zikawei (the ancestral home of Ricci's great colleague, Paul Hsü) in the suburbs of Shanghai. The Jesuit, Lazarist, Dominican, and other European missionaries, with their Chinese colleagues, vigorously revived the Catholic communities in nearly every province. This still illegal but extensive Catholic activity in the interior was more massive and better organized than the Protestant missionary effort, and yet represented a less acute cultural challenge to Chinese society. The Catholic priests dressed and lived in Chinese style, and

CANTON FACTORIES, CA. 1854. *The 15-man fast-boat (foreground) seems to be vying with two Westerners out for exercise in a shell (center). The American side-wheeler* Riverbird *lies off the open space in front of the factories, each of which has its own flagstaff. (Oil painting by a Chinese artist)*

their schools did not teach European languages, whereas the Protestants brought more of their secular culture along with them and attacked Buddhist and Taoist "idols" and Chinese religious and social customs more directly. Thus Catholic missions penetrated much further among the Chinese population, yet in the end the Protestants had the more revolutionary impact.

The Role of the Cantonese. Western influence was felt most directly through the Cantonese. Household servants, Chinese merchants in foreign legal trade, Chinese opium distributors, and Christian colporteurs (distributors of religious writings), all came at first from the regions of longest contact in the far south, particularly Canton. Speaking a strange "dialect" (actually a different language) and organized in their own community, the Cantonese who accompanied foreign merchants to Shanghai or Amoy constituted in themselves an unassimilable foreign element in competition with the local people. If they had established residence in Singapore or Hong Kong, they might carry certificates giving them the status of British subjects. If so, or if they were part of the foreign merchant "establishments" permitted at the ports by treaty, they could claim foreign protection under extraterritoriality. Often they wore Western-style clothes to advertise their privileged position.

In the late 1840's these Chinese in contact with foreign merchants helped to develop still another social evil in the form of the coolie trade, through which male laborers were shipped under contract, mainly from Amoy but also from Macao and other ports, to meet the demand for cheap labor in newly developing areas overseas, such as Cuba, Peru, Hawaii, Sumatra, and Malaya. Chinese emigration to Southeast Asia had been going on for centuries, but several factors now combined to speed it up. One was the worldwide effort to abolish slavery, which created a demand for contract labor as a substitute; another was the introduction of foreign shipping, both sail and eventually steam, which could transport large cargoes of coolies at very little cost. In this new trade under foreign flags, Chinese "crimps" (procurers of laborers) inevitably committed excesses while recruiting and keeping in depots (barracoons) the human cargoes for shipment, just as some foreign vessels came near to duplicating the conditions of the earlier African-American slave trade. The British government tried to prevent abuses by consular inspection of ships. The Ch'ing policy was at first to maintain the traditional ban on emigration.

Abolition of the Cohong at Canton led to the rise of a new type of Chinese merchant, the comprador, who was employed on contract to handle the Chinese side of a foreign firm's business with Chinese merchants, securing commercial intelligence and buying and selling. All this trained him to become a modern entrepreneur in the new Chinese business class which grew up within the protection of the treaty ports. Thus Chinese from the first participated in the modern economy of international trade that began to take shape on the coastal fringe of the Chinese empire.

The Rise of Rebellion

After 1850, peasant-based rebellions covered much of the eighteen provinces for the greater part of two decades. Considering the restricted scope of the Western impact before 1850, one can hardly conclude that it was the chief cause of these vast disorders. Their origins lay in the general condition of China, which by the late 1840's was plainly conducive to rebellion. Population, if we accept the trend of the official estimates, had continued to increase. Administration, judging by selected cases, had continued to deteriorate under the pressure of widespread official self-seeking in the face of ever-mounting problems. Thus, for example, the accumulation of silt in the Yellow River and Grand Canal was not offset by the maintenance of dikes. The canal became less usable for grain transport. In 1852 the Yellow River finally broke loose and began a long,

Northern course, 1852
to 1938 and 1947 to date

Yellow R.

SHANTUNG PENINSULA

Tsingtao

YELLOW

SEA

Grand Canal

Yellow R.

Kaifeng

flood area

Approximate southern course
during Yüan, Ming and Ch'ing
periods to 1852

Southern course,
1938-47

Yangtze R.

Shanghai

COURSES OF THE YELLOW RIVER

disastrous process of shifting its main stream from the south to the north of the Shantung peninsula, the first major shift since 1194. Pressure of numbers, flood, famine, poverty, corruption, and the resulting ineffectiveness of government were demonstrated in the increase of banditry, riots, and minor outbreaks in many areas.

As the Ch'ing power grew less effective, opposition was organized by secret societies. In general, these bodies were called *chiao* in North China, meaning a religious sect or doctrine, and *hui* in the South, meaning a society or association. Offshoots of the White Lotus Society (and forerunners of the Boxers of 1900) appeared in North China in 1813 and were quickly suppressed, but subversive activity was less easy to control in South China, where the main vehicle of unrest was the Triad Society, also known as the Heaven and Earth Society or Hung League and by several other names. According to legend, this society was founded in 1674 by militant Buddhist monks of a monastery near Foochow who had been victimized by corrupt officials. Under the slogan "Overthrow the Ch'ing and restore the

SECRET SOCIETIES. *Stages in the initiation ceremony for Triad Society members.*

Ming," it developed an elaborate secret ritual and became a blood brotherhood whose members were sworn to exterminate Manchu rule. The day-to-day functions of the Triad Society were more peaceful and prosaic, however. Like the Masonic orders of the West, it was a fraternal organization pledged to high moral principles and mutual help among members. It was particularly useful for persons who moved from place to place—traveling merchants, boatmen, transport coolies, petty officials, or smugglers. Use of the secret Triad signs and passwords could secure one protection in strange places on the routes of trade or in overseas centers like Singapore and Batavia.

Disorder became most widespread in the late 1840's in South China where imperial control was diminished by two factors. First, it was the part of China conquered last and least dominated by the Ch'ing, garrisoned by Manchu bannermen only at Canton. Second, it included the region which had been longest subjected to the disturbing influences of foreign trade and contact, culminating in the opium traffic and the war with Britain. Indeed, Canton was the seedbed of modern Chinese nationalism, the focal point most stimulated by the Western example of patriotism and nationalistic interests. Cantonese militia, armed to repel the British, felt in 1841 that they had done so. When later dispersed by the Ch'ing government, they harbored resentment against both the British and the Manchu appeasers of the British. Because Shanghai was closer to the districts of tea and silk production, its opening in 1843 had thrown transport gangs out of work on the routes to Canton. Finally, when the British navy began a program of pirate suppression in 1849, its success forced pirate gangs to move inland from the coast, up the West River and into Kwangsi province.

The Taiping Kingdom.   As in most popular rebellions, a religious cult provided the fanatical basis of organization for the rebel movement that finally emerged in Kwangsi. The founder, Hung Hsiu-ch'üan (1814–1864), and his chief collaborators were Hakkas, that is, members of a distinct linguistic group descended from North Chinese migrants who had settled centuries earlier in large communities in South China. They were not fully assimilated and sometimes became involved in local feuds with the "native" population. Hung was also a frustrated scholar, who had failed more than once in the Canton examinations. He was, finally, a mystic or, at any rate, an unstable personality, whose illness and religious experience convinced him that he was a new messiah. Hung's religious cult was based on the Protestant Bible, which reached him first in 1836 in the form of Chinese tracts written by the early convert Liang A-fa. Hung had a long delirium and saw visions. Subsequent reading of these tracts gave him the explanation: he had seen God and his own Elder Brother, Jesus Christ, for whom he, as the Heavenly Younger Brother, must now save mankind. Hung had some brief contact with Protestant missionaries at Canton, but he put together his own religion, borrowing chiefly the militant teachings of the Old Testament rather than the loving-kindness of the New. The Ten Commandments were taken intact, but not the Sermon on the Mount.

The military organization of Hung's followers, after he had spent several years preaching his new faith, was carried out in conditions typical of the period. As imperial officials lost their capacity to suppress bandits and settle disputes, local militia corps were commonly organized to maintain order. Usually they were paid and led by members of the gentry as the natural local leaders, but they could also be formed by secret societies or religious cults, who could develop sources of revenue from forced contributions, taxes, or rackets. The continued decline of central authority, however, soon set these local forces in competition against one another. Somewhat like tribes of the steppe before the rise of a Chinggis Khan, these militia units were susceptible to being swept up into a great expanding "horde."

The unit organized by Hung's followers in the late 1840's, called the "God Worshippers Society," attracted all manner of disaffected persons—Hakkas, Triad Society members, pirates, and homeless peasants. They began their armed resistance to imperial troops in July 1850 at a village near the West River in Kwangsi. Expanding rapidly, in September 1851 they captured the departmental city of Yung-an to the north and raised the banner of dynastic revolt. Hung took the title of Heavenly King of the "Heavenly Kingdom of Great Peace" (*T'ai-p'ing t'ien-kuo*). The term

"Great Peace" (*T'ai-p'ing*) had been used in the Classics, by earlier rebels, and as a reign title in several Chinese dynasties, in addition to its new use to translate a Biblical phrase. Another leader emerged in the person of a former charcoal dealer, Yang Hsiu-ch'ing (died 1856), who became the Eastern King and commander-in-chief, while others became the Northern, Western, Southern, and Assistant Kings.*

Besieged at Yung-an by imperial forces, the Taipings broke out in April 1852 and went north, acquiring cohorts as they went. Lacking artillery, they failed to take the provincial capitals of Kwangsi (Kweilin) and Hunan (Changsha) but seized the capital of Hupei (Wuchang) early in 1853 and descended the Yangtze in a great flotilla to Nanking, the second city of the empire, which they captured by assault in March 1853.

This remarkable military success was followed by a mixed record of ups and downs. An expeditionary force was sent toward Peking but it was forced westward to Shansi and back into Chihli, harassed by the North China winter, and was finally turned back near Tientsin late in 1853. Meanwhile the Taipings had not set up administrative control over the regions they traversed from Kwangsi northward. They lacked qualified personnel to install as local magistrates. Their forces entered sixteen of the eighteen provinces and captured some six hundred walled cities. But they could not administer what they conquered. Established in the rich heartland along the Yangtze, they set up the traditional Six Ministries of central government at Nanking, but they seem to have had little more than a military administration in the countryside.

In their military-religious society, during the early period, men and women were for a time strictly segregated in separate barracks. Chastity was prescribed for both sexes. Women were organized into labor and even military battalions. Equality of the sexes was manifest in the abolition of foot-binding and the appointment of women as officers and administrators. The Taipings' puritanical zeal also set them against slavery, adultery, witchcraft, gambling, alcohol, opium, and tobacco. Their religion and ideology were a fascinating mixture of Christian and Chinese elements. God's second son, Hung, was hailed as a new Son of Heaven, appointed by the Mandate of Heaven. His followers preached to crowds and offered sacrifices to God; they destroyed idols and temples, Taoist, Buddhist, and Confucian; and their first moral precept was reverence for God, Jesus, and Hung. But their second moral precept was filial piety. The brotherhood of men was combined, paradoxically, with a society of hierarchy and status.

Much of the Taiping system came in fact from Chinese tradition. Since the Bible did not provide a detailed blueprint, Hung and Yang found a

---

Wang, the ancient term for king, had come to be used at Peking for imperial princes, as well as foreign rulers. In English the Taiping "kings" (*wang*) are sometimes called "princes."

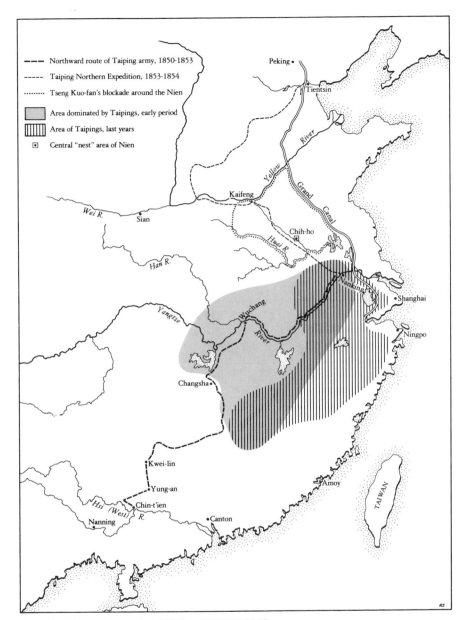

THE TAIPING AND NIEN REBELLIONS

model in the classic *Rituals of Chou* (*Chou-li*), a work cited by radical reformers like Wang Mang (in power 9–23 A.D.) and Wang An-shih (1069–1074). The Chinese utopian tradition was reflected in a primitive economic communism. All persons were to contribute their possessions and services to a common treasury and receive their support from it. Both land and people were to be redistributed. Landholdings were to be classified in nine grades according to productivity, and farming households were to have equally productive allotments according to the number of household members. Every twenty-five families were to form a unit with a church and a public treasury under an officer who would be in charge of payments, as well as religion, education, the judgment of disputes, and the military organization. Ideally every farmer was also a soldier and the government hierarchy was at once both civil and military. (Equal land-holdings, the groupings of families into mutually dependent units, and a peasant militia were of course all old Chinese institutions.) Since in fact the Taipings did not set up a territorial administration, it is uncertain how far the equalization of land use was carried out. Their blueprint was given effect mainly in the early years at Nanking. The egalitarian ideal was limited, for each king built up his own palace, administration, and military forces.

Since Hung stressed the role of a personal and transcendent deity, he envisioned something quite different from the traditional Chinese state, with its rather rational claim to be based on the immanent order of nature. The Taipings' fanaticism reduced their appeal. Their anti-Manchu attack was combined with attacks on Confucianism and the whole social order. They repelled the conservative scholar-gentry class yet failed to achieve an alliance with the rebellious Triad Society. The Taipings borrowed some Triad terminology and many Triads joined the ranks. But Nanking did not help Triads who engineered local rebellions at Amoy and Shanghai in 1853. The Taiping leaders underestimated the value of Shanghai as a source of foreign aid and made little effort to develop foreign trade.

Meanwhile, jealousy among the original founders of the movement proved its undoing. The Machiavellian Yang Hsiu-ch'ing had from the first gained power partly by going into trances and receiving visitations from God. The less devious Hung Hsiu-ch'üan, though he claimed to be the Son of God, did not claim to receive similar communications. At length Yang challenged Hung's superiority and in 1856 Hung got the Northern King (Wei Ch'ang-hui) to assassinate Yang. Wei went further and killed Yang's family and thousands of his followers. Hung soon felt obliged to have Wei assassinated in turn. His original lieutenants having been removed, Hung now appointed mediocre relatives to govern his kingdom. The movement gave way to profligacy and corruption and was kept going only by the emergence of a new military genius (Li Hsiu-ch'eng) who was given the title of Loyal King in 1859 and commanded the Taiping forces in their last years in the lower Yangtze.

With rebellion in every province in the 1850's, the Ch'ing dynasty was able to reassert itself because it continued to monopolize the trained administrative talent of those who knew how to govern in the Chinese Empire. The loyalty of these men was a tribute to the tradition of scholar government and to the achievement of K'ang-hsi and his successors in

Defeat of Taiping forces by superior firepower of Ch'ing inland navy (on left). A battle near Kiukiang reported by Tseng Kuo-fan in January 1855.

forging the unity of state and culture. The scholar class preferred Manchu rule on traditional lines to Chinese rule by heterodox rebels. In the end, the Taipings were suppressed by new Chinese armies under Chinese scholar-official leadership, notably from Hunan.

The principal leader was Tseng Kuo-fan (1811–1872), whose career illustrates the whole process. Tseng became a metropolitan graduate in 1838 and spent the next decade in high official and scholarly circles at Peking. In 1852 he was given the task of organizing a militia army to defend Hunan, his native province. He built his Hunan Army on Confucian principles, to defend China's traditional society. Tseng had been an eclectic scholar and an advocate of practical "statecraft" in administration. Not brilliant, but persistent, he first enlisted local gentry as officers personally loyal to himself. Then by discipline, training, and paternalism he built up the morale of their troops, inculcating as cardinal virtues (1) respect for superiors, (2) concern for the common people, and (3) cultivation of good habits. The Hunan Army first grew from a defensive into an offensive force when sent to save situations in other provinces. Second, it built and trained a naval arm for use on the Central China waterways. Third,

Tseng refused to move out of Hunan prematurely, until in 1854 his forces recaptured Wuchang. Yet even at this date there was still no unity of imperial command and rebellion was still spreading.

The Nien and Moslem Rebellions.   Stimulated by the Taiping invasion of the Yangtze Valley in 1853, a separate rebellion emerged in that year in the area west of the Grand Canal between the Huai and Yellow Rivers. This region on the borders of four provinces (see map, page 471) had long harbored secret-society bandit gangs called simply *nien* ("bands"), whose origins can be traced back to the White Lotus Society. Lacking major cities but with easy access in all directions, the area had been plagued by salt smugglers, and by clan and village feuds, often involving a bellicose minority of Chinese Muslims, as well as by flood, famine, and refugees. The *nien* bands finally achieved a degree of coordination after 1853 by selecting a top leader. Several hundred local groups, based on their fortified, earth-walled villages, under clan and village leaders, supplanted the central government officials over a wide area. They accumulated arms and horses, levied their own taxes, and soon began cavalry raids to plunder adjoining regions. By 1855 the Nien movement was organized as an alliance of five main bands under yellow, white, blue, black, and red banners. It used secret symbols, blood oaths, and elaborate rituals in the secret-society fashion and also imitated the Taipings in wearing long hair. Nien and Taiping forces cooperated on many occasions. Yet the movement remained decentralized and never attempted to expand and take over big cities or set up a rival dynastic government. By degrees, however, the Nien leaders created an effective army, mainly cavalry, and established firm control, first over the local militia bands and then over the population and the food supply, in an area of perhaps 100,000 square miles. By 1860 they confronted the imperial government with the danger that the Nien and Taiping movements might join together.

An even more long-continued revolt against the Ch'ing arose in distant Yunnan. Islam had been firmly rooted in both Northwest and Southwest China ever since the Mongol period. The Chinese Muslim minority in Yunnan still formed a distinct religious community and not infrequently fought with their non-Muslim neighbors, particularly in mining areas, where the dwindling resources of copper, tin, lead, and precious metals extractable by premodern methods were a bone of contention. The Ch'ing officials in this faraway mountain plateau were few and impotent, quite unable to check disorders which began in 1855 under the leadership of the chief priest, a devout and learned man who had made his pilgrimage to Mecca and saw the Islamic faith as compatible with Confucian social teachings. In 1861 he was induced to return to an uncertain allegiance to the Ch'ing, but in western Yunnan the revolt continued for another dozen years under a vigorous fighter, Tu Wen-hsiu. In 1856 he had made Tali (once capital of the medieval kingdom of Nan-chao) the capital of his new Islamic kingdom, taking for himself the title of sultan. His regime managed to get some arms through Burma (it is sometimes called the Panthay Rebellion, using a Burmese term meaning Muslim), and in 1872 even sent a vain mission to London seeking British help. Meantime another violent Muslim rising, beginning in 1862, had convulsed Northwest China, while primitive Miao tribesmen in the mountains of Kweichow had been in rebellion ever since 1854.

Although these smaller movements—Nien, Muslim, and Miao—all lacked the size of the Taiping kingdom, they were a similar index to the collapse of the central power. The Ch'ing dynasty was now caught between the twin forces of "internal rebellion and foreign aggression." But while these inland rebels were proving unable to create institutions to supplant the traditional system, the Westerners in the treaty ports were energetically seizing the opportunity to create a new order on the coast.

Final Establishment of the Treaty System

Compared with the fratricidal slaughter of millions and the wholesale destruction of cities and farming capital (such as the mulberry trees essential for silk culture) which attended the great rebellions, the Opium War with its few thousands of casualties had been a very small affair indeed. Similarly the early opium trade, the missionary movement, and the first treaty ports all were on a small scale. They did not directly affect the lives of ordinary Chinese, but by calling the old order into question they began the long-term process of undermining the institutions of Chinese society. In the short term, however, the foreign diplomatic influence was not always revolutionary. On the contrary, one of the issues of China's modern history is the question how far the Western powers after 1860 may have inhibited political change by propping up the faltering Ch'ing dynasty. In the decade from the rise of rebellion in 1851 to 1860, the Western powers moved from a policy of negotiation with Peking to one of coercion and then, having secured a second treaty settlement, from coercion to cooperation with the dynasty.

During the 1850's the disintegration of the central government's control over the local scene, in the treaty ports as in the provinces of the vast interior, led to the rise of local power-holders. In the case of the ports, however, the foreign consuls, instead of creating Chinese-type administrative agencies of the kind set up by the various rebel regimes or the gentry leaders of the interior, created new Western-type agencies of their own. At Shanghai the foreign settled areas were flooded with refugees from the Taipings. In 1853, when Triads seized the walled city, the imperial custom house was put out of action and the imperial officials, from the taotai (intendant of circuit) on down, were ousted. The foreign settlement organized its own local militia of Western merchants, the Shanghai Volunteer Corps. In July 1854 the consuls of Britain, the United States, and France joined in getting the taotai's consent to regulations which set up a degree of self-government and formed the basis for the later growth of the International Settlement and French Concession, with their own powers of local taxation and upkeep of roads and municipal police. Thus the future center of China's modernization at the entrance to the Yangtze Valley became a semiforeign city run by the local foreign land-renters under the protection of their treaty rights of extraterritoriality.

Meanwhile, in the absence of the imperial custom house, the British consul had maintained the collection of duties due by treaty, so as to forestall Chinese collection of duties on foreign trade in the interior. The idea of a treaty tariff, known to all and equally enforced, had proved unworkable in the face of collusion between Chinese customs collectors and competing foreign merchants. Yet without equal taxation, free trade and the secure growth of legal commerce would be jeopardized. In July 1854, the British, American, and French consuls therefore arranged that their nominees should serve the taotai as his customs collectors, seeing to it that the foreign merchants were impartially assessed and also ensuring that the taotai would receive the revenue. From this beginning grew the Foreign Inspectorate of Customs. From 1855 an Englishman (Horatio Nelson Lay) was employed by the Chinese government, as a private individual, to assess the duties from China's foreign trade. Neither the International Settlement nor the Foreign Inspectorate would have been created in more normal times of strong Chinese administration. Under pressure of a crisis, they were a product of the British instinct for *ad hoc* arrangements and of Chinese resilience in cooperating with powerful aliens on the frontier.

The Anglo-French War with China. China's foreign trade in tea, silk, and opium increased even as rebellion spread more widely, but Canton lost its pre-eminence in trade and antiforeign feeling there mounted. Westerners were still excluded from the walled city, and this became an issue of "face" between Britain and China. By 1851 Britain was ready to coerce China again to gain broader trading privileges, but recognized that foreign agression might add to domestic disorder and so hinder foreign trade. It appeared unlikely that the Taipings would foster Western trade any more than the Ch'ing, and the Western powers therefore maintained neutrality toward the rebellion.

In 1854 Britain, the United States, and France tried to negotiate treaty revisions with Peking in pourparlers at Canton, Shanghai, and off Tientsin. But negotiation was refused or evaded, while occasional popular attacks

on Western nationals raised the issue of foreign prestige. The Western nations, which at this same time were forcing trade treaties on Japan and
other Asian countries, were in a mood to press their claims for further contact with China on Western terms. Convinced that the treaty system would
deteriorate if not reaffirmed and extended, Britain found a pretext in 1856,
when the consul claimed a British flag was disregarded on a Chinese-owned
vessel registered at Hong Kong, the lorcha *Arrow*. (A lorcha was a vessel
with Western hull and Chinese rig.) When a French missionary, seized as
a foreign subversive in an area of rebellion, was executed in Kwangsi, the
French found this a basis for cooperation with Britain to coerce the Chinese Empire.

The British knew what they wanted—the acceptance by the Son of
Heaven of the Western concept of international trade and relations—but
it took them four years to get it. After some delay, they captured Canton
early in 1858 and installed the Chinese governor of Kwangtung as a puppet to govern the city under an allied commission.

Aiming at the emperor, the Anglo-French negotiators took their forces
direct to Tientsin and there in June 1858 secured their treaties, which
provided that their ministers could reside at Peking on terms of diplomatic
equality. American and Russian plenipotentiaries went along to Tientsin as
"neutrals" and secured almost identical treaties. Since permanent Western
legations at Peking would end the ancient tradition of China's superiority,
the Ch'ing court became increasingly determined not to concede this point,
even though it had been accepted in treaty drafts. When the British and
French ministers arrived off Tientsin a year later, in June 1859, to go to
Peking and exchange treaty ratifications, they were refused passage. Trying
to force a passage up the river, they were repulsed. Four British gunboats
were unexpectedly sunk with many casualties. The British and French
therefore had to return again in 1860 with stronger forces. For this final
showdown the British brought to North China 41 warships, 143 troop
transports, 10,500 troops, and a coolie corps of 2500 Cantonese. The
French brought 6300 troops and more than 60 ships. The allies defeated
much larger imperial forces under the Mongol commander-in-chief, Prince
Senggerinchin, and entered Peking in October, while the emperor fled beyond the Wall to Jehol.

In the settlement at Peking, Anglo-French friction arose over the French
thirst for national glory, in the absence of any commercial interest in China,
while the British negotiator (Lord Elgin) had to restrain also the expansionist demands of the "old China hands." But when the chief British negotiator was seized while under a flag of truce and some twenty men in his
party were executed before he was released, Elgin took reprisal against the
emperor personally by destroying his summer palace of some two hundred
buildings northwest of Peking (the Yüan Ming Yüan), which had already

been looted by the invading forces and Chinese villagers. Short of ammunition and faced with the onset of winter, the allies had to get a quick settlement and withdraw. They signed new conventions with the emperor's brother, Prince Kung, who now represented the dynasty. These documents confirmed the treaties of 1858, increased their indemnities, and added certain other concessions. For example, Britain secured the Kowloon Peninsula opposite Hong Kong. France obtained by a subterfuge the right for Catholic missions to hold property in the interior.

This second treaty settlement had the general effect of opening the Chinese Empire to Western contact. Without introducing any radically new principles, it enlarged the scope of the foreign privileges that had been developed under British leadership at the five early treaty ports.

The Russian Advance in Manchuria.   By the most-favored-nation principle, Russia also secured these privileges, but meanwhile her envoys had also been active elsewhere. By the Sino-Russian treaties of 1689 and 1727 the Ch'ing emperors had succeeded in keeping the Russians out of the Amur watershed and on the far outer frontier of Mongolia. This had diverted Russian expansion to other parts of Asia. Bering discovered Alaska in 1741, Russian posts were established on Kamchatka, and Russian contact began with Japan. In 1799 the Russian-American Company was chartered to keep up with the British East India Company by monopolizing Russian trade in the Pacific. From 1812 to 1839 it even maintained an outpost in California, not far north of that of the Mexicans at San Francisco. Meanwhile, from 1727 until after 1860, a regular Sino-Russian trade was carried on at the Chinese border town of Mai-mai-ch'eng in Outer Mongolia opposite the Russian town of Kiakhta (see page 252). Although trading missions ceased going to Peking, the Russian ecclesiastical mission had continued there with four priests and half a dozen language students. This mission became a center of Chinese studies, and was also a point of semiofficial contact.

The opening of the treaty ports had coincided with a continued Russian advance into Central Asia in the area soon to be known as Russian Turkestan (as opposed to Chinese Turkestan east of the Pamir massif). During the eighteenth century the Russians had steadily advanced, setting up fortified lines of outposts against the mobile Kirghiz and Kazakh tribes of the steppe. These outposts soon extended from the Caspian north to Orenburg and thence east along the Irtysh River. By degrees this arc was steadily pushed southward. On this frontier Russian trade developed with Chinese Turkestan as well as with the khanates of Khiva, Bokhara, and Samarkand (see map on page 598). In 1851 a Sino-Russian treaty was signed at Kuldja, the main city of the Ili region, to regulate trade there along the lines already established at the more easterly mart at Kiakhta. Russian trading caravans were to be carefully regulated as to routes, seasons, factories, residences, and the like, but were to be under the control of their own consul at Kuldja. The agreement was on terms of equality and reciprocity, such as seem to have characterized the contact between the Ch'ing and Russian Empires, particularly on this far frontier where both were conquering powers and had some community of interest against the warlike local tribes.

Stimulated by the British success in China, the Russians also began a second invasion of the Amur watershed, from which they had had to withdraw after 1689. This move was led by a vigorous proconsul, Nikolai Muraviev, who was appointed governor-general of Eastern Siberia in 1847. He sent Russian flotillas of barges down the Amur in 1854 and the years following, founding posts on the north bank all the way down to Khabarovsk, where the Ussuri enters the Amur. Russian troops and settlers soon created a position of strength. On May 16, 1858, even before the treaties were concluded at Tientsin, Muraviev secured a treaty at Aigun, which ceded to Russia the north bank of the Amur and left China and Russia in joint possession of the territory between the Ussuri and the sea, pending its further disposition. Muraviev's program of occupying sparsely populated frontier areas now won support from his own, hitherto reluctant, government in St. Petersburg (see map, page 252).

The Russian Treaty of Tientsin in June 1858, though it gained all the Western trading privileges, left the question of the east coast of Manchuria unsettled. It remained for a clever diplomat, General Nikolai Ignatiev, to consolidate Russia's East Asian gains in 1860 (all the more necessary after Peking in 1859 had rejected the Treaty of Aigun). In his negotiations Ignatiev used several stratagems. Reaching Peking in June 1859 after the Ch'ing victory over the British gunboats outside Tientsin, he took up residence at the Russian ecclesiastical mission and negotiated fruitlessly for several months. In 1860 he went to Shanghai and by his knowledge of Peking ingratiated himself with the other Western plenipotentiaries. After the allies had fought their way to the capital, with Ignatiev in their train, he was in a position to mediate between them and the Ch'ing court. The Sino-Russian Treaty of Peking of November 1860, signed after the British and French had departed, was his reward for mediating. It confirmed the Treaty of Aigun and in addition gave Russia the Maritime Province between the Ussuri and the Pacific, where Muraviev had already founded Vladivostok (meaning in Russian "Rule of the East") in July 1860. Thus the Ch'ing Empire had barely been opened to trade and evangelism by the Western powers when Russia began the process of its territorial dismemberment.

The Restoration of the Ch'ing Government

To overcome the evils of domestic disorder and foreign invasion, the Chinese state required strong leadership at the top, but for this exacting task the Taiping rebels had early proved unprepared and ineffective—Heaven's Mandate never really came within their reach. By 1860 the only hope of re-establishing peace and order seemed to be at Peking. Here a genuine "restoration" occurred, a revival of dynastic leadership such as had taken place before in Chinese history after devastating rebellions, notably in the founding of the Eastern Han and in the middle T'ang (see pages 85 and 120). This revival of imperial leadership coincided with several turning points in the struggles of the time—first of all, in the campaign against the rebels.

In 1860 the Great Camp of the imperial forces below Nanking was destroyed for a second time, by the vigorous Taiping commander Li Hsiu-ch'eng, and this disaster forced the Ch'ing court finally to give the Hunan scholar-general Tseng Kuo-fan unified command over the whole campaign of suppression. In August 1860 he was appointed governor-general and imperial commissioner with top military and civil authority over the middle and lower Yangtze provinces. He installed other Chinese scholar-generals as governors of provinces and finally began to hem in the rebel forces. Another corner was turned when the Anglo-French capture of Peking broke the back of the die-hard antiforeign party within the Ch'ing court, and the emperor's brother, Prince Kung, emerged to conclude the treaty settlement. Appeasement of the invaders by accepting the treaty system was now acknowledged to be the only possible way to save the dynasty. Finally, the Hsien-feng emperor died in August 1861, and by a *coup d'état* his brother, Prince Kung, and the young Empress Dowager, Tz'u-hsi, mother of the new boy-emperor, came into power. Executing rival princes who had been more antiforeign, they gave the new reign strong Manchu leadership along two main lines: to cooperate warily in the working of the treaty system and to give full support to the Chinese gentry leaders under Tseng Kuo-fan in the suppression of rebellion. As Prince Kung put it, the rebels were a disease in China's vitals, the barbarians an affliction only of the limbs. The new reign was called *T'ung-chih*, meaning "Union for Order."

Foreign Aid and the End of the Taiping Kingdom.   To assist his Hunan Army, Tseng had his able young disciple Li Hung-chang (1823–1901) build up the Anhwei Army, a similar regionally-based gentry-led striking force. Whereas the Hunan Army was already declining because of its long-continued losses and inadequate financial support, Li succeeded in April 1862 in moving his new Anhwei Army into Shanghai on foreign-rented steamers and with gentry-merchant support. Confirmed as governor of

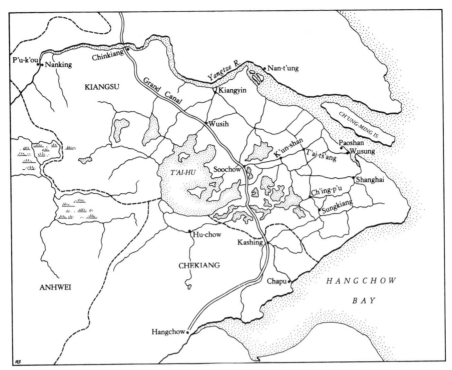

THE YANGTZE DELTA

Kiangsu, he gradually entrenched himself in the Yangtze delta. In addition to the tribute grain collections, he got some control over the new Maritime Customs revenues and other taxes on the commerce of the Shanghai area. Thus financed, he purchased foreign arms and built his Anhwei Army up to seventy thousand men, the most powerful force in China. He and Tseng set up arsenals to make Western guns and steamships and, in the process first of suppressing rebels and second of "self-strengthening," got their own personal supporters into power in a bureaucratic machine.

One impetus for adopting Western arms was given by the example of a foreign-officered mercenary force at Shanghai. This began as a local corps of foreign adventurers, paid by Chinese merchants and led by Frederick Townsend Ward of Salem, Massachusetts. When the last great outbreak of the rebellion brought Taiping forces to the outskirts of Shanghai early in 1862, Britain and France now abandoned neutrality in defense of the treaty ports of Shanghai and Ningpo. Instead of a foreign legion, Ward now trained a small Chinese force of about four thousand men, whose Western arms and use of amphibious tactics of maneuver on the waterways of the Yangtze delta won more than a hundred engagements and brought them the name of "Ever-Victorious Army." After Ward's death in 1862, Major Charles George Gordon, lent from the British army, eventually succeeded to the command, receiving, like Ward, Chinese military rank under Governor Li Hung-chang. "Chinese" Gordon and his small Sino-foreign army helped capture Soochow. A similar Franco-Chinese force helped re-capture Hangchow.

Finally, in July 1864, Nanking was taken by Tseng Kuo-fan's younger brother, with no foreign assistance, after desperate fighting. Thus the rebel kingdom came to a bloody end. This massive movement, with all its early vigor and idealism, had lacked adequate leadership and had stumbled blindly into dissension, corruption, and final defeat. For several years the Taipings had had the opportunity to enlist foreign aid while the Western powers were, part of the time, actually at war with the Ch'ing government; yet the opportunity was never taken. In the end it was the large Chinese armies mobilized under Tseng that did the great bulk of the fighting against the rebels. Chinese use of foreign forces was kept carefully limited. As an imperial edict put it in 1862, "For the time being, we have to make use of foreigners to train our soldiers, as a scheme for self-strengthening...." Western aid to the Ch'ing cause came less through the intervention of foreigners than through the Chinese leaders' own use of foreign trade revenues and of Western guns, ships, and training, in the spirit of "self-strengthening." The Manchu dynasty was saved by Chinese scholar-officials who were loyal to it as part of the Confucian order, and who found Western aid useful for their own purposes in the final years of their long-continued effort. The other mid-century rebellions—of the Nien (1853–1868) and of the Muslims in the Southwest (1855–1873) and in the Northwest (1862–1873)—were all suppressed without Western participation but with some use of modern arms.

The Opening of China. China's acceptance of the second treaty settlement gave the Western powers a stake in the established order, for they were now part of it. In the early 1860's they moved to develop their opportunities. Eleven more treaty ports were eventually opened, including places in North China and Manchuria, on Taiwan, and up the Yangtze as far as Hankow. Foreign vessels continued to participate in the domestic carrying trade among China's coastal and river ports, a right denied foreigners in most countries. The import of opium was legalized on payment of a moderate duty. Foreign imports of all kinds were allowed to pass freely in the interior on payment of a further transit duty of 2½ per cent, which was roughly half the import duty. Thus they could compete with native products. The regulating of foreign trade was handled by an extension of the Shanghai Foreign Inspectorate, which created the Chinese Imperial Maritime Customs Service as a foreign-staffed arm of the Peking government. Travel in the interior under passport now gave the missionaries access to the entire population. Both Catholics and Protestants soon began to acquire and use new property in the interior.

Behind all these opportunities for merchant and missionary expansion stood the power of the Western nations, led by Britain. Their ministers at Peking, backed by gunboats in the ports, had the primary function of enforcing treaty rights. The result was a great intensification of the Western challenge. The new "barbarians" were now truly within the gates. The Chinese people, however, had not yet responded to this threat in nationalistic terms. The tribute system had been destroyed, but the treaty system, only a part-way step toward modern international relations, was curiously reminiscent of the Chinese traditional polity—under extraterritoriality, treaty-power nationals were added to, but did not displace, the privileged Manchu-Chinese ruling class. The traditional Chinese state and social order, which had accommodated alien rulers so often before, remained intact. The very competitiveness of the Europeans seemed to give the dynasty a chance to manipulate these aggressors against one another. After 1864 the Ch'ing dynasty thus had a reprieve and China an opportunity to modernize in self-defense with Western help.

17. Japan's Response to the West

The Impact of the West

Early Pressures. The Japanese by 1639 had so successfully closed their doors to the outside world that subsequently Japan all but dropped out of the consciousness of Europeans. Even the Catholic missionaries eventually gave up their attempts to re-enter the country, and few Western ships came near Japan. The only important exception was the annual Dutch vessel from the East Indies to the Dutch trading post on the island of Deshima in Nagasaki harbor. Occidentals simply accepted the inaccessibility of the islands as a fact of political geography, and, absorbed in their expansion into other, much larger areas in Asia, came to regard Japan as a remote, poor country of little interest. But increased Western activity in the Chinese area in the late eighteenth and early nineteenth centuries drew attention once again to Japan. Western ships started to frequent Japanese waters, and demands began to grow in the West that Japan follow China's lead in opening its doors to commercial and diplomatic contact.

The Russians were the first to exert pressure on Japan. During the eighteenth century Russian and Japanese explorers and traders sometimes encountered one another in the Kuril Islands and Sakhalin, north of Japan's northern island of Hokkaidō. In 1809 the Japanese explorer Mamiya Rinzō (1780–1845) had even ventured up the Amur River. Russian representatives attempted to open official relations in Hokkaidō in 1792 and at Nagasaki in 1804, but both times they were firmly, though courteously, refused. The Russians in pique raided Japanese outposts in the islands north of

Hokkaidō in 1806 and 1807, and the Japanese retaliated by capturing some Russians in 1811 and holding them imprisoned for two years.

Meanwhile the British too were beginning to return to Japanese waters. English vessels visited Hokkaidō in 1797, Nagasaki in 1808 in search of Dutch ships under Napoleonic control, and Edo Bay in 1818. An armed clash occurred in 1824 between British sailors and Japanese on a small island south of Kyūshū.

By the middle of the nineteenth century, the United States had replaced both England and Russia as the nation most interested in opening Japan. Large numbers of whaling vessels from New England frequented the North Pacific, and the great circle route across the Pacific brought American clipper ships close to the shores of Japan on their way to and from Canton. The American crews were naturally interested in obtaining supplies in Japanese ports and in reducing the dangers of capture and mistreatment by the hostile Japanese. As steam came into use, moreover, coaling stations in Japan appeared an attractive possibility. For these various reasons, opening the ports of Japan became increasingly important to Americans, just at the time when westward expansion overland was bringing them to the Pacific and "manifest destiny" seemed to beckon them on across the seas.

As early as 1791 two American ships had entered Japanese waters, and in 1797 another visited Nagasaki, chartered by the Dutch authorities in the East Indies to replace their own ships, cut off from them by the Napoleonic wars. An American businessman in Canton dispatched a small vessel, the *Morrison,* to Japan in 1837 to repatriate seven Japanese castaways and, through this act of good will, to open up relations with Japan, but the unarmed ship was fired on by the Japanese and driven off. In 1846 Commodore Biddle entered Edo Bay and tolerated various indignities from the Japanese in a vain effort to open negotiations. In 1849 Commander Glynn took a stiffer attitude at Nagasaki but proved no more successful, though he was able to pick up fifteen stranded American seamen.

Japanese Reactions.   The Japanese reacted sharply to these invasions of their cherished seclusion. Following the Russian raids in the north, the shogunate for a while took over the Hokkaidō domain of Matsumae in order to strengthen defenses in that area. In 1806 it also issued instructions to local authorities to drive off all foreign ships and in 1825 strengthened this stand by ordering that they destroy foreign intruders with "no second thought," although in 1842 it realistically relaxed these orders to permit the local authorities to provide foreign ships with supplies when this was deemed necessary to avoid violence.

The Japanese leaders thus remained firmly determined to maintain the traditional policy of isolation and opposed to any capitulation to what seemed to them to be Western affronts to Japan's national dignity. Men from the collateral Tokugawa domain of Mito, which had long been a center of strong nationalist sentiment with pro-emperor overtones, led in advocating a hard line. In 1825 Aizawa Seishisai (1782–1863), in a document called *New Proposals,* urged the shogunate to "smash the barbarians whenever they come in sight." He argued that foreign trade was economically injurious to Japan, that foreign contacts would undermine Japanese morale, and that the only sound defense was to build national strength through greater unity and the judicious use of Western techniques, while excluding Westerners themselves. This general position was subsequently developed further by Fujita Tōko (1806–1855), another influential Mito intellectual. In 1830 Tokugawa Nariaki (1800–1860), the daimyo of Mito, called for political reform, emphasizing these Mito views. He argued for continued isolation to be backed up by greater national unity and military renovation. Specifically he urged the shogunate to relax the controls which had kept the daimyo militarily weak and financially impotent. He started vigorous reforms within his own domain, borrowing Western military techniques to strengthen the domain army.

It was clear to some Japanese, however, that foreign naval power was too strong for Japan to resist. Scholars of "Dutch Learning" in particular could see that blind resistance was dangerous. Their voices were not as inconsequential as they had been in the past, since the increasing menace of the West had drawn attention to Western science and military technology. In 1811 the shogunate itself had established an office for the translation of Occidental books, which in 1857, under the name of Institute for the Investigation of Barbarian Books, became a school of Western science and languages. Similar schools were established by several of the larger domains, notably Mito, Satsuma, Chōshū, Tosa in Shikoku, and Hizen (Saga) in Kyūshū, all of which were to play significant roles in the following years. (See map, pages 402–403.) Some scholars of "Dutch Learning" spoke out boldly. In 1838 Takano Chōei (1804–1850) issued a pamphlet urging the opening of Japan to foreign contact, but was imprisoned for his audacity and eventually was forced to commit suicide. Sakuma Shōzan (1811–1864), an expert on Western-style gunnery, in an effort to justify the technological changes that he realized were necessary, coined the slogan "Eastern ethics and Western science," a concept which, like its counterpart developed in China, was to prove comforting to a whole generation of modernizers.

The Opening of Japan.   The United States eventually determined to take decisive action to open Japan's ports. It chose for the purpose Commodore Matthew C. Perry and assigned him three steam frigates and five other ships—a quarter of the American navy. Perry, proceeding by way of the Indian Ocean, reached Japan in July 1853. After several days of diplomatic sparring at Uraga near the mouth of Edo Bay, he forced the Japanese to accept a letter from the president of the United States to the emperor of Japan and then departed, promising to return the next spring for the answer. Perry never discovered what had been well known in the Occident two centuries earlier—that the "emperor" he was attempting to deal with was actually only the shogun.

The Japanese realized that their small vessels and antiquated shore batteries were no match for the fleet at Perry's command or the still larger British naval forces in Asian waters. Edo lay exposed to the superior guns of the West, and the water-borne food supply of this city of over a million was completely vulnerable to blockade. The shogunate authorities were also aware of what had happened to the Chinese in the recent Opium War, and the Dutch had repeatedly advised them through Nagasaki that they would have to give way to foreign demands.

One might imagine that, since the exclusion policy had been created by the Tokugawa shoguns in the seventeenth century, they could abandon it with impunity in the nineteenth. But the policy meanwhile had become sacrosanct and the shogunate flabby and irresolute, pulled in a variety of directions by the "house" daimyo who staffed its higher posts, the collateral domains which controlled much of its military power, and the "public opinion" of its own retainers. Being divided itself on this intensely controversial problem, the shogunate could present no united front to the rest of the nation or to the West.

Since 1845 the chief figure among the shogunate "elders" had been Abe Masahiro, an able, young "house" daimyo. Abe realized that general understanding would be necessary for the extremely unpopular but unavoidable policy of opening the country to more foreign contact. He therefore referred the problem posed by Perry to all of the daimyo. This was a momentous step, unprecedented in two and a half centuries of shogunate rule. It opened the door to discussion and criticism of all shogunate policies, thus starting a rapid erosion of Tokugawa prestige and authority. The last years of Tokugawa rule, from 1853 until the ultimate collapse in 1868, are fittingly known as the *bakumatsu,* or "end of the shogunate."

Abe's appeal to the daimyo produced no national consensus. The replies were overwhelmingly antiforeign but often ambiguous. About a third of the leading domains realized that Japan must make some concessions on trade, the profits of which could then be used to strengthen defenses. Some opposed trade but advised making enough concessions to give time for further military preparations. The rest demanded that no concessions be made and the Americans be driven off. The shogunate's Confucian scholars, who had also been consulted, took the same line, and the imperial court, insulated from foreign pressures in its inland capital of Kyōto, was also known to be strongly isolationist.

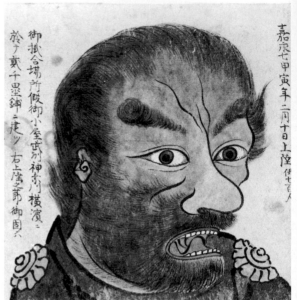

*An 1854 woodblock print giving a "true image" of Commodore
Perry of the "North American Republican State" and a picture of
Adams, his second-in-command, from a (1854) scroll depicting
the American expedition.*

Perry returned in February 1854 and insisted on conducting negotiations
further up Edo Bay at Kanagawa, now part of the great port city of Yokohama. The Japanese finally accepted what they felt were the minimum
American demands. In the Treaty of Kanagawa, signed on March 31, they
agreed to open two quite unimportant and isolated ports to American ships
for provisioning and a limited amount of trade. These were Shimoda at the
end of the mountainous Izu Peninsula and Hakodate in Hokkaidō. They
also agreed to the stationing of an American consul at Shimoda and
promised to give good treatment to shipwrecked American sailors. One
element of the Chinese treaty system was included, the most-favored-nation
clause, stipulating that additional privileges granted to other nations would
automatically come to the United States as well. The shogunate concluded
similar treaties with the British on October 14, with the Russians at
Shimoda on February 7, 1855, and subsequently with the Dutch. The
Russian treaty added Nagasaki as an open port and another aspect of the
Chinese treaty system—extraterritoriality.

These treaties were hardly the full commercial agreements the Western
powers desired, and so they kept up their pressures for increased trade
relations. The outbreak of the Anglo-French War in China in 1856 and
the announcement by the British that they intended to negotiate a com-

mercial treaty with Japan made the shogunate realize that the Perry treaty had given only a brief respite. To forestall greater demands, it signed agreements with the Dutch and Russians in October 1857 for carefully regulated trade at Nagasaki and Hakodate, but it was left to the American consul, Townsend Harris, to force Japan fully open to trade.

Harris, who had arrived in Shimoda in 1856, gradually convinced the shogunate authorities that it would be better to conclude a full commercial treaty with a relatively peaceful and friendly United States before a less favorable treaty was wrung from them by the stronger and more demanding European powers. The resulting treaty, signed on July 29, 1858, called for an exchange of ministers; the immediate opening to trade of Kanagawa and Nagasaki in addition to Shimoda and Hakodate; the opening between 1860 and 1863 of Niigata on the west coast and Hyōgo (the modern Kōbe) to trade and Edo and Ōsaka to foreign residence; moderate limitations on import and export duties; and extraterritorial privileges for Americans. Within the next several weeks the Dutch, Russians, British, and French made similar treaties, but heightened the inequities of the treaty relationship by fixing Japanese import duties at relatively low levels.

Even before the Harris treaty went into effect in the summer of 1859, foreign traders began to settle in large numbers at the harbor of Yokohama, close to Kanagawa, and this unimportant fishing village soon grew into the chief port for foreign trade. Since the gold-silver ratio in Japan was 5 to 1, in contrast to the worldwide 15 to 1 ratio, and also because the value of Japanese coinage was fixed by the shogunate and was not dependent on the metallic content of the coins, the injection of foreign currency thoroughly disrupted the Japanese monetary system. This together with the heavy foreign demand for certain export commodities, particularly silk and tea, the inflow of cheaper foreign manufactures, particularly cotton textiles, frantic efforts to increase armaments, and growing political disruption resulting from the foreign threat, set off a severe inflationary spiral. The shogunate did its best to limit foreign trade by every possible tactic but was frustrated by the determination of the Westerners and the eagerness of commercial groups in Japan for quick profits.

The most serious consequence of the treaties was the presence in Japan of considerable numbers of Westerners, whom most Japanese regarded with great distrust and hostility. Troubles inevitably resulted between fervid samurai activists and Western diplomats and traders. There were several assassinations in 1859, and in 1861 Harris' Dutch interpreter, Heusken, was cut down. The British legation in Edo was attacked that same year and burned down in 1863. In 1862 four Britishers riding in the hills back of Yokohama were attacked by samurai in the procession of the daimyo of Satsuma, and one of them, Richardson, was killed. Such incidents resulted in heavy indemnities, which strained the shogunate's finances, and they further eroded Edo's authority, ground as it was between the arrogant, demanding Western powers and intransigent native isolationists.

Political Ferment in Japan

Japanese Responsiveness.   To observers at the time, Japan's position seemed even more precarious than that of China. Divided among more than 260 autonomous feudal regimes and united only under a shogun whose authority and power were fast disintegrating, Japan seemed politically more backward and less capable of effective action than the centralized and thoroughly bureaucratic Chinese government. Its feudal class society seemed ill prepared to respond to the challenge of more modernized Western nations. Its pre-industrial economy was no match for European machine production. It lacked the great continental solidity of the vast Chinese Empire, and its small islands were pathetically exposed to Western sea power.

And yet, Japan responded to the challenge of the West with much greater speed and far more success than China. No wars were fought, no smuggling trade developed, no territory was lost. There was turmoil, but out of it soon emerged a radically changed political system under which the Japanese moved rapidly toward becoming a modern power. Obviously Japan in the mid-nineteenth century, even though it had derived a large part of its higher culture from China, was a very different country, capable of very different responses to the Western challenge.

One clear and crucial difference lay in the respective attitudes toward the outside world. The Chinese, long accustomed to the idea that China was the unique land of civilization, could not accept the multi-state international concepts of Europe, did not believe that there was much of value to be learned from "barbarians," and, although outraged by Western presumptions, could not really see the seriousness of the challenge, assuming that these new "barbarians," like others before them, would come to comprehend the superiority of China and accept it. The Japanese, on the other hand, were linguistically, culturally, and geographically distinct enough from the Chinese to have developed a strong feeling of separate identity and, because of their acute awareness of China, also had a clear sense of the plurality of nations. The European system of equal and independent states was easy for them to accept. Well aware of all that they had learned over the ages from China and even from Korea and India, they could readily see that there was much of great importance to be learned from the West too. Accustomed to thinking of China as far larger, much older, and more advanced than Japan, they had no sublime sense of cultural superiority but rather a nagging fear of inferiority. Thus, when menaced by the West, they did not react with disdain but rather with that combination of fear, resentment, and narrow pride that one associates with nationalism. In fact, their reaction proved extremely nationalistic. Despite the intensity of rivalries among the various domains, most Japanese leaders in the face of the foreign menace seem to have placed national interests ahead of old feudal loyalties.

The very decentralization and diversity of the Japanese political and social system also permitted a greater variety of responses than appeared in China, and out of this diversity, through a rough process of trial and error, some responses emerged that proved successful. For example, while most of the domains were too small or too politically divided to react effectively, enough could to provide a variety of responses. Sharp class divisions had the same effect. While the samurai, with their feudal military background, showed a much keener appreciation of the superior military power of the West than did the Chinese civil bureaucracy, Japanese peasant entrepreneurs and city merchants, with their emphasis on personal economic goals, responded quickly to the new opportunities for foreign trade. The broad and functionally stratified samurai class, constituting around 6 per cent of the total population and including many men close to the grubby minor details of the economy and administration, also produced a much wider spectrum of responses than did the relatively narrow higher bureaucracy and elite of gentry degree-holders in China.

Another Japanese advantage was its extraordinary cultural homogeneity and economic and intellectual centralization. This was in part the result of Japan's geographic isolation and much smaller size in terrain and population than China. But homogeneity and centralization were even more the product of the whole Tokugawa system of control, particularly the institution of "alternate residence" of the lords at Edo. Unlike China, where inland areas were often quite unaware of the foreign threat, all parts of Japan responded immediately, even if in diverse ways. This situation, together with the relatively large size of the Japanese ruling class and the high levels of political administration and economic integration, which rising standards of living and high literacy rates had made possible, meant that Japan was far more capable than China of carrying out a unified, effective response to the West, once one had been decided upon.

Ironically, the very erosion of the foundations of the Tokugawa system also proved advantageous for the Japanese. In China, dynasties had come and gone, but the basic political, social, intellectual, and even economic system had remained extraordinarily stable for a millennium. It was hard to imagine, much less adopt, any other system. But in Japan the feudal social and political structure of the early seventeenth century was clearly outmoded by the nineteenth. The economy, society, and culture had evolved beyond it. Both the Confucian concept of the right of the man of personal merit to political leadership and the ancient Japanese tradition of imperial rule were fundamentally subversive to the Tokugawa polity. Thus other systems of political organization were not only imaginable but were secretly desired by some. There was a certain restiveness in society, particularly among the lower samurai. The rigid political structure was seriously undermined, and, beneath the surface calm, pressures were building up along dangerous fault lines within the society. A relatively light external blow thus could set Japan in motion in a way that much heavier blows could not move a basically far more stable China. As a consequence, Japan got off to a more speedy start in adjusting to the new world conditions, and this in turn gave it a decisive advantage during the following century.

The Emergence of the Imperial Court.   Abe had placed the shogunate in an anomalous position when he was forced to conclude the treaty with Perry against the expressed opinions of most of the daimyo and the known disapproval of the imperial court. To strengthen his position he took the novel step of having the court give formal sanction to the treaty. He also brought powerful collateral and "outside" daimyo into the inner councils of government, putting Nariaki of Mito in charge of coastal defenses.

The "house" daimyo, who traditionally dominated the Edo government, resented the role of these outsiders. Under Hotta Masayoshi, who replaced Abe late in 1855, they reduced Nariaki's influence and attempted to regain full control over the government. They also moved toward further concessions to the Western powers because, being more fully involved in the situation at Edo, they were more aware of Japan's serious plight than were the great lords from less exposed areas.

Before concluding the commercial treaty with Harris in 1858, Hotta again asked the daimyo for their opinions. Again the response was largely negative, even if somewhat more realistic than in 1853. Hotta also took the unprecedented step of going to Kyōto to obtain the emperor's approval in advance. But the imperial court was awakening from its long political slumber. The revived interest during the Tokugawa period in Japan's ancient history and the growing emphasis on the unbroken imperial line as the chief source of Japan's assumed superiority over other countries, had gradually called attention to the emperors and built up their prestige. Now both the shogunate and many of the domains were turning to Kyōto at this moment of crisis in the nation and uncertainty in Edo. Bolstered by the opposition of some of the largest domains to Hotta's policies, the court gave an ambiguous reply, which amounted to a refusal.

At this juncture, on May 30, 1858, Ii Naosuke, the lord of Hikone, the largest domain among the "house" daimyo, assumed the post of "great elder," the shogunal premiership which was filled only in times of crisis, usually by the head of the Ii family. Ii adopted a strong stance in an effort to regain control over the country. He signed the treaty, refused to go to

The first Tokugawa embassy sent abroad, in Washington in 1860.

Kyōto when summoned by the court, forced it to give its approval to the treaty, and decided a dispute over the shogun's heir in favor of the immature daimyo of the collateral domain of Wakayama over Nariaki's adult and able son, Keiki, who was the candidate of a faction that looked toward reform of the shogunate. When these acts were greeted by violent criticism and an upsurge of subversive, pro-emperor agitation, he responded by placing Nariaki, Keiki, and a few other major daimyo in domiciliary confinement, punished several court nobles and shogunal officials, and carried out a purge of pro-emperor intellectuals in Mito.

Ii's effort to restore Edo's authority seemed for a while to be succeeding, but it collapsed when a group of extremist Mito samurai assassinated him on March 24, 1860. It has been argued that, had Ii lived, the shogunate might have survived under his strong leadership to play a major role in Japan's subsequent modernization, but this seems improbable, because the shogunate, heavily burdened by tradition, was less capable of revolutionary change than were other groups. And Ii's reassertion of Tokugawa absolutism was more apparent than real. Actually, Edo's prestige and authority had both been greatly reduced. All over the country samurai activists were expressing their opinions freely on all matters of national policy. Despite long-standing prohibitions, daimyo and their agents, and even samurai acting on their own initiative, now felt free to approach the court in Kyōto to win it over to their views. Imperial sanction was becoming necessary for any major policy decision.

The imperial court thus emerged as the focus not only for opposition to Edo's foreign policies but for efforts to reform the government and society in the face of the foreign menace. The slogans of "honor the emperor" (*sonnō*) and "expel the barbarians" (*jōi*) became the twin rallying cries of the opposition. Both had strongly anti-shogunate overtones and were therefore taken up with particular enthusiasm by the samurai of some of the "outer" domains that had always nurtured resentment of Tokugawa rule. So strong was the appeal of these slogans that even Ii had been forced to give to the court vague promises that the "barbarians" would be expelled as soon as Japan was strong enough.

There was also a definite breakdown of feudal discipline as the domains began to assert their independence of Edo and restless samurai acted independently of their domain governments. Many samurai became "masterless samurai" in order to be free to agitate in Kyōto or elsewhere in behalf of the policies they supported. Known as *shishi,* or "men of determination," it was activists of this sort who killed Ii and went on to leave a wide trail of political assassination throughout Japan.

The shogunate was clearly in a hopeless position. Edo could not withstand foreign pressures for trade, yet was forced by public opinion to make promises to "expel the barbarians." Its authority over the domains and control over the individual samurai was fast ebbing. The shogunate had been forced to recognize the ultimate political authority of the imperial court. Both the political order and the economic system on which it stood were giving way under the Western impact. Ii had sought to shore up the tottering structure, and his death removed its last firm support.

The Rise of Satsuma and Chōshū.   No new "great elder" was appointed, and the shogunate floundered around indecisively. The initiative was lost to the imperial court and some of the "outer" domains. In particular Satsuma in southern Kyūshū and Chōshū at the western tip of Honshū came to the fore. They were among the largest domains, being ranked officially as the second and ninth in income. Their samurai forces were proportionately even larger, since both domains had been drastically reduced in geographic area but not in retainers as a result of the wars at the end of the sixteenth century.

Chōshū and Satsuma—particularly the latter—were relatively backward areas economically and socially, being located on the periphery of the nation, but this was an advantage rather than a handicap. It meant that the morale and cohesiveness of their samurai were less eroded than in the more advanced central parts of the country, where the bulk of Tokugawa power lay. They also had the advantage of strong anti-Tokugawa traditions dating back to their defeats more than two and a half centuries earlier. Mito, in contrast, being part of the Tokugawa power structure, faded from the political scene after the death of Nariaki in 1860, when the anti-Edo movement started to become truly revolutionary. Some other great domains were also inhibited from taking a strong stand because of traditional loyalty to the Tokugawa.

Another reason for the emergence of Satsuma and Chōshū was their financial strength at a time when most domains were seriously in debt and their samurai under heavy financial pressures. Satsuma and Chōshū had the money not only to bolster samurai morale but to buy Western arms and finance decisive action. Although in the early nineteenth century Satsuma had been burdened by a crushing debt, it had started vigorous reforms in 1830, at the very beginning of the so-called Tempō Reforms. It had canceled the domain's debts and strengthened its commercial monopolies, particularly of cane sugar, of which Satsuma, for climatic reasons, had a virtual monopoly in Japan. Both efforts had succeeded in large part because of the relative backwardness of the area.

Chōshū's Tempō Reforms had started in 1838 and had featured the reduction of samurai debts and the slashing of domain expenditures, in part through the reduction of monopolies, which was more typical of the Tempō Reforms than Satsuma's strengthening of monopolies. But the chief reason for Chōshū's financial solvency seems to have been an unusual institution known as the "nurturing office." Founded in 1762 as an emergency fund to help the domain's government and samurai in times of need, it had become an investment organ, particularly successful as a merchandiser of the surplus rice of the domain and as a storer of goods and provider of funds to other domains engaged in transport activities on the Inland Sea. By regularly investing part of the domain's revenues through this office, instead of devoting all its financial energies to repaying its debts, Chōshū stumbled into a system of deficit financing. Thus, during this period of creeping inflation, it profited from the gradual diminution of the value of its debt and the enhancement of the value of its investments.

Politics in Chōshū, as in many other domains, had become a matter of rivalries between samurai factions, which alternated in power by winning the support of the daimyo and his major retainers, the so-called house elders. In 1857 a moderate reform faction replaced the conservative faction in power and decided that Chōshū should take part in national politics. But it was not until 1861 that it took a specific step, proposing to the Kyōto court that the emperor should order the shogan to embark on a policy of "expansion across the seas," thus achieving a "union of court and shogunate" (*kōbu gattai*). Both Kyōto and Edo were agreeable, the one because the proposal was an open recognition of the emperor's political primacy, the other because it won the court's support for the shogunate's foreign policy.

Nothing, however, came of Chōshū's effort to mediate between Kyōto and Edo, and it was soon eclipsed by a more specific set of proposals for a "union of court and shogunate" put forward by Satsuma in May 1862. As a result, Satsuma was authorized by the court to bring order to Kyōto by suppressing the many extremist "masterless samurai" who were active there. It also persuaded Edo to make Keiki the guardian of the young shogun and appoint the collateral lord of Echizen, Matsudaira Keiei, as a sort of acting prime minister. Matsudaira, in an effort to win a broader national consensus, relaxed the last shogunate controls over the domains, abandoning the old hostage system and reducing the presence of daimyo at Edo under the "alternate attendance" system to a meaningless one hundred days every three years.

Meanwhile Chōshū had become more radically pro-emperor in its stance. This was largely because of the influence of a young teacher of military tactics, Yoshida Shōin (1830–1859). Yoshida had studied "Dutch Learning" in both Nagasaki and Edo and had been deeply influenced by the pro-emperor Mito thinkers. He had also attempted to smuggle himself out of the country on one of Perry's ships in 1854 but was imprisoned instead. Back in Chōshū, he opened a school and implanted his radically pro-emperor thoughts in a number of young men who were to play an important role in building the new Japan. Although he himself was executed in 1859 for having planned to assassinate the Edo representative in Kyōto, one of his disciples, a high-born samurai named Kido Kōin (1833–1877), became an important figure in the domain government and helped swing it toward an openly "honor the emperor" and "expel the barbarian" policy.

Because of Chōshū's new radicalism, the court shifted its support away from Satsuma to Chōshū, which started to organize a rudimentary government in Kyōto as well as small bodies of "imperial troops." Chōshū was supported for a while in its strong pro-emperor stand by Tosa, a major "outer" domain in Shikoku, but a more moderate Tosa faction regained control of the domain early in 1863 and adopted a more cautious policy. Swarms of activist "masterless samurai" in Kyōto, however, gave strength to the imperial cause by assassinating moderates, and meanwhile a body of some two thousand peasants, the so-called Heavenly Chastising Force, aroused by samurai radicals, attacked the shogunate authorities in the Nara area south of Kyōto.

The Resort to Military Force

Trials of Strength.   The Chōshū-dominated court induced the shogun in the spring of 1863 to come to Kyōto, where he was forced to set June 25, 1863, as the date when the "barbarians" would be expelled. This placed the shogunate in a humiliating position, because it was obviously unable to carry out this promise, but it also put Chōshū out on a limb. When the appointed day arrived, the shogunate did nothing, but the Chōshū forts along the Strait of Shimonoseki, at the western end of the Inland Sea, started to fire on foreign ships. In response, an American warship shelled the forts on July 16 and sank two Chōshū gunboats recently bought at Nagasaki, while four days later French warships sent ashore landing parties which destroyed the forts and their ammunition.

Chōshū's impractical foreign policy had undermined its prestige and alarmed other Japanese. On September 30, 1863, troops from Satsuma and Aizu, a collateral domain in northern Honshū, whose lord had been appointed by Edo to be the military governor of Kyōto, carried out a *coup d'état* at the court, driving the Chōshū forces out of the city. The long Tokugawa peace had at last been broken. A group of moderate nobles was put in control of the court, and its incipient government organs and "imperial troops" were disbanded. Early in 1864 six "outer" and collateral lords were made a body of "participating daimyo" to aid the court, but, lacking any unity of policies or effective administrative organs, they soon broke up in futility.

Since Chōshū had reconstructed its forts and continued to fire on Western vessels, a combined fleet of seventeen British, French, Dutch, and American ships demolished the forts again in September 1864. The Western powers then made Chōshū agree not to refortify the straits and extorted a promise of an indemnity of $3 million from the shogunate. Subsequently, in June 1866, the powers agreed to a postponement of the payment in return for various new trade concessions, including a drastic lowering of import duties from around 20 per cent to a mere 5 per cent.

Chōshū's repeated military defeats at the hands of the foreign powers forced its leaders to recognize the impracticality of their foreign policy. They also came to see the inadequacy of their military strength in the domestic contest. Chōshū troops had marched on Kyōto in the summer of 1864 but had been defeated on August 20 at one of the gates of the imperial palace by the forces of Satsuma and Aizu. It was clear that Chōshū would have to redouble its efforts to build up and modernize its military strength.

Chōshū had started to form rifle units in 1857, and in 1860 it had embarked on a program of purchasing Western ships and guns. In 1863 it began to form a peasant militia and to organize rifle units composed of both samurai and commoners, such as the famous Kiheitai ("Irregular Troops Unit"), and these programs were now expanded. The use of peasant soldiers was a revolutionary departure from the whole Tokugawa system— socially and politically as well as militarily. The new units were officered in large part by young extremists, including former disciples of Yoshida Shōin, and thus gave added strength in domain politics to the extremist faction and new routes to power for its humbler members. For example, two young samurai, Inoue Kaoru (1835–1915) and Itō Hirobumi (1841–1909), who two years after participating in the attack on the British legation in

Edo in 1861 had gone to England to study, rose to influence as commanders of two of the new mixed units and went on to become major figures in the modernization of Japan. In fact, Itō, who was a peasant by birth but the adopted heir of a family of the lowest samurai status, was to become perhaps the most important architect of the new government, illustrating by his career the large role of lowly but ambitious samurai in the revolutionary transformation of Japan.

Satsuma too had learned much the same lesson as Chōshū about the inadequacy of traditional Japanese military power. Following the assassination of the Englishman, Richardson, by Satsuma samurai in 1862, the British exacted an indemnity of £100,000 from the shogunate and subsequently sent a fleet to Kagoshima, the Satsuma capital, to force punishment of the culprits and the payment of an indemnity by the domain. The Satsuma forts fired on the British ships on August 15, 1863, and the latter responded by leveling much of the city. Satsuma ended up with an indemnity payment of £25,000, largely borrowed from the shogunate, and a profound respect for and interest in the British navy. It immediately set about procuring Western ships with British aid, thus laying the foundations for what was to grow into the Imperial Japanese Navy.

The Chōshū Wars.   The Chōshū attack on Kyōto in August 1864 induced the shogunate at last to take firm action, and it dispatched against Chōshū an army of 150,000 men made up of levies from a large number of domains. The series of disasters that befell Chōshū in 1864 discredited the reformist clique, and its conservative opponents, who had consistently opposed the policy of involving Chōshū in national politics, came back into power in November of that year. Faced with the overwhelming might of the shogunate, the conservatives capitulated on January 24, 1865, accepting the mild demands for an apology, the execution of three "house elders" held responsible for Chōshū's policies, and promises to return seven extremist court nobles who had fled to Chōshū and to disband the new mixed units that had attacked Kyōto. The leniency of the shogunate's terms were a reflection of its own weakness. The domains that made up its army were not willing to bear the costs of a long campaign, and some of them, like Satsuma, were not ready to see the shogunate's power enhanced through the complete elimination of Chōshū.

Although the Chōshū government bowed to the shogunate, the extremist leaders of the mixed rifle units were unwilling to see their base of power destroyed. They refused to disband their units, and even before Chōshū capitulated to the shogunate they started armed resistance against the domain government. Winning skirmish after skirmish, they finally seized the Chōshū capital on March 12 and set up with the reformist faction a coalition regime in which Kido proved to be the dominant figure. The victory of the mixed units in the Chōshū civil war was a turning point in Japanese social and military history. Samurai of humble birth had defied with impunity their domain government, and mixed peasant and samurai forces had proved superior to its aristocratic, class army.

The outcome of the civil war in Chōshū also nullified the results of the shogunate expedition against Chōshū. Edo, buoyed by its assumed success in the campaign, had ordered the restoration of the "alternate attendance" system, but the daimyo simply ignored its orders. Now the shogunate saw that it would have to start all over again to bring a rebellious Chōshū into line. When a year of maneuvering to build up support for its policies and overawe Chōshū into accepting its terms failed to produce results, it finally dispatched a second army against Chōshū in August 1866. But this time the shogunate lacked the military superiority it had enjoyed before. Its army was less well organized and less united in purpose. Satsuma and some other powerful domains refused to participate. And Chōshū was now more unified, led by more determined men, and militarily stronger, having in the meantime improved and standardized its weapons and reorganized the whole of its forces into modernized military units. Though outnumbered, the Chōshū soldiers outfought the shogunate army; some of the participating domains withdrew their support; and by October the shogunate was compelled to sue for peace.

The Collapse of the Shogunate.   A single domain had defied and defeated Edo. The end of the shogunate seemed only a matter of time, and its downfall was now hastened by the decision of Satsuma and Chōshū to cooperate with each other. The whole Tokugawa system depended on mutual antagonisms among the domains. Satsuma and Chōshū by tradition were as unfriendly toward each other as toward the shogunate, an attitude sharpened by their rivalry for leadership in Kyōto after 1861 and by Chōshū's more intransigent stand on foreign policy. But these differences gradually lessened, as Chōshū was forced toward Satsuma's more realistic approach to the "barbarian" problem and both came to feel greater fear of restored shogunate power than jealousy of each other. They began to see that a league of major domains under the emperor would be a more effective and safer political system for themselves and for Japan than any patched up union between the court, the domains, and the shogunate.

The Satsuma leaders, Ōkubo Toshimichi (1830–1878) and Saigō Takamori (1827–1877), a man of dominating personality though of lowly samurai birth, were becoming increasingly suspicious of the shogunate's intentions. Some Edo officials were advocating a policy of reform and military modernization to be followed by the complete crushing of Chōshū and the subsequent suppression of other domains, such as Satsuma. They were strongly backed by the French Minister, Léon Roches, who hoped for increased French influence through a restored shogunate. Through his efforts, a French school was opened at Yokohama, a naval dockyard was built at Yokosuka nearby, and large quantities of weapons were imported. Not to be outdone, the British Minister, Sir Harry Parkes, who had played a large role in opening China, supported Satsuma with information and arms, while Satsuma itself moved toward a rapprochement with Chōshū. Two pro-imperialist "masterless samurai" from Tosa, who had taken refuge in Satsuma and Chōshū from the moderates in their own domain, acted as intermediaries in bringing these two mutually suspicious and hostile domains together. Finally on March 7, 1866, Saigō and Ōkubo concluded with Kido in Kyōto a secret alliance.

Keiki, who had been the unsuccessful candidate for shogun a decade earlier, succeeded the young, childless shogun in January 1867 and immediately set about modernizing the shogunate's forces and reorganizing its administration. Late in 1866 he had tried to organize a council of leading daimyo, through which the shogunate would retain its primacy while surrendering its monopoly of power, but the effort failed when only five of the twenty-four invited daimyo came. Tosa now proposed that the shogun return his political power to the emperor and head a council of daimyo under the latter. This solution would have relieved the shogun of the burden of full responsibility for national and foreign affairs while leaving him his source of income and power—his personal domain which was at least seven times the size of the largest daimyo domain. Keiki accepted the proposal on November 8, 1867, but this "imperial restoration" came to naught when the other daimyo again ignored his invitation to join the council.

Meanwhile Satsuma and Chōshū had decided on more radical action. Through Iwakura Tomomi (1825–1883), a court noble with close associations with Ōkubo, they obtained an entirely irregular "imperial rescript," calling for the destruction of the shogunate. Then on January 3, 1868 (the ninth day of the twelfth month of 1867 according to the Japanese calendar), the Satsuma and Chōshū forces, aided by those of the collateral domains of Echizen and Nagoya and the "outer" domains of Tosa and of Hiroshima in West Honshū, seized the palace and announced another "imperial restoration."

Keiki was inclined to accept the results of this *coup d'état* and retreated with his troops from Kyōto to Ōsaka to avoid clashes with the "imperial forces." But some of the collateral and "house" daimyo and many of the officials in the shogunate were not prepared to acquiesce meekly to this power grab by their old rivals. The shogunate forces marched from Ōsaka on Kyōto but were defeated south of the capital on January 27. They outnumbered the "imperial forces," but once again victory went to the side with technological superiority.

*Satsuma soldiers fresh from victory in the war against the shogunate.
All wear Western-style uniforms and two have Western-style
haircuts, but they carry samurai swords. (Their rifles are not shown
in the picture.)*

The "imperial forces" then moved on Edo. Keiki, who himself came
originally from pro-imperialist Mito, decided to capitulate, but die-hard
shogunate supporters put up a fight in Edo, principally on July 4 at what
is now Ueno Park. Aizu in northern Honshū desperately resisted the "imperial forces" but was crushed by November. The Tokugawa navy, which
slipped out of Edo Bay, continued the fight in Hokkaidō. When it finally
surrendered in May 1869, the whole of Japan came under the control of
the revolutionaries.

The Creation of the New Government

The New Leadership.   The overthrow of the Tokugawa had proved relatively easy. While the shogunate was immobilized by its own inner divisions
and most of the rest of Japan, divided into units too small or too indecisive
to take effective action, stood by and watched, a handful of able young
samurai from Chōshū and Satsuma had gained control over their own domains and then, through a bold use of the power of these two domains, had
seized control over the whole nation with great speed and relatively little

bloodshed. But to transform this military victory into lasting political power was another matter.

In theory an "imperial restoration" had taken place on January 3, 1868, but this was largely a matter of symbolism. The Japanese were much too accustomed to figurehead emperors, shogun, and daimyo to return easily to personal imperial rule. Nor were the emperor and his court prepared for actual political leadership. The Emperor Kōmei, who had been a foe of the extreme pro-imperial faction, had died early in 1867, to be succeeded by his son Mutsuhito, then only fourteen. Mutsuhito, who reigned until 1912, was in time to grow into an impressive and possibly influential figure. Known as the Meiji emperor for the new "year period" of Meiji ("Enlightened Rule") adopted in 1868, he became the personal symbol of the modernization of Japan, and the great political change became known as the Meiji Restoration. But in 1868 he was obviously too young to rule, and he seems never to have been more than one among many determiners of policy. Nor were the courtiers around him, the descendants of the ancient Fujiwara aristocracy, able to guide the nation. Iwakura and a few others, controlling as they did the imperial source of legitimacy, did become powerful figures in the new government. But most of the courtiers continued in merely symbolic roles as before.

Since the extremists of southwest Japan had acted in the name of their respective daimyo, it was natural for these daimyo to figure in the new government, but their role too was largely symbolic, as it had usually been in their own domains, and in time they were dropped even from titular posts. The real leadership was largely in the hands of the samurai who had engineered the revolution, although it had to be exercised tactfully by them through layers of daimyo, court nobles, and the emperor. Such a cumbersome structure led to anonymity and vagueness in leadership, but it was a system long familiar to the Japanese.

The new leaders were a remarkably young group of men. Iwakura, the oldest, was forty-three in 1868. The three most powerful men of samurai origin, Kido, Ōkubo, and Saigō, ranged between thirty-five and forty-one while Itō was a mere twenty-seven. For the most part they were of relatively humble birth. Kido was among the few who might have attained local, but scarcely national, political leadership under the old system. Iwakura, though a court noble, could never have hoped for real political power, and most of the others could have been nothing more than petty functionaries or possibly scholars. Clearly they had few emotional commitments to the *ancien régime.* They also were obviously men of exceptional talent, resilience, and daring to have risen so rapidly to the top.

The New Policies.   The new leaders had two decided advantages over their predecessors. They were freer of the yoke of tradition and thus more capable

*The Meiji emperor as a young man and Ōkubo Toshimichi as a
leader in the Meiji government.*

of drastic innovation. More important, the turbulent fifteen years since the
coming of Perry had helped clarify what course Japan would have to take
to retain its independence. It was obviously impossible to "expel the
barbarians." Instead Japan would have to try to match Occidental military
power and industrial skills. Only then could it hope to be secure against
the West, regain control over its tariffs, and eliminate the other unequal
features of the treaties. It was also becoming clear that, before Japan could
match Occidental military and economic power, it would first have to
create a much more centralized and modern government and would have
to carry out major economic and social reforms.

   Already on April 8, 1868, the revolutionaries had the emperor issue a
"Five Articles Oath" (or "Charter Oath"), which indicated the course they
hoped to follow. One article stated that "deliberative assemblies shall be
widely established and all matters decided by public discussion." This was
probably not so much a promise to create democratic institutions, of which
the new leaders knew little, as an assurance that other samurai groups not
yet represented in the new government would not be frozen out. Two of
the articles promised a revolutionary break with the feudal class restrictions
of the past: "The common people, no less than the civil and military
officials, shall each be allowed to pursue his own calling so that there may
be no discontent"; "Evil customs of the past shall be broken off and everything based on the just laws of Nature."

   The last article propounded what was to prove the basic philosophy of
the whole effort: "Knowledge shall be sought throughout the world so as

to strengthen the foundations of imperial rule." Japan was to be modernized and strengthened through the use of Western knowledge, because the only defense against the West lay in the creation in modern form of the ancient Chinese ideal of "a rich country and strong military" (*fukoku kyōhei*), which could best be achieved through Western technology.

This was a surprisingly frank disavowal of the crude "expel the barbarian" concept with which most of the revolutionaries had started and which had helped them so much in their overthrow of the Tokugawa. But now that they were in power, this sort of simplistic xenophobia was an embarrassment, and they severely suppressed its continuing advocates. Would-be assassins of the British minister were treated as common criminals, and the leaders of friendly forces which clashed with French marines and sailors in Ōsaka early in 1868 were forced to commit suicide. The whole change in attitude was symbolized by an audience with the emperor arranged in March 1868 in Kyōto for the representatives of the foreign powers.

The Organs of Government.   It was easier to establish general policies than to carry them out. The new government had fallen heir to the position of the shogunate, which faced insoluble foreign problems, was financially bankrupt, had never exercised direct rule over most of Japan, and had lost much of the control it had once possessed. What organs of centralized government there were had been largely destroyed by the revolution. The new regime, like the old, was virtually powerless before Western military might, and the 5 per cent tariff rates imposed by the 1866 agreement left the country without economic defenses against the cheap manufactured goods of the West.

None of the new leaders had had any experience in operating a national regime, but by trial and error they evolved a system of government that worked, however makeshift its elements. On January 3, 1868, the day they assumed power in Kyōto, they created "three offices" to constitute the new government. On June 11, they reorganized the government under a Council of State, named after the ancient Grand Council of State and divided into legislative and executive branches, in apparent imitation of the division of powers in the American government. On August 15, 1869, the Council of State was reorganized with six ministries under it. Because of the archaic relationship between Shintō and the imperial family, however, it was outranked by an Office of Shintō Worship (actually the same name as the ancient Office of Deities). The old system of court ranks for government officials was also revived. Finally on September 13, 1871, the Council of State was divided into three chambers for legislative, administrative, and judicial functions, and the Office of Shintō Worship was realistically downgraded to the level of an ordinary ministry.

Such rapidly changing government bodies were less important than were the men who staffed them. The top posts, normally held by court nobles or daimyo, were largely symbolic. Attempts to draw into the administration the representatives of the various domains through representative assemblies, as promised in the "Five Articles Oath," proved unworkable, because the whole concept was not clearly understood, and the effort was abandoned after 1870. The important members of the government had proved throughout to be the samurai activists themselves, who usually filled the posts of Councilors and subordinate positions in the ministries. Gradually they moved up to positions of titular responsibility. This first happened in 1871 when Ōkubo became minister of finance, and by 1873 it had become the rule for the heads of ministries to be the young samurai who actually ran them.

Meanwhile the imperial capital had been moved to Edo, which had been the real political capital of Japan for two and a half centuries. On September 3, 1868, it was renamed Tōkyō ("Eastern Capital'"), and the next May the emperor was moved into the old shogunal castle, which thenceforth became the imperial palace.

The Centralization of Power.   Central organs of government did not themselves create centralized rule. To do this, the new government had to establish its authority over the more than 260 separate domains, which in theory were autonomous and some of which had become all but independent during the final years of the shogunate. The daimyo and the great bulk of the samurai in all the domains, including those who had engineered the "imperial restoration," were scarcely prepared to see their domains swallowed up into a new and more centralized form of government, but this is precisely what the new leaders achieved in an amazingly short time, and with great enhancement of their own power. This surprising turn of events was possible only because of three factors: the leaders saw clearly the need for a fully centralized government if Japan were successfully to resist the West; they were themselves already in control of the domains whose military power underlay the imperial government; and the other domains had no basis for unified action and, although unclear as to what was happening, were eager not to be left out in the great reshuffle of political power that was obviously underway.

The new government divided the shogun's territory into prefectures for administrative purposes, and from the start it asserted rights of taxation and control over the domains, making the administration of the domains approximate that of the prefectures and in 1869 abolishing the barriers on highways and custom duties some of the domains had maintained. The key move, however, came when Kido and Ōkubo persuaded their respective daimyo in Chōshū and Satsuma and also the lords of Tosa and Hizen (in Kyūshū) to return their domains to the emperor on March 5, 1869. Many other daimyo followed suit, not wishing to be discriminated against by the new government, and the remainder were ordered to do likewise in July. This "return of the *han* registers" was accomplished so easily because it was a largely symbolic act, and the daimyo, as expected, were reappointed as governors. The stage, however, was now set for the complete abolition of the domains on August 29, 1871. Most of the daimyo and samurai were thunderstruck, but all complied meekly. Confused, bankrupt, and divided by mutual suspicions, the domains could put up no effective resistance against the new government, which was able to command support from all over Japan by championing the now popular concepts of "imperial rule" and "national unity" in the face of the foreign menace. Thus the domains, some of which had existed as effective political units for three or more centuries, were wiped out at one bold stroke, and all of Japan was divided into three urban prefectures (*fu*) and seventy-two other prefectures (*ken*). The number was reduced to a total of forty-five in 1889—exclusive of Hokkaidō and the Ryūkyū Islands—and has remained unchanged since.

The leaders in Tōkyō saw clearly that military strength was a crucial factor not only for the central government's control over the nation but in the effort to defend Japan from the West. At the time of its victory over the shogunate, the new government had only a few small volunteer units under its direct control and had been forced to rely on the support of domain armies, principally those of Chōshū and Satsuma. A much larger and more centrally controlled military was an obvious necessity. In 1871 the government formed an Imperial Force of ten thousand men drawn from the domain armies of Satsuma, Chōshū, and Tosa and trained along French lines. Then in 1872 it divided the ministry of military affairs into army and navy ministries.

The new navy was made up of ships from the shogunate fleet and from the various domains but was largely officered by men from Satsuma, who were to dominate it for the next several decades. Meanwhile the new army came under the leadership of men from Chōshū, particularly Yamagata Aritomo (1838–1922). Born into a family of the lowest samurai rank in Chōshū, Yamagata had studied under Yoshida Shōin, had commanded the Kiheitai in the Chōshū civil war, and after a year of study in Europe had returned to Japan in 1870.

The most important military innovation came with the issuance on January 10, 1873, of a conscription law, carefully prepared by Yamagata, who soon thereafter became army minister. All men, regardless of social background, were made liable for three years of active military service followed by four in the reserves. Universal conscription which had been prefigured by the use of commoner volunteers in the mixed units in Chōshū a decade earlier, was probably the most revolutionary step in the modernization of Japan. For almost three centuries commoners had been denied the right even to possess swords. The whole class system had depended on the clear functional division between them and the samurai. Now the weaponless masses suddenly became the foundation of a greatly expanded and entirely centralized and modernized military system. Naturally it took several years to put universal conscription fully into effect, but as it gradually became a reality the new government established unchallengable control over the country.

Consolidating the New Regime

Finances. The ease with which the central government had pushed the domains into oblivion in 1871 is to be explained in part by the generous financial settlement it provided the feudal classes. The daimyo were particularly well treated. When they had been made governors over their old domains in 1869, they had been given one-tenth of the former domain taxes as their private income, and this they retained in 1871. Since the central government took over the costs of local government and the old domain debts, the daimyo were better off financially than before. The samurai were treated less well. Their stipends were continued, but reduced between 1869 and 1871 to about two-thirds of what they had been before.

It has been argued that the new government needlessly complicated its financial problems by paying off the daimyo and samurai so generously, but this is doubtful. The samurai class constituted around 6 per cent of the total population, or about ten times the percentage of the privileged classes in France at the time of the French Revolution, and it would have been difficult and dangerous to attempt to dispossess so large a group that had long monopolized the martial arts and political leadership. Moreover, loyalty to the daimyo remained strong, and the new leaders were themselves mostly men of samurai origin with close ties to their own daimyo and domains. A less generous settlement might not have been possible in the early 1870's. As we shall see, the new government, as it grew stronger, did reduce the terms of its settlement to the point where serious revolts resulted. Actually, the government seems to have steered a successful course between the twin perils of financial bankruptcy and the danger of pushing the daimyo and samurai to unified rebellion or creating, as in France, a permanent resistance by supporters of the *ancien régime*.

There is no denying, however, the serious financial plight of the new government. It had no sources of revenue beyond those that had proved inadequate for the shogunate and domains, but it was burdened with the costs of the campaigns it had fought to come to power, the accumulated debts and indemnities of the shogunate and domains, and many new costs involved in trying to modernize the country, as well as the normal expenses of government and the payments to the daimyo and samurai. Little help could be expected from custom duties because of their limitation to 5 per cent in the agreement of 1866, which had also saddled Japan with an expensive program of building lighthouses and setting out buoys and lightships.

Today technologically backward regimes can often count on financial aid from abroad in the form of loans on easy terms or outright grants, but this was unthinkable in the nineteenth century. The Japanese, in their fear of Western encroachments, were reluctant to place themselves under the financial wing of any foreign nation, and the Western nations and bankers, looking upon Japan as a poor risk, required especially high interest rates and firm guarantees. Except for loans floated in London in 1869 to finance railroad construction and in 1872 to help cover the costs of the liquidation of the domains, borrowing abroad was not important in financing the new government.

The seriousness of the government's financial situation can be seen from the fact that receipts in 1868 were hardly more than a third of expenditures, and more than a third of these were in the form of forced loans, which, in the fashion of the shogunate, the new government exacted from the great merchant houses. The situation was only a little better in 1869, and the government had to resort to issuing large quantities of paper notes, which naturally fell in value and contributed to an already chaotic currency situation left over by the previous regime. But in the early 1870's the government's financial position improved. As it got full control over the country, its tax income rose to 60 per cent of expenditures by 1872, and, more important, confidence in its future increased so greatly within Japan that the government had little difficulty in borrowing what it needed domestically.

Meanwhile Tōkyō was carrying out a series of monetary, banking, and tax reforms, which helped stabilize its financial position. The prime movers in these reforms were Ōkuma Shigenobu (1838–1922), a Hizen samurai of iconoclastic temperament who became vice-minister of finance in 1869, and Itō, who had been sent to the United States to study currency systems and served as his assistant. The two set up a modern mint, adopted the American system of national banking, which never worked well in Japan and was subsequently abandoned, and established a uniform decimal currency in 1871 with the *yen* as its unit.

In July 1873, a few months before Ōkuma became minister of finance, a thorough revision of the agricultural tax system was begun. The land tax was the chief source of government income, constituting as late as 1880 four-fifths of all tax revenue. Before the tax reforms of 1873, agricultural taxes had been figured as percentages of agricultural yields, as they had been in feudal times, but, since the amount paid varied with the harvest, government budgeting had been difficult. Hence in 1873 these percentages were changed to a fixed tax in money based on land values. With the intention of taking half of the productivity of the land as taxes, the government at first set the tax at 3 per cent of assessed land values, but when this proved unrealistically high, it reduced the tax in 1876 to 2.5 per cent.

To carry out the new tax system, the ownership of all land had to be clearly established. This was done in 1872. Hitherto cultivators, feudal lords, and in many cases an in-between group of nonfeudal landlords had all had rights to the land, but now it was established that the man who paid the taxes, usually a cultivator or landlord, was the owner. Thus in modern Japan, unlike most of postfeudal Europe, there were no remaining feudal estates, but there was considerable tenancy from the start. The fixed money taxes contributed to an increase in tenancy, because in years of bad harvest poorer peasants could not meet these fixed payments and had to mortgage their land. About a quarter of the land was farmed by tenants even before the change in the tax system, and this figure shot up to 40 per cent in the next two decades and to 45 per cent by 1908.

The Abolition of Feudal Privileges. The young samurai leaders, who had themselves risen to power in defiance of feudal restrictions, had promised in the "Five Articles Oath" to remove feudal social limitations, and they lived up to this promise with remarkable speed. They abolished class restrictions on professional fields of activity in 1869 and the next year permitted commoners to assume family names. In 1871 even the *eta* and other outcast groups, who at the time constituted between 1 and 2 per cent of the population, were given full legal equality, although social discrimination against them remains strong even today.

The samurai were still distinguished from commoners, but their separate classification carried no legal privileges and in time became a matter of only historical interest. Some of the abler samurai became officials in the new government, but most lost their functional positions in society when the domains were abolished and the military was turned from a closed class profession into a mass conscript system. Their pride was further hurt when they lost their distinctive badge of prestige. In 1871 they were permitted to discard the long and short swords they traditionally wore, and in 1876 they were ordered to do so.

Another serious blow was their loss of economic privilege. Even before 1868 most had eked out only an impoverished existence on their small stipends, and these had been reduced considerably since then. In 1873 the government offered the poorer samurai the option of a final lump-sum payment, and in 1876 it commuted into government bonds all samurai stipends on a sliding scale that gave proportionately more to the poorer samurai. On average the samurai received only 264 *yen* apiece, roughly half the value of their already reduced stipends. Most of them, unable to adjust to the new conditions, sank into poverty and disappeared as a class. The financial settlement with the daimyo at this time was again much more generous. The government bonds they received in 1876 in lieu of further annual payments made them relatively wealthy capitalists and the source of a large proportion of the banking capital of the period.

These swift social and economic changes naturally were not accomplished without considerable turmoil. More capable and enterprising persons were able to find enticing new opportunities, but most people found it difficult to adjust. A large proportion of the big urban merchant firms, accustomed to privileged patronage from the shogunate and domains, went bankrupt. Many peasants were bitterly opposed to the fixed monetary tax and to conscription, which was defined as a "blood tax." Peasant uprisings, which had doubled in number during the troubled last years of the shogunate, became even more frequent after 1868, rising to a crescendo in 1873 following the conscription law. But disaffection among former samurai was, of course, a much more serious threat and a matter of far greater concern to the new leaders than urban unrest or peasant disturbances. They made special efforts to settle indigent samurai on new lands as farmers or to absorb them into the government, the military, and the new industries.

Foreign Policy.   To some of the more traditional new leaders, foreign wars seemed a solution to the problem of samurai unemployment and a means of restoring feudal military virtues. Korea had insultingly rebuffed Japanese efforts to modernize relations between the two countries and modify the treaty of 1606 under which trade had been conducted at Pusan on the south coast of Korea by the Sō, the daimyo of Tsushima. Taking advantage of this situation, the group in charge of the government in the summer of 1873 decided on a military expedition to chastise Korea.

This decision had been made possible by the absence from Japan of many of the stronger and more enlightened members of the government. In November 1871 Iwakura had led abroad a mission of forty-eight members to see the West at first hand and persuade the foreign powers to modify the unequal treaties inherited from the shogunate. Two other leading figures in the administration, Kido and Ōkubo, and a number of rising stars such as Itō had gone with Iwakura. The Iwakura Mission went first to the United States and then to various countries in Europe. Although it proved of great educational benefit to its members, it failed completely to induce the Western powers to modify the treaties.

While Iwakura and the others were abroad, the government had been left largely in the hands of Ōkuma, Saigō, who had been the chief general in the campaigns of 1868, and Itagaki Taisuke (1837–1919), a Tosa soldier-samurai who had become disgruntled by the predominance of men from Satsuma and Chōshū in the new government. These three made the decision for a Korean campaign, but Iwakura and his colleagues, who re-

Saigō Takamori.

turned to Japan in September 1873 fully conscious of Japan's weakness as compared with the West, were appalled at the plan and managed to have it overruled. This split the ruling group, and Saigō and Itagaki resigned in disgust.

To mollify the defeated party, a less hazardous expedition was agreed upon. The Ryūkyū Islands, inhabited by a people who in language and culture are a variant of the Japanese, had their own line of kings, who for centuries had been tributary to China but since 1609 had been tightly controlled vassals of the daimyo of Satsuma. In 1872 the Tōkyō government had extended its control over the islands, and now it decided to send a punitive expedition of thirty-six hundred men against the aborigines of the east coast of Taiwan for having killed fifty-four shipwrecked Ryukyuans in 1871. The expedition was successfully accomplished in 1874 but raised a diplomatic crisis with China. Peking, unaware of the niceties of Western international law, settled the dispute by paying Japan an indemnity for the costs of the expedition and for the murdered Ryukyuans, thus recognizing in Western eyes Japan's claims to the islands, which in 1879 were made Okinawa Prefecture, named for the largest island.

Relations with Korea were settled by borrowing a page from Perry's book. The Japanese made a show of naval power in 1875 and, after a brief military encounter, forced the Koreans to sign the Treaty of Kanghwa on February 27, 1876. Two ports were opened to Japanese trade in addition to

Pusan, where Japanese already resided, and Korea's independence was asserted, though China continued to claim suzerainty.

The Suppression of Samurai Opposition.   The Taiwan expedition and other measures did little to relieve the financial plight of most samurai, some of whom began to resist the new policies by force of arms. The outbreaks occurred principally in the domains in western Japan from which the new leadership had largely been drawn, perhaps because the samurai there were not much awed by these new upstart leaders who had once been their own comrades. A mutiny occurred among the mixed units of Chōshū as early as 1870. When Saigō resigned from the government in 1873, a large proportion of the Satsuma soldiers in the new imperial forces returned with him to Satsuma, leaving the central army all the more in the hands of Chōshū men. In February 1874, two thousand former samurai of Hizen, under the leadership of Etō Shimpei, a disillusioned member of the new government, rose in revolt and seized the domain capital of Saga. Smaller revolts followed in various parts of Kyūshū and in Chōshū in 1876.

The most serious samurai uprising, however, occurred in Satsuma. There discontented samurai had clustered around Saigō, and hotheads among them forced him in January 1877 into the position of leading an armed revolution against the government he had done so much to create. Saigō's forces at their height numbered around forty thousand, but Tōkyō sent against them all its military power—the new conscript army, the navy, and the national police force, which had been built up mainly of former samurai as a major bulwark of the central government. In bloody fighting the Satsuma forces were finally crushed, and in September Saigō and his chief lieutenants met their end. The peasant army, backed by better weapons and superior transport facilities, had won the day. Once again modernized organization and technological superiority had proved decisive. Saigō himself became in retrospect the most popular and romantic hero of the Meiji Restoration, but his defeat spelled the end of the old order. The new government had met its last great domestic challenge. Henceforth it could push ahead to modernize Japan and build up its power against the outside world, free of any fear that reactionary forces would overthrow it at home.

18. Modernization in Meiji Japan

Economic Development

The Roles of the Government and the People. The new leaders, even when struggling with the problems of creating a centralized administration and staving off attacks by outraged samurai, never lost sight of the need to develop a "rich country" if Japan were to have the "strong military" that could win it equality with the West. They approached the problem of modernizing Japan's economy and society with remarkable breadth of understanding and openness of mind. They could expect no foreign aid, but they were at least free of foreign ideologies of modernization. In contrast to the often unrealistic assumptions of the twentieth century, no one in Japan or abroad thought that the Japanese should or could suddenly convert their feudal society into a full-fledged democracy or their backward agricultural economy into a fully industrialized one. The lower level of expectations permitted a much more pragmatic, step-by-step approach to the problem than is common in developing countries today.

Perhaps in part because of this sounder approach, the results were more spectacular and came more quickly than anyone could have foreseen. Within a mere half-century, the Meiji leaders achieved their goals, creating a relatively sound and modernized economy, on the basis of which Japan was able to win the national security and equality they longed for. In terms of their own objectives, their achievements constitute the national Cinderella story of modern times, even though, as in Bismarckian Germany, their emphasis on military power and national, as opposed to individual, prosperity bequeathed serious problems to later generations.

513

The question of the respective roles of the government and people in the economic development of Meiji Japan is of special interest today, when the proper balance between the two is an issue in many developing countries. In Japan, the government provided a favorable environment for economic growth by removing feudal restrictions on trade within the country and on individual activities, by assuring internal stability, and by providing sound currency, adequate banking facilities, a reasonable tax system, and efficient government services. It also took a direct role in industrial development. It pioneered many industrial fields and sponsored the development of others, attempting to cajole businessmen into new and risky kinds of endeavor, helping assemble the necessary capital, forcing weak companies to merge into stronger units, and providing private entrepreneurs with aid and privileges of a sort that would be considered corrupt favoritism today. All this was in keeping with Tokugawa traditions that business operated under the tolerance and patronage of government. Some of the political leaders even played a dual role in politics and business. Inoue of Chōshū, for example, became a sort of arbiter of the affairs of the great house of Mitsui.

Still, all these efforts would have meant little if there had not been an eager response by thousands of private Japanese to the new economic opportunities. In the long run, it was private initiative that produced the bulk of Japan's economic modernization and growth. A host of petty entrepreneurs appeared and also exceptional men who dared to experiment on a large scale with modern Western techniques of economic organization.

Although private individuals at first showed reluctance to enter the hazardous and little understood field of machine production, which grew in any case only very slowly, they responded vigorously to the opportunities created by foreign trade and the new government policies in the more traditional areas of the economy. As a consequence, during the first two decades of the Meiji period, growth in agriculture, commerce, and traditional forms of manufacturing quite overshadowed the development of new industries. In the decade of the 1880's alone agricultural acreage increased by 7 per cent and average yields per acre by 21 per cent. Total agricultural production doubled in the next twenty-five years. The economy as a whole thus developed a sound foundation for the modern industries which the government sought to foster at the top of the economic pyramid. This was probably one of the chief reasons for the difference between Japan's subsequent rapid industrialization and the less successful efforts in China and other Asian countries, where modern industry initiated from the top often sank into the quagmire of a stagnant local economy.

Early Industrialization. Regardless of the growth of the traditional economy, however, modern industry was still essential to Japan if it was to

Train on the Tōkyō-Yokohama railway, a favorite subject for early Meiji woodblock artists.

withstand the Western menace. The government leaders were particularly interested in developing the strategic industries on which modern military power depended. The shogunate and some of the stronger domains, such as Hizen, Mito, and Satsuma, had led the way in borrowing Western technology to smelt iron and cast cannon. They had also started to build Western-style ships, and by the time of the Restoration the shogunate and domains together possessed 138 such vessels, either built in Japan or bought abroad. They had also started to master Western navigational techniques. In 1860 the shogunate had been able to send an entirely Japanese-manned steamer, the *Kanrin-maru,* across the Pacific to accompany a shogunate embassy to the United States.

The new government inherited from the shogunate two modern shipyards, at Yokosuka and Nagasaki, and added another at Hyōgo (the modern Kōbe). It also operated large factories in Tōkyō and Ōsaka for making cannon, rifles, and ammunition, and three small gunpowder plants. Though Western models were used, foreigners themselves were not employed in these five arsenals for security reasons.

The government also took the lead in developing modern communications, because of the public nature of this undertaking and its great cost. Internal transportation within Japan was extremely backward and expensive since there were few navigable rivers or good roads. It was said to cost as much to move goods fifty miles inside Japan as all the way from Europe. Consequently, railways, once constructed, proved immensely profitable.

A nineteen-mile line was laid between Yokohama and Tōkyō in 1872, and a similar line from Kōbe to Ōsaka, completed in 1874, was extended to Kyōto in 1877. Telegraph lines, which were cheaper to construct and important for administrative control over the nation, linked all the major cities by 1880.

The nonstrategic industries had to be developed too if Japan was to compete successfully with the West and eliminate the dangerous imbalance that had developed in its foreign trade. Actually a silk blight in Europe in the 1860's had produced such a strong demand for Japanese silk and silk-worm eggs that Japan enjoyed a favorable balance of trade for a decade, but the recovery of the European silk industry and the lowering of tariffs in 1866 combined to produce large deficits after 1869. The imbalance was heightened by charges for shipping, insurance, and other services the Japanese were still too inexperienced to provide. The inflow of foreign manufactured goods disrupted many handicraft industries on which peasants depended for much of their livelihood, and the outflow of specie undermined the value of paper money and credits, thus contributing to the economic plight of the samurai. New industries were desperately needed to stem the inflow of foreign goods and give employment to peasants and samurai.

The government established a ministry of industry in December 1870. The next year Itō took charge of it as vice-minister and in 1873 became minister, remaining in this key post until 1878. The ministry encouraged the private development of manufacturing and industries through technical assistance, easy credit, and subsidies, but the results were meager, and many of the new ventures went bankrupt. Capital was scarce and interest rates as a result high, usually above 10 per cent. Moreover, the Japanese themselves had had little experience with machinery, and foreign technicians were inordinately expensive.

The government, therefore, became increasingly involved in industrial and mining ventures. By 1873 its bureau of mines employed thirty-four foreigners. In 1874 it bought out a coal mine started in 1869 by Hizen with English technical and financial aid, and it went on to develop eight other modern coal mines and invested heavily in a modern iron mine in 1881. It also built a machine tool factory in 1871, a cement plant in 1875, a glass factory in 1876, and a brick factory in 1878, all in Tōkyō. Most Japanese coal, iron, and copper mines, however, remained unmodernized and in private hands, although private capital did introduce modern methods into such relatively simple processes as match and paper making.

The Textile Industry.   The most important industrial field was textiles, since these made up half of Japan's imports between 1868 and 1882.

Woolens had become significant for the first time in Japan because soldiers and government functionaries now wore Western-style woolen uniforms and many other men were adopting Western dress. Since this was an entirely new industry for Japan, the government was forced to develop it itself, building a mill in 1877–1878, which remained the chief producer until after 1900.

Cotton yarn and goods constituted a much bigger industry. In attempting to compete with foreign production, however, domestic manufacturers found themselves handicapped by a more costly and inferior local cotton fiber, and eventually the Japanese were forced to give up growing cotton. The industry also lacked mechanical experience and adequate capital for the large scale of production needed to make costs competitive with those of the West. As a result, the government was forced to play a large role initially. An Edo merchant had ordered American spinning machinery as early as 1864, and Satsuma set up a textile factory with British spindles and looms in 1868 and built another in Osaka in 1870. The latter was taken over in 1872 by the government, which also built two other mills in 1880 and 1881. A more important step was the creation in 1878 of a fund of 10 million yen to provide loans on easy terms to private entrepreneurs. As a result, private interests began to move cautiously into the cotton textile field.

Silk reeling, on the other hand, was mechanized with relative ease, and the government's role was limited to providing technical advice and operating a few pilot plants. Turning the silk reel by steam or water power, which produced much finer silk than reeling by hand, was a simple process requiring only modest capital, while all the other steps in silk filature remained hand processes at which the Japanese were already expert.

The first mechanical silk-reeling plant was established in 1870 by a collateral daimyo in the silk-producing area of central Honshū, and the government established three pilot plants between 1872 and 1877. Government plants, however, accounted for only a tiny fraction of mechanical silk reeling in Japan. The rest was developed by private entrepreneurs. The house of Ono built a silk-reeling plant in Tōkyō late in 1870 and seven more in 1872–1873. Local businessmen in the silk-producing areas of central Honshū followed suit. By 1880 some 30 per cent of Japanese silk exports were machine-reeled products which outclassed the hand-reeled silk of the rest of Asia and competed well with European silk. Silk accounted for some 43 per cent of Japanese exports, and, chiefly because of the brisk demand for it abroad, Japan's foreign trade began to show a favorable balance in the mid-1880's. Thus the industry that contributed most to the balancing of foreign trade was developed almost completely by private capital and enterprise.

The Development of Hokkaidō.   Japan's only unexploited frontier was in Hokkaidō, and its development seemed important to the Meiji leaders for both economic and strategic reasons. The Japanese had exercised some control over this cold, inhospitable island since about the eleventh century, but in the early nineteenth century the Japanese population was still limited chiefly to the coast and the extreme south, while the rest of the island and the small ones to the north were inhabited for the most part by Ainu aborigines. The Japanese, however, had surveyed and mapped the islands and waters north of Hokkaidō and were exploiting their fisheries.

Because of the opening of Hakodate to foreign ships through the Treaty of Kanagawa in 1854, the shogunate took over direct control of Hokkaidō from the Matsumae daimyo, as it had on certain previous occasions. It also agreed in 1855 to Russian demands for a rough delimitation of the northern boundary, with Kunashiri and Etorofu, the two large southern islands in the Kurils, assigned to Japan and the two countries continuing their joint occupation of Sakhalin. A clearer settlement of the northern boundary was reached in 1875 when Japan ceded its interests in Sakhalin in return for Russia's relinquishment of its claims to the central and northern Kurils.

The new government embarked on an ambitious program of colonizing Hokkaidō. In 1869 it gave the island its present name, meaning "Northern Sea Circuit" (previously it had been known as Ezo, meaning "barbarian"), and it created a Colonization Office under a Satsuma samurai, Kuroda Kiyotaka (1840–1900). Kuroda in 1870 went to the United States, where, on President Grant's advice, he hired the United States Commissioner of Agriculture, Horace Capron, at the princely salary of $10,000 plus expenses, and a staff of American experts to advise on the development of Hokkaidō. Remaining in Japan until 1875, these men left an unmistakably American cast—dairy herds and silos—to the rural landscape of Hokkaidō.

Between 1869 and 1881 the population of Hokkaidō more than quadrupled, reaching 240,391, agricultural acreage increased more than tenfold, and the fishing industry more than doubled. In 1883 the island was given a normal prefectural system of local government, though it continued to be called a "circuit" (*dō*), rather than a prefecture (*ken*). By 1918 a further tenfold increase in population had taken place, and Hokkaidō had become securely Japanese and an important part of the economy.

Financial Retrenchment.   The development of Hokkaidō, though valuable in the long run, added to the financial drain on the central government during the 1870's. Meanwhile the government's many industrial enterprises were for the most part losing money. These costs on top of the heavy expenses for liquidating the old regime, especially the bond payments of 1876 and the Satsuma Rebellion the next year, severely strained the government's financial credit. By 1880 its paper currency had fallen to hardly more than half its face value, and a serious inflation had set in. Rice prices more than doubled between 1877 and 1880, and inflation drastically cut the real value of the fixed land tax on which government finances depended.

In the face of this financial crisis, the government decided on a policy of economic retrenchment and deflation. The first major step, announced on November 5, 1880, was the sale of all nonstrategic government industries. A prime advocate and the chief executor of this retrenchment policy was Matsukata Masayoshi (1835–1924), a Satsuma man of humble samurai origin, who was appointed minister of finance in 1881 and remained in that key post until 1892.

Because of the weakness of private capital and the unprofitability of most government industries, Tōkyō had difficulty in finding buyers for its industrial ventures and eventually had to dispose of most of them at very reduced rates, ranging between 11 and 90 per cent of the original investments. Most were sold, sometimes without competitive bids, to insiders, that is, to businessmen or government officials already closely associated with the leaders. As Japan's industrialization began to overcome its initial handicaps in the next few years and return handsome profits, particularly on the basis of the reduced prices at which the government industries had been bought, the few who had been in a position to purchase these enterprises grew wealthy and came to control a large share of Japan's modernized economy. All this contributed to the eventual concentration of much of Japanese industry in the hands of a few giant corporations—the zaibatsu, or "financial cliques," as they were later called pejoratively.

This outcome of the retrenchment policy has given rise to Marxist interpretations that the chief motive for the sale of government industries was the commitment of the government leaders to large-scale capitalism. There is no real evidence for this theory, however, and it assumes an understanding by the Japanese leaders of the long-range effects of their actions and a preference for capitalism over government ownership that seem altogether improbable. All the contemporary documents show that the political leaders were desperately trying to cut government expenditures, and the sale of the industries was but one aspect of a drastic reduction in the budget. Their favoring of insiders is also understandable. They were interested primarily in the nation's economic growth. Selling the industries at reasonable prices to men they felt were competent seemed the best way to ensure their continued development. This was far more important to the national interest than the payment the government received. As it turned out, most of the industries sold did not for a decade or more make profits comparable to the return in other economic fields. The purchasers' faith in the future of industry in Japan is, in fact, more surprising than the low prices they paid.

Matsukata's retrenchment policies were successful, and by 1886 he had the government back on an even financial keel. New taxes were instituted,

and a centralized, European-style banking system, under the newly founded
Bank of Japan, was substituted in 1882 for the earlier American system.
The whole economy, too, although temporarily depressed by the deflationary
policies, soon recovered and surged ahead even more rapidly than before.
Deflation had weeded out the unsound speculative ventures that had
flourished under the inflationary conditions of the late 1870's, leaving only
the sounder enterprises. These profited from the return to hard money and
the drop in interest rates from around 15 per cent to around 10. Private
management of the former government industries, being free from cumbersome bureaucratic control, seems also to have been more efficient. The
Japanese were in the meantime beginning to overcome initial handicaps,
such as the high cost of internal transport and inexperience with machinery.
In short, Japan was ready for an industrial "breakthrough"—at least in
certain fields.

The Business Community.   The men who led the rapid development of the
Japanese economy in the next few decades were as remarkable a group as
the Meiji political leaders themselves and in many ways much like them.
They too were obviously men of exceptional talent, flexibility, and daring
to have emerged so successfully from the economic confusion of the preceding years. Like the political leaders, they were often motivated as much by
patriotism as by personal ambition. They realized that they too were
strengthening the country and establishing its security. The government
leaders concurred, and society accorded them a surprising degree of respect
and prestige, considering the traditional Japanese contempt for economic
activities.

One might suppose that the urban merchants, who had so dominated
the culture as well as the economy of the late Tokugawa period, would
have comprised the bulk of the new business leadership, but their role
actually was relatively small. Their past experience of subservience to the
shogunate and domains seems to have inhibited them from developing new
entrepreneurial skills. They stuck for the most part to traditional merchandising and banking activities. Those who attempted to branch out into
new fields often went bankrupt, as happened to the houses of Shimada and
Ono. The once great house of Kōnoike survived but gradually lost ground.

Among the bigger concerns, only the house of Mitsui made the transition
with complete success. This it did under the leadership of Minomura
Rizaemon (1821–1877), an orphan of obscure origin, whose appointment
as general manager was unprecedented in Mitsui history. He established a
close relationship with Inoue, moved the firm from Kyōto to Edo, sent five
members of the Mitsui family and two employees to the United States to
study modern business methods, and separated the rest of the firm from its
merchandising branch, which in time was modernized into Mitsukoshi, one

of Tōkyō's great department stores. Mitsui eventually developed into the
largest of the zaibatsu firms. The third largest zaibatsu company, Sumitomo,
also grew out of an old merchant firm, which like Mitsui dated back to the
seventeenth century but had specialized in copper mining.

Men of samurai background played a much larger role in developing the
new economy than did the urban merchants. This may seem strange in view
of the traditional samurai contempt for business and the profit motive, but
it can be explained by samurai traditions of leadership, their high standards
of education, the tremendous interest in economic problems among samurai
intellectuals during the second half of the Tokugawa period, the managerial
skills some samurai had developed as domain or shogunate officials, and the
severe financial difficulties in which most samurai found themselves in the
1870's.

In the large samurai class, however, it was only a few rather untypical
figures who distinguished themselves as successful businessmen. The more
affluent samurai, together with the daimyo, provided much of the new
banking capital out of their government bond payments, but the banks
were closely supervised by the government and did not represent significant
samurai entrepreneurial activity. Actually most of the many companies
founded by samurai failed because of their business inexperience.

The most outstanding example of a successful samurai entrepreneur was
Iwasaki Yatarō (1834–1885). He had been the supervisor of Tosa's
mercantile operations in Nagasaki and, after the dissolution of the domain,
managed to make its commercial and shipping interests his private firm,
subsequently named Mitsubishi. He was much favored by the government,
which saw in him a person who could develop a Japanese shipping line
that would eliminate dependence on foreign ships. During the Taiwan
expedition of 1874 the government had him operate the thirteen ships it
had bought and subsequently gave them to him. He was again put in
charge of marine transportation during the Satsuma Rebellion and was
given nine more ships. His line began to operate abroad in 1879, and
eventually Mitsubishi grew to be the second largest of the zaibatsu.

Even men of peasant origin became important business leaders. The
lowering of the land tax in 1876, together with the continuing inflation,
brought the tax burden in rural Japan below what had been normal levels.
This resulted in considerable rural prosperity and a chance for the wealthier
peasants to invest in agricultural improvements and in expansion of their
traditional industrial and commercial enterprises. The mechanization of silk
reeling, for example, was largely the work of enterprising peasants. Others
ventured further afield. Yasuda Zenjirō (1838–1921) ran away from his
peasant home to Edo, where he became a successful banker and the founder
of the fourth largest zaibatsu firm. Another man of rural origin, Asano
Sōichirō (1848–1930), acquired control and then ownership of the cement

factory that the government had built and turned this hitherto financially disastrous undertaking into a great success.

The most outstanding businessman of peasant origin was Shibusawa Eiichi (1840–1931). Born near Edo into a rich peasant family engaged in the indigo-dyeing business, Shibusawa was given a good education and developed great ambitions. He left home in 1863, determined to achieve samurai status, became enrolled as a samurai under Keiki, and accompanied Keiki's younger brother to Europe on an official mission in 1867. After Keiki's abdication, Shibusawa started a banking and trading company for his former lord but was soon drafted to serve in the new central government. Under the patronage of Ōkuma and Inoue he rose rapidly, becoming one of the major figures in the finance ministry. However, he resigned from the government in 1873 and became president of the First National Bank, which he had helped found by forcing Mitsui and Ono banking interests into a merger. In 1880 he organized the Ōsaka Spinning Mill, which soon became Japan's first major industrial success. From this beginning he went on to become one of the nation's greatest entrepreneurs, having a hand in the creation and management of more than a hundred companies.

Industrial Success.   Under the leadership of men of this sort, Japanese industry began to overcome its initial handicaps and to grow at an accelerating pace. Shibusawa's Ōsaka Spinning Mill spearheaded the new industrial advance. It was much larger than earlier mills, thus cutting overhead costs, and Shibusawa had trained a young man in England to run it with the most up-to-date techniques. The mill had already proved a great financial success by 1884, in the midst of the deflationary depression. In the next few years there was a rush of entrepreneurs into the spinning industry, particularly in Ōsaka, the old center of the cotton trade.

The boom in spinning was followed by a more general boom. New firms prospered in such diverse fields as mining, weaving, cement, beer, chinaware, gas, and electricity, but the greatest growth came in cotton spinning and railway transportation. Between 1883 and 1890, government railways expanded from 181 to 551 miles and private railways from 63 to 898 miles. Cotton spindleage almost tripled between 1882 and 1887 and production grew tenfold in the next five years. By 1894 the Japanese spinning industry had become so efficient that its products began to venture into the world market on a significant scale, and in 1897 Japan became a net exporter of cotton yarn. By the end of the century cotton spinning and weaving employed 247,117 persons, or 63 per cent of all factory workers.

The 1880's also saw the emergence of a trend toward mergers and cartel-like organization among Japanese business concerns, in place of sharp competition. Such trends have been common in mature industrial economies but perhaps appeared so early in Japan because of the government's eagerness for economic efficiency and the long tradition among Tokugawa businessmen of forming monopolistic associations under official sponsorship. In 1885 the competing steamship lines of the Mitsubishi and Mitsui interests were merged into the Japan Mail Line (Nippon Yūsen Kaisha, or N.Y.K.), under Mitsubishi domination. Under Shibusawa's leadership a tight cotton-spinners cartel was also organized to allocate the inadequate supply of skilled labor, to arrange for noncompetitive purchase of raw cotton and the sale of cotton yarn abroad, to assign quotas in times of overproduction, and to arrange mutually advantageous compacts with shipping lines and merchandising firms. Thus by the 1890's the pattern had been set for the development of industry-wide cartels and of "combines" of interlocking business interests in finance, commerce, and manufacturing.

Industrial growth in Japan, as in other countries, was not a straight-line development. The boom years of the 1880's were followed by a period of slower expansion, but Japan's victory in the Sino-Japanese War in 1895 set off another upsurge in all the established industrial fields and in certain new ones such as chemical fertilizers. Another slowdown followed in which existing companies were amalgamated into larger and stronger units. Then the Russo-Japanese War of 1904–1905 brought a third and bigger boom. Cotton weaving began to catch up with cotton spinning; the electric industry grew as railways were electrified and cities installed street lighting and streetcars; shipping tonnage and services abroad expanded rapidly; the production of coal almost tripled in the decade after 1904; the Yawata Iron Works, founded by the government in 1901 at the northeastern tip of Kyūshū, helped Japan to meet a significant proportion of its iron and steel needs; and a few other heavy industries began to join the simpler light industries as important components of the economy. Thus, during the two and a half decades following Matsukata's financial reforms, one industry after another came of age, and Japan, with its industrial base now diversified and soundly established, entered on a period of sustained industrial growth.

The Transformation of Society

Westernization.   Industrialization as well as political and military modernization depended on new skills, new attitudes, and broader knowledge. The leaders had realized from the start that social and intellectual modernization was prerequisite to successful innovation in other fields. But in the social and intellectual areas, as in economics, the responsiveness of thousands of individuals from all classes was more important in the long run than the planning of the authorities.

Many innovations were not really necessary to modernization but were merely imitations of Western customs. At the time, however, the distinction between fundamental features of modern technology and mere Occidental pe-

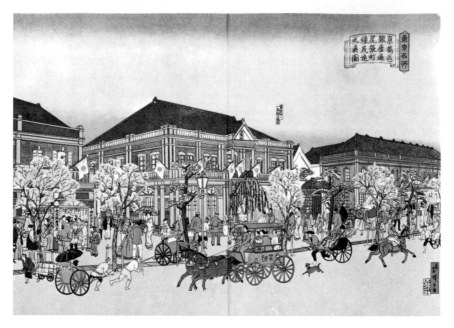

*An 1877 woodblock print showing the Ginza in downtown Tōkyō,
with modern brick buildings, rickshaws, and a horse-drawn
streetcar.*

culiarities was by no means clear. If it was necessary to use Western weapons,
there might also be virtue in wearing Western clothes or shaking hands in the
Occidental manner. Moreover, the Meiji Japanese had good reason to adopt
even the more superficial aspects of Western culture. The international
world of the nineteenth century was completely dominated by the Occident,
and in view of the arrogant Western assumption of cultural superiority, the
Japanese were probably right in judging that they would not be regarded
even as quasi-equals until they too possessed not only modern technology
but also many of the superficial aspects of Western culture. The resulting
effort to borrow almost anything and everything Western may now seem
amusingly indiscriminate, but it is perfectly understandable.

Some innovations were inspired by mixed desires for technological progress and cultural conformity. For example, Western hygienic practices were
introduced, and Japanese in time became enthusiastic wielders of tooth-
brushes and consumers of patent medicines. The Gregorian calendar, together with the seven-day week and Sunday holiday, was adopted and the
sixth day of the twelfth month of 1872 (the fifth year of Meiji) was made
January 1, 1873 (Meiji six). Mail service was introduced the same year,
and in 1886 Japan joined the international metric agreement, adopting the
metric system for general use in 1924. A curious hybrid of East and West
was the rickshaw, invented in Japan in 1869. It was an ingenious combina-

tion of superior Western-style wheels with cheap Eastern labor and spread widely throughout Asia before giving way in Japan itself in the twentieth century to motorized transport.

Many innovations were only for psychological effect—on Westerners or on the Japanese themselves. Western-style haircuts, in place of the samurai shaved pate and long peripheral hair tied in a top knot, were a major symbol of Westernization. Soldiers and functionaries were put in Western-style uniforms, and men of prominence often adopted Western clothes and even the full beards then in style in the Occident. Western dress was prescribed for all court and official ceremonies in 1872. In the latter part of the Meiji period the cutaway (called *mōningu* for "morning coat") became so entrenched that it is still in general use for formal occasions, and *haikara* ("high collar") became a popular word for "fashionable." Meat eating was encouraged, although previously it had been considered immoral because of Buddhist attitudes, and the beef dish of *sukiyaki*, developed at this time, became a popular hallmark of Japanese culture. Western art and architecture were adopted, producing an ugly Victorian veneer in the cities and depressing "Western rooms" in the mansions of the wealthy.

The craze for Westernization reached its height in the 1880's. There were even efforts to make social relations between the sexes conform to Western practice. Women of good families were taught foreign languages and ballroom dancing. In 1883 the government erected in Tōkyō an elaborate social hall, called the Rokumeikan, where dances were held every Sunday night for the political elite and the diplomatic corps. A great fancy-dress ball was held there in 1887, with the chief government dignitaries in attendance.

This, however, proved to be the last straw for more conservative Japanese. There was a general revulsion against unnecessary imitation of the West, accompanied by a re-emphasis of native values and traditions. Many superficial aspects of Western culture, such as ballroom dancing, were dropped, permitting significant technological innovations to free themselves of the onus of association with useless and irritating peculiarities. The same cycle of enthusiastic and somewhat indiscriminate adoption of Western ways, followed by the rejection of certain less essential aspects of these innovations, was to repeat itself more than once in subsequent Japanese history and can also be discerned in other Asian countries.

Legal Reforms. To win acceptance by the West, it was essential that the Japanese reform their legal institutions along Occidental lines. Extraterritoriality was among the most galling features of the unequal-treaty system, but there was no hope of eliminating it until the Western powers had full confidence in Japanese legal processes. Legal renovation was also fundamental to technological modernization and was necessitated by the abolition of the old class structure and the other great changes taking place.

Western concepts of individual rather than family ownership of property were adopted, although for purposes of formal registration of the population the law continued to recognize the old extended family, or "house," consisting of a patriarch and those of his descendants and collateral relatives who had not legally established a new "house." Concepts of legal rights, as opposed to the traditional emphasis on social obligation, came to permeate the new laws. The structure and procedures of the courts were made to conform to those of the West, and torture as an accepted legal practice was abolished in 1876. But some innovations, such as the prohibition of prostitution and mixed bathing, which were adopted simply to placate Western prejudices, proved ineffective and were subsequently abandoned.

Most of the legal reforms ware instituted piecemeal, and a thorough recodification of the laws proved a difficult and slow task. Drafts, drawn up largely under French influence, were submitted in 1881 and again in 1888. A complete code, revised largely on the basis of German legal precedent, finally went into effect in 1896.

Religion.   One feature of Western civilization which the new government made no move to adopt was Christianity, even though this would have created a more favorable impression on Westerners than any other step it could have taken. Prejudices against Christianity ran much too deep in Japan. In fact the new government re-established in 1868 the old Tokugawa bulletin boards proscribing the religion, and it aroused a storm of protest from the foreign diplomats by rooting out a clandestine community of some three thousand Christians which had remained in the Nagasaki area from the period of Catholic missions in the sixteenth and seventeenth centuries. Not until the members of the Iwakura Mission had seen how strongly Westerners felt about their religion did the government in 1873 drop the old ban on Christianity, and even then only indirectly by removing the public bulletin boards on the grounds that their content was already well known.

But Christianity had in the meantime re-entered Japan. As early as 1859, American Protestant missionaries had taken advantage of the Harris treaty to come to the open ports. One of them, Dr. J. C. Hepburn, a medical missionary of the American Presbyterian Church, compiled a Japanese-English dictionary, published in Shanghai in 1869, which established the standard system for romanizing Japanese that still bears his name. Catholic missionaries also started to regather their remaining flock in the Nagasaki area. A Russian Orthodox monk, Nikolai (1836–1912), came to Hakodate in 1861 and moved in 1872 to Tōkyō, where he became the bishop and later the archbishop of a flourishing missionary church.

Gradually hostility toward Christianity abated, and the government in the 1880's adopted a clear policy of religious toleration, tacitly accepting

Christianity, together with Buddhism and Shintō, as one of the three major religions of Japan. Aided by its association with Western civilization, which many Japanese felt to be the obvious "wave of the future," Christianity also attracted many inquiring Japanese intellectuals from the samurai class, who saw in it the key to Western progress and strength. They also saw in Protestant Christianity a new code of personal ethics and loyalty that would strengthen Japan at this time of confusion over the old codes of conduct.

Niishima Jō (1843–1890), a samurai from central Honshū who had gone to America in 1864, where he had graduated from Amherst College and become an ordained Congregational minister, founded a school in Kyōto in 1875 that grew into Dōshisha University. A group of young samurai from the Kyūshū domain of Kumamoto, who had been converted by an American teacher of English, transferred to this institution in 1876 and later became prominent Christian leaders. The influence of Dr. William S. Clark, the president of the Massachusetts Agricultural College, who had gone to Japan in 1876 to take charge of the newly founded Sapporo Agricultural College (later Hokkaidō University), led to the conversion of several able young samurai, including Nitobe Inazō (1862–1933), who became a leading scholar and educator, and Uchimura Kanzō (1861–1930), who reacted to the sectarian divisions and close national affiliations of the Protestant missionaries by founding a "No Church" (Mukyōkai) movement.

Christianity thus had a strong impact among Japanese intellectuals, but its popular appeal remained small. Although Christians had constituted close to 2 per cent of the Japanese population in the early seventeenth century, in 1889 they numbered less than a quarter of 1 per cent, divided among forty thousand Catholics, twenty-nine thousand Protestants, and eighteen thousand Orthodox, and the number of Christians in recent times has never reached as much as 1 per cent of the population.

The lack of popular interest in Christianity did not mean a return to native religions and philosophies. Despite the Confucian background of the leaders, Confucianism, as the orthodoxy of the Tokugawa system, stood discredited in their eyes. While Confucianists were the most effective critics of Christianity and in time won acceptance from the government leaders for some of their attitudes, many of the fundamental concepts of Confucianism were obviously not suited to the new situation.

Shintō was in better repute because a revived interest in it had been a key element in the intellectual trends that led to the "imperial restoration." The creation in 1869 of the Office of Shintō Worship above the organs of civil government was an effort to establish a Shintō-oriented government, modeled on the semi-theocratic state of more than a millennium earlier, but this proved impractical. Despite the official favor shown to Shintō, this simple nature worship did not have much to offer men of the new age, institutionally or intellectually. The attempted revival had little inner life and soon faded away. The government continued to control and support the more important Shintō shrines, but the Shintō cults themselves lapsed into their traditional passive state, forming no more than a quiet ground swell in the emotional life of the people. Only the so-called popular Shintō Sects, such as Tenrikyō, which were recently founded, eclectic religions, popular among the lower classes, continued to show much vigor.

The favored status of Shintō contributed to a violent disestablishment of Buddhism in the first years of the new regime. The Buddhist clergy had gained administrative control over a large proportion of the Shintō shrines almost a thousand years earlier, and under the Tokugawa most Japanese had been forced to register for census purposes as members of Buddhist parishes. Now this latter practice was discontinued, the administrative association of Buddhist and Shintō institutions was dissolved, and Shintō properties were restored to their own priests. These measures inspired a general anti-Buddhist outburst, in which church property and many artistic treasures were destroyed.

Buddhism thus was hard hit, but the persecution together with the challenge of Christianity actually helped it shake off some of its lethargy of recent centuries. There was a gradual revival of Buddhist scholarship. The large True Sect (Shinshū) showed particular vitality, and adopted in time some of the organizational techniques of the Christian churches, including foreign missions to the nearby continent, Hawaii, and the West Coast of the United States.

Secular Thought.   The failure of the Japanese to accept Christianity and the superficiality of much that they did borrow has given rise to the assumption that only the externals of Western civilization were accepted and that native traditions were impervious to the ideals and values of the West. Thus some observers have felt that Sakuma was right in his slogan of "Eastern ethics and Western science," which many of the Meiji leaders endorsed. In practice, however, no clear line could be drawn between the external aspects of Western civilization and its internal value system. The legal forms of the West, for example, inevitably brought with them the concepts and value judgments on which they were based. Moreover, the Japanese of the early Meiji period, although naturally influenced by the feudal and Confucian elements in their past, remained nonetheless open to the ideas and institutions of the West. Scientific techniques and external fashions were easier to understand and adopt than were Western ideas and values, but these too seeped in and profoundly influenced society.

The Meiji leaders were themselves thorough-going utilitarians and pragmatists. They were neither doctrinaire traditionalists nor blind followers of the West. All of them were ready to champion Western ideas when these seemed useful or an inevitable trend or to defend traditional points of view when these seemed of continuing value. They took advantage of any idea or technique that gave promise of helping to build "a rich country and strong military."

These attitudes were perhaps a natural outgrowth of the pragmatism of Tokugawa thought and the secular and agnostic tendencies of Confucian philosophy, but they were also influenced by Western ideas. The Meiji leaders, while ignoring Christianity, found encouragement for their points of view in the growing secularism, nationalism, and materialism of the nineteenth-century West. They easily adopted the Occident's confidence in science as the panacea for all problems. They found the utilitarianism of Jeremy Bentham and John Stuart Mill very appealing, and Herbert Spencer became the idol of many Japanese intellectuals. A little later Social Darwinism, which seemed to explain the success of the Meiji leaders themselves and to justify Japan's rise as an imperialist power, became a popular theory.

The pragmatism of the Meiji leaders thus was an easy blend of Tokugawa traits and Western attitudes. It also helps explain the extraordinary moderation and flexibility of the revolutionaries who remade Japan. The wave of political assassinations of the 1860's and 1870's shows how violent Japanese can be in espousing causes, but the Meiji leaders were interested in finding formulas that worked, not in proving some dogma. They had the advantage of being completely united on what the ultimate goal was, but they were remarkably open-minded as to how it should be reached. They also had behind them the long Japanese tradition of group responsibility and decision through consensus. Though all were strong personalities, none ever sought to monopolize authority by eliminating the others. When the policies of one failed or lost support, he readily stepped aside in favor of another who might have a new approach or better represent the consensus. The result was extraordinary flexibility in policy for a government that had no formal mechanism for deciding differences of opinion, and a surprising ability to correct mistakes before they became irreparable.

Seeking New Knowledge. The Meiji leaders clearly recognized the need for new skills and knowledge: in the "Five Articles Oath" they had stated, "Knowledge shall be sought throughout the world." One obvious way to acquire this knowledge was by sending students abroad. The shogunate and some of the domains had started doing this before the Restoration, and the new government continued the effort. No less than fifty-four students accompanied the Iwakura Mission abroad in 1871. Students returned from study in the West had important careers as political, intellectual, and economic innovators and leaders, and some, such as Yamagata, Itō, and Inoue, were among the chief architects of the new Japan.

Importing foreign experts was another way to get knowledge of the West and mastery of its technology. In the closing years of the old regime, foreign experts had been used in various industrial undertakings, and the new government greatly expanded the use of such hired talent. As we have seen, foreigners were extensively used in the development of Hokkaidō and in the bureau of mines, and by 1879 the ministry of industry employed 130 foreigners, whose salaries accounted for nearly three-fifths of the ministry's fixed expenditures.

Since the "Dutch Learning" of the late Tokugawa period had proved to be a half-century or more out-of-date, a new start in Western science and scholarship was made through the use of foreign scholars. A series of German doctors, starting in 1871, gave Japanese medicine a strong German cast. English and American scholars were more important in other sciences. Professor E. S. Morse of Harvard, who arrived in 1877, is remembered as the founder of modern zoological, anthropological, archaeological, and sociological studies, and the Japanese still feel a strong sense of debt to Ernest Fenollosa of Boston, who came as a professor of philosophy in 1878 and by his own enthusiasm helped to revive an interest in the native artistic tradition.

Foreign experts and scholars were inordinately expensive, since they required what were by Japanese standards fabulous salaries and a luxurious style of living. But perhaps just because they were so costly to the Japanese, they seem to have been more esteemed and better put to use than is often the case in developing countries today, where the costs for foreign experts have commonly been met by foreign countries or international agencies. But the great expense also made the Japanese eager to replace foreigners as soon as possible by the Japanese they had trained or students returned from abroad. This was already happening in the late 1870's, and the process was speeded by Matsukata's retrenchment policies in the 1880's. By the turn of the century, few foreign experts remained, except as language teachers. There was one exception, however. Foreign missionaries, who came at their own expense, increased in numbers and often proved valuable teachers of English and transmitters of other knowledge.

The printed word had been the chief source of knowledge of the West for the scholars of "Dutch Learning" during the Tokugawa period, and translations and books played an even greater role in the new age. The leading popularizer of knowledge about the West was Fukuzawa Yukichi (1835–1901), the most influential man in Meiji Japan outside of government service. A samurai from northern Kyūshū, he studied "Dutch Learning" in Nagasaki and Ōsaka, taught Dutch in Edo, and then switched to English when he discovered that English was the language of the foreigners flocking to Yokohama after 1859. He accompanied shogunate embassies to the United States in 1860 and Europe in 1862 and founded a school in Edo which eventually grew into Keiō University, one of Japan's two leading private universities and the source of many of its top business leaders. But

A print from the early 1870's showing the old-style "unenlightened man" in samurai garb, the "half-enlightened man" with Western-style cap, umbrella, and shoes, and the "enlightened man" in Western costume complete with a cane and dog.

his first fame came from his writings. In 1869 he published *Conditions in the West,* in which he described in simple and clear terms the political, economic, and cultural institutions of the Occident, making plain his preference for the British parliamentary form of government. This work sold 150,000 copies in its first edition. Fukuzawa followed it in the next decade with a number of others, including *The Encouragement of Learning,* which is said to have sold over 700,000 copies.

Many other private scholars shared with Fukuzawa the task of spreading Western knowledge. Fifteen intellectual leaders joined him in 1873 in founding the Meirokusha ("Sixth Year of Meiji Society"), which had a brief but influential existence, holding public lectures and publishing a magazine. The translating of Western books was perhaps the chief literary activity of the period. Samuel Smiles' *Self-Help* and Mill's *On Liberty,* appearing in 1870 and 1871, were both immensely popular. There was also a flood of translations of Western literature of all types, from *Robinson Crusoe* (1859) to Jules Verne.

Education.   The new leaders clearly saw that an organized system of education was a fundamental aspect of a modernized society and as early as 1871 created a ministry of education to develop such a system. This effort was of course aided by relatively high literacy rates and the Japanese familiarity with schools and formal education, but the various Tokugawa educational institutions did not themselves prove capable of adjusting to the new conditions. The Confucian-oriented domain schools for the samurai and the so-called "temple schools," where commoners had learned to read and write, all withered away. The only exceptions were the shogunal schools. The Confucian "University" in Edo, the medical school, and the language programs at the Institute for the Study of Barbarian Books were united in 1869 into a single government institution. The non-Western aspects of the curriculum were dropped in 1871, and in 1877 the school was renamed Tōkyō University, under which name it has remained ever since the pinnacle of the Japanese educational system.

The disappearance of most earlier schools left the government free to develop a thoroughly modernized system of education. It never had to contend with the entrenched relationship between religion and education that existed in most Western countries. It was thus able to put into practice Western concepts of a uniform, government-operated educational system more fully than was possible in much of the West itself in the nineteenth century.

The ministry of education at first adopted a highly centralized system of education along French lines. Sixteen months of schooling were made compulsory for children of both sexes. Compulsory education was extended to three years in 1880 and to six years in 1907. It was no easy matter, however, to carry out such plans because of the insufficiency of both funds and teachers. As late as 1886 only 46 per cent of the children of statutory school age were in school, but by 1905 the figure had risen to 95 per cent, and subsequently crept up still higher.

In the meantime the original centralized French system had been somewhat decentralized and remodeled partially along American lines. This was done under the influence of men like Fukuzawa, Mori Arinori (1847–1889), a Satsuma samurai, who after serving as minister to Washington, became minister of education, and Dr. David Murray of Rutgers College, who served as an adviser in the ministry from 1873 to 1879. A further liberalization of education was also fostered by the rapid development of a great number of private schools. Many were founded by missionaries, and Christian schools were particularly important in the field of secondary education for girls, which was somewhat neglected by the government. Quite a few of the missionary institutions later grew into large universities. There were also many secular private schools. Keiō, founded by Fukuzawa, was joined in 1882 by an institution set up by the former government leader Ōkuma. This grew into Waseda University, the other great private university and a prime source later for parliamentary politicians. Other private secular schools followed, some of which became in time huge even if not very distinguished universities.

*An 1877 print showing a first-grade class learning from a
vocabulary chart produced by the ministry of education in 1875.*

A shift back toward a more centralized, authoritarian educational system came in the 1880's and reached its height in the issuance in 1890 of an Imperial Rescript on Education. This brief document made only passing reference to education itself but showed the revived influence of Confucian ideology in its stress on harmony and loyalty to the throne. Its central concept of mass indoctrination through formal education, however, was an entirely modern emphasis. Part of the new educational policy was a desirable return to Japanese and Chinese literature, history, and thought, to balance the hitherto almost exclusive concern with Western subjects. Other aspects of the new policy were an increasing emphasis on indoctrination in education, standardization of the curriculum, and increased government control over private institutions, especially at the lower educational levels. Still another aspect was the expansion of the government school system and the enhancement of its prestige over the private schools. As a result, private elementary and secondary schools shrank to relative insignificance.

Tōkyō University was reorganized into a genuine multifaculty university in 1886 and became the principal training center for future government officials. Until 1893 its graduates were accepted directly into government service without examination. An inevitable result of this policy was the domination of the higher ranks of the bureaucracy by graduates of the Law Faculty of Tōkyō University, a tradition which still persists. Other government universities, thereafter known as Imperial Universities, were added—

Kyōto in 1897, Tōhoku (in Sendai) in 1907, Kyūshū (in Fukuoka) in 1910, Hokkaidō (in Sapporo) in 1918, and others later.

Early in the twentieth century, the new Japanese educational structure was almost complete. At the bottom were compulsory six-year coeducational elementary schools, designed to produce a literate citizenry for efficient service in the army, factories, and fields. On the level above these were three types of institutions: (1) five-year academic middle schools for boys; (2) various lower technical schools, which produced the lower levels of technical skills; and (3) girls' higher schools, which were supposed to provide all the education needed even by girls from better families. Above this level stood three-year academic higher schools for boys, inaugurated in 1896, and higher technical schools for more advanced technical skills, started in 1903. At the top of the pyramid were the three-year universities (four-year in medicine), which produced the elite leadership.

This was a beautifully logical system, more rationally conceived and uniformly carried out than in most Western countries of that period. It also worked on the whole very well. The unchallenged prestige of the government institutions, which had the lowest tuition rates, gave Japanese education a more egalitarian flavor than the schools of the English-speaking countries. An educational system that was remarkably open to all who had the desire and ability to make use of it became the chief device for selecting the leaders of the nation. As a result, a society which had only shortly before been organized along strictly hereditary feudal lines became within a generation or two less class-bound than England or many other European countries.

The system, however, had serious drawbacks too. It was so carefully tailored to fit the needs of the state, as these were envisioned by its leaders, that it did not adequately meet all the educational needs of Japanese society as it developed. Women's higher education, for example, grew up largely outside the official educational structure, and the rapid growth of private universities showed that there was a demand in Japanese society for much more higher education than that deemed adequate by the government. There was also a cramping conformity and a possibility of uniform indoctrination that were to prove extremely damaging to Japan in the long run.

The Creation of the Constitution

Early Interest in Representative Institutions.   The Meiji leaders realized that their early political reforms were largely makeshift. Once they had established their unchallengeable control over the whole nation through the suppression of the Satsuma Rebellion, they turned their attention to devising some more permanent form of government. Coming from a society which had enjoyed for more than two centuries a clearly defined, fully accepted, and almost unchanging political order, they longed for an equally clear, unchanging, and unchallengeably legitimate political system. Influenced by Western ideas, they thought of it as embodying some form of representative institutions.

Their willingness to consider creating representative political bodies was a surprising departure from Japanese traditions, but it can be explained by the obvious prestige of Western institutions at the time and the assumption that, since the most advanced and powerful nations of the day had constitutions embodying representative government, there must be something in constitutions and representative institutions that produced progress and strength. They saw the specter of the French Revolution or the backwardness of Russia as the fate of regimes that were too autocratic. It was also clear to the Japanese leaders that a constitution and a parliament would greatly enhance Western respect for Japan and bring nearer the day when it would be accepted by them as an equal.

Another factor in the situation was that the government leaders were not dealing just with downtrodden peasants and politically apathetic townsmen. The whole samurai class was well educated and full of men who felt themselves rightful participants in government. Such men insistently demanded a share in the administration, and, as we have seen, the promise in the "Five Articles Oath" that "deliberative assemblies shall be widely established and all matters decided by public discussion" was probably meant as an assurance to them that they would find a place in the new political order. However, "deliberative assemblies" and "public discussion" were quite unfamiliar techniques to the Japanese at that time. The four attempts between 1868 and 1870 to create a deliberative assembly made up partly of domain representatives seemed to add nothing of value, and there was no great outcry when the effort was quietly dropped.

Interest in representative institutions revived in the autumn of 1873 when Itagaki of Tosa, after leaving the government because of the disagreement over Korean policy, founded with other Tosa leaders and Etō of Hizen a political club they subsequently named the Public Party of Patriots (Aikoku Kōtō). This was a daring step, because the word "party" had bad connotations, being associated with the bureaucratic factionalism of Chinese history. The new group, however, did not hesitate to denounce the arbitrariness of the government and call for the establishment of "a council chamber chosen by the people." Itagaki refused to become embroiled in Etō's revolt in Saga the next year but instead founded a new political group called the Risshisha, or "Society to Establish One's Moral Will," a name based on the Japanese title for Smiles' widely read book, *Self-Help*. The Risshisha aimed at the economic rehabilitation of the samurai class as well as the creation of a popular assembly. It spread widely in Tosa and early in 1875 it was renamed the Society of Patriots (Aikokusha) and began to penetrate to other areas.

It is hard to say why Itagaki among the new political leaders took this unusual turn toward democracy or why there was so ready a response to his ideas in his native Tosa. Tosa was a relatively backward, peripheral area and Itagaki a particularly soldierly samurai. One factor may have been the resentment of Tosa men at the predominant role of Satsuma and Chōshū in the new government, but of course other domains had even more to resent on this score. A more basic reason may have been that a class of "village samurai" in Tosa, together with village headmen and merchants who had been allowed to purchase samurai status, had long constituted a rural opposition to the urban administration of the domain, and their attitudes of popular opposition were easily transferred to the new government.

The government leaders were not particularly shocked by Itagaki's demands and continued to regard him as one of them. In fact, they themselves studied various proposals for a constitution and in 1875 had the emperor promise that in due time a national assembly would be formed. Itagaki was persuaded to return to the government in 1875 on the basis of an agreement that had been worked out in Ōsaka between Ōkubo and Kido to induce the latter to rejoin the government after he too had resigned in a huff the year before. The Ōsaka agreement called for a reorganization of the government. A Supreme Court was created to protect the independence of the judiciary, and a Senate was set up and given the task of preparing for a national assembly. When it finally presented the fruits of its toil in 1880, Iwakura and Itō, who were then the chief powers in the regime, shelved the draft as too closely modeled on English institutions.

Another point in the Ōsaka agreement was the calling of a conference of prefectural governors. It first met in June 1875, and at its second meeting in 1878 it decided on the establishment of elected prefectural assemblies. Although the franchise was restricted to males who paid five yen or more in taxes and the powers of the assemblies were limited to discussing tax and budgetary matters put before them by the governors, these bodies, convened in March 1879, were the first popularly elected political organs to operate successfully anywhere in the non-Western world. They were followed in 1880 by similar elected assemblies in city wards, towns and villages.

The "People's Rights" Movement.   Itagaki resigned again from the government late in 1875, ostensibly because one point in the Ōsaka agreement had not been carried out. He and his closest associates managed to avoid involvement in the Satsuma Rebellion and in 1878 renewed their efforts to create a nationwide popular movement. This time there was a tremendous response to their demand for a parliamentary form of government. One reason for the popularity of this so-called "movement for freedom and people's rights" (*jiyū minken undō*) was the dissatisfaction with current conditions among many samurai. But the most numerous and enthusiastic members of the movement actually were prosperous peasant landowners and petty entrepreneurs, probably because they, rather than the impoverished samurai, constituted the chief tax-paying group. Men of samurai origin usually remained the top leaders and intellectual guides, but peasants and businessmen provided the chief financial support and the bulk of the members of the new political associations.

Another reason for the spread of the parliamentary movement was the growing knowledge of democratic institutions among Japanese intellectuals, largely because of Fukuzawa's books and those of other writers. For example, Nakae Chōmin (1847–1901), a Tosa samurai by origin, popularized the ideas of Rousseau. Nakae also helped found in 1881 the *Tōyō Jiyū Shimbun* (*Oriental Free Press*), which became an influential organ in the movement. The first real Japanese newspaper had been started in 1870, and by 1875 there were more than a hundred. Newspapers and other periodicals were usually journals of opinion, reflecting the political views of their backers. Unemployed samurai and other political outsiders flocked into newspaper work and thus helped create in Japanese journalism a strong tendency toward political protest, which has survived to the present day.

Because of the lack of traditions of democracy and freedom of expression in Japan, the line between political agitation and opposition through rebellion was not at all clear to the people of the time. Even political assassination, the chief weapon of the "men of determination" (*shishi*) of the preceding decade, seemed legitimate to some would-be champions of "freedom and people's rights." Ōkubo, the most powerful figure in the government, was killed in May 1878 by extremists who had the curiously mixed motives of avenging Saigō's death in the Satsuma Rebellion and defending "people's rights." Itagaki attempted to control the mushrooming political movement through national conventions of the Society of Patriots. The first was held in September 1878, and at the fourth held in April 1880 the name of the organization was changed to the League for Establishing a National Assembly.

The government leaders were naturally apprehensive about the growth and occasional violence of the movement. In 1875 they adopted new press, publication, and libel laws, designed to prevent newspaper attacks on the government. A running fight resulted between journalists and officials, with the government imprisoning and fining editors, and the newspapers setting up dummy editors as a defensive tactic. In 1880 the government adopted a stringent law on public gatherings. This law required police permission for any public meeting, prohibited soldiers, policemen, teachers, and students from participating in political activities, and gave the authorities such general and vague powers that they could suppress almost any form of political agitation.

The Crisis of 1881.   The government leaders were not so much opposed to the creation of some sort of parliament as determined to do this in their own way. Opinions among them were divided between those who admired British institutions and those who looked instead to the more restrictive Prussian model, and between gradualists and those who felt some step should be taken at once. To clarify the situation, all the Councilors were asked to submit their views to the emperor in writing. The responses were predominantly moderate. By this time the three most powerful leaders of the original Restoration were gone—Kido through tuberculosis in 1877, Saigō because of his revolt the same year, and Ōkubo at the hands of an assassin in 1878—and the former second line of slightly younger samurai had taken their place. Yamagata, the builder of the army, decried the popular demands for "freedom," but even he felt that some sort of national assembly should be formed by starting with the better men from the prefectural assemblies and then, through slow trial-and-error methods, creating a true national assembly. Only Kuroda, the developer of Hokkaidō, felt that all talk about an assembly was premature.

It is hardly surprising that the government leaders, already accustomed for more than a decade to guiding the destinies of the nation as they saw fit and certain that they knew best what was good for Japan, were not prepared to bow to the demands of what must have seemed to them a rabble of ill-informed agitators. What is surprising is that most of them were willing to consider forming some sort of elected body that would have at least a small share in political decisions and that one of their number, Ōkuma, proposed in March 1881 the immediate adoption of the full British parliamentary system.

Itō was thunderstruck by Ōkuma's extremism and seems to have felt that Ōkuma was trying to get ahead of him in their rivalry for leadership in the government by jumping on the "people's rights" bandwagon. In other words, he suspected Ōkuma of conniving with outsiders against his colleagues in the government. This impression was strengthened by a clamorous outburst in the press against the sale (in Matsukata's deflationary program) of the assets of Kuroda's Hokkaidō Colonization Office at a scandalous 3 per cent of investment value—a policy Ōkuma had opposed. These suspicions were probably not justified, and Ōkuma may merely have been trying to establish an extreme position for bargaining purposes with the other leaders. If so, he made a great error in tactics. Itō and his colleagues decided Ōkuma must be dropped from the government. In October they had him dismissed from office and at the same time canceled the Hokkaidō sale as a sop to the opposition. They also issued an Imperial Rescript promising a national assembly, but not before 1890.

The gradualist point of view thus won out in the crisis of 1881, and Itō emerged as the most influential man in the government. The whole top leadership also consolidated into a group exclusively from Satsuma and Chōshū.

Itagaki and other Tosa men had already withdrawn; so had Etō and other men from Hizen; and now Ōkuma of Hizen had also been forced out. Iwakura, the one truly influential court noble, died in 1883. For the next decade and a half, the leadership was in the hands of such Chōshū men as Itō, Yamagata, and Inoue and such Satsuma men as Kuroda, Matsukata, and Saigō's younger brother Tsugumichi, who had led the Taiwan expedition in 1874. There were rising complaints that the government had become a two-domain oligarchy, or a "Sat-chō clique" as it was pejoratively called.

The Party Movement.   Ōkuma, when he left the government, took with him several able young officials, including Inukai Tsuyoshi (1855–1932) and Ōzaki Yukio (1859–1954), two men of samurai origin who were to have very distinguished careers as democratic politicians. The next March, Ōkuma and his followers founded a political party, called the Constitutional Progressive Party (Rikken Kaishintō), which was oriented toward English parliamentary concepts and initially drew its chief support from urban intellectuals and businessmen. Fukuzawa and the products of his Keiō University were among its most important supporters, as was Iwasaki, head of the great Mitsubishi interests.

Meanwhile Itagaki had once again reorganized his political following under the new name of Liberty Party (Jiyūtō)—although the accepted English translation of its name has always been Liberal Party, a title more consonant with its later history. Drawing on radical French doctrines, the party proclaimed that "liberty is the natural state of man" and advocated a constitution decided upon at a national convention.

These two parties, though repeatedly disbanded, reorganized, merged, and renamed, were to remain two major political streams in Japan, and they are in fact the twin sources and the reason for the split name of the post–World War II Liberal Democratic Party. Although they were frequently able to stir up enthusiastic mass support, they had few enrolled members— at most a few thousand in the early years. Most Japanese remained too close to the feudal past to commit themselves openly by joining political parties. Both retained feudal features in their leader-follower organization and readily split into smaller leader-follower factions. While both parties supported the imperial institution as the symbol of Japan's political unity, they argued that a popularly elected parliament could better represent the emperor's will than a Satsuma-Chōshū oligarchy. Each, however, was quick to accuse the other of being a self-seeking faction merely attempting to replace the "Sat-chō clique." In particular, the Progressives would accuse the Liberals of being at the service of Mitsui interests, and the Liberals would reply by accusing the Progressives of being controlled by Mitsubishi.

The government opposed the parties by strengthening the laws on public meetings in 1882. It also got Itagaki out of the country by persuading

Mitsui to finance a trip for him to observe European governments. While he was abroad his party fell into serious difficulties. Some of its members became involved in peasant uprisings, protesting the drastic drop in prices and resultant increase in the burden of taxes caused by Matsukata's deflationary policies. The government had no trouble in suppressing the disturbances, but the Liberal Party was so disrupted and discredited by its involvement that it dissolved itself in October 1884. The faction-ridden Progressives also soon fell apart.

Another effort was made in 1887 to rally the opposition groups against the government. This time the movement was directed less toward advocacy of democratic institutions than against the government's foreign policies. In order to persuade the Western powers to relinquish extraterritoriality, Inoue, as foreign minister, had proposed a transitional period in which mixed courts of foreign and Japanese judges would try cases involving Westerners. This proposal and the planned opening of all of Japan to foreign residence were both very unpopular, and the parties seized on these issues to attack the government. Such xenophobia was frequently to characterize the stand of the parties. While advocating Western parliamentarianism, they could be as chauvinistically anti-Western on other matters as the government and, lacking political responsibility, considerably less realistic.

To counter this latest attack, the government issued on December 25, 1887, a Peace Preservation Law, which gave it the right to expel from the Tōkyō area any person felt to be "a threat to public tranquillity." In the next few days some 570 persons were removed from the capital. The revived party movement was shaken by this blow and soon collapsed completely when some of its leaders were inveigled back into the government. Ōkuma became foreign minister in February 1888 and thus replaced the Satsuma-Chōshū oligarchs as the object of popular indignation at the failure to get revision of the unequal treaties. In October 1889 he lost a leg when a fanatic threw a bomb at him.

Preparation for the Constitution.   While the parties were attempting with relatively little effect to influence political decisions, Itō and his colleagues methodically went about preparing for the promised national assembly and the writing of a constitution. Even before Ōkuma had been ousted from the government in 1881, Itō had won acceptance of several basic points, which were embodied in the final results. He was determined that, while the Constitution should not slavishly reproduce any Western system and would be adapted to Japan's special needs, it should at the same time be based on the best constitutional theory and practice of the West, so that it would stand the double test of Western judgment and Japanese use. In March 1882 he led a study mission to Europe, which visited the leading capitals but concentrated on study in Berlin and Vienna, where Itō knew he would find the theories and practices he felt were most appropriate for Japan.

Itō returned to Japan in August 1883 and the next spring was made chairman of a special commission to draft the constitution. But before setting about this task, he started creating the organs of government he felt would be needed before the risky experiment in elective institutions was inaugurated. First he created in 1884 a new peerage to populate a projected House of Peers, designed to serve as a brake on an elected House of Representatives. The new peerage, divided into the five ranks of prince, marquis, count, viscount, and baron (named after the titles used in ancient Chou China), was made up largely of the former daimyo, graded according to the size of their former domains and the latters' services in the "imperial restoration." The peerage also included the old court nobles and some of the new leaders, who kept promoting themselves until Itō and a few others ended up as princes.

Itō's most important innovation was the introduction in December 1885 of a cabinet based on the most up-to-date European models. Replacing the Council of State, in which court nobles had lingered on as official intermediaries between the emperor and the oligarchs, the cabinet was made up of the heads of the various ministries, who were mostly the chief oligarchs themselves. Thus at one stroke the leaders were consolidated into a more effective executive body. Itō himself took the post of prime minister. When he relinquished it in 1888, it went to Kuroda of Satsuma, who, following the bomb attack on Ōkuma in 1889, passed it on to Yamagata of Chōshū, just returned from a second trip to Europe. The whole system of bureaucratic appointments was also modernized, and in 1887 a civil service examination system was adopted on German models.

Itō and his colleagues saw the authority of the emperor as central to the whole system of government they were designing. After all, their own revolutionary seizure of power had been justified as an "imperial restoration," and they seem to have been to a considerable extent believers in the myth they had themselves helped create. They also probably realized that imperial prerogatives were the best bulwarks behind which the oligarchs could take refuge from the rising popular demands for a share in political power. Itō therefore did his best to enhance imperial prestige and protect the throne from popular pressures. In 1885 he revived the ancient title of Naidaijin, or inner minister, commonly translated "lord keeper of the privy seal." He also placed the imperial household ministry outside of the cabinet. In April 1888 he created a Privy Council to pass judgment in the emperor's name on the constitution being drafted, and he characteristically took the presidency of this body himself, so that he could ensure the approval of his own handiwork.

Itō Hirobumi as a young official in the finance ministry in the 1870's and with his family as a leading minister in later years.

As Itō and his colleagues gradually established what they hoped would be the permanent political pattern for modern Japan, there was a decided hardening of the official philosophy. Perhaps this was inevitable in any case, because the leaders were no longer young revolutionaries but were veteran administrators entering middle age. It was at this time that education was put under strict centralized controls, and the imitation of Western social customs was dropped. The Confucian and feudal emphasis on loyalty and obedience came back into fashion and found expression, as we have seen, in the Imperial Rescript on Education in 1890.

While Itō was setting up the chief organs of the new political order, Yamagata was pursuing a somewhat different course. He seems to have had a more literal concept of imperial rule than Itō, and as the chief architect of the army, he placed more emphasis on the armed services as a bulwark of strong executive power. He consequently devoted himself to building up the army's morale and technical competence and to developing a degree of autonomy for the armed services within the government.

In December 1878 Yamagata adopted the German general staff system and established the principle that the chief of staff in matters of military command, as opposed to financial and administrative affairs, was independent of the army minister and the civil government, acting only under the command of the emperor and with the right of direct access to the throne. To emphasize the importance of the chief of staff, Yamagata resigned as army minister and assumed this new post. In the same year Yamagata put out an "Admonition to the Military," emphasizing the old virtues of loyalty, bravery, and obedience, and in 1882 he had the emperor issue an "Imperial Precept for the Military" (sometimes called the "Rescript to Soldiers and Sailors"). The text made clear that "the supreme command" of the army and navy was in the hands of the emperor, thus strengthening the independence of the armed services from the civil organs of government.

Yamagata, as home minister between 1883 and 1888, also had a chance to build up strong executive power in other fields. He reorganized the police into a more centrally controlled and efficient force, and the Peace Preservation Law of 1887 was largely his handiwork. He also undertook a reorganization of local government into an efficient but highly centralized and authoritarian system, embodied in laws promulgated in 1888 and 1890.

The Meiji Constitution. The actual work of drafting the constitution and its supporting legislation did not get under way until 1886. Among the chief participants, under Itō's direction, was a German, Hermann Roesler. The finished document was promulgated on February 11, 1889, the official anniversary of the supposed founding of the Japanese state in 660 B.C.

The constitution made good the promise to create a national assembly by 1890. There was to be a bicameral parliament, called in English the Diet. The House of Peers was to be made up largely of the higher ranks of the nobility, elected representatives of the lower ranks, and some imperial appointees, who turned out to be usually men of scholarly distinction. The lower house was to be chosen by an electorate limited to adult males paying taxes of fifteen yen or more—some 450,000 persons in 1890, only about 5 per cent of the adult male population. The Diet was given a real share in power in that the budget and all permanent laws required favorable action by both houses. The constitution also guaranteed a whole series of popular rights, such as freedom of religion and of "speech, publication, public meetings, and association" and rights to property and due process of law, although these were all hedged by phrases such as "except in cases provided for in the law" or "within limits not prejudicial to peace and order."

These were daring innovations in Japan, but the leaders felt that they had adequately safeguarded imperial prerogatives, and in this way their own power. The constitution was presented as the gift of the emperor, who reserved the exclusive right to initiate amendments—none in fact were ever made. It declared the emperor to be "sacred and inviolable" and the locus of sovereignty as the descendant of a dynasty "which has reigned in an unbroken line of descent for ages past." It made clear that the emperor exercised all executive authority and also "the legislative power with the consent of the Imperial Diet." It specifically stated that "the emperor has the supreme command of the army and navy." It made the individual ministers directly responsible to him, rather than collectively responsible as the cabinet, which was not even mentioned in the constitution. The budget of the imperial household remained entirely free of Diet control. The emperor could at any time prorogue (i.e., temporarily suspend) the Diet or dissolve the lower house, necessitating new elections. When the Diet was not in session he could issue imperial ordinances which temporarily took the place of laws. The oligarchs also reserved what they felt was the trump card to prevent undue Diet control over the purse strings: if the Diet failed to pass the new budget, the previous year's budget would remain in effect.

The constitution was a blend of many conflicting ideas, but it turned out to be a reasonably successful balance among the various political forces of the time. It has often been condemned in recent years for having provided too little democracy, but this is the perspective of a later age. At the time most Western countries themselves had limitations on the electorate and parliamentary power, and the advice to the Japanese of most Occidentals, including such disparate figures as President Grant and Herbert Spencer, was to go slow on democratic experimentation. Considering the feudal background and authoritarian experience of the men in control of the government and the unfamiliarity of the Japanese public with democratic ideas and institutions, the constitution defined perhaps as liberal a system of government as could have operated successfully at the time. While disappointing to the opposition groups, it met their minimum demands, without at the same time completely alienating more conservative forces.

THE POLITICAL SYSTEM UNDER THE MEIJI CONSTITUTION

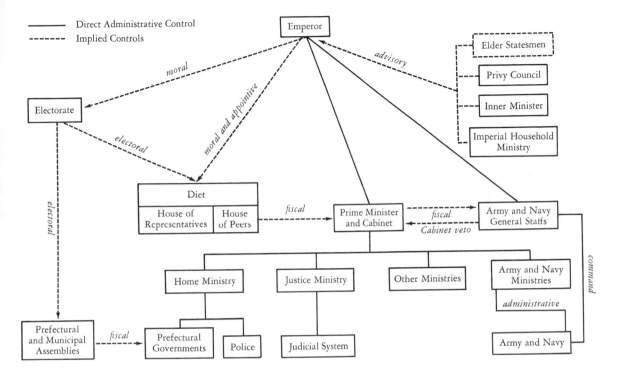

Because of this balance and the sanctity of its supposed imperial origin, the constitution was never seriously challenged from either side.

A more valid criticism could be directed against the ambiguities of the constitutional system. The pretense of broad imperial authority, when in fact the emperor remained essentially a symbol, caused no serious trouble so long as the oligarchs acted in his name. However the group of oligarchs was nowhere mentioned in the constitution, nor were provisions made for some successor body. When these men did pass from the scene, two serious problems arose. It was not clear which organs of government should exercise the imperial prerogatives. For example, who was to choose the prime minister when there were no longer oligarchs around to fill the post or appoint someone else? The almost unlimited imperial powers, moreover, could be abused by individuals or organs of government which lacked the overall jurisdiction and breadth of vision of the oligarchs. Who, for example, was to keep an independent military in line with the civil government when there was no longer an oligarchy to supervise both?

It may never be known whether Itō was blind to these problems, unconsciously assuming the continuation of people like himself in control, or purposely left the constitution ambiguous in order to make room for further evolution. In any case, the very ambiguities of the constitution probably made possible a more healthy political evolution than could have occurred under a system rigidly defined in terms of the political perceptions of the 1880's, and the failure in the long run to find successful answers to the questions Itō had left should be blamed not on him so much as on the generations that followed.

The Early Years of Constitutional Government

The First Diet Session.   The first national elections were held on July 1, 1890, and the Diet was convened in November. It soon became clear that Itō and his colleagues had made some serious miscalculations about the working of the system they had created, and the process of constitutional government started to evolve rapidly away from the picture they had in mind. For one thing, the party politicians had acquired considerable experience, both in electioneering and in parliamentary techniques, in the prefectural assemblies that had been in existence since 1879. Some had developed strong constituencies among the local electorate, which, to the consternation of the government, consistently preferred party politicians over announced supporters of the government. Of three hundred members of the first House of Representatives, 130 belonged to the newly reconstituted Liberal Party and 41 to the Progressives, while some of the independents were obviously prepared to vote with these opposition parties against the government.

The party men, wanting to establish Diet control over the cabinet, made immediate use of the one substantial power the constitution had given the Diet. They slashed the budget by about 11 per cent, concentrating on the salaries and perquisites of the bureaucratic followers of the oligarchs. Itō's trump card proved of little value. In a rapidly expanding economy, last year's budget was never enough. More control over the purse strings had been given to the Diet than had been intended, and as a consequence far more concessions had to be made to the party politicians than had been envisaged.

The oligarchs were united in feeling that the cabinet must remain "transcendent"—that is, above Diet politics. Yamagata who was among those least inclined to tolerate dictation by the Diet, was the prime minister at the time, and he did his best to override the opposition through intimidation and bribery. Eventually Itagaki and some of his Liberals agreed to restore about a quarter of the funds cut by the Diet, and the cabinet had to settle for this compromise.

Compromises of this sort were to prove the main pattern of Diet politics for the next several years. They were satisfactory neither to the Diet politicians, who hungered for official status and control over the cabinet, nor to the oligarchs, who resented this encroachment on their hitherto almost unlimited powers. The question arises as to why either side tolerated this situation. The answer for the parties is easy enough: they lacked the power to do anything else. For the oligarchs it is more difficult. Part of the answer may lie in pride of authorship in the constitution: Itō in particular desperately wanted the system to work. Another reason was the supposed imperial origin of the document, which made it difficult to flout. A still more important reason was the attitude of the Western nations: an obvious failure in this attempted "Westernization" of Japanese political institutions would have brought ridicule and further delayed the acceptance of Japan as an equal. But the most important reason probably lay in the nature of the oligarchs. They had a fairly wide spread of views, tended to operate by consensus, and were by life-long experience pragmatic men. They reacted flexibly to this new problem, presenting no monolithic stand against the Diet, which itself was divided among mutually hostile and selfishly ambitious groups. A more clear-cut confrontation between a unified popular democratic movement and a unified dictatorship would have quickly come to grief. As it was, the Japanese tendencies toward ambiguity, consensus, and compromise permitted an evolutionary development that moved with remarkable speed along the parliamentary paths blazed long before in England.

The Struggle Between the Diet and the Cabinet (1891–1898).   Yamagata resigned in disgust from the prime ministership in May 1891, and Matsukata of Satsuma succeeded him. By then the pattern of alternation in power between Chōshū and Satsuma oligarchs had become well established, and it was to continue unbroken until 1898. Matsukata attempted to carry out a strong repressive policy against the Diet, which Yamagata also had advocated. When the Diet tried to slash the budget again in November 1891, he dissolved the lower house. In the elections of February 15, 1892, the home minister, who was in charge of the police and local government, used all the powers of bribery and force he could muster to defeat opposition politicians in what was to prove the bloodiest and most corrupt election in Japanese history. But this frontal attack failed. The opposition forces again won a clear majority of 163 seats, and both houses passed resolutions condemning the government.

Matsukata was under attack from two sides. The lower house voted a cut of a third in the supplementary budget, and the army and navy ministers withdrew from the cabinet in protest against the punishment of officials who had intervened in the elections. Matsukata was forced to resign in May 1892, and Itō now took a turn at trying to deal with the Diet. He was inclined to a more flexible approach than his predecessors and early in 1892 had even suggested the formation of a government party to capture the

Diet. This startling idea, which would have ended the concept of "transcendental" cabinets, had been rejected by his colleagues, but Itō had other tricks up his sleeves.

In response to the usual attack on the budget, Itō had the emperor surrender some of his own income and order the high officials to follow suit, and through this voluntary reduction of part of the budget, he obtained enough support to pass the rest. In the Diet session of November 1893 he managed to win the cooperation of the Progressives for his foreign policies, thus dividing the opposition. But in the face of continued obstreperousness on the part of the Diet over foreign policy, he was finally forced to dissolve the lower house in January 1894 and, after March elections, again in June. The Sino-Japanese War (see pages 553–554) broke out on August 1, before the new Diet was elected, and popular enthusiasm over Japanese military successes greatly eased the conflict between the Diet and the cabinet. Reacting to a war situation in the same way as most Western parliaments have, the Diet voted all the war budgets unanimously and almost without debate.

When the Diet resumed the attack on the cabinet following the forced return to China in 1895 of one of the fruits of victory, the Kwantung (also called Liaotung) Peninsula in Manchuria, Itō took a long step away from the concept of "transcendental" cabinets. He made a deal with Itagaki and his Liberal Party, rewarding them for their support with the key post of home minister for Itagaki in April 1896 and several other official plums for his henchmen.

The coalition between Itō and the Liberals induced the Progressives, under Ōkuma, to band together with other Diet elements to form a new party, named Shimpotō, also best translated as Progressive Party. When this group started to form ties with Matsukata, Itō tried to bring both Matsukata and Ōkuma into his cabinet, but Itagaki objected. Itō then in disgust turned over the prime ministership to Matsukata in September 1896.

Matsukata, following Itō's lead, assigned Ōkuma the post of foreign minister in return for support by the Progressive Party in the Diet. This new coalition, however, fell apart when Ōkuma resigned from the cabinet in November 1897. Matsukata in pique dissolved the lower house and then resigned in January 1898. Itō returned as prime minister, but failing to get the support of either the Progressives or the Liberals, followed Matsukata's lead by dissolving the lower house and then resigning in June.

Two Unsuccessful Experiments.   The confrontation between the cabinet and Diet had reached an impasse. None of the oligarchs was willing to assume the prime ministership under these conditions. Itō proposed that either he be allowed to form a government party or else the cabinet be entrusted to the two former members of their group, Ōkuma and Itagaki, who had just merged their political followings as the Kenseitō, or Constitutional Party. The oligarchs chose the less odious of the two suggestions, and Ōkuma became prime minister with Itagaki as home minister. But the parties were not ready for such heavy responsibilities. The army and navy ministers, who were always military men, held themselves disdainfully aloof from the rest of the cabinet, and the bureaucracy as a whole proved uncooperative. Moreover the old factional divisions remained strong within the new party, and Itagaki was disgruntled that only two of his henchmen were in the cabinet, as compared to four of Ōkuma's. The cabinet broke up in November after only four months in office, and the Constitutional Party redivided into its component elements, with the Liberals retaining the name of Constitutional Party and the Progressives calling themselves the Real Constitutional Party (Kenseihontō).

Yamagata then came back as prime minister and attempted to turn the political clock back. He had been in Europe when Itō had formed his coalition with the Liberals in 1896, and he heartily disapproved of this step. When Ōkuma had become prime minister, Yamagata had insisted that the army and navy ministers be appointed separately from the rest of the cabinet. But he was realistic enough to realize that he must have Diet support, and he worked out a joint legislative program with the Constitutional Party, even though he stubbornly refused its members a place in his cabinet. One result of this cooperative arrangement was the reduction in 1900 of the tax qualification for voting from fifteen yen to ten yen and the expansion of the House of Representatives to 369 members. Another result was the passage, with the aid of considerable bribery, of Yamagata's budgets and his bills for increased taxation.

Yamagata's chief efforts, however, were devoted to increasing the autonomy of the armed services and the freedom of the bureaucracy from penetration or influence by the parties. In 1899 he revised the civil service system to keep politicians out of the topmost ranks, which hitherto had been open to political appointees. In 1900 he extended the powers of the Privy Council and issued a ruling that only officers of the top two ranks on active duty could serve as army or navy ministers, thereby ensuring that the army and navy general staffs would have complete control over these two vital posts.

Yamagata, however, could not permanently hold back the currents of the time. As he devised ways to freeze the party men out of administrative posts, they wearied of their union of convenience with him. Without Diet support, of course, he could not continue effectively in office, and he resigned in October 1900.

The Seiyūkai-Supported Cabinets (1900–1912). The Constitutional Party had meanwhile approached Itō, who, finally winning the grudging approval

Yamagata Aritomo as a
genrō, *aged 78, during*
World War I.

of his colleagues for his old idea of organizing a government party, founded in September 1900 a new party, called the Rikken Seiyūkai, or Friends of Constitutional Government, formed out of the old Liberals in the Constitutional Party and his own supporters in the bureaucracy. Drawing from the largest of the popular political streams and a major factional element in the bureaucracy, the Seiyūkai enjoyed uninterrupted pluralities, and often an outright majority, in the House of Representatives for the next two decades.

Itō became prime minister in October 1900 with a cabinet made up largely of genuine party men or ex-bureaucrats who had joined the party. He had smooth sailing in the House of Representatives with the support of the Seiyūkai, but some of his colleagues in the oligarchy remained critical of his tactics, and the House of Peers actually voted down his tax bills. Faced with bickering in the cabinet and weary of his fourth term as prime minister, Itō resigned in May 1901.

Yamagata proved unwilling to re-enter the political maelstrom, and the choice of prime minister finally went to his protégé, Katsura Tarō (1847–1913), like him a Chōshū general. This marked the end of the original oligarchs' titular responsibility for the government. Itō and Yamagata occupied the post of president of the Privy Council between them from 1903 until Yamagata's death in 1922, but neither they nor any other men of their generation, with the exception of the outsider Ōkuma, ever became prime minister again or held a cabinet post. Instead they let their slightly younger protégés take over, retaining only indirect and gradually fading control as *genrō,* or "elder statesmen," as they came to be called.

Katsura established a purely bureaucratic cabinet, in the tradition of his patron Yamagata. At first he had little difficulty with the Diet, because Itō, as party president, made the Seiyūkai support him. But Katsura ran into trouble when Itō, whose party following represented primarily the rural tax-payers, refused to support his bill for an increased land tax to pay for further naval expansion. Finally Katsura was forced to compromise, agreeing to pay for naval expansion by loans rather than increased taxes. He ran into more serious trouble late in 1903, after Itō had left the presidency of the Seiyūkai. He was forced to dissolve the Diet in December, but was saved from the usual consequences by the outbreak of the Russo-Japanese War the next February (see pages 555–556) and the enthusiastic response it produced in the Diet.

The peace terms concluding the war in September 1905, however, proved disappointing to the Japanese public. The government was accused of having snatched defeat from the jaws of victory, and there was widespread rioting. More than a thousand police and citizens were killed or wounded in Tōkyō before order was restored through martial law. Ōkuma's faction— the Real Constitutional Party—took advantage of the situation to press its attack against the government, and Katsura resigned in January 1906.

Itō had resigned the presidency of the Seiyūkai in July 1903 because of pressure from Yamagata, who found Itō's double role as party president and elder statesman too anomalous and perhaps too threatening to his own influence. Itō, however, had been replaced as party president by a man whose position was almost equally anomalous. This was Prince Saionji Kimmochi (1849–1940), a high member of the old court nobility, who had studied for ten years in France, had become a liberal newspaperman on his return to Japan, and had been forced by the court to abandon this shocking career for the bureaucracy. There he had become a protégé of Itō and had followed him into the Seiyūkai. Saionji was the obvious choice to succeed Katsura, but the oligarchs selected him ostensibly not as party president but as a noble and bureaucrat. He, however, appointed two of his party colleagues to the cabinet and naturally enjoyed full Seiyūkai support in the Diet.

With the formation of Saionji's cabinet in 1906, a fairly stable, though ambiguous, solution of the Diet problem had been reached—at least for the time being. The prime ministership was passed back and forth with relative ease between Saionji and Katsura until 1912, and neither was again forced to dissolve the Diet. The two proved able to cooperate with less open friction than had their respective patrons, Yamagata and Itō. Katsura was more flexible and conciliatory in dealing with the Diet than

Yamagata had been, and Saionji, though a more genuine supporter of parliamentary government than Itō, moved only very cautiously toward party control of the cabinet. At the same time, he was as successful as Itō in maintaining Seiyūkai support for his own cabinets and the party's co-operation with those of Katsura. The Seiyūkai politicians were at least temporarily satisfied with their share in power and access to patronage through cabinets that clearly relied on their votes for necessary legislation, and Saionji and Katsura were ready to give them this much in return for needed support in the Diet.

The Fulfillment of the Meiji Dream

Security and Imperialism. Thus by the first decade of the twentieth century, a reasonably successful, semiparliamentary form of government had been achieved. In fact, a number of small steps and a host of shifting compromises had produced a much larger beginning in democracy than most Meiji leaders would have desired, and universal education and a rapidly expanding university system were soon to carry Japan much further toward democracy. But this was scarcely the real objective of the Meiji oligarchs. Parliamentary institutions, like industrialization or universal education, were only means to an end—mere by-products of what they really sought. This was the double objective of security from the nations of the West and acceptance by them of Japan as an equal, and this they achieved with complete success, though not without creating problems for future generations.

Two key steps in the achievement of security and equality were the Japanese victories over China and Russia. These two wars proved more clearly than anything else that Japan had indeed developed the "rich country and strong military" on which security and equality seemed to depend. But they also started Japan on a course of foreign conquest and empire that was to end a half-century later in catastrophe. One naturally wonders why Japan, which was attempting to defend itself from Western imperialism, should in the process have become an imperialistic power itself.

After internal stability had been assured through the suppression of the Satsuma Rebellion in 1877, Yamagata had turned his attention abroad, arguing with increasing vehemence that the geographic line of national advantage Japan should defend lay far beyond the line of sovereignty. Such imperialist concepts might be traced to Yamagata's old teacher, Yoshida Shōin, or to the whole military mystique of the samurai class. But expansion abroad was not an important part of the Japanese tradition. There had been only two nationally organized efforts in Japanese history—the campaigns in southern Korea up until the seventh century and Hideyoshi's invasion of

Korea in the late sixteenth century. Isolation had been the usual rule for Japan.

A much more obvious source of Yamagata's line of reasoning was the example of Western imperialism. Imperialistic expansion and domination seemed an inherent part of the Western-dominated world Japan had joined. Yamagata was merely a typical military man of his day in the ideas he expressed. And Japan's foreign conquests of the next few decades received as much praise from the West as any of its other efforts at "modernization." The generally accepted ideas and practices of the time almost inevitably drew any strong military power, and particularly one in Japan's geographic position, into imperialistic adventures.

The Sino-Japanese War.   Japan's opening of Korea in 1876 led to increasing embroilment with China over the peninsula. Peking adamantly insisted on its suzerainty over Korea, which Japan refused to recognize, and Korean reformers began to look to Japanese liberals like Fukuzawa for inspiration and to the Japanese government for support. When a conservative, antiforeign mob in Seoul attacked the Japanese legation in the summer of 1882, both China and Japan responded by sending troops to the aid of opposing sides. In 1884 a coup by Korean liberal elements ended with a clash between Chinese soldiers and the Japanese legation guard. To calm the situation Itō and the Chinese statesman Li Hung-chang met in Tientsin in 1885 and agreed that both countries would withdraw their troops from Korea and notify the other before sending them back.

During the next decade the Chinese intensified their efforts at modernizing their military forces, particularly the navy, while the Japanese became increasingly involved in Korea, thus setting the stage for an even more serious confrontation. When the Tonghak ("Eastern Learning"), a popular religious organization with a strongly antiforeign bias, broke out in revolt in southern Korea in 1894, China sent a small body of troops at the Korean king's request, and Japan then sent in a larger force, demanded reforms of the Korean government, and finally seized control of it and had it declare war on China. War followed between Japan and China on August 1.

The ensuing hostilities were the first real test of the efforts at military modernization both China and Japan had been making for a whole generation. Most Westerners assumed that the Chinese giant would win through sheer size, but Japan quickly proved that its modernization had been more successful. Its armies seized the whole of Korea and then invaded Manchuria. But victory was largely determined by sea power, which in the absence of railways controlled even China's access to Korea. While the Chinese fleet was larger, the Japanese was qualitatively much better. On September 17 off the mouth of the Yalu River, the Japanese, using modern British naval tactics, severely crippled the Chinese fleet, which came out

like cavalry, lined abreast. The Japanese then captured the naval base of
Port Arthur in South Manchuria and besieged Weihaiwei on the northern
coast of Shantung, where the remainder of the Chinese fleet was bottled up.
Weihaiwei fell, the fleet surrendered, and China had to sue for peace.

The terms of the Treaty of Shimonoseki, signed between Itō and Li on
April 17, 1895, were relatively severe, though perhaps less so than they
might have been had not a Japanese fanatic shot and wounded Li. China
was obliged to cede Taiwan, the nearby Pescadores Islands, and the Kwantung Peninsula in South Manchuria; recognize Korea's independence; pay
200 million taels indemnity; open more ports; and negotiate a commercial
treaty. The latter, signed in 1896, gave Japan all the privileges that the
Western powers had in China and added the further privilege of carrying on
"industries and manufactures," using the cheap labor in the treaty ports.

Japan's triumph, however, was soon tarnished by a blatant power play
by the Western nations. Russia, which itself had ambitions in both Manchuria and Korea, was alarmed by Japan's success. It persuaded Germany
and France to join in a diplomatic intervention on April 23, 1895, "advising" Japan to give up the Kwantung Peninsula. Bowing to *force majeur,*
Japan complied, receiving in compensation 30 million taels of additional
indemnity. There was naturally a strong reaction of indignation among the
Japanese public, which became further embittered when the same three
powers appropriated pieces of China for themselves in 1898, the Russians
taking, under a twenty-five year lease, the Kwantung Peninsula that Japan
had been forced to disgorge only three years earlier.

The Achievement of Equality.   Still, Japan's victory over China greatly
impressed the West, and the British in particular, disillusioned with the
incompetence of the Chinese government, began to show a decidedly more
pro-Japanese attitude. Even before the war they had been enough impressed
by Japan's internal order and legal reforms to agree to relinquish extraterritoriality. For years, the Japanese effort to revise the unequal treaties
had been fruitless, despite increasingly explosive demands by the political
parties and the public. By 1888 only one nation—Mexico—had surrendered
its extraterritorial privileges. But finally Britain, in a treaty signed in London
on July 16, 1894, just a few days before the outbreak of war with China,
agreed to relinquish extraterritoriality as of 1899, and the United States
and the other powers quickly followed. Subsequently Japan regained complete control over its own tariffs through a treaty signed with the United
States on February 21, 1911.

When the fervently antiforeign Boxer uprising broke out in North China
in 1900 and many foreigners were killed and the legations in Peking were
threatened (see pages 634–640), Japan acted as one of the consort of
"Western" powers to save the legations and safeguard foreign treaty rights.

Almost half of the relief expedition of twenty thousand men which marched on Peking was made up of Japanese troops, who, in contrast to some of the Western contingents, conducted themselves in exemplary fashion.

Japan also achieved equality with the nations of the West in another more dramatic way. On July 30, 1902, the Anglo-Japanese Alliance was signed—the first military pact on equal terms between a Western and a non-Western nation. The British, seeing their long dominance of the eastern seas threatened by the rise of new naval powers, bolstered their position in East Asia by allying themselves with the only strong naval power in the area. They also forestalled by this pact any Russo-Japanese agreement to partition Northeast Asia and instead secured Japanese support for the maintenance of the treaty system in China. The Japanese, faced with growing rivalry with Russia over Korea and Manchuria, needed the alliance to ensure that, if war broke out, Russia would not be joined by other European powers, as it had been in its intervention over the Kwantung Peninsula in 1895. The wording of the alliance made clear that in such a case Britain would come to Japan's aid. The alliance also secured Britain's blessing for Japanese ambitions in Korea, recognizing that Japan was interested in that country "in a peculiar degree politically as well as commercially and industrially." Itō had favored an agreement with Russia which would give Manchuria to Russia and Korea to Japan, but Yamagata and Katsura were convinced that war with Russia was inevitable and therefore wanted the British alliance. Since they were in control of the government in 1902 their view won out.

The Russo-Japanese War.   The event that really won for Japan full status as a world power and equality with the nations of the West was its victory over Russia, the biggest, even if not one of the more advanced, of the Western powers. Russia in 1896 had obtained from Peking the right to build the Chinese Eastern Railway across Manchuria to its port of Vladivostok on the Sea of Japan, thus shortening the Trans-Siberian Railway, the rail link it had started in 1891 to construct across Siberia to the Pacific. When Russia obtained the lease of the Kwantung Peninsula in 1898, it also got the right to connect this line by a southward extension, the South Manchurian Railway, to the ports of the peninsula, Port Arthur and Dairen (Ta-lien in Chinese). These railway concessions gave Russia considerable control over Manchuria, and the Boxer crisis allowed it to overrun the whole area militarily. Its efforts to take Manchuria over completely, however, ended in diplomatic frustration, and it agreed to a phased withdrawal of its forces.

Mutual suspicion and enmity steadily mounted between Japan and Russia. In negotiations between August 1903 and February 1904, Japan won a fairly free hand in Korea but offered to recognize Russian rights only in the zones along the new railways in Manchuria. Meanwhile the Russians had been slow in withdrawing their troops and had begun transporting large reinforcements over the Trans-Siberian system, which had been completed in 1903. Japan broke off relations on February 6, 1904, started hostilities on February 8 with a night torpedo-boat attack on the Russian fleet in Port Arthur, and only two days later declared war.

In May Japanese forces crossed the Yalu River from Korea into Manchuria, while sea-borne forces seized Dairen and besieged Port Arthur. The naval base finally fell in January 1905. Meanwhile Japanese armies had been driving the Russians back in Manchuria and in March captured Mukden, the capital of the region. The Russians' last hope was their Baltic fleet. Denied by Britain the use of the Suez Canal and Britain's worldwide system of ports, the Russian fleet of forty-five ill-assorted, poorly prepared vessels, surmounted all difficulties and eventually reached East Asian waters. In its final dash to make the relative safety of Vladivostok, however, it was intercepted by the Japanese fleet on May 27 in the Straits of Tsushima and was annihilated. Both countries were exhausted by the war, and the Russians were plagued at home by revolution. They both readily accepted President Theodore Roosevelt's diplomatic initiative and met to discuss peace terms in Portsmouth, New Hampshire.

The Treaty of Portsmouth, signed on September 5, 1905, recognized Japan's "paramount interest" in Korea, restored at least in theory China's sovereignty and administration in Manchuria, and gave Japan the Russian lease on the Kwantung Peninsula and the Russian-built South Manchurian Railway as far north as Changchun. The Japanese were eager to extract an indemnity from the Russians, but the latter were adamant on this point, and eventually Japan settled for the southern half of Sakhalin instead. It was the failure to win an indemnity that the Japanese public found so disappointing.

Japan was now free of all foreign competitors in Korea. Itō took on the task of working out a new relationship between the two countries and in November secured a convention making Korea a Japanese protectorate and ending its diplomatic contact with other powers. He himself became resident general. In 1907 he extended Japanese control over the Korean government, arranged that Japanese could serve as Korean officials, and disbanded the Korean army. Widespread rioting which greeted these moves was severely repressed in 1450 armed engagements between 1908 and 1910. Meanwhile Itō, after resigning as resident general, was assassinated by a Korean patriot in October 1909 on a trip to Manchuria. In August 1910 Japan quietly annexed Korea. There was no protest from the powers, which generally approved what was judged at the time to be an inevitable step in world progress. Called Chōsen, the Japanese pronunciation of the ancient Korean name of Chosŏn, Korea was governed for Japan's strategic and economic purposes by Japanese officials under a military governor-general.

Japan thus had become not just a modern nation but a major imperialist power with important colonies in Korea and Taiwan and predominant rights in South Manchuria. It entered World War I in 1914 as Britain's ally and, although playing only a minimal military role, picked up the German colonial possessions in East Asia and the Pacific—Kiaochow Bay and the port of Tsingtao on the south coast of Shantung, which the Germans had obtained in 1898 following their intervention over the Kwantung Peninsula in 1895, and the German North Pacific Islands, which Japan was assigned at the end of the war as a Mandate under the League of Nations. Japan sat at the Versailles Peace Conference as one of the victorious Five Great Powers—the only non-Western nation to be accepted as a full equal by the West. Thus the Meiji leaders had succeeded far beyond their fondest dreams. This was already clear before Itō died in 1909. It was even clearer by the time the last members of the group passed from the scene as venerable octogenarians—Yamagata in 1922 and Matsukata in 1924.

19. China's Response to the West

Early Westernization in Self-Defense

The success story of Meiji Japan from 1868 to 1912 highlighted China's contemporary failure. Both countries had been saddled with unequal treaties that impaired their sovereignty and threatened their economic independence. For Japan to catch up with the modern Western world in all its complexities, and finally to defeat one of the major world powers in a full-scale modern war—all in the space of a single lifetime—was an almost incredible feat. China's inability to do this is more understandable than Japan's success. Plainly one reason for Japan's achievement was its capacity to act as a nation with the same degree of patriotic mobilization that nationalism called forth among Western peoples.

As in Western countries, this intense nationalism also had its influence on the writing of history and our understanding of what happened. The Meiji period has been well documented by Japanese historians with a natural pride in Japan's accomplishments. In China of the same period the collapse of the old order left only a few loyal chroniclers and only a prolonged tragedy for them to record. Undoubtedly the parallel stories of Japan's rise and China's decline have come to us with a certain bias—or at least a fuller record—in favor of those who succeeded. Late Ch'ing history has remained less fully developed since 1912 also because revolutions, though they make history, give little opportunity to write it. In short, Japanese historical writing modernized with Japan, while in China, historiography, like so much else, remained longer in traditional channels.

For these and other reasons, we may expect our picture of China's response to the West to change as research progresses.

Our own view is that the major determinants of China's response lay within Chinese society, not outside it. Inertia, the most important of these, made efforts at Westernization superficial—temporary responses to immediate dangers, diminishing whenever danger receded. More broadly, we think traditional China never could have achieved modernization as Japan did because Chinese society was both so massive in size and so firm in organization that it could not be rapidly shifted to Western models of organization. In this view a modernized China could not be built up until much of the durable even if decaying structure of the old society had been torn down. This process was much slower than in Japan, which was far smaller and far more responsive, in addition to having characteristics that made Western institutions and ideas more readily accepted.

This explanation of China's slowness to modernize is sociological and institutional. It differs from the alternative explanation that traditional Chinese society was not distinctively different from the West, and that the slowness of modernization was primarily due to the baneful, depressive influence of Western "imperialism." In an extreme form this view regards all Western contact as having been injurious and a form of "imperialism." But this does not explain why so overwhelming an influence as "imperialism" produced such different results in China and Japan. We suggest that in both countries Western influence was at first slight, a stimulant more than a depressant, and that it stimulated Japan to respond rapidly and successfully. China's response was impeded by its size and inertia and also by certain distinctive features of the Confucian state-and-society such as the culturalism already described. By the time the depressive and exploitative influences of "imperialism" had grown and accumulated later in the century, it was too late for China to respond successfully. Even so, some of China's early efforts to modernize were vigorous and impressive. The contrast with Japan appeared only later. In the 1860's an outsider might well have bet the other way.

Two significant changes were made in 1860 in the Ch'ing political structure: first, the Anglo-French invasion of Peking forced the Son of Heaven to accept foreign potentates as equals, fatally undermining the monarchy's ancient claim to a universal kingship; second, the renewed Taiping threat in the lower Yangtze forced the Manchu court to entrust the military suppression of the rebels to the Chinese gentry leadership under Tseng Kuo-fan, which built up regional Chinese military power and weakened Manchu control. These were constitutional changes that led in the same direction Japan would soon be moving in: to make the Chinese Empire behave internationally like one nation among equals and base its military strength

Prince Kung (personal name, I-hsin; 1833–1898), brother of the Hsien-feng emperor, signer of the unequal treaties of 1860, head of the Grand Council and Tsungli Yamen.

upon the Chinese common people. Yet these results, so quickly to be achieved in Japan, were not realized until much later in China. Unlike the Meiji Restoration, which was a revolutionary fresh start, the Chinese reforms of the early 1860's were only the first step on a long road with many turnings.

"Self-Strengthening" and the Cooperative Policy. Since the Taiping campaign of 1860–1862 was defeated with Anglo-French aid around Shanghai and Ningpo, China in the early 1860's was quite aware of the military superiority of the West, and military Westernization was seen as a solution to both domestic and foreign problems. Tseng Kuo-fan quoted Mencius, "If you can rule your own country, who dares to insult you?" Prince Kung (see figure above) proposed to use suppression of the rebels as a means for securing Western arms. China's conventional wisdom invoked by Wei Yüan in the 1840's—use barbarians to control barbarians— was now seen to be inadequate. Instead, stress was put on Wei Yüan's statement, "Learn the superior technology of the barbarians in order to control them." Thus emerged the movement for "self-strengthening," which after 1861 followed several lines—diplomatic, fiscal, educational, and military. This program now began to supplant the outworn tribute system.

China's new foreign policy was welcomed by the Western ministers at Peking, who were now committed to a policy of cooperation both among

Britain, France, the United States, and Russia and between all of them and China. Diplomats like Rutherford Alcock (British minister 1865–1869), who had been a chief architect of the treaty system, tried to keep a balance between foreign treaty rights and China's legitimate interests and to check the aggressive demands of British merchants in the treaty ports. Alcock recognized that China's modernization involved "such a revolution as has never been seen since the world began." Progress could not be rapid. The "cooperative policy" of the 1860's was designed to help China modernize gradually.

To handle diplomatic relations with the West there was created in March 1861 a new "Office for General Management" or Tsungli Yamen, headed by Prince Kung. This was not actually a new ministry but only a subcommittee of the Grand Council which took the place of a foreign office until one was created in 1901. Decisions on foreign policy still had to come from the emperor, and the Tsungli Yamen was in charge of foreign relations only at Peking. In the coastal provinces there were appointed two commissioners for foreign affairs, who were also the governors-general at Nanking and Tientsin, reporting directly to the emperor. This decentralization suited the growth of regional power that had occurred during the struggle against the Taipings.

The Maritime Customs Service. Creation of the new order in foreign affairs was much influenced by the British negotiators. Horatio Nelson Lay (see page 476) had been since 1855 the Chinese-paid "foreign inspector" vigorously administering the assessment of duties at Shanghai. His intimate knowledge of treaty relations and of the Chinese language had helped him play the key role, while on leave from his customs post, in browbeating the Ch'ing treaty negotiators at Tientsin in 1858. Later he had helped expand the new customs service. He was appointed Inspector General of Customs by Prince Kung and the Tsungli Yamen in January 1861, and soon after was instructed to procure for the Chinese government the ultimate weapon of the day, a fleet of steam gunboats. But Lay in England not only procured a fleet of eight ships with British crews, he also went further and tried to keep control of the fleet in his own hands. When this powerful flotilla reached China in 1863, both Prince Kung and Tseng Kuo-fan refused to accept Lay's arrangements, he was paid off, and the fleet was disposed of by the British. Lay had grandly considered himself to be working *for* the Chinese authorities, not *under* them. "The notion," he said, "of a gentleman acting *under* an Asiatic barbarian is preposterous."

Robert Hart (see page 562) who succeeded Lay in 1863 built the Customs Service on an entirely different basis. Hart was from northern Ireland and had come to China in the British service in 1854. He told his foreign Commissioners of Customs that "those who take the pay, and who

Sir Robert Hart at work. A drawing from a London periodical, ca. 1890, shows the Inspector General of Customs at his famous standing desk.

are the servants of the Chinese Government... are the brother officers" of the native officials and "in a sense, the countrymen" of the Chinese people. He had his foreign Commissioners oversee all aspects of customs procedure but they were nominally subordinate to the Chinese Superintendents of Customs (usually the local taotais) at each port, who received the actual payments of duties. Hart himself remained responsible for the entire foreign staff, which by 1875 included 252 employees from Britain and 156 from sixteen other Western countries. Thus he created with great tact, patience, and foresight an administrative arm of the Ch'ing central government which used foreign employees to handle the foreign merchants and also assisted China's efforts at modernization.

The new customs revenue, as well as Hart's discreet advice, supported a new institution at Peking, the Interpreters College (T'ung-wen Kuan) which aimed to free China's diplomats from dependence on foreign interpreters. As the Tsungli Yamen argued, "In any negotiations with foreign nations, the prerequisite is to know their nature and feelings." Or as Li Hung-chang said, "First understand their ambitions, be aware of their desires, and... their points of strength and weakness." Similar small schools were opened in Shanghai, Canton, and Foochow, but results were disappointing because the students appointed were mainly middle-aged Manchu bannermen.

A demand for Western scientific learning was created by the setting up of arsenals and shipyards. Tseng and Li finally combined all their efforts in the Kiangnan Arsenal at Shanghai in 1865. By 1868 its Chinese work-men had produced their first steamship, though they used a foreign-built engine. Translation of Western scientific treatises and manuals was an essential part of this development. At Foochow another arsenal and navy yard were set up in 1866 with French assistance.

Nearly all these steps in Westernization were dealt with at Peking through the new Tsungli Yamen rather than through traditional channels. The policy pursued during the 1860's was thus a mixture of old and new. The Western aggressors were appeased with trade and contact under the treaties, the secrets of their military strength were learned in order to ward off foreign attack and suppress domestic rebellion, but meanwhile efforts were made to revive the old Confucian type of government. Restoration of the traditional order, with its unity of state and culture, had actually been the major aim, Westernization in self-defense a minor aim.

The Restoration of Confucian Government

We have suggested that the Chinese state-and-society had achieved such an equilibrium and self-sufficiency among its political, economic, social, ideological, and other elements, that the whole might decline in vigor and yet remain impervious to outside influence. In the processes of government the need for order, the vested interests of the scholar-official and landown-ing classes, and the conservative ideology of Confucianism all met and reinforced one another. Consequently, China's basic response in the 1860's to the dual menace of foreign aggression and domestic rebellion was to reaffirm, or "restore," the old Confucian system rather than modernize it. The new was neither expected nor prized, least of all from abroad. As one arch-conservative put it, "Why must we learn from the barbarian foreigners? . . . They are our enemies."

To this institutional and psychological inertia was added the political weakness of the Ch'ing central power after 1860. The Restoration, as a come-back of dynastic rule after serious rebellion, aimed in the traditional fashion at revival more than innovation. But the dynasty had been severely shaken. The emperor had to lead the way but the T'ung-chih emperor (reg. 1862–1875) was a weak boy, under a regency dominated by his mother, the Empress Dowager (1835–1908). This remarkable woman, usually called Tz'u-hsi from the first two characters of her long title, was clever and strong-willed but narrow-minded. As coregent for her son, she soon learned how to use the imperial prerogatives of appointment, promotion, praise, censure, dismissal, and punishment of officials to make herself the real ruler of the empire. She became entrenched in power, governing with the aid of palace eunuchs and trusted high officials, but she had no grasp of

China's problem of modernization. Consequently the revival of Confucian government on Chinese lines was energetic and partially successful, but steps toward modernization ran into trouble.

Suppression of the Rebellions.   The capture of Nanking in 1864 had extinguished the Taiping Kingdom, the only real competitor for dynastic power, but large areas were still in revolt. The Nien rebels had developed a defensive strategy of "strengthening the walls and clearing the countryside" (see page 474), based on the fortified earth-walled villages of their "nest" area. This strategy concentrated both the farming population and the harvested crops from the fields within the earth-walled villages, so that invading imperial forces would find neither manpower nor food supplies. Meanwhile the Nien cavalry made hit-and-run raids into provinces to the north. The addition of Taiping remnants to the Nien forces prompted the appointment in 1865 of Tseng Kuo-fan to suppress the Nien.

Occupation of the nest area and leveling of its earthen walls had twice been achieved, but to no avail; the populace and chiefs of village militia corps had continued to support the Nien, and the earthen walls had been rebuilt. Tseng now tried a traditional strategy. He proscribed the Nien leaders, listing them for execution, but promised to pardon and protect their followers and the village chiefs who surrendered. Isolating the nest area by setting up four strong points and blockade lines (see map, page 471), Tseng's forces invaded it and carefully screened one earth-walled village after another, registering the populace in five-family groups for mutual guaranty and formally appointing village chiefs. Meanwhile they revived cultivation in devastated areas, recovered control of the people and food supply, and so cut off the Nien raiding forces from their source of manpower and provisions. "Strengthening the walls and clearing the countryside" was thus used against the rebels.

Late in 1866 Li Hung-chang took over the task of suppressing the Nien, since the principal force involved was the Anhwei Army which he had built up. Tseng Kuo-fan had formally disbanded his Hunan Army after the defeat of the Taipings, to get rid of urgent problems of finance, leadership, and discipline among the troops. Li's Anhwei Army took its place as the chief modern force in China. Supplied with arms from the new arsenal at Shanghai and with tribute rice from the rich Yangtze delta, the Anhwei Army soon had thirty thousand or more muzzle-loading rifles for its seventy thousand troops, together with cannon on barges, and seven thousand cavalry. After 1866 the Nien split into two mobile bands in the eastern and western sectors of the North China Plain. They were kept apart by blockade lines a thousand miles long, manned by 100,000 troops, along the Grand Canal and Yellow River, on the west and northwest borders of

Shantung. Gradually hemmed in, the eastern band was destroyed in January and the western in August 1868.

Southwest China, where Tu Wen-hsiu had set up his own Muslim state in 1856 (see page 475), saw an even longer struggle to reassert the central authority. Tu as a Muslim religious partisan apparently offered little leadership to the non-Muslim Chinese. The Ch'ing cause seems in the end to have offered a greater degree of orderly administration and nonpartisan justice to all elements of the mixed population. Some Ch'ing generals came from the local gentry as commanders of militia corps. Even Muslim Chinese found it advantageous to take the Ch'ing side. Through death and migration the population meanwhile had been reduced by more than one-half. Walled cities like Yunnanfu (modern Kunming) underwent long sieges. Muslim power at one time was based on fifty-three walled cities, which the imperial forces captured one after another, often with bloody massacres. Tali was finally captured in 1873, and Tu Wen-hsiu killed himself. In the same year the Miao tribesmen in Kweichow were also suppressed.

In Northwest China, in the arid "panhandle" strip of Kansu province that forms the corridor for communication with Turkestan, risings of Chinese Muslims had occurred in the 1780's, inspired partly by the fanatical sect known as the New Teaching. In the mid-nineteenth century a new rebellion seems to have arisen not against the Ch'ing so much as against corrupt local officials. A revolt broke out near Sian in 1862 and spread westward. The principal leader of the militant New Teaching built up his base near Ning-hsia. This northwestern region was of great strategic importance but its recovery had to wait upon the subjugation first of the Taipings in 1864 and then of the Nien in 1868. The task was given to one of the victorious gentry-generals of Hunan, Tso Tsung-t'ang, whose recovery of Shensi and Kansu took five years (1868–1873), precisely as he foresaw. His management of subordinates, maintenance of extended lines of supply, and revival of local civil administration all seemed to prove the efficacy of traditional methods. Systematic and indomitable, he advanced slowly, reducing rebel strongholds and killing as many rebels as possible. By 1871, as he wrote a friend, his wife had died, his hair was white, he had lost most of his teeth, he suffered from dysentery and malaria, and he was being criticized for his slowness. However, by 1873, though the population had been greatly reduced, peace reigned over the Northwest.

The Restoration of the 1860's was a triumph both of warfare and of civil government in the traditional manner. Tseng, Li, and Tso were pre-eminently scholar-administrators. Their success was due not only to hard fighting but also to their application of Confucian moral and political principles, encouragement of economic recovery, effective taxation and, in addi-

A PEKING HOUSEHOLD. *Peking official (ca. 1872) seated in his
garden courtyard with his son; ladies, children, and servants
above. Unidentified lady at far left.*

tion, some use of Western technology. Yet the Restoration did not bring
China back to the status quo ante but rather to a new equilibrium in which
the leading officials at the top of their provincial administrations, though
loyal to the dynasty, had strong regional power. The dynastic central power
owed its survival to, and henceforth had to contend with, this growth of
regionalism.

The Economic Aftermath of Civil War.   Like the United States, China
in the late 1860's confronted an enormous task of reconstruction. Fighting
had occurred over a longer period and in a larger area than in the United
States, but the Middle Kingdom lacked a modern industrial capacity to bind
up the nation's wounds. Serious losses of capital had occurred—for example,
irrigation works in the Northwest and mulberry trees, essential for silk-
worm culture, in Central China. Great numbers of homeless persons had
to be fed and put to work. These problems were met principally by the
fortitude and hard work of the common people. Leadership was exercised
in each locality mainly by the gentry, with official encouragement. Transport and distribution of relief grain, establishment of soup kitchens, orphan-

ages, refugee centers, as well as public works—"using work in place of charity"—were managed by gentry and officials together. Government action was mainly in the form of moral exhortation and direction, widespread remission of the land tax, reduction of tax rates, and occasionally the resettlement of farmers with seeds and tools. On the whole, these measures aided landlords more than tenants; the former might pay less land tax, but the latter seldom secured reductions of rent.

After the outbreak of civil war in the 1850's, the central government's treasury had been quickly exhausted, and land taxes from rich provinces were cut off. Peking increased the sale of rank and even office, thus inflating the gentry class, and issued new iron cash, paper, and other cheap forms of money, thus inflating the currency. But the revenue crisis could not be met by increasing the land tax, which had been set in established quotas for each area ever since the emperor in 1712 had optimistically decreed that tax quotas should "never thereafter be increased." Ch'ing finance had thus been cursed by inelasticity.

To meet this fiscal crisis there was instituted in Kiangsu in 1853 a small tax on merchants and traders, which became known as likin (*li-chin,* "a tax of one-thousandth"). This new tax had three important features: it was too small to be worth a great effort to avoid and hence was easy to collect; it was collected on articles of consumption, either as a transit tax on goods as they passed a likin barrier or as a sales tax where the goods were sold; and finally the likin revenues were mainly retained within the provinces, where the local gentry participated in administering the likin system. By 1860 it had spread to almost every part of China. Gentry and officials who were mobilizing troops collected likin to support them. By the time peace was restored, it could not be dispensed with.

The central government revenue before 1850 had been collected mainly from the agricultural sector of the economy (see table, page 568). By the end of the century the new taxes on commerce had more than doubled the revenue. Among these the portions of likin made available to Peking were at first the most important. But the new Maritime Customs revenue rose in the 1860's to about 7 million taels a year and subsequently much higher. It included the tax on foreign opium still being imported in increasing amounts from India. The government of China could no longer be financed by the ancient methods of a superficially centralized agrarian-bureaucratic state. The growth of regional armies and the spread of the likin system began a trend toward decentralization or regionalism which could not be reversed, although it was held in check by the reaffirmation of the Confucian ideology.

The Philosophy and Leadership of the Restoration. Western ideas played a remarkably small part in the revival of the 1860's. On the contrary, the

ESTIMATES OF CENTRAL GOVERNMENT REVENUES

(receipts nominally expected at Peking, in millions of taels)

	Pre-1850	Early 1890's	Early 1900's
Land tax and grain tribute	30	32	33
Salt gabelle	5 or 6	13 (a)	13 (a)
Old-style customs	4	1	4
New Maritime customs	0	22	35
Likin	0	15 (b)	14 (b)
Sale of rank or office, misc.	1	5	4
Rough total	40	89	103

(a) including salt likin
(b) including native opium likin

Restoration leaders reaffirmed China's ancient morality and stressed its application to practical affairs through "statecraft" (see pages 445–446). The main ideas of this morality in action may be compressed into a series of propositions: that the harmony of Chinese society depended on hierarchic organization and performance of proper roles from top to bottom; that each individual should follow the social norms of conduct, the ancient Confucian *li* or "principles of social usage"; that the virtuous example of the superior man gave him moral authority; and that legal punishments and the use of force only supplemented government by virtuous moral example. Rebels had to be chastised, and either reformed or eliminated, but the use of force had to be followed up by an incorrupt, just, and benevolent government. Domestic harmony thus restored, prosperity would ensue. This philosophy was strongly elitist and hierarchic, opposed to the egalitarian trend of modern times. It looked for its model to the golden age of antiquity and had nothing like the modern concept of progress. The main emphasis of economic policy was not on increased production and revenue but on frugality, and the proper use of fixed taxes and resources. The Restoration's ideal was static harmony, not dynamic growth. Its vision was limited to the ancient Confucian model. This included a doctrine of cyclical change or "change within tradition," which could be invoked to sanction reform. But reform remained essentially conservative, restricted by two beliefs: that agriculture, providing the "people's livelihood" (*min-sheng*), was the basis

MILITARY MODERNIZATION. *Manchu bannermen with a small cannon, assigned to guard the British consulate at Canton, ca. 1870.*

of the state, and that a carefully selected elite of "men of talent" was the basis of good government.*

In the 1860's, the interests and ideas of Manchu and Chinese leaders became nearly identical, for both were bent on making the traditional system work again. Up to 1850 Manchus had supplied roughly half the officials at Peking, two-thirds of the governors-general and one-third of the governors in the provinces. But in the subsequent suppression of rebellion the new talent that emerged was almost entirely Chinese. They had always staffed the lower levels of bureaucracy. Now Manchus became even scarcer in the provinces. Meanwhile by the 1860's Manchuria was no longer tightly closed to Chinese migration, the Manchu banners were no longer a potent military force, the Manchu language was hardly used, and the ban on Manchu-Chinese intermarriage was no longer effective. The Manchu leadership had almost merged into the Chinese upper class. Until the new Chinese nationalism in the 1890's brought the dynasty under attack as racially alien, it functioned as a traditional Chinese institution. Modern critics who say that Chinese leaders, by remaining loyal to the Ch'ing in this era, "sold out" to alien rulers are applying a nationalist standard of loyalty anachronistically.

*See Mary Clabaugh Wright, *The Last Stand of Chinese Conservatism: The T'ung-chih Restoration, 1862–1874* (Stanford, Calif.: Stanford University Press, 1957).

The first step in finding the "men of talent" needed for the Restoration was to revive the regular examinations, reopen local academies, and get standard works reprinted. Another effort was to relate the examination questions to real problems of the day—for example, how could troops best be trained, distributed, and maintained? This element of practicality followed the school of "statecraft," stressing the more skillful use of traditional methods. One necessary measure was to restrain the sale of degrees. This practice, used in moderation, had had a double value: it provided quick revenue in times of emergency, and it assured the loyalty of the wealthy but nonscholarly man, by letting him buy his way into the scholar class without destroying the scholar's supremacy. "Irregular" degrees obtained by purchase were clearly distinguishable from "regular" examination degrees. In the first half of the nineteenth century the sale of degrees had regularly taken in more than a million, and often 2 million, taels a year. The "irregular" gentry by purchase, at the lowest level of rank, had formed roughly three-tenths of the whole gentry class, which up to 1850 totaled in any given year about 1,100,000 men throughout the empire.

The Restoration tried with some success to prevent any sale of office and to limit the sale of rank. But here again, it was not possible to go back to the status quo ante. The "regular" gentry had grown by an increase in the quotas of first-level degrees to be awarded by examination in the various provinces. As rewards for contributions, quotas were gradually raised during the Rebellion by about 18 per cent. Richer areas, by securing higher quotas, could get more of their young men into the gentry class. During most of the Ch'ing period the rich and cultured urban centers of the lower Yangtze had furnished a high proportion of the winners in the Peking examinations. About two-fifths had come from Kiangsu alone, where the Manchu court got its rice supply and most needed to have allies.

Meanwhile the "irregular" gentry increased even faster than the "regular." By the late nineteenth century the gentry totaled about 1,450,000, more than a third of them qualified only by purchase, an index no doubt of the movement of merchants into gentry status. Thus despite the revival of the examination system, its position as the font of Confucian government eventually grew weaker. Finally, the Restoration was least effective on the lowest level, that of the petty functionaries who normally lived on customary fees or "squeeze." Here the traditional morality was weakest. One could not select and train "men of talent" at this level, nor provide the technical specialization that modern government required.

The Reaction to Christian Missions

One positive result of the restoration of Confucian teachings, though similarly defensive in aim and spirit, was the anti-Christian movement aroused by increased missionary activity. Roman Catholic and Protestant missions were very different movements. The Catholics still had some 150,000 communicants scattered through the provinces in 1800, a foundation for the growth that came with the treaties. By 1870 their community numbered nearly 400,000 souls, ministered to by some 250 European Jesuits, Franciscans, Lazarists, Dominicans, and others, and by many Chinese priests and catechists. The Sino-French convention of 1860 promised the missionaries complete toleration and restitution of former properties, and through a French ruse, the Chinese text of the agreement also permitted them (and therefore all other foreigners too) to lease or buy land and erect buildings anywhere. Thus the Church became a landlord, renting out its properties, in addition to managing schools, seminaries, and orphanages. After its long history in China, Catholicism had become firmly rooted in Chinese society. Impressive ceremonies marked the stages through which a convert became first an adorer, then a catechumen, and finally was baptized. Festivals and pilgrimages, family worship, the teaching of moral conduct, the Church's support of its own, all bound the faithful into the Catholic community. The whole effort, tempered by the persecutions of the past, was carefully adjusted to Chinese ways.

The Protestant missionaries, in contrast, were still on the periphery of China. In 1850 they totaled only about 80 persons, representing a score of mission societies, and confined almost entirely to the five treaty ports, Macao, and Hong Kong. Lacking the tested methods of the Catholic fathers, the Protestant missionaries and their wives, many of whom were also missionaries, remained clearly a part of the Sino-Western treaty-port society (see figures on page 595). By 1870 there were 350 or more Protestant missionaries, but their converts probably totaled fewer than 6000 persons. No single agency, comparable to the Propaganda at Rome, coordinated their efforts, which were almost as fragmented as those of the Western merchants. Pioneer agencies like the London Missionary Society and the American Board of Commissioners for Foreign Missions (Congregationalist) had been joined by others in great profusion—Dutch Reformed, Gospel Baptist, Wesleyan Methodist, and many more. Protestant missionaries from northern European countries and North America were sharply marked off from the Catholic missionaries, who came mainly from Latin countries and regarded the results of the Reformation as dangerous heresy. To Protestants, Rome was anti-Christ, the Catholic faith a rival religion. Cooperation and even contact between the two branches of Christianity were minimal.

In 1866 a remarkable English organizer, Hudson Taylor, began the China Inland Mission, which eventually grew into the largest of all mission agencies, wholly devoted to the spreading of the gospel. Taylor had a straightforward belief in salvation through faith in Christ as the only alternative to eternal hellfire, and China had seemed to him a big problem. "*A million a month* were dying in that land," he said later, "dying without God." He recruited missionaries of any Protestant denomination, from any country, guaranteed them no fixed salaries, asserting "the Lord will provide," and sent them to inland centers to live simply among the people, dress in Chinese style, and lead Chinese souls to salvation. Making it widely known that he would not solicit support except by prayer, Taylor found contributions and recruits steadily forthcoming. Protestant mission stations gradually began to appear in the interior provinces where the Catholic Church had long been established.

Gentry Hostility.   Since the days of Yang Kuang-hsien in the seventeenth century (see page 250), Confucians had criticized Christian doctrine as superstitious and heterodox: why, they asked, had an all-powerful and merciful God permitted original sin? Having been proscribed as heterodox in 1724, Catholicism remained so down to 1846. All this did not commend Christianity to the Chinese scholar class on intellectual grounds. To this were added urgent political considerations: the Taiping rebels claimed to be Christians, while the powerful barbarian invaders from the West also professed the Christian religion. Finally, the Chinese gentry now found the missionaries beginning to confront them as would-be rivals in the performance of their social functions.

First of all, the missionaries came as teachers, offered religious instruction, and set up schools, thus laying claim to membership in a scholar class which, however, was not Confucian. To convey the Christian message, missionaries found it necessary, at least by implication, to question the social order of which the gentry were the local protagonists. They competed with the gentry in practical affairs such as shelter of orphans, relief for the destitute, and aid in time of famine or disaster, thus tending to supplant the gentry in certain of their customary functions. Another important cause of friction was the privileged status claimed by missionaries, or thrust upon them, under extraterritoriality. Just as the gentry were set off from the Chinese populace by their immunity from corporal punishment and their privileged access to and influence with officials, so the missionaries were untouchably privileged, immune to official coercion, able to intercede with Chinese officialdom and, failing that, to call upon their own governments. Catholic bishops in particular assumed a quasi-official status with much pomp and ceremony. Having a privileged position, missionaries, like leading gentry, were often obliged to defend the interests of Chinese, primarily their converts, who regarded them as patrons and protectors. As friction developed between communities of Chinese Christians and non-Christians, missionaries were called upon to intervene with local officials, demanding punishment of culprits and payment of reparations. Hostility was not lessened by the fact that converts were sometimes opportunistic "rice Christians," or from among the underprivileged, those least committed to Confucian scholarship as a path of advancement. Christianity seemed bent on mobilizing the discontented.

Judging by modern standards of nationalism, it would be hard to imagine a more solid basis for gentry hostility to the incoming priest or evangelist, with his strange speech, uncouth ways, and apparently subversive aims. The missionary's purpose, expressed in terms of succor and salvation of his fellow men, was inevitably subversive of the traditional Chinese order. The hostility of the Chinese scholar class is not surprising. Chinese opposition was sufficiently violent to provoke thousands of small incidents and some 240 riots or attacks on missionaries between 1860 and 1899. Yet it was not adequate to check the missionary movement or to figure largely in the missionary literature that poured back to the West.

The anti-Christian movement was led sporadically by gentry here and there, who used traditional means to arouse popular hostility. Their first device was the printed word, which carried authority in a land where literacy was still an upper-class hallmark. Many traditional accusations were reprinted—that Christianity was only an offshoot of Buddhism and Islam, that communicants engaged in immoral and perverse practices, that priests administering extreme unction used the opportunity to extract a dying person's eyeballs for alchemic uses, and the like. In the 1860's scatological compilations vividly described the sexual promiscuity of Christian priests and believers in mixed congregations. This outright pornography attracted readers and discredited Christianity at the same time. Anti-Christian zealots next had recourse to the ancient practice of posting anonymous handbills in public to arouse action, especially in administrative cities at examination time, when thousands of tense degree candidates were concentrated for a week or more. Local issues might arise from missionary attempts to lease property, or build structures which adversely affected the local *feng-shui,* the geomantic "spirits of wind and water."

Disputes were seldom lacking, as well as rumors that exaggerated the facts. The most inflammatory were touched off by the willingness of Catholic Sisters of Charity (see page 574) to accept waifs and orphans and sometimes even to pay a small fee to encourage delivery of such unfortunates to their care. This charity, misinterpreted by popular suspicion, could be linked with the ancient folklore concerning kidnapers who mesmerize small children and lead them off. A few orphanages may actually have been exploited by Chinese kidnapers for the small fees involved. This was social dynamite. Overt action could be touched off by placards mobilizing all defenders of propriety to demonstrate at a given time and place. The local riffraff could be counted upon to create a mob. Riot, destruction, burning, beating, and even death might result. The more numerous and

*A Roman Catholic orphanage in transit. A nun (center) inspects
babies in process of transportation. Photographed in or near
Kiukiang, ca. 1891, in the period of anti-Christian riots.*

more vulnerable Chinese converts usually suffered more than the missionaries themselves. This pattern of events, repeated in many parts of China
over many decades, must be seen as a largely unorganized defense of the
old order, led by the less respectable members of that upper class which
felt itself most threatened by Western contact.

The Tientsin Massacre, 1870.   This incident undid the work of a decade
by revealing the opposed and irreconcilable nature of Western and Chinese
aims and attitudes. The British aim had been to put the responsibility for
enforcing the treaty system on the Ch'ing central government, while helping it to inaugurate modernization. Yet peaceful suasion could not entirely
supersede the threat of force, especially to protect the treaty rights of missionaries. For example, when Hudson Taylor, who had opened a station
of the China Inland Mission at Yangchow on the Grand Canal just north
of the Yangtze, was mobbed in August 1868, Minister Alcock had eventually sent four gunboats to Nanking to press Tseng Kuo-fan into cashier-
ing the negligent Yangchow authorities. There were other cases of this
sort, and Sino-French relations were much worse. Having no commercial
interests to protect, French officials in China tended to use the protection
of Christian missions as a means of expanding French political influence.

In asserting this protectorate, they used gunboats and negotiated missionary cases directly with the provincial authorities.

At Tientsin French Sisters of Charity had offered fees for orphans. Rumors spread and tension rose. On June 21 a mob gathered. The truculent French consul, demanding that it disperse, fired on the magistrate, missed him, and was himself torn to pieces. The mob then killed twenty other foreigners, mainly French, including ten nuns, and destroyed the Catholic establishments. The outraged and fearful foreign powers mobilized gunboats off Tientsin.

The crisis was laid in the lap of Tseng Kuo-fan, now old and ill, who nevertheless demonstrated once again his character and courage. He investigated and announced to his countrymen the unwelcome facts as he found them: that there was no real evidence of kidnaping by Chinese, or of scooping out eyes and hearts by missionaries. Simultaneously he resisted severe French demands and was finally helped by events in Europe, where France's defeat in the Franco-Prussian War left her powerless. Later in 1870 Li Hung-chang took over at Tientsin as governor-general of Chihli, backed by his Anhwei Army. The Tientsin massacre left Sino-Western relations even more embittered by resentment and fear.

Economic Developments under the Treaty System

The Western economic invasion was conducted so largely by Chinese merchants that it did not provoke as immediate and concrete a defensive response as did the earlier invasions of Western armed forces or the influx of missionaries. Yet China was slow to imitate Western forms of industrial development and the reasons for this pose a chief problem in the history of this period.

Extraterritoriality and the Treaty-Port Establishment. In the treaty ports, areas of land were leased in perpetuity by the British and French governments, which paid modest ground rents annually to the Chinese government; these were known as "concessions." In the 1860's, there were British concessions at Canton, Amoy, Chinkiang, Kiukiang, Hankow, Tientsin, and Newchwang; and French concessions at Canton, Shanghai, Hankow, and Tientsin. As time passed the number increased. Within these leased areas the foreign consulates in turn granted ninety-nine-year leases to land-renters. Under extraterritoriality they also exercised legal jurisdiction over their own nationals, and by degrees developed taxation, police forces, and other features of municipal government. Thus China's sovereignty, without being destroyed, was put largely in abeyance in the foreign quarters of the major ports. Meanwhile Shanghai created its own unique city government when

CHINESE LAW AND ORDER.
*A culprit in a cangue
sealed by the Shanghai
magistrate, 1872.*

in 1863 the British and American areas coalesced to form the Shanghai International Settlement. Among its two thousand or more foreign residents, the British were dominant with the Americans second. The foreign land-renters (or "rate-payers") were represented by an elected council which derived its authority from the foreign consuls and their extraterritorial powers. By degrees the Shanghai Municipal Council came to deal with all the problems of a large city—roads, jetties, drainage, sanitation, police, and recreation facilities such as the race course. Taxes were levied on Chinese residents without representation, as under a Chinese regime. Shanghai remained Chinese territory, but it was free from Chinese taxation and under foreign consular control within the treaty system.

With Western control came Western law with its special utility for commerce, such as legal incorporation and proceedings for enforcement of contract. Western nationals were subject to their country's consular court and could be sued by Chinese plaintiffs only in that court. Britain transferred her Supreme Court for China and Japan from Hong Kong to Shanghai to hear appeals from all her consular courts. But appeals from the French consular court had to go to Saigon, and those from the Spanish, Dutch, or Russian consulates to Manila, Batavia, or Vladivostok, respectively. This made it difficult for Chinese plaintiffs to appeal consular judgments. A new invention in 1864 was the Shanghai Mixed Court, presided

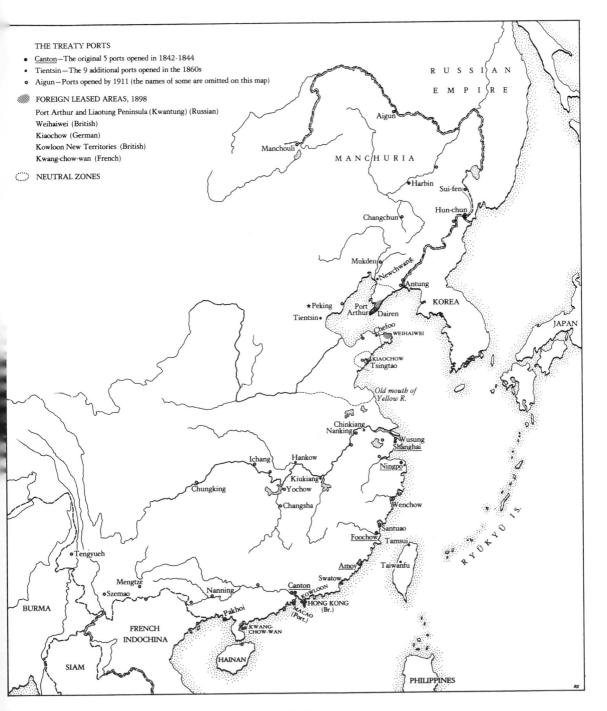

THE TREATY PORTS

● Canton—The original 5 ports opened in 1842-1844

● Tientsin—The 9 additional ports opened in the 1860s

○ Aigun—Ports opened by 1911 (the names of some are omitted on this map)

▨ FOREIGN LEASED AREAS, 1898

    Port Arthur and Liaotung Peninsula (Kwantung) (Russian)

    Weihaiwei (British)

    Kiaochow (German)

    Kowloon New Territories (British)

    Kwang-chow-wan (French)

⬭ NEUTRAL ZONES

RUSSIAN EMPIRE

Aigun

Manchouli

MANCHURIA

Harbin

Sui-fen

Hun-chun

Changchun

Mukden

Newchwang

Antung

KOREA

★ Peking

Port Arthur   Dairen

Tientsin

Chefoo

WEIHAIWEI

JAPAN

KIAOCHOW

Tsingtao

Old mouth of Yellow R.

Chinkiang

Nanking

Wusung

Shanghai

Ichang

Hankow

Ningpo

Chungking

Kiukiang

Yochow

Changsha

Wenchow

Santuao

Foochow   Tamsui

Tengyueh

Amoy

Taiwanfu

RYUKYU IS.

Mengtze

Nanning

Canton

Swatow

Szemao

KOWLOON

HONG KONG (Br.)

BURMA

Pakhoi

MACAO (Port.)

FRENCH INDOCHINA

KWANG-CHOW-WAN

SIAM

HAINAN

PHILIPPINES

FOREIGN ENCROACHMENT ON CHINA

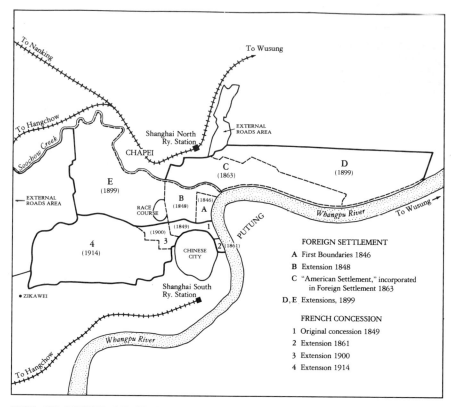

THE GROWTH OF SHANGHAI

over by a Chinese magistrate but with a foreign consular "assessor" sitting
with him as a cojudge. Using Western procedure, it handled cases between
local Chinese and cases in which Chinese were the defendants. Thus both
foreign and Chinese defendants had rights of trial before judges of their
own nationality, by the laws of their own countries.

Shanghai's business developed on the basis of extraterritoriality. As Chinese crowded in and real estate values rose, the foreign land-renters got
high profits by subrenting the land they had leased. As Shanghai, Canton,
Tientsin, Hankow, and other centers grew into great modern cities, the
vested interests dependent on extraterritoriality grew correspondingly.
What had begun as a legal device mainly to protect Western individuals
against the Chinese custom of judicial torture became even more a device
to protect foreign firms and corporations from Chinese taxation. Nationals
of countries that lacked treaty relations with China secured extraterritorial
privileges by becoming protégés of foreign treaty-power consuls. Thus,
for example, the French consuls, instead of the Chinese government, exercised jurisdiction in China over citizens of Memel, Monaco, Persia, and
Rumania. The most-favored-nation clause continued to give every treaty

power all the privileges that any one of them acquired. What had begun in the 1840's as a system to control 350 foreigners in five ports would eventually, in the twentieth century, come to include some ninety treaty ports or open ports, some twenty-five ports of call (for steamships), and about a third of a million foreign residents. The Westerners in the new treaty-port cities developed the municipal institutions of the urban West—newspapers, schools, libraries, hospitals, sewage and water systems, paved streets, and illumination. They also brought their higher standard of living with its meat diet, leather shoes, spring beds, and modern plumbing. All this made foreigners a kind of upper class in China, as privileged and powerful in its way as the Chinese upper class itself.

The Failure of Treaty Revision.   In the late 1860's the hope of both the Western and the Ch'ing officials who were active in the "cooperative policy" at Peking was that China could gradually adjust to the outside world without further disaster. Each side had its opponents to contend with. The treaty-port merchants demanded increased privileges—opening the interior to foreign steamers, railways, and mining enterprises, abolition of likin and transit taxes, permission for foreign residence anywhere, and so on. At the opposite extreme, the antiforeign die-hards were buoyed up by the Ch'ing government's success in suppressing rebellion; some were ready to try to expel the missionaries by force, relying on the sovereign strength of Chinese popular sentiment. Between these two camps—the one insatiable and the other irreconcilable—the Western diplomats and the high Ch'ing officials tried to construct peace and security.

Proposals for reform to strengthen China were submitted in 1865–1868 particularly by Hart of the Customs and by Wade of the British legation. They put forward arguments which Chinese reformers were to use more fully in later decades. Western contact had created an unprecedented foreign problem which required an unprecedented solution by domestic modernization. "If policies are altered," wrote Hart, "China can become the leader of all nations; if policies are not altered, she will become the servant of all nations." Increased contact with the West seemed one of the best ways to help China remake her civilization. In 1868 the retiring American minister, Anson Burlingame, who had been a pillar of the "cooperative policy" since 1861, was sent as China's first envoy to the Western world. As an imperial appointee of the first civil rank, he and his retinue toured the Western capitals. In Washington he concluded a treaty on rather egalitarian terms. But Burlingame was also an orator. His proclamation that a new day of Westernization and Christianity had dawned in the ancient Middle Kingdom was premature and misleading. His mission ended with his sudden death in Russia in 1870.

Meanwhile, since the treaties could be revised after ten years, Alcock with Hart's help had conducted lengthy negotiations in 1868–1869, trying to reach agreement on concessions which would partly meet the demands of the British merchants and yet not be utterly rejected by Chinese conservatives. Signed in October 1869, subject to later ratification, the Alcock Convention's statesmanlike provisions would have put the British expansion and the whole treaty system in China on a more equitable basis for the future. But because Alcock was trying to restrict and so to stabilize the foreign impact on China, his draft treaty was violently attacked by the China trade interests in Britain. Consequently the British government refused ratification. On the Chinese side Prince Kung had consulted the court and Grand Council and high provincial officials. The Convention seemed a diplomatic victory for China and the imperial approval was considered final. Britain's unexpected rejection of it was therefore a damaging blow to the moderate "cooperative policy" of the 1860's. This setback, along with the more spectacular missionary incident at Tientsin in 1870, indicated how great was the gulf between Chinese and foreign interests in China.

Growth and Change in China's Foreign Trade.   As the British position in China grew steadily stronger in the last decades of the century, the Maritime Customs Service under Hart performed a many-sided role facilitating trade under the treaties and also aiding Chinese efforts at modernization through new institutions. First of all, the Customs ensured to Peking a growing, reliable, and uncommitted source of new revenue and preserved the restricted imperial tariff against smuggling and corruption. To check the large-scale Chinese smuggling of opium, salt, and other commodities from the free port of Hong Kong into nearby Chinese territory, two measures were necessary: first, the old Portuguese port of Macao was formally ceded to Portugal in 1887, making it foreign territory; and second, the Customs set up offices in Kowloon and Lappa (close to Macao) to check the smuggling in Chinese junks. The Customs also completed the charting of the China coast, installed lighthouses, beacons, markers, and other modern aids to navigation, handled all the management of port facilities, and published trade statistics and commercial and scientific reports. Its foreign commissioners in the ports, like Hart at Peking, mediating between foreign treaty rights and Chinese interests, often performed quasi-diplomatic functions, while its Chinese staff provided a modern training ground for civil servants. From four hundred Western and fourteen hundred Chinese employees in 1875, the staff grew to seven hundred and thirty-five hundred in 1895, more than half the Westerners being British. In brief, Hart and the Customs were at the core of the treaty system, and their work was one of its most constructive aspects, however the whole system may be judged.

With the growth of the treaty ports into modern cities came the advances

*A Maritime Customs Assistant and his staff, 1892. W. Hancock
(Chinese name, Han Wei-li) rose from Third Assistant, Class B, in
1877, to Acting Commissioner in 1904. This photograph was
probably taken in Hanoi on his journey from Hong Kong
to the Yunnan border. Mr. Hancock's Chinese teacher, Mr. Lo,
on right, is with his two wives and their maids.*

in technology that brought China constantly closer to the outside world. In
1869 the Suez Canal halved the distance to Europe. In 1870–1871 cables
were laid connecting Vladivostok, Nagasaki, Shanghai, Hong Kong, and
Singapore, whence telegraphic communication went on around the world
via London to San Francisco. China was thus drawn further into the world
economy and became more subject to the vicissitudes of international prices,
business crises, and foreign competition. During the latter part of the nineteenth century the China trade was affected by the worldwide fall in the
value of silver, as silver output rose and many countries went on the gold
standard, demonetizing their silver. The treaty tariff had been set at fixed
monetary rates which in many cases represented 5 per cent in 1858 but
generally became lower as prices rose in subsequent decades. Foreign imports
and Chinese exports, as they passed in either direction between treaty ports
and the interior, were to pay an additional 2½ per cent (half the tariff
duty) as transit dues, and be subsequently free from all the likin and other
taxes that goods in China's purely domestic commerce might have to pay.
Similarly an additional 2½ per cent could be paid as "coast trade" duty to

*Commissioner of Customs H. F. Merrill (Harvard '74) at Ningpo,
about 1894, with his wife, daughter, and household staff: (from left)
amah, nurse-girl, number-one boy (in charge), number-two boy,
gateman, cook, number-two cook, wash boy, and four chairbearers.*

avoid all further taxes on Chinese goods carried in foreign ships from one
Chinese port to another. These arrangements prevented China from imposing a protective tariff, a considerable impairment of sovereignty, and
gave the foreign merchant a privileged advantage over his Chinese
competitor.

Foreign merchants, having looked forward to a rich opportunity, were
correspondingly frustrated when this Eldorado failed to materialize. During
the 1870's and 1880's China failed to provide the expected market for
Western products. By 1890 the total value of the China trade, both in and
out, was only 50 million pounds sterling, less than that of many small countries and was already surpassed by Japan's foreign trade. The chief reasons
for this stagnation were no doubt China's poverty, self-sufficiency, and conservatism. But British merchants ascribed it to a mandarin conspiracy
whereby transit taxes still prevented the "opening" of the China market.

In the content of the trade, the great staples of mid-century, opium
imports and tea exports, both reached their highest volume and then declined. Legalized and taxed under the treaty settlement of 1858–1860,
opium imports reached a peak of 87,000 chests in 1879, but thereafter
declined because production of opium within China (several times the quantity imported) increasingly supplied the still growing Chinese market.

Similarly tea exports to Britain rose, from 30 million pounds in the 1830's, to a peak of 150 million pounds in the 1880's but thereafter declined because tea from India and Ceylon, transplanted there from China in mid-century, began to take over the British market. China failed to modernize her tea industry. Indian tea was produced by large-scale methods on big plantations created by capital investment. It was carefully standardized and exported free of duty. Chinese tea was collected from individual farmers on a small-scale basis, its quality was not protected against adulteration by get-rich-quick dealers, and it was taxed both in transit and on export. China's silk, her most famous product, began to suffer a similar decline after 1900 because in Europe and in Japan scientific prevention of silkworm disease, mechanization of silk reeling, and modern market organization produced a higher quality standardized product. The Ch'ing government was unable to perform functions of commercial leadership and regulation which governments were performing elsewhere.

China's production of cotton, mainly in the Yangtze Valley, had supplied a large handicraft industry. After the second treaty settlement, imports of cotton goods up to 1890 failed to achieve the great increase that Britain hoped for. The principal growth was not in cotton textiles, but in cotton yarn, imports of which, mainly from India, increased twentyfold from 1872 to 1890. This was because machine-spinning of yarn was some eighty times as productive as hand-spinning, while machine-weaving of cloth was only about four times as fast as hand-weaving. Thus the cheaper cotton yarn from abroad crippled the native Chinese spinning industry but supplied Chinese weaving, which still continued for many years on hand looms in peasant households as before.

Opinions differ as to the net effect of foreign trade on nineteenth-century China. The classic Marxist concept, of machine-industry products disrupting the handicraft industries of a backward country's farm economy, seems to apply to China only in a limited degree, for China's involvement in the world economy was less than that of fully colonial areas in Southeast Asia. As tea and silk exports declined, China began to export diverse products (vegetable oils, tung oil, pig bristles, hides and skins, and soybeans) which were mainly by-products of cheap labor on small farms rather than on plantations or in factories.

Compradors, Bankers, and Entrepreneurs.   Unlike the rivalry of foreign missionaries and Chinese gentry, foreign and Chinese merchants needed one another. In the Canton trade the hong merchants had been the chief intermediaries between foreign traders and the great Chinese domestic market. In the treaty ports after 1842 their place was taken by the compradors. But where the hong merchants had been Chinese-style brokers licensed by government, the compradors were contractual employees of foreign trading firms who handled the Chinese side of their business. The compradors bridged the cultural, linguistic, and institutional gap between East and West. One of the most famous was Tong King-sing, who like most early compradors came from the Canton delta. Having got an English-language missionary education, he served as a Hong Kong government interpreter and then as a Maritime Customs clerk at Shanghai and in 1863 became Jardine, Matheson and Company's comprador there. Typically, he purchased degree status and so acquired membership in the official class, while also becoming a capitalist investor in treaty-port enterprises.

Comprador-merchants were only the most visible element in the growth of China's domestic trade. Another consisted of private banking that developed through chains of money shops centered in the coastal region at Ningpo and also, curiously enough, in certain cities of Shansi in the landlocked Northwest. Shansi had long been a strategic center of imperial control and a crossroads of trade routes—between Mongolia and Szechwan and between North China and Central Asia—as well as a transfer area between camel caravans and the canal transport of North and Central China. Shansi merchants already had widespread connections and a pawnshop business in other provinces, and had also begun to guarantee silver shipments by employing private mounted troops to convoy them. As the spread of banditry endangered the shipping of silver bullion, shippers began to use banking facilities. Where an armed convoy of silver would cost 2 or 3 per cent of its value, these private remittance banks charged a rate of only three-tenths of 1 per cent for drafts.

The pioneer Shansi banker in the period around 1800 was a dye-shop merchant, who had a shop in Tientsin, set up an office to buy materials in Chungking, and so got into the remittance business. The number of banking chains eventually grew to between twenty and thirty, organized in three main groups based in central Shansi. In order to be licensed by the Board of Revenue at Peking, new banks had to get a guarantee from others already in the business. The Shansi firms maintained a near monopoly by withholding their guarantee from extra-provincial capitalists. High provincial authorities, who were some of the greatest shippers of funds and who normally accumulated their personal fortunes through "squeeze," came to rely upon these private bankers in many unofficial ways. The banks not only transmitted their official funds to Peking, but specialized in dealing with the greedy functionaries who lined the route from the provincial treasuries to the Board of Revenue. The banks also advanced funds to officials expecting lucrative appointments. From the second quarter of the nineteenth century they helped the Canton trade transfer funds by draft to purchase teas and silks in Central China and pay for opium imports.

In the distribution of foreign imports Chinese dealers were aided by their guild organization and superior knowledge of local conditions. Foreign firms, which had originally set up branches in every port, began to close them and concentrate their business in major shipping centers like Hong Kong and Shanghai. In the interport trade, that is, from one treaty port to another in China's domestic commerce, Chinese merchants became the principal users of the foreign shipping, which was more secure and reliable than native shipping. In short, Chinese capitalists could also benefit from the security and facilities of the treaty system. Compradors who left foreign employment and became treaty-port entrepreneurs were only the most prominent representatives of this trend.

Shanghai's rise as the capital market of China was marked by the formation in 1865, mainly by British firms, of the Hong Kong and Shanghai Banking Corporation. It and other foreign banks financed Chinese merchants and Chinese banks, transferred funds between ports, handled remittances from Chinese overseas, and even issued their own banknote currency. Chinese capital was attracted to the ports by the security of investment in real estate, as well as by the need for local industries—to process goods; to provide public utilities and urban housing; and to support the shipping industry. This cooperative Sino-foreign growth attracted Chinese capital and talent. For example, in 1862 Russell and Company organized a steamship line by securing capital in roughly equal portions from partners in the United States, from foreign merchants in China, and from Chinese merchants and compradors. By securing shallow-draft American side-wheeler steamboats and setting up a regular twice-weekly service between Shanghai and Hankow, this American-led, Chinese-backed enterprise inaugurated the great era of steamboating on the Yangtze.

After 1870, economic growth in the treaty ports was creating resources of investment capital and entrepreneurial skill which, in favorable circumstances and in due time, might have been used to bring China through that critical phase of industrialization, the breakthrough into self-sustaining growth. But the treaty ports were only one sector of the Chinese economy. Contemporary experience in Japan showed that success in industrial modernization would have required more central support and more comprehensive scope. It would have needed a whole set of circumstances that were lacking in China outside the treaty ports—more clearly defined national political goals, a more stable framework of law and monetary practice, stronger leadership from the government, and a more independent style of entrepreneurship.

The Difficulties of Early Industrialization

During the quarter-century after 1870 the rate of China's economic modernization, though considerable, fell behind that of Japan and the West. Steamboating on the Yangtze imitated that on the Mississippi, but a subsequent era of railroading did not ensue, as it did in the American West. While industrialization was beginning to spread throughout Japan, it remained limited to a few small enclaves in China. China's slowness to industrialize may be attributed to a complex of factors—intellectual, psychological, social, economic, political, and administrative.

The Inadequacy of Government Leadership. The idea that the unequal treaties prevented China's industrialization, if we can judge by the Japanese example, is over-simple and does not explain what happened. Decision lay first with the Chinese government; only the government's default gave the treaty port its later dominant role. The restrictive effect of the treaty system was cumulative, and evils visible in its later years were by no means inevitable from the start. In short, the incapacity of government to take the lead was the first great fact in China's slowness to industrialize.

This incapacity of Peking was most evident in two sectors, finance and policy. Peking's antiquated fiscal system was still based on tax-farming— that is, provincial officials were expected to make certain tax quotas available to Peking while maintaining themselves and their administrations on the remainder of what they collected. Budgeting, accounting, central planning, and control were impossible. About 1890, Peking listed annual revenues totaling roughly 89 million taels (see table, page 568), but of these reported collections, only a part ever reached Peking, the greater part being allotted for provincial uses. However, the unreported collections were probably three to five times as great as those listed for the Peking record. Mobilization of fiscal resources was thus beyond the power of the central government.

In the provinces, industrialization was hindered by the purblind opposition of the official class. This intellectual conservatism was evident, for instance, in the economic views of Tseng Kuo-fan. In 1867 he noted with distaste that Western nations for centuries had been squabbling greedily over material gains; their merchants in the treaty ports sought profit at the expense of China; modern steamers, railways, and telegraphs, if managed by foreigners or by Chinese attached to foreigners, would threaten the livelihood of the common people (*min-sheng*); Confucian government must protect the people's livelihood, lest the wrath of the multitude be provoked. Tseng, though a leader in "self-strengthening," had no concept of modern economic development. Advocates of Westernization in the late nineteenth century are now blamed by some in retrospect for their failure to industrialize. At the time, however, they were attacked for attempting too many changes too rapidly. Their attackers, ignorant of the outside world, saw much innovation at home but could not see the larger paradox, that in spite of her considerable rate of change, China was steadily falling behind other nations. The Chinese upper class accepted neither the concept of progress (implying con-

The infant emperor Kuang-hsü (born 1871) on horseback.

tinual change and rejection of stability) nor the concept of nationalism (implying international competition on an equal basis).

Behind the inertia of the Ch'ing leaders lay their vested interests in maintaining the power structure of the day and in using modernization only for personal and political aims within that structure. During most of the period up to 1894 the court remained firmly under the control of the Empress Dowager Tz'u-hsi, who steadily built up her bureaucratic machine. She dominated the young emperor, and according to legend even encouraged him in a life of excess that brought on his death in January 1875 at the age of nineteen. To maintain herself in power the Empress Dowager now broke the sacred dynastic law of succession, which required that a new emperor always be chosen from the succeeding generation in order to maintain the ritual observances demanded by filial piety. Instead, she shocked propriety by having her own nephew (the son of her sister), a four-year-old boy of the same generation as his predecessor, selected emperor with the reign title of Kuang-hsü ("Glorious Succession," 1875–1908). Until he took on the imperial functions in 1889, she continued to rule. She removed Prince Kung from power in 1884. Officeholders all over the empire quietly contributed to her personal fortune.

The Empress Dowager's forceful personality was devoted to a conservative end, the maintenance of the dynasty by keeping an equilibrium between the traditional central power and the new regional interests. Regionalism was buttressed by the modernization projects of leading officials, their new arsenals and industries in provincial centers. The Empress Dowager could maintain the Manchu dynasty only by cooperating with and manipulating the regional leaders, all of whom with proper Confucian reverence still looked up to the Ch'ing throne for official appointment and for final answers, with no thought as yet of exercising the independent power of warlords.

Li Hung-chang's Industrial Empire.   Li Hung-chang's career (see page 480) illustrates the delicate balance between regional power and dynastic loyalty. During the quarter-century after 1870 he remained continuously in power at Tientsin, as governor-general of Chihli and commissioner for the northern ports, quite contrary to the tradition that even the highest official should be shifted every three, or at most six, years. Li's position was based on three elements: first, on his Anhwei Army, between twenty-five and forty thousand strong, stationed in Chihli and Shantung and for many years also in Kiangsu, supplied by arsenals at Tientsin, Nanking, and Shanghai; second, on his bureaucratic machine of some two hundred younger commanders, officials, and technical specialists, many of them from Li's native place (Ho-fei) in Anhwei, who worked under him as their patron; and third, on local provincial revenues plus those collected for defense of the metropolitan province of Chihli, mainly from lower Yangtze sources. In bringing Li to North China the Empress Dowager had evidently decided to join forces with, rather than oppose, his growing power. The two came to depend upon one another in matters both of policy and of profit. Li Hung-chang's machine, like that of an American city boss, utilized the flow of public funds through private hands. Thus his long leadership in Westernization had mixed motives, patriotic and personal, ideological and pecuniary.

In organizing new economic projects, Li and others used the formula "government supervision and merchant operation" (*kuan-tu shang-pan*), meaning that these were profit-oriented enterprises operated by merchants but controlled by officials. This followed the tradition of the salt monopoly, a fiscal device for milking official taxes and private squeeze from a monopolized staple for which there was an inelastic demand. This static, tax-farming tradition was antithetic to that of the dynamic, risk-taking entrepreneur who founds modern industries. It made for distribution of profits rather than their reinvestment, for profiteering rather than industrialization.

Li's first venture was naturally in steamships. Peking's food supply still depended on the lower Yangtze tribute rice which came by barge up the decaying Grand Canal and by seagoing junk around Shantung. Accordingly, the China Merchants' Steam Navigation Company which Li set up in 1872 was financed partly by an annual government subsidy for haulage of tribute rice. Li first appointed as managers men experienced, quite inappropriately, in the junk transport of tribute rice; but he soon turned to Jardine's English-speaking comprador Tong King-sing, who had been directing the operation of their steamships as well as some owned by himself and other Chinese. In the new company under Tong, the merchant shareholders generally became managers, with official titles. They secured perquisites and patronage, appointing relatives and friends to the staff. The enterprise was neither government-run nor private in modern terms, but a hybrid in which officials and merchants cooperated to get rich. Aided by the tribute rice subsidy, the China Merchants' line competed successfully with the foreign lines in Chinese waters. In 1877, it bought the larger fleet of Russell and Company, thus became the biggest, and thereafter maintained monopolistic rate agreements with the British lines. However, the latter reinvested their profits more prudently, while the China Merchants' managers took out the profits and let the fleet deteriorate. British ships eventually recovered their dominance in China's domestic carrying trade.

This company served as a prototype for other enterprises. The system of "government supervision and merchant operation" demonstrated in one enterprise after another that it was a traditional, not a modern, institution. First, it suffered from nepotistic and cliquish favoritism, squeeze, and lack of risk-taking initiative. Second, being under government control, managers were motivated to share profits immediately, rather than to save them for reinvestment in their enterprises, lest they be taken by the government. Finally, "government supervision" usually brought certain monopoly rights, originally granted to assist competition with the foreigner, but soon used as props to compensate for inefficiency.

Impelled by the logic of one industry demanding another, Li with Tong King-sing as his manager began in 1876 to develop a modern coal mine at Kaiping north of Tientsin. This aimed to supply fuel for China Merchants' ships and to give them a southbound cargo after they had brought tribute rice north. The use of modern pumps, fans, and hoists soon yielded profits from coal seams that old-style Chinese pit-miners had abandoned. With a dozen Western engineers and modern equipment, the new Kaiping Mining Company by 1883 had set up machine shops, produced its own engines, railway cars, and tugboats, and installed local telephones, telegraphs, and a railroad line seven miles long. It was soon producing 250,000 tons of coal a year. However, Tong King-sing died in 1892 and his successor was a Chinese bannerman close to the Manchu court, an expert in the art of squeeze, who milked the company of its resources. It became increasingly dependent on foreign loans and in 1900 was taken over by a British company, represented by an American engineer (later President), Herbert Hoover. After 1912 Kaiping was absorbed into the Sino-British Kailan Mining Administration.

Thus in North China, the steamship brought the coal mine, which required in turn a railroad. Early railway projects had been vetoed by officials determined to forestall foreign exploitation. A small, unauthorized Shanghai-

*China's first railway, Shanghai-Wusung, a 30-inch narrow-gauge
track built in 1876 by Jardine, Matheson and Company and
others. At left: the first engine, the British-made "Pioneer"; note
Chinese attendant wearing queue. Center: the 9-ton engine
"Celestial Empire," with six 27-inch wheels. Line was purchased
and destroyed by Chinese authorities in 1877.*

Wusung line, opened by foreigners in 1876 (see figure above), was
purchased the next year by the Nanking governor-general, who promptly
had it torn up. The railway begun for Kaiping coal was extended only
slowly—south to Tientsin in 1888, northeast to Shanhaikuan in 1894, and
to the outskirts of Peking in 1896, about 240 miles in all. Except for a
short line in Formosa, this was the sum of China's response to the railroad
age after thirty years of agitation. The reasons for this retardation are in-
structive. First, the water transport network was well developed and offered
severe competition except in North China. Steamships had penetrated China
on waterways that went far into the interior, but railroads had to invade
Chinese life much more directly, crossing canals and rice fields and disturbing grave mounds. Popular superstitions and xenophobic opposition could
be easily aroused. High land values, when combined with popular sentiment,
made any right of way a costly investment. Capital was not easily mobilized; government finances were weak, while bond issues and other devices
for the creation of credit were underdeveloped. Peking's defensive strategy
was to oppose both foreign-run railroads and big foreign loans for Chinese
lines.

The mandarin-industrialist who rose to the top of Li Hung-chang's industrial empire was Sheng Hsüan-huai (1844–1916). After being assistant

manager of the China Merchants' line, Sheng organized another "government-supervised, merchant-operated" enterprise, the Imperial Telegraph Administration. Despite its official-sounding name, this company built up its capital of some two million dollars by selling shares to "merchants," particularly to Sheng and others in the management. The government made loans and policed the telegraph lines, to protect them against irate farmers fearful of the effect of the tall poles on geomantic forces of "wind and water"; but the profits went into annual returns of as much as 20 per cent to the shareholders. Until after 1900, when the company's lines were gradually nationalized, Li Hung-chang through his deputy, Sheng, controlled the telegraph administration all over the country, appointing its personnel and protecting them against charges of corruption.

In the industrialization of many countries, machine production of cotton goods had been the leading industry. Cotton mills were proving very successful in Japan in the 1880's. As early as 1878 Li began to sponsor a Chinese textile mill, the Shanghai Cotton Cloth Mill, to compete with foreign imports. The throne granted it tax exemption and a ten-year monopoly to produce cotton cloth and yarn; foreign machinery and engineers arrived. But merchant shares were subscribed in inadequate amounts, and the first manager invested the funds unwisely. After Sheng Hsüan-huai took over the project in 1887, he financed the mill with loans from the China Merchants' Company, which he also headed, and from Li Hung-chang's provincial government in Chihli. Beginning in 1890, some four thousand factory workers were soon turning out excellent cloth and yarn, and some 25 per cent was paid on shares in 1893, when the mill unfortunately burned down uninsured. Undaunted, Li and Sheng planned to set up eleven more mills, monopolize a new Chinese textile industry, and eliminate foreign imports. They had five mills in operation when the Sino-Japanese War of 1894–1895 cut short their hopes.

The Slow Progress of Modernization

The material growth of the treaty ports with their commerce and industry was of course accompanied by intellectual and cultural innovation. Yet the new ideas and attitudes got from Western contact remained minor elements in the broad stream of Chinese tradition. The wearing of the queue, the long gown of the scholar, the bound feet of women, marriage and funeral processions and the palanquins of officials passing through the crowded streets—the whole appearance of Chinese life remained unaffected by any vogue for things Western such as was sweeping contemporary Japan. Ideas of change were spreading, but very slowly. If we look at such new developments as the modern post office, the press, and the training of students abroad, we see a common pattern: in each case China's modernization was inspired by Western examples and yet had to be superimposed upon old indigenous institutions, which persisted so strongly as to slow down the need or demand for innovation.

Postal Services and the Press.   Robert Hart early began to work toward setting up a nationwide modern postal service, but it took him thirty years because he found China's needs already met, though at a premodern level of efficiency. First, there were the sixteen hundred or so official horse-post stations on the five main routes radiating from Peking over the empire. This ancient system moved official persons, correspondence, goods, and money but only for government purposes. Second, for the postal needs of the common people, commercial "letter hongs" forwarded private mail for small fees according to the distance and profitability of the route, without attempting, however, to reach all parts of China. By the end of the century there were some three hundred letter hongs registered in the twenty-four treaty ports and many more in the country as a whole. Finally, Western governments set up their own postal services between major cities in foreign trade and opened this facility to foreign residents. Eventually dozens of these foreign post offices operated in China.

To develop a modern national post, in the midst of all these vested interests, Hart used the resources of the Maritime Customs. Given the task of transmitting legation mail overland to Peking in wintertime, the Customs gradually built up a postal department. Eventually it got foreign steamers in Chinese waters to carry only the mail of the imperial post office, which was formally set up as part of the Customs in 1896. It became the agency for all steamer shipment of the mails of the private letter hongs and began to put its old-style competitors out of business.

The rise of professional journalism, another index of modernization, also had its venerable antecedents. The famous *Peking Gazette* dated back at least to the T'ang and reproduced official documents made public at the court, but it was not an official publication nor did it appear in one single form: private firms in Peking produced and distributed the so-called gazette on a commercial basis, disseminating court news and imperial documents among the scholar-gentry class all over the empire. In the cities news was also spread by commercial handbills or newsprints, produced as a sideline by printing shops and hawked in the streets. Price lists distributed by guilds and book publishing, usually under official or scholar-gentry auspices, were other traditional mechanisms for spreading printed information.

Protestant missionaries injected a revolutionary element into these ancient channels. Barred from the interior until the 1860's, they early resorted to print to spread the gospel in Chinese translation and in the vernacular, not the classical style. The London Missionary Society set up a press at Malacca in 1815 and published a monthly magazine in Chinese. Other missionaries followed this example. Besides the missionary periodicals in Chinese, there were English-language newspapers like the *China Mail* (Hong Kong, 1845–   ) and the *North China Herald* (Shanghai, 1850–   ) which served the trading community and became the immediate models for modern-style Chinese newspapers.

Chinese journalism finally rose above the purely factual level when men of literary talent began to publish editorial opinion—an activity strictly discountenanced by the dynasty and therefore possible only under treaty-port protection. The pioneer in this field, Wang T'ao, began life as a classical scholar, spent the 1850's in Shanghai as Chinese editor of the London Missionary Society press, and in the 1860's helped James Legge complete his monumental translations of the *Five Classics* (see pages 41–42). Two years of this period Wang spent with Legge in Scotland. After this long apprenticeship, Wang T'ao became in the 1870's an independent journalist, founding and editing his own daily newspaper in Hong Kong and publishing his own comments, enriched by his travels in Europe and Japan. Wang T'ao was a forerunner—at heart a nationalist, intellectually a critic of the Chinese scene. His Western contact generated ideas both of patriotism and of reform.

Training Abroad.   A still greater stimulus for reform came from the experience of education in the West. The pioneer "returned student" was a poor boy from Macao, Yung Wing, who learned English in missionary schools and was sent by missionaries to the United States. He became a Christian and an American citizen and graduated from Yale in 1854. His Yale education revealed to him, he said, "responsibilities which the sealed eye of ignorance can never see." He conceived that "through Western education China might be regenerated, become enlightened and powerful." But not until 1872 was Yung Wing finally able, with the support of Tseng Kuo-fan and Li Hung-chang, to realize his long-cherished dream of sending an educational mission to the United States. Under this scheme 120 long-gowned Chinese boys, mainly from poor Cantonese families, went in four classes of 30 each to Hartford, Connecticut, where they were boarded out with families up and down the Connecticut Valley but came periodically to the mission headquarters for Chinese classical studies. Soon, however, they underwent "a gradual but marked transformation" in speech and dress, hiding their queues and developing athletic, exuberant, undecorous ways—becoming, in short, Americanized. Yung Wing, who had by now married an American girl and was more Congregational than Confucian in outlook, encouraged this acculturation but his conservative colleagues were appalled, and their outrage reverberated in Peking. The mission was expensive and an anti-Chinese movement had been growing in California, where Oriental exclusion was already a political issue. In 1881 the educational mission, for a variety of reasons, was given up. The students from Hartford who arrived

THE CHINESE EDUCATIONAL MISSION TO THE UNITED STATES.
*Above: Students on arrival in San Francisco en route to Hartford,
Connecticut, 1872. Below: Chinese students' baseball team
("The Orientals"), Hartford, 1878. The mission was recalled in
1881.*

AMERICAN PRESBYTERIAN PIONEERS: THE REV. CALVIN W. AND
MRS. JULIA B. MATEER. *In Tengchow, Shantung, Calvin Mateer
founded a secondary school, helped translate the Bible,
published many textbooks including the widely used* Mandarin
Lessons *(1892), and advocated higher education from the West to
undergird Christianity in China.*

back in Shanghai to kowtow before the taotai were greeted with suspicion as
a threat to the vested interest of all scholars in the unreformed classical
examination system. Consequently Yung Wing's boys contributed to China's
modernization mainly through Western technology or management, in the
navy, the telegraph and railroad administrations, the diplomatic service, and
the Kaiping mines. Only twelve became regular officials.

Protestant Missions and Modernization. The same record of vigorous
pioneering and modest results, of great effort and much frustration, typified
the missionary movement. Foreign Catholic priests numbered about 250 in
1870 and about 750 in 1896, whereas numbers of Protestants arriving in
China roughly doubled every decade. Protestant mission stations increased
accordingly—from 35 in 14 places in 1860, to 498 in 356 places in 1900.
Yet by 1890, when the 1300 Protestant missionaries outnumbered the Catholics two to one, they had only 37,000 Protestant communicants, compared
with the half-million Catholics. The Protestant missionary force was composed for the most part of Americans and Britishers in roughly equal

numbers, mainly from the middle class or rural areas, and often without much higher education. While most Protestants remained committed to evangelism, an increasing minority began to see that good works might be more fruitful than evangelism alone. Reform came naturally to them. Their efforts to change individual conduct set them vigorously against many social customs—polygamy, child marriage, foot-binding, gambling, fortune-telling, the idolatry of other religions, and even Confucian reverence for ancestors, as well as infanticide and the opium evil. Literacy and therefore schooling were necessary to the reception of the gospel, and an educated native pastorate to its propagation. By 1877, when the first General Conference of Protestant Missionaries surveyed the scene, there were twenty theological schools with 231 students. Protestant primary schools gradually grew to secondary level, came to be called "colleges" (like St. John's College at Shanghai after 1879), and in time became counterparts, if not offshoots, of the denominational colleges in New England and the Middle West. Thus the missionary band from Oberlin College, in 1881, were forerunners of the Student Volunteer Movement for Foreign Missions that began to recruit American college youths for mission work. There was a parallel growth of medical missions, dispensaries, hospitals, and medical schools for Chinese doctors. By 1890, when the second General Conference of Protestant Missionaries met, they had a "Medical Missionary Association of China" in action parallel to their "Educational Association of China." There was no limit to the Christian opportunity for good works.

One Baptist who fought the terrible famine of 1877–1879 in Shansi was Timothy Richard, a Welshman of broad imagination who believed that Christianity, as the dynamic of Western civilization, could win China more effectively in proportion as China accepted the fruits of Western civilization in general. Human progress, Western-style, was part of God's plan, and good works, especially education, were necessary to progress. From 1891, as secretary of the SDK (Society for the Diffusion of Christian and General Knowledge among the Chinese), Richard sought to spread ideas of reform among the scholar and official classes. He had an ally in Young J. Allen from Georgia who had become a translator and editor, publishing from 1868 a weekly "mission news" for the Chinese Christian community. Allen expanded this into *The Globe Magazine* (later translated *Review of the Times*). This journal, ably edited by Chinese scholars, presented in literary Chinese a wide selection of Western ideas and information. It became in fact one source of the Reform Movement of the late 1890's.

Yet like Wang T'ao's editorials and Yung Wing's educational mission, missionary espousals of reform were peripheral to Chinese life, products of the new Sino-Western community in the port cities, remote from the peasants or scholar gentry. Until Japan's smashing victory of 1895, Chinese thinking remained for the most part firmly in the grip of tradition.

20. Imperialist Encroachments on China, Vietnam, and Korea

Foreign Aggression on China's Periphery

Imperialist rivalry, nibbling at the periphery of the Chinese world, intensified after 1870 for a number of reasons. In Europe economic nationalism moved the democracies, Britain and France, to lead the way in colonial expansion. The literate citizenry of every European power, newly in contact with world events through the growth of the urban press, developed varying degrees of enthusiasm for national exploits overseas. These were rationalized by the doctrine of Social Darwinism—that races and nations necessarily compete for survival, and only the fittest survive. The religious enthusiasm of missionaries was echoed in the idealism of administrators conscious of the "white man's burden." Newspaper-reading publics became, psychologically, men-on-the-spot, alarmed or elated by the day's events and likely to clamor for action.

As the competition for colonies developed, it became apparent that the Chinese Empire had uncertain or unstable frontiers. Maps were usually unreliable, historical claims often conflicted, and the limits of Ch'ing authority came increasingly into dispute. To the uncertainties of terrain were added the vagueness and timidity of Peking's claims to suzerainty over tributary states. After all, the tribute system was mainly a defensive institution, based less on treaty law than on Confucian ethics, less on military domination than on cultural supremacy. When called upon either to take responsibility for disorders in tributary areas and recompense aggrieved foreigners or else to renounce suzerain jurisdiction, Peking's first impulse was to avoid responsibility and payment of indemnities. Thus the Ryūkyū

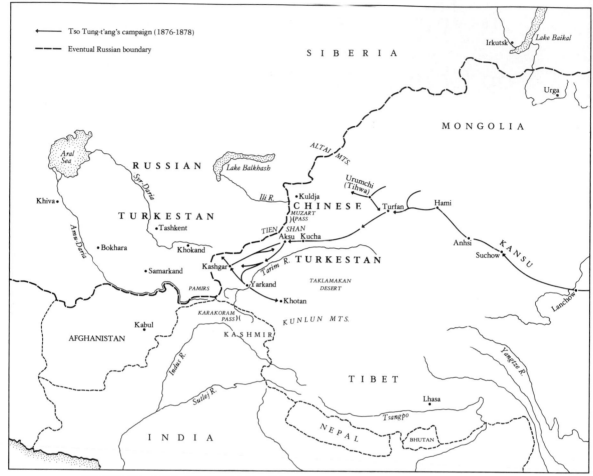

CENTRAL ASIA IN THE NINETEENTH CENTURY

(Liu-ch'iu) Islands, Taiwan, Vietnam, Korea, and areas of Central Asia gradually became fair game for foreign colonial expansion.

Russian Pressure in Central Asia.   The territorial integrity of the Ch'ing Empire was endangered in the 1870's on its farthest northwestern frontier, in Chinese Turkestan. Of the three principal areas there of concern to Ch'ing strategists, the first was the region around Hami (or Komul), which was the key point of ingress to Central Asia across the desert road from China's northwest province of Kansu. The Hami region and other nearby centers to the west, had been the Manchus' logistic base for military expeditions farther west and also a source of Turkic-speaking allies and administrators to assist in the Ch'ing conquest and rule of Central Asia.

The second strategic area centered on the grazing land of the Ili River valley, between the Altai Mountains on the north and the T'ien Shan on the south. This was the former homeland of the Zungar tribe of the Western Mongols, and after their annihilation in the 1750's, it had been populated by penal colonies and military garrisons, ruled by a military governor at the chief city, Kuldja. In this and other Ch'ing outposts, Chinese tea, silk, and cotton textiles were traded for horses from the Kazakh tribal lands to the northwest.

The third region, least firmly under Ch'ing control, consisted of the oasis cities in the Tarim River basin south of the T'ien Shan and east of the Pamir massif, a region sometimes called Kashgaria after the principal oasis and focus of the trade routes. In these centers the population was predominantly Turkic-speaking and Muslim, much the same as in the trading oasis states west of the Pamirs. The two Central Asian regions east and west of the Pamirs were closely connected by language, religion, culture, trade, and politics, for they both had been ruled in succession by the Mongol Khanate of Chaghadai; by the empire of Tamerlane in the thirteenth and fourteenth centuries (see pages 165, 200), and then from the fourteenth to the seventeenth centuries by the Moghuls, warriors who claimed Mongol descent though Turkic in language and Muslim in religion.

Latest in this sequence of rulers were the members of a religious clan descended from the Prophet Muhammad, the Khoja family, who had risen to power in many of the oasis cities in the late seventeenth century. Khoja rulers in Kashgaria thus had close ties west of the Pamirs and could find support there. When driven out by the Ch'ing some of their descendants took refuge in Khokand across the mountains to the west. The Khokand khanate became a center of commercial expansion and developed a tributary trade with the Ch'ing. It was also a base for anti-Ch'ing rebels. The Ch'ing governors in Kashgaria had conferred the title of *beg,* together with lands and serfs, on some 270 local chiefs who thus formed a local ruling class nominally beholden to Peking. Nevertheless, being on the farthest fringe of the Chinese world, they could not easily be kept under control.

By 1860, after only a century of Ch'ing rule, Chinese or Eastern Turkestan was of increasing interest to the expanding empires of Russia and Britain. The Russians in particular, encroaching steadily southward and southeast across the Kirghiz and Kazakh steppe, were about to take over Western or Russian Turkestan with its cotton production and its strategic access to the northern fringes of British India. Meanwhile Peking kept a tenuous hold on Kashgaria and Ili, at a distance of 3500 miles and six weeks by horse-post. This was dictated by a strong tradition of strategic, rather than economic, concern for the western borders of Mongolia.

In 1862 the Muslim rebellion in Northwest China led to a rising in Chinese Turkestan which got Khoja support from Khokand. A Khokandian general, Yakub Beg, soon seized power and ruled much of the Tarim basin as an independent Muslim state from 1865 to 1877. In 1871, to forestall Yakub and British influence, the Russians moved troops into the strategic Ili River valley and occupied the commercial center of Kuldja, where they had had a consul and a regulated trade since 1851 (see page 479). The Russians promised Peking they would withdraw from Ili whenever Ch'ing control should be re-established.

By the mid-1870's Peking thus faced a crisis. Although Tso Tsung-t'ang's forces had suppressed the Northwest Muslims in 1873, his men were in Kansu province, roughly as far from Yakub's capital at Kashgar as Kansas City is from Los Angeles, on a route that crossed many hundred miles of desert and required ninety days' travel by caravan. At the same time China was embroiled with Japan over the Taiwan issue (see page 511).

This crisis evoked two schools of strategy. Li Hung-chang, and others concerned with "self-strengthening" and coastal defense against seaborne aggression, opposed the financing of a costly effort by Tso Tsung-t'ang to reconquer unproductive territory in far-off Central Asia. After a great debate in memorials presented to the throne, Tso won out and went ahead. Central Asia had bulked large in the dynasty's traditional strategy of defense against the Mongols; its recovery was necessary to show reverence for the imperial ancestors. Tso raised foreign and Chinese loans in Shanghai to buy Western cannon and operate an arsenal and a woolen mill at Lanchow. Meanwhile he fed and clothed his troops partly by making them farmers to grow grain and cotton. He built up a base area in Kansu, with advanced bases farther west. In 1876, Tso's troops dashed across the desert route, seized Urumchi and other strategic centers and mercilessly slaughtered the Chinese-speaking Muslim rebels of the northern region, treating them as domestic traitors. They then invaded the Tarim basin, treating the Uighur Turkish population more leniently as frontier rebels. Yakub died in 1877. By 1878 Tso had recovered all Chinese Turkestan except the Ili region.

This spectacular achievement led Peking to demand that Russia evacuate Ili. The first Manchu negotiator fatuously conceded so much to Russia that he was threatened with beheading. A great diplomatic furor and war scare ensued. But the crisis passed. Another treaty in 1881 exacted a larger indemnity from China but restored most of Ili to the Ch'ing. In 1884 Chinese Turkestan was made a province under the name Sinkiang, "The New Dominion." This happy outcome fostered a resurgence of Chinese self-confidence and confirmed the conservatives in their easy talk of fighting off foreign aggression while complacently opposing Westernization.

China's Slow Diplomatic Response. Why was Peking so slow to send abroad envoys who could observe the enemy's home circumstances and defend China's interests? Western ministers resided in Peking from 1861, but no Chinese diplomatic mission functioned abroad until 1877. This inertia had its roots in both psychology and politics. Traditionally, envoys had gone abroad in times of strength to spread the imperial prestige, but in times of weakness to beg peace from barbarian tribes. Once the imperial prestige had been shattered by the stationing at Peking of Western ministers who need not kowtow, foreign relations had become humiliating. This wounded pride was utilized in politics. The power of Westernizers like Li Hung-chang grew with Western contact but could best be checked and balanced by tolerating the shrill accusations of die-hard conservatives who condemned all association with foreigners as simple treason. The Empress Dowager accordingly gave ear to both sides and profited from the stalemate.

Foreign expansionists could also profit from Peking's indecisiveness, as the Japanese did in the case of the Ryūkyū Islanders killed by aborigines in Taiwan (see page 511). Foolishly, the Tsungli Yamen did not contest Japan's suzerainty over the Ryūkyū Islands, which had been formally tributary to China although controlled by the Satsuma *han* of Japan since 1609. Worse still, to avoid paying Japan compensation, the Yamen disclaimed responsibility for the Taiwan aborigines, and so the restive Japanese samurai sent their punitive expedition to Taiwan in 1874. War was averted, but China had to pay an indemnity to get the Japanese to withdraw. Li and others made the point that a Chinese envoy in Japan might have averted this costly incident.

Another incident occurred when a British expedition went from Burma into Yunnan in 1875 to open a new overland trade route, and a British interpreter was murdered by armed Chinese. Britain demanded indemnity, apology, refinement of rules for Sino-foreign intercourse, and trade concessions, all of which were embodied in the final capstone of the treaty system, the Chefoo Agreement of 1876. As one result China's first resident minister abroad, Kuo Sung-tao, was sent to London in 1877 to apologize. Kuo was from Hunan, a Hanlin scholar and a friend of Tseng Kuo-fan. His reports from London praised railways, telegraphs, and mines and admired the two hundred Japanese whom he found learning British technology. Kuo's outspoken advocacy of Westernization roused the die-hards, whose denunciations forced him into retirement in 1879. By that time China had legations in the United States, Germany, France, Japan, and Russia as well as Britain.

China's predicament—not wanting to acknowledge the equality of foreign rulers by sending envoys to them—became a crisis when foreign powers took over states tributary to China. This happened especially in Vietnam, where all the elements of Western aggressiveness, the weakness of the tributary state, and China's incapacity to assert a Western type of suzerainty combined to destroy the old order of the tribute system.

Vietnam's Absorption by France

The weakness of the Vietnamese state in the nineteenth century was due to many factors—first of all, to its size and elongated shape. The Hanoi delta in the North had been the ancient center of population, production, and power. The Mekong delta south of Saigon had been recently taken over and was less developed, a frontier of Vietnamese expansion, while the new capital at Hué, perched on the thin coastal strip of arable land, had the task of forging North and South into a unified state. Socially, unity was impeded by the presence of non-Vietnamese ethnic minorities, both the primitive hill tribes of the interior and remnants of the Cham and Khmer (Cambodian) peoples in the south. Lying on the cultural boundary between the Chinese and the Indian-influenced Southeast Asian civilizations, Vietnam had not attained the same degree of ethnic and social homogeneity as China, much less Korea or Japan. The Confucian state and its mandarinate overlay the rather different society of the villages, but could not rely on a classically indoctrinated rural elite or gentry class to dominate the countryside while remaining loyal to the throne. Syncretic religious sects easily arose and flourished, while regional overlords still maintained personal armies and ran their local administrations with only lip service to the court.

In their attempt to unify the country after its two and a half centuries of division north and south, the emperors of the new Nguyen dynasty vigorously reconstructed their regime on the contemporary Ch'ing model. Minh-mang (1820–1841) in particular adopted the Chinese methods of bureaucratic centralization. He built up the territorial administration of centrally appointed magistrates, conducting land surveys and collecting taxes in the South. He installed military colonies in the new frontier areas, and fostered the examination system to recruit talent widely. He also established a pervasive control over the Buddhist church. But his successors Thieu-tri (1841–1847) and Tu-duc (1848–1883) ran into serious problems of inflation and natural disaster which generated rebel movements.

French Encroachment. In particular the Nguyen rulers found no way to keep out foreign influences, since the long coastal frontier was impossible to control, and this facilitated the steady growth of Roman Catholic Christianity aided by French missionaries. After two centuries of active proselytism, the Christian church had become an indigenous sect with more adherents in Vietnam than in all of China, deeply involved in Vietnamese politics, inter-village feuds, and occasional dissidence. As a regime based on Confucian principles of moral leadership through the imperial orthodoxy, the Nguyen rulers and their conservative supporters felt increasingly threatened by the foreign religion. They moved against it. In the dozen years up to 1860, some twenty-five European and three hundred Vietnamese priests and perhaps thirty thousand Vietnamese Christians were killed in persecutions. This gave French empire-builders the opportunity they had been seeking.

After much frustration in trying to keep up with Britain, when France lacked a comparable interest in foreign trade, the ambitious Napoleon III found an active East Asian role in championing Catholic missions. While joining with Britain against China 1857–1860 (see pages 476–478). France also used her forces against Vietnam and in 1859 seized Saigon and then took over the three provinces around it. Emperor Tu-duc, hard pressed at the time by a rebellion in Tongking, signed in 1862 a treaty ceding France these three provinces and promising her trade, religious freedom, and a vague protectorate over Vietnam's foreign relations.

To the Vietnamese rebellion against Tu-duc in the North were now added Vietnamese risings against the French in the South. The local mandarins fled; hence the French, instead of being able to rule through them had to undertake direct rule themselves and create their colony of Cochin China. Eying the possibility of trade with China up the Mekong, they also established a protectorate over nearby Cambodia in 1863–1864: first they offered their help to King Norodom (reg. 1860–1904), who was also beset by rebels; and then with a show of force at his capital, Pnom Penh, they obliged him to give up his dependence on Siam. In 1867 a Franco-Siamese treaty confirmed this arrangement. In the same year the French occupied the three southernmost provinces to round out their colony of Cochin China.

This French lodgement in South Vietnam was mainly the work of the navy, with missionaries playing only a secondary role and merchants almost unrepresented. Since the home government was preoccupied elsewhere, French admirals ruled Cochin China largely on their own. The geographical exploration of the Mekong in 1866–1868 stirred the French public's appetite for an Indo-Chinese empire. An expedition explored the ruins of Angkor, and went through Vientiane and Luang Prabang to Yunnan. It proved that the Mekong could never rival even the Irrawaddy as a trade route leading to Southwest China, and French interest now shifted to the Red River (Song Koi) route through Tongking. On this frontier, French expansionists saw themselves reasserting France's vitality, competing with Anglo-American dominance, and helping lesser peoples.

The Sino-French War. By the 1880's sovereignty over "Annam" (as Vietnam was called in China and in the West) was claimed both by France, on the basis of a Franco-Vietnamese treaty of 1874, and by China, on the basis of some fifty tribute missions sent to Peking by rulers of Vietnam since 1664, most recently in 1877 and 1881. France, however, had control over her colony of Cochin China in the South and a preponderant

FRENCH INDO CHINA

influence at the Vietnamese capital, Hué. Franco-Chinese hostilities developed on the Chinese border in the North, where Tongking had been in disorder for a decade. There was not only disaffection here against the ruling Nguyen dynasty of Vietnam, but also an infiltration of Chinese irregulars, remnants of the Taiping and Panthay rebels. The resulting turmoil prevented the French from using their new treaty rights, such as that of trade on the Red River. The Vietnamese ruler encouraged the irregulars against the French and invited in the Chinese army against both. Finally, in 1882 the French seized Hanoi, set up by treaty a protectorate over Annam, and at once had to send for reinforcements. China in 1883 sent regular troops from Yunnan and Kwangsi across the border into Tongking, where they met the French in pitched battles.

The concurrent Sino-French hostilities and negotiations in 1883–1885 confused observers at the time and have confused historians since. One complicating factor was the multiplicity of authorities, while the negotiators of both sides were harassed by compatriots whose clamor for war increased every time their side was defeated. A war party had emerged in the councils of the Ch'ing government during the Ili crisis with Russia. The suppression of rebels in the 1860's and 1870's had left the Chinese bureaucracy sprinkled with old soldiers in the garb of civil officials, who took heart at the Ch'ing success in Central Asia. The most bellicose intransigence in foreign affairs was advocated at Peking by half a dozen younger scholars who were known as the "purification clique." Brilliant memorialists and sycophants of the Empress Dowager, they attacked the older advocates of "self-strengthening" as appeasers and supported a militant posture against Russia and France. In 1884 when French victories led to the dismissal of Prince Kung and the Grand Council, the "purification clique" came briefly into positions of power, only to suffer defeat and eclipse in turn through France's further victories. The most able member of this clique, and the only one to survive in power, was Chang Chih-tung (1837–1909), who became governor-general of Kwangtung and Kwangsi in 1884 and proved his practical capacity in support of the war effort.

Sino-French negotiations began almost as early as the hostilities. Finally Li Hung-chang in May 1884 drew up with a French naval officer a settlement, known as the Li-Fournier convention, which provided that China should withdraw her troops and admit French trade through Tongking while France should keep Annam and her treaty rights there and claim no indemnity from China. For this deal the war party excoriated Li in forty-seven memorials, the court refused to accept the loss of suzerainty, and hostilities continued, sporadically but more violently, along with abortive negotiations. Robert Hart, being in the councils of Peking but not its politics, began secret talks. In 1885 he sent his London agent of the Maritime

Customs to Paris and with the court's authority settled peace terms there on the basis of the Li-Fournier convention. Li signed the peace in June 1885.

The extra year of hostilities was costly for China. One French fleet attacked northern Taiwan in August 1884; another anchored in Foochow harbor alongside eleven small Foochow-built wooden steam warships, the Fukien fleet of the new Chinese navy. The eight French armor-clad vessels were bigger and had heavier guns. When, after five weeks' indecision, Peking let a French ultimatum expire on August 23, the French destroyed nine Chinese vessels in a few minutes and also the shipyard that had been founded in 1866 with the aid of French engineers.

On the land French superiority was less marked. Overconfident French troops were occasionally ambushed by Chinese with Remingtons in the Tongking jungle. The French took the delta around Hanoi and, advancing on the main route north to the Kwangsi border, eventually took Langson just south of Chen-nan-kuan. The unexpected Chinese recovery of this strategic spot in March 1885 caused the fall of the French cabinet and somewhat salved Chinese pride.

The war against France was China's first defensive action against a modern enemy since the beginning of the "self-strengthening" movement in the 1860's. It disclosed one major fact: modern arms are relatively ineffective without modern organization and leadership. The best European guns were useless in Chinese hands without adequate training, tactics, supply, communication, strategy, and command. The harbor at Foochow, for example, was some twenty miles from the sea through a narrow passage past forts armed with new Krupp and Armstrong cannon. Yet the command was so ill-informed, disorganized, and indecisive that neither the modern armament nor even traditional tactics of blockage and harassment were used with any vigor against the French. Again, China in 1884 had more than fifty modern warships, a majority built in Chinese yards, but they were of many sorts and under four separate commands. The Nanyang and Peiyang fleets, respectively under the Southern and Northern Commissioners at Nanking and Tientsin, were larger than the Kwangtung and Fukien fleets, but stayed defensively in their home waters. Caution and bureaucratic rivalry, each official saving his own, prevented a national war effort.

One result of the French war, however, was to call forth vigorous manifestations of nationalism, particularly in Kwangtung, the chief base area for the forces in Tongking. The long-standing antiforeignism of the Cantonese was heightened by several things—fear of a French attack, China's declaration of war after the Foochow debacle, and Chang Chih-tung's old-style offer of cash rewards for dead Frenchmen. Even without an invasion of the area, widespread riots and pillaging occurred, especially of Catholic and Protestant missions. The modern Chinese-language press in Hong Kong, which was now purveying inflammatory news to a social stratum of readers

*The Thành-thái emperor,
seated in a determined pose
among his three brothers,
reigned from 1889 to 1907
but was not completely
submissive to the French,
who in 1907 deposed and
exiled him to Reunion
Island as "insane."*

much broader than the scholar-literati class, seems to have helped this growth of an urban-centered mass nationalism.

Colonial Indo-China. The Sino-French war established French rule over four regions: Cochin China, governed directly as a colony, and Cambodia, Annam (i.e., central Vietnam), and Tongking, ruled more indirectly as protectorates. These regions were combined in the Indo-Chinese Union in 1887.

French residents had been governing Cambodia on behalf of King Norodom since the 1860's, but the Nguyen throne of Vietnam now posed greater difficulties. After Tu-duc's death in 1883, three of his successors met untimely ends and the fourth, the boy-emperor Ham-nghi, fled in 1885 to lead a resistance in the hills until captured three years later. The French finally installed a compliant emperor of their own choice so as to rule through the Nguyen dynasty, and suppressed rebellion with networks of posts and punitive flying columns. Nevertheless a sporadic resistance continued until about 1895, led by loyalist mandarins (like the chief censor, Phan Dinh Phung) or guerrilla fighters (like Hoang Hoa Tham in Tongking; died 1913).

Meanwhile the French in Indo-China inherited with enthusiasm the old Vietnamese claims to areas lying between the expanding states of Vietnam and Siam. Cambodia, formerly under joint suzerainty, had already been taken over in the 1860's, and energetic French empire-builders, even before the conquest of Tongking, had pursued intensive explorations of Laos and adjoining areas on the upper Mekong. Laos had been split in 1707 into two hostile parts with capitals at Luang Prabang and Vientiane, and the latter had been absorbed by Siam in 1828 while the former remained a tributary kingdom. With disorder in Tongking, Chinese bandits entered Luang Pra-bang, Siamese forces came in to suppress them, and the French began to intervene against this Siamese "expansion."

In the 1890's French imperialism, already confronting Britain in Africa and elsewhere, became aroused to "recover" for Vietnam all areas east of the Mekong. Frontier incidents threatened to bring on a Franco-Siamese war. In 1893 the French sent gunboats and an ultimatum to Bangkok, whereupon the British urged moderation on France and compliance on Siam. Thus pressed, Siam ceded to France Laos and the whole east bank of the Mekong and evacuated the old Cambodian areas around Angkor (which were eventually ceded to France in 1907). French expansion, stimulated by this absorption of Laos in 1893, was not stabilized until the Anglo-French agreement of 1896, which averted war and guaranteed the independence of Siam in the area of the Menam Valley. This was the real heart of the country and also the main area for British trade. The French expansionists had in effect been bought off with large territories which, however, had little economic value.

The French administrators in Indo-China believed that French culture was of universal value and superiority. In Cochin China they followed a general policy of "assimilation," training Vietnamese in French ways and incorporating them in the lower levels of a single bureaucracy. In the other protectorate areas they also tried a superficial policy of "association," bring-ing cooperative Vietnamese, Cambodian, and Laotian officials at higher levels into a parallel though powerless structure of native agencies of gov-ernment, so that French rule would be indirect in appearance. For this purpose an imposing façade of rulers was maintained—the emperor of Vietnam and kings of Cambodia and Laos (at Luang Prabang) together with courts, councils, and consultative assemblies. This served to make French rule more palatable. Yet in fact the aim was only assimilation, for to the French the imposition of their culture seemed the only genuine means of modernization available.

Paul Doumer, governor-general from 1897 to 1902, laid the fiscal and administrative foundations of a self-supporting centralized regime, instead of trying to build a modern government indirectly through the protectorate system. From his capital at Hanoi the governor-general ruled Cochin China through its governor, and the four protectorates of Cambodia, Annam, Tongking, and Laos through French *résidents supérieurs,* under whom French residents in turn ruled the provinces through the native officialdom. This use of Vietnamese mandarins, though indirect rule in form, left no doubt as to who held power. In the Napoleonic fashion, major central minis-tries were now built up to direct a unified tax collection, including govern-ment monopolies of salt, opium, and alcohol, as well as public services and

The Duy-tan emperor was enthroned in 1907 at the age of seven but in 1916, implicated in a plot for military rebellion, was dethroned and exiled to Reunion Island.

programs of public works—port facilities, canals, roads, and railways. This created a framework for a national government and for economic expansion. French investment opened coal mines and plantations.

The general effect of French rule was to weaken if not liquidate traditional institutions of law, ethics, family, and village community, without as yet creating a new social order to take their place. While breaking down the village commune, French rule built up landlordism with its attendant evils of sharecropping, usury, and inefficient production on fragmented holdings, so that the rice-farming economy, especially of the northern delta, soon became overpopulated and undercapitalized. Both the social order and the standard of living suffered.

Korea's Response to the Outside World

Korea, like Vietnam, was a small kingdom by Chinese, though not by European, standards. Neither country could fend off foreign encroachment without Chinese support. But where Vietnam temporarily fell victim to a European power expanding far overseas, Korea was fated by geography to lie at the focal point where the three empires of China, Japan, and Russia met and clashed. Moreover, the blighting influence of imperial Confucianism in general and its tributary system in particular was even more marked in Korea than in Vietnam. For centuries the foreign relations of Korea had been limited to the sending of regular tribute missions to China and some other missions to Japan. The Korean kings, though weak as domestic rulers, were vigorously hostile to all Western contact. They maintained a rigid policy of seclusion until it was almost too late to learn the art of diplomacy. The reluctance and confusion of aim in Korea's response to the imperialist menace were major reasons for the disastrous outcome. For here, as elsewhere, imperialist expansion, though irresistible in its later phases, had seemed at first to be little more than an intellectual challenge on the outer horizon.

Rebellion and Restoration.   The Korean state in the 1860's met a challenge on two fronts, foreign and domestic, just as China and Vietnam had done a few years earlier. On the domestic front a large-scale peasant-based rebellion, led by a religious cult, broke out in southeastern Korea in 1862–1863, the most serious revolt in several hundred years. Although primarily a protest against poverty and *yangban* misgovernment, this rising was also inspired by the upsetting news of the Taiping rebellion and foreign invasion in China. In Korea, however, domestic rebellion and foreign religion had a different relationship from that they had in China.

Catholic Christianity had reached Korea first in the form of Chinese writings from the Jesuits at Peking and became known as the "Western Learning." The first Chinese Catholic missionary penetrated Korea only in the late eighteenth century. Gaining adherents, Christianity was soon persecuted, in 1801 and later, as a heterodox sect and also a foreign menace. It became perforce a secret society, ministered to by Chinese priests and, after 1836, by French priests who were smuggled into the country.

In the 1860's a syncretic religious cult known as the *Tonghak* or "Eastern Learning" arose in violent opposition to this "Western Learning," but also partly inspired by its example. The founder, Ch'oe Che-u (1824–1864), was the guilt-ridden son of a poor village scholar of North Kyŏngsang province. He suffered repeated frustrations in the official examinations, much like his Chinese contemporary the Taiping leader, Hung Hsiu-ch'üan. After years of study and meditation, Ch'oe felt impelled, partly by the news of the Taiping movement and the Anglo-French attack in China, to seek the mandate of the Lord of Heaven. This he claimed to have received on May 25, 1860, in the form of divine instructions to found a religion that could make the East as strong as the West. His teachings used concepts from Taoist, Buddhist, Neo-Confucian, and even Catholic cosmology, but with a strong admixture of native Korean shamanism and an apocalyptic emphasis on the spiritual union of the believer with the Creator. In the "new era," a "world of new creation," the *Tonghak* "way," would overcome the Westerners by its magic and supersede Confucianism and Buddhism to begin a new cycle, enriching the poor and exalting the lowly. The new

N. = pukto (northern part of province)
S. = namdo (southern part)

CHINA

CHANGKUFENG

Tumen R.

Ch'ŏngjin

YANGGANG

Yalu R.

CHAGANG

HAMGYŎNG

S. N.

Antung   Sinŭiju

PYŎNGAN

N.

S.

Hamhŭng

Hŭngnam

Taedong R.

SEA   OF
JAPAN

P'yŏngyang

Wŏnsan

Chinnampo

HWANGHAE

KANGWŎN

— 1953 Truce line

38°

Kaesŏng

— 38° 1945 Occupation line

KANGHWA IS.

Seoul
Inchŏn
(Chemulpo)

Han R.

KYŎNGGI

YELLOW

S. N.

CH'UNGCH'ŎNG

Naktong R.

SEA

Kongju
Taejŏn

KYŎNGSANG

Taegu

N.
S.

CHŎLLA

N.
S.

Masan

Mokp'o

Pusan

TSUSHIMA IS.

JAPAN

KOREA IN RECENT TIMES

sect naturally appealed to the poverty-stricken peasantry, spread rapidly, and contributed to risings in southeast and south Korea. Though Ch'oe, when arrested and tried in 1864, maintained that the *Tonghak* aimed to defeat Catholicism, he was decapitated as a subversive. Presumably his teaching seemed to be too similar to Taiping Christianity. Under his successors the *Tonghak* faith spread quietly into every province.

The rulers of Korea in the 1860's met domestic rebellion and the Western challenge by an anti-Christian policy of seclusion and a revival and reform of traditional institutions. A vigorous conservative reform program was pursued by the Korean regent of the decade 1864–1873, who was known by his title as the Taewŏngun or Grand Prince. This man's personal name was Yi Ha-ŭng (1821–1898) and he was father of the boy-king Kojong (reigned 1864–1907); he was also quite prepared to challenge the whole establishment. He met the crisis in the domestic fortunes of the Yi dynasty by seeking reforms which would effect a "restoration" of the golden age of the dynastic founder (Yi Sŏng-gye), a bit like the contemporary T'ung-chih Restoration in China. These reforms aimed to restore the proper functioning of the traditional Korean "three systems" of land tax, relief grain, and military service, all of which had become thoroughly corrupted. The Taewŏngun used many devices to strengthen the central administration, the monarchy, and the royal family. He tried to wipe out factionalism by closing almost all the private academies which nurtured factional adherents, by depriving the censoring organs of their power in the government, and by directly taxing the *yangban* class. He recruited talent much wore widely, reorganized the central administration, and revised the law codes. He also tried to create military strength by giving more prestige to the military class, building fortresses, and training some twelve thousand riflemen with modern arms.

Despite all this effort to revitalize tradition and even use modern means to defend it, the Taewŏngun was vigorously exclusionist. When his execution of French priests brought on a French naval attack in 1866, his commander sternly lectured the invaders with Confucian righteousness: "How can you tell us to abandon the teachings of our forefathers and accept those of others?" After the French had left (in defeat, as the Koreans assumed), the Taewŏngun redoubled the persecution of Christians, but in keeping with established customs he left Korea's foreign relations for Peking to handle.

The Opening of Korea.   During all the alarms of the Ili crisis with Russia and the Tongking fighting with France, Li Hung-chang had kept his eyes on the danger closest to North China, the growth of Japanese power, particularly in Korea. Japanese trade had continued at Pusan on a restricted basis somewhat like the Dutch trade at Nagasaki, and occasional diplomatic missions went from Seoul to the shogun at Edo. Other than this, Korea kept her borders tightly sealed. The annual tribute ritual, conducted at Peking with the Board of Rites, continued down to the 1860's to be the only regular foreign contact.

In the nineteenth century, Western vessels, surveying or in stress of weather, more frequently visited the Korean coast. Korea regularly succored the shipwrecked, expelling them to China, but resisted violently all efforts to open trade or even negotiate. This excited a degree of rivalry to see who could emulate Commodore Perry and "open" Korea. In 1871 the American minister to China was sent with five warships to the river mouth below the capital. His surveyors proceeded up river. Two Americans were wounded. He demanded an apology, in vain. In retaliation the American fleet destroyed five forts and killed perhaps 250 Koreans, yet in the end it could only sail away. Korea adamantly refused to negotiate and felt confirmed, by her apparent victories, in the old policy of seclusion.

Expanding powers in adjacent territory now began to pose more serious threats than Westerners who came from afar. By the mid-1870's some four thousand Koreans, refugees from hard times and harsh government, had defied the seclusion policy by settling in the newly formed Russian Maritime Province to the north. Meanwhile the provoking of a war with Korea had become a fixed aim of frustrated Japanese samurai. In 1873 their plans for invasion were forestalled by cooler heads in Japan (see pages 510–511), but Tōkyō was determined to try to open Korea and draw it away from China.

In 1875 a party of Japanese, landing from warships surveying the Korean coast, was fired upon. The Tōkyō government, still strongly opposed to an invasion of Korea, now determined to "open" Korea peacefully through moderate demands for intercourse backed by a show of superior force. The Tsungli Yamen and Li Hung-chang stuck to the old Sinocentric concept of China's moral but inactive suzerainty over a tributary state— "though Korea is a dependent country of China, it is not a territorial possession; hence in its domestic and foreign affairs it is self-governing." They finally advised Korea to negotiate. The Japanese warships and transports that anchored off Inchon thus secured in February 1876 an unequal treaty modeled on the Western treaties with China and Japan. It opened three ports for Japanese trade—Pusan, Inchon (then known as Chemulpo), and Wonsan—and declared Korea to be an "independent state."

Sino-Japanese Rivalry in Korea.   The growth of foreign contact had violent repercussions within Korea, and China was soon obliged to play a more active role in Korea's government and politics. But China's reluctant intervention brought a Chinese program of moderate reform into competition with more radical modernizing influences from Japan.

Reform was complicated by the fact that both the Chinese and Japanese influences were violently opposed by die-hard conservatives like the Taewŏn-gun. Though out of power since 1873, he helped foment an antiforeign rising in 1882, during which a mob attacked the Japanese legation. Both China and Japan sent troops, but China sent larger numbers, kidnaped the Taewŏngun, and held him for three years in China. Japan was mollified by an indemnity, and Li Hung-chang now tried to develop preferential Sino-Korean trade relations, appoint advisers, and dominate Korean politics.

From 1880 China's relations with Korea had been removed from the control of the Ministry of Rites, which had traditionally handled tribute relations, and put under Li Hung-chang, who with Chinese and British advice had been developing a comprehensive policy. First, Li hoped through Chinese intervention in Korea's domestic affairs to foster "self-strengthening" concurrent with China's own development of naval and military power. Second, he hoped to protect Korea against Japanese or Russian absorption by getting her into treaty relations with all the trading powers, whose commerce would create vested interests in Korea's independence, a strategy of "using barbarians to offset barbarians." This new policy was followed when a United States naval diplomat (Commodore R. W. Shufeldt), again following the Perry tradition, tried first through Japan to negotiate a treaty, without avail, and then succeeded in doing so through Li Hung-chang at Tientsin in 1882. Li negotiated for Korea but failed to get into the treaty a clause describing Korea as "a dependent state of the Chinese Empire." Instead, the American treaty recognized Korea's independence. So did the treaties that followed in 1883–1886 with the other Western powers.

During the early 1880's the main threat to Korea seemed to come from Russia, which was also the power most feared by Britain. But as time went on, the basic rivalry for domination of Korea developed between China and Japan. At first China with British encouragement seemed to be ahead. But within Korea, the more radical reformers gravitated to the Japanese camp, because Japan was modernizing more vigorously than China. Korea's domestic struggles between radical and traditional reformers thus reflected the progress of modernization within her two big neighbors. But Korean conservatism and factional rivalries were still basic problems. China's removal of the Taewŏngun had left in power his enemies, the entrenched Min family, who were represented at court by King Kojong's queen (often referred to as "Queen Min"). The queen and her Min family faction now cooperated with China, undid some of the Taewŏngun's reforms, and similarly opposed the modernization efforts of those who wanted to follow the Japanese example. The lack of national unity, manifested in the curse of factionalism, continued to upset Korean efforts to achieve independence and modernization.

The Korean reformer, Kim Ok-kyun.

Foreign influences flooded into Korean politics. After cultural missions went in 1881 to both China and Japan, a Korean mission visited the United States in 1883, and another set up a legation in Washington in 1888. American influence, strong in Japan in the 1880's, also reached Korea through missionary-educators and sympathetic diplomats, who espoused Korean independence even though, as later with the "integrity of China," the use of force to support the idea was never contemplated in Washington.

Paradoxically, during the era of Chinese ascendancy at Seoul from 1882 to 1894, it was mainly contact with Japan that inspired a growing number of patriots with Western ideas of nationalism and reform. Japanese liberals, like Fukuzawa Yukichi who advised the young reformers Kim Ok-kyun and Pak Yŏng-hyo in the early 1880's, saw Japan inaugurating a new day in Korea much as the United States had done in Japan. But these Korean reformers, who wanted to Westernize on the Japanese model, found their hopes blocked by the ruling Min faction and the dominant Chinese influence, and so attempted a *coup d'état* in 1884. With the knowledge of the Japanese legation, they assassinated conservative ministers and seized the king, only to be thwarted by the vigorous young Chinese commander, Yüan Shih-k'ai, who defeated the Japanese legation guards and rescued the king. This crisis was settled in 1885 when Li and Itō Hirobumi negotiated at Tientsin the Li-Itō Convention, a mutual abstention agreement by which the two countries agreed to withdraw their troops and military advisers from Korea and in case of trouble notify the other party before sending them back.

Behind this stalemate lay a Japanese decision, following a great debate in Tōkyō, to build up further national strength before becoming involved in hostilities abroad. Itō believed that time was on Japan's side, that to fight for Korea prematurely would only benefit Russia. Li, on his part, felt that historical tradition and geographical proximity favored China. Li went ahead with an active program of modernization, urging upon Korea many of the reforms that Britain had urged upon China twenty years before: a Korean Customs Service headed by Westerners lent from the Chinese Maritime Customs; an American adviser on foreign affairs; telegraph lines; and military training. Li's lieutenant in Seoul as Resident from 1885 to 1894, the young and overbearing Yüan Shih-k'ai, sought to preserve the forms of Chinese suzerainty, while American diplomats and missionaries, among others, benevolently fostered Korean independence. Meantime the decade after 1885 saw a steady increase of Japanese influence among young Korean patriots.

During this period, however, the Korean government's halting efforts at reform did little to alleviate the misery of the populace, and the *Tonghak* movement, venerating its martyred founder, continued to appeal to the oppressed. As in the ancient tradition of shamanism, *Tonghak* members worshiped at altars in the hills with chanting and ritual dancing in order to ward off illness. Occasionally they organized demonstrations with bells and drums at the royal palace, seeking a posthumous pardon in traditional fashion so as "to claim redress of grievances for the cult founder." In 1894 conservative elements associated with the *Tonghak* movement and utilizing its popular organization rose in rebellion in South Korea, demanding reform of the corrupt and inefficient local administration under which the people were suffering. This rebellion precipitated Chinese and Japanese intervention, which then led to the Sino-Japanese War (see pages 553–554). Japan's decisive victory and the resultant peace treaty established the independence of Korea from China.

Japan's Absorption of Korea.   By 1894, Japanese of all camps had been involved in Korean politics. Militant expansionists came to help the *Tonghak,* just as liberals like Fukuzawa publicly mourned the assassination of his disciple Kim Ok-kyun. It was one thing, however, to expel Chinese influences and declare Korea independent, and quite another to set the Korean government on the path of Japanese-type modernization.

Three successive Japanese ministers to Korea failed in this task. The first, after Japanese troops took over Seoul in July 1894, installed in power the Taewŏngun, of all people, to head a sweeping reform program; but the Japanese soon found the old man interested "only in grasping power and purging his opponents." The second minister then brought the exiled reformer of 1884, Pak Yŏng-hyo, and other pro-Japanese modernizers into power in a government of all parties, but Pak was forced to flee again. The third Japanese minister finally conspired with the Taewŏngun in October 1895 to effect at last the brutal murder of the old man's daughter-in-law, "Queen Min," whose body was burned in her palace grounds. After this, Japanese influence was eclipsed for a couple of years by that of Russia —especially after the king fled for safety to the Russian legation (February 1896), where he stayed for more than a year.

Dynastic weakness and foreign aggression inspired at Seoul in 1896–1898 a Korean counterpart of the Reform Movement then blossoming at Peking (see pages 629–634). The main protagonist, Sŏ Chae-p'il, had been a leader of the attempted coup of 1884 but then had got safely away. He came to the United States and as "Philip Jaisohn" acquired an American wife, citizenship, and a medical degree. Returning in 1896 as a government adviser, he founded two reformist institutions: a newspaper, *The Independent (Tongnip Shinmun)*, which used only the vernacular *han'gŭl* without Chinese characters, and an embryonic political party, the Independence Club (*Tongnip Hyŏphoe*), which began to debate political issues and soon organized large demonstrations to promote national independence through governmental reforms. Like their Chinese contemporaries, the Korean reformers had no contact with peasant-based movements like the *Tonghak,* but they endangered the vested interests of dominant court conservatives, who therefore suppressed the reform movement at the end of 1898.

The weak Korean king, though he took the title of emperor in 1897, was incapable of holding power. Japan's victory had ended the influence of China, which had been backed by Britain, and so Korea's fate was now left poised between Japan and Russia. They made agreements over Korea in 1896 and 1898, but this did little to check their rivalry, and only Japan's victory over Russia in the war of 1904–1905 finally established her domination of the peninsula as a protectorate (see page 556).

Korea's response to foreign contact in the nineteenth century had thus been doubly handicapped. Within the protecting cocoon of the Chinese tribute system the country's leaders had been less well prepared for outside relations than those of Vietnam. But by the time Korea was opened, the pressures emanating from great-power rivalries had become much greater. Not one power but five pushed their way into Seoul—Chinese and Japanese troops, Russian, British, and American diplomats, together with Catholic and Protestant missionaries, all exerted their several influences in this hermit kingdom that lacked any tradition or experience of multistate foreign relations. The Koreans were caught off balance from the beginning.

After Japan defeated Russia in 1905, her aim in Korea was originally not so extreme as it later became. Itō Hirobumi took on the task of working out the relationship between the two countries. Backed by Japanese troops, he secured in November 1905 a convention making Korea a Japanese pro-

tectorate and ending its diplomatic contact with other powers. He set up a
Residency General to administer the Japanese protectorate, exercising wide
powers immediately under the Meiji emperor but leaving the Korean emperor still reigning. Itō aimed at a modernizing, benevolent administration
capable of winning Korean collaboration and good will while making
Japan's dominance secure.

This moderate approach met difficulties. When the Korean emperor sent
a secret mission to the Second Hague Peace Conference of 1907 to protest
Japan's domination, he was forced to abdicate in favor of his feeble-minded
son. Itō assumed wider powers, arranged that Japanese could serve as
Korean officials, and disbanded the Korean army. Widespread "riots" ensued, amounting in fact to a nationwide rebellion, which the Japanese
vigorously suppressed by burning villages and killing some twelve thousand
"rioters" in the course of twelve months. In this war the Japanese reported
1450 engagements in 1908, 900 in 1909, and 147 in 1910. Itō attempted
to work with a Korean ministry, including would-be reformers of the
1890's, and held out against immediate annexation, which was advocated
by Yamagata and Katsura, as well as by ultranationalist pressure groups.
But Itō was assassinated in Manchuria by a Korean patriot in October 1909,
after his resignation as resident-general; and the annexation of Korea which
followed in August 1910 was generally approved by Japanese opinion,
liberal and otherwise.

Now called Chōsen, Korea was governed for Japan's strategic and economic purposes by Japanese officials at the middle and higher levels, as a
colony outside the Japanese constitutional process. Korean nationhood was
thus suppressed at the very time when conservative *yangban* (the Japanese
had abolished their class status), reformist students, disbanded soldiers, and
impoverished peasants, rebelling alike against foreign rule, were developing
a common sentiment of nationalism.

Meanwhile by 1895 the Chinese Empire had lost its traditional, rather
passive suzerainty over the two countries of Vietnam and Korea that had
been its closest cultural satellites. Two industrializing nations from overseas, France and Japan, had posed a foreign threat that soon grew larger
and affected the Chinese people more directly.

21. The Heyday of Imperialism in China

Power Politics Over China

China's Effort at "Self-Strengthening."   After the conclusion of the Sino-French war in 1885, China enjoyed a decade of comparative tranquillity in her foreign relations. Her positive program in Korea was an offshoot of a more general effort to build up military and naval strength in response to the encroachments of Russia, France, and Japan in peripheral areas. These had roused a degree of nationalism and inspired many efforts to modernize in self-defense, yet in the absence of a strong central leadership, these efforts remained dependent upon the continuity of a reforming official in one post and the comparative weakness of local vested interests arrayed against him.

The vulnerability of this kind of personally sponsored development was illustrated in Taiwan, which was separated from Fukien and made a province in 1885. Gentry-based conservative interests were relatively weak, and the first governor, one of Li Hung-chang's lieutenants (Liu Ming-ch'uan), was able to get some impressive results during his six-year term: an arsenal at the capital, Taipei; a naval force based on the Pescadores Islands between Taiwan and the mainland; land-tax reform based on a land survey and population registration; and other modern services. Unfortunately, this governor was not a genuine Confucian scholar; rather, he had risen from the peasant-bandit level as an able commander against the mid-century rebels. Conservative critics effected his removal in 1891.

A more powerful regional reformer was Chang Chih-tung. Converted to modernization by bitter experience in fighting the French, he emerged after 1885 as Li Hung-chang's chief rival in regional influence and bureaucratic

WESTERNERS THROUGH CHINESE EYES. *Four sketches from a*
  Shanghai picture magazine (Tien-shih-chai hua-pao) *founded in*
  1884. Illustrated are Western sports (boat racing and a paper
  chase), a cautionary tale of a French opium addict, and an instance of
  foreign medical skill. The Chinese explanations are summarized.

*"In the fair weather of spring and
autumn, Westerners regularly
hold boat races for high stakes.
The little oars fly by like
swallows crossing a screen; the
shallow boats are like leaves,
light as seagulls playing on
water. Amid the waves the
high-spirited participants don't
mind getting wet. Spectators on
both banks cheer them on.
Their whole country is mad
about it."*

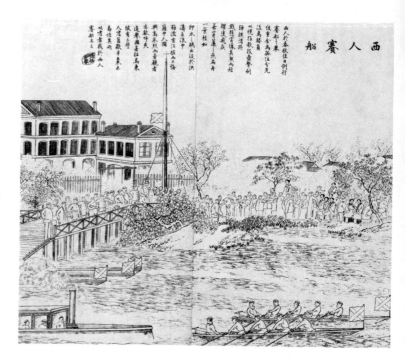

*"In the fine weather of spring and
autumn, on two occasions in
each season and each time on
three days only, Westerners
compete in racing on horseback
with high wagers. This autumn
at Shanghai they have added
paper-chasing: up to 50 or 60
riders gather in one place,
one goes ahead scattering
multi-colored paper strips, and
the others follow, racing madly.
Whoever first gets over the paper
course is the winner."*

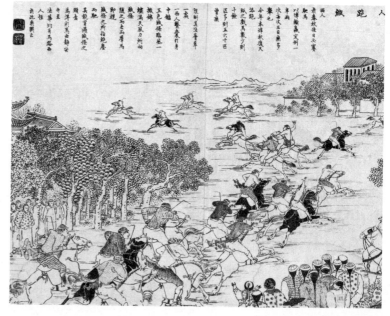

"Opium coming to China has become an evil beyond control. If it is not Heaven's will to stop it, there is no other way to save the situation. Heretofore it has been said that only we Chinese are opium smokers. Not so. A French addict in the prime of life, traveling with his wife, an English friend, and a French servant, lay down to smoke in a Singapore hotel but next morning became ill and died—the doctor said from smoking too much. How can one not be afraid!"

"A foreign woman doctor, specialized in women's ailments and also in surgery, examined at the T'ung-jen Hospital in Hongkew a woman patient with a huge growth. Saying, 'This can be cured,' she took out a sharp knife, cut it off (it weighed one-fourth as much as the patient) and applied medicine, and after a month it was cured. The patient was fortunate to find this doctor, and the doctor fortunate to find this patient on whom to demonstrate such miraculous skill, which leaves Chinese doctors speechless and ashamed."

politics. Although governor-general at Canton in 1885–1889 and at Nanking in 1894–1896, Chang found his main regional base at the Wuhan cities (the joint name for Wuchang, Hanyang, and Hankow where the Han River enters the Yangtze). He served there as governor-general of Hunan and Hupei for fifteen years, 1889–1894 and 1896–1907. This long tenure helped him build up the appurtenances of regional power—his own staff of subordinates, local sources of revenue, military forces, industries, and political patronage. His scholastic brilliance and his record of antiforeignism made Chang less vulnerable than others to conservative attack when he embarked on modernization. Becoming a regional leader twenty years later than Li Hung-chang, he showed a less wide-ranging ability but a greater fiscal probity and a burning desire to establish a philosophical sanction for modernization and to fit it theoretically into China's classical tradition.

As Chang set up one modern institution after another, he confronted the fact that "self-strengthening" steadily eroded the underpinnings of the Confucian order. Defense, for example, required literate officers trained in academies, military men who also qualified as scholars. This broke down the ancient supremacy of *wen* over *wu*, civil over military. Again, the fact that military command required a mastery of practical military technology blurred the old distinctions between superiors (scholar-officials who "labor with their minds") and inferiors (artisans and other small men who "labor with their strength"). As Chang's defense effort took in more and more of Western technology, he constantly tried to preserve China's traditional learning and values. He became the leading spokesman for China's salvation through conservative reform by "self-strengthening," the use of Western devices for Chinese ends.

A major Chinese defense effort was to build a navy. After the French destroyed the Fukien fleet in 1885, a Board of Admiralty or "Naval Yamen" was set up at Peking as a gesture acknowledging that a navy must function as a centralized unit, but in fact the centrifugal forces of regionalism still perpetuated four fleets in four regions of the China coast. Li Hung-chang at Tientsin, as Northern (Peiyang) Commissioner, created the principal fighting force, known as the Peiyang fleet. He contracted with foreign firms to build forts and bases in North China, including a naval base at Port Arthur and a fortified depot at Weihaiwei. Instead of building his own vessels as Foochow continued to do, Li bought from the big British and German arms firms. A British naval officer served as his chief adviser until 1890. By then Li's Pciyang fleet of some twenty-five vessels had nine modern warships.

This late Ch'ing naval effort was starved by the court, which decided instead to build up the new Summer Palace northwest of Peking as a retreat for the Empress Dowager on her retirement in 1889. The famous marble barge in the big lake there epitomizes this story. It is reminiscent of the palatial extravagance of the Wan-li emperor that undid the Ming dynasty just four centuries earlier. The chief eunuch and other courtiers encouraged these expenditures in order to line their own pockets. The Imperial Household Department misused large levies from the provinces as "naval funds." It also borrowed from Jardine, Matheson and Company. The result was that millions of taels went into the Summer Palace and no additions were made to the Peiyang fleet in the early 1890's, while intensive naval development was occurring in Europe and nine fast ships were being added to the Japanese navy. The fleet's smaller units even took to carrying passengers between Port Arthur and Chefoo. By 1894 Li realized that his fleet was inefficient and did his best to avoid a showdown with Japan.

The Impact of Japan's Defeat of China. When the new Japanese navy unexpectedly defeated Li's Peiyang fleet off the Yalu in September 1894, it upset the power balance both within China and internationally. Li Hung-chang, now 72, had to negotiate with Itō Hirobumi at Shimonoseki the humiliating treaty that gave Japan Taiwan and a large indemnity. Japan's victory had worldwide repercussions and inspired a rivalry among imperialist powers competing to expand at China's expense.

The rise of modern nationalism and industrialism in Europe and Japan had now reached the flash point where modern steam navies and railways, the ultimate devices of the day in firepower and logistics, could dominate distant areas of the globe. The great power rivals, expanding outward from Europe, had already laid claim to much of Africa and the Near East. The sudden rise of Japan as a military and naval power spotlighted the final collapse of the Ch'ing tribute system and the vulnerability of Britain's informal commercial empire based on the unequal treaty system. And so international relations in East Asia entered upon a full decade of ominous instability.

One way to bring some order into the confusing kaleidoscope of great power politics in the 1890's is to look at the Anglo-Russian rivalry all across the Asian continent, from the Near East and the Afghan border on the northwest approach to India, through Central Asia, Tibet, and Mongolia, to Manchuria and Korea. Britain was entrenched on the south as ruler of India, Malaya, and Burma and as the dominant trading power in Siam, China, and adjacent areas. Britain's particular rival in Siam and Burma had been France, and Anglo-French rivalry, which had been especially bitter in Africa, was compounded after 1893 by the Franco-Russian alliance. Thus one element intensifying European rivalry in the Far East was Russia's accelerated expansion as a land power across the north of Asia.

After Muraviev's successful mid-century invasion of the Amur and the acquisition of the Maritime Province in 1860 (see page 479), Russian expansion had run into serious difficulties of food supply and transportation.

LI HUNG-CHANG ON HIS
WORLD TOUR, 1896.
*Li at the age of 72
visited Russia, Germany,
France, England, and
the United States. Here
he stands between the
British prime minister,
Lord Salisbury (left),
and the later Viceroy of
India, Lord Curzon.*

The cossacks in the sixty villages that formed a communication route along the Amur could not grow enough crops in the unfavorable climate to feed themselves; in summer they could navigate upstream only with difficulty, and in winter they lacked draft animals for transport on the ice. With the sale of Alaska to the United States in 1867 and the decline of the sea-otter fur trade in the Pacific, even the Russian garrisons and naval forces in Northeast Asia were reduced. Finally, after 1869 the Suez Canal wrecked the Russian hope of developing trade via the Amur between China and European Russia. By 1880 the population of the Russian Far East was still less than 100,000; the combined immigration of Chinese, Tungus from Manchuria, and Koreans exceeded that of Russians; trade was mainly in non-Russian hands. The area's connections with European Russia were maintained more by sea than by land. Russia's position was weak and her policy passive. After the settlement of the Ili crisis in 1881 the Russians felt on the defensive in East Asia, where they faced the Ch'ing Empire's active colonization of Manchuria, Li Hung-chang's build-up of his Peiyang fleet and Port Arthur naval base, and the contemporary growth of the Japanese fleet.

However, in 1886 Tsar Alexander III concluded that all these weaknesses in the Russian position—in population, food supply, land transport, and naval power—could be overcome by building a trans-Siberian railway which would strengthen Russian land power in East Asia. Diplomatic isolation and frustration elsewhere made it easier to turn eastward again, and French capital was available. In 1891 work was started on the Trans-Siberian Railway from both ends, with completion scheduled for 1903. It became a key element in the Russian state program of heavy industry. Once under way, Russia's turning to the east was justified by ideologists of the time as a sacred "historical mission" to spread Western culture to the Orient.

As Russia's interest and power thus increased, her East Asian policy became more vigorous. Japan's victory in 1895 roused her to immediate action. After leading France and Germany in obliging Japan to restore the Liaotung Peninsula to China (see page 554), Russia pressed her advantage. In 1895 she got French and Russian banks to loan China about half the funds needed to pay China's indemnity to Japan. In 1896 Russia got Chinese permission to build the Chinese Eastern Railway 950 miles across Manchuria to Vladivostok, in order to avoid by this short-cut the costly tunnels and bridges which the trans-Siberian line would require on the 350-mile longer Amur route. Li Hung-chang in St. Petersburg negotiated in June 1896 a secret Russo-Chinese treaty of alliance. It committed China and Russia to fight together against any Japanese expansion on the continent. After much maneuvering and confusion, Russia followed up this treaty by sending a naval squadron into Port Arthur in December 1897 and getting from China in March 1898 a twenty-five year lease of the southern tip of Manchuria, the Liaotung (or Kwantung) Peninsula, with the right to connect it with the Chinese Eastern Railway by a north-south line 650 miles long, the South Manchurian Railway.

The Scramble for Concessions.　　This Russian success in acquiring her long-sought ice-free port, to be connected with Europe by rail, illustrated the novel methods of a new phase of imperialist penetration in China. The new approach used loans, railways, leased areas, reduced land tariffs, and rights of local jurisdiction, of police power, and of mining exploitation to create in effect a "sphere of influence." Great-power rivalry chiefly motivated the rapid maneuvers by which Britain, France, Germany, Russia, Japan, and to some extent the United States variously challenged, assisted, forestalled, and cooperated with one another to take advantage of the expected breakup of China.

The sequence of major events in the scramble went roughly as follows: because two German missionaries had been killed by bandits in Shantung, a German fleet occupied the harbor of Tsingtao in Kiaochow bay on the Shantung promontory in November 1897. Almost at once a Russian fleet seized Port Arthur on the south Manchurian (Liaotung) peninsula in December, as already mentioned. By April 1898 a French fleet had occupied the harbor of Kwangchow, south of Canton and near Indo-China. Britain responded by leasing both the New Territories opposite Hong Kong and a naval base at Weihaiwei on the Shantung coast opposite Port Arthur.

All these demands and seizures were legalized by treaties with China, usually through ninety-nine year leases, and created what were called "spheres of interest" or "influence." Chinese sovereignty and customs collections were preserved but foreign domination and exploitation of key areas were also arranged. While the details of these maneuvers are almost as confusing to historians today as they were to diplomats at the time, certain patterns do emerge.

First of all, no power followed a single, straight course of action, because each was influenced by all the others and often by conflicting pressures at home. The Russian moves summarized above, for example, were only one thread in the tapestry and were partly responses to the moves of others. Thus both Germany and Britain in 1895–1896 had actively encouraged Russia to press forward in East Asia in order to lessen her pressure elsewhere; and Russia occupied Port Arthur in December 1897 only after Kaiser Wilhelm II had offered encouragement and set an example by sending his ships into Tsingtao in November. Russia's counsels were often divided, many of her efforts failed, events were often unforeseen, and bold action alternated with worried hesitation. So it was with the other powers.

Secondly, there was a certain degree of alignment among the European powers. The Franco-Russian allies, having little sea trade, encroached on China from their land-based positions on the south and north in Indo-China and the Russian Far East. France actually was the first to act, in June 1895, extorting a concession to open mines in Southwest China and to extend her railways there from Tongking. This success, after decades of Anglo-French competition in planning the railway penetration of Yunnan, was eventually followed by French construction of the narrow-gauge line from Hanoi up the Red River to Yunnan-fu (Kunming), completed in 1910. On their land frontiers, moreover, France and Russia secured reductions in the Chinese customs tariff. Working through a Belgian syndicate, they also secured in May 1897 the concession for a Peking-Hankow railway through the Chinese interior.

Britain and Germany, on the other hand, being trading and naval powers without important land frontiers with China, sought their spheres in the Yangtze Valley and Shantung, respectively. They also had greater capital resources, and their bankers lent most of the funds that China required to pay the Japanese indemnity. Of these two maritime powers, however, the British were defending a long-established commercial position which gave them four-fifths of the foreign trade of China, while the Germans were newcomers and already Britain's chief trade competitors, aggressively seeking markets and naval bases. The Kaiser kept on friendly terms with his cousin the Tsar and, after prospecting for a naval base elsewhere, had won the latter's tacit consent for the German occupation of Kiaochow in November 1897. This move precipitated the general scramble.

In the ensuing melee, the British government, under vigorous pressure from the China Association and other spokesmen for the China trade and imperial expansion, pragmatically followed a policy of "compensation." While still espousing the traditonal principle of the integrity of China, the Open Door, and equal opportunity for the trade of all comers, Britain nevertheless carved out her own "sphere," applying in effect the same two-power standard that she was applying in the naval race to keep abreast of any combination of two competitors. Thus, as it turned out, France acquired a "sphere" in Kwangtung-Kwangsi-Yunnan with a naval base at Kwang-chow Bay (April 1898), while Russia got a "sphere" in Manchuria, and Germany one in Shantung, each with a leased territory enclosed by a neutral zone and with railways projected from the main port. But meanwhile Britain had kept pace with France by opening Southwest China to trade up the West River from Canton and by a projected Burma railroad (February 1897). Moreover, through a nonalienation agreement (that China would not cede the territory to any other power) Britain had got a claim to the entire Yangtze Valley—the whole hinterland of Shanghai, half the China market. Britain also got concessions to build some 2800 miles of railways, roughly equal to the combined length of the French (420 miles), Russian (1530 miles), and Belgian (650 miles) concessions. In addition Britain leased Weihaiwei, opposite Port Arthur, as a naval base and increased eightfold the territory leased on the mainland next to Hong Kong. She also tried to ensure the survival of the treaty system, which had been so largely a British creation, by securing the opening of more treaty ports in the southwest and northeast and a promise that the office of Inspector General of Customs would remain British-held as long as Britain's share of the China trade remained the largest. Yet this outcome tended to weaken Britain's position in China, since her taking "compensation" only confirmed the special positions of the other powers in Yunnan, Shantung, and Manchuria, contrary to her interests there.

The results of the scramble of 1898 were most evident in the political scene. It inaugurated a new and more ominous phase of the treaty system, because "spheres of influence" were plainly part-way steps toward making China into a congeries of outright European colonies. Up to this time the trading powers led by Britain had dominated China's foreign trade, ports of access, and internal waterways. Now, Germany and Russia were moving in to dominate entire provinces with new railways, mines, industries, and seaports. The leased territories and railway zones, to be governed and policed by foreigners in Manchuria and Shantung, would become quasi-colonial areas, much more extensive and more menacing to China's integrity than the old treaty-port concessions. In short, imperialism threatened the Ch'ing Empire with extinction. It directly inspired both the Reform Movement and the Boxer uprising.

The Reform Movement

No one had been more surprised by China's defeat in 1894 than the conservatives who had opposed modernization. Remote from the scene of battle, shaken by its unexpected outcome, they were equally violent in accusing Li Hung-chang of treachery and in opposing the peace settlement. They clamored for the war to continue. Within a twenty-day period the throne received 130 memorials signed by some 2500 persons. This unprecedented outpouring of patriotic concern stressed that the indemnity, three times Peking's annual revenue, would put the empire in debt to foreigners while the other terms would weaken its prestige and power almost to extinction. In this atmosphere of consternation, a radical reformer from Canton, K'ang Yu-wei, led a group of more than 1200 provincial graduates, who were at Peking for the triennial examinations, in presenting on May 2, 1895, what became known as the "Ten Thousand Word Memorial" or "Memorial of the Examination Candidates." It advocated rejecting the peace treaty, moving the capital inland for prolonged warfare, and instituting a multitude of reforms. This inaugurated the Reform Movement which absorbed the attention of the scholar-official class during the next four years, while the imperialists' demands became constantly more menacing.

With China's defeat the dam had broken. The foreign powers moved toward dismembering the empire, "cutting up the Chinese melon," while the ruling class strove to save the traditional state-and-culture by something more than "self-strengthening"—namely, the "reform of institutions." The Reform Movement was an institutional innovation, for it led to political discussion by scholar-gentry who were not in office, quite contrary to the Ch'ing dynasty's established regulations. As early as 1652, mindful how factionalism had weakened the Ming, the emperor had forbidden degree-holders to put forward views on policy, or "to associate with large numbers of others, or to form alliances or join societies." The Yung-cheng and Ch'ien-lung emperors had denounced all associations of officials as self-seeking "factions" (*tang*), incapable of any distinterested concern for policy, and had demanded that each official be personally loyal in the sense of taking the emperor's "likes and dislikes as his own will."

Although the nineteenth century had seen this authoritarianism modified in practice, the memorial of the examination candidates advocating myriad reforms was almost unprecedented. Even more revolutionary was the rise of scholar-gentry political associations or "study societies" (*hsüeh-hui*). The most famous was the "Society for the Study of Self-Strengthening" founded at Peking in August–September 1895. Branches of it and similar societies were soon set up in Shanghai and other major centers, with financial support from reform-minded high officials like Chang Chih-tung and Yüan Shih-k'ai. Scholars once in politics quickly became journalists. The study societies began to publish journals and newspapers. When K'ang's junior colleague, Liang Ch'i-ch'ao, began in August 1895 to edit a daily for the Self-Strengthening Society, he at first borrowed the title of a missionary monthly (*Wan-kuo kung-pao* or *The Globe Magazine*) and reprinted many articles from it; indeed, the young Liang for a time actually assisted the reform-minded missionary, Timothy Richard. The Reform Movement began to use group organization, discussion meetings, and an active press, strongly reminiscent of missionary methods. With the spread of literacy, these methods could bring more than simply the scholar class into participation in political life.

The Ideology of Reform.   For scholars indoctrinated by their studies in the all-embracing social theory of Confucianism, change had to be sanctioned by ideas. The theory of reform had developed slowly over two generations, ever since men like Commissioner Lin Tse-hsü, believers in the administrative reforms of the school of "statecraft," had first urged the use of Western arms during the Opium War. But as the pressure to adopt Western ways in self-defense increased, so did the need to justify the process. How could one defend Chinese ways by adopting Western ways?

One answer was to make a distinction between what was defended and what was adopted, as between ends and means. Japanese reformers had used the phrase, "Eastern ethics and Western science." For China, the sanction for "self-strengthening" was finally summed up in the slogan popularized by Chang Chih-tung in the 1890's: "Chinese learning for the essential principles; Western learning for the practical applications." To a critical mind, however, this slogan was specious and misleading. It invoked a Sung philosophical distinction between *t'i* "substance" (literally, "body") and *yung* "function" (literally, "use"). This pair of terms designated the interdependence between the inner substance of any one thing and its outward functioning. It had been applied, for example, to the superior man's inner self-cultivation and outward governing of others, to the ruler's being a sage in spirit and a king in action. But Chang was now stretching the old ideology of Neo-Confucianism to cover the new practice of Westernization. This was decried by critics like Yen Fu, who in the 1890's was translating J. S. Mill, T. H. Huxley, Herbert Spencer, and other Western writers on evolution and utilitarianism and so knew something of both civilizations. Yen pointed out that "Chinese learning has its substance and function; Western learning also has its substance and function." The *t'i-yung* formula was a snare, for techniques will affect values, and means that are adopted will determine ends.

Another approach was to find the sanction for Westernization within China's own tradition. This was a variant of the customary practice of "finding in antiquity the sanction for present-day changes." Thus in the 1860's, Western studies in the Interpreters College at Peking had been justified by alleging that "Western sciences borrowed their roots from ancient Chinese mathematics." In the 1880's a vulgar apologetics for Westernization developed along this line—for example, tracing the origin of chemistry to the ancient theory of the "five elements" (see page 50), so as to make chemistry part of China's cultural heritage.

A further step was to find a doctrine of change in China's past. Thus the ancient idea of "change of method" (*pien-fa*) was gradually stretched by expanding the meaning of the term *fa,* which meant literally "method" but also, more broadly, "law" or "institution." The innocuous phrase "change of method" now began to cover "institutional change" of the most basic kind. For example, writers in the early 1890's advocated the inauguration of a parliament, which they justified by quoting classical aphorisms about "ruler and people being one body, superior and inferior being of one mind." But still there was no equivalent in Chinese tradition for the dynamic idea of progress, so dominant in contemporary Western works.

K'ang Yu-wei's Reinterpretation of Confucianism. K'ang Yu-wei, the radical petitioner of 1895, finally supplied the reinterpretation by which the Classics could sanction Westernization and Confucianism could include progress. He had been born into a distinguished scholar-official family of Canton and became a precocious student of the Classics. But soon he found them "all empty and lacking in substance." K'ang said later that his teacher "often cautioned me about my undue feelings of superiority," but nevertheless, at the age of twenty-one, while meditating upon the world, "in a great release of enlightenment I beheld myself a sage...." He proceeded to act like one and remake the classical tradition.

First of all, he carried further the "new text" movement which had questioned the authenticity of the orthodox "ancient text" versions of certain Confucian Classics (see pages 66 and 444). To reformers committed to working within the classical tradition, the "new text" school of interpretation was very appealing because it broke the monopoly of the Neo-Confucian orthodoxy. K'ang synthesized the studies of the "new text" school, and in 1891 attacked the authenticity of several Classics. He concluded that the "Han Learning" was wrongly based, while "the Classics honored and expounded by the Sung scholars are for the most part forged and not those of Confucius." His devastating attack is not now generally accepted by scholars, but it was erudite, persuasive, and therefore most unsettling to the scholarly world of the 1890's. High officials had the printing blocks of his books burned in 1894, but they could not prevent K'ang's becoming a metropolitan graduate and Hanlin academician in 1895. He was now at the top of the establishment.

Having brushed aside the orthodox view, K'ang pushed further certain "new text" interpretations and in 1897 claimed that Confucius had himself created, rather than merely edited, the principal Classics as a means of invoking antiquity in order to make institutional reforms. This view, if accepted, would allow a near-revolution invoking the name of the Sage himself. Inspired by the example of Christianity, K'ang also proposed to exalt Confucius as the focus of a Chinese national religion. This was not all. Combining two classical sources, K'ang derived an evolutionary sequence, consisting of the Three Ages of (1) Disorder, (2) Approaching Peace and Small Tranquillity, and (3) Great Peace (*t'ai-p'ing*) and Great Unity (*ta-t'ung*). In this analysis, the world had been struggling in the Age of Disorder and with K'ang's reforms would now enter the Age of Approaching Peace and Small Tranquillity. Thus China's classical learning was made to encompass a theory of evolution and progress.

The Radical Reformers' Rise to Power in 1898.   Although K'ang Yu-wei had supplied the philosophic groundwork, the Reform Movement did not at once gain the ascendant. The panic that followed defeat in 1895 soon died down; the Self-Strengthening Society was suppressed in both Peking and Shanghai, though reform activities were pushed by officials and gentry in some provinces. Hunan, for example, though its gentry had held out against both Taiping rebels and Christian missionaries, now saw many innovations. With the blessing of Chang Chih-tung as governor-general, the provincial officials promoted modernization at the capital, Changsha—paved and lighted streets, steam launches on the river, telegraph lines to the outer world, a modern police system, colleges with modern curricula, a study society with lectures and discussions. These achievements of gentry-official cooperation were symptomatic of a growing movement in many parts of China.

When the imperialist powers revived the atmosphere of crisis in late 1897, K'ang Yu-wei got his chance. He was recommended to the emperor as a young expert on reform by moderates committed to orthodox "self-strengthening." By mid-1898, with the imperialist powers apparently ready to tear China apart, action seemed essential, K'ang was full of proposals, and the ardent young emperor, then twenty-seven, finally gave him his confidence. K'ang's first audience lasted five hours. "China will soon perish," he said. "All that is caused by the conservatives," replied the emperor. "If Your Majesty wishes to rely on them for reform," said K'ang, "it will be like climbing a tree to seek for fish."

K'ang's program called for the restructuring of internal administration on the grounds that China's traditional checks and double-checks, diffusion of power and surveillance of power-holders, had been developed to preserve the ruling dynasty against enemies arising from within. Now, against enemies from without, this cumbersome machinery was worse than useless. He therefore proposed a cabinet type of domestic administration, with a dozen ministers employing modern-trained experts, to supplant the clumsy Six Ministries and Grand Council. Like the Japanese, K'ang was impressed with the usefulness of parliaments not only to raise taxes, check corruption, and promote popular welfare as in Western countries, but also to strengthen the Confucian bond between ruler and people. He called for a national assembly, a constitution, and even local "bureaus of people's affairs" to carry out reforms with scholar-gentry participation. Among his followers all manner of wild ideas were current—democracy, simplification of the written language, even equality of the sexes and Western dress.

During the hundred days between June 11 and September 21, 1898, Kuang-hsü, with K'ang Yu-wei, Liang Ch'i-ch'ao, and others as advisers behind the scenes, issued forty or more reform edicts dealing with almost every conceivable subject: setting up modern schools and remaking the examination system; revising the laws as a preliminary to getting rid of extraterritoriality; promoting agriculture, medicine, mining, commerce, inventions, and study abroad; and modernizing the army, navy, police, and postal systems. Few of these orders were carried out, except in Hunan. Officials waited to see how the Empress Dowager, in retirement since 1889, would respond to this radical program. Conservative opposition was of course vociferous. All the reformers except the emperor were Chinese; the emperor's abolition of sinecure posts threatened many Manchu incumbents; and some feared he would dismiss all Manchus. The proposal to transform monasteries into schools terrified the monks, who had friends among the palace eunuchs. Military reform threatened the ancient Manchu banners and the Chinese constabulary of the Green Standard. The attack on the old examinations as qualification for office threatened all degree-holders who aspired to become officials. The attack on corruption affected nearly everyone in office. In short, as his program unfolded, the emperor found himself at war with the whole establishment, not least with his adoptive "mother," the Empress Dowager, who was still vigorous at sixty-three.

The issue in 1898 was not between reform or no reform, but between K'ang Yu-wei's radicalism and a continuation of the moderate "self-strengthening," which was now in its fourth decade of creeping Westernization. The aims of the latter were summed up in Chang Chih-tung's book, *Exhortation to Study,* which he published during the Hundred Days to state the antiradical position. This influential work, distributed by imperial order, aimed first of all to preserve the Manchu dynasty by a revival of the Confucian social order. It therefore upheld the "three bonds" (three of the *Mencius'* famous five relationships, namely, those between emperor and official, father and son, husband and wife) and vigorously opposed egalitarianism, democracy, constitutional monarchy, the doctrine of the "people's rights" (*min-ch'üan*), parliaments, the freedom of the individual, and civil liberties of the Western sort. Second, Chang aimed to save China by education. He proposed to reform the examination system; to set up a hierarchy of schools and colleges and an imperial university at Peking; and in the curriculum to stress both the Confucian Classics and Western technology. This program was modeled on Japan's. It would include the sending of students abroad and universal military service. Third, Chang hoped to save China by industrialization. For this his military "self-strengthening" effort at Wuhan was setting a practical example. One of its aims was to make China less dependent on imported steel. Having begun an iron foundry and arsenal at Hanyang (1890) and an iron mine at Ta-yeh in Hupei (1894), Chang advocated construction of a Peking-Hankow-Canton railway through China's heartland, by a central railway administration.

The Empress Dowager found her entire world threatened by K'ang Yu-wei's attack on those twin pillars of her regime, classical learning and organized corruption. She bided her time while opposition grew. Finally on September 21, 1898, with the help of the top Manchu military commander, Jung-lu, she seized the Kuang-hsü emperor in a *coup d'état* and began her third regency. K'ang and Liang escaped to Japan; but six of the reformers, including the brilliant young eclectic philosopher from Hunan, T'an Ssu-t'ung, were executed. The emperor remained in forced seclusion, and when the Empress Dowager finally died in 1908, he mysteriously predeceased her by one day.

The abrupt end of the Hundred Days restored most of the status quo ante, yet some moderate reform measures continued, such as the abolition of certain sinecures and the establishment of modern schools. The chief significance of 1898, however, was that the radicals' attempt at a revolution from above, in the pattern of the revolution effected in Japan by the Meiji Restoration, had failed. The Empress Dowager's countercoup, though it was followed by another decade of moderate reform, suggested that any really revolutionary change would have to come from below, presumably by violence. Thus gradualism, by being too gradual, made violent revolution more certain. Yet it was still in the future. The ease of the Empress Dowager's *coup d'état* suggests that China as a whole was far from ready for revolution in 1898. After sixty years of attack and stimulus from the Western world, the traditional Chinese order was still strong and capable of violent protest against modernization.

The Boxer Rising

The Boxer Movement. The radical reforms of 1898 had been a daring effort by Chinese scholars at the very top of the ruling class to respond to the foreign menace by modernizing the whole Ch'ing government. After its failure, the initiative shifted to a popular movement that was led by a traditional type of secret society. Its name *I-ho ch'üan,* crudely translated by Westerners as "Righteous and Harmonious Fists," or more simply as "Boxers," indicates that this society under the name of Righteousness and Harmony (*I-ho*) practiced its own form of so-called Chinese "boxing" (*ch'üan*), which, through a sequence of postures and exercises, aimed to harmonize mind and muscle in preparation for combat. This was a magic art using Taoist sorcery and a prescribed ritual—members thrice recited an incantation, breathed through clenched teeth, foamed at the mouth, and became possessed by spirits who made them happily impervious to foreign bullets. The Boxers found their heroes in semifictional, semihistoric, operatic characters like those in *All Men Are Brothers,* in the ancient tradition of popular rebellion. Their original slogan early in 1899 was "overthrow the Ch'ing; destroy the foreigner."

Anti-Christian hostility was one obvious factor inspiring the Boxer movement, for the steady growth of missionary activity in the 1890's exacerbated all the problems that had accumulated during the previous decades. Some Christian converts flouted the sacred family relationships, refused to support the local festivals and deities, and got the missionaries to intervene and help them in their disputes. With French support, Catholic prelates could coerce local officials. Scurrilous anti-Christian diatribes continued to circulate.

The sudden rise of the Boxer movement was also fostered by economic and political conditions. Yellow River floods had led to widespread famine in Shantung in 1898. North China suffered generally from drought. Destitute country people were moving about as vagrants. To some degree the importation of foreign cotton goods and oil depressed local industries, while plans for new railways seemed to threaten the livelihood of carters and canal bargemen. The late 1890's, in fact, saw disorder, riots, banditry, or local risings in every one of the eighteen provinces, rather reminiscent of the late 1840's just before the Taiping upheaval. In sum, the Boxer movement emerged as a direct-action response to a deepening crisis in the lives of the whole Chinese people.

The movement received its prodynastic impetus in 1899 from the patronage of Manchu and Chinese officials. The hard core of conservative Manchu princes in the Ch'ing court had been educated in the palace with little experience of actual government or the outside world. These men accepted in 1899 the same purblind slogan that had roused the samurai of Japan forty years earlier—"Expel the barbarians!" In trying to use the Boxers against the foreigners, they were invoking the ancient idea, China's equivalent of Western "popular sovereignty," that the righteous indignation of the common people was the final arbiter of politics. An alliance between antiforeign officials and prodynastic Boxers began to take shape in the autumn of 1899, after government troops had defeated and seized some of the antidynastic Boxer rebels in Shantung. The Boxer slogan shifted to "support the Ch'ing; destroy the foreigner," which was pleasantly different from the usual anti-Ch'ing battle cries of secret societies.

Ch'ing officialdom was split into an ardent pro-Boxer faction, which eventually became dominant, and a much larger but frustrated anti-Boxer element, which despised the Boxers' superstitious fanaticism, and yet sympathized with their aims. In Chihli during the first five months of 1900, Boxer bands of hundreds and even thousands spread over the countryside, burning missionary establishments and slaughtering Chinese Christians. The Manchu princes seem to have persuaded the Empress Dowager that the Boxers' magic invulnerability was real. When repeated notes came from the diplomatic corps, demanding suppression, the edicts issued in response, in January and again in April 1900, were highly equivocal—the groups that attacked missionaries and their converts were "of different kinds"; officials suppressing them must "discriminate" between the good and bad elements. The diplomatic corps, so confident of Western superiority, was slow to recognize that the Empress Dowager, after decades of enforcing foreign privileges under the unequal treaties, was finally prepared to let this popular movement challenge the West by force.

The Siege of the Peking Legations and Its Aftermath.   With the court thus determined to appease rather than suppress the Boxer terror, further foreign provocation was hardly necessary to trigger the final explosion; the foreigners had been provocative for sixty years already. The final outbreak was precipitated from both sides. In June 1900 Boxers besieged the foreign communities in both Tientsin and Peking. The foreign powers concentrated naval forces and mounted a relief expedition. The Ch'ing dynasty declared war against them. In North China outside the capital some 250 foreigners were killed, most of them missionaries and mainly in Shansi province. Chinese Christians died in far greater numbers, although scattered communities succeeded in defending themselves.

This midsummer madness astounded the world. After a month of no news from the diplomats, the missionary leaders, Sir Robert Hart, and the others besieged in the Peking legations, they were credibly reported all massacred. The decentralized nature of the Ch'ing government meantime had proved of some practical use. While the benighted Manchus at court were trying extermination, the worldly-wise Chinese regional officials resorted to diplomacy to mitigate the catastrophe. Li Hung-chang, now governor-general at Canton in concert with Liu K'un-i at Nanking, Chang Chih-tung at Wuhan, and Yüan Shih-k'ai in Shantung decided to ignore the dynasty's declaration of war. They proposed that if the foreigners would send no more warships into the Yangtze area, the governors-general there would maintain order. The effect of this was to neutralize all of China ex-

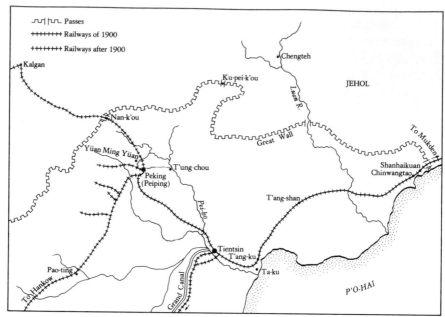

Passes
Railways of 1900
Railways after 1900

THE APPROACHES TO PEKING

cept the northern provinces. The convenient fiction was accepted that the Boxer outbreak was in fact a "rebellion," as it has since been called, and not an act supported by the dynasty.

Thus the Boxer War, the fourth and largest which China fought against Western powers in the nineteenth century, remained localized in North China while the provincial authorities elsewhere loyally represented the dynasty's interest in peace, corresponding by telegram with the court at Peking and letting the Empress Dowager eat her cake and have it too. She pursued simultaneous policies of extermination, as demanded by the Manchus dominant at court, and peace, as vigorously sought by her envoys abroad and her officials in South China. This ambivalence of Ch'ing policy was also evident in Peking. Seventy-six foreigners died defending the legations; the rest survived because the commander of one part of the imperial forces, though maintaining a noisy bombardment, did not use available artillery or press home the attack. International forces relieved the siege of the Tientsin concessions on July 14, and of the Peking legations on August 14.

As the Western invaders with the usual local assistance began to loot the city, which the Boxers had already despoiled, the Empress Dowager and the emperor left Peking by cart in disguise. At the age of 65, the Empress Dowager now had her closest contact with her people's problems of securing shelter, food, and protection against bandits and lawless troops. The court reached Sian and stayed there for more than a year. Li Hung-chang

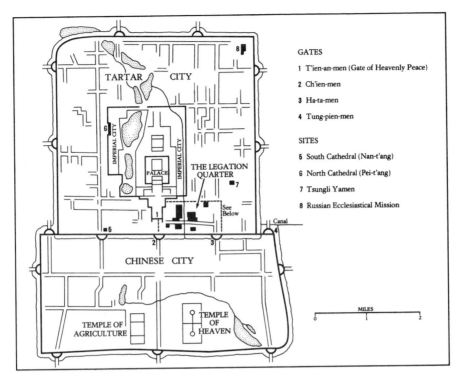

GATES

1 T'ien-an-men (Gate of Heavenly Peace)

2 Ch'ien-men

3 Ha-ta-men

4 Tung-pien-men

SITES

5 South Cathedral (Nan-t'ang)

6 North Cathedral (Pei-t'ang)

7 Tsungli Yamen

8 Russian Ecclesiastical Mission

PEKING IN 1900

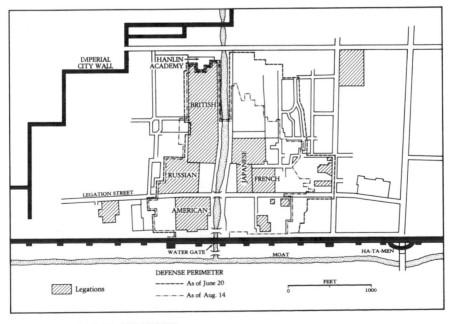

THE LEGATION QUARTER

大清國當今聖母皇太后萬歲萬歲萬萬歲

DYNASTIC DECLINE AT PEKING.   *Left: The Empress Dowager
transported by palace eunuchs in court dress, as photographed in
1903. In a mat-roofed Summer Palace courtyard under a
dragon-embroidered umbrella, the Empress wears small shoes
raised on gilt platforms. At right front is the chief eunuch,
Li Lien-ying. Right: After the Boxer Incident, the Empress
Dowager had to conciliate the foreigners. Here she is photographed
with ladies of the diplomatic corps, who stand close about and
over her, Western fashion. The Empress holds hands with the
American minister's wife, Sarah Pike Conger, who had survived
the siege of the Peking legations and was now deeply impressed
by the Ch'ing ruler's "womanly tenderness" and "intuitive ability."*

at the age of 77 was looked to as usual to save the situation. He temporized skillfully with the foreigners, who accepted his fiction that the hostilities had not been a war at all but a joint effort to suppress rebellion. Although the German minister had been the only German killed, the Kaiser demanded the right to name a commander-in-chief for the allied forces. The latter reached Peking only in October and devoted himself largely to punitive expeditions to dozens of North China cities, which continued for six months afterward. By late 1900, around 45,000 foreign troops were in North China, and Russia in a separate war had long since occupied Manchuria.

The Boxer Protocol was finally signed September 7, 1901, by a Manchu prince, Li Hung-chang (who died two months later), and the plenipotentiaries of eleven powers. It required the execution of ten high officials and the punishment of a hundred others; formal apologies; suspension of examinations in forty-five cities, half of them in Shansi, to penalize the gentry class; expansion of the Legation Quarter, to be fortified and permanently garrisoned; destruction of forts and occupation of railway posts to ensure foreign access to Peking from the sea; raising of import duties to an actual 5 per cent; and a staggering indemnity.

A British commercial treaty of 1902 tried with only modest success to improve various conditions of trade and evangelism. But abolition of likin taxes, which impeded trade, establishment of a national coinage, passage of legal reforms that would pave the way for abolishing extraterritoriality, and many other steps toward modernization which Japan had taken in the 1870's, all proved impossible to achieve. The Boxer rising and the Protocol marked the nadir of the Ch'ing dynasty's foreign relations and left little hope for its long continuance. Yet no alternative had emerged.

Imperialism and the Chinese Response

Foreign Financial Exploitation of China.   After 1901, the new imperialist domination was not confined to "spheres of influence" but extended to Peking's entire financial structure. Up to 1893, some twenty-five loans had been made to Chinese government agencies by foreign sources in China. But the total indebtedness still outstanding, all secured on the Maritime Customs revenue, had been inconsiderable. The Sino-Japanese war indemnity (230 million taels) came to about $150 million, and the big loans used to meet it in 1895, 1896, and 1898 were secured from the foreign banks on onerous terms: China received less than the face value to begin with (e.g., 94 per cent), had to pay rather high interest for as long as forty-five years, and also had to pay in gold, at the mercy of the gold/silver exchange rate. The Boxer indemnity of 450 million taels (about $333 million) was to be paid in bonds which bore interest at 4 per cent in gold, so that by the conclusion of payments in 1940, interest and principal repaid would total 928 million taels (or $739 million).

These Japanese and Boxer indemnities, unlike productive loans, were complete losses to China. Their payment drained off the Ch'ing government's revenue collected from foreign trade by the Maritime Customs, which had previously provided funds for armament and modernization. (Even this limited revenue had been further cut as the rise of prices gradually reduced the percentage value of tariff duties fixed in money terms in 1858). Henceforth even large portions of the provincial revenues and of the likin and salt revenues on domestic trade would have to be added to the Maritime Customs revenue, just to pay the foreign bondholders.

To be sure, imperialism's bark was sometimes worse than its bite. The Boxer indemnity illustrates this: in the end, the eclipse of Tsarist Russia and Imperial Germany during World War I and the remission of American, British, and other portions of the indemnity, as well as other changes, reduced actual payments to less than a third of the original assessment. Similarly, Japan's claim to a sphere in Fukien, obtained through a non-alienation agreement in April 1898, was never followed up. Italy's demand for a sphere in Chekiang in March 1899 was successfully refused. A number of the railway concessions made in the late 1890's were never actively pursued. That the "breakup of China" did not occur was partly owing to Chinese dexterity, as yet little studied, in balancing one imperialist power against another. Yet this era of financial imperialism, with its insatiable great-power rivalries and exploitative demands, has tended to overshadow the preceding decades of quieter commercial penetration and economic growth and has given patriotic Chinese ever since an indelible hatred for the whole treaty system as a "foreign imperialist yoke."

American Expansion and the Open Door.   Many Americans in the 1890's were righteously proud that the United States, unlike European powers, had never fought wars and seized colonies in Asia. To be sure, American missionaries and traders had enjoyed the special privileges secured and maintained there in large part by the British navy. Yet the fact remained that American activity, at least in the American view, had avoided "imperialism" in East Asia just as it avoided "entangling alliances" in Europe. By invoking Britain's own doctrine of most-favored-nation treatment and equal opportunity, the United States had got the benefits of Britain's free-trade empire without its odium or responsibilities. However, as the European race for colonies developed, new expansionist tendencies together with certain accidents of history brought the United States onto the East Asian scene as a great power also. The American people were more susceptible to the imperialist virus than they liked to think.

The expansion of the United States, like that of the European powers, was due to a mixture of causes—in its case, the rise of industries manufacturing cheap export products, the disappearance of the frontier at home, and a missionary tradition abroad. As the navy's great proponent of sea power, Captain A. T. Mahan, put it, America was "looking outward" in an era when doctrines of Social Darwinism and Nordic racial superiority provided a sanction for keeping up with other nations in the search for markets, colonies, and naval bases. Mahan's advocacy of bases overseas coincided with the decision of the Congress in 1890 to build a first-class battle fleet and with public agitation for a canal across Nicaragua so that the fleet could operate in both oceans. Meanwhile there had been a long-continued commercial interest in Hawaii, where the white sugar planters sought annexation to the United States.

The American expansion of 1898 in East Asia was triggered by the coincidence of the war with Spain over Cuba. Theodore Roosevelt, assistant secretary of the navy, had prepared Commodore Dewey and his American Asiatic Squadron at Hong Kong to attack the Spanish fleet at Manila. Dewey did so at dawn on May 1; by lunchtime the Spanish fleet was sunk or burning. Seeing no alternative, the United States occupied Manila with a force of eleven thousand in the summer of 1898, received the Philippines from Spain by a peace treaty in December, and at once became involved in suppressing a full-fledged Filipino struggle for independence. Hawaii had been annexed by Congressional action in July, and the western Pacific island of Guam had been taken from Spain. These American acquisitions, outstripping those of any imperialist power in China, gave the United States potential naval bases at Pearl Harbor, Guam, and Manila, as well as the Hawaiian Islands and the entire Philippine archipelago. It was right in the middle of this period, in September 1899, that Secretary of State John Hay issued his first Open Door notes.

Hay had recently been minister to London, where the British early in 1898 had consulted him on how to preserve the tradition of equal opportunity, an open door for trade, in the face of imperialist "spheres of influence" in China. He now got the advice of one of Robert Hart's chief commissioners in the Chinese Maritime Customs. As a result, the first American Open Door notes reflected the specific interest of Hart and the Customs in maintaining that original principle of the treaty system—the equal taxation of foreign trade in all treaty ports, inside as well as outside the new "spheres of influence." They requested, first, that each power not interfere with "any treaty port or any vested interest" within its "sphere"; second, that only the Chinese government should collect duties on trade at such ports, and only according to the treaty tariff; and third, that no preferential harbor dues or railroad charges should benefit the subjects of a power having a "sphere." In short, these first Open Door notes sought to preserve equality of trade in China, not the Chinese state. Britain, Germany, France, Italy, and Japan all agreed to accept these provisions if everyone else did. The Russian reply was rather negative and Hay's success was limited, but he made the best of it by blandly notifying all concerned that their unanimous acceptance of his notes had been "final and definitive."

As the Boxer rising brought foreign armies into North China and Manchuria in the summer of 1900, China's chances of survival as a state seemed more dubious than ever. Hay's second note, a circular of July 1900, therefore stated the American desire for a solution that would bring "permanent safety and peace to China, preserve Chinese territorial and administrative entity, protect all rights guaranteed to friendly powers by treaty and international law, and safeguard for the world the principle of equal and impartial trade with all parts of the Chinese Empire." Everyone agreed, and the Open Door became publicly established as the traditional American policy toward China. In time its essential concept became the preservation, not merely of foreign commercial opportunity, but of China's integrity as a nation. But in origin it was an effort by a maritime power at a distance to maintain the treaty system against the spread of colonialism. It was a statement of principle in words, put forward as a good thing in itself, without thought of forceful action to back it up. The United States was simultaneously acquiring a colony in the Philippines. It is safe to say that the Open Door policy seemed grander in the United States than elsewhere.

China's Weaknesses and Strengths. When we try to interpret the events of 1900 it seems plain that the imperialist powers kept the reactionary Ch'ing dynasty in power the better to enjoy their special privileges; they had in fact cooperated with the established order throughout the six decades of the unequal treaties. Much evidence can be marshaled to show the inveterate stubbornness, if not rapacity, of foreign groups in defense of their interests in China—witness the failure of the Alcock Convention of 1869 (see page 580) or of the British treaty of 1902 to reform the treaty system for China's benefit. Great changes seldom seemed to the foreigners to be in their interest. They preferred to prop up the old order.

It is plain enough that China was victimized by the foreign powers. This theme is naturally attractive to modern Chinese patriots. It leaves unanswered, however, the underlying question: why did China not respond to foreign encroachment earlier and more vigorously? Where were those Chinese revolutionaries who could have met the Western aggression by modernizing the traditional Chinese state and expelling the imperialists? In the twentieth century such leaders appear; where were they in the nineteenth century?

The mid-century rebels, being anti-Manchu, were potentially nationalistic but lacked modern ideas. The strongest of them, the Taipings, after ten years' development proved themselves old-fashioned rivals for power and showed little capacity for remaking the traditional order. The "self-strengthening" movement thereafter was more defensive than creative, a conservative compromise avoiding radical modernization. The reformers of 1898, though their plans were potentially revolutionary, viewed themselves as loyal ministers of the dynasty, entirely dependent on the ruling power of the Son of Heaven. The empire's bankruptcy of leadership was finally demonstrated by those Manchu grandees who took up the inane atavism of the Boxers. Talent on a large scale was simply not devoted to purposes of real revolution or reform before 1900. No one appeared under the old order who had any solid prospect of making drastic changes in it. This weakness of the forces of change within China was less an achievement of Western imperialism than a tribute to the strength of the Chinese social order, state, and culture. It was the overall cohesion and structural stability of Chinese civilization that basically inhibited its rapid response to the Western menace.

In maintaining this Chinese momentum in established ways, no single factor was all-important. China's remarkable imperviousness to foreign stimuli resulted from a complex of factors, just as did Japan's equally remarkable and opposite capacity for change and modernization. At the highest level of generality, we have suggested that Japan already had the essential ingredients of modern nationalism, in a people ready to strive together for national ends, while China did not. Beneath this level of abstraction, each observer can select his own balance among many interacting factors.

On the material plane, for example, China had vast resources but they were being exploited in traditional ways. Modern methods could not easily be substituted. Japan, as it turned out, was far poorer in raw materials, like iron, necessary for modernization, but her people met the challenge with vigor and adaptability. The great size of the Chinese Empire, which made it potentially a world power, also retarded its response in many ways. Economically it was almost self-sufficient. Strategically it was well-nigh invulnerable to conquest, if not to defeat; sea power, to which Japan was so exposed, could dominate many Chinese cities but not the vast interior. The dense populations of interior areas like Hunan and Szechwan remained beyond foreign contact, reservoirs of traditional attitudes and of talent trained in the old style; instead of reading newspapers, the elite in these areas still studied the Classics and grew up intellectually almost untouched by the treaty ports.

Institutions, however, made an even greater difference than material circumstances. Japan's feudal order, as noted in Chapter 17, had already produced the loyal *han* administrators, the merchant capitalists, the scholars of Dutch learning, the patriotic individual samurai, who could create a nation-state to compete with other nation-states. China was in a different mold, above such competition. Her ancient institutions were finely balanced and well tempered to preserve an equilibrium among three strata—the monarch and his officials, the landlord-scholar-gentry class, and the illiterate farming populace. In this predominantly agrarian empire neither merchant-capitalists nor artisans, neither traders abroad nor inventors and investors at home, could create centers of disequilibrating growth. The Chinese people, in short, were in the grip of their past. Their national religion was in fact the worship of the past. The prime virtue of filial piety led to reverence for ancestors. The world of thought fostered reverence for the Confucian Classics. Rulers could not counter the injunctions of their dynastic founder. Precedent dominated administration. Social and economic life was ruled by old custom. Even rebels invoked the past, incapable of real revolution. China was under the spell of her own great historical tradition and ancient learning, both kept alive by the written language.

This backward-looking self-sufficiency of intellectual life gave China's leaders two major characteristics. First, trained to concentrate on the affairs of the Middle Kingdom, they were willfully ignorant and correspondingly contemptuous of things abroad. Pride of culture, absorption in the Chinese universe, made them unresponsive to "barbarian" ideas. Secondly, as supporters of a universal state, China's leaders were immune to nationalism. The great empire of continental East Asia, though centered on the dense population of China, had long since had to take in the peripheral peoples of Inner Asia, particularly the nomads and seminomads of the steppe, whose warrior horsemen had played an ever greater role in China's domestic power politics. The Mongol and Manchu conquests were fundamental, not superficial, phenomena of the great empire's political life—despite the insouciance regarding them affected by some Chinese chroniclers. As the most sophisticated example of Sino-barbarian administration under an alien dynasty of conquest, the Ch'ing regime vigorously suppressed racist-nationalist sentiment. Through the examination system it recruited talented bureaucrats who had indoctrinated themselves in upward-looking loyalty; it avoided any formal doctrine that officials should represent bottom-level constituencies. Until the rise of treaty-port newspapers and missionary education, presenting a comparative view of other nations, the whole process of government remained highly elitist and lacking in the symbolism, vocabulary, and practices of modern nationalism. Among other things, the elite, trained in loyalty to the ruler and to the past, lacked a common sense of national purpose in making changes, and this inhibited the strong central leadership necessary for modernization. The Manchus could not afford to mobilize the Chinese people for participation in political life lest the dynasty become more obviously alien and dispensable and so be rejected.

大清光緒三十一年崇佑庭七十有四小照

尚書銜軍功花翎
福州將軍閩海關監督船政大臣
兼署閩浙總督東福建鹽政大臣世襲罔替奉恩將軍

NON-CHINESE OFFICIALS IN CHINA. *Above: A Manchu official: Ch'ung-shan of the Bordered Red Banner. Inscription on right: "Tartar General of hereditary rank by receipt of Imperial Grace, with brevet rank of Board President and Peacock Feather bestowed for military merit," etc. On left: "Portrait of Ch'ung Yu-t'ing at 74 sui, 1905" (with his seals, "Yu-t'ing" and "Ch'ung-shan of the imperial family"). Below: Sino-foreign officials, Foochow, ca. 1905. Front row, from left: Customs Commissioner E. B. Drew (American); Salt Intendant Lu; Japanese Consul; Tartar General Ch'ung-shan; American Consul (Dr. S. L. Gracey); Grain Intendant Ch'i-yüeh; French Consul. In the back row are interpreters and officials.*

In this specific and seldom understood political situation, China's response to the West was affected positively by one unusual and nonnationalistic factor, the tendency to admit "barbarians" to a peripheral participation in Chinese civilization and even to cooperate in joint enterprises with powerful invaders on the frontier. By their treaty-based privileges, special capacities and resources, the foreigners became a new element added into the old Chinese ruling class. This produced the long-continued role of the treaty ports, which is otherwise inexplicable. The ports were truly semicolonial phenomena in the sense that foreign governments dominated them locally while the dynasty continued to rule the broad interior of the empire as a whole. Sea power and land power, foreign ways and interests, and Chinese ways and interests, met in the treaty ports in a peculiar, stalemated harmony that modern nationalism would never have tolerated. The Chinese and foreign officials divided their authority while the merchants shared their profits. In time the Chinese state, without changing its own nature, met its problems of Western contact by employing foreign administrators and advisers in the Maritime Customs and elsewhere. In the absence of a nationalistic spirit, this employment of foreigners was not used as an opportunity to learn from them quickly and get rid of them, as in Japan; it was more like those inveterate arrangements on the Inner Asian frontier where powerful "barbarians" who could not be defeated were given recognized status in the empire and so used, if possible, to control their fellows beyond the frontier. In their nineteenth-century foreign relations, as elsewhere, the Chinese were drawing on their past.

As a result, the antinationalistic Ch'ing regime, approaching the end of its dynastic cycle, was thoroughly on the defensive—strong enough to cling to tradition and suppress rebellion, yet too weak to provide leadership for change. The late Ch'ing record in diplomacy, dealing with the imperialist powers with considerable success from a position of weakness, is therefore all the more remarkable. China used her obvious weakness to motivate the foreigners to stultify one another's ambitions. The Ch'ing negotiators spread rumors and leaked secrets. They appeared panic-stricken and helpless. They accepted bribes while granting concessions. But China survived, and their diplomacy deserves re-examination as having been more effective than outsiders have realized.

22. Imperial Japan: Economy and Society

Japan's rise from semicolonial status under the unequal treaties to the level of a great power and ally of Britain was an unparalleled success story. For this new Japan the early decades of the twentieth century were a golden age. Having successfully met the great challenge presented by the Western powers in the nineteenth century—in fact having been the only non-Western nation to do so—why should Japan not overcome the seemingly simpler problems ahead?

Indeed, Japan in the first quarter of the twentieth century gave every promise of living up to this optimistic prospect. The nation moved ahead rapidly in all fields, continuing with amazing speed to close the technological gap between itself and the West that had so terrified the Japanese only a generation or two earlier. By 1925 Japan was a far more modernized country and much more of a world power than at the close of the Russo-Japanese War.

The next two decades saw a continuation of the same rapid technological progress, growth of power, and modernization of institutions, but meanwhile a profound change had come over the country. The brilliant successes of earlier years had somehow turned into staggering new problems. Confidence had been replaced by new fears, the old unity of purpose by inner conflict. Japan continued to rush forward, but the Japanese themselves began to wonder apprehensively where they were going. And their worries proved to be justified. Japan became involved in wars of increasing magnitude, until in 1945 its newly won empire and ancient homeland both

648

fell in ruins in perhaps the largest single catastrophe to overwhelm any nation in modern times. Japan's unparalleled success had turned to ashes.

This second great phase in Japan's modernization is doubtless pregnant with meaning. But no one is as yet sure just what this reversal of fortune fully signifies. We have some idea of the dynamics of Japan's modernization in the nineteenth century, and the disaster that struck in the 1930's and 1940's may be clear enough, but how and why did the one so quickly turn into the other? The few who have attempted to answer the question have usually treated the disaster as if it were a direct outgrowth of the imperfections of the Meiji system, but we must remember that two generations separated the original Meiji leaders from the men who led Japan to its great defeat. One whole generation of relative stability lies between the Meiji oligarchs and the later crisis.

In transforming their society to meet the problems they faced in the nineteenth century, however, the Japanese undoubtedly did create new ones to be faced in the twentieth. A spurt in population accompanied the modernization of the economy and the introduction of modern medical science. Hence Japan, long self-sufficient and even an exporter of food in the nineteenth century, became increasingly dependent on imports of rice and raw materials. Thus the quest for economic security led to dependence on foreign markets. Similarly the quest for military security resulted in a rapid build-up of military might, which led to expansion abroad. The Japanese now found themselves embroiled in imperialistic rivalries and the difficulties of colonial rule that beset all colonial powers in the twentieth century.

Equally serious were less understood social and intellectual problems. The new economy, universal education, and many other factors were producing a vastly more complex society. Urban Japan had changed more rapidly than the countryside, and the gap in thought and attitudes was widening between the masses, who received only elementary schooling, and those who underwent the new, Western-oriented higher education. Even among the more educated, divergencies of attitude were becoming greater: professional military men, civil administrators, educators, men of letters, businessmen, and politicians were living different kinds of lives and thinking different thoughts.

There were also fresh stirrings of discontent among the lower classes. Tenancy had grown steadily in the countryside, and the new urban proletariat of factory workers, as it gradually became divorced from its peasant origins, became more vulnerable to fluctuations in the industrial economy. Living standards for the Japanese as a whole had moved steadily upward, but economic expectancies rose even faster. The unhappy conditions of life among tenant farmers and factory workers posed a major social problem.

Still another problem was leadership. The Meiji leaders had been a close-knit group, united on their goal: to achieve security and equality for Japan by using Western technology. Now professional military men, who were much more narrowly specialized than their predecessors, might argue that Japan's future lay in increased military strength in order to seize a larger empire, whereas business leaders or the politicians they helped elect might feel that such a course was both costly and dangerous and that Japan would do better to invest in industrial expansion. Such divisions of opinion are not infrequent in modern societies, and their resolution requires either strong leadership or an effective mechanism for settling disagreements—both of which Japan lacked. The Meiji oligarchs created a government which they could direct from above. They assumed the continuation of a strong and unified leadership group like themselves. The second and third generation of leaders, however, were the heirs and not the architects of the system. They were in it, not above it.

Behind the political ambiguities was a growing diversity of values. The guiding spirit of the Meiji transformation was an emperor-oriented nationalism. This had been expressed in a driving ambition to make Japan into a powerful state. But once Japan achieved power, its goals became diverse and the earlier political consensus became gravely fragmented, even though the core elements of nationalism remained strong.

Japan's political life in the late nineteenth and early twentieth centuries was partly free and partly unfree. As Japan's society became more modern, demands for greater freedom were created by new streams of Western thought, heightened social mobility, more and better education, and wider participation by the people in the political control of society. This reflected the major trend in Japanese politics through the 1920's: the step-by-step increase in the power of the Diet and in the strength of the political parties in relation to the other governmental elites. Yet during the same period the potential for greater authoritarian controls also increased. When crises arose in the early 1930's that Japan's leaders could not solve, a shift occurred in the balance of elites and Japan became a militarist state. The shift to military control demonstrated that the evils as well as the benefits of modernization could appear in non-Western as in Western nations.

The Maturing of The Economy

The base for Japan's modern industrial development was formed during the last thirty years of the nineteenth century. The first development occurred in the traditional sector of the economy. Freed from Tokugawa restrictions and given impetus by institutional innovations and reforms, Japan's traditional small industries underwent a notable expansion. The second wave of advance came in the modern sector during the late 1880's and the 1890's. But we must keep this nineteenth-century growth in proper perspective. In spite of its qualitative brilliance, it was small. In a quantitative sense Japan's "takeoff" period really began only after the Russo-Japanese War. At the end of the nineteenth century the country was still technologically backward, exporting for the most part raw or semiprocessed materials such as silk.

The rate of economic growth after 1900 was spectacular. The upsurge of the late nineteenth century continued almost without interruption for the next four decades. Between 1900 and the late 1930's the production of raw materials more than tripled, and the output of manufactured goods increased well over twelvefold. By the late 1930's the Japanese economy was relatively mature even in its heavy industries. Close to 60 per cent of the export trade, which had grown about twentyfold in the meantime, was made up of fully manufactured goods, and certain industries within the great manufacturing nations of the West had become almost hysterically afraid of Japanese competition.

Many scholars have attributed this economic growth to Japan's exploitation of its new colonial empire. The Japanese certainly wrested from their colonies what they could, and control over the agricultural products and mineral resources of Korea and Taiwan proved to be of strategic advantage. But however exploitative the empire was in human terms, it was probably more an economic drain than an asset. More was spent in the colonies than was derived from them, even if we disregard the greatly increased military outlay required for their seizure and defense.

Other scholars have stressed the role of foreign markets (of which colonial markets were but a very small part) to explain Japan's economic growth. They have argued that the inequities of landlordism and zaibatsu concentration of wealth limited domestic consumption and forced Japan to turn outward for markets. This hypothesis also is not borne out by the facts. As a source of raw materials and advanced machinery, foreign trade was necessary. But it accounted for a smaller percentage of Japan's total economic activity than was true of most European countries during the same period. Japan's economy was dominant, not satellitic. Its growth was largely self-generated.

Some of the growth was used up by an increase in the population, which came close to doubling—from 43,847,000 in 1900 to 73,100,000 in 1940. Much went into investment in the new empire and into increased military expenditures. And a high percentage was plowed back as capital investment, perhaps 15 per cent or more of net income in boom years. Yet despite these claims on Japan's total product, enough remained to effect a substantial rise in per capita consumption during the first four decades of the twentieth century. At all levels of society, standards advanced somewhat, although relative disparities between different groups also increased.

As the Japanese economy developed, it became closely integrated with the world economy. Japan lacked extensive mineral resources and so, as industrial output rose, it became necessary to import ever increasing amounts of raw materials, which could be paid for only by a corresponding expansion in exports. Most of the time these were easily obtained; but the psychological awareness of dependence became more and more intense. Moreover, while foreign trade was not the motor of Japan's economic growth, it bulked large enough to make the difference between an economy running in high or in low gear. In the 1950's and 1960's it was said that when New York sneezes, Tōkyō comes down with a cold. The beginnings of this situation were already visible in the 1920's and 1930's.

The Pattern of Growth.   A boom began after 1905 that continued until 1913. The three types of demand that contributed to this advance typify the forces that sustained Japan's growth into the 1930's. The first was continuing expansion of the traditional sector of the economy. As wages rose, consumer taste, remaining relatively constant, demanded more of traditional goods, rather than the products of new industry. The second type of demand, domestic and foreign, was for cottons, bicycles, and other products of Japan's light industries. The third type of demand was that created by government expenditures, which increased sixfold in the two decades before 1913. Most of this increase was military. Throughout the period 1887–1940 government investment in the economy, as a proportion of total investment, averaged well over 40 per cent. This created a steady market for the products of Japan's heavy industries at a time when these were not yet competitive with those of the West.

Japan's rate of government expenditure and industrial investment in the years after 1905 proved too high for it to maintain, and by 1911 it faced a serious financial crisis. This was ended by the First World War which produced a strong new impetus for economic expansion. This was the "best" war in Japan's history: its military participation was minimal, orders for munitions poured in from its allies, and there was a vast increase in demand for Japanese manufactured goods in Asian and other markets cut off from their usual European sources of supply. Between 1915 and 1920 the Japanese economy grew by leaps and bounds. The destruction of European shipping played into the hands of the Japanese merchant marine, which almost doubled in size and increased its net income about ten times. The number of factory workers almost doubled, as did the export of cotton goods. Profits were huge and, despite a sharp rise in prices, permitted a rate of capital investment in industry that was unusually high even for Japan. In addition, Japan became for the first time a creditor nation, with gold reserves of more than 2 billion yen, a sixfold increase in six years.

A spiraling inflation kept Japan's war boom going for more than a year after the armistice, but prices collapsed in March 1920. The next twelve years were economically among the least impressive of Japan's modern history. One reason was that Japanese agriculture and the domestic production of raw materials reached a plateau. This leveling off accentuated the growing gap between rural and urban income levels, and put the burden of absorbing the expanding population on the industrial sector, which had problems of its own. A second reason for the poor performance of this period was a relative decline in government expenditures. Earlier such expenditures had buffered fluctuations in the economy. During the 1920's, a time of peace and democratic tendencies, military expenses were cut without a compensatory increase in other expenditures. The result was to leave the Japanese much more exposed to the ups and downs of internal and foreign markets. A third reason was that the price structure of most countries had been more thoroughly deflated after World War I than had that of Japan. This led to an unfavorable balance of trade during the early 1920's and to the loss of gold reserves. Japan's exports were buoyed up by the prosperity of the United States during the later twenties, but were dealt a disastrous blow by the economic consequences of the Great Depression.

Other domestic factors also contributed to the checkered pattern of Japan's economic life in the twenties. The postwar depression had begun to lift in 1922, but on September 1, 1923, a great earthquake occurred in the Tōkyō area in which more than 130,000 persons died and billions of dollars' worth of property was destroyed. This set off a construction boom financed in part by foreign borrowing. After 1924 Japan temporarily went off the gold standard, letting the yen depreciate, which stimulated foreign trade. An inflationary expansion of the economy ensued; but this was checked by a bank crisis in the spring of 1927, when a number of important banks failed, and deflation once more set in. Then, after springing back briefly, the economy experienced an even greater shock in 1930. In January, Inoue Junnosuke, the orthodox-minded finance minister, unwisely put Japan back on the gold standard, just two months after the American crash and at a time when world prices had already started to drop. As a result the yen rose, exports dropped and Japan sank into a serious depression.

Despite these difficulties, the Japanese economy was not stagnant between 1920 and 1930: advances were made in technology, industry was diversified more widely, manufacturing came close to doubling in output, and the gains of World War I and of the period of inflationary expansion from 1922 to 1927 were consolidated by the elimination of unsound enterprises. But the cost in human suffering and social unrest was high. The price of rice, which had risen 174 per cent in the preceding six years, fell by more than half within a year after the 1920 deflation, recovered almost to the old high by 1925, and then sank almost to the 1914 level by 1931. The price of silk, the chief export and the most important secondary product of Japan's agriculture, fell by more than two-thirds between 1925 and 1929.

Recovery and the Rise of a War Economy.   Although the depression lasted for many years in the United States, Japan was already recovering by 1932. The major factor contributing to this recovery was an expansion of foreign trade. Japan went off the gold standard in December 1931, and the yen sank from 50 cents to 30 cents. This devaluation produced a boom in exports. Cheaper Japanese goods captured many markets in Asia and Africa that were not sealed up within European empires. A second factor responsible for Japan's rapid recovery was the return to military adventure in 1931, restoring the high level of military expenditures that had been lacking during the previous decade. Since there was slack in the economy, these two factors were complementary: trade helped build industrial strength which served the military, and military demand contributed to the recovery from depression. By 1936 industry was more diversified; technological advances had occurred in the metallurgical, machine, and chemical industries; the volume of exports abroad and to the colonies had doubled in six years; and the net national product had increased by half.

The reaction in the West to the expansion of Japanese exports was negative: tariffs were raised, restrictions were sought, and voices were lifted against "dumping" and cheap Oriental labor. When one considers that Japanese exports were only 4 per cent of world exports, and that Japanese imports from the United States and Europe were greater than exports to those areas, such fears seem hypochondriac—reflecting grave doubts in the West regarding the viability of the international economic order.

The reaction of the West provided support for those in Japan favoring expansion. Other industrial powers had either extensive colonies or vast internal resources. Japan, the Britain of Asia, was deficient in both respects. It appeared that the only way to fulfill the national destiny in the face of Western restrictions was to create an economically self-sufficient empire. Events as they unfolded after 1936, however, show that these arguments were fallacious. Despite raised tariffs abroad, Japan had successfully recovered from the depression. This recovery was based on a multilateral pattern of trade: Japan sold more than it bought in Asia and Africa, and bought more than it sold in the United States and Europe. This geographical imbalance in trade was possible because currencies could be converted.

After 1936, however, more and more of Japan's exports went to its colonies. This led to diminishing foreign credits and forced Japan to impose controls on dollar imports. Also by 1936 the Japanese economy was taut. The expansion of the early thirties had brought about full employment and few resources were idle. Hence there was little possibility of another round of growth when Japan went to war, first with China in 1937 and then with the United States and the Western Allies in 1941. Japan could increase its strategic economic potential only by imposing strict controls to reduce consumption and shift productive capacities to war industries. Dependence on foreign raw materials further limited its economic potential, thus heightening the discrepancy between Japan and the United States, which possessed vast sources of raw materials and, at the beginning of the war, was far from enjoying full employment.

The Zaibatsu System.   The scarcity of capital in early Meiji Japan, the government's willingness to give financial aid and privileges to entrepreneurs who gave promise of building up the economy, and the sale in the 1880's of government industries to the few who were able to buy them enabled a relatively small group of business leaders to gain control of much of the modern sector of Japan's economy, just before industrialization started to pay off. The concerns they established in the late nineteenth century grew faster than the economy as a whole and by the 1920's controlled a large part of the nation's economic power. In the industrial upsurge of World War I, these industrialists expanded enormously, and during the economic uncertainties that followed the war they fastened their hold on the economy even more firmly. At least half of Japan's banks were eliminated during this period, leaving the financial power needed for large-scale industrial expansion concentrated in the hands of a few giant institutions.

The leading financial and industrial groups had from the start cooperated closely with the government, but now a greater equalization of roles began to take place. Businessmen were no longer dependent on the government for their capital requirements. And while continuing as an instrument of government policy, big business, by its ties within the bureaucracy and by its financial influence on the political parties, came to have a growing voice in the formation of policy. To many Japanese it appeared that the tail was beginning to wag the dog. The term zaibatsu, or "financial clique," which came into common use for these business giants, had a strongly pejorative flavor.

There has never been any clear agreement on which companies constituted the zaibatsu, but the top four are always listed, in order of their size, as Mitsui, Mitsubishi, Sumitomo, and Yasuda. In addition, no one would dispute the inclusion of other giants such as the Furukawa, Kuhara, and Kawasaki interests, as well as Aikawa's Nissan interests and other "new zaibatsu" which emerged in the 1930's by building armaments and by aiding the army to exploit Manchuria.

The greatest difference between a zaibatsu firm and a Western corporation was that the former usually spread over a variety of fields, constituting

ORGANIZATION OF THE MITSUI COMBINE
(based on specific examples among major units in the combine)

Arrows indicate percentage of stock ownership. Numbers in parentheses are paid-up capital in millions of yen (roughly 3 to the dollar).

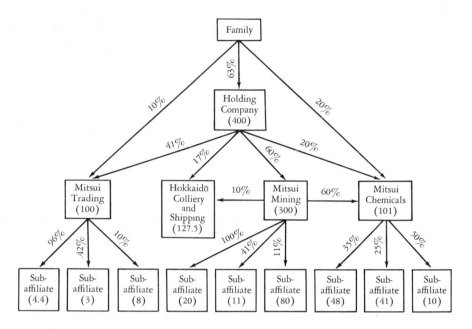

a "combine" of business enterprises, or what might be called a conglomerate today, rather than a single great company. Such a combine might spread horizontally through a variety of manufacturing or mining industries and vertically through the different stages of production of a single product. Thus one of the Mitsubishi mining companies might extract the minerals which one of the Mitsubishi manufacturing companies then fashioned into a product which a Mitsubishi trading firm marketed abroad, transporting it in ships of another Mitsubishi affiliate, and the whole process would be financed through the Mitsubishi bank.

During the 1920's and 1930's, Mitsui and Mitsubishi were probably the two largest private economic empires in the world. In 1941, the sprawling Mitsui interests consisted of a main holding company, with 70 direct corporate affiliates. The two largest, Mitsui Trading and Mitsui Mining, controlled respectively 126 and 31 other affiliates, while 108 other companies were under the control of the remaining 68 direct affiliates. At their peak the Mitsui interests probably employed about a million people in Japan proper and another million in the empire and abroad.

Mitsui was owned by the Mitsui family, which held some 90 per cent of their wealth jointly and were strictly controlled in their actions and expenditures by family laws. The family held shares directly in many of the Mitsui companies and owned a majority interest in the central holding company. This distinction between family and holding company did not exist in the more recently risen zaibatsu firms. Another difference between Mitsui and most of the others was that, while the actual business control of the Mitsui combine had long since passed into the hands of managers, the original entrepreneur or his immediate descendants might still be in control in the newer zaibatsu firms. In addition to family ownership, the internal cohesiveness and power of the zaibatsu was augmented by interlocking directorates, by the use of financial and marketing power to control affiliates in which the combine held only a minority stock interest, and by an almost feudal sense of corporate loyalty. The staff of affiliate companies regarded themselves as part of the whole organization and were loyal to it.

There has been a heated debate over the efficiency of the zaibatsu system. Today most economists agree that the system was very efficient and in its era something like it was almost inevitable. When any backward country industrializes, there is a shortage of capital, skilled labor, and technological know-how. To obtain rapid growth, these must be brought together in a concentrated form. During the second half of the nineteenth century, when free enterprise was strong and there existed no historical model of socialist development, it was natural for this to occur in private hands. The zaibatsu system afforded entrepreneurial strength to the Japanese economy: the profits from established enterprises were used by the combines as risk capital to pioneer new fields. Even the concentration of wealth in the few controlling families was probably a net economic gain—permitting the bulk of the profits to be reinvested for further expansion. There were of course tendencies toward monopoly, but the importance of foreign markets and raw materials helped to keep zaibatsu prices competitive.

It is more difficult to evaluate the social and political effects of the system. While offering a career opening to talent, the zaibatsu were bureaucratic, hierarchical, and not supportive of individualism. Whether they were more undemocratic than Japanese society in general is open to question. Some have criticized the zaibatsu concentration of wealth as an obstacle to the development of a strong middle class. Would not a wider distribution of corporate stock have been better? On the other hand, the middle management of the zaibatsu concerns (along with the professions, small businessmen, landlords, and upper levels of the bureaucracy) did constitute a recognizable middle class even during the 1920's, with homes, savings, a high concern for their children's education, and so on. Did not rapid economic growth, which the zaibatsu system promoted, do more to strengthen this class than economic concentration did to weaken it?

The relations between the zaibatsu, political parties, and the government have not been adequately studied. To what extent did zaibatsu contributions to election campaigns influence party policies? Might the parties otherwise have adopted different policies or been politically more healthy? Whatever the answers may be, there is no question that the political activities of the zaibatsu early became a target for popular criticism and helped to tarnish the concept of parliamentary government in many Japanese minds.

Although nondemocratic, the zaibatsu did not fit in very well with militarism, the other political trend then developing in Japan. Their ties to the conservative political parties led them to favor representative government as it existed during the 1920's. The higher education and foreign experience of their managers, together with an awareness of the importance of foreign trade, tended to give the zaibatsu an international outlook. Before the war it was the supporters of militarism who were the most violent critics of the zaibatsu. For example, the officer bureaucrats of the Japanese Kwantung Army in Manchuria, viewing the zaibatsu as Western, urban, liberal, and corrupt, shut them out of the early phase of Manchurian development after 1931. As Japan slipped deeper into war after 1937, the zaibatsu industries inevitably became the core of the war economy. Even then they proved difficult to control. The zaibatsu represented such aggregates of economic power that it was more expedient for the government to seek their cooperation than to force their submission. What the pattern of cooperation was has not yet been studied.

The Double Structure of the Japanese Economy.   Another distinctive feature of the Japanese economy was the tremendous number of small concerns with fewer than five workers. In 1930, for example, more than half (2,772,183) of Japan's manufacturing labor force (4,759,921) was employed in such small businesses. It is difficult to estimate their productive capacity since their tax reports grossly underestimated their actual role in the economy. It is clear that they were less efficient than the big modern factories, and that the value of their output was considerably less than their numerical strength would indicate. They cannot, however, be dismissed as merely the declining sector of traditional small industries. Relative to medium and large industry, their percentage of total production was slowly declining, yet in Tōkyō alone their number increased phenomenally from about 3000 in 1923 after the Tōkyō earthquake to almost 26,000 in 1932.

Bimodality thus marked the Japanese economy: a handful of giant combines, thousands of tiny workshops, and in between relatively few medium-sized industries. Japanese economic historians refer to this pattern as the "double structure" of the economy. In part it was a result of a split technology: zaibatsu engineers versed in Western science as contrasted with the owners of small shops rooted in the artisan tradition of Tokugawa Japan. The availability of capital was also bimodal. Zaibatsu banks catered to industries within the same combine, but small business could be started

SILK SCREENING. *Some traditional techniques survive into the modern era as artisans gradually become artists.*

with private savings or a loan from a patron. The two extremes also reflect clear differences in social organization: the zaibatsu, although paternalistic, were recognizably modern or "Western"; the workshops held to traditional Japanese small-group organization. By the late 1930's some of these distinctions had begun to blur. Universal education and ties to larger industries led to a rising level of technology in the small businesses. And changes were also taking place in social organization. In general, however, the relative differences continued into the postwar period, along with a double standard of wages.

Among the small concerns with fewer than five workers were traditional handicrafts, woven textiles, shops producing daily necessities, and repair shops, all areas of expanding demand as standards of living rose. Yet the small businesses also were integrated with the most advanced sector of the economy. Probably over half of Japan's small concerns subsisted entirely on subcontracts from zaibatsu-type industries. The time-consuming assembly of an electrical device, for example, might take place in a village shop one hundred miles from the factory.

The meaning of this double structure is controversial. Was the low efficiency of small business a drag on the economy, or did small shops perform the easy jobs, enabling the modern sector to direct all of its energies to the more complex and capital-intensive tasks of technological production and thus expand the total economy more rapidly? If the former position is taken, one can go on to see the relation between the zaibatsu and small business as exploitative: putting out simple tasks to the workers in these shops kept cheap labor cheap and maintained repressive social patterns. Had the total productive process been brought into the factory, a greater equalization of wages, more favorable conditions for labor organization, and new social patterns might have developed. In human terms, the system was obviously exploitative: working conditions in the small shops were poor.

On the other hand, the use of such shops was the cheapest way to produce, and it was this economic consideration, rather than any zaibatsu social policy, that led to the putting-out of work. Moreover, the double structure developed not because of zaibatsu planning, but in spite of zaibatsu growth. That it was not destroyed by rapid industrial growth was due to the high rate of population growth, which kept up the supply of cheap labor. In the postwar period, the same type of economic growth in the modern sector —in combination with a sharply decreased rate of population growth— pulled labor out of small industries and out of the farm villages. This situation forced small concerns to raise wages, gradually eroding the prewar double structure.

Social Change

The Japanese Family.   The family continued to be of political as well as social importance in Japan during the early decades of the twentieth century. It was seen as the building block of the unique Japanese "national polity." Its ideal virtues of harmony, solidarity, and loyalty were projected onto the Japanese state. It was the last stronghold in Japan of Confucian social practices. Even the city dweller, whose life was modern in many respects, participated in a still vital area of Japan's premodern tradition in his family life.

In the family as it existed in the late nineteenth century, lineage, not matrimony, was holy. The line extended from the ancestors to the parents to their eldest son and heir. Marriage was for the purpose of obtaining heirs for the "house." The position of the daughter-in-law was partly defined by the saying, "The womb is borrowed." If a marriage was childless the "bride" might be returned, or an heir might be adopted, or in a well-to-do family a concubine might be set up. Both the eldest son and his wife, as well as other unmarried sons and daughters, lived with the parents. The ideal family was three generations under a single roof.

Change in an institution as basic as the family proceeds very slowly. Even after World War II the pattern described above was still recognizable in most areas of rural Japan. Yet in urban Japan changes were already under way during the late nineteenth century. The expanding population that accompanied Japan's early industrialization produced a great number of second and third sons who moved to cities and formed nuclear families, centered on the husband-wife relationship rather than the line of a "house." As the economy developed, more time was spent away from the family, and for increasing numbers of wage earners the economic significance of the family as the unit of production began to disappear. The women's rights movement, the doctrine of political rights, romantic literary currents, Protestant Christianity, socialism, and other influences also contributed to the shift from lineage to the conjugal tie. All stressed the ideal of equality between the sexes. The transition to the nuclear family was not complete. Even in cities most marriages were still arranged by parents and go-betweens, although the future partners were consulted and exercised veto powers. The result was the Japanese-type conjugal family: different from the West, but also different from the traditional family system.

Rural Society.   Japanese rural society by the turn of the century was in no sense a simple peasant society. Primary education was on the point of becoming universal. Children of the well-to-do often went on to intermediate and higher education. Newspapers were read. Many Japanese had traveled as soldiers in the army. Most had relatives in the proliferating cities. New agricultural methods had been accepted. As railway lines were built, agricultural markets became nationwide. Government influence was pervasive, and rural hearts thrilled to Japanese military victories. A degree of "openness" had developed that made the village qualitatively different from the Tokugawa village. Yet it was not a modern society. In many important ways the "cake of custom" remained unbroken. Religiously, socially, politically, the practice of community solidarity that derived from the "traditional society" of Tokugawa Japan remained in force.

The unit of the local "organic" society was the hamlet—a grouping of households, from about ten to seventy in number, such as dot the Japanese countryside today. The social cohesion within such groupings had several sources. One was the ethic of harmony, the etiquette found in most face-to-face groups in Japan. Another was the rituals of hamlet shrines or temples which stressed community solidarity. Irrigation in most areas required community decisions regarding the allocation of limited water resources. And from the Tokugawa era most hamlets possessed communal pastures or wooded hills; decisions concerning these were made by a hamlet council to which each household sent one representative. This council also handled collections, aid to families in time of crises, and even plans for community recreation.

Within the hamlet one principle of organization was kinship. A lineage or related families might act as a block within the hamlet council. Another

Three generations on the farm.

more important factor was the pattern of land ownership. At the time of the Meiji Restoration about 25 to 30 per cent of the land was worked by tenants. The proportion slowly rose to 45 per cent in 1908 and was maintained at this level until after World War II (46 per cent in 1941). Most Japanese landlords were small landowners, with a few more acres than they could work themselves. Even those with larger holdings almost invariably lived on their land. And there were infinite gradations in the size and patterns of holdings. Only 20 per cent of farm families were pure tenants; 35 per cent were part owners, part tenants; and 45 per cent owned all the land they worked.

In areas where landlordism was extensive community solidarity was hierarchical. (In a fishing village, boat ownership was the equivalent of land ownership in an agricultural village.) There were always more people willing to work the land than land available to be worked. This gave the landlord the upper hand. Tenants were protected by custom, but written contracts were rare. The power of the landlords was bulwarked by ideologies such as "agrarianism," a Confucian-tinged concept stressing the virtues of obedience, loyalty, harmony, and frugality. Landlordism gave rise to serious inequities within rural society. Taxes that took about 35 per cent of the value of the crop during the early Meiji period dropped by 1902 to about 20 per cent as a result of tax cuts and creeping inflation. But rents collected from tenants remained at almost Tokugawa levels, about 50 per cent of the crop. Cities grew and prospered, but the farmers, who even in the late

1930's constituted 44 per cent of the total population, received a shrinking proportion of the national wealth. The prosperity of urban life made the hardship of the countryside, where expectations also rose with education, less tolerable than before.

After World War I tenant unions (called farmers unions) began to form, first in perfectures about Tōkyō and then in the northeast and other areas. These paralleled the rising labor unions in the cities, and for the most part were founded by city intellectuals. A major role was played during the early years by Christian socialists, but by the mid-twenties Marxists were dominant. A national organization of these unions was formed in 1922. It is possible to exaggerate the importance of these unions. Even in the peak year of 1927 they had only 365,000 members, while almost 4 million families were wholly or partially tenants. After the Manchurian Incident of 1931 the tenant movement was suppressed. Yet it is symptomatic of the new openness of rural society that ideas so at odds with tradition could have entered and been accepted at all.

Political power in rural Japan was vested in two interlocking, national hierarchies: the bureaucracy and the organizations of the party politicians. The latter began with Diet members and reached down through prefectural assemblymen to local "men of influence." Such influential local figures, often landlords or small businessmen, were brokers who could deliver blocks of votes in exchange for favors, public or personal.

Local bureaucracy began in the Home Ministry and extended downward through prefectures to cities, towns, and villages. Appointments were made from above, and the chain of authority was marked by a high degree of submissiveness and by a responsibility toward higher authority. An adjunct of the officialdom was the police, also under the Home Ministry. The political role of the Home Ministry changed with time. It was early used by the government against the parties. Then, as party men gained power in the government and as the bureaucracy was headed by party appointees, it was used by the party in power for the advancement of its candidates. At all times, but especially during the 1930's, the Home Ministry was the watchdog on guard against "dangerous thought."

The village, which usually consisted of a number of scattered hamlets, was the lowest administrative level in the bureaucratic hierarchy. Here modern bureaucracy with its records, directives, and impersonality met the hamlet society in which personal ties, the family, and collective solidarity were paramount. Village organization itself was a compromise between the two. The rules by which it operated and most of its responsibilities were imposed from above. Yet the headmen or mayors were elected; those chosen were usually men of influence in their communities, men of good family with a better than average education, men with experience in farming and farm finance. Under the mayor was an elected village council. This decided on matters of local importance, and its expression of local sentiment was expected to guide the mayor in the execution of government directives.

Urban Society.   The traditional city in Japan was freer than the country-side. Restrictive organizations did exist, such as ward associations, shrine groups, guilds, and fire-fighting groups; and in crowded areas where houses adjoined, privacy was slight and immediate neighbors were close and familiar. But personal ties could not be formed among all residents in a city district. Movement in and out of communities was frequent. And in the absence of the cooperation demanded by agriculture and communal property, the sense of community solidarity was weak.

The modern city in Japan grew out of the traditional city, following Japan's economic growth. In 1895 only 12 per cent of the 42 million Japanese lived in cities or towns of more than 10,000 persons. By the mid-1930's over 45 per cent of the 69 million Japanese lived in such urban areas, and over a quarter of the population lived in cities of more than 100,000 persons. By 1940 Tōkyō was rivaling London and New York with a population of 6,779,000, while Osaka, Kyōto, Nagoya, and the new port cities of Yokohama and Kōbe together accounted for an equal number.

Cities were the centers of Japan's modern cultural transformation. During the 1870's and 1880's material signs of the new times appeared first in Tōkyō: horse-drawn streetcars, gas lamps, meatshops selling beef, Western-style buildings, barbershops offering a nonsamurai cut, Western dress, and the new schools and colleges. Change was uneven. As late as 1901 an ordinance was issued in Tōkyō against going barefoot. Yet by this time primary school education was almost universal, and those moving in from the rural areas as well as those growing up in the cities were for the most part literate. When one considers that Japan's school-age population increased from 4.2 million in 1873, to 7.2 million in 1893, to 11.3 million in 1935, the magnitude of this accomplishment becomes apparent. The cities also became the centers for higher education that spread the new culture of modern Japan. Enrollments in universities and technical colleges increased from 22,910 students in 1900 to 223,477 in 1940.

By the end of World War I the changes in city life had become even more conspicuous. Standards of living had risen; workers drank beer and soft drinks; weekly magazines, movie houses, bars, restaurants, and other manifestations of popular culture had appeared. The *narikin,* the *nouveau riche* who had risen during the war, were much in evidence. This was the age of the *mobo* and *moga* (*modan boi* [modern boy] and *modan garu* [modern girl]) who strolled on the Ginza of Tōkyō or the main thorough-fares of Osaka, boys who wore Harold Lloyd glasses and girls who drank, smoked, and read literature. These were the years of the permanent wave,

PERCENTAGE OF SCHOOL AGE CHILDREN ATTENDING PRIMARY SCHOOLS

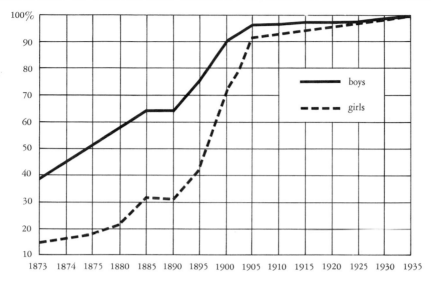

the bathing suit, the bare-legged chorus line, the dance hall and cabaret. It was a time when students not concerned with the leftist political movement became engrossed in the "three S's"—sports, screen, and sex. During the early 1930's Japan Victor and other gramophone companies suddenly expanded, selling hundreds of thousands of sad songs suggesting the transiency of life, the indistinguishability of tears and *sake,* the pleasures of jazz, liquor, and dancing, the passing of time, and the languid beauty of willows along the Ginza. Sales of records jumped from 10,483,000 in 1929 to 16,895,000 in 1931.

Although this popular culture was tame by European standards it seemed outrageous to many in Japan. Some essayists called the period culminating in 1931 and 1932 the era of *"ero, guro,* and *nansensu"* (the erotic, the grotesque, and the nonsensical). That Japan's urban culture had reached this point made the gulf between city and village seem almost unbridgeable. In 1931 and 1932 Japan was at the pit of its depression, and rural conditions were particularly bad. As a result, the cities and their mode of life were castigated by rightist spokesmen as the antipode of what was truly Japanese.

Another effect of social change in Japan was to produce wide generation gaps. In the 1930's there were many families in which three generations lived together: grandparents in their eighties, parents in their fifties, and children in their twenties. The grandparents had been born in Tokugawa Japan. The second generation had come of age just after the turn of the century when Japan's modern culture was beginning to appear. Many had come to the cities from rural areas bringing with them the social reflexes of the countryside. The third generation became adults amid the democracy, jazz, depression, and crises of the late 1920's and early 1930's. Even when three such generations were bound by close personal ties, they were in many ways three different kinds of people, far more so than in Europe or the United States where the tempo of change had been slower.

Industrial Labor.   The shift from an agricultural to an industrial economy was accompanied by a number of social ills, from which urban labor suffered more than any other group except tenants. The government was controlled from the start by men who thought in terms of national strength rather than human welfare. Even in the political parties the interests of property owners were dominant. As a result, Japan was slow to adopt social legislation to protect urban workers. Vast slums grew up in the cities, and until 1926 there were few limits on the conditions or hours of factory work. Children sometimes worked fourteen hours or more a day, and large numbers of overworked laborers suffered from tuberculosis.

Labor was abundant and cheap. In textile factories many girls worked only a few years and then returned to their rural homes. Other workers returned to the farm in time of depression. Farm families easily provided the needed industrial recruits to match industrial growth. Because of these ties the modernization of labor was slow: even in the 1930's urban labor still stood with one foot planted in the stagnant economy of the paddy field. Advances in technology also meant that the demand for labor rose less rapidly than industrial growth. Still the picture was not all black. Though unskilled labor had little bargaining power, the real wages of industrial workers increased by more than half between 1914 and 1929.

Under such conditions the labor movement remained small. By 1897 there were 400,000 workers in factories employing more than five; and by 1907, 600,000. Under the influence of the Christian and early socialist movements a few unions were formed. They soon came under police pressure, tended toward anarcho-syndicalism, and were suppressed after 1911. A second phase began during World War I under moderate Christian leadership. By the end of the war there were 1,700,000 factory workers and by 1920, 86 unions. The 1918–1920 period in particular was marked by spiraling inflation, rice riots, and labor disputes. From 1920 unionism turned toward Marxist socialism. (See pages 679–681.) To combat this the government legalized moderate unions and passed some industrial laws. At the same time it stepped up its pressure against the revolutionary left. The result was a plethora of small unions on the extreme left associated with the more radical of the political parties, and one or two large federations, headed by moderate socialists and containing the majority of organized labor. In the peak year of 1936, 973 unions had 420,589 members—a small

RICE RIOTS IN NAGOYA IN 1918. *The spiraling price of rice led to large-scale riots against rice merchants in many cities. Police and then army troops were called in to suppress them.*

percentage of the total industrial labor force of 6,090,116. The following year, under various pressures, the major federation switched from socialism to national socialism.

Currents of Thought

Intellectuals in Japan today are the heirs not of the early Meiji thinkers but of the generation that came to maturity just after the turn of the century. Where the Meiji thinkers were morally, socially, and even politically akin to the Restoration leaders, intellectuals after the turn of the century became increasingly alienated both from society and from the late Meiji political order.

To Western eyes, the advanced intellectuals of the early decades of the twentieth century seem almost to have bridged the cultural chasm and to be contemporary with their Western peers. Romanticism gave way to realism and then to naturalism; socialism and anarchism were issues of the day. The 1909 diary of the poet Ishikawa Takuboku reveals a life that is strikingly modern: detached introspection, reading Turgenev in bed, commuting to work on the streetcar, listening to the talk of the Kyōto University tennis team from the room next door. Even his poetic images are drawn from the modern world: "If I could...throw away this garment of obligation my body would become as light as hydrogen." Partly because he was so modern, his feeling of isolation and estrangement in the Japan of his day was profound:

Do not be loved by others, do not accept their charity, do not promise anything. Do nothing which entails asking forgiveness. Never talk to anyone about yourself. Always wear a mask. Always be ready for a fight—be able to hit the next man on the head at any time. Don't forget that when you make friends with someone you are sooner or later certain to break with him.*

The social and cultural reasons for the appearance of this sense of alienation are several. One reason was that there were more graduates than jobs, especially in the government. Another reason was that the new Western-oriented generation reacted against the neo-traditionalism of the government. But an even more basic source of alienation was the problem of Japan's cultural identity. What did it mean to be Japanese and to have abruptly borrowed so much of the culture of the modern West? Intellectuals after the turn of the century faced this problem on a much deeper level than had the previous generation. Natsume Sōseki (1867–1916), a professor at Tōkyō Imperial University (hereafter Tōkyō University) and then Japan's greatest modern novelist, wrote that Japan had only superficially mastered the teachings of the West; what would be the consequences, he asked, if Japan could complete its enlightenment in fifty years:

If, then, by our physical and mental exertions, and by ignoring the difficulties and suffering involved in our precipitous advance, we end by passing through, in merely one-half the time it took the more prosperous Westerners to reach their stage of specialization, to our stage of internally developed enlightenment, the consequences will be serious indeed. At the same time we will be able to boast of this fantastic acquisition of knowledge, the inevitable result will be nervous collapse from which we will not be able to recover.†

Before examining some of the positions taken by major Japanese thinkers, we must first ask what the Japanese tradition was at this time. For an understanding of Japan's modern history, the most important locus of tradition was the several interpretations of state philosophy that together constituted orthodoxy in Japan between 1890 and 1945.

The Orthodox Philosophies of the Japanese State.   The creation of a strong state structure had been the aim of Japan's leaders since the Meiji Restoration. Other world powers had constitutions, and the political "outs" demanded a constitution, so the Meiji Constitution was written. Though the constitution itself was based on a German model, it included certain

*Translated by Donald Keene. From *Modern Japanese Literature:* An Anthology Compiled and Edited by Donald Keene; Copyright © 1956 by Grove Press, published by Grove Press, Inc. (British publisher, Thames & Hudson).
†Kōsaka Masaaki (ed.), *Japanese Thought in the Meiji Era* (Tōkyō: Pan Pacific Press, 1958), pp. 447–448.

elements from Japanese tradition. Perhaps the key concept was the *kokutai,* the unique Japanese "national polity." This centered on the imperial house, described in the Meiji Constitution as "a single lineage for ages eternal." At the end of the lineage was the emperor, "sacred and inviolable." Also a part of the *kokutai* were the Japanese people who possessed virtues lacking in the peoples of other nations—loyalty that bound the people to the emperor, and filial piety that undergirded the family units of which the nation was composed. Integrated by such moral principles, Japanese society was viewed as a harmonious whole. During World War II a Tōkyō University economist lecturing on "Japanese capitalism" was reproved by a member of his audience who said that Japan could not be called capitalist since, harmonious and tranquil, it had never experienced the class conflict present in other industrial societies.

The essential problem for constitutional interpretation up until 1945—and thus for validation of this or that program of political action as well—was how to reconcile the real legal rights and privileges conferred by the constitution with the absolute religious authority of the emperor. Depending on whether the stress was put on Japan's Shintō tradition or on German law, and depending on which school of German law was used, the constitutional scholar would arrive at a more authoritarian position or at a position more supportive of parliamentary government.

One constitutional interpretation, which offered an explanation of Japan's imperial lineage and moral qualities, was propounded by Itō Hirobumi. Following German organic theories of the state, he saw these qualities as products of the historical evolution of the Japanese *volk.* The imperial institution had developed within the body politic as the brain had evolved within the physical body. Itō was perfectly aware that he and his colleagues made the actual decisions. His attribution of absolute authority to the emperor was in part the conscious act of a social engineer. "In Europe," he reported to the Privy Council in 1888, "religion is a common principle that penetrates and unites the hearts of the people." But does there exist in Japan a comparable basis for the national unity that a parliamentary system requires?

In our country religion is weak. There is not one that could serve as a principle of state. Buddhism today has fallen into decline. Shintō is based in the precepts of our forefathers and transmits them, yet as a religion it has little power to move men's hearts. In our country, as a common principle, there is only the Imperial House.

The most rational elements in Itō's view of the state were further developed by Minobe Tatsukichi, a professor at Tōkyō University between 1900 and 1932. Minobe accepted the core elements of *kokutai* theory. But Minobe superimposed upon this a newer German theory that described the

*Minobe Tatsukichi, professor
of law at Tōkyō Imperial
University, who saw
the emperor as an "organ"
of the government.*

state as a legal person possessing both sovereignty and the authority to rule. The emperor was the highest organ of this person with the ultimate right to carry out the executive functions of the state. The differences between this view and Itō's were slight. Yet the consequences were important. In Minobe's eyes the emperor was clearly less than the state and subordinate to its laws. This reduced the absolute character of the emperor's authority, and balanced against it the authority of other organs of the state. This interpretation weakened the sanction for autocratic rule by the bureaucracy (in the name of the emperor), opening the way for increased Diet power. It is no exaggeration to say that Minobe's theory furnished the theoretical scaffolding for the movement to establish party cabinets during the 1910's and 1920's.

Minobe's interpretation never obtained a monopoly even in academic circles. It was, however, the dominant legal interpretation of the constitution from World War I until 1935 when Minobe came under attack. It not only influenced scholars and intellectuals, but also became the prescribed subject matter in constitutional law for the higher civil service examinations, the door to the Japanese bureaucracy. The considerable rationality of the functioning of the government during those two decades was not unrelated to the rationality of this theory. Unfortunately for Japan, the bureaucrats were unwilling to have others taught what they believed themselves. Within the state system of education other less liberal views predominated.

One such view combined elements from Japanese tradition with some of the less rational elements of nineteenth-century German thought. The *kokutai* had been viewed in Confucian terms as an immanent and eternal order, and the imperial house as "coeval with Heaven and Earth." Hozumi Yatsuka, another professor at Tōkyō University (between 1888 and 1912), added the notion that Japan was a "family-state" since all Japanese were descended from a common folk ancestor, identical with the imperial ancestor. All Japan was thus a single racial and spiritual family. From the second decade of the twentieth century, passages such as the following began to appear in school texts on moral education:

Our country takes as its base the family system: the nation is but a single great family, the imperial family is our main house. We, the people, worship the unbroken imperial line with the same feeling of respect and love that a child feels toward his parents.... The union of loyalty and filial piety is truly the special character of our national polity.*

This conservative vision of society did not change thereafter; but revisions of textbooks during World War I did introduce complementary materials of a more liberal and international outlook.

A further development in the religious view of the *kokutai* was the union of history and Shintō myth. This amalgam also entered textbooks toward the end of the first decade of this century; one Japanese historian has called it "Japan's myth of the twentieth century." Once history is linked to myth, the emperor is sacred not simply as the embodiment of a moral order, but also as a lineal descendant of the Sun Goddess. To this theory Uesugi Shinkichi, still another Tōkyō University professor (between 1903 and 1929), appended a theory of absolute monarchy in which the emperor was identified with the body of the state. This theory opposed Minobe's during the second, third, and fourth decades of the twentieth century. Its adherents in academic circles and at the higher levels of the bureaucracy were generally less successful than their opponents, but they came into their own during the late 1930's as the ideologists of a military Japan.

In short, although the range of orthodox belief was narrow at the turn of the century, by 1914 there had developed bitterly antagonistic positions within the orthodoxy: the liberal, constitutional monarchism of Minobe versus the absolute, Shintō-tinged monarchism of Uesugi. In spite of the support the latter received from patriotic societies, military groups, rural groups, and others, it lost ground during the early 1920's to more liberal, international opinions. Yet two points should be noted. The generation that came to maturity in the 1930's had begun its education in the very years

*Ishida Takeshi, *Meiji seiji shisōshi kenkyū*, pp. 7–8.

when this "Shintō" view of Japanese tradition entered the school texts, and in the conservative nationalism of the 1930's and 1940's there can be found little that had not already developed thirty years earlier.

It is also worth noting what these strains of orthodox thought had in common. For one thing, like their Meiji predecessors, they rejected the earlier Confucian view of a changeless society. Most of the social content was stripped from the Tokugawa *kokutai,* leaving only a few fixed points —the emperor, loyalty, filial piety, and harmony. As a result, orthodox ideology was not an obstacle to many kinds of social change. Second, in keeping with earlier thought, they showed no clear distinction between nature and society. In the organic view of the state, social evolution was seen as a natural process. In the Shintō view, this world of men merges with an irrational god-world in which the transitions from myth to history, from half-human deities to half-divine humans, are imperceptible. It was this sense of a spiritual continuum between the human and the divine that permitted the attribution of divinity to the emperor until 1945. Third, in orthodox ideology there was only a weak distinction between society and self. Ethics taught self-realization through the fulfillment of one's duties to society, not through the development of a sense of independence or personal integrity. There were no grounds on which the individual could withhold loyalty to the social order: the claims of family, school, work-group, or nation always had a higher priority than those of their component members.

Perhaps because of this orthodoxy modern Japanese thinkers have shown a particularly deep concern with the problem of self. This has at times taken the form of a search for philosophic principles that will enable the individual to stand up against society. Some answers have been found in Western culture, others by transforming elements of Japanese tradition. Yet, at a time when the ultimate value of the individual was being increasingly questioned in the West itself, the search was difficult. Against the background of Japanese orthodox thought it was far easier to stress equality within the social group than independence from it.

Literature.   During the 1880's and early 1890's the novel was romantic and liberal. It paralleled the idealism of the political party movement. But with the involvement of the parties in the exchanges of power politics, the rise of alienation among intellectuals, and the influence of new currents of literary thought, Japanese writers turned away from public concerns to concentrate on the private lives of individuals. The literature they wrote was apolitical; it ignored the emperor, the army, politics, and business. It was consciously antitraditional—preoccupied with the individual and opposed to the old family system. Yet in spite of this iconoclasm, few works of literature portrayed alternatives to the old society.

The turn-of-the-century naturalist writers, for example, identified the true self with the forces of nature. Man learns what he is by liberating his natural desires, especially sex, from the constraints of an artificial society. Yet "natural man" was not so much dynamic as submissive to the internal and external demands of time, age, death, sickness, hunger, and sex. He was not a man of determined will, engaging in purposive action. Rather, great stress was put on the moods evoked by changing circumstance and on a sensitive description of the feelings of those caught up by these natural forces. The delicate, introspective, moody character of the works of the naturalists is reflected even in their titles: *Mediocrity, Dust, Mildew, Loneliness, Indulgence.**

The novelist Natsume Sōseki held that the progress of modern Japan was the result of an "external enlightenment" which had led Japan to sever its ties with tradition, to lose its "ancestral energies," and to become engrossed in "mere appearances." A true understanding of Western culture, he stressed, would lead to an independent spirit based on individually-held internal values. This standpoint led Natsume Sōseki to touch on politics. He held that individual morality was higher than state morality, and he ridiculed those who justified every action in terms of patriotism:

When the bean curd man peddles his wares he is not doing it for the state. His basic purpose is to gain the means by which to live . . . though indirectly this may benefit the state. . . . But, wouldn't it be awful if he always had to keep that in mind and eat his meals for the state, wash his face for the state, and go to the toilet for the state?

The affirmative, individualistic side of Sōseki's thought was further developed by others. Abe Jirō (1883–1959) developed a neo-Kantian ethical individualism, stressing universal principles of conscience. Popular among students, Abe emphasized the ethical nature of the self. He criticized the sensual individualism of the naturalists and the family-state ideal of the government, and he supported women's rights. The well-born, romantically individualistic writers of the White Birch School formed another such affirmative group. They extolled genius and idealism. One wrote: "Had I not known Tolstoi I might have become a politician, living from day to day without faith or a reason for existence." Contrasting the artificiality of the old society with the natural altruism of man, they attempted to define a new morality for Japan.

But predominant in modern literature were darker, pessimistic strains. In the later novels of Natsume Sōseki, the complete development of the indi-

*Howard Hibbett, "The Portrait of the Artist in Japanese Fiction," *Far Eastern Quarterly,* Vol. 14 (1955), p. 350.

Natsume Sōseki, novelist and critic, seated in the book-filled room of the Japanese scholar.

vidual led, not to freedom, but to a bleak world of fear, despair, and absolute loneliness. In *The Gate* the hero, having stolen the wife of a friend, spends the rest of his life in secluded misery with her, each suffering from the loneliness and pain of the other. At the end he attempts to find an answer in Zen Buddhism, but without success. The "gate" does not open. In *Passers-by* the protagonist is beset with even greater fears and anxieties until at the end only religion, madness, or death remains. But for Sōseki, neither religion nor madness was a live option. In *Kokoro* (*Mind*) the end is suicide, in *Grass by the Road* it is resignation to an answerless fate. Natsume Sōseki differs from the naturalists primarily in that suffering, in his view of life, affirms the ethical character of man—even though man's lot is hopeless.

Throughout Sōseki's writings runs the problem of what values to live by. The character Ichirō in the novel *Passers-by* reflects the crisis of the individual in a modernizing society:

He suffers because nothing he does appears to him as either an end or a means. He is perpetually uneasy and cannot relax. He cannot sleep so he gets out of bed. But when he is awake, he cannot stay still, so he begins to walk. As he walks, he finds that he has to begin running. Once he has begun running he cannot stop. To have to keep on running is bad enough, but he feels compelled to increase his speed with every step he takes. When he imagines what the end of all this will be, he is so frightened that he breaks out in a cold sweat. And the fear becomes unbearable.

Ichirō's friend, trying to assuage his anxiety, replies:

"This uneasiness of yours is no more than the uneasiness that all men experience. All you have to do is to realize that there is no need for you alone to worry so much about it. What I mean to say is that it is our fate to wander blindly through life."

Not only were my words vague in meaning but they lacked sincerity. Your brother (Ichirō) gave me one shrewd, contemptuous glance; that was all my remarks deserved. He then said:

"You know, our uneasiness comes from this thing called scientific progress. Science does not know where to stop and does not permit us to stop either. From walking to rickshaws, from rickshaws to horsedrawn cabs, from cabs to trains, from trains to automobiles, from automobiles . . . to airplanes—when will we ever be allowed to stop and rest? Where will it finally take us? It is really frightening."

"Yes, it is frightening," I said.

Your brother smiled.

"You say so, but you don't really mean it. You aren't really frightened. This fear that you say you feel, it is only of the theoretical kind. My fear is different from yours. I feel it in my heart. It is an alive, pulsating kind of fear."*

Ichirō's friend typifies the Japanese majority, who are pleased with trains, airplanes, science, their rising standard of living, and the rest of their modern life. He is representative of the student who proceeds successfully from higher school to university law school to a job in government or industry. Ichirō, however, speaks for the alienated intellectual unable to integrate, or find meaning in, the elements of his life.

Another writer hailed as the genius of his age during the 1920's was Akutagawa Ryūnosuke (the author of the short story *Rashōmon*). A disciple of Natsume Sōseki, Akutagawa continued his master's concern with the problem of what Western culture meant in Japan. Yet where Natsume Sōseki felt that "internal modernization" would come in time, Akutagawa was doubtful. In *The Faint Smiles of the Gods* Akutagawa writes from the point of view of a Portuguese priest in Japan during the late sixteenth century, struggling to sustain his faith in the power of God while beset by strange animistic forces that hinder his mission. The priest is spoken to by an old man, a god of Japan in human form:

Perhaps even God will become a native of this country. China and India changed. The West must also change. We exist in the midst of trees, in the flow of shallow water, in the wind that passes through the roses, in the evening

*From Edwin McClellan, "An Introduction to Sōseki," *Harvard Journal of Asiatic Studies,* Vol. 22 (December 1959), pp. 205–206.

light lingering on the wall of a temple. Everywhere and at all times. Watch out for us!

As a part of East Asian culture, Japan had far more to its tradition than animism. Yet after the explicit rejection of Buddhism and Confucianism during the early Meiji period, it is not strange that Akutagawa should use this symbol to contrast with the universal values of the West. Elsewhere Akutagawa likened Japan to an Olympics run by the insane. Projecting his own uncertainties onto Japan, he suggested that even Dante's hell would be better: at least it had law, fixed rules. Akutagawa's suicide in 1927 was hailed by Japanese leftist critics as the end of bourgeois literature, symbolic of the impasse reached by "middle-class culture."

It would be an exaggeration to say that religion, or its lack, was central as a literary concern in twentieth-century Japan. The dominant genre was the autobiographical novel—confessional or contemplative—in which the author appears as his own, often dissolute, hero. With this was combined a *haiku*-like description of the texture of sensual experience, often of great beauty. Yet one can say that literature reflected cultural anxieties that were widespread among intellectuals. These were not unrelated to the fact that Japan had jettisoned most of its own philosophic tradition without finding anything to replace it more substantial than emperor-centered nationalism.

Philosophy.   The philosophical history of Japan in modern times is incredibly complex. Virtually every school of thought in Europe or America, not to mention schools of Buddhist philosophy and the like, has been represented in one form or another. Yet the strongest current of Western philosophical thought in Japan, beginning in the late nineteenth century and gaining ground in the twentieth, was German. A song sung by higher school students in the late Meiji period began:

> *Dekanshō (Descartes, Kant, and Schopenhauer)*
> *Dekanshō*
> *Half the year we live with them,*
> *The other half we sleep.*

By the 1920's the most popular Western philosophy was German idealism, the most popular philosopher, Hegel. That this type of thought should have found acceptance is related to the earlier interest in German state philosophy. In part, too, there was an affinity between intellectual life in twentieth-century Japan and the anguish of German metaphysics. As student types in Japan, the "literary youth" and the Werther-like "philosophic youth" replaced the "political youth" of the late nineteenth century. Within this broad current of thought, the most original synthesis with Japanese tradition was that of Nishida Kitarō.

Nishida was born in 1870, only three years after Natsume Sōseki. His graduation from the philosophy department of Tōkyō University in 1894 was followed by a period of hardship. He taught in high schools and junior colleges, receiving little recognition. He began the practice of Zen Buddhism, but his diary tells of years of frustration. Although he meditated, he found it difficult to concentrate, his body ached, he daydreamed about traveling abroad or becoming famous, and his mind remained clouded. Not until 1905 does the entry appear: "Zen is music, Zen is art, Zen is action; beyond this there is nothing that need be sought to give peace of mind." From this time Nishida's task was "to provide a philosophic foundation" for "the vision of the shapeless shape, the voice of the voiceless reality" which was the "basis of oriental culture."*

To accomplish this task Nishida drew on a wide range of Western philosophers such as Hegel, James, and Bergson, all of whom were concerned with the philosophic expression of religious experience. Nishida's first concern was to find universal categories for the "moment of true existence" he had found in Zen. In his first work, *A Study of the Good*, published in 1911 after he had become an assistant professor at Kyōto University, he termed this "pure experience," experience before the differentiation of knower and known. Nishida's second concern was to relate this insight to the universe of existence. Nishida's third concern was to apply the Buddhist "logic of nothingness" to define the position of Japanese culture in relation to world culture.

The meaning of Nishida's philosophy for prewar Japan was ambiguous. On the one hand, it appears to be a philosophy with no social implications, since once the self is unified in "pure experience," all conflicts are resolved and further action is unnecessary. Nishida stressed the importance of harmony, community, and other values found in orthodox thought, and some of his followers became scholarly propagandists for the Greater East Asia Co-Prosperity Sphere during World War II. They argued that the contradictions inherent in modern culture could be transcended only by a return to the unique spirituality of Japan. On the other hand, Nishida himself spoke up in 1938 and 1939 to criticize those who attacked science and free inquiry in the name of patriotism. He stressed that Japanese culture, though unique, was meaningful only as a part of a universal, world culture composed of unique particulars. Likewise, his emphasis on the Japanese state was in a context of a world society of nations. Cast in the concepts of Western philosophy, his experience of religious individuality took on implications lacking in traditional Zen.

Christianity in Modern Japan. During the Meiji era Christianity entered Japan as a part of Western culture, and gradually spread in both the cities

*Ueyama Shumpei, "Nishida Kitarō," in *Nihon no shisōka II*.

and the countryside. Then during the 1890's, as the new nationalism took hold, Christianity declined in rural areas and became concentrated among the urban middle class and among intellectuals. The percentage of Christians remained small and even in the early 1970's constituted only one-half of 1 per cent of the population.

Christianity was clearly incompatible with the dominant intellectual tendencies during Japan's century of modernization. For one thing, Christianity was seen as unscientific, as unsuited to the temper of a secular age. For another, Christianity did not fit in well with the values of orthodox Japanese thought. When an early samurai convert, Ebina Danjō, "took God as his feudal lord," he described the change within himself from world-immanent loyalties to a transcendental loyalty as "Copernican." The transcendental negation of the family-state ideal is reflected in the words of Niishima Jō, the founder of Dōshisha University: "God, not my parents, created me." Another Christian, Uchimura Kanzō, opposed Japan's actions in the 1905 war against Russia on the grounds of Christian pacifism, while also opposing the missionary churches of his day.

Thus a corollary of the observation that Christianity was incompatible with orthodox thought is that, when it was accepted, it could effect at times a radical change. Christians initiated many social welfare projects, an area in which the Meiji government had little interest. They were concerned with women's higher education, opened orphanages, aided outcast communities, worked with the poor in the slums, helped rehabilitate prostitutes, and were active in women's rights movements. They were politically active in the early phase of the labor and socialist movements, and many worked for democracy in government.

Yoshino Sakuzō (1878–1933), for example, became a Christian while in higher school. While at Tōkyō University he helped edit a Christian journal and associated with Christian socialists. In 1916, when a professor of law at Tōkyō University, he wrote "The Essence of Constitutional Government," a manifesto for parliamentary reform. Working within the framework of Minobe's constitutional interpretation, he advocated universal suffrage, reform of the House of Peers, the subordination of the army to the cabinet, and so on. His second concern was social democracy; he favored a gradual evolution toward socialism by parliamentary means.

One Japanese historian has written that while "Europeans and Americans find it difficult to understand" the degree to which Marxism has entered the consciousness of the Japanese intellectual, "Japanese intellectuals have not understood the extent of the attraction held by the word 'liberal' in the historical life of Europe and America."* Why did Yoshino maintain his liberal position? Why did he not only support social equality,

*Tsurumi Shunsuke, in *Gendai Nihon no shisō*, p. 55.

Yoshino Sakuzō, political liberal and professor at Tōkyō Imperial University.

but also stress the value of the individual? The answer seems to be that these commitments derived from his Christian belief and his German idealistic philosophy. German philosophy provided him with an abstract humanistic ideal. Christianity made this concrete and gave it life. "To realize democracy thoroughly, humanism must function as a living concept," he wrote. Yoshino found this in the Christian belief that "sees all men as the children of God, and recognizes in all men a spark of divinity." Or more briefly: "Christian belief, as it asserts itself in every aspect of society is democracy."*

Marxism in Japan.   Socialism as a theory entered Japan in the last decade of the nineteenth century. In 1901 a Social Democratic party was formed —mainly by Christian socialists—and banned the same day. In the next ten years Marxist socialism and anarcho-syndicalism also became known. The entire movement, however, was suppressed after 1911 when a plot to assassinate the emperor was discovered.

A second wave of socialist thought arose in the years after World War I: the age of liberalism and internationalism. The economy had leaped ahead during the war, the number of workers and students increased, and the Rice Riots of 1918 turned the thoughts of many toward the new social problems within Japan. Also influential were the Russian Revolution and new cur-

*Takeda Kiyoko, "Yoshino Sakuzō," in *Nihon no shisōka II.*

rents of European socialism. By the mid-twenties liberalism, syndicalism, and anarchism had largely been replaced by Marxism.

The government reaction to socialism was to suppress the revolutionary left while, tacitly at least, recognizing the parliamentary left. This policy in large measure shaped the course of the movement. The largest political parties and their associated unions were moderate. They were usually Marxist in doctrines, even if led by Christian socialists, but they accepted parliamentary means. This was the force that by 1937 had won 10 per cent of the vote at the polls. Inevitably the moderate socialists were also most vulnerable to the appeal of nationalism.

On the revolutionary left were a great number of student "social science study groups," splinter parties, and radical unions. These were usually small in size, and were reorganized so frequently that it is almost impossible to treat them by name. Police pressure on the Japanese Communist Party, founded in 1922, was so great that there were often more leading Communists in jail than out. In the revolutionary left a key role was played by the universities. After each purge a new generation of graduates would revitalize the leftist parties. Even after 1933 when the parties and unions of the extreme left had been almost completely suppressed, university study groups continued to read and produce Marxist writings. The re-emergence of Marxism after World War II was largely due to this prewar generation of academicians.

A clear sign of the intellectual vitality of Marxism was its strength in literature. From 1927 till 1932 the proletarian school dominated Japanese letters until writers of other persuasions protested at the "tyranny of the left." The proletarian school believed that the purpose of literature was social enlightenment. It portrayed the aimless, frivolous character of bourgeois existence. It described the heroism of the worker. It attacked the effeteness of Japanese tradition, as in the following poem:

> *Don't sing*
> *Don't sing of scarlet blossoms or the wings of dragonflies*
> *Don't sing of murmuring breezes or the scent of a woman's hair*
> *All of the weak, delicate things*
> *All the false, lying things*
> *All the languid things, omit.*
> *Reject every elegance*
> *And sing what is wholly true,*
> *Filling the stomach,*
> *Flooding the breast at the moment of desperation,*
> *Songs which rebound when beaten*
> *Songs which scoop up courage from the pit of shame*
> *These songs*
> *Sing in a powerful rhythm with swelling throats!*

> *These songs*
> *Hammer into the hearts of all who pass you by!* *

Why did Marxism spread as it did? What did it mean in Japan? What were its limits? One reason it spread, certainly, was that the twenties were more open and tolerant than any other decade in prewar Japan and at the same time the least impressive decade in terms of economic growth. Some Japanese scholars have suggested that Marxism grew because of its resonance with Japanese tradition: would Japan evolve, they asked, from a premodern (collective) society to a postmodern (socialist) society without ever developing a modern (individualistic) society? And did not Marxism appeal to the moral sense of many Japanese, offering an opportunity to sacrifice self for the "good of the people" as they had been taught to sacrifice "for the good of state"? Others have pointed out that Marxism in Japan was opposed to both tradition and nationalism. It taught that family, state, and the economy were exploitative, and demanded heroic action against them. Some have even compared it to Christianity, saying that the spiritual function of both was to reject the imperial cosmology. Certainly the appeal of Marxism in Japan was different from that in most other Asian countries. In the latter the spread of Marxism depended on Lenin's theory of imperialism and on the idea of industrialization through socialism. But in Japan, itself an imperialist power, it was Marx's analysis of the ills within capitalist society that was central.

Finally, the fact that Japan was a fairly modern state made the objective situation in which revolutionary Marxists found themselves discouragingly different from the situation in other Asian countries. The intellectual vitality of Marxist groups in the universities had little impact on the larger society. Nonstudent organizations had little staying power in the face of strong governmental and business bureaucracies. The centralized police system was highly efficient: it blanketed Japan far more thoroughly than any Western police system. Nor were there any "ungoverned" mountain redoubts in Japan in which revolutionaries could group their forces beyond the reach of government authority.

*Translated by Donald Keene. From *Modern Japanese Literature:* An Anthology Compiled and Edited by Donald Keene; copyright © 1956 by Grove Press, published by Grove Press, Inc. (British publisher, Thames & Hudson).

23. Imperial Japan: Democracy and Militarism

The Growth of Parliamentary Influence

The Political Elites.   Government in Japan between 1890 and 1945 was constitutional, but it was not mainly parliamentary. The constitution gave different powers to different bodies. These bodies may be termed the elites of the system.

One pair of elites was the army and navy. They had two kinds of power in the structure of government. First, the chiefs of staff of the services were directly under the emperor and not responsible to the cabinet. This was their "right of autonomous command." At certain critical moments it was hard to define where this right ended and foreign policy began. Second, the services had leverage over cabinets, for, by withdrawing their ministers they could cause a cabinet to collapse and by withholding a minister they could prevent the formation of a new one. On the other hand, the cabinet and Diet could exert pressure on the services through the service ministers and by control of military appropriations.

Another elite was the civil bureaucracy, the "officials of the emperor." Its power derived not from the constitution but from its responsibility in carrying out the executive function. Within the bureaucracy the top men in the central ministries were of particular importance. Graduated in most cases from the Law School of Tōkyō University, they were the cream of the educational cream who had passed the difficult examination for a career in state service. Their ability was great and their social status high. Designed to be a neutral body, they were conservative by inclination, though some sectors of the bureaucracy became politicized as time went on. They influenced government by such means as drafting the legislation presented in the Diet, access to the cabinet ministers, administration of laws, and the holding of high policy-making positions by their more influential members after retirement from the regular bureaucracy.

Another elite consisted of various persons or groups close to the emperor. The emperor had the right to name the prime minister, but someone else always did it for him. At first it was the oligarchs, an entirely extra-legal body. After 1922, the year in which Yamagata died, it was Saionji or a group of ex-prime ministers. The right to name a prime minister was extremely important, since the person named could form a cabinet, call an election, and usually win it. Other influential officials near the emperor were the Inner Minister, Imperial Household Minister, and the members of the Privy Council. The latter had the constitutional authority to ratify treaties; its real power was that it was composed of influential men, ex-officials and ex-ministers.

Still another influential group, if not a constitutional elite, was the zaibatsu combines. These were politically powerful because elections cost money, particularly as the size of the electorate increased. Between 1915 and 1924 campaign expenditures rose from about 5 to 22 million yen. During the same period cases of bribery and election offenses doubled. Campaign contributions meant influence on legislation—when such influence seemed necessary. The question is sometimes asked: did the zaibatsu run the Diet? The answer seems to be that the functions of state and economic enterprises were largely separate. Their goals—state power and growth—were largely compatible. The compatibility of goals made cooperation easy. Not till the social criticism of the 1920's and the depression years of the early 1930's did the question arise of whether the interests of the two were in fact the same.

Another elite was the Diet which had an appointed House of Peers and an elected House of Representatives. The former body of nobility and eminent men was intended as a conservative check on the lower house. It performed this function well and there is little else to say of it. The House of Representatives was powerful because only the Diet could pass permanent laws and any increase in the budget required its approval. The latter prerogative made the lower house more powerful than Itō had intended, because he had not realized that increased budgets would always be needed. From 1890 on the big question in Japanese government was how to control the lower house. No good answer was found, so the parties which dominated the lower house gradually won out in competition with the other elites and moved toward the control of the cabinet, the central stage of government.

The Workings of Government by Compromise.   But the elites did not merely compete. They also cooperated. The constitution gave different but real powers to the various elites. In order for the work of government to be done the elites had to work together. Looking closely, we see that each elite was not self-contained and united. Rather, within each elite there existed rival cliques: coteries competing within the Peers, bureaucratic factions within the ministries, a Chōshū clique versus non-Chōshū officers within the army, a Satsuma clique versus opposing cliques in the navy, parties within the Diet, Mitsui versus Mitsubishi among the zaibatsu, and Itō and Saionji versus Yamagata and Katsura among the oligarchs. Therefore coalitions of cliques that cut across the different elites emerged to rule in Japan.

The ties joining a faction of one elite with a party or faction of another were personal and sometimes antedated the formation of the Diet. For example, Hoshi Tōru, a politician in the party that became the Seiyūkai, was a friend of Mutsu Munemitsu. Mutsu was a protégé of Itō. This led to Itō's leadership of Hoshi's party after 1900. Itō in turn was a friend of Inoue Kaoru who had close ties to the Mitsui house. This led the Mitsui to become the angel of the early Seiyūkai. A comparable inter-elite coalition was also put together—drawing on the aid of the Mitsubishi zaibatsu—about the second major party formed in 1913.

Up until 1905 cooperation among the elites was obtained by oligarchic control at the top. It is only a slight exaggeration to think of the oligarchs as puppeteers at a constitutional Punch and Judy show. Yamagata in particular was powerful. Men loyal to him ran the army, staffed the higher bureaucracy—especially the Home Ministry which in turn controlled local government and the police—and also sat in the House of Peers and Privy Council. Pulling the right strings, Yamagata and the other oligarchs (or *genrō* as they are called in their later years) coordinated the work of the various elites. Even with these resources the Yamagata "machine" proved unable to control the lower house in the period 1890–1900. Consequently Itō in 1900 coopted the Liberal Party and formed the Seiyūkai. Using its connections with power, the Seiyūkai became the majority party. But until 1905 it depended on its oligarchic connection and was largely manipulated from above like the other elites.

The year 1905 was a turning point. In the economy there began a boom that marked the start of sustained economic growth in Japan's modern sector. The victory over Russia expanded Japan's colonial empire and made it the pre-eminent power in East Asia. The war also marked the awakening of a nationalism far stronger than that of the preceding decades, and was a turning point in politics. Itō had proved a failure as a party leader. He could not dominate the party as he wished and could not stand the deals, petty machinations, and abuse that he met in dealing with the party rank and file (he was once pissed on during a party caucus). Saionji had succeeded him but was no more successful. While Saionji served twice as

Unlike the earlier Meiji leaders, Hara was a man of compromise who built his power amid competing elites, factions, and coalitions.

prime minister between 1905 and 1912, he actually conducted himself more as a *genrō* than as a party president after 1905, while Hara Kei became the real party leader.

Hara, born in 1856, was of a different generation from the Meiji leaders. He was also from an area in northeastern Japan that played no role in the Restoration. As an "outsider," his career was accordingly different: at twenty-three he became a newspaper reporter, then a profession close to politics; he entered the Foreign Office at twenty-six and advanced steadily until fifteen years later he became ambassador to Korea. He then went on to become the editor of one of Japan's great daily papers, a bank official, the president of a company, and a member of the Diet. He also helped Itō to found the Seiyūkai in 1900. Patient, intelligent, hard-working, and paternalistic, Hara was the most able politician in the Japan of his day. The national ends for which he worked were enunciated in a later program: "the perfection of national defense, the expansion of education, the encouragement of industry, and the expansion of communications." Hara's goals, perhaps, were not too different from those of Yamagata during his later years. Yet he felt that they should be achieved by a government led by the political parties, not the oligarchy. From 1905 Hara worked sedulously to build the power of the Seiyūkai. The inner history of Japanese government during much of the next sixteen years was the struggle of Hara's machine against that of Yamagata.

One means Hara used to build power was to create a vertical party organization. For a Diet member to win an election required support by politicians in the prefectural assembly and local support by influential men. In some regions there were personal political organizations like the "iron constituency" in Okayama Prefecture which sent a member of the Inukai family to the Diet in every election from 1890. From this region 76 per cent of the votes went to Inukai or to candidates designated by him in the decade after 1890, 47 per cent of the votes after 1932 when the son inherited the "fief" from the father, and 35 per cent, still enough to win a Diet seat, in the years immediately after World War II.

But such constituencies were exceptional. In most areas the local bosses would swing their blocks of votes from one party to another to get patronage from the party in power. A block of votes was an expression of local solidarity: a higher percentage of rural voters turned out for elections than city voters. In rural Japan there was a feeling against wasting votes; a vote counted if it joined other votes to elect a candidate who would get schools, roads, dams, bridges, or tax relief for the area concerned. Hara's tactic was to win these blocks of swing votes by pork barrel politics. He served as Home Minister three times and used the resources of his ministry to favor those districts that supported the Seiyūkai. Communities that aligned themselves with the Seiyūkai got schools and roads, and those that did not were overlooked. Railways, nationalized in 1906, were another area of patronage. The military wanted to change Japan's railways over to the same broad-gauge lines used on the continent. Hara defeated this plan in order that available funds could be spent in laying down new narrow-gauge track into Seiyūkai constituencies.

A second means used by Hara to extend party power was to politicize the bureaucracy. The heights of the bureaucracy were still manned by men appointed by the oligarchs in pre-examination days. The civil service examination system and the regulations governing the bureaucracy had been drawn up by Yamagata to make sure that the next generation of officials would also stay free from party influence. In practice "neutrality" meant loyalty to superiors who were loyal to the oligarchy—who in turn saw themselves as standing above the ruck of partisan interests and concerned only for the good of all Japan. In Hara's eyes the bureaucracy and particularly the influential Home Ministry was the heart of the Yamagata machine.

Hara in time gained the right of some patronage appointments in the bureaucracy. More significant, however, was his success in winning over regular civil service bureaucrats to the party cause. The bureaucracy grew from 29,000 in 1890 to 72,000 in 1908. By 1905 new men from the examination system were starting to replace oligarchal appointees at the top of the system. When Hara became Home Minister in 1906 he established a working relation with some of these new men, appointing them to strategic positions in the police and in the offices controlling public

PRIME MINISTERS 1898–1921

Yamagata	November 1898–October 1900
Itō	October 1900–June 1901
Katsura	June 1901–January 1906
Saionji	January 1906–July 1908
Katsura	July 1908–August 1911
Saionji	August 1911–December 1911
Katsura	December 1912–February 1913
Yamamoto	February 1913–April 1914
Ōkuma	April 1914–October 1916
Terauchi	October 1916–September 1918
Hara	September 1918–November 1921

works, railway construction, and local affairs. These were the men who implemented the pork barrel policy described earlier. Hara also made changes at the prefectural level, firing "unpopular" governors who would not carry out his policies and appointing in their place "effective" men more in tune with his ideas. By the second decade of the twentieth century there were many civil service officials who stood to gain high office under cabinets associated with the Seiyūkai and lose their positions when the Seiyūkai was out of power. That is to say, portions of the bureaucracy had been penetrated by the parties.

A third means of extending party power was to penetrate the other elites. This proved more difficult. As the oligarchy weakened, some younger Peers became more independent of it and some new Peers appointed through party influence became aligned with a party. In the 1920's Hara's party thus succeeded in establishing a working alliance with the largest faction in the Peers. But this was of short duration. At certain times the cabinet also succeeded in bringing pressure to bear on the Privy Council, but it too was in the main successful in resisting party influence. With the military the parties were even less successful. Thus the advance to power of the parties continued to depend heavily on compromises with the other elites.

The Taishō Political Crisis of 1912–1913. The years between 1905 and 1912 were on the surface like those from 1900 to 1905. Katsura and Saionji alternated as prime ministers as had their mentors Yamagata and Itō in an earlier period.

For both Katsura and Saionji, support in the Diet was provided by the Seiyūkai. It was furnished, of course, for a price. This arrangement broke down in the winter of 1912–1913 in what Japanese historians call the Taishō Political Crisis, named after the reign name chosen for the new emperor who had ascended the throne in the summer of 1912. The Crisis is worth examining in some detail since it exemplifies some of the forces in Japanese government at this time.

Saionji became prime minister for the second time in the summer of 1911. In line with the demands of the Seiyūkai and in response to Japan's needs, he was determined to enforce a policy of retrenchment. But the army and navy pressed for increased appropriations. After months of negotiations the demands of the services were refused. The army minister, therefore, after conferring with Yamagata, sent his resignation to the emperor without previously informing Saionji. With this, Saionji's cabinet fell.

The oligarchs, faced with finding a new man, first asked Saionji to form another cabinet. He refused. Yamagata wanted General Terauchi, but the others refused, feeling that an army man would not be accepted by the parties. The oligarch and financial authority Matsukata was asked, but he too refused, as did another one of Yamagata's favorites. Admiral Yamamoto Gombei of Satsuma also turned down the post, saying in effect that the Chōshū army clique should clean up its own mess. Finally, as a last resort, Katsura was asked to form his third cabinet and he accepted.

Katsura was a Chōshū man and an ex-general. He had risen in the army at a time when it was led by men with great breadth of vision (unlike the narrower, professional officers of the thirties). At the turn of the century he shared Yamagata's view that cabinets should be "transcendent," above party control. But by 1912 he was used to cooperating with the Seiyūkai and was ready to form a party of his own. He saw himself not as a soldier but as a statesman, and he accepted the post of prime minister with the intention of continuing the retrenchment policy of his predecessor. Nor was he simply a pawn of Yamagata. In 1911 he had recommended Saionji as his successor in direct opposition to Yamagata and he had been reported to the old man as having said, "When I come back [from a trip to Europe] I will push into retirement such people as Yamagata."

In the eyes of the public and parties, however, Katsura had arranged for the army to overthrow Saionji's cabinet in order to get the post for himself. He was viewed as a Chōshū general attempting to perpetuate oligarchic rule. The first problem facing Katsura was the navy's demand for battleships. It too threatened to withhold a minister if its demands were not met. Countering this, Katsura had an imperial rescript issued directing the navy to furnish a minister. Newspapers and the political parties interpreted this not as opposition to the services, but as an undemocratic and high-handed action in making use of the emperor's supreme authority.

The opposition parties, some businessmen, some intellectuals, and a few professional men had formed in 1912 a League for the Protection of the Constitution. It called for a "Taishō Restoration": just as the early years of the Meiji emperor had witnessed sweeping reforms toward a modern

*Katsura began as a Chōshū
general, but the demands of
the age forced him to attempt
to become a party politician.*

Japan, so the reign of the Taishō emperor must open with similar changes
toward a democratic Japan. The League staged massive protest rallies against
Katsura's use of the imperial rescript. Orators at meetings in the main
cities of Japan shouted, "Destroy the Satchō leaders and off with Katsura's
head." Newspapers supported the movement and local Seiyūkai politicians
joined in. For a time the ex-bureaucratic leadership of the Seiyūkai remained
neutral, but, since Katsura was moving to form his own political party, they
felt released from their earlier pledge to support his cabinet and joined in
the opposition movement. Katsura's party lacked a majority in the Diet.
His ministry was so unpopular that he had little hope of winning at the
polls. The Diet was often surrounded by jeering crowds. Perceiving that
the situation was hopeless, Katsura resigned and died later in the year, a
broken man.

A new cabinet was formed by Admiral Yamamoto, who had earlier refused the post. It marked a temporary return to the pattern of pre-Crisis
days—of government by a cabinet of moderate ex-bureaucrats with the support of the Seiyūkai in the Diet. Most of the ministers joined the Seiyūkai
when they entered the Yamamoto cabinet. Much legislation favorable to
the parties was passed by this cabinet. It continued the earlier policy of
retrenchment, cutting the budget by more than 13 per cent and reducing
the bureaucracy by more than ten thousand persons. It was at this time that
some party men were first appointed to influential posts in the bureaucracy.
The Yamamoto cabinet also opened the posts of army and navy minister,

heretofore limited to active-service generals and admirals subject to the discipline of the services, to retired general-rank and flag-rank officers. None were ever appointed, but the fact that they could be deterred the services from further attempts to overthrow cabinets.

Domestic Politics during World War I. A by-product of the Crisis was the formation in 1913 of Japan's second major political party, the Dōshikai (which through mergers became the Kenseikai in 1916 and the Minseitō in 1927). After almost thirteen years of Seiyūkai monopolization of power and patronage, the other groups in the Diet were hungry. Thus when Katsura set about to form a second party that could effectively compete for a partnership role in government (like that of the Seiyūkai), many members of the lower house of the Diet flocked to join. The oligarchs were also unhappy with the burgeoning strength of the Seiyūkai and its almost effortless resumption of power during the Yamamoto cabinet. They saw in the Dōshikai a potential counterweight. When a scandal caused the Yamamoto cabinet to collapse in 1914, Ōkuma—who had founded the distant predecessor of the Dōshikai in 1881—was asked to form a new cabinet. Ōkuma naturally relied on the Dōshikai for support in the Diet and appointed the president of the party, Katō Kōmei, to be foreign minister in his cabinet.

Ōkuma dissolved the Diet and called an election in March 1915. This election saw the first of the modern political campaigns in Japan. Ōkuma and his ministers spoke at rallies throughout the country. A speech by Ōkuma on "The Power of Public Opinion in Constitutional Politics" was recorded and played from gramophones on platforms all over Japan. On election morning telegrams were sent in Ōkuma's name to voters in critical districts. At the same time the Dōshikai showed that it too could use effectively those techniques that the Seiyūkai had developed earlier: it mobilized the police and local officials to aid Dōshikai candidates and it promised patronage to districts in which it hoped to gather the swing vote. The Dōshikai won an absolute majority in the Diet. This victory was the only break in Seiyūkai control of the Diet from the time of its formation in 1900 to 1924.

Once the election was won and the Seiyūkai put down, the interests of the oligarchs and the Dōshikai diverged. The oligarchs found it no easier to deal with the Dōshikai than the Seiyūkai. In control of the Diet, both parties acted much the same, pushing for increased party power in the government. Yamagata was angered especially by the actions of Foreign Minister Katō. It earlier had been the custom to circulate secret diplomatic documents to the oligarchs. Katō put an end to this. Instead, when requested by the oligarchs, he sent officials to explain matters. Katō sent the ultimatum to Germany that brought Japan into World War I on the side of the Allies without informing Yamagata beforehand. He was called on the carpet for this and promised to behave in the future. But in 1915 when he imposed the Twenty-One Demands on China (see page 755), he again failed to consult the oligarchs. Yamagata's reaction was that Katō was worse than Hara. A deep rift developed between the two men, and as long as Yamagata lived he saw to it that Katō was not asked to form a cabinet. These were lean years for Katō's Kenseikai, as the Dōshikai had been renamed in 1916.

In the meantime, Hara had become aware in the election of 1915 that all of the gains of the Seiyūkai could be washed away if the opposition party came to power. He therefore set about to mend his fences, approaching those who had the ear of Yamagata and eventually meeting with Yamagata himself. As a result when the Ōkuma cabinet fell in 1916 and General Terauchi, a protégé of Yamagata, was appointed as the new prime minister, it was Hara to whom he turned for support in the Diet. But Hara kept a distance between himself and the "bureaucratic" prime minister: he gave his support on issues favorable to the party cause and withheld it when he pleased. The Seiyūkai re-established its position as the largest party in the election of 1917. When the cabinet fell in the aftermath of the rice riots of 1918, the process that had begun in 1905 reached its logical conclusion: Hara was appointed prime minister.

Hara's three-year ministry between 1918 and 1921 achieved many of the ends for which he long had been striving. He abolished the subprefectural district offices, thus reducing bureaucratic control over towns and villages and increasing the autonomy of municipal governments which were normally under party influence. He established small electoral districts (one-seat districts like those of the United States) in place of multiseat districts which left room for representation by minority political groups. This gave the advantage in elections to the major parties. He continued his pork barrel policy, building schools and undertaking an 800-million-yen railroad expansion program. He obtained some openings for political appointees in the colonial bureaucracy. He enfranchised the rural small landowners—the Seiyūkai was especially strong in rural Japan—by reducing the tax qualification from ten to three yen. (Members of the more urban-based Kenseikai saw this not as a democratic advance but as "the perpetuation of class despotism" in the Diet.)

What Hara did not do was to change the structure of government. To attempt more than minor modifications would have produced conflicts with the other elites and would have rocked the foundations of the "Hara machine." In Hara's eyes structural changes were not necessary. It was better to manipulate the other elites and attain party goals by compromise. As Hara's biographer puts it, "Prime Minister Hara in 1918 was still Home Minister Hara," both in his goals and his tactics. Another thing that Hara did not do was to advance social legislation; he was economically conservative and opposed to the rising social movement.

Taishō Democracy

Hara's assassination in 1921 by an ultranationalist brought a sudden tragic end to his brilliant career, but the years after his death saw continued steps in the direction of constitutional government. These new developments, though of course reflecting economic, social, and intellectual changes within Japan, were also responsive to new influences from the West where liberal tendencies were in the ascendant during the twenties. This period is rather loosely called the time of "Taishō Democracy" after the reign period that extended from 1912 to 1926.

The Diplomacy of Empire.   Japan's foreign policy from the Taiwan Expedition of 1874 to the annexation of Korea in 1910 had been consistent. Actions were carried out by a government unified under the oligarchs for the sake of commonly held objectives. The objectives were security, autonomy, and big-power status. Security was obtained by industrial and military development. Autonomy was regained in the mid-nineties when the unequal treaties were revised. Big-power credentials came with the victories over China and Russia in 1895 and 1905, which gave Japan an empire. The empire was bulwarked by bilateral agreements with other imperialist powers. The Anglo-Japanese Alliance of 1902, renewed in 1905 and 1911, was a key agreement. Between 1907 and 1916 Japan also entered into four pacts with Tsarist Russia which protected Japan's special position in Korea and Manchuria. The United States, too, acknowledged Japan's empire; Taft and Katsura in 1905 gave mutual assurances regarding the Philippines and Korea, and the Lansing-Ishii Agreement of 1917 recognized that "territorial propinquity" gave Japan special interests in China. Expansion against other Asian peoples was rationalized within Japan by the doctrines of Social Darwinism, by notions of the superiority of Japan's unique national polity, and by the idea of a Japanese national mission to bring progress and modernity to its backward neighbors.

A second brief period in the history of Japanese imperialism was from World War I to 1922. During the first half of this period the European powers were involved in the business of war, leaving a power vacuum in East Asia. Japan took advantage of this. As an ally of Britain, Japan declared war on Germany and took over the German position in Shantung. The following year, 1915, Japan issued the so-called Twenty-One Demands to China—an attempt to strengthen the position it had won in Manchuria as a result of the Russo-Japanese War and to make new advances in China. The first fourteen demands asked for Chinese confirmation of the newly gained Japanese position in Shantung, economic concessions in Manchuria and Mongolia, and so on. The last group of demands, successfully resisted by the Chinese, were for extensive rights within China proper, including the

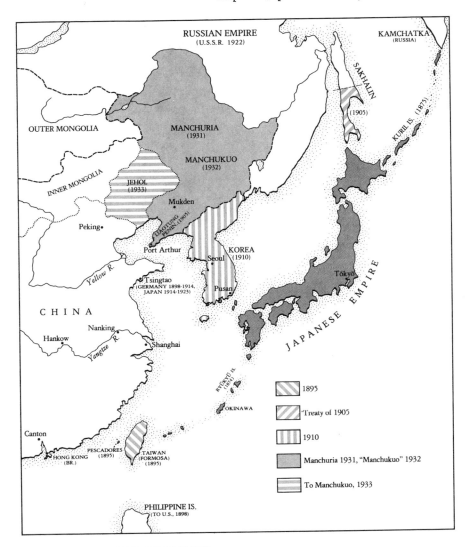

GROWTH OF JAPAN'S EMPIRE

appointment of Japanese advisers within the Chinese government. A third attempt to fish in troubled waters came in 1918 when Japan at the behest of the Allies sent troops to eastern Siberia to join an Allied intervention. Once the government had committed troops, the army took advantage of its "autonomy of command" and sent in many times the number of troops originally agreed on and kept them there long after the other Allies had withdrawn. This action was enormously expensive and enormously unpopular within Japan. It contributed to the declining prestige of the military, and the troops were finally withdrawn in 1922 with nothing to show for their efforts.

In the meantime international relations were entering a new postwar phase. Parallel to the victory of the democracies in World War I was the rise of the Wilsonian "new diplomacy" that emphasized self-determination and the sovereign rights of each people. The thrust of the new diplomacy was to shift from wartime armaments to a peacetime system of limited disarmament, and from a prewar system of bilateral treaties to a postwar system of multilateral treaties. The system was embodied in three treaties reached at the Washington Conference between November 1921 and February 1922. The "Four Power Pact" among Japan, Britain, the United States, and France replaced binational security arrangements with a weaker collective agreement for mutual consultation in case of threats to insular possessions. The "Five Power Pact" established a military equilibrium in the Pacific, stipulating that Britain and the United States would not build fortifications east of Singapore or west of Hawaii, and that the ratio of capital ships between Japan's one-ocean fleet and the two-ocean fleets of Britain and the United States would be 3-5-5. France and Italy, the other two of the "five powers," agreed to a 1.75 ratio. The intention of this agreement was to make Japan secure in its own waters, but unable to wage war against either the United States or Britain. The "Nine Power Treaty" dealt with China. On the one hand it recognized unequal-treaty rights in China and tacitly recognized Japan's position in Manchuria. On the other hand it confirmed the "sovereignty, the independence, and the territorial and administrative integrity of China." In effect it was a statement of principles intended, first, to prevent the powers from taking advantage of Chinese disunity to further dismember China, and second, to apply when a goverment worthy of the name should emerge in China.

The Washington Conference system was, thus, not opposed to the colonial status quo. One could say, even, that it protected a stable colonial order in the hands of the victors in World War I. It was understood, however, that there was to be no new aggression, no new grabbing of colonies, that would upset this diplomatic order.

In keeping with this pattern of big-power relationships, Japan changed over to a foreign policy of internationalism, sometimes called "Shidehara diplomacy" after Shidehara Kijūrō, foreign minister in 1924–1927, and 1929–1931. Indeed, internationalism characterized all of Japan's foreign relations during the 1920's. It was supported by the parliamentary coalition in the Diet, the bureaucrats, and the businessmen, who were international in culture and whose ascendancy paralleled Japan's close ties with the United States, England, and France, the democratic victors in World War I. It was associated in the public mind with the rise to power of the parliamentary coalition.

The New Liberalism.   The postwar internationalist climate affected Japan internally too. When Itō went to Europe in the 1880's in search of a consti-

A rally in 1919 at Ueno Park in support of universal manhood suffrage.

tution, he found German principles most to his liking. In 1918, however, the democracies were strong and victorious. The popular Japanese image of the war was that of the *Punch* stereotypes: the bearded Kaiser of German militarism fighting the beautiful goddess of liberty, who represented the Allied cause. The influence of this democratic current was felt as early as 1916–1917 when school texts were revised to include (alongside the religious view of the emperor) an emphasis on internationalism. Needless to say, this was oriented toward the West; few in Japan at this time were intellectually concerned with the nationalistic stirring in neighboring China, not to speak of changes in the rest of the non-Western world.

Liberal intellectual currents within Japan, always sensitive to Western opinion, blossomed at this time. Yoshino Sakuzō (1878–1933), a professor at Tōkyō University, presented in various magazine articles his plans for the reorganization of government structure so as to subordinate the various elites to a party cabinet. The spirit of the age was reflected in the romantic individualism of the novelist Mushakōji Saneatsu, who wrote that "only a country without authorities is livable" and hoped that at last Goethes and Emersons would be born in Japan.

A Japanese writer has described a universal suffrage rally he attended as a youth in 1919. It was held under the auspices of the Yūaikai, the labor union which had risen after 1912 under the moderate leadership of the Christian, Suzuki Bunji. The three hundred who went to meet the speaker, the veteran Diet member Ozaki Yukio, sang a song written by the pioneer Christian social worker Kagawa Toyohiko as they marched through the streets of Kyōto: "Realizing that labor is a sacred vocation, let our spirits bravely advance, aiming at a distant ideal...." The lecture hall was packed, and the crowds that were turned away broke windows and doors in order to hear Ozaki's oration. The manifesto passed that day amidst tumultuous applause pointed out "the misery of the proletariat and their oppression by the propertied classes," and, while "pledging loyalty to the sacred Emperor," demanded universal suffrage as a means of "extirpating the injustices of the [present] socio-economic system."

Here in microcosm we see a temporary union of labor, an incipient leftist political movement, the Christian social movement, liberal party politicians, journalists, and scholars that characterizes the brief span between 1917 and 1920. The same ideological variety can be found in various student societies established at this time in Tōkyō. A magazine put out by one carried pictures of Lincoln, Rousseau, Kropotkin, Marx, Lenin, and Rosa Luxemburg. A writer described the intellectual content of the era as a melange of different ingredients "swallowed whole without sufficient chewing," and his own position in his student years as a "leftist, emperor-oriented faith in democracy." Born of wartime prosperity and ideological ferment the "social movement," as it was called, was buoyed by the participation of intellectuals. Appealing to new democratic symbols and influenced by egalitarian doctrines, they campaigned for universal suffrage, social legislation, and women's rights. Workers' and tenants' organizations mushroomed overnight. A variety of leftist political groups were also formed. As early as 1918, Hara said that radical thought was the most serious problem he had to deal with. The movement was strong, in part, because it was diffuse enough to draw support from every group that opposed some aspect of state orthodoxy.

The political parties were also affected by this change in the spirit of the times. The Kenseikai, continuously out of power after 1916, not only played the role of an opposition party, but was somewhat changed in character by the "social movement." The election of 1917 appears to have been a turning point in this respect. The Kenseikai lost the election of 1917 to the Seiyūkai, but it won in certain urban districts that had previously gone to the Seiyūkai, and many of its successful candidates were a new type of men—journalists, professors, or lawyers—more liberal than the party leadership. Many of these men joined in the universal suffrage movement in 1917 and 1918 in alliance with the social movement. In the Seiyūkai, too, new men appeared who recognized that they would have to represent new interests if they were to win sufficient votes. Such tendencies were accelerated by the factional wrangling that broke out within the Seiyūkai after the death of Hara in 1921. Hara's successor as party president and prime minister was unsuccessful at maintaining unity within the party. His ministry was followed between 1922 and 1924 by three nonparty cabinets of varied character. As a consequence, some of the more liberal factions of the Seiyūkai allied themselves with the Kenseikai and in 1923 launched the Second Movement for the Protection of the Constitution.

If this movement had had support from the new white-collar class and from the students' and workers' groups that were appearing at this time in urban Japan, and if the alliance of liberal Diet members and the social movement that characterized the universal suffrage movement had continued, then the history of the next two decades might have been different. As it was, however, by the early months of 1920 the principal components in the social movement had abandoned the idea of political action within the framework of the constitution. The main reason for this was the 1920 defeat of the universal suffrage movement. But they also were angered by the antilabor, antiunion stance of Hara's Home Ministry. Labor groups were hurt by the recession of 1920. And more generally, these new idealistic groups were disillusioned by the realism with which the parties had compromised their way to power. As a result, labor unions, political groups, and student organizations turned left to anarcho-syndicalism and direct action, and then to Marxism, and, except for a few journalists, the Second Movement for the Protection of the Constitution lacked the support of intellectuals. Even the liberal Yoshino Sakuzō was cool toward it, pinning his hopes for the future democratization of Japan on labor groups. Rallies were held in the major cities of Japan, but the turnout was not enthusiastic.

The lack of support did not mean that the parties were weakened at the polls; the coalition of parties that supported the Second Movement for the Protection of the Constitution won the election of 1924 handily. This caused the resignation of the cabinet, and a new party cabinet under Katō Kōmei as prime minister was formed. Yet the alienation of "progressive intellectuals" from the two main parties meant that social elements which in other advanced countries defended parliaments from attacks by the right were in Japan critics of the parliamentary state. The significance of this situation was not to become clear until the early 1930's.

The Era of Party Governments. The high-water mark of party government in prewar Japan was the cabinet of Katō Kōmei in 1924–1926. It inaugurated an eight-year period in which the post of prime minister went to the president of one or the other of the two major parties. It was not party government in the British sense, since the president of the majority party in the Diet did not automatically have the right to form a cabinet. At times the post was given to the head of the minority party, who then went out and got his majority in an election. But government was by party leaders, and majority support in the Diet was recognized as necessary for rule.

PRIME MINISTERS 1924–1932

Seiyūkai	*Kenseikai-Minseitō*
	1924–1926 Katō Kōmei
	1926–1927 Wakatsuki
1927–1929 Tanaka	
	1929–1930 Hamaguchi
	1931 Wakatsuki
1931–1932 Inukai	

Katō Kōmei has been aptly described as the very model of a modern Meiji bureaucrat. Born in 1860, he got his start (like his successors in the Minseitō, Wakatsuki and Hamaguchi) as a graduate of Tōkyō University. He entered Mitsubishi at twenty-one, married the boss's daughter, spent some time in England, entered the Foreign Ministry (unlike Wakatsuki and Hamaguchi, who rose in the Ministry of Finance), and at the age of forty became foreign minister. Like Hara he was a man of parts, becoming in rapid succession a Diet member, the president of a large newspaper, several times foreign minister, ambassador to England, and from 1914 on served as president of the Dōshikai and its successor the Kenseikai (after 1916). His last cabinet office prior to 1924 was that of foreign minister in Ōkuma's cabinet at the time of the Twenty-One Demands to China. As a man Katō was blunt, cold, haughty: a purist respected if not popular. He has been called an "enlightened conservative," a term that might be applied to his government as well. An Anglophile, he both understood and staunchly supported party government on the British model.

The accomplishments of the Katō cabinet were considerable, although each seems to have had a darker side. One major achievement was the passage of a universal manhood suffrage bill in 1925. With this the electorate increased from 3 to more than 12 million. When one considers that the national electoral system had begun only in 1890, this marked an amazingly rapid advance. Coupled with this was the re-establishment of the middle-sized election district which has continued ever since. Yet earlier in 1925 Katō agreed to pass a strengthened antisubversive measure, the so-called Peace Preservation Law, which prohibited the formation of groups that advocated a change in the Japanese "national polity" or the abolition of private property. Penalties up to ten years in prison were provided for membership in such a group; these terms were made even more harsh in 1928 for use against the Japanese Communist Party. The conjunction of this law with the suffrage act indicated a willingness to recognize the political potential of every man, as well as a conservative desire to limit the range of political alternatives to which he would be exposed. Also involved in the bargaining for this bill was the restoration of diplomatic relations

GROWTH OF THE JAPANESE ELECTORATE

The Criteria of Eligibility	Election Year	Size of Electorate	Total Population
1889: male subjects 25 and over, paying 15 yen or more in taxes	1890	453,474	40,072,000
1900: male subjects 25 and over, paying 10 yen or more in taxes	1902	983,193	45,227,000
1919: male subjects 25 or over, paying 3 yen or more in taxes	1920	3,069,787	55,963,000
1925: all male subjects 25 and over	1928	12,409,078	63,863,000
1947: all citizens 20 and over	1949	42,105,300	78,100,000

with the Soviet Union (eight years before a similar action by the United States).

A second accomplishment of the Katō ministry was a program of social legislation favorable to labor. Article 17 of the Public Peace Law, which had been used against unions, was abolished. A National Health Insurance Law and a Labor Disputes Mediation Law were enacted, and the Factory Law enacted in the late Meiji period was revised. These, together with the suffrage bill, in effect, legalized union support for the nonrevolutionary socialist movement that was rising at this time. Against the revolutionary left, that is, those who advocated the overthrow of the emperor, the Katō cabinet was draconian; but toward those who were willing to work within the Japanese constitutional framework, Katō was permissive.

A third reform dealt with the Peers. This body, heavy with the post-1885 nobility, was a thorn in the side of party government, often blocking bills passed by the lower house. Katō originially had wanted to change the constitution so as to curtail the functions of the Peers. This proved impossible, but he was able to change the Peers' composition, limiting the number of members from the nobility and increasing the number of imperial appointees, who were usually men of legal, academic, or other achievement.

The ascendancy of the parties, the rise of democratic currents in the cities, and the foreign policy of internationalism led to a decline in the prestige of the services. Army officers took to wearing civilian clothes when off duty. Four divisions were cut out of the army in 1924 as part of a broader retrenchment program that cut the civil bureaucracy by twenty thousand men. Military expenses, which were 42 per cent of the budget in

1922, were pared to 29 per cent in 1925 and 28 per cent in 1927. Yet the army was by no means out of the picture altogether. This was the period during which it was mechanized. Military training was introduced into middle and higher schools, and local training units were set up for youths who did not continue their education. Many officers of the eliminated four divisions became instructors under this program. At the height of party power in December 1925 the moderate army minister, General Ugaki, could write in his diary:

More than 200,000 troops in active service, more than 3,000,000 in the veterans' organization, 500,000 or 600,000 middle and higher school students, and more than 800,000 trainees in local units: all of these will be controlled by the army, and their power will work as the central force aiding the Emperor in war and peace alike. The right of autonomous command over the Emperor's army is, in a time of emergency, not limited to the command of troops, but contains the authority to control the people.

The Troubled Years of Party Government 1927–1932.   Katō Kōmei died in 1926 and was succeeded by Wakatsuki of the same party. Shidehara continued as foreign minister and there was little break with the policies of Katō. The Seiyūkai, however, returned to power in 1927, its fortunes revived by General Tanaka Giichi, who had become its president in 1925. Tanaka was born in Chōshū in 1863. Entering the army, he rose to become army minister in the Hara cabinet in 1918. His association with party politicians was so close that some generals distrusted him, feeling that his ambition might work against the interest of the army. Tanaka was neither a military oligarch nor a real party politician, but he was broader in outlook and more astute than the narrowly professional generals of the late 1930's who were to follow.

As prime minister, Tanaka spoke of a "positive foreign policy," of strengthening Japan's position in Manchuria, and of taking a tougher attitude toward the Chinese. In fact, Japan's relations with China remained by and large the same as under Shidehara, but Tanaka's bellicose tones provoked an anti-Japanese reaction in China. This boomeranged on the Tanaka cabinet when in 1928 officers of the Japanese Kwantung Army in Manchuria assassinated Chang Tso-lin, Japan's client warlord in the area, in the hope that his son would be less nationalistic and more compliant to Japanese suggestions. Tanaka tried to cover up the incident, even telling the young Shōwa emperor, who had succeeded his father in 1926, that the army was not responsible. When the truth came out, the emperor called Tanaka a liar. This led to his resignation.

The return of the Minseitō to power in 1929 (the cabinets of Hamaguchi and Wakatsuki with Shidehara as foreign minister in both) was a return to a government more committed to party rule. One of the major accomplishments of Hamaguchi's cabinet was Japan's participation in the London Naval Conference of 1930, which saw the Washington Conference formula of 5-5-3 for capital ships extended to heavy cruisers, and a 10-10-7 formula applied to light cruisers. Basing his policy on friendship with the United States and Britain and on a determination to avoid an arms race, Hamaguchi used moderate admirals to override majority opinion in the navy. The Naval General Staff declared that he had infringed on its right of supreme command. The Privy Council, the Peers, and the Seiyūkai attacked the concessions made at London. The Seiyūkai was unaware that criticism of the Minseitō at this critical juncture had the effect of weakening party power in general. Hamaguchi successfully stood up to this barrage of criticism until November 1930 when he was shot by a rightist "patriot."

In addition to the furor over the cruiser ratio, the political mud-slinging at times, as in the elections of 1928 and 1930, was such that it almost seemed as if the two major parties themselves were intent on hastening the downfall of party government. The Minseitō called the government of the Seiyūkai between 1927 and 1929 a "Mitsui cabinet," since the bank crisis of 1927 had been settled on terms highly favorable to the Mitsui. In reply, in 1930 the Seiyūkai called the government of Hamaguchi a "Mitsubishi cabinet." Whether the Japanese politicians of this period were in fact more venal than those in the West can be questioned. But the very size of the zaibatsu made the sources of their campaign donations more obvious, and infractions of the highly restrictive election laws were legion. Furthermore, there was probably a higher level of ethical expectation regarding government morality (deriving from the same Confucian assumptions that lay behind Yamagata's belief that government should be above parties and other private interest groups). Corruption, magnified by suffering due to the depression and by slashing attacks from both the left and the right, thus attracted much attention, and faith in party government weakened even during the era in which the parties' gains seemed irreversible.

Reviewing the history of the 1924–1932 period, we note first that it occurred within the constitutional structure of multiple elites. The power balance shifted in favor of the lower house, society became more open, mass media became more influential, the economy became more diversified, and yet no breakthrough to a new political structure occurred. Even the enactment of universal suffrage did not disrupt the usual workings of the system. The intermediate institutions—prefectural organizations, veterans' associations, shrine and temple associations, business groups, the police and lower bureaucracy, and the system of education—that served as the transmission belt between town or village and nation remained firm. The newly enfranchised were accommodated within the existing political scheme.

Universal suffrage did affect the socialist movement. It gave new strength to moderate unions and political organizations. Even many organizations that were Marxist in ideology adopted parliamentary tactics after 1925. Their rosy hopes for gains at the polls were dashed by the elections of 1928, 1930, and 1932, when, to their chagrin, the newly enfranchised gave most of their votes to the two old parties. To some extent it was the inability of the moderate left to attract voters that fed the revolutionary fringe. The weak showing at the polls underlines the point that the significance of prewar socialism was more intellectual than numerical.

The inability of the two main parties to change the political structure may have stemmed from the conservative character of the leaders, who usually entered the parties only after serving long apprenticeships in other more conservative elites. But it is also possible to say that the parties were as liberal as they could have been, if they were to cooperate effectively with the other elites and avoid a possibly violent reaction from the right. The two parties were alike in most respects, at least when they were in power. The choice between them was rarely such as to inspire a voter with democratic fervor. But their essential similarity was the precondition for the gains that were made; the slight difference between them at any one time—such as the Kenseikai stress on universal suffrage before 1924—defined the next goal for legislative advance. Had the Kenseikai been conspicuously more advanced than its opposition, the government might have formed a stable alliance with the Seiyūkai, permanently excluding the Kenseikai from power.

Comparative history is still in its infancy, but a contrast between Japan and pre-Weimar Germany with its comparable government of plural elites offers a relief from the perspective that comes from interpreting Japanese government in terms of the Anglo-American democracies. Both Japan and Germany were late developers and both had semifeudal survivals, such as the power of the family head and the prestige of the military. Both had imperial consitutions, Prussian in inspiration, that limited the powers of the legislature. Both were run by academic, elitist bureaucracies, and the armed services in both were directly under the monarchy. One significant difference between them was that Japan's society was much more homogeneous: there were no politically significant religious splits, no strong regional loyalties, no Junker class with its own party, and no powerful socialist party with widespread political support. The pace of evolutionary change was so even that both major parties represented, by and large, the same social groups—rural landlords, "men of influence" in the rural political structure, and urban industrial interests. A comparison with the underdeveloped parliamentary state of Germany before World War I also suggests a higher evaluation of Japan's gains under the Meiji constitution—especially when one considers that Japan not only had to build its parliamentary organization, but also to implant the very vocabulary necessary for its articulation.

The Rise of Militarism

Had Japan not been subject to new outside influences after 1929 it might have continued its earlier pattern of slow gains in a parliamentary direction within the framework of the constitution. It is possible, even, that the principle of automatically selecting the head of the majority party in the Diet as prime minister might have been established. But this trend came to an end. There was no reversion to the pre-1913 pattern of oligarchic control; nor were there revolutionary changes in the post-1890 structure of government. Rather, what happened was a small shift in the balance between the elites, the advantage passing from the parties to the military. This small shift produced an enormous change in political climate and policy, setting Japan upon the course that led to disaster in World War II. The three most important outside influences were: the world depression that began in the United States in 1929, the march north of the Kuomintang troops together with the emergence of a strong Chinese nationalism that threatened Japan's position in Manchuria, and the rise to power of Hitler and Mussolini in Germany and Italy.

The Depression.   In Japan the domestic depression of 1926 led to the bank crisis of 1927 in which a number of weak banks were wiped out. These developments took place against the economic backdrop of the relatively weak showing of the Japanese economy during the 1920's. These minor crises were followed by a major catastrophe when the world depression hit Japan early in 1930.

Objective indices show that the value of Japanese exports dropped 50 per cent from 1929 to 1931. Workers' real incomes dropped, from an index of 100 in 1926, to 81 in 1930, to 69 in 1931. Unemployment rose to about 3 million, with much of the burden falling on farm families. Rural Japan bore the brunt of the depression suffering; for example, between September 1929 and September 1930 the price of silk cocoons fell 65 per cent. In 1930 the "bumper crop famine" occurred. On October 2 a crop 12 per cent greater than that of the previous years was predicted; by the following day the price per unit (five bushels) of rice had fallen to sixteen yen, although the cost of production was seventeen yen. By October 10 the price had fallen to about ten yen. In 1931 the evil of too much was followed by the greater evil of too little. An unprecedented crop failure occurred in northeastern Japan and Hokkaidō. Images of the depression in Japan were formed by this event: children begging for food outside the dining-cars of trains, starving peasants stripping off the tender inner bark of pine trees or digging for the roots of wild plants, the agents for city brothels bargaining with farmers who had nothing left to sell but their daughters. Between 1926 and 1931, rural cash incomes fell from an index of 100 to 33, and

A hamlet discussion during the depression year of 1934 in Aomori.
Topic is how to survive without selling daughters.

by 1934 were back only to 44. Because of lower prices, the peasants' real
income, never high, was down about one-third. The condition of tenants
and poorer farmers, at near-subsistence levels even in good times, was
far worse.

The blame for the depression fell on the parties. This was because party
leaders, in the public mind, were intimately associated with the zaibatsu,
the bureaucracy, the landlords, and the urban white-collar class. All the
groups of this "parliamentary coalition," with the possible exception of the
landlords, had a common vision of economic growth by participation in the
international, economic order that paralleled the comity of democratic nations. This was the 1920 outgrowth of the Meiji vision of limited democracy
and paternalistic capitalism at home working in cooperation with the great
powers abroad. The depression called into question the validity of the international economic order; this in turn cast doubts on the worth of the comity
of democratic nations and Japan's parliamentary government. At the same
time the emergence of the Fascists in Italy and the Nazis in Germany contributed to the rise of antidemocratic forces in Japan. It seemed particularly
significant to many that Germany, the most admired of Western states and
the constitutional model for Japan, had turned its back on democracy and
was looking to authoritarian and militarist policies as the wave of the future.

These developments revived the unsolved question of the Meiji constitution: Who would rule in Japan? Who best represented the will of the
emperor and the interests of the people? Was it the party politicians, the

lackeys of the zaibatsu who worked cheek by jowl with the self-satisfied higher bureaucracy, under whose government the farmers had suffered so much? Or was the imperial army, which had preserved untarnished its honor and sense of duty, best fitted to rule? Some in the army, at least, saw the question in these terms. Those who advocated a greater role for the army at home asked further whether Japan could afford to depend on the world economy in view of rising tariff barriers, protests against cheap Japanese goods, and the problem of finding adequate raw materials and markets. They argued that military expansion abroad could create an autonomous empire within which Japan could insulate itself from the vagaries of the world economy—a controlled imperial economy within which the livelihood of farmer and worker would be guaranteed.

Party government acted effectively, if late, to counter the depression. Inukai Tsuyoshi became prime minister of a Seiyūkai cabinet in December 1931 and took Japan off the gold standard. This led to the boom in exports that made Japan the first nation to recover. By 1936 domestic consumption was up 20 per cent. Some of this was taken up by a 7 per cent rise in population to 70 million, but a rise greater than 10 per cent in real incomes occurred for the nation as a whole. This was not evenly distributed. The salaried classes benefited the most. But unemployment dropped, and the real wages of workers rose from an index figure of 155 for 1925–1929 to 174 for 1930–1934, and then declined to 166 for 1935–1939 as moderate inflation set in. Rural incomes also recovered somewhat, but, since new debts made even heavier the earlier burden of taxes and rents, few gains were made. Economic recovery, however, came too late to benefit the parties.

The Army in Politics: The Manchurian Incident.   Ever since the decline of the oligarchy, the army had had the capacity for independent action. This was guaranteed by the position of the General Staff directly under the emperor. The use of this autonomy was not new in 1931. The army had used its powers to prolong the Siberian Expedition in the early 1920's, and to fight for military appropriations at other times. Examples also can be found of independent actions by field-grade officers that, when successful, tended to commit the army as a whole to some policy that it might not otherwise have chosen. In general, however, a decline in the army relative to the other elites, combined with moderate leadership by a transitional generation of generals willing to cooperate with the parties, had kept the army in line until the late twenties.

The attachment of the army and of Japan as a whole to Manchuria was of long standing. In popular sentiment Manchuria was viewed as a recompense for the 100,000 Japanese lives lost in the Russo-Japanese War. Army planners saw Manchuria as a buffer against Russian power in the north.

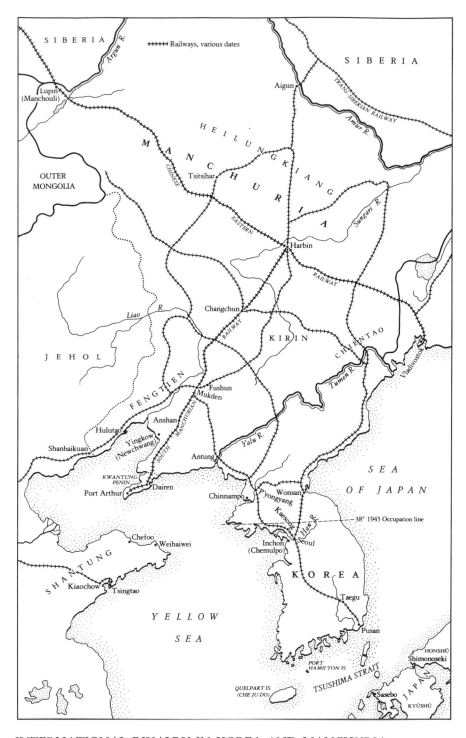

INTERNATIONAL RIVALRY IN KOREA AND MANCHURIA

Military considerations were strengthened after 1918 by a policy of containment of Communism. Of foreign investment in Manchuria, 75 per cent was Japanese; particularly important was the South Manchurian Railway Company. There were a million Japanese subjects in Manchuria, mostly Korean, and 40 per cent of Japan's China trade was with this area. Arguments in favor of the expansion of this economic position had been powerfully bolstered by the depression.

In spite of these various interests, Japan did not have a policy of reducing Manchuria to a colony. It was content to maintain a façade of Chinese sovereignty under a semipuppet warlord, a balance possible because of Chinese disunity. By the late 1920's, however, this balance had been upset by the unification of China by the Nationalists in 1926–1928 and the rise of Chinese nationalism, which increasingly challenged the Japanese position in Manchuria. Faced with this new situation, no important group in Japan considered withdrawing. Japan's party leaders, such as Wakatsuki and Shidehara, argued for peaceful diplomacy and international trade, but the status quo was crumbling. Action was necesssary if Japan's position in Manchuria was to be maintained. Even many in the parties recognized this, and all groups in the army favored some kind of action. In August 1931, Minami, the most powerful of the moderate generals, drew up a plan. While predicated on cooperation with the Foreign Office, it aimed at the formation of a "fundamental policy for Manchuria" to obtain practical results by the spring of 1932. A second group, the army's China experts, under General Tatekawa, favored direct action by the army, as did many field-grade officers both in Tōkyō and in the Japanese military in Manchuria (known as the Kwantung Army).

The Mukden incident that led to the Japanese takeover in Manchuria has often been described as a coup carried out by junior officers without the knowledge of their superiors. This is not true. The architects of the plot were indeed only field-grade officers, Colonel Itagaki and Lieutenant-Colonel Ishiwara of the Kwantung Army, but late in August 1931, Ishiwara told General Tatekawa of the General Staff and others of his plan to provoke an incident that would lead to a Japanese takeover of Manchuria. No one objected. He also told General Honjō, the commanding general of the Kwantung Army, who is said to have replied that he would take "immediate action" in case of a crisis. When the chief of staff of the Kwantung Army heard of the plot, he asked the army in Tōkyō to send someone to inform the Kwantung Army of Tōkyō's policy. Tatekawa was sent, but before leaving dispatched a cable to alert the plotters. Tatekawa arrived in Manchuria on the evening of September 18 and went straight to a geisha house, his message undelivered. On the same night a bomb exploded on the tracks of the Japanese railway north of Mukden. Colonel Itagaki ordered a full-scale attack against the Chinese troops in Mukden, and General Honjō, hearing of the crisis, called out the whole Kwantung Army. Once action had begun, no one in the army was willing to consider a return to the earlier situation.

The effects on the government of the army's aggression were disastrous. On the day after the fighting began the Wakatsuki cabinet decided on a policy of "nonexpansion of hostilities." But on September 21 the army advanced into areas beyond the South Manchurian Railway zone. On September 24 the Japanese government announced that "the action of the Japanese army was taken in self-defense and hence unavoidable," but that "the army was already returning to the railway zone." Actually the army continued to advance and the Japanese government was unable to control it. By early 1932 the conquest of all Manchuria had been completed. In March 1932 Manchuria was proclaimed an independent state under the last Ch'ing ruler (P'u-yi). The Lytton Commission of the League of Nations visited Manchuria in the spring of 1932 and condemned Japan as an aggressor. The report was adopted by the League of Nations, from which Japan withdrew in protest the following year. By this time the Japanese armies had already moved west from Manchuria to occupy about five thousand square miles of the Inner Mongolian province of Jehol.

The Wakatsuki cabinet was unable to take effective action because it was split. Several ministers supported the action of the Kwantung Army; most disapproved silently; only two were openly critical. Divided, the cabinet vacillated for several months and finally resigned in December. The next cabinet was formed by Inukai, the last party prime minister in prewar Japan. Inukai's Seiyūkai was also disunited. One faction favored military expansion. The majority, including the prime minister, accepted the conquest of Manchuria but opposed further army expansion into China. Long a fighter for party rule, Inukai was particularly enraged by the army's usurpation of the decision-making functions of the cabinet. He therefore attempted to negotiate directly with the Chinese. According to his son, Inukai also sought, unsuccessfully, to obtain an imperial rescript to restrain the army in Manchuria. But such moves were without effect, and Inukai was assassinated by ultranationalists on May 15, 1932.

At this point the parties became the victims of the methods which they had used so successfully for four decades. They had risen to power by manipulating other elites and by compromise. In 1932 compromise could lead only to a weakening of party power. The parties needed strong leaders who could dig in their heels and fight. But none was forthcoming. Had Saionji been a stronger person, had he spoken resolutely against the army in the name of the emperor, the "parliamentary coalition" might have rallied. The rationale of the army's defiance of the cabinet was the fiction that the army acted on the direct orders of the emperor. But Saionji saw as his first duty the protection of the emperor from involvement in political controversy; this took precedence over his weaker concern for parliamentary government.

The year 1932 was the pit of the depression and the peak of agitation by the revolutionary right. Stirred by the conquest of Manchuria, by the fighting between Japanese and Chinese forces that had broken out in Shanghai in January and February, and by the "patriotic assassinations" of establishment figures, many hoped that an army general would be chosen prime minister. In this situation the best that Saionji could do was to appoint as prime minister Saitō Makoto (1858–1936), a moderate admiral, in the hope of reconciling the services and moderate elements within the parties. Wakatsuki, the president of the Minseitō, was too liberal to be acceptable to the services. The new president of the Seiyūkai was an expansionist who might have encouraged the army in its continental policy. As military men, both Saitō (prime minister May 1932–July 1934) and his successor Admiral Okada (prime minister July 1934–March 1936) were not unacceptable to the army in spite of their moderate character. Saitō's cabinet of "national unity" was made up of ex-bureaucrats and politicians appointed from both parties. Split into factions and jealous of each other, the parties were willing to accept their reduction to a ministerial role in government. The parties continued a vigorous criticism of the military from the floor of the Diet, but in general the four years of the Saitō and Okada cabinets saw a steady drift away from the policies of the 1920's.

The Rise and Fall of the Revolutionary Right, 1931–1936. Until the mid-1920's there had been few civilian patriotic societies, but then they began to proliferate, and they became extremely numerous during the 1930's and 1940's. Charts drawn by Japanese scholars to show their lineages and interrelationships look like computer wiring diagrams. Most groups were small. Ideologically, all were committed to the emperor, the "national polity," and to the Japanese virtues of harmony and duty. Most opposed internationalism and favored Japanese expansion and pan-Asianism. Some advocated direct action against the "traitors at the side of the emperor."

A second component in the revolutionary rightist movement of the 1930's consisted of certain groups of young army and navy officers. Educated in army schools after leaving middle school, officers were more traditional in outlook than most other segments of society. They were sympathetic to the postdepression plight of rural Japan from which most service recruits were obtained. Some were therefore susceptible to the traditional idea of morally pure direct action to overthrow the corrupt government of party politicians. Mixed in with these feelings were animosities against the monopolization of army control by Chōshū generals or against the domination of the army bureaucracy by graduates of the elite War College.

In 1931 military and civilian ultranationalist groups joined in two plots to overthrow the government and establish a "national defense state" under an army-led cabinet. Both plots fizzled. Early in 1932 the civilian League of Blood assassinated a party politician and then a Mitsui executive. On May 15, 1932, a group of junior officers in the army and navy, acting in concert with a rural patriotic group, murdered Prime Minister Inukai and attacked the Seiyūkai headquarters, the Bank of Japan, various official residences, and the Tōkyō Police Headquarters. In 1934 a lieutenant-colonel killed one of the triumvirate of top generals, who belonged to an opposing clique. The last and greatest coup by the revolutionary right was the rebellion of the First Division on February 26, 1936. Young officers led fourteen hundred troops into the streets of Tōkyō. They attacked government offices, killed cabinet ministers and members of the Imperial Household Ministry. For three days the center of the city was in a state of seige, with soldiers occupying the Diet, the Army Ministry, the General Staff Headquarters, and other government centers. At first some army generals wanted to placate the rebels. But the high officials around the throne had the emperor stand firm, and the other elites—including the navy—joined in opposition to the rebellion. On the 29th the insurgents were branded as rebels and put down by soldiers brought in from outside commands.

The rebellion was followed by purges of generals who had been involved in clique politics within the army. It was at this time that power came into the hands of officers, including General Tōjō, who were later to lead Japan into World War II. The leaders of the rebellion were quickly tried and executed, and the powers of the military police to root out those who advocated "direct action" were augmented. The re-establishment of discipline within the army did not mean that the army as an elite had become depoliticized. If anything its voice in Japan became greater: the threat of renewed violence if the army were not given its way became a potent argument in political councils and a determining factor in foreign policy.

A second consequence of the period of terror was the suppression, first of the left and then of liberals. Under attack by the right, many in the government, including some party politicians, intensified their persecution of the left to demonstrate their own patriotism. The lack of a tradition of civil rights for minority groups proved fatal. The revolutionary left, openly heretical in its attacks on the emperor, was the first to go. In 1932, fifteen hundred socialists, Communists, and union organizers were arrested and as many again in 1933. Many were sent to prison, a few were killed. From 1933 liberal professors came under fire. Some lost their jobs. In 1935 Minobe was attacked in the Diet for having suggested that the emperor was an organ of the state; he was dismissed from all his posts and his works were banned. From this time, what had been orthodox constitutional theory became heresy, and the religious interpretation of the state became official.

Cross-Currents, 1936–1937.   The period after the February Rebellion of 1936 and before the beginning of the China war in the summer of the following year was politically confused. In it two cross-currents appeared: a stronger voice for the army in a government thinking of war, and a resurgence of the political parties in opposition to the army-dominated government.

The Okada cabinet resigned after the rebellion, and a new cabinet was formed by Hirota Kōki, the former foreign minister, a career diplomat and an advocate of a stronger foreign policy. The army interfered from the start, vetoing as cabinet ministers a leading Foreign Office official, Yoshida Shigeru (prime minister 1946–1947, 1948–1954), and several others on the grounds that they were too liberal. In the end, only four party men were able to enter the cabinet. The policies carried out by this cabinet, and that of General Hayashi which followed it, form a logical bridge between the conservatism of the years 1934–1936 and the intensified militarism after the onset of the China war.

One act of the Hirota cabinet was the passage of more stringent laws for the control of dangerous thoughts. Another was the passage of a greatly augmented budget for military expenditures. This provided the funds for army modernization that the military had long been advocating. In foreign policy the cabinet aligned its policies with those of the army, calling for the neutralization of five northern Chinese provinces. It also stressed, for the first time, Japan's concern with the regions to the south of China. And in December 1936 Japan signed the Anti-Comintern Pact with Germany.

The Hirota cabinet also re-established the ruling that only generals and admirals on active duty might be appointed as service ministers. One purpose of this was to prevent the generals ousted after the 1936 rebellion from re-entering politics by the side door. The result, however, was to make cabinets clearly dependent on the good will of the military services, as they had been before 1913. This became obvious early in 1937 when General Ugaki was asked to form a cabinet. Because of his close ties with the political parties, his association with cliquism in the army, and his responsibility for the 1924 reduction of four divisions, the army refused to furnish an army minister. As a retired general Ugaki was unable to become his own army minister and was forced to withdraw. In his place, General Hayashi Senjūrō, who faithfully followed the army line, became prime minister. The character of the four short months of his cabinet is summed up in the slogans it used: "Respect the gods and honor the emperor," and "The union of government and religion."

The second cross-current during this period was the revival of the parties and their opposition to the army. In the election of February 1936 (one week before the rebellion), the Seiyūkai, with its more nationalistic "positive" foreign policy, entered with 301 incumbent Diet seats to the Minseitō's

PRIME MINISTERS 1932–1945

Moderate Admirals	Saitō	May 1932–July 1934
	Okada	July 1934–March 1936
Growing Militarism	Hirota	March 1936–February 1937
	Hayashi	February 1937–June 1937
China War	Konoe	June 1937–January 1939
	Hiranuma	January 1939–August 1939
Diplomatic Pause	Abe	August 1939–January 1940
	Yonai	January 1940–July 1940
Axis Pact	Konoe	July 1940–July 1941
	Konoe	July 1941–October 1941
World War II	Tōjō	October 1941–July 1944
Ending the War	Koiso	July 1944–April 1945
	Suzuki	April 1945–August 1945

146. Yet the Minseitō, using slogans such as "What shall it be, parliamentary government or fascism?" won a notable victory at the polls, coming out of the election with 205 seats to the Seiyūkai's 174. Such a result was not simply habitual voting by a lethargic populace. Rather, it shows a positive awareness of the problems of the day.

Increasingly ignored by the bureaucratic-military cabinets, the parties gradually came to oppose the government. In January 1937 a Seiyūkai Diet member made an impassioned speech attacking the army's interference in government. The army minister replied; a bitter debate followed; the Diet member recommended that the army minister commit hara-kiri; the army minister wanted to dissolve the Diet. The navy minister and others refused, and therefore the Hirota cabinet resigned. The Hayashi cabinet, which lasted only four months, was also brought down by the parties. Like Yamagata at the turn of the century, Hayashi felt that cabinets should be above the factional strife which the parties represented. He demanded that those who entered his cabinet renounce their party ties. To attain the unity he desired, he dissolved the Diet shortly after getting the budget passed and threw the support of the government behind the Shōwa-kai, a pro-militarist party. Apparently his idea was to realize in Japan the "one country, one party" formula of the Nazis. Yet in the election of April 1937 the Shōwa-kai won only 19 seats out of a total of 466 and Hayashi was forced to resign. It had been made plain, as in the late Meiji period, that government parties could not win an election.

The 1937 election reveals the extent to which, in spite of the drift to the right in the balance of governmental elites, the Japanese people had maintained a moderate, antimilitary position. Devotion to the emperor and

Japan did not automatically lead them to favor the more extreme forms of nationalism in politics. The bulk of the people, as in the elections of 1930, 1932, and 1936, stayed with the two major parties, which, although severely factionalized, made a common front against the Hayashi government. These parties received over 7 million votes and won 354 seats in the Diet. Progovernment parties won only 40 or so seats. By and large, the voting pattern of the 1930's represents not a break with that of the 1920's but a continuation. This also can be seen in the gradual growth of moderate socialism, which won 8 Diet seats in 1928, 5 seats in 1930 and 1932, 18 in 1936, and 37 in 1937 (receiving over 900,000 votes). Since the Social Mass Party (formed in 1932) was plagued by a national-socialist fringe on one side and antiparliamentary Marxism on the other, it cannot simply be described as a democratic force. Yet it was led by moderates such as the Christians Abe Isoo and Katayama Tetsu (prime minister 1947–1948), and its slogan, "Anticommunism, antifascism, anticapitalism," had a genuinely democratic appeal. Votes for this party were concentrated in the cities and represented elements that would emerge in much stronger force in postwar Japan.

To resolve the conflict between the parties and the government, and to promote a "Shōwa restoration" of national unity, Prince Konoe Fumimaro was asked to form the next cabinet. Konoe had ties with the army, the political parties, and the Japanese financial world. A civilian, a descendant of the ancient court aristocracy, a protégé of Saionji, a skillful and popular writer, a man who in his youth had gone to Kyōto University expressly to study with the philosopher Nishida and the Marxist economist Kawakami Hajime, Konoe had some appeal for every group. His appointment was greeted enthusiastically in all quarters. Certainly the parties expected from him a greater liberality than had existed under Hayashi. Yet, whatever potential he might have had in peacetime, in the course of the war that broke out a month after the formation of his cabinet, he proved too weak to resist the demands of the military and belligerent civilians whose hold on the government became stronger and stronger.

Japan at War

The China War. In 1937 all Japanese army planning was predicated on the assumption that the Soviet Union was Japan's only serious enemy in East Asia. By 1935 Russia had more troops in its Far Eastern Provinces (about 240,000) than Japan had in Manchuria (160,000), as well as more planes and greater mechanized strength. At the Seventh Comintern Congress of 1935 it was proclaimed that the fascist states of Germany and Japan were the enemies of the Soviet Union. In March 1936 the Soviet Union concluded a mutual defense pact with Outer Mongolia, and it obviously benefited from the united-front policy which brought the Kuomintang and

Chinese Communists together after 1936. To match the military strength of the Soviet Union in East Asia, the Japanese army in the summer of 1937 drew up a "Five-Year Plan for the Production of War Material." To fulfill this required time and peace; the last thing Japan needed was a full-scale war with China.

Indeed, apart from Manchuria, Japan's strategic concern in China was limited to the formation of buffer zones in North China to protect Manchuria from surprise attack during a possible war with Russia. These limited objectives in the main had been achieved by the end of 1935, although Japan still wanted the Nationalist government to recognize formally the special importance of the North China provinces to the security of Japan's continental empire. A few among the army's China experts and some radical officers in the Kwantung Army in Manchuria argued that the Nanking Government should be crushed before it had time to enter into an alliance with the Soviet Union and menace Manchuria from the south. But such a tactical emphasis represented a minority opinion within the overall strategy directed against the Soviet Union. Nevertheless, when on July 7, 1937, a local, unplanned clash took place between Chinese and Japanese troops in the Peking area, it quickly spread into a general war.

One reason for the spread of war was a Sino-Japanese difference in moral assumptions. Japan saw its position in China as based on national destiny, economic need, and history. Most Japanese felt their actions since 1931 were necessary to protect legitimate imperial interests. They judged events in terms of a status quo that was being disturbed by Chinese nationalism. China, on the other hand, saw its entire modern history as one of continuous aggression by foreign powers. Japan's encroachments were the most recent and outrageous. Rising Chinese nationalism could tolerate these no longer. A second reason was a crisis of mobilization: generals on both sides sent in troops so they would not be forced to negotiate from weakness, and once troops were on the ground they were committed to battle to improve their positional strength. A third reason was that within the Japanese government the question of what policy should be made became entangled with the question of who should make it. As military men and jingoistic bureaucrats won out in power struggles, policy became more aggressive. Several times armistices were reached by armies in the field only to be overturned by decisions made in Tōkyō.

As the fighting increased so did sentiment in favor of a knockout blow against Nationalist China. The General Staff argued that if the Chinese capital of Nanking fell, the Chinese government would give in to Japanese demands. Nanking was captured in December, and the willingness of army commanders to see this former center of anti-Japanese agitation punished led to days of wanton slaughter. The Nationalist leader Chiang Kai-shek, however, held out, so in January 1938 it was decided to launch an all-out offensive in China in order to set up a new central government favorable to the Japanese. By October 1938 Hankow and Canton had been captured. The threat of the Soviet Union in the north led Japan to limit its involvement in China to the control of railroads and major cities. On November 3 Konoe announced the establishment of Japan's New Order in East Asia. For a while, Japan hoped that Chiang Kai-shek would give up and head a government under Japanese control. When this hope proved futile Japan turned to Chiang's rival Wang Ching-wei who, reviving the pro-Japanese writings of Sun Yat-sen, the founder of the Nationalist movement, became the head of a puppet government at Nanking in March 1940.

The Background of the Pacific War. In the China War the army was central, but in the events leading to the Pacific War the navy was perhaps the more important service. The 1930 London Disarmament Conference had galvanized opinion within the navy. In the years that followed, those who had been opposed to the Treaty became dominant and used their power 1) to purge many of those in the navy who had supported the Treaty, 2) to push a program of weapons development (new submarines, airplanes, ships, and torpedoes) that would strengthen the navy without infringing on the 5-5-3 capital ships ratio, and 3) to force Japan to withdraw from the international disarmament system by presenting a demand for complete naval parity that of course proved unacceptable to the other powers at the Second London Conference in 1935. Free from the Treaty, Japan began in 1937 a larger program of naval construction. This was carried on secretly so as not to alarm the United States and Britain. As a result, by 1940 the Japanese navy was strong. Its leaders felt that, though it was not a many-ocean fleet, it was more than the equal of any other power in its own waters of the western Pacific.

Following Japan's withdrawal from the disarmament system, which like its earlier withdrawal from the League of Nations weakened its ties to the United States and Britain, Japan moved closer to rapprochement with Germany and Italy. This proved to be a diplomatic blunder, for the problem of Germany was uppermost in the minds of American and British leaders, and only when the problem of Japan become connected with the problem of Germany did United States–Japanese relations begin to worsen decisively. Events in China alone would not have produced the same result.

It is not surprising that militarist Japan eventually became allied with Nazi Germany and Fascist Italy, the only two states in the West that were dissatisfied with the international disarmament system and not critical of Japan's aggression in China. Japan had been culturally close to Germany since the late Meiji period, and there were many who admired the accomplishments of the Nazis. Japan's "New Order in East Asia" almost sounded like a translation from the German. Moreover, the 1936 Anti-Comintern

Pact expressed a common animus against the Soviet Union that prefigured later, more compelling ties. In addition, among the great powers, Japan, Germany, and Italy, were have-not nations, covetous of the riches in the empires of the Western democracies. Still, even given the above factors, there was no straight line linking the Japanese situation in 1937 to the 1941 attack on Pearl Harbor.

Japan's concerns were Asian, not European. From the end of 1938, Japan's main problem was how to settle the mess in China. Each new cabinet proclaimed its intention to extricate Japan from China. Obviously this was to happen on terms favorable to Japan. Much of Japan's diplomatic and military strategy during the late 1930's was directed toward bringing about a situation in which the Chinese government would give in to Japan. A second problem was relations with the Soviet Union. The Soviet potential for action in Asia was in inverse proportion to its involvement in Europe. The threat to Russia in Europe was Germany. This made relations with Germany extremely important to Japan. A third problem was the American Pacific fleet. The Japanese navy viewed this as its most dangerous potential enemy, hence the navy was disposed not to antagonize the United States, if this could be accomplished without weakening the navy. A fourth concern was Southeast Asia, rich in the raw materials needed by Japan for the formation of an autarkic economy. Here Japan was faced by the colonies of France, Holland, and Britain.

Throughout the early part of 1939 Japan sought to strengthen its position against the Soviet Union and to bring pressure to bear on the Chinese government by establishing an alliance either with Germany and Italy or with Britain. Most of the army and many civilian bureaucrats, including Hiranuma (prime minister January–August 1939), leaned toward Germany. But Germany was not willing to ally itself with Japan against Russia alone and insisted that Japan commit itself against Britain and the United States as well. The Foreign and Naval Ministries resisted an alliance based on these terms.

Pro-German groups in Japan were gaining ground when in August 1939 Germany signed a nonaggression pact with the Soviet Union and turned to war on the West. The reaction of the Japanese was that the Germans had made fools of them. Hiranuma said on resigning as prime minister: "Japan's foreign policy is in a state of having been practically betrayed." Japan had wanted an alliance as protection against Russia. Concern with this had mounted during 1938 as Russia extended aid to China, and during the summer months from May to September 1939, even as Germany was concluding the pact, Japanese troops were battling several Russian divisions in a large-scale battle near Nomonhan on the Mongolian-Manchurian border. An armistice was signed in September, but victory had gone to the more highly mechanized Soviet forces. Now Germany had freed the Soviet Union to take an even stronger stance in Asia and had gone to war with Britain.

This brought about a reorientation of Japanese policy. Hiranuma was succeeded as prime minister first by General Abe and then by Admiral Yonai, the latter noted for his pro-British and pro-American leanings. During this period (August 1939–July 1940) German diplomatic advances were repelled by the Japanese, and many leaders attempted to improve relations with the United States and Britain. China remained the stumbling block. The United States Secretary of State, Cordell Hull, was not willing to countenance aggression by abandoning China; hence negotiations in this direction came to nothing. Some have argued that this was a critical moment: had the United States been more flexible, it might have reached an agreement with Japan that would have precluded the later Japanese pact with Germany and Italy. Yet even if the Japanese Foreign Ministry had concluded an agreement with Britain, France, and the United States, the agreement subsequently might have been undone by the Japanese military services.

By late spring of 1940 the situation was changing again. Japan was amazed by the German victories in Europe. The fall of Britain appeared at hand. Again voices were raised in favor of an alliance with Germany. In July the army withdrew its minister, overthrowing the Yonai cabinet. The second Konoe cabinet that replaced it was the most militant yet formed. General Tōjō came in as the representative of the army. Hoshino, a former economic planner in Manchuria, entered as minister without portfolio and head of the Planning Board. And Matsuoka, blunt, erratic, contradictory, and American-educated but wildly pro-German, became foreign minister.

This government signed a Tripartite Pact with Germany and Italy in September 1940. The Pact provided that the signatories would go to war against any nation attacking one of their number—excepting those already at war at the time the Pact was signed. Japan hoped to get four things from this Pact: 1) It wanted better relations with the Soviet Union. Germany, ostensibly on good terms with Russia, offered to act as a go-between. The negotiations took time, but in April 1941 Japan got a neutrality pact with the U.S.S.R. 2) Japan wanted assurances that the colonies in Asia of the colonial powers that Germany was defeating in Europe would enter its New Order. 3) Japan wanted to end the war in China. It felt that China would collapse if materiel and moral support from outside were cut off. It hoped that a Eurasia divided into spheres among Germany, Russia, and Japan would bring about this end. 4) Japan felt that this pact would isolate the United States more than ever, and therefore make it less likely to intervene in China or elsewhere.

Party celebrating the signing of the Tripartite Pact. General Tōjō (in knee boots) watches while Foreign Minister Matsuoka (facing left in the right foreground) proposes a toast, calling the document a "pact for peace."

United States policy in East Asia in the years between 1931 and Pearl Harbor espoused the principles of the Open Door, China's territorial integrity, and nonaggression, but avoided supporting these principles by military action. In part the United States was incapable of action: its army was small and its navy was divided between two oceans. Confronted by Japanese aggression, the United States could only disapprove. Public indignation at Japanese actions in China slowly rose. The bombing of Chinese cities—with bombs made from American scrap, and planes using fuel bought from American companies—was viewed with horror. But, on the whole, the American people were firmly behind the government policy of noninvolvement. The election campaign of 1940 saw each candidate outpeacing the other. When Japan began to move southward in spite of American warnings, the most the United States could do was to invoke economic sanctions. When the Germans overran France, Japanese army observers were sent to Tongking in northern Indo-China in June 1940, and in September army units followed. In response the United States adopted a licensing system to limit exports of aviation gasoline, steel, and scrap iron to Japan. Until this time the United States had been preoccupied with Europe. It had only a secondary concern with East Asia and wished to avoid any Asian entanglement that would weaken its power in the Atlantic. But when the Tripartite

Pact was signed in September 1940 the European crisis merged with the Far Eastern crisis. The slowly rising public opinion against Japan merged with the greater antipathy already felt toward Germany. Consequently, far from isolating the United States as Japan had intended, the Tripartite Pact made the United States more anti-Japanese than before.

The months between the signing of the pact in September 1940 and mid-1941 were in Japan a time of preparation for a further move to the south. Japan wanted to cut off the Chinese government from southern supply routes and to obtain strategic resources. It was felt in Japan, especially in naval circles, that a total embargo might be put into effect by the United States at any moment and that therefore a self-sufficient empire, including the oil-rich Dutch East Indies, was a military necessity. Some favored a move south even at the risk of war. Many, however, were hesitant about moving against Dutch and British colonies while Britain still stood. They did not want war with the United States, which through Lend-Lease and joint military planning, was increasingly involved on the British side.

In June 1941 Japan again found itself betrayed by Germany. Instead of finishing off Britain, and thus facilitating a Japanese move to the south, Germany attacked Russia, giving its ally Japan little advance notice. The German attack put Japan in the humiliating position of having just concluded a neutrality pact with the Soviet Union through the good offices of Germany, while Germany was preparing to invade that country. Germany then compounded the insult by asking Japan to attack the Soviet Union in the east. This occasioned a fierce debate in the army between those who favored war with Russia and those who wanted to move to the south. At an Imperial Conference on July 2, 1941, it was decided to fight Russia if the German armies proved victorious in the west. By September the German armies had been stopped short of Moscow. Japan therefore decided to honor its neutrality pact with Russia and ignore the German request. Instead, with its northern flank in Manchuria now safe from a Soviet attack because of German pressure in Europe, Japan decided to proceed south even at the risk of war with Britain and the United States, unless the United States through last minute negotiations could be persuaded to accept Japan's objectives in China.

Preparation for southward expansion, however, ruined what little chance for success the negotiations might have had. Japanese troops entered southern Indo-China in July 1941, and the United States reacted by placing a total embargo on all exports to Japan. This cut Japanese oil imports to 10 per cent of their previous volume and produced the "crisis of the dwindling stockpile." The Navy General Staff, not averse to war, said that Japan's oil reserves would last only two years. If no action were taken by October, any later action would become impossible and Japan would be forced to retreat step by step until all its gains were lost. This concept was embodied in "an outline plan for carrying out the national policy of the empire" submitted to a meeting of the Liaison Council on September 3, 1941. Faced with the either-or logic of this plan, Japan's leaders decided to go to war with the United States if an agreement regarding oil was not reached by early October. Two days later at a briefing for an Imperial Conference, the emperor said, "This would seem to give precedence to war." Konoe replied that such was not the case; war would come only if diplomacy failed. The naval chief of staff, when asked what a war would mean, compared Japan to a patient critically ill, an operation, though extremely dangerous, might save his life. At the Imperial Conference held the next day that approved this fateful decision, the emperor read a poem by the Meiji emperor:

> *Since all are brothers in the world,*
> *Why is there such constant turmoil?*

What did Japan have in mind when considering the possibility of war? During World War II some fantastic reports of Japanese aims were circulated in the United States: that Japan expected to dictate the terms of peace from the White House or to reduce the United States to the original Thirteen Colonies. This was nonsense. No person in a position of responsibility in Japan held such views. The strategy was to carve out an area within which economic self-sufficiency would be possible and to defend it until the United States tired of war. This was to be achieved by sinking America's Pacific fleet—a stroke in which Japan succeeded, missing only the aircraft carriers. The Japanese plan assumed the victory of Germany in Europe, the defeat of England, and the collapse of the Chinese government, all of which seemed probable in late 1941. It further assumed that, with these conditions fulfilled, Japan could fight the United States on a one-to-one basis in East Asia. It bet the land-based airpower, shorter supply lines, and supposed greater will power of Japan against the greater productivity of America. Beyond war were vague schemes for the division of the world into spheres (Japanese, German, Russian, and American) and the transformation of international relations into intersphere relations.

Yet, though the decision had been taken to go to war if oil were not obtained through negotiations, most Japanese leaders still felt that diplomacy would win out. Japanese efforts to this end began seriously in July 1941 and continued frantically even after the September decision and the formation of the Tōjō cabinet in October. (Of course, the negotiations for peace were accompanied by the move into Indo-China mentioned earlier and by preparations for the Pacific war—Pearl Harbor was rehearsed for months in advance at Kagoshima Bay in southern Kyūshū.)

In July 1941 the second Konoe cabinet was dissolved and the third Konoe cabinet formed in order to get rid of the pro-German foreign minister,

Matsuoka. Concessions were planned. The reasoning of Japan's leaders was that the United States had little effective power in the western Pacific. If Japan pledged minor withdrawals, then the United States ought to be willing to rescind its embargo on oil. War would be averted, and the long-term political outcome in East Asia would depend on the result of the war in Europe. Konoe pressed for a meeting with Roosevelt. He apparently was willing to stipulate that Japan would not go to war with the United States under the provisions of the Axis Pact even if American actions involved it in a war with Germany. More than this the "peace party" in Japan could not offer. Had negotiations been successful, it is conjectural whether the Japanese military services would have accepted this much. The army was clearly not willing to give up its conquests in China, or even to return to the status quo ante of 1937. The navy was aware that the United States' ship-building program, launched by Roosevelt in 1940, would gradually diminish Japan's naval superiority in the western Pacific. Perhaps Japanese military planning had progressed so far that these negotiations were little more than window-dressing—however seriously they were intended by civilian leaders.

In contrast to Konoe's realism, the reasoning of Secretary of State Cordell Hull, the dominant voice in shaping American Far Eastern policy, was sternly moral. Japan was an aggressor. Any compromise would sanction aggression. The United States should not negotiate unless Japan underwent a change of heart. The last chance to put off the war came in November when Japan offered as a temporary *modus vivendi* to turn the clock back to June 1941: withdrawal of Japanese troops from southern Indo-China in return for oil and a United States "hands off" policy toward China. Roosevelt was interested, but Hull blocked acceptance. He feared that any sudden change in American policy would endanger the network of relations that had been established between the United States and Britain, Holland, Australia, and China. He countered by submitting to the Japanese a ten-point program requiring the withdrawal of all Japanese armed forces from Indo-China and China. Behind this uncompromising stand was a calmness and a sense of the ampleness of time that ultimately rested on the belief that Japan would not dare to attack the United States, and that, if it did, it could be quickly and easily defeated.

The Japanese took Hull's program as the rejection of further negotiations. Possessed by the vision of an East Asia dominated by Japan and trapped in a timetable of their own making, they attacked Pearl Harbor on December 7, 1941.

The Nature of Japanese Militarism.   Modern society has both democratic and totalitarian potentials. Industrialization, universal education, the nationalism that enables a government to tap the political energies of the masses, communications and transport, and even modern weapons can be used to create new freedoms or to suppress human rights. Both Nazi Germany and the Soviet Union of Stalin exemplified the totalitarian potential of modern, or modernizing, societies. Postwar Japanese historians, viewing their own history in terms of world experience, have been almost unanimous in terming the changes of the thirties as the growth of fascism in Japan. There were indeed many points of similarity.

Both Japan and Germany moved away from parliamentary government. In both countries a narrow-minded nationalism and the use of terror by a revolutionary right contributed to the rise of authoritarianism. Both limited the freedoms of speech, press, and assembly; and in both, liberals and leftists who attempted to speak out against aggression or oppressive legislation were persecuted. Both were expansionist, aggressive states. Thus, at a high level of abstraction it is possible to combine these features of Japan and Germany with their common historical character as late modernizers (see page 702) and construct a "fascist model" of political change. Yet the differences between Japan and Germany seem as important as the similarities.

First, their governmental structures were basically dissimilar. Germany had undergone the Weimar change; its government was completely parliamentary and power was in the hands of the dominant coalition of parties in the Reichstag. To gain power the Nazis had to obtain a plurality of the votes in a national election. Japanese government in the 1930's was still at the "pre-Weimar" stage. As in Germany before World War I, the Diet was only one of several elites. A shift could occur in the character of the government without a shift in the balance of party power in the Diet. Victory at the polls was not a prerequisite for the rise of authoritarian government.

Second, not only was Japanese government in the 1930's more like that in Germany before World War I, but its society was also considerably less "modern" than that of Hitler's Germany. In Germany there was an almost point-to-point correlation between economic change and political polarization. After the runaway inflation of 1922–1923 both the Nazis and the Communists rose from very small beginnings to become major parties in the elections of 1924—at the expense of the centrist parties. The economic stabilization achieved by 1928 caused both parties to decline sharply at the polls. Then, in the wake of the world depression both spurted ahead in the early thirties and the numerically superior Nazis maneuvered themselves into power. Of this pattern one can say that the direct relation between the individual's awareness of his predicament and his reaction to politics at the national level was pathological, not normal. It reflected the breakdown of intermediate institutions—business, welfare, judiciary, police—that ordinarily buffered the relation between the individual and the state. The Weimar framework was used to carry out what amounted to direct plebiscites between two extreme, antiparliamentary programs.

In contrast, the traditional (post-1890) social structure was relatively firm in Japan. The two major parties were both centrist, and they were never seriously challenged by an extremist mass party. They continued to get the bulk of the votes, and often the votes went to the more parliamentary of the two. The revolutionary extremist groups that came to prominence in 1931–1936 had little influence on the support given to the Seiyūkai and the Minseitō at the polls. And these two parties totally defeated the government-supported parties in the 1936 and 1937 elections. The only other tendency visible in the elections of the 1930's was the slow secular trend in favor of semiliberal socialist parties. Behind the stability in Japanese voting was the fact that intermediate institutions—as in the 1920's —were in good condition. They "contained" the misery of the poorer peasants and workers in the worst years of the depression. The Japanese middle class, such as it was, was also in better shape than its German equivalent. War and inflation wiped out the savings of the middle class in Germany; when the depression came there was nothing for it to fall back on. The Japanese middle class did very well during the war and the 1920's without encountering any serious inflation. The depression hurt small and medium-sized businesses, but bank savings and salaries were worth more than ever. Many remember the early thirties as the "best" period in prewar Japan.

Third, because the government structures and societies were different, the process by which the "antiparliamentary forces" rose was also very different. The Nazis rose as a mass party with a revolutionary program. Taking over the government, the Nazi party remade it in its own image, step by step establishing authoritarian controls. Having created a totalitarian regime, it then made war. Without exaggerating its efficiency, there is no denying its dynamism. But in Japan the antiparliamentary forces were not a dynamic, purposive, united group. It is hard even to characterize those who in the 1930's gradually replaced the party leaders in the cabinets, except to say that they were ex-bureaucrats and ex-military men, former members of the Peers and former members of the Privy Council. Those men did not plot to seize power. Rather, they were appointed in the hope that they would be more effective than the parties in controlling the army. The times were not propitious for the parties, so nonparty prime ministers and then more and more nonparty ministers were appointed. Behind this "drift" within the establishment were the disputes, maneuvers, and compromises among the multiple elites of government. Communications were often poor and actions uncoordinated. One Japanese scholar has described Japan's path to war as a gradual nervous breakdown within the system. The most dynamic groups

724 East Asia: Tradition and Transformation

Ceremonial send-off given by schoolmates for a student entering the army.

were the military services, which tended to confuse military strategy with national policy. Military services tend to be politically strong in early modernizing states and weak in fully modern states. Japan was not fully modern. Within a relatively modern state structure, the power of the Japanese army and navy stemmed from the fact that legally they had never been fully subordinated to civil control. By the summer of 1937 Japan was less parliamentary than in 1931, but was not yet totalitarian in the Nazi sense.

The first turning point came when Japan blundered into war with China. The second turning point was Pearl Harbor. War led to wartime controls. A Liaison Council was formed to coordinate policy making between the cabinet and services. A Planning Board was established to direct wartime economic expansion and administer economic controls over resources, labor, trade, prices, wages, and public services. The economy became laced and overlaced with regulations, moving largely in response to government direction. Finally an Imperial Rule Assistance Association—patterned after the Nazi "one country, one party" model—was set up for spiritual mobilization and all of Japan's major political parties were brought within it as well as unions, veterans organizations, and many others. Such control made Japan into something more of a totalitarian state by 1941. Moreover, official controls were reinforced by community and family pressures far greater than those in the West. These demanded "right thoughts" as well as "right actions," and led to the ethical climate in which university students could be recruited as suicide pilots in the last desperate years of the war. But Japan in this period is better labeled militarist than fascist. The basic state apparatus was not new or revolutionary, but merely the old "establishment," now dominated by the military elite, overlaid by controls, and swept up in a spiritual nationalism. When the war ended, opinion shifted and the controls were removed, and until the reforms of the Occupation took hold, the basic state structure was much the same as it had been earlier.

Finally, the spiritual difference between Nazi Germany and militarist Japan was immense. In Germany Teutonic myths were used as a vehicle for values that would sanction aggression, but the myths were never presented as literal truth. The problem of reconciling myth with science did not arise. The break with the past was with the moral position of Christianity, liberalism, and socialism. The enormity of the break necessitated concentration camps for those who opposed Nazi power. In Japan it was not necessary to disinter archaic myths. They were still alive in the traditional sector of Japan's cultural double-structure and could be used to justify Japanese expansion.

Moreover, along with myths, there was a rational dimension to the Japanese position in the 1930's. Certainly the colonial powers of the West were hypocritical in condemning Japan's takeover of Manchuria. In the depression world of rising tariff barriers and preferential markets, arguments for economic autarky were reasonable, even if the means taken to obtain it were not. As a result, most Japanese could make the transition from the liberal orthodoxy of the 1920's to the wartime orthodoxy of the late 1930's with little sense of a moral break. Many persons were sent to prison, but concentration camps were unnecessary. And after the war, although antimilitarism (the total rejection of the policies of the former leadership) was strong, there was little sense of individual guilt—except in the attitudes of intellectuals toward the countries overrun in Asia.

24. China: From Monarchy to Warlordism

The Late Ch'ing Reforms

China in the early twentieth century was still absorbed in a process of incipient revolution such as Japan had gone through in the 1860's. The old order had begun to crack after Japan's attack in 1894–1895, but its political structure remained standing for another fifteen years.

The final decade of the Ch'ing dynasty from 1901 to 1911 was less a period of collapse than of new beginnings. Institutional and social change began early, political disaster came only at the end. Up to 1911, in fact, the Chinese state pursued a gradual reconstruction along lines that had been advocated unavailingly in the 1890's. The Empress Dowager and her conservative supporters, having thrown the Kuang-hsü emperor and K'ang Yu-wei out of power in 1898 (see page 634), proceeded to give effect after 1901 to most of their radical reform program. In truth, they had no alternative. The Boxer War had shown the bankruptcy of mere antiforeignism, while the threat of anti-Ch'ing rebellion goaded the regime into constructive action to save itself. Conservative reform was thus the principal movement on the Chinese public scene. The republican revolutionary effort grew up on the periphery, fragmented and inconsequential until 1905, and afterward still a minor eddy in the stream of change.

It was reformers, not revolutionaries, who mainly prepared the ground for revolution. Great changes were at last under way in Chinese life, and the alien Ch'ing dynasty, trying to guide these changes, could not avoid nurturing anti-Ch'ing and centrifugal forces that would eventually destroy it. Students the government trained abroad, new armies it trained at home, merchants it encouraged in domestic enterprise, political assemblies it convoked in the provinces, all sooner or later turned against the dynasty. In political quicksand, the more the dynasty struggled to save itself, the deeper it sank. For modernization now meant Chinese nationalism, which implied the end of Manchu rule.

Along this one-way street leading to political disaster, however, the late Ch'ing reforms deserve study as attempted solutions to China's peculiar problems of modernization. Chang Chih-tung and Liu K'un-i, the Yangtze "viceroys" (governors-general respectively of Hunan-Hupei and of Kiangsi-Anhwei-Kiangsu), who in 1900 had dexterously remained both at peace with the foreigners and loyal to the dynasty, presented three memorials to the Empress Dowager in July 1901, outlining a broad program reminiscent of the Hundred Days of 1898. They understated a few blunt truths: "... popular feelings are not the same as thirty years ago. The people admire the wealth of foreign countries and despise the poverty of the Middle Kingdom." They admire foreign troops, the "fair play" of the Maritime Customs Service, the strict orderliness of foreign concessions. "Rebels are slowly emerging" and spreading subversive doctrines. Their catalogue of needed reforms was longer than ever, but it is significant that education, to create a new elite, was still first on the list.

Education: New Schools, New Scholars. The general aim of the educational program was to train and select officials more effectively. Its aim was not mass education of the Chinese people, nor was it liberal education of the Chinese individual. The main problem was how to appease the contemporary generation of scholar-officials in office and the classically trained aspirants for office, all of whom had a vested interest in the classical examination system. The solution was a compromise: to set up a hierarchy of schools at all the territorial levels of government—county, prefecture, province, and imperial capital—parallel to and feeding into the traditional examinations. In time, after about ten years, the new schools, supported by contributions from the public, would supplant the old examination system. Meantime, it was hoped, the two systems could be used side by side. Candidates prepared in the new schools and candidates prepared privately in the traditional way would alike take the regular examinations, which would be somewhat modernized in content. As first steps, the "eight-legged essay" (see page 190) was abolished and the old-style academies (*shu-yüan*) were ordered converted into government schools.

Unfortunately it soon appeared that the traditional route to office of private preparation for the examinations would continue to be cheaper, easier, and more attractive than the new route, which led through years of costly schooling. The majority of old-style aspirants for office would shun the new government schools. On the other hand, among the restive, modern-minded youth, the new government schools faced competition from Christian missionary education in strategic urban centers. By 1905, Protestant missions had some 389 "intermediate and high schools and colleges" with fifteen thousand students. These institutions were setting a revolutionary example by fostering Christianity, individualism, education of women, and Western ways generally, all under the protection of extraterritoriality. They refused to have their students pay homage to Confucius or the emperor, as required in government schools. (Peking countered by barring mission school graduates from official careers.) Private Chinese modern education was also beginning. In 1904 an able young graduate of the Peiyang naval academy, Chang Po-ling, opened at Tientsin a middle school which acquired a campus and by 1909 grew into Nankai University.

Faced with this competition from the old-fashioned, who clung to the examinations, and the modern-minded, who flocked to missionary and private schools, Chang Chih-tung concluded in 1903 that the new school system could secure neither students nor popular financial support until the examination system ceased to exist as an alternative. In 1905 the leading provincial officials urged its immediate abolition, which was ordered to take effect the next year. The government's educational hopes now lay entirely with the new schools. A Ministry of Education was created in 1906 to supervise them.

The new system, modeled on the Japanese, called for specialization after middle school to produce specialists for government service. The massive and detailed regulations issued in 1904 followed Japan's example in leading students through higher elementary school (four years), middle school (five years), and higher school (three years, achieving the degree of *chü-jen*) to the Imperial University (three years, achieving the degree of *chin-shih*). The Imperial University had been created in 1898 with W. A. P. Martin, the American who had been head of the Interpreters College (T'ung-wen Kuan) from 1869 to 1895, as first dean of Western studies. In 1902 the university absorbed the Interpreters College. But below this top institution the new school system across the land lacked modern-trained faculties, buildings, equipment, funds, and leadership. It was easier to found colleges than middle schools, easier to inaugurate middle schools than primary schools. The system remained weakest at the base.

Provincial educators also found their chief inspiration in Japan. Chang Chih-tung sent two missions to study the Japanese system and buy textbooks. He began to see the need for general public education, in order to find talent among the people. Soon he imported Japanese professors, who could communicate with their Chinese colleagues and students at least in writing. He began to look to Japan as the best training ground for the new generation of Chinese schoolteachers—cheaper than the West because Japan was near at hand, easier because Japan's "language, literature, and customs" were close to China's and because many Western books had already been translated into Japanese. In addition, Chinese students could be supervised more easily in Japan by Chinese government inspectors.

The flow to Tōkyō of Chinese youth seeking modern education had begun by 1896. After the suppression of the 1898 reform movement, Chinese students in Japan rose to about two hundred in 1899, one thousand in 1903, thirteen hundred in 1904, roughly eight thousand by the end of 1905, and thirteen thousand or more in 1906. But the number who went exceeded by far the number who enrolled in serious academic studies, which in turn far exceeded the number who eventually graduated. Indeed, the Chinese graduates from reputable Japanese institutions before 1912 never exceeded seven hundred a year. Among the many thousands who went to Japan in the last decade of the Ch'ing, something like one-half were supported by Chinese government funds, mainly from provincial governments. They often prepared in new provincial schools and usually were sent in annual delegations to Tōkyō. There they followed the Chinese practice of organizing associations or guilds (*hui*) among fellow provincials, reminiscent of the regional guilds organized by officials, gentry, and merchants in Peking and other major cities over the centuries. As a result the new educational system brought young men and even some young women together more intimately, over a longer period and in circumstances more stimulating to group cohesion, than the old examinations had ever done. Just as the new student life in China nurtured provincial consciousness and provincial loyalties, so life in Tōkyō nourished nationalism.

In this way Chinese education was quietly revolutionized. Classical studies gave way to a mixed Sino-Western curriculum. Private preparation for triennial examinations on traditional themes gave way to school life day by day, a broader range of ideas, more social and intellectual contact. Instead of indoctrinated scholar-gentry loyal to Confucius and the Son of Heaven, the new system produced revolutionists. Chang Chih-tung could carefully prescribe light-blue gowns, hats with red tassels, a multitude of rules to foster decorum among his students, and an edifying song: "The Holy Son of Heaven plans for self-strengthening.... Hygiene makes the people strong and healthy.... Honor parents, respect rulers...." But once the examination system had been washed away, there was no checking the tides of change.

The intellectual content of the new education, in China as in Japan, now contained much from the West. Despite so many decades of increasing Western contact, it was only after 1900 that the Chinese scholar class really began to absorb Western ideas. A famous popularizer of Western fiction, Lin Shu, had already been turning out by hearsay (i.e., by listening to oral translations) his Chinese versions of Dickens, Dumas, Scott, Balzac, and others—156 works in all. To this continuing literary fare were now added Yen Fu's translations and interpretations of the classics of Western liberalism. Having joined the Chinese navy, Yen saw the world, especially England, in the 1870's and concluded that the secret of Western power was Western thought. He became a convert to Herbert Spencer's Social Darwinism: the individual's energetic self-realization must help his nation to compete and survive. Liberal principles, Yen Fu felt, were needed more to augment China's national wealth and power than to foster individual freedom. Democratic self-government would be premature. The translator tried especially to convey those ideas of Victorian Britain that seemed most meaningful for late-Ch'ing China. T. H. Huxley's *Evolution and Ethics* appeared in classical Chinese with Yen's commentaries in 1898, followed in the next decade by works of Adam Smith, J. S. Mill, Montesquieu, and others. Yen Fu's translations and commentaries, by exalting Western logic, law, science, and evolution, severely indicted China's sages as the cause of her backwardness, yet did it as an inside job, in classical Chinese addressed to the literati.

New Armies: The Rise of Yüan Shih-k'ai.   By 1901 China had inherited from her distant and recent past three main types of military organization. The Manchu banner forces, still subsisting on their inadequate stipends, together with the decentralized Chinese constabulary ("Army of the Green Standard"), were effete and useles. A few thousand bannermen had been given modern guns and formed into the Peking Field Force in 1862. Later, selected units of the constabulary, especially around Peking, had received arms and training. But the officers were still chosen by their prowess in mounted and dismounted archery, sword-brandishing, pulling a powerful bow, and lifting a heavy stone, an antic ritual of no modern use. The old-style military examinations were abolished in August 1901, and new military academies ordered established.

The second type of military formation was the regional armies commanded by Chinese civil officials. Their prototype had been the precedent-breaking Hunan Army (see page 473) built up by Tseng Kuo-fan after 1852. Its peasant recruits had been officered by gentry and organized in battalions of 500 soldiers plus some 180 carriers for logistic support—nominally, one porter for every three soldiers. Despite Tseng's formal disbandment of the Hunan Army (see page 564), it had continued to exist, along with the Anhwei Army created by Li Hung-chang and similar forces organized by Tso Tsung-t'ang and others against the mid-century rebels. These gentry-led, regionally recruited armies were composed not of mere militia (*t'uan-lien*), in the sense of part-time farmer-soldiers, but rather of professional fighting men (*yung,* "braves"). With their own personal networks of leaders and sources of local support, they became vested interests, supplanted the bannermen and constabulary in the provinces, and came to be known generically as the Defense Army. The Anhwei Army (under Li at Tientsin) and the Hunan Army (led by Liu K'un-i at Nanking) had been the dominant rivals among these forces. Although usually equipped with modern rifles and artillery instead of the old matchlocks and smooth-bore cannon, they still lacked standardized armament as well as modern-trained officers and staff specialists, to say nothing of engineer, signal, quartermaster, modern transport, or medical services.

The third and most recent type of military organization had developed in response to Japan's aggression. Both Li and Chang Chih-tung had set up military academies in the 1880's and hired German instructors to train a new officer corps. Chang created a Self-Strengthening Army at Nanking in 1895 on the German model. Its three thousand men were carefully selected, well-paid country boys. A more significant unit developed under Yüan Shih-k'ai, a military more than a civil official, who had risen as Li's pro-consul in Korea (see page 616). Appointed in 1895 to train a new imperial army with German instructors to be financed by the Board of Revenue, he soon had seven thousand men in training near Tientsin, recruited from several provinces and well paid, with precautions against the usual cor-ruption. Through his personal leadership of this new force, which came to be known as the Peiyang Army, Yüan laid the foundation of the "Peiyang clique" and became the "father of the warlords." Among his early officers were at least ten men who after the revolution were to become military governors of provinces, and five (in addition to Yüan himself) who became presidents or premiers of the Peking government under the republic.

The deaths of Li Hung-chang (1901) and Liu K'un-i (1902) left Yüan Shih-k'ai, in his mid-forties, the chief army-builder in the empire. Inheriting Li's position as governor-general of Chihli from 1901 to 1907, he worked closely with the top Manchu, the notoriously corrupt Prince Ch'ing, who had held the highest positions in foreign affairs at Peking ever since the dismissal of Prince Kung in 1884. Yüan's build-up of six divisions of his Peiyang Army, with its half-dozen diversified military schools, miniature general staff, well-drilled troops, and impressive maneuvers, was imitated, incompletely and less effectively, in most of the provinces.

For the Ch'ing Empire, still fragmented by regional-provincial interests, genuine military centralization was politically impossible. A reorganization in 1904 left China's armies still controlled essentially at the provincial level. The New Army blueprint called for thirty-six divisions, but it lacked the essential ingredients of centralized direction, adequate financing, and industrial support. The chief innovation was that new military academies, like that at Paoting near Peking, now produced a new class of scholar-officers, military activists imbued with patriotism, who combined modern military skills with the scholar's sense of responsibility for putting the empire in order. Japanese instructors, cheaper than Germans, were hired in increasing numbers, and Chinese officer candidates were sent to military

BOAT-TRACKING ON THE YANGTZE. *Photographed in the 1940's. The second junk is held inshore by four lines and hauled upstream by one line attached to 19 or more trackers, who pull with right arm and left shoulder-band.*

MAN-TRANSPORT IN SZECHWAN. *Porters resting with 298- and 317-pound loads of brick tea en route to Tibet, 1908.*

academies in Japan, where their patriotism was further aroused by the example of a foreign land. Chiang Kai-shek, of Chekiang, aged eighteen, attended Paoting in 1906 and went to Japan in 1907.

Administrative Reform: The Central-Provincial Power Balance. The Ch'ing administration, inherited from the early Ming and refined during more than four centuries, had served the agrarian-based Chinese Empire well enough until about 1800. But just as the mounted archer had been supplanted rather suddenly by the railroad and rifle, and the sailing junk by the steamship, so the imperial government had become outmoded. China now needed dynamic central organs to perform new functions with unwonted initiative and speed, apply new laws and fiscal procedures, and be more fully acknowledged by the provinces as their superior and coordinator. But such a unitary national government would upset the ancient balance between Peking and the provinces. The provincial administrations still were a separate echelon parallel to the metropolitan administration, and they still reported directly to the emperor. The provinces were merely supervised and serviced, rather than directed and controlled, by the Six Ministries at the capital. Unfortunately for Peking, the late nineteenth-century growth of regionalism that began with Chinese gentry-led suppression of the rebellions, had also been helped by the growth of treaty-port industries, local trade revenues, regional armies, and personal bureaucratic machines. All these new things had strengthened the major provincial governments in the power structure, quite contrary to the increasing need for stronger government at the center. Centralization consequently faced both the bureaucratic inertia of old vested interests and the restive jealousy of new provincial interests.

Reforms at Peking were generally begun by new agencies set up along-side, within, or under the ancient organs of government; as the new organs grew stronger, the ancient ones withered. In 1901, as required by the Boxer Protocol, the Tsungli Yamen became a full-scale Ministry of Foreign Affairs (Wai-wu Pu). In 1905 a Ministry of Police was inaugurated, forerunner of a Ministry of Internal Affairs. In the reorganization of 1906, the new Ministry of Education took over the examining function of the Ministry of Ceremonies, while the old Ministry of War, customarily headed by civil officers, was expanded into the Army Ministry, headed by ambitious Manchu generals. Innovations started by "bureaus" (*chü*) in the coastal provinces also began to be pursued by committees or new ministries at Peking. After bureaus of commercial affairs had first promoted chambers of commerce, commercial newspapers, and business and industrial schools in leading provinces, a Ministry of Commerce was set up at Peking in 1903. It eventually absorbed the old Ministry of Works and became a Ministry of Agriculture, Industry, and Commerce, trying to promote railroad-building, industrial exhibits, standard weights and measures, registration of firms, mining regulations, company law, farmers' associations, and other modern measures. Typically, it offered official rank as a reward for economic achievement.

New structures at Peking were easier to inaugurate than new processes over the empire. Legal reform, for example, was held by the foreign powers to be prerequisite, as in Japan, to any abolition of extraterritoriality. In 1904 a law-compilation bureau began work under Shen Chia-pen, a sixty-five-year-old scholar-veteran of the Ministry of Punishments. He began by trying to give modern expression to traditional social values but ended up proposing revolutionary changes. In 1907 Shen put forward a draft criminal code based on Japanese and German models which would have distinguished law from morality—that is, it would have made the Confucian rules of propriety, such as filial piety, legally unenforceable. By also making all persons outside the imperial family equal before the law, Shen would have dealt a blow to the five relationships and the whole hierarchic social order based on distinctions of status, age, and sex. His draft was rejected.

He also presented, however, a less drastic revision of the Ch'ing code which was finally promulgated in 1910 and remained in force until after 1928. It contributed to modernization by reducing corporal punishment and torture; abolishing branding, slicing, slavery, and public exposure of heads and corpses; substituting individual for collective responsibility; distinguishing between civil and criminal law; and enunciating certain general principles to guide the application of the numerous specific regulations or "supplementary laws" (*li*). These had accumulated during the dynasty to a total of about nineteen hundred items, a corpus of rather concrete but often mutually contradictory rules which magistrates could not apply with any degree of consistency or predictability. This ambiguity and uncertainty as to the law applicable to a case, added to the fact that law had been neither primary nor pervasive in Chinese society, had left the judicial function of magistrates stunted and undeveloped, to say nothing of the whole world of legal philosophy and phraseology and the legal profession itself. Though he reduced the number of *li*, Shen Chia-pen could not remake this situation.

Financial reform was even more difficult, not only because it threatened so many "rice bowls" (individual incomes) but also because the inherited fiscal system was so superficial and weak to begin with. Actual tax collections over the empire remained largely unknown, unbudgeted, and unaccounted for. Local tax collectors, as well as the provincial regimes above them, still had to live on what they collected. Moreover, the tax quotas officially received were not centralized in a "common purse." Instead, they were listed as fixed sums due from a multitude of specific sources and allotted to a multitude of specific uses. Revenues from a province were allotted in bits and pieces to meet needs in it or elsewhere. Of the eighteen provinces, thirteen regularly forwarded fixed allotments for specific purposes to other provinces. For example, the 7 million taels to maintain the bannermen in Peking came from fifty-two different sources over the empire. This *ad hoc* procedure tied the imperial revenues to an infinite number of vested interests, mainly the support of officials and soldiers. Finally, even at Peking there was no single fiscal authority. The imperial revenues about 1905 totaled on the books roughly 70 million United States dollars, a small sum for so large a country. Yet the new trade taxes—customs and likin—were earmarked for foreign indemnity payments, while the traditional land tax quotas remained inelastic. The Ministry of Finance, although reorganized in 1906, still could not achieve central control. Other ministries continued to receive and expend their traditional revenues and even set up their own banks, like the Bank of Communications (1907).

A novel effort to make a national budget began with nationwide revenue surveys in 1908 and the compilation of budget estimates in 1910, in which central-and-provincial government revenues and expenditures were differentiated from local. This produced estimates of total revenues (297 million taels) and expenditures (national-including-provincial, 338 million taels; local, 37 million taels) which presaged a sizable deficit (78 million taels). Unfortunately, planning and budgeting, collecting statistics, and setting tax rates, went on uncoordinated in both the central ministries and the provinces, with the provinces not subordinate to the ministries and yet expected to supply the revenues. This basic lack of centrality was deeply rooted in Chinese custom, political values, and social structure. It became apparent that the Ch'ing government, which had been superficial, passive, and indeed parasitic for so long, could become modern only by greatly expanding its functions and asserting central leadership. For an alien dynasty in an era of rising nationalism, this was impossible.

Constitutionalism, Provincialism, and Nationalism. When Japan's constitutional monarchy defeated Russia's tsarist autocracy in 1905, constitutionalism seemed to have proved itself as a basis for unity between rulers and ruled in a national effort. Even Russia now moved toward parliamentary government. Constitutionalism in China, it was hoped, might give the rising provincial interests a meaningful share in the dynastic government and so keep them loyal to it. Between 1906 and 1911 Peking actively pursued a dual program to combine administrative modernization and constitutionalism. Such changes, however, precipitated a struggle for power, both within the central government and between it and the provinces. At the capital, the Manchu princes succeeded in maintaining, or even enlarging, their grip on key posts while preventing really fundamental reforms. This pro-Manchu and therefore anti-Chinese coloration at Peking antagonized the rising spirit of nationalism in the rest of China.

The new nationalism produced in 1905 China's first modern boycott, against the United States' discriminatory treatment of Chinese, particularly the total exclusion of laborers. In this boycott, the old tradition of cessation of business by local merchant guilds was expanded nationwide to most of the treaty ports, especially Shanghai and Canton, where students joined merchants in mass meetings and modern press agitation. American trade was damaged for some months, and Peking hesitated to repress this popular antiforeign movement lest it become antidynastic also.

Under the pressure of rising nationalist sentiment, the court sent two official missions to study constitutionalism abroad in the first half of 1906. One visited mainly the United States and Germany; the other, Japan, England, and France. Prince Itō lectured the visitors to Japan on the necessity of the emperor's retaining supreme power, not letting it fall into the hands of the people. On their return they recommended following this Japanese view, that a constitution and civil liberties including "public discussion," all granted by the emperor, could actually strengthen his position because he would remain above them all. In September 1906 the Empress Dowager promised "a constitutional polity" after due preparation. In August 1908 she proclaimed a set of principles to guide a nine-year program to prepare for constitutional self-government. Consultative provincial assemblies were to be convened in 1909 and a consultative national assembly in 1910. Even this idea of a nine-years' tutelage imitated Japan, where in 1881 the Diet had been promised for 1890.

The Ch'ing regime was grievously weakened by the death of the Empress Dowager on November 15, 1908. For half a century the "Old Buddha" (*Lao Fo-yeh*), as she was respectfully called in common parlance, had been at the center of power, exerting a tremendous influence that is still almost unstudied. She was a great patron, for example, of the colorful, northern-style "Peking opera" but lacked the ability of a K'ang-hsi or Ch'ien-lung, in far different times, to be a leading connoisseur of art and patron of literature. On her death, the demise of the hapless but not unhealthy Kuang-hsü emperor was announced as having occurred on the preceding day. His mysterious death at thirty-seven destroyed China's best chance for a transition to a constitutional monarchy and left the throne in the hands of ignorant and vainglorious Manchu princes. The Empress Dowager had named as his successor her three-year-old grand-nephew, Pu-yi, who reigned as the Hsüan-t'ung emperor (1909–1912), with his father, the second Prince Ch'un, as regent. Sir Robert Hart, the Inspector General of Customs, returned to England in 1908, Yüan Shih-k'ai was forced to retire in January 1909, and Chang Chih-tung died in October.

The dynasty's reform effort, too grudging and too slow, now faced more problems than it could solve. For example, the new central administration reorganized under eleven ministries in 1906 needed coordination through a cabinet. But such an agency, if packed and dominated by the prime minister, might eclipse the throne as the source of executive action. The Ch'ing regency feared to create it.

By February 1910, representatives of all the sixteen new provincial assemblies gathered at Peking. Representing a vociferous, nationwide movement, they petitioned the throne to set up a national parliament. This was rejected, but the petitioning continued. The demand for government by a genuine parliament and cabinet became intensified after the consultative national assembly, consisting of one hundred appointees of the throne and one hundred of the provincial assemblies, convened in October 1910. Thus pressed, the regent promised a parliament for 1913 and meanwhile, in April 1911, at long last established a cabinet, but with incredible ineptitude he appointed eight Manchus, one Mongol bannerman, and only four Chinese!

The Railway Controversy.   Provincial conflict with the central power came to a head over railway-building. China's late nineteenth-century policy of avoiding foreign-financed and foreign-run railways had been smashed in the scramble of 1898. Foreign-controlled lines—Russian and Japanese in Manchuria, German in Shantung, and French in Yunnan—had now become tools of economic imperialism, preliminary to opening mines, extracting resources, and exploiting markets. Other lines, though nominally owned by the Ch'ing government, had been financed under contract by foreign banking syndicates, which commonly floated bond issues to raise funds as foreign loans to the Chinese government. They then built the lines and managed them as trustees for the foreign bondholders, holding a first mortgage on the railway as security for the original loan. China was thus entering the railway age with foreign financiers awaiting the profits.

Consequently a patriotic "rights recovery" movement arose in most provinces, where local groups demanded redemption of the foreign lines and formed companies to build Chinese provincial lines. With the moral support of provincial leaders in Hupei, Hunan, and Kwangtung, Chang Chih-tung got a British loan in 1905 and redeemed the American China Development Company's contract of 1898 to build the Hankow-Canton railway. But provincial resources proved inadequate to finance construction. Though doubly inspired by patriotism and hope of profit, these merchant-gentry railway companies found it difficult to raise the capital needed to purchase a right of way, pay the land tax on it, and buy foreign rolling stock. Speculation and corruption also handicapped their efforts, which in any case ran counter to the technological need for central planning and direction of any railroad network.

The chief proponent of railway centralization was Sheng Hsüan-huai, who had risen under the patronage of Li Hung-chang and Chang Chih-tung in turn (see pages 588 and 605) and by 1908 had got control over both the China Merchants' steamship line and Chang's industrial base around Hankow. In that year Sheng combined the Han-yang arsenal, the Ta-yeh iron mines (80 miles away in Hupei), and the coal mines at P'ing-hsiang (250 miles south in Kiangsi) to form the Han-Yeh-P'ing Coal and Iron Company. To finance it he had already become dependent on Japanese loans, just as Japan's steel works at Yawata, begun in 1896, had become dependent on iron ore from Ta-yeh. Already illicitly rich from his "official supervision" of textile mills, telegraphs, and other enterprises, Sheng now worked with the Manchu minister of finance at Peking to float foreign loans, in particular to build railways from Hankow to Canton and from Hankow into Szechwan. These were the so-called "Hukuang railways" (the line from Hankow to Peking had been completed in 1905). Thus railway-building had become a major political issue. Peking's technically necessary leadership in railway development, and the foreign loans needed for it, had got thoroughly embrangled with Sheng Hsüan-huai's well-known corruption, provincial opposition to central power, and anti-Manchu feeling in general.

Since railroad loans had become a chief tool of imperialist encroachment, the United States now became quixotically involved under the Taft administration in defending the Open Door through the contradictory method of "dollar diplomacy." Secretary of State Philander C. Knox made a vague proposal in November 1909 for "neutralization" of the railways in Manchuria. This, however, ran counter to the British policy after 1907 of acquiescing in the Russo-Japanese expansion in Manchuria. Knox's ill-conceived proposal only stimulated Japan and Russia to reaffirm secretly in 1910 their division of spheres in the Northeast. Meanwhile, in July 1909 President Taft had intervened in the Hukuang railway loan negotiations with a personal telegram to the regent at Peking, demanding "equal participation by American capital" so that it could promote "the welfare of China and...her territorial integrity." This got the Morgan group of banks included in a four-power (French, British, German, American) banking consortium set up in 1910.

The final contract of the consortium, signed with Sheng in May 1911, coincided with an imperial decree, which Sheng had advocated, to nationalize, buy out, and put under Peking's control all provincial railway projects. This rebuff to provincial interests threw the fat in the fire. To patriots in the provinces it seemed that the Manchus and their corrupt henchmen were selling China to foreign bankers for their own profit. A "railway protection" movement sprang up, particularly in Szechwan, with mass meetings and anguished petitions to Peking, all in vain. The Szechwan movement intensified. Shops and schools were closed. Tax payments were stopped. Peasant support was mobilized. In September the government moved

MEMORIAL ARCH TO A
VIRTUOUS WIDOW. *Near
Chiung-chou, Szechwan, 1908.
Topmost inscription:
"Chaste and filial."*

troops, shot down demonstrators, and seized the gentry leaders. Typically, these men were degree-holders of means, with landlord-merchant backgrounds, who had studied in Japan, were now prominent in the provincial assembly, and had invested heavily in railway projects. Their antiforeign slogan, "Szechwan for the Szechwanese," represented the interest of the provincial ruling class, which had now become violently antidynastic.

Thus the decade of late Ch'ing reforms had seen the beginning of a social and institutional transformation. After the Boxer fiasco, the modern world began to flood into China and the pace of change accelerated. Missionary education and the Y.M.C.A. began to reach upper-class and city youth. The attack on footbinding marked the beginning of the emancipation of Chinese women. Two traditionally disesteemed professions, the merchant and the military, acquired new prestige. The nineteenth-century treaty-port mandarins and compradors who had specialized in dealing with foreigners at the ports began to be superseded by officials trained abroad and by merchant-capitalist entrepreneurs of broader background. Some landlord gentry, no longer oriented toward official examinations and imperial preferment, had developed local commercial and industrial interests. Basically conservative, this provincial elite had supported the constitutional movement in hopes that a parliament at Peking could link them with the ruling power, and that a cabinet responsible to parliament, holding the bureaucracy responsible in turn, could modernize China's finances, administration, and

public services. After 1909 the provincial assemblies had become new
political institutions, centers of policy discussion and political organization.

The modern press in the urban centers, most of which were treaty ports,
served as the bloodstream of this new life of politics. Chinese periodicals had
been started in large part by missionaries up to 1895, but most of the sixty
or so publications begun during the next fifteen years down to 1911 were
purely Chinese ventures that combined commercial journalism with reformist ideas. New dailies sprang up in Shanghai to join the pioneer *Shun
Pao,* founded in 1872, which had reached a circulation of fifteen thousand by
1895. The Commercial Press, another pioneer in modern publishing, was
founded in 1897 and spread new textbooks among the schools. By 1911 the
provincial assemblies and the press provided a forum for both the "gentry"
interests and the new class of young students and military officers—"Young
China." Constitutional monarchy was still the slogan of the day, but the
dynastic order had been fatally undermined by revolutionary ideas.

The Revolution of 1911

The Japanese Influence. New regimes in China have often started their
conquest from an external base—witness the Khitan, Jurchen, Mongol, and
Manchu conquerors between the tenth and the seventeenth centuries. In the
early twentieth century the treaty ports, the Overseas Chinese communities
in Southeast Asia and elsewhere, and the Japanese Empire all gave shelter
to Chinese rebels. In fact, the Revolution of 1911 was largely made in
Japan.

This idea of the formative role of Japan has been unpalatable and rather
disregarded, both among Western peoples, whose forebears stimulated
China's Westernization, and among Chinese patriots, who have suffered
from later Japanese aggression. Nevertheless, the period from 1898 to 1914
saw a major Japanese impact on the course of Chinese history. Japan was
alike the model of Ch'ing government reformers and until about 1907 the
home base for anti-Ch'ing revolutionaries. Republican China went to school
in Tōkyō. The Japanese stimulus to modern education, militarism, and constitutionalism in China, already noted, was part of a broader contribution
to the rise of Chinese nationalism in general. Japan's influence in this brief
period was more direct, profound, and far-reaching than that of Britain in
the nineteenth century or of the United States from 1915 to 1949, or even,
one may suspect, of the Soviet Union in the 1950's. One reason for this was
Japan's cultural as well as geographical propinquity. Another reason was the
historical circumstance that, in this dawn of their modern age, China was
most eager to learn and Japan most eager to teach, as yet without serious
conflicts of national interest.

Japan's coming of age as a great power between 1895 and 1905 made her the model for Asia in the eyes of patriots not only in other Asian lands but also in Japan. It fortified the dream of Japan's pan-Asian leadership toward modernization and against Western imperialism. Japanese interest in contemporary China was expressed in organizations like the East Asian Common Culture Society (Tōa Dōbun Kai) founded by political, cultural, and expansionist leaders in 1898. China was studied historically at Tōkyō and Kyōto, centers of contemporary research were established in Taiwan, at Mukden by the South Manchurian Railway Company, and at Shanghai. To promote Japan's continental expansion beyond Korea and against Russia, the ultrapatriotic Amur River Society (lit., "Black Dragon Society" from the Chinese name for the Amur), founded in 1901, encouraged Japanese adventurers to penetrate East Asia as students, travelers, and businessmen. The opposition leaders of the Liberal and Progressive parties also regularly demanded from the government, as a domestic political tactic, a more vigorous foreign policy. Some of them became actively interested in reform and revolution in China.

Japanese protection and shelter were accordingly given K'ang Yu-wei and Liang Ch'i-ch'ao in 1898 (see pages 629–634). K'ang stayed for a time with the Progressive Party founder, Ōkuma, who had been prime minister briefly in 1898 and who formulated Japan's growing interest in China in his so-called "Ōkuma doctrine": that Japan, having modernized first, should repay her ancient cultural debt to China by now guaranteeing her freedom and aiding her modernization. Ōkuma's follower, Inukai, cultivated the groups of Chinese political exiles. In 1898 he got Liang and the revolutionary leader Sun Yat-sen together to discuss cooperation between the radical reformers led by K'ang Yu-wei and the anti-Ch'ing revolutionaries represented by Sun. K'ang, however, not only refused to meet Sun unless he became a disciple; he also remained a monarchist, stubbornly loyal to his Kuang-hsü emperor. In 1899 he began to visit Overseas Chinese communities around the world to set up units of his Protect-the-Emperor Society, collect funds, and stimulate a reformist press. In his teacher's absence, Liang for a time contemplated joining forces with Sun, but K'ang prevented it. The Japanese effort at unity failed; and after 1900 the two Chinese exile groups, reformers and revolutionaries, though both patriotic and both proscribed by Peking, became bitter rivals. Of the many leaders who emerged in these years, two became especially well-known and have been most studied.

Two Protagonists: Liang Ch'i-ch'ao and Sun Yat-sen. Liang visited Honolulu and Southeast Asia in 1900–1901, and the United States in 1903, but spent most of the decade in Japan. Already a master of classical learning,

he absorbed modern ideas voraciously and wrote upon all manner of sub-
jects in an eloquent, clear, and forceful style that soon made him the most
influential writer of the period—the Chinese students' window on the world.
The titles of his successive journals indicate the trend of his thinking—
"Public Opinion" (1898–), "The Renovation of the People" (1902–),
"The National Spirit" (1910–). Still only thirty in 1903, Liang soon left
his teacher behind. K'ang Yu-wei was then forty-five, past changing, and
Liang had already put him in his place by praising him as "the Martin
Luther of Confucianism" and a great thinker of the period "before Darwinism came to China." As he absorbed modern learning in Japan, Liang began
to put China's problems in a context of world history. To justify reform, he
took up the then worldwide doctrine of Social Darwinism. He compared
China's long development with that of other nations, compared Columbus
and Vasco da Gama with Cheng Ho, Immanuel Kant with Wang Yang-
ming, and looked back on the "new text" movement, of which he had been
an ardent member in the nineties, as comparable to the revival of Greek
learning in the Renaissance. In short, he got outside China's classical learning
and began the modern reappraisal of Chinese history that is still going on.

Liang's hope for China lay in popular education for nationalism, a moral
"renovation of the people." Echoing Fukuzawa and other Westernizers in
Japan, he espoused an Anglo-Saxon ideal of self-respect, enterprise, and
public-spirited citizenship. Denouncing China's political decadence, he urged
the transfer of loyalty from ruler to nation, from Confucian personal relationships to principles of law and the establishment of new institutions—"a
constitution, a parliament, and a responsible government." He also sponsored literary magazines, the writing of short stories and other fiction, and
translations of world literature, mainly from Japanese versions, into Chinese.
In politics, however, Liang refrained from blaming China's ills on the
Manchu dynasty. Like any member of the gentry elite as well as most foreign
observers, he believed his people unprepared for representative democracy.
He remained therefore a gradualist and a constitutional monarchist, anti-
republican and not actively revolutionary until the very end of the decade.
The Political Culture Association (Cheng-wen She) which he organized in
1907 advocated orderly political processes and had great influence in the
constitutional movement, although it fell into the usual liberal position—
attacked from opposite sides by both the Ch'ing government and the anti-
Ch'ing revolutionaries.

While Liang was an upper-class aristocrat of the intellect and a leader of
thought more than of action, his fellow Cantonese Sun Yat-sen (formal
name: Sun Wen) was one of the early professional revolutionaries of
modern times. The two men approached China's problems from opposite
social contexts, with antithetic preconceptions, and through different media.

While Liang was expounding the ideology of Chinese nationalism, Sun built up the structure of the early revolutionary movement. Sun had, or acquired, a remarkable list of qualifications for revolutionary leadership. He came from the district next to Macao, longest in touch with Westerners, farthest from Peking's control, home of the original "returned student" Yung Wing, of the early comprador Tong King-sing, and of countless emigrants to the Overseas Chinese communities abroad. Socially as well as geographically, Sun's origin was opportune. Son of a peasant, he was schooled by an uncle who had fought for the cause of the Taipings; its leader Hung Hsiu-ch'uan was his boyhood hero. Sun's early career was equally unoriented toward the emperor at Peking, for at thirteen he joined his elder brother in Honolulu, where he stayed three years and studied an English curriculum in a Church of England boarding school. He sang in the choir and accepted Christianity. Returning to his native village an iconoclast, he broke local idols and was sent away. He studied in Hong Kong, supported by his overseas brother, and after another visit to Honolulu, spent five years (1886–1892) in Canton and Hong Kong studying chemistry, physiology, surgery, and the like for his medical degree from a British misson hospital. In 1892 he began to practice in Macao but was forced out for lack of a diploma from Portugal. Having been concerned over the fate of China ever since her defeat by France in 1885, Sun submitted a reformist petition to the chief Westernizer of the day, Li Hung-chang, but got no reply. Thwarted as a doctor, disregarded by those in power, he now turned to a new calling—neither merchant, peasant, scholar, nor medical practitioner, but revolutionist, a man of no class, ready to work with all classes.

Sun had already made contact with that traditional rebel body, the Triad Society (see page 467). By 1894 he had a secret society of his own, the "Revive China Society" (Hsing-Chung Hui), with branches in Hawaii as well as in the Macao–Hong Kong–Canton area. In 1895 its first plot, to seize the Canton government offices, was discovered, and several of his fellow conspirators were executed. But Sun escaped to Japan, cut his queue, grew a mustache, and in Western-style clothes soon passed for a Japanese under the name of Nakayama (lit., "central mountain," which in its Chinese form, Chung-shan, would later be applied to public parks and thoroughfares, educational institutions, and even a style of clothing in Nationalist China). Now "wanted" by Peking, Sun went by way of the United States to London. There in 1896 he was recognized at the Chinese legation, "kidnaped," and held for twelve days preparatory to being shipped back to China for execution; but his old teacher of medicine (Sir James Cantlie) who had also taught him cricket in Hong Kong, mobilized British opinion and got him released. Thus at the age of thirty, already world-famous as the leading anti-Ch'ing revolutionary, Sun felt himself a man of destiny.

THE GROWTH OF HONG KONG.   *Top: Harbor, City of Victoria,
and the Peak seen from Kowloon on the mainland side of the
harbor in a painting of 1856. Bottom: The reverse scene one
hundred and twenty years later—from the Peak looking down
on the city and across the harbor to Kowloon, a photograph
of 1976.*

By the time he returned to Japan in 1897, and received the aid and advice of expansionists there, Sun had put together several ingredients of rebellion, some new, some old. New elements included financial support from Overseas Chinese communities which had grown up outside the traditional mainland society with nonconformist, commercial values, nationalistic but frustrated in their political loyalties; and leadership from a small group of semi-Westernized, sometimes Christian, patriotic youth who came like Sun from the Canton area, on the modernizing fringe of Chinese life. Old-style ingredients included the bands of armed rebels that could be assembled by the mainland secret societies; and the simple antidynastic aim of seizing local power somewhere by force, hoping thereby to set off a chain reaction that would topple the imperial government. In October 1900 a two-week rising was engineered with Triad Society aid at Waichow north of Hong Kong, but it petered out when Japanese arms and men from Taiwan failed to materialize. Combining traditional and modern means, Sun joined the American lodge of the Triad Society in Hawaii in 1903 and through it sought funds from Chinese all over the United States.

By this time, he faced a new problem: how to compete with other revolutionaries by appealing to the new generation of Chinese students, especially in Japan. For this purpose he needed a rationale of revolution. K'ang Yu-wei still had most of the support of the rather conservative Overseas Chinese merchants in Southeast Asia, and Liang Ch'i-ch'ao's writings were forming the ideas of the new student class. Meanwhile risings had been attempted by others, and revolutionary societies, schools, and journals were springing up in the treaty ports as well as in Japan. A group in Shanghai, led by classical scholars like Chang Ping-lin and Ts'ai Yuan-p'ei, attacked K'ang and Liang. In 1903 their inflammatory anti-Manchu paper (*Su-pao*) was suppressed amid great notoriety, and Chang was imprisoned for three years. In Hunan, Huang Hsing founded his "China Revival Society" (Hua-hsing Hui) in 1903 and tried to unite army officers, students, and secret society members for a rising, but as so often happened, the plot was discovered and broken up. Revolutionary activity was thus growing, but it lacked coordination, specific ideology, and a long-term program.

Facing this competition and opportunity, Sun Yat-sen now developed his own ideological appeal. In 1903 he wrote his first newspaper articles in Tokyo and Honolulu. By mid-1905, after organizing Chinese student groups in Brussels, Berlin, and Paris, he was back in Tōkyō again. Dedicated in aim but flexible, if not indeed opportunist, as to means, Sun now put together from his multicultural background from China, Japan, the United States, and Europe a set of ideas to justify and guide a republican revolution. This was the Three Principles of the People (*San min chu-i*): nationalism (*min-tsu chu-i,* a term connoting both people and race); democracy (*min-ch'uan chu-i.* literally, "people's rights"); and "people's livelihood" (*min-sheng chu-i,* a classical term that some later equated with socialism). These three protean concepts summed up much of the ferment of the age and yet could undergo much change in specific content. Nationalism was at this time both anti-Manchu, hence prorepublican, and anti-imperialist, though this latter aspect was not stressed by those seeking foreign aid for the revolution. Democracy implied an anti-Confucian egalitarianism to be guaranteed by a constitution (which stole Liang's thunder) with five powers—executive, legislative, and judicial as in the United States, plus examination and censorial or "control" powers drawn from Chinese tradition. This "five-power constitution" was apparently Sun's own invention. Finally, his "people's livelihood," to meet the new problems of industrial growth, involved no Marxist class struggle but instead followed Henry George's then popular idea of a single tax to appropriate future unearned increase of land values and thus check the enrichment of speculators and monopolists. Thus the ancient term "people's livelihood" in 1905 meant principally this urban "equalization of land rights" in the specific Western single-tax sense, not an agrarian land redistribution. The latter would as yet have kindled little enthusiasm among the sons of merchants and landlords, eager though they might be for a political revolution.

The T'ung-meng Hui and Its Vicissitudes.   All these ingredients—Overseas Chinese funds, secret society contacts, new student leadership, and revolutionary ideology—were finally combined in 1905 under Japanese encouragement. Bringing rival groups together, Sun's friends in Japan introduced him to Huang Hsing and others of the Hunan group. At a big Tōkyō meeting in August the T'ung-meng Hui ("United League," a typical secret society name) was founded with Sun as chief executive, Huang Hsing second in command, and Chang Ping-lin and others named to key posts. Overseas offices in Singapore, Brussels, San Francisco, and Honolulu were to be co-ordinated with branches in seventeen provinces. Among roughly a thousand early members, the largest group was from Hunan and Hupei (so long governed by that modernizer of education, Chang Chih-tung), while the Cantonese were second, and the Szechwanese and lower Yangtze contingents third and fourth in size.

Felt by many to be a magnetic personality, Sun at thirty-nine was not only the eldest but also the most famous, the most widely traveled, and the most experienced among this revolutionary band, with the greatest number of contacts in Japan and elsewhere abroad, although not in the Yangtze provinces. On the other hand, as a foreignized Chinese and not one of the scholar elite, a man known for conspiracy and desperate action rather than for literary production, and indeed intellectually rather superficial, he could not assume the role of modern sage to guide the thinking of his generation. And yet, given the multicultural confusion produced by the collapse of

China's great tradition and the variety of foreign models, probably no systematic thinker could have had even as much success as Sun Yat-sen.

The new ideology of republicanism was expounded by Sun's literary lieutenants in the T'ung-meng Hui journal *The People (Min-pao)*. Attacking Liang's ideas of gradualist reform and constitutional monarchy, writers like Wang Ching-wei and Hu Han-min largely succeeded in winning Chinese student support for the attractive thesis that China could catch up with and indeed surpass the West by a quick revolution. "Men of determination," providing strong leadership (as in Japan), could intervene to speed up modernization. Gradual evolution and popular education to prepare for modern political life were unnecessary. *The People* backed Sun's three-stage program: (1) three years of military government, with local self-government beginning county by county; (2) six years under a provisional constitution, which later came to be known as a period of "tutelage"; and (3) eventual constitutional government with an elected president and parliament. These optimistic assumptions and over-simple promises soon proved more popular than the cooler rationality of Liang Ch'i-ch'ao, whose espousal of benevolent monarchy was in any case torpedoed by the death of the Kuang-hsü emperor in 1908.

Despite its new unity, the revolutionary movement suffered repeated frustrations. In the most rebellious province, Hunan, an independent revolt of the secret Society of Brothers and Elders (Ko-lao Hui) in October 1906, caused partly by famine, was joined by coal miners at P'ing-hsiang in Kiangsi but was suppressed in a month by government troops from four provinces. In 1907, Ch'ing protests led Japan to expel Sun Yat-sen. He and Huang Hsing moved to Hanoi in French Indo-China and in 1907–1908 staged six outbreaks in Kwangtung, Kwangsi, and Yunnan. But the friendly French soon found that the Chinese example stimulated Vietnamese unrest. They in turn expelled the T'ung-meng Hui conspirators. By 1909, Ch'ing arrests and executions, combined with the revolutionists' failure of coordination and lack of success, had discouraged Overseas Chinese financial support and led to dissension within the movement. It practically came to a standstill, and Sun went to the West again seeking funds. Others took up anarchism, advocated especially by a group of students from Paris, and, like Russian anarchists, resorted to assassination to dramatize their cause. In 1910 the handsome Wang Ching-wei tried to bomb the prince regent in Peking but was caught and imprisoned. Anti-Manchu feeling was rising, but the revolutionary movement seemed thoroughly frustrated.

Huang Hsing pursued the most hopeful course of subverting imperial New Army troops. An army revolt engineered at Canton in February 1910 was suppressed, but another overseas fund drive collected 187,000 Hong Kong dollars, mainly from Southeast Asia and Canada, and financed the smuggling of arms and "dare-to-die" attack forces into Canton in April 1911.

Like most earlier plots, this "Canton Revolution" was doomed, despite individual heroism, by a sequence of difficulties—inadequate secrecy, government precautions, last-minute changes of plan, lack of coordination, and general confusion. Huang Hsing's men in several groups tried as usual to seize the government offices, but one group mistook another's identity, and they dispersed each other with gunfire. Sun Yat-sen listed this as the tenth failure of his forces since 1895. Huang Hsing concluded that "in instigating revolution, dictatorship is imperative. Once a dissenting voice is permitted, the revolution is bound to fail."

All these risings had been more political than military in their ulterior purpose, to destroy the dynasty's prestige and claim to power. Outbreaks and assassinations, funds and arms from abroad, had been used for their destructive effect on that tacit popular acquiescence which constituted Heaven's mandate. But this was equally endangered by worsening economic conditions, manifested in peasant rice riots (as in Hunan in 1910) and by the frustration of gentry interests, which supported provincial "railway protection" movements (as in Szechwan in 1911). Both contributed to a rapid decline of the Ch'ing dynasty's central authority and therefore of the monarchy as an institution. By 1911 Heaven's mandate had indeed been withdrawn from the Manchus; they had lost the confidence and active support of the great part of the Chinese establishment—local officials and police, modern troops, and even their commanders.

The End of the Ch'ing Dynasty. When the denouement came, it was partly accidental, locally improvised, and out of T'ung-meng Hui control. Students and soldiers had organized a succession of revolutionary study societies in Hupei, the better to plot a rising. Their plot was as usual discovered (on October 9), and some of the New Army soldiers in Wuchang revolted in order to save themselves on October 10 (since celebrated as the "Double Ten," i.e., tenth day of the tenth month). Although fewer than three thousand out of a much larger body of troops rebelled, the Manchu governor-general fled the city, as did his military commander. Wuchang fell to the rebels. The foreign consuls declared neutrality. Since no revolutionary leader was on the scene, a brigade commander (Li Yüan-hung) was pressed into leadership. This anti-Manchu rebellion received spontaneous popular support locally. Within a few weeks it inspired anti-Manchu declarations in some two dozen other centers, usually backed by the T'ung-meng Hui, the New Army, and provincial assemblies. By early December all the southern and central and even the northwestern provinces had declared their independence, usually under Ch'ing army officers who became military governors and held power jointly with provincial assembly leaders of the constitutional movement. Fighting occurred in only half a dozen places.

LEADERS OF THE CHINESE REPUBLIC. *At Nanking, early 1912 (front, left to right): Ts'ai Yüan-p'ei, Minister of Education; Huang Hsing, Army Minister; Sun Yat-sen, Provisional President.*

The Ch'ing court now recalled Yüan Shih-k'ai to power since the best troops were loyal to him, but he came on his own terms, as prime minister of a new cabinet government as well as commander of the armed forces. Meanwhile the rebellious provinces and the T'ung-meng Hui revolutionists joined forces in setting up a provisional government at Nanking. Sun Yat-sen, who had read of the Wuchang revolt in a Denver newspaper, had gone on to England seeking a loan and British help to prevent Japan's giving financial or military aid to the dynasty. He reached Shanghai just in time to be elected, as a senior figurehead, to the provisional presidency of the Chinese Republic. He was inaugurated at Nanking on January 1, 1912, but at the same time offered to resign in favor of Premier Yüan Shih-k'ai whenever the latter would support the new republic.

Although some sharp fighting occurred, particularly at the Wuhan cities, the 1911 revolution was singularly unviolent. It was also inconclusive, because its main aim was purely negative, to get rid of Manchu rule. There was a widespread consensus on a few positive points—that the provinces must be represented in a parliament; that Chinese unity was essential to forestall foreign, probably Japanese, intervention; and that Yüan Shih-k'ai was the one man with sufficient experience, ability, and backing to head a new government. Sun Yat-sen, Huang Hsing, and other revolutionists had generally agreed by late December that Yüan represented the chief hope of avoiding civil war, chaos, and foreign intervention. On his part, Yüan, backed by his military commanders, negotiated both publicly and secretly on various levels, from a central position, with the Ch'ing court on the one hand and with the revolutionists and their Nanking provisional government on the other, and gradually engineered a general settlement: on February 12, 1912, the infant Hsuan-t'ung emperor (later known as Pu-yi) bowed to "the Mandate of Heaven . . . manifested through the wish of the people" and abdicated, ending the Ch'ing dynasty, as well as the ancient Chinese monarchy and empire. Sun Yat-sen then resigned as provisional president and Yüan was elected his successor at Nanking. A violent army mutiny at Peking, however, necessitated Yüan's presence, and so he avoided moving the capital south. He was inaugurated on March 10 in his own bailiwick at Peking, to govern under a provisional constitution until a parliament should be elected and full constitutional government be established.

Yüan as president was later to "betray" the revolutionists who had elected him, just as he had "betrayed" the Ch'ing court that had made him prime minister. But in 1912 he had no rival of equal stature capable of holding power at that unprecedented moment when the Chinese leviathan had been decapitated and no Son of Heaven was left to perform the crucial imperial functions at the apex of state and society. In this great political crisis the Manchus might have tried to fight rather than be pensioned off; the northern armies might have been used against Nanking; and the Japanese, who were soon to become aggressive, might have seized this earlier opportunity. As it happened, however, Yüan had the skill and chicanery to oust the Manchus, court foreign recognition, beguile the revolutionists, and maintain an administration through a time of great uncertainty. The Japanese, with divided counsels, were unable to agree on an active policy. Britain pressed for Chinese unity. Sun and his republican colleagues, having neither armed forces nor large constituencies in the provinces, knew that China needed strong and unified rule, and that they could not provide it. With nationalist sentiments of every type calling for unity under a strong man, Yüan emerged as the sole candidate.

Thus when China's immemorial monarchy was abolished, the emergence of a power-holder cushioned the shock. But Chinese political life without the Son of Heaven inevitably deteriorated, because the chief of state now lacked the traditional ideological and ceremonial sanctions for the exercise of supreme power. While not exactly theocratic in Western terms, the Chinese ruler had been indubitably placed above mankind, as Yüan was not. Lacking the traditional sanctions and not yet having developed modern ones, the Son of Heaven's successors—both Yüan and the warlords—had to rely increasingly on military force. When new sanctions were eventually established, years later, they were not those of the Anglo-Saxon model of government, which the revolutionists had vaguely had in mind. In this way 1911 marked the beginning of a prolonged crisis of central power in the world's most ancient government.

The Republic's Decline into Warlordism

The great modern transformations of economy, politics, society, thought, and culture, which have swept about the world like tidal waves, had by 1912 begun to smash China's traditional civilization to bits and pieces. Chinese who have lived through the unprecedented era since that time have thus experienced chaos on every level, private and public, practical and theoretical. Nowhere has the search for a new order, a revival of national power, a remaking of the national life, been more prolonged or more frustrating.

Domestic Politics: Yüan vs. the Kuomintang. The new provisional president, Yüan Shih-k'ai, having taken over the principal administrative functions of the extinct monarchy, soon became involved in a power struggle with the revolutionary leaders. To keep power from 1912 to 1916, he used bribery, military force, and assassinations, coerced the parliament, revised the constitution at will and finally tried to revive the monarchy. All these manipulations branded him an enemy of the people and their republic.

In March 1912 Yüan inaugurated the republican system of government by appointing his protégé T'ang Shao-i, a nephew of Tong King-sing who had been educated in Connecticut under Yung Wing (Tong and T'ang are variant romanizations of the same surname), to be prime minister and form a ten-man cabinet. It contained four T'ung-meng Hui members, among them Sung Chiao-jen of Hunan, a close colleague of Huang Hsing and a leading drafter of the new provisional constitution. This document had divided authority between president and parliament, and disagreement soon arose over which should control the cabinet and its administration. Prime Minister T'ang had no party organization, no patronage, no budget, and no control over his cabinet ministers. When he found that Yüan would not let him run the administration, he and the four T'ung-meng Hui members resigned (June 1912), and the cabinet thereafter became responsible to the president, not the parliament. President Yüan, however, avoiding a rupture, invited Sun Yat-sen and Huang Hsing to Peking, where each spent almost a month. Yüan saw them frequently, expressing agreement with their views, and appointed Sun director of railways to mastermind a great national railway system, all on paper. These older revolutionary leaders, unskilled in government, were unable to create or even demand party rule. Their ideas about it were vague, their aims uncertain, their counsels divided; the institution itself was untested on the Chinese scene. Political parties in fact were just taking shape, emerging out of two traditions.

One tradition was that of the clique or faction (*tang*) of scholar-officials, like K'ang Yu-wei's Self-Strengthening Society and the other political study groups formed after 1895. This element had contributed to the nationwide constitutional movement and now in May 1912 took shape in a Republican Party which generally supported Yüan's administration. After Liang Ch'i-ch'ao returned from Japan to a hero's welcome, he formed a Democratic Party and in May 1913 amalgamated these Republicans, Democrats, and other small groups into the Progressive Party, still generally in support of the government in power. The other source of party tradition came from the secret societies whose example had inspired the conspiratorial societies of revolutionists. Many political groups partook of both traditions. Some politicians belonged to several parties. No party was more than a congeries of upper-class individuals who were drawn together by personal ties or common background, but who lacked reliable electoral constituencies, political status, and experience. In short, the adaptation of Western methods of political association and agitation, such as had begun in Japan in the 1870's, was barely starting in China. Genuine issues of party policy could not be seriously debated because the institutional role of parties was itself still an issue.

Instead of a separation of powers under the supremacy of law as the central myth of the state, the Chinese monarch had traditionally integrated in his person all the powers of government. Yüan had got control over the cabinet and civil administration and was expanding it over the provincial military governors. Bearing these burdens of personal responsibility, he was unprepared by experience or tradition to countenance a "loyal opposition" that might attack his policies and thwart his power while professing a higher loyalty to the Chinese Republic. Nevertheless this was precisely what the Western model of parliamentary government seemed to call for; the way seemed open for an opposition party to try to dominate the parliament, and the attempt was made. This next phase of the power struggle was led by Sung Chiao-jen, who now ranked just after Sun and Huang among the revolutionists. He persuaded four small political groups in August 1912 to join with the T'ung-meng Hui in forming an open party, the Kuo-min Tang or "National People's Party." National elections, held on the basis of a very restricted and indirect franchise in each province, gave the Kuomin-tang a majority in the bicameral parliament by February 1913. Sung Chiao-jen thereupon campaigned widely in Central China, criticizing the adminis-tration and demanding that the Kuomintang should now control the cabinet, though Yüan should remain president.

This was a high point of parliamentary democracy in modern China, but Sung Chiao-jen's inauguration of electioneering had a denouement that spectacularly blighted this promising development. Yüan hired assassins, as the Shanghai Mixed Court later documented in detail, and on March 20, 1913, at the Shanghai railway station Sung Chiao-jen, not yet thirty-one, was shot down. Yüan temporarily confused the public with fabricated charges against Huang Hsing. Assassination had heretofore been a weapon of the anti-Ch'ing revolutionists out of power, but President Yüan had now developed its use in power, having already had various prorevolutionist generals assassinated or executed. The strategic murder of Sung asserted a principle (that the power-holder is above the law) and demonstrated a tactic (that an opposition movement can best be checked by eliminating its leader) which have been used to strangle democracy in China ever since.

The revulsion against Yüan was heightened by his getting money and recognition from the imperialist powers on onerous terms: while blasting party government at home, he seemed to be mortgaging China's revenues to the foreigners. This stemmed from his urgent financial needs. Although he now had personal control over the military governors who commanded most of the armies, having been their old commander, he was no more able than his Ch'ing predecessors to augment the land tax and other meager revenues flowing to Peking. The Ch'ing had staved off bankruptcy by borrowing 10 million pounds sterling in April 1911 for "currency reform and Manchurian industrial development" from the four-power consortium of British, French, German, and American banks. To this group Russian and Japanese banks were added in June 1912 to make a six-power consortium. Yüan had early begun to seek massive foreign funds, but the consortium, while maintaining its virtual monopoly over loans to China, demanded that China's salt taxes be the security and that they be collected, like the maritime customs, by a joint Sino-foreign administration. Patriotic Chinese of all persuasions protested these terms. President Wilson in March 1913, reversing Taft's position of 1909, refused to support American participation on the grounds that the conditions of the loan threatened China's administrative independence. But after fourteen months of negotiation the consortium contract for the Reorganization Loan of 25 million pounds sterling was nevertheless signed (April 26, 1913). This was done with the remaining five-power group banks, without the parliament's approval, and on the same day that the evidence was published concerning Sung's assassination. Since the bonds were floated at only 90 per cent with 6 per cent commission to the banks, China actually received only 84 per cent, or £21 million, and yet would have to repay principal and 5 per cent interest until 1960, a total of £67,893,597.

Yüan's success in smashing the idea of an opposition party and in borrowing foreign money to pay his armies was largely due to the widespread belief that only he could keep China united and at peace. In mid-1913 he was still backed by the Progressive Party, tolerated by much of the Kuomintang, and supported by the northern military governors, his own men of the Peiyang clique. He therefore spurned various concessions offered by the Kuomintang, dismissed the military governors who supported it in Central and South China, and moved troops against them. Reacting to Yüan's aggressiveness, during July and August 1913 seven provincial governments, though ill-armed, again declared their independence of Peking in the short-lived "second revolution." This movement lacked popular or foreign support and was suppressed within two months with little fighting. Sun Yat-sen, Huang, and other leaders, fleeing to Japan, found themselves back where they had started, while Yüan's generals of the Peiyang clique expanded their control over most of the remaining provinces.

The final phase of parliamentarism began when the Progressive Party, with moderate Kuomintang help, formed a cabinet at Peking in September 1913 which included some of Yüan's henchmen and also Liang Ch'i-ch'ao as minister of justice. Yüan's aim, now becoming more clear, was to get himself at last formally elected president by the parliament, by the agreed-upon procedure, and then dispense with it. Bribery and strong-arm intimidation bent the parliament to his will. On October 6 it finally elected him president. On the 7th he succeeded through diplomatic bargaining in getting the major powers to recognize the Chinese Republic. On October 10 he was formally inaugurated as its first president. Soon he destroyed it. In November he ordered the Kuomintang dissolved and excluded 438 members or former members from the parliament. In January 1914 he suspended the parliament and then the provincial assemblies. In February the cabinet resigned. Yüan, at fifty-four, was now dictator.

Though execrated by patriots of a later day, Yüan's piecemeal dismantling of the thin façade of parliamentarism seems to have been of great concern only to a minor part of the public, for the most part the sprinkling of would-be parliamentarians who had just begun to emerge in the treaty ports and provincial capitals. Neither the foreign powers nor the inarticulate common people nor the city merchant class offered much objection, while the administrative bureaucracy, the army, and most of the provincial governors simply favored stability under the one man at the top. Unlike the diffusion of responsibility in Japanese politics, the Chinese polity was accustomed to a single head who could balance the many conflicting interests and give final decisions. Yüan now did so, ruling through appointed organs and under a new document, the Constitutional Compact promulgated on May 1, 1914, which gave him comprehensive dictatorial powers. He muzzled the press, encouraged local "self-government" by gentry and elders, and revived the censorate and the state cult of Confucius. Alighting from his armored car, he conducted the ancient imperial rites at the Temple of Heaven. By the end of 1915 he was president for life.

Foreign Relations: The Republic vs. the Foreign Powers.   The new Chinese Republic began by losing control over two outlying regions of the old Ch'ing Empire. Tibet and Outer Mongolia broke away and became oriented more to Britain and Russia, respectively, than to Peking. Having cast out the Manchus in the name of national-racial self-determination, the Chinese revolution had little claim to Inner Asia. But Yüan Shih-k'ai, inheriting power at Peking, maintained the traditional claim nevertheless. Russia, Outer Mongolia, and China soon agreed on the formula: Chinese suzerainty and Outer Mongolian autonomy (which permitted actual Russian domination). Britain followed a similar formula: Chinese suzerainty and Tibetan autonomy (allowing a British permanent interest). Both Russia and Britain finally recognized Yüan's government on November 7, 1913.

This expansion of great-power influence in China's borderlands was paralleled by a further growth of foreign control over China's revenues at home. Hart's British successor as Inspector-General of Customs got the imperial government's agreement in November 1911 to a fundamental change in the handling of the Maritime Customs revenue, now fully pledged to meet China's foreign loan and indemnity payments. Previously the foreign commissioners had reported to Peking their accounts of revenues collected, but the Chinese superintendents of customs had actually received the funds. Now, as most of the provinces declared their independence, the unity of the Customs Service and China's foreign credit and debt payments were all preserved by arranging that the foreign commissioners should for the first time receive the revenue funds and transmit them through the Inspector-General to an International Commission of Bankers at Shanghai representing foreign creditors. The foreign position at Shanghai was further strengthened in the face of revolution when the consular body in late 1911 took control over the Mixed Court (see pages 576 and 578). This expansion of foreign control over Shanghai and the customs revenues, together with the modernization of the new Salt Revenue Administration under a British chief inspector, had the same ambivalence as many earlier aspects of the unequal-treaty system—infringing further upon China's sovereignty and yet in the short run helping its government. China's credit was sustained, facilitating foreign loans, and the salt revenues were greatly increased.

Another ambivalent merit of the treaty system had been that the rapacity of any one power was somewhat checked by the jealousy of all the others. World War I, however, diverted the powers' attention and let Japan embark on a course of aggression. In August 1914 China declared her neutrality, but the Ōkuma government declared war on Germany, flouted China's neutrality by landing troops on her territory, and took over the whole German position in Shantung. Japan followed this on January 18, 1915, by secretly presenting to Yüan Shih-k'ai Twenty-One Demands in five groups. The fifth group would have given Japan control over the Chinese government through a system of advisers and specific control over the police, arms purchases, arsenals, and the development of Fukien province. By the usual device of leaking these outrageous terms to the foreign press, Yüan obliged Japan to leave group five for "future discussion," but under a

Japanese ultimatum of May 7 he was forced to accept most of the first four groups. No Western power came to his aid, although the British minister opined that "Japan's action toward China is worse than that of Germany in the case of Belgium." The Sino-Japanese treaties of May 25, 1915, embodying these demands, confirmed Japan's dominant position in Shantung, and in South Manchuria and Eastern Inner Mongolia, long recognized as her sphere. In addition Japan was acknowledged to have a special interest in the Han-Yeh-P'ing industrial base in Central China, which had long been used as security to get Japanese loans, even by Sun Yat-sen in 1912. Although never ratified by a Chinese parliament, these treaties served Japan as a charter for continental expansion. The aim of the Twenty-One Demands, presented by a cabinet that represented Japan's new industrial interests, was basically economic. But the effect in China was mainly political, for they roused a new spirit of nationalism, expressed in mass rallies, strikes, boycotts of Japanese goods, and vigorous protests in the press.

Yüan's Monarchical Fiasco.   Yüan's stout anti-Japanism, for which he had been famous ever since his start in Korea, won him nationwide support in 1915, but his effort to govern China floundered in an ideological vacuum: the ancient Confucian ethical sanctions and the ceremonial forms of imperial rule had lost their potency, while modern beliefs and institutions of popular government, either parties in competition or party dictatorships, had not yet become established. Since Chinese society now lacked a clear political creed, Yüan governed in a rather "Legalist" tradition, by force and manipulation, with little faith even in himself, knowing only that human beings "fear weapons and love gold," as Liang phrased it.

This poverty of political belief was illustrated in Yüan's effort to revive the monarchy. In August 1915 he launched from behind the scenes a monarchical movement complete with a Yüan-for-emperor association to "plan for peace," nationwide "people's petitions," a unanimous vote by "elected" representatives, old-style memorials, and similar contrivances, all demanding his enthronement. In response to the demand thus manufactured, Yüan, after appropriate hesitation, consented in December 1915 to accept the throne. His reign title would be "Grand Constitutional Era" (*Hung-hsien*), to begin with 1916. All this came to nothing.

One factor in his failure was the disaffection of his generals, who bore him no love. Another was the opposition of the Japanese government, which mobilized an almost unanimous treaty-power opinion and "advised" against the monarchy. The precipitating factor was military opposition within China, sparked by men like Liang Ch'i-ch'ao, the antirevolutionist who still saw history as irreversible and now advocated the continuity of the Chinese Republic. He plotted with one of his Hunanese students, who had been military governor of Yunnan, the province farthest from Yüan's control, and on December 25, 1915, Yunnan declared its independence. There followed six months of limited fighting and intensive negotiation. By degrees eight southern and western provinces turned against Yüan, while he first postponed his enthronement, then renounced the throne, and finally died on June 6, 1916, a broken man.

In the background other forces, both ideological and geopolitical, had worked against the idea of monarchy. The sanction of power in China no longer came from an impersonal heaven, expressed in portents and in the tacit acquiescence of the populace. On the contrary, the idea had taken hold that the people, the body politic of the nation, were the active makers of history. The Son of Heaven as an institution had been gradually discredited in the long years leading up to 1911. For Heaven's Mandate had been substituted the concept of the people's will, the consent of the governed. The apotheosis of "the people" (*min*) permeated the new nationalist thinking—the "people's army" (*min-chün*), the "national people's party" (*Kuomintang*), the "three people's principles." Yüan the strong man had been too scornful of the modern idea of representation, even though it was demanded only by the upper classes, not the common mass. In traditional terms he had also been too disloyal to his followers to command their loyalty in return.

Geopolitics too worked against him because the provinces, distinct geographic, cultural, and administrative regions, had grown steadily more independent of Peking, in a process under way since the 1850's. There were also the ineradicable climatic, economic, and historical differences that produced divergent interests and outlooks between South and North China, such as had plagued every dynasty. After Yüan's death still other, foreign influences inhibited China's unity and continued to checkmate his successors in the struggle for power: first, the political sanctuary and strategic resources available to local power-holders in the treaty ports, beyond central control; second, the interests and capacities of the imperialist powers in their respective spheres of influence, which enabled them almost to dominate whole provinces; third, the power of the foreign banks, both in and outside the consortium, to make and unmake Chinese governments by giving or withholding loans; and finally, the constant inflow from abroad of new ideas and techniques, ranging from the anarchism of Kropotkin and the individualism of Ibsen to armored trains and bicycles, all of which contributed both to China's ongoing cultural revolution and to the disintegration of the old order.

The Nature of Warlordism.   Between 1916 and 1928 and in peripheral areas even longer, China was divided among a number of competing warlords, or local military leaders. These were essentially men in between. They were not in a dynastic interregnum, where "change within tradition" would bring forth a new dynasty. Yet they were not modernizers with a new order in mind. Their armies, newly swollen and modern-armed, using the new railways and river steamers, could now more easily dominate the terrain, yet they could not create a new polity. In 1911 the revolutionists, with a party but no army, had failed to gain power. Now the warlords, with armies but no parties, were equally incapable. Their repeated use and misuse of parliaments and slogans only highlighted their lack of adequate principles and institutions. Since 1913 the armies had proliferated and the parties had splintered. No one could integrate the new military power with a new political organization. Under the warlords, China's government deteriorated, the people suffered, and Chinese society after a century of decline reached a nadir of demoralization.

Behind the surface parade of hundreds of bemedaled commanders leading their shambling legions across the historical scene in these years, certain typical characteristics emerge. First of all, a warlord had to have a strong personality, subordinate officers, and troops. His problem was first to train them and win their personal loyalty, then to feed and supply them all. For this he needed support from the revenues of a great city, a province, a trade route, or railway, or from other militarists or a foreign power. The geography of a region might give him a strategic advantage, but its land and people could provide only food and manpower to be requisitioned, not a true territorial base in the modern guerrilla sense, with support among the peasantry. The typical warlord army had no roots among the local people but was a scourge upon them, exacting taxes, living off the villages, feared and despised. An army moving to a new province might therefore better itself, at least temporarily. It might be both parasitic and peripatetic.

In the second place, because military force created political power only when legitimized and mediated through institutions, the warlords sought formal appointments, seals of office, and documents properly signed by others, and also justified their every move by pronouncements in favor of the public welfare and patriotic principles. In short, they needed the help of civilian politicians and civil government. Warlordism did not substitute military force for the other elements of government; it merely balanced them differently. This shift in balance came partly from the disintegration of the sanctions and values of China's traditional civil government, already noted. Partly it came from the warlords' new technical military capacities, greater mobility and fire-power, which were not balanced by an equilibrating growth of new political institutions. This has become, of course, a major motif in modern world history—material technology, especially military, outrunning the growth of popular participation in government. In this respect warlordism was less an old Chinese custom, as foreigners have generally assumed, than a result of unbalanced modernization, armaments growing faster than political agencies capable of controlling them.

Finally, the nature of warlord politics has seemed remarkably confusing to everyone at the time and since, partly because the warlords were so venal and treacherous, so given to sudden shifts of allegiance and wily stratagems reminiscent of operatic characters in the *Romance of the Three Kingdoms.* However, while the old power structure was decapitated, its lower, regional levels continued to function, and tried to create nationwide organs at higher levels. The ultimate aims of the warlords were political, and they sought all manner of institutional means to bolster and expand their power, working with parliaments and assemblies, even convoking conferences of military governors. Being deficient in their capacity for modern political organization, the competing warlord groups could not rise above the regional level. Nevertheless they always acknowledged the existence of the Chinese state. Throughout this period the Peking government continued to function abroad diplomatically and maintained many of its services. No one ventured to proclaim a new dynasty. Times had changed. The struggle among the warlords, among the politicians in the parliament, and between the warlords and the politicians went through a sequence of phases with a general trend toward the weakening of the parliament and fragmentation of the country. In the first phase Liang Ch'i-ch'ao and others of the former Progressive Party formed a "Research clique," which generally tried to work with the Peking government and was opposed by the Kuomintang remnants from the South. As the Peiyang military governors who dominated a dozen northern and central provinces got more and more control over the government and parliament, this estranged the southern provinces. In the second phase, the defection of the Southerners from the Peking parliament in 1917 marked a turning point, for it gave another opportunity to Sun Yat-sen.

In Japan Sun had reverted to his earlier secret-society approach to revolution and in July 1914 had founded the "Chinese Revolutionary Party" (Chung-hua Ko-ming Tang) as a disciplined underground elite who were to be fingerprinted and sworn to personal loyalty to Sun. His aim was to overcome "that lack of party discipline . . . the cause of our failure." Huang Hsing and many others, however, refused to take the oath; this revived conspiratorial effort was plainly not democratic, nor did it appeal to the rising patriotism of the time, for Sun Yat-sen omitted from his new party platform of 1914 the principle of nationalism. Originally anti-Manchu, this principle (incredible as it may seem) apparently no longer held significance for him; his thinking was now pan-Asian, directed toward cooperation with Japan, not against imperialism. Out of tune with the times, Sun had contributed little to the frustrating of Yüan Shih-k'ai in 1916.

In 1917, however, Sun Yat-sen re-emerged and jumped into the warlord-parliamentary fray. In July he went to Canton along with other former Kuomintang colleagues and most of the Chinese navy. He convened some

WARLORDS. *Top: The quondam "Christian General," Feng Yü-hsiang, addressing his troops in 1928. Bottom: The "Marshal of Manchuria," Chang Tso-lin (in winter hat), saluted by the Fifteenth Regiment, U.S.A., then stationed in Tientsin, ca. 1927.*

250 members of parliament and formed a military government with himself as generalissimo, but the local warlords were the real power-holders. Sun at Canton, trying to team up with the local men in power, was like Liang Ch'i-ch'ao at Peking, trying to provide a civilian component for the warlord government there. After the Peking government declared war on Germany in August 1917, it financed its domestic warfare by borrowing enormous sums from Japan, the so-called "Nishihara loans," partly on the excuse of preparing to fight Germany. Peking now made a military alliance with Japan, imported Japanese military instructors, and worked closely with a pro-Japanese group of politicians and militarists known as the An-fu (Anhwei-Fukien) clique. Many patriots protested that the power-holders were again selling China to the foreigners in order to build their own military power. Liang Ch'i-ch'ao finally withdrew from politics in frustration.

In the South Sun Yat-sen's Canton parliament was also split. One element in it (the Political Study clique), cooperated with the warlords, who nevertheless began to assassinate Sun's men and forced him to retire to Shanghai in May 1918. A Kwangsi clique of militarists now dominated the South, much as the An-fu clique controlled the North. The end of World War I put North and South under pressure to patch things up, and in 1919 the two factions negotiated at Shanghai in a fruitless peace conference. During 1920, however, China's fragmentation entered a third phase: minority elements both north and south, seeking allies wherever possible, ousted the groups in power but still could not stabilize their own control.

After 1922 the disintegration of China's civil government entered still another phase and began to produce divergent results north and south. In the North the warlord melee cast up new leading personalities, less directly indebted to Yüan Shih-k'ai for their early careers. Three men eventually stood out; in the course of their triangular relations, each allied himself in turn with each of the other two against the third, and thus each was double-crossed by the others. These three were:

(1) Chang Tso-lin (died 1928), "Warlord of Manchuria," an ex-bandit who had risen as Japan's ally against Russia and been military governor at Mukden since 1911, buttressed by the resources of the Three Eastern Provinces and their strategic defensibility vis-à-vis North China.

(2) Wu P'ei-fu (1872–1939), who had been trained in the Confucian Classics and then by Japanese officers at the Paoting military academy, and who became the repository of many Chinese and British hopes for peace and order in Central China.

(3) Feng Yü-hsiang (1882–1948), a big, burly man of peasant origin, a soldier from the age of eleven and a graduate of Paoting, who was baptized by a Y.M.C.A. leader in 1913 and was known to his foreign missionary friends as the "Christian General" because he urged his well-disciplined troops to pursue Protestantism, austerity, practical education, and social

reform. Seizing Peking in 1924, Feng broke the power of the Peiyang warlords and finally destroyed their façade of parliamentary government.

The intricate relations among these and other warlord figures defy detailed description. From 1922 to 1926 half a dozen inter-provincial wars erupted. They produced incalculable suffering among a populace oppressed by systematic pillaging and over-taxation. The material results of warlordism included inflation of the currency, disruption of trade, deterioration in railways and in public works for flood control and irrigation, and the recrudescence of the opium evil. The Ch'ing government in 1906 had begun a concerted attack on opium production and smoking, with such widespread patriotic support that the British Indian importation, already down to fifty thousand chests a year, was gradually reduced and stopped at the end of 1917. The much larger Chinese production, well on the way to extinction, was then revived by the simple warlord device of levying such high taxes on land suitable for poppy-growing that nothing but opium could meet the payments.

But the impact of warlordism with all its evils was greatest perhaps on the minds of patriotic youth. "In China today only cunning, crooked, vile, and ruthless people can flourish," wrote Liang Ch'i-ch'ao. Out of the desperation and humiliation of the period came a new revolution which began among the intellectual class.

25. The Rise and Decline of

Nationalist China

The Revolution in Thought and Culture

Modern China has experienced demoralization and decline followed by revival and regeneration on a scale much larger than a mere dynastic cycle. If we compare the social ills of the early nineteenth century (of which increasing opium addiction was a symptom) with the moral fervor and dedication of the Maoist revolution of recent decades, we must conclude that an entire civilization has not only waned but also been remade. The decline reached its political nadir with warlordism after 1916, and revival began with the institution of party dictatorship. Ideologically the waning of Confucianism eventuated in Mao Tse-tung's adaptation of Marxism-Leninism. But in both politics and ideology there was a crucial transition period in which Western liberal models and ideas had an influence.

The warlord era was both chaotic and creative. This was no paradox, for in China's tradition-bound society, new ways could be tried out only after old patterns had been broken. In the decade after 1916 all sorts of ideas and practices, fads and experiments, bubbled forth unrestrained by authority. With political decline came a pluralism of intellectual, economic, and social developments. Underlying the intellectual ferment were processes of economic growth in the cities and of general social change.

The Economic and Social Background. While the decline of central power permitted the rise of disorder in the countryside, the decline of Western imports into China during and after World War I facilitated the rise of native industry in the foreign-administered treaty ports, protected from the warlordism which flourished in the provinces. A new merchant class, outside

763

the ancient guild system, had been fostered by government policies after 1901. By 1914 there were over a thousand local chambers of commerce with 200,000 members. Large-scale enterprises, however, had been mostly British, but also American (particularly in Shanghai) and German (in Shantung until 1915). For example, China's paucity of petroleum resources had given a clear field to foreign imports of kerosene, to supplant vegetable oils for illumination, and of fuel oil, to compete with coal. These imports were dominated by Standard Oil subsidiaries and by the Asiatic Petroleum Company (A.P.C.), an affiliate of the Anglo-Dutch combine, Royal Dutch–Shell, formed in 1907. The long-continued import of cotton yarn and then of textiles had stimulated Chinese cotton-growing to supply British, Chinese, and Japanese mills in China. The market for cigarettes was first developed by an American-organized, London-based combine, the British-American Tobacco Company (B.A.T.), formed in 1902, which soon began through its compradors to lend seed and credit to North China tobacco cultivators. It set up a network of collecting points and curing factories to supply Chinese tobacco to half-a-dozen big B.A.T. cigarette factories, but Chinese firms, like Nanyang Brothers formed in 1905, were soon competing.

By 1914 a modern Chinese administrative and entrepreneurial class had emerged. (It was later stigmatized, anachronistically, as the "comprador class.") To be sure, it grew up under the wing of foreign educators, civil servants, and businessmen. This new class acquired experience in mission and other schools with mixed Sino-Western curricula, in the Maritime Customs, in the Post Office (which was separated from the Customs in 1911 and by 1918 employed a hundred foreigners and 27,000 Chinese), in the steamship lines, mills, shops, and general commerce of old treaty-port firms like Jardine, Matheson or Butterfield and Swire, or in new specialized concerns like the A.P.C. and B.A.T. This nascent middle class had learned modern economic ways in the treaty ports and from association with foreigners. They had accumulated the attitudes and skills necessary for economic development, and World War I gave them their opportunity.

Of the other ingredients needed for industrialization, Chinese capital had accumulated both in overseas communities and in the ports. It was now handled through modern Chinese banks, some of which grew up under government auspices and some as private concerns. These modern banks increased from 17 in 1914 to 102 in 1926, and put the old-style Shansi remittance banks out of business. Yet many factors still retarded the growth of financial resources. As an alternative to productive investment, old-fashioned moneylending, for instance, could still bring 12 per cent or often much more per year. Efforts at currency reform and unification had still not succeeded in abolishing the variable unit of account, the silver tael, even though silver dollars from government mints had come into general use under Yüan Shih-k'ai, most of them bearing his image.

A labor force meanwhile had been drawn to urban centers where cheap labor was needed to tend cotton spindles or sort tobacco, or to work in factories producing matches, flour, canned food, cement, and other mass-produced commodities. These opportunities for employment, newly accessible by railway and steamship, opened up alternatives to the closed routine of peasant life. Warlord taxation and conscription, population increase (presumably), and natural calamities stimulated migration to the cities. Urban life and factory work broke the bonds of the old family system. As wage-earning sons and womenfolk became financially independent, the family ceased to be a self-contained economic and social unit controlling the individual. Instead, the impersonal, universalistic criteria of function, not those of status or specific kinship ties, were applied in the urban labor market. In crowded slums and sweatshops, new values began to take over, and true proletarian factory workers began slowly to accumulate. By 1919 they numbered over a million, perhaps a million and a half.

Social change was evident not only in the rise of new capitalist and labor classes but also in a new status for youth and women. Young men had led the Revolution of 1911, and students now claimed the old privileged status of the scholar class. By 1915 the Ministry of Education listed 120,000 government schools of all sorts with about four million students—an increase over the old days, although only a few thousand reached the college level. Catholic and Protestant mission schools had perhaps half a million students in 1919. Protestant colleges set new standards in higher education. Missionaries had also pioneered in teaching girls, who were a sizable proportion of the thirteen thousand students in Protestant middle schools. In 1915 the first women's institution of higher education, Ginling College, opened at Nanking.

The emergence of these new social classes—merchant-entrepreneurs, factory laborers, and modern-style students—fostered the metamorphosis of Chinese society. Classical degree-holders (gentry in the narrow sense) gave way to younger men, students trained in the cities or even abroad. Landlords tended to become absentee city-dwellers, no longer presiding over the rural society. In short, the rise of city life, with its classes responsive to mass movements, was accompanied by a corresponding decline of rural life, where the leadership of the big households disappeared at the top and the peasant masses met grievous problems in the villages. Through improvements in transport and public health, China's rural population was probably increasing in numbers, but its standard of living was probably falling. Tenantry seems to have grown, as well as the landless peasantry—illiterate, rootless, jobless, and so available for banditry, warlord armies, or dirt-cheap coolie labor.

This collapse of the old society pressed the new student class to stand forth as leaders and saviors. Having inherited the tradition that scholars should advise the power-holders and serve the state-and-culture, they felt uniquely qualified by their studies to modernize and "save" the nation. Their motives and ideas sprang increasingly from foreign contact. Japan still took the largest number of students abroad (about two-fifths), but one-third now went to the United States. The remission to China in 1908 of $12 million (about two-thirds) of the American share of the Boxer indemnity had led to the establishment of Tsing Hua College at Peking, whence a steady flow of scholarship students to the United States began in 1911. (In 1924 the remainder of the indemnity was remitted, and the China Foundation for the Promotion of Education and Culture was established to use the remitted payments as they fell due.) To provide a labor force during the war in Europe, some 140,000 Chinese contract workers were recruited in 1916–1918 and sent to France, where Chinese student workers like James Yen (Yen Yang-ch'u) of the Y.M.C.A. began to develop methods of mass education. In France a work-and-study movement among Chinese students had already been initiated by Ts'ai Yüan-p'ei and others. All this experience fostered the long process of dissolving the ancient barrier between scholarship and labor.

France more than America became a source of political movements and doctrines among returned students in China. The industrial capitalism and factory labor class which gave socialism its *raison d'être* in Europe were still small-scale in China. But European theories of anarchism, especially the anarcho-communism of Peter Kropotkin, found a wide response. Kropotkin's *Mutual Aid: A Factor of Evolution* (1902) argued that mutual aid was as much a law of nature as mutual struggle, although restraints upon freedom must of course be destroyed before cooperation could flourish. Chinese students in Tōkyō and especially in Paris applied the anarchist teachings to China by opposing all elitist organizations and all government (hence nationalism itself), while advocating egalitarianism, mass movements, and direct action including assassination. This anarchist line of thought, combining puritanism, self-sacrifice, and the destruction of the established order with a utopian faith in the public will and voluntary association, was taken up by anarchist groups in major centers.

The New Thought at Peita.   The intellectual revolution centered at Peking National University (usually abbreviated as Peita) because of its prestige as the top of the educational system—only two other government universities as yet existed—and because of the faculty collected there in 1917 by the new chancellor, Ts'ai Yüan-p'ei. As a classical scholar, T'sai had risen to the Hanlin Academy at twenty-five, but later had joined the T'ung-meng Hui, studied Kant and other Western philosophers in Germany, and served as minister of education in the first republican cabinet under Sun and then Yüan in 1912. Returning from further study in Germany and France, he now set about converting Peita from a bureaucrat-ridden school that prepared officials to hold sinecures into a center of learning where ideas from all over the world might compete. His clarion call in 1912 for "education above politics . . . beyond political control," had been silenced by Yüan Shih-k'ai's authoritarian effort to revive Confucianism, and it would be muffled again by the rise of party dictatorship; in the long run, China's reconstruction would seek a new orthodoxy to buttress a new polity. But in the warlord era the very weakness of the political order (not its strength, as under a pluralistic rule of law) permitted freedom of thought to flourish for a time in a genuinely liberal fashion. Ts'ai encouraged the most divergent views at Peita and even the activity of professors and students, as individuals, in politics. The resultant intellectual flowering was a counterpart, on the plane of ideas, to the political revolution in 1911. This revolution in thought was carried on by men of a rare transitional generation, born generally in the 1880's, who had acquired a grounding in Chinese classical studies and then immersed themselves in Western culture abroad. They stood astride two worlds, as few have done before or since, and rejected China's traditional orthodoxy out of knowledge, not ignorance.

Ts'ai brought to Peita to be Dean of Letters a leading revolutionary journalist, Ch'en Tu-hsiu. Coming from a well-to-do official family, Ch'en had passed the classical examinations, studied in Japan and France, and participated in the 1911 revolution. He had become a zealous advocate of individual freedom in the style of the French Revolution—"liberty, equality, fraternity." He attributed China's decay to Confucianism: its family obligations enervated the individual; its disdain of commerce impoverished the economy. In the monthly he founded in 1915, *New Youth* ("La Jeunesse," *Hsin ch'ing-nien*), Ch'en called upon Chinese youth to "be independent, not servile . . . progressive, not conservative . . . dynamic, not passive . . . cosmopolitan, not isolationist . . . utilitarian, not emptily formalistic . . . scientific, not (merely) imaginative." At Peita, Ch'en continued to edit *New Youth,* which became a wide-open forum for discussion, printing letters to the editor, distributing as many as sixteen thousand copies, stirring up the student class all over the country.

Ch'en's principal ally at Peita was a younger man, Hu Shih, also from a scholar-official family and with an early training in the Classics. He had turned to philosophy at Cornell and under John Dewey at Columbia picked up the idea advocated by many revolutionists of using vernacular speech (*pai-hua*) for literary writing instead of the classical style (*wen-yen*). The vernacular novels of the Ming and Ch'ing (see pages 236–237) and also the missionary tracts had paved the way for writing *pai-hua.* Hu Shih, reflecting the "New Tide" in American poetry, pioneered in writing Chinese poetry in everyday words. He and a brilliant specialist in linguistics (Y. R. Chao) stated the case for written *pai-hua* and the movement was launched

*Dr. Hu Shih in 1946, at Cornell University, lecturing on the history
of Chinese philosophy. He was China's ambassador to the
United States in the early war years 1938–1942.*

with Ch'en Tu-hsiu's support in the pages of *New Youth,* which soon was
written entirely in the vernacular.

This "literary renaissance" had several aims—first of all, to create a new
written style to go with modern thought. "A dead language," declared Hu
Shih, "cannot produce a living literature." His advocacy of Dewey's pragmatism and the scientific method led him to seek precision of statement, a new
written language as a tool for critical thinking. A second aim was to reach
the common people, both by making literacy easier for them and by creating
a popular literature directly relevant to their lives. Ch'en Tu-hsiu wanted to
abandon "stereotyped and over-ornamental" classicism in favor of "fresh
and sincere" realism, to overthrow the "unintelligible literature . . . of the
aristocratic few" and create a "plain, simple, and expressive literature of the
people." A further aim of the movement was to emancipate the individual,
by destroying the written language that had been "the repository of Confucian morality and Taoist superstition." A new literature of protest soon
emerged. *New Youth* published in May 1918 a satirical short story, "The
Diary of a Madman." In it the madman is convinced that people want to
kill and eat him. He examines a history book: "Over every page were
scrawled the words 'benevolence, righteousness, truth, virtue.'" Looking
closer, however, he "discovered all over it a succession of two words between
the lines: 'Eat men!'" This bitter indictment of the old society was typical
of the author, Lu Hsün, whose short stories and essays soon made him the
great pioneer figure in China's modern literature.

Thus by 1919 Peking University had become a meeting ground for manifold influences from abroad and from China's classical tradition. *New Youth* had been joined by other journals of discussion. In the resulting ferment, all the social and philosophical theories then current in the Western world and Japan were given expression, whether or not fully grasped—realism, utilitarianism, pragmatism, liberalism, individualism, socialism, anarchism, Darwinism, materialism, etc. Utilizing this armory of ideas, the wholesale criticism of the old society supported two principal protagonists, called by Ch'en "Mr. Democracy" and "Mr. Science." "Only these two gentlemen," he wrote, "can cure the dark maladies in Chinese politics, morality, learning, and thought." The ground was prepared, in ideas and means of communication, for a great explosion of intellectual energy in politics and learning.

The May Fourth Incident. The phrase "May Fourth" derives from the 1919 student demonstration of that date in Peking, but has been taken in the Chinese numerary fashion to designate the whole intellectual movement roughly from 1917 to 1921 or even later, of which we have noted the beginning. The May 4 incident marked the emergence of nationalism as the dominant force in politics. This patriotic concern had been mounting ever since Japan's seizure of Shantung in 1914 and her subsequent Twenty-One Demands. China's entrance into World War I in August 1917 had been urged by some as a means of ensuring China's presence at the peace settlement in order to counter Japan's wartime expansion. However, Japan by secret notes had got British, French, and Italian agreement beforehand to her retaining the ex-German rights in Shantung, which also seemed implicit in the Lansing-Ishii agreement of November 1917 with the United States. The end of World War I in November 1918 brought jubilation in the West at the victory of democracy over militarism. But the Chinese delegation representing both Peking and Canton at the Paris Peace Conference in January 1919 soon found, like President Wilson, that his doctrine of self-determination and open diplomacy did not apply to East Asia. It developed that in 1918 the warlord government at Peking also had signed secret agreements confirming Japan's Shantung position. The arguments of China's able young diplomats were unavailing. Chinese public concern became unprecedentedly aroused. Hundreds of associations of Overseas Chinese, students, merchants, educators, labor unions, and political groups telegraphed their protests to Paris. As student indignation mounted at the Peking government's secret sell-out, news came of the Paris decision to leave Japan in Shantung. On May 4, over three thousand college students from thirteen institutions in Peking assembled at the Gate of Heavenly Peace (T'ien-an Men) and endorsed a manifesto. The subsequent demonstration erupted into violence when students beat one pro-Japanese official as a "traitor" and burned the house of a cabinet minister.

The historical impact of the May Fourth incident came from the students' subsequent program of political agitation. The Peking students organized a union, including girls as well as boys. They quickly secured nationwide support from the press and the merchants, from Sun Yat-sen and the Canton government, and from warlord rivals of the An-fu clique. Students in other cities, similarly organized, staged demonstrations, began boycotts of Japanese goods, and mobilized support with speeches in the streets. They stimulated a similar organization of the modern scholar class—professors, teachers, writers, journalists—for political action. In late May and early June student strikes closed the schools in more than two hundred cities. The students proved themselves a new force in politics, under the banner of anti-Japanese patriotism. The warlord Peking government, true to its belief in force, tried early in June to suppress the movement by imprisoning some 1150 student agitators, turning part of Peita into a jail. In response, girls now joined the boys in the streets. Shanghai merchants sympathetically closed their shops in a week-long patriotic strike. Workers struck for patriotic reasons in some forty Shanghai factories. This truly national movement, involving major classes and reaching a new level of popular activity, won the day. The Peking students marched victoriously out of jail. Three pro-Japanese "traitor" officials were dismissed. The cabinet resigned. China refused to sign the Versailles Treaty.

The New Culture Movement.   Out of the political activity of the May Fourth incident came China's new nationalism of the 1920's, to be marked by the rise of party dictatorship, the growth of socialist thinking, and the struggle against imperialism. Meanwhile the intellectual ferment, out of which political activism had been generated, went steadily on—media of communication increased, Western ideas were eagerly sought after, old evils were more vigorously attacked and new values debated. This intellectual activity, in the year or two following May 4, 1919, generally stopped short of social and political action and was given the name "New Culture Movement." As its medium, several hundred new periodicals in the written vernacular made their appearance, though some only briefly. Newspapers, too, catered to the new thought and its re-examination of all values. Publication of books, including translations of Western works, rose sharply. By these means the intellectual revolution, begun by young professors in their thirties and students in their twenties, spread from Peita all over the country. Associations for innumerable purposes sprang up everywhere. Leading foreign scholars came to lecture. John Dewey spent two years in China and lectured frequently, often with Hu Shih interpreting. Bertrand Russell came for almost a year and, advocating state socialism, found a wide audience.

The attack on the old Confucian order of hierarchy and status denied the validity of the ancient "three bonds," the subordination of subject to ruler, of son to father, and of wife to husband. It denounced the three corresponding virtues—loyalty to superiors, filiality, and female subjection—as props of despotism in both state and family. The anti-Confucianists attacked the tyranny of parents, their arrangement of marriages, and the subordination of youth to family. The emancipation of women made great strides in this period, parallel with the movement for women's suffrage and equal rights in the West. The many conservatives who wanted to make Confucianism a state religion, which K'ang Yu-wei still advocated as he had in 1898, provoked increasing opposition. The Confucian proprieties or principles of social usage were denounced as fetters on the individual. Social harmony based on inequality of roles was anathematized. "Chinese culture," wrote Lu Hsün, "is a culture of serving one's masters, who are triumphant at the cost of the misery of the multitude."

The attack on Confucianism stimulated a critical re-evaluation of Chinese antiquity. Scholars at Peita, "antiquity-doubters," reappraised the authenticity of the Classics. Liang Ch'i-ch'ao, now retired from politics, and Hu Shih among others led a wide-ranging "reorganization of the national heritage," winnowing the grain from the chaff within the great tradition. Thus they restudied the ancient philosopher Mo-tzu, the history of Buddhism in China, the vernacular novels, the thought of the Ch'ing period. This concern for the national heritage was heightened by disillusionment with European "materialism" after World War I. Liang returned from the Paris Peace Conference convinced of the spiritual bankruptcy of Western civilization, which had become materialistic, withered, dry, and sick from a "spiritual famine." A whole series of controversies argued the merits of one issue after another. Religion was debated, defended, and widely decried. When the World Student Christian Federation met in Peking in 1922, a nationwide antireligious and anti-Christian movement was organized among students.

In proportion as the intellectual and cultural revolution triumphed over the traditional order, it lost its unity of aim. A split occurred between those inclined toward academic studies, reform, and gradual evolution and those inclined toward political action, rebellion, and violent revolution. People sorted themselves out, partly according to background and personal temperament. The pragmatic approach to recreating China's civilization was led by Hu Shih, who inveighed against "isms," both the various forms of socialism and other all-embracing creeds. Instead, he urged a concentration on "problems," to be analyzed by the "genetic method" and with "a critical attitude": "There is no liberation *in toto,* or reconstruction *in toto.* Liberation means liberation from this or that institution, from this or that belief, for this or that individual; it is liberation bit by bit, drop by drop." To many, this seemed inadequate to meet China's problems and emotionally unsatisfying as well. Hu's long-term program of education had no short-term political method. It could only produce liberal manifestoes asking warlord governments to guarantee civil liberties, all in vain. Chinese supporters of individualism could not appeal to a positive doctrine of individual rights and freedoms like that of Western liberalism. The latter had derived from the Western doctrines of natural rights and the supremacy of law, but these had no counterparts in China capable of supporting a genuine Chinese liberalism. Instead, the would-be liberal in warlord China, before he could "selfishly" demand his own civil liberties, had to help create a modern nation-state, as his new loyalty to country also demanded. For a time the focus of concern had been how to emancipate the individual. But after 1921 it shifted back to the more customary theme, how to strengthen the state. Nationalism took precedence over liberalism. Political movements soon arose that would again try to mobilize and control the individual and his cultural activity.

The Introduction of Marxism-Leninism. The May Fourth incident had shown what students could accomplish when organized for political action. This potentiality was plain to Sun Yat-sen, then in Shanghai, and he set about recruiting students as part of his general reorganization of the Kuomintang. Political action also appealed to the romantic temperament of Ch'en Tu-hsiu. Just at this point, the example and the doctrines of Soviet Russia came to hand in practical form. One whole wing of the New Culture movement, like some major Kuomintang leaders, soon felt they had found the action program they had been seeking.

The intellectual appeal of Marxism lay partly in its claim to being "scientific," in an age when science seemed to be the secret of Western superiority. Marx's concept of "historical materialism"—that society progresses through a sequence of stages (primitive, slave-owning, feudal, capitalist, socialist) by virtue of "class struggle" between ruling and exploited classes for control of the "means of production"—appealed to students in need of a system to explain "progress" and simplify the confusing events of history. The optimistic belief that class struggle and exploitation could be obviated by abolishing private ownership of the means of production was particularly attractive in an underdeveloped country where industrialization and all its problems were just beginning. Moreover, Marxism had been capped by Lenin's concept of the revolutionary vanguard, the disciplined intellectual elite of the Communist Party, and by his explanation of colonial imperialism as due to the growth of international monopoly capitalism. While European Marxism, originally prescribed for advanced industrial societies, had thus far been a very minor motif in China's intellectual history, Marxism-Leninism was something new. In the China of 1919 its messianic vision was made more credible by the startling Soviet success in seizing power. It seemed to offer an all-embracing solution to China's problems. On the theoretical plane, it provided a self-consistent, universalistic, and "scientific" view of world history which enabled one to reject the imperialistic West in the name of Western "scientific thought" and explain China's humiliating backwardness as due to her bondage to "capitalist imperialism" (e.g., Japan and the Western treaty powers), which had allied itself with "warlord feudalism" (e.g., the An-fu clique). On the political level, Leninism offered a new and tighter method of party organization and a technique for seizing power and using it to mobilize the populace and recreate society —actually, the latest step in borrowing political technology from the Western world. For the individual, finally, Leninism claimed to offer a way toward self-discipline and sacrifice for patriotic ends.

While these appeals would grow stronger with time, they made their appearance at a propitious moment, when patriotic fervor was seeking organized expression. China's "betrayal" at Versailles offered dramatic proof that the real national enemy was "imperialism." Henceforth nationalism and anti-imperialism seemed interlinked, just as Lenin said. Some leaders of the New Culture movement proceeded to political action. In the pages of *New Youth,* Li Ta-chao, a professor of philosophic bent much concerned for the Chinese peasants' liberation, had already hailed "The Victory of Bolshevism"; in May 1919 he edited a whole issue on Marxism. Study groups in Peking and Shanghai took up various kinds of socialist theory. (A Hunan student, Mao Tse-tung, who had assisted Li in the Peita library, returned to Changsha in March 1919 and led another such group.) By mid-1920 Ch'en Tu-hsiu and Li Ta-chao had wholeheartedly accepted Marxism-Leninism. Ch'en met with others in September to plan the founding of a Chinese Communist Party. By the time Mao and eleven others attended the Shanghai meeting of July 1921, now regarded as the founding First Congress of the Chinese Communist Party, small party branches existed also in Peking, Changsha, Wuhan, Canton, and Tsinan.

The Soviet contribution to this sudden development had begun with an offer to give up all privileges under the old tsarist unequal treaties, which aroused widespread pro-Soviet enthusiasm. Agents of the Communist International (Comintern, organized in March 1919) helped set up the first Communist organization in Shanghai, with its news agency, publications, and branches and also assisted at the First Congress of the Party. At this stage Comintern know-how was an essential ingredient. Activists among the worker-students in postwar France, many of them from Hunan, in 1921 set up their own Young China Communist Party in Paris. Chou En-lai, a graduate of Nankai University, became the most famous of the group of Communist leaders who returned from France.

After 1921 the growth of party organizations, both Communist and Kuomintang, confronted intellectuals with a painful choice, to pursue scholarship eschewing politics, or to subordinate learning to political action. When Hu Shih and Ch'en Tu-hsiu parted company early in 1921, after four years' collaboration, they symbolized the alternatives.

Writers soon faced a similar choice. As in the European Renaissance, the written speech of everyday life was just beginning to be used, tentatively and experimentally, in all the forms of literature. New styles and themes for novels, stories, essays, poetry, drama, criticism, all awaited fresh creation in Chinese. Many beginnings were made, many of them not yet studied. But for most writers the overwhelming preoccupation became the social revolution—the evils of the old order, the struggle to remake it. Writers believed that theirs was a didactic social function, to instruct their fellow countrymen and save China. Those who individualistically pursued romanticism or "art for art's sake," often on Anglo-American models, were soon overshadowed by those with a social purpose, like Lu Hsün, desirous of serving their country as spiritual physicians.

The most influential early group, the Society for Literary Studies, took over the editing of *Short Story* magazine published by the Commercial Press. They advocated a varied and realistic "humane literature," stressed the translation of Western fiction, and encouraged new talent, including several women. A rival group was the Creation Society formed by Kuo Mo-jo and others in Japan, dedicated at first to an all-out, rebellious romanticism. It published candid autobiographic confessions in which sexual desire and patriotic sentiment alike met frustration and left the hero usually remorseful and guilt-ridden. In the mid-1920's, however, the Creation Society turned with equal energy to Marxism. As Kuo Mo-jo wrote on his conversion in 1924, "I am now able to impose order on all the ideas which I could not reconcile; I have found the key to all the problems which appeared to me self-contradictory and insoluble"—a statement which epitomized the appeal of Marxism-Leninism and augured ill for the liberal-individualist approach to literature as art. Lacking a modern tradition and established artistic canons in a new medium, writers perhaps more readily accepted a primarily social function in the revolutionary process.

The Background of the Nationalist Revolution

The 1920's saw the height of warlord disorder and the rise of a revolution to overcome it. The first aim of the revolution was national reunification. Beyond this were other goals, foreign and domestic. In foreign relations, the revolution aimed to abolish foreign privileges and influence under the unequal treaties. Every patriot was anti-imperialist. On the domestic scene, however, interests diverged. Social revolution, through mass organization of factory labor and even of peasants in the villages, emerged as a possibility. But the main leadership eventually turned against social revolution, suppressed the mass movements, and consolidated its power on a platform of national unity and anti-imperialism. As a process the revolution first accumulated its various elements during a preparatory period from 1921 to mid-1925, came to high tide for two years thereafter, and then receded. As a step in China's political modernization, the rise of the Kuomintang meant that a new form of government, party dictatorship, had finally been devised to supplant the dynastic system. The treaty system also took on its final form, modified to permit more exercise of Chinese sovereignty. Yet both these developments stopped part way. The Kuomintang dictatorship did not get firm control over all the provinces of China. The revolution which brought it to power, mainly in the cities, also stopped short of the countryside. Similarly China's recovery of sovereignty failed to abolish extra-territoriality. Thus the Nationalist Revolution, like the Revolution of 1911, got limited results.

The influence of the West was also meeting its inevitable limitations. Neither Western entrepreneurs in the ports nor missionaries in the interior could deal with the problem of China's political order. No treaty-power government could offer China a model for her reorganization, or show how to harness her new nationalism for purposes of industrialization. The West had helped destroy the old order, but how could it now help build a new one? This question underlay the post–World War I diplomatic settlement of 1921–1922.

The Slowness of Treaty Revision. The treaty powers looked forward to China's developing a stable central government like any other nation. The treaty system had always kept open the possibility of its own liquidation, since the treaties were all made between two sovereign powers, one of which (China) accepted limitations on its sovereignty. Foreign diplomats and Chinese nationalists disagreed less on the desirability of China's recovering full sovereignty than on the speed and procedures with which to accomplish it. The principal effort by the powers to deal with the China problem was made at the Washington Conference (November 12, 1921–February 2, 1922). The settlement was in four main categories, although it lacked any means of enforcement, either in sanctions and operative clauses or in binding commitments of power politics.

In the first place, the Anglo-Japanese alliance, which might embroil Britain and the Commonwealth in any Japanese-American conflict, was now abolished, with no equally firm alliance to take its place. Second, limitation of naval armament in capital ships, one primary purpose of the conference, was accepted on a five-five-three ratio for Britain, the United States, and Japan, with the proviso that no British or American naval bases would be developed east of Singapore or west of Hawaii. Third, Japan agreed to withdraw from Shantung and also withdraw her forces from the Northeast Asian mainland, where intervention against the Bolshevik revolution in mid-1918 had brought Allied forces, especially Japanese, into the Maritime Province, northern Manchuria, and eastern Siberia. Thus, in return for an assurance of her naval domination of the western Pacific, Japan withdrew on the Asian mainland to her territorial position in 1905, except for Korea. Finally, the Nine-Power Treaty formally proclaimed everyone's support of the Open Door and the territorial integrity and administrative independence of China and moved toward gradual liquidation of the treaty system by calling for conferences on the Chinese customs tariff and on extraterritoriality.

As a consequence of these agreements, Japan withdrew from Shantung, and Britain eventually restored Weihaiwei. But the tariff conference was not held until 1925–1926, and even then failed to agree except on the important point that China might exercise tariff autonomy by 1929. Similarly the extraterritoriality commission, meeting in Peking only in 1926, achieved no result. Inhibiting this international effort to facilitate China's growth as a nation-state was the lack of an effective central government. Banditry and warlord excesses endangered foreign lives and property. The inability of the Chinese authorities to perform their international obligations undercut their claims to exercise rights of sovereignty. Thus China's internal disorder checked the proposed revision of the unequal-treaty system.

The Soviet Approach to the Chinese Revolution.   The Soviet impact on China in the 1920's was still another phase of Western influence. But in contrast with the treaty powers' halfhearted efforts at a gradual reform of China's foreign relations, Moscow offered China a working model of domestic revolution. As early as 1912, Lenin had suggested that the Communist-led proletarian revolution of industrialized Europe should support Asian nationalist revolutions that might be led by "bourgeois-democratic" movements against colonialism and imperialism. At the second Comintern congress in 1920 Lenin's "theses on the national and colonial question" argued that, just as Western capitalism had prolonged its life by exploiting the cheap labor and raw materials of its Asian colonies, so the Western proletariat could now, by a "flank attack," ally with the Asian bourgeoisie against their enemy, "capitalist imperialism," which was the economic exploiter of the colonial peoples and the political ally of the reactionary "feudal" ruling class in Asia. Lenin's theory of imperialism thus unified the world scene. It gave historical significance, within a single cosmology, to all the elements in Chinese politics. One's military rivals could be stigmatized as "warlords" representing the "feudal reaction" of a dying order. Urban merchants and middle-class individuals could be classified as the "national bourgeoisie," representing the capitalist stage of history, which it would now be possible to "leap over." With the use of Soviet aid and of the Chinese peasantry, a "united front" could be developed, led by the "proletariat" in the Communist Party. By this tactic the "bourgeois nationalist" movement could be supported to defeat foreign "imperialism" while at the same time (and this was essential) the "proletarian party" could be organized to seize power from within. Lenin foresaw a wide range of opportunities—Communist parties in Asia could make "temporary agreements and even alliances" with "bourgeois nationalist" movements in a united front, or alternatively, they could develop their own communist "soviets of workers and peasants" as centers of independent power.

This range of theoretical alternatives was inherited by Lenin's successors. Trotsky advocated independent soviets in China, while Stalin advocated a united front with the Kuomintang. In Marxist thinking a true party must represent a class, and so Stalin had to argue that the Kuomintang was only a coalition or "bloc of four classes": proletarian workers, peasants, petty bourgeoisie, and capitalists, later called national bourgeoisie. These alternatives gave the Soviet approach to China a built-in dualism—it could stress either a united front of all revolutionary classes against foreign imperialism and its "lackeys," or a class struggle within China, with soviets of proletarians and peasants fighting the Chinese bourgeoisie plus the feudal reactionaries, landlords, militarists, and their imperialist supporters. Between these two tactics lay a middle ground of coalition with some classes against others, for example, with the "petty bourgeoisie" but against the "national bourgeoisie."

In addition to this flexibility of doctrine, the Soviet government pursued a dual approach to China on the two levels of open diplomacy and revolutionary subversion. Diplomacy conducted by the Soviet foreign ministry had begun with the offer to give up the former tsarist privileges. Several missions to Peking led to hard bargaining and an actual reassertion of former tsarist aims in Northeast Asia. The eventual Soviet treaty with Peking in May 1924 provided for joint administration of the Chinese Eastern Railway and a dominant Russian influence in Outer Mongolia. Simultaneously, under the Soviet program of subversion, Comintern agents helped develop the Chinese Communist Party apparatus and a Communist-led labor movement, and also made contact with leading warlords in the North and with Sun Yat-sen in the South. By this time events in Russia had necessitated Lenin's introduction in 1921 of the New Economic Policy of retrenchment, a "temporary retreat" from Communism. This was the less extreme and less fearsome Soviet image presented to Sun and his followers.

The Kuomintang Reorganization and Comintern Alliance. Sun Yat-sen was groping for a party organization that could make the transition from a seizure of power to a civil government exercising "political tutelage" over the unsophisticated Chinese masses. The Soviet party dictatorship now seemed to be part of a broad trend of history, while fascism in Italy after 1919 offered an example of party dictatorship not based on class war. The May Fourth incident inspired Sun to revive and reorganize the Kuomintang, and new general regulations, party principles, and a manifesto, were all three issued on January 1, 1923. Reorganization was formally completed at the party's First Congress in January 1924. As part of this process, Sun gradually developed a working alliance with the Comintern.

Sun was pushed in this direction by several circumstances. The treaty powers had dealt only with the Peking government and had done little to liquidate the treaty system. His demand in September 1923 that they let his Canton government use the local Maritime Customs surplus was sharply refused; the treaty powers concentrated naval vessels at Canton to prevent his seizing the Customs. His repeated requests for Western aid got no response. His domestic vicissitudes had been equally disappointing. The Kuomintang rump parliament at Canton was as prone to splintering as the warlord parliament at Peking. Sun's uneasy cooperation with a local warlord had collapsed, forcing him to flee to Shanghai. He needed help.

The Kuomintang-Comintern alliance meant cooperation with the nascent Chinese Communist Party (CCP). The Second Congress of the CCP in mid-1922 favored an alliance with the Kuomintang (KMT) on a parallel or equal basis. However, instead of an alliance between parties, it was arranged on Comintern orders that Communist Party members would join the Kuomintang as individuals, and keep their own separate organization, thus forming a "bloc within" instead of a "bloc without." Sun permitted Li Ta-chao to retain his CCP membership when he joined the KMT. Ch'en Tu-hsiu then joined on similar terms and was given high KMT positions. Others followed.

With Soviet advice Sun now began the creation of a party army and sent his devoted military assistant, Chiang Kai-shek, to the Soviet Union to study its methods. The KMT began to be represented at Comintern meetings. After returning to Canton early in 1923 Sun began using CCP members in important posts. He took the technical guidance of an able Soviet adviser, Michael Borodin, who drafted the KMT's new constitution and soon had a political institute teaching propagandists how to organize mass support. On the Soviet model the KMT now set up local cells which in turn elected delegates at higher levels (county and province), each of which elected an executive committee, up to the national party congress, which chose a central executive committee, whose standing committee could now by "democratic centralism" dominate a centralized Leninist-type party.

On the Communist side of this marriage of convenience, the Third CCP Congress, in June 1923, by a bare majority acquiesced in the "bloc within" type of alliance. It agreed that the KMT should be the "central force of the national revolution." Mao Tse-tung, for example, as head of the CCP organization department, cooperated for a time with a KMT stalwart in "coordinating" the two party organizations. But the small CCP, with fewer than a thousand members, opposed close coordination as giving the KMT too much control over its membership. Their dual strategy was now to

*Sun Yat-sen and his young wife,
Soong Ch'ing-ling, a graduate
of Wesleyan College for
Women (Macon, Georgia), en
route to Peking at the end
of 1924.*

capture the KMT from within while developing their own mass organizations outside it.

Sun Yat-sen's attitude in welcoming individual Communists into his party was both self-confident and practical. He saw how effectively students could organize workers and peasants. The few hundred members of the CCP were a mere handful compared with the scores of thousands of the KMT. While Lenin is said to have referred to Sun Yat-sen's "inimitable, one might say, virginal naiveté," Sun felt certain that his party could remain the principal Chinese partner of the Russians, who he felt would "not be fooled by these youngsters" of the CCP.

Kuomintang Ideology and the Party Army. To go with the new party apparatus, Sun Yat-sen needed as always a revolutionary ideology. While on the sidelines in Shanghai in 1918 and later, he had developed a theory of "psychological reconstruction." This included the idea that "knowing is more difficult than doing," an acknowledgment that the revolution thus far had lacked in ideas. In his own mind Sun did not accept the Leninist thesis that capitalism inevitably produces imperialism. He favored the struggle of oppressed nations against oppressing nations, but he did not link this with a class struggle inside each nation. Instead, in response to Borodin's request that the KMT be given a more formal ideology, he put forward his own

Chiang Kai-shek as
superintendent of the
Whampoa Military Academy
in 1925, aged 38.

revised statement of the *Three Principles of the People.* In these rather
discursive lectures in the winter of 1922–1923, the principle of nationalism,
which in 1905 had been anti-Manchu and in 1914 had been disregarded
in Sun's platform, now stressed anti-imperialism. It also included self-
determination both for the Chinese people and for minorities within China.
The principle of people's rights, often translated as democracy, distinguished
between popular sovereignty and the administrative capacity of the government. Sun piously hoped to "make the government the machinery, and the
people the engineer," but this was to be done only through the devices of
election, initiative, referendum, and recall (copied from the American
Progressive movement of a bygone era), which had never become operative
in China. The principle of people's livelihood (*min-sheng*) remained the
vaguest of all, since Sun specifically denied the Marxist thesis of class struggle and reiterated his earlier concepts of the limitation of capital and the
equalization of landholdings on the single-tax basis advocated by Henry
George. Of the three principles, nationalism was the dominant core around
which unanimity could be achieved.

Just as important as the party apparatus and its ideology was the indoctrinated party army. After Chiang Kai-shek's return from four months
in the Soviet Union, he became head of a new military academy at Whampoa below Canton, aided by a corps of Soviet advisers. The leading CCP

representative, Chou En-lai, was deputy head of the political education department, which Communists steadily infiltrated but without ultimate success. Soon two regiments of cadets constituted a KMT "party army," trained to fight for Sun Yat-sen's ideology.

Sun died unexpectedly on March 12, 1925, and his figure became the object of a revolutionary cult reminiscent of the ancestor reverence accorded a dynastic founder. His writings became a creed of "Sun Yat-senism." To carry on his cause, the Nationalist Government (Kuo-min cheng-fu) was formed at Canton on July 1 as a military-party dictatorship with Wang Ching-wei, one of Sun's principal political heirs, as its chairman, just as the revolution developed into a great mass movement.

The Kuomintang's Rise to Power

Labor Organization.   By the summer of 1925 the two revolutionary parties, the dominant KMT and the small CCP, faced an explosive opportunity: an upsurge of patriotic anti-imperialism combined with a militant anticapitalist labor movement. Each of these movements had its own rationale. Six years after the May Fourth movement, the treaty powers still exercised nearly all their accumulated privileges: the Japanese Kwantung leased territory and South Manchurian Railway dominated southern Manchuria. The South Manchurian Railway and the British-owned Kailan Mining Administration policed China's biggest coal mines. At Tientsin, concession areas were still governed by the British, French, Japanese, and Italians. Legation guards still paraded through Peking. Most of Shanghai was governed by the foreign (mainly British) rate-payers through the Shanghai Municipal Council. The trade of South China was largely dominated by Hong Kong. Foreigners still held the top posts in the Chinese Maritime Customs, Salt Revenue, and Post Office administrations, revenues from which went chiefly to pay China's foreign creditors. Foreign steamship lines and gunboats plied China's inland waters all the way into Hunan and Szechwan. Many modern industrial enterprises were foreign-owned.

Any middle-school student could add details to this humiliating picture of semicolonialism, which the competing warlords of North and Central China and Manchuria could not alter, some of them indeed being part of it. The stimuli for anti-imperialism were most visible in the great port cities— Shanghai, Canton, Hong Kong, Wuhan, Tientsin—where the new factory labor class was also heavily concentrated. The evils of factory work in China had become as great as the unlimited supply of manpower: a twelve-hour day, more or less; a seven-day week with a very few festival holidays; unskilled peasants paid by piece-work, with a high rate of turnover; child labor exploited along with that of mothers, their nursing babies often parked under the basins of boiling water in the silk filatures; uncontrolled hazards to body and health; friction with Chinese labor contractors and foreign managers and foremen; and pay so low that all family adults had to work—such conditions, reminiscent of Europe a century earlier, gave the Chinese labor movement its own impetus.

A modern labor movement required, of course, new forms of labor organization. In China's traditional handicraft guilds, shop masters still dominated the artisans and apprentices, and craft solidarity was stressed, not working-class solidarity. Nor were the old secret societies suited to leading a labor movement; in Shanghai the powerful "green gang" (*Ch'ing-pang*) and "red gang" (*Hung-pang*) could not rise above the underworld level of opium smuggling, prostitution, crime, and protection rackets. Some workingmen's benefit associations had been formed, mostly among miners or railway workers, but the most efficient early union was built up after 1914 among Chinese seamen in international shipping. With the May Fourth movement had come a wave of strikes. Thereafter the organizing efforts of anarchist, KMT, and other political groups were gradually overshadowed by those of the CCP, which initiated the first all-China congress of labor organizations at Canton in May 1922 and fomented strikes in Hunan, Hupei, and along the North China railways.

By 1925 the foreign treaty-port establishment and the provincial military governors seemed to much of the articulate Chinese public to constitute an evil partnership of "imperialism" and "warlordism." KMT and CCP alike saw these twin evils as the enemies of "nationalism." Chinese industrialists were the more ready to oppose them because of the recrudescence of foreign competition since World War I. In Shanghai early in 1925 union organization and strikes increased, and at the same time merchants in the Chinese General Chamber of Commerce protested against regulation and "taxation without representation" under the Shanghai Municipal Council. When its British-officered police killed thirteen demonstrators on Nanking Road on May 30, there ensued a nationwide multiclass movement of protests, demonstrations, strikes, boycotts, and militant anti-imperialism. This "May Thirtieth movement" dwarfed all previous antiforeign demonstrations. In similar fashion, on June 23, a demonstration on the Shaki bund, the roadway facing the consular island of Shameen at Canton, led to shooting between Whampoa cadets and Anglo-French troops and to the death of fifty-two Chinese. There then ensued a great fifteen-month strike and boycott against Hong Kong, crippling British trade in South China. These tumultuous events, with many smaller incidents and issues, afforded a great opportunity for student agitation and for mobilizing all classes in a great national cause. The CCP exploited this opportunity. Its young enthusiasts moved into the center of affairs. Its membership, including the Youth Corps, rapidly increased to about twenty thousand by late 1925. It bade fair to capture the leadership of the mass movement in the cities.

TREATY PORT LIFE. *Top: Returned students from Britain, France, and the United States. Bottom: Sikh policeman directing Shanghai traffic.*

The Northern Expedition and the KMT-CCP Split.   The nationwide response to the May Thirtieth movement of 1925 marked the onset of high tide for the Nationalist Revolution. It also raised the question of the revolution's ultimate aims and began to strain the unity of the disparate groups that were working together at Canton. The growth of the CCP, which was abetted by the ambitious leaders of the left-wing KMT who now dominated the Canton government, put the right wing of the KMT on the defensive. Its major interest was anti-imperialism on a united, national basis rather than through class warfare. It wanted an ideology of national unity which would be multiclass and both anti-imperialist and anti-Communist. For the CCP and the Comintern, which controlled its party line, the choice was difficult —either to break with the KMT entirely, facing the danger of being overpowered by it, or to keep working with the still dominant left KMT against the right, hoping to split the two. The Communists were developing independent power in the labor movement, and were also leading peasant movements.

On balance, however, the trend of events seemed still to justify the KMT-CCP united front, and Stalin chose to continue it. The Second Kuomintang Congress of January 1926, at which the left KMT held the balance of power, also continued the alliance. It kept leading Communists in the KMT secretariat and organization bureau, and seven (constituting 20 per cent) on the central executive committee. This arrangement was approved by both Wang Ching-wei, the leader of the left wing, and Chiang Kai-shek, the principal military commander. Chiang's Whampoa cadets had already defeated local forces in the Canton area, but the militant organization for the Hong Kong strike and boycott had been taken over by the CCP and was creating at Canton an armed, Communist-led government-within-a-government. Communist influence was expanding within the KMT apparatus and mass organizations and practically took over the navy. Allegedly in self-defense, Chiang on March 20 staged a *coup d'état* at Canton, ousting part of the CCP leadership and some Soviet advisers, while simultaneously reaffirming his loyalty to the Canton-Moscow alliance. Thus in the spring of 1926 Chiang Kai-shek emerged as the principal proponent of China's military unification, and the CCP again faced the choice of continuing to work with the KMT or turning against it. Once again Moscow favored collaboration: Stalin needed his alliance with Chiang as a means of arguing against Trotsky, just as Chiang still needed a united revolutionary effort with CCP and Soviet support for a great Northern Expedition.

This great military campaign, long planned by Sun to smash the warlords and reunify China, was also aimed at rising above local conflicts at Canton and expanding the revenue area of the government. Launched in July 1926, the expedition, preceded by its newly trained propagandists, advanced rapidly and absorbed some thirty-four warlord armies or contingents by the time it reached the Yangtze. The Nationalist troops showed respect for the people and were welcomed. Only one regiment eventually proved to be under Communist control; CCP cells had not been widely established in the military forces. At the end of 1926 the Nationalist Government, still dominated by the left KMT, moved from Canton to Wuhan. The Comintern in Moscow followed Stalin's lead and ordered the CCP to stay with it. The CCP therefore continued as a "bloc within," largely prevented from exploiting peasant unrest or building independent military power.

As the Northern Expedition in the spring of 1927 continued its successful take-over of Central China, the Nationalist Revolution entered a phase in which the military forces played a larger role, and purely political manipulation of the movement as a result became less feasible. The preponderant anti-Communist view of the military soon fostered a split in which first Chiang and the KMT military joined the right KMT in turning against the left KMT and the CCP, and then the left KMT also turned against the CCP, eventually rejoining the right. Thus the Nationalist drive for unity and a new political order purged itself of the divisive Communist program for class struggle and social revolution.

These developments took place after Chiang Kai-shek had moved down the Yangtze to take over the rice basket and industrial base of the region around Shanghai. Just at this point, on April 6, 1927, Peking authorities raided the Soviet Embassy and seized incriminating evidence of subversion (Li Ta-chao and other Communist leaders were later executed). Then at Shanghai, on April 12, Chiang's forces with foreign concurrence supported local anti-Communist elements who destroyed the armed CCP organization and labor movement by a sudden coup and reign of terror. On April 18 Chiang set up his own government at Nanking with the support of most of the KMT central executive committee in defiance of Wuhan. In this crisis the Comintern representatives and CCP leaders at Wuhan were still instructed from Moscow to follow Stalin's line of cooperation with the left KMT. But the latter, finally disillusioned and alarmed, broke in July with its Communist colleagues and expelled them. On August 1 an uprising of Communist troops at Nanchang began an open civil war between the two parties. The Comintern blamed Ch'en Tu-hsiu, as secretary-general of the CCP, for the "opportunism" which had led to failure, "in complete contradiction to the instructions of the Comintern." (He was expelled in 1929, a scapegoat for Stalin's misjudgments.) Mao Tse-tung, who in a February 1927 report on the peasant movement in Hunan had advocated a peasant rising contrary to the Moscow directive of that period, now led a so-called "Autumn Harvest" insurrection in Hunan. It was soon suppressed. Communist putsches at Swatow and Canton both failed. The youthful CCP leadership was executed, driven underground in the cities, or forced into the countryside.

The way was open for Chiang Kai-shek and the right-wing KMT, with the support of the Chinese bankers and businessmen of Shanghai, to make peace with the left KMT and build up their Nanking regime as the central government of China. Warlordism was not yet wiped out, but China was more united than it had been for a decade. At last it had a government intent on building a modern nation-state and reasserting the national dignity.

The Revolution and the Foreign Powers.   The response of the treaty powers to China's dramatic awakening to nationalism was to give ground and acknowledge many of its claims. After the May Thirtieth movement of 1925, Chinese were added to the Shanghai Municipal Council; municipal parks were eventually opened to Chinese residents; and the Shanghai Mixed Court was supplanted by a purely Chinese district court. The powers in 1926 permitted Canton to collect the customs surtaxes they had refused to Sun Yat-sen in 1923. Britain gave up concessions in Hankow and Kiukiang.

The fighting in 1925–1927 forced most of the Protestant missionaries to withdraw from the interior, while an international force of forty thousand troops gathered to defend Shanghai. When Nationalist troops, taking Nanking in March 1927, killed six foreigners, British and American gunboats laid down a protective barrage but later a settlement was worked out. Considering the passions and fears of the day, rather little Sino-foreign violence erupted. Like Britain, the American State Department maintained neutrality and refused to be obsessed by the Bolshevik menace, despite the conviction of the Shanghai foreign community that Chinese antiforeignism was a Moscow plot. The Western powers did little to prevent the rise or precipitate the fall of Soviet influence on the revolution.

Another Nationalist Northern Expedition in 1928 occupied Peking ("Northern Capital") and renamed it Peiping ("Northern Peace"). By the end of 1928 the Nationalist Government had received international recognition. The "Young Marshal" of Manchuria (Chang Hsueh-liang, son of the old warlord Chang Tso-lin), brought the Three Eastern Provinces into political union with the rest of China. China's unity was nominally complete. Led by a new generation of "returned students" who had studied mainly in the West, the government strove to consolidate national resources and abolish the unequal treaties. Extraterritoriality for the major powers continued, but Nanking issued new law codes and secured new treaties placing many minor foreign nationalities under Chinese jurisdiction. Tariff autonomy was fully recovered by 1933, as well as control over the Maritime Customs, the Salt Revenue Administration, and the Post Office. Foreign concession areas were reduced from thirty-three to thirteen.

This vigorous Nationalist foreign policy, whittling away treaty privileges, slowed down after 1931 because Japan's new aggression gave China and the Western powers a common defensive interest in preserving the Western legal position in China. As Nanking turned against Marxist-Leninist class struggle and confronted Japanese aggression, it toned down its attack on foreign privilege and found a community of interest with the foreigners, particularly the British, Americans, French, and Canadians, who continued to participate in Chinese life as privileged persons, maintaining colleges and hospitals, banks, trading firms, and investments.

The Comintern strategy of the 1920's seems in retrospect to have had little if any chance of success. The political organization of urban labor, in order to seize power as in Europe, was still a forlorn hope in China. Labor unions could develop strength only in the few port cities where the new Nationalist leadership and foreign interests were also most heavily concentrated. Lacking a party army, the CCP could not seize the cities. Nor could it seize the KMT from within, since the Comintern had given the KMT a centralized Soviet-style party structure, difficult to subvert. The peasantry meanwhile remained largely unexploited for political purposes in the 1920's. With the CCP so small and inexperienced and Moscow's directives coming from such an obfuscating distance, a Communist success was hardly to be expected. From their victory the KMT and Chiang Kai-shek drew the fatal conclusion, typical of the time, that national political power depended fundamentally on professional armies supported by industries. They remained blind to the potentialities of peasant organization as another source of political power, also capable of lending support to armies. This was the view of an entire generation, older than the Communists, with more ties to the cities and the landlord class than to the peasantry, whose ambitions did not include a social revolution in the villages.

The Decade of the Nanking Government

The Nanking period, from 1928 to the time of the full-fledged Japanese attack of 1937, forms a distinct epoch during which China faced toward the Western world, while the latter, unfortunately, was absorbed in its own problems. This decade saw the onset of Stalinism in the Soviet Union, the Great Depression in the United States, and Nazism in Germany. Japan's aggression against China was unchecked from outside the East Asian scene. Nanking thus balanced precariously among three major influences—the pervasive though somewhat superficial Western contact; the mounting aggression of Japan; and the unresolved problems of the Chinese countryside. The Nationalist regime looked for inspiration both to the modern West and to the Chinese past, but remained stuck in between. This bifocal dilemma, with all its false hopes and frustrations, may be typical of new nations modernizing late on the ruins of ancient empires. The old regimes and traditions seem bankrupt, but Western models do not fit the local scene—patriotic leaders look to both, but in vain.

One striking feature of Nationalist China was the comparatively small size and underdeveloped condition of the modern government and economy. Even at the end of the Nanking decade, the 400 or possibly 500 million Chinese were served by about the same mileage of modern highways as the 25 million people of Spain, less railroad mileage than Italy or the state of Illinois, less than a third the telegraph lines of France, less industrial production than the 8 million people of Belgium.

In seeking to promote China's national development, the generation of the 1930's for the most part turned to Western models, for neither Japan nor the Soviet Union were friendly sources of inspiration. This dependence upon Western models, which created the community of interest between Nanking and the West, helps to explain the superficial character of the regime. Its program of modernization verged upon Westernization, for Western-trained officials naturally tried to apply what they had learned abroad, and their efforts reflected the administrative institutions, technology, and values of life in the industrialized nations, where agricultural backwardness and peasant discontent were not dominant problems. Consequently Nanking often understood modern finance, foreign trade and exchange, transport and telecommunications better than it understood its own hinterland. Its modern-minded officials seldom felt at home in the villages.

The Kuomintang's weakness derived also from the way it came into power, first by absorbing into its ranks most of the time-serving local officialdom in areas taken over, second by killing off its younger and idealistic rivals in the CCP. Once in power the KMT abandoned the Soviet-type organizations through which it had begun to mobilize workers, peasants, youth, and women. It turned against student movements, ceased to scrutinize local administration, and lost its sense of mission. In short, the party became a wing of the bureaucracy, antirevolutionary.

Chiang Kai-shek. Despite the end of the monarchy two decades earlier, Chinese politics still required a single power-holder at the top to give final answers, which neither a presidium nor a balance of constitutional powers could supply. Unification (against warlords) and resistance (against Japan) were the dominant needs of the day; the power-holder had to be a military leader. Chiang Kai-shek became indispensable. He was a man of patriotic dedication and strong-willed determination, politically astute but with certain backward-looking intellectual limitations. To his early landlord background in Chekiang and an abiding respect for the virtues of Tseng Kuo-fan had been added some of the samurai ideals of the Japanese Military Cadets Academy and finally the experience of warlord politics in a period when armies counted heavily. From Soviet Russia, Chiang had learned more about armies than about mass movements. He did not believe in the efficacy of popular mobilization vis-à-vis military force. In any case, he faced the

GENERALISSIMO AND WARLORDS. *Chiang Kai-shek (center) in late 1928, after taking over North China, with two of his army commanders: the "Model Governor" Yen Hsi-shan (right), and the "Christian General" Feng Yü-hsiang (left, in common soldier's uniform). In 1930 Yen and Feng fought Chiang for power but were defeated.*

continuing problem of all holders of power: how to keep on holding it. Dealing with all possible rivals required the constant and jealous manipulation of personnel and resources. Chiang's dual task was to stay on top and simultaneously build up the military strength of the state.

After his marriage in 1927 to Soong Mei-ling, a Wellesley graduate and sister of Sun Yat-sen's widow, Chiang became like her a confirmed Methodist and maintained contact with the West through his wife, her brother T. V. Soong (a Harvard graduate), and her brother-in-law H. H. Kung (an Oberlin graduate). He used these relatives with American background in top financial posts, and long-time colleagues of Japanese background in military posts. In party politics, Chiang's major problem, as an outsider not of the old guard, was how to cooperate with and divide the KMT leaders descended from the early days of the party, especially Wang Ching-wei of the left wing and Hu Han-min of the right. During 1927 Chiang cooperated at different times with each against the other. Then for three years, he worked with Hu, leaving Wang out of power. When the two of them briefly joined up against him in 1931, Chiang proved more than ever indispensable as military commander against the Japanese. He then joined with Wang for four years. Hu died in 1936, and Chiang became Party Leader in 1938. Wang, who had considered himself Sun Yat-sen's heir, survived an assassination attempt in 1935, and in 1939 went over to the Japanese, evidently out of both personal and patriotic frustration (see Chapter 22).

In time the supremacy of the "Generalissimo" (the title used for Chiang Kai-shek by the foreign press) came to rest on a tripod of army, party, and government, in each of which he balanced his personal bureaucratic machine against regional or rival groups. The army was dominated by the "Whampoa clique" of officers who had been his students at Canton. They controlled the great military bureaucracy and the secret military police and held the balance against the Kwangsi militarists and other regional forces. In the party, Chiang relied on the "Organization clique" headed by the brothers Ch'en Kuo-fu and Ch'en Li-fu (hence commonly called the "CC clique"), who built up the Central Political Institute for training civil servants and the KMT central secretariat and Organization Ministry, with their personnel files, financial resources, and secret party police. Their major rivals were the "Political Study (or Science) clique" (Cheng-hsueh Hsi), a looser-knit group of politicians and administrators with business connections, partially descended from Liang Ch'i-ch'ao's "Research clique."

The Kuomintang never achieved a tight discipline over its members, whose effective number remained somewhere between 2 and 4 million. In its power structure a gradual expansion of membership was offset by a continual concentration of power at the top. The First Party Congress of 1924 had had 150 delegates; the Sixth in 1945 had 600, a catch-all of prominent personalities. The Central Executive Committee had begun in 1924 with 24 regular members and 17 reserves, but by 1945 totaled 222 regular members with 90 in reserve. Since it had only two or three meetings a year, power gravitated to its Standing Committee, which began as 8 persons but increased to 50, meeting more or less weekly. There being no institution of a loyal opposition, the tendency was to bring everyone of importance under the KMT aegis into a personal relationship with the leader. Since the party, not the people, controlled the government during the "period of tutelage" (1928–1948), the Political Council which usually headed the government was really a subcommittee of the Central Executive Committee of the party. Some party ministries—Organization, Information, Social Affairs, Overseas Affairs—functioned as part of the central administration. Party and government thus interpenetrated and became practically indistinguishable. China's first experiment in party government thus echoed many aspects of dynastic government—the separate military and civil bureaucracies were united only at the top, under a ruler chosen from a continuing body (the party) which retained the statutory power, and he was aided by open and secret supervisory personnel at all levels.

The Growth of Militarism. Much can be said for the thesis that Japan's aggression changed China's history by necessitating military defense and distracting attention from domestic reform. When Japanese militarism was finally destroyed after continual aggression in China during fourteen years (1931–1945), the Chinese government, or what was left of it, had little but militarism with which to reconstruct the country. The Japanese militarists had forced it to go in the same direction, negating the Western influence of the 1920's and 1930's and destroying all chance of gradualism, reform, and evolution in meeting the problems of the Chinese people.

While not denying the validity of this view, one can also see domestic reasons for Chiang Kai-shek's rise as a military politician. After the 1927 split, Nanking was committed to unification and national development without class war. Kuomintang labor unions ("yellow" unions in Communist parlance) were promoted to compete with leftist unions, but peasant associations were generally suppressed. Forgoing mass mobilization at the village level as a source of power, the Nationalist Government had to compete with the remaining warlords pretty much on their own level. A post-unification conference in 1929 to disband the swollen armies reached no agreement. Warlordism died only slowly, and military unification was never achieved. An anti-Chiang wing of the KMT centered at Canton. In Yunnan, Szechwan, Shansi, Sinkiang, and other provinces, local militarists gave only lip service to Nanking. The Communists in Kiangsi until 1934 and in Shensi thereafter constituted a regionally based rebel power. The Japanese in Manchuria from 1931 and in Jehol and part of Hopei from 1933 became a foreign-based regional power. Year after year central government forces fought or negotiated in some part of the country in the name of national unity. Nanking's comparative success in this task was Chiang Kai-shek's success. Under him the Nationalist military establishment became less a Soviet-type party army controlled by the Kuomintang than a semigovernment under its own leader who had created it.

Having dispensed with the Soviet military mission in 1927, Chiang shifted to German advisers and aid and the German military structure, similar to that of Japan. The general staff was autonomous and separate from the minister of war under the Executive Yuan. The Nationalist forces remained independent of civil government and free from legislative interference. The Military Affairs Commission created more and more ministries for economic and political as well as strictly military purposes. In this enormous bureaucracy, Whampoa graduates held top posts without further training and expended the larger part of the Nationalist revenues on an unbudgeted basis. The central army, the best troops in China, soon grew to a crack force of 300,000. The Yangtze delta between Shanghai and Nanking was fortified. Arsenals produced German-type weapons. The German specialists got results, although they did not envisage cooperation with the peasantry or the eventual war of maneuver and "scorched earth."

The Economy.   During the Nanking decade the chief models of economic growth were provided by nations that were in varying degrees "totalitarian" —Nazi Germany, the Soviet Union, and Japan. However, the Nationalist Government, trying to inaugurate budgeting and auditing with the military out of hand, was never sufficiently in control of its finances, let alone the national economy, to pursue a plan of development. The United States was absorbed in the depression and the New Deal, and as yet had no concept of government-to-government programs of foreign aid.

Finance was the first focus of the government's economic effort. More than thirty foreign banks still operated in the treaty ports, monopolizing foreign exchange transactions, in some cases issuing their own bank notes, and generally serving as repositories for the private funds of Chinese politicians, militarists, businessmen, and speculators. Sometimes they held half the silver stock in Shanghai, where silver was the basic medium of exchange. The biggest foreign bank was the Hong Kong and Shanghai Banking Corporation, with assets of half a billion dollars. The hundred or so modern Chinese banks—government, provincial, or private—issued great quantities of depreciating bank notes and chiefly financed short-term commercial transactions or made loans to government agencies.

To finance the revolution, the Kuomintang had established the Central Bank of China at Canton in 1924 with T. V. Soong as manager. From 1928 it acted in Shanghai as a central bank of issue and a government treasury. Soon it was joined by the Bank of China (descended from the Board of Revenue Bank of 1905), the Bank of Communications (dating from 1907) and the Farmers Bank of China (1933). These four government banks now monopolized the issue of bank notes and formed a quadripartite equivalent of a European-type central government bank, dominating the scene with two-fifths of the capital and reserves, and over half the deposits, of all the modern Chinese banks.

As finance minister until 1933, T. V. Soong carried through a fiscal revolution—recovery of tariff autonomy and increase of customs revenue, suppression of likin taxes, and abolition of the ancient unit of account, the tael. These reforms brought the modern sector of the economy increasingly under the government's financial influence and made it possible to move toward government control of credit. From 1934 the American silver-buying program siphoned the silver currency out of China most disastrously. In self-defense China carried through a monetary reform in 1935 which substituted a managed paper currency for silver and backed the paper currency partly with reserves of foreign exchange. The effort was to stabilize the international value of China's money, and so build a banking system independent of foreign powers.

Despite this progress in the modern sector, it proved well-nigh impossible, even through credit cooperatives or the Agricultural Credit Administration set up in 1937, to make credit readily available to the farming population. Rural bank credit had still to be used for seasonal short-term needs, not for long-term productive investment, and merely competed with the usury of old-style moneylenders. Many fine rural programs were blueprinted, and some begun, for everything from land reclamation, reforestation, irrigation, and water conservancy to pest control, improved seeds and tools, and crop and animal breeding. Farm extension work, American-style, was introduced. But no sustained effort could be mounted at the critical level of the village to increase the farmer's productivity nationwide.

Public finance showed the same concentration of activity in the modern, treaty-port sector of the economy. Partly this was necessitated by the important fact that the Nanking Government had given up any claim to the land tax and left it for provincial administrations to exploit, thus making a virtue out of its initial inability to control large regions of the interior. This renunciation of the tax which had been the main resource of most dynasties was symptomatic of Nanking's tendency to avoid disturbing the rural scene. Instead, the National Government got about 50 per cent of its revenue from the Maritime Customs (as compared with about 1 per cent in the United States). In addition, it taxed the consuming public through consolidated excise taxes on staples like tobacco, kerosene, and flour, as well as through the salt monopoly. Since there was no income tax, this regressive taxation fell on the average consumer as heavily as on the wealthy and so tended to reduce mass purchasing power. Constant deficits were met by borrowing from the four government banks about 25 per cent of what the government expended. The four banks in turn sold bonds on the domestic market, debt payments on which soon exceeded the large payments still due to foreign creditors. Servicing all these debts took about a third of all expenditures. The domestic bondholders included many Nanking bureaucrats, and they often got high interest rates (up to 20 to 40 per cent if one allows for discounts they received on the purchase price). Such ill-gotten gains, paid to Chinese within the Chinese scene, were no doubt a good deal less odious than the enormous indemnity payments extorted by foreign powers after 1901. But Nanking's policy did not encourage production at home or capital loans from abroad, and achieved little saving and investment for long-term industrial growth. The nation's capital was not mobilized, while the available resources went mainly to support the military or to benefit what the Marxists called "bureaucratic capitalists."

Cultural Life and American Influence. Though living in the shadow of rebellion suppression and imminent invasion, those Chinese in the 1930's who felt themselves the intellectual inheritors of the May Fourth period re-

LIBERALS IN SHANGHAI 1933. *From left, the American journalist Agnes Smedley, George Bernard Shaw, Madame Sun Yat-sen (Soong Ch'ing-ling), Ts'ai Yüan-p'ei, then head of Academia Sinica, and Lu Hsün. Shaw was visiting China. The others had been founders of the short-lived China League for Civil Rights.*

mained divided into two main wings—reformist and revolutionist. Representative of the former were academically inclined scholars who fostered science, technology, and learning divorced from politics. Typical of the latter were activist-minded writers who tried to produce a literature of social revolution.

In literary circles Lu Hsün became a senior figure, encouraging younger writers, denouncing the Nationalist censorship and persecution of left-wing literature, and at the same time deploring the lowered, propagandist standards of the leftists. "Good literary works," he asserted, "have never been composed in accordance with other people's orders." As a rebel against social injustice, he became emotionally converted to the Communist cause although never a party member. In 1930 he joined with others to form the League of Left-Wing Writers. This broad organization with its many subsidized publications and polemical tactics marked the beginning of Communist ascendancy in the literary scene under the recently unfurled Soviet banner of "socialist realism." The KMT could neither prevent nor compete with this development, which increasingly gave student youth its view of the world.

American reformist influence in the 1930's was greatest among the non-revolutionary wing of the intelligentsia, those who were foreign-trained and worked in academic and scientific institutions. The dozen Christian colleges now got more than half their income from Chinese sources, and were controlled locally by Chinese boards of directors, with faculties two-thirds Chinese though largely foreign trained. Although they had only 6500 students, as compared with 41,000 in the hundred or so government institutions of higher education, they still were pacesetters in instruction as well as in standards of living and social life. The big national universities like Peita and Tsing Hua also had staffs largely trained abroad, mostly in the United States. American influence was similarly evident in the Geological Survey of China, the dozen research institutes of the central government's Academia Sinica, the National Agricultural Research Institute at Nanking, and the big Rockefeller-supported Peking Union Medical College at Peiping, as well as the national health service which benefited from its pioneer work. This institutional growth was the fruit of training Chinese students in the West. Some 2400 had entered American universities between 1901 and 1920; 5500 did so between 1921 and 1940, studying altogether in 370 institutions, primarily in branches of engineering or business economics—practical subjects. Returning to work in Shanghai firms or Nanking agencies or in institutions like those just listed, these modern-trained graduates were a new elite, who lived on a material and intellectual plane far above the poverty and illiteracy of the Chinese village. In the 1920's and 1930's, a new generation of Chinese scholars, stimulated by study abroad, achieved creative beginnings in many lines—for example, discovering Peking Man and the Shang dynasty capital at An-yang (see pages 5 and 19–20), finding previously unknown architectural monuments, publishing and using Ch'ing archives, and in general assimilating into Chinese the vocabularies and concepts of modern science.

The missionary response to China's problems, while still evangelical, had also taken on many practical forms. The thousand or so American missionaries of 1900, representing twenty-eight societies, had increased by 1930 to more than three thousand representing sixty societies. With the rise of nationalism, the effort now was to make the Christian church in China indigenous, led by a Chinese pastorate and partially self-supporting, with the foreign missionary only advising and assisting. With its lesser stress on the gospel and its direct concern for social service, the Y.M.C.A. attracted an able young Chinese leadership and now developed programs for literacy and social work among factory laborers. Christian compassion found other outlets. The North China famine of 1920–1921 led to the creation of the China International Famine Relief Commission. By 1936 it had used $50 million in foreign contributions for pioneer programs of rural improvement in cooperation with local authorities in famine areas—building wells, roads,

*A Chinese Christian community leader of the Society of the Divine
Word, Lanchow vicariate, Kansu, among paintings, scrolls,
and statues of Chinese Christian art.*

and river dikes, and setting up farm credit cooperatives in North China
with some 200,000 members. As Christianity in China became increasingly
concerned with social welfare, an interdenominational Protestant conference
of 1922 organized the National Christian Council, partly to apply the
social gospel, partly to promote the "indigenous" Chinese Christian church.
In addition to its urban program, this body began to develop a rural program and encouraged agricultural research and extension activities. Christian
missions were thus by the 1930's approaching the problems of "rural reconstruction."

A pioneer in this movement, James Yen, a graduate of Yale and the
Y.M.C.A., began work at Ting-hsien near Peking in 1926 with subsequent
support from the Rockefeller Foundation. Here his Mass Education Movement began with foreign assistance to attack the problems of the Chinese
peasantry, pioneering in the application of agricultural science and the
spread of elementary education. It soon confronted questions of farm credit,
marketing, cooperatives, and farmers' associations. This last type of organization, when combined with literacy, could give voice to peasant grievances
and eventually raise questions of land tenure and local politics. At this
point, the gradualist approach of the social worker and educator ran into
the vested interests of local power-holders, those remnants of the erstwhile
"gentry" who now often functioned with the military support of militarists
or secret societies. Thus "rural reconstruction" threatened the status quo.

Instinctively, government authorities moved to control and use it. Chiang Kai-shek through Madame Chiang, who was in close touch with church and Y.M.C.A. leaders, invited American missionaries to set up a model county administration among the peasantry in a part of Kiangsi recovered from the Communists, but little could be achieved in religious or community work in the midst of so much poverty. Chiang mounted his own program for China's regeneration in the New Life Movement, stressing the ancient virtues of moral conduct—propriety, righteousness, integrity, and the sense of shame—and using Y.M.C.A. methods. It exhorted the public through a network of thirteen hundred branches during 1934–1937. Behind this movement but unknown to the public was Chiang Kai-shek's secret Blue Shirt organization modeled on European fascism and devoted to militarizing the nation under his leadership.

Largely beneath the level of public notice or statistical knowledge in this period, the disintegration of China's ancient rural society was still proceeding apace. The great mass of the Chinese farming population in the million villages remained beyond the reach of the Nationalist Government or missionary reform efforts. Farm handicrafts were now suffering the full impact of factory production. Drawn inexorably into the money economy, farming remained undercapitalized. The cultivator was too poor to store his crops, improve his seeds or tools, or avoid borrowing from the usurer. Poverty and demoralization worsened in the villages, while the non-Communist prescriptions and programs for their remaking, largely Western-inspired, remained scattered and ineffective. The hope for rural reconstruction was in any case cut short by invasion and warfare.

Japan's Aggression in China

Japan in Manchuria and China's Response.   Manchuria, China's Northeast, was a big, new frontier area, a quarter the size of China proper, yet containing less than a tenth as many people. Population had tripled from perhaps 11 million in 1900 to 34 million in 1930, partly through migration from North China, and was 95 per cent Chinese. But the Japanese military in Manchuria felt a sense of imperial mission (see pages 705–707). The rise of the Nationalist Government and its patriotic claims to Manchuria as racially, historically, and legally part of China clashed head on with the explosive militarism of the Japanese Kwantung Army. When Japanese officers arranged the "Mukden incident," of September 18, 1931, and proceeded to take over Manchuria, the Chinese patriotic reaction and boycott led to an "undeclared war" outside the foreign concession area at Shanghai (January 28–March 3, 1932). After seventy thousand Japanese troops had battled a surprisingly vigorous Chinese resistance, both sides accepted an armistice rather than expand the fighting. But meanwhile the successful coup in Manchuria had shattered the collective security system of the League of Nations. Neither the League nor the American policy of "non-recognition" of gains made by force could now stop the momentum of Japan's expansion.

Mindful of the old tradition of barbarian conquest of China with Chinese help, the Japanese set up a puppet government in Manchuria with Japanese advisers in indirect control. The state of Manchukuo ("Manchu-land") was proclaimed on March 1, 1932. Soon the last Ch'ing boy-emperor, Pu-yi, was enthroned as emperor. Local Chinese were brought into "self-government committees" proclaiming "national independence." The fiction of an independent state justified the exclusion of foreign interests as long as the powers did not recognize the new government. The army program for Manchukuo stressed industrialization. New companies were chartered with special inducements to mobilize private capital. A badly needed unification of the currency was achieved under a central bank; and communications, transport, and hydroelectric power developed rapidly. Strategic railroads were pushed toward the Soviet frontiers of Manchuria, and the formerly competing Chinese lines parallel to the South Manchurian Railway were incorporated with it into a single system. All this created in Manchuria an industrial base in competition with the Japanese homeland and required a heavy capital investment. Japan's economic gains were minimal, but the new strategic base on the continent provided the satisfactions of imperial glory and also a vested interest in further expansion.

Moving inexorably on North China, the Japanese created a demilitarized zone, just south of the Wall between Peiping and Tientsin, from which a Chinese puppet regime fostered infiltration of smuggled goods and narcotics into North China. In 1935 North China was made a neutral zone by agreement, whereupon Japanese officers tried to incite a separatist movement to make its five provinces into a puppet "North China-land" (*Hua-pei kuo*). This effort collapsed in December in the face of Peiping student demonstrations which dramatized Nanking's dilemma—when and where to resist by force.

China's nonmilitary resistance in the form of a boycott after the Mukden incident had been very effective, spreading over the whole country and overseas, inhibiting Japanese sales and even contact with Japanese banks or business concerns. The boycott was coordinated by the Kuomintang with much initiative from students and merchants. It operated underground in the treaty ports, using terrorism when necessary, and enforced its program elsewhere by public meetings, propaganda, inspection, fines, and actual punishment of malefactors. Japanese exports to China proper were cut in half. Japan's aggression was provoking a national response at a new level of public participation. Nanking, however, discounted the capabilities of nonmilitary and paramilitary (guerrilla) resistance. The Nationalist experts in firepower knew that unarmed civilians could not stop Japan's tanks and planes. The indubitable correctness of this view was confirmed by common sense as well as by military opinion in most of the world. Yet it overlooked what was later demonstrated in many countries: the effectiveness of popular resistance when mobilized in support of, and coordinated with, conventional firepower. Chiang Kai-shek expressed the conventional wisdom in his strategy of building up his German-trained army before committing it to battle. For almost six years after September 1931, with skill and tenacity, he temporized, negotiated, withdrew, and avoided a showdown with Japan. This was plainly a harsh necessity. Yet alongside his new army Chiang had little success in using mass organizations to mobilize the nation. On the contrary, opposed to the class war by which the Communists were rallying peasants against landlords (see pages 895–902), Chiang used his new army to follow a strategy of "unification before resistance" and so mounted five anti-Communist "extermination campaigns" in 1931–1934. Nanking's policy of fighting Chinese rebels but not Japanese invaders outraged noncommunist patriots and put the government under heavy pressure.

By 1936 the Communists had survived their Long March of 1934–1935 from Kiangsi and now had a territorial base in the Northwest. Both the CCP and the Comintern had proposed a second united front in August 1935, this time for national defense against Japan. This tactical shift aimed to take Japanese pressure off the Soviet Union and Nationalist pressure off the CCP. In late 1936 the formation of the Rome-Berlin Axis and the German-Italian-Japanese Anti-Comintern Pact heightened the danger of aggression. When Chiang was forcibly held or "kidnaped" in December at Sian by Chinese troops from Manchuria, who were more eager to resist Japan than to exterminate CCP rebels, Chou En-lai mediated to release him, whereupon the second united front gradually took shape.

The Second Sino-Japanese War. Japan's full-scale aggression in 1937, first near Peiping on July 7, then at Shanghai in August, really opened World War II, which in China lasted a full eight years, longer than the war in Europe. During the first four years, moreover, down to December 8, 1941, Free China fought alone while isolationist America until mid-1941 continued with a growing sense of guilt to sell essential oil and iron to Japan's war machine. By that time the Nationalist Government and its leader had shown both inspiring fortitude and the same limitations that had characterized their rule at Nanking. The regime, oriented toward foreign trade and contact, was progressively cut off from them and confined to the hinterland whose problems it had hardly begun to face. Chiang assumed, correctly, that Japan's fanatical aggressiveness would sooner or later bring other powers to China's aid. The war became a test of stamina. At Shanghai the new Nationalist armies fought the Japanese to a standstill but suffered severely. Once outflanked in late 1937, they withdrew westward, "trading space for time" and using "scorched earth" tactics to destroy many industrial installations that could not be transported inland. After a pause at Hankow in 1938 the Nationalist Government moved up above the Yangtze gorges to Chungking in the mists of Szechwan. Whole arsenals and factories, and faculties and student bodies of universities, migrated beyond the reach of Japan's tanks, though not of her planes.

Occupied China was soon divided between two puppet regimes, each with its own currency. In North China the Japanese forces, using the rail lines as invasion routes and seizing the cities, rather quickly overcame resistance except in the densely populated plains inside the rail network, where guerrilla movements began to take shape. Japan's North China army kept ahead of its Central China rivals by setting up a puppet Provisional Government of China at Peiping, using as figureheads old men who had been Japan-oriented in the warlord era. They urged a return to the classical virtues and pan-Asian cooperation, in press and school propaganda that was both anti-Western and anti-Communist. In Central China, Japan also installed a puppet Reform Government at Nanking in March 1938. After the fall of Canton and Hankow in October, Japan announced the creation of her New Order in East Asia (see page 715) which would substitute Japan's over-lordship in China for the Western treaty system. This induced the frustrated patriot and one-time student in Japan, Wang Ching-wei, to seek peace by defecting from Chungking and Chiang Kai-shek; and on March 30, 1940, after much negotiation, Wang became head of a Reorganized Nationalist Government at Nanking, a shadowy replica of the former Nanking Government, under the nominal control of the "Orthodox Kuomintang," a rump group of anti-Chiang KMT members who had defected along with Wang. These puppet façades at Peiping and Nanking, like Manchukuo, rested on force and fooled no one. Yet, as in Europe a bit later, the invaders' superior arms made urban resistance suicidal and collaboration almost unavoidable. Collaborators, moreover, could mitigate the conqueror's harshness even while working under him, and so were not wholly unpatriotic. The relative ease with which Japan recruited collaborators and governed a large part of China in the 1930's suggests that not all the Chinese people were as yet ready for mobilized popular resistance.

Beyond the southwestern periphery of Japan's invasion, the Nationalist Government survived in the less developed hinterland. This brought it into competition with the Communists. From mid-1937 began another period of KMT-CCP collaboration and scarcely veiled competition. Soon the KMT could see that the CCP would gain more from the social transformations of wartime, especially mass mobilization and the arming of peasants. It turned against such developments in the area under its control, and Nationalist troops, eventually 200,000 or more, blockaded the CCP in its base in the

MANPOWER TAXIS. *A family wheelbarrow with front and rear handlers, Hankow, late nineteenth century. A rickshaw puller evacuating a Nationalist officer from Nanking, 1949. A pedicab on Nanking Road, Shanghai, 1966.*

Northwest. The united front continued only as a façade of unity, to paper over the fact that two armed party dictatorships were rivals for ultimate power.

The Nationalist Government, while avoiding social change in the countryside, took measures to buttress its political power. A People's Political Council, chosen of broadly representative public figures, was created in 1938 to meet the demand for representative government, although it was given advisory powers only. Its questions did not have to be answered. From 1939 to 1947 the San-min chu-i Youth Corps under Chiang as chief built up a pyramidal structure parallel to the party. However, as the youthful membership grew older, it became a rival of the party, with no new ideas, and finally had to be absorbed back into it. A Central Training Corps, set up at Chungking as an indoctrination mill, brought together group after group of assorted magistrates, officers, professors, and administrators from all over the country. Each group, in two or three weeks of tightly scheduled lectures, calisthenics, and other exercises became informed on the Kuomintang's principles and heard and saw the Party Leader. Meantime in local government a "new county (*hsien*) system" was introduced in 1939. It aimed to invigorate economic and welfare activities at the county level, which proved difficult, and also to revive the ancient *pao-chia* mutual-responsibility and surveillance system, which proved of some effect in maintaining local order. This revival featured "self-government" through election of *pao* representatives in village administration, but there is little record of the election process taking hold in the back country.

All these measures, like Chungking's indomitable wartime performance as a whole, betrayed a poverty of ideas. The original leaders of the KMT still clung to power. The Military Affairs Commission took over more and more of the civil government's functions and had as many as 5 million troops under arms at one time. Yet the intellectual leadership of this massive effort was confined to the meager set of ideas put forth in *China's Destiny,* a treatise Chiang Kai-shek published in 1943. Its first theme was anti-imperialism, stressing the humiliations of foreign aggression, the manifold evils of the unequal treaties. The patriotic sense of grievance is plain whether or not one agrees that the many strains of modernization have all been due to Western victimization of China. The second theme was Chiang's proposal to revive the ancient virtues of the Confucian social order and subordinate the individual properly to the state. At the same time he would industrialize on a grand scale for national defense and collectivize the peasants to make them farmer-soldiers.

The sufferings of the government civil servants, the people from "down river," who had migrated to the crowded housing and consumer-goods shortages of wartime Szechwan, were capped by the continuing inflation, which destroyed their government stipends and living standards by a process

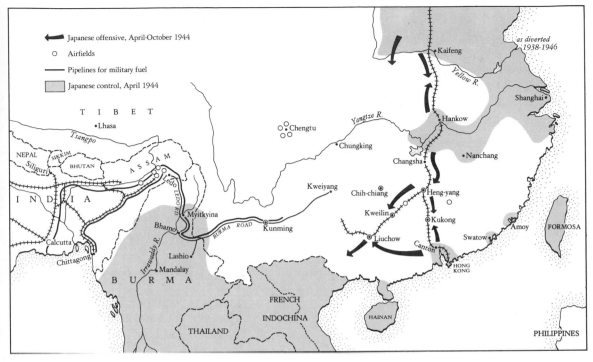

THE CHINA-BURMA-INDIA THEATER IN WORLD WAR II

of slow strangulation. Although it was in a self-sufficient agricultural region with a considerable food supply, the government failed to develop its tax revenues and relied heavily on note-issue to finance its needs. This left the rural subsistence economy relatively unaffected, but put the government's urban stipendiaries, the whole modern element in Free China, through an inflationary wringer. White-collar salaries never kept up. Books, clothing, furnishings went for food. Malnutrition produced skin disease, stomach ailments, tuberculosis. Poverty led many to the humiliation of surviving by corruption. The privileged few in business tended to hoard commodities or gold rather than invest their untaxed profits, but most of the modern stratum of Free China was enervated and demoralized, and eventually blamed the regime in power. This coincided in the universities with the KMT effort to both expand and control higher education for political purposes. The academic wing of the intelligentsia began to question the KMT leadership.

American Aid to China.   In the first two and one-half years of China's struggle, the Nationalist Government received far more help from the Soviet Union than from America, Britain, and France. An entire Soviet "volunteer" air force fought Japan in China. But Soviet aid died away after the onset of World War II in September 1939. At first Free China's cause

MANPOWER FOR AIRPLANES. *Thousands of peasants moving earth and crushing rock to build an airfield near Chengtu for B-29's to bomb Japan, 1942.*

won American public acclaim but little help. Except for the Indo-China rail route from Haiphong to Kunming (until the fall of France in 1940) and the Burma Road truck route over high mountains and deep gorges from the rail-head in Burma to Kunming, Free China was practically cut off.

When the Japanese attack at Pearl Harbor in 1941 made an active ally of Chungking, the United States Government through its military aid began for the first time to play a major role in China's domestic affairs. The wartime alliance brought to its highest point the American participation in Chinese life that had been growing for a century past. Revision of the British and American treaties in January 1943 formally ended the unequal-treaty system; yet, ironically, the war effort created an American presence— manifest in air forces and bases, training schools, supply and transport services, and other wartime agencies with their radio networks and airlines —greater than ever before. Most spectacular was the success of the Four-teenth U.S. Air Force under General C. L. Chennault in checking the Japanese bombing of Free China's cities.

But American aid suffered a series of handicaps. First, Japan's quick seizure of Burma in early 1942 cut the Burma Road supply route. The only substitute was an airlift from India over the mountainous "hump" of

Generalissimo and Madame Chiang Kai-shek with Stilwell at Maymyo in Burma, April 1942.

northern Burma to Kunming—a costly route of very limited capacity (see map). Second, the Allied strategy, to defeat Germany before Japan, gave the distant China–Burma–India theater a low priority. Lend-lease aid to China amounted by early 1946 to $1.5 billion, but this was only about 3 per cent of the $50 billion lend-lease aid given to all countries in World War II. China was neither easy to help nor strategically of first importance. General Joseph Stilwell, designated Chiang Kai-shek's "chief of staff," tenaciously set about the difficult reconquest of North Burma to reopen a land route to China as the putative base for attacking Japan. By early 1945 a road and a pipeline accomplished this, but the naval campaign in the Pacific had long since carried the war directly to Japan.

Thus warfare outpaced diplomacy. The initial American policy aim, to help China become a "great power" capable of stabilizing East Asia after Japan's defeat, had been joined with a parallel military aim, to help the Nationalist Government build up its military capacity. If the Allied attack on Japan had indeed gone through China, conditions there after the war might have been more viable and less inviting to Communist rebellion. In fact, however, China was bypassed and became a sideshow. This exacerbated the inevitable frictions of any alliance and produced bitterness and recrimination between the Americans and the British, between Stilwell and Chennault, between Chiang Kai-shek and his allies—eventually between

America and China. The American war effort, so concentrated on defeating Japan, expressed the outlook of a people accustomed to peace in a stable society, who had never themselves suffered invasion and who viewed the war overseas as a brief interlude. In China, on the other hand, the principal war effort had already been expended, to survive Japan's aggression since 1937. The KMT ideal of unifying China militarily and the CCP hope of seizing power for social revolution underlay Chinese politics. Americans eager to win the war pressed for a more unified KMT-CCP war effort, only to meet frustration. Partly over this issue, General Stilwell was recalled in November 1944. Once Japan was defeated in August 1945, the United States quickly demobilized its powerful forces. But the arms it had provided made the Nationalist commanders overconfident of their capacity to suppress the Communists. Their government emerged from World War II economically debilitated and politically insecure but with superior firepower. This combination of circumstances led it into a civil war that proved its undoing (see pages 902–904).

The decline and fall of the Kuomintang, after its early promise, was a tragedy hotly disputed in the United States. Certain points may be suggested. First, the KMT-CCP rivalry was continuous from the very moment in 1923 when the KMT was reorganized as a Leninist-style party dictatorship. The potentialities for revolutionary change, such as the mobilization of the peasantry to take part in war and politics, steadily increased, yet the Kuomintang did not succeed in grasping and using them. Second, Japan's aggression after 1931 was an ever present fact in China's national life, even more immediately pressing than the potentialities of revolution. It diverted the government from many constructive tasks and led to its militarization. Third, American aid to the Nationalist Government after 1941, though it climaxed a century of American help toward meeting China's problems, came too late. If in the early 1930's substantial United States Government aid had gone to Nanking, as it has gone to so many regimes since 1941, Chinese history might have been altered. But American aid in wartime, coming late to a hard-pressed regime, served more as a crutch to lean on than as a means to cure its ailments.

Finally, Nationalist China's deterioration during eight years of wartime attrition reflected both the impact of overwhelming circumstance and an inadequacy of leadership, in proportions still being debated. For the Nanking Government, based on the coastal cities, removal inland was all but fatal. The Chinese Communists' comparatively successful wartime expansion was accomplished without the oppressive burden of frontal resistance and national responsibilities that exhausted Chungking's energies. Nationalist forces tied down most of Japan's troops in China, roughly half her armies overseas, and suffered the great part of China's 3 million or more battle casualties. Meanwhile the CCP regime built up its power on a more primitive level (see pages 895–902). Chinese tradition sees history in more personal terms than does modern social science. Chiang Kai-shek, who took responsibility as the holder of power, has been blamed by many for losing it. Study should show, however, that he was seldom master of Free China's circumstances. His inflexible rectitude mirrored the inertia of a whole political tradition, still in the shadow of the Confucian Empire. On the other hand, just as Western aid was unable to prevent Free China's deterioration, so Western models were of little use to the Chinese republic in wartime. Out of the war in China came something new, the greatest of all its revolutions.

26. The New Japan

World War II in East Asia

History at times seems to work by the yin-yang concept that any action, pushed to an extreme, will result in an opposite reaction. World War II in East Asia was begun by men who wished to preserve Japan's position in Manchuria and gain a new empire, men dedicated to the conservative "national polity" and opposed to Communism in Asia. The result of the war was the total loss of Japan's colonial empire, the destruction of the old polity, and the rise of Communist China.

One of the lesser themes espoused by the Japanese during the war was the liberation of Asian colonies from the yoke of European imperialism. "Asia for the Asians," said Japanese spokesmen, proclaiming their own Monroe Doctrine for the continent. The countries "liberated" by Japan found its New Order to be harsher and in some ways more distasteful than the former colonial regimes. Still, changes occurred during the Japanese occupations which made it impossible for the colonies to be re-established after the war. In long perspective, this may prove to have been the most significant outcome of the Pacific War.

Pearl Harbor and Japan's Blitzkrieg in East Asia. On the morning of December 7, 1941, a Japanese surprise attack by carrier-based planes sank seven battleships, many lesser vessels, and destroyed over half of the American aircraft at Pearl Harbor and the other American bases in Hawaii. This was a brilliant tactical victory for Japan. Yet public opinion in the United

States, so long divided by isolationism, immediately became unified. While continued Japanese expansion in Southeast Asia might have left the American people divided and uncertain, Pearl Harbor shocked them into an all-out war effort.

The shock became greater when it was realized that the losses at Pearl Harbor were due to unpreparedness of mind more than of materiel. Ambassador Grew had warned from Tōkyō that Japan might attack with dramatic suddenness, as in previous wars. Decoding Japanese secret messages, Washington had for weeks been expecting an attack somewhere. At Pearl Harbor, enemy submarines had been sighted and depth charges dropped, and the approaching planes had actually been detected by radar well before the attack. Yet the American forces on that Sunday morning were not alert to the danger.

The Pearl Harbor disaster was lessened by the fact that three aircraft carriers of the Pacific Fleet were at sea, unharmed, and the sunken battleships had been close to obsolescence. But a second disaster, in some ways greater though less publicized, followed in the Philippines. Despite the imminence of war, United States bases under General Douglas MacArthur were undermanned, poorly armed, and inadequately linked by communications. Their bombers and fighters took to the air but landed for lunch and refueling. Eight or nine hours after Pearl Harbor, Japanese air attacks caught them on the ground, lined up wing to wing. A third disaster occurred the following day when the British battleship *Prince of Wales* and the battlecruiser *Repulse,* lacking air cover, were sunk off Malaya by carrier-based planes.

The crippling of the United States Pacific Fleet, the destruction of American air power in the Philippines, and the sinking of the British ships pulled the cork from the Southeast Asian bottle. The way lay open for Japanese amphibious drives through the Philippines, Borneo, and the Celebes, and through Malaya and Sumatra to Java. This was followed by a Japanese offensive from Indo-China through Thailand to Burma. Victory followed upon victory. Japanese troops advanced through "impenetrable" jungles to take Singapore from the rear. The great naval base, its only defenses facing the sea, fell on February 15, 1942. By March the Dutch East Indies were completely in Japanese hands. The Philippines were invaded on December 10; Manila fell on January 2; after bitter battles on the mountainous Bataan Peninsula fighting came to an end on April 9, 1942. By the end of May Japanese troops had pushed far into northern Burma, closing the Burma Road and cutting off most supplies to China.

Elated by success, the Japanese army favored concentrating on the Asian continent to subdue China and deal with Russia, while the navy proposed to take Hawaii and cut American-Australian communications in the South and Southwest Pacific. Guam had been taken on December 13 and Wake

Island on the 20th; and in the early months of 1942 the Japanese moved into the Solomon, Ellice, and Gilbert island chains, and into northern New Guinea. In the summer the western Aleutian islands of Kiska and Attu were occupied. By this time Japan possessed a vast oceanic and continental empire stretching from Sakhalin four thousand miles south almost to Australia, and from Burma six thousand miles east to the Gilberts.

Japan's Attempt to Consolidate Its Conquests.   In the second phase of the war, from mid-1942 to mid-1944, Japan tried to develop its empire and exploit it economically, while the Allies assailed its periphery.

The area overrun by Japan was culturally diverse. Burma, Cambodia, and Thailand had Theravada Buddhist cultures. Vietnam had a mixture of Mahayana Buddhism and Confucianism. Malaya and most of the Dutch East Indies were Muslim, and the Philippines had an American-Spanish Catholic culture with an admixture of indigenous elements. Each area had different languages, different ethnic origins, and different national histories. With the exception of Vietnam, Japan's new conquests were not a part of the East Asian culture zone. For this reason and also because of wartime pressures, only a weaker and severely modified form of the "Japanese colonial pattern" that had developed in Taiwan, Korea, and Manchuria could be applied in these areas.

Within these limitations, the Japanese attempted to supplant the long-established Western colonial governments and meet the need for raw materials and markets that had emerged from the depression and politics of the thirties and had inspired the whole push southward. Japan sought to solve both problems simultaneously by the creation of a Greater East Asia Co-Prosperity Sphere, an autarkic and mutually beneficial economic community. To deal with the national governments within the sphere—and to forestall Foreign Ministry meddling in the affairs of the army—a Greater East Asia Ministry was established in Tōkyō in November 1942. Staffed by civilians, it was responsible for a variety of cultural exchange programs as well as for foreign relations within the new empire. But the real power in the conquered areas was held by military administration teams which were responsible, through the local army commanders, to the Army General Staff in Tōkyō.

Japanese occupiers, as in Taiwan and Korea, attempted to implant a new cultural and moral order—that is, their particular blend of the East Asian tradition and the Japanese pattern of modernity. Their occupation policies embodied the ambivalence toward the West so strong in wartime Japan itself: the utilization of Western technology and cultural forms that made Japan the most advanced and Westernized Asian nation, together with an attack on Western materialism, Communism, and liberal, individ-

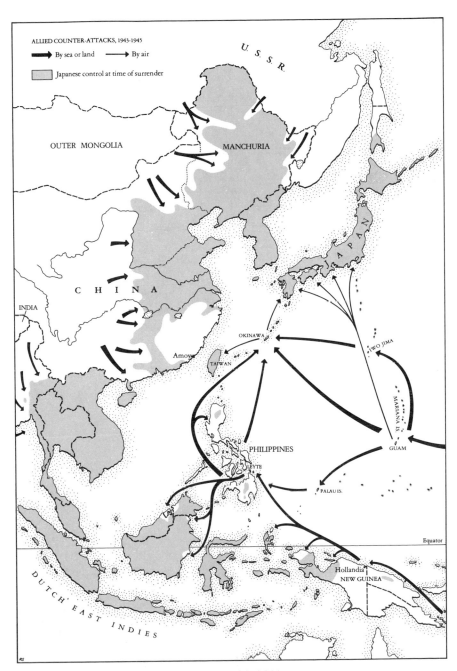

ALLIED COUNTER-ATTACKS, 1943-1945

By sea or land   By air

Japanese control at time of surrender

U.S.S.R.

OUTER MONGOLIA

MANCHURIA

C H I N A

INDIA

Amoy

OKINAWA

TAIWAN

IWO JIMA

JAPAN

MARIANA IS.

GUAM

PHILIPPINES

LEYTE

PALAU IS.

Equator

D U T C H   E A S T   I N D I E S

Hollandia
NEW GUINEA

WORLD WAR II IN GREATER EAST ASIA

ualistic values. To found its "New Order" Japan tried to revitalize traditional forms of social authority—to strengthen the power of the family head, to subordinate women to male authority, and to stress filial piety, loyalty, and group responsibility. Japan also supported the local religious traditions as conservative forces promoting order. Just as Confucianism and the "Kingly Way" had been promoted in Manchukuo and North China, so in Thailand and Burma the Japanese encouraged Buddhism, in Malaya and the Dutch East Indies, Islam, and in the Philippines, Catholicism. Religious and cultural leaders and local dignitaries were invited to visit Japan, and teachers were sent from Japan to make Japanese the second language of each area and the medium for intra-sphere communication. Under the wartime conditions, not learning the language became a form of passive resistance.

Although the occupations went smoothly enough during 1942 and 1943 when the Allies were still unable to mount a dangerous counteroffensive, in the end Japan's New Order was unsuccessful. In Southeast Asia Japan had neither the time nor the resources to carry out programs of mass education, develop communications and transportation, achieve striking advances in agricultural productivity, or integrate the diverse areas into its own economy, as it had done in Taiwan and Korea. Even if there had been time, Japan was no substitute for the world economy: it could neither absorb all the tropical exports of Southeast Asia nor could its strained wartime economy supply the needed industrial products. As Japanese shipping dwindled in the last years of the war, Japan was unable even to obtain the raw materials which these countries produced, and the occupied areas were thrown back onto a stagnant, subsistence economy, subject to maldistribution, shortages, and inflation. The hardships of the local populations became particularly severe during the last years of the war.

The response to the Japanese conquests took the form of nationalism. Prior to World War II nationalism had been rising in all of the colonial states of Asia. Yet nowhere was it strong enough to oust the colonial power. Billing themselves as the champions of Asia against Western imperialism, the Japanese occupiers attempted to encourage and use nationalism to obtain local cooperation. Thus Japan called its takeover of one area a "liberation," in another it granted "independence" to a native government, or it set up a native government where none had existed. This policy worked well in the early years, but as the local economies deteriorated and as it became clear that the Allies would win the war, the nationalist movements turned against Japan. There was, however, no uniform pattern. Thailand, for example, had been independent before the war, it was given new territories by the Japanese, and it kept considerable autonomy during the war. A "Free Thai" movement arose in the last years of the war, but there was little fighting, Japanese troops were well-disciplined, and no anti-Japanese feelings persisted after the war. In contrast, in the Philippines where independence had been promised by the United States and pro-American sentiment was strong, a strong anti-Japanese resistance movement arose that was harshly suppressed. In addition, during the fighting to recapture the Philippines, Japanese military discipline broke down and many atrocities were committed. This left a residue of feelings that embittered Philippine attitudes toward Japan in the postwar era. In most of the occupied countries there was continuity between wartime nationalist leaders and postwar leaders. In Indonesia the Dutch had ruled through minorities. The Japanese established a government of the Muslim majority which, after the war, was successful in winning independence from the Dutch. In Indo-China the contradictions in the Japanese attitude toward nationalism were particularly sharp. On the one hand the Japanese army, short of military administrators, ruled through the Vichy French officials and tried to suppress the nationalist movement. The Viet Minh policy was to avoid clashes with Japanese troops. On the other hand Japanese generals in Saigon denounced European imperialism, younger Japanese officers were openly contemptuous of the French, and early in 1945 when the French officials became restive, the Japanese put them in jail and proclaimed Vietnamese independence. Then, when the war ended, the Japanese acquiesced when Ho Chi Minh moved to establish the "Democratic Republic of Vietnam." This became the basis of the anticolonial movement in the postwar period.

The Allied Drive on Japan.   Despite Japan's strenuous efforts to exploit its vast conquests, its military leaders missed the lesson of their own victory: they failed to give top priority to building air power. Their military technology, quite advanced at the start of the war, lagged behind as the United States developed new planes, radar, homing torpedoes, proximity fuses, and other novel devices. Their economy had already been stretched taut by the China war and lacked the capacity for rapid expansion that the American economy possessed. Moreover, Tōkyō and Berlin, unlike the Allies, failed to coordinate their efforts or even exchange adequate intelligence.

The American counterattack was slowed by two factors: the Anglo-American decision to defeat Germany first, and the time lag between the beginning of the war and the full conversion of the American economy to war production. The first successful major engagement for the Allies was the naval Battle of the Coral Sea fought to the northeast of Australia on May 7–8, 1942. Losses were about equal, but since American production was greater, this meant an Allied gain. A greater victory occurred in the Battle of Midway a month later. A major Japanese armada approached Midway Island, the westernmost of the Hawaiian chain, with hopes of annihilating the remainder of the United States Pacific Fleet. But Japanese naval codes had been broken by a special unit in Washington, and American planes

Japanese soldiers on Guadalcanal carrying equipment by hand.

were able to intercept and destroy the four aircraft carriers of the superior Japanese fleet. Having lost its striking force, Japan's far-flung empire was henceforth on the defensive.

In the final phase of the war two great island-hopping, amphibious offensives brought Allied troops to the doorstep of Japan. One of these returned MacArthur to the Philippines (Leyte, October 1944), where one of the most destructive campaigns of the war was fought. By June 1945 the Philippines were in Allied hands. The other offensive pushed straight across the South Pacific. Beginning in the Gilbert Islands (Tarawa, November 1943), then moving onward to the Marshalls and the Carolines, it next took a thousand-mile jump to the Marianas (Saipan, June 1944) and then to Iwō Jima. Saipan and Tinian brought Japan within range; Iwō Jima was taken as a haven for disabled bombers returning from raids over Japan. In April 1945 the two offensives converged on Okinawa, which fell in June. These offensives required the development of new amphibious techniques that combined air superiority, naval barrages, landing craft, and men. Considering the small size of the islands that were fought over, the losses were enormous. On the Japanese side more than 85 per cent of the defenders on Okinawa were killed; on the Allied side there were 49,100 casualties, about a fifth of which were at sea where massed attacks by suicide planes called *kamikaze* sank 34 ships and damaged 368 others.

Two factors were crucial in the strategy of the war. By the destruction of Japan's merchant marine, navy, and naval air power, the Allies succeeded in isolating Japan from its empire. At the start of the war Japan had a merchant marine of 6 million tons. Conquest and new construction brought this to a total of over 10 million. By the end of the war all but 1.8 million tons, mostly small wooden ships plying coastal waters, had been sunk. Attacks by surface ships accounted for 10 per cent of the Japanese losses; aircraft for 30 per cent; and submarines, a major offensive weapon, for 60 per cent. As Japan became less able to transport men, equipment, food supplies, or raw materials, its economy began to weaken and its empire to wither on the vine. Once cut off, Burma, Malaya, Thailand, Indo-China, the Dutch East Indies, China, and Japanese military bases on Pacific islands became irrelevant to the course of the war. Nevertheless, fighting continued on many fronts. Anglo-American-Chinese forces launched offensives in Burma (March 1944 to July 1945), Russia invaded Manchuria in the last days of the war, and Chinese forces, both Nationalist and Communist, attacked Japanese positions in China along a front of several thousand miles. These actions affected the situation in postwar Asia, but they contributed little to the defeat of Japan.

A second factor was the destruction by firebomb raids of Japan's industrial facilities and civilian housing. Begun during the last half of 1944, the raids mounted in intensity and culminated in saturation bombing by thousand-plane flights in the months preceding surrender. Fearful destruction was wrought in Japan's densely populated cities built largely of wood. The worst raid of the war occurred on March 10, 1945, when 130 B-29's dropped incendiary bombs in parallel swathes through Tōkyō, killing over 100,000 persons and burning out most of the city. In all, 668,000 civilians were killed in Japan and 2.3 million homes were destroyed. By the last days of the war, railroads were breaking down, coal production was falling, oil was almost gone, aircraft production was dropping, nonmilitary industrial production was nil, and the average civilian was consuming less than fifteen hundred calories a day. The horror of war had become a part of the daily life of millions of Japanese. Japan was beaten, yet would not acknowledge defeat.

The Politics of War and Defeat. At the outset of war, Tōjō was both prime minister and his own army minister. Wearing two hats, he could oversee both civil and military affairs. He donned a third in February 1944, becoming chief of the General Staff to coordinate administrative and command functions within the army. In a general election in April 1942, the government-sponsored Imperial Rule Assistance Association secured the election of a pro-Tōjō Diet, which assured him of support in that quarter as well. Controlling the top posts and with this broad base, he continued in power until July 1944.

Yet Tōjō was no dictator. Unlike Hitler or Mussolini, he was but the first among many generals and admirals who led the military services, the most powerful elites of wartime Japan. Above Tōjō was the emperor, and around the emperor were the senior statesmen—the inner minister, the president of the Privy Council, and various former prime ministers such as Konoe, Yonai, and Hiranuma—who maintained extensive contacts with officials of the numerous wartime ministries.

From the start, Japan planned to negotiate a peace when the United States grew tired of fighting. As the tide of battle turned against Japan after 1943, those about the emperor began to favor immediate negotiations: if Japan could not fight its enemies to a standstill, then it would make peace before all was lost. In the minds of several, pessimism about the war was mingled with fear that radicals in the army would impose a system of "imperial communism" if conditions in Japan grew worse.

The senior statesmen were ambiguous in their objectives, their meetings were secret, and their actions were indecisive, for they feared assassination by army fanatics. After years of "spiritual mobilization" even these men of high prestige could not openly speak out in favor of peace. Finally the fall of Saipan and the resultant vulnerability of Japan to bombing created a crisis. Ministerial opposition to Tōjō joined with the influence of the senior statesmen to force his resignation. The senior statesmen wanted to appoint in his place Admiral Yonai (prime minister January–July 1940), who had opposed war with the United States and Britain. But Yonai was too moderate to be accepted by the army; he became, instead, deputy prime minister and navy minister in the cabinet of General Koiso Kuniaki (July 1944–April 1945). Koiso's cabinet was in turn toppled by the invasion of Okinawa in April. The senior statesmen selected as his successor an old but prestigious admiral, Suzuki Kantarō, former head of the Privy Council, hoping that under him peace could be achieved. Suzuki appointed as his foreign minister Tōgō Shigenori, who favored an early peace. Yet the Allies had repeatedly demanded an unconditional surrender which would have left the fate of the emperor unclear, and under these circumstances even Tōgō could not bring himself to speak of surrender. In public all reaffirmed Japan's intention to fight to the end.

At the Yalta Conference in February 1945 the United States and Great Britain had obtained a pledge from the Soviet Union to enter the war against Japan within three months after the surrender of Germany, which came in May. In July the Allied declaration at the Potsdam Conference in Germany bid Japan choose between an "order of peace, security, and justice" if it would surrender, or "utter destruction" if it refused. The official Japanese response was a decision "to press forward resolutely to carry the war to a successful conclusion." In the face of the casualties expected in an autumn invasion of Japan, the American high command decided to use the atomic bombs that had been developed too late to use against Germany. Hiroshima was obliterated on August 6. Russia, which had been moving troops from Europe to Asia since the German surrender, declared war on Japan on August 8, and began to invade Manchuria. The following day Nagasaki was destroyed by a second atomic bomb.

Even after these catastrophes the military remained adamant, unmoved by those in the cabinet and Supreme Council who favored surrender. An Imperial Conference was therefore called at which the emperor, breaking the deadlock, made the decision to surrender. All insisted, however, on one condition: the prerogatives of the emperor as "sovereign ruler" must not be prejudiced. The allied reply was that he would be under Allied control and his fate would be determined by the Japanese people. On the morning of August 14 a second Imperial Conference was called; opinion split three to three, the two chiefs of staff and the army minister opposing Navy Minister Yonai, Prime Minister Suzuki, and Foreign Minister Tōgō. Again the emperor, saying that "the unendurable must be endured," gave his support to the group favoring unconditional surrender. It was a final commentary on the orthodoxy that had emerged in Japan after 1890 that, although Japan was smashed and beaten, only the emperor could force acceptance of a surrender that put the imperial system in jeopardy.

The Occupation of Japan

Japan's history was significantly changed by America's postwar occupation of the country. Although it lasted only seven years, it was decisive for Japan's subsequent development. The Occupation succeeded because it built on some earlier trends, yet in crucial respects it broke with the prewar system in ways that were revolutionary. It made changes that would not have occurred had not Japan been briefly subject to a foreign power.

Japan in September 1945 was open to change to a degree that is unusual in history. Cities were gutted by fires and bombings, factories were damaged or destroyed, railroads were disrupted, the people were hungry and ill-clothed. The civilian populace had been girding for a final "battle of Japan" when the emperor's surrender speech was broadcast. This shattered the sense of national mission, leaving the Japanese psychically benumbed and without direction. Most Japanese were relieved that the war was over but apprehensive at what might follow.

Expecting a cruel and harsh Occupation, the Japanese found it benevolent. Fearing a vindictive rule, they found it constructive. Under these conditions the sense of duty that had enabled them to bear the sacrifices of war turned to positive, and at times even enthusiastic, cooperation with the new authorities. The rejection of wartime policies and the shift toward democracy were reinforced by the discovery that, contrary to what the Japanese people had believed during the war, their nation was reviled in all the countries that had been a part of its Co-Prosperity Sphere. Some Japanese writers, comparing Japan's receptivity to change at this time to the years after Perry, have labeled this the "second opening" of Japan.

It was of great significance that the Occupation was American. In 1945

Japan had both democratic and totalitarian potentials. On the one hand was the post-1890 parliamentary tradition; on the other, the prewar factors that had stifled this tradition, and the wartime structure of economic controls and national mobilization. Had Japan been occupied by the Soviet Union, Japanese capabilities for national planning and collective endeavor would doubtless have made it a model Communist state. Occupied by the United States, however, it built on the parliamentary institutions of its modern tradition to move in the direction of a more open society. The basic American assumption was that a democratic Japan would be less likely to disturb the world's peace again. At the same time it has been argued that it was also in America's strategic interest to remake Japan in its own image, strengthening its representative system of government and making its capitalist economy more competitive, and thus building up its own side in the cold war with the Soviet Union that after the war spread rapidly from Europe to East Asia. There is undoubtedly some truth in this too. Like the action of the Soviet Union in building a Communist state in North Korea, the reforms in Japan contributed to the subsequent polarization of political forces in the postwar era.

The Structure of the Occupation.   In theory the Occupation was international, and after an agreement reached in Moscow in December 1945, its guiding bodies were supposedly a thirteen-nation Far Eastern Commission in Washington and a four-power Allied Council in Tōkyō. Accordingly, General Douglas MacArthur was given the title of Supreme Commander for the Allied Powers (SCAP) and the whole Occupation administration under him also came to be known as SCAP. In fact, the Occupation was American throughout. It was carried out almost entirely by MacArthur, his staff, and the American and some British troops under his command. MacArthur was in many ways the ideal man for the post. He viewed himself as a man of destiny acting on the stage of history. Self-confident and speaking in broad historical themes, he inspired the Japanese during the hard early postwar years, giving them hope for a better future. He was also the ideal commander from the point of view of American politics: as a confirmed Republican under a Democratic administration, he could carry out the most radical reforms without arousing criticism at home.

Unlike Germany, Japan was not governed directly by foreign troops. The army of occupation ruled through the Japanese administrative structure. In Tōkyō under MacArthur was the General Headquarters of SCAP, which contained various staff sections roughly parallel to the ministries of the Japanese government. In the prefectures were "military government" teams, which acted as an inspectorate to ascertain that reforms enacted into law were carried out. Liaison between the SCAP sections in which policy was

The Japanese emperor visits General MacArthur. In his 1946 New Year's rescript Emperor Hirohito reaffirmed the Meiji Charter Oath, including the "elimination of misguided practices of the past" and "love of mankind," and referred to "the false conception that the emperor is divine." MacArthur commented that the emperor "squarely takes his stand for the future along liberal lines. His action reflects the irresistible influence of a sound idea."

formulated and the Japanese government was undertaken by the Central Liaison Office, staffed chiefly by Foreign Ministry personnel.

After 1948 the liaison arrangement was eliminated in favor of direct contact with government ministries. Some criticized the pattern of SCAP rule, saying that the same bureaucracy which had formerly followed the dictates of the Japanese military now followed the American military, and pointing out that this was poor preparation for democracy. In the early years there was an uneasy tension between the supposed power of a democratized Diet and the actual power of SCAP. Yet in practice, after the initial reforms, SCAP gradually turned over the reins of government to the Japanese.

The assumptions of the Occupation were based on a devil theory of history: that Japan's leaders since the early 1930's had been engaged in a giant conspiracy to wage aggressive war. This view was clearly brought out in the indictment of the Tōkyō war crimes trials. The leaders had attained their ends because Japanese society was "feudal," its values militaristic, its huge financial combines "merchants of death," and its political system reactionary. So faulted was Japan's character that only the most radical action could reform it. This theory of conspiracy was partly false and partly a gross exaggeration, but it was responsible for the thoroughness of the early wave of reforms. American conservatives became radical, and reforms were enacted that would have been impossible without this climate of opinion. The

Occupation's enthusiasm for the job of democratizing Japan at times outran its grasp of the situation, but it was dedicated and largely successful.

Demilitarization and Reform.   The Occupation began with the liquidation of the apparatus of Japanese militarism The empire was dismembered and all Japanese abroad, soldiers and civilians alike, were returned to Japan. The military services were demobilized; paramilitary and ultranationalist organizations were dissolved. Shintō was disestablished. Armaments industries were dismantled. The Home Ministry was abolished. The police were decentralized, their powers curtailed, and their authority to regulate speech and "thought" revoked. Political prisoners were released from jail.

The Occupation next acted to remove the old leadership. Twenty-five of the top leaders were brought to trial for having begun the war. Seven of these, including Tōjō, were hanged in December 1948. Most of the others were given long prison sentences. In retrospect it is clear to all that Japanese militarism was not of the same genus as National Socialism (it ran no Dachaus) and that the application of the principles of the Nüremberg trials at Tōkyō was winner's justice. In another action taken against the old leadership about 200,000 former military officers or high officials in government or business were purged, that is, forbidden to hold office or continue in their business. This brought to the fore a younger generation of Japanese, better able to adjust themselves to the reforms of the Occupation.

The most significant reform was the enactment of the 1947 constitution. The Meiji constitution had begun:

Having, by virtue of the glories of Our Ancestors, ascended the Throne of a lineal succession unbroken for ages eternal; desiring to promote the welfare of, and to give development to the moral and intellectual faculties of Our beloved subjects ... We hereby promulgate ... a fundamental law of the State, to exhibit the principles, by which We are to be guided in Our conduct, and to point out to what Our descendants and Our subjects and their descendants are forever to conform.

The new constitution began:

We, the Japanese people, acting through our duly elected representatives in the National Diet, determined that we shall secure for ourselves and our posterity the fruits of peaceful cooperation with all nations and the blessings of liberty throughout this land, and resolved that never again shall we be visited with the horrors of war through the action of government, do proclaim that sovereign power resides with the people and do firmly establish this Constitution.

The 1947 constitution transformed Japan's political life, making Japan into a truly parliamentary state. Some of the major changes were:

1. The prewar multiple elites (the services, Privy Council, and special officials close to the emperor) were either abolished or strictly subordinated to the cabinet.
2. The Cabinet became a "committee" of the majority party or coalition in the Diet—on the British model.
3. Both houses of the Diet became fully elective, and the franchise was extended to all men and women aged twenty or over. The 466 (later increased to 491, and then to 511) members of the more powerful House of Representatives were chosen from 124 electoral districts, which usually had 3 to 5 seats each, allowing a certain degree of proportional representation. The 250 members of the House of Councilors were to be chosen 150 from prefectures and 100 from the nation at large.
4. The judiciary was made independent, and the Supreme Court was given the power to pass on the constitutionality of Diet legislation.
5. Governors of prefectures, as was already the case of mayors of municipalities, were made elective and local government was given increased powers.
6. Human rights were guaranteed. Among these were the classic Western rights of assembly, a free press, and life, liberty, and the pursuit of happiness, but also included were newer rights such as "the right to maintain the minimum standards of wholesome and cultural living," "academic freedom," and the right of workers to bargain collectively.

The position of the emperor was also changed. Formerly sacred as well as sovereign, he was stripped of all "powers related to government" to become "the symbol of the state and of the unity of the people, deriving his position from the will of the people with whom resides sovereign power." The change in the actual political role of the emperor was small, because, except for the surrender decision, he had not been a decision maker. But the change in theory was immense. That the emperor was not thrown out altogether eased the transition to the postwar world. Yet the effect of his changed position, going far beyond the political restructuring demanded by Yoshino Sakuzō in the 1920's, was to weaken myth and secularize the state. This was a decisive break with Japan's long Shintō tradition and the form it had taken in the Meiji constitution. The minority of conservatives who lamented the change usually cared less for the imperial institution itself than for the traditional moral order associated with it. They sensed in the emperor a special kind of power by which the Humpty Dumpty of tradition might be put back together again. Those who fought to preserve the present constitution saw their struggle as directed against the total prewar syndrome of emperor, state, family system, and the obligations associated with each.

That Japan was ready for the new constitution was made clear in the subsequent decades of parliamentary government. Yet the difficulty of effecting this reform illustrates clearly the nature of the Occupation as a revolution from outside. SCAP informed the prime minister of the importance of constitutional change in September 1945. The cabinet produced a draft constitution little different from that of Meiji. Thereupon the Government Section of SCAP prepared its own draft for use as a "guide." A slightly modified version of this draft was then adopted, ostensibly in accordance with "the freely expressed will of the Japanese people," as an amendment to the Meiji constitution. One Japanese journalist wrote that some passages in the new constitution "by Japanese literary standards, sound quaintly and exotically American." His comment, like all references to the Occupation's direction of government reforms, was censored by SCAP.

Another achievement of the Occupation was land reform. All land owned by absentee landlords and all land held by others above 10 acres per family was bought by the government and sold to former tenants on extremely easy credit terms. This left a maximum holding of 7½ acres farmed by the owner himself and 2½ acres more to rent out. Since the land was paid for at pre-inflation prices, this was tantamount to expropriation. The percentage of land worked by tenants dropped from 46 to 10 per cent and rents were limited to modest levels. Because farmers prospered in hungry postwar Japan, debts were quickly paid off, and there emerged a countryside of small, independent, relatively prosperous, and politically conservative farmers.

In the modern sector of the economy the target of the reformers was the zaibatsu. The first wave of reforms dissolved eighty-three zaibatsu holding companies, froze the assets of zaibatsu families, and then wiped out their fortunes with a capital levy. This broke the giant combines into their component sub-combines, companies, and banks. To prevent their re-establishment, antimonopoly laws were passed and new inheritance and income taxes were instituted. In December 1947 further deconcentration of twelve hundred companies was planned, but this was abandoned as Occupation policy swung from reform to recovery.

Critics have argued that these reforms meant little and that the post-Occupation Japanese government ignored the antitrust laws. It is true that former zaibatsu companies tended to re-establish relations with the banks of their former combines. Depending heavily on these banking resources, and benefiting also from centralized marketing facilities and other business advantages, loose coalitions of industries, each centering on a bank and a marketing company, emerged and in some cases readopted the old names— Mitsui group, Mitsubishi group, and so on. But there were differences too. The new coalitions were less hierarchical and much less closely knit than before the war. The degree of control was very much less, as competing banks might be used. Some companies did not re-establish connections at all. And many important new companies emerged outside the zaibatsu tradition.

Along with "zaibatsu-busting," the Occupation helped labor unions. Workers were given the right to organize, bargain, and strike. Laws were passed to better the conditions of employees. Within this changed climate men who had been active in the prewar labor movement again began to recruit workers; by 1949, 6.5 million had joined unions and the number rose steadily thereafter. More of the total Japanese labor force was unionized than in the United States, and only a little less than in England.

The vigor of labor's response at first delighted Occupation reformers. Their enthusiasm waned, however, when, instead of becoming an American-type labor movement, it became political and Marxist like prewar Japanese unionism. As the emphasis shifted toward economic recovery, the Occupation took the position that further wage gains must await increases in production. In 1949 earlier labor laws were revised and a more restrictive Taft-Hartley type of legislation was passed. In 1950 Communist leaders were driven from the unions in the so-called "red purge." These measures, however, had little effect on the continuing vitality of the movement.

The surge of the labor movement within the new framework underlines a larger thesis that applies to the Occupation as a whole: though the Occupation was a revolution from outside, the response of the people, desiring more freedom and democracy, made the reforms successful. Without this, the changes would not have stuck, and the swing away from the Occupation reforms after 1952 would have been far greater.

Another vital reform was in education. Prewar education had been compulsory for only six years; this was extended to nine years and most students went for twelve. Prewar education had special channels leading to vocational schools, normal schools, higher technical schools, or universities. Once under way a student found it hard to alter his course. This was changed: levels were standardized so that the completion of any level kept all channels open at the next level. The content of education also changed. Emphasis was placed on democracy and individual rights in the textbooks, classroom projects replaced rote learning, and social studies replaced "national history" in the lower grades; in every area an attempt was made to end indoctrination and promote independent thought. Prewar higher education had been elitist. Under the Occupation a variety of lesser schools were made over into multi-faculty universities on the American pattern: the first two years given over to "general education," followed by two years of specialization. Junior colleges also proliferated, but were attended largely by women. Despite a vast increase in higher education, however, the academic hierarchy remained sharply differentiated, with Tōkyō University and the other older national universities soaring far above the others in influence and prestige.

The Conservative Phase of the Occupation and the Peace Treaty.　By the end of 1947 the primary goals of the Occupation had been achieved. The continued presence of foreign troops in Japan's cities, of censorship, and of SCAP direction of government, could only provoke a negative reaction. The

United States wanted to get out. The Soviet Union, unhappy at the prospect of continuing American influence over Japan, demanded a veto in the negotiations for a peace treaty. This blocked a treaty and the Occupation drifted on for five more years. Decision making, however, increasingly passed into Japanese hands. When a peace treaty was finally signed the transition was almost imperceptible to the average citizen.

The cold war also contributed to the change. By the middle of 1948 it was clear that the Communists would win in China. This made the potential industrial and military strength of Japan an important counter in American East Asian policy. At the same time it was hoped that democracy would flourish in Japan. Thus the foe of 1945 became the friend of 1948. For Japan to succeed as a parliamentary state economic stability was necessary. American policy therefore turned from reform to reconstruction. This conservative tendency was accelerated when North Korea invaded the South in June of 1950. As American and then United Nations troops fought to repel the invasion, Japan became a staging ground and workshop for the United Nations forces. A last object lesson of the power of civilian government in a democracy was given to the Japanese when in April 1951 General MacArthur was dismissed after disagreeing with President Truman over the conduct of the war.

On September 8, 1951, the United States and forty-seven other nations signed a peace treaty with Japan, by which Japan regained its independence on April 28, 1952, but renounced its claim to former colonies. China, India, and the Soviet Union did not sign, but as the Occupation was American their abstention had no effect. India signed a separate treaty shortly thereafter as did the Nationalist Chinese government on Taiwan.

On the same day as the peace treaty, Japan signed a security treaty with the United States which provided for the continuation of American bases in Japan and committed the United States to defend Japan in case of need.

The Economy and Society

Reconstruction and Economic Growth.   At the end of the war with its empire lost, its population swollen to 72 million, its foreign relations severed, and its industries smashed, dismantled, or stopped for lack of raw materials, Japan's prospects appeared bleak. The Occupation's purges and program of economic deconcentration inhibited economic planning. While businessmen waited uncertainly, inflation, an effective capital levy in itself, wiped out the savings of the prewar middle class. In 1947 production was only 37 per cent of the prewar level. All economic predictions regarding Japan's future were pessimistic.

SCAP began to emphasize economic recovery in 1948. American aid to Japan had begun in 1947, much of it foodstuffs to prevent starvation in the

The bullet trains leave Tōkyō for Ōsaka every fifteen minutes and travel at 125 miles per hour.

cities, and by 1952 2 billion dollars had been given. Inflation slowed the growth of foreign trade, so in 1949 SCAP forced Japan to adopt a politically unpopular austerity program to bring it under control. The reduction of prices led to a small spurt in exports. The first major boom in manufacturing came between 1950 and 1953 when 4 billion dollars' worth of military procurement orders were placed in Japan during the Korean War. This coincided with the quiescent phase of the Occupation, the peace treaty, and the first Japanese governmental and private plans for industrial development. The surge during the Korean War was followed by a recession in 1953–1954, a new export boom in 1955–1957, and then other deflationary pauses and rounds of renewed growth. By the mid-1950's Japan had regained its prewar economic levels and during the 1960's it forged rapidly ahead to become one of the great industrial and trading powers of the world. The Occupation had carried out the first revolution in postwar Japan; economic growth produced the second.

By 1970 even the casual visitor to Japan was assaulted with evidences of well-being—television antennas sprouting from tile roofs, new buildings with air conditioning and automatic doors, men wearing dark blue suits and women stylishly dressed, the bustle of the cities and the whirr of farm equipment in the countryside. The railways were the best in the world: fast, clean, and frequent. The old trunk road between Tōkyō and Ōsaka, the once scenic Tōkaidō known to us through Hiroshige's woodblock prints, had become an almost continuous industrial belt through which ran the "bullet train" that other nations talked of imitating. The life expectancy had risen to 68.7 years for men and 73.7 for women. Per capita income had risen from $146 in 1951 to $395 in 1960, and rose to over $2000 in 1972. This put Japan ahead of Italy, Austria, and England, but still well behind West Germany.

One economist has argued that postwar Japan was "the most extraordinary success story in all economic history." It is important to grasp its magnitude. The gross national product rose from a stuporous $1.3 billion in 1946 to $15.1 in 1951, to $51.9 in 1962, to about $290 billion in 1972—as measured in the revalued yen. Moreover, as the modern sector, which always had the highest growth rate, became proportionately larger in the total economy, the rate of economic growth in real terms (that is, after inflation has been subtracted) accelerated.

ANNUAL PERCENTAGE GROWTH IN GNP

1951–1955	8.6
1955–1960	9.1
1960–1965	9.7
1965–1970	13.1

This growth made the Japanese economy the third largest in the world following the trillion dollar economy of the United States and the 400 million dollar economy of the Soviet Union. Perhaps more significantly, its GNP had become greater than the combined GNP's of all the rest of East Asia (China, Korea, and Vietnam) together with that of India.

The Dynamics of Japan's Economic Success.   There is no single explanation for Japan's growth in the early postwar decades. Rather, it was the result of a great variety of factors working together. Japanese workers were hardworking, literate, and technically advanced. A German industrialist visiting Japan in the late 1960's commented that Japanese workers work the way German workers used to work. The Japanese had a high rate of savings. A 1970 advertisement for a Japanese bank on a Tōkyō billboard showed a smiling family—a mother, a father, and a single child (a boy). The caption read: "Happiness is a bank account with a million yen (about $3300)."

At the end of World War II there was a gap between the technology of the most advanced nations and that of Japan. Importing new equipment, Japan could take advantage of the technological progress which it embodied, and this eventually made its industries among the most efficient in the world. Japan had the engineers and scientists that were necessary to utilize this backlog. In many cases they improved on the technology that was brought in. Still, one lesson that all but the most developed countries can draw from Japan's experience is that it is cheaper to license or buy new technology from the most developed countries than to develop it yourself. Even in 1970, as research outlays increased, the amount spent on research in Japan was lower than in other advanced economies.

Another factor in Japan's economic advance was the relatively light

Left: Toyota plant near Tōkyō. Flowers were brought from a worker's garden. Right: Girls on Sony assembly line.

burden of nonproductive military spending, made possible by the security treaty with the United States. Where the United States and the Soviet Union spent close to 10 per cent of their GNP on defense, and Western European countries about 5 per cent, Japan consistently spent less than 1 per cent. The difference was available for productive uses.

Even agricultural productivity increased. Japan's original agricultural revolution (1868–1920) was contemporary with its industrialization. By the 1920's the import of foodstuffs from the colonies led to a leveling-off of productivity. After World War II fresh advances were made, based on chemical fertilizers, new insecticides, and light farm machinery. Because of these advances and a government program of price supports, Japan became self-sufficient in rice production. Its own production of other foodstuffs such as wheat, fruits, or meat, however, had to be supplemented by imports.

Another critical condition for growth was the resumption of multilateral world trade. Japan's exports grew from 820 million dollars in 1950 to over 25 billion in 1971. Imports grew from 974 million in 1950 to over 18 billion in 1971. As Japan is poorly endowed with the raw materials required by an industrial economy, about three-fourths of its imports consisted of ores, oil, coking coal, steel scrap, rubber, cotton, wool, lumber, and other raw materials. Without these, Japan's industries could not have run. That they were obtainable only through peaceful trade powerfully conditioned Japanese attitudes to international relations.

A sampling of Japanese exports in 1970 reveals the fecundity of its manufacturers. Japan was the world's leading ship-builder. Japan bought iron ore and coking coal from the United States and sold steel to the United States in return. The Japanese ability to move rapidly from a new technique to a finished product to a marketing effort was remarkable. Honda and Suzuki motorcycles, Toyota and Datsun cars were found in most countries of the world. In the light precision industries Sony, Matsushita, and other companies sent out tape recorders, television sets, binoculars, electronic calculators, electron microscopes, and a growing flood of other modern products. Among German camera manufacturers in 1970 a paralysis of will resulting from Japanese competition was called the "Japan complex." Where before the war the words "made in Japan" had meant cheap ten-cent-store goods, they increasingly came to suggest a quality product. The international organs of the giant Mitsui and Mitsubishi combines could build hydroelectric plants, chemical factories, or harbors anywhere in the world. Japan was already participating in the development of Alaska, Australia, and the Philippines, and had begun arrangements to participate actively in the development of Siberia.

Japan's most important trading partners in 1970 were the United States, which took 30.8 per cent of its exports, and the non-Communist countries of Asia, which took 25.4 per cent. Since more than half of United States sales to Japan were of raw materials or agricultural products and virtually all Japanese sales to the United States were of finished goods, critics of this trade argued that the United States had become an economic colony of Japan. Critics on the Japanese side turned this argument around, saying that Japan had become a factory producing goods for the benefit of the United States with its rich natural resources and more efficient agriculture. Japan's trade with Asia was spread evenly over a number of countries. The main problem in this trade was that the Asian countries wanted Japanese cars and machinery but, except for those endowed with raw materials, they had little to sell that Japan wanted to buy. Europe took 15 per cent of Japanese exports, a small amount considering Europe's economic size. Europe feared Japanese competition, and it matched Japan in carrying out protectionist policies. Trade with China and the Soviet Union gradually rose during the sixties, though with some political fluctuations. In 1970 trade with the Communist states took 5.4 per cent of Japan's exports.

To stress the importance of foreign trade is not to say that the Japanese economy was oriented primarily to foreign markets. Japanese exports as a percentage of GNP (9.8) were smaller than those of any European country —France 12.3, United Kingdom 16.6, West Germany 18.8. Even more than before the war, growth depended on the expansion of the domestic consumer market—which was marked by the acceptance of new patterns of consumption. New giants such as Matsushita, Tōshiba, or Hitachi arose to produce new goods for the Japanese masses. It was the size of the domestic market which made possible the "economies of scale" that made Japan so effective a competitor abroad.

The manufacturing process itself during the fifties and sixties was characterized by a high degree of teamwork between labor and management. This occurred, of course, against a backdrop of steadily rising wages. In spite of an ideology of class struggle that colored union pronouncements and the display of red flags in May Day parades, in spite of hard labor bargaining in the annual "spring offensives," there were few crippling strikes in Japanese plants. Unions were organized on the basis of companies, not trades. Most workers in companies enjoyed the security of lifetime employment and showed a high degree of loyalty toward their company.

A final factor of great importance for economic growth was the particular Japanese combination of free enterprise and government guidance that businessmen from other countries sometimes referred to as "Japan Inc." A number of points may be noted: 1) Banking credit, backed ultimately by the government, made heavy capital investment possible—on the assumption that increases in productivity would provide surpluses to cancel out debts later on. The system worked. Where roughly two-thirds of the capital requirements of the average American company were met by stock and one-third by debt, in Japan the percentages were reversed. Commercial banks lent out a high percentage of their funds for purchases of fixed capital with the tacit backing and guidance of the Bank of Japan. This type of "overextended" bank credit, channeling both government and private capital into development, refinanced industry during the 1950's and 1960's. 2) The government was more deeply involved in planning than the government of any other nonsocialist state and guided the economy probably with greater skill than any socialist state. The Finance Ministry and the Ministry of International Trade and Industry (commonly called MITI in English) coordinating their efforts through the Economic Planning Agency, cooperated in charting Japan's future growth. Growth industries were targeted, production goals were set, and foreign markets were estimated. Growth was rewarded with high depreciation allowances, cheap loans, subsidies, and light taxes. Some businesses benefited as well from research carried out in government laboratories that was then turned over to companies for commercial development. 3) The government successfully carried out a policy of protection. Foreign competition was permitted mainly in areas where foreign companies could not compete or where Japanese production was not planned. Infant industries, particularly in new technologies, were protected by successive walls of tariffs, quotas, currency controls, foreign investment controls, and bureaucratic red tape. Foreign investment was not welcome, except when it brought in new technology, and then only as a minority interest. From the late sixties to the early seventies as Japan grew to super-power proportions this protectionism could no longer be justified. To maintain its access to other markets, Japan was forced to "liberalize," opening its own markets to the imports of other nations. By this time, however, relatively few of the manufactured products of other countries were able to compete effectively. 4) Japanese businessmen often chafed at bureaucratic regulations and government interference and argued that it was their own efficiency and hard work that was responsible for their success. This was not untrue. In spite of the large government role in the economy, Japan was not a socialist country. Most economic decision making occurred within the company unit. Each company had to suffer the consequences of wrong decisions. Each company "rested on its own bottom" financially. Yet the attitude of businessmen toward the government took for granted a favorable and supportive business climate such as did not exist in most other countries.

Social Change. Perhaps the most significant change in postwar Japanese society was the decline in the growth rate of the population. During the years from 1868 to 1945 it was the reduction of the death rate through modern hygiene that led Japan's population to more than double. After 1950 it was the decline in the birth rate that caused the population to begin to level off.

POPULATION GROWTH

Year Period	*Population at End of Period*	*Percentage Increase during Period*
1920–1925	59,179,200	6.8
1925–1930	63,872,496	7.9
1930–1935	68,661,654	7.5
1935–1940	72,539,729	5.6
1940–1945	71,998,104	−0.7
1945–1950	83,199,637	15.6
1950–1955	89,275,529	7.3
1955–1960	93,418,501	4.7
1960–1965	98,274,961	5.2
1965–1970	103,720,060	5.5
1970–1975	111,933,818	6.9

The immediate postwar years witnessed a baby boom, and as the girls born during the boom began to have babies, the rate again rose in the years between 1970 and 1975. But the overall rate of natural increase was down. The percentage of the aged in the population increased from 4.9 in 1950 to 7.9 in 1975 and is expected to reach 12.4 in 1995. (The percent in the United States is 10.3, in Britain 13.7.) As women of child-bearing age become a smaller component in the total population, the rate of natural increase will decline further. Present estimates suggest that Japan's population in the year 2000 will be 135 million. Considering that Japan is already the most densely populated country in the world in terms of the ratio between population and utilizable land, it is clear that Japan's future would be brighter if the population were much less. On the other hand, in comparison with many countries where population growth is wildly out of control, Japan is moving in the direction of a stabilized population.

One explanation for the decline in the birth rate stresses government policy. In 1945 Japan faced the specter of becoming so overcrowded that the quality of life would seriously deteriorate and further industrialization could only fractionally improve the lot of its people. Consequently the government in 1948 passed a Eugenics Protection Law, legalizing abortion for economic as well as medical reasons. This produced immediate results: for a time in the 1950's abortions exceeded live births. Public and private efforts were made to spread birth control practices: post office posters, for example, contrasted small families of well-fed, happy children with large families of ill-fed, poorly clothed, cheerless children. The government set up family planning clinics and some factories cooperated in establishing family planning groups. Such policies contributed to changes in attitudes: public opinion polls in the early seventies revealed that younger couples were more strongly in favor of family planning than older ones.

A second explanation contends that government policy alone would not have succeeded in reducing the birth rate, and sees as the critical factor institutional changes parallel to those that had occurred slightly earlier in the advanced nations of the West. Some of these changes were: a more educated populace; later marriage due to longer years of education, the postponement of marriage to avoid living with in-laws, and a spreading desire to prolong the independence and pleasures of the single life into the early twenties; a higher level of medical knowledge and facilities; and the acceptance of the two-child ideal.

A third explanation maintains that neither government policy nor institutional changes would have reduced the birth rate if couples had not perceived that it was in their self-interest to have fewer children. It points out that until the 1930's, at least, children left school early, more often than not to work for the family enterprise or farm, and sons supported their parents in their old age. Children were a valuable commodity, and having many was the best form of insurance. By the 1950's Japan had reached the stage of development where children became increasingly expensive and contributed little in economic terms. They went to school for many years, and then to work for a company, marrying and establishing a separate household. (A further marked advance in the nuclear family was noted in the 1975 census.) Unless there was a special need they would not regularly aid their parents who, more and more, came to depend in old age on savings and retirement benefits. Two children met the parents' human needs; more made savings difficult.

A second major change was the redistribution of population within Japan. The combination of a rapidly expanding economy and a slowly growing population produced a labor shortage. Men and then women were drawn willy nilly from agriculture and small and medium industry into the new large industries of the cities. During the 1960's this flow of workers to better jobs began to erode the "double structure" characteristic of the prewar economy. Small and medium sized businesses were forced to pay higher wages to compete for manpower with the higher wages, greater security, and extra fringe benefits offered by the modern sector. During the 1960's an accelerating rate of bankruptcies appeared among smaller businesses. A similar shift took place from the farm to the city. In 1950 there were 6.18 million farm households in Japan, almost the same number as during the early Meiji era; by 1970 the number had declined slowly to 5.34 million households, while the farm population as a percentage of the total population declined from 85 per cent in the early Meiji to about 50 per cent in 1945 to less than 20 per cent by 1970.

During the early postwar era, changes in the village were not apparent on the surface. The tiled or thatched roofed houses, the green terraced fields, and the ubiquitous shrines and temples had an air of timelessness. But by the 1960's even the physical setting had begun to change. Factories were built in rural areas to take advantage of cheaper labor costs. New concrete buildings appeared—schoolhouses, warehouses, or sales outlets for automobile and tractor concerns. Roads were improved; trucks and farm machinery appeared in the most remote villages; small hills were bulldozed to provide sites for new housing; and new houses were often roofed with sheets of bright blue plastic. In the new countryside temples and shrines often looked like intruders from another age.

Beneath the surface, changes were even more profound. Far more than before the war, farming became commercialized with considerable amounts of capital involved. It was carried out for profit, not subsistence: if pigs were in oversupply, they were slaughtered and chickens were raised, and the same attitude extended to agricultural crops. Members of farm families commuted to work in nearby cities, while those in more remote areas commuted to smaller towns to replace others who migrated to cities. Often the bulk of farmwork was performed by the wife, with the help of grandparents or older children. In 1960 slightly less than half of the average farm household's income of $1133 came from nonagricultural pursuits. By 1970 the income of the average farm household had risen to $3880, surpassing that of urban

Scenes of Tōkyō, at the end of World War II and now.

worker families, and about 60 per cent of this came from nonfarm sources.

Village society also changed drastically. The hamlet dweller began to look outward. Administrative amalgamation consolidated villages into "cities," where the decisions governing hamlet life were made. Television sets in every household brought in world news and the gamut of Japanese and American programs (with Japanese expertly dubbed in). Farm boys went to high school and then off to jobs in the cities, and farm girls did not want to become farmers' wives. As family heads and other able-bodied men left the countryside during the working day, the fabric of traditional society wore thin, and hamlet solidarity began to crumble. Men with land and an outside job had little interest in spending their weekends on communal functions, which in regions near cities were close to collapse. Only in the exceptional village were old patterns of human relations renewed in more egalitarian forms, perhaps centering on farmers' cooperatives or on some village project.

Japan's farms were still small, averaging about 2½ acres. But Japan had arrived at the point where further gains in productivity could be achieved only by getting the marginal farmer off the farm and consolidating landholdings. With this end in mind the government began in 1970 to remove the legal restrictions on land concentration that the Occupation had set up to prevent a recrudescence of landlordism. It is ironic that had it not been for the land reform of the Occupation—so necessary at its time—this consolidation would already have been well underway. Even by the early seventies, however, consolidation had hardly begun, for not only did farming furnish a second income, but land was seen as valuable, as insurance to fall back on in time of trouble, or as a speculation for future real estate gains. Still, the capital base for consolidation had already begun to appear in the more prosperous farms, farm machinery was available, and economists predicted that the emigration of the young from the countryside to city jobs would gradually lead to the sale of smaller landholdings.

The new Japan was basically urban. In 1972 one of every nine Japanese lived in Tōkyō, and one out of four lived in the Tōkyō-Osaka industrial belt. Tōkyō was to Japan what Paris was to France: the center of government, finance, business, industry, and the arts and letters. Tōkyō was the center of a huge net of feeder electric railways, the terminuses of which intersected with a constantly growing internal web of subway lines. At such intersections there developed, in addition to the old downtown of the Ginza, eight or nine newer "downtowns," each with magnificent department stores, shopping areas, business offices, banks, movie houses, coffee shops, restaurants, bars, and night clubs. So crowded were the commuter trains that since the late fifties students were hired as "pushers" to help pack in passengers or as "pullers" to remove passengers whose attempted entry prevented car doors from closing. In the heart of the city were areas of private homes and

*Pushers packing in the
passengers on the Tōkyō
rapid transit.*

increasing numbers of "mansions," high-rise condominium apartments that
were luxurious by Japanese standards. Surrounding the inner city were older,
middle class residential areas which expanded outward to envelop what in
prewar times had been farm villages. And farther out along rail lines were
aggregates of residential developments *(danchi)*—drab rows of five to six
story concrete buildings with tiny crowded apartments often set down
incongruously in the middle of the rice fields in areas under cultivation since
the dawn of Japanese history.

In this urban society the twin revolutions of the Occupation and economic
growth had sweeping consequences. The status of women rose. As most girls
went to high school and many to college, the legal rights of women were
increasingly a matter of practice. The ideal of the conjugal family advanced.
(Newspapers occasionally received letters complaining of brides who were
cruel to their mothers-in-law.) In the new climate of religious freedom,
popular religious sects proliferated. There were freer social relations between
boys and girls. The pursuit of happiness—or of pleasure—in coffee houses,
movie theaters, and pinball parlors, at symphonies, or on ski slopes, beaches or
camping grounds became an accepted goal, especially for youth. These
changes can be seen as quantitative advances along lines laid down in prewar
Japan, yet the changes were not simply linear. Rather they created a new
social configuration, a new way of life. The older generation recognized this
by saying that the *a-pu-re (après la guerre)* generation was entirely different—more relaxed, franker, less polite, and perhaps more egoistic. They
regretted the change, viewing juvenile delinquency and other urban phenomena as signs of moral decay, and they criticized the postwar system of
education. Yet the old themselves accepted and participated in a way of life

that had not been foreseen at the end of World War II.

Considering the rapid pace of change, one would expect to find in Japanese society deep dislocations and considerable social unrest. These were not entirely absent. There were the old who lived on fixed incomes and were hard hit by rising prices. Among the middle-aged there were shopkeepers, small-boat fishermen, and others who missed out on Japan's modern prosperity. There were the universities, storm centers for recurrent waves of unrest among the youth.

One illustration of how the strains and dislocations of rapid economic growth were met was the Sōka Gakkai (Value Creating Association). The most successful of Japan's "new religions," it rose from a membership of a few thousand families in the early 1950's to claim 4.3 million families in 1964. After that its growth leveled off. (The Japanese Communist Party paid it the supreme compliment of studying its organizational techniques.) Probably about one of every twelve Japanese was a member. The sect attracted urban Japanese who felt uprooted, who missed the traditional community, or who did not share in Japan's new prosperity. First spreading among shopkeepers, taxi drivers, coal miners, and unskilled labor, it then began to spread to other groups as well; its successes among younger Japanese were notable. Its appeal was down-to-earth. Members asked potential converts: "Why are you living? Are you satisfied with your life?" To the problem of the atomization and alienation of the individual in postwar society it gave a traditional answer: that only the Nichiren Sect of Buddhism and faith in the Lotus Sutra could bring salvation to the individual, the nation, and the world. Teaching faith healing and mutual assistance, it brought its members together in warm, tightly knit, supportive, local associations. Although a Buddhist-based sect, in its early years it placed a heavy emphasis on profit in this world as a sign of the efficacy of belief. By the early seventies profit had become less important. Because the Sōka Gakkai used paramilitary terminology to describe its hierarchy of local and regional branches, because of its traditional cultural content, and because of its predilection for parades, pageants, and mass convocations, some saw it as a dangerous reaction against modernity. Another view, more sympathetic, stressed the degree to which it provided a sense of community and belongingness for immigrants from the countryside or the city poor, similar to what others obtained from the factory, company, or government office.

Other Japanese centered their lives on their possessions, their homes, or their jobs. Where before the war more traditional goods were desired, the modern husband and wife wanted new products. The "three sacred treasures" of Japan, anciently the mirror, the jewels, and the sword, became in the late 1950's the television, the refrigerator, and the washing machine. In the early 1960's a new set of consumer "treasures" were designated the "three C's," the car, the color television, and the "room cooler," and by the

late 1960's there were the "three V's," the villa, the vacation, and the visit
to a foreign country. The Japanese media described the new privatistic orientation toward home and possessions as "my-home-ism" and "my-car-ism."
Over fourteen thousand married couples were asked in a 1969 poll: What
have you to live for? Almost 83 per cent of the women and over 57 per
cent of the men replied "home and children." The rest of the men, and a
much higher percentage among those with a university education, gave first
place to their work. In a sense "my-job-ism" was an orientation of such long
standing that it was not necessary to coin a new phrase to describe it. Opinion
polls showed a shift from traditional loyalty to the company toward the desire for personal gratification in work. Loyalty, however, was still strong.

Viewed comparatively, Japanese society in the early seventies lacked many
of the ills that plagued other industrialized societies. There was no drug
problem in Japan, nor had there been one in the past. Gun laws were severe
and strictly enforced: hunting rifles were tightly controlled and civilians
were not permitted to own handguns. Japan had no conscription system, no
soldiers abroad, and no involvement in foreign wars. There were vestigial prejudices in Japan against the *eta,* the outcast community of the
Tokugawa period whose social assimilation, even in the postwar era, was
incomplete. And there were strong prejudices against the 600,000 Korean
residents in Japan, a national as well as ethnic minority. But these groups
were both so well behaved and so small a part of the total population that
they did not constitute a major social problem in the eyes of most Japanese.
Japan also appeared to lack a "culture of poverty." Even the poor and the
marginal maintained the ethic of endurance, forbearance, and making do.
Thus even poor districts seemed somehow middle class in character. There
was no city in Japan where it was dangerous to walk the streets at night.
Moreover, except among students, there was no widespread questioning of
social, religious, and political authority. The lack of such ills, and the awareness that they existed elsewhere, made many Japanese increasingly satisfied
with their own society.

But Japanese society had problems too. For years social investment had
been sacrificed for the sake of maximum economic growth. Housing was poor
by Western standards. Welfare programs for the sick and old were inadequate. Education was underfinanced. Sewage disposal methods were antique.
The sudden blossoming of an automobile economy in an already constricted
living space with inadequate roads and parking produced the world's worst
traffic jams. Yet perhaps the greatest internal ill was pollution. It was as if
half the population of the United States and one-fourth of its industry had
been crammed into the single state of California. The skies of Tōkyō were
often grey, the sun dimmed to a pale moon-like orb, and Tōkyō Bay was
sludgy with the voided effluents of industry. Traffic policemen, though rotated every two hours, suffered from lead poisoning. In 1970 Japan suddenly

woke up to this problem—partly in response to the rise of ecological concern in the United States. Magazines and papers were filled with articles asking: "Where are we going?" and "What are we doing to ourselves?" Some in Japan felt that the extreme pro-business stance of Japanese government would prevent it from attacking this problem head-on. Others felt that the dynamism of the "task-force approach" that the highly centralized government had brought to the Tōkyō Olympics and the 1970 Ōsaka Exposition also could be applied to this more serious concern.

Intellectual Currents.   In the process of modernization Japan destroyed a large part of its tradition in order to build a strong nation. A few traditional concepts, however, were enshrined at the core of the new nationalism so as to preserve symbolically what was being destroyed in fact. Mesmerized by the emperor ideology as a "teaching... infallible for all ages and true in all places," the Japanese marched into the modern world. The most important ideological change in postwar Japan was the destruction of this emperor-state orthodoxy.

National self-consciousness as a distinctive people and culture (*kokumin-shugi*) was not lost. The Japanese sense of "we-ness" versus "they-ness" remained stronger than in any other modernized country. A Japanese victory in sports or the conquest of a Himalayan peak was hailed enthusiastically by the whole nation. The admission of Japan to the United Nations brought a sense of national fulfillment. A steel company in Kyūshū mounted a poster on the inner wall of a rolling mill: "In quantity and quality let us lead the world." But nationalism in the sense of devotion to the state (*kokkashugi*) came under a dark cloud. The Japanese flag was rarely flown in the first two decades after the war. Actions could no longer be justified "for the sake of the nation." Or if a sanction was sought, it was "for the sake of a new Japan," implicitly international in outlook and democratic in practice. And militarism or anything pertaining to war was viewed by intellectuals and by most of the people as anathema.

The rejection of the old orthodoxy left many in a state of aimlessness. One reaction to this was a vogue of existentialism and existentialist literature— with roots in Japan's prewar tradition of German philosophy. *The Stranger* by Albert Camus became a best seller. Many intellectuals felt that this novel depicted their predicament and sense of estrangement as accurately as did the writings of Japanese authors. The brilliant writer Dazai Osamu, indulging in women, alcohol, and drugs, continued the "negative identity" of Akutagawa that had become all the more palatable as the result of a meaningless war and a crushing defeat. The "hero" of Dazai's *The Setting Sun* speaks. "It is painful for the plant which is myself to live in the atmosphere and the light of this world. Somewhere an element is lacking which would permit me to continue." Dazai died in a double suicide in 1948.

Another reaction to the aimlessness and uncertainty in intellectual circles in the late forties was the revival of Marxism. It was particularly strong in universities, but also influenced unions and the parties of the left. Some scholars who repudiated it during the 1930's picked it up again after Japan's defeat. To many students it seemed the antithesis of militarism, offering a historical schema in terms of which the upheavals of modern Japan could be interpreted in a worldwide perspective. Conditions in the universities also contributed to its spread. There was tremendous pressure on high school students to get into a good university. Once in, many experienced a feeling of letdown. Most Japanese universities were physically depressing. Students lived at a subsistence level. Classes were large, contact with instructors was minimal, and the teaching was often no more than rote learning. If students had cause to complain at universities in the West, they had far greater cause in Japan. Moreover, while students had a very high status in their home communities, in the universities they found themselves in a social limbo.

Even under these conditions the majority of students were apolitical or only mildly leftist in their politics. The minority joined activist groups which soon took over the student self-government organizations that had been established by the Occupation. Known by the name of their national federation, the Zengakuren, these students held periodic protest meetings, rallies, and demonstrations. They filled their university grounds with political posters. And when the national political situation enabled them to mobilize wider student support, they demonstrated outside of the universities as well. Such demonstrations reached a high pitch in the early fifties and again in 1960.

After 1960 the student movement disintegrated into a variety of factions. On the right the dominant faction was associated with the Japanese Communist Party. It followed the party policy of building organizational strength without engaging in the kind of disorder that would invite repression. On the left were a number of anti-Communist factions that became extremely violent during the late sixties—occupying university buildings, demonstrating at airports, tossing fire-bombs in subways, and clashing with the police. These groups were Marxist in their political criticism of the government. Yet they were also anarchic and existentialist. They sought to achieve self-realization through open opposition to the status quo; they derided their professors as purveyors of "dead learning"; they compared their lives in the tightly ordered Japanese society to ball-point pens—at any time they could look at the transparent barrel and tell how much ink was left. A 1970 poll found that 79 per cent of university students were not favorably disposed toward any faction of the student movement; 6 per cent favored the Communist faction; and 10 per cent the anti-Communist factions.

In society as a whole the bleakness of the immediate postwar era had passed by the early 1950's. Japan returned to more normal patterns of life and thought. Characteristic of its intense and varied intellectual life, Japan became one of the leading book publishing nations in the world. The Japanese also read more newspapers per person than any other people in the world (a single subscription covers both the morning and evening paper). Literature was marked by ample variety. Proletarian literature revived and continued as one small stream. An antiwar literature arose, describing the brutality of army life or the horror of Hiroshima. Popular literature abounded with tales of samurai and contemporary stories with sad-happy endings. "SF" (science fiction) and detective stories, called "novels of deduction," were widely read. Younger writers generally were sympathetic to the left, yet not so blindly sympathetic as to take contemporary Russian or Chinese novels as models. In form and content they built directly on Japan's prewar syncretism of the European and the traditional. Serious novels continued the prewar themes of family, sex, loneliness, death, man's inability to communicate, mental aberrations, an aesthetic view of life, and the dissolute lives of novelists themselves.

In quality, too, the postwar years were marked by great creativity in the arts. Tanizaki's *The Makioka Sisters,* banned during the war, was published, and he continued to write till his death in 1965. Nobel Prize winner Kawabata wrote *The Sound of the Mountain* and other of his best works. Younger writers of stature, Mishima Yukio and Ōe Kenzaburō, emerged as well. Architects such as Tange and sculptors such as Nagare or Noguchi Isamu attained world repute. The films of Kurosawa, Ozu, or Naruse were shown in art theaters around the world. In painting, along with the works of modernists like Okada Kenzō, there were the sensuous Buddhist figures of the Munakata prints and the black ink paintings of modern calligraphers who turned Chinese ideographs into forms of abstract art.

From the early sixties two new tendencies began to appear in Japanese intellectual life. One was that Japanese Marxism began to thaw. The revelation of Stalin's crimes, followed by the Sino-Soviet split, produced schisms in the leftist movement. One writer who repudiated his Marxism in 1964 suggested that these revelations had the effect in Japanese intellectual circles that the 1936 Russian purge trials had on the European intelligentsia. Some magazines that had been Marxist in orientation began to accept other types of writing as well. Marxist scholars at universities became in many cases more eclectic. Marxism remained an influential intellectual current in Japan in a way that was true only of Italy or France in Western Europe. Even Japanese businessmen often unconsciously used categories derived from it. But as a total system of thought it slowly began to lose ground, its insights enveloped in other, newer ideas.

A second tendency of the middle sixties was the re-emergence of national self-confidence in Japan. The Japanese came to realize how successful they had been in economic growth and took pride in it. They were also gratified by the plaudits they received from abroad for their staging of the 1964 Tōkyō Olympics and the 1970 Osaka Exposition. The latter, in which space technology bordering on science fiction was a hands-down winner over traditional themes, reflected the same optimism about a technological future that was invariably revealed in public opinion polls. From the late 1960's there began, too, to appear books and movies about the heroism of the Japanese forces in World War II.

This new nationalism, however, was diffuse—like that of other modern states. There was no significant revival of emperor ideology. Individualism—seen as egotism in much prewar thought—continued to be a conscious goal among students and younger Japanese. Students wanted jobs that would permit them self-expression. The old lineal family ideal continued to decline and no one viewed the state as an aggregate of families. And, as Japan's Shintō past became less and less meaningful, the myth of the emperor continued to decline. The emperor was a popular figure, but he had lost his awe. In a 1970 poll 81 per cent favored keeping the emperor as a symbol, 9 per cent (26 per cent of those age sixteen to twenty) favored abolishing the throne, and only 8 per cent (18 per cent of those sixty or over) wanted to increase the emperor's authority.

In retrospect the most significant change in Japanese culture after 1945 was its openness and receptivity to new influences from the West and the strong re-emergence of the universalistic tendencies of Japan's own modern tradition. After having been secluded from new Western intellectual influences since the start of the China War in 1937—and some would even say since the rise of the emperor orthodoxy in the 1890's—Japan quickly made up for lost time. Particularly influential were new intellectual currents from the United States. American texts became widely used in medicine, law, the sciences, and engineering; economics faculties translated books on business management. American anthropology, psychology, and sociology entered to mix with Marx, Weber, and English social science. Perhaps only in the arts and letters did the European influence continue dominant, but here too Japan was open to English and American influences. These multiple influences were not doctrinally coherent. Yet on the whole, combining with liberal ideas that existed in the penumbra of the prewar orthodoxy, they reinforced the democratic pluralism that marked Japanese intellectual life.

Some of those thinkers in Japan who were most committed to parliamentary democracy felt keenly the lack of a doctrinally coherent, democratic consensus rooted in Japan's history. They lamented the shallowness of Japanese liberalism—in contrast to Western nations which, having experienced a Renaissance, Reformation, and Enlightenment, were able to fashion their own democratic institutions. They argued that the postwar changes are even more of an "external enlightenment" than those so designated by Natsume Sōseki at the turn of the century. Some critical Japanese thinkers pointed to the dramatic suicide of the novelist Mishima Yukio in 1970 as a sign of a crisis of meaning in Japanese culture. Mishima's last work was titled *The Sea of Fertility*. The name was taken from a "sea" on the moon and conveyed Mishima's view of contemporary Japanese culture as sterile because it was cut off from its own tradition. Other Japanese, however, argued that important elements of Japanese tradition were still alive. They cited as evidence both arts and institutions that were modern, yet different from those of the modern West. Some argued further that the Japanese tradition had been successfully fused with elements of the Western tradition, and that, since the values and experiences that had shaped the West were implicit in modern Japanese culture, their social realization would gradually unfold.

Politics

The Yoshida Period.   The first period of postwar politics lasted from 1945 through 1954. This was the period of politics under the Occupation and the years immediately following the peace treaty. It might also be called the "Yoshida Years."

When the war ended there was great flux and no one was sure what kind of government Japan would have. Alongside the major prewar parties, which were all immediately revived, was a welter of smaller groupings and independent candidates, who in the 1946 election garnered more than a third of the votes. Of those elected to the lower house in 1946, 81 per cent were new members. By the 1947 election most of the fringe groups had been absorbed into the major parties. It was apparent that the major prewar parties would continue to dominate the postwar scene. The old Seiyūkai became the Liberal Party (Jiyūtō); the Minseitō became the Progressive and then the Democratic Party (Minshutō); and the Socialist Mass Party, that had gotten 9.1 per cent of the vote in the 1937 elections, became the Socialist Party, gaining 26.2 per cent of the vote in 1947.

In the early postwar years the two conservative parties, the Liberals and the Democrats, competed with each other as in the prewar era—even to the point that in 1947 the Democrats joined with the Socialists and another small party to form a government under Katayama Tetsu, the Socialist Party leader. This coalition, however, did not work well, for the conservatives and socialists could not pull together in harness, the socialists could not carry out their policies under the Occupation, and the moderate socialist leaders were attacked by the party's left wing for their compromises with the Occupation and the conservatives. When the second cabinet based on this coalition fell in 1948, Yoshida Shigeru, who had been prime minister 1946–1947 and was head of the Liberal Party, again became prime minister. He called an election, won an absolute majority of Diet seats for his party, and was able to maintain himself as prime minister until December 1954.

Yoshida's personal history embodies many of the elements in Japan's modern century. He was born in 1878, the year after the Satsuma rebellion. One of fourteen children of a Tosa loyalist, he was adopted nine days after his birth into the wealthy Yoshida family where he was raised as a "young master." He went to a Confucian school, to the elite Peers School, and then transferred to the Law School of Tōkyō Imperial University. After graduation he entered the Foreign Ministry; his career, one biographer notes, coincided with the era of Japanese Empire, his consciousness was that of the great empire of Japan. A conservative at home, he took the British Empire as the model for Japan, and he was a constant advocate of close ties between Japan, England, and the United States. From this standpoint, and because of an independence of character rare among Japanese bureaucrats, he criticized the Twenty-one Demands during World War I, he criticized the military during the thirties—refusing the post of ambassador to Washington in 1932 because of his opposition to Japan's politics in Manchuria—and he worked tirelessly to better relations between Japan, Britain, and the United States in the late thirties. During World War II he became the center of a high-ranking conservative group which, fearing that war would lead to a revolution in Japanese society, worked to promote a negotiated peace; for these peace activities he was imprisoned for over two months in the spring of 1945. This opened the way for his role under the Occupation.

Yoshida's actions during his ministries were consistent with his background. He worked well with SCAP and saw this not as collaboration with a foreign conqueror but as the re-establishing of those ties with the United States and England that had been broken by the rise of the militarists. He offered full cooperation with the United Nations during the Korean War—short of any Japanese involvement in the war; he represented Japan at the signing of the Peace Treaty and Security Treaty in 1951. He was responsible for the formation of the National Police Reserve in 1950, the addition of a National Safety Force in 1951, and the transformation of these into the Self Defense Forces in 1953. Favorably disposed toward business, unsympathetic to labor, and bitterly anti-Communist, Yoshida carried out the anti-inflationary program that, while politically unpopular, contributed to Japan's initial postwar growth. Enjoying the backing of SCAP as well as an absolute majority in the Diet, Yoshida was autocratic toward his party and cabinets—so much so that his admirers and detractors alike called him "one man Yoshida." Yoshida saw himself as the builder of a new Japan—while preserving the virtues of the old—like the Meiji oligarchs whom he admired above all other figures in Japanese history.

Confrontation Between the Conservatives and Socialists. The second period of postwar politics was from 1955 to 1960: a period of post-Occupation and post-Yoshida politics, during which prominent prewar or wartime leaders

Yoshida Shigeru in 1954.

headed the major political parties. It was also a period of two-party politics: the left and right wings of the socialists, divided since 1951, joined in October 1955 to form a single socialist party; in the face of a united opposition the two conservative parties could not afford to remain apart so they merged a month later, forming the Liberal-Democratic Party (commonly abbreviated as Jimintō, or LDP).

The conservatives were the party in power, the party of those who had been in power since 1948. During these years they formed close ties with bureaucrats, bankers, and businessmen. Together these constituted the "establishment" of postwar Japan. Since there was no longer a House of Peers or a Privy Council, officials who reached the limit of possible advancement in the bureaucracy often joined the conservative party and ran for a Diet seat (if they did not join a business firm). Such ex-bureaucrats figured importantly in cabinets and on Diet committees because they were familiar with administrative procedures and had personal ties within the central ministries. They coordinated the work of the economic ministries which, in turn, were the government bodies that cooperated closely with the industrialists and financiers from whom the conservative Diet members obtained their campaign funds.

As the heirs of a prewar elite, the conservatives were the most affected ideologically by the demise of emperor thought. In its place, for lack of a clear-cut alternative philosophy, they depended on a more diffuse nationalism. The most visible component of this was what might be labeled "economism," an emphasis on strengthening Japan's economy and improving the livelihood of its people. A second goal, also to be obtained by economic means, was to re-establish Japan in the eyes of the world. Although rightfully called "conservatives," the leaders of the LDP were not conservatives in a contemporary Western sense of the term. Rather, they were extremely competent managers, men who could make the system run. They favored highly centralized and efficient government. They were opposed to much "local autonomy" on the grounds that it needlessly complicates the tasks of government. They believed in free enterprise, but, Keynesian in theory and paternalistic by instinct, they also felt it was the job of the government to keep the economy running in high gear. They were closer to the French "planners" than to the laissez-faire posture of either American party. Internationally, they were pro-Western and anti-Communist. They had absolutely no hesitation, however, about encouraging trade with China or Russia. The LDP attitude to this was that business is business.

Another characteristic of the LDP was the lack of a grass-roots party organization at the village or ward level. What counted was the "machine" of the individual Diet candidate, his ties to influential local figures and to prefectural politicians. (The exception was the one hundred members of the upper house elected from a nationwide constituency.) The sense of party at the local level was further weakened by the fact that candidates had to compete with members of their own party as well as with the opposition in the three-to-five-man election districts. Once elected, however, the Diet member discovered that the only way to advance in the party, the only way to obtain advantages for his district, the only way to get further campaign funds, was to attach himself to an influential leader within the party. This led to the formation of personal cliques which the Japanese spoke of as "semifeudal" in character. The factional leaders jockeyed for position, formed alliances, and vied for a chance to be prime minister and win cabinet posts for their followers. They also maintained strict party discipline in Diet votes over their clique members.

A trend that became clear during the second period of postwar politics was the gradual decline in the conservative vote at the polls and the rise of the socialist vote.

Elections	Conservative Votes	Socialist Votes (without Communists)
1952	66.1 per cent	21.9 per cent
1953	65.1	27.6
1955	63.2	30.2
1958	57.8	32.9
1960	57.6	36.3

The very success of the conservative government in transforming the economy diminished those groups that voted conservative and increased those who voted socialist. About 75 per cent of farmers voted for the LDP, and they were kept prosperous by substantial crop subsidies, but farmers were an ever smaller component in the total population. The rapidly growing and youthful white-collar class as often as not voted for socialists—because a large part of it had only recently left the universities, because it read magazines of a Socialist orientation, because it felt trapped and powerless in a huge machine, and because it wanted to counterbalance the conservative vote for the sake of democracy. Labor unions more than doubled their membership to over 11 million between the early fifties and early seventies; the majority of their votes could be delivered to socialist candidates. On the left was the largest and most powerful federation of unions, Sōhyō. It represented government employees and white-collar workers as well as factory workers. To the right of Sōhyō, upholding a more bread-and-butter approach to unionism, were Dōmei and other smaller federations, which supported candidates from the moderate wing of the party. These were made up mainly of industrial workers and continued to grow in size even after Sōhyō membership leveled off in the 1960's. Socialist candidates with support from several federations tended to run well; those without union support did poorly. So dependent were the socialists on the unions for campaign funds and other support, and so weak was their local party organization, that they were called a one-pressure-group party. Heartened by their gradually rising vote, the socialists in the late fifties began to hope that one day they would come to power by parliamentary means.

The socialists were the heirs of the prewar socialist tradition, Marxist, and to a lesser extent, Christian. They were a permanent opposition after 1948:

PRIME MINISTERS SINCE YOSHIDA

Hatoyama	December 1954–December 1956
Ishibashi	December 1956–February 1957
Kishi	February 1957–July 1960
Ikeda	July 1960–November 1964
Satō	November 1964–June 1972
Tanaka	July 1972–November 1974
Miki	December 1974–December 1976
Fukuda	December 1976–

as such they suffered from the irresponsibility and inability to attract talent that often affects political parties separated from power. Their most effective leaders have been drawn from the labor union movement, often men who rose from the ranks or, less frequently, men with a university education. Ideologically the socialists spanned a gamut of positions from revolutionary Maoism to a moderate reformism scarcely distinguishable from the liberal wing of the conservative party. There were two modal points. One to the left of center was Marxist and revolutionary in theory, if not in practice. It was sympathetic to China; it talked of a class party; it argued about whether Japan's greatest enemy was American imperialism or Japanese monopoly capitalism. The other position, more to the right, was basically reformist in character and committed to parliamentary forms of government.

The period between 1955 and 1960 saw greater tensions and more confrontations between the two major parties than at any other time in postwar Japan. In part this was because prewar and wartime animosities continued to rankle. The socialists were led by men who had suffered persecution or had been jailed for their beliefs. The conservatives were led by the type of men who had done the persecuting and then had been purged themselves during the Occupation. Hatoyama Ichirō, Yoshida's successor as prime minister, was the education minister who had purged liberals from the Kyōto Imperial University faculty during the thirties. Kishi Nobusuke, prime minister from 1957 to 1960, had been a minister in the Tōjō Cabinet that declared war on the United States.

A second reason for the confrontation between the LDP and the socialists was a post-Occupation, post-Yoshida swing away from the reforms imposed by SCAP. This trend was especially strong during the ministry of Hatoyama who came to power on an anti-Yoshida platform. Some of the changes were: 1) The police law was revised in 1954, in effect recentralizing the police. During the late 1950's the police were further strengthened to cope with riots and matters of internal security. 2) Elected education boards were made appointive by a law passed in 1956, increasing the influence of the Ministry of Education. The ministry also strengthened its control over textbooks. 3) In 1956 the Local Autonomy Office was given greater power in overseeing local government, and in 1960 it became a cabinet ministry. The opposition called this the revival of the prewar Home Ministry. During these years budgetary deficits made the prefectures more and more dependent on the central government. 4) In 1956 a commission was appointed to make recommendations for a revision of the constitution. The conservatives were particularly unhappy at the changed status of the emperor and the article which stated that: "The Japanese people forever renounce war as a sovereign right of the nation and the threat or use of force as a means of settling international disputes. . . . Land, sea, and air forces, as well as other war potential, will never be maintained." The constitution could not be amended, however, since after the election of 1956 the conservatives lacked the necessary two-thirds vote in the Diet. 5) The government continued an extremely slow buildup of its armed forces, despite the clear prohibition in the constitution. It justified this on the grounds that defensive forces do not constitute a war potential. Since the Supreme Court was docile and unwilling to find governmental actions unconstitutional, there was no way for this buildup to be blocked.

In comparison with the massive reforms of the Occupation era these shifts back to a more conservative direction were small. Yet, occurring in politically sensitive areas, they were viewed by the socialists as the beginning of a return to the repressive system of prewar Japan. Unable to defeat these measures in the Diet, the socialists frequently resorted to demonstrations or even violence. Confrontation politics reached a climax in the spring and early summer of 1960 over the issue of the revision of the Security Treaty with the United States.

The 1952 Security Treaty enabled the United States to use bases in Japan as staging areas for actions elsewhere in Asia. It also provided that American troops could be used "to put down large-scale internal riots and disturbances in Japan" on request of the Japanese government. By 1958 both sides were willing to scrap such provisions. The new 1960 treaty was more favorable to Japan. It made prior consultation with the Japanese government necessary before American bases could be used for actions elsewhere in Asia or before the United States could bring nuclear weapons into Japan. The socialists, however, favored abolishing the treaty altogether, holding that any treaty at all might lead to Japanese involvement in an American war in Asia. All of the tensions of five years came to a head over this issue.

Other factors also contributed to the confrontation at this time: anxiety over increased Soviet-American tensions, the critical treatment of the treaty by most Japanese newspapers, the unpopularity of Prime Minister Kishi who was viewed as a narrow bureaucrat by the public and labeled "war criminal Kishi" by the socialists, and, finally, the manner in which the treaty was ratified at a special night session of the Diet without the customary "democratic debate." Massive demonstrations were held to protest the treaty.

At times over 100,000 persons took to the streets of Tōkyō; included among the demonstrators were unionists, housewives, professors, and members of cultural, professional, and women's organizations as well as unusually large numbers of students. Most of the demonstrations were peaceful, but some radical students clashed with police at the Diet and the residence of the prime minister. At the time the conservatives saw the demonstrations as a kind of mass hysteria. The socialists hailed them as the dawn of a revolutionary consciousness and the beginning of a new age in Japanese politics.

The Relaxed Sixties. Once the ratification of the new treaty was completed, however, Kishi resigned, the demonstrations came to an end, and a more peaceful, third period of politics began. One major reason for the change

*Students demonstrating in 1960 against the Security Treaty, Prime
Minister Kishi, United States spy flights over the Soviet Union,
and a proposed visit of President Eisenhower to Japan.*

was the decline of "confrontation politics" in the Diet. The new prime
minister, Ikeda, a former minister of finance who captained a middle-of-the-
road faction within the LDP, adopted what was called in Japanese a "low
posture." This meant he was careful not to offend the feelings of the opposition, and he made at least token compromises on legislative issues. The
degree of confrontation was also lessened by the emergence of a new generation of leaders on both sides—men who, not having been leaders in
prewar or wartime Japan, were less concerned with the battles of the past.

PERCENTAGES OF VOTES IN NATIONAL ELECTIONS FOR THE HOUSE OF REPRESENTATIVES

	Liberal Democratic Party	Socialist Party	Democratic Socialist Party	Kōmeitō	Communist Party	Inde-pendent Candidates	New Liberal Club
1960	57.6	27.6	8.8		2.9	3.1	
1963	54.7	29.0	7.3		4.0	4.8	
1967	48.8	27.8	7.4	5.4	4.8	5.7	
1969	47.6	21.4	7.7	10.9	6.8	5.5	
1972	46.9	21.7	7.0	8.5	10.5	5.1	
1976	41.8	20.7	6.3	10.9	10.4	5.7	4.2

Tensions in the Diet were also reduced by the absence of new legislation designed to roll back the Occupation reforms. The new conservative leaders saw no need for further changes.

A second reason for the relaxed politics of the early sixties was the growing realization by leaders and people alike of the magnitude of Japan's economic success. Japan had made giant strides forward in the fifties, yet the almost uniformly gloomy predictions of economists had led many to discount the gains. By the early sixties the acclaim given to Japan abroad together with the abundant evidence of prosperity within Japan forced the Japanese to recognize their own achievement. It contributed to the Japanese sense of national pride. It cut the ground from under the critique of Japanese society by the socialist left. And it made the conservative leaders more confident in their own abilities. Prime Minister Ikeda's 1960 plan to double the income of the Japanese within ten years—which was over-fulfilled within seven years—was an early indication of this new attitude.

Within this climate of opinion two new trends appeared in Japanese politics after 1960: the strengthening of the conservative party, even while its total vote continued to decline, and the fragmentation of the opposition. The LDP percentage of the total vote declined an average of about 1 per cent a year over the decade of the sixties. As during the fifties, this was by and large the result of sociological erosion, the shift of population away from those sectors that supported the conservatives. The decline occurred in spurts and pauses. In the 1960 election there was virtually no decline in the conservative vote and a gain of nine seats in the lower house. This strong showing was probably due to a popular reaction against the violence of the riots earlier in the year. In 1963 the vote dropped by 3 per cent and the conservatives lost 13 seats. In 1967 the vote dropped by another 6 per cent for the loss of another 6 seats—reflecting the lesser popularity of Prime Minister Satō, who was somewhat to the right of his predecessor. In the 1969 election, however, after renewed student violence at universities throughout Japan, the vote declined by only 1 per cent and the conservatives gained 23 seats in the lower house (11 in the election and 12 independents who joined the party after the election). This gave the conservatives 300 of the 491 seats, the largest majority since the mid-fifties. It increased the preponderance of the conservatives in Japanese politics, and it enabled Satō to remain prime minister longer than any other figure in Japan's modern history. Some analysts went further and suggested that new qualitative patterns were emerging in the voting—support for the conservatives from younger Japanese who in previous elections had tended to vote for the socialists.

The socialists broke into two parties before the election in 1960. The lines along which the split occurred were partly ideological—the socialists were deeply divided over the issue of the Security Treaty—partly those of personal cliques, and partly a reflection of cleavages within the labor movement.

Those moderate socialists whose backing came predominantly from Zenrō (later Dōmei), the smaller of the two largest federations, formed the Democratic Socialist Party. This remained a stable splinter party during the sixties, committed to achieving socialism by parliamentary means. Those socialists, including some moderates, who were supported by the largest federation, Sōhyō, for the most part stayed within the Socialist Party. During the early sixties when Ikeda was prime minister the Socialist Party took a moderate public stance.

Eda Saburō, the secretary-general of the party, advocated evolutionary "structural change" (a concept borrowed from Italian Communists) rather than revolution, and presented his "vision" for the socialist future of Japan, combining Japan's no-war constitution, British democracy, the Soviet welfare system, and the American standard of living. The left wing of the party was unhappy with this formulation. It was able in the mid-sixties to win control of the party and push a much more radical line. (It was not accidental that this shift to the left occurred only five months after the LDP had moved from Ikeda to the more conservative Satō.) The fierce ideological contention within the Socialists weakened the party in the eyes of the public, which also felt, according to polls, that the party lacked men of ability in its leadership. As a consequence its percentage of the vote dropped from almost 28 per cent in 1967 to 21.4 per cent in 1969. In the same election it lost 50 seats in the lower house, dropping from 140 to 90. It remained the largest opposition party, but it no longer could hope to gain control of the government. This exacerbated the tensions within the party: each wing blamed the party's decline on the policies of the other.

Benefiting from the declining vote of the conservatives and socialists were two other parties, both of which were particularly strong in large cities where many voters were opposed to the conservatives and disillusioned with the socialists. The Japanese Communist Party had been a strong splinter party in the late forties; it won 35 seats in the Diet in 1949. In 1950, however, it dropped its slogan of "a lovable Communist party" in favor of violence, and as a result lost popular support and virtually dropped out of sight in electoral politics. In the elections of the fifties it averaged only a single Diet seat. During the sixties it adopted a more pragmatic policy, its candidates skillfully seized on local issues, and it conducted effective local campaigns. As a result in 1969 it received 6.8 per cent of the vote and 14 Diet seats. The second party to gain was the Kōmeitō, the political wing of the new religion, the Sōka Gakkai. It first entered local elections and those for the upper house. Then in 1967 and 1969 it entered candidates for the lower house, gaining 25 and then 47 seats. The name "Kōmei" has been translated as the "Clean Government" Party. Its appeal was moral: end corruption, stop rising prices, improve living conditions, and work for international peace. Much of its foreign policy was borrowed from the moderate left. Japanese

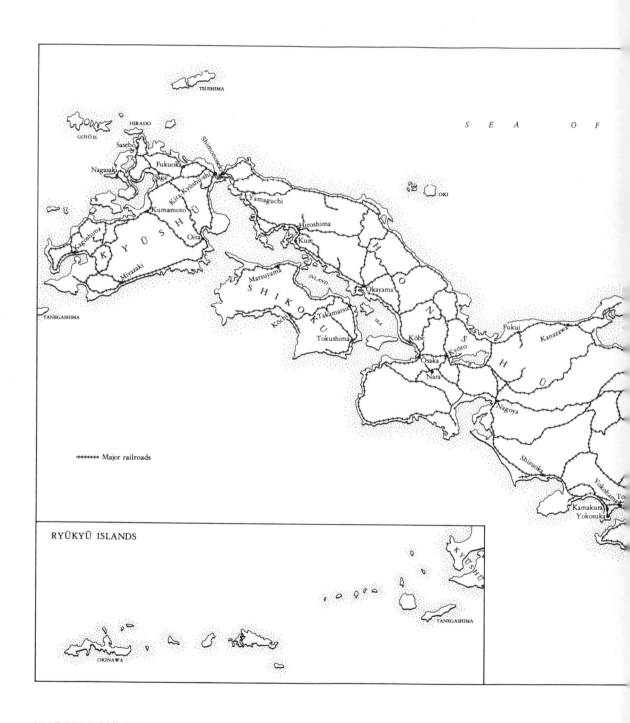

S E A   O F

TSUSHIMA

HIRADO

GŌTŌ IS.

Sasebo

Nagasaki

Fukuoka

Saga

Kita Kyūshū-shi

Shimonoseki

Yamaguchi

OKI

Kumamoto

K Y Ū S H Ū

Ōita

Hiroshima

Kagoshima

Kure

Miyazaki

Matsuyama

INLAND

Okayama

H
O
N
S
H
Ū

TANEGASHIMA

S H I K O K U

Kōchi

Takamatsu

SEA

Fukui

Kanazawa

Tokushima

Kōbe

Ōsaka

Kyōto

Nara

Nagoya

+++++ Major railroads

Shizuoka

Yokohama   To

Kamakura

Yokosuka

RYŪKYŪ ISLANDS

KYŪSHŪ

TANEGASHIMA

OKINAWA

MODERN JAPAN

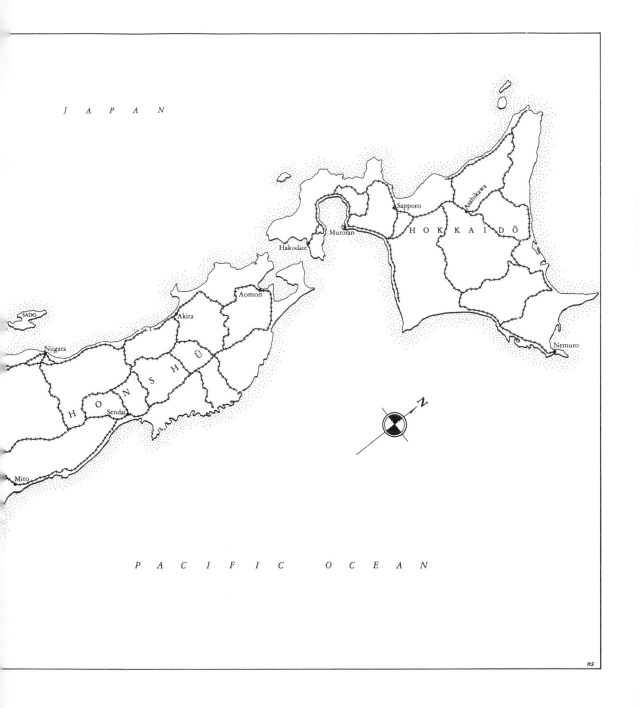

J A P A N

Sapporo

Asahikawa

Muroran

H O K K A I D Ō

Hakodate

Aomori

SADO

Akita

Niigata

Nemuro

H O N S H Ū

Sendai

Mito

P A C I F I C   O C E A N

RS

analysts believed that the election gains of the Kōmeitō reached a limit in the 1969 election—just as the membership of the Sōka Gakkai began to level off—and viewed its future as a possible swing party in a coalition government.

Underlying the voting patterns of the 1960's was a new mood, a new consensus. The Japanese people were more moderate, more middle-of-the-road, than the rhetoric of either major party suggested. In the early seventies this center position, slightly to the left of the conservatives but far to the right of the socialists, became stronger. In a 1970 poll 51 per cent of students who had graduated and entered companies wanted a reformed capitalist society, 24 per cent were for the status quo, 7 per cent were for a socialist system.

In the eyes of its supporters Japan's bureaucratically centralized democracy already had proved itself as one of the most stable parliamentary governments in the world. Japanese critics, however, continued to view it as a "good-time democracy," arguing that it had yet to meet the tests of adversity. What would happen, they asked, if economic growth came to a stop, or if a crisis in international relations left Japan isolated? Certainly in the early seventies the kinds of checks and balances that made some Western democracies stable were lacking in Japan. On the vertical axis prefectural and local governments had little real autonomy vis-à-vis the central government. On the horizontal axis, there was no separation of powers: the legislative and executive were fused (in the British fashion) and the judiciary was subordinate. There did not exist counter-balancing regional blocs. Nor did there exist the same degree of separation between government and large companies that was found in the West. Finally, the "opinion leaders" in Japan were a smaller, more centralized group, just as the media for which they wrote were for the most part centered on Tōkyō. Supporters of the system countered that the socialist critique of the government was one kind of check that Japan had and that was missing, for example, in the United States, and that the emergence of a vigorous middle class in the postwar era gave to Japanese democracy the kind of social base that existed elsewhere only in Europe and the United States.

Certainly, growing out of Occupation reforms, there had occurred a quiet revolution in education that had changed fundamentally the nature of Japanese society in a pluralistic and democratic direction. In prewar Japan traditional values and mores were perpetuated not only by the conservative agrarian sector of the society, but also by a system of primary education that reinforced the traditional content of the Meiji modernization. Only a small elite carried their studies beyond middle school, and university graduates constituted only 3 per cent of the population. University professors—an important channel through which Western ideas reached Japan—often studied at a German university for several years after graduating from a university in Japan, and then returned to spend the rest of their lives working in a narrow field of specialization. Universities were hierarchical and compartmentalized, and their faculties were isolated from society at large. Such a pattern of education was not enough to destroy what the Japanese term "the inwardness and isolation of an island people." By the mid-seventies, however, there were 420 universities and 513 junior colleges. About 92 per cent of Japanese go on to senior high school and 34 per cent to college or university. Half of those who go to college are women—who have the greatest influence on the next generation. University professors go abroad often during their careers. In 1975 over one-fourth of the faculty of Kyōtō University was abroad at one time or another. Professors write for magazines and appear constantly on television—much more so than in the United States. During the depression year of 1975 the Japanese spent over $3 billion on books and magazines. This flowering of what might be called a mass university culture produced a populace incomparably more cosmopolitan than that of the prewar era. It is the kind of base needed for a parliamentary state.

International Relations.   For Japan as for most of the countries in the world, foreign relations in the postwar era developed within the overarching nuclear balance between the United States and the Soviet Union, in the context of the cold war. From 1964 China, becoming a nuclear power, entered this balance in a very minor way as had England and France in Europe.

One central principle of Japan's foreign policy during these years was to maintain close ties to the United States. This policy ran parallel to its domestic politics. From 1945 to 1954 Japan's foreign policy was either in American hands or a continuation of Occupation policy under Yoshida. In the fifties and sixties there was talk of greater independence, and some new initiatives were made, but by and large Japan decided to maintain close ties with the United States. Cultural and educational interchange between the two countries was far more extensive than between Japan and Germany before the war. The United States was a great open market for Japanese exports, as well as a source of new technology. Japan's defense depended on the Security Treaty.

The very closeness of these ties produced some problems and criticism. Conservative Japanese who were opposed to certain kinds of social change often saw it as the Americanization of Japanese culture—not unlike the reaction of European conservatives. American military bases in Japan were a frequent source of irritation. If an airfield was lengthened, a political demonstration invariably was held. American atom bomb testing in the Pacific was an extremely sensitive issue in Japan. Because American bombs had leveled Hiroshima and Nagasaki, because of Japan's close association with the United States, and because the left in Japan was highly vocal, there was far more criticism in Japan of American bomb tests than of those by the Soviet Union or China. Okinawa was another major problem. Conservatives saw it as an affront to Japanese sovereignty. The left saw it as an outpost on Japanese territory of the United States military policy in Asia. The Okinawans themselves, who had been second-class citizens in Japan before the war, became quite nationalistic in reaction to the American control of the island. Some in Japan were critical of Japan's close postwar ties with the United States, arguing that Japan lacked a foreign policy of its own and merely coasted along behind its American ally. Others pointed out that Japan had pursued a superbly successful foreign policy of expanding its trade without the costs of political involvement or military spending.

The second guiding principle of Japan's foreign policy was support for an open, stable, peaceful world trading order. This can be seen, for example, in the pattern of Japan's developing relations with Southeast Asia. In the late forties and early fifties Japan had no relations with the countries in its former Greater East Asia Co-Prosperity Sphere. The question of reparations for war damages was pending. From about 1950 there developed a balance in Asia between the continental Communist power of China, North Korea, and shortly afterward North Vietnam, and an arc of peripheral, non-Communist states from Thailand to South Korea that were backed by the United States. In the mid-fifties Japan began to reach agreements on reparations in order to re-establish diplomatic and trading relations with these countries, and reparations were followed by aid, credits, and loans. Japan also invested heavily in these countries, sometimes building factories, but more often securing sources of raw materials—oil, ore, or timber. By the mid-sixties Japan had become the dominant economic power in the area. Neon signs in Bangkok advertised Japanese products. The streets of Saigon were filled with Japanese motorscooters. A cynic observed that the United States was at war in Vietnam to protect Japanese markets. By the early seventies Southeast Asia's balance of trade with Japan was so unfavorable and Japanese traders were so numerous that anti-Japanese sentiment—of the sort that the United States had long experienced in South America—had begun to rise. Moreover, by the early seventies other changes were underway that presaged a change in Japan's future role in the area. Britain had withdrawn its military forces from Southeast Asia and the Indian Ocean. Australia was only partially capable of replacing Britain. The United States, while unlikely to withdraw completely, was steadily reducing its military commitment in support of these nations. The leaders of Southeast Asia began to wonder if Japan would not play a larger political role in the future than it had in the past. But they were uncertain and apprehensive as to what the role would be.

Of all of the countries in the arc of peripheral states, Japan's nearest neighbor was South Korea. The two countries had certain interests in common: had there been no Japan, South Korea would not have been viable as a non-Communist state, and Japan, too, felt more comfortable in having South Korea between it and the rest of the continent. For a long time, however, Japan found it difficult to establish ties with South Korea. The Koreans hated the Japanese and feared economic domination by Japan. The Koreans demanded higher reparations than the Japanese were willing to pay, they barred the more efficient Japanese fishing boats from their waters, and they resented the willingness of the Japanese government to let Japan's 600,000 Koreans choose for themselves which Korea they would acknowledge. The political left in Japan also opposed the establishment of relations with South Korea on the grounds that it would deepen the rift between North and South Korea and harden Japan's anti-Communist stance. These difficulties were overcome sufficiently to normalize relations between the two countries in 1965. This led to aid, loans, investments, and increased trade, touching off great economic growth in South Korea. After 1965 the Korean fears of Japanese domination and their animosity toward Japanese began to subside, but attitudes on both sides remained mixed and ambiguous.

Japan's attitude toward Taiwan and China was also complex. Japan recognized the Nationalists on Taiwan in 1952 at American insistence. It could not also recognize China proper. Yet for the most part it tried to maintain a colorless, apolitical stance that would enable it to relate simultaneously to both Chinas. Taiwan was an important trading partner of Japan, usually more important than mainland China. Japanese investments in Taiwan were considerable. Using these as a lever, the Nationalist government repeatedly put pressure on Japan not to recognize the government in Peking or to extend to it economic credits. A minority of conservative party leaders in Japan felt that a Taiwan ruled by Peking might strategically endanger Japan, and therefore advocated stronger ties with Taiwan. Relations between the two countries were also helped by the fact that anti-Japanese feelings were weaker among the Taiwanese population of Taiwan than in any other part of East Asia. Yet Japan very carefully avoided the kind of political or military involvement that would interfere with a future improvement of relations with China.

In the early years after the Communist revolution Japan's image of China was not unfavorable. Many in the universities felt that China would forge ahead of Japan. But after the failure of the "Great Leap Forward" and the political turmoil of the "Cultural Revolution" Japan's image of China became much less favorable. Even on the political left, all but the most extreme groups dismissed China as a possible model for Japan. In spite of this, China continued to hold a special fascination for the Japanese—as the fount of inspiration for Japan's traditional culture, as a people of the same race, as a potential source of raw materials, as a potential trading partner, as an experimental society run by revolutionary leaders, and as a nuclear power lying just across the China Sea. Trade with China rose and fell depending on the political mood of Peking, but by 1970 had risen to slightly over 2 per cent of Japan's total trade (and about 22 per cent of China's). In addition to trade there was also a considerable range of officially sanctioned unofficial cultural contacts. Japanese on the whole were eager for better economic and political relations with China. Even those in the government wanted to regularize relations with China, but not at the risk of damaging other more important economic and political relations.

The Soviet Union was not a popular country in Japan, except among a small segment of the left. When asked to list three countries they liked, only 4.5 per cent of respondents in a September 1971 poll listed the Soviet Union. The top favorite was Switzerland with 35.9 per cent, followed by France 28.5, and the United States 27.5. In contrast 32 per cent listed the Soviet Union among their choices of the countries they disliked, followed by North Korea 24.6, China 21, South Korea 14.1, and the United States 13.2. (The last figure, higher than usual, reflected the immediate Japanese reaction to the shocks of the summer of 1971.) The antipathy for Russia went back to 1905, to the sudden Soviet sweeps into Manchuria a week before the end of World War II, to the experiences of Japanese prisoners of war in Siberian prison camps, and to the Soviet occupation of the Southern Kuriles. Yet, since Japanese foreign policy was realistic, Japan was as concerned to have closer and better ties with the Soviet Union as it was with China. It carefully avoided a cold war stance that would prevent this. The result was an increase in trade with the Soviet Union and talks regarding Japanese participation in the development of Siberia. The Soviet Union wanted technological assistance and long-term loans from Japan. It offered in return lumber and the possibility of oil, gas, and other raw materials. Behind these negotiations was the desire of the Soviet Union to strengthen Siberia against a possible Chinese attack and to balance off Japan's ties to China with ties to itself.

The Seventies.   The years between 1945 and 1970, in retrospect at least, have a kind of unity. The national concern to rebuild a more prosperous Japan ran through the Occupation into the fifties and sixties. The continuous rapid growth of both the economy and the standard of living saw the realization of this goal. A world economy based on free trade and open access to markets was another factor. The role of the United States was still another—as a source of new technology, as Japan's chief trading partner, and as the guarantor of Japan's defense. The unquestioned supremacy of the LDP as the party-in-power gave an unusual consistency to government policy.

There was no sharp break after 1970. Japanese exports continued to rise, from $19 billion in 1970 to $55 billion in 1975. The GNP reached $500 billion in the same year. The American market share of these exports dropped from 35 per cent in 1970 to less than 25 per cent in 1975, but the United States remained far and away the largest importer of Japanese goods. By any assortment of indices, Japanese material well-being also advanced. The savings of an average family rose from slightly over a million yen to slightly more than 2 million ($6700) in 1974. Households with air conditioners increased from 6.8 to 23.3 per cent. There was slightly more than one color television per household. Better than one out of two families had a car—with a higher percentage in the countryside than in the cities. One family in eleven had a piano. And the life expectancy rose to more than seventy-one years for men and seventy-six for women.

Yet beginning in 1971 Japan experienced a series of shocks and changes that raised serious questions about the existing order. Out of these emerged a configuration of new issues such as often marks the start of a new era. It was a token of the magnitude of the new issues that politicians in all camps, conservatives and the left alike, formed study groups, drew in intellectuals, and began to draft policies to deal with them.

The changes began in the summer of 1971 when a crisis was produced in Japan by two American actions. In one the United States placed a 10 per cent surcharge on all imports and floated the dollar in an attempt to overcome an intolerable deficit in its balance of trade. This was primarily directed against Japan and Germany. The United States blamed Japan for the unfavorable balance and demanded that Japan revalue the yen, dismantle protectionist barriers, and accelerate the opening of its markets to American products. Japanese businessmen saw the unfavorable balance as the result of cost-push inflation in the United States that drove up prices faster than productivity, making American goods too expensive to compete in world markets. They also saw inflation as a consequence of Vietnam war spending. They criticized American marketing techniques, pointing out that Japanese businessmen could think in inches, but American businessmen were unwilling to think in centimeters. They argued that the United States, instead of resorting to neo-protectionism, ought to set its own house in order. The confrontation over trade ended when the Japanese government agreed to a stiff revaluation of the yen and the opening of Japan to new categories of American products. Japanese exports, however, continued to gain. The favorable balance was larger in 1972 than it had been in 1971.

The other action by the United States—the two together were called the "Nixon shocks" in Japan—was the announcement in July 1971 that the American President would visit Peking in 1972. Polls taken later in the year showed that the majority of Japanese welcomed this move. All parties in Japan had held, at least privately, that America's China policy had been extremely unrealistic. Yet the suddenness of the American move undercut the government of Prime Minister Satō. Why had its closest ally made a major change in its foreign policy in Asia without consulting or even forewarning Japan? What did it mean that this change occurred just as the United States was withdrawing from Vietnam and reducing its military presence in the rest of Asia? Did statements about a new American policy based on relations among the five world powers (Europe, the Soviet Union, Japan, China, and the United States) prefigure a turn to neo-isolationism? How would this change affect the fortunes of the perimeter nations of Asia, and how would subsequent changes in these countries affect Japan? In the eyes of some, not only had Japan been slighted, but the basic assumptions on which its foreign policy rested had been called into question.

The United States—after the fact—moved quickly to assuage the consternation felt by the Japanese. President Nixon invited Prime Minister Satō to the San Clemente White House before going to Peking. At their meeting he stated that no agreement would be reached with China that would prejudice America's relation to Japan. The two leaders also specified the date, May 15, 1972, for the return of Okinawa to Japan. This marked the final settlement of an issue that had vexed the relations of the two countries since 1945.

In spite of these reassurances, the Japanese felt anxious. Would they in the future become isolated as the only major non-Communist power in the western Pacific? One effect of this anxiety was to make the Japanese feel that they could no longer take for granted their special relation to the United States, but had to work to preserve it. A range of actions illustrates this concern. The government put limits on the rates at which some exports could be expanded. It encouraged improvement of English language training in Japan. It expanded offices in the United States to promote better public relations. A Japanese prime minister gave $10 million to ten universities in the United States for the support of Japanese studies, and private firms gave many millions more. In addition a Japan Foundation was established, under the sponsorship of the Foreign Ministry, to bring foreign scholars to Japan for a period of study and to promote Japanese studies abroad. Underlying these moves was an only slightly altered conservative vision of a continuing partnership between the two largest economies in the non-Communist world. As a parliamentary state and as a country which, with some perturbations, would continue to support free trade, Japanese leaders viewed the United States as their best ally. They also saw the United States and Japan as having a common interest in the development and stability of perimeter nations of Asia.

Another effect of the new anxiety over foreign relations was to add fuel to the ongoing debate over national defense. By 1970 Japan's Self-Defense Force had about a quarter of a million troops and an air force of about one thousand jet planes. Defenders of the Force pointed out that it cost less than 1 per cent of the GNP and was, for a nation of Japan's size, the smallest military establishment in the world. Critics replied that the figure of "less than 1 per cent" concealed the fastest growth of any military in the world, that the Force was over-officered and therefore capable of rapid expansion, and that, being technologically advanced, it was more powerful than its size would indicate. The "Nixon shocks" led some to question the adequacy of the existing defense arrangements. Should not Japan build its own defense industries, they argued, instead of remaining dependent on the United States for its most advanced weapons? And what about atomic weapons? Because of Hiroshima, a taboo had prevented even discussion of the subject during the fifties and early sixties. By the late sixties it was openly discussed, but the government flatly stated that it would not develop nuclear weapons in spite of the emergence of China as a nuclear power. A 1970 white paper entitled "Japan's Defense" reiterated this position: "Japan is a great power economically, but it will not become a great power militarily. Rather it will become a new kind of state with social welfare and world peace as its goals." It was clear to all, however, that the development of facilities for the peaceful use of atomic energy and of space rockets gave Japan the capacity to go nuclear in short order were the situation to change. From 1971 some Japanese writers began to question the credibility of the American "nuclear umbrella" provided by the Security Treaty. If the chips were down would the United States risk the destruction of its cities to protect Japan? Behind such a question was an unvoiced doubt: could the United States accept an Asian nation as an ally on the same basis as a European nation?

The rapprochement between the United States and China opened the way for a dramatic change in Japan's China policy. Satō Eisaku resigned as prime minister in July 1972—after having held that post even longer than Itō Hirobumi. In fact he had hung onto the office for so long that he had alienated both public and party opinion; in the election that followed, the conservative party rejected his handpicked successor (an ex-bureaucrat and graduate of Tōkyō University Law School) and picked instead Tanaka Kakuei, the first prime minister in Japanese history who was neither a university graduate nor a general. Born the son of a poor farmer, Tanaka's formal education ended at sixth grade. He then became an apprentice in a Tōkyō construction firm, attended night school, served with the imperial army in China, founded his own construction company, and won a Diet seat in the election of 1947. Thereafter he rose steadily within the conservative party until he reached ministerial rank. With this rags-to-riches background, as a youthful figure of fifty-four in a party long dominated by age, as the author of *Remodeling the Japanese Islands,* which advocated the decentralization of industries and government, and as a man of great vigor with a reputation for getting difficult jobs done, Tanaka came to office on a surge of popularity.

At the end of August 1972 Tanaka met with Nixon in Hawaii. A month later he met with Chou En-lai in Peking, establishing diplomatic relations with the People's Republic and recognizing it as the sole legal government of China. The accord stated: "Although the social systems of China and Japan are different, the two countries should and can establish peaceful and friendly relations." This led to a rupture of diplomatic ties with Taiwan, although economic and cultural relations seemed certain to continue. Journalists in Tōkyō, aware that Japan's recognition of Peking went far beyond the American initiative in China and conveniently forgetting the Hawaii talks in their desire to stress Japan's new independence of action, labeled the event the "Tanaka shock." This accord was given substance with an exchange of ambassadors, an airlines agreement in April 1974, a maritime agreement in November of the same year, and a fisheries agreement in August 1975. Trade between the two countries more than tripled from $1.1 billion in 1972 to $3.8 billion in 1975. This amounted to only 3.3 per cent of Japan's total trade, but it was over 25 per cent of China's. China wanted to buy high technology from Japan, Japan wanted Chinese oil, yet China was reluctant to become simply an exporter of raw materials. Between 1974 and 1976 talks were also held regarding a treaty of peace and friendship. China insisted that the treaty include a clause directed against third powers seeking "hegemony" in Asia—by which China meant primarily the Soviet Union. Japan, desiring to continue a more even-handed diplomacy, was unwilling to join with China against the Soviet Union. As of late 1977 the stalemate on this issue continued.

The recognition of China necessarily led to the rupture of diplomatic relations with Taiwan. Taiwan denounced the Japanese action, asserting that it was one of the three worst mistakes in the history of Japanese diplomacy, the other two being the 1937 Sino-Japanese War and Pearl Harbor. In fact, however, economic and cultural ties continued much as before. Japanese investment in Taiwan continued to grow. Trade increased from $1.6 billion in 1972 to $2.6 billion in 1975. In July 1975 a Japanese airline (a front company for JAL) reopened service to Taiwan, which had been broken off in 1972. In effect, however much the Kuomintang leadership on Taiwan had been embittered by the Japanese recognition of Peking, it could not afford to end these ties with Japan. And however much China may have disliked Japan's economic two-China policy, it was willing, for the short term at least, to overlook it.

The willingness of China to receive a United States president while American troops were still fighting in Vietnam was remarkable. Whereas China earlier had supported revolutionary movements and left-wing factions within Communist parties around the world, it now soft-pedaled revolution and turned to better its relations with major powers. Earlier China had castigated United States imperialism as the greatest danger to the world; now it did an about-face and sought United States support against the threat of "social imperialism" from across China's northern frontier. This did not necessarily indicate a basic change in China's perception of the United States as capitalist and imperialist. But as the United States sought to extricate itself from Vietnam, the immediate threat of the United States appeared to China very much less than that of the Soviet Union. As a major world power closely allied with the United States, Japan's support was sought. Japanese visitors to Peking were told—to the consternation of left-wing socialists in Japan—that China "understood" Japan's ties with the United States and felt that the Security Treaty was only natural.

The last American troops left Vietnam in February 1973, demonstrating the inability of the United States to maintain a non-Communist government in South Vietnam. Conservatives and moderates in Japan had viewed the war as a bad mistake; the left had seen it as an imperialist adventure. All Japanese were glad when the United States pulled out. Yet many wondered what effect it would have on America's Asian policy. Did it signal a return to isolationism? Would the withdrawal from Southeast Asia affect the Security Treaty and relations with Taiwan and Korea? The United States assured Japan that it would not. Watergate and the events leading to the resignation of President Nixon in August 1974 added to such worries. At the same time, the majority of Japanese saw both the withdrawal from Vietnam and the fall of Nixon as the affirmation of America's democratic polity.

As international relations in East Asia were changing, a series of economic crises occurred. The first was the "oil shock" of 1973. Japan had gone to war in 1941 when its oil supply was cut off. The 1941 yearly supply of oil would fuel the Japan of 1976 for only three days. Japan was entirely dependent on imports of oil, 80 per cent of which came from the Middle East. The formation of OPEC and the fourth Middle East war in October 1973 led to successive hikes in the price of oil, the curtailment of production, and cuts in exports to nations seen as friends of Israel, which included Japan. The problem of supply was solved in time, but the 450 per cent rise in the price of oil during 1973 coupled with other inflationary forces in the world economy jolted the Japanese economy, which was geared to cheap oil. Prices spiraled. The commodity price index, which had risen from 80 in 1966 to only 100 in 1970, jumped to 180 by early 1976. Much of the rise occurred during the "two-digit inflation" of 1973 and 1974.

Expensive oil alone Japan could adjust to; Europe, if not the United States, was no less dependent. But OPEC raised the possibility of other raw materials' cartels. Importing close to 100 per cent of its iron ore, bauxite, wool, rubber, and phosphates, about 96 per cent of wheat and soybeans, and high percentages of the other raw materials needed for an industrial nation, Japan was one of the least well-endowed countries in the world. Would the supply of natural resources in the future be politicized? Would prices be manipulated for the benefit of producers, forcing Japan into an ever more disadvantageous position? Japan's response to such fears was labeled a "raw materials diplomacy." It aimed at long-term agreements or joint ventures with producing countries and a wide variety of investments—especially in politically safe areas like Australia, Canada, or the United States. Above all it was based on continued support for a free-trading world economy.

The problem of inflation was compounded by the world recession during 1974 and 1975. Japan had maintained the highest sustained growth rate in the world for over two decades, but in 1974 its real growth was a negative 1.8 per cent, and in 1975 it grew only 3.1 per cent. Conditions in Japan were not bad. Industrial wages increased from an index figure of 100 in 1970 to 232 in 1975. Unemployment rose only from 1.2 per cent to about 2 per cent, with a million or so unemployed. Yet this was the first real recession since the postwar recovery had begun, and the Japanese found it unsettling. Layoffs raised questions about the durability of Japan's system of "lifetime employment." In 1975 an unprecedented 21 per cent of university graduates could not find jobs. And retired persons living on pensions or savings were hard hit by inflation. The short-term answer to recession was renewed growth; Japan mounted an export drive and by mid-1976 the yen had firmed and the Toyotas were flowing to America.

But in the meantime there arose a larger debate about the goals of national policy. One question was how much Japan could grow in the future. Most felt that two-digit growth was neither attainable nor desirable, that 7 or 8 per cent was attainable but not desirable, and that 5 or 6 per cent would be just about right. A few felt that even this was too much. A second question was what kind of growth; the consensus was that there should be a shift from smokestack industries such as heavy chemicals or steel to clean industries such as computers, optical goods, or electronics. An emphasis on developing high technology industries had already characterized the economy, even before the debate began. Yet to produce a substantial change would require far greater government interference in the economy than has prevailed hitherto.

A third and thornier question was how the fruits of a future growth should be distributed. Earlier it had been largely a question of the division between reinvestment and wage increases. These continued to claim a large share of profits. Substantial reinvestment would be required if the economy were to be given a new direction. Wages had risen so rapidly and for so long that there was an expectation of ever higher wages. Five per cent growth would not suffice to meet these claims. Wage demands may moderate. During 1974 and 1975 labor unions, acting for the good of their companies, settled for small increases in real wages. But 1975 also witnessed the largest strike in Japanese history: the walkout by transportation workers mirrored the highly political character of government employees' unions and suggested what might occur should a catalyst develop that would weaken the bonds of company loyalty.

A plethora of new and competing demands emerged during the early seventies along with those for wages and capital reinvestment. The populace wanted better housing, health care, public transportation, sewage systems, and government support for private universities. The strongest new claims were for welfare and for action against pollution. By the mid-seventies the Japanese realized that pollution was not just a question of the crippling Minamata disease in a few areas and the dirty air of Tōkyō, but of quantitatively higher levels of a great variety of pollutants throughout Japan and its surrounding seas. Residents' movements influenced local elections in areas where clam beds were blighted or local crops ruined. Japan had the technology to reduce pollution, but the equipment was expensive and constituted a levy on profits. As of 1977 Japan's environmental laws were among the most progressive in the world, but their implementation was only beginning. The strength of the new claim for a government program of welfare to aid the aged and the weak was reflected in Prime Minister Miki's "Life Cycle Plan," which proposed that there should be a guarantee for a minimal level of well-being for every Japanese at each stage in his life cycle. The existing level of welfare spending in Japan was so low, however, that any major undertaking would not only absorb the surplus of future growth, but require some redistribution of present income as well.

How these claims would be melded was not clear during the mid-seventies. That so many more claims than in the past had arisen just as growth was beginning to slow down suggested that Japan faced a difficult period of reexamination of national goals.

Politics also were changing during the seventies. Until the mid-seventies the Liberal Democratic Party had been almost unchallenged. However much the party may have been rent by clique strife over the question of who would be prime minister or who would get cabinet and party posts, it was united in the Diet and capable of clear-cut decisions on policy.

But difficulties began in the mid-seventies. In the July 1974 Upper House election the Liberal Democratic Party lost its majority. It won only 62 seats of the 130 up for election, giving it 126 seats, exactly one-half of those in the Upper House. Domestic issues, especially the soaring prices of consumer goods, were central in the election. The turnout, in spite of bad weather, was the highest for any postwar Upper House election: over 73 per cent of eligible voters. After the election an independent joined the Liberal Democratic Party and two other conservative independents supported it in the Diet, so it could continue in power without entering into a coalition. Yet the election cast a shadow over the future of the party. "The authority of money in politics" in particular became the target of journalistic criticism.

Fukuda Takeo, attacking the role of money in elections, observed that $10 million of campaign funds would lose a seat but $17 million would gain one.

In the months that followed, criticisms of moneyed politics became entangled with questions about the personal finances of Prime Minister Tanaka. These led to his resignation in November 1974 and to the selection in December of "Clean Miki" as the new Prime Minister with a mandate to reform the party. Like Tanaka, Miki was a maverick in Japanese politics. Born in 1907, he had attended a California college and was a graduate not of Tōkyō University but of the less prestigious Meiji University. Unlike most Liberal Democratic Party leaders who were ex-bureaucrats, Miki went directly from the university to politics. He was elected to the Japanese Diet at the age of 30 in 1937 and became the youngest cabinet minister in Japanese history in 1947. He formed his own political party, which then became a faction within the Liberal Democratic Party. Viewed as a weak but liberal figure, he was seen as a man who might restore the image of the conservative party.

Miki's first year as prime minister was spent fighting inflation and coping with recession. At the start of his second year, in January 1976, the "Lockheed scandal" broke. During a hearing in Washington a Lockheed official testified that payoffs had been made, among other countries, in Japan. Throughout the year this was front-page news in Japan. The Japanese as always were extremely sensitive about the American connection. Bribes are not a usual part of business in Japan. That they had occurred in connection with military equipment and that they were disclosed just when there was rising criticism of "moneyed politics" made the impact all the greater. During the summer a handful of Japanese businessmen who had received the money were arrested, and then ex-Prime Minister Tanaka and other political leaders were arrested as well. Some praised the conservative government for not attempting a coverup. Others saw the arrest of Tanaka as the continuation of factional strife. Even some conservatives began to argue that their party could not remain as closely associated with business in the future as it had been in the past.

Another setback for the Liberal Democratic Party, if not for conservatism in Japanese politics, came in the general election of December 1976. The Liberal Democratic Party lost 16 Diet seats, dropping from 265 to 249, and this in a Lower House newly enlarged by 20 seats to 511. Eleven independents subsequently joined the Liberal Democratic Party, giving it a five-vote majority, enough to keep it in power but not enough for it to retain complete control over all Diet committees. Shortly after the election Miki, taking responsibility for the poor showing, resigned as prime minister. He was succeeded by Fukuda Takeo, a graduate of the First Higher School and the Law Faculty of Tōkyō University, an ex-bureaucrat of the Ministry of Finance, a Diet member, and the leader of a powerful faction within the

Liberal Democratic Party. Though Fukuda was seventy-one, some welcomed his leadership as a skilled economic technocrat who could steer Japan's economy through troubled times. Others saw him as the personification of all they disliked in the Liberal Democratic Party.

The left did not do much better in the election. The Communist Party dropped from 39 seats to only 17. The Socialist Party, expecting major gains, advanced only 11 seats for a total of 123. As measured in Diet seats, it was the center that benefited the most. The Kōmeitō (Clean Government Party) leapt ahead from 30 seats to 55. The Democratic Socialists advanced from 19 seats to 29. The most dramatic gain from 5 to 17 seats was achieved by the New Liberal Club. This group of ambitious younger Diet members had splintered off from the Liberal Democratic Party the previous June in protest against the continued domination of their party by elderly factional leaders. Ideologically the New Liberal Club was more conservative than centrist, but tactically it assumed a centrist stance in the Diet to maintain an identity separate from the Liberal Democratic Party.

If the election is analyzed in terms of the popular vote, however, a different picture emerges. The vote did not correlate directly with Diet seats because of the electoral district system. The Communist Party, in spite of its disastrous showing, saw its popular vote decline only one-tenth of 1 per cent, from 10.5 to 10.4. The Socialist Party vote declined 1.2 per cent—while it gained additional seats. The vote of the Democratic Socialists declined by seven-tenths of 1 per cent. The Kōmeitō vote rose 2.4 per cent, over the vote of the 1972 election, but only to regain the 10.9 per cent of the vote it had received in the 1969 election. And if the 4.2 per cent vote of the New Liberal Club is added to the 41.8 per cent of the Liberal Democratic Party, then the total conservative vote dropped only eight-tenths of 1 per cent— one of the smallest conservative declines in any recent election. Overall the voting demonstrated the stability that has characterized postwar Japanese elections.

Stability also characterized the Upper House election in July 1977. The LDP's popular vote was markedly lower than it had been three years earlier, when it was deemed to have done very badly. It ended the campaign with 124 seats, 3 short of a majority. But 3 independents joined the party, giving it the edge needed to stay in power. Since the LDP had campaigned against the widespread expectation that it would lose its majority, it hailed the result as a victory. As for the opposition, moderates gained a few seats, while the radical left suffered a setback. The results suggested that the LDP would remain the chief factor in Japanese politics over the near future.

Whatever the perturbations of the seventies, it would not do to lose sight of the strengths of Japan. It was something new in the world—a major economic power without a commensurate military force. What others spent on guns, Japan had available for other needs. Even recent changes in inter-

Fukuda Takeo, who became Japan's prime minister in December 1976.

national relations did not lead to significantly larger military budgets: military spending in 1976 remained about eight-tenths of 1 per cent of the GNP. The Japanese people have in abundance the skills needed to operate a modern society. Since the end of World War II they have enjoyed as great an intellectual freedom as that existing anywhere in the world. The Japanese have a long experience in parliamentary politics. A change away from rule by a single party would not be detrimental to it.

Conclusions about the only non-Western state to have successfully industrialized are not difficult to reach. Economic and educational statistics, census returns, and the results of public opinion polls are sufficiently numerous that even foreigners may know more about certain aspects of Japan than the leaders of other Asian nations know about their own countries. Like other parliamentary states, Japan since the end of World War II has been a goldfish bowl open to scrutiny by all.

Yet the very openness may deceive: faced with an overwhelming amount of data we are forced to ask which aspects are fundamental and which indices pivotal. Unlike other neighboring states in which an apparatus of modern government has been imposed on societies that are still predominantly agricultural, Japanese society is complex. The blurring of class lines, the ideological diversity, the release from the restraints of tradition, the range of choices open to individuals in society, the vigor of its modern culture make appreciations possible from differing, or even conflicting, points of view.

Since many of these same characteristics are found in Europe and America, Westerners find Japan more intelligible than the rest of Asia. In contrast, the impact of revolutionary organization and doctrines on hitherto tradition-bound, immobile people is almost beyond Western understanding. Yet there is a danger in finding Japan too easily intelligible, too Western. For just as the modern West continues to be inspirited by its Judeo-Christian-Greek tradition, so the influence of Japan's recent non-Western past remains within its modern life. This invites questions whose answers are not to be found in the study of the West. As the only non-Western modern nation Japan may be an archetype with which developing non-Western nations may fruitfully be compared. The study of this archetype has only just begun.

27. Vietnam and Korea:
Colonialism and Nationalism

Colonialism in East Asia

The two larger components of the ancient Chinese culture area, China and Japan, were subjected in the mid-nineteenth century to an unequal-treaty system of Western privileges which was at most only semicolonial. We have stressed the contrasting torpor and rapidity with which these two peoples got rid of the unequal treaties—Japan within fifty years but China only after a hundred. Meanwhile the two smaller components of East Asian civilization, Vietnam and Korea, initially subjected to similar unequal treaties, soon suffered the much more grievous experience of full colonialism. French rule over Vietnam lasted some eighty years and Japanese rule over Korea about forty.

Despite great differences, the Vietnamese and Korean peoples have shared certain patterns of experience. As noted in Chapter 20, the foreign challenge was met first by an effort to reaffirm the Confucian principles which integrated state and society, and therefore the rulers violently opposed Christianity with its egalitarian teachings and foreign orientation. As tributaries of the Ch'ing, they also sought and accepted Chinese help, only to find it inadequate. Both countries were plagued by peasant poverty and rebellion, which their dynasties lacked the capacity to alleviate by modern means of economic growth. It became increasingly apparent that modern arms, technology, and means of production could be secured only from abroad, and this split the leadership into xenophobic conservatives and modernizers who favored foreign contact. This in turn exacerbated the factionalism of domestic politics and weakened the ruling houses.

Once the French and the Japanese had taken control, their colonial administrations discredited the traditional ruling class. In Vietnam the Nguyen emperors and mandarinate were maintained as vestigial puppets while in Korea the royal house disappeared into the Japanese nobility. Modernization, particularly education and new skills, was made available by the alien rulers, who came in as a new ruling class. The two countries were thus deprived of native leadership, not only in politics but also in letters, thought, and culture generally. The social order was decapitated. As a result, these colonial populations suffered a grievous hiatus in indigenous leadership, in the period between the discrediting of the old regimes and the slow and niggardly training of modern leaders. In this respect Vietnam and Korea suffered as Japan and China did not.

The similarities between Vietnam and Korea do not stop there. After a bitter experience of modern colonialism, both peoples after World War II were pulled apart by rival great-power blocs that fostered separate regimes north and south. Both peoples have experienced the disaster of civil war while yearning for national reunification, and in both countries American intervention has played an important role.

Nationalism and Communism in Vietnam

The Retardation of Vietnamese Nationalism. Vietnam's response to the French, like that of China to the West, was retarded by the need to supplant Confucian social values with a new concern for the nation as the focus of loyalty and for technological skills as the means of progress. After the French take-over, many Vietnamese continued for another generation to find their foreign model in China. True to the pattern of imitating the Ch'ing, Vietnamese scholars who traveled abroad in the 1860's and the 1870's had vainly advocated Westernization in self-defense, and Emperor Tu-duc (reigned 1848–1883) had attempted a "restoration" of his dynasty's vigor. By the end of the century a succeeding generation of scholars, still versed in Confucianism, was ready to respond to K'ang Yu-wei's reform program of 1898 and the subsequent Chinese movements of reform and revolution. These Vietnamese scholars, like their Chinese counterparts, eventually centered in Tōkyō, but they used ideas of Rousseau, Montesquieu, Adam Smith, Mill, Spencer, and Huxley, among others, as intellectual substance. Only later would the spread of French education in Vietnam give another, more direct channel of access to the Western national-revolutionary tradition.

Japan's victory in 1905 drew some two hundred young Vietnamese to Tōkyō in an "exodus to the East." A leader among them was Phan Boi Chau (died 1940), who became acquainted with Liang Ch'i-ch'ao, Sun Yat-sen, and those Japanese patrons of pan-Asianism, Okuma and Inukai. Inspired by works of K'ang and Liang, Chau* wrote a *History of the Destruction of the Vietnamese State* and formed a political association to aim at Vietnam's independence under a constitutional monarchy. Unfortunately, Japan's great-power friendship with France caused Chau, like Sun Yat-sen earlier, to be expelled from Tōkyō by 1909. The success of the Chinese revolution of 1911 and contact with the T'ung-meng Hui leader, Hu Han-min, at Canton inspired him to organize a Society for the Restoration of Vietnam, aiming now at a republic. But Chau's efforts to foment anti-French risings led to his imprisonment for some years after 1913 amid the general suppression of all revolutionary efforts.

Would-be reformers fared no better. Scholars who tried to develop Sino-French-Vietnamese education, and to push for national modernization within a framework of cooperation with France, made little headway. This failure was partly due to the disconcerting oscillations of French policy: conservative administrators might crack down on schools and reform groups which their liberal or socialist predecessors had permitted. It was also true that anti-French feeling remained so strong among the scholar class that any reform venture might get out of hand. Nationalistic scholar gentry, attempting to develop modern education in Vietnam on their own, opened the Tonkin Free School at Hanoi in 1907, frankly imitating Fukuzawa Yukichi's Keiō school in Japan. The French closed it the same year and exiled its leaders. In 1918 they permitted a tame substitute, the University of Hanoi, to replace it.

All this reflected the fact that the French had seized power from a ruling class steeped in traditions of government by scholar-officials, loyalty to the emperor, and rebellion against foreign rule. Young Vietnamese scholars regarded themselves as the future ruling class and therefore as natural saviors of their oppressed country. As late as 1916 the young Nguyen emperor (Duy-tan) helped organize a rebellion, and fled to the mountains when it was prematurely discovered (see page 609).

Against this upper-class rebelliousness, French rule was maintained by force and manipulation, principally by keeping Indo-China divided and by utilizing the old mandarinate as a bulwark of authority. The French preserved the façade of the traditional government, instead of destroying it; at the same time, for logical reasons, they delayed the creation of a new system of popular government. This amounted to using the past against the future, letting the strength of tradition stifle new growth. There was little native participation at the lower administrative levels in Cochin China. Meanwhile the mandarinates in the other "protectorate" areas were staffed with compliant functionaries who depended on the French. The enforced

---

*Vietnamese names are written in the Chinese order, surname first, but it is customary to use the personal name which is written last as though it were the surname. This is said to result from the fact that a few surnames like Nguyen are so prevalent as to lack particularity.

The Bao-dai emperor, flanked by the French resident superior and his own prime minister, returns to his country at the age of 20 after ten years in France. When he tried to be an active constitutional monarch, French opposition deflected him into an idle life, until the Viet Minh forced his abdication in 1945.

collaboration of the Nguyen dynasty with French rule robbed it of nationalist influence at the top. The Nguyen emperor who came to the throne in 1925 at the age of twelve with the reign title Bao-dai was left only ritual functions to perform. When a Grand Council of Economic and Financial Interests was created in 1928, it included Vietnamese but remained French-dominated. Even at lower levels, Frenchmen staffed much of the civil service. As late as 1942 there were fifty-one hundred French officials and only twenty-seven thousand Indo-Chinese, the highest proportion of Europeans in any Asian colonial government. Indigenous political activity was smothered by French police control over travel, mail communication, and publication, and by the repression of free assembly, labor organization, and political movements. Suspects were summarily shipped to the island of Pulo Condore.

Among many anachronisms in education, the classical examinations, inculcating an outworn orthodoxy, were preserved until 1915–1918, a decade longer than in China. Modern education for a new order developed slowly. Modern research on Indo-China's several cultures and complex history, although brilliantly pursued by the Ecole Française d'Extrême Orient at Hanoi, remained a matter of nonpolitical antiquarianism. Only in 1941 did patriotic scholars known as the "Know the New" group begin writing popular biographies of "heroes of the people" like the Tay-son brothers of the eighteenth century, in order finally to enlist history in the cause of nationalism. Meanwhile the old Sino-Vietnamese classical education, using Chinese characters, had died out in some areas, but lingered in others. In Cochin China, where classical influences had been weakest historically and the French colonization was heaviest in the 1860's, the Saigon colonial government decided to use the romanized script in order to break the barrier that the "Chinese language" interposed between the French and the "natives." In Annam and Tongking the Chinese writing system preserved its grip much longer. But early Vietnamese revolutionaries there correctly perceived that in the long run the use of the romanized script might help them reach a larger audience more quickly. By 1915 there were daily newspapers in romanized Vietnamese serving all three regions.

Education for the people as a whole, even French education, remained minimal. In all of Indo-China in 1939 there were only about 500,000 pupils in "general education," the bulk of them being confined to the first and second grades of elementary school; and there were only about 600 university-level students. Among the Southeast Asian colonies of the West, only the Netherlands East Indies (Indonesia) showed a poorer record. Until 1930, therefore, Vietnam remained very much a "Confucian village society," despite the ferment among segments of the intelligentsia. After 1930, urbanization began to have more effect, and new urban occupational groups— doctors, teachers, lawyers, mill owners—began to lose the enthusiasm of the preceding generation for compromise solutions between Western culture and "Confucius and Mencius." There was no exact equivalent of the Chinese May Fourth Movement in Vietnam, but there did emerge coteries of writers, with specific programs of social reform, who published their own journals. The most famous of these was the Self-Reliance Literary Group. It electrified literate Vietnamese in 1933 with its heroic call—reminiscent of Peking in 1919—for simplified literature, egalitarianism, individualism, patriotism, scientific methods, and an assault upon outmoded Confucian ideas. The French suppressed its first journal, *Phong Hoa (Reform of Customs)*, in 1936.

By these various traditional, divisive, diversionary, and repressive measures, the French maintained their control during the early decades of modernization. The old order was clearly bankrupt. French energy was creating, in the attractive new capital cities like Saigon, a new administration with modern services. In the 1920's, when revolutionary Vietnamese leadership had not yet emerged, there was a great investment of French capital, an expanded production, and some interest on the part of French socialists in Franco-Vietnamese collaboration. But meanwhile French achievements in public health, another of the two-edged benefits of modernization, helped the population to increase even faster than the food supply.

The crowded delta around Hanoi in the North, like similarly ancient areas of intensive cultivation in China, suffered the most from population growth. More and more people on the same plots of land meant greater poverty and insecurity. Meanwhile in the newly settled and less crowded South, French rule created a plantation economy like that in Burma or the Netherlands East Indies, not paralleled elsewhere in East Asia. The French land policy, beginning in Cochin China in the 1860's, had not maintained the ancient tradition of the communal lands. These had formed something like a fifth of the cultivated area and had been a resource that could be relied upon by poorer villagers. Instead, the French pursued a program of land expropriation and granted large concessions to French colonists, much of which passed on into the hands of the new class of their Vietnamese landed collaborators. In the course of time roughly half the land was taken over to form large estates or plantations, on which peasants worked as landless laborers to produce rubber and other crops for export. The big French rubber-plantation, coal-mining, and other export concerns, together with the Banque de l'Indochine and the Chinese rice traders and money-lenders, increasingly dominated the colonial economy and formed an interest group wedded to colonialism, while the condition of the populace worsened, certainly in their own minds and probably also in material terms.

Revolution, not reform, seemed to many Vietnamese the only answer to this economic exploitation, political repression, and cultural stagnation. Of the 100,000 Vietnamese soldiers and laborers who were sent to France during World War I, many returned with "dangerous" thoughts. The ideas of national self-determination, revolutionary class struggle, and party dictator-ship which flourished in China in the early 1920's had immediate reper-cussions south of the border. Revolution began in Vietnam through similar nationalist and communist organizations.

The Communist Movement. The Vietnam Nationalist Party founded in 1927 was indebted to the Kuomintang of China for much of its ideology, method, and support. Denied any chance to function in an established electoral process, it turned in the late twenties to terrorism. Meantime a more highly trained professional revolutionary movement was being set in motion by Ho Chi Minh (ca. 1892–1967), who like Sun Yat-sen began as a national-ist (using the name Nguyen Ai Quoc, "Nguyen the patriot") but, being a generation younger than Sun, turned to communism. Getting to France before World War I, he helped found the French Communist Party in 1920, and was sent by it to Moscow in 1923 to study at the University for the Toilers of the East. He participated in the Comintern Fifth Congress of 1924, and arrived in Canton in 1925 to work under Borodin. There he

*Ho Chi Minh, president of the Democratic Republic of
Vietnam, being welcomed in India.*

recruited Vietnamese to form the Vietnam Revolutionary Youth League as
a first step toward a Communist Party, and published a paper, *Youth
(Thanh Nien)*. Through this indoctrination in Leninism he began to create
for the first time a centralized subversive movement, based on secret cells in
Indo-China capable of surviving French police repression. Some members
were trained at the Whampoa Military Academy. After the Kuomintang-
Communist split in China, Ho Chi Minh as a principal Comintern agent
succeeded at Hong Kong in 1930 in uniting regional splinter groups into
the Communist Party (Cong-san Dang) of "Vietnam," a title soon broad-
ened to "Indo-China." It soon had some fifteen hundred members and
Comintern support.

The first phase of the Vietnamese revolution began in 1930 partly because the world depression then began to hit the Indo-Chinese export economy while simultaneous crop failures and famines intensified the popular
suffering in the crowded delta regions. The Vietnam Nationalist Party attempted a military rising, starting in February with a mutiny of troops at
Yen Bai on the Chinese border, which the French crushed with such
severity that the party was all but destroyed. The newly unified Communist
network, however, receiving a great influx of ardent revolutionaries, proceeded to stir up many strikes, demonstrations, incidents, and even peasant
risings. The French used their Foreign Legion in a small-scale war to get
the situation under control in 1931, and as a result thousands were killed,
tried, executed, or deported. Ho Chi Minh was jailed in Hong Kong (1931–

1933) and the Communist Party structure and Comintern contact were temporarily broken.

This defeat fostered among some Vietnamese Communists the Trotskyist view that any united front with "bourgeois nationalists" was inherently "reactionary" and unreliable—as witness the 1927 disaster to the united front in China. Later in the 1930's, however, the orthodox Stalinist party, rebuilding its underground apparatus with help from Moscow via Siam, joined with Trotskyists and others in local Saigon politics during the period of the Popular Front. When the united-front policy ended after the outbreak of World War II, Vietnamese Communists as well as nationalists again staged risings against French rule and were again ruthlessly suppressed. Nevertheless the Communist movement had clearly become a major vehicle of Vietnamese nationalism.

Communists became leaders of the national revolution in Vietnam for a variety of reasons. In China the Kuomintang or Nationalist Party had the advantage of age and experience over its Communist rivals; in Vietnam, it was the other way round. Older and wiser than Nguyen Thai Hoc, the rash young leader of the Vietnamese Nationalists who was guillotined in 1930, Ho Chi Minh and his confederates adroitly escaped the consequences of their own party's "soviet movement," which had been bloodily repressed in central Vietnam in the early 1930's, by remaining cautiously on the periphery or even outside Vietnam. More important, to a nation whose elite had a long tradition of cultural borrowing, international Communism offered an intelligible system of political and philosophical ideas and organizational methods that had been domesticated in China and could be adopted by Vietnamese revolutionaries in the same creative way that Vietnamese rulers had adopted Chinese bureaucratic blueprints a century before. Tragically for them, non-Communist Vietnamese revolutionaries could turn to no external model of equal potency. In the 1930's the Chinese Kuomintang lost its momentum as a trail-blazing political movement capable of inspiring young Vietnamese. It no longer gave much practical attention to the pan-Asian ideals that had moved Sun Yat-sen and Hu Han-min. In the meantime, Vietnamese Communists assiduously maintained contact with Yenan. One senior Communist ideologue even admiringly adopted as his pseudonym the Vietnamese version of the Chinese term for "Long March" (Truong Chinh) in honor of the CCP feat of 1935.

As a revolutionary problem Vietnam was politically and socially somewhat less complex, if militarily more difficult, than China. First, on the level of theory, the imperialism of the treaty powers in the Chinese treaty ports was many-headed and limited; only indirectly could it be blamed for the domestic problems of Chinese poverty, warlordism, and political disunity. In Vietnam imperialism was embodied solely in the French regime, which bore direct responsibility for domestic affairs; every evil could be denounced in terms of the Marxist-Leninist doctrine of imperialism. The anti-French aims of nationalists and Communists almost coincided. Second, on the practical level, the centralized French regime, controlling all the communications and the police, financial, and military powers of the state, represented a unified imperialism in full possession of the country, not confined to treaty ports on the periphery—an antagonist very different from the rival imperialist powers in China. This made regional power bases impossible and external aid important, if not essential, for revolutionaries in Vietnam; in this respect the Comintern apparatus could outdistance all rivals.

A multiclass coalition on united-front lines was also an indicated tactic in Vietnam, where so little proletariat as yet existed. Revolt was just beginning in the 1920's when Ho Chi Minh in Moscow and Canton made his Vietnamese translations and applications of Marxism-Leninism. He then envisaged a two-stage revolution—first a "bourgeois-democratic" struggle of all revolutionary classes to achieve independence, then the "proletarian revolution" itself. As he said in 1927, no one in Vietnam "as yet understood the significance of the word Communism." In the end Communism in Vietnam was nourished from both France and China and was no doubt sustained by its own sophisticated techniques; yet even so it hardly more than survived French repression into the period of World War II.

In her wartime expansion, Japan made no effort to "liberate" the Vietnamese nation. Quite the contrary. She continued to recognize French sovereignty represented by the Vichy governor, who skillfully maintained France's position on a diplomatic tightrope until the Japanese military take-over near the end of the war. Nationalist China, however, gave Ho Chi Minh and his Vietnamese followers active support and a staging area across the border, where in the spring of 1941 the Vietnamese Communists led the way in creating a united-front organization, the League for the Independence of Vietnam or Viet Minh ("Viet League"), with Ho Chi Minh as secretary-general. By 1945 Vo Nguyen Giap (1912–   ), a young Vietnamese teacher-turned-general, trained by the Chinese Communists at Yenan, was in command of guerrilla forces in Tongking.

When the Japanese forcibly seized power from the French administration in March 1945, they created another regime like that the French had maintained. Nominally it was under Emperor Bao-dai and other dignitaries, but actual control rested with Japan. The Viet Minh established a "liberated zone" on the Chinese border, not unlike the Chinese Communists' "liberated areas" farther north. From this territorial base they steadily infiltrated the Red River delta and even the puppet regime of Bao-dai. On Japan's sudden surrender in August 1945, the Viet Minh and Vo Nguyen Giap's small army found themselves for the moment the only effective power in Vietnam. The Japanese remained neutral, and Emperor Bao-dai abdicated at Hué on

August 26 in favor of the Democratic Republic of Vietnam. Its independence was joyfully proclaimed at Hanoi by Ho Chi Minh on September 2.

Vietnam after Independence. Japan's surrender created immediate problems of public order, especially in Cochin China where rival, armed religious sects (the syncretic Cao Dai sect with its own church and pope, and the Hoa Hao, a Buddhist revival society) had their own anti-Communist forces and challenged the Viet Minh united front, which was broadly inclusive in form although dominated by the orthodox or Stalinist Indo-Chinese Communist party.

The Allied take-over to disarm and repatriate the Japanese was divided between Chinese forces north of the sixteenth parallel and British forces south of it. With the British in mid-September 1945 came the Free French, concerned for the twenty thousand French civilians still in Saigon, and determined like General de Gaulle not to diminish the national glory by giving up the empire. Under local British orders the rearmed French forcibly retook control of Saigon (September 23), and by January 1946, when the British left, they had reoccupied principal cities, routes, and plantations in Cochin China, although resistance continued sporadically in the countryside. In Tongking, on the other hand, the Nationalist Chinese forces arriving in mid-September had let the Viet Minh go on functioning at Hanoi, while the French representatives looked on in impotence. Having removed the Japanese and got French agreements in favor of Chinese commercial interests, Nationalist China withdrew her forces during the spring of 1946. By that time the Viet Minh was well entrenched.

The Vietnamese nationalists were handicapped by having had little experience of actual government; Japan had used French collaborators rather than Vietnamese to run the administration during most of the war. The rather simple unifying aims of xenophobic anticolonialism, to expel the French and achieve independence, were also cut across by the aims of domestic social revolution. The poverty and inequalities of the crowded North Vietnam delta country fostered a combined social and national movement, such as Ho Chi Minh advocated. To pursue both these revolutions at once involved a struggle on two fronts, a united national struggle of patriots against foreigners and a divisive class struggle mobilizing the poor and insecure mass against the propertied and well-to-do minority. The Communists, with their tighter organizational methods, had survived better than other groups against Franco-Japanese repression; and Ho Chi Minh despite his years in Moscow had emerged as the senior figure in the national revolution with something of Sun Yat-sen's capacity for bringing rival groups together. Finally, the success of Communism in China in the form of Mao's "New Democracy" in the late 1940's naturally strengthened the sister movement south of the border. In this period the Vietnamese Communists made continual efforts to minimize the Communist core of their united front. They formally dissolved the Indo-Chinese Communist Party in November 1945, held an election for the first time, brought more non-Communists into the Hanoi government, and set up a popular front (the Lien Viet) with a program of "independence and democracy."

Ho Chi Minh was beset by rival groups, such as the anti-Communist patriots supported by Nationalist China, and saw no prospect of aid to Vietnamese independence from China or the United States. He made an agreement with the French on March 6, 1946. France recognized the Democratic Republic of Vietnam as "a free state with its own government, parliament, army, and finances, forming part of the Indo-Chinese Federation and the French Union"—a formula that put the Republic into a colonial federation which would in turn form a "union" with the metropolitan power. In return, French troops came back to Hanoi unopposed. General promises were made on both sides, subject to further working out of specifics; but continued negotiations including a conference in France (at Fontainebleau in July–August) proved only how irreconcilable were the differences of aim and attitude. The French unilaterally put Cochin China under a puppet regime, detached from the rest of Vietnam. A French naval and air bombardment of Haiphong on November 23 killed 6000 or more civilians. The Vietnamese made a surprise attack on the French in Hanoi on December 19, and a full-scale war ensued, with the Viet Minh organizing a national resistance against 115,000 or more French troops.

As this Franco-Vietnamese colonial war continued month after month during 1947 and 1948, it gradually became a focus of the international power politics of the cold war. In brief, as the Chinese Communists began to gain the upper hand in China and the Communist risings of 1948 erupted in Burma, Malaya, the Philippines, and Indonesia, anti-Communist resistance also stiffened in many countries in a worldwide tendency toward polarization. The Communist core of the Viet Minh became more overt; and the French finally succeeded in 1949 in setting up a Vietnamese regime at Hué and Saigon under the ex-emperor Bao-dai as chief of state and a rallying point for nationalist anti-Communists.

Attracting nationalists to an "independent" Vietnam that would still be French-controlled was not easy. The anti-Communist Catholic ex-mandarin, Ngo Dinh Diem, who had been Bao-dai's chief minister in 1933, now refused to head Bao-dai's new government, even though the French had at last agreed to make Cochin China part of a united Vietnam "associated" with France. The French colonial regime could not relax its grip, least of all with a war on its hands. By the time the French National Assembly in January 1950 finally confirmed the treaties making Bao-dai's Vietnam and also Cambodia and Laos into independent but "associated" states, the war in

Vietnam was escalating to a new level. Communist China, now on the border of Tongking, and the Soviet Union recognized Ho Chi Minh's government; the United States and Britain recognized Bao-dai's. American arms were soon flowing in great quantity to the French in Vietnam, while Chinese economic aid, arms, and training (based in South China) henceforth bolstered the Viet Minh forces.

During the seven-year struggle with France, economic shortages and political regimentation overtook North Vietnam. The regime became more thoroughly Communist on the Chinese model. A successor to the Indo-Chinese Communist Party (dissolved in 1945) reappeared early in 1951 in the form of the Vietnam Workers (Viet Nam Lao Dong) Party. As mobilization of men and materiel proceeded, the French forces totaling some 420,000 men, including a Vietnamese army of 200,000, met a constantly more formidable military challenge from a Viet Minh army almost as large, entrenched in mountain bases and among the populace. When a Communist-led "Free Laotian" (Pathet Lao) movement invaded Laos to the west, the French finally decided to block the main route by airborne buildup of the mountain-ringed post of Dien Bien Phu. In April–May 1954 Vo Nguyen Giap unexpectedly transported artillery to this area and destroyed the French Empire. The surrender of this post on May 7, 1954, pushed an international conference already in session at Geneva to recognize an explicitly temporary partition into North and South Vietnam, divided a little north of Hué on about the seventeenth parallel: the Communist-controlled Democratic Republic of Vietnam ruled the North from Hanoi; France withdrew in favor of the Bao-dai government of the Republic of Vietnam with Ngo Dinh Diem as premier at Saigon. He vigorously suppressed the armed religious sects and other corrupt elements, and in late 1955 won elections which ousted Bao-dai and made himself president of the Republic. With United States support, Diem refused to join in the nationwide elections promised at the Geneva conference and by 1960 a campaign of rural insurgency and terrorism was under way against his regime in the South, aided from the North.

Further American involvement in South Vietnam was seen in Washington as a necessary response to the expansion of international Communism, in the cold war era of confrontation between the American-led "free world" and the presumed ambitions of Russia and China. Moreover, presidents, officials, and congressmen, remembering the political agonies of the right-wing investigation of the "loss" of China in the early 1950's, resolved not to "lose" Vietnam as well. In 1961 such resolution seemed to call, inexpensively, only for the sending of arms and a handful of advisers to help the Diem government. In 1965, after four chaotic years which had seen Diem's overthrow and murder in a military coup in 1963 and declining prospects, under the generals who succeeded him, the stakes were dramati-

An unexploded bomb in a Vietnamese farmyard.

cally, and disastrously, raised. More than half a million American troops
were sent to salvage the Saigon government, and American air power was
used for systematic, selective bombing of North Vietnam. By 1968, this
policy of intervention had reached a state of publicly acknowledged bankruptcy. It had produced inflation at home, as well as widespread popular
revulsion; and it had not destroyed the Communists' position in Vietnam,
as their explosive offensive of February 1968 sharply demonstrated.

Americans in responsible positions seem to have understood the Vietnamese whirlpool in which they were caught in the 1960's even less well than
their predecessors had understood the Chinese ordeal of the 1940's. Many
of them confidently presumed that an appropriate technology could be
found to defeat political revolutionaries. The Vietnamese Communists, endowed with the will power of a dynamic, romantic nationalism as well as a
knowledge of the countryside, were not intimidated by this presumption.
In fact they used it against the United States, skillfully dramatizing the
theme of a disadvantaged peasantry struggling against the latest devices of
scientific warfare. In addition to this misplaced American faith in military
technology, ambassadorial reporting from Saigon showed little knowledge
of Vietnamese or East Asian history. It focused excessively upon leaders
like Diem, without looking at the institutional and historical limits of their
ability to carry out reforms or mobilize popular support. There was little
recognition, for example, of the heritage left by the ancient Confucian
monarchy—that the ruler's need for a monopoly of virtue made him fear
to accept the legitimacy of opposition. In the meantime ugly scenes from an

increasingly dirty war flashed upon the television screens of millions of American homes, showing that Vietnamese values were being ignored and American values badly compromised. Unlike the previous American military engagements with the three other East Asian societies—Japan in the 1940's, Korea and China in the 1950's—this East Asian war produced a profound crisis of the American spirit. President Johnson gave up seeking reelection in 1968. President Nixon, while steadily withdrawing the American forces from June 1969, spread the war to Cambodia and bombed Hanoi but was finally able to negotiate in January 1973 only a ceasefire and American withdrawal in defeat. In 1975 Saigon's forces collapsed and the American embassy departed. In 1976 Vietnam was united under Hanoi.

Japanese Colonialism in Taiwan and Korea

In no respect did Meiji Japan catch up with the West more quickly than in colonialism. Within a decade of the final French conquest of Indo-China, Japan took over Taiwan. In another decade she had Korea. Given her late start compared with the French, Japan's achievements, both in integrating the colonial economies of Taiwan and Korea into that of the homeland and in suppressing nationalist political developments, are all the more noteworthy.

Several factors obviously favored Japan's empire-building—not only geographic proximity and easy communication by sea with an island and a peninsula which sea power could control, but also (and equally important) cultural proximity. Japan, Taiwan, and Korea were all parts of the Chinese culture area. Chinese characters, used in all three writing systems, still provided a common medium of communication, so that a literate Korean or Taiwanese could understand a Japanese official's orders written in classical Chinese. The devices of indirect rule, which blunted the efficiency of other colonial regimes, were thus less necessary. Moreover, the traditional phraseology and concepts of imperial Confucianism—benevolent rule, family morality, the social order—could be utilized by the new masters, who by the same token were not imbued with alien ideas like individualism, Christianity, or the White Man's Burden. This common background made it easy for Japan to update and use the *pao-chia* system of collective responsibility, for example, in Taiwan. The Chinese cultural tradition even in its Korean variation tended to support established authority. Japan could thus work from the inside; moreover she did so in the East Asian area where ideas and methods of authoritarian rule had gained maturity, balance, and sophistication through a long development. Cultural proximity made it easier for some Taiwan-Chinese and Koreans to become Japanized collaborators and for Japanese police to oversee the populace. Japan was close enough culturally, in fact, to envision an actual absorption and assimilation of her colonial subjects, more complete than France could contemplate.

Japan's Development of Taiwan.   The mountainous island of Taiwan, 250 miles long by 60 to 80 miles wide, offered Japan a golden opportunity for economic development. A short sea haul from the home islands, Taiwan was comparatively underpopulated by some 3 million industrious Chinese peasants and a small minority of about 120,000 aborigines of Malay origin. The island was underdeveloped but could produce semitropical food crops to meet Japan's needs.

Politically, Taiwan was still almost a Chinese frontier area. It had been settled principally since the late Ming, and was accustomed to being governed from a distance, as it did not become a separate province until 1885. In 1895 Chinese nationalism had not yet produced even the Reform Movement that culminated in 1898 on the mainland, and the Ch'ing dynasty's helpless surrender of Taiwan to Japan bequeathed no irredentist heritage to future patriots. Japan took over a largely prenationalistic polity as well as a premodern economy.

Japanese development of Taiwan got under way only in 1898 with the appointment of General Kodama Gentarō as governor-general and Gotō Shimpei, a doctor of medicine, as head of the civil administration. These two leaders in Japan's modernization inherited a chaotic situation, for the traditional subsistence economy was plagued by disorder, and the central administration had largely broken down. They set out to make the colony economically self-supporting, and a strategic bulwark of Japan, come peace or war. They established order, then conducted thorough surveys of the land, people, and customs, and pressed for scientific development of resources.

To establish peace and order Gotō rebuilt the old *pao-chia* system and integrated it with a modern police network, so that local police officers worked closely with the household groupings of mutual responsibility in the villages. Meantime, offering amnesty or liquidation, the regime extinguished the patriotic, bandit-type resistance by mid-1902. The rank and file of the police force were recruited more and more from Taiwanese, who received special education and training under Japanese administrators. Well paid and disciplined, the police assisted in many kinds of administration—registration of households, collection of taxes, sanitation, water control, even afforestation.

Next, the Japanese administration reorganized the land tenure system. Cadastral surveys reduced the confusion of land rights. Prior to this time large landowners had rented to smaller landowners who had subrented in turn, so that several parties might receive rents from a single piece of soil. Furthermore, the Chinese government land tax had remained stationary and much new land remained untaxed. The Japanese had new land registers and maps drawn up and in 1904 bought out the noncultivating landowners by giving them public bonds. This move created a society of owner-farmers

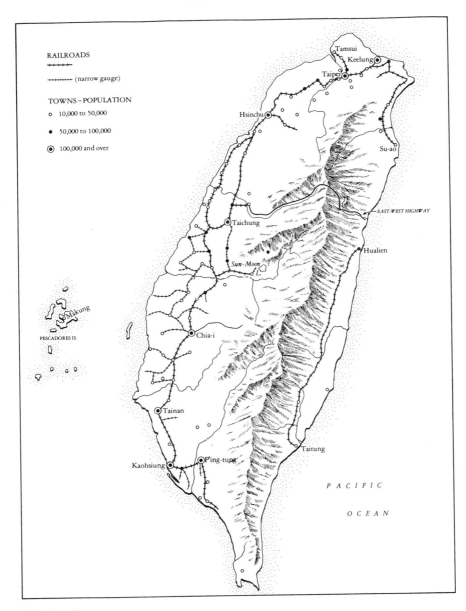

RAILROADS
+++++
++++++++ (narrow gauge)

TOWNS – POPULATION
○ 10,000 to 50,000
● 50,000 to 100,000
◉ 100,000 and over

TAIWAN

responsible for taxes on their own private property, and more than tripled the land tax revenue.

On the social plane, Japanese superiority was asserted and enforced with many forms of discrimination to keep the Chinese populace subordinate. The Japanese language was widely promoted for administrative purposes and technical education. After World War I, Japanese was taught in the elementary schools to further the policy of assimilation, but higher education for Taiwanese remained very limited.

Material development came rapidly, mainly through government leadership and investment. Public health measures eliminating epidemic diseases and malaria contributed to a doubling of the population between 1905 and 1940. By 1903 the railway linked up the north and south of the island, and some six thousand miles of roads eventually reached the countryside.

Production efforts centered on rice, tea, and especially sugar cane. Agricultural experiment stations, importing Hawaiian cane, encouraged production for new Japanese-financed sugar mills, which invested in land improvement, irrigation, fertilizer, and transport. Labor was attracted, and cultivators were persuaded to plant new, free land, on condition that part of it produce cane. Standards and marketing methods were scientifically developed. By monopolizing the sugar mills, Japanese capital controlled this new export industry. Fostered by heavy early investment and a protectionist policy (Taiwan sugar entered Japan duty free), Taiwan's sugar industry by 1914 had increased about fourfold—a triumph of capitalist development—and supplied a great part of Japan's needs.

Taiwan-Chinese political resistance in terms of nationalism developed rather slowly. For one thing, Japanese rule did not require the suppression of a local ruling house or the entire discrediting of the traditional civilization. Nor did it break up the rural community. On the contrary, the Japanese regime sponsored farmers' associations to promote agrarian improvements (thereby laying a foundation for the later success of rural reconstruction in the 1950's), and the Taiwan farmer's brick house and use of electricity and scientific technology testified to his comparative welfare in the Asian scene. Thus economic progress, reinforced by police controls, discouraged anti-Japanism. During World War I, however, Taiwanese political associations were formed to seek Taiwan-Chinese equality with the Japanese. Taiwan students in middle schools and private universities in Japan, where some two thousand were seeking education, readily responded to liberal ideas of personal freedom and political reform. The 1920's brought repeated petitions for representative government, the organization of cultural and youth groups, and some abortive Communist activity. But Japan's aggression in China after 1931 was accompanied by intensified police repression in Taiwan, and comparatively few incidents erupted before Japan was ousted in 1945.

Korean Nationalism under Japan.   In Taiwan after 1895, a rather new Chinese province had been brought under Japanese control before the rise of the Chinese nationalist movement. In the ancient kingdom of Korea, in contrast, Korean nationalism was already active among the upper class by

1910. Indeed the crucial fifteen years between 1895 and 1910 had been the watershed between traditional xenophobia and modern nationalism in most of Asia. Korea thus presented a very different political problem.

As one stimulant of Korean nationalism, Christian missionaries, especially American Presbyterians and Methodists, had made great progress in the decades after the opening of Korea to Western contact in 1882. They founded hospitals and schools, including facilities for educating women and for training a Korean pastorate. By 1910 there were some 200,000 Korean Christians under about 50 foreign Catholic priests and more than 300 Protestant missionaries, most of whom were American. The missionaries, with their religious, medical, and educational institutions, although repeatedly enjoined by their governments from "intermeddling" in Korean politics, nevertheless constituted a vested interest averse to Japanese imperialism and sympathetic to Korean modernization following Western models. By the same token, Japanese administrators after the 1910 annexation found Christianity and Western liberalism subversive. In 1911, they accused more than a hundred leading Korean Christians of conspiring to assassinate the governor-general. They were arrested, hung by the thumbs or otherwise pressured into confessions, and sentenced to prison terms. Christian protests, mainly from the United States, in time got many of them released. Missionaries continued to give the small but elite Christian community a sustaining contact with the outside world. By identifying itself with nationalist aspirations, Christianity found more adherents in Korea than in most parts of Asia.

The nature and limitations of American missionary support of Korean nationalism were illustrated in the long career of Syngman Rhee (Yi Sungman, 1875–1965). Rhee got his start in the English language, in Western studies, and in Christianity at an institution established by the Methodists in Seoul in 1885 and recognized by the Yi dynasty government as a source of modern-trained officials. The journalism and debating activities in which he became a student leader were also a training for revolutionary politics. During Korea's mounting domestic crisis in 1896 (see page 617) he joined the Independence Club and helped organize mass demonstrations in the traditional manner. After seven years' imprisonment, he came to the United States, an emigré nationalist, studied at leading universities and returned to Korea as a Y.M.C.A. worker. Forced out by the Japanese pressure against Christians in 1911, he then settled for twenty-five years in Hawaii, becoming the leader of an expatriate faction of Korean nationalists and remaining unreconciled to the Western missionaries' acquiescence in Japanese rule.

The Japanese attitude of superiority toward the Koreans, so evident in their military administration after 1910, was like that of most colonial rulers over less developed societies. The efficiency of Japan's exploitation was unchecked by ideas of representative government or self-determination.

Japan's experience in Taiwan suggested that the Koreans should be ruled paternalistically but rigorously, as an inferior, subject people, with elementary mass education to enhance their productivity but no political training for future independence. Thus the bureaucracy—in the government-general at Seoul, in the provinces, counties, and municipalities, and in education—became three-fifths Japanese (52,000 Japanese to 35,000 Koreans in 1936). All political activity was prohibited and all publication tightly controlled.

Japan developed in Korea an exemplary network of railways and roads, as well as postal services and telecommunications, hydroelectric plants, mines, and a few modern industries. Aided by public health measures and peace and order, the Korean population increased by about five-sixths between 1910 and 1940. But Japanese large-scale landlordism increased several times over, while Korean living standards remained very low. By the 1930's half the rice crop was being exported to feed Japan, but the per capita consumption of rice in Korea had reportedly dropped 45 per cent—a clear sign of lowered welfare.

The spread of poverty went hand in hand with new ideas. Modern education, in the schools established by the Japanese regime, produced a literate population that would prove capable of rapid economic growth later in the century. But private Korean schools and those of foreign missionaries also nourished patriotic discontent. Korean students in Japan became ardent nationalists. Christian and liberal attitudes grew stronger after World War I. They included a Wilsonian belief in the self-determination of peoples and in the moral influence of world opinion. This faith underlay the great March First *(Samil)* movement of 1919, a nationwide unarmed demonstration of Korean nationalist sentiment. (The May Fourth movement was to be launched in Peking a few weeks later in a similar atmosphere although with very different results.)

Hoping to impress the statesmen reshaping the world at Versailles, Korean patriots fixed on their late emperor's commemoration day as the occasion for a protest, secretly organized and dramatically made public. On March 1, thirty-three cultural and religious leaders and their co-conspirators in every township over the country, read an eloquent "Proclamation of Independence." A million or so demonstrators marched, shouting for independence. In brutally suppressing them, the frightened Japanese recorded nineteen thousand persons jailed and two thousand casualties.

The nationalist movement thus launched suffered severely from factionalism. This had been the bane of traditional Korean politics for centuries; the bureaucracy had become fractured into long-lasting, almost hereditary factions which commonly enlisted the individual official's primary loyalty. In the modern nationalist movement this factional tradition was kept alive by the dispersion of Korean patriots to many foreign lands, especially to

Russia, China, Japan, and the United States, where they acquired different ideas, conflicting approaches, and discordant allies. Influences from these larger countries pulled Korean nationalists in different directions. But the failure of the March First movement and the survival of the Soviet revolution now favored the rise of Communism as the chief vehicle for Korea's anti-Japanese patriots in the 1920's.

Since the late nineteenth century an expatriate community of Korean emigrants had grown up across the Tumen River in the Chientao region of eastern Manchuria near the Korean-Russian border (see map, page 706). Other Korean emigrants had formed communities in Siberian cities along the Trans-Siberian Railway. Koreans were consequently the first East Asians to participate in the Soviet revolution, both in the armed forces and under the Comintern. As Lenin turned to the East, Korean patriots were the most readily available allies—and the most anti-Japanese. More Koreans than Chinese attended the Congress of the Toilers of the East held in Moscow in January 1922 to counter the Washington Conference (see page 694). Yet organization within Korea proved difficult. A Korean Communist Party was finally inaugurated in Seoul in 1925, but its dissidence was continually suppressed by the Japanese police, who actually knew more about the Korean Communist movement than any of its members. Meanwhile, among the exiled patriots seeking aid from non-Communist powers, Syngman Rhee negotiated during the 1930's in Washington, Geneva, and Moscow; but by World War II the Korean factions in China and in Washington were small and ineffective compared with the troops and cadres secretly prepared over the years in the Soviet Union—although all had been equally frustrated by the Japanese police in Korea.

The postwar wave of liberalism in Japan in the 1920's had produced a movement for conciliation and reform of the Korean administration, but these liberal beginnings were choked off when militarism swept the Japanese Empire in the 1930's. Japan's heightened dominance in Korea produced a sullen and restive though largely helpless people, whose resentment was nourished by the belief that their increasing poverty was due to Japanese exploitation. Police controls, backed by the army, were well developed and ever alert against all expressions of nationalism. Even the Korean language was banned in the late 1930's. Koreans were expected to take Japanese surnames, and the Korean language press was almost eliminated. Korean of course remained the language of the home, while Christianity continued to hold its small share of converts—half a million in 1938 in an increased total population. But under the pressure of Japan's war effort, Korean agriculture continued to deteriorate, while tenancy and landlordism (especially Japanese landlordism) increased. As Japan's power grew in Manchuria and spread into China, Korea became even more abjectly submerged in the Japanese Empire.

Korea Since World War II

The Postwar Occupations.   Unlike Vietnam, Korea suffered no reoccupation by former rulers after World War II. Instead, she was taken over and bisected by two victorious powers, one of which (the U.S.S.R.) had prepared for this with more foresight than the other (the U.S.A.).

The American idea of self-determination, more an attitude than a concrete program, was reflected in the Cairo Conference statement of December 1, 1943, by Roosevelt, Churchill, and Chiang Kai-shek, that "in due course Korea shall become free and independent." The phrase "in due course" expressed Allied uncertainty as to how Korean self-government might be achieved. International trusteeship by Britain, China, the United States, and the Soviet Union was subsequently agreed to. But in contrast to the distant American overseas interest in the principle of independence of small nations, the continental Soviet interest across a common border (albeit only a dozen miles long) reflected long-term strategic concerns expressed in the very different ideology and procedures of Soviet Communism. Soviet troops entered North Korea on August 9, 1945, just before Japan's surrender on August 15; but American troops, unprepared for the task, arrived only on September 8. By arranging to take Japanese surrenders north and south of the 38th parallel, the two powers, as it turned out, created two countries. International trusteeship was never achieved. Unification proved impossible.

In the North the Russian aim to create a Communist state was comparatively definite and was achieved in successive stages. Communist elements got control of the "people's committees" that were being organized at each level of government—county, municipal, and provincial—while opponents were got rid of in one way or another (about a million North Koreans migrated to the South). Mass organizations were set up to mobilize workers, farmers, youth, women (now "emancipated"), and others in a national front. Finally, the powers having failed to agree on means for reunification, elections were held in the North in November 1946, with almost everyone voting, followed by a Convention of People's Committees at the capital, P'yongyang, in February 1947, which in turn set up a People's Assembly. This at once elected a People's Committee to run a provisional Korean government. At its head was the original Soviet nominee, Kim Il-song, a young man now bearing the name of a former guerilla leader. The whole process of political indoctrination and mobilization was managed by the dominant Labor (i.e., Communist) Party, supported by Korean "people's militia" numbering 150,000 or more and guided by Soviet advisers in the background. Along with this political structure went vigorous programs for rural reorganization in the guise of land reform, beginning with confiscation and redistribution of landlords' estates, together with nationalization of industry and a planned economy in general.

Organized forcibly from the top down, the North Korean Communist Party dictatorship seems to have displayed most of the strong and weak points typical of such regimes. Being Korean in form, although actually under Soviet guidance, it was less offensive to nationalist sentiment than Japanese rule; and its reforms had attractions for various groups, particularly in the early stages of the totalitarian metamorphosis.

In the South the American aim to foster the growth of an independent, self-governing nation was immensely more complex and difficult. Unlike the Russians in the North, the Americans had made no preparations to take over South Korea even temporarily. Drawn suddenly into a power vacuum, they arrived three weeks after the war's end to find that the Japanese governor-general had prompted formation of an interim government headed by a moderate. This regime had organized local "people's committees" all over the country and proclaimed a "People's Republic" with a broad economic and political reform program. Its potential for becoming a non-Communist regime was never tested, for the American military government, taking responsibility, refused to recognize it. Instead the Americans incurred odium by dealing initially with the Japanese, all of whom were soon repatriated, however.

While trying to postpone political decisions, the United States Occupation faced urgent economic problems. The Korean economy had been enervated by the war, yet it was integrally tied to that of Japan and suffered when the tie was cut. The Americans generally assumed in 1945 that Korea would soon be unified. But their hopes of peaceful reconstruction by international cooperation were increasingly frustrated as the two super-powers moved toward cold war confrontation. In December 1945 the Moscow conference of foreign ministers, seeking a way out of this impasse, agreed that a Soviet-American joint commission should superintend creation of a unified Korean government, under a four-power trusteeship for five years. But the Koreans themselves, except those under Communist control, opposed trusteeship. This scheme was clearly hopeless by mid-1946.

The American military government in the South therefore proceeded to give steadily increasing responsibility to its Korean personnel and inaugurated in December 1946 a partly elected legislative assembly. Trying to establish a rule of law as a basis for political and economic freedom, the United States' policy was more intent on political than on economic ends. The aim was to get a stable, representative government established as soon as possible without attempting basic economic reforms. As a result, land reform to aid the mass of impoverished tenant cultivators by redistribution of Japanese holdings was delayed until 1948. This delay was partly due to the fact that in the meantime the nascent political process, in the shadow of Communism across the border, had become dominated by landlord-minded conservatives.

Syngman Rhee, now seventy after a long career of emigré agitation, had reappeared to save his people like a latter-day Moses. Rhee espoused ultra-nationalism—independence without delay and unification at any price—against the current American policy of trusteeship and settlement by negotiation. Touring the provinces in an eloquent bid for support, while quietly organizing a strategic following among the police, Rhee used whatever political methods served his cause. He soon built up a political party, complete with mass demonstrations and strong-arm squads. As Communist intransigence became more obvious on the left, including a resort to terrorism in South Korea, anti-Communism gained strength on the right. In this polarized political scene the moderates gradually lost out while the extremists took over.

Meantime in September 1947 the United States placed the Korean problem before the United Nations, which set up a Commission on Korea to aid Korean unification and to observe Korean elections for the creation of a national assembly and government. Rhee's party won the elections in South Korea in May 1948; he headed the new assembly and on August 15 became president of the new Republic of Korea with wide executive powers, thus terminating the American military government.

Having excluded the United Nations election commission, the North Korean regime hastily held its own elections and on September 9, 1948, proclaimed itself a Democratic People's Republic. Within a year Soviet and American forces had been largely withdrawn from the divided peninsula. By June 1950, when North Korea mounted its attack on the South, the North was the stronger state, both industrially because of its mineral and hydro-power resources and militarily because of Soviet armament for offensive warfare.

The Korean War and After. The North Korean surprise attack on June 25, 1950, was at once condemned by the United Nations Security Council. (The Soviet Union, having boycotted the Council for six months as a protest against the presence of Nationalist China, was not present to cast a veto.) President Truman, mindful of the historical lesson of the 1930's in China and Europe—that aggression unchecked fosters more general warfare—interpreted the North Korean attempt at unification by force as a case of aggression by one sovereign state against another (much as the Americans were later to do in Vietnam). He committed United States forces to defend South Korea and at once secured the support of the United Nations in the name of collective security. Forces were sent from Britain, Turkey, and thirteen other member countries, although South Korea supplied two-fifths of the ground forces and the United States one-half, as well as most of the naval and air power. All were put under the unified command of General Douglas MacArthur. The 142,000 casualties suffered by

New elevated highways in downtown Seoul.

the United States made the Korean War the fourth largest in American history. (South Korean casualties were estimated at 300,000, North Korean at roughly 520,000, and Chinese at perhaps 900,000.)

The war had four phases. First, under the well-prepared, Soviet-armed North Korean assault, the outnumbered Korean-American forces initially were forced back southeast of the Naktong River to protect a rectangular fifty-by-fifty mile perimeter around Pusan in the extreme southeast. They beat off violent North Korean attacks while gathering strength from abroad. In the second phase, MacArthur demonstrated the offensive power of modern military technology with a massive amphibious landing on September 15 at Inchon, the port for the capital, Seoul—a gamble that succeeded brilliantly and was soon followed by recovery of Seoul and destruction of the North Korean invasion (see map, page 604).

The war entered a third phase when United Nations forces crossed the 38th parallel in early October and, expanding their aim from repulse of the Northern invasion to an ill-advised effort to reunite Korea by force, pushed north toward the Yalu. The two main American thrusts were under separate commands, divided by fifty miles of "impassable" mountains. In mid-October massively organized Chinese Communist "volunteers" began to cross the Yalu into North Korea to defend China's interest in this region on the frontier of its Northeast industrial base. Marching long distances through the mountains by night, lying hidden from air reconnaissance by day, they waited until by late November they totaled 300,000 or more.

Unexpected Chinese flank attacks then forced the American columns into a costly retreat of 275 miles in the winter cold, all the way south of Seoul. But China's attempt to use her vast resources of manpower to unify Korea by force was now contained by United Nations firepower that eventually produced a stalemate on about the 38th parallel. General MacArthur wanted to carry the war to China; his increasingly public disagreement with the fixed American policy of no more than a limited war led to his dismissal by President Truman in April 1951. In the fourth phase of the war, truce talks began in July 1951 and dragged on at Panmunjom for two years. An armistice was finally signed July 27, 1953; in 1976 it was still in effect, with a closed border across the peninsula.

To the political inexperience and economic problems of South Korea were now added the burdens of a postwar rehabilitation. President Syngman Rhee's autocratic methods put nationalism ahead of democracy in a newly emerging state threatened by subversion and invasion. Police repression, corruption, and rigging of elections finally touched off spontaneous student demonstrations in Seoul in April 1960, and Rhee was obliged to retire, leaving Korean politics to an uneasy contest between a faction-ridden national assembly and army rule. In 1961 a military junta seized power and inaugurated a series of five-year plans for economic development; in 1965 a treaty with Japan allowed a resumption of Japanese investment. In 1963 and later General Chung-hee Park won election as head of a civil government, but in 1972 he revised the constitution to permit his ruling indefinitely as a dictator backed by the army, police, and the Korean CIA. Increasingly he jailed cultural, religious, press, and political leaders in an effort to suppress all dissent. Meanwhile American economic aid ended while Seoul and other centers saw rapid material development; but rural poverty induced by population pressure could not quickly be relieved.

Mountainous North Korea, building upon the basic structure left from the Japanese period, had forged ahead industrially after 1945, but by the late 1960's was outdistanced by South Korea, with its greater population and resources including food supply and capital. The North remained militantly regimented under the fulsome personality cult of Kim Il-song, and warlike acts continued. American military aid to the South, including two United States divisions, also continued. The last Chinese forces in the North had been withdrawn in 1958, but the uneasy truce did not develop into a Korean peace settlement.

28.   The People's Republic in China

The Rise of the Maoist Leadership

The Chinese Communist Party (CCP) like the Comintern had at first regarded peasants in orthodox Marxist-Leninist fashion as capable only of auxiliary action. But Mao Tse-tung's famous report on the peasant movement in Hunan in February 1927 asserted heretically that the "revolutionary vanguard" in China was not the proletariat but the "poor peasantry." Mao soon learned from experience the necessity of combining peasant mass organization with military power. With Chu Teh as military commander and a few thousand men he took refuge in the winter of 1927–1928 in the mountainous Ching-kang-shan region on the Hunan-Kiangsi border, where he developed a territorial base in the traditional fashion of rebels. But Mao kept his movement ideologically orthodox in terminology. The Chinese Soviet Republic was proclaimed at Juichin, Kiangsi, in November 1931 as a "democratic dictatorship of the proletariat and peasantry," using Lenin's formula of 1905 in utterly different circumstances. The nonexistent "proletariat" was favored by excellent labor laws on paper. The Red Army was specially privileged as a political class army. Land was violently redistributed, but collectivization was not pushed.

Mao Tse-tung's ascendancy to leadership came only by degrees. It was delayed when the CCP Central Committee, dominated by young Moscow-returned students, abandoned Shanghai for Kiangsi in the autumn of 1932. Chiang Kai-shek's first four extermination campaigns, in late 1931, May–June and July–October 1932, and again in 1933 were checked by guerrilla tactics that drew KMT columns into the mountains. In late 1933–1934,

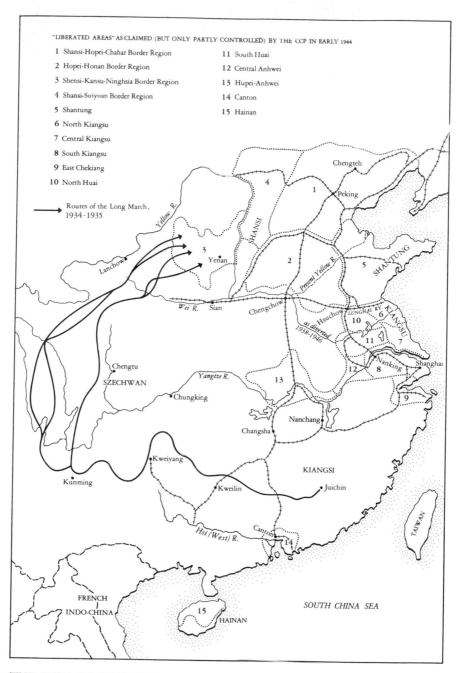

"LIBERATED AREAS" AS CLAIMED (BUT ONLY PARTLY CONTROLLED) BY THE CCP IN EARLY 1944

1 Shansi-Hopei-Chahar Border Region
2 Hopei-Honan Border Region
3 Shensi-Kansu-Ninghsia Border Region
4 Shansi-Suiyuan Border Region
5 Shantung
6 North Kiangsu
7 Central Kiangsu
8 South Kiangsu
9 East Chekiang
10 North Huai

11 South Huai
12 Central Anhwei
13 Hupei-Anhwei
14 Canton
15 Hainan

→ Routes of the Long March, 1934-1935

THE RISE OF THE CHINESE COMMUNISTS

however, a systematic, German-devised, KMT blockade and penetration along lines of blockhouses began to invade the Communist area. As a result, over 100,000 CCP personnel broke out of their Kiangsi redoubt in October 1934, moving swiftly by night on the Long March, a great and now legendary feat of human endurance that took them in one year some six thousand miles on foot, fighting continual battles along the way. Only in January 1935, when Chinese Communism was out of touch with Moscow, was the Moscow-trained element in the party obliged to acknowledge Mao's leadership. Even so, they continued to oppose his line in party councils for several years more.

The Yenan Period.   The CCP leaders and less than twenty thousand troops reached northern Shensi in 1935, making their headquarters at Yenan from the end of 1936. This arid, sun-drenched, dusty region of loess soil, fragmented by eroded gullies and not easily penetrated by wheeled vehicles, was defensible but generally lacking in water supply, surplus crops, and landlords. It formed a natural setting for a simple, egalitarian, do-it-yourself way of life, far from the ills of urbanism. The ten-year Yenan period gave Mao his opportunity and he put his stamp on a whole generation of the CCP leadership. When an enterprising American journalist, Edgar Snow, interviewed Mao and his colleagues after the Long March, he found a self-confident and even jovial band of veteran revolutionaries, whose homespun earthiness and evident devotion to the peasant's cause, brilliantly portrayed in *Red Star over China,* captured the imagination of readers around the world.

By 1937 it was plain that Chinese resistance to Japan would divert Japan from attacking Russia and Nanking from attacking the CCP. The Chinese Communists therefore joined the Nationalist government in a new united front, following Japan's attack near Peiping on July 7, 1937. This second effort at KMT-CCP cooperation was little more than an uneasy armed truce that began in an atmosphere of patriotic enthusiasm but soon deteriorated. CCP power now expanded in the wholly new context of a national war of resistance that in itself provided an urgent sanction for peasant mobilization in patriotic self-defense. The bases for organized resistance were centered in the less accessible border areas between provinces, beginning with the Shansi-Hopei-Chahar Border Region set up in 1938. By 1945 there were said to be nineteen such bases, mostly called "liberated areas," with a total population of 70 to 90 million, protected by about 2 million militia and by Communist armies claimed to total 910,000 troops. The Chinese Communists had expanded as the most effective leaders of peasant resistance to Japan in North China. The Nationalist government at Chungking, unable to compete on this level, blockaded the Yenan area.

During wartime the Communists temporarily abandoned their program of land confiscation in favor of rent reduction. Landlords were generally

WOODCUTS FROM NORTH
CHINA IN WARTIME: THE
ARMY AND THE PEOPLE.
*"Support Our Common
People's Own Army."
From top:
Peasants bring in flocks for
food and pack animals for
transport. They welcome
soldiers with music and a
banner, stand guard, provide
hot water to drink, carry the
wounded, give new recruits a
send-off, and care for the
disabled. Matching placards
at the serviceman's door
read, "Fine clothing and
sufficient food; a
well-established household."*

*"Marriage Registration." A couple arrange their own marriage in
modern style and sign the register on the k'ang-table of a local
official. Right: brick cooking stove, folded quilts.*

left in possession, guaranteed a reduced rent, and also allowed to vote in local elections. Instead of their former soviet system, the Communists announced direct elections by the so-called three-thirds system. They would confine their own representation to one-third of the offices and seek to retain Kuomintang and independent participation in the other two-thirds. The Communist movement and its Eighth Route Army prospered in proportion as the common people would willingly give them support in the free political competition of the war years, when the Japanese and their Chinese puppets as well as the Kuomintang offered some alternative to the Communist regime. The CCP's economic program included production drives both by troops and by farmers to achieve the self-sufficiency of each area in food supply. The improved seeds and techniques of Western-style scientific farming were largely lacking, but the Communists made up for this by their emphasis upon cooperation in land reclamation, labor exchange among farmers, mutual aid in transport, and small-scale industrial cooperatives. By bringing the farmers into associations for common ends and controlling these associations through leadership and propaganda, the CCP found a new road to political and military power.

Ideological Development.   Mao's three stated goals in 1940 were the pursuit of the united front with the KMT, armed struggle against Japan, and party-building in the CCP area. A fourth goal, less advertised, was to build a million-man army. The overall problem was to maintain long-term revolutionary aims while finding as many allies as possible in the effort to compete with the Nationalists, fight Japan, and reform China. The CCP united-front tactics became sophisticated, flexible, and efficient. They tried to isolate enemies, separating out all possible allies and neutrals, appealing to their interests and caring for their specific needs almost like ward politicians, and yet never compromising the ultimate independence of the CCP. "United-front cadres" in the KMT areas posed as non-Communists and never expected CCP help. Free China's cultural and political life was infiltrated by able, dedicated, and hard-working members who kept their secret faith in China's Communist future. Similarly the "friendly armies" program penetrated the KMT forces with military men who rose by merit. But the united front also fostered a wartime attitude of friendly cooperation and exemplary sacrifice in the common cause. Armed struggle could be integrally combined with the united front, against either Japanese invaders or KMT diehards, once they had been sufficiently isolated.

The third ingredient of CCP power was party-building. Membership grew from 40,000 in 1937 to 1,200,000 in 1945. Strenuous efforts were required to keep the CCP a disciplined, centrally controlled Leninist party. It was less than ever a party of the proletariat, even though peasants were now called "rural proletarians." Its activities were spread over a quarter of a

TROOPS AT FARM WORK. *Soldiers threshing with flails and a stone roller, stacking the straw, and storing bags of grain. Note basketball hoop, right rear.*

EXPLAINING NEW METHODS OF CHILDBIRTH. *An instructress points to the chart, stressing principles of hygiene and proper preparation for delivery.*

million square miles. Control could be exercised only by Communists working with proper ideological coordination, and so it was essential to indoctrinate the new cadres. For this purpose party schools processed thousands of students at Yenan.

In 1942 Mao inaugurated an ideological reform movement for "correcting unorthodox tendencies" *(cheng-feng)* in thought, in personal relations inside and outside the party, and in speech and writing. Prolonged criticism and self-criticism in small groups, confessions of guilt and repentance in public meetings, became standard procedures. The aim was to maintain the party's militancy during a united-front period and so keep it prepared for future tasks. This took a strenuous effort to re-educate and discipline new followers still contaminated by a liberal background, an individualistic temperament, or traditional morality.

This rectification campaign also marked the final elimination from CCP councils of the Moscow-returned "internationalists," trained by the Comintern, who had opposed Mao's leadership. It was now agreed that Marxist-Leninist theory had to be tested in action, be applied to rural China's concrete realities, and become a Marxism that had "taken on a national form." This became the basis of "Mao Tse-tung thought." It represented the Sinification of Communism in China, two decades after the Party's founding, in a period of wartime nationalism and minimal Russian influence. Henceforth it was no longer an alien creed. The principal achievement had been to build a Leninist party on a peasant base, demonstrating (contrary to Marxist theory) that the Communist order is in fact independent of the proletariat. This inversion of Marxism implied that a man's ideological tendencies did not come from his class affiliation, as posited by historical materialism. His class was now determined by his ideology; a bright peasant could become a "proletarian." This was a triumph of subjective and political considerations over the Marxist emphasis on the economic mode of production.

Mao's essay of 1940, "On the New Democracy," was a persuasive propaganda document that justified the united front as a temporary phase and yet reaffirmed the party's long-term mission. For the benefit of his non-Marxist audience Mao Tse-tung blandly claimed to have inherited the mantle of Sun Yat-sen and the May Fourth movement, while for Marxists he implicitly put himself on the level of Marx, Engels, Lenin, and Stalin as an original contributor to Communist theory. In actual fact Mao's "innovations" had been in the realm of practice, not theory. All his dicta could be found in earlier literature. His real contribution had been the creation of a party, an army, and mass support in a rural territorial base.

A new cult of the common people, stressing their "liberation," aimed at the awakening and activation of the Chinese peasant masses. The cultural movement stressed pictorial art in the form of the woodcut, which could be cheaply reproduced. Choral singing was combined with an ancient type of country dance to create a new art form in the *yang-ko* ("seedling song"), a poor man's opera that used folk tunes, a chain dance step, and the subject matter of everyday life to provide entertainment which indoctrinated as it liberated. The new creed of the common man embraced the revolutionary ideal that modern technology and a new social organization could be used to remake and enrich the life of the peasant. This cult of the common people animated the cadres and the military forces. The party worker had to live in the village, work with the peasant, eat his food, lead his life, think his thoughts. Only thus could he lead the masses in their regeneration. "Liberation" by the inexorable logic of events became also the sanction for the new party dictatorship: 1) the revolution aimed to give the masses a new life; 2) this could be achieved only through absolute political power, sufficient to change the old order; 3) political power could be achieved only through organization in a centralized party; 4) a party could be effective only if its members submitted to absolute party discipline. The party took on the character of an ongoing, living entity with a historic mission, transcendent over individuals.

The CCP's Seventh Congress in April–June 1945, the first since 1928, perfected its strategy for the postwar period by adopting the flexible line of "coalition government." After the New Fourth Army incident of January 1941, when Nationalist troops had fought a CCP force south of the Yangtze, the government had blockaded the CCP area more intensively. A general fear arose in China that World War II would be followed by civil war. Mao now declared that China needed a "new democratic government of a coalition nature embracing all parties and nonpartisan representatives." Depending on expediency, this could mean a coalition including the Kuomintang, as was to be proposed in 1946, or a coalition with minor parties and liberals against the Kuomintang, as was to be achieved in 1949. Meanwhile this line appealed particularly to modern-minded but frustrated intellectuals.

The KMT-CCP Civil War. During World War II, General Joseph Stilwell as Chiang Kai-shek's nominal chief of staff had trained Chinese troops in India for the reconquest of North Burma, while United States airpower supplied by the Hump airlift had protected cities and harassed Japanese forces in China. But the Allied attack on Japan by-passed China, going more directly by sea, and the main result of American aid was to give the politically enfeebled Nationalist government superior armaments and a sense of overconfidence with which to face the CCP after 1945. General George C. Marshall as a special envoy to China mediated during 1946 to arrange a coalition government, but the Nationalist generals (and Stalin too) overrated the efficacy of Nationalist firepower, while Mao and the CCP pushed ahead with popular mobilization and civil war. After 1946 Ameri-

THE PROBLEM OF
DISTRIBUTION IN
CHINA IN THE 1940's.
*The well-nourished
woman sits in front of a
grain shop; the beggar
boy has come into
town from a famine
area.*

can forces were withdrawn, and Secretary of State Marshall in Washington abstained from intervention.

The Chinese civil war from 1946 to 1949 was one of the big struggles of modern times. At the beginning the Nationalists had about 3 million troops, mostly with modern arms including American-supplied trucks, tanks, and planes. The main lack was a cause to inspire the common soldier. Chiang Kai-shek, contrary to experienced advice, persisted in reoccupying provincial centers in the North and Northeast, where his garrisons were soon cut off and dependent on air supplies. The Communists meanwhile began with about a million men, but gained steadily in men and American equipment from Nationalist surrenders. Maneuvering in the countryside, mobilizing the villages, destroying Nationalist rail communications, but avoiding unfavorable terms of battle, the CCP field armies grew in size and power. They were aided by the mobilized logistic support of some millions of peasants who could both destroy railways and substitute for them, as well as dig tank traps and report the results.

The Nationalist debacle in 1947–1949 was a failure less of arms than of aims. Chiang's forces had superior arms but no capacity for economic revival, no program for popular mobilization, no new vision of China's future. Urban populations in the KMT areas were increasingly demoralized by skyrocketing inflation. Collapse came from many causes: Whampoa-Kwangsi jealousies among commanders, defensiveness and hoarding of resources in warlord style, corruption in handling of supplies, distrust between officers and men, the Generalissimo's determination to mastermind tactics from a distance. By mid-1948 the Communists equaled the Nationalists in numbers. In October they forced the surrender of the large garrisons in the Northeast, and, by January 1949, of large forces surrounded on the Hsuchow plain north of Nanking. In January the Communists entered Tientsin and Peking, in April Nanking, in May Shanghai, in October Canton, in November Chungking. By May 1950 their victory was complete. Chiang Kai-shek and part of the KMT leadership withdrew to Taiwan. In the midst of these events the People's Republic of China was proclaimed at Peking on October 1, 1949.

Founding the People's Republic

Political Organization. After twenty-eight years of trial and error on the road to power, the CCP had acquired the experience, vision, and self-confidence to start creating a new China. The early 1950's recalled the great epochs of reorganization when a new dynasty like the Ming swept out foreign influence, surveyed the land and people, and put the empire in order. Continuities with the past, however, were less striking than innovations, creative adaptations of what the modern world, especially the Soviet Union, had to offer.

The military take-over left in office most local administrators. The Communist cadres gave it a festive air, dancing the *yang-ko* in the streets, proclaiming peace and liberation. It was a hopeful honeymoon period, devoted to getting rid of the residual Kuomintang influence, supplanting it with a coalition government, and reforming China's armies, foreign relations, and economic system.

Mao defined the new government as a democratic coalition under Communist leadership at the same time that it was a dictatorship directed against the reactionary classes or "enemies of the people." Thus the Chinese "people's democratic dictatorship" would attempt in united-front style to line up the broadest possible support for the regime and at the same time eliminate its foes. Any individual could be transferred by a stroke of the pen to the category of enemy of the people; this provided a flexible basis for sifting out dissident members of the population.

The new central administration under Chou En-lai as prime minister left several minor parties in existence, though without much following, and gave posts of prominence to non-Communists in order to carry out the idea of coalition government. It was essential to use the training and ability of that major part of the upper class that had never been Communist.

Liberal intellectuals were therefore given scope for their talents and placed in high positions, interlarded in the ministries with party members who lacked their abilities but were more reliable. The larger part of the Western-returned scholars, as patriots, were devoted to their country's future. Long since estranged from the Kuomintang, they saw no alternative but to co-operate with the CCP.

The Communists, like the Kuomintang, set up a tripod of power—party, government, and army, each forming a separate echelon but tied together by the Communist leadership. The party grew to 2.7 million members by 1947, to 6.1 million by 1953, to 14 million by 1959, to 17 million by 1961, and some 28 million by 1973. The Central Committee grew to include ninety-four members and ninety-three alternates as of 1962, but power was exercised by its Political Bureau of nineteen members and ultimately by this bureau's Standing Committee of some seven persons. Below the Central Committee the party structure descended through roughly eight levels, the principal ones being 6 regional bureaus; 28 provincial or big-city committees; 258 special district committees; 2200 county *(hsien)* or similar committees; some 26,000 commune committees after 1958; and more than 1 million branch committees in the villages, factories, schools, army, or other units.

The party structure was paralleled by the government structure that its members interpenetrated. People's Representative Congresses were set up in a hierarchy from the village on up to the National People's Congress at Peking, first convened in 1954. These congresses provided an arena for popular participation in "democratic centralism" but had no real power. The government structure was reorganized in 1954 when the new constitution (to be distinguished from the new party constitution of 1956) diminished the role of non-Communists and strengthened that of the prime minister. Chou En-lai now headed a State Council which included as many as sixteen vice premiers and the heads of some seventy ministries or similar bodies. Administration was divided into major functional systems which handled political and legal (internal) affairs; propaganda and education (cultural matters); agriculture, forestry, and water conservation (rural work); industry and communications; finance and trade. Each of these systems was supervised both by an office of the State Council and by an office of the party Central Committee. "Vertical rule" extending downward through lower-level branch agencies was balanced by "dual rule" when such branch agencies were also coordinated through committees operating laterally at a given level in the hierarchy. Foreign affairs and military affairs were also handled by functional systems.

In all operations the party set the policy and the government agencies carried it out. The party also had its members in most of the key administrative posts, and its regional, provincial, and local party committees could supervise as they coordinated action at the various levels. Within each government agency party members had their own organization in committees and branches, and the leading party members formed a top group or "party fraction."

Parallel to the party and government were the new nationwide mass organizations. These had originated during the KMT-CCP collaboration of the 1920's, but the KMT had let them wither away. For example, the All China Federation of Trade Unions founded in 1922 claimed a membership of over 13 million in 1956. Similar organizations were set up for Democratic Women (76 million members in 1953); Democratic Youth (34 million in 1957); Cooperative Workers, that is peasants in cooperatives (162 million in 1956); and for intellectuals, students, Young Pioneers, and so on. These mass organizations reached the individual in his professional or social role, among his peers, in ways that the government could not. Each had broad programs and an extensive administrative apparatus. Half the adult population was thus brought into one or another action group and its program of meetings, study, and agitation. Big training programs with schools and indoctrination centers served to recruit activist personnel. The mass organizations, bridging the immemorial gap between populace and officialdom, helped to politicize the formerly apolitical populace and applied the concept of the "mass line": that the CCP leadership must be guided by constant contact with the worker-peasant masses, first securing from the party workers full and accurate reports as to the masses' problems and opinions, then issuing policy directives to meet these problems, and finally getting the masses to adopt the policies as their own and carry them out. In effect, this was an effort to indoctrinate and manipulate the climate of opinion. When coordinated in each locality, this whole apparatus could bring to bear upon every individual a pervasive and overwhelming public pressure.

The mechanism to apply this pressure was the campaign or movement, which might appear to start spontaneously but developed only as the Central Committee decreed. Campaigns quickly set in motion the enormous new apparatus of party, state, and mass organizations and directed hammer blows against one target after another among the various classes and their habits and institutions.

Standing behind this apparatus for revolutionary change were well-paid security forces and secret services. Local police stations also supervised the street committees, whose duty it was to promote not only welfare measures but also mutual surveillance and denunciation among neighbors and within families. The street committees disposed informally of conflicts arising among individuals. The police stations settled more serious cases or if necessary passed them on to the hierarchy of "people's courts," where criminal cases normally came to trial only after the accused had been thoroughly interrogated, without benefit of counsel, had fully confessed, and had denounced any others concerned. Since law expressed the revolutionary policy of the party, it remained largely uncodified and changeable. The legal profession was not developed. Justice was weighted on the side of the state, to be secured by applying universal principles to the circumstances in each case, with a minimum of procedure. Litigation was disesteemed, legislation unimportant. Although law codes remained unpublished, the norms of conduct were of course made known through political indoctrination. In all this there were many echoes of Chinese tradition. "Reform through labor" in state factories and work camps followed Soviet organization but reflected the ancient Chinese belief that individual conduct could be reformed through indoctrination and social pressure.

Economic Reconstruction. In 1949 Mao proclaimed a "shift to the cities" and the need to learn from the Soviet example in industrialization. The CCP had inherited three economic sectors: the subsistence economy of the countryside, the separately based, foreign-trade-and-industry economy of the treaty ports, and finally the Northeast (which foreigners had called Manchuria) as a heavy industry base created by the Japanese in an underdeveloped area. One task was to organize these three economies into one.

A first aim was to get production back to its prewar level. In the Northeast, the Soviet occupation had removed more than half the capital equipment, worth at least 2 billion American dollars. In China proper, railroads had been torn up, urban labor demoralized. Wartime blockades between city and country had increased rural self-sufficiency; market crops like cotton had to be revived. Some 9 million persons were on government rations or payrolls (including minor Nationalist administrative and military personnel). The regime still had to expand its note issue to meet a budget deficit of perhaps 75 per cent. Shanghai prices rose seventy times in nine months from May 1949 to February 1950.

The first move toward quelling the inflation was to get the budget more or less balanced by increasing revenue, first in the countryside by collecting agricultural taxes in kind, then in the cities through devices like a sales tax on each major commodity and business taxes set by "democratic appraisal" of trade associations to squeeze money out of the more monetized sector of the economy. Secondly, the entire fiscal administration was reorganized to give the central government control over formerly local taxes, to eliminate the handling of official funds by private banks, and generally to reduce expenditures. By taking over the banks, the government got control of money and credit and it set up six government trading corporations to dominate prices in major consumer commodities.

One device for restoring confidence was to express wages, salaries, bank deposits, some government payments, and bond issues in terms of commodity units (commodity "basket" values), defined in quantities of goods

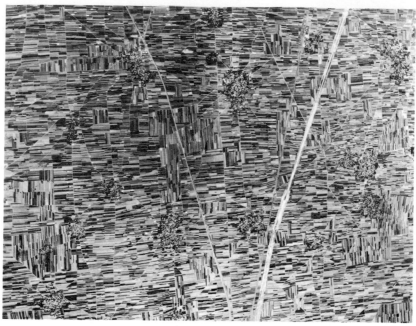

PATTERNS OF TRADITIONAL LAND USE, NORTH AND SOUTH. *Top: Aerial view of villages, fields, footpaths, and cart roads on the densely populated North China Plain, before the land reform of the 1950's. Curved railway on left avoids the villages. Bottom: Aerial view of long, narrow, irrigated rice fields in Kiangsu, north of Yangtze River. Village houses and trees are in strips on dikes along major canals. Transportation is by water.*

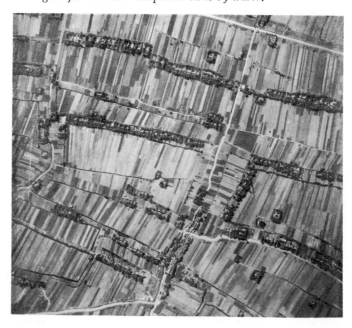

of daily use rather than in monetary prices. A typical unit might be composed of certain quantities of rice, flour, coal, and white shirting. As prices rose, the commodity-based unit would rise accordingly in money terms. Paid in this unit, one was protected against further inflation. Thus, in brief, by a variety of methods designed to achieve a balance between the supply of goods and the flow of money income, the inflation was conquered by mid-1950. It was an impressive achievement.

By 1952 the three sectors of the old economy had been given greater unity than ever before. Railway track had been rebuilt and even expanded from about 10,000 miles to 15,000, and highways had been reopened to make a total of about 75,000 miles. A centralized banking system and single uniform currency now covered the country. Budgeting could be attempted realistically for the first time. Private enterprise was permitted to continue in form, but in fact it was brought increasingly under state control. By controlling credit and raw materials and monopolizing key commodities, the state could now dominate production and commerce, in addition to having outright control of most heavy industry, railways, and foreign trade. The one other thing necessary was to achieve the traditional goal of controlling the surplus production of the land.

The nationwide land reform, begun in mid-1950 and completed by early 1953, was not merely economic in aim but also social and political. A work team of cadres coming to a village first identified out-and-out enemies, if necessary got them out of the way, and then explained the desirability of land reform to the poor peasantry and identified active elements to lead the forthcoming movement. After this preparation a period of "class struggle" was inaugurated. In "struggle meetings" the accumulated grievances of the populace could be brought forth in "speaking bitterness" or "settling accounts." Unpopular landlords or "local despots" could be either killed, expelled, or brought to confess and reform, while the entire community committed themselves to the new order by taking violent measures.

The next phase was to create peasants' associations that by a process of community assent could work out the definition of class status for each individual as landlord, rich peasant, middle peasant, poor peasant, or farm laborer and could carry on the classification, confiscation, and redistribution of landholdings. The resulting "equalization of land tenure" was in the old tradition of peasant rebellions. Generally the remnants of the landlord gentry were wiped out either in person or in status, while the party representatives established their authority. The tiller now had title to his land.

This "new democracy" phase of private ownership had been advertised in 1950 to last for a "rather long time," but in fact it lasted no longer for the farmer than it had for the capitalist. The regime moved without delay toward the construction of the new collectivist agrarian system. The reform moved gradually from north to south through a series of planned phases, first setting up temporary, usually seasonal, small-scale mutual-aid teams, then larger permanent ones, and then agricultural producers' cooperatives in which the peasants began to cultivate in common and share a common product in proportion to their pooled contributions of land, equipment, and labor. The cooperatives were still posited on private ownership of land and voluntary cooperation for mutual benefit. However, the goal began to shift. Soon it was argued that only full-scale collectivization could effect the increase in agricultural product necessary to pay for industrialization.

Social Change.   China's traditional ancestor reverence, family-clan cohesiveness, and filial piety had long been eroding. Communist "liberation" furthered the process. By the new marriage law of 1950, women were given full equality with men in rights of marriage, divorce, and property ownership. This acknowledged the portentous but little studied emancipation of Chinese women, a secular change that had been accelerating throughout the century. As a symbolic deathblow to the old family system, children were now commended for denouncing their parents, thus spectacularly reversing the ancient stress on filial piety as the highest virtue. Extended family ties were disparaged as feudal, and romantic love as bourgeois. The new state tried to displace the Chinese extended family system as the focus of one's primary loyalty, leaving the nuclear family as the norm, much as in industrial-urbanized societies.

Mobilization of the populace was made easier in late 1950 by the Korean War. Reports of China's early victories and later of alleged germ warfare by the United States provided a useful sanction for destroying the generally favorable Chinese image of America. Two major campaigns were mounted, to "resist America, aid Korea," and to "suppress counterrevolutionaries." They called for patriotic spying on relatives and neighbors, public denunciation even of parents, and consignment of enemies of the people to "reform through labor." Execution of such enemies, together with persons condemned by "people's courts" in the land reform, were in the hundreds of thousands, some say many millions. The honeymoon was over.

In this context of terror and patriotism, foreign missionaries were denounced as spies and jailed or expelled. A "three-self" movement was set going, for "self-government, self-support, and self-propagation" of the Christian church in China, free of the missionaries' alleged "cultural imperialism." "National churches" free of foreign ties were finally set up. By 1958, the "three-self" movement unified the worship of all Christian denominations in each locality.

The campaign mechanism for mobilizing public pressure against designated types of individual conduct was used more and more plainly for refashioning China's social structure. The "three-anti" and "five-anti" movements of 1951–1952 were organized very thoroughly with standardized methods. The "three-anti" campaign was directed against officialdom, and was anticorruption, antiwaste, and antibureaucratism—plainly an attempt to weed out and invigorate the vast administrative apparatus inherited from the KMT and rapidly added to since 1949. The "five-anti" movement was a similarly concerted attack on merchants and manufacturers (the bourgeoisie) and was specifically against bribery, tax evasion, theft of state assets, cheating in labor or materials, and stealing of state economic intelligence. As in all campaigns, the public was mobilized, committees established, and appearances created of great popular initiative, righteous anger, and enthusiasm for the triumph of virtue. Confessions, apologies, and the reform or elimination of culprits by suicide, execution, or labor camp followed. Large sums were also squeezed out of the business class.

Building upon methods used in Yenan to Leninize the party (as well as to convert Japanese war prisoners), Liu Shao-ch'i and other organizers developed empirical procedures of thought reform to deal with every type of enemy or supporter. When Americans taken prisoner in the Korean War "confessed" to germ warfare and collaborated with their Chinese captors, they were responding to techniques developed through use with Chinese of all sorts, including party members. These so-called "brainwashing" procedures applied to prisoners were the extreme example of what in a more normal form was the real Communist effort at revolution, to change Chinese thinking and behavior.

Thought reform generally had certain common features: control of the individual's personal environment and of the information available to him (this was now true of the whole country); the stimuli of idealism and of terror intermixed; and a grim psychological experience, undergone with guidance through successive phases and intensified by the manipulation of one's sense of guilt or shame. The Chinese slang term "brainwashing" imparted perhaps too much mystery to a process faintly visible elsewhere in religious crusades of the past, only now more thoroughly organized. Psychologists can explain how privation, prolonged insecurity, and tension, combined with extended fatigue and repetitive indoctrination, can shatter the individual's sense of inner identity and create pressures from which the only escape for many is submission to authority. For the Chinese student class, from whom the CCP had to get its cadres, this intellectual-emotional reconditioning was carried out in the big revolutionary colleges set up as part of the new educational system.

A center of this type containing about four thousand students might be subdivided into classes of one or two hundred and then into study groups of six to ten persons. A typical six-month course of thought reform might consist of three stages. First, group identification, a period of togetherness and considerable freedom and enthusiasm. During this stage major Marxist-Leninist-Maoist concepts were studied and a free exchange of views, with a feeling of common effort, led the trainee to expose himself freely in a "thought mobilization."

The second phase was one of induced emotional conflict within each individual. The daily schedule continued to be physically exhausting. The milieu, carefully controlled behind the scenes, now seemed to close in. The individual began to feel under pressure as criticism and self-criticism intensified and the dangers of being rejected became apparent. The evils within the old individual were now attacked, not merely the old society in the abstract, and the student strove to dig up his failings and correct them. He might struggle with himself and be "struggled with" by his group-mates over an excess of subjectivism or objectivism, of opportunism or dogmatism, of bureaucratism or individual heroism, and so forth. Each participant, whether or not he resisted, felt completely alone. He soon felt guilt (he should be punished) and also a sense of shame. He was thus prepared to achieve a psychological catharsis through confession and self-condemnation.

The third phase was that of submission and rebirth. When his final thought summary or confession had been gone over and accepted, the individual was likely to feel exhilarated, cleansed, a new person. He had been manipulated so that the wellsprings of his own nature had put him under intense emotional pressure, and the relief from this self-induced tension was associated with the external authority of the party, on whom he should henceforth be dependent. The party's aim was not only to secure control over disciplined activists but also to raise the quality of their performance by changing their goals and values. They renounced family and father, and accepted the party and the revolution in their place.

In the case of older intellectuals, particularly returned students from the West, criticism, self-criticism, and confession could only be an overlay of the formative experience of a mature person. When Peking professors denounced the corrupting influence of the bourgeois West, the net effect was perhaps less to change these individuals than to align them in the public eye as supporters of the new order. Thus the one class who might have represented a Western non-Communist influence neutralized themselves.

Out of the Chinese inheritance, authoritarian traditions could be invoked for modern purposes. One point of resonance was the concept of the unity of theory and practice. Lenin held that theory must be applied in activity, as an effort not only to understand the world but to change it. Or as Mao said, "We must unify appropriately the general truth of Marxism with the concrete practice of the Chinese revolution." Confucian scholars, particularly Wang Yang-ming (1472–1529), had attacked the dualism of knowledge and action, holding that the completely sincere man must express his moral perceptions in equally moral conduct. Confucianist self-cultivation meant that knowledge is realized in action and action contributes to knowledge.

While Confucian self-cultivation was not a group affair, it stressed the possibility of morally improving human nature, the ancient Chinese belief that through proper ethical instruction and exhortation, man can be made into a more social being. The gap between individual self-cultivation and group self-criticism is a very broad one in fact but the two have something in common. Thought reform at Yenan made use of traditional Chinese terminology and invoked Confucian sanctions. The good Communist, according to Liu Shao-ch'i, must discipline himself through self-cultivation, through "watching himself when alone," so as to become flexibly and resourcefully obedient to the party's leadership. Thus where Confucianism had instilled loyalty to family, father, and emperor, Maoism now diverted it to the people, the party, and the leader. The Classics were quoted for this purpose.

Soviet Aid.   Having early in 1949 proclaimed his policy of "leaning to one side" against "capitalist imperialism," Mao Tse-tung spent nine weeks of hard bargaining in Moscow and in February 1950 signed a thirty-year Sino-Soviet alliance treaty. It seems unlikely that Peking expected to join in the Soviet-armed North Korean aggression of June 1950 against South Korea. Instead, the CCP evidently hoped to seize Taiwan from the Nationalists, but this was prevented when President Truman ordered the American Seventh Fleet to stop invasion either way across the Taiwan Strait. Impelled by strategic concern for the industrial base in Manchuria, Peking entered the Korean War in force only after the American–United Nations forces had advanced northward across the 38th parallel. Divisions of General Lin Piao's Fourth Field Army, labeled as "volunteers," crossed the Yalu in late 1950. As we have noted in the preceding chapter, they were able to catch the Yalu-bound American columns in the flank and force a precipitous American retreat from North Korea. While truce negotiations began in July 1951 and went on for two years until July 1953, fighting continued and the Chinese forces in Korea, now under General P'eng Te-huai, were built up with heavy Soviet weapons. The People's Liberation Army also invaded Tibet in October 1950 and in a year-long campaign reasserted Chinese control. Afterward, China's military modernization used Soviet models and assistance. A professional officer corps was created in Soviet style to run a regular army of about 2.5 million men.

Soviet aid came only at a price. In 1950 Sino-Soviet "joint-stock" companies were set up, on the model used in Eastern Europe, for the development of mining in Sinkiang and similar purposes. However, after the death of Stalin in 1953 these were liquidated, and the Soviets also gradually gave up their special position in the Northeast on the main railway and at the Port Arthur naval base.

In industrialization the Soviet example and expertise were at first China's greatest inspiration. Thousands of Chinese trainees went to the U.S.S.R., and thousands of Russian technicians came to help with hundreds of industrial projects. Aided by Soviet loans, China's prewar pattern of foreign trade was reversed, flowing to the Soviet bloc instead of to the West and Japan. China received essential help in technology, unknown amounts of military hardware, and capital equipment but went into debt accordingly. The loans were repaid in raw materials.

China's capacity to follow the Stalinist Russian industrial model was inhibited by certain specific conditions. China in the early 1950's was actually closer to the Russia of 1900 than to the Soviet Union of 1928 when the five-year plans began. Russia in 1900 already had a higher per capita production of pig iron, steel, and cotton goods, and more railroad track per square mile, than China in 1952, together with a larger corps of modern-educated technical and professional manpower and a more developed educational system. The Soviet model, which stressed heavy industry at the expense of the peasant, was thus not really suited to China's situation. China's superabundance of people (estimated by the census of 1953 at 583 million and increasing about 12 to 14 million yearly), together with the comparative lack of new land for cultivation, meant that China's population would press upon the food supply even more than Russia's had.

The Struggle Toward Socialism

China's revolution has tried, most basically, to make peasants into citizens, to bring the masses into politics. But the Chinese village is not yet part of automobile civilization. Its concerns have come down from a simpler age: how to produce enough and how to distribute it. Next to famine and disease, the ancient enemy has been the ruling class—the privileged few whose education and connections gave them access to land and office. Since the ruling class generally governed the villages from the towns and cities, Mao's problem after taking power was how to reach the village to revolutionize it. If he could not reach and change them, the villagers would retain the ancient ideas that sanctioned the ruling class—for example, that acquiring an education qualifies one to rule others—and thus the old village would remain ready to accept a new ruling class. The Maoist revolution, to remake the society by remaking the people, thus became a semicontrolled process of struggle, between ideas, behavior patterns, and the interests of classes.

One feature of the revolution was the fusion of morality and politics, such that a policy mistake was a moral crime, on the ancient Confucian assumption that conduct is character made manifest or, in Marxist terms, that theory and practice interact. This unity of ideas and action could be achieved (or at least aimed at), in the People's Republic as under imperial Confucianism, because moral-ideological authority and political power were combined. Since theory and practice in this Chinese view interpenetrate, ideology must also constantly shift in its application to events as they unfold.

Another feature of Mao's thought was a stress on contradictions as the stuff of the dialectical process of conflict: for example, contradictions of socialism and imperialism in the outer world, of the needs of industry and those of agriculture within China, of proletarian and bourgeois tendencies within oneself, of freedom and discipline, democracy and centralism, and so on in all aspects of life. Contradictions when perceived lead to struggle, eventual polarization, and resolution in a new unity. Thus one struggle only led to another without any end to the process, which Mao aptly called "continuing revolution," a way of life. What a contrast with the old Confucian ideal of harmony!

Agriculture versus Industry. Land reform together with controls over the urban and industrial sector put Peking by 1953 in a position to plan for both industrialization and agricultural collectivization. The swelling cities would increase their demand for agricultural products. Industrialization would also necessitate imports of Soviet-bloc capital goods, to be paid for again by agricultural products. To extract more from the farm economy, a squeezing mechanism had to be created in the form of true collectives. While these might lower incentives, they seemed the only sure way to enforce saving and check the revival of a "rich peasant" class.

The initial move toward collectivization got results faster than anticipated. Fifteen per cent of the farm land and families were in agricultural producers' cooperatives by mid-1955. Mao Tse-tung spent several weeks touring major provinces, testing local sentiment, and then called for 250 million peasants to form 2 million agricultural producers' cooperatives of fifty families each (say two cooperatives in each of a million or so villages). This bold plan, pushed by eager cadres, again went faster than expected. By May 1956, nine-tenths of the peasantry were reported to have joined cooperatives. They were quickly asked to move on to the higher level of socialized agriculture by giving up their shares in the cooperatives (which had varied according to their contributions) and becoming wage laborers on full collective farms. Unlike the disastrous Soviet collectivization of 1929–1932, collectivization in China did not lead directly to state ownership but to ownership by the individual cooperatives, which bought the land from the peasant owners. The program at its successive stages had evidently produced sufficient results to obviate resistance—at least very little was reported. China's peasantry saw no alternative but to have faith in Chairman Mao and the party, even though the New Democracy had now run its course in only five years. Unlike Lenin, Mao had begun with the villages, not the cities, and all anti-Communist leadership had been eliminated.

The cooperatives developed forthwith into fully collective farms. One or two to a village, they now served as the new focus of village life, undertaking the local public works and welfare activities which under the empire had been the function of gentry leadership. Where the local Confucian degree-holders of the big families—a conservative-minded and often exploitative elite—had traditionally taken the initiative to repair temples and bridges or maintain schools and charities, it was now the local cooperative or collective farm chairman, usually an enthusiastic party appointee, who initiated projects for reforestation, combating erosion, care of the aged, improving the local dispensary, introducing pumps or new plows, or pushing literacy. Ambitious plans set forth bright promises: to see cultural amenities introduced, the multitude of diseases and all flood and drought eliminated, forests widely planted, labor fully employed. Equally ambitious was the long-term plan to control the Yellow River by a "staircase" of forty-six dams on the main stream, plus hydroelectric power and multipurpose projects. For the farm boy just learning to read, this confident vision was undoubtedly inspiring. For doubters and dissenters there was plainly announced "reform through labor."

Meanwhile preparation for a Soviet-type forced-draft industrial development had gone forward with the nationalization of banking, industry, and trade. The conflict between the development of agriculture and industry, and the consequent subordination of the former, was apparent in the first five-year plan targets announced in 1955 (for the five years 1953–1957): steel to be quadrupled, power and cement doubled, but cotton piece goods to be increased by less than one-half and food grains by less than one-fifth. The farmer's product would be taken from him indirectly as well as by outright collection of crops and taxes. Just as men had been cheaper than armament in Chinese warfare, so in her agricultural development China would have to stress capital-cheap, labor-intensive projects like flood control dikes and irrigation ditches. Pigs could be multiplied to provide both food and manure, but chemical fertilizers were likely to be limited. Meanwhile capital investment was to be concentrated in heavy industry. The Maoist enthusiasts who now dominated the CCP Central Committee envisioned that the people's productive energies would be psychologically liberated and incentive devices such as emulation campaigns would achieve "quantity, speed, quality, and economy" of production all at once. This forced-draft industrialization eventually did channel something like 30 per cent of the Chinese people's gross national product through the government, which used approximately one-half of it for investment. China's industrial growth seemed rapid and formidable—as of 1957, the fastest of any underdeveloped Asian country.

In this period also, the railroad was extended in the Northwest to Outer Mongolia and over the desert road to Turkestan. These lines, accompanied by migration, opened up the arid Inner Asian frontier for greater exploitation and also had political-strategic importance, strengthening the revived Chinese grip on Inner Mongolia and Sinkiang.

Intellectuals and Cadres. "Socialist construction" required the mobilization of everyone, including the thin stratum of about 100,000 technical, professional, and academic "higher intellectuals" who were still mainly Western-oriented. The party heads believed, optimistically, that they had by this time "spiritually transformed" this stratum and won its allegiance; but they were concerned that the new party apparatus had stifled intellectual life. Campaigns were therefore mounted in 1956–1957 to manipulate these two strategic elements, intellectuals and cadres.

A campaign for freer criticism of the cadres and bureaucracy was begun in May 1956 under the classical slogan, "Let a hundred flowers bloom together; let the hundred schools of thought contend." This was not a clarion call for free speech. Criticism was not to overstep the implicit limits of complete devotion to the party's final authority. In the aftermath of the Hungarian rising of October–November 1956 and its suppression by Russia, which coincided with signs of discontent in China, Mao announced in 1957 his doctrine of contradictions—some "antagonistic" as between the regime and its "enemies," and some "nonantagonistic," normal and arguable, as between the bureaucracy and "the people." Within this framework he hoped that a continuing struggle over the execution of policy, using his method of "unity-criticism-unity," could be healthily pursued and yet contained. As in the Yenan period, this dialectical process would call forth criticism and then would meet it. Repeated invitations eventually released a surprising torrent of publicly expressed dissatisfaction on the part of intellectuals and the professionally trained elite with the CCP's totalitarian political system, its ideas, aims, and methods. This startled the party in the late spring of 1957 and was harshly suppressed. The recent critics were soon obliged to accuse themselves publicly and condemn one another in an "antirightist" campaign.

Meanwhile the Central Committee faced the even more serious problem of controlling the enormous apparatus of cadres that executed its policies. The twin drives in agriculture and industry had achieved spectacular results. The face of the country was changed with new roads, factories, cities, dikes, dams, lakes, afforestation, and cultivation, for which the 650 millions of China had been mobilized in nationwide efforts of unparalleled intensity and magnitude. An enormous apparatus of many millions of activists was needed to do the party's work, yet it was largely unseasoned and inexperienced. Four-fifths of the party members probably lacked a high school education. Young cadres fresh from their indoctrination might easily fall into the evils of "blind optimism," "dogmatism," and "commandism," or of "conservatism," "empiricism," and "blind opportunism," instead of manipulating the peasantry correctly through discussion, logic, and persuasion. Cadres could be stimulated by Mao's ideological pronouncements more easily than they could be given wisdom, or saved from the corruption and false reporting that has inveterately characterized peasant-official relations in the past. Agricultural collectivization had in fact proceeded with considerable friction. The peasantry had been widely misled by the cadres' false promises.

Roused by the danger of being "out of touch with the masses," the CCP inaugurated in April 1957 a great ideological campaign for "rectification" of the party cadres' working style, parallel to the campaign to induce criticism from the intellectuals. Both groups were also brought into a big campaign for "downward transfer," *hsia-fang,* to move teachers, students, and city cadres and functionaries into the countryside so that by manual labor among the villagers they could avoid "separation from the masses" and could also help agricultural production.

The Frenzy of 1958. When the Central Committee met in September 1957, it faced a crucial problem. "Socialist transformation" had given the new state-and-party apparatus an effective control over the economy, and party committees at all levels now made economic decisions. But red tape had grown faster than production. Collectivization had not actually increased the agricultural product received by the regime, which faced a dire problem of agricultural stagnation. During 1952–1957 city population grew about 30 per cent, but government grain collections hardly grew at all. The Soviet model of taxing agriculture to build industry was facing a dead end.

To meet this crisis, the strategy of a Great Leap Forward was adopted in 1958 to achieve development in the modern industrial sector and the rural agricultural sector as two distinct though related processes. In the villages, mass mobilization would make use of rural labor never before fully employed: first, for irrigation, flood control, and land reclamation; second, to raise productivity per unit of land by using more hands; and third, to expand small-scale rural industries with materials and equipment locally available. It was hoped that this rural development, using China's abundance of manpower, would not need much help from the modern industrial sector, which would put its product into exports for securing capital goods or into investment in further plant construction.

The Great Leap was to take advantage of China's rural backwardness and manpower surplus and realize the Maoist faith that ideological incentives could get economic results, that a new spirit could unlock hitherto untapped sources of human energy. Since the professional economists, like other intellectuals, had suffered downgrading as a result of the Hundred Flowers Campaign, the overambitious targets of the Great Leap were formulated in each locality, not by economists, but by cadres inspired by emulation and often contemptuous of experts. One spectacular way to localize industry was to set up small backyard iron smelters that would involve farmers in metallurgy (even though the metal produced often turned out unusable). As the campaign developed, there was a general decentralization of economic planning and management. The central statistical bureau was broken up and

FARMERS IN INDUSTRY. *Small-scale local iron smelters such as were widely constructed during the Great Leap Forward of 1958.*

localized. As a result of reporting by untrained local enthusiasts, the statistical bureau claimed that in 1958 production of food crops and cotton had nearly doubled in one year. The leadership became a captive of its own claims. The incredible figures that the Central Committee trumpeted abroad had to be humiliatingly withdrawn in the late summer of 1959.

The Great Leap got mixed results. Through sheer muscle power, it changed the face of China with tens of thousands of reservoirs, thousands of hydroelectric power stations, hundreds of miles of railways, bridges over the great rivers, new canals and highways, more mines, more irrigated land. But this all-out effort at instant growth led to massive errors, such as the salinization of newly irrigated land, and a tremendous wasting of manpower, which was withdrawn from agriculture.

The commune was an integral part of the Great Leap, based on the mass-line idea of the release of the "spontaneous initiative of the masses." A typical commune was formed by amalgamating a number of agricultural producers' cooperatives of the higher stage, that is, collective farms. The commune included local government functions, both military and security, as well as local trade, finance, taxation, accounting, statistics, and planning, all under party control. It was divided into production brigades and teams, a production team corresponding to the old cooperative, perhaps half a village. Private plots were taken over. Peasants were to eat in large mess halls, although this was apparently seldom achieved, and all labor to be controlled. Farmer battalions marched like shock troops to attack new production goals while women took their places in the fields. This grandiose concept was pursued with great fanfare and utopian fervor. The result, it was hoped, would be agricultural cities with the peasants proletarianized and uprooted from their own land.

This revolution collapsed from general overwork and exhaustion, the damaging of incentives, and the incapacities of management. When an egalitarian wage system was instituted, paying each according to his needs, it lowered productivity. So did shifting labor about like military platoons within the commune. In December 1958 the Central Committee had to transfer the center of decision making from the commune down to the level of the production brigade. Wages were paid again according to labor done and work points acquired. As the agricultural crisis worsened in 1960, the commune was further decentralized and the production team with an average membership of about forty households that could work together became the basic unit. Private garden plots were reintroduced. The economic recession and industrial standstill after 1960 were greater than any that had occurred in the better-off Soviet economy. In the early 1960's China suffered both from adverse weather, producing poor harvests, and also from the withdrawal of Soviet technicians and aid. As a result China underwent several years of serious economic dislocation. Gross national product declined by perhaps one-third in 1960. Malnutrition was widespread. The people were exhausted and apathetic. Transportation broke down. Industry stagnated. The regime acknowledged that agriculture, shortchanged for a decade, must now receive top priority. Mao and the CCP, using their political power, had made economic errors on a truly gigantic scale.

The mounting extremism of the Chinese revolution during the 1950's, the feverish tendency to accelerate campaigns and revise targets upward, had been continually encouraged by Mao and the Central Committee in the faith that the masses would respond to a Marxist-Leninist leadership that knew how to unleash the latent "productive forces" of society and free the "creative capacity" of the Chinese working class that had previously, it was believed, been held in check by domestic and foreign exploiting classes. This faith was not entirely frustrated but neither was it vindicated. By the 1960's the Chinese people had learned how to coexist with the CCP regime, as they had with autocracies in the past, but the initial enthusiasm of the revolution had been spent. Worse still, the rift had widened between the party's top organizers and their charismatic leader. In mid-1959, smarting from the economic debacle of the Great Leap, members of the Central Committee denounced Mao's romantic and extremist policies. Mao weathered their criticism, since he was still indispensable, but his infallibility was gone and he had to remove himself from day-to-day administration of affairs. From this time the domestic policy battle was joined; soon it was complicated by foreign relations.

Foreign Policy. The ethnocentric tradition that the Chinese Empire was all-under-heaven *(t'ien-hsia)* or mankind's "central country" *(chung-kuo)* had stressed China's self-sufficiency and nonexpansiveness, except on its strategic Inner Asian frontier. The revolution during the 1950's created a new Chinese nation that expanded over Inner Asia to include Tibetans, Uighur Turks, Inner Mongols, and two score other minorities within a vast realm that comprised the unheard-of total of 700 million or more persons. The preponderant Han Chinese majority had inherited an ideal of unified central government as the only guarantor of peace and prosperity against civil war and foreign incursion. Unlike European nation-states that all arose within the culture of Christendom, the Chinese had a sense of cultural or ethnic nationalism that demanded the unity of the whole Chinese realm. One principal aim of foreign policy was therefore the recovery of Taiwan, which Peking claimed to be an integral part of China "occupied" by American imperialism. Its recovery would end the Nationalist-Communist civil war and complete China's reunification.

The revolution at home fostered a militant attitude toward the outside world, stressing the universalistic theme of "American imperialism" as the enemy and China's "liberation" as the model for all ex-colonial and underdeveloped countries in a great worldwide struggle of the progressive "socialist camp" against the reactionary "imperialist camp." In these terms China's newly heightened nationalism found expression in a broader universalism, in which People's China relied upon the Soviet Union as its "elder brother." In this spirit, Peking during the 1950's utilized both coercion and persuasion in foreign policy, as on the home front.

The first phase, 1950 to 1954, began belligerently in an interaction with the United States containment policy, which was triggered specifically by the Soviet-backed North Korean invasion of South Korea in June 1950. As we have noted, this precipitated both the American-backed United Nations defense of South Korea and a resumption of American military-naval support of the Nationalist government on Taiwan. Soon after Chinese troops intervened in Korea and entered Tibet, Chinese military support aided the Viet Minh in Indo-China. After two years of negotiation, the Korean armistice was signed in July 1953; and after the defeat of the French at Dien Bien Phu, France's withdrawal from Indo-China was agreed upon, with China participating as a great power, at Geneva in July 1954. This expansion of Peking's influence, however, was paralleled by an expansion of American commitments. On this front of the Cold War, both sides sought security through militant action. In September 1954 a joint defense system, the Southeast Asia Treaty Organization (SEATO), was created by the United States to include Britain, France, Australia, New Zealand, the Philippines, Thailand, and Pakistan. Washington also signed defensive alliances with Seoul (January 1954) and Taipei (December 1954). Thus, by the time

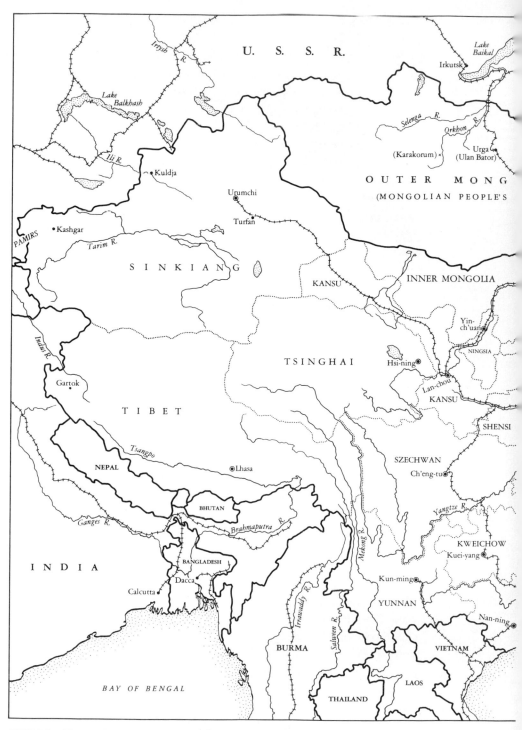

CHINA: THE PEOPLE'S REPUBLIC

U. S. S. R.

SAKHALIN

Chita

TRANS- SIBERIAN RAILWAY

Khabarovsk

Amur R.

HEILUNGKIANG

Harbin

OLIA
REP.)

INNER MONGOLIA

Vladivostok

Ch'ang-ch'un
KIRIN

SEA OF JAPAN

Hu-ho-
hao-t'e

HOPEH

LIAONING
Shen-yang

NORTH
KOREA

JAPAN

Tōkyō

Peking

P'yŏngyang

Tientsin

Shih-chia-
chuang

T'ai-
yuan

Seoul
SOUTH
KOREA

SHANSI

SHANTUNG

Tsinan

Tsingtao

Yellow R.

SHENSI

YELLOW SEA

Sian

Loyang

Cheng-
chou

KIANGSU

HONAN

Nanking

Shanghai

HUPEH

Ho-fei

Wu-han
(Wu-ch'ang)

ANHWEI

Yangtze

Hangchow

CHEKIANG

EAST CHINA SEA

Nan-ch'ang

Ch'ang-sha

HUNAN

KIANGSI

FUKIEN

Foochow

Taipei

Kweilin

KWANGSI

KWANGTUNG

Canton

*Hsi (West)
R.*

TAIWAN

PACIFIC OCEAN

HONG KONG
MACAO

⊙ Provincial capitals

HAINAN

SOUTH CHINA SEA

PHILIPPINE
IS.

RS

the Communist-Nationalist confrontation over the offshore island of Que-moy in Amoy harbor led to a crisis in early 1955, China's activity concerning four contiguous areas was matched by an American-led and financed anti-Communist effort at containment.

After the militancy of these early years came a phase of greater reliance on diplomatic persuasion. At the Geneva conference of April–July 1954, Chou En-lai joined the foreign ministers of the other powers in an effort to create stability in Indo-China as France withdrew. In negotiating at this time with India and Burma, Chou enunciated five principles of "peaceful coexistence." These also formed his main theme at the conference held in April 1955 at Bandung in western Java by leaders of twenty Asian and African states. In tune with the "Bandung spirit," American and Chinese ambassadors began in August 1955 to hold periodic talks—in all they held seventy-three at Geneva and then fifty-eight during 1958–1966 at Warsaw.

Yet this soft line soon yielded to a hard one. Imperialism seemed to be on the defensive after Russia launched the first intercontinental ballistic missile (ICBM) in August 1957 and its first satellite orbited the earth in October. In November Mao went to Moscow, leaving China for the second time, to celebrate the fortieth anniversary of the Bolshevik revolution. Declaring that "the east wind prevails over the west wind," he called for a new belligerency in East-West relations. This soon became evident in the Taiwan Straits, where the American buildup of Nationalist military power had been re-sumed in 1951. The Nationalists increasingly harassed the mainland by espionage, reconnaissance and leaflet-dropping flights, and commando raids. They also strengthened the fortification of "the front" on Quemoy, commit-ting to it a third of the Nationalist forces. Eventually, Communist bombard-ment in August–September 1958 created a second Quemoy crisis, which subsided but left Quemoy a bone of contention, still held by the Nationalists as a recognized part of the mainland.

Another area of renewed belligerency was Tibet, whose people were pressed toward a socialist revolution that would amount to Sinicization. A rising at Lhasa in March 1959, when the Dalai Lama fled to India, led to harsh repression by the Chinese. During the following summer Sino-Indian friction increased on both ends of the Himalayan frontier and finally erupted in brief hostilities in October 1962. China asserted control of the strategic route between Tibet and Sinkiang through the Aksai-Chin region. Although it later appeared that India had provoked China's brief but crush-ing counterattack, the People's Republic seemed to the Western public at the time to be the aggressor.

The Cultural Revolution

The Emergence of Two Lines.   Socialist transformation had bureaucratized Chinese life, but neither it nor the Great Leap and communes had met the

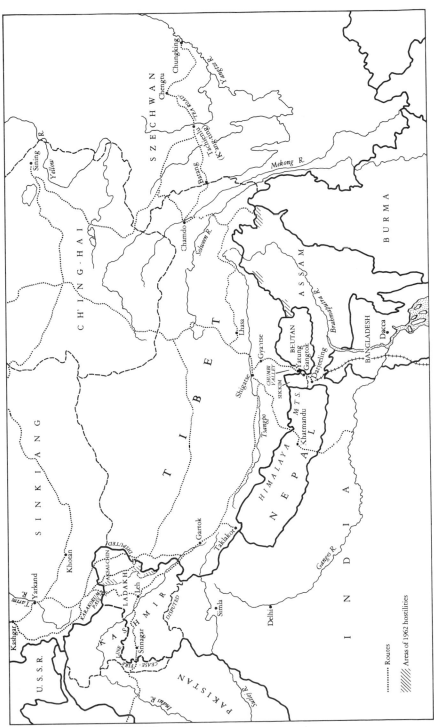

TIBET AND ENVIRONS

people's economic expectations. As popular dissatisfaction mounted, it inspired within party counsels a sharper struggle between alternative lines of policy. Once the CCP leadership had established its control of China, its unity began to suffer from the strain of decision making, and this strain increased when the Soviet model of industrialization had to be abandoned. The alternative policies inherent in the situation began to be represented by protagonists, Mao on one side and eventually Liu Shao-ch'i on the other.

Mao's early career had confirmed in him certain special traits—independence of view and concern for the common peasant. In the early and mid-1920's he had collaborated with the KMT and after the split of 1927 he had learned the importance of military force and guerrilla tactics. In neither period was he an organization man working primarily within the Communist Party. The twenty years of his leadership after 1935 had seen the repeated success of his style of militant struggle. The personal dominance of Mao Tse-tung was steadily built up by the revolutionary movement's need for personal leadership, yet within the spectrum of alternatives he was distinctly the protagonist of one line against another.

Two views of revolution were of course inherent in the European origins of Marxism. One saw history as a moral drama and revolution as a moral crusade. The other saw the progress of the arts, especially technological development in material terms, as the agent of revolution enabling new forces of production to create new classes. Pursuing these cognate themes, Mao could stress the moral pursuit of social equality and selfless virtue while Liu Shao-ch'i could stress the practical need of specialized skills and material progress. This latter strain of "scientific Marxism" assumed that a society's "superstructure" of political, social, and cultural life reflected its material base, the relations of production; and that these had to be changed before the superstructure could be changed. In contrast, the voluntarism (willfulness, not "volunteering") and populism espoused by Mao asserted that the will of the masses, once energized, could conquer all. In Mao's background one can also see the peasant's ancient hatred of ruling class privilege and special status. Early in the century, Chinese students had responded to the anarchist ideal, to abolish all government and capitalism, and create a free society based on mutual cooperation. In his background were other vestiges of China's past: the Chinese Classics assert that all men are potentially good and only need teaching to realize their potentialities, and leadership must be taken by an ethical elite whose moral superiority can transcend their environment. This residual strain of Confucianism fostered the supreme role of a sage hero, whereas the more Soviet-oriented Liu Shao-ch'i and his colleagues omitted the "thought of Mao" from the new CCP constitution of 1956 and opposed a cult of Mao's personality.

The dualism of these inherent alternatives was expressed under several rubrics: *Leader versus commissar.* Mao had been the distant symbol of

Chairman Mao talking to peasants at Yang-chia-ling near Yenan about 1940.

paternal compassion, whereas the party commissars under Liu had had to exercise local discipline. Mao stood above his colleagues, a figure apart. *The mass line versus party-building.* Mao stood for struggle. He wanted the cadres to serve the people, stir them up, and respond to their stirrings in the spirit of the mass line. Liu and other party-builders preferred to keep struggle subordinate to party unity, and stressed the training of cadres to be a new elite that could guide China's transformation. *Village versus city.* Mao's concerns harked back to the simple existence of Yenan. He disdained city life. His ideal was the omnicompetent man of the soil, a combined farmer, craftsman, and militia soldier in a self-sufficient countryside. Organizers in the Central Committee, in contrast, saw the need of special skills for industrialization, the importance of the urban elite, the necessity of technical education. *Voluntarism versus planning.* Most of Mao's contemporaries favored the systematic effort of Five-Year Plans, the accumulation of investment capital and building-up of industry. But Mao was less concerned with economics than with politics. Voluntarism was Mao's personal faith. It led him to favor decentralized local initiative versus central control, the people versus bureaucratism, the peasantry versus any revival of a ruling class. Finally, the most publicized of all these contrasts was that of *red versus expert,* the politically indoctrinated versus the professionally trained.

These different paths to China's future had not always been mutually exclusive but had been advocated as cognate principles (like the ancient *yin* and *yang*) in many Central Committee pronouncements. Liu Shao-ch'i had backed the utopianism of the distinctly Maoist Great Leap Forward. But its failure precipitated a hardening of attitudes. After December 1958, Mao "voluntarily" gave up his position as chief of state to Liu. The CCP leadership now confronted the question that comes to every revolution: When should change give way to stability? Alternatively, how can the revolutionary spirit be kept alive? In the final analysis, this was the problem of revisionism, a dilemma which the Soviet Union had also faced. This made the impact of Soviet revisionism on Chinese politics all the greater.

The Sino-Soviet Split. Since the Chinese and Russian peoples had very different histories, self-images, needs, and goals, it is not surprising that a major split developed between them on several levels at once. Memory made them suspicious of each other: the Mongol horde of the thirteenth century had enslaved South Russia; Tsarist imperialists had encroached on China's Northeast, Mongolia, and Turkestan. Behind the Communist fraternal rhetoric, history provided few bonds of mutual admiration. Their collaboration, chiefly in the form of Soviet aid paid for by China, had followed the desires of their leaders, who could as easily disrupt it. Ideology had been the original bond, so it became the point of fracture.

Mao knew no foreign languages. By the time he acquired a Marxist concept it had often been a bit Sinicized in the process of translation. Moreover, Mao had begun with revolutionary action; he acquired ideology as he went along. He had to bend Communist doctrine to fit it to local needs. Russia had created a "dictatorship of the proletariat" as the only path to socialism. But the CCP set up a "people's democratic dictatorship" and claimed that a mere "hegemony of the proletariat" at the head of a united front and coalition government representing all "revolutionary classes" could lead China to socialism. Moreover, the CCP claimed to do it by a gradual, persuasive, non-violent transformation, quite unlike the abrupt and violent change postulated by Lenin and Stalin.

In 1956 Soviet "de-Stalinization" embarrassed the CCP at a time when it was still invoking Stalin's name. To be sure, Soviet premier Khrushchev's recognition of "many paths to socialism" accepted Peking's claim to be the model for Asia, but this concession also cut the ground from under Marxist-Leninist doctrine. From this time on, the split widened. Peking like Moscow was now an autonomous center of doctrinal authority. International Communism was no longer monolithic. Friction, if not rupture, was inevitable. Khrushchev, on the crest of the Soviet success in launching the first sputnik, denounced the Great Leap and the communes, with which Mao claimed to be surpassing Moscow, as left deviations, dangerous fanaticism. In return, Soviet "revisionism" was attacked by Peking as an opportunist sell-out to capitalism. Although Moscow had promised Peking nuclear weapons assistance in 1957, it was stopped. The Soviet technicians with their blueprints were suddenly withdrawn from China in 1960. The two parties engaged in public denunciations in 1963. A lively fear of Chinese fanaticism and expansion grew up in the Soviet Union, and by 1969 armed border clashes arose both along the Amur and in Central Asia. The Chinese built air-raid shelters on a massive scale while Soviet striking forces massed on the border.

As the Sino-Soviet split widened, Peking sought at first to capture the leadership of the Communist world revolution, exporting cultural missions and militant propaganda and supporting "national liberation movements" in Asia and Africa. Mao and his principal supporter in this period, General Lin Piao, pictured how the Chinese model of revolution could be applied to the underdeveloped two-thirds of mankind against the industrialized imperialist powers. The metaphor used in September 1965 was to "surround the cities from the countryside," but the advocacy of self-reliance for all people's revolutions meant that China could point the way but not itself achieve the world revolution by its own expansion. (One is reminded of the ancient theory of tributary relations: China was a model which other countries should follow but on their own initiative.)

Lin Piao's do-it-yourself prescription for world revolution was issued partly to forestall any effort by the professional military to intervene in Vietnam under Soviet nuclear protection, because this would sidetrack the Maoist effort at continuing revolution. In February 1965, the United States had begun continuous bombing of North Vietnam (see page 882); this aggression on China's doorstep was accompanied by promises not to invade North Vietnam on the ground; and so Peking suffered the humiliation of impotence, unable to protect a neighboring ally. Meanwhile, 1965 brought other setbacks in Peking's foreign relations. China's effort to organize an Afro-Asian conference excluding the Soviet Union failed in June. And in October, an abortive coup in Indonesia was followed by the slaughter of the pro-Peking Indonesian Communist Party. These and other failures abroad helped turn China inward.

Problems within the Party.   Behind the civil strife of the late 1960's were deep strains and stresses. The first was among the people, where there was a gap between China's poverty and the expectations of her citizens, newly active in politics. To destroy the old order, the CCP had roused a whirlwind and now had to ride it. Where the KMT had been a small, superficial regime, the CCP had asserted its authority down to the very rice roots. Shortages before, in the old free market economy, had been no one's fault. Now they reflected poor planning.

Having taken on this staggering burden, the CCP had built enormous structures of administration. But administrators of collective units had tended to become bureaucrats, less concerned with common manual labor, closer to being an upper class. Opportunists interested in their own careers and families reappeared, seeking connections and special privileges, better education, private property. For example, party leaders of the Long March generation were not averse to special schools for their children. In short, "liberation" of the common peasant had intensified rather than diminished the competition for elite status. The new party-government-army power structure was an elite organization, intensely status- and security-conscious, controlled from the top down. The upper incumbents became more cautious and less revolutionary while the lower levels felt boxed in and frustrated. The axiom that revolutionaries supplant an *ancien régime* only to inherit its evils was evidenced in the wide gap between the cadres and the Chinese public. A new ruling class was taking shape, abetted by organization men like Liu Shao-ch'i and the CCP Secretary-General Teng Hsiao-p'ing.

Within the bureaucratic structure were further problems of morale and motivation. The party was responsible for the thought and behavior, loyalty and discipline, of all party members. They were set apart from nonparty members and deeply involved in the "party life" of constant meetings, criticism and self-criticism, reporting on subordinates, and trying to maintain a good record in the secret files of the personnel, control, and supervisory offices. Whether in the party or not, a cadre's personal dossier was almost more important than himself. He never saw it, but he knew it contained his own statement of his personal history and background, his ideological views, and all his family and other associations. Dubious individuals would be systematically investigated, and in campaigns, of course, a vulnerable individual might become a target. Where the ancient examination system had made for self-indoctrination, the Communist system made for self-intimidation. Quite aside from the specific evils attacked by a campaign, the eventual selection of certain human targets for systematic denunciation and public humiliation was sufficient to remind all observers that, but for the grace of the party, they too might be pilloried. These unnerving public spectacles strikingly reaffirmed the party's authority. Typically they moved individuals who felt threatened to denounce their pilloried colleagues with unusual vehemence.

As a result of all this, campaigns, the engines of social change, began to lose their efficacy in the 1960's. Cadres learned how to go through the proper motions in meetings without thorough commitment. They learned to avoid close friendships lest they involve themselves in subsequent denunciations in intimate detail. An activist discovered how to ride out campaigns, feigning a progressive enthusiasm in the mobilization phase, and becoming properly prudent and self-critical in the consolidation phase. The party establishment, in short, had learned how to protect itself against Mao's methods of continuing revolution, but it was thereby losing its capacity really to mobilize the people.

Thus the issue of revisionism arose from the fact that too many party members had lost faith in Mao's romantic, Heaven-storming approach to China's problems. Party bureaucrats like Liu and Teng opposed the Maoists' fanaticism and zealotry because they would only hinder economic recovery. Wrestling with practical problems, the bureaucrats dragged their feet when Mao called in late 1962 for yet another campaign, for "socialist education." The inadequate response to this campaign led Mao to turn to the army.

Bureaucratism had also appeared in the Soviet-type professional officer corps, established in 1955. The officers challenged the political commissar system and "politics in command," and favored the Soviet principle of unity of command. Party committees in the armed forces declined as did party membership. But after Defense Minister P'eng Te-huai was ousted in 1959, for criticizing the Great Leap and having had contact with the Soviets, he was succeeded by General Lin Piao, who now worked closely with Mao. New party members were recruited into the armed forces, and company party committees were re-established. A separate echelon of party members now had its own organization at successive levels down to the company and the squad. Indoctrination and surveillance were both pushed. Political officers kept this system functioning and prevented the formation of groups of like-minded dissidents. The army was thoroughly indoctrinated, so well that by 1964 it was possible to launch a nationwide emulation campaign to "learn from the People's Liberation Army." The army by the fall of 1965 provided the base from which Mao was able to move toward a new campaign that he called the Great Proletarian Cultural Revolution, or more accurately, great revolution to create a propertyless class culture.

Chairman Mao's Crusade. The Great Proletarian Cultural Revolution was a super-campaign that ran roughly from May 1966 to April 1969. But it turned out to be a second revolution more than a controlled program. As Mao moved against outspoken critics, he found more party support for them than he had foreseen. As with the Hundred Flowers criticisms of 1956, opposition proved surprisingly widespread, but this time it was within the party. Mao responded with a vast new effort to mobilize support from outside the party. The public scene was soon filled with mass meetings, parades, and propaganda displays exalting Mao as "the red sun in our hearts." Tremendous excitement, even hysteria, among millions of youth led to exhaustion, apathy, and further surges of effort. Out of it all came a purge of the party by the leader. But where Stalin had purged his party from within, secretly and using the party apparatus, Mao purged the CCP from without, publicly and using mass organizations such as the Red Guard youth. Where Stalin used his secret police and killed millions of people,

Mao relied on the People's Liberation Army and used methods of public humiliation.

Mao's first move was to ensure his control of the mass media at the center by attacking cultural and educational commissars and the Peking Party Committee. He went outside the party apparatus to field groups of teen-agers as Red Guards, calling upon them in a poster written in his own hand to "bombard the headquarters." They were to "learn revolution by making revolution." Also outside party channels, he set up a nationwide Cultural Revolution organization headed by a committee that included his wife, Chiang Ch'ing. During the fall of 1966 with logistic support from the army, some 11 million Red Guards came to Peking for a succession of mass rallies and then dispersed over the country to link up with others and carry out their own "Long Marches." In the public scene they violently attacked people and things that seemed to represent the "four olds" (old ideology, thought, habits, and customs). In January 1967, Mao escalated the Revolu-tion still further to attack the party structure itself, inciting the "revolution-ary masses" to seize power from below as in the Paris Commune of 1870. Many million copies of a little red booklet, *Quotations from Chairman Mao Tse-tung,* brought every activist a wide range of axioms to ponder and a talisman to wave in devotion. The cult of Mao dominated the media. The party powerholders were attacked piecemeal and had no way to organize among themselves. As a result, the party establishment was thoroughly shaken up, if not shattered.

To take the place of the old structure of authority, Mao eventually called for "revolutionary committees" at all the levels of government. They were to include "revolutionary masses" (new blood), army men, and old party cadres who had been adequately revolutionized. The party establishment fought back bitterly in one place after another, fielding their own Red Guards, proclaiming their loyalty to Mao but defeating his forces. Eventu-ally, local factions began to use firearms in their struggles. Civil strife reached a point where the army had to be called in more and more to restore order. By January 1968 revolutionary committees had been set up in all the twenty-nine provinces and major cities, but an effective core of administra-tion had not been built up within them. In the end, the attack on the party gave civil power to an increasing number of army men, who were brought into key administrative positions.

In the midst of all this frenzied turmoil, the universities and schools had remained closed while intellectuals and experts were being attacked and students revolutionized in factional fighting. In the fall of 1968, millions of student youth including erstwhile Red Guards were sent down to the farms. The Ninth Party Congress of April 1969 elected a new Central Committee with a preponderance of military personnel. A new party con-

GROUP WORK AND STUDY. *Top: A team of girls preparing for planting near Nanking. Bottom: A group reading in an afternoon study session near Canton.*

SCHOLARS ON THE FARM. *Peking Aeronautical Institute teachers
and students helping Tungpeiwang Commune members with
their July harvest, 1967. A hundred people using hand tools.*

stitution named Lin Piao as Mao's successor. By degrees China turned back
to the continuing task of material development.

In the aftermath of the Cultural Revolution universities slowly reopened
with student bodies selected not by competitive examinations, which would
still create an elite, but by popular nomination from their production units.
Candidates for higher education had to have worked for two years after
middle school and were expected to return to serve the communities whence
they had come. This effort to inject higher education into the villages was
paralleled by giving elementary public health training to "barefoot doctors"
who would work among the common people. Urban functionaries were
meanwhile rotated regularly to "May 7 schools" (really farms) that gave
them an experience of study coupled with manual work on the land, in a
continuing effort to break down the ruling class tradition. Social change
was also evident in a new spirit of egalitarianism and the submersion of
intellectuals.

The Cultural Revolution left behind a degree of public morale and self-
confidence in a more relaxed atmosphere. Many of its victims were quietly
brought back into responsible posts. But one of its long-term results was to

leave the CCP leadership fractured into radical and pragmatic factions. The violent denunciation and recrimination of the late 1960's had split the leadership. Many veteran officials who had been dragged out and denounced by Red Guards remained resentful and even defiant.

Suddenly in September 1971 Lin Piao, who had risen so high during the Cultural Revolution and the subsequent ascendancy of the military, was reported killed in a plane crash in Outer Mongolia. By degrees the story was put out that he had plotted usurpation and even the assassination of Mao and had attempted to flee when his dastardly plot was discovered. Whatever may have been the facts of this bizarre episode, the subsequent circumstantial exposure of Lin Piao's long-term perfidy made him a traitor to the revolution much like his predecessor as the number two, Liu Shao-ch'i, and posed again the question how one so evil could have risen so high. To outside observers the need to blacken the moral character of policy losers seemed a curious holdover from Confucianism.

Sino-American Relations

While the Chinese people had been going through the Cultural Revolution, the American people had found themselves involved in a different turmoil, the Vietnam War. The American defeat in Vietnam after an expenditure of 56,000 lives and $150 billion coincided with several other factors to make possible President Nixon's dramatic renewal of Sino-American relations. First of all, from June 1969 to January 1973 he systematically removed the American forces from Vietnam under a policy of "Vietnamization" of the military effort. In the process he extended the destruction to Cambodia in 1970 and finally terror-bombed Hanoi, vainly trying to use overwhelming force to mitigate political defeat. In January 1973 Washington and Hanoi agreed to a ceasefire, prisoner exchange, and American withdrawal from the war, which continued, however, between North and South Vietnam for another two years.

Second, the American withdrawal from the Indo-China area (Vietnam, Cambodia, and Laos) followed the inauguration of a policy of detente, or negotiation, rather than military confrontation in the continuing competition between Washington and Moscow. The resulting Soviet-American collaboration-cum-rivalry in trade, arms limitation under the SALT agreement (May 1972), and cultural exchanges modified the cold war posture of these two super-powers. This in turn made Chinese-American contact highly desirable on the third side of the Sino-Soviet-American triangle.

Third, the American defeat in South Vietnam, where the war effort had always been limited by the necessity not to invade North Vietnam lest it provoke China's entrance as in Korea, led Mao Tse-tung to conclude that American capitalist imperialism was for China a "minor contradiction" as compared with the "major contradiction" of Soviet "socialist imperialism." This appraisal of Russia as the main menace led Peking to respond positively to the Nixon administration's measured efforts to restore relations. From 1970 to 1973 these various trends converged to restructure China's foreign relations.

The breakthrough, after twenty-two years of estrangement, was dramatic. In April 1971 Peking unexpectedly welcomed American table-tennis players and journalists in a gesture of "people-to-people diplomacy." Suddenly in July Nixon announced that his foreign policy adviser Dr. Henry Kissinger (later Secretary of State) had secretly visited Peking to prepare for a presidential visit. In October the Republic of China on Taiwan was expelled from the United Nations and the People's Republic admitted. In February 1972 President Nixon visited Peking, saw Chairman Mao, and with Prime Minister Chou En-lai signed at Shanghai a joint communiqué. This document stated the two parties' divergent views on several matters but agreed on a joint effort to develop commercial and cultural contact and to move toward normal relations. In May 1973 the two governments opened embryo embassies in the form of liaison offices headed by ambassadors in Peking and Washington.

Under this new order trade developed, dozens of delegations passed back and forth (mainly in fields of technology), and thousands of Americans (mainly ethnic Chinese) visited the People's Republic. On the Chinese side this was a large-scale government program of controlled contact which brought Americans into the channels of tourism within China that had already been established for other foreigners from all over the world. This foreign tourism was in fact added onto the massive domestic program by which Chinese delegations were brought to exemplary demonstration sites where they could learn from model achievements such as those of the Shansi province Tachai brigade in agriculture and, in the northeast, of the Taching oil field in industry. American contact was thus fitted into the ongoing effort to remake China.

The Shanghai communiqué also defined the status of Taiwan when the American side acknowledged "that all Chinese on either side of the Taiwan Strait maintain there is but one China and that Taiwan is a part of China." The United States sought "a peaceful settlement of the Taiwan question by the Chinese themselves." Accordingly it would reduce American forces on Taiwan with the ultimate objective of their complete withdrawal. Implicit in this document and its acceptance of the one-China concept was the idea that Washington would eventually withdraw diplomatic recognition from Taipei in order to achieve "normalization," full diplomatic relations, with Peking. However, since two separate regimes had existed since 1949, each claiming to be the one China, it was plain that this potent phrase represented an ideal (in fact the central myth of the traditional Chinese state) rather than an actuality. This made the history and circumstances of Taiwan peculiarly important.

The Republic of China on Taiwan.   After 1949 the Nationalist government of the Republic of China in exile, still dominated by the Kuomintang (although since 1948 under a constitution instead of "party tutelage"), considered itself only temporarily superimposed upon Taiwan as one of its provinces and maintained a posture of militant readiness for "counterattack" to recover the mainland. Political life on Taiwan reflected the psychology of rulers in exile, proudly determined not to give up claims that sustained their hopes and sense of historical consistency. As a consequence, the Nationalist government in the early 1950's continued, as on the mainland although in different circumstances, to devote itself in large part to military preparation for counterattack, rather than concentrating its energies on more general development. In this garrison atmosphere under martial law, the tradition of an almost monarchic, one-man leadership died slowly. After all, it was barely fifty years since the abdication of the Son of Heaven.

Relations between the ruling minority from the mainland and the Taiwan-Chinese majority met an initial disaster in March 1947. The flagrant corruption of the Nationalist take-over authorities, before the arrival of most of their compatriots, provoked widespread demonstrations that were countered by the systematic killing of several thousand leading Taiwanese. A whole generation of local leadership was decimated. As time passed, most of the 2 million or so political leaders, civil servants, teachers, and soldiers who came from the mainland had to depend on modest stipends from the Nationalist government, while the 10 million or more Taiwan-Chinese in agriculture and trade began to participate more directly in the island's economic growth. On the other hand, the Taiwanese at first participated in political life for the most part only under the provincial government. Under it an election process gradually developed. Taiwanese became the majority among students in higher education and held most of the offices in local government, while the "mainlanders" continued to run the Nationalist government.

Economic growth was assisted by American aid, both military and economic, as well as by land reform. The Sino-American Joint Commission on Rural Reconstruction, after beginning on the mainland in 1948 by simply fostering agronomic technology, found that rent reduction, improvement of tenant contracts, and eventually land ownership by the cultivator (achieved by 1964) were all needed to settle the age-old landlord-tenant problem. Helped through farmers' associations (inherited from the Japanese era), the combination of technical education, rural handicrafts, credits, and cooperatives soon set an example of rural development that fostered Nationalist programs of aid to many developing countries.

As industrialization got under way, the island's earlier reliance on sugar and rice production for the Japanese market had to be followed by a considerable reorientation to achieve greater self-sufficiency and to push industrial growth in the face of rapid population increase. The 3 million population of 1905 had approached 7 million by 1940; with an influx of 2 million or more from the mainland, the total by 1958 was about 11 million, and by 1976 16 million. Compared with the mainland, however, Taiwan had a higher living standard and a much higher dependence on foreign trade. Development proceeded within a general framework of government domination or monopolies in industry. American assistance of some $2 billion fostered growth until the mid-1960's, with such success that industrialization then continued apace without outside aid, and attracted increasing amounts of Japanese as well as American investment.

The American attitude in 1949 was to refuse responsibility for the island, but to continue economic aid without military aid, as part of an attempted disengagement from China. But the North Korean aggression of 1950 led to the United States Seventh Fleet's patrolling the Formosa Strait, while an American military mission assisted in a military aid program, after 1954 under a mutual defense treaty.

In the late 1960's the American warfare in Indo-China used Taiwan as a staging area. After its expulsion as the representative of China from the United Nations in October 1971, the government of the Republic of China lost diplomatic relations with most countries, yet its foreign trade continued to expand. The Nixon-Chou communiqué of February 1972 stated, on the Chinese side, that Taiwan's status crucially obstructed the normalization of relations with the United States. Yet American trade and investment in Taiwan thereafter increased and the mutual defense treaty of 1954 continued in force. When Chiang Kai-shek died in 1975, his son Chiang Ching-kuo as prime minister became the principal government leader. Thus Taiwan, or rather the American recognition of the Nationalist government, which was still at war with the vastly greater People's Republic, continued to be a major unresolved issue in Chinese-American relations.

Relevant to an American solution of this problem—how to deal with one China but two governments—was the Japanese example. The secret and unexpected reversal of American China policy in July 1971 produced a very understandable "Nixon shock" in Tōkyō and inspired Japan to quickly normalize relations with Peking. The Sino-Japanese treaty of September 1972 restored diplomatic relations and reaffirmed the one-China principle that Taiwan was part of China. But while Japan-Taiwan diplomatic relations ceased, trade and travel relations continued with the aid of newly created private "associations" staffed by the former diplomats. Peking's claim to sovereignty over Taiwan was thus publicly affirmed while the fact of Taiwan's separate autonomy continued largely unchanged.

In the years following the Shanghai communiqué, American progress toward normalization was slowed by the distraction of the Watergate investigation climaxed by the resignation of President Nixon in August 1974. Dr. Kissinger made repeated visits to Peking, and in December 1975 President Ford went to China, reaffirming the normalization policy. Yet Peking and Taipei both continued to be represented in Washington, as they were in no other capital city or international body in the world.

The Revolution in Transition

Mao's attack on "capitalist-roaders" in the party establishment during the Cultural Revolution of the late 1960's left China's leadership in the early 1970's severely split. An ardent radical wing based partly in Shanghai was carrying on Mao's moral crusade against self-seeking materialism in order to "serve the people" with true socialist dedication. Its witch-hunting approach was evident in the slogan "the bourgeoisie are within the Communist Party." The more pragmatic wing, composed of the great majority of administrators in office, remained concerned about material incentives to inspire economic production and technical skills to aid China's material progress. For a time in Chairman Mao's last years "radicals" dominated the media while "pragmatists" ran the administration. (These terms were foreign labels for a murky situation.)

After the fall of Lin Piao in September 1971, the role of the military in government had been reduced and the party reconstructed. The Tenth Party Congress met in August 1973 with 1200 or more delegates representing 28 million party members. It was held in secret and lasted only four days. Younger faces appeared in the leadership to represent the protagonists of the Cultural Revolution. The new Central Committee was more broadly based. In 1973–1974 a study campaign was mounted to "criticize Lin Piao and Confucius" in order to expose their reactionary views, despite the 2500 years that separated them historically. In January 1975 the Fourth National People's Congress convened in Peking briefly with 2800 delegates to adopt a new constitution. This congress strove to symbolize the restoration of party unity in preparation for the change of leadership, for both Chou En-lai as prime minister and Mao Tse-tung as party chairman were by this time seriously ill.

After seven years in obscurity, the one-time secretary-general of the party, Teng Hsiao-p'ing, who had been denounced as the number two "capitalist-roader" and target of the Cultural Revolution, was rehabilitated in 1973 and soon restored to power. He evidently helped diminish the military role in government. By 1975 he was a party vice-chairman and a member of the politburo, as well as army chief of staff and senior vice-premier of the government. When Chou En-lai died in January 1976 Teng was acting premier—a blunt little man intent on getting results. But Mao outlived Chou, and in April the politburo dismissed Teng from all his posts and made the relatively unknown Hua Kuo-feng acting premier. Following the terribly destructive Tangshan earthquake of August 1976, Mao Tse-tung died on September 9. Hua was soon made party chairman in his place, and almost immediately the four Cultural Revolution protagonists at the top of the Central Committee, including Mao's widow Chiang Ch'ing, were out of power. Their control over the media, the Peking radio and the *People's Daily (Jen-min jih-pao),* came to an end, and they were systematically denounced as anti-party renegades, while Teng Hsiao-P'ing reappeared. This did not mean, however, that the moral crusade of the Cultural Revolution would not be heard from again.

These shifts of leadership represented a struggle over policy and between interest groups more than the naked individual "power struggle" so often assumed by the foreign press. The Central Committee, no matter how selfless and dedicated, faced hard choices on which honest disagreement was unavoidable. Devoted to large-scale planning in terms of revolutionary doctrine, China's leaders were obliged to agree on a national party line in a comprehensive fashion inconceivable to laissez-faire capitalists or welfare-state legislators in the West. The most demanding or at least vociferous interest group in the early 1970's carried on the spirit of the Cultural Revolution as a sacred trust. It stood for Mao Tse-tung's continuing moral revolution to liberate the common people and change their motivation, to combat the ancient evils of bourgeois selfishness, bureaucratism, and special privilege, and to give opportunity especially to the frustrated younger generations of party activists. This was the cause of social revolution. Against it stood the competing practical demands of modern development, stated in terms more easily intelligible to outsiders—how to keep food supply ahead of population growth, how best to use China's newly discovered and very extensive oil reserves such as those on the Hopei-Shantung coast and offshore, how to balance the desires for self-sufficiency and for foreign technology and capital, and a host of similar problems. Behind them all lay the question of how to reconcile the patriotic desire to make China a great power with the Maoist drive to serve the people. Policy makers faced a constant choice between investing in the power of the state and investing in the livelihood of the Chinese people on the land.

The death of Chou En-lai and Mao Tse-tung in 1976 marked the passing of the revolutionary leadership that had turned to Marxism-Leninism as the salvation of China about 1921, fifty-five years before. The achievements of the movement they led are still largely beyond present-day capacity to appraise: for example, the people of China have doubled in numbers and become a nation; they have created enormous new structures of government and industry. China has undergone tremendous ups and downs. During the active lifetime of this generation, the Nationalist revolution to unify China against foreign imperialism (1923–1928), the efforts of the Nanking government in modernization (1928–1937), and the destructiveness of Japan's invasion (1937–1945), all set the stage for the Communists' buildup of a new order at Yenan (1936–1946), their victory in civil war (1947–1949), and the subsequent remaking of China under the People's Republic. While Mao and Chou functioned from 1949 to 1976 as successors to the traditional Son of Heaven and his chief minister at the top of state and society, they did it as revolutionaries intent on social change as well as on economic growth. Their achievement was that of a whole people, prepared by long years of disaster to mobilize their collective energies in a great national regeneration. But the new order thus created remained still to be consolidated, with priorities still disputed between the claims of China's industrial revolution and China's social revolution.

Because of her population density, China's special problem in economic development was how to build up industry without shortchanging the rural sector, that is, how to create strong state industries and still bring the village masses out of their material poverty.

During the first quarter-century, central planning and control of state enterprises' profits for reinvestment had helped China's industrial output increase rapidly, as high as 10 per cent a year, doubling every seven years. For this purpose producers' goods were imported at first from the socialist bloc ($6.5 billion worth of machinery between 1952 and 1973) in spite of the Western embargo on such shipments to China, which lasted until 1960. In fact from 1949 to 1973 the machine-building industry grew 20 per cent a year, as did the output of iron and steel and, after 1965, oil production. China became the world's largest producer of machine tools. But transportation remained a bottleneck: 50,000 km of railways and 650,000 km of highways in the 1970's were minimal for so vast a country.

The other bottleneck was agricultural production. How could it be modernized to increase productivity? Mechanization of agriculture began with electric pumps for the age-old task of moving water; by 1973 two-fifths of the arable land was irrigated. At the same time small tractors were being used both in the fields and on the roads, and dozens of chemical fertilizer plants had been imported. Decentralized scattering of small-scale rural industries—iron foundries, chemical plants, flour mills, cement factories, brick kilns—reduced the rural sector's dependence on transport and augmented its strategic self-sufficiency. But meanwhile per capita consumption of rationed grain, cloth, and other consumer goods had not risen appreciably, nor had prices or wages. The hard-working populace had been given security and social services but only a very gradual rise in material living standards. Assuming an annual population growth rate of about 1.5 per cent, food supply would have to grow at about 2 per cent in order to achieve even a slight rise in living standards. Grain imports would still be necessary. Rapid improvement was thus not to be expected—the world's largest country would continue to be one of the poorest per capita.

One byproduct of construction under the People's Republic was a revolution in archaeology. Many neolithic and Shang Dynasty sites were excavated. Tombs of the First Emperor of the Ch'in and of the Han, T'ang, and other periods yielded surprising and dazzling works of art in bronze, sculpture, ceramics, textiles, tomb paintings and even literary texts, accurately located and dated for almost the first time. In the mid-1970's magnificent exhibitions were sent abroad to Japan, Western Europe, and North America.

China's foreign policy tried to lead the developing countries of the "third world" in opposition to the alleged domination or "hegemony" of the two "super-powers" (U.S.A. and U.S.S.R.). As a model of foreign aid in Africa, China completed in 1975 the building of the Tanzania-Zambia railway. Her industrial growth at home continued apace, making her industrial production in the mid-1970's comparable to that of Japan fifteen years before. Meanwhile China's satellites circled the earth, her nuclear tests slowly continued, a large coastal defense navy took shape—a great power was in the making. In August 1977, the Eleventh Party Congress, representing 35 million party members, confirmed the reinstatement of Teng Hsiao p'ing in the top leadership. This seemed plainly to usher in a period of industrial modernization. The Cultural Revolution was officially at an end.

Illustration Acknowledgments

TEXT ILLUSTRATIONS

Chapter 1   p. 10, G. B. Cressey, *China's Geographic Foundations;* p. 13, *P'ei wen chai kung-chi-tu;* p. 14, *Tien-kung k'ai-wu* collection of 1637; p. 15, *T'ien-king k'ai-wu.*

Chapter 2   p. 23, East Asian Library, Columbia University; p. 29, (left) Courtesy Museum of Fine Arts, Boston, (top right) Courtesy Museum of Fine Arts, Boston, (bottom right) Courtesy of the Smithsonian Institution, Freer Gallery of Art, Washington, D.C.

Chapter 3   p. 39, W. C. White, *Tomb Tile Pictures of Ancient China,* pl. LXXII; p. 43, American Museum of Natural History; p. 45, (top) *Han Wu Liang Tz'u,* (bottom left) Shanghai woodblock, 1873, (bottom right) Sung painting by Chao Ming Chien.

Chapter 4   p. 58, restored by Wilma Fairbank from a rubbing; p. 64, Courtesy of the Royal Ontario Museum of Art, Toronto, Canada; p. 67, restored by Wilma Fairbank from a rubbing; p. 70, restored by Wilma Fairbank from a rubbing; p. 74, *T'ien-kung k'ai-wu;* p. 77, restored by Wilma Fairbank from a rubbing.

Chapter 5   p. 89, Courtesy Museum of Fine Arts, Boston; p. 90, Osvald Siren, The Museum of Far Eastern Antiquities, Stockholm; p. 92, Nelson Gallery—Atkins Museum, Kansas City, Missouri; p. 97, Collections of the University Museum of the University of Pennsylvania; p. 110, Paul Pelliot; p. 113, (top and bottom) Nelson Gallery—Atkins Museum, Kansas City, Missouri; p. 114, Laurence Sickman and Alexander Soper, *Art and Architecture of China,* Penguin Books, 1936.

Chapter 6   p. 133, *Fa yüan chu-lin,* compiled by Tao-shih in 668, printed in 1124; p. 141, *Ch'ing-ming shang-ho t'u-chuan,* Peking, 1958; p. 144, Courtesy of the Smithsonian Institution, Freer Gallery of Art, Washington, D.C.; p. 145, Courtesy Museum of Fine Arts, Boston.

Chapter 7   p. 155, American Museum of Natural History; p. 156, The Museum of Far Eastern Antiquities, Stockholm; p. 175, *Shui-hu-chuan.*

Chapter 8   p. 183, *Chao Tzu-ku erh-shih-ssu hsiao shu-hua bo-pi;* p. 189, Sidney Gamble; p. 199, *Ming-jen hsiang-chuan;* p. 194, *Pin-feng-kuang-i.*

Chapter 9   p. 219, by permission of the Houghton Library, Harvard University; p. 221, (top) Charles Cutting, (bottom) slide in John K. Fairbank's collection; p. 224, *Ch'ing-tai ti-hou-hsiang;* p. 233, Nan-hsün sheng-tien; p. 236, *Ch'ing-tai ti-hou-hsiang;* p. 239, by permission of the Houghton Library, Harvard University; p. 247, (both) Nieuhof, *An Embassy from the East India Company of the United Provinces to the Grand Tartar,* Rare Book division, the New York Public Library, Astor, Lenox, and

Tilden Foundations; p. 248, (top) Musée Guimet, Paris, (bottom) by permission of the Houghton Library, Harvard University.

Chapter 10   p. 261, Photographie Giradoux; p. 270, *Bulletin de la Société des Etudes Indochinoises,* Saigon, 1934.

Chapter 11   p. 283, Pl. X, H. Ikeuchi and A. Umehara, *T'ung-kou,* vol. 2, Tōkyō, 1940; p. 285, (both) National Museum of Korea; p. 288, Fine Arts Department, Duksoo Palace, Seoul, Korea; p. 290, U.S. Army Photograph; p. 291, Bureau of International Relations, Ministry of Foreign Affairs, Republic of Korea.

Chapter 12   p. 304, T. Sekino, *Chōsen koseki zufu,* Korean Government Library, 1915; p. 308, National Museum of Korea; p. 309, United Nations; p. 321, National Museum of Korea.

Chapter 13   p. 328, (top) Courtesy Museum of Fine Arts, Boston, Edward S. Morse Memorial Fund, (bottom left) Asian Art Museum of San Francisco, The Avery Brundage Collection, (bottom right) Tōkyō National Museum; p. 333, (top) Norman F. Carver, Jr., Kalamazoo, Michigan, (bottom) Editoriale Fotografico; p. 341, (both) Asuka-en, Nara; p. 355, Tōkyō National Museum.

Chapter 14   p. 360, Metropolitan Museum of Art, Rogers Fund; p. 367, Tōkyō National Museum; p. 371, Tokyo National Museum; p. 373, Asuka-en, Nara; p. 374, Tōkyō National Museum; p. 385, *Japanese Architecture and Gardens,* Kokusai Bunka Shinkokai; p. 387, Tōkyō National Museum; p. 388, Consulate General of Japan; p. 389, *Japanese Architecture and Gardens,* Kokusai Bunka Shinkokai; p. 390, Consulate General of Japan.

Chapter 15   p. 395, Japan Tourist Association; p. 404, *Illustrations of Famous Places in Edo;* p. 415, *Illustrations of Famous Places in Edo;* p. 421, Nagami Tokutarō, *Nagasaki no bijutsu shi;* p. 427, *Collection of Illustrations for the Cultivation of Ethics;* p. 428, The Art Institute of Chicago; p. 430, Courtesy Museum of Fine Arts, Boston.

Chapter 16   p. 441, *Shanghai Gazetteer,* 1871; p. 447, (top and bottom) *Hai-kuo wen-chien lu,* ca. 1730; p. 449, (both) *Huang Ch'ing chih-kung t'u,* Palace Edition, 1761; p. 459, Radio Times Hulton Picture Library; p. 463, Courtesy of the Peabody Museum of Salem; p. 465, Courtesy of the Peabody Museum of Salem; p. 468, *Ming-jen hsiang-chuan;* p. 473, by permission of the Houghton Library, Harvard University.

Chapter 17   p. 488, (left) Exhibition circulated by the Smithsonian, (right) Honolulu Academy of Arts, Gift of Mrs. Walter P. Dillingham in memory of Alice Perry Grew, 1960; p. 493, Time-Life Picture Agency; p. 501, *Utsusareta bakumatsu,* vol. 3, Asoka Shobō Book Co.; p. 503 (both) *Kensei hiroku,* Yamada Shoin Publishing Co.

Chapter 18   p. 524, *Meiji bunka zenshū, zasshi-hen,* vol. 18; p. 531, Kanagaki Robun, *Seiyō dōchū hizakurige;* p. 533, *Meiji bunka zenshū, kyōiku-*

hen, vol. 10; p. 542, (bottom) Library of Congress; p. 550, International Society for Educational Information, Inc., Tōkyō.

Chapter 19 p. 560, Radio Times Hulton Picture Library; p. 562, Drew Collection, Harvard-Yenching Library; p. 566, Thomson, *Illustrations of China and Its Peoples,* vol. 4, London, 1874; p. 574, Drew Collection, Harvard-Yenching Library; p. 581, Drew Collection, Harvard-Yenching Library; p. 582, Mrs. Helen Merrill Groff-Smith; p. 587, Courtesy of Essex Institute, Salem, Mass.; p. 590, Courtesy of Essex Institute, Salem, Mass.; p. 595, Drew Collection, Harvard-Yenching Library.

Chapter 20 p. 607, Historical Pictures Service Inc., Chicago; p. 609, Historical Pictures Service, Inc., Chicago; p. 615, slide, Harvard-Yenching Library.

Chapter 21 pp. 620–621, (both) *Tien-shih-chai hua-pao,* 1884; p. 624, Radio Times Hulton Picture Library; p. 639, Oriental Collection of the late Ernst von Harringa; p. 646, (top and bottom) Drew Collection, Harvard-Yenching Library.

Chapter 22 p. 659, Rene Burri, Magnum; p. 662, Carl Mydans, Time/Life; p. 667, Tokugawa-Reimeikai Foundation; p. 670, *Nihon hyakunen no kiroku,* Kodansha Publishers; p. 679, International Society for Educational Information, Inc., Tokyo.

Chapter 23 p. 685, *Kensei hiroku,* Yamada Shoin Publishing Co.; p. 689, Radio Times Hulton Picture Library; p. 695, *Nihon hyakunen no kiroku,* vol. 2, *Sekai to Nihon;* p. 704, *Nihon hyakunen no kiroku,* Kodansha Publishers; p. 718, Kyodo Photo Service, Tōkyō; p. 724, *Nihon hyakunen no kiroku,* Kodansha Publishers.

Chapter 24 p. 732 (bottom) Wilson, Arnold Arboretum; p. 739, Arnold Arboretum; p. 744, (top) Courtesy of the Peabody Museum of Salem, (bottom) Government Information Services, Hong Kong; p. 749, China Photo Service; p. 760, (top) Wide World Photos, (bottom) U.S. Signal Corps.

Chapter 25 p. 768, Cornell University; p. 779, Wide World; p. 780, Radio Times Hulton Picture Library; p. 783, Marc Chadourne, *China,* copyright 1932, reprinted by permission of Crown Publishers; p. 789, Radio Times Hulton Picture Library; p. 794, Eastphoto; p. 796, The Bettmann Archive; p. 801, (top) Courtesy of Essex Institute, Salem, Mass., (bottom left) H. Cartier-Bresson/Magnum, (bottom right) Emil Shulthess/Black Star; p. 804, General Library, University of California at Berkeley; p. 805, U.S. Army Photograph.

Chapter 26 p. 814, *Nihon hyakunen no kiroku,* vol. 2, *Sekai to Nihon;* p. 819, International Society of Educational Information, Tōkyō; p. 825, UPI; p. 827, (left) Scheler/Black Star, (right) Eiji Miyazawa/Black Star; p. 833, *Japan of Today;* p. 835, UPI; p. 844, UPI; p. 849, Hamaya/Magnum; p. 868, Wide World Photos.

Chapter 27   p. 873, Historical Pictures Service, Inc., Chicago; p. 876, The Bettmann Archive; p. 882, Marc Riboud/Magnum; p. 893, UPI.

Chapter 28   p. 903, George Silk/ *Life* magazine © Time Inc.; p. 908, (top) University of Chicago Press, (bottom) Air Force Photo/Defense Mapping Agency, Aero Space Center; p. 919, Cartier-Bresson/Magnum; p. 927, Eastphoto; p. 933, (top) Marc Riboud/Magnum, (bottom) Scheler/ Black Star; p. 934, Eastphoto.

COLOR PLATES

Plate 1   William Rockhill Nelson Gallery of Art, Kansas City

Plate 2   *Wen-hua ta-ko-ming ch'i-chien ch'u-t'u wen-wu,* vol. 1

Plate 3   National Museum of Korea

Plate 4   Courtesy Museum of Fine Arts, Ross Collection, Boston

Plate 5   Courtesy Museum of Fine Arts, Chinese-Japanese Special Fund, Boston

Plate 6   Courtesy Museum of Fine Arts, Gardner and Hough Funds, Boston

Plate 7   William Rockhill Nelson Gallery of Art, Kansas City

Plate 8   Courtesy Museum of Fine Arts, Chinese-Japanese Special Fund, Boston

Plate 9   The Fogg Museum of Art, a gift of Charles Coolidge, Harvard University

Plate 10   The Metropolitan Museum of Art, anonymous gift, 1942

Plate 11   Courtesy Museum of Fine Arts, Charles B. Hoyt Collection, Boston

Plate 12   Asian Art Museum of San Francisco, The Avery Brundage Collection

Plate 13   William Rockhill Nelson Gallery of Art, Kansas City

Plate 14   William Rockhill Nelson Gallery of Art, Kansas City

Plates 15 and 16   Courtesy Museum of Fine Arts, Fenollosa-Weld Collection, Boston

Plate 17   Courtesy Museum of Fine Arts, William Sturgis Bigelow Collection, Boston

Plate 18   Asian Art Museum of San Francisco, The Avery Brundage Collection

Plate 19   Courtesy Museum of Fine Arts, gift of Denman Waldo Ross, Boston

Plate 20   Metropolitan Museum of Art, Rogers Fund

Plate 21   Honolulu Academy of Arts, Honolulu, Hawaii

Plate 22   Metropolitan Museum of Art, Purchase 1918, Joseph Pulitzer Bequest

Plate 23   George Silk/*Life* Magazine © Time Inc.

Plate 24   Eastphoto

Charts on pp. 545, 656, 665, and back endpaper by Contis Studios

Maps by Richard Sanderson

Index

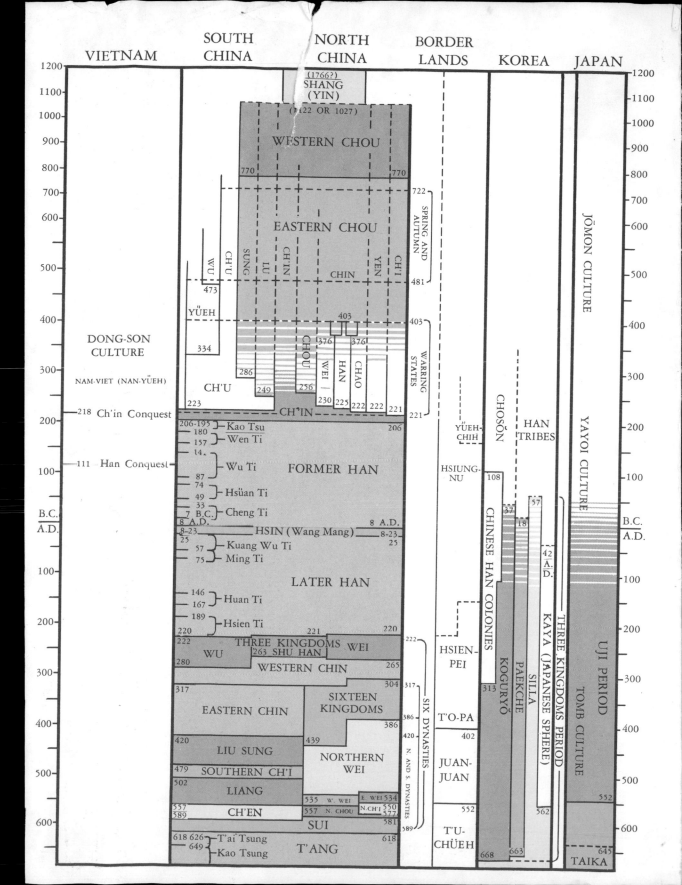